# The BASIC Newbury House DICTIONARY of American English

Heinle & Heinle Publishers
20 Park Plaza
Boston, MA 02116 USA

Thomas Nelson Australia
102 Dodds Street
South Melbourne, 3205
Victoria, Australia

Nelson Canada
1120 Birchmont Road
Scarborough, Ontario
Canada M1K5G4

International Thomson Publishing GmbH
Königwinterer Straße 418
53227 Bonn
Germany

International Thomson Publishing Japan
Hirakawacho-cho Kyowa
Building, 3F
2-2-1 Hirakawacho-cho
Chiyoda-ku, 102 Tokyo
Japan

International Thomson Publishing Asia
60 Albert Street #15-01
Albert Complex
Singapore 189969

International Thomson Editores
Seneca 53
Col. Polanco
11560 Mexico D.F.,
Mexico

The publication of ***The Basic Newbury House Dictionary of American English*** was directed by the members of the Newbury House Publishing Team at Heinle & Heinle:

*Chief Editor:* Philip M. Rideout

*Editorial Director:* Erik Gundersen
*Managing Developmental Editor:* Amy Lawler
*Market Development Director:* Jonathan Boggs
*Senior Production Services Coordinator:* Kristin M. Thalheimer
*Vice President and Publisher:* Stanley J. Galek

Also participating in the publication were:

*Activity Guide Author:* Cheryl Pavlik
*Assistant Editors:* Heide Kaldenbach-Montemayor, Jill Kinkade
*Channel Manager:* Amy Terrell
*Associate Market Development Director:* Mary Sutton
*Manufacturing Coordinator:* Mary Beth Hennebury
*Cover Designer:* Kim Wedlake, Ha Nguyen
*Interior Designer:* Remo Cosentino
*Thematic Artists:* James Edwards, Grace Hsu, Gary Undercuffler
*Spot Artist:* Gary Undercuffler
*Maps:* Charles Martin
*Compositor:* Datapage Technologies, Inc.

For Asian bilingual and other special Asian editions, contact:

Amy Lee, President
Creative Transaction Corporation
17 Stepping Stone Lane
Greenwich, CT 06830
USA



Heinle & Heinle Publishers is a division of International Thomson Publishing, Inc.

Manufactured in the United States of America.

ISBN: 0-8384-6015-1

10 9 8 7 6 5 4 3

# The Newbury House Family of Dictionaries

Explore the first family of learner's dictionaries developed from an American English vocabulary base.

*The Basic Newbury House Dictionary* is a 15,000-word reference tool that encourages the development of basic vocabulary with an abundance of graphics and full-color art. With the inclusion of an Activity Guide, this resource eases and motivates the transition from picture and bilingual dictionaries to more complete learner's and standard dictionaries.

ISBN: 0-8384-6015-1

***The Newbury House Dictionary of American English***, our classic 40,000-word reference volume, is the ONLY learner's dictionary to be updated annually. This year's additions include the following entries and many more: *debit card, DVD, home page,* and *sport utility vehicle*. In addition, each copy of the *The Newbury House Dictionary* is bundled with a value-adding CD-ROM that offers easy electronic access and provides pronunciation for all words in the dictionary.

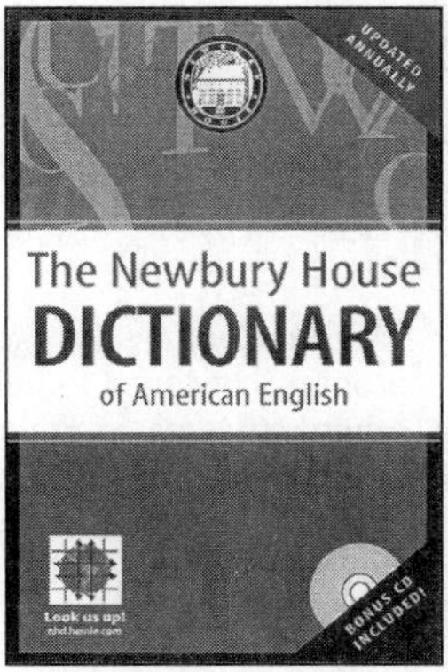


Paperback ISBN: 0-8384-7812-3
Hardcover ISBN: 0-8384-5191-8
Activity Guide ISBN: 0-8384-5614-6

***The Newbury House On-line Dictionary*** is the ONLY on-line, interactive learner's dictionary. Join thousands of others who visit our website weekly at: **http:\\nhd.heinle.com.** Continuously updated and fully-searchable, this on-line resource provides clear explanations, sample sentences, and full-color photos to help you understand new words.

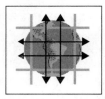

**Look us up!**

# Correlating *The Basic Newbury House Dictionary* with *Making Connections, Voices in Literature, Crossroads Café,* and *Collaborations*

"Teachers use dictionaries in the classroom all the time, and I support them completely in this regard."

—Lydia Stack, *San Francisco Unified School District*

Simply stated, the teaching of dictionary skills has become part of the curriculum. Toward this end, we have correlated *The Basic Newbury House Dictionary* with four of the most popular textbook series available. All of the critical vocabulary in *Making Connections, Voices in Literature, Crossroads Café,* and *Collaborations* has been carefully addressed in *The Basic Newbury House Dictionary.* Here is a brief profile of these four series:

*Making Connections* is a three-level program designed to help secondary school students communicate in English through motivating themes from content areas such as math, science, social studies, and literature.

*Voices in Literature* is a three-level series that integrates authentic multicultural literature and fine art with rich, interactive classroom learning activities.

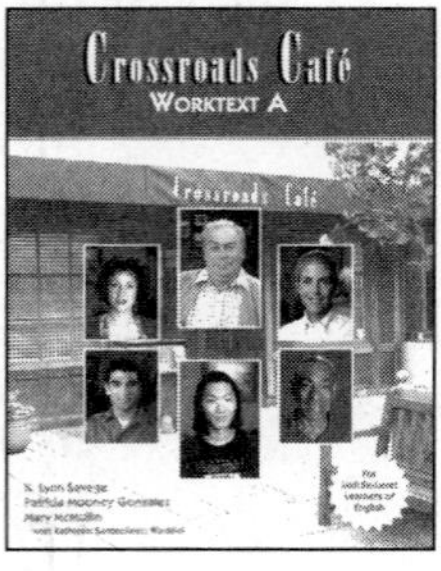


*Crossroads Café* is a four-skills, video-based program that focuses on the lives of an ethnically diverse cast who frequent a neighborhood café.

*Collaborations* is a four-skills series for adult learners organized around authentic immigrant stories that serve as springboards for the development of language skills, vocabulary, and lifeskills competencies.

# CONTENTS

# ACKNOWLEDGMENTS

The Chief Editor and the Newbury House Team would like to thank the following individuals who have offered their years of teaching expertise and thoughtful insights and suggestions to the development and production of the family of *Newbury House Dictionaries*. Their enthusiastic support, shown in attending focus groups, answering questionnaires, and editing portions of manuscript, is much appreciated.

## CONTENT EDITORS

- Linda Butler
- Mary Jane Curry *University of Massachusetts, Boston*
- Marisa Garman
- Joann Kozyrev, *Ohio University*
- Robin Longshaw, *Brown University*
- Melanie May
- Steve Murray
- Lois Poulin, *Mount Ida College, Massachusetts*
- Laura Rideout
- Caroline Schwarzwalder, *North Shore Community College, Massachusetts*
- Jane Selden, *LaGuardia Community College,City University of New York*
- Paula Woolley

## BUSINESS EDITOR

- Laurie Winfield, *Department of Education, State of Texas*

## TECHNOLOGY EDITOR

- Deborah Healey *Oregon State University*

## USAGE NOTES EDITORS

- Eleanor Jones, *American Language Institute, Lisbon, Portugal*
- Linda Lee
- Helen Solorzano, *Northeastern University*

## CONSULTANTS

- Linda Abe, *Indiana University*
- Kathryn Amrani-Joutey, *Boring Public Schools, Oregon*
- Carol Anatasi, *Boston Public Schools, Massachusetts*
- Michelle Beatty, *Palo Alto, California*
- Myron Berkman, *Mission High School, California*
- Bob Betts, *University of California, Irvine Extension*
- Haydee Bidot, *Austin, Texas*
- Susan Bland, *Ithaca, NewYork*
- Ana Bocorny, *Pontifica Universidade Catolica do Rio Grande do Sol, Brazil*
- Deborah Bradford, *Pine Manor College, Massachusetts*
- Christina Brooks, *Framingham Public Schools, Massachusetts*
- Eric Burton, *Community College of San Francisco*
- Sharon Carey, *Project Place, Massachusetts*
- Judy Clark, *Trimble Technical High School, Texas*
- Sarah Cogliano, *Boston Architectural Center, Massachusetts*
- Greg Dahlstron, *Harlingen High Schools, Texas*
- Brian Damm, *Kanda Institute of Foreign Language, Japan*
- Karen DeNitto, *Mercy College, New York*
- Marie diTargiani, *Catholic Migration Services, New York*
- Gloria Dove
- Greg Dowd, *Tokai University, Japan*
- Jane Ellis, *Carlsbad High School, California*
- Anne Erde, *Brookline Adult Education, Massachusetts*
- Michael Feher, *Quincy Community Schools, Massachusetts*
- Judith Gex, *LaGuardia Community College, New York*

- Marcia Gherardi, *Yazigi International, Brazil*
- Deborah Gordon
- Aida Greenberg, *West Contra Costa Unified School District, California*
- Mary Gugich, *Portland Public Schools, Oregon*
- Stacey Hagen, *Edmonds Community College, Washington*
- Maria Heimpel, *Felix High School, California*
- Lee Hewitt, *Adult Learning Programs, Massachusetts*
- Helen Jarandillo, *New York City Board of Education*
- Jean Bernard-Johnston, *Western New England College, Massachusetts*
- Catherine Kann, *Roxbury Community College, Massachusetts*
- Maidy Giber Kiji *Konan Women's University, Japan*
- Casey Kopec, *Education Development Center, Massachusetts*
- Cynthia Hall Koure, *SCALE, Massachusetts*
- Sylvia Laborde, *Alianza Cultural Uruguay—Estados Unidos*
- Joan Lamacchia, *World Education, Massachusetts*
- Mark Landa, *University of Minnesota*
- Eileen LeVan, *Oakland, California*
- Helen Liferber, *New York City Board of Education*
- Martha Grace Low, *University of Oregon*
- Lois Maharg, *Community College of San Francisco*
- Anne Marazziti, *Taft High School, New York*
- Mary Lou McCloskey, *Educo Atlanta*
- Thelma Mejia, *Dallas Public Schools*
- Bruce Mitchell *EF International, Massachusetts*
- Denise Myers, *Adult Learning Center Family Literacy Program, Massachusetts*
- Marisa Olivera, *Alianza Cultural Uruguay—Estados Unidos*
- Mary Pierce, *Connecticut Board of Education*
- Meredith Pike-Baky *University of California, Berkeley*
- Karen Price, *Graduate School of Education, Harvard University*
- Marcia Reeves, *ETS (Educational Testing Services)*
- Michael Reynolds, *Brookline Adult Education, Massachusetts*
- Freebie Rivera, *Auxiliary Services, New York City Board of Education*
- Karen Rosa, *San Lorenzo High School, California*
- Eric Rosenbaum, *Bronx Community College, New York*
- Cecilia Ryan, *West Hills High School, California*
- Jennifer Sarofeen, *Temescal Canyon High School, California*
- Joan Sawyer, *Brookline Adult Education, Massachusetts*
- Renalt Shepherd, *Boston Public Schools*
- Lydia Stack, *San Francisco Unified School District*
- Betty Stone, *SCALE, Massachusetts*
- Elsy Suttmiller, *Dallas Public Schools*
- Rosemarie Tejada, *Carlsbad High School, California*
- Christina Terranova, *Malden Public Schools, Massachusetts*
- Patricia Thompson, *Maxwell High School, Georgia*
- Carole Thurston *Northern Virginia Community College*
- Marjorie Vai, *The New School for Social Research, New York*
- Janet Waters, *University High School, Irvine, California*
- Ken Zimmerman, *New England School of English, Massachusetts*
- Sarah Zovich, *LaGuardia Community College, City University of New York*


## CONTRIBUTORS


- Anne Albarelli-Siegfried *North Harris College, Texas*
- Chris Antonellis *Boston University*
- Louise Beyer, *Middlesex Community College, New Jersey*
- Merilee Brand, *Bickford Adult ESL Centre Ontario, Canada*
- Suzannah Bray, *Glendale Community College, California*
- Milada Broukal, *Glendale Community College, California*
- Dorothy Burak *University of California, San Diego*

- Metta Callahan, *The New School for Social Research, New York*
- Barrie Chi
  *Union County College, New Jersey*
- Effie Cochran, *Papatzikov Baruch College, City University of New York*
- Sue Dicker, *Hostos Community College, City University of New York*
- John DiFiore
  *Union County College, New Jersey*
- Olga Drapanos
  *ELS Language Centers, Boston*
- John Dumicich, *New York University*
- Ardis Flenniken
  *California State University, Northridge*
- Kathleen Flynn
  *Glendale Community College, California*
- Helen Kalkstein Fragiadakis
  *Contra Costa College, California*
- Marjorie Friedman
  *ELS Language Centers, St. Petersburg*
- Hyacinth Gaudart
  *Universiti Malaya, Kuala Lumpur*
- Linda Griffith
  *Glendale Community College, California*
- Patty Heiser, *University of Washington*
- Cecil Hill, *American Academy of Language Arts, Phnom Penh, Cambodia*
- Kathy Hitchcox
  *International English Institute, California*
- Elliot Judd, *University of Illinois, Chicago*
- Grazyna Kenda
  *Technical Career Institute, New York*
- Victoria Kimbrough, *The New School for Social Research, New York*
- Suzanne Koons
  *West Valley College, California*
- Alice Lawson, *Rice University, Texas*
- Candace Matthews
  *The George Washington University*
- Kevin McClure
  *ELS Language Centers, San Francisco*
- J.V. McKenzie
  *California State University, Northridge*
- Martha McNamara
  *University of Akron, Ohio*
- Maureen McNerney
  *York University, Ontario, Canada*
- Loretta Meaker
  *Peel Board of Education, Ontario, Canada*
- Jane Merivale
  *Centennial College, Ontario, Canada*
- Lise Minovitz, *Indiana State University*
- Betsy Morgan, *Eastern Michigan University*
- Dale Myers, *University of Tennessee*
- John Myers
  *Coast Language Academy, Oregon*
- Jill Neely, *Merritt College, California*
- Linda Pelc, *LaGuardia Community College City University of New York*
- Margene Petersen
  *ELS Language Centers, Philadelphia*
- Eva Ramirez, *Laney College, California*
- Alison Rice, *Hunter College City University of New York*
- Eric Rosenbaum, *Bronx Community College, City University of New York*
- Janine Rudnick, *El Paso Community College*
- Tim Rushing, *University of Akron, Ohio*
- Howard Sage, *New York University*
- Brett Sherman, *Pace University, New York*
- Lorraine C. Smith, *Queens College, City University of New York*
- M.E. Sokolik
  *University of California, Berkeley*
- Anne Sokolsky
  *Golden Gate University, California*
- Robert Stein, *Bronx Community College City University of New York*
- Robby Steinberg, *Harvard University Division of Continuing Education*
- Deborah Stewart, *La Guardia Community College, City University of New York*
- Jerome Su, *Bookman Books, Taipei, Taiwan*
- Sandra Taverner
  *Sheridan College, Ontario, Canada*
- Maria Thomas-Rŭzíc
  *University of Colorado, Boulder*
- Andrea Tobias
  *showa Women's Institute, Massachusetts*
- Nancy Tulare, *School for TESOL, Washington*
- Connie Vernon
  *University of Evansville, Indiana*
- Linda Vinay, *Fisher College, Massachusetts*
- Susan Weil, *City College, City University of New York*
- Jennifer Wharton, *EF International, Boston*
- Hoda Zaki
  *Camden Community College, New Jersey*
- Ladislav Zgusta, *University of Illinois, Champaign-Urbana*

# FOREWORD

*The Basic Newbury House Dictionary of American English* is a 15,000-word reference tool that encourages the development of basic vocabulary with an abundance of graphics and full-color art. With the inclusion of an Activity Guide, this resource eases and motivates the transition from picture and bilingual dictionaries to more comprehensive learner's and standard dictionaries. Like the longer *Newbury House Dictionary of American English*, the *Basic* is written under the guidance of an experienced lexicographer and by ESL and EFL teachers who put themselves into the minds of their students.

## Look us up!

Based upon their extensive teaching experience, the teachers incorporated many features into *The Basic Newbury House Dictionary* that are tailored to the English language learner's special needs:

- **Definitions are clear and concise.** They are written in a controlled vocabulary of 2,500 high-frequency, everyday words so they are easy to understand.
- **Sample sentences** are provided for nearly every headword to show how the word is used in actual writing or in speaking. These sentences are composed of a limited vocabulary for easy comprehension.
- **Pronunciation** is presented in the International Phonetic Alphabet (IPA) system.
- **Up-to-date vocabulary items** — terms such as *fanny pack* and in-line skates — are included along with contemporary basic business and technology terms.
- **A wealth of expressions,** including idioms and phrasal verbs that Americans really use, add to the reader's ability to expand his or her knowledge of English.
- **Antonyms and synonyms** add variety to the learner's perspective on language.
- **Culture and usage notes,** plentiful throughout the dictionary, provide useful information about American English and about life in the United States.

- **Cross-referencing** between entries encourages learners to explore the connections between related words.
- **Artwork!** A wealth of spot illustrations instantly help users to understand and appreciate words more fully. Here are some examples:

ATM

orbit

measure

- **Full-color art pages,** illustrating such relevant scenes as an office, a classroom, and a supermarket, appeal to visual learners by giving new vocabulary a clear context.
- **Helpful appendices** contain maps, irregular verb charts, citizen test information, lists of countries and their corresponding nationalities and languages... and more!

As chief editor, I express my gratitude to those colleagues who made *The Basic Newbury House Dictionary* a reality. At Heinle & Heinle, to Charles Heinle, president, and to Stanley Galek, publisher, who once again with generosity and goodwill provided the extensive resources necessary to write and produce this demanding work; to Erik Gundersen, editorial director, for extending his creativity in shaping the work into an intellectual partnership with ESL/EFL teachers and publishing colleagues alike; to Amy Lawler, managing developmental editor, for moving the project forward with cheerful perseverance; to Kristin Thalheimer, production services coordinator, for her equally pleasant persistence in bringing the book to light of day; and to Gary Undercuffler, artist extraordinaire, for the twinkle in his eye, reflected to all in his illustrations. I especially wish to thank Amy Lee for her decade-long encouragement and for bringing our work into partnership with major Asian publishers in bilingual editions.

Philip M. Rideout, M.S. in TESOL
Chief Editor/Lexicographer

# GUIDE TO THE DICTIONARY

## I. Notes on Spelling

**1. The English alphabet**

The English alphabet has 26 letters arranged in the following order:

Capital or uppercase letters:
A B C D E F G H I J K L M N O P Q R S T U V W X Y Z
Lowercase letters:
a b c d e f g h i j k l m n o p q r s t u v w x y z

The word list in the dictionary is arranged in alphabetical order.

The preferred spelling is given first, then the alternative spelling if one exists:

**judg•ment** or **judge•ment**

**2. Irregular verbs** are shown when the spelling of a verb changes in different tenses.

Most verbs add **-ed** for the past tense and for the past participle, **-ing** for the present participle, and **-s** for the third-person singular. For example:

**jump, jumped, jumping, jumps**
The children **jump** rope every day.
They **jumped** rope for four hours yesterday.
They have **jumped** rope many times.
They are **jumping** rope right now.
My daughter **jumps** rope after school every day.

Whenever a form of the verb does not follow this pattern, the irregular spelling is shown:

- **go** /goʊ/*verb* **went** /wɛnt/, **gone** /gɔn;gɑn/, **going**, **goes**
- **operate** /ˈapəˌreɪt/*verb* **operated, operating, operates**
- stab /stæb/*verb* **stabbed, stabbing, stabs**

Also, the ending **-es** is included where necessary to show where it must be added in the third person singular if a verb ends in **sh, ch, s, x,** or **z.** For example:

wash, washes

**3. Irregular plural of nouns**

Usually the plural of a noun is formed by adding an **s** at the end of the word, as in **car, cars** or **hat, hats.** However, if the noun ends in **sh, ch, s, x,** or **z,** an **-es** must be added. We have provided this plural form after the part of speech:

**church** /ˈtʃɜrtʃ/*noun, plural* churches

If the noun ends in a **y** preceded by a consonant, the **y** must be changed to an **i** and **-es** must be added. For example:

**city** /ˈsɪti/ *noun, plural* **cities** an area with many thousands of people living and working close together: *Many tourists visit the city of London.*

The forms of these and other irregular nouns, such as **child, children** and **knife, knives** are also shown.

### 4. Adjectives

In English, when we want to express the idea of a greater or a stronger quality, the comparative and superlative forms are used. These forms are usually made by adding **-er** or **-est** at the end of short adjectives. The spelling of these forms changes if the adjectives are of one syllable, or if they are of two syllables and the second syllable ends in a **y** preceded by a consonant. These spelling changes are shown after the part of speech:

**hot** /hɑt/ *adjective* **hotter, hottest**

Some adjectives of two syllables and all adjectives of three or more syllables do not change their spelling in the comparative and superlative. For example:

**honest,** more honest, most honest
**beautiful,** more beautiful, most beautiful

These forms are not included as part of the entry.

A few adjectives have irregular comparative and superlative forms. These are included as part of the entry.

**good** /gʊd/ *adjective* **better** /ˈbɛtər/, **best** /bɛst/

## II. Notes on Pronunciation

**See Appendix 13, p. 561, for a handy guide to the pronunciation symbols used in this dictionary.**

### 1. Symbols

The pronunciation symbols used in this dictionary are based on the International Phonetic Alphabet, adapted for American English. They are shown in the list on p. 561.

## 2. American English and the choice of pronunciations

The pronunciations shown are the most common in American English. There is no single "best" pronunciation in American English, and often a word has more than one pronunciation. Not all pronunciations of a word are shown — only the most common one. For example, many Americans pronounce the **wh** in words like **what** and **when** with the sound /hw/. This dictionary shows only /w/, the more common pronunciation. Speakers of some dialects do not generally make a distinction between the sounds /ɑ/ in many words where this dictionary shows /ɔ/, such as **cost** or **bought**; to save space, only /ɔ/ has been shown. As another example, many Americans add a sound like /ə/ between a vowel and /r/ in the same syllable, as in **here** or **care,** pronouncing these as /hɪər/ and /kɛər/; this is a predictable variation and is not shown in the dictionary.

## 3. Entries with no pronunciation shown

### a. Compound words

Some entries are compounds, formed from two separate words that are combined to form a new word. The pronunciation of a compound that is written with a space or a hyphen between the parts is not generally given if the words that form it are entered in the dictionary. For example, the pronunciation of **junk food** or **air-condition** can be found by looking up the individual words **junk** and **food** or **air** and **condition** elsewhere in the dictionary. Compounds, especially compounds used as nouns, typically have primary stress on the first element and secondary stress on the second: **junk food** /ˈʤʌŋkˌfud/, **hot dog**/ˈhɑtˌdɔg/, **post office** /ˈpoʊstˌɔfɪs/, **swimming pool** /ˈswɪmɪŋˌpul/.

### b. Inflected words

Pronunciations are not shown for regular inflected forms that follow the normal rules for pronunciation. For compound words in which one part of the compound is an inflected form, such as **air-conditioned**, the pronunciation is not shown.

### c. Derived words

Words that appear in bold type at the end of an entry are derived from the main entry word. If the pronunciation follows the same pattern as the entry word, with only a common suffix added, no separate pronunciation is shown.

# III. Notes on Entries

## 1. Headword

This is the word or phrase being defined, set in boldface at the beginning of the entry, as in **act** as shown below.

**2. Meanings** are given in simple controlled English vocabulary that is easy to understand. Words and expressions often have more than one meaning, and each meaning begins with a number (**1, 2, 3,** and so on) as shown below.

> **act** /ækt/ *verb* **1** to take action: *He acted on my ideas.* **2** to behave, to show, especially emotion: *He acts as though he is pleased.* **3** to perform a role: *He acted in a television program.*

## 3. Sample sentences and phrases

Sample sentences and phrases are also written in a controlled vocabulary for ease of understanding. The sentences are provided to aid the reader in understanding the word's meaning or meanings and to show how the word can be used in everyday speech or writing. See in **act** above: *He acted on my ideas; He acts as though he is pleased.*

Two sample sentences are sometimes given for a definition when shades of meaning need to be known, as in:

> **payable** /'peɪəbəl/*adjective* that is to be paid (by a certain date or to a certain person or business): *The loan is payable on the first of each month.*||*Make the check payable to me.*

## 4. Special vocabulary

New words dance onto the stage of American English with great regularity, inspired by all domains of life. For example, the world of technology has produced **gigabyte** and **virtual reality** and contemporary culture has given us **Generation X** and **grunge.**

This dictionary includes a careful selection of those new words likely to remain for readers of periodicals, recent literature, and for participants in American cultural life. These words are presented generously throughout the dictionary, both as specific entries and in the context of the many sample sentences provided.

Workplace, contemporary American terms, and technology terms are the three chief areas under which special vocabulary items have been included in this dictionary. Following is a brief overview of the ways in which vocabulary from these special areas has been included.

### a. Workplace terminology

Workplace terms are presented in various ways. Words used in daily living are defined, such as **money, cash, credit card, paycheck,** and **bill.** "Second-level" terms that apply both to daily living and to basic business, such as **contract, savings account, down payment, deed,** and so on, are also included.

### b. Technological terms

The computer is common both in society at large and in many schools and households. Therefore, useful computer terms like **PC, laptop computer, Internet,** and **World Wide Web** are defined without becoming too technical. Terms in everyday use that touch on the world of technology, such as **VCR, CD (compact disc),** and **cable TV,** abound in the dictionary. For example:

> **Internet** /ˈintərˌnɛt/*noun* a huge computer network of electronic mail and information, used by millions of people and organizations all over the world *See:* Email; information superhighway; World Wide Web USAGE NOTE.

### c. Contemporary American terms

There is an ever-changing nature to the language that we hear in daily conversation and read in newspapers and magazines. Some words go in and out of style very quickly, while others have staying power. We have included those terms and expressions that are likely to become a permanent part of our vocabulary such as **Generation X, fanny pack,** and **HMO.**

> **fanny pack** *noun* a small bag worn around the waist for carrying money, keys, etc.: *When Pedro rides his bike, he puts his money and some crackers in his fanny pack.*

In addition, we have included numerous American cultural terms that students of English are likely to be curious about, such as **ATM, delicatessen, FBI, Fourth of July, Super Bowl,** and **World Series.**

## IV. Grammar Notes

**1. Parts of speech** are given in full spelling such as *noun* for noun, *verb* for verb, and *adjective* for adjective. Some words change their meaning when they are used as more than one part of speech. These definitions start on a new line, starting with the new part of speech, as in **flap** as both *verb* and *noun:*

> **flap** /flæp/ *verb* **flapped, flapping, flaps** to move up and down, or sideways: *Birds flap their wings.*
>
> **flap** /*noun* **1** an up-and-down or side-to-side motion:*The bird took off with a flap of its wings.* **2** a piece of material used as a covering: *The flaps of my jacket pockets keep things from falling out.*

**2. Derived Words**

Words that are part of the same word family as the headword are often placed at the end of the entry. If the word is pronounced differently from the headword, its pronunciation is provided.

> **abdomen** /'æbdəmən/ *noun* the stomach area: *My abdomen hurts. -adjective* **abdominal** /æb'damənəl/.

**3. Labels**

Labels are sometimes placed after the parts of speech to give additional information about a word, such as *slang* or *informal.*

See Appendix 14, p. 562, to find the abbreviations for all parts of speech as well as other important labels and terms used in the dictionary.

> **junkie** or **junky** /'ʤʌŋki/ *noun slang, plural* **junkies** a person who cannot stop taking drugs

**4. Countable and uncountable nouns**

In English, most nouns are either countable or uncountable. Some nouns are countable in some contexts and uncountable in others. Plurals of countable nouns that form simply by adding an ***s*** are not given. If a noun is countable, you can count it with numbers, as in **three cups** or **two ideas.** Plurals of irregular countable nouns, as in **junkie** above, are given.

However, uncountable nouns do not have plurals. If a noun is uncountable, you cannot count it with numbers. It has only a singular form — it has no plural. For example, **luggage, literature,** and **junk mail** are uncountable. I bought some **luggage** (uncountable). I bought **two suitcases** (countable). When a noun is uncountable, it is labeled as follows:

> **junk mail** *noun, (no plural)* letters and other printed material received in the mail that try to sell you things you usually don't want: *I get a lot of junk mail every day and I just throw it in the trash.*

## 5. Synonyms and antonyms

Synonyms, which are words that have a similar meaning to the headword, are included, as with, for example, *ablaze*:

> **on fire:** burning, in flames, *(synonym)* ablaze: *The house next door is on fire.*

Antonyms, which are words that mean the opposite of the headword, are also included, as with *subtract:*

> **add** /æd/ *verb* **1** to put numbers together into a total: *The waiter added up the food check.* **2** to increase the size or amount of something: *We added a room to our house. (antonym)* subtract

**6. Expressions** are presented and defined after the main meanings. Expressions provide additional meanings using the main headword together with other parts of speech, such as *prepositions, adjectives, verbs,* and other *nouns.* Many idioms are included. Here are examples of some expressions, which begin with **on fire** after the main definition of **fire:**

> **fire** /faɪr/ *noun* the process of burning, which produces heat and light: *The fire in the stove is hot enough to cook.*||*We sat around the fire to keep warm.*||*The restaurant was closed because of a fire.* **on fire:** burning, in flames, *(synonym)* ablaze: *The house next door is on fire.* **to be under fire:** to be under attack: *The soldiers are under fire from enemy guns...* **to fight fire with fire:** to use the same methods as someone else: *He complains to the boss about us, so we'll fight fire with fire and complain to the boss about him.*

## 7. Cross references

Cross references are placed at the end of entries; the word *See:* directs the user to see another entry for additional information:

**vaccine** /væk'sin/ *noun* a medicine taken to prevent diseases: *She takes a vaccine against influenza every fall. See:* serum.

## 8. Culture and Usage Notes

Numerous usage notes are presented at the ends of entries. They explain the proper use of a word or present important information on American culture. One that does both is the following:

**yes** /yɛs/*adverb* **1** used to express agreement: *Would you like to go? Yes, I would.* **2** very much so: *Would you like to drive my new car? Oh, yes, I would!*

USAGE NOTE: The use of *yes, yes, sir* and *yes, ma'am* is formal. *Yeah, uh-huh, mm-hmm, yep,* and *yup* are informal, and commonly used in everyday conversation: *"Do you know Ann?" "Uh-huh." "Have you seen her today?" "Mm-hmm." "Will she be at the meeting?" "Yup."* The body language for *yes* is a small, forward nod of the head.

# DICTIONARY ACTIVITY GUIDE

## CONTENTS

# INTRODUCTION

How many of these things can you find in ***The Basic Newbury House Dictionary?***

- ❐ full-color pictures of many delicious fruits
- ❐ a description of Halloween
- ❐ idioms and expressions like *to keep one's fingers crossed* and *like crazy*
- ❐ a map of North America
- ❐ how to pronounce the word *socialize*
- ❐ a synonym for the word *pocketbook*
- ❐ the language spoken in Brazil
- ❐ information on becoming a U.S. Citizen

If you put a check mark next to each item, you're absolutely right. All of these things are in your dictionary!

People sometimes forget how much information is included in a dictionary, so we put together this ***Activity Guide*** to introduce you to ***The Basic Newbury House Dictionary***. As you complete the activities in the guide, you will learn how to find many different kinds of information with your dictionary.

The ***Activity Guide*** contains 12 lessons, each taking about 30 minutes to complete. At the beginning of each lesson, you will see a box with the dictionary skills covered in that lesson. On the next page, there is a summary of all of the skills covered in this ***Activity Guide***. Finally, a complete answer key is provided beginning on page 30 GUIDE so that you can check your work.

# QUICK GUIDE TO DICTIONARY SKILLS

Learning a few key dictionary skills will help you become a much better reader and writer. But what *is* a dictionary skill? It's a quick idea or strategy that helps you take advantage of important information in the dictionary. For example, "using the pronunciation guide" can help you pronounce a difficult word like *vaccine.*

This ***Activity Guide*** introduces you to 12 dictionary skills. Here is a list of these skills with questions to help you learn how to use them.

1. Finding antonyms
   - *What's the opposite of "get"?*
2. Finding the correct spelling
   - *How do I spell "success"?*
3. Finding synonyms
   - *What's another word for "attractive"?*
4. Finding words in the dictionary
   - *How do I use the guidewords at the top of each page?*
5. Using pictures for meaning
   - *What's a "tangerine"? Oh, there's a picture of a tangerine on p. 3a!*
6. Using the pronunciation guide
   - *How do you pronounce the word "beautiful"?*
7. Using sample sentences
   - *Do Americans say "make a cake" or "do a cake"?*
8. Understanding cultural information
   - *When do I say "Miss Jones" and when do I say "Ms. Jones"?*
9. Understanding definitions
   - *How many meanings does the word "in" have?*
10. Understanding formal and informal usage
    - *Is having lunch with my boss a formal event?*
11. Understanding grammar
    - *Is "elegant" a noun or an adjective?*
12. Understanding idioms
    - *What does "to fight fire with fire" mean?*

# I CLOTHING

**In this unit you will practice:**
finding words in the dictionary • understanding grammar • finding the correct spelling

## FINDING WORDS IN THE DICTIONARY

**1.** Look at the picture of the clothing on page 12a. Choose six words and write them in alphabetical order below.

a. *belt* ______ d. ______

b. ______ e. ______

c. ______ f. ______

**2. Guidewords** help you find words in the dictionary. You can find them at the top left and right corners of the pages. For example, the guidewords on pages 52-53 are **calm** and **capital.**

**3.** Look at pages **208-209**. Write the guidewords below.

______ ______

**4.** Look at these words. Circle the word that is on page **243.**

**jungle** **jacket** **jersey** **jewel**

## UNDERSTANDING GRAMMAR

**5.** The dictionary tells you if a word is a noun, a verb, or an adjective. Look up these words. Mark an **(X)** in the columns for all the forms you find.

| | **noun** | **verb** | **adjective** |
|---|---|---|---|
| a. hat | X | | |
| b. dress | | | |
| c. iron | | | |
| d. suit | | | |
| e. belt | | | |

## FINDING THE CORRECT SPELLING

**6.** The dictionary can help you with spelling. Sometimes you can spell a word in more than one way. What is another way to spell *T-shirt?*

______________________________

# 2 SCHOOL DAYS

**In this unit you will practice:**
finding words in the dictionary • understanding definitions • finding the correct spelling

## FINDING WORDS IN THE DICTIONARY

**1.** Remember you can find guidewords at the top left and right corners of every two pages. Find the guidewords on these pages. Write them on the lines.

a. 56 – 57 *cartoon* *cautious*
b. 100 – 101 ______ ______
c. 134 – 135 ______ ______

**2. Compound words** are made of two different words:

**tooth + brush = toothbrush**

Some compound words are written as one word: **goldfish**
Some are hyphenated: **good-looking**
Some are two separate words: **rubber band**

Match the puzzle pieces to make compound words. Use the dictionary to help you.

## UNDERSTANDING DEFINITIONS

**3.** Write the names of the schools in the proper columns.

| | | |
|---|---|---|
| **elementary school** | **community college** | **high school** |
| **junior high school** | **grammar school** | **graduate school** |

a. *elementary school* ______ b. ______ c. ______

______ ______ ______

## FINDING THE CORRECT SPELLING

**4.** The dictionary tells you how to spell the different forms of the verbs. The verbs in these sentences are misspelled. Look up the verbs and correct the spelling.

*example:* Our class ~~visitted~~ an art museum.
***visited***

a. Carl studyed with Luisa.

b. My mother teachs in an elementary school.

c. The students are siting in the classroom.

d. The bus stoped at the school.

# 3 FOODS AND COOKING

**In this unit you will practice:**
finding words in the dictionary • using pictures for meaning • finding the correct spelling • understanding grammar

## FINDING WORDS IN THE DICTIONARY

**1.** Look at the picture of the foods on page 17a. Choose your six favorite foods and write them in alphabetical order below.

a. ______________________ d. ______________________

b. ______________________ e. ______________________

c. ______________________ f. ______________________

## USING PICTURES FOR MEANING

**2.** Write each food from Activity 1 in the correct column below. (*Hint*: Some foods may go in more than one column.)

| a. Foods that you keep in the refrigerator. | b. Foods that you can bake in an oven. | c. Foods that are sweet. |
|---|---|---|
| *milk* | ______ | ______ |
| ______ | ______ | ______ |
| ______ | ______ | ______ |
| ______ | ______ | ______ |

| d. Foods that you keep in the freezer. | e. Foods that you can cook on a stove. | f. Foods that you must cook before eating. |
|---|---|---|
| ______ | ______ | ______ |
| ______ | ______ | ______ |
| ______ | ______ | ______ |
| ______ | ______ | ______ |

## FINDING THE CORRECT SPELLING

**3.** Write the correct spelling of each verb form.

| | 3rd person present tense | past tense |
|---|---|---|
| *example:* fry | *fries* | *fried* |
| a. mix | ______ | ______ |
| b. cut | ______ | ______ |
| c. chop | ______ | ______ |
| d. freeze | ______ | ______ |
| e. beat | ______ | ______ |

## UNDERSTANDING GRAMMAR

**4.** Look up the comparative and superlative forms of these adjectives and write them in the correct columns. Some are regular and some are irregular.

| | comparative | superlative |
|---|---|---|
| *example:* sweet | *sweeter* | *sweetest* |
| a. salty | ______ | ______ |
| b. delicious | ______ | ______ |
| c. sour | ______ | ______ |
| d. spicy | ______ | ______ |
| e. bland | ______ | ______ |

# 4 IN THE LIVING ROOM

**In this unit you will practice:**
finding words in the dictionary • finding synonyms • understanding definitions

## FINDING WORDS IN THE DICTIONARY

**1a.** Choose one word from each column to make compound nouns. Write them on the lines below.

| | |
|---|---|
| **easy** | **table** |
| **lamp** | **shade** |
| **end** | **case** |
| **window** | **chair** |
| **coffee** | |
| **book** | |
| **night** | |

*example:* ___*window shade*___ ______________________

______________________ ______________________

______________________ ______________________

**1b.** Look at the picture on page 6a. Which item in the list above is NOT usually found in the living room?

______________________

## UNDERSTANDING DEFINITIONS

**2.** Look up the word *in.* Write the definition number that matches the meaning of *in* on the lines below.

| | | definition number |
|---|---|---|
| *example:* | My sister was born **in** 1964. | 3 |
| | a. The sofa is **in** the living room. | ________ |
| | b. I'll be back **in** a month. | ________ |
| | c. I put the keys **in** the drawer. | ________ |
| | d. This chair was made **in** Italy. | ________ |
| | e. I don't like driving **in** the snow. | ________ |
| | f. His address is **in** the telephone book. | ________ |
| | g. Thanksgiving is **in** November. | ________ |

## JUST FOR FUN!

**3.** Follow the directions to draw a living room on a separate piece of paper.

a. Draw a window.
b. Draw a window shade on the window.
c. Draw a bookcase under the window.
d. Draw an easy chair next to the bookcase.
e. Draw an end table beside the easy chair.
f. Draw a table lamp on the end table.
g. Draw a sofa next to the end table.
h. Draw a rug in front of the sofa.
i. Draw a coffee table on top of the rug.
j. Draw a cat in the easy chair.

# 5 TALL OR SHORT?

**In this unit you will practice:**
finding words in the dictionary • understanding grammar

## FINDING WORDS IN THE DICTIONARY

**1.** Find and circle the adjectives below. An example has been done for you. Then put the words in alphabetical order on the lines that follow.

wavyhandsomeuglyprettyoldtallshortfatoverweight

beautifulthinyoungbaldcurlyslimsmall

| | | |
|---|---|---|
| a. *bald* | g. | m. |
| b. | h. | n. |
| c. | i. | o. |
| d. | j. | p. *young* |
| e. | k. | |
| f. | l. | |

**2.** Look at pages 24-25. Circle the words you find on those pages.

**blue** **brown** **beautiful** **bald** **banjo** **big**

## UNDERSTANDING GRAMMAR

**3.** Look for these words in the dictionary. Write the word in the correct column.

**pretty** **hair** **mustache** **beard** **elderly** **short** **elegant**

| | noun | adjective |
|---|---|---|
| *example:* | ________ | *pretty* |
| | ________ | ________ |
| | ________ | ________ |
| | ________ | ________ |

**4.** Choose words from the list in Activity 3 to complete these sentences.

*example:* She works at a home for *elderly* people.

a. That man has blond ________.

b. When I was young, my father had a long ________.

c. All of my sisters are ________.

d. The ________, ________ woman walked across the street.

## JUST FOR FUN!

5. Complete the faces with the features listed.

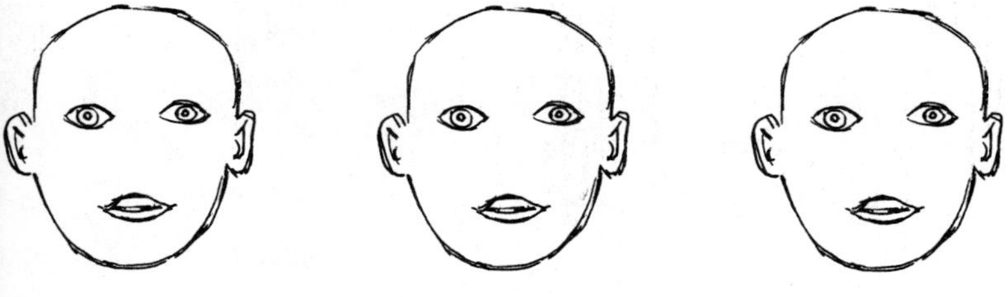

a. bangs
a mole on left cheek
curly hair
big nose

b. sideburms
a scar on forehead
bald
small nose

c. a mustache
a goatee
straight hair
big nose

# 6 MAKING AND DOING

**In this unit you will practice:**
using sample sentences • understanding idioms

## USING SAMPLE SENTENCES

**1.** Look up the words *do* and *make.* Use the information in the sample sentences to make phrases by connecting the words.

**do** ........................................ homework

**make**

a living
homework
laws
the cooking
a cake
50 kilometers per hour
money
a mistake
well

**2.** Is it *make* or *do?* Make your best guess!

*example:* ___*make*___ a guess

a. ______________ furniture

b. ______________ math

c. ______________ a friend

d. ______________ your homework

e. ______________ five dollars

f. ______________ the dishes

## UNDERSTANDING IDIOMS

**3.** There are many idioms with *make* and *do*. Replace the words in bold with a word or words that mean the same thing.

*example:* He **made up the story**. He ___*lied*___.

a. Don't **make fun of** them. Don't ________________.

b. You'll have to **do** it **over.** You'll have to ________________.

c. This book **doesn't make sense**. This book ________________.

d. You'll **make it** if you work hard. You'll ____________ if you work hard.

e. She likes to **make believe** that she has a sister. She likes to ________________ that she has a sister.

## JUST FOR FUN!

**4.** Can you guess the names of the people who do these things? Complete the sentences with the words in the box.

| | | | |
|---|---|---|---|
| **teacher** | **cashier** | **student** | |
| **travel agent** | **baker** | **surgeon** | **scientist** |

*example*: a person who **makes change** ___*cashier*___

a. a person who **makes bread** ________________

b. a person who **does operations** ________________

c. a person who **makes tests** ________________

d. a person who **does homework** ________________

e. a person who **does experiments** ________________

f. a person who **makes airline reservations** ________________

# 7 TIME FOR WORK

**In this unit you will practice:**
understanding grammar • finding the correct spelling • understanding definitions

## UNDERSTANDING GRAMMAR

**1.** Circle the word that doesn't belong in each group of words below. (*Hint*: Think about "parts of speech." Are all words *nouns? Adjectives?*)

| | | | | |
|---|---|---|---|---|
| *example*: | salary | timecard | payroll | (promote) |
| a. | manage | employee | supervise | work |
| b. | later | teller | carpenter | waiter |
| c. | hire | job | fire | pay |
| d. | occupation | work | difficult | job |
| e. | slowly | hard | fast | quick |

**2.** Most nouns are either countable **(count)** or uncountable **(non-count)**. If a noun is countable, you can count it with numbers, as in **three cups** or **two ideas**. **Uncountable nouns** cannot be counted with numbers; they have only a singular form, as in **luggage, literature,** or **junk mail**.

Are the words below **count** or **non-count** nouns? Write each word in the correct column.

| | | | | |
|---|---|---|---|---|
| **job** | **work** | **secretary** | **information** | **machine** |
| **tax** | **salary** | **unemployment** | **equipment** | **boss** |

| **count noun** | **non-count noun** |
|---|---|
| *job* | ______ |
| ______ | ______ |
| ______ | ______ |
| ______ | ______ |
| ______ | ______ |

## FINDING THE CORRECT SPELLING

**3.** Write the plurals of the count nouns in Activity 2.

____________________ ____________________

____________________ ____________________

____________________ ____________________

## UNDERSTANDING DEFINITIONS

**4.** Which of these words are people? Which are machines? Which can be a person or a machine? Complete the sentences with the correct words.

| | | |
|---|---|---|
| **calculator** | **carpenter** | **computer** |
| **dishwasher** | **helper** | **plumber** |
| **supervisor** | **typewriter** | **waiter** |

*example*: A *dishwasher* can be a person or a machine.

a. A ____________________ is a person.

b. A ____________________ is a person.

c. A ____________________ is a person.

d. A ____________________ is a person.

e. A ____________________ is a person.

f. A ____________________ is a machine.

g. A ____________________ is a machine.

h. A ____________________ is a machine.

# 8 GREETINGS AND EXCLAMATIONS

**In this unit you will practice:**
finding synonyms • understanding formal and informal usage

## FINDING SYNONYMS

**1.** Find synonyms for these words and phrases. Write them on the lines below.

*example:* **so long** ***good-bye***

a. y'all ____________________

b. hi ____________________

c. nope____________________

d. see you later____________________

e. pardon me ____________________

## UNDERSTANDING FORMAL AND INFORMAL USAGE

**2.** Some situations are more formal than others. Read these situations and mark an **(X)** in the correct column.

| | | **formal** | **informal** |
|---|---|---|---|
| *example:* | a wedding reception | X | ________ |
| | a. a job interview | ________ | ________ |
| | b. a neighborhood barbecue | ________ | ________ |
| | c. lunch with your boss | ________ | ________ |
| | d. meeting your friend's parents for the first time | ________ | ________ |
| | e. a movie with friends | ________ | ________ |

**3.** Read the words and phrases below. Decide if they are formal or informal and mark an **(X)** in the correct column.

| | | formal | informal |
|---|---|---|---|
| *example:* | hi | ________ | X |
| | a. How do you do? | ________ | ________ |
| | b. yeah | ________ | ________ |
| | c. y'all | ________ | ________ |
| | d. I beg your pardon. | ________ | ________ |

**4.** For each word or phrase marked informal, write a more formal version below:

*example:* **hi ➔ hello**

a.______________________ ➔ ______________________

b.______________________ ➔ ______________________

# JUST FOR FUN!

**5.** Some words are used to show emotions like surprise, fear, or disgust. We call these words **exclamations.**

Look at the pictures below. Write the word that fits each picture. (*Hint:* More than one answer may be correct.)

**darn golly gee ha ooh hey oops good oh**

a.

b.

c.

_______*oops*_______ ______________________ ______________________

d.

e.

f.

______________________ ______________________ ______________________

# 9 TAKING, GETTING, AND GIVING

**In this unit you will practice:**
finding words in the dictionary • understanding definitions • understanding grammar

## FINDING WORDS IN THE DICTIONARY

**1.** Match the verbs with the words in the box. Make as many pairs as you can. Check your answers in the dictionary.

**get**

**give**

**take**

| | |
|---|---|
| away | in |
| back | off |
| behind | over |
| ahead | into |
| on | up |

a. *take off*

b. ______

c. ______

d. ______

e. ______

f. ______

g. ______

h. ______

i. ______

j. ______

## UNDERSTANDING DEFINITIONS

**2.** Use the words in the box in Activity 1 to complete the sentences below.

*example:* He gets ____*up*____ at 6:00 every morning.

a. He is very stubborn. He never gives ____________________.

b. The plane took ____________________ on time.

c. Take ____________________ your clothes before you go swimming.

d. I study every night so I won't get ____________________.

e. Hurry! Get ____________________ the bus before it leaves!

f. Mary took ____________________ the class when the teacher got sick.

g. Please give me ____________________ my pen. I need it.

h. I am planning to take ____________________ golf this summer.

## UNDERSTANDING GRAMMAR

**3.** Find the other forms of these verbs.

| | | **past tense** | **past participle** |
|---|---|---|---|
| *example:* | **go** | **went** | **gone** |
| | a. give | ____________________ | ____________________ |
| | b. take | ____________________ | ____________________ |
| | c. get | ____________________ | ____________________ |

## FINDING ANTONYMS

**4.** Find the **antonyms** of the words and write them on the lines below. (*Hint*: Antonyms are opposites: *hot* is an antonym of *cold.)*

a. give ______________________________

b. take ______________________________

c. get ______________________________

# 10 HAPPY OR SAD?

**In this unit you will practice:**
using the pronunciation guide • using sample sentences

## USING THE PRONUNCIATION GUIDE

**1.** Find the number of syllables in each word below. Write them in the correct columns.

| | | | |
|---|---|---|---|
| **tired** | **cold** | **excited** | **frightened** |
| **stressed** | **angry** | **confused** | **jealous** |
| **happy** | **disgusted** | **embarrassed** | **interested** |
| **comfortable** | **intelligent** | **scared** | |

**one syllable**

*cold* ____________

____________

____________

____________

**two syllable**

____________

____________

____________

____________

**three syllable**

*disgusted* ____________

____________

____________

____________

**four syllable**

____________

____________

____________

____________

**2.** Rewrite the two-, three-, and four- syllable words in Activity 1 above, marking the syllables.

*example*: **ex-ci-ted**

| **two syllable** | **three syllable** | **four syllable** |
|---|---|---|
| ____________ | ____________ | ____________ |
| ____________ | ____________ | ____________ |
| ____________ | ____________ | ____________ |
| ____________ | ____________ | ____________ |
| ____________ | ____________ | ____________ |

**3.** Where's the stress? Look at the words in Activity 2. Write the words in the correct columns. Write the stressed syllable in capital letters.

| | **first syllable stress** | **second syllable stress** |
|---|---|---|
| *example*: | ANG-ry | ex-CI-ted |
| | ____________ | ____________ |
| | ____________ | ____________ |
| | ____________ | ____________ |
| | ____________ | ____________ |
| | ____________ | ____________ |

## USING SAMPLE SENTENCES

**4.** Sample sentences help you understand the meaning of each word. Sometimes they can also help you with grammar.

Look at the sample sentences for the underlined words. Choose the correct preposition (*of, by, in,* etc.), then complete the sentences with your own ideas.

*example*: The students were <u>confused</u> *by* *the instructions*.

a. I am <u>interested</u> __________ baseball.

b. I am <u>frightened</u> __________ ____________________.

c. They are <u>jealous</u> __________ me because ____________________.

d. The students were <u>confused</u> __________ ____________________.

e. She was <u>embarrassed</u> __________ ____________________.

# II SPORTS

**In this unit you will practice:**
understanding grammar • finding the correct spelling • understanding definitions

## UNDERSTANDING GRAMMAR

**1.** Which of these sport words have *-ing* forms? Write them on the lines.

*example:* **swim** **swimming**

a. baseball ______________________ f. jog ______________________
b. basketball ______________________ g. ski ______________________
c. bicycle ______________________ h. soccer ______________________
d. football ______________________ i. tennis ______________________
e. golf ______________________ j. volleyball ______________________

## FINDING THE CORRECT SPELLING

**2.** All of these signs have a misspelled word. Correct the spelling in the line below.

Skiiers MUST
Register

Swiming
from 12-6 p.m. ONLY.

Jogers Only.
No bikers allowed.

a.____________________ b.____________________ c.____________________

No night sking.
permitted.

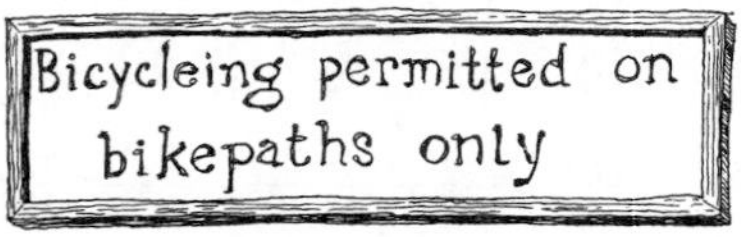
Bicycleing permitted on
bikepaths only

d.____________________ e.____________________

# UNDERSTANDING DEFINITIONS

**3.** Match the places and the equipment with the sports.
(Some words can be used more than once.)

| **place to play** | **sport** | **equipment** |
|---|---|---|
| court | baseball | racket |
| course | basketball | helmet |
| field | football | ball |
| diamond | golf | club |
| | tennis | bat |

# JUST FOR FUN!

**4.** Eleven sports words are hidden in this puzzle. Can you find them?

| | | | |
|---|---|---|---|
| **ball (2)** | **basketball** | **bicycle** | **club** |
| **football** | **golf** | **jog** | **net (2)** |
| **racket** | **soccer** | **tennis** | **volleyball** |

| | | | | | | | | | | | | |
|---|---|---|---|---|---|---|---|---|---|---|---|---|
| A | C | A | G | J | O | G | S | P | Y | N | L | K |
| B | V | S | O | X | T | V | T | W | V | O | L | M |
| I | O | B | L | C | C | J | E | L | O | L | C | Y |
| C | L | H | F | C | L | T | N | E | L | W | B | P |
| Y | L | E | W | N | U | H | N | T | L | A | A | X |
| C | E | A | L | I | B | E | I | O | E | W | O | S |
| L | R | A | C | K | E | T | S | J | Y | N | E | T |
| E | B | X | S | I | F | O | O | T | B | A | L | L |
| W | M | O | N | O | Q | O | K | F | A | P | R | V |
| L | A | S | O | G | C | P | U | V | L | L | M | S |
| F | G | E | A | T | Y | C | U | O | L | W | J | R |
| T | K | H | B | A | S | K | E | T | B | A | L | L |
| R | C | M | N | T | L | P | U | R | A | F | B | V |

# 12 NAMES AND NICKNAMES

**In this unit you will practice:**
finding words in the dictionary • understanding cultural information

## FINDING WORDS IN THE DICTIONARY

**1.** Look for these abbreviations in the dictionary. Write out their full names.

a. CD ______________________

b. YMCA ______________________

c. MPH ______________________

d. NAACP ______________________

e. NASA ______________________

f. P.O. ______________________

**2.** How do you pronounce these abbreviations?

a. MPH

b. NASA

c. NAACP

d. YMCA

e. CD

## UNDERSTANDING CULTURAL INFORMATION

**3.** Answer these questions about the abbreviations in Activity 1.

a. Which is used in addresses? ______________

b. Which sends people into space? ______________

c. Which is related to a car? ______________

d. Which plays music? ______________

e. Which is an organization? ______________

**4.** Look up the abbreviations in the box below. Write them in the correct columns. *(Hint:* Some words can go in more than one column.)

| | | | |
|---|---|---|---|
| **Mr.** | **Miss** | **Ms.** | **Mrs.** |

| unmarried man | unmarried woman | married man | married woman |
|---|---|---|---|
| __________ | __________ | __________ | __________ |

**5.** Some people do not like to use the words below because they are about one gender only. For example, many people say *chairperson* instead of *chairman.* What is another word for *postman? Mankind?*

a. postman ______________________________

b. mankind ______________________________

c. fireman ______________________________

d. policeman ______________________________

# ANSWER KEY TO ACTIVITY GUIDE

## Lesson 1, pp. 6 Guide

**1.** Answers will vary. Here are some possible ones:
- a. belt / cap
- b. dress / jacket
- c. hat / purse
- d. necktie / sneakers
- e. pants / socks
- f. sweater / t-shirt

**2.** helicopter, him

**3.** jungle

**4.** a. hat - noun
- b. dress - noun, verb, adjective
- c. iron - noun, verb
- d. suit - noun, verb
- e. belt - noun

**5.** Yes: 'tee-shirt'

## Lesson 2, pp. 8 Guide

**1.** b. defense / demand
- c. enclose / enter

**2.** blackboard, cardboard, classroom, dress code, extracurricular, homework, notebook, report card, textbook

**3.** Answers may vary.
- a. elementary school / grammar school
- b. community college / graduate school
- c. junior high school / high school

**4.** a. studied
- b. teaches
- c. sitting
- d. stopped

## Lesson 3, pp. 10 Guide

**1.** Answers will vary. Here are some possible responses:
- a. bagel / cereal
- b. cheese / milk
- c. eggs / muffin
- d. fish / noodles
- e. steak / rice
- f. yogurt / spaghetti

**2.** Answers will vary. Here are some possible responses:
a. butter, cheese, milk, eggs, yogurt
b. bread, muffin, chicken, fish, ham
c. muffin, cereal
d. bacon, chicken, hot dogs
e. rice, noodles, spaghetti, eggs,bacon, fish, hamburger, hot dog
f. rice, noodles, eggs, chicken,bacon, hamburger, hot dog, steak

**3.** example: fries / fried
c. mixes / mixed
d. cuts / cut
e. chops / chopped
f. freezes / froze
g. beats / beat

**4.** example: sweeter / sweetest
d. saltier / saltiest
e. more delicious / most delicious
f. more sour / most sour
g. spicier / spiciest
h. blander / blandest

## Lesson 4, pp. 12 Guide

**1.** a. window shade, bookcase, end table, coffee table, easy chair, floor lamp
b. night table

**2.** example: 3
b. 2
c. 4
d. 5
e. 2
f. 6
g. 1
h. 3

## Lesson 5, pp. 14 Guide

**2.** a. bald
b. beautiful
c. curly
d. fat
e. handsome
f. old
g. overweight
h. pretty
i. short
j. slim
k. small
l. tall
m. thin
n. ugly
o. wavy
p. young

2. bald, banjo
3. Nouns: hair, mustache, beard; Adjectives: elderly, short, elegant
4. a. hair
   b. beard
   c. (Answers will vary.) pretty, short, elegant
   d. (Answers will vary.) short, elderly OR elegant, pretty
5. (Students draw their answers according to the list of features.)

## Lesson 6, pp. 16 Guide

1. **'do':** homework, the cooking, 50 kilometers per hour, well;
   **'make':** a living, laws, a cake, money, a mistake
2. a. make
   b. do
   c. make,
   d. do
   e. make
   f. do
3. a. laugh at
   b. redo / do again
   c. isn't logical
   d. succeed
   e. pretend
4. a. baker
   b. surgeon
   c. teacher
   d. student
   e. scientist
   f. travel agent

## Lesson 7, pp. 18 Guide

1. a. employee
   b. later
   c. job
   d. difficult
   e. slowly
2. **count:** boss, job, salary, secretary, tax, machine
   **non-count:** information, work, equipment, unemployment
3. bosses, jobs, salaries, secretaries, taxes, machines
4. a. waiter
   b. plumber
   c. helper
   d. carpenter
   e. supervisor
   f. computer
   g. typewriter
   h. calculator

## Lesson 8, pp. 20 Guide

**1.** a. 'you all'
b. 'Hello'
c. 'no'
d. 'Good bye' / 'Until we meet again.'
e. 'I'm sorry.' / 'I beg your pardon.'

**2.** Answers may vary.
formal: a,c,d
informal: b,c,e

**3.** formal: a,d
informal: b,c

**4.** example: 'Hi' / 'Hello'
b. 'yes'
c. 'you all'

**5.** Answers may vary.
a. darn, oops, oh
b. golly, gee, ooh
c. darn, oops, oh
d. ooh, good
e. ha
f. hey

## Lesson 9, pp. 22 Guide

**1.** Here is a list of ALL the possible answers:
get ahead, give away, get away, give back, get back, give in, get behind, give off, get in, give up, get into, take in, get over, take off, get up, take up

**2.** a. in
b. off
c. off
d. behind
e. in / into
f. over
g. back
h. up

**3.** a. gave / given
b. took / taken
c. got / gotten

**4.** a. take
b. give
c. give

## Lesson 10, pp. 24 Guide

**1.** **One syllable:** cold, stressed, scared
**Two syllable:** tired, happy, frightened, angry, confused, jealous
**Three syllable:** excited, disgusted, embarrassed, (interested)
**Four syllable:** comfortable, intelligent, (interested)

**2.** **Two syllable:** ang-ry, con-fused, fright-ened, hap-py, jeal-ous, ti-red
**Three syllable:** dis-gus-ted, em-barr-assed, ex-ci-ted, in-terest-ed
**Four syllable:** com-for-ta-ble, in-ter-est-ed, in-tel-li-gent

**3.** **First syllable stress:** ANG-ry, FRIGHT-ened, HAP-py, JEAL-ous, TI-red, IN-terested,COM-for-ta-ble;
**Second syllable stress:** ex-CIT-ed, con-FUSED, dis-GUS-ted, em-BARR-assed, in-TEL-li-gent

**4.** Answers will vary.
a. in / baseball
b. of / snakes
c of / I have a boyfriend
d. by / the spot on her shirt

## Lesson 11, pp. 26 Guide

**1.** a. —, b. —, c. bicycling, d. —,
e. golfing, f. jogging, g. skiing, h. —,
i. —, j —

**2.** a. skiers
b. swimming
c. joggers
d. skiing
e. bicycling

**3.** court / basketball / ball
court / tennis / ball, racket
course / golf / ball, club
diamond, field / baseball / ball, bat
field / football / helmet, ball

**4.** (See below)

| | | | | | | | | | | | | |
|---|---|---|---|---|---|---|---|---|---|---|---|---|
| A | C | A | G | J | O | G | S | P | Y | N | L | K |
| B | V | S | O | X | T | V | T | W | V | O | L | M |
| I | O | B | L | C | C | J | E | L | O | L | C | Y |
| C | L | H | F | C | L | T | N | E | L | W | B | P |
| Y | L | E | W | N | U | H | N | T | L | A | A | X |
| C | E | A | L | I | B | E | I | O | E | W | O | S |
| L | R | A | C | K | E | T | S | J | Y | N | E | T |
| E | B | X | S | I | F | O | O | T | B | A | L | L |
| W | M | O | N | O | Q | O | K | F | A | P | R | V |
| L | A | S | O | G | C | P | U | V | L | L | M | S |
| F | G | E | A | T | Y | C | U | O | L | W | J | R |
| T | K | H | B | A | S | K | E | T | B | A | L | L |
| R | C | M | N | T | L | P | U | R | A | F | B | V |

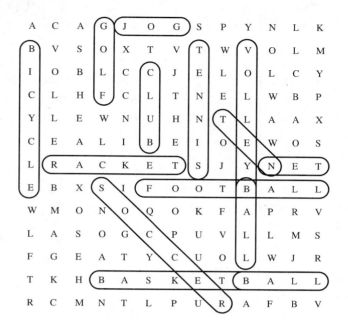

## Lesson 12, pp. 28 Guide

**1.** a. compact disc
   b. Young Men's Christian Association
   c. miles per hour
   d. National Association for the Advancement of Colored People
   e. National Aeronautics and Space Administration
   f. post office

**2.** a. 'miles per hour'
   b. (see dictionary entry for phonetic spelling)
   c. (see dictionary entry for phonetic spelling)
   d. (see dictionary entry for phonetic spelling)
   e. (see dictionary entry for phonetic spelling)

**3.** a. P.O.
   b. NASA
   c. MPH
   d. CD
   e. NAACP

**4.** Mr. / Miss, Ms. / Mr. / Mrs.

**5.** a. letter carrier
   b. humanity/ humankind
   c. firefighter
   d. police officer

# GUIDE TO PRONUNCIATION SYMBOLS

## Vowels

| Symbol | Key Word | Pronunciation |
|---|---|---|
| /ɑ/ | **hot** | /hɑt/ |
| | **far** | /fɑr/ |
| /æ/ | **cat** | /kæt/ |
| /aɪ/ | **fine** | /faɪn/ |
| /aʊ/ | **house** | /haʊs/ |
| /ɛ/ | **bed** | /bɛd/ |
| /eɪ/ | **name** | /neɪm/ |
| /i/ | **need** | /nid/ |
| /ɪ/ | **sit** | /sɪt/ |
| /oʊ/ | **go** | /goʊ/ |
| /ʊ/ | **book** | /bʊk/ |
| /u/ | **boot** | /but/ |
| /ɔ/ | **dog** | /dɔg/ |
| | **four** | /fɔr/ |
| /ɔɪ/ | **toy** | /tɔɪ/ |
| /ʌ/ | **cup** | /kʌp/ |
| /ɜr/ | **bird** | /bɜrd/ |
| /ə/ | **about** | /ə'baʊt/ |
| | **after** | /'æftər/ |

## Consonants

| Symbol | Key Word | Pronunciation |
|---|---|---|
| /b/ | **boy** | /bɔɪ/ |
| /d/ | **day** | /deɪ/ |
| /ʤ/ | **just** | /ʤʌst/ |
| /f/ | **face** | /feɪs/ |
| /g/ | **get** | /gɛt/ |
| /h/ | **hat** | /hæt/ |
| /k/ | **car** | /kɑr/ |
| /l/ | **light** | /laɪt/ |
| /m/ | **my** | /maɪ/ |
| /n/ | **nine** | /naɪn/ |
| /ŋ/ | **sing** | /sɪŋ/ |
| /p/ | **pen** | /pɛn/ |
| /r/ | **right** | /raɪt/ |
| /s/ | **see** | /si/ |
| /ʃ/ | **shoe** | /ʃu/ |
| /ʒ/ | **vision** | /'vɪʒən/ |
| /t/ | **tea** | /ti/ |
| /ð/ | **they** | /ðeɪ/ |
| /θ/ | **think** | /θɪŋk/ |
| /ʧ/ | **cheap** | /ʧip/ |
| /v/ | **vote** | /voʊt/ |
| /w/ | **west** | /wɛst/ |
| /y/ | **yes** | /yɛs/ |
| /z/ | **zoo** | /zu/ |

## Stress

/'/ **city** /'sɪti/

used before a syllable to show primary (main) stress

/ˌ/ **dictionary** /'dɪkʃəˌnɛri/

used before a syllable to show secondary stress

# A,a

**A, a** /eɪ/ *noun* **A's, a's** or **As, as**
**1** the first letter of the English alphabet
**2** the highest grade in school: *I got an A on my history exam.*

**a** /ə;eɪ/ or **an** *indefinite article*
**1** used to show one person or thing: *A man asked me what time it was.*
**2** used before words that show a number or amount: *A lot of people are in this class. See:* an, **USAGE NOTE.**

**abandon** /ə'bændən/ *verb*
to leave someone or something completely: *The people abandoned the village before the soldiers came. –noun* **abandonment.**

**abbreviate** /ə'brivi,eɪt/ *verb* **abbreviated, abbreviating, abbreviates**
to make shorter, especially a word: *Many dictionaries abbreviate the word "noun" by using "n." –noun* **abbreviation** /ə,brivi'eɪʃən/.

**abdomen** /'æbdəmən/ *noun*
the stomach area: *My abdomen hurts. –adjective* **abdominal** /æb'damənəl/.

**ability** /ə'bɪləti/ *noun, plural* **abilities**
the skill and the power to do something: *She has the ability to speak four languages.*

**able** /'eɪbəl/ *adjective*
having the skill and power to do something: *After the operation, he was able to walk again. –adverb* **ably.**

**abnormal** /æb'nɔrməl/ *adjective*
unusual: *The high temperatures are abnormal for this time of year.–adverb* **abnormally** *(antonym)* normal.

**aboard** /ə'bɔrd/ *preposition*
on a ship, train, airplane, or other vehicle: *The conductor says "All aboard" before the train leaves the station.*

**abolish** /ə'bɑlɪʃ/ *verb*
to end or stop something, usually forever: *The government abolished the tax on food. –noun* **abolition.**

**about** /ə'baʊt/ *preposition*
related to, concerning: *We had a meeting about a new product.*

**about** *adverb*
**1** around: *About 20 people came to the meeting.*
**2** ready to: *I'm just about to go to work.*

above

**above** /'ə'bʌv/ *preposition*
higher than: *She put her hands above her head. (antonym)* below.

**abridge** /ə'brɪʤ/ *verb* **abridged, abridging, abridges**
to take out parts, especially from a written work: Reader's Digest *abridges long books so that people can read them quickly. –noun* **abridgment;** *–adjective* **abridged.**

**abroad** /ə'brɔd/ *adverb*
out of the country: *Our company ships farm machinery abroad.*

**abrupt** /ə'brʌpt/ *adjective*
**1** quick and unfriendly: *He talks to everyone in an abrupt manner.*

A

**2** happening by surprise: *The bus came to an abrupt stop.* –*adverb* **abruptly.**

**absence** /'æbsəns/ *noun*
a situation of not being somewhere: *His absence from work was because of his illness. (antonym)* presence.

**absent** /'æbsənt/ *adjective*
not present: *The student is absent from class. (antonym)* present.

**absolute** /'æbsə,lut/ *adjective*
complete, definite: *She told you the absolute truth.* –*adverb* **absolutely.**

**absorb** /əb'sɔrb/ *verb*
**1** to take in: *The towel absorbed water from the sink.*
**2** *figurative* to learn and remember: *She absorbs new ideas very quickly.* –*adjective* **absorbent.**

**abstract** /æb'strækt/ *adjective*
about ideas, feelings, etc. (not physical things): *"Beauty" and "truth" are abstract ideas.* –*adverb* **abstractly.**

**absurd** /əb'sɜrd/ *adjective*
foolish, stupid: *He made an absurd comment about taxes being too low.*

**abundance** /ə'bʌndəns/ *noun*
many or much of something: *Flowers grow in abundance in our garden.* –*adjective* **abundant;** –*adverb* **abundantly.**

**abuse** /ə'byuz/ *verb* **abused, abusing, abuses**
**1** to use in a harmful way: *She abuses alcohol by drinking too much.*
**2** to hurt: *The man abused his wife by hitting her often.*

**abuse** /ə'byus/ *noun*
bad treatment: *The boy was beaten and starved; he lived through much abuse.* –*adjective* **abusive.**

**AC** /,eɪ'si/
**1** *abbreviation of* alternating current: *Household electricity in the USA is AC.*
**2** *abbreviation of* air conditioner: *Will you turn on the AC?*

**academic** /,ækə'dɛmɪk/ *adjective*
related to studying and school: *His academic work is excellent.* –*adverb* **academically.**

**academy** /ə'kædəmi/ *noun*
**1** a private school that prepares students for college: *That academy is very expensive.*
**2** a school for special training: *My daughter attends the police (military, naval, etc.) academy.*

**accelerate** /ɪk'sɛlə,reɪt/ *verb* **accelerated, accelerating, accelerates**
to move faster: *The car accelerated to a speed of 100 miles (160 km) per hour.*

**accent** /'æk,sɛnt/ *noun*
a sound in one's speech typical of a country or area: *He speaks English with a Spanish accent.*

**accent** /'æk,sɛnt/ *verb*
to show the importance of something: *The teacher accented her wish for quiet in the classroom by speaking louder.*

**accept** /ɪk'sɛpt/ *verb*
**1** to take willingly: *He accepted my apology for being late.*
**2** to say "yes," that you will do something: *Are you going to accept his invitation to the party? (antonym)* refuse.

**acceptable** /ɪk'sɛptəbəl/ *adjective*
**1** satisfactory: *We received an acceptable price for our house.*
**2** all right to do: *Wearing a shirt without a tie is acceptable dress for dinner here.*

**acceptance** /ɪk's ɛptəns/ *noun*
approval: *his work received acceptance by his boss.*

**access** /'æk,sɛs/ *noun*
entrance, permission to use: *Everyone has access to the public library.*

**accident** /'æksədənt/ *noun*
something harmful or unpleasant that happens by surprise: *He had an accident on the way to work; he fell and broke an ankle.* –*adjective* **accidental;** –*adverb* **accidentally.**

**accompany** /ə'kʌmpəni/ *verb formal* **accompanied, accompanying, accompanies**
to go with someone: *I accompanied my friends to the party.*

**accomplish** /ə'kɑmplɪʃ/ *verb*
**1** to finish: *We accomplished the job in an hour.*
**2** to achieve, do important things: *She has accomplished much in her short career.* –*noun* (act) **accomplishment.**

**according to** *preposition*
**1** in agreement with: *According to the law, you must stop at a red light.*
**2** as said by: *According to John, Sue was home at 8:00 P.M.*

---

**USAGE NOTE:** *According to* is not used with *me.*

---

**accordion** /əˈkɔrdiən/ *noun*
a musical instrument played with the hands by forcing air out through holes that are opened and closed with the fingers: *My father plays country music on the accordion.* *See:* art on page 15a.

accordion

**account** /əˈkaʊnt/ *noun*
**1** money kept in a bank: *I have a checking account at Metropolitan Bank.*
**2** a description, story: *The police wrote an account of the accident.*
**on account of:** because of: *On account of bad weather, the picnic was cancelled.*

**accountant** /əˈkaʊntnt/ *noun*
a person who keeps and gives information about a company's or person's money: *My accountant works on my taxes every year.* *–noun* (business) **accounting.**

**accuracy** /ˈækyərəsi/ *noun*
**1** something that is correct and true: *the accuracy of a report*
**2** the ability to hit a target: *Her accuracy with the gun surprised everyone.*

**accurate** /ˈækyərɪt/ *adjective*
exact, correct: *The numbers in the report are accurate.* *–adverb* **accurately.**

**accusation** /ˌækyəˈzeɪʃən/ *noun*
a charge of crime or wrongdoing: *Her accusation that I ate the last piece of cake was false.*

**accuse** /əˈkyuz/ *verb* **accused, accusing, accuses**
to blame: *The police accused him of theft.* *–noun* (person) **accuser.**

**ace** /eɪs/ *noun*
in the USA, a playing card marked with a letter "A" for "Ace": *In card games, the ace often has the highest number of points.*

ace

**ache** /eɪk/ *noun*
a dull pain: *I have an ache in my leg from walking too much.*|| *a toothache, headache, etc.* *–verb* **to ache.**

**achieve** /əˈʧiv/ *verb* **achieved, achieving, achieves**
to reach, gain (success, happiness, etc.): *He achieved his goals in life by having a good job and a family.* *–noun* (act) **achievement.**

**acid** /ˈæsɪd/ *noun*
a substance or liquid that has a sour taste
**acid** *adjective*
having a sour taste: *Vinegar has a strong acid taste.* *–noun* **acidity.**

**acknowledge** /ɪkˈnɑlɪʤ/ *verb* **acknowledged, acknowledging, acknowledges**
**1** to answer: *She acknowledged my smile with a wave of her hand.*
**2** to admit: *He acknowledges the fact that he is wrong.* *–noun* **acknowledgment.**

**acne** /ˈækni/ *noun*
a skin condition of red spots, especially on the face

**acorn** /ˈeɪˌkɔrn/ *noun*
the nut of the oak tree: *"Mighty oaks from little acorns grow."*

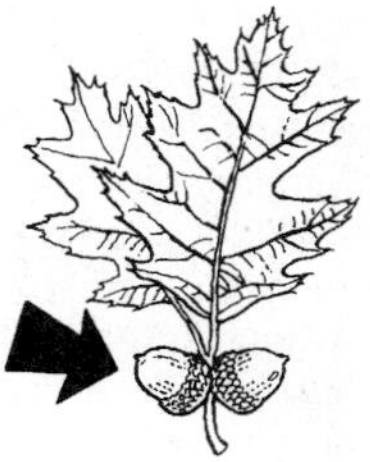
acorn

**acquaintance** /əˈkweɪntns/ *noun*
a person whom one knows, but not well: *She is an acquaintance that I see on the bus to work.*

**acquire** /əˈkwaɪr/ *verb* **acquired, acquiring, acquires**
to buy or get: *She acquired a knowledge of Spanish while living in Latin America.* *–noun* (act) **acquisition.**

**acre** /ˈeɪkər/ *noun*
a square piece of land measuring 69.57 yards (63.57 m.) on each side: *Our house is on an acre of land which gives us a nice big backyard for our garden.*

**acrobat** /'ækrəˌbæt/ *noun*
a person who performs special gymnastic movements, usually in the air

acrobats

**across** /ə'krɔs/ *preposition*
moving on or over something: *We walked across the bridge.*

**across** *adverb*
from one side to the other: *We walked across.*

**act** /ækt/ *verb*
**1** to take action: *He acted on my ideas.*
**2** to behave, to show, especially an emotion: *He acts as though he is pleased.*
**3** to perform a role: *He acted in a television program.*

**act** *noun*
**1** an event, happening: *The flood was an act of God.*
**2** a part of a play: *We especially enjoyed the third act of the play.*
**to put on an act:** to make believe, pretend: *He put on an act of being a horse to make his little brother laugh.*

**acting** /'æktɪŋ/ *noun*
performing in plays or movies: *She chose acting as a career.*

**action** /'ækʃən/ *noun*
happenings, movement: *The action of the waves hitting the beach washed away the sand.*
**to take action:** to do something quickly: *The police officer took action when he saw the robber and arrested him.*

**active** /'æktɪv/ *adjective*
busy: *She never sits down to relax; she is very active.* –*adverb* **actively.**

**activity** /æk'tɪvəti/ *noun, plural* **activities**
**1** a planned event: *The activities at the school include sports and dances.*
**2** movement: *People were running everywhere; there was a lot of activity.*

**actor** /'æktər/ *noun*
a person who performs in plays or movies: *My son is an actor in the movies.*

**actress** /'æktrɪs/ *noun, plural* **actresses**
a female actor

**actual** /'æktʃuəl/ *adjective*
real, exact: *Our actual expenses for food and clothes for last year were lower than we thought.*

**actually** /'æktʃuəli/ *adverb*
in fact, really: *Actually, that student needs to study more to pass the exams.*

**A.D.** /ˈeɪ'di/
*abbreviation of* anno Domini: (Latin for) the year of Jesus Christ's birth: *The United States became independent from England in 1776* A.D. *See:* B.C.

**ad** /æd/ *noun informal*
*short for* advertisement

**adapt** /ə'dæpt/ *verb*
to change to work in a new way: *She adapted quickly to her new job.* –*noun* **adaptation** /ˌædəp'teɪʃən/.

**add** / æd/ *verb*
**1** to put numbers together into a total: *The waiter added up the food check.*
**2** to increase the size or amount of something: *We added a room to our house. (antonym)* subtract.
**to add up:** to make sense, seem true: *What he says does not add up.*

**addict** /'ædɪkt/ *noun*
a person who is dependent on a drug or other substance: *He is a drug addict.* –*verb* **to addict** /ə'dɪkt/; –*noun* **addiction.** *See:* drug.

**addition** /ə'dɪʃən/ *noun*
the process of adding things or numbers: *the addition of 2 + 2 = 4*–*adjective* **additional;** –*adverb* **additionally** *(antonym)* subtraction.

**address** /ə'drɛs/ *noun, plural* **addresses**
**1** the location of a person, business, or institution: *My business address is 2 Wall St., New York, NY 10002.*
**2** a speech: *She gave an address to the United Nations.*

address

**address** /'ə'drɛs/ *verb*
to write an address: *The secretary addressed the envelopes before mailing them.*

**adequate** /'ædəkwɪt/ *adjective*
enough, *(synonym)* sufficient: *He makes an adequate salary, enough to pay his bills. –adverb* **adequately.**

**adjective** /'ædʒɪktɪv/ *noun*
a word that tells something about a noun: *In the sentence "The boy made a large sandwich," the word "large" is an adjective.*

**adjust** /ə'dʒʌst / *verb*
to change: *I adjusted the air conditioner to stay cool. –adjective* **adjustable.**

**administration** /əd,mɪnə'streɪʃən/ *noun*
**1** in the USA, the executive branch of the federal government, especially the President
**2** control of something, management

**admiral** /'ædmərəl/ *noun*
the highest rank of naval officers: *He is an admiral in the US Navy.*

**admire** /əd'maɪr/ *verb* **admired, admiring, admires**
to respect, approve of: *I admire how quickly she learned English. –noun* **admiration** /,ædmə'reɪʃən/.

**admission** /əd'mɪʃən/ *noun*
**1** entrance fee, the right to enter a place: *Admission to the concert was $10 per person.*
**2** acceptance at a university or school: *She was offered admission to the university.*

**admit** /əd'mɪt/ *verb* **admitted, admitting, admits**
**1** to confess, tell something: *He admitted that he had made a mistake. (antonym)* deny.
**2** to allow to enter, pass through: *We were admitted to the club by the owner.*

**adolescent** /,ædl'ɛsənt/ *noun*
a youth, especially ages 13–17

**adopt** /ə'dɑpt/ *verb*
**1** to become legal parents to a child: *We adopted two children.*
**2** (in law) to make into a law *–noun* **adoption.**

**adorable** /ə'dɔrəbəl/ *adjective*
cute: *That little girl is adorable!*

**adore** /ə'dɔr/ *verb* **adored, adoring, adores**
to worship, to love deeply: *He adores his wife.*

**adult** /ə'dʌlt/ *noun*
a person or animal who has finished growing: *At 21 years of age, he is now an adult. –noun* (condition) **adulthood** /ə'dʌlt,hʊd/.

**advance** /əd'væns/ *noun*
an improvement: *Advances in medicine make health care better.*

**advance** *verb* **advanced, advancing, advances**
to make progress: *The hikers advanced up the mountain. –noun* (condition) **advancement.**

**advantage** /əd'væntɪdʒ/ *noun*
**1** having more ability or strength than someone else: *Our experience gives us an advantage over others.*
**2** a good thing about something, a benefit: *The house is new and near a good school; it has many advantages.*
**to take advantage of: a.** to use an opportunity: *I will take advantage of my business trip to Paris to see the beautiful sights.* **b.** to cheat someone

**adventure** /əd'vɛntʃər/ *noun*
an exciting time or event: *Our camping trip turned into an adventure when we got lost.*

**adverb** /'æd,vɜrb/ *noun*
a word that describes a verb, adjective, or another adverb: *The word "really" in the sentence "I really like her" is an adverb.*

**advertise** /'ædvər,taɪz/ *verb* **advertised, advertising, advertises**
to give out information to sell a product or service: *Our company advertises on television and in newspapers. –noun* **advertisement** /,ædvər'taɪzmənt/, (business) **advertising.**

**advice** /əd'vaɪs/ *noun*
directions or opinions as given to someone about what to do: *She took my advice and did not drop out of high school.*

**advise** /əd'vaɪz/ *verb* **advised, advising, advises**
to give someone an opinion about what to do: *My teacher advised me to go to college.*

**advisor** or **adviser** /əd'vaɪzər/ *noun*
a person who gives opinions on what to do: *My college advisor said I should take courses in mathematics.*

**aerobics** /ɛ'roʊbɪks/ *noun plural*
a type of dance exercise to music: *She does aerobics for 45 minutes every morning in order to stay healthy and fit.*

aerobics

**affair** /ə'fɛr/ *noun*
**1** a business matter: *Our company lost money in that affair.*
**2** a social event, such as a party: *I have to go to a social affair this evening.*

**affect** /ə'fɛkt/ *verb*
to change: *Very hot weather affects how people feel and act.*

**USAGE NOTE:** The verb *affect* means to have an influence or cause a change. The noun *effect* means the result of this change: *The flood affected the town. The effects were homelessness and disease. See:* effect.

**affection** /ə'fɛkʃən/ *noun*
**1** a feeling of warmth for someone: *He feels affection for his grandchildren.*
**2** holding and sometimes kissing someone: *The child needs his mother's affection.* –*adjective* **affectionate.**

**afford** /ə'fɔrd/ *verb*
to be able to do or pay for something: *We can't afford to buy that expensive car; we don't have enough money.*

**affordable** /ə'fɔrdəbəl/ *adjective*
not too expensive: *There are not many affordable apartments in big cities.*

**afraid** /ə'freɪd/ *adjective*
fearful: *The child is afraid of dogs and cries everytime one comes close by.*

**African-American** /'æfrɪkən/ *noun*
an American whose ancestors were African: *He is an African-American.* –*adjective* **African-American.** *See:* black.

**USAGE NOTE:** Compare *African-American* and *black.* In the USA, the terms *African-American* and *black* are both used to talk about Americans of African descent. Some people use the term *African-American,* others prefer the term *black.* Both are acceptable.

**after** /'æftər/ *preposition*
**1** in back of, behind: *I told my dog to stay home, but he came after me.*
**2** later in time: *We had dinner after the movie.*

**after** *conjunction*
later than: *She came to the party after I did. (antonym)* before.

**afternoon** /ˌæftər'nun/ *noun*
the time between noon and evening: *At school, we play sports in the afternoon until it gets dark.*

**afterward** /'æftərwərd/ or **afterwards** *adverb*
after an event: *We went for a walk, and afterward we ate lunch.*

**again** /ə'gɛn/ *adverb*
another time, once more: *Oh, it's raining again!*

**against** /ə'gɛnst/ *preposition*
**1** next to, near: *The bookshelves are against the wall.*
**2** in contact with: *Strong winds hit against the buildings.*
**3** in opposition to: *The people voted against that new tax.*

**age** /eɪʤ/ *noun*
**1** how many years someone has lived: *The boy is 15 years of age.*
**2** a time period in life: *Some say middle age starts after 40.||My grandmother died of old age.*

**age** *verb*
to get older: *He is 60 years old but has aged well.||Wine ages in barrels.*

**agency** /'eɪʤənsi/ *noun, plural* **agencies**
**1** a part of government: *The Environmental Protection Agency tries to stop bad air and poisoned earth.*
**2** a business that helps people do something: *She found a job through an employment agency.*

**agent** /ˈeɪʤənt / *noun*
a person who does business for others, representative: *A travel agent makes airline and hotel reservations.*

**aggravate** /ˈægrəˌveɪt/ *verb* **aggravated, aggravating, aggravates**
to annoy, bother: *He aggravates me by complaining all the time.* –*noun* **aggravation.**

**aggressive** /əˈgr ɛsɪv/ *adjective*
**1** unfriendly: *That dog always barks at strangers; he's very aggressive.*
**2** competitive: *Our company has many aggressive salespeople.* –*adverb* **aggressively;** –*noun* (act) **aggression.**

**ago** /əˈgoʊ/ *adverb*
in the past: *We met for the first time five years ago.*

**agree** /əˈgri/ *verb* **agreed, agreeing, agrees**
to have the same idea: *He agreed with what I said.* –*adjective* **agreeable.**

**agreement** /əˈgri mənt/ *noun*
a decision that two or more people make: *We have an agreement not to talk about some things.*

**agriculture** /ˈægrɪˌkʌlʧər/ *noun*
the science of keeping animals and growing food: *Agriculture is a big business in North America.* –*adjective* **agricultural** /ˌægrɪˈkʌlʧərəl/.

**ahead** /əˈhɛd/ *adverb*
**1** forward: *The traffic is bad, but I am moving ahead slowly.*
**2** to a better position: *She works hard to get ahead in life. (antonym)* backward.
**ahead** *preposition*
**ahead of:** in front of: *He went ahead of everyone in line.*

**aid** /eɪd/ *verb*
to help: *I aided my friend by giving him some money.*
**aid** *noun*
help, assistance: *The Red Cross gives aid to people after floods and fires.*

**AIDS** /ˈeɪdz/
*abbreviation of* acquired immune deficiency syndrome

**aim** /eɪm/ *verb*
**1** to direct something at a point: *He aimed the basketball at the net.*
**2** to plan to do something: *She aims to go to college.*

**air** /ɛr/ *noun*
the gases around the earth, which we breathe: *The air in the country is cleaner than the air of the city.* –*verb* **to air.**

**air-condition** *verb*
to cool the air with an air conditioner: *We air-conditioned our house during the hot summer.*
–*noun* (machine) **air conditioner.**

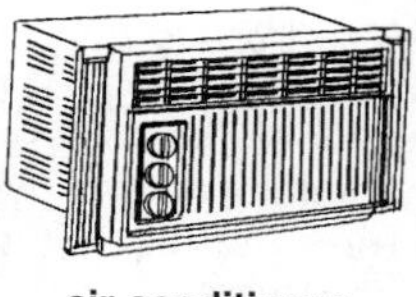
air conditioner

**air conditioning** *noun*
a machine or a system used to cool air in buildings: *The air conditioning wasn't working so our offices got very hot.*

**aircraft** /ˈɛrˌkræft/ *noun, plural* **aircraft**
an airplane, glider, or other flight vehicle: *The Air Force maintains many kinds of aircraft.*

**airfare** /ˈɛrˌfɛ r/ *noun*
the cost of an airline ticket

**airline** /ˈɛrˌlaɪn/ *noun*
a business that carries passengers and cargo by airplane: *We took American Airlines from Colombia to New York.*

**airmail** /ˈɛrˌmeɪl/ *noun*
letters, packages, etc. sent by air: *A letter sent airmail will get to Europe in a week.* –*verb* **to airmail.**

**airplane** /ˈɛrpleɪn/ *noun*
a machine for flying: *The airplane allows people to travel very far quickly.*

**airport** /ˈɛrpɔrt/ *noun*
a place where airplanes take off and land that has buildings for passengers and cargo

**aisle** /aɪl/ *noun*
an open path between rows of seats: *We walked down the aisle to our seats in the theater.*

aisle

**alarm** /əˈlɑrm/ *noun*
a warning call, bell, siren, or buzzer: *A*

A

*prisoner set off an alarm as she tried to escape.* –*verb* **to alarm.**

**alarm clock** *noun*
a clock that can be set to give a signal at a later time: *I set the alarm clock to wake me up at 7:00 A.M.*

**album** /ˈælbəm/ *noun*
a book with blank pages for saving photographs and other things: *We have a photo album of family pictures.*

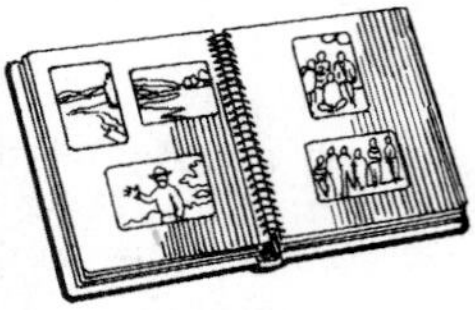
album

**alcohol** /ˈælkəˌhɔl/ *noun*
beverages made from grains and fruits, such as wine, beer, and gin: *You should not drink alcohol and then drive.*

**alcoholic** /ˌælkəˈhɔlɪk/ *adjective*
related to alcohol: *alcoholic beverages*

**alcoholic** *noun*
a person who has problems with drinking alcohol –*noun* **alcoholism** /ˈælkəˌhɔˌlɪzəm/.

**alert** /əˈlɜrt/ *adjective*
aware, ready to act quickly: *The guard stayed alert to watch for anything unusual.*

**algebra** /ˈælʤəbrə/ *noun*
a branch of mathematics using signs and symbols to show unknown numbers in a problem: *The letter x stands for 4 in the algebra problem x + 3 = 7.* –*adjective* **algebraic** /ˌælʤəˈbreɪɪk/.

**alibi** /ˈæləˌbaɪ/ *noun*
proof that a person was not near a crime scene and therefore could not have committed the crime: *The police think that he committed the crime, but his alibi proves he was out of town when it happened.*

**alien** /ˈeɪliən/ *noun*
a stranger, *(synonym)* a foreigner: *He is an alien in this country; he is here on a student visa. (antonym)* native.

**alike** /əˈlaɪk/ *adjective*
similar: *The two dresses look alike but one is more expensive.*

**alimony** /ˈæləˌmoʊni/ *noun, (no plural)*
payments a person makes to his or her former wife or husband: *He paid alimony to his former wife.*

**alive** /əˈlaɪv/ *adjective*
living, having life: *After the bad accident, he was barely alive.*

**all** /ɔl/ *adjective*
of a total: *All the students came to class.*

**all** *adverb*
**1** totally, completely: *Jack was upset because the soda was all gone.*
**2** for a given time period: *It rained all night (day, week, etc.).*

**all right: a.** well, healthy: *I feel all right today.* **b.** OK, yes: *"Would you like to join us?" "All right."* **c.** satisfactorily: *The motor in the car works all right.*

**allergic** /əˈlɜrʤɪk / *adjective*
sensitive to some plants, chemicals, dust, or foods: *When I go near plants that I'm allergic to, I start to sneeze.* –*noun* **allergy** /ˈælərʤi/.

**alley** /ˈæli/ *noun, plural* **alleys**
a path between buildings: *We walked down an alley and entered the building from the back door.*

**alligator** /ˈæləˌgeɪtər/ *noun*
a large animal (reptile) of the crocodile family, but with a shorter, wider head: *Both alligators and crocodiles have long bodies, short legs, and sharp teeth.*

alligator

**allocate** /ˈæləˌkeɪt/ *verb* **allocated, allocating, allocates**
to plan to use money for a specific purpose: *The city government allocated money for schools and the police in this year's budget.* –*noun* **allocation** /ˌæləˈkeɪʃən/.

**allow** /əˈlaʊ/ *verb*
to let, permit: *We allowed our son to use the family car.*–*adjective* **allowable** *(antonym)* forbid.

**allowance** /əˈlaʊəns/ *noun*
money for everyday expenses: *We give our daughter a weekly allowance.*

**ally** /ˈælaɪ/ *noun, plural* **allies**
a partner: *The United States of America and England were allies in World War II. (antonym)* enemy.

**ally** *verb* /əˈlaɪ/ **allies**
to combine, unite: *Two political parties allied with each other to reduce taxes.*

**almost** /'ɔlmoʊst/ *adverb*
nearly, not quite: *I have almost finished my homework.*

**alone** /ə'loʊn/ *adverb*
by oneself, without anyone else: *He is not married and lives alone.*

**along** /ə'lɔŋ/ *preposition*
**1** by the side of: *Cars are parked along the sides of the street.*
**2** in the path of: *Trucks are moving along the highway at high speed.*
**along** *adverb*
**1** forward, into the future: *I have to move along now; see you later.*
**2** with another person: *Joe brought his girlfriend along to the party.*
**to get along: a.** to leave: *I have to get along now; see you later.* **b.** to be friendly with, to be on good terms with: *My boss and I get along just fine together.*

**aloud** /ə'laʊd/ *adverb*
out loud, spoken: *The student read her poem aloud in class.*

**alphabet** /'ælfəˌbɛt/ *noun*
the letters in a language: *The English alphabet has 26 letters.*

**alphabetical** /ˌælfə'bɛtɪkəl/ *adjective*
in order of the alphabet (from A to Z): *He put the words in the list in alphabetical order.* –*adverb* **alphabetically;** –*verb* **to alphabetize** /'ælfəbəˌtaɪz/.

**already** /ɔl'rɛdi/ *adverb*
earlier: *She was already at work when her boss got there in the morning.*

**also** /'ɔlsoʊ/ *adverb*
in addition, too: *We bought a new sofa and also a new coffee table.*

**altar** /'ɔltər/ *noun*
a high flat surface like a table, for religious ceremonies: *The priest said a prayer at the altar.*

**alter** /'ɔltər/ *verb*
to change: *The tailor altered my pants because they were too tight.* –*noun* **alteration.**

**alternate** /'ɔltərnɪt/ *noun*
something different: *If that restaurant does not make what we want, we can find an alternate one that does.*

**alternate** *verb* /'ɔltərˌneɪt/ **alternated, alternating, alternates**
to move back and forth: *We alternate visiting my two grandmothers every weekend.*

**alternative** /ɔl 'tɜrnətɪv/ *noun*
another choice: *We can take a boat to Florida or, as an alternative, we can fly.*
**alternative** *adjective*
different: *An alternative way would be to travel by railroad.* –*adverb* **alternatively.**

**although** /ɔl'ðoʊ/ *conjunction*
even though: *Although he is heavy, he can still run fast.*

**altitude** /'æltəˌtud/ *noun*
distance above sea level: *Our airplane is flying at an altitude of 35,000 feet (10,660 meters).*

**altogether** /ˌɔltə'gɛðər/ *adverb*
completely: *He is altogether wrong in what he says.*|| *Altogether, 200 people went to the wedding.*

**aluminum** /ə'lumənəm/ *noun*
a lightweight, silver gray metal: *Beer and soda cans are made of aluminum.*

**always** /'ɔlweɪz/ *adverb*
**1** forever: *I will love you always.*
**2** whenever, anytime: *If you don't like that shirt, you can always wear another one.*
**3** every time: *We always go to the mountains for our vacation. (antonym)* never.

**am** /m/ *verb*
first person singular present tense form of *to be: I am ready to go now.*

**A.M.** /ˌeɪ'ɛm/
*abbreviation of* ante meridiem, the time between 12:00 midnight and 11:59 in the morning: *My meeting was at 9:00* A.M. *today. See:* P.M.

**amateur** /'æmətʃər/ *noun*
a person who does activities, such as sports, for pleasure and without pay: *He is an amateur at golf, but he loves the game.*–*noun* **amateurism.** *(antonym)* expert.

**amaze** /ə'meɪz/ *verb* **amazed, amazing, amazes**
to surprise or impress: *She plays tennis*

*so well that she amazes me!* –*noun* **amazement;** –*adverb* **amazingly.**

**ambassador** /æm'bæsədər/ *noun*
the highest level representative of a government in a foreign country: *The United States ambassador to France works in Paris.* –*noun* (job) **ambassadorship;** –*adjective* **ambassadorial.**

**ambition**
/æm'bɪʃən/ *noun*
**1** desire to succeed, *(synonym)* drive: *He has ambition and works hard to get a salary increase.*
**2** a goal, objective: *Her ambition is to become a chef.* –*adjective* **ambitious.**

**ambulance**
/'æmbyələns/ *noun*
a vehicle used to bring sick people to a hospital: *An ambulance came to the car accident in two minutes. See:* art on page 11a.

ambulance

**ambush** /'æm,bʊʃ/ *noun, plural* **ambushes**
an attack made from a hidden place or position: *A soldier hid in a tree and set an ambush for any enemy soldiers passing below.* –*verb* **to ambush.**

**American** /ə'mɛrɪkən/ *noun*
a person from the United States: *Maria is an American from Los Angeles.*

**American** *adjective*
related to the Americas: *The Central American beaches are very beautiful.*

**American dream** *noun singular*
in the USA, success, measured by having one's own house and automobile, a good education and job, as well as the promise of an even better life for one's children: *As immigrants, they achieved the American dream when their daughter became a doctor.*

**Americas** /ə'mɛrɪkəz/ *noun plural*
North, Central, and South America

**ammonia** /ə'moʊnyə/ *noun*
a strong-smelling gas that is mixed with water and used as a cleanser: *He used ammonia to wash the bathroom floor.*

**ammunition** /,æmyə'nɪʃən/ *noun*
things that can be fired from a gun or exploded, such as bullets, cannon shells, etc.

**among** /ə'mʌŋ/ *preposition*
included within: *Among her many friends, John is her favorite. See:* between.

**amount** /ə'maʊnt/ *noun*
a total, sum: *The amount of the doctor's bill is $100.*

**amount** *verb*
to add up: *The bill amounts to $20.*

**ample** /'æmpəl/ *adjective*
more than enough –*adverb* **amply** /'æmpli/.

**amputate** /'æmpyə,teɪt/ *verb*
to cut off in surgery: *The doctor amputated the patient's leg.* –*noun* **amputation.**

**amuse** /ə'myuz/ *verb*
**1** to please: *Our friend's jokes amused us.*
**2** to hold the attention of someone: *The little girl amuses herself for hours by playing with her toys.* –*adjective* **amusing** /ə'myuzɪŋ/.

**amusement** /ə'myu zmənt/ *noun*
entertainment, fun: *For amusement, we go to the movies once a week.*

**an** /ən/ *indefinite article*
one, some: *I have an idea for a good vacation; let's go to the mountains.*

---

**USAGE NOTE:** Use *an* before vowel sounds: *an apple*/*an expensive gift.* Use *a* before consonant sounds: *a door*/*a good book.* Note that the sound of the following word, not its spelling, shows whether to use *a* or *an: an umbrella* but *a unit*; *an hour* (h is silent) but *a historical novel* (h is sounded).

---

**analysis** /ə'næləsɪs/ *noun, plural* **analyses** /-,siz/
work done to find facts and solutions to problems: *We did an analysis of the problem and proposed solutions to it.*

**analyze** /'ænl,aɪz/ *verb* **analyzed, analyzing, analyzes**
to examine something to understand it: *A doctor analyzed a patient's X-rays.*

**anatomy** /ə'nætəmi/ *noun, plural* **anatomies**
the structure of a living thing: *Is the anatomy of a human similar to that of a monkey?* –*adjective* **anatomical** /,ænə'tamɪkəl/; –*adverb* **anatomically.**

**ancestor** /ˈæn,sɛstər/ *noun*
the persons from whom one's family comes (great-grandmother, father, etc.): *She can name her ancestors all the way back to sixteenth-century Spain.* –*noun* **ancestry;** –*adjective* **ancestral.**

**anchor** /ˈæŋkər/ *noun*
**1** a heavy metal device that keeps boats from moving: *Sailors put the ship's anchor into the water.*

anchor

**2** the main person on TV news –*verb* **to anchor.**

**ancient** /ˈeɪnʧənt/ *adjective*
very old: *In school, we studied the ancient Greek and Roman civilizations.*

**and** /ənd/ *conjunction*
in addition, plus: *She likes to fish and to play tennis.*

**anemia** /əˈnimiə/ *noun*
a condition of not having enough oxygen-carrying red cells in one's blood: *Anemia can come from not eating the right foods.* –*adjective* **anemic.**

**anesthesia** /,ænəsˈθiʒə/ *noun*
the loss of feeling in the body, especially because of a drug: *I was under anesthesia when I had an operation.*

**angel** /ˈeɪnʤəl/ *noun*
a spiritual being: *Many kinds of angels are found in the Bible.* –*adjective* **angelic** /ænˈʤɛlɪk/; –*adverb* **angelically.**

**anger** /ˈæŋgər/ *noun*
a strong negative feeling: *After their argument, he showed his anger by hitting the other man in the face.*

**anger** *verb*
to make angry: *Her critical words angered me.*

**angle** /ˈæŋgəl/ *noun*
the figure formed by straight lines coming together at one point: *A 90-degree angle has one line that is straight up and another line that is level with the floor.* –*verb* **to angle.**

**Anglo** /ˈæŋgloʊ/ *noun, plural* **Anglos**
a white-skinned North American not of Hispanic heritage *See:* white.

**angry** /ˈæŋgri/ *adjective* **angrier, angriest**
feeling anger: *Someone stole his wallet and he is very angry about it.* –*adverb* **angrily** /ˈæŋgrəli/. *See:* art on page 18a.

**animal** /ˈænəməl/ *noun*
any creature that is not a plant: *Horses are animals.*

**ankle** /ˈæŋkəl/ *noun*
the joint connecting the foot and lower leg: *She fell on the sidewalk and broke her ankle. See:* art on page 21a.

**anniversary** /,ænəˈvɜrsəri/ *noun, plural* **anniversaries**
one or more years after the date on which an event took place: *Our first wedding anniversary was last Tuesday.*

**announce** /əˈnaʊns/ *verb* **announced, announcing, announces**
to say something in public: *The parents announced the wedding of their daughter in the newspaper.* –*noun* **announcement** /əˈnaʊnsmənt/.

**annoy** /əˈnɔɪ/ *verb*
to cause a little bit of anger: *The noise from the street traffic annoyed me.* –*noun* **annoyance.**

**annual** /ˈænyuəl/ *adjective*
happening once every year: *The annual rainfall in this area is light.* –*adverb* **annually.**

**anonymous** /əˈnɑnəməs/ *adjective*
not named, unknown: *An anonymous person called the police to say who the car thief was.*

**another** /əˈnʌðər/ *pronoun*
a different or additional person (animal, thing): *He ate one hamburger, then ordered another.*

**another** *adjective*
different: *She loves another man now.*

**answer** /ˈænsər/ *noun*
a spoken or written response, reply: *I got an answer to my letter yesterday.*

**answer** *verb*
to reply: *The company answered that it is interested in my offer.*

**ant** /ænt/ *noun*
a small black insect: *There were many ants on the picnic table in the park.*

ant

**antacid** /æntˈæsɪd/ *noun*
a liquid used to stop an acid, burning

A

feeling: *He took an antacid for his upset stomach.*

**antelope** /ˈæntl̩ˌoʊp/ *noun*
fast, four-legged animal with horns

antelope

**antenna** /ænˈtɛnə/ *noun, plural* **antennas**
**1** a wire, dish, etc., that receives or sends electronic signals: *The antenna for my car radio is broken.*
**2** *plural* **antennae** /-ni/**:** a thread-like feeler on the heads of some animals: *An ant has two antennae on its head.*

**antibiotic** /ˌæntɪbaɪˈɑtɪk/ *noun*
a medicine that fights off disease: *I took an antibiotic for my ear infection.*

**anticipate** /ænˈtɪsəˌpeɪt/ *verb* **anticipated, anticipating, anticipates**
to await, expect: *I anticipate that the weather will change soon. –noun* **anticipation** /ænˌtɪsəˈpeɪʃən/.

**antidote** /ˈæntɪˌdoʊt/ *noun*
something that stops a poison: *The doctor gave an antidote for the poison the boy had eaten.*

**antifreeze** /ˈæntɪˌfriz/ *noun*
a liquid used in engine radiators in the winter: *Because he forgot to put antifreeze in his car radiator, it wouldn't start in the cold weather.*

**antihistamine** /ˌæntɪˈhɪstəˌmin/ *noun*
medicine that stops the symptoms of allergies and colds

**antiperspirant** /ˌæntɪˈpɛrspərənt/ *noun*
something put under the arms to stop sweating and odor

---

**USAGE NOTE:** Compare *antiperspirant* and *deodorant.* An *antiperspirant* stops a person from sweating, but a *deodorant* stops sweat from smelling bad.

---

**antique** /ænˈtik/ *noun adjective*
something that is valuable because it is old: *The clock in the hallway is an antique.*

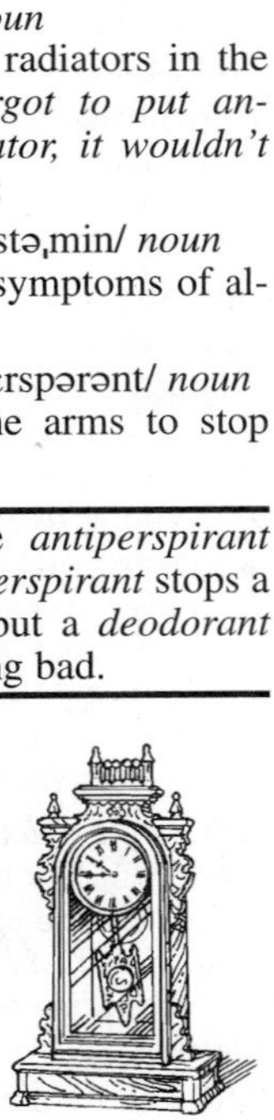
antique

**antiseptic** /ˌæntəˈsɛptɪk/ *noun*
a chemical that stops bacteria from causing disease: *I put antiseptic on the cut.*

**antonym** /ˈæntəˌnɪm/ *noun*
a word that means the opposite of another word: *"Happy" is an antonym of "sad." (antonym)* synonym.

**anxiety** /æŋzaiəti/ *noun, plural* **anxieties**
worry, nervous fear: *As the man waited for his wife to come out of a hospital operation, his anxiety increased.*

**anxious** /æŋkʃəs/ *adjective*
impatient, worried: *The examination was difficult, and the student was anxious about failing it.–adverb* **anxiously.** *(antonym)* relaxed.

**any** /ˈɛni/ *pronoun*
**1** some, an amount of something: *My friend asked me for money, but I didn't have any with me.*
**2** all, a total amount: *I told him he could have any money that I have at home.*

**any** *adjective*
**1** the question and negative form of some: *I don't have any money.*
**2** all: *I'm going fishing, and I will give you any fish that I catch.*

**any** *adverb*
at all: *I was ill yesterday and I don't feel any better today.*

**anybody** /ˈɛniˌbɑdi/ *pronoun*
anyone: *Anybody can say what they think.*

**anyhow** /ˈɛniˌhaʊ/ *adverb*
**1** in any way: *He can pay for the purchase anyhow he wants: with cash, check or credit card.*
**2** no matter: *Anyhow, I don't care what grade I get, if I pass.*

**anymore** /ˌɛniˈmɔr/ *adverb*
now, any longer: *They moved away; they don't live here anymore.*

**anything** /ˈɛniˌθɪŋ/ *noun*
any object, occurrence, or matter: *I would give anything to be beautiful. –pronoun* **anything.**

**anytime** /ˈɛniˌtaɪm/ *adverb*
whenever, at any time: *We can leave anytime you are ready.*

**anyway** /ˈɛniˌweɪ/ *adverb*
**1** in any way or manner: *You can pay the bill any way you want: cash, check or credit card.*

**2** and so (to continue a discussion): *Anyway, we finally found out what the problem was.*
**3** either, in addition: *It's OK that we can't go for a walk because I didn't feel like going anyway.*

**anywhere** /'ɛni,wɛr/ *adverb*
at any place: *You can sit (walk, go, etc.) anywhere you want.*

**apart** /ə'pɑrt/ *adjective*
not together: *If my parents are apart, they telephone each other every day.*

**apart** *adverb*
in parts or pieces: *The mechanic took the engine apart.*

**apartment** /ə'pɑrtmənt/ *noun*
a room or set of rooms for living in a building or house: *We have a two-bedroom apartment.*

**ape** /eɪp/ *noun*
a gorilla, monkey, or similar animal

ape

**apiece** /ə'pis/ *adverb*
each: *Those tennis balls cost $1 apiece.*

**apologize** /ə'pɑlə,ʤaɪz/ *verb* **apologized, apologizing, apologizes**
to say one is sorry for doing something: *The man apologized to the woman for spilling coffee on her dress.*

**apology** /ə'pɑləʤi/ *noun, plural* **apologies**
an expression of regret for doing something wrong: *The woman accepted his apology for spilling coffee on her dress.*

**apostrophe** /ə'pɑstrəfi/ *noun*
the punctuation mark ('): *An apostrophe is used in contractions ("isn't," "doesn't") and possessives ("that man's wife").*

**apparent** /ə'pærənt/ *adjective*
clear: *He's very unhappy, and it is apparent that he wants to leave now.* –*adverb* **apparently.**

**appeal** /ə'pil/ *verb*
**1** to please: *The idea of spending two weeks on vacation appeals to me.*
**2** to ask for help: *The Red Cross appealed for money to help people after the hurricane.* –*noun* **appeal.**

**appear** /ə'pɪr/ *verb*
**1** coming into view: *The sun suddenly appeared from behind a big cloud.*
**2** to seem, to be likely: *It appears the weather will be nice.*

**appearance** /ə'pɪrəns/ *noun*
how one looks and dresses: *The woman has such a nice appearance.*

**appendix** /ə'pɛndɪks/ *noun, plural* **appendixes** or **appendices** /-də, siz/
**1** in the body, an organ located on the right side of the abdomen
**2** something added on, especially to the end of a book

**appetite** /'æpə,taɪt/ *noun*
desire for food, drink, or pleasure: *Our son is a football player and has a big appetite for meat.*

**applaud** /ə'plɔd/ *verb*
to show approval by striking one's hands together, (*syn.*) to clap: *The audience applauded the singer's performance.* –*noun* **applause** /ə'plɔz/.

**apple** /'æpəl/ *noun*
a round fruit with red, green, or yellow skin and a sweet, juicy flesh: *I ate an apple for dessert. See:* art on page 3a.

apple

**applesauce** /'æpəl,sɔs/ *noun, (no plural)*
apples crushed and cooked into a soft state: *Before they get teeth, babies enjoy eating applesauce.*

**appliance** /ə'plaɪəns/ *noun*
an electrical machine used for a specific purpose in the home: *Major appliances include stoves, refrigerators, washing machines, and dishwashers.*

**applicant** /'æplɪkənt/ *noun*
a person looking for a specific job: *We have ten applicants for the job of secretary.*

**application** /,æplɪkeɪʃən/ *noun*
a form for writing down information for a purpose, such as a job or a loan: *I filled out an application for a job at the store.*

**apply** /ə'plaɪ/ *verb* **applied, applying, applies**
**1** to ask for admission or assistance: *I applied to the state university to study.*
**2** to be meaningful to, to relate to: *This letter does not apply to you.*

A

**appointment** /ə'pɔɪntmənt/ *noun*
a time, place, and date to see someone: *I have an appointment tomorrow with my teacher.*

**appreciate** /ə'priʃiˌeɪt/ *verb* **appreciated, appreciating, appreciates**
to be thankful for: *The student appreciated the extra help from her teacher.*

**appreciation** /əˌpriʃi'eɪʃən/ *noun*
gratitude, thankfulness: *The man showed his appreciation to the waiter by giving him a big tip. –adjective* **appreciative** /ə'priʃətɪv/.

**apprentice** /ə'prɛntɪs/ *noun*
one who is learning a skill or trade: *My son is an apprentice in a furniture maker's workshop. –noun* **apprenticeship** /ə'prɛntɪˌʃɪp/.

**approach** /ə'proʊʧ/ *noun, plural* **approaches**
**1** a way of handling a situation: *She took a friendly approach in talking with her neighbors about the problem.*
**2** a way or path toward something: *The pilot made a slow, gradual approach to the airport runway.*

**approach** *verb* **approaches**
to move toward: *As I approached the house, I saw that the door was open.*

**appropriate** /ə'proʊpriɪt/ *adjective*
correct, right: *It was not appropriate for her boss to ask her to babysit for his children.*

**approval** /ə'pruvəl/ *noun*
**1** permission, consent: *The owner gave his approval for a raise in pay for all employees. (antonym)* refusal.
**2** admiration, praise: *I hope my new girlfriend gets my parents' approval. –verb* **approve** /ə'pruv/

**approximate** /ə'prɑksəmɪt/ *adjective*
estimated, not exact: *The builder gave an approximate cost for fixing the roof.*

**approximate** *verb* /'ə'prɑksəˌmeɪt/ **approximated, approximating, approximates**
to estimate, guess: *The mechanic approximated the cost of a new engine for my car. –adverb* **approximately;** *–noun* **approximation** /əˌprɑksə'meɪʃən/.

**apricot** /'æprɪˌkɑt/ *noun*
a small, peach-like fruit *See:* art on page 3a.

**April** /'eɪprəl/ *noun*
the fourth month of the year, the month between March and May: *April has 30 days.*

**apron** /'eɪprən/ *noun*
a cotton covering worn over one's clothes to keep them clean

**aptitude** /'æptəˌtud/ *noun*
ability to do something easily: *That student has an aptitude for mathematics.*

**aquarium** /ə'kwɛriəm/ *noun, plural* **aquariums**
a glass tank used to keep fish

aquarium

**arc** /ɑrk/ *noun*
a curved path or a section of a curve: *The diagram showed an arc between the two points.*

**arcade** /ɑr'keɪd/ *noun*
a building with shops or amusements

arcade

**arch** /ɑrʧ/ *noun, plural* **arches**
(in architecture) a curved structure: *The arches inside a big church are marvelous to see. –verb* **to arch.**

**architect** /'ɑrkəˌtɛkt/ *noun*
a trained professional who does plans for buildings: *The architect drew the floor plans for the new school. –noun* **architecture.**

**are** /ər/ *verb*
*present plural of* to be

**area** /'ɛriə/ *noun*
**1** a place, location: *The picnic area is near the parking lot.*
**2** one's field of knowledge: *Marketing is not my area; I'm in accounting.*
**3** the size of a flat surface measured by multiplying the length by the width: *What's the area of your garden?*

**area code** *noun*
in the USA and Canada, the first three numbers of a telephone number, used in making a long-distance call: *My tele-*

*phone number in Michigan is 555-6543, area code 313.*

**arena** /ə'rinə/ *noun*
a large building for sports and events such as concerts: *The sports arena has basketball games and rock concerts.*

arena

**argue** /'ɑrgyu/ *verb* **argued, arguing, argues**
to disagree, to fight with words: *His parents argue every day.*

**argument** /'ɑrgyəmənt/ *noun*
a difference of opinion, verbal disagreement: *Every discussion with him turns into an argument. –adjective* **argumentative** /ˌɑrgyə'mɛntətɪv/.

**arise** /ə'raɪz/ *verb formal* **arose** /ə'roʊz/, **arisen** /ə'rɪzən/ , **arising, arises**
to get out of bed, awaken: *He arose at noon.*

**arithmetic** /ə'rɪθməˌtɪk/ *noun*
addition, subtraction, multiplication, and division

**arm** /ɑrm/ *noun*
**1** the part of the upper human body that goes from the shoulder to the hand: *The mother put her arms around her child.*
**2** the parts of objects that are similar to human arms: *The arms of the chair were too high. See:* art on page 21a.

**arm** *verb*
to give someone weapons: *The military arms its soldiers with modern weapons.*

**armadillo** /ˌɑrmə'dɪloʊ/ *noun, plural* **armadillos**
an animal that digs for food and shelter in the ground and has tough skin made of hard plates: *The armadillo is found in the American South and in Central America.*

armadillo

**armchair** /'ɑrmˌʧɛr/ *noun*
a chair with parts for one's arms

**armed** /ɑrmd/ *adjective*
having a weapon: *The criminal is armed with a pistol and is dangerous.*

**armor** /'ɑrmər/ *noun*
a covering worn by a soldier or on a piece of military equipment for protection: *Armor stopped the bullet. –noun* (military building) **armory.**

**armpit** /'ɑrmˌpɪt/ *noun*
the place under the arm where it joins the shoulder: *He puts deodorant on his armpits after he showers.*

**army** /'ɑrmi/ *noun, plural* **armies**
soldiers and tanks that fight on land: *The army gathered on the border to attack its neighbor.*

**aroma** /ə'roʊmə/ *noun*
a pleasant smell, especially of cooking: *The aroma of coffee filled the air. –adjective* **aromatic.**

**around** /ə'raʊnd/ *preposition*
**1** in a circular motion: *The teacher told the student to turn around in his seat and pay attention.*
**2** *informal* approximately, about: *I'll meet you at the restaurant around noon.*

**around** *adverb*
about: *We visited the shopping center and just looked around.*

**arouse** /ə'raʊz/ *verb* **aroused, arousing, arouses**
to awaken or excite *–noun* **arousal.**

**arrange** /ə'reɪnʤ/ *verb* **arranged, arranging, arranges**
to make plans, to organize: *The manager arranged the papers on her desk and then began work.*

**arrangement** /ə'reɪnʤmənt/ *noun*
agreement, understanding: *Our arrangement with our neighbor is to take turns shoveling snow from the sidewalk.*

**arrest** /ə'rɛst/ *noun*
the taking or holding of a person, by police, for breaking the law: *She was put under arrest after robbing the store. –verb* **to arrest.**

A

**arrival** /ə'raɪvəl/ *noun*
**1** the coming to a place, appearance: *The arrival of my airline flight is at gate 10.*
**2** a person who has recently reached a new destination: *That student is a new arrival on campus. (antonym)* departure.

**arrive** /ə'raɪv/ *verb* **arrived, arriving, arrives**
to reach a place: *We arrived in town yesterday.*

**arrogant** /'ærəgənt/ *adjective*
self-important: *Ever since he got a new job, he's been arrogant. –adverb* **arrogantly;** *–noun* (attitude) **arrogance.**

**arrow** /'æroʊ/ *noun*
a long thin piece of wood, metal, or plastic with a point at one end and feathers at the other: *People shoot arrows at targets.*

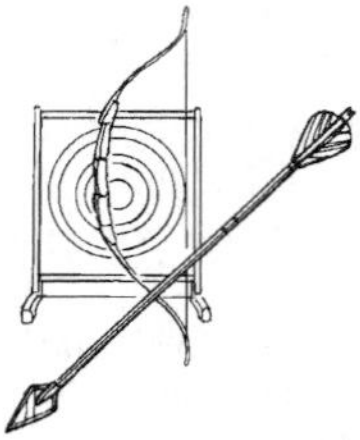
arrow

**arson** /'ɑrsən/ *noun*
the setting of fires on purpose: *The store burned down, and the police suspected arson. –noun* (person) **arsonist.**

**art** /ɑrt/ *noun*
making or expressing beauty by painting, sculpture, architecture, music, literature, drama, dance, etc.: *That museum has a great collection of art.*

**artery** /'ɑrtəri/ *noun, plural* **arteries**
one of the large blood vessels going from the heart: *One of the patient's heart arteries is blocked.*

**arthritis** /ɑr'θraɪtɪs/ *noun*
the painful swelling of joints such as in the hands, hips, and knees *–adjective* **arthritic.**

**article** /'ɑrtɪkəl/ *noun*
**1** a thing, object: *Articles of clothing are kept in the drawer.*
**2** a short written piece: *I read a magazine article on a new type of medicine.*
**3** (in grammar) one of a set of adjectives used to limit a noun: *The English definite article is "the"; the English indefinite articles are "a" and "an."*

**artificial** /ˌɑrtə'fɪʃəl/ *adjective*
made by humans, not made from natural things: *Artificial sweeteners are used in soft drinks. –adverb* **artificially.**

**artist** /'ɑrtɪst/ *noun*
a person who creates art, such as a painter or musician *–adjective* **artistic.**

**as** /əz/ *adverb*
to the same amount as someone or something else: *He is just as willing to discuss the problem as you are.*

**as** *conjunction*
**1** to the same degree, amount: *She is as intelligent as she is pretty.*
**2** because: *He fell asleep on the sofa, as he was so tired.*
**3** in the same way: *Walk as fast as I am walking.*

**as** *preposition*
**1** in the role of: *He works as a cook.*
**2** in the same way: *We agree as a group on how to handle the problem.*

**ASAP** or **asap**
*abbreviation of* as soon as possible: *Call me ASAP.*

**ash** /æʃ/ *noun, plural* **ashes**
the powder left after something has burned: *He dropped his cigarette ash in the ashtray.*

**ashamed** /ə'ʃeɪmd/ *adjective*
feeling guilt: *He failed the test and was ashamed of himself because he did not study for it.*

**ashore** /ə'ʃɔr/ *adverb*
on shore, on land: *After arriving in port, the ship's passengers went ashore to see the sights.*

**ashtray** /'æʃˌtreɪ/ *noun*
a type of dish for tobacco ashes: *I put my cigarette out in the ashtray.*

**Asian** /'eɪʒən/ *adjective*
related to Asia: *Asian products are sold all over the world.*

**Asian** *noun*
a person from Asia: *She is an Asian from Korea.*

**aside** /ə'saɪd/ *adverb*
to one side, away: *He put his newspaper aside and watched TV.*

**aside** *adverb*
**aside from:** except for: *Aside from the rainy weather, our vacation was fun.*

**ask** /æsk/ *verb*
to question: *I asked my friend how she feels.*

---

**USAGE NOTE:** *To ask* is the most common verb used to request information or an answer from someone. *To inquire* is more formal and often used in writing. *To question someone* suggests doubt, such as in: *The police questioned a man about the theft.*

---

**asleep** /ə'slip/ *adjective*
sleeping: *The baby is asleep now. (antonym)* awake.

**asphalt** /'æs,fɔlt/ *noun*
a black coal-based covering for roads or roofs: *a road made of asphalt*

**aspirin** /'æsprɪn/ *noun, plural* **aspirin** or **aspirins**
a painkiller in tablet form: *I had a headache and took two aspirin(s).*

aspirin

**ass** /'æs/ *noun, plural* **asses**
a donkey: *The ass is often used to carry things over the mountains.*

**assassinate** /ə'sæsə,neɪt/ *verb* **assassinated, assassinating, assassinates**
to murder someone important in a planned way: *President Kennedy was assassinated in 1963.* *–noun* (killer) **assassin** /ə'sæsən/ (act) **assassination** /ə,sæsə'neɪʃən/.

**assault** /ə'sɔlt/ *verb*
to attack: *A thief assaulted me with a club.* *–noun* **assault.**

**assemble** /ə'sɛmbəl/ *verb* **assembled, assembling, assembles**
to put or come together: *The workers in that factory assemble trucks.*||*Students assembled on the classroom.*

**assembly** /ə'sɛmbli/ *noun, plural* **assemblies**
**1** putting parts of something together: *The assembly of a gun by a soldier can be done in seconds.*
**2** a gathering of people: *The assembly of students takes place in the auditorium.*

**asset** /'æsɛt/ *noun*
an important person, thing, or quality: *She is very talented and is a real asset to our company.*

**assign** /ə'saɪn/ *verb*
to give a job to someone to do: *My boss assigned me the job of finding new offices to rent.* *–noun* **assignment.**

**assignment** /ə'sa ɪnmənt/ *noun*
a job, duty, etc. given to someone by another person: *Our teacher gives a lot of homework assignments.*

**assist** /ə'sɪst/ *verb*
to help someone: *My friend assisted me in moving to a new apartment.*

**assistance** /ə'sɪstəns/ *noun*
help in doing something: *I really needed my friend's assistance in helping me to move.*
**public assistance:** (welfare); money or food given by the government to the homeless and other people in need of financial aid

**assistant** /ə'sɪstənt/ *noun*
a person who helps someone else at work: *Her assistant types letters and answers the telephone.*

**associate** /ə'soʊʃiɪt/ *noun*
a coworker or partner: *My associates and I work for the city government.*
**associate** *verb* /'ə'soʊʃi,eɪt/ **associated, associating, associates**
to work, socialize with: *We associate with our neighbors at church.*

**associate degree** *noun*
in the USA, a rank one earns after a two-year program at a college or university *See:* B.A., USAGE NOTE.

**association** /ə,soʊsi'eɪʃən/ *noun*
a group of people with shared interests: *Our company belongs to the National Association of Manufacturers.*

**assorted** /ə'sɔrtɪd/ *adjective*
of different kinds, mixed: *The bowl has assorted candies.* *–noun* **assortment.**

**assume** /ə'sum/ *verb* **assumed, assuming, assumes**
to believe something is true without knowing: *I assume that the moving truck will be here this morning. –noun* **assumption.**

**assure** /ə'ʃʊr/ *verb* **assured, assuring, assures**
to promise that something is true: *I assure you that I'm telling you the truth. –noun* **assurance.**

**asterisk** /'æstərɪsk/ *noun*
the symbol (*) often used in writing to show that there is a comment at the bottom of the page or that something has been left out

**asthma** /'æzmə/ *noun*
a medical condition that makes it hard to breathe: *My friend has asthma.*

**astonish** /ə'stɑnɪʃ/ *verb*
to greatly surprise: *I am astonished at how expensive the rents are in this city.*

**astrology** /ə'strɑləʤi/ *noun*
belief in the influence of stars, planets, sun, moon, etc. on human affairs and events *–noun* (person) **astrologer.**

**astronaut** /'æstrəˌnɔt/ *noun*
a person who goes into outer space: *The astronauts trained for years in how to use their spacecraft.*

astronaut

**astronomer** /ə'strɑnəmər/ *noun*
a scientist who studies the planets, stars, sun, etc., of outer space: *Many astronomers work at night, looking at the stars. –noun* **astronomy.**

**at** /ət/ *preposition*
**1** toward, in the direction of: *I looked at her and smiled.*
**2** during, while: *He works at night.*
**3** located in, in the position of: *The information is at the bottom of the page.||She is at her office.*
**4** related to time: *He leaves work at five o'clock.*
**5** doing, engaged in: *She is hard at work on a project.*
**6** in the condition of: *The country is at peace now.*
**7** in a superlative description: at most, at least, at best, at worst, etc.: *I've been waiting at least three hours!*

**ate** /eɪt/ *verb*
*past tense of* to eat: *This morning, I ate eggs for breakfast.*

**athlete** /'æθˌlit/ *noun*
a person trained in or who is good at exercises and sports: *His son was an excellent athlete who played several team sports.*

**athletic** /æθ'lɛtɪk/ *adjective*
related to sports: *She entered many athletic competitions. –adverb* **athletically;** *–noun plural* (sports) **athletics.**

**Atlantic** /ət'læntɪk/ *noun*
the ocean located between Europe and Africa on one side and North and South America on the other: *New York is on the Atlantic (Ocean). –adjective* **Atlantic.**

**atlas** /'ætləs/ *noun, plural* **atlases**
a collection of maps in a book: *Our world atlas has maps of every country.*

**ATM**
*abbreviation of* automated teller machine *See:* art on page 10a.

ATM

**USAGE NOTE:** *ATMs* are found in business districts and shopping malls. People use them to get cash from their bank accounts.

**atmosphere** /'ætməsˌfɪr/ *noun*
**1** the air above the earth
**2** the special feeling created in a place or by a thing: *A reading room in a library has a quiet atmosphere.*

**atom** /'ætəm/ *noun*
the smallest unit of matter: *Atoms form molecules that make up matter. –adjective* **atomic.**

**attach** /ə'tæʧ/ *verb* **attaches**
to put something on: *I attached a note to my report. (antonym)* detach.

**attachment** /ə'tæʧmənt/ *noun*
something added on: *A vacuum cleaner has attachments such as a brush.*

**attack** /ə'tæk/ *verb*
**1** to strike: *The criminal attacked his victim with a knife.*
**2** to criticize strongly: *The critics attacked the writer's latest book as weak.* –*noun* (person) **attacker;** –*verb* **to attack.**

**attempt** /ə'tɛmpt/ *verb*
to try: *He attempted to pass the examination, but failed.*

**attempt** *noun*
an effort: *She made an attempt to call, but no one was home.*

**attend** /ə'tɛnd/ *verb*
to be present at: *I attended the wedding at the church.*

**attendance** /ə'tɛndəns/ *noun*
presence: *My attendance at my brother's wedding was required.*

**attention** /ə'tɛnʃən/ *noun*
looking and listening: *His attention to his work was interrupted by the telephone.*

**attic** /'ætɪk/ *noun*
a space under the roof of a house: *We put old furniture and books in our attic.*

attic

**attitude** /'ætə,tud/ *noun*
feelings or ideas about someone or something: *She has a good attitude toward work; she's always cheerful.*

**attorney** /ə'tɜrni/ *noun*
a lawyer: *The attorneys for the company were in court today.*

**attract** /ə'trækt/ *verb*
to create interest: *San Francisco attracts millions of tourists each year.*

**attraction** /ə'trækʃən/ *noun*
**1** appeal: *Disneyland is a popular attraction.*
**2** the ability and quality in a person to attract, *(synonym)* charm: *His smile and easy manner were attractions that drew the public to him.*

**attractive** /ə'træktɪv/ *adjective*
**1** appealing, interesting: *I have an offer of a new job at an attractive salary.*
**2** causing interest, *(synonym)* charming: *She is a very attractive woman with many admirers.* –*adverb* **attractively.**

**auction** /'ɔkʃən/ *noun*
a public sale of things that people offer bids on: *When the old woman died, her son held an auction of her furniture.* –*verb* **to auction.**

**audience** /'ɔdiəns/ *noun*
the people who come to listen to and watch an event: *The audience at the rock music concert was very loud.*

audience

**audio** /'ɔdi,oʊ/ *noun*
related to sound and sound equipment (radio, stereo, etc.): *The audio of the TV was not good.* –*adjective* **audio.**

**audiovisual** /,ɔdioʊ'vɪʒuəl/ *adjective*
related to teaching aids, such as charts, films, television and other forms of non-written instruction: *Some students prefer audiovisual learning to using books.*

**audit** /'ɔdɪt/ *noun*
an official examination of an individual's or company's business records: *An accountant did an audit of our records.* –*verb* **to audit.**

**auditorium** /,ɔdə'tɔriəm/ *noun*
a large room with seats and often a stage for lectures and entertainment

auditorium

**August** /'ɔgəst/ *noun*
the eighth month of the year, between July and September

**aunt** /ænt/ *noun*
the sister of one's father or mother, or the wife of one's uncle: *My aunt Betty is my mother's sister. See:* art on page 13a.

**author** /'ɔθər/ *noun*
a person who writes a book, article,

poem, etc.: *Cervantes is one of the most famous authors in the Spanish language.*

**authority** /ə'θɔrəti/ *noun*
**1** power, control: *The company's owner gave each manager the authority to spend up to $10,000 on travel.*
**2** expert, master: *Professor Smith is an authority on chemistry.*
**3** *plural* **authorities:** people in charge, specifically government: *Government authorities arrested a thief.*

**authorization** /ˌɔθərə'zeɪʃən/ *noun*
the giving of permission (authority, the right, etc.): *The company gave authorization to all managers to spend money as they wished.* –*verb* **to authorize.**

**autobiography** /ˌɔtəbaɪ'ɑgrəfi/ *noun, plural* **autobiographies**
the story of a person's life written by that person

**autograph** /'ɔtəˌgræf/ *noun*
one's signature: *The boy asked a famous baseball player for his autograph.*

**automatic** /ˌɔtə'mætɪk/ *adjective*
working by itself: *The doors to the department store are automatic.* –*adverb* **automatically.**

**automated teller machine** *noun*
an ATM, a computerized bank machine for obtaining cash, seeing one's account balances, and making deposits: *Automated teller machines are very convenient, especially on weekends.*

**automobile** /ˌɔtəmə'bil/ *noun*
a car: *The automobile gives us a lot of personal freedom to go places.* –*adjective* **automotive.**

**autopsy** /'ɔˌtɑpsi/ *noun, plural* **autopsies**
a medical examination of a dead human body to find out what caused death

**autumn** /'ɔtəm/ *noun*
the season between summer and winter: *The weather is a little cold in autumn.*

**available** /ə'veɪləbəl/ *adjective*
free: *I am available tomorrow to see you.* –*noun* **availability** /əˌveɪlə'bɪləti/.

**avenue** /'ævəˌnyu/ *noun*
a wide street, often a main street: *People love to walk down the avenues of Paris. See:* street, USAGE NOTE.

**average** /'ævrɪʤ/ *noun*
the number that comes from adding all items in a group then dividing the total by the number of items: *The average of 10, 16, and 4 is 10; that is, 10 plus 16 plus 4 equals 30, and 30 divided by 3 is 10.* –*verb* **to average.**

**average** *adjective*
ordinary, neither very good nor very bad: *He's not excellent; he's just an average child.*

**avoid** /ə'vɔɪd/ *verb*
to stay away from: *She avoids walking on dark streets at night.* –*adjective* **avoidable;** –*noun* **avoidance.**

**await** /ə'weɪt/ *verb*
to wait for something: *I am awaiting an answer to my application for the job.*

**awake** /ə'weɪk/ *verb* **awoke,** /əwoʊk/ or **awoken, awaking, awakes**
to get someone up from sleep: *The mother awoke the baby from its afternoon nap.*

**awake** /ə'weɪk/ *adjective*
not sleeping: *The baby is awake now and wants to eat.*

**award** /ə'wɔrd/ *verb*
to give a prize (honor, praise, etc.): *The school principal awarded a prize in history to the best student.*

**award** *noun*
a prize honor, etc. given to someone for outstanding performance: *The teacher gave her best student an award.*

**aware** /ə'wɛr/ *adjective*
having an understanding of: *A newspaper reporter must be aware of current events.* –*noun* **awareness.**

**away** /ə'weɪ/ *adverb*
somewhere else: *When no one answered the doorbell, the stranger went away.*

**awesome** /'ɔsəm/ *adjective*
creating great admiration: *The size of the Grand Canyon is awesome.*

**awful** /'ɔfəl/ *adjective*
bad: *We are having awful weather this week, cold and rainy.* –*adverb* **awfully.**

**awhile** /ə'waɪl/ *adverb*
for a short time: *I'll stay awhile; then I must leave.*

**awkward** /'ɔkwərd/ *adjective*
not smooth, embarrassing: *He runs with an awkward movement.* –*adverb* **awkwardly;** –*noun* **awkwardness.**

**awning** /ˈɔnɪŋ/ *noun*
a shade usually hung outside to keep the sun out of a window: *Stores and restaurants in our neighborhood use awnings on sunny days.*

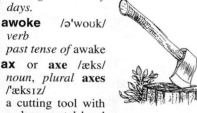

awning

**awoke** /əˈwoʊk/ *verb*
*past tense of* awake

**ax** or **axe** /æks/ *noun, plural* **axes** /ˈæksɪz/
a cutting tool with a sharp metal head on a long wooden handle: *He chopped the tree down with an ax.* –*verb* **to ax** or **axe.**

ax

**axis** /ˈæksɪs/ *noun, plural* **axes** /ˈækˌsiz/
**1** a straight line on which points are marked: *I drew a horizontal and a vertical axis on a sheet of paper.*
**2** a straight line around which an object turns: *The earth rotates on its axis.*

axis

**axle** /ˈæksəl/ *noun*
a metal pole on which wheels turn: *My car's rear axle needs grease.*

# B, b

**B, b** /bi/ *noun* **B's, b's** or **Bs, bs**
**1** the second letter of the English alphabet
**2** the grade in school, below an A, the highest: *She got a B on her mathematics exam.*

**B.A.** /ˌbi'eɪ/
*abbreviation of* Bachelor of Arts degree: *He received his B.A. in June. See:* associate degree, USAGE NOTE.

**USAGE NOTE:** A *B.A.,* like a *B.S.* (Bachelor of Science), is often called a *bachelor's degree* and is given after one finishes four years of college. Two-year colleges give *associate's degrees (A.A.).*

**baboon** /bæ'bun/ *noun*
a large monkey that lives mainly in Africa

**baby** /'beɪbi/ *noun, plural* **babies**
a child or offspring younger than two, an infant: *His wife had a baby.*

**baby** *verb* **babied, babying, babies**
to treat carefully: *This plant can break easily; you have to baby it.*

**babysit** /'beɪbiˌsɪt/ *verb* **babysat, babysitting, babysits**
*informal* to take care of a child while the parents are away: *She babysits her friends' daughter.* *–noun* (person) **babysitter.**

**bachelor** /'bætʃlər/ *noun*
an unmarried man

**back** /bæk/ *noun*
**1** the side of the human body opposite the stomach and chest: *I hurt my back when I lifted a heavy box.*
**2** the rear part of something, opposite the front: *The back of the house needs to be painted.*
**in back of:** behind, at the back of: *The garage is in back of the house.*

**back** *adverb*
in the direction from which one came: *A tree fell across the road and we had to drive back home.*

**back** *verb*
to support someone, especially by giving money: *Some rich people backed a politician running for mayor.*
**to back up: a. something:** to copy computer records: *She backed up her day's work on the computer.* **b. someone** or **something:** to go backwards: *The driver backed up his car and stopped.*

**backbone** /'bækˌboʊn/ *noun*
**1** the bone that goes from the neck to the lower back, *(synonym)* the spine
**2** courage: *He has a lot of backbone; he always tells the truth.*

**background** /'bækˌgraʊnd/ *noun*
**1** something behind something else: *The hunter waited in the background of the trees for deer to go by.*
**2** a person's family, education, and experience

**backpack** /'bækˌpæk/ *noun*
a type of bag carried on the back: *Backpacks are used to carry things like books, clothes, or food.*

**backpack** *verb*
to walk in the country wearing a back-

pack: *We backpacked for two weeks in the mountains.* –*noun* (person) **backpacker,** (action) **backpacking.** *See:* art on page 12a.

backpack

**backward** or **backwards** /ˈbækwərdz/ *adverb*
**1** in the direction opposite to the one in which one is moving: *She looked backwards over her shoulder.*
**2** in the opposite or wrong order: *He got the directions backwards: He drove south instead of north.*

**backward** or **backwards** *adjective*
not modern: *They live in a backward part of the country.*

**backyard** /ˈbækˈyɑrd/ *noun*
the land behind and belonging to a house: *We have a flower garden in our backyard.*

**bacon** /ˈbeɪkən/ *noun*
salted, smoked meat from a pig's side: *Bacon with eggs is good for breakfast. See:* art on page 17a.

**bacteria** /bækˈtɪriə/ *noun plural, singular* **bacterium** /-ˈtɪriəm/
very small living things: *Many bacteria cause diseases. See:* virus.

**bad** /bæd/ *adjective* **worse** /wɜrs/, **worst** /wɜrst/
**1** evil: *He lies and steals and does many other bad things.*
**2** poorly behaved: *She was bad, so her mother would not let her go out with her friends.*
**3** not of good condition or quality: *He has some bad teeth.*
**4** not good to eat or drink: *The milk has gone bad; it is sour.*
**5** with a feeling of guilt: *I feel bad about the nasty things I said to you.*
**6** with a feeling of sympathy: *I feel bad that you are sick.*
**7** something extreme, severe, especially very sick: *She has a bad sore throat.*
**It's too bad:** to feel sorry: *It's too bad that you have to leave now.*

**badge** /bædʒ/ *noun*
a sign or mark that shows honor or membership, position, etc. in a group: *The police officer wore a badge showing her rank.*

badge

**badger** /ˈbædʒər/ *noun*
an animal that digs and lives in the ground: *Badgers have a wide long body, short legs, and front claws.*

**badly** /ˈbædli/ *adverb* **worse** /wɜrs/, **worst** /wɜrst/
**1** in a bad way, not well: *He sings badly.*
**2** very much, a lot: *He badly wants to study at the university.*

**bag** /bæg/ *noun*
a container made of paper, plastic, cloth, etc.: *I carried the food home in a shopping bag.*

**bag** *verb* **bagged, bagging, bags**
to put things in bags *See:* art on page 10a.

**baggage** /ˈbægɪdʒ/ *noun, (no plural)*
bags, suitcases, etc. used to carry clothing while traveling: *I carried my baggage onto the train.*

**baggy** /ˈbægi/ *adjective* **baggier, baggiest**
loose fitting (clothes): *His pants are so baggy that they are almost falling off.*

**bail (1)** /beɪl/ *noun*
money left with a court of law that lets a person awaiting trial be released from jail: *If someone released on bail does not come to trial, the bail is lost.*

**bail** *verb*
**to bail someone out:** to help someone out of a bad situation, especially jail: *The protesters were taken to jail; a friend bailed out several of them.*

**bail (2)** *verb*
to take water out of a boat: *As the water came into the boat, we bailed it out with buckets.*

**bait** /beɪt/ *noun, (no plural)*
animal food used to catch animals and

fish: *A fisherman used pieces of fish as bait on his hooks.* *–verb* **to bait.**

**bake** /beɪk/ *verb* **baked, baking, bakes**
to cook in an oven: *She bakes fresh bread every morning.* *–noun* (person) **baker,** (business) **bakery.**

**balance** /'bæləns/ *noun*
the ability to stand, walk, etc. without falling down: *She lost her balance and fell down.*

**balance** *verb* **balanced, balancing, balances**
to keep something from falling: *For fun, he balanced a ball on his nose.*

**balcony** /'bælkəni/ *noun, plural* **balconies**
**1** a platform, built on the outside of a building: *The rooms of that hotel have balconies where people can sit outside.*
**2** rows of seats upstairs in a theater or hall

**bald** /bɔld/ or **bald-headed** /'bɔld,hɛd/ *adjective*
with little or no hair on the head: *His bald head shines in the light.* *–noun* **baldness.**

bald

**ball (1)** *noun*
**1** a round object used in games: *The football player kicked the ball.*
**2** something shaped into a ball: *She made a sweater from balls of yarn.*

**on the ball:** (a person) intelligent, knowledgeable, and hard-working: *Mary did the job fast and accurately; she's really on the ball.* *See:* art on page 9a.

**ball (2)** /bɔl/ *noun*
a formal dance party: *Men and women put on their best clothes to go to a ball.*

**ballet** /bæl'eɪ/ *noun*
a type of dancing: *We went to see the ballet last evening.* *–noun* (person) **ballet dancer,** (female) **ballerina.**

ballerina

**balloon** /bə'lun/ *noun*
a bag of thin rubber filled with a gas: *Children have fun with balloons at birthday parties.*

balloons

**ballot** /'bælət/ *noun*
a piece of paper used in a secret vote: *People vote for politicians by marking ballots.*

**ballpark** /'bɔl,pɑrk/ *noun*
baseball stadium, a place where ball games are played

**ballpoint pen** /'bɔl,pɔɪnt/ *noun*
a writing instrument with a ball-shaped tip

**ballroom** /'bɔl,ru m/ *noun*
a large hall for dances

**ballroom** *adjective*
a type of formal dancing

**baloney** or **boloney** or **bologna** /bə'loʊni/ *noun*
**1** a type of sausage: *She sliced baloney for sandwiches.*
**2** *slang* nonsense: *What she says is baloney.*

**bamboo** /bæm'bu/ *noun*
a tall plant used in houses and furniture: *Bamboo is lightweight and strong.*

**ban** /bæn/ *noun*
a stop, block: *The government put a ban on the sale of that drug.*

**ban** *verb* **banned, banning, bans**
to block, *(synonym)* to forbid: *The sale of alcohol to people under age 18 is banned.* *(antonym)* allow.

**banana** /bə'nænə/ *noun*
a long, yellow-skinned (when ripe) fruit with soft insides *See:* art on page 3a.

**band** /bænd/ *noun*
**1** a group of something: *There was a great musical band at the party.*
**2** a strip of material (rope, tape, cloth): *A worker put metal bands around a box.*

**band** *verb*
to group together: *The workers banded together to stop the sale of the company.*

**bandage** /'bændɪʤ/ *noun*
a piece of fabric that covers an injury: *A nurse put a bandage over the cut.*

**bandage** *verb* **bandaged, bandaging, bandages**
to cover a wound with bandages *See:* art on page 11a.

**Band-Aid™** /ˈbændˌeɪd/ *noun*
a small bandage that sticks by itself: *He put a Band-Aid™ over a cut on his finger.* *See:* art on page 11a.

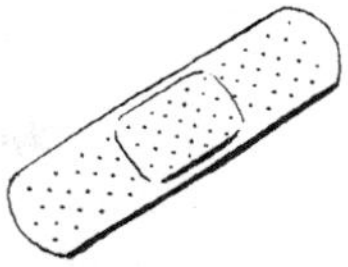

Band-Aid™

**bandana** /bænˈdænə/ *noun*
a colorful handkerchief: *That cowboy wears a red bandana around his neck.*

**bang** /bæŋ/ *noun*
**1** a loud noise: *The gunshot made a loud bang.*
**2** a hard blow, bump: *The cars crashed into each other with a bang!*

**bang** *verb*
to make a loud noise or hit: *The door banged shut.*

**banjo** /ˈbænʤoʊ / *noun, plural* **banjos** or **banjoes**
a musical instrument with strings: *A banjo is played like a guitar in country-western music.*

**bank (1)** /bæŋk/ *noun*
a safe place to put one's money that also makes loans: *Both individuals and businesses put their money in banks.*

**bank** *verb*
to put or keep money in a bank: *She banks at the Liberty Bank on the corner.* *See:* deposit; withdraw.

**bank (2)** *noun*
the land at the edge of a river, lake, etc.: *We walked along the river bank. See:* shore.

**bank account** *noun*
an amount of money in a bank that one adds to or subtracts from: *She has two bank accounts: a savings account and a checking account.*

**bankrupt** /ˈbæŋkrəpt/ *adjective*
without money or credit, unable to pay one's bills: *That company is bankrupt.* –*noun* (act) **bankruptcy.**

**banner** /ˈbænər/ *noun*
a large flag or piece of cloth or plastic with writing on it used for decoration or business: *The company banner is displayed at meetings.*

**banquet** /ˈbæŋkwɪt/ *noun*
a formal dinner with many people: *There were 200 people at the wedding banquet.*

**baptism** /ˈbæptɪzəm/ *noun*
a religious ceremony in which a person is touched by water to join a church and thought to be cleansed of sin –*verb* **to baptize** /bæpˈtaɪz/.

**bar (1)** /bɑr/ *noun*
a public place that serves liquor: *Where is the bar in this hotel?*

---

**USAGE NOTE:** A *bar* is the counter where liquor is served inside a *barroom* but is also a general term for any business that serves alcohol; a *pub* often also serves light food, such as sandwiches; a *tavern* usually offers food and sometimes bedrooms for travelers; a *nightclub* (or club) offers live music or other entertainment. A *snack bar* serves only food.

---

**bar (2)** *noun*
**1** a flat, hard piece of metal: *That bank keeps bars of gold in its safe.*
**2** anything shaped like a bar: *She put a bar of soap on the sink.*

**bar** *verb* **barred, barring, bars**
**1** to lock with a bar: *I barred the door.*
**2** to block someone or something: *Police barred entrance to the building.*

**barbecue** /ˈbɑrb ɪˌkyu/ *verb* **barbecued, barbecuing, barbecues**
to cook food on a metal grill over an open fire, usually outside: *We're going to barbecue chicken tonight. See:* grill.

**barbecue** *noun*
a party where food is grilled: *On July 4, we ate hamburgers and hot dogs at a family barbecue. See:* charcoal; cookout.

**barbed wire** /bɑrbd/ *noun*
wire with sharp points on it used as a fence: *Farmers use barbed wire to keep cattle in their fields.*

**barber** /ˈbɑrbər/ *noun*
a person who cuts hair: *He goes to the barber every two weeks.* –*noun* (place) **barber shop.**

B

**bare** /bɛr/ *adjective*
**1** uncovered: *The baby lies in bed as bare as the day he was born.*
**2** plain, simple: *She earns only enough money to buy the bare necessities of food and clothes.*

**bare** *verb* **bared, baring, bares**
to show: *He took off his shirt and bared his chest.*

**barefoot** /ˈbɛrˌfʊt/ *adverb*
without shoes: *Holding hands, the couple walked barefoot on the beach.*

**barely** /ˈbɛrli/ *adverb*
almost not at all, just, hardly: *I hurt my foot and can barely walk.*

**bargain** /ˈbɑrgɪn/ *noun*
**1** a low price for something: *I got a bargain when I bought that suit for half price.*
**2** an agreement: *If you will sell me the car for $10,000, we have a bargain.*

**bargain** *verb*
to ask for a lower price

**bargain** *adjective*
very inexpensive: *The shoes were for sale at a bargain price.*

**barge** /ˈbɑrʤ/ *noun*
a long, low boat that carries heavy loads: *The load of wheat was carried up the river by a barge.* –*verb* **to barge.**

**bark (1)** /bɑrk/ *noun*
the covering of a tree: *The bark of a birch tree is white and black.*

**bark (2)** *noun*
a sound a dog makes

**bark** *verb*
to make sounds like a dog: *The dog barked at the neighbors.*

**barn** /bɑrn/ *noun*
a building for keeping animals and their food: *We keep horses, sheep, and chickens in the barn.*

**barracks** /ˈbærəks/ *noun plural*
building where soldiers live: *Barracks are simple buildings.*

**barrel** /ˈbærəl/ *noun*
a large, round container made of metal or wood: *Oil is sold by the barrel.*

**barren** /ˈbærən/ *adjective*
**1** having no life, no animals, plants, or people: *Some deserts are barren, with no life.*
**2** not able to have children: *Because of an illness, she is barren.*–*noun* **barrenness.** *(antonym)* fertile.

**barrier** /ˈbæriər/ *noun*
something that blocks the way: *A tree fell across the road and made a barrier to traffic.*

**barrier**

**barrio** /ˈbɑrio/ *noun, plural* **barrios**
a mainly Spanish-speaking neighborhood in an American city: *There are many barrios in Los Angeles and Miami.*

**bartender** /ˈbɑr tɛndər/ *noun*
a person who makes alcoholic drinks as a job: *She is a bartender at a Mexican restaurant.*

**base** /beɪs/ *noun*
**1** the lower part of something: *That vase sits on a wooden base.*
**2** the point where a part of something connects to the whole: *The lamp is broken at its base.*
**3** the main place where one works or lives: *They use their apartment in New York as a home base from which they travel often.*
**4** a military camp, building, airport, etc.: *The Air Force planes flew back to their base.*
**5** (in baseball) one of four squares touched by runners

**base** *verb* **based, basing, bases**
**to base something on something:** to use as a reason for doing something: *She based her decision to marry him on love, not money.*

**base** *adjective* **baser, basest**
**1** basic: *These are the base numbers for the house's value.*
**2** low: *That man works from base desires: sex, drugs, and greed.* –*adverb* **basely.**

**baseball** /ˈbeɪsˌbɔl/ *noun*

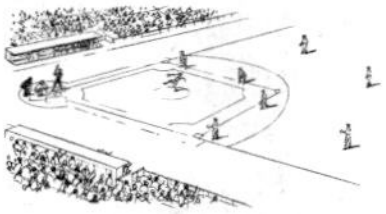

baseball

**1** a hard ball about the size of an adult's closed hand
**2** a game played on a field by nine players on each team who hit the ball with a bat and run around four bases to score

**USAGE NOTE:** The game of *baseball* is called America's pastime, meaning the favorite sport of the country.

**basement** /ˈbeɪsmənt/ *noun*
rooms under a building: *They keep old furniture in their basement.*

**bash** /ˈbæʃ/ *noun, plural* **bashes**
**to throw a bash:** a lively and usually expensive party: *For her 50th birthday, her husband threw a bash for 100 friends.*

**bash** *verb* **bashed, bashing, bashes**
to hit with a heavy instrument: *Firefighters bashed in the door.*

**bashful** /ˈbæʃfəl/ *adjective*
afraid to talk to people: *He was too bashful to ask her for a date.* –*noun* **bashfulness;** –*adverb* **bashfully.**

**basic** /ˈbeɪsɪk/ *adjective*
having the simple facts or ideas about something: *He has a basic understanding of the problem.* –*adverb* **basically.**

**basin** /ˈbeɪsɪn/ *noun*
**1** a hollow pan (for liquids): *He put water in the basin to wash his hands.*
**2** a sink

**basis** /ˈbeɪsɪs/ *noun, plural* **bases** /ˈbeɪˌsiz/
the main reason(s) for something: *What is the basis of your opinion?*

**basket** /ˈbæskɪt/ *noun*
**1** an open, lightweight container made of straw, or strips of wood: *She put dirty clothes in a laundry basket.*
**2** a round, metal tube with a net (used in basketball). *See:* wastebasket.

basketball

**basketball** /ˈbæsˌkɪtˌbɔl/ *noun*
a game played by two teams who throw a ball through a basket to make points *See:* art on page 22a.

**bat (1)** /bæt/ *noun*
a flying animal active at night: *Bats eat insects and fruit.*

bat

**bat (2)** *noun*
**1** a thick, wooden stick
**2** a long, rounded piece of metal or wood used to strike a baseball

**bat** *verb* **batted, batting, bats**
**1** to use a bat to hit a baseball: *He batted first in the game.*
**2** to open and close the eyelids quickly: *She batted her eyes when dust got in them.*

**batch** /bætʃ/ *noun, plural* **batches**
**1** a group of persons or things: *He made a batch of cookies.*
**2** an amount of something made at one time: *Computers can work on a number of jobs in a batch.*

**bath** /bæθ/ *noun, plural* **baths** /bæðz/
**1** washing, especially all of one's body: *I took a hot bath last night.*
**2** a bathtub in which to wash oneself

**bathe** /beɪð/ *verb* **bathed, bathing, bathes**
to wash oneself: *He bathes daily in the bathtub.* –*noun* (person) **bather.**

**bathing suit** /ˈbeɪðɪŋ/ *noun*
clothing worn to go swimming: *She wears a one-piece bathing suit at the beach.*

**bathroom** /ˈbæθˌrum/ *noun*
a room with a bath and toilet: *"Excuse me, I have to go to the bathroom."*

**USAGE NOTE:** In the USA, *bathroom* usually means a room with a toilet and bathtub or shower in a house, but *restroom* refers to a toilet in a public building. *See:* ladies' room; men's room.

**bathtub** /ˈbæθˌtʌb/ *noun*
a large basin for bathing: *a white bathtub*

**batter (1)** /ˈbætər/ *noun*
a mixture of foods to be cooked, such as flour, sugar, butter, and milk: *He put the cake batter in the oven to bake.*

**batter (2)**
(in baseball) the person who hits the ball

**batter** *verb*
to hit someone many times: *A man battered his girlfriend, and she called the police.*

**battery** /'bætəri/ *noun, plural* **batteries**
a storage container for electricity: *I put two new batteries in my flashlight and the beam was bright again. See:* assault and battery.

**battle** /'bætl/ *noun*
**1** a fight between enemy soldiers (airplanes, warships, etc.)
**2** *figurative* a struggle: *Our company is fighting a legal battle.*

**battle** *verb* **battled, battling, battles**
**1** to fight: *Two armies battled for days.*
**2** to struggle against: *She has been battling cancer for years.*

**bay** /beɪ/ *noun*
a large body of water around which the land bends: *Fishermen work in the bay.*

**B.C.** /'bi'si/
*abbreviation of* Before Christ: the years before the birth of Christ in the Christian calendar *See:* A.D.

**be** /bi/ *verb*
used as an *auxiliary verb, a helping verb,* or with another verb: *I am* (helping verb) *shopping* (main verb) *for a new coat.* The tenses of *to be* are:

**Present Tense**

| **Singular** | **Plural** |
|---|---|
| *I am* | *We are* |
| *You are* | *You are* |
| *He/she/it is* | *They are* |

**Present Participle:** *being*
**Past Tense**

| **Singular** | **Plural** |
|---|---|
| *I was* | *We were* |
| *You were* | *You were* |
| *He/she/it was* | *They were* |

**Past Participle:** *been*
**Negative Contractions:**
**Present Tense**

| | |
|---|---|
| *He/she/it isn't* | *You/they aren't* |

**Past Tense**

| | |
|---|---|
| *He/she/it wasn't* | *You/they weren't* |

**1** used with present participles (*-ing* forms) of other verbs: *I am shopping for a new coat.*||*Are you going with me?*
**2** used with a past participle (often *-ed* forms) of other verbs: *I was stuck in traffic.*||*You are invited to the party.*
**3** used with infinitives (*to* + verb form) to show **a.** the future: *We are to go on vacation in July.* **b.** intention: *We are to be married next month.* **c.** obligation: *She is to be in class at 9* A.M.

**beach** /bitʃ/ *noun, plural* **beaches**
a sandy area by a lake or ocean: *We spend summers at our friend's house on the beach*

**beacon** /'bikən/ *noun*
a strong light usually on a tower: *Tall buildings near airports have red beacons to warn airplanes away at night.*

beads

**bead** /bid/ *noun*
a small round piece of material with a hole: *Her necklace is made of red glass beads.* –*verb* **to bead.**

**beak** /bik/ *noun*
the nose and mouth of a bird, turtle, etc.: *Some birds have long, colorful beaks.*

beak

**beam** /bim/ *noun*
**1** a long, thick piece of metal or wood used to make buildings, bridges, etc.: *Steel beams are put together to make the insides of buildings.*
**2** a ray of light: *Beams of light came from the car's headlights.*

**beam** *verb*
**1** to shine: *Stars beam at night.*
**2** to send a signal, *(synonym)* to broadcast: *Radio stations beam their programs to listeners.*

**bean** /bin/ *noun*
a seed of many plants: *I like to eat lima beans and black beans.*

**bear (1)** /bɛr/ *noun, plural* **bears** or **bear**
a large animal with thick fur, sharp teeth, and claws: *Grizzly bears are big and can be dangerous. See:* art on page 14a.

**bear**

**bear (2)** *verb* **bore,** /bɔr/ **bearing, bears**
**1** to carry something heavy: *Steel beams bear the weight of buildings.*
**2** to feel bad: *He cannot bear the pain of a toothache.*
**3** to give birth to: *After having five daughters, she hoped to bear a son.*
**4** to go in a certain direction: *Go to the corner, then bear right and you will find the grocery store.*

**bearable** /'bɛrəbəl/ *adjective*
able to be survived: *The hot weather is uncomfortable but bearable. –adverb* **bearably.** *See:* unbearable.

**beard** /bɪrd/ *noun*
hair on the face: *My father has always worn a beard and mustache. –adjective* **bearded.**

**beard**

**beat** /bit/ *verb* **beat, beating, beats**
**1** to hit again and again: *A man beat another man with a club.*
**2** to mix or blend: *She beat the eggs with a spoon.*
**3** to win: *Our team beat the other team.*
**4** to make a regular rhythm or sound: *He could hear the beating of his heart as he ran.*

**beat** *noun*
tempo, rhythm of music: *The beat of the music makes me want to dance.*

**beautiful** /'byutəfəl/ *adjective*
pleasing to the senses or the mind: *The mountains are beautiful in the summer. See:* handsome, USAGE NOTE.

**beauty** /'byuti/ *noun, plural* **beauties**
something pleasing to the senses or the mind: *People see beauty in nature and art.–verb* **to beautify.**

**beaver** /'bivər/ *noun*
an animal that looks like a large rat with a long flat tail: *Beavers cut down trees with their sharp teeth.*

**beaver**

**because** /bɪ'kɔz/ *conjunction*
for the reason that, as: *I cannot go to work today because I am sick.*

**because** *preposition*
**because of:** by reason of: *I studied late because of a test tomorrow.*

**become** /bɪ'kʌm/ *verb* **became,** /-'keɪm/ **becoming, becomes**
to grow, come to be: *She wants to become a doctor.*

**bed** /bɛd/ *noun*
a piece of furniture for sleeping *–verb* **to bed.** *See:* art on page 22a.

**bed and breakfast** *noun*
a private home that rents rooms to guests and serves breakfast: *We stayed at a bed and breakfast last night. See:* room and board.

---

**USAGE NOTE:** A *bed and breakfast* (or *B & B)* is a private home that offers guests a bedroom, bathroom, and a full breakfast. B & Bs are usually located in the countryside.

---

**bedroom** /'bɛd,rum/ *noun*
a room for sleeping: *The house has two bedrooms.*

**bedspread** /'bɛd,spr ɛd/ *noun*
a bed covering put over the sheets and blankets: *a yellow bedspread See:* art on page 22a.

**bee** /bi/ *noun*
an insect with wings that stings and makes honey: *Bees live in beehives.*

**bee**

**beef** /bif/ *noun*
the meat of cattle: *We had roast beef for dinner.*

B

**beehive** /'bi,haɪv/ *noun*
a home for bees: *I put my hand in the beehive and was stung three times!*

**been** /bɪn/
*past participle of* to be

**beeper** /'bipər/ *noun*
an electronic device that beeps to tell you to call someone: *He wears a beeper when he is away from his office in case someone needs to reach him.*

beeper

**beer** /bɪr/ *noun*
**1** an alcoholic drink usually made from grain: *She had a sandwich and a beer for lunch.*
**2** a drink made from a plant or root: *ginger beer, root beer*

**beet** /bit/ or **beet root** *noun*
a plant with a thick red root eaten as a vegetable

**beetle** /'bitl/ *noun*
a hard-shelled insect with wings

**before** /bɪ'fɔr/ *preposition*
in front of: *He stood before me. (antonym)* behind.

**before** *adverb*
**1** earlier than: *It is ten minutes before 12 o'clock.*
**2** ahead of: *The child ran before her classmates. (antonym)* after.

**before** *conjunction*
ahead of in time: *I hope he quits his job before it makes him crazy.*

**beg** /bɛg/ *verb* **begged, begging, begs**
to ask for something strongly: *He begged her to stay with him, but she left.*

**began** /bɪ'gæn/
*past participle of* begin

**beggar** /'bɛgər/ *noun*
a poor person who asks for money

**begin** /bɪ'gɪn/ *verb* **began** /-gæn/, **beginning, begins**
to start: *We began our vacation on August 1. –noun* **beginner.** *(antonym)* finish.

**beginning** /bɪ'gŋ/ *noun*
a start: *At the beginning, our business grew slowly. (antonym)* end.

**begun** /bɪ'gʌn/
*past participle of* begin

**behalf** /bɪ'hæf/ *noun*
**on behalf of:** as the representative of: *As her lawyer, I act on behalf of Mrs. Jones by going to court.*

**behave** /bɪ'heɪv/ *verb* **behaved, behaving, behaves**
**1** to act in a certain way: *As a manager, she behaves professionally.*
**2** to act well: *Children, behave yourselves! –noun* **behavior.** *See:* misbehave.

**behind** /bɪ'haɪnd/ *adverb*
**1** last, in back of: *Runners must run fast or be left behind by the others. (antonym)* before.
**2** late in doing something: *The doctor is running behind today. She has many patients waiting.*

**behind** *preposition*
**1** at the back of: *She sat behind me.*
**2** below in rank, grade, etc.: *She was behind the other students.*

**behind** *noun informal*
part of the body on which one sits

**being** /'biɪŋ/ *noun*
**1** in existence: *The United States of America came into being in 1776.*
**2** a living thing: *Every being on earth depends on the environment.*

**belief** /bɪ'lif/ *noun*
a strong feeling or idea that something is true or right: *She is a woman with strong religious beliefs.*

**believable** /bɪlivəbəl/ *adjective*
capable of being thought true: *His description of the crime was believable. –adverb* **believably.**

**believe** /bɪ'liv/ *verb* **believed, believing, believes**
**1** to know or feel that something is true: *She believed her son when he said he didn't start the fight.*
**2** to think: *I believe he is coming on Friday.*
**to make believe:** to pretend: *The boys make believe they are cowboys. –noun* (person) **believer.**

**bell** /bɛl/ *noun*
a hollow metal object that makes pleasant sounds when hit: *The mail carrier rang the doorbell.*

**belly** /'bɛli/ *noun, plural* **bellies**
the stomach: *I lay on my belly all day at the beach and sunburned my back.*

**belong** /bɪ'lɔŋ/ *verb*
**1** to be the property of, be owned by: *That car belongs to me.*
**2** to go together naturally: *That couple belongs together; they really get along well.*
**3** to be a member of a group: *He belongs to the health club.*
**4** to be part of something: *That part belongs to the engine.*

**belongings** /bɪ'l ɔŋɪŋz/ *noun plural*
personal property, such as clothes, etc.: *He packed his belongings in a suitcase for his vacation.*

**beloved** /bɪ'lʌvɪd/ *adjective*
(someone who is) highly loved: *a beloved daughter*

**below** /bɪ'loʊ/ *preposition*
lower than, under: *The foot is below the knee.*

**belt** /bɛlt/ *noun*
**1** a piece of leather worn around the waist: *Belts hold up pants. See:* art on page 12a.
**2** an endless strap used as part of a machine: *The fan belt on my car broke.*

**bench** /bɛnʧ/ *noun, plural* **benches**
a long seat: *People sit on benches in the park.*

**bend** /bɛnd/ *noun*
a turn, curve: *I followed the bend in the road.*

**bend** *verb* **bent** /bɛnt/, **bending, bends**
**1** to turn, make curved: *I bent a stick and broke it in two pieces.*
**2** to lean over at the waist: *She bent over and picked up a piece of paper.*

**beneath** /bɪ'niθ/ *preposition*
below, under: *A dog lies beneath the porch. (antonym)* above.

**beneath**

**benefit** /'bɛnəˌfɪt/ *noun*
gain, positive result: *She received a benefit for her good work, a large raise.* –*adjective* **beneficial;** –*adverb* **beneficially.**

**benefit** *verb* **benefited, benefiting, benefits**
to gain: *The company benefited from selling a new product.*

**bent** /bɛnt/ *adjective*
not straight: *That piece of metal is bent.*

**berry** /'bɛri/ *noun, plural* **berries**
a small fruit: *I baked a cake with berries in it.*

**beside** /bɪ'saɪd/ *preposition*
**1** next to: *He sat down beside her.*
**2** apart from, other than: *The fact that you like your car is beside the point; it is so old that it does not work.*
**3** compared with: *Beside me, she seems tall.*

**beside** *adverb*

**besides:** *adverb* also, in addition to: *Besides talking to him, she wrote him a letter.*

**best (1)** /bɛst/ *adjective*
*superlative of* good: of the highest quality or ability: *She is the best student in the class. (antonym)* worst.

**best** *noun*
the highest quality: *He buys only the best in clothes.*

**at best:** the most one can expect: *At best, you will get only a small increase in salary.*

**best (2)** *adverb*
*superlative of* well: in the most positive way: *I feel best in cool weather.*

**bet** /bɛt/ *noun*
an agreement that the person who wins receives something, such as another person's money: *People place bets on sports games.*

**bet** *verb* **betted, betting, bets**
to say something as in a bet: *I bet it's going to rain.*

**betray** /bɪ'treɪ/ *verb*
to be disloyal to the trust of a person or group: *The soldier betrayed his friends by telling the enemy where they were hiding.* –*noun* (act) **betrayal,** (person) **betrayer.**

**better (1)** /'bɛtər/ *adjective*
comparative of good higher quality, skill, achievement, etc.: *He is a better runner than I am.*

**better** *adverb*
*comparative of* well: *My mother was sick, but she's feeling better now.*

**better** *verb*
to improve: *She has bettered herself by getting a good education.*

**between** /bɪ'twin/ *preposition*
in the space separating two things: *Airplanes fly people between New York and Washington every half hour.*

**beverage** /'bɛvrɪʤ/ *noun formal*
a drink, usually not water: *Restaurants serve hot beverages, such as coffee.*

**beware** /bɪ'wɛr/ *verb*
to be careful about something dangerous: *"Beware of the dog" means that a dog might attack you.*

**beyond** /bɪ'yɑnd/ *preposition*
**1** on the other side of: *The campground is beyond the next field.*
**2** to a greater amount: *She is educated beyond everyone in her family.*
**3** too difficult for: *Understanding mathematics is beyond him.*
**4** further in time than, later: *Looking beyond this year, I see a good future.*
**5** besides, in addition: *I don't know anything about him beyond what I've told you.*

**bias** /'baɪəs/ *noun, plural* **biases**
**1** a general belief against doing something: *She has a bias against wasting money.*
**2** prejudice: *He has a bias against people who wear glasses.*

**biased** *adjective*
inclined: *He is biased against people with glasses.*

**bib** /bɪb/ *noun*
a cloth with strings to tie around the neck: *Babies wear bibs when they eat.*

bib

**Bible** /'baɪbəl/ *noun*
(*cap.*) the holy writings of Christianity and Judaism: *She reads the Bible every day.* –*adjective* **biblical** /'bɪblɪkəl/.

**bicycle** /'baɪsɪkəl/ *noun*
a two-wheeled vehicle moved by moving the feet on it: *I bought a new bicycle.*

**bicycle** *verb* **bicycled, bicycling, bicycles**
to travel by bicycle –*noun* (action) **bicycling,** (person) **bicyclist.** *See:* art on page 24a.

**bid** /bɪd/ *verb formal* **bid, bidding, bids**
**1** to ask or command: *She bid the child to stand still.*
**2** to make an offer of money –*noun* (act) **bid.**

**big** /bɪg/ *adjective* **bigger, biggest**
**1** large in size, shape, etc.: *She has big feet.*
**2** important: *Our company has a big meeting next month. (antonym)* small.

**bigot** /'bɪgət/ *noun*
someone who has strong, unreasonable opinions about other people because of their race, religion, etc: *He is a bigot who hates everyone who is not like him.* –*noun* **bigotry.** *See:* prejudiced.

**bike** /baɪk/ *noun*
bicycle or motorcycle –*noun* (person) **biker.** *See:* bicycle.

**bike** *verb* **biked, biking, bikes**

**bilingual** /baɪ'lɪŋgwəl/ *adjective*
**1** able to communicate well in two languages: *She is bilingual in English and Chinese.*
**2** something written or spoken in two languages: *a bilingual dictionary*

**bill (1)** /bɪl/ *noun*
**1** a printed piece of paper that lists things and their price: *Our company sends out bills each month.*
**2** paper money: *She paid with a $100 bill.*
**3** (in government) a new law or plan that lawmakers vote to accept or refuse: *Congress worked on an anticrime bill.*

**bill** *verb*
to send out bills to customers: *The company bills its customers every month.*

**bill (2)** *noun*
a bird's beak

billboard

**billboard** /'bɪl,bɔrd/ *noun*
a large, flat board for advertisements, usually by the side of the road

**billion** /ˈbɪlyən/ *noun*
(in the USA) 1,000,000,000: *That company sells a billion dollars of shoes a year.* –*adjective* **billionth.**

**Bill of Rights** *noun*
(in the USA) rights given by law, such as freedom of speech, freedom to meet in public, etc.: *The Bill of Rights is part of the Constitution.*

**bin** /bɪn/ *noun*
a large, open container: *That store keeps nails and screws in bins.*

**bind** /baɪnd/ *verb* **bound** /ˈbaʊnd/, **binding, binds**
to wrap with bandages: *Doctors bind wounds.*

**bingo** /ˈbɪŋgoʊ/ *noun*
a gambling game with numbered cards: *When he had five numbers in a row, the player shouted "Bingo!" and won a prize.*

bingo

**binoculars** /bənɑkyələrz/ *noun, plural*
glasses that make distant objects seem closer and larger: *The nature lover looked through her binoculars to see birds far away.*

binoculars

**biography** /baɪɑgrəfi/ *noun, plural* **biographies**
the history of a person's life: *He read a biography of a baseball player.* –*noun* (person) **biographer;** –*adjective* **biographical** /ˌbaɪəˈgræfɪkəl/; –*adverb* **biographically.** *See:* autobiography; fiction USAGE NOTE.

**biology** /baɪˈɑləʤi/ *noun*
the science and study of life: *In the biology class students looked at leaves under a microscope.* –*adjective* **biological** /ˌbaɪəˈlɑʤɪkəl/; –*adverb* **biologically;** –*noun* (person) **biologist.**

**bird** /bɜrd/ *noun*
an animal with feathers, wings, and a beak: *Most birds can fly.*

**a bird in the hand is worth two in the bush:** something of small value is worth more than something that is unsure

**to kill two birds with one stone:** to do two things with one effort: *I had a business appointment in the city, then met my friend for lunch, so I killed two birds with one stone. See:* art on page 14a.

**birth** /bɜrθ/ *noun*
**1 a.** the time and act when a baby or an egg comes out of its mother: *Our cat gave birth to three kittens. (antonym)* death. **b.** to cause or produce something: *The woman's actions gave birth to a movement for freedom in her country.*
**2** one's origin (or ancestry, parents, grandparents, etc.): *He is German by birth, but is now a citizen of Venezuela.*

**birth certificate** *noun*
legal document stating when and where one was born

**birthday** /ˈbɜrθˌdeɪ/ *noun*
the date when one was born: *She bought me a present for my birthday.*

**birthplace** /ˈbɜrθˌpleɪs/ *noun*
where one was born: *Her birthplace is San Francisco.*

**biscuit** /ˈbɪskɪt/ *noun*
small bread: *He had biscuits and gravy for breakfast. See:* bun.

**bisect** /ˈbaɪˌsɛkt/ *verb*
to cut, cross, or divide into two equal parts: *That road bisects a farm.*

**bishop** /ˈbɪʃəp/ *noun*
**1** a high-level official in some Christian religions
**2** a piece in the game of chess

**bit** /bɪt/ *noun*
**1** a small amount: *She cleaned a bit of dirt off of her pants.*
**2** in computers, a unit of information in a language that has two units: *Eight bits is equal to one byte.*

**bite** /baɪt/ *verb* **bit** /bɪt/, **biting, bites**
to cut with the teeth: *Some dogs will bite you.*

**bite** *noun*
**1** an act of biting: *The cat's bite hurt my hand.*
**2** a small amount of food: *I had a bite to eat for breakfast.* –*noun* **biter.**

**bitter** /ˈbɪtər/ *adjective*
**1** having a sharp, acid taste: *Lemons taste bitter.*
**2** giving pain: *It was a bitter cold winter.*
**3** angry: *The two friends became bitter enemies.* *–adverb* **bitterly;** *–noun* **bitterness.**

**biweekly** /baɪˈwi kli/ *adjective*
every two weeks (14 days): *They publish a biweekly newspaper.*

**black** /blæk/ *noun*
a person of African descent: *North American blacks sometimes prefer to be called African-Americans.*

**black** *adjective*
very dark, like the color of coal: *She wore a black dress today.* *–noun* **blackness.** *See:* art on page 16a.

---

**USAGE NOTE:** The term *black* is used to refer to people whose ancestors were Africans. Some people prefer to use the term *African-American* or *person of color* instead of *black.* All three terms are acceptable.

---

**blackboard** /ˈblæk,bɔrd/ *noun*
a flat surface to write on in classrooms: *The teacher wrote on the blackboard with white chalk.* *See:* art on page 8a.

**blackmail** /ˈblæk, meɪl/ *verb*
to demand actions or money by threatening to tell a harmful secret about someone *–noun* (person) **blackmailer;** (act) **blackmail.**

**blacksmith** /ˈblæk, smɪθ/ *noun*
a worker who makes things of metal: *A blacksmith can make horseshoes.*

**bladder** /ˈblædər/ *noun*
a small bag of skin that holds and forces out liquid waste from the body: *My bladder is so small that I have to go to the bathroom often.*

**blade** /bleɪd/ *noun*
narrow, flat piece of something: *a knife blade*

blade

**blame** /bleɪm/ *verb*
**blamed, blaming, blames**
to say someone is responsible for something bad: *I blame him for the accident.*

**blame** *noun*
a charge of wrongdoing: *I put the blame on him for causing the accident.*

**bland** /blænd/ *adjective*
**1** having little flavor: *Some foods, like white rice, taste bland.*
**2** mild, boring: *He has a very bland personality.*–*noun* **blandness;** *–adverb* **blandly** *(antonym)* tasty.

**blank** /blæŋk/ *adjective*
**1** clear, without writing or markings: *I wrote a letter on a blank piece of paper.*
**2** without expression, interest, or understanding

**blanket** /ˈblæŋkɪt/ *noun*
**1** a bed covering: *To keep warm, she has two blankets on her bed.*
**2** *figurative* any type of covering: *A blanket of snow covered the ground.* *See:* art on page 22a.

blanket

**blanket** *verb*
to cover completely: *A heavy rain blanketed the fields with water.*

**blast** /blæst/ *verb*
**1** to explode: *A bomb blasted a hole in the road.*
**2** an explosion: *You could hear that blast for miles.*

**blaze (1)** /bleɪz/ *verb* **blazed, blazing, blazes**
to burn strongly: *A fire blazed in the fireplace.*

**blaze** *noun*
**1** a big fire: *The blaze lasted for three hours.*
**2** a very bright light: *They played baseball at night under the blaze of spotlights.*

**blazer** /ˈbleɪzər/ *noun*
a type of jacket that does not match the pants worn, especially by men: *He wore a blue blazer to the party.*

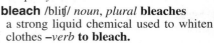

blazer

**bleach** /bliʧ/ *noun, plural* **bleaches**
a strong liquid chemical used to whiten clothes *–verb* **to bleach.**

**bleak** /blik/ *adjective*
**1** cold, gray: *On a cold, rainy day the beach area looks bleak.*
**2** with little or no hope: *He has no job and his future is bleak. (antonym)* bright.

**bleary** /ˈblɪri/ *adjective* **blearier, bleariest**
unable to see well, unclear: *When she wakes up in the morning, her eyes are bleary.*

**bleed** /blid/ *verb* **bled** /blɛd/, **bleeding, bleeds**
**1** to lose blood
**2** *figurative* to feel pain at another person's suffering: *My heart bleeds for those people in a war.*
**3** (of colors) to run together: *My red shirt bled onto my white socks in the washing machine; now my socks are pink.*

**blend** /blɛnd/ *verb*
to mix: *I blended milk and butter into the flour.*

**bless** /blɛs/ *verb* **blessed, blessing, blesses**
to make holy, especially by asking God: *The priest blessed the people in church. (antonym)* curse.

**blessing** /ˈblɛsɪŋ/ *noun*
**1** an act of making something holy: *She asked for God's blessing for her new baby.*
**2** a good event (situation or condition): *It is a blessing to have good health.*

**blew** /blu/ *verb*
past tense of *blow*

**blimp** /blɪmp/ *noun*
a long, rounded aircraft filled with gas: *In the USA, blimps with advertising on them fly over outdoor sports events.*

blimp

**blind (1)** /blaɪnd/ *adjective*
unable to see

**blind** *verb*
to make someone lose sight: *An injury to his eyes blinded him for life.* *–noun* **blindness;** *–adverb* **blindly.** *See:* disabled, USAGE NOTE.

**blind (2)**
a covering for a window: *She closes the blinds when the afternoon sun shines in.* *See:* art on page 20a.

**blindfold** /ˈblaɪndˌfoʊld/ *noun*
a piece of cloth tied over the eyes so a person cannot see *–verb* **to blindfold.**

**blink** /blɪŋk/ *verb*
**1** to open and close the eyelids rapidly: *If you don't blink, your eyes will dry out.*
**2** to go on and off quickly: *The car blinked its lights to signal me.* *–noun* **blink.**

**blinker** /ˈblɪŋkər/ *noun*
a light that goes on and off such as a directional signal on a car

**bliss** /blɪs/ *noun*
extreme happiness: *After they got married, they lived in bliss.* *–adjective* **blissful;** *–adverb* **blissfully.** *(antonym)* sorrow.

**blister** /ˈblɪstər/ *noun*
a pocket of skin filled with liquid: *A burn caused blisters on her hand.*

**blizzard** /ˈblɪzərd/ *noun*
a bad snowstorm

**bloated** /ˈbloʊtɪd/ *adjective*
too big: *After a big meal, his stomach felt bloated.*

**block** /blɑk/ *noun*
**1** a hard substance with flat sides: *She carved a statue out of a block of ice.*
**2** land with buildings on it between two streets: *I walk ten blocks to work each morning.*
**3** a group of something: *He bought a block of 100,000 shares of IBM stock.*

**block** *verb*
**1** to prevent from happening: *Congress blocked the President's plan.*
**2** to stand in the way: *A big tree fell and blocked the road.*

**blockage** /ˈblɑkɪʤ/ *noun*
something that prevents flow or movement: *That man had a blockage in his heart and almost died.*

**blond** /blɑnd/ *adjective*
having light, yellowish hair: *That man has blond hair.* *–noun* (man) **blond,** (woman) **blonde.**

**blood** /blʌd/ *noun*
the red liquid pumped by the heart through the body

**blood pressure** *noun*
measurement of the force with which blood moves through the body: *High blood pressure can cause heart attacks. See:* art on page 11a.

**bloom**

**bloom** /blum/ *verb*
to flower: *Our apple tree bloomed last week. (antonym)* wither.

**blossom** /ˈblɑsəm/ *noun*
a flower as it opens: *The blossoms on the apple tree appeared last week.*

**blossom** *verb*
to flower: *The roses blossomed last week. See:* bloom.

**blot** /blat/ *noun*
a spot that makes something dirty: *an ink blot*

**blot** *verb* **blotted, blotting, blots**
to soak up a liquid: *She blotted water off the table with a towel.*

**blouse** /blaʊs/ *noun formal*
a woman's shirt: *She wears white silk blouses. See:* art on page 12a.

**blow (1)** /bloʊ/ *verb* **blew** /blu/, **blowing, blows**
**1** to force air, such as through pipes or the mouth: *She blew out the candles on her cake.*
**2** to move (air) through space: *The wind blows hard during a storm.*
**3** to sound a horn or whistle: *I had to blow the horn to warn another car.*

**to blow something up: a.** to explode: *Soldiers blew up the bridge.* **b.** *figurative* to become very angry: *He's so irritable that he blows up at any little mistake.* **c.** to make something larger by filling it with air: *She blew up balloons for the party.* **d.** to make bigger: *He blew up some photographs.*

**blow (2)** *noun*
**1** a hard hit as with a fist: *He died from a blow on the head by a club.*
**2** a shock, upset: *The sudden death of her husband was a bad blow to her.*

**blue** /blu/ *adjective*
**1** having the color of: *My car is blue.*
**2** *figurative* sad: *She feels blue today. See:* art on page 16a.

**blueberry** /ˈbluˌbɛri/ *noun, plural* **blueberries**
small, dark berries: *Blueberries taste delicious with cream and sugar. See:* art on page 3a.

**blue-collar** *adjective*
of people who work with their hands in jobs that need some training: *Most blue-collar workers in the USA do not belong to unions. See:* white-collar.

---

**USAGE NOTE:** *Blue collar* refers to people who work at manual jobs and belong to the *working class. White collar* workers generally work in office jobs and form the middle and upper-middle classes of North American society.

---

**blue jeans** *noun*
blue pants made of a thick cloth, usually cotton *See:* jeans.

**bluff (1)** /blʌf/ *verb*
to pretend: *I think that he is bluffing about quitting his job so he will get a raise in salary.*

**bluff (2)** *noun*
a cliff

**blunt** /ˈblʌnt/ *adjective*
**1** direct, sometimes unfriendly in manner: *She is blunt because she tells people exactly what she thinks.*
**2** not sharp, dull: *a knife with a blunt edge*

**blur** /blɜr/ *verb* **blurred, blurring, blurs**
to make someone unable to see clearly: *Her headache was so bad it blurred her eyesight.*

**blur** *noun*
something unclear: *Time has gone so quickly; this summer was just a blur.*

**blush**

**blush** /blʌʃ/ *verb* **blushed, blushing, blushes**
to become red in the face: *Some boys blush when a pretty girl smiles at them.*

**blush** *noun*
**1** a reddened face
**2** red makeup for the cheeks

**boa** /ˈboʊə/ or **boa constrictor** *noun*
**1** a long, powerful snake: *Boa constrictors wrap themselves around animals and crush them.*
**2** a piece of clothing with feathers worn around the neck: *The actress wore a boa to the party.*

boa

**boar** /bɔr/ *noun*
a wild male pig

**board** /bɔrd/ *noun*
**1** a thin, flat piece of wood: *Workers nail boards together to build a house.*
**2** a group of people that directs a business or institution: *the company's board of directors, the school board*
**3** meals: *The cost of room and board at the university is high.*
**on board:** on a ship, airplane, train, etc.: *There are 150 passengers on board this jet.*

**board** *verb*
**1** to cover with boards: *During the storm, we boarded up the windows.*
**2** to enter a ship, train, etc.: *Sailors boarded their ship.*

**boarder** /ˈbɔrdər/ *noun*
a person who pays to live in another person's house: *She has three boarders in her large house. See:* tenant.

**boast** /boʊst/ *verb*
**1** to say good things about oneself: *He boasted about how strong he is.*
**2** to be proud of: *He boasted about his three grandchildren.* *–noun* **boasting.**

**boat** /boʊt/ *noun*
a small ship: *We went fishing on the river in a boat.*

**bobcat** /ˈbɑbˌkæt/ *noun*
a wild cat native to North America

**body** /ˈbɑdi/ *noun, plural* **bodies**
**1** the physical form usually of a human or animal: *The old man's body is healthy, but his mind is weak.*
**2** the main part of something: *The body of the newspaper article is long.*

**bodyguard** /ˈbɑd iˌgɑrd/ *noun*
a person whose job is to keep another person from harm

**boil** /bɔɪl/ *verb*
**1** to heat a liquid until it reaches the temperature of 212°F or 100°C: *I boiled the water to cook the eggs.*
**2** to cook: *I boiled the vegetables.*

**boil** *noun*
**1** liquid when boiling: *I heated the water to a boil.*
**2** a painful inflammation of the skin: *I have a boil on my back.*

**boiler** /ˈbɔɪlə r/ *noun*
a large container (a tank) for heating water: *Our boiler is in the cellar.*

**bold** /boʊld/ *adjective*
**1** courageous: *Business leaders like to think of bold plans.*
**2** strong and clear (in art, buildings, ideas): *a building with bold lines* *–adverb* **boldly;** *–noun* **boldness.**

**bolt (1)** /boʊlt/ *noun*
**1** a metal bar used to lock doors, etc.: *I shut the bolt on the bathroom door.*
**2** a thin piece of metal that twists into a circle (a nut) to hold things together: *The parts of the car are held on by strong bolts.*

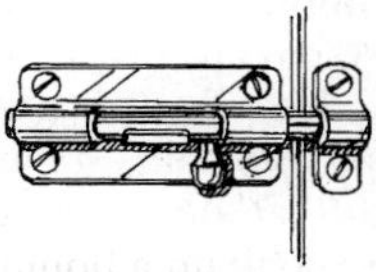

bolt

**bolt (2)** *noun*
**1** a roll of cloth fabric: *A tailor made a suit from a bolt of wool.*
**2** a flash of lightning

**bolt** *verb*
to close or lock with a bolt

**bomb** /bɑm/ *noun*
**1** an explosive device
**2** *informal* a failure: *The play was a bomb; everyone left at intermission.*

**bomb** *verb*
to damage or destroy with a bomb: *Terrorists bombed the mayor's office.*

**bond** /bɑnd/ *noun*
**1** a relationship of trust (cooperation, friendship, love): *There is a strong bond between the two sisters.*
**2** (in chemistry, physics) the forces that hold matter together: *a chemical bond*

**bond** *verb*
to become friends, especially to trust, like, or love someone: *People often bond when they face danger together.*

**bone** /boʊn/ *noun*
a hard, white part that makes up the frame of the body (the skeleton): *Our bones give us our shape.*

**bone** *verb* **boned, boning, bones**
to take out bones: *She boned the chicken before cooking it.*

**bonfire** /ˈbɑnˌfa ɪr/ *noun*
a large fire made outside: *We built a bonfire to celebrate Independence Day.*

**bonus** /ˈboʊnəs/ *noun, plural* **bonuses**
**1** a payment, usually in addition to regular wages or salary: *Our company pays everyone a bonus at the end of the year.*
**2** something unexpected but good: *I didn't think anyone would remember my birthday, so when my friends sent cards it was a bonus.*

**bony** or **boney** /ˈboʊni/ *adjective* **bonier, boniest**
**1** having many bones: *That fish is bony and difficult to eat.*
**2** very thin, showing bones: *He eats so little that he is bony.*

**boo (1)** /bu/ *verb* **booed, booing, boos**
a sound of disapproval: *The audience booed the football player when he made a bad play.* –*noun* (act) **boo.**

boo

**boo (2)** *noun*
a sound made to frighten or surprise someone: *When she walked up behind him and shouted "Boo!" he jumped.*

**booby trap** /ˈbubi træp/ *verb* **booby-trapped, booby-trapping, booby-traps**
a hidden device or situation meant to harm or kill someone: *A soldier was killed because the enemy booby-trapped the path.* –*noun* (bomb) **boobytrap.**

**book** /bʊk/ *noun*
**1** pages kept together with a cover: *We read two books for our English class.*
**2** things in book form: *a book of stamps*

**book** *verb*
to charge with a crime: *The police booked her for stealing from the shop. See:* art on page 8a.

**bookcase** /ˈbʊkˌke ɪs/ *noun*
shelves with sides and usually a back: *My bookcase holds almost 100 books. See:* art on page 6a.

**bookkeeper** /ˈbʊk ˌkipər/ *noun*
a person who maintains the accounts of a business, accountant –*noun* **bookkeeping.**

**bookstore** /ˈbʊkˌs tɔr/ *noun*
a shop that sells books *See:* art on page 4a.

**boom** /bum/ *verb*
**1** to make a deep, loud noise: *Big guns boom when they shoot.*
**2** to grow rapidly: *Our business is booming this year.*

**boom** *noun*
**1** a deep, loud noise: *Fireworks make a loud boom when they explode.*
**2** a time of rapid growth in business

**boomerang** /ˈbumə ˌræŋ/ *noun*
a flat, curved piece of wood used as a weapon that will return to the thrower

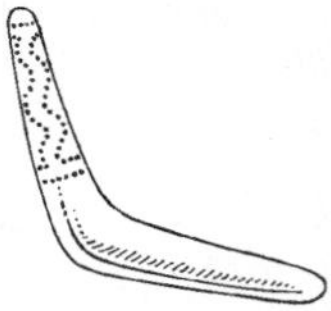
boomerang

**boost** /bust/ *verb*
to lift or push up: *The mother boosted her child into a high chair.* –*noun* (act) **boost.**

**boot** /but/ *noun*
a strong shoe with a tall top: *Cowboys wear leather boots. See:* art on page 12a.

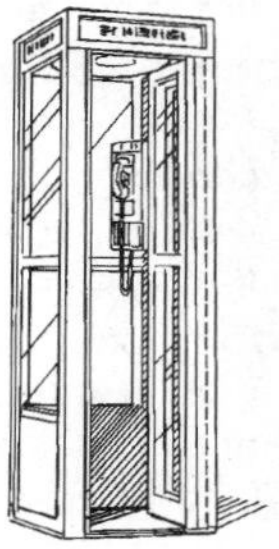
booth

**booth** /buθ/ *noun*
**1** a small place with a door: *She went into a telephone booth to make a phone call.*
**2** in a market, a table that shows products: *That booth sells silver jewelry.*
**3** in a restaurant, a table with soft seats on either side

**border** /ˈbɔrdər/ *noun*
**1** the edge of something: *The border of that rug is torn.*
**2** the legal line separating two states or countries: *We crossed the Mexican bor-*

*der into the United States of America.*

**border** *verb*
to make a line: *Trees border the road on both sides.*

border

**bore (1)** /bɔr/ *verb* **bored, boring, bores**
to make someone feel tired: *That movie about the war bored me; I almost fell asleep.*

**bore** *noun*
a dull event or person: *He talks all the time and is a bore.* –*noun* **boredom.**

**bore (2)** *verb*
to cut a hole in something: *Workers bore a hole in the ground for an oil well.*

**boring** /'bɔrɪŋ/ *adjective*
uninteresting: *He is so boring; he never says anything interesting but talks a lot.*

**born** /bɔrn/
*past participle of* to bear
given life: *The child was born on December 25.*

**born** *adjective*
having a natural ability to do something: *She is a born athlete.*

**borne** /bɔrn/
*past participle of* to bear

**borrow** /'bɑroʊ/ *verb*
to receive a loan of something with the promise to return it: *She borrowed $2,000 from the bank.* –*noun* **borrower.**

**boss** /bɔs/ *noun, plural* **bosses**
the person in charge of others: *She is a great leader and the clear boss at that publishing company.*

boss

**boss** *verb*
to give orders: *She bosses everyone around.*

**bossy** /'bɔsi/ *adjective pejorative* **bossier, bossiest**
telling others what to do: *He is bossy with everybody.* –*noun* **bossiness.**

**botany** /'bɑtni/ *noun*
the study of plant life: *I took botany classes in college and now I do research on plants in the rain forest.* –*adjective* **botanical** /bɑ'ţænɑkɑ/; –*noun* (person) **botanist.**

**both** /boʊθ/ *adjective*
of two things or people: *Both friends arrived at the same time.*

**bother** /'bɑðər/ *verb*
**1** to give unwanted attention: *She told him to stop bothering her.*
**2** to hurt: *My back is bothering me today.*

**bother** *noun*
an annoyance: *For him, details are a bother.*

**bottle** /'bɑtl/ *noun*
a round container for liquids: *I bought a bottle of wine.*

**bottle** *verb* **bottled, bottling, bottles**
to put into bottles: *That company bottles soft drinks.*

**bottom** /'bɑtəm/ *noun*
**1** the lowest part of something: *There is mud on the bottom of the lake.* *(antonym)* top.
**2** *informal* the buttocks: *She fell on her bottom.*

**bottom** *verb*
to reach the lowest level: *A submarine bottomed on the ocean floor.*

**boulder** /'boʊldər/ *noun*
a large rock: *A boulder came down the mountain and crushed the car.*

**boulevard** /'bʊlə,vɑrd/ *noun*
*abbreviation:* Blvd. a wide major street in a city *Santa Monica Blvd. is a famous street in Los Angeles. See:* street.

**bounce** /baʊns/ *verb* **bounced, bouncing, bounces**
**1** to go quickly off a surface: *A ball bounces off the sidewalk.*
**2** to move up and down: *The mother bounced her little boy on her knee.*

**bounce** *noun*
**1** a spring: *a bounce of a ball off the wall*
**2** energy: *She walks with a bounce in her step.* –*adjective* **bouncy.**

**bouncer** /'baʊnsər/ *noun*
a strong person who makes people leave bars if they act badly

**bound (1)** /'baʊnd/ *noun*
a jump: *The dog jumped over the fence in one bound.*

**bound** *verb*
to jump, leap: *The dog bounded over the fence.*

**bound (2)** *adjective*
**1** tied up: *Her hands were bound with rope.*
**2** going toward: *I am bound for home.*
**3** required to do something: *He was bound by the contract to make monthly car payments.*

**boundary** /'baʊnd ri/ *noun, plural* **boundaries**
**1** a legal line dividing two places: *The boundary between the two towns is shown by a line on the map.*
**2** a limit: *Some things are beyond the boundaries of human knowledge.*

**boundless** /'baʊndlɪs/ *adjective*
unlimited, endless: *She is a worker with boundless energy.*

**bountiful** /'baʊntəfəl/ *adjective*
much of something, abundant: *The harvest of wheat and corn was bountiful this year.*

**bouquet** /boʊ'keɪ/ *noun*
a bunch of flowers

**bout** /baʊt/ *noun*
**1** a fighting match: *The boxer fought a 12-round bout.*
**2** *figurative* a short, difficult time, especially with illness: *Every winter, I have a bout of the flu.*

**boutique** /bu'tik/ *noun*
a small shop: *He owns a women's clothes boutique.*

**bow (1)** /boʊ/ *noun*
**1** a piece of ribbon tied into loops: *I tied the package with a red bow.*
**2** a curved piece of wood (metal, etc.) and a string used to shoot arrows: *He hunts deer with a bow and arrow.*

bow

**bow (2)** /baʊ/ *noun*
**1** the front part of a ship: *The bow moves through the water.*
**2** bending at the waist: *The singer came on stage and took a bow to the audience.*

bow

**bow** *verb*
to bend at the waist: *She bowed to the audience.*

**bowel** /'baʊəl/ *noun*
the tubes from the stomach where wastes are prepared to go out of the body
**bowel movement:** a pushing out of solid waste from the body

**bowl** /'boʊl/ *noun*
a dish with upward curved sides: *I'd like a bowl of soup, please.*

bowling

**bowl** *verb*
to roll a ball on a flat surface (bowling alley): *We bowl every Thursday night.* –*noun* (game) **bowling.**

**box (1)** /bɑks/ *noun, plural* **boxes**
**1** a square or rectangular container: *I put my books in a box.*
**2** the amount in a box: *The family ate a box of cereal.*

**box** *verb* **boxed, boxing, boxes**
to put in a box

**box (2)** *verb*
to fight with fists –*noun* (person) **boxer.**

**boy** /bɔɪ/ *noun*
**1** a young human male: *When he was a boy, he loved sports.*
**2** a son, especially young

**boy** *exclamation* of delight, surprise, or disgust: *Boy! This hot weather is too much for me!* –*noun* **boyhood;** –*adjective* **boyish.**

**boycott** /'bɔɪˌkɑt/ *verb*
deciding for political reasons not to buy products or do business with a company

**boyfriend** /'bɔɪˌfrɛnd/ *noun*
male friend, usually romantic: *Her boyfriend brings her flowers. See:* girlfriend.

**USAGE NOTE:** A *boyfriend* can describe a man of any age who has a romantic friendship with someone. *Girlfriend* can describe both a romantic friend and a non-romantic friend who is female.

**Boy Scouts** *noun plural*
*used with a singular verb* an international organization for boys, 11 or older, to develop character and outdoor skills

**bra** /brɑ/ *noun*
*short for* brassiere

**brace** /breɪs/ *noun*
**1** a support, such as a heavy piece of wood, for part of a building, etc.
**2** medical equipment used as support: *She wears a brace on her bad knee.*
**3** *plural* wires made of metal or plastic used to straighten teeth

**brace** *verb* **braced, bracing, braces**
to put up a support: *Workers braced the falling roof with metal poles.*

**bracelet** /'breɪslɪt/ *noun*
jewelry worn around the wrist or arm: *She wears gold bracelets. See:* art on page 12a.

**brag** /bræg/ *verb* **bragged, bragging, brags**
to praise one's own successes: *He brags about his own strength and good looks.*

**braid** /breɪd/ *verb*
to put pieces of hair (rope, etc.) around and between each other: *She braids her hair every morning.*

**braid** *noun*
a length of woven hair, rope, etc.: *She has gold braid on her uniform.*

**braid**

**braille** /breɪl/ *noun*
a system of reading and writing for the blind that uses raised dots to show letters, numbers, and symbols

**brain** /breɪn/ *noun*
**1** the organ in the head used for thinking and feeling: *Humans have large brains.*
**2** *figurative* intelligence: *She is so bright; she's a real brain.*

**brainstorm** /'breɪnˌstɔrm/ *verb*
to think of as many ideas as possible without criticizing them: *Every month, we brainstorm ideas for new products.*

**brake** /breɪk/ *noun*
a device that stops a wheel from turning: *I stepped on the brakes and slowed the car down.*

**brake** *verb* **braked, braking, brakes**
to put on the brakes

**branch** /bræntʃ/ *noun, plural* **branches**
**1** a tree limb: *A bird is standing on a branch of a tree.*
**2** *figurative* a smaller office of a company or institution

**branch** *verb* **branched, branching, branches**
to divide into two or more directions: *The river branches into two smaller rivers south of here.*

**brand** /brænd/ *noun*
**1** the commercial name of a product: *Ivory™ is a well-known brand of soap.*
**2** a mark put on animals to identify their owner *–verb* **to brand.**

**brand-new** /'bræn'nu/ *adjective*
new and never used before: *That is a brand-new television, not secondhand.*

**brandy** /'brændi/ *noun, plural* **brandies**
an alcoholic drink made from boiled wine or fruit juice: *She likes apple brandy.*

**brash** /bræʃ/ *adjective pejorative*
rude: *She is brash about asking for the best table at the restaurant. –adverb* **brashly;** *–noun* (act) **brashness.**

**brass** /bræs/ *noun*
a hard bright metal

**brassiere** /brə'zir/ *noun formal*
a piece of clothing that supports a woman's breasts

**brat** /bræt/ *noun pejorative*
a badly behaved child: *Her children act like brats; they won't listen to anyone. –adjective* **bratty.**

**brave** /breɪv/ *adjective*
unafraid of danger: *Firefighters are*

*brave in saving people from burning buildings.* –*adverb* **bravely;** –*noun* **bravery** /ˈbreɪvəri/. *(antonym)* cowardly.

**bread** /brɛd/ *noun*
a food made of baked flour, water or milk (and yeast): *I baked a loaf of bread.* *See:* art on page 17a.

**breadth** /brɛdθ/ *noun*
the size of something from side to side *See:* length; width.

**break** /breɪk/ *noun*
**1** the act or result of cracking something: *A break in the pipe caused water to leak out.*
**2** a stop or interruption of something: *The light went out because of a break in the supply of electricity.*
**3** an escape from prison: *There was a break at the jail last night; two prisoners escaped.*

**to get a break:** to have good or bad luck: *The factory fired 300 workers; they got a bad break. But I got a break* (or) *they gave me a break; I still have my job.*

**to take a break:** to relax for a short time

**break** *verb* **broke** /broʊk/, **breaking, breaks**
**1** to crack into pieces or damage: *The dish broke when it hit the floor.*||*The refrigerator broke because it was so old.*
**2** to push through: *The child's tooth broke through the skin.*
**3 a.** to stop activity: *Bad storms break the flow of electricity to buildings.* **b.** to pause to relax: *Let's break for lunch now.*
**4** to disobey the law: *She broke the law by stealing that money.*

**to break something** or **someone down: a.** to stop working: *This old car breaks down all the time.* **b.** to lose control of one's feelings: *When his mother died, he broke down and cried.*

**to break in: a.** to enter a building by force, *(synonym)* to burglarize: *A thief broke in and stole my TV.* **b.** to interrupt: *She broke in on the conversation.*

**to break out: a.** to develop a disease, especially a rash: *The child broke out with red spots (the measles, etc.).* **b.** to escape: *The prisoner broke out of jail.*

**to break up: a.** to laugh or cry: *His girlfriend made funny faces, and he broke up (laughing).* **b.** to separate: *Their marriage broke up after a year.*

**breakdown** /ˈbreɪkˌdaʊn/ *noun*
**1** a stopping: *The truck had a breakdown on the highway.*
**2** unable to live normally because of bad emotions: *She had a nervous breakdown.*

breakdown

**breakfast** /ˈbrɛkfəst/ *noun*
the morning meal: *We ate bacon and eggs for breakfast.*

**break-in** /ˈbreɪkˌɪn/ *noun*
a forced entry into a building: *During a break-in in our apartment, the TV was stolen.* –*verb* **to break in.**

**breakthrough** /ˈbreɪkˌθru/ *noun*
**1** the act, result, or place of pushing past something that blocks one's way: *We had a breakthrough in talks with management.*
**2** an advance: *The discovery of penicillin was an important breakthrough in stopping many diseases.*

**breakup** /ˈbreɪkˌʌp/ *noun*
a coming apart: *Mark was very sad after his breakup with Laura.*

**breast** /brɛst/ *noun*
**1** one of two organs on a woman's chest that make milk: *The baby drank milk from her mother's breast.*
**2** the front part of the body, between the neck and the stomach: *The baby slept next to her father's breast.*

**breath** /brɛθ/ *noun*
**1** a taking in of air: *She opened her mouth and took a deep breath.*
**2** the air taken in or let out while breathing: *His breath smelled like coffee.*

**breathe** /brið/ *verb* **breathed, breathing, breathes**
to take air into and out of the lungs: *She breathes deeply while she sleeps.*

**breed** /brid/ *noun*
a type of animal with characteristics passed down from its parents to its babies: *A French poodle is a breed of dog.*

**breed** *verb* **bred** /brɛd/, **breeding, breeds**
to have babies: *Animals breed in the springtime.* *–noun* (person) **breeder.**

**breeze** /briz/ *noun*
a light wind *–verb* **to breeze;** *–adjective* **breezy;** *–adverb* **breezily;** *–noun* **breeziness.**

**brew** /bru/ *verb*
**1** to make a drink by boiling, mixing, or soaking solids, such as tea leaves or coffee beans: *I brewed a pot of coffee in the coffeemaker.*
**2** to make beer

**brew** *noun*
a mixture, especially a heated one *–noun* (person) **brewer,** (place) **brewery.**

**bribe** /braɪb/ *noun*
money or actions given illegally for something: *She gave the official a bribe, so she could get a driver's license in another state.* *–noun* (act) **bribery;** *–verb* **to bribe.**

**brick** /'brɪk/ *noun*
a block of hard clay used as building material: *Apartment buildings are made of thousands of bricks.*

**bride** /'braɪd/ *noun*
a woman who is getting married: *She became a bride at age 24.* *–adjective* **bridal.**

**bridegroom** /'braɪd,grum/ or **groom** *noun*
a man who is getting married

**bridesmaid** /'braɪdz,meɪd/ *noun*
an unmarried woman who helps the bride: *There were six bridesmaids at the wedding.*

**bridge** /brɪʤ/ *noun*
**1** a structure that crosses rivers, roads, etc.: *Trains go across a bridge over the river.*
**2** the round top of the nose between the eyes *–verb* **to bridge.**

**brief** /brif/ *adjective*
short, to the point: *The manager made a brief statement to open the meeting. (antonym)* long.

**brief** *verb*
to inform: *The generals briefed the President on the military situation.* *–noun* **briefing;** *–adverb* **briefly.**

**briefcase** /'brif,keɪs/ *noun*
a soft, flat piece of luggage for holding books and papers: *She put her papers in her briefcase. See:* art on page 12a.

briefcase

**bright** /brait/ *adjective*
**1** having a strong shine or glow: *The sun is so bright that it hurts my eyes.*
**2** having strong colors: *She wears bright red dresses.*
**3** intelligent: *a bright student* *–adverb* **brightly;** *–noun* **brightness.**

**brighten** /'braitn/ *verb*
to become lighter: *The clouds left and the sky brightened. (antonym)* darken.

**brilliant** /'brɪlyənt/ *adjective*
**1** having a very bright surface: *Diamonds are brilliant. (antonym)* dull.
**2** extremely intelligent *(antonym)* dumb.
**3** perfect: *The violinist gave a brilliant performance.* *–noun* **brilliance;** *–adverb* **brilliantly.**

**brim** /brɪm/ *noun*
**1** the top of a glass, pot, etc.: *She filled the glass full to the brim.*
**2** the bottom outer edge of a hat: *His hat has a wide brim.*

**brim** *verb* **brimmed, brimming, brims**
to be full to the top: *The baskets were brimming with wheat and potatoes.*

**bring** /brɪŋ/ *verb* **brought** /brɔt/, **bringing, brings**
**1** to carry: *I bring an umbrella with me if it rains.*
**2** to go with: *She brought a friend to the party.*
**3** to cause to happen, *(synonym)* to initiate: *He brought the conversation to a close (the water to a boil, happiness to his parents).*
**4** to sell for: *That house will bring $100,000.*

**to bring something about:** to make happen, *(synonym)* to achieve: *She brought* *about a major change in the way her company sells its products.*

**to bring someone** or **something in:** to arrest: *The police brought in three criminals.*

**to bring something out:** **a.** to take outside: *I brought out the trash.* **b.** to improve: *Adding salt brings out the flavor in some foods.* **c.** to show a hidden quality: *She was a good student in high school, but going to college brought out the best in her.*

**to bring someone** or **something up:** to raise someone and care for until fully grown (children): *Parents bring up children.*

**brink** /brɪŋk/ *noun*
the top edge of a something, such as a cliff: *She looked over the brink at the water below.*

**brisk** /brɪsk/ *adjective*
**1** fast and energetic: *We took a brisk walk around the block.*
**2** sharp and cool: *A brisk wind blew through our hair.* *–adverb* **briskly.**

**brittle** /ˈbrɪtl/ *adjective*
hard and easy to break: *The bones of old people are brittle and break easily.* *–noun* **brittleness.**

**broad** /brɔd/ *adjective*
**1** big from side to side; wide: *The avenues of big cities are often broad.*
**2** covering a large amount, many topics, etc.: *That professor has a broad knowledge of history.* *–adverb* **broadly.**

**broadcast** /ˈbrɔdˌkæst/ *verb* **broadcast** or **broadcasted, broadcasting, broadcasts**
to send over the air (radio, TV): *Some radio and TV stations broadcast programs 24 hours a day.* *–noun* **broadcast,** (person) **broadcaster.**

**broccoli** /ˈbrɑk əli/ *noun*
a vegetable with thick green flowers and stems *See:* art on page 2a.

broccoli

**brochure** /broʊˈʃʊr/ *noun*
a small, printed booklet: *The travel agency mails out brochures about trips.*

**broil** /brɔɪl/ *verb*
to cook over direct heat: *She broiled a steak over a fire.*

**broke** /broʊk/
*past tense of* break

**broke** *adjective informal*
without money: *I am broke.*

**broken** /ˈbroʊkən/ *adjective*
**1** cracked, smashed, or not working: *His arm is broken.*
**2** not kept: *He reminded her of her broken promise.*

**bronze** /brɑnz/ *noun*
a gray to reddish-brown metal (made of tin and copper): *a bronze statue*

**bronze** *verb* **bronzed, bronzing, bronzes**
to make or cover with bronze

**brood** /brud/ *noun*
a group of young, especially of birds: *There is a brood of chickens in the barn.*

**brood** *verb*
to think deeply and worry: *He brooded over whether to quit his job.*

**brook** /brʊk/ *noun*
a small stream: *A brook runs in front of their house.*

**broom** /brum/ *noun*
a cleaning tool made of long, stiff threads (bristles) attached to a handle: *He used a broom to sweep the floor.*

**broth** /brɔθ/ *noun*
a clear soup: *On a cold day, he likes to eat a bowl of beef broth for lunch.*

**brother** /ˈbrʌðər/ *noun*
the male of two or more children of the same parents: *My brother, Richard, lives in New York.* *–adjective* **brotherly.** *See:* art on page 13a.

**brother-in-law** /ˈbrʌəərɪnˌlɔ/ *noun, plural* **brothers-in-law**
a brother of one's husband or wife or the husband of one's sister

**brow** /braʊ/ *noun*
the front upper area of the head between the eyes and hairline: *He has wrinkles in his brow.*

**brown** /braʊn/ *adjective*
the color that is a mixture of red, yellow, and black: *Chocolate and dirt are both brown. See:* art on page 16a.

**browse** /braʊz/ *verb* **browsed, browsing, browses**

to look over in a relaxed way: *She browsed through books in the library.*

**bruise** /bruz/ *noun*
a change in skin color that is made by a blow to the skin: *He fell on the sidewalk and got a bruise on his arm.*

**bruise** *verb* **bruised, bruising, bruises**
to make bruises: *He bruised his knee.* *See:* art on page 11a.

**brunch** /brʌntʃ/ *noun*
(*a combination of* breakfast *and* lunch) a meal in the late morning: *We had brunch on Sunday at 11:00 A.M.*

**brunet** or **brunette** /bru'nɛt/ *noun*
a person with dark hair *See:* blond; redhead.

**brunt** /brʌnt/ *noun*
the main part of something, usually unpleasant: *The sales manager took the brunt of the criticism for low sales.*

**brush** /brʌʃ/ *noun, plural* **brushes**
**1** a tool made of stiff threads (bristles of nylon, wire, hair, etc.) on a hard back: *Brushes can be used to clean, polish, smooth, or paint.*
**2** a light touch in passing

**brush** *verb* **brushed, brushing, brushes**
**1** to use a brush: *She brushed her teeth with a toothbrush.*
**2** to touch or bump someone lightly while passing: *Her coat brushed me as she ran past.* *See:* art on page 19a.

**brutal** /'brutl/ *adjective*
violent without feeling: *It was a brutal murder.* *–noun* **brutality** /bru'tæləti/; *–verb* **to brutalize** /'brutl,aɪz/; *–adverb* **brutally.**

**B.S.** /'bi'ɛs/
*abbreviation of* Bachelor of Science, a type of four-year college degree: *She graduated with a B.S. in physics.* *See:* B.A., USAGE NOTE.

**bubble** /'bʌbəl/ *noun*
a small ball of gas, especially air, covered with a liquid: *Bubbles in soft drinks don't last long.*

**bubble** *verb* **bubbled, bubbling, bubbles**
to make bubbles: *Boiling water bubbles.* *–adjective* **bubbly.**

**buck (1)** /bʌk/ *noun*
the adult male of some animals, especially deer: *A hunter shot a buck.* *See:* doe.

**buck (2)** *noun*
*slang* a US dollar: *I need ten bucks to go to the movies tonight.*

**bucket** /'bʌkɪt/ *noun*
a round container with an open top: *He filled a bucket with water.*

**buckle** /'bʌkəl/ *noun*
a metal fastener, especially for a belt

**buckle** *verb* **buckled, buckling, buckles**
to close a buckle: *I buckled the seat belt in the car.*

**bud** /'bʌd/ *noun*
a young, not fully grown leaf or flower

**bud** *verb* **budded, budding, buds**
to grow buds: *Trees and flowers bud in the springtime.*

**buddy** /'bʌdi/ *noun, plural* **buddies**
a friend: *My buddies and I go fishing every Saturday.*

**budge** /'bʌdʒ/ *verb* **budged, budging, budges**
to move a little: *This door is stuck; it won't budge.*

**budget** /'bʌdʒɪt / *noun*
a plan of income and expenses over time: *I have a budget that includes the cost of food, rent, clothes and fun.*

**budget** *verb*
to plan how much money to spend *–adjective* **budgetary.**

**buffalo** /'bʌfəloʊ/ *noun, plural* **buffalos** or **buffalo**
a large, four-legged, hoofed animal: *In Asia, farmers use water buffalos to pull plows.*

buffalo

**buffet** /bə'feɪ/ *adjective noun*
food put on a table for people to serve themselves: *For lunch we had a buffet.*

**bug** /bʌg/ *noun*
**1** an insect: *There are bugs in that dirty kitchen.*
**2** *figurative* a hidden listening device: *The spy hid a bug in the lamp.*
**3** *figurative* a problem in an electrical or mechanical device or system: *My computer program has a bug in it that makes my computer crash everytime I try to run it.*

**bug** *verb* **bugged, bugging, bugs**
**1** *informal* to annoy: *His boss keeps bugging him to work faster.*
**2** *figurative* to use a listening device: *Police bugged the criminal's telephone.*

**build** /bɪld/ *verb* **built** /bɪlt/, **building, builds**
**1** to make something: *Workers built a house of wood.*
**2** to base on: *Theories should be built on facts.*

**build** *noun*
the shape of a person's body: *He has a strong (fat, short, weak, etc.) build.*

**building** /'bɪldɪŋ/ *noun*
**1** a permanent structure: *She owns some office buildings in this area.*
**2** growth: *The building of a country (business, career) can take many years.* –*noun* **builder.**

**bulb** /bʌlb/ *noun*
an electric light: *The bulb in that lamp has burned out.*

**bulge** /bʌlʤ/ *verb* **bulged, bulging, bulges**
to stick out: *Her stomach bulged because she was expecting a baby.*

**bulk** /bʌlk/ *noun*
**1** large size: *Big animals, such as elephants and whales, have huge bulk.*
**2** the most of something: *The bulk of the students passed the exam.*

**bulky** /'bʌlki/ *adjective* **bulkier, bulkiest**
large and difficult to handle: *A mattress is bulky for one person to carry.*

**bull** /bʊl/ *noun*
the male of cattle and some other animals that can produce young

**bulldozer** /'bʊl,doʊzər/ *noun*
a large, powerful machine with a shovel or a blade in front: *Bulldozers move earth for the building of roads, etc.* –*verb* **to bulldoze.**

**bullet** /'bʊlɪt/ *noun*
a round, usually pointed piece of metal shot out of a gun

**bulletin** /'bʊlətn/ *noun*
short, public news information: *A TV news bulletin said there is a big earthquake in California.*

**bulletin board** *noun*
**1** a board on a wall where people put notices, information, etc.: *I saw our class schedule on the school bulletin board.*
**2** an electronic mail system that allows computer users to leave messages for anyone *See:* art on page 8a.

**bulletproof** /'bʊ lɪt,pruf/ *adjective*
capable of stopping bullets: *The police wear bulletproof vests.*

**bull's-eye** /'bʊlz,aɪ/ *noun*
the center of a circular target: *People shot arrows at the bull's-eye.*

**bully** /'bʊli/ *noun, plural* **bullies**
a person who makes others do things by using fear or strength: *That big boy is a bully in the schoolyard.* –*verb* **to bully.**

**bum** /bʌm/ *noun*
*pejorative* a bad person: *He drinks and does not take care of his family; he's a bum.*

**bumble** /'bʌmbəl/ *verb*
**bumbled, bumbling, bumbles** to do something in a stupid, awkward way –*noun* (person) **bumbler,** (act) **bumbling.**

**bumblebee** /'bʌmb əl,bi/ *noun*
a large, flying insect that makes honey: *Bumblebees fly from flower to flower.*

**bump** /bʌmp/ *noun*
a rounded, raised piece of something (earth, skin, etc.): *There is a bump on my arm where a mosquito bit me.*

**bump** *verb*
to hit with force: *I bumped my leg on the table.* –*adjective* **bumpy.**

**bumper** /'bʌmpər/ *noun*
a bar on the back or front of a vehicle to protect it: *The car bumper hit the wall.*

**bun** /bʌn/ *noun*
a small, roundish bread: *I had an egg on a bun for breakfast. See:* biscuit.

**bunch** /'bʌnʧ/ *noun, plural* **bunches**
a group of something: *She bought a bunch of bananas at the store.*

**bunch** *verb*
to crowd together: *People bunched together* (or) *up in the crowded bus.*

**bundle** /'bʌndl/ *noun*
things close together, usually tied: *I put a bundle of clothes in the washing machine.*

**bundle** *verb* **bundled, bundling, bundles**
to put together, to wrap up: *She bundled dirty clothes in a bag.*
**to bundle up:** to dress warmly: *Bundle up; it's cold outside!*

**bungle** /ˈbʌŋgəl/ *verb* **bungled, bungling, bungles**
to do something badly: *He bungled a report; it had many mistakes.*

**bunk** /ˈbʌŋk/ *noun*
a narrow bed, often placed one above the other: *Soldiers sleep in bunks.* –*verb* **to bunk.**

**bunny** /ˈbʌni/ *noun informal, plural* **bunnies**
a baby rabbit: *She touched the bunnies in the children's zoo.*

**buoy** /ˈbui/ *noun*
a marker floating in the water used to warn of danger or mark a passageway: *Don't swim beyond the red buoy.* –*verb* **to buoy;** –*adjective* **buoyant.**

**burden** /ˈbɜrdn/ *noun*
a heavy weight: *Elephants can carry heavy burdens, such as tree logs.*
**burden** *verb*
**1** to weigh down: *He was burdened with two big suitcases.*
**2** *figurative* to worry, trouble: *She is burdened by money troubles.* –*adjective* **burdensome** /ˈbɜrdnsəm/.

**bureau** /ˈbyʊroʊ/ *noun, plural* **bureaus**
**1** a piece of furniture with drawers: *She keeps her towels and sheets in a bureau. See:* art on page 22a.
**2** a government agency: *the Federal Bureau of Investigation*

**bureaucracy** /byʊˈrɑkrəsi/ *noun, plural* **bureaucracies**
government or business departments with complex rules and slow decision making: *Her application for citizenship has not gotten through the bureaucracy.* –*noun* (person) **bureaucrat** /ˈbyʊrəˌkræt/; –*adjective* **bureaucratic** /ˌbyʊrəˈkrætɪk/.

**burglar** /ˈbɜrglər/ *noun*
a thief who illegally enters a building: *A burglar broke the door lock and stole my TV.* –*verb* **to burglarize** /ˈbɜrgləˌraɪz/; –*noun* (act) **burglary.**

**burn** /ˈbɜrn/ *verb* **burned** or **burnt** /ˈbɜrnt/, **burning, burns**
**1** to be on fire: *The house is burning.*
**2** to hurt with fire: *The fire burned her hand.*
**to burn something down** or **up:** to destroy by fire: *A fire burned down the house.*||*The fire burned the car up.*
**burn** *noun*
an injury or wound caused by fire or sunlight: *She had a burn on her hand. See:* sunburn.

**burnout** /ˈbɜrnˌaʊt/ *noun*
**1** the breakdown of a machine, especially because of heat: *Don't run the engine without oil, or you'll have a burnout.*
**2** extreme tiredness: *Many students have burnout after taking exams.*

**burp** /bɜrp/ *verb*
gas coming from the stomach through the mouth: *The man burped after eating lunch.* –*noun* **burp.**

**burrow** /ˈbɜroʊ/ *verb*
to dig into the ground: *Some animals burrow with their paws.*

**burst** /bɜrst/ *noun*
**1** a sudden outpouring: *There was a burst of laughter from the audience.*
**2** a fast action: *She ran by me in a burst of speed.*
**burst** *verb* **burst, bursting, bursts**
to break open suddenly, especially because of inside pressure: *A pipe burst, shooting water into the air.*

**bury** /ˈbɛri/ *verb* **buried, burying, buries**
**1** to put a dead person in a grave: *He buried his father yesterday.*
**2** to hide, especially in the ground: *A dog buried a bone.* –*noun* **burial.**

**bus** /bʌs/ *noun, plural* **buses** or **busses**
a large, often public vehicle used to carry passengers: *He takes the bus to work every day. See:* art on page 4a.

**bush** /bʊʃ/ *noun, plural* **bushes**
a plant shorter than a tree, usually with branches and leaves: *I cut the rose bushes in the front yard.*
**to beat around the bush:** to talk about something without getting to the point: *Say what you have to say and stop beating around the bush.*

B

**bushel** /ˈbʊʃəl/ *noun*
a unit of dry measure equal to 2,150.42 cubic inches (35.24 liters) in the USA

**business** /ˈbɪznɪs/ *noun, plural* **businesses**
**1** activities of people buying and selling goods and services: *Business is good in today's economy.*
**2** an organization of people, buildings, and products or services: *The businesses on Main Street include a supermarket, a candy store, and a dry cleaners.*
**to mean business:** to be serious: *They really mean business. If you don't pay them by next week, they're going to take you to court.*
**to mind one's own business:** not to interfere in the lives of others: *You mind your own business and stay out of mine!*
**none of your business:** not of concern to you

**businessman** /ˈbɪznɪsˌmæn/ *noun, plural* **businessmen** /-ˌmɛn/
a man who does business: *Businessmen travel all over the world.*

---

USAGE NOTE: *Businessperson* is used to discuss both men and women in business.

---

**businesswoman** /ˈbɪznɪsˌwʊmən/ *noun, plural* **businesswomen** /-ˌwɪmən/
a woman who does business: *Businesswomen can earn a lot of money in Los Angeles.*

**bust** /bʌst/ *noun*
**1** a statue of the head and upper part of the chest and shoulders: *There are busts of famous writers in the library.*
**2** a woman's chest area: *The dressmaker measured her bust and waist to make her wedding dress.*

**bustle** /ˈbʌsəl/ *verb* **bustled, bustling, bustles**
to do something with energy: *At lunchtime, that restaurant bustles with activity.*

**busy** /ˈbɪzi/ *adjective* **busier, busiest**
**1** active, working: *I'm busy writing a report now, but I can talk to you later.*
**2** on the telephone: *Her line is busy now.*
*–verb* **to busy;** *–adverb* **busily.**

**but** /bət/ *conjunction*
**1** in contrast, on the other hand: *She is pretty, but he is ugly.*
**2** except for: *No one but John saw the accident happen.*
**3** except that: *We wanted to buy that house, but the price was too high.*
**4** instead of the expected: *It rained all day, but we still had a good time.*
**5** without the result that, *(synonym)* unless: *It never rains but it pours heavily.*

**but** *preposition*
except: *I want nothing but the truth from you.*

**but** *adverb*
only: *She's but a baby.*

**butcher** /ˈbʊʧər/ *noun*
a person or business that cuts and sells meat: *I went to the butcher to buy a chicken.*

**butcher** *verb*
to kill animals and cut their meat *–noun* (act) **butchery.**

**butler** /ˈbʌtlər/ *noun*
the main male servant in a household: *The butler poured the wine.*

**butt (1)** /bʌt/ *verb*
to hit or push with the head or an animal's horns: *Two goats butted each other.*

**butt (2)** *noun*
**1** the unsmoked end of a cigarette or cigar: *She put the cigarette butt into the ashtray.*
**2** *slang* the buttocks or bottom: *She fell on her butt.*

**butter** /ˈbʌtər/ *noun*
a yellowish fat made from milk or cream: *I put some butter on my bread.*

**butter** *verb*
to put butter: *She buttered her toast.* *See:* art on page 17a.

**butterfly** /ˈbʌtərˌflaɪ/ *noun, plural* **butterflies**
an insect with a narrow body and four wings: *There are many types of butterflies, most of which are very colorful.*

**butterfly**

**buttermilk** /ˈbʌt ərˌmɪlk/ *noun, (no plural)*
the thick, sour milk left over after butterfat has been removed from whole milk

**buttocks** /ˈbʌtəks/ *noun plural*
the part of the body where one sits: *See:* bottom; rear end; butt.

**button** /ˈbʌtn/ *noun*
**1** a small round fastener for holding clothing together: *A button on his shirt fell off.*
**2** a part like a button on a machine
**button** *verb*
to fasten a button: *He buttoned his shirt.*
**to button something up:** to fasten with buttons: *He buttoned up his shirt.*

**buttonhole** /ˈbʌt nˌhoʊl/ *noun*
an opening in fabric for a button

**buy** /baɪ/ *noun*
**1** a purchase
**2** *informal* something bought at a low price: *That car is a great buy.*
**buy** *verb* **bought** /bɔt/, **buying, buys**
to pay for: *I buy a newspaper every morning.* *–noun* (person) **buyer.**

**buzz** /bʌz/ *noun, plural* **buzzes**
a low sound of zzz's, like that made by a fly: *The buzz of the bee around me was annoying.*
**buzz** *verb* **buzzed, buzzing, buzzes**
**1** to make a low humming sound: *Bees buzz as they fly.*
**2** to have a lot of energy: *That office buzzes with activity.* *–noun* (device) **buzzer,** (action) **buzzing.**

**buzzard** /ˈbʌzərd/ *noun*
a large bird that eats dead meat: *Buzzards stood around the dead animal.*

**by** /baɪ/ *preposition*
**1** next to: *The chair is by the door.*
**2** through the action of something: *She was hit by a car.*
**3** across or past: *The bird flew by the window.*
**4** not later than: *You must wake up by 8 o'clock.*
**5** during: *They traveled by night.*
**6** according to: *He's five minutes late by my watch.*
**7** adding one direction of measurement to another: *The room is 8' by 10', meaning that it is eight feet long and ten feet wide.*
**by** *adverb*
**by the way:** introducing a new topic of conversation

**bye** /baɪ/ *interjection*
good-bye, so long: *Bye, I'll see you tomorrow.*

**bypass** /ˈbaɪˌpæs/ *noun, plural* **bypasses**
a temporary road around a road being repaired
**bypass** *verb*
to go around, avoid

**bystander** /ˈbaɪˌstændər/ *noun*
someone near but not participating in something: *My brother was an innocent bystander when he saw a robbery happening across the street.*

**byte** /baɪt/ *noun*
a unit of measurement for computer data, equal to eight bits: *One character (such as the letter "a") takes up one byte of space.*

# C,c

**C,c** /si/ *noun* **C's, c's** or **Cs, cs**
**1** the third letter of the English alphabet
**2** a school grade below B and above D

**cab** /kæb/ *noun*
**1** a car that carries passengers for a fare (price), a taxicab: *Let's take a cab.*
**2** a section where the driver sits in a large vehicle or piece of machinery: *Trucks, train engines, etc., have cabs.*

**cabbage** /ˈkæbɪʤ/ *noun*
a large, round, green or purple leafy vegetable similar to lettuce *See:* art on page 2a.

**cabdriver** /ˈkæbˌdraɪvər/ *noun*
a person who drives a taxicab

**cabin** /ˈkæbɪn/ *noun*
**1** a small, simple house
**2** a room for sleeping on a ship
**3** an enclosed section of a boat or plane: *The passengers and crew are in the cabin.*

**cabinet** /ˈkæbənɪt/ *noun*
**1** a piece of furniture with shelves and doors used to store things: *We keep dishes and canned food in the cabinets over the kitchen sink.*
**2** a group of high-level government officials: *the President's cabinet See:* art on page 7a.

**cable** /ˈkeɪbəl/ *noun*
**1** strong, thick rope, usually made of many wires twisted together: *Steel cables support that bridge.*
**2** a covered bunch of wires that carries electronic messages: *electric cable See:* cable television.

**cable** *verb* **cabled, cabling, cables**
to send a message electronically: *The newspaper reporter cabled a story to the newspaper.*

**cable television** or **cable TV** *noun*
a type of television service that sends its programs to customers who pay for the service: *The TV pictures sent by cable television are very clear.*

**cacao** /kəˈkaʊ/ *noun, plural* **cacaos**
a tree of Latin America that bears beans from which chocolate and cocoa are made

**cactus** /ˈkæktəs/ *noun, plural* **cacti** /-ˌtaɪ/ or **cactuses**
a green desert plant with sharp needles

cactus

**cafe** or **café** /kæˈfeɪ/ *noun*
**1** a restaurant that serves simple food and drinks: *We went to a cafe for coffee.*
**2** a restaurant that serves alcoholic drinks, and sometimes provides entertainment, a bar, nightclub

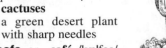

---

**USAGE NOTE:** *Café* is one of several words used to describe kinds of *restaurants. Cafés* and *coffee shops* usually serve drinks such as coffee, tea, and soda, but cafés serve simple meals, and coffee shops usually serve dessert foods. A *coffee house* is like a café or coffee shop except that people at coffee houses often listen to poetry or music while they drink and eat. *Cafeterias* and *diners* are inexpensive restaurants that serve hot meals. At a cafeteria, customers walk along a line of food, choose their food, and pay at the end of the line. Diners are informal restaurants that serve home-style food, and are often open from the early morning until late at night.

**cafeteria** /ˌkæfəˈtɪriə/ *noun*
a restaurant where customers serve themselves: *Our college has a big cafeteria. See:* café, USAGE NOTE.

**caffeine** /kæˈfin/ *noun*
an ingredient in coffee and tea that energizes the heart and breathing: *The caffeine in coffee makes me nervous.*

**cage** /keɪʤ/ *noun*
an area enclosed with metal bars to keep animals from escaping: *At the zoo, you can see many animals in cages.*

**cage** *verb* **caged, caging, cages**
to close an animal in a cage: *Birds are caged to keep them from flying away.*

**cake** /keɪk/ *noun*
**1** a sweet baked food made of a mixture of flour, eggs, milk, sugar, etc.: *He ate some chocolate cake.*
**2** something shaped like a cake: *She bought a cake of soap.*

**a piece of cake:** something that is simple to do, an easy task: *That job is so easy; it's a piece of cake! –verb* **to cake.**

**calcium** /ˈkælsiəm/ *noun*
a white mineral that is found in bones, shells, and milk: *People need calcium to have strong bones.*

**calculate** /ˈkælk yəˌleɪt/ *verb* **calculated, calculating, calculates**
to do math (to add, subtract, etc.) *–noun* **calculation.**

**calculator** /ˈkælkyəˌleɪtər/ *noun*
a small electronic device for doing math: *Calculators let you do calculations fast and accurately. See:* art on page 20a.

calculator

**calendar** /ˈkæləndər/ *noun*
a chart of the days and months of a year or years: *She writes the times of her meetings on her appointment calendar. See:* art on page 8a.

**calf** /kæf/ *noun, plural* **calves** /kævz/
a baby cow or bull: *The young of some large animals, such as the cow and hippopotamus, are called "calves."*

**call** /kɔl/ *noun*
**1** a loud voice, a shout: *He gave a call to his friend across the street.*
**2** a telephone conversation: *I will give you a call at home tonight.*
**3** a short visit: *I made a call at my aunt's house before going home.*
**4** a sound made by animals: *Bird calls filled the air.*

**call** *verb*
**1** to telephone: *I called you yesterday.*
**2** to name someone or something: *We live in a town called San Marcos.*
**3** to shout or say something loudly: *She called her friend's name.||A swimmer called out for help.*
**4** to ask someone to come to you: *The mother called her children inside the house.*
**5** to order to appear: *He was called before a court of law.*

**to call for:** to need: *This situation calls for immediate action.*

**to call someone up:** **a.** to telephone someone: *I called up the police for help.* **b.** to tell someone to come for military duty: *He was called up for duty last week.*

**to call something off:** **a.** to order away: *The owner called off his dog when it barked at the child.* **b.** to stop or put off, *(synonyms)* to cancel, postpone: *We called off the picnic when it began to rain.*

**caller** /ˈkɔlər/ *noun*
**1** a person who telephones another person: *The caller on the phone is from your bank.*
**2** a visitor: *Come downstairs, you have a caller.*

**callus** /ˈkæləs/ *noun, plural* **calluses**
a hard place on the skin: *I have calluses on my hands from working in the garden.*

C

**calm** /kɑm/ *adjective*
**1** peaceful: *I feel calm now that my exams are over.*
**2** almost or totally motionless: *The ocean is calm today; it looks like a mirror.*
**calm** *noun*
peace: *At night, a calm settled over the battlefield.*
**calm** *verb*
to make quiet, peaceful: *She calmed her nerves with a cup of tea.* –*adverb* **calmly;** –*noun* **calmness.**

**calorie** /'kæləri/ *noun*
**1** a unit used to measure the amount of heat in something
**2** a unit used to measure the amount of energy produced by food: *Potatoes with gravy and butter have a lot of calories.*

**calves** /kævz/ *noun plural of* calf

**camcorder** /'kæm,kɔrdər/ *noun*
a hand-held TV camera and recorder whose tapes can be played on a videocassette recorder (VCR): *We used our camcorder to tape our vacation.*

**came** /keɪm/ *verb*
*past tense of* come

**camel** /'kæməl/ *noun*
a large, four-legged animal with a long neck and hump(s) on its back: *Camels can live in the desert without water for a long time.*

**camera** /'kæmrə/ *noun*
a device used to take pictures, such as photographs, movies, or pictures for TV: *She used her camera to take pictures on her vacation.*

**camp** /kæmp/ *noun*
**1** a place outdoors where people live in tents: *Lisa and Rumi set up camp in the woods.*
**2** a cabin in the countryside: *Her parents have a camp by a lake in Canada.*
**camp** *verb*
to set up a camp and sleep outdoors: *People camp* (or) *camp out in the woods in the summer.*
**to go camping:** *They like to go camping.*

**campaign** /kæm'peɪn/ *noun*
an organized effort by people to reach a goal: *A politician runs a political campaign to get elected to office.*

**camper** /'kæmpər/ *noun*
**1** a person who goes camping: *Campers enjoy the outdoors.*
**2** a vehicle used for camping trips that usually includes a place to sleep

camper

**campus** /'kæmpəs/ *noun*
the land and buildings of a college, university, or some business headquarters: *I study on campus in the college library.*

**can (1)** /kæn/
*auxiliary verb*
**1** able to do something: *She can run fast.*||*He can speak English and Spanish.*
**2** to have the right or power to do something: *We can vote.*
**3** to have or not have permission: *You can go to the movies tonight. See:* auxiliary verb.

**USAGE NOTE:** Compare *can* and *may. Can* is used to talk about the ability to do something: *The little boy can tie his own shoes now. May* is used to talk about permission: *You may sit down now.*||*May I go to the bathroom?* Some people use *can* to ask for permission as in *"Mom, can I go to the movies?"* but *"May I go to the movies?"* is more formal English.

**can (2)** /kɑen/ *noun*
a metal container, usually with flat ends and rounded sides, sealed without air to keep foods and drinks fresh and pure: *I opened a can of soup.*

**canal** /kə'næl/ *noun*
**1** a waterway for boats to carry goods and passengers: *The Erie Canal connects the Great Lakes with New York Harbor.*
**2** (in medicine) a tube in the body that holds or carries fluid: *the ear canal*

**canary** /kə'nɛri/ *noun, plural* **canaries**
a small, usually yellow bird that sings

**cancel** /'kænsəl/ *verb*
to stop something previously agreed on or planned: *I canceled my airline reservations.* –*noun* **cancellation.**

**cancer** /'kænsər/ *noun*
a disease that causes lumps (tumors) to grow in the body and often kills people: *Smoking causes lung cancer.*

**candidate** /'kænd ə,deɪt/ *noun*
**1** a person running for a political office: *She and two other politicians are candidates for mayor.*
**2** a person or thing ready for something: *He is a candidate for a job.* *–noun* **candidacy** /'kændədəsi/.

**candle** /'kændl/ *noun*
a round, usually long piece of wax with a wick (piece of string) that is burned for light: *The candles lighted the dining room with a soft glow.* *See:* art on page 5a.

**candy** /'kændi/ *noun, plural* **candies**
sweet food made with sugar and often with chocolate, nuts, or fruits: *I ate some chocolate candy.*

**cane** /keɪn/ *noun*
a stick made of wood or metal used to help a person walk

**cannibal** /'kænəbəl/ *noun*
a person who eats other people

**cannon** /'kænən/ *noun, plural* **cannons** or **cannon**
a large gun used to fire shells long distances: *A ship fired its cannons against soldiers on land.*

cannon

**cannot** /'kæ,nɑt/ *verb negative of* can
**1** to be unable to do something: *I cannot play the piano.*
**2** to not have permission: *Her boss told her that she cannot take the day off from work.* *See:* can't.

**canoe** /kə'nu/ *noun*
a light, narrow type of boat: *Native Americans used canoes to travel on rivers.* *–verb* **to canoe.** *See:* kayak.

**can't** /kænt/ *verb*
*contraction of* cannot: *I can't speak French.*

**cantaloupe** /'kæn tl,oʊp/ *noun*
a round melon with rough skin and sweet, light-orange insides *See:* art on page 3a.

**canvas** /'kænvəs/ *noun, plural* **canvases**
**1** a thick, rough cloth used for ships' sails, tents, and coverings
**2** cloth stretched over a wooden frame for painting pictures: *She paints with oil on canvas.*

**canyon** /'kænyən/ *noun*
a long, deep hole in the earth's surface: *The Colorado River flows through the Grand Canyon.*

**cap** /kæp/ *noun*
**1** a removable top to a bottle, jar, etc.: *Please put the cap back on the medicine bottle.*
**2** a soft hat: *a baseball cap*

**cap** *verb* **capped, capping, caps**
to cover with a cap: *Workers capped an oil well to prevent oil from spilling.* *See:* art on page 12a.

**capability** /,keɪpə'bɪləti/ *noun, plural* **capabilities**
the ability or power to do something: *He has the capability to speak four languages.* *–adjective* **capable.**

**capacity** /kə'pæsəti/ *noun, plural* **capacities**
**1** the ability to contain, hold, or absorb: *That restaurant has a 100-seat capacity.*||*a tank with a 100 gallon capacity*
**2** the ability to do something: *He has the capacity to work long hours.*

**cape** *noun*
an area of land stretching out into the sea: *Cape Cod, Massachusetts, is a popular vacation area.*

**capital (1)** /'kæpətl/ *noun*
the official place where a state, provincial, or national government is located: *Washington, DC is the capital of the USA.*

**USAGE NOTE:** In the USA, the building(s) where a state's or the country's elected officials meet is called the *capitol,* spelled with an "o."

**capital (2)** *noun*
wealth, such as money, land, buildings, etc., owned by a person, business, or institution (church, government)

**capital (3)** *noun*
a letter written in tall form, *(synonym)*

upper-case: *This sentence begins with a capital T.*

**capitalism** /ˈkæpətl,ɪzəm/ *noun*
an economic system based on private ownership, competition, and a free market: *After the Soviet Union broke up, the government there began to move from communism toward capitalism.* –*adjective* **capitalistic** /ˌkæpətlˈɪstɪk/. *See:* communism; socialism.

**capital punishment** *noun*
the legal act of putting to death criminals who commit very serious crimes: *Some states in the USA allow capital punishment; others do not.*

**capitol** /ˈkæpətl/ *noun*
the building in which the governing body of a state meets: *Elected representatives discussed new laws in the capitol.* *See:* capital (1), USAGE NOTE.

capitol

**capsule** /ˈkæpsəl/ *noun*
medicine inside a soft gelatin coating: *Capsules dissolve in your stomach, releasing the medicine.*

**captain** /ˈkæptən/ *noun*
**1** the top officer in command of a ship: *The captain went on board the ship.*
**2** in the USA, a military officer above below major
**3** general head of a group or team: *The captain of the football team encouraged the players.*

**captive** /ˈkæptɪv/ *noun*
someone taken and held by force against their will, (*synonym*) a prisoner: *Soldiers put an enemy captive in prison.* –*noun* **captivity.**

**capture** /ˈkæptʃər/ *verb* **captured, capturing, captures**
**1** to take someone or something by force: *The police captured a criminal.*
**2** to keep information: *Cameras capture special memories in photos.*

**car** /kɑr/ *noun*
**1** an automobile: *I drive my car to work every day.*
**2** a vehicle that runs on tracks or wires: *a railroad car, a subway car, a cable car* *See:* art on page 24a.

**caramel** /ˈkærəməl/ *noun*
a candy made with sugar, butter, and milk or cream: *Caramel candy is smooth, rich, and chewy.*

**carat** /ˈkærət/ *noun*
a measurement of the weight of precious stones (diamonds, rubies, etc.) or gold equal to 200 milligrams: *Her diamond is five carats.*

**caravan** /ˈkærə,væn/ *noun*
a group of people making a trip together: *A caravan of people and their camels crossed the desert.*

**carbohydrate** /ˌkɑrboʊˈhaɪ,dreɪt/ *noun*
any of a group of substances (nutrients) such as sugar and starch, that provide the body with energy: *Grains and fruits are high in carbohydrates.*

**carbon** /ˈkɑrbən/ *noun*
the chemical element found in coal, graphite, and diamonds: *The black lead in pencils is made of soft carbon.*

**carbon dioxide** /daɪˈɑk,saɪd/ *noun*
a gas formed when people and animals breathe: *About 1% of the air around the earth is made up of carbon dioxide.*

**carbon monoxide** /məˈnɑk,saɪd/ *noun*
an extremely poisonous gas

**carburetor** /ˈkɑrbə,reɪtər/ *noun*
a device on an engine that mixes fuel and air so the engine can burn it

**card** /kɑrd/ *noun*
**1** a piece of stiff paper or plastic used for many purposes, such as a credit card, business card, greeting card, or postcard
**2** a playing card: *There are 52 cards in a deck.*

**to lay one's cards on the table:** to say what one thinks: *After many meetings, she finally laid her cards on the table and offered me the job.*

**cardboard** /ˈkɑrd,bɔrd/ *noun*
flat, stiff, thick paper: *The gift arrived in a cardboard box.*

**cardinal** /ˈkɑrd nəl/ *noun*
**1** a Roman Catholic clergyman ranking below the Pope
**2** a red songbird

**cardinal** *adjective*
related to numbers used in counting: *Some cardinal numbers are 1, 2, 3, and 200. See:* ordinal.

**care** /kɛr/ *verb* **cared, caring, cares**
**1** to feel concern about the health and safety of others: *She cares about everyone; she cares about people.*
**2** concerned about something, to worry: *She cares about the quality of her work.*

**not to care for:** not to like or love: (love) *I don't care for her.*||(like) *He doesn't care for carrots or beans.*

**to care for someone** or **something:** to look after someone's health: *When she was sick, he cared for her day and night.*

**care** *noun*
**1** concern for others: *He shows care for every one of his children.*
**2** supervision of someone's health or well-being: *The nurses and doctors took good care of me in the hospital.*
**3** close attention: *She did her school report with great care.*

**career** /kəˈrɪr/ *noun*
a life's work, especially in business or in a profession: *She has a career in teaching high school English.*

**careful** /ˈkɛrfəl/ *adjective*
**1** being aware of danger: *Be careful when you cross the street.*
**2** wanting to be accurate, correct: *He was very careful to say exactly what he meant in his report.* *–adverb* **carefully;** *–noun* **carefulness.** *(antonym)* careless.

**caress** /kəˈrɛs/ *noun, plural* **caresses**
a gentle touch or pat, showing love: *She gave the baby a caress on the cheek.* *–verb* **to caress.**

**caretaker** /ˈkɛr,teɪkər/ *noun*
a person who takes care of a piece of property: *Large houses often have a caretaker who does the gardening and repairs.*

**cargo** /ˈkɑrgoʊ/ *noun, plural* **cargoes** or **cargos**
goods usually in large amounts: *Cargo is carried on ships, airplanes, and trucks.*

**carnival** /ˈkɑrnəvəl/ *noun*
a celebration with singing, dancing, and usually a parade: *The carnival in Rio in Brazil is world-famous. See:* festival.

**carol** /ˈkærəl/ *noun*
a song of joy and praise, for Christmas: *We sang carols in church.* *–verb* **to carol.**

**carpenter** /ˈkɑr pəntər/ *noun*
a person who earns a living by making and building things with wood: *A team of 12 carpenters built that house.* *–noun* (skill) **carpentry** /ˈkɑrpəntri/.

**carpet** /ˈkɑrpɪt/ *noun*
a floor covering of woven fabric or other material, a rug: *The carpet needs cleaning; someone dropped food on it.* *–verb* **to carpet.**

**car pool** *noun*
a travel arrangement to and from work (school, etc.) in which the riders share a car and travel expenses: *My high-school son goes in a car-pool to school with two of his friends.* *–verb* **to car-pool.**

**carrot** /ˈkærət/ *noun*
a plant whose orange-colored root is eaten as a vegetable *See:* art on page 2a.

**carry** /ˈkæri/ *verb* **carried, carrying, carries**
**1** to hold and move someone or something from one place to another: *The bus carries people to work.*||*I carried food home from the store.*
**2** to support weight: *Those thick wires carry the weight of that bridge.*
**3** to be important: *The boss always listens to her; her opinions carry a lot of weight with him.*
**4** to include a guarantee or penalty: *That car carries a five-year warranty.*||*The parking ticket carries a $50 fine.*

**to become** or **get carried away:** to do too much of something and lose control of oneself: *He got carried away and talked for hours.*

**cart** /kɑrt/ *noun*
a small, light vehicle: *Shopping carts are pushed by hand. See:* art on page 10a.

**carton** /ˈkɑrtn/ *noun*
a container made of stiff, thick paper or cardboard: *I bought a carton of milk.*

C

**cartoon** /kɑr'tun/ *noun*
**1** a picture or group of pictures, often with words, drawn to make people laugh: *I like to look at the cartoons in the morning newspaper.*
**2** a short usually funny film *–noun* (person) **cartoonist.**

**cartridge** /'kɑrtrɪʤ/ *noun*
**1** a bullet with gun powder inside a round, metal case: *She loaded the cartridges into the gun.*
**2** a small, removable container in a larger device: *I changed the ink cartridge in my ballpoint pen.*

**carve** /karv/ *verb* **carved, carving, carves**
**1** to cut (meat, vegetables) into pieces: *She carved the turkey at the table.*
**2** to shape something by cutting: *She carves jewelry out of precious stones.* *–noun* (person) **carver.**

**car wash** *noun, plural* **washes**
a business where cars are washed: *We took our car to the car wash to have it cleaned and waxed.*

**case (1)** /keɪs/ *noun*
**1** a protective cover for other things: *a suitcase, cigarette case, a bookcase*
**2** a container holding a certain number of cans, bottles, etc.: *I bought a case of canned beans (beer, shampoo, baby food).*

**case (2)** *noun*
**1** an example, particular event, or condition: *The accident was a case of being in the wrong place at the wrong time.*
**2** convincing arguments or proof (in law): *His lawyer told him that he had a good legal case.*

**in case** (or) **in case of:** should something happen: *In case of fire, call the fire department.*

**cash** /kæʃ/ *noun*
paper money, such as dollar bills, or metal coins used in making daily purchases: *I am going to the bank to get some cash.*||*Will you pay in cash or by credit card?* ||*I will pay cash.*

**cash** *verb* **cashes**
to give a check for paper money: *I cashed a $100 check at the bank.*

**cashier** /kæ'ʃɪr/ *noun*
a person who takes payment from customers in a store, restaurant, etc.: *The cashiers at the supermarket ring up sales, take your money, and give you change. See:* teller; art on page 10a.

**Cash on Delivery**
*See:* COD.

**casino** /kə'sinoʊ/ *noun, plural* **casinos**
a large hall, especially for gambling: *The casinos in Las Vegas are as big as football fields.*

---

**USAGE NOTE:** Each state in the USA makes its own laws about *gambling,* so in some places casinos are legal and in other places they are not. The most famous cities with *casinos* are *Las Vegas, Nevada,* and *Atlantic City, New Jersey.*

---

**casserole** /'kæsəˌroʊl/ *noun*
a deep dish for baking and serving mixed foods: *a casserole of pasta and cheese*

**cassette** /kə'sɛt/ *noun*
a container (cartridge) with photographic or sound tape used to record or play back sights or sounds: *I put a cassette in the tape player to listen to jazz.* *–noun* (device) **cassette player.**

**cast (1)** /kæst/ *noun*
the group of actors in a play or movie or the characters in a book

**cast (2)** *verb* **cast, casting, casts**
to throw something (a net, line, rope): *A fisherman cast a net into the water.*
**to cast a** or **one's ballot:** to vote: *She cast her ballot in the election.*

**cast** *noun*
(in medicine) a hard covering used to keep a broken bone still while it heals: *The doctor put a cast on the football player's broken leg. See:* art on page 11a.

**castle** /'kæsəl/ *noun*
a large building or group of buildings with thick walls against attack: *Europe has many old castles.*

**casual** /'kæʒuəl/ *adjective*
informal: *In the summer, people dress in casual clothes, like T-shirts and shorts.* *–adverb* **casually;** *–noun* **casualness.**

**cat** /kæt/ *noun*
**1** a general term for a group of four-legged, furry animals with sharp teeth and claws: *Cats include lions, tigers, leopards, house cats, etc.*
**2** a small cat with soft fur: *People love cats as pets.*

**the cat's meow:** the very best: *They love their new house; they think it's the cat's meow.* *See:* art on page 14a.

**catalog** or **catalogue** /'kætl ˌɔg/ *noun*
a booklet containing information about products, school courses, etc.: *Businesses mail out catalogs of their products to customers.*

**catastrophe** /kə 'tæstrəfi/ *noun*
a great disaster: *Strong earthquakes are catastrophes that kill thousands of people.* –*adjective* **catastrophic.**

**catch** /kæʧ/ *noun, plural* **catches**
**1** an act of taking hold of something in motion: *One player threw the ball and the other made a good catch.*
**2** a fastener: *I opened the catch on a door.*
**3** a hidden difficulty or unpleasant requirement: *There is a catch in that contract where you have to pay all the money now, but wait six months for delivery of the product.*

**to play catch:** to throw a ball back and forth between people: *The children are playing catch in the playground.*

**catch** *verb* **caught** /kɔt/, **catching, catches**
**1** to stop and hold something in motion: *Here, catch the ball.*
**2** to close the distance between you and someone else: *A runner caught up with the others and passed them.*
**3** to get somewhere on time: *Hurry, we've got a plane to catch!*
**4** to stop and hold: *The police catch criminals every day.*
**5** to hook on something: *His coat caught on the door handle.*
**6** to get a sickness: *I catch a cold every winter.*

**to catch on:** **a.** to understand: *She is a bright student; she catches on to new things quickly.* **b.** to become popular: *That new product (actor, film, etc.) has really caught on.*

**to catch one's breath:** to begin to breathe normally: *The runner stopped and caught her breath.*

**category** /'kætəˌgɔri/ *noun, plural* **categories**
a group or type of thing (idea, problem, etc.): *I place him in the category of an excellent student.* –*verb* **to categorize.**

**caterpillar** /'kætəˌpɪlər/ *noun*
a small fuzzy worm-like creature with many legs: *A caterpillar turns into a butterfly or moth.*

**cathedral** /kə'θidrəl/ *noun*
a great church

**Catholic** /'kæθlɪk/ *adjective*
of or belonging to the Roman Catholic Church –*noun* (person) **Catholic,** (religion) **Catholicism** /kə'θɑləˌsɪzəm/.

**catsup** /'kɛʧəp/ *noun*
*variation of* ketchup

**cattle** /'kætl/ *noun plural*
cows, bulls, and oxen as a group: *Cattle are raised for meat, milk, and leather.*

**Caucasian** /kɔ'ke ɪʒən/ *noun*
a white person: *The criminal was a male Caucasian.*

**caught** /kɔt/ *verb*
*past tense and past participle of* catch

**cauliflower** /'kɔlɪˌflauər/ *noun*
a plant in the cabbage family whose white, flowered head is eaten as a vegetable *See:* art on page 2a.

cauliflower

**cause** /kɔz/ *noun*
**1** a reason something happens: *The cause of fire was a broken electric wire.*
**2** an effort centered on a goal: *She works for a political cause against higher taxes. See:* movement.

**cause** *verb* **caused, causing, causes**
to make something happen: *His carelessness caused the car accident.*

**caution** /'kɔʃən/ *noun*
**1** concern about not making a mistake: *He uses caution when he crosses a busy street, not to get hit by a car.*
**2** warning about danger: *A big sign blocking the road says, "Caution! Danger Ahead."* –*verb* **to caution.**

**cautious** /'kɔʃəs/ *adjective*
**1** careful: *He has a cautious attitude about spending money.*
**2** concerned about danger: *She is very*

*cautious when she goes out alone at night.* –*adverb* **cautiously.**

**cave** /keɪv/ *noun*
a hole in the ground, usually with an opening in the side of a hill or mountain: *People lived in caves long ago.*

C

**cavity** /'kævəti/ *noun, plural* **cavities**
a hole or hollow place: *I went to the dentist to have two cavities in my teeth filled.*

**cc** /'si'si/ *noun abbreviation of*
**1** carbon copy: *I sent a letter to a company with a cc to my lawyer.*
**2** cubic centimeter

---

**USAGE NOTE:** This abbreviation is often put at the end of a business letter to let the receiver of a letter know who else received a copy of the letter: *I see that you sent a cc of this letter to my boss, so she should already know about our meeting.*

---

**CD** /ˌsi'di/ *noun*
*abbreviation of* compact disc: *I bought two new CDs today.*

**CD-Rom** /ˌsi'di'rɑm/ *noun*
a compact disc with a read-only memory

**cease** /sis/ *verb formal* **ceased, ceasing, ceases**
to stop an action: *The government ordered the company to cease selling the bad medicine.*

**ceiling** /'silɪŋ/ *noun*
**1** the top part of a room: *The ceilings in our house are covered with plaster.*
**2** an upper limit: *The Congress put a ceiling on government spending. See:* art on page 6a.

**celebrate** /'sɛləˌbreɪt/ *verb* **celebrated, celebrating, celebrates**
to do something special (like having a party) for an occasion: *I celebrated my birthday with friends in my favorite restaurant.* –*noun* **celebration** /ˌsɛlə'breɪʃən/.

**celebrity** /sə'lɛbrəti/ *noun, plural* **celebrities**
a famous, living person: *Popular movie stars are celebrities.*

**celery** /'sɛləri/ *noun*
a green plant eaten as a vegetable: *Celery makes noise when you eat it raw. See:* art on page 2a.

**cell** /sɛl/ *noun*
**1** the basic unit of living things: *Our bodies are made up of cells.*
**2** a small room locked from the outside: *The police put the thief in a prison cell.*
**3** a unit for making or storing electricity: *Some cells change chemical energy into electrical energy.*

**cellar** /'sɛlər/ *noun*
the space below ground under a building: *Please put the old clothes in the cellar.*

**cello** /'ʧɛloʊ/ *noun, plural* **cellos**
a stringed musical instrument held between the knees and played with a bow *See:* art on page 15a.

cello

**cellular** /'sɛlyələr/ *adjective*
of the cell: *Doctors must study the cellular type of a disease in order to cure it.*

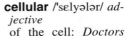

**Celsius** /'sɛlsɪəs/ *noun*
a system of measuring temperature that places the boiling point of water (at ground pressure) at 100 degrees, and the freezing point at 0 degrees, *(synonym)* centigrade. *See:* Fahrenheit.

**cement** /sɪ'mɛnt/ *noun*
**1** a building material that can be poured or spread when mixed with water, then hardens like rock: *That sidewalk is made of cement.*
**2** a soft substance that holds things together when it hardens, *(synonym)* glue: *rubber cement* –*verb* **to cement.**

**cemetery** /'sɛməˌtɛri/ *noun, plural* **cemeteries**
a burial place for the dead, *(synonym)* a graveyard: *His parents are buried in a cemetery near the center of town.*

**censor** /'sɛnsər/ *verb*
**1** to remove parts of printed or filmed materials that are considered offensive: *School officials disapproved of certain parts of the book and censored it.*
**2** to stop publication: *Some governments censor books that point out faults in the government.* –*noun* (person) **censor,** (act) **censorship.**

**census** /ˈsɛnsəs/ *noun, plural* **censuses**
a count of the people in a country by the government: *The census is taken in the USA every ten years.*

**cent** /sɛnt/ *noun*
1/100 of a dollar, a penny: *That pen costs just 20 cents to make.*

**centennial** /sɛnˈtɛniəl/ *noun*
a year that is 100 years after the date that something happened or began, a 100th anniversary

**center** /ˈsɛntər/ *noun*
**1** a point that is equally far from all the points on the outer limits of something, *(synonym)* the middle: *the center of the earth*
**2** the main location of some activity: *Hollywood is the center for American filmmaking.*
**3** (in sports) a player that occupies a middle position: *He's the center on that football team.*

**center** *verb*
to put something in a central position: *She centered the picture on the wall.*

**centigrade** /ˈsɛntəˌgreɪd/ *noun*
*See:* Celsius.

**centimeter** /ˈsɛntəˌmitər/ *noun*
a unit of length in the metric system equal to 1/100 of a meter: *One centimeter is .3937 inch long. – abbreviation of* **cm.** *See:* art on page 16a.

**central** /ˈsɛntrəl/ *adjective*
in, at, near, or forming the center: *That store is in a central place where everyone can get to it.* *–adverb* **centrally.**

**century** /ˈsɛntʃəri/ *noun, plural* **centuries**
**1** a time period of 100 years
**2** one of the 100-year time periods before or after the birth of Christ: *Many scientific discoveries were made during the twentieth century (1901-2000). See:* A.D.; B.C.

**cereal** /ˈsɪriəl/ *noun*
grain, like wheat and oats, or food made of it: *Many people in the USA eat cereal for breakfast. See:* scrambled egg, USAGE NOTE; art on page 17a.

**ceremony** /ˈsɛrəˌmoʊni/ *noun, plural* **ceremonies**
a formal event, usually with rituals: *The priest performed a marriage ceremony.* *–adjective* **ceremonial** /ˌsɛrəˈmoʊniəl/.

**certain** /ˈsɜrtn/ *adjective*
**1** definite, without doubt: *She has so much talent that she is certain to be a success.*
**2** sure to happen: *If he jumps off the bridge, he goes to a certain death.*
**to make certain:** to make sure: *I made certain that I had my keys before I left the house.*

**certainly** /ˈsɜrtnli/ *adverb*
**1** of course, yes: *"Will you help me with my homework?"—"Certainly, I will."*
**2** for sure, definitely: *It is so cold outside that you will certainly freeze unless you wear a heavy coat.*

**certificate** /sərˈtɪfɪkɪt/ *noun*
a formal document that states, under oath, a fact, qualification, or promise: *I showed my birth certificate when I applied for a passport.* *–verb* **to certify.**

**certificate**

**cesarean** /sɪˈzɛriən/ or **cesarean section** *noun*
an operation in which a baby is delivered by cutting open the mother's stomach and uterus: *The doctor delivered the baby girl by cesarean.*

**chain** /tʃeɪn/ *noun*
**1** a line of (usually metal) rings locked inside each other: *The dog pulled on its chain but could not get loose.*
**2** a group of stores, restaurants, etc., owned by the same person or company: *McDonald's™ is a large chain; you can find it in cities everywhere.*

**chain** *verb*
to stop with a chain: *The owner chained her dog to a fence.*

**chain saw** *noun*
a saw driven by a motor: *Workers use chain saws to cut down trees.*

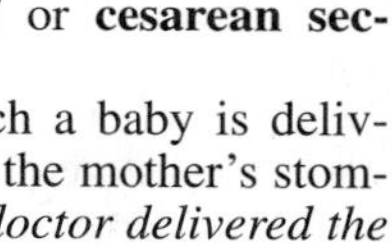
**chain saw**

**chair** /tʃɛr/ *noun*
**1** a piece of furniture with a back, for one person to sit on: *We bought some new chairs for the apartment.*

**2** an office or seat of authority and importance *See:* chairperson; art on page 5a.

**chairperson** /'ʧɛr,pɜrsən/ *noun, plural* **chairpersons**
a head of a meeting, committee, or school faculty: *She is the chairperson of the history department.* –*noun* (person) **chairman** /'ʧɛr,mən/, (job) **chairmanship, chairwoman** /'ʧɛr,wʊmən/.

**chalk** /'ʧɔk/ *noun*
a stick (of chalk) used for writing and marking: *The teacher writes on the blackboard with chalk.* –*adjective* **chalky.** *See:* art on page 8a.

**challenge** /'ʧæləndʒ/ *verb* **challenged, challenging, challenges**
**1** to ask or dare someone to play a game or sport: *I challenged her to a game of tennis.*
**2** to test one's abilities: *The difficult courses at school challenged his ability to make good grades.*
**3** to question: *The police challenged the thief's story.*

**challenge** *noun*
**1** an invitation to play a game or sport: *I accepted her challenge to a tennis match.*
**2** a difficult job: *She found her new sales job to be quite a challenge.* –*noun* (person) **challenger.**

**chambermaid** /'ʧeɪmbər,meɪd/ *noun*
a cleaning woman, especially in a hotel: *Chambermaids in hotels make the beds.*

**champ** /ʧæmp/ *noun informal*
*short for* champion: *Joe Louis was boxing champ of the world for many years.*

**champagne** /ʃæm'peɪn/ *noun*
a type of wine with bubbles in it: *People drink champagne to celebrate New Year's Eve.*

**champion** /'ʧæmpiən/ *noun*
the winner of a final contest: *She is the national champion in tennis.*

**championship** /'ʧæmpiən,ʃɪp/ *noun*
the last in a series of contests, the winner of which will be champion: *He won the championship in golf.*

**chance** /ʧæns/ *noun*
**1** the way some things happen for no obvious reason, by accident, etc.: *When she arrived late for her train, chance was on her side; the train had not yet left.*
**2** an opportunity: *I had the chance to go to San Francisco on vacation.*
**by chance:** accidentally, not planned: *We met by chance at the library.*
**games of chance:** games of luck: *Some people like to play games of chance, such as cards, dice, and slot machines.*
**to take a chance:** to take a risk: *She took a chance by crossing the busy street against the traffic light, but was not hurt.*

**change** /ʧeɪndʒ/ *verb* **changed, changing, changes**
**1** to become something different: *I changed my life by going back to college and then getting a better job.*
**2** to exchange: *The two people changed places with each other.*
**3** to give or receive an equal amount of money for bills or coins that are smaller: *"Can you change a $20 bill?"—"Yes, I have two $10's."*
**4** to give one country's money for an amount of another's: *I changed my dollars into French francs at the bank.*
**to change one's mind:** to think differently: *I changed my mind and stayed home instead of going out.*

**change** *noun*
**1** something different: *There was a change in the weather from sun to rain.*
**2** coins: *I have a lot of change; can you give me dollar bills for these quarters?* –*noun* (person or machine) **changer.**

**channel** /'ʧænl/ *noun*
**1** a television station's place on the TV between others: *We can get channels 2, 7, and 9 on our TV.*
**2** a waterway: *The English Channel separates England from France.*

**chant** /'ʧænt/ *noun*
**1** a short, simple song, often religious in nature
**2** a short saying: *"No more war! No more war!" is a war protesters' chant.* –*verb* **to chant.**

**Chanukah** /'hɑnəkə/ *noun*
*variation of* Hanukkah

**chaos** /'keɪ,ɑs/ *noun*
extreme confusion: *After the earthquake, the area was in chaos: no electricity, roads blocked, injured people every-*

*where.* *–adjective* **chaotic** /keɪˈɑtɪk/. *(antonym)* order.

**chapel** /ˈʧæpəl / *noun*
a small church: *At that school, students go to chapel every evening.*

**chapter** /ˈʧæptər/ *noun*
a part of a book: *I read Chapter 11.*

**character** /ˈkærɪktər/ *noun*
**1** the general goodness or badness of a person's behavior, such as honesty: *He is a man of good (bad, strong, etc.) character. See:* integrity.
**2** a single letter or mark used in writing: *"Letter" is a word with six characters.*
**3** a person in a novel, play, or film: *I didn't like the main character in that book.*

**charge** /ʧɑrʤ/ *noun*
**1** the price of something: *What is the charge for a night in that hotel?*
**2** a purchase with a credit card: *Will you pay cash or will this be a charge?*
**3** a fast move forward
**4** a measure of the amount of electricity in something
**5** a statement of blame against someone: *the charge of drunk driving.*
**to be in charge (of):** to be in control or command (of): *I'm leaving you in charge of the office while I'm gone.*

**charge** *verb* **charged, charging, charges**
**1** to put a price on: *They're charging $25 for these jeans.*
**2** to buy with a credit card: *I charged a new pair of shoes on my credit card.*
**3** to ask for payment from: *The store is charging her for the glass that she broke.*
**4** to blame someone for something, *(synonym)* to accuse: *She was charged with drunk driving.*
**5** to rush forward: *Soldiers charged at the enemy.*
**6** to put the ability to produce electricity back into something, *(synonym)* to energize: *to charge a dead battery* *–adjective* **chargeable.**

**charge card** *noun*
a type of credit card that must be paid completely each month: *American Express offers a charge card. See:* credit card.

**charge card**

**charitable** /ˈʧærətəbəl/ *adjective*
**1** giving help or money to those who need it, *(synonym)* generous: *He gives his time and money to helping poor children; he is a very charitable man.*
**2** of or for charity: *Charitable organizations help the poor.* *–adverb* **charitably.**

**charity** /ˈʧærəti/ *noun, plural* **charities**
an organization that helps poor people: *People give money to charities to help the homeless.*

**charm** /ʧɑrm/ *noun*
**1** the ability to please, *(synonym)* attractiveness: *She is a woman with great charm.*
**2** something worn because it is thought to be magical: *He wore a charm to protect himself from evil.*

**charm** *verb*
to please someone with warmth and pleasantness: *He charms everyone he meets.* *–noun* (person) **charmer.**

**charming** /ˈʧɑrmɪŋ/ *adjective*
pleasing, attractive, delightful: *We vacationed in a charming little village.*

**chart** /ʧɑrt/ *noun*
**1** a map, especially one of the oceans
**2** a display of information in the form of a diagram, graph, etc.: *My math book is full of charts of numbers.* *–verb* **to chart.**

**chase** /ʧeɪs/ *verb* **chased, chasing, chases**
to hurry quickly after someone or something to catch them: *The police chased the thief and caught her.*
**to chase someone** or **something away** or **off:** to frighten or force away: *The farmer used a gun to chase off hunters from his farm.*

**chase** *noun*
an act of chasing: *The movie began with a police chase through the streets.*

**chat** /ʧæt/ *noun*
casual, friendly talk: *My friend and I have a chat every day.* *–verb* **to chat.**

**chatter** /ˈʧætə r/ *noun*
informal talk about unimportant matters: *The teacher told her students to stop their chatter.* *–verb* **to chatter.**

**cheap** /ʧip/ *adjective*
**1** costing very little, *(synonym)* inex-

pensive: *The hotel room was cheap, so we stayed an extra night.*
**2** of poor quality: *The clothes from that store are cheap; they fall apart.*
**3** not generous with money: *Everything that he buys has to be a bargain; he's really cheap. –adverb* **cheap, cheaply;** *–noun* **cheapness.**

**cheapen** /ˈʧipən/ *verb*
to lower the quality of something: *The manufacturer used lower quality cloth in the dresses and cheapened them.*

**cheat** /ʧit/ *verb*
**1** to do something dishonest for one's personal interest: *She cheated on her examinations; she is a cheat.*
**2** to take from someone unfairly: *That store cheated me out of $10 on that sweater by charging me too much. –noun* (person) **cheat.**

**check** /ʧɛk/ *noun*

check

**1** a piece of printed paper used as an order to a bank to pay someone the amount of money one writes on it: *Every month, I write checks to pay my bills.*||*I pay them by check.*
**2** the bill in a restaurant or bar: *The waiter handed me the lunch check.*
**3** a mark as with a pen or pencil, usually (√): *I put a check by each item on my grocery list as I took it from the shelf.*
**4** an examination to see that something is correct or in good condition: *I added up some figures, then asked my coworker to give my answer a check (for accuracy).*
**5** **a.** a pattern of small squares **b.** material with such a pattern on it: *Her dress was a black and white check.*

**check** *verb*
**1** to test to see if something is correct or O.K.: *I checked my report for any errors.*||*Oh, I was just checking to see how you are feeling.*
**2** to put a checkmark beside something: *I checked (off) each item on the list.*
**to check in** or **into something:** to sign in at a hotel, motel, airport, etc.: *The tourist checked into the hotel.*
**to check out: a.** to pay the bill and leave a hotel: *He checked out (of his hotel) in the morning.* **b.** to find to be true: *The police said the man's story checked out; he really was in the hospital at the time of the murder.* **c.** (of library books, tapes, etc.) to borrow: *I checked out two books from the library. –noun* (person) **checker.** *See:* checkers (game); check-in; checkout.

**checkbook** /ˈʧɛkˌbʊk/ *noun*
a folder containing checks: *I list checks I write in my checkbook. See:* art on page 10a.

**checkered** /ˈʧɛkə rd/ *adjective*
divided into squares

**checkers** /ˈʧɛkər z/ *noun plural*
*used only with a singular verb* a game played by two people, each with 12 small, round black or red pieces (checkers) moved on a board divided into squares of two different colors: *Checkers is easy to learn and fun to play. –noun* **checkerboard** /ˈʧɛkərˌbɔrd/.

**check-in** *noun*
an area or counter, where you sign into a hotel or present yourself at an airport: *The hotel check-in is near the front door.*

**checking account** *noun*
an account at a bank against which checks can be written: *I opened a checking account with $500. See:* savings account.

**checklist** /ˈʧɛkˌlɪst/ *noun*
a list of items to be done: *I use a checklist when I go to the store for eggs, milk, butter, bread, etc.*

**checkout** /ˈʧɛkˌaʊt/ *noun*
an area for making payment before leaving a hotel or store: *The checkout counter is near the front door. See:* art on page 10a.

**checkup** /ˈʧɛkˌʌp/ *noun*
a medical examination of a person by a doctor: *I am going to my doctor for a checkup.*

**cheek** /ʧik/ *noun*
either side of the face, from below eye level to the chin: *The little boy has red cheeks in the winter.*

**cheer** /ʧɪr/ *verb*
to shout with delight, admiration, or sup-

port: *The crowd cheered when their team scored. (antonym)* boo.
**to cheer up (someone):** to make someone feel happier: *Her visit to the hospital cheered up her sick boy. –verb* **to cheer.**

**cheerful** /ˈʧɪrfəl/ *adjective*
happy, pleasant: *She is a cheerful person. –adverb* **cheerfully;** *–noun* **cheerfulness.**

**cheese** /ʧiz/ *noun*
a solid or soft food made from the thickest part of milk: *She likes melted cheese on her hamburger. See:* art on page 17a.

**cheetah** /ˈʧitə/ *noun*
a large, fast African cat with spotted fur: *Cheetahs are among the fastest animals in the world.*

**chef** /ʃɛf/ *noun*
a cook, especially the head cook in a restaurant: *The chef changes items on the menu each day. See:* art on page 5a.

**chemical** /ˈkɛmɪkəl/ *adjective*
having to do with chemicals: *There was a chemical fire at a warehouse last night.*

**chemical** *noun*
a substance made from or used in a chemical process: *Many household cleaners contain dangerous chemicals. –adverb* **chemically.**

**chemistry** /ˈkɛməstri/ *noun*
the science of matter, how it is structured, and how it combines and changes: *She took a course in chemistry in college. –noun* (scientist) **chemist.**

**chemotherapy** /ˌkimoʊˈθɛrəpi/ *noun*
strong chemical medications given especially as a treatment for cancer

**cherry** /ˈʧɛri/ *noun, plural* **cherries**
a small, round, usually dark-red fruit that grows on a tree: *Cherries taste sweet. See:* art on page 3a.

**chess** /ʧɛs/ *noun*
a board game for two players

**chest** /ʧɛst/ *noun*
**1** the front of the human body above the stomach
**2** a strong box used for storing or shipping goods
**3** a small cabinet, usually hanging on a wall: *There's some aspirin in the medicine chest in the bathroom.*

**chestnut** /ˈʧɛsˌnʌt/ *noun*
a tree and its brown nut: *Many people like to roast chestnuts and eat them.*

**chew** /ʧu/ *verb*
to move the lower jaw to break up (food) with the teeth: *She chewed on a piece of meat. –noun* (person) **chewer, chewiness;** *–adjective* **chewy.**

**chewing gum** *noun*
a soft, sweet substance made for chewing: *She put a stick of chewing gum in her mouth.*

**Chicano** /ʧɪˈkɑnoʊ/ *noun, plural* **Chicanos**
a person of Mexican parents living in the USA: *Many Chicanos live in southern California. –noun* (woman) **Chicana** /ʧɪˈkɑnə/.

**chick** /ʧɪk/ *noun*
a baby bird, especially a baby chicken

**chicken** /ˈʧɪkə n/ *noun*
**1** a farm bird raised for its eggs and meat: *We had fried chicken for dinner.*
**2** *slang* a person without courage, *(synonym)* a coward:
**to chicken out:** to agree to do something, then not do it because of fear: *He said he would go skiing, but he chickened out at the last minute.* See: chick; hen; rooster; art on page 14a.

**chicken pox** *noun*
a mild disease, mainly of children, with fever and itchy, red, pus-filled spots (a rash) on the skin: *Our little girl had the chicken pox for ten days.*

**chief** /ʧif/ *noun*
the top person in an organization: *He is the chief in the fire department.*

**chief** *adjective*
most important: *What is that country's chief product?*

**chiefly** /ˈʧifli/ *adverb*
most importantly, especially: *We are chiefly concerned for your safety.*

**child** /ʧaɪld/ *noun, plural* **children** /ˈʧɪldrən/
**1** a very young person, about 2 to 12 years old who is no longer a baby but not yet a teenager

**2** a son or daughter: *The couple has three children, all married and in their thirties now.*

**childhood** /'ʧaɪldˌhʊd/ *noun*
the period from birth to about age 13: *She had a happy childhood.*

**children** /'ʧɪldrən/ *noun*
*plural of* child

**chili** /'ʧɪli/ *noun, plural* **chilies** or **chili pepper**
**1** a pepper with a hot, spicy taste, used fresh or dried in cooking
**2** a dish made with beans in a hot, spicy sauce made with chili powder

**chill** /'ʧɪl/ *noun*
**1** a cold temperature, but not freezing: *In the morning, there is a chill in the air.*
**2** a cold feeling: *She got a chill and now has a bad cold.*

**chill** *verb*
to cool: *He chilled the wine in the refrigerator.* –*adjective* **chilly.** *(antonym)* heat.

**chime** /ʧaɪm/ *noun*
**1** a set of bells
**2** an electronic device that produces a bell-like sound: *I heard the chime of the doorbell.* –*verb* **to chime.**

**chimney** /'ʧɪmni/ *noun, plural* **chimneys**
the large metal pipe or hollow brick structure for passing smoke from a fire or furnace into the open air

chimney

**chimpanzee** /ˌʧɪmpæn'zi/ *noun*
a type of African ape with long arms: *Chimpanzees are intelligent animals.*

**chin** /ʧɪn/ *noun*
the front of the lower jaw beneath the lips

**to keep one's chin up:** to have courage: *Keep your chin up; you will do well on the exam. See:* art on page 21a.

**china** /'ʧaɪnə/ *noun*
fine dishes, cups, plates, and bowls: *We use our best china for Sunday dinner.*

**chip** /ʧɪp/ *noun*
**1** a piece of wood, paint, etc. knocked or fallen off something: *Chips of paint fall on the floor from the old wall.*
**2** thin pieces of fried potatoes: *a bag of potato chips*
**3** a round piece of plastic used for money in gambling
**4** *short for* microchip, the part of an electronic device that controls it –*verb* **to chip.**

**chipmunk** /'ʧɪpˌmʌŋk/ *noun*
a small squirrel-like animal with brown fur and black stripes on its back: *Chipmunks like to eat seeds and nuts.*

**chiropractor** /'kaɪrəˌpræktər/ *noun*
a licensed professional who lines up people's bones, especially your back –*noun* **chiropractic.**

**chirp** /'ʧɜrp/ *verb*
to make a high, short, sharp sound: *Birds chirped in the early morning.*

**chisel** /'ʧɪzəl / *noun*
a metal tool with a V-shaped point for cutting wood or stone –*verb* **to chisel.**

**chocolate** /'ʧɔklɪt/ *noun*
a light to dark brown candy, powder, or syrup made from roasted cacao beans: *He sent a box of chocolates to his sweetheart.*

**choice** /ʧɔɪs/ *noun*
**1** the power or right to choose: *I have a choice between two job offers.*
**2** someone or something chosen: *His first choice for a vacation is Disney World.*

**choice** *adjective* **choicer, choicest**
special, very desirable: *They bought a choice piece of property near the water.*

**choir** /'kwaɪər/ *noun*
a group of singers: *Our neighbors sing in the church choir.*

choir

**choke** /ʧoʊk/ *verb* **choked, choking, chokes**
**1** to stop breathing because of a block in the air passage in the throat: *He choked on a piece of meat.*
**2** to cut off someone's air supply by squeezing the neck: *The murderer choked a man to death. See:* strangle.

**cholera** /'kɑlərə/ *noun*
a serious, often deadly disease of the stomach and intestines found mainly in

tropical countries: *Those people caught cholera from bad drinking water.*

**choose** /ʧuz/ *verb* **chose** /ʧoʊz/ or **chosen** /ˈʧoʊzən/, **choosing, chooses**
**1** to pick out of a greater number, to make a choice: *I had to choose between two job offers.*
**2** to decide: *I chose to go to the movies alone.*

**chop** /ʧɑp/ *verb* **chopped, chopping, chops**
**1** to cut with hard, sharp blows: *She chops wood for the fire with an ax.*
**2** to cut into small pieces: *She chopped carrots with a knife.* *–noun* **chop.**

**chopsticks** /ˈʧɑpˌstɪks/ *noun plural*
two thin sticks of wood, ivory, etc., used to take hold of food and put it in the mouth: *Chopsticks are commonly used in China and Japan.*

**chord** /kɔrd/ *noun*
(in music) three or more musical notes played together *See:* cord.

**chore** /ʧɔr/ *noun*
a boring but necessary act: *I have to do the chores at home, like taking out the garbage and washing the dishes.*

**chorus** /ˈkɔrəs/ *noun, plural* **choruses**
a large group of singers, *(synonym)* a choir: *My daughter sings in the high-school chorus.* *–adjective* **choral.**

**chose** /ʧoʊz/ *verb*
*past tense of* choose

**christen** /ˈkrɪsən/ *verb*
(in some churches) to make someone, usually a child, a Christian and/or give them a first name in a church ceremony: *The minister christened our son and we named him Joseph.* *–noun* **christening.**

**Christian** /ˈkrɪsʧən/ *adjective*
**1** related to Jesus Christ and his religious teachings
**2** of Christianity, its churches, beliefs, etc.: *the Christian religion*

**Christian** *noun*
a believer in Christianity: *He became a Christian at age 17.*

**Christmas** /ˈkrɪsməs/ or **Christmas Day** *noun*
(in Christianity) Christ's birthday, celebrated on December 25th: *She spends Christmas with her family.*

**chrome** /kroʊm/ *noun*
a shiny, hard metal *–verb* **to chrome;** *–adjective* **chrome-plated.**

**chuckle** /ˈʧʌkə l/ *verb* **chuckled, chuckling, chuckles**
to laugh softly: *He does not laugh out loud; he only chuckles.*

**chummy** /ˈʧʌmi/ *adjective* **chummier, chummiest**
friendly: *They are very chummy with each other.*

**chunk** /ʧʌŋk/ *noun*
a thick piece: *He cut off a chunk of meat from the roast turkey.* *–adjective* **chunky.**

**church** /ˈʧɜrʧ/ *noun, plural* **churches**
a building for worship, especially a Christian one: *I go to church every Sunday.*

---

**USAGE NOTE:** Jews go to worship in a *synagogue* or *schul,* and Muslims go to a *mosque*.

---

**cider** /ˈsaɪdər/ *noun*
juice squeezed from fruit, especially apples

**cigar** /sɪˈgɑr/ *noun*
a round, wrapped roll of tobacco leaves made for smoking: *Some cigars are very expensive.*

**cigarette** /ˌsɪgəˈrɛt/ *noun*
a round roll of finely cut tobacco wrapped in paper for smoking: *She smoked a cigarette.*

**cinema** /ˈsɪnəmə/ *noun formal*
**the cinema:** the industry of making movies

**cinnamon** /ˈsɪnəmən/ *noun*
a brown spice from Asia

**circle** /ˈsɜrkəl/ *noun*
**1** a closed curved line whose every point is equally far from the center: *The teacher drew a circle on the blackboard.*
**2** a group of people with the same interest: *a circle of friends*

**circle** *verb* **circled, circling, circles**
to draw a circle around: *The student cir-*

*cled the answers on the test. See:* art on page 16a.

**circuit** /ˈsɜrkɪt/ *noun*
**1** a closed path of wires for an electrical current: *electrical circuits*
**2** a route with regular stops: *That truck driver makes a circuit of the stores.*

**circular** /ˈsɜrk yələr/ *adjective*
having a round shape or design: *The dancers made circular movements.*

**circulation** /ˌsɜrkyəˈleɪʃən/ *noun*
**1** the movement of the blood as it is pumped through the body by the heart: *For an old man of 92, he has good circulation.*
**2** the number of copies of a newspaper, magazine, etc., sold at one time: *The circulation of the Sunday newspaper is over one million. –verb* **to circulate.**

**circumference** /sərˈkʌmfrəns/ *noun*
**1** the distance around a circle
**2** the distance around the outside of something round: *The circumference of the earth is over 40,000 km (nearly 25,000 miles).*

**circumstance** /ˈsɜrkəmˌstæns/ *noun*
a condition that affects something else: *Ice on the roads and a bad storm are circumstances that lead to car accidents. –adjective* **circumstantial.**

**circus** /ˈsɜrkəs/ *noun, plural* **circuses**
a traveling show of performers (clowns, acrobats) and trained animals

**citizen** /ˈsɪtəzən/ *noun*
a legal member of a country: *She is a US citizen. –noun* **citizenry.**

**citizenship** /ˈsɪtəzənˌʃɪp/ *noun*
the legal condition of belonging to a country, usually including the right to vote: *I had to wait five years, but I now have my US citizenship.*

**citrus** /ˈsɪtrəs/ *noun*
**1** a general term for trees bearing citrus fruits
**2** the fruits themselves, such as oranges, lemons, and grapefruit: *Lots of citrus is grown in Florida and California.*

**city** /ˈsɪti/ *noun, plural* **cities**
an area with many people living and working close together: *Many tourists visit the city of London.*

**city hall** *noun*
a building where a city's government is located

**civil** /ˈsɪvəl/ *adjective*
**1** (in law) of a citizen's rights and responsibilities: *Civil courts deal with cases like divorce and business disagreements, not criminal matters.*
**2** polite, especially without being friendly *–adverb* **civilly;** *–noun* **civility.**

**civilian** /səˈvɪlyən/ *noun*
someone who is not a member of the military or police forces, an ordinary citizen: *He has left the army; he's a civilian again.*

**civilization** /ˌsɪvələˈzeɪʃən/ *noun*
a high level of government, laws, written language, art, music, etc., within a society or culture *–verb* **to civilize.**

**civil rights** *noun plural*
in the USA, the rights of each citizen guaranteed by the Constitution, such as the rights to vote and not suffer prejudice because of race, nationality, etc.: *The political movement for civil rights was strongest during the 1960s. See:* non-violent, USAGE NOTE.

**civil war** *noun*
a war between groups in a country
**the Civil War:** in the USA, the war between the North and South: *The Civil War lasted from 1861 to 1865.*

**claim** /kleɪm/ *noun*
**1** a demand for something that one has a right to: *He filed an insurance claim after his car was stolen.*
**2** a statement that something is true: *The police believe her claim that she knows who the thief is. –verb* **to claim.**

**claim check** or **ticket** *noun*
a paper ticket or piece of plastic with the same numbers on both parts, one attached to an item, the other held by the owner: *I showed my claim check at the airport luggage area and claimed my bags.*

claim check

**clam** /klæm/ *noun*
a sea creature with two hard shells: *Many people like to eat fried clams.*

**clap** /klæp/ *verb* **clapped, clapping, claps**
to strike the hands together in approval, *(synonym)* to applaud: *The audience clapped after the concert.*

**clarify** /ˈklærəˌfaɪ/ *verb* **clarified, clarifying, clarifies**
to make clear, *(synonym)* to explain: *The student was confused and the teacher clarified the idea.* *–noun* **clarification.**

**clarinet** /ˌklærəˈnɛt/ *noun*
a wooden musical instrument shaped like a long, narrow black tube with a bell-shaped end *See:* art on page 15a.

**clarity** /ˈklærəti/ *noun*
**1** clearness of ideas, writing, or situations: *She speaks with great clarity on difficult matters.*
**2** clearness or purity of physical things: *the clarity of a diamond*

**clash** /klæʃ/ *verb* **clashed, clashing, clashes**
**1** to hit together violently: *the clash of armies in battle*
**2** to argue: *The man and woman clashed over spending too much money.*
**3** to not look good with: *That bright red tie clashes with his green suit.*

**clasp** /klæsp/ *noun*
a fastener made of two parts that lock together: *She fastened the clasp on her necklace.* *–verb* **to clasp.**

**class** /klæs/ *noun, plural* **classes**
**1** a level in society based on money, education, and family standing: *There are four social classes in the USA, the upper class, middle class, working class, and lower class.*
**2** a group whose members have at least one similarity: *A motorcycle belongs to a different class of vehicle from cars and trucks.*
**3** a group of students who will finish school in the same year: *He graduated with the class of 1995.*

**classic** /ˈklæsɪk/ *noun*
**1** an object regarded as an example of the best of something: *That 1950 car is a classic.*
**2** a musical or literary work (novel, play, etc.) that has been considered as important for a long time: *The novel* The Adventures of Huckleberry Finn *by Mark Twain is a classic.* *–adjective* **classic, classical.**

**classification** /ˌklæsəfəˈkeɪʃən/ *noun*
a grouping of things by their similarity to each other: *The classification of steel is as a metal.* *–verb* **to classify.**

**classified ad** *noun*
a brief advertisement printed in a newspaper or magazine offering or asking for goods or services, jobs, etc.: *I looked in the classified ads for an apartment.*

**classmate** /ˈklæsˌmeɪt/ *noun*
a student with whom one attends school: *She was one of my classmates in high school.*

**classroom** /ˈklæsˌrum/ *noun*
a room where students are taught by a teacher: *My classroom is on the fourth floor.*

**classy** /ˈklæsi/ *adjective slang* **classier, classiest**
among the best in appearance or behavior: *They live in a very classy neighborhood.*

**clause** /klɔz/ *noun*
**1** a part in a document that requires something to be agreed on and/or done: *The rent clause in my apartment lease says I must pay on the first of each month.*
**2** one part, with its own subject and verb, of a complex or compound sentence: *There are two clauses in this sentence, and they are divided by a comma.*

**claw** /klɔ/ *noun*
one of the sharp nails on an animal's paw or toe: *a bear claw, a lion's claws* *–verb* **to claw.**

**clay** /kleɪ/ *noun*
material from the ground that can be shaped when wet, and will hold the shape when dried or baked: *She likes to make dishes out of clay.*

**clean** /klin/ *adjective*
free of dirt, dust, or soil: *I have clean clothes.*||*Please get me a clean piece of paper to write on.*

**clean** *verb*
**1** to free from dirt, such as by washing: *She cleaned her eyeglasses with a handkerchief.*
**2** to put in order: *The boy cleaned his room by putting his toys and clothes back where they belong.*

**cleaner** /'klinər/ *noun*
**1** a substance, like strong soap, used to clean surfaces
**2** a cleaning business for clothes, *(synonym)* a dry cleaner: *I took my suit to the cleaner to be cleaned and pressed.*

**clear** /klɪr/ *adjective*
**1** easy to understand: *clear writing, clear instructions*
**2** easy to see through: *clear glass*
**3** having no rain or snow and few clouds: *clear weather*
**4** free of objects that block the way: *The road is now clear after the storm.*
**to make it clear** or **oneself clear:** to state strongly so that there is no misunderstanding: *He made it clear what he wanted.*

**clear** *verb*
**1** to remove things that block the way: *Workers cleared fallen trees from the road.*
**2** to get approval for or from: *He cleared the project with his boss.||She cleared customs at the airport.*
**to clear (something) up: a.** to become free of bad weather: *The sky is clearing up.* **b.** to clarify or explain something: *She cleared up the misunderstanding.*

**clear** *noun*
**in the clear:** free of danger or blame: *The judge said that she is not guilty, and she is now in the clear.*

**clearance** /'klɪrəns/ *noun*
**1** a statement that something will be allowed, *(synonyms)* approval, permission: *The airport gave the airplane clearance to land.*
**2** enough space: *There was enough clearance for the big truck to go under the bridge.*

**clearly** /'klɪrli/ *adverb*
without being blocked or unclear: *After I hit my head, I could not see clearly.*

**clergy** /'klɜrʤi/ *noun plural*
the group of ministers, priests, rabbis, mullahs, etc., as a whole: *The government asks advice from members of the clergy.*

**clerical** /'klɛrɪkəl/ *adjective*
**1** of basic office work, such as answering the telephone, writing down orders, etc.: *He is a clerical worker with a clerical job.*
**2** of the clergy: *A minister wears a clerical collar.*

**clerk** /klɜrk/ *noun*
**1** a person who keeps records, accounts, etc., in an office
**2** a salesperson in a store: *My friend is a (sales)clerk in a store.* *–verb* **to clerk.**

**clever** /'klɛvər/ *adjective*
**1** intelligent and quick at understanding: *She is a clever student.*
**2** skillful, especially in solving problems: *He solves computer problems that no one else can; he has clever ideas.* *–adverb* **cleverly;** *–noun* **cleverness.**

**click** /klɪk/ *noun*
a light, sharp sound: *the click of a camera shutter*

**click** *verb*
**1** to make a clicking sound: *The key clicked as it turned in the lock.*
**2** to move something that makes a click: *He clicked the light switch on.*

**client** /'klaɪənt/ *noun*
a customer of someone who provides a service, such as a lawyer, tailor, hairdresser, etc.: *He likes to take his clients to lunch. See:* customer, USAGE NOTE.

**clientele** /ˌklaɪ ən'tɛl/ *noun plural*
a group of customers: *That expensive store has a rich clientele.*

**cliff** /klɪf/ *noun*
the top and side of a hill that drops down sharply: *She stood on the cliff and looked down at the ocean below.*

cliff

**climate** /'klaɪmɪt/ *noun*
the type of weather that a place has: *Places can have cold, warm, or hot climates.* *–adjective* **climatic.**

**climax** /ˈklaɪˌmæks/ *noun, plural* **climaxes**
the most exciting or final point in a series of events: *The game came to a climax with our team winning in the last second of play.*

**climb** /klaɪm/ *verb*
to move upward: *The airplane took off and climbed above the clouds.*

**climb** *noun*
an upward movement on land or into the air: *Our group made the climb up the mountain.* –*noun* (person) **climber.**

**clinic** /ˈklɪnɪk/ *noun*
a medical building: *In that health clinic, doctors treat patients who are sick.* –*adjective* **clinical.**

**clip** /klɪp/ *noun*
a device that holds things together: *a paper clip, a hair clip*

**clip** *verb* **clipped, clipping, clips**
**1** to fasten with a clip: *I clipped my papers together with a paper clip.*
**2** to cut with short strokes: *The hairdresser clipped her hair with scissors.*

**clipboard** /ˈklɪpˌbɔrd/ *noun*
a flat board with a clip at the top to hold papers

**clock** /klɑk/ *noun*
an instrument for showing the time (that is not a wrist or pocket watch): *an alarm clock, a wall clock*

**around the clock:** all day and night: *Rescue workers worked around the clock to help victims of the earthquake.*

**clock** *verb*
to measure time: *Officials clocked the races at the Olympics.*

**clockwise** /ˈklɑkˌwaɪz/ *adverb*
in the direction that the hands of a clock move: *Starting at 12, looking at the clock, the hands move clockwise to the right. See:* counter-clockwise.

**clog** /klɑg/ *noun*
**1** a blockage: *a clog in a water pipe*
**2** a type of shoe, usually with a thick wooden bottom

**clog** *verb* **clogged, clogging, clogs**
to block: *My nose is all clogged up from a cold.*

**close (1)** /kloʊs/ *adjective* **closer, closest**
**1** with little space between, nearby: *Her chair is close to the wall.*
**2** near in time: *It's close to 5:00.*
**3** very friendly: *They are a close family with a few close friends.*

**a close call: a.** something that is difficult to judge: *The two runners crossed the finish line together, so who won was a close call.* **b.** a narrow escape from danger or death: *The speeding taxi nearly hit him; that was a close call.* –*adverb* **closely;** –*noun* **closeness.** *(antonym)* far.

**close (2)** /kloʊz/ *verb* **closed, closing, closes**
**1** to shut or cause to shut: *The store closes at 6:00 on Saturdays.*||*I closed the window.*
**2** to come to an end: *The movie closed with a love scene. (antonym)* open.

**closet** /ˈklɑzɪt/ *noun*
a small room for keeping clothes, towels, etc.: *We keep our coats and umbrellas in the closet by the front door. See:* art on page 22a.

**cloth** /klɔθ/ *noun, plural* **cloths** /klɔðz, klɔθs/
material made of threads of cotton, wool, etc.: *That suit is made of woolen cloth.*

**clothe** /kloʊð/ *verb* **clothed** or **clad** /klæd/, **clothing, clothes**
to provide with clothing: *Parents feed and clothe their children.*

**clothes** /kloʊz/ *noun plural*
coverings for a person's body: *She likes to wear expensive clothes. See:* clothing; garment.

**clothing** /ˈkloʊðɪŋ/ *noun*
clothes in general: *Food and clothing are basic necessities.*

**cloud** /klaʊd/ *noun*
**1** a mass of water droplets in the sky: *The sky is full of gray clouds today.*
**2** a mass of smoke, fog, or dust: *a dust cloud*

**on cloud nine:** very happy: *They are in love and on cloud nine.*

**cloud** *verb*
to become covered with clouds: *The sky is clouding up now.*

**cloudy** /ˈklaʊdi/ *adjective* **cloudier, cloudiest**
covered with clouds: *The weather is cloudy today.*

**clover** /ˈkloʊvər/ *noun*
a small green plant, usually with three heart-shaped leaves

**clown** /klaʊn/ *noun*
a performer in colorful clothes who does funny things: *She liked the circus clown with the big red nose. –verb* **to clown.**

**club** /klʌb/ *noun*
**1** a group of people who meet because of a common interest: *He belongs to a book club.||They joined a tennis club.*
**2** a long, round, thick stick used to hit people: *Police officers carry clubs.*
**3** in the USA, a playing card with black cloverleafs on it

**club** *verb* **clubbed, clubbing, clubs**
to strike with a club

**clue** /klu/ *noun*
a thing or fact that helps answer a question: *Police look for clues at the scene of a crime, like the criminal's gun.*

**clumsy** /ˈklʌmzi/ *adjective* **clumsier, clumsiest**
not able to do things in a careful way: *He is so clumsy that he is always bumping into people. –noun* **clumsiness.**

**clung** /klʌŋ/ *verb*
*past tense and past participle of* cling

**cluster** /ˈklʌstər/ *noun*
a tight grouping of something: *a cluster of grapes –verb* **to cluster.**

**clutch** /klʌʧ/ *verb* **clutches**
to hold tightly with the hand(s): *She clutched her purse as she walked.*

**clutch** *noun*
a device in a vehicle for changing speeds: *the clutch in a car*

**clutter** /ˈklʌtər/ *verb*
to mess up: *People have cluttered the street with papers and cans. –noun* **clutter.**

**c/o** /ˈkərˌʌv/
*abbreviation of* (in) care of (used in an address so that someone will pass it on to the right person): *You can write to Mr. Jones in care of his company. Address the letter: Mr. John Jones, c/o XYZ Company, 123 Main St., Anywhere.*

**coach** /koʊʧ/ *noun, plural* **coaches**
**1** a person who leads, teaches, and trains people in sports or in acting, singing, etc.: *a football coach||a voice coach*
**2** a railroad passenger car

**coach** *verb* **coaches**
to lead, train, and teach others in sports, singing, etc.: *He coaches a baseball team.*

**coal** /koʊl/ *noun*
a mineral made of carbon, black or dark brown, taken from the ground and burned for heat, that also provides gas for burning: *That stove burns coal, not wood.*

**coarse** /kɔrs/ *adjective* **coarser, coarsest**
**1** of poor quality: *The poor woman could only afford coarse clothing.*
**2** rough, not smooth: *coarse sand*

**coast** /koʊst/ *noun*
land near the ocean: *the coast of Panama*
*See:* coastline.

**coast** *verb*
to move without power: *I coasted down the hill on my bicycle. –adjective* **coastal.**

**coastline** /ˈkoʊstˌlaɪn/ *noun*
the land along an ocean: *The Maine coastline is beautiful on a sunny day.*

**coastline**

**coat** /koʊt/ *noun*
**1** an outer garment: *She is wearing a fur coat.*
**2** a covering spread over a surface: *A worker put a coat of paint on the walls.*

**coat** *verb*
to cover with something: *The furniture was coated with dust.*

**coax** /koʊks/ *verb* **coaxes**
to try patiently to ask someone to do something, *(synonym)* to persuade: *The mother coaxed her child to take some bad-tasting medicine.*

**cobra** /ˈkoʊbrə/ *noun*
a very poisonous snake of Asia and Africa: *A bite from a cobra can kill in minutes.*

**cockroach** /ˈkɑkˌ roʊʧ/ *noun, plural* **cockroaches**
a brown, flat-bodied insect found in dark wet places: *We kill cockroaches with traps and a spray.*

**cocktail** /ˈkɑkˌteɪl/ *noun*
an alcoholic drink made by mixing liquor: *She likes to have a cocktail before dinner.*

**cocoa** /ˈkoʊkoʊ/ *noun*
a hot chocolate-flavored drink: *She had some cocoa for breakfast.*

**coconut** /ˈkoʊkəˌnʌt/ *noun*
the large nut of the palm tree: *The juice inside coconuts is called coconut milk. See:* art on page 3a.

**cod** /kɑd/ or **codfish** /ˈkɑdˌfɪʃ/ *noun, plural* **cod** or **cods**
a fish found in the North Atlantic Ocean

**C.O.D.** or **COD** /ˌsioʊˈdi/ *noun*
*abbreviation of* cash on delivery, meaning that one pays the person who delivers the goods for the goods, and for the cost of sending them: *I paid for the shoes C.O.D.*

**code** /koʊd/ *noun*
a set of rules of behavior or laws: *That school has a dress code requiring boys to wear shirts and ties, no jeans.*||*the legal code in a country*

**code** *verb* **coded, coding, codes**
to put something into a secret code: *A spy coded a message.*

**coed** /ˌkoʊˈɛd/ *adjective*
*short for* coeducational

---

**USAGE NOTE:** Most schools and universities in the United States are *coed*, but there are some single-sex schools and universities. These are usually *private schools* and they are referred to as boy's schools and men's colleges or girl's schools and women's colleges.

---

**coeducational** /ˌkoʊɛʤəˈkeɪʃənəl/ *adjective*
referring to the education of both male and female students in the same school or college: *My son and daughter both go to coeducational schools. –noun* **coeducation.**

**coffee** /ˈkɔfi/ *noun*
a dark brown, energy-giving drink made by putting hot water with powder of beans of a tropical tree: *She drinks coffee for breakfast each morning. See:* art on page 5a.

**coffin** /ˈkɔfɪn/ *noun*
a box-like container in which a dead person is put for burial: *Workmen lowered the dead man's coffin into a grave.*

**coil** /kɔɪl/ *noun*
something wrapped in a circle or spiral: *a coil of wire –verb* **to coil.**

**coin** /kɔɪn/ *noun*
a piece of metal money, usually small, round, and flat: *She has some old silver coins.*

**coincidence** /koʊˈɪnsədəns/ *noun*
the happening of two or more events at the same time by chance: *By coincidence, she met an old friend on the street whom she had not seen in years. –adjective* **coincidental** /koʊˌɪnsəˈdɛntl/; *–adverb* **coincidentally.**

**cola** or **kola** /ˈkoʊlə/ *noun*
**1** the seeds from a tree that give energy (caffeine) used to make soft drinks, like Coca-Cola™, Pepsi™, etc.
**2** a drink made with cola: *He drank cola with lunch.*

**cold** /koʊld/ *adjective*
**1** having a low temperature: *Many people do not like cold weather.*
**2** feeling uncomfortable because of a lack of warmth: *I feel cold in winter.*

**cold** *noun*
an illness, usually with a blocked nose, fever, and aches, also called the common cold: *He has a bad cold.*
**to catch cold** or **a cold:** to get this illness: *She caught cold yesterday.*
**the cold:** a condition of low temperature: *I don't like the cold. –adverb* **coldly;** *–noun* **coldness.** *(antonym)* hot. *See:* art on page 11a.

**cold-blooded** /ˈkoʊldˈblʌdɪd/ *adjective*
**1** having a body temperature that goes up and down with the outside temperature: *Snakes and insects are cold-blooded animals.*
**2** having no feeling or emotion: *a cold-blooded murder*||*a killing in cold blood See:* warm-blooded.

**cold cuts** *noun plural*
cold slices of meat, such as balogna, salami, or beef: *She put some cold cuts on the table for sandwiches.*

C

**collapse** /kəˈlæps/ *noun*
**1** a falling into ruin: *Heavy rainfall caused the collapse of the roof.*
**2** a loss of strength: *She worked so hard that she suffered a collapse.*
**collapse** *verb* **collapsed, collapsing, collapses**
**1** to fall into ruin
**2** to lose strength and fall down: *The runner collapsed at the finish line.*
**3** to fold up something so it needs less space: *to collapse an umbrella*

**collar** /ˈkɑlər/ *noun*
**1** the material around the neck of a shirt, coat, etc.
**2** a round leather or cloth strap or chain: *He puts a collar on his dog before walking it.*

**colleague** /ˈkɑˌl ig/ *noun*
a person with whom one works, especially in a profession: *My colleagues in the office agree to the proposal.*

**collect** /kəˈlɛkt/ *verb*
**1** to come or bring together as a group: *The teacher collected the homework.||A crowd collected in front of the burning building.*
**2** to get and keep things for fun as a hobby: *He collects stamps.*
**to call collect:** to telephone someone who pays the cost: *The student called her mother collect from school.*

**collection** /kəˈlɛkʃən/ *noun*
a group of similar objects brought together by someone as a hobby or by a museum: *I have a coin collection.* –*noun* (person) **collector.**

**college** /ˈkɑlɪʤ/ *noun*
in the USA, an institution of higher or professional education: *a four-year college||a community college* –*adjective* **collegiate** /kəˈliʤɪt/. *See:* university.

**collide** /kəˈlaɪd/ *verb* **collided, colliding, collides**
to hit against something with force, to crash: *Two cars collided on the street.*

**collision** /kəˈlɪʒən/ *noun*
a crashing together: *Two cars were involved in a collision.*

**cologne** /kəˈloʊn/ *noun*
a type of light perfume: *He puts cologne on his face after he shaves.*

**colon** /ˈkoʊlən/ *noun*
**1** the lower intestine: *He had cancer of the colon.*
**2** the punctuation mark (:): *Colons are used in this dictionary to introduce the sample sentence.*

**colonize** /ˈkɑləˌnaɪz/ *verb* **colonized, colonizing, colonizes**
**1** to send people to live in another area of land or country, while governing them from the home country: *The Spanish, British, and French colonized the Americas.*
**2** to go live in a colony –*noun* **colonization.**

**colony** /ˈkɑləni/ *noun, plural* **colonies**
**1** a group of people who have moved to another area, but are still governed by their home country
**2** a region, country, or land of colonization, especially one controlled by a foreign power: *the (former) French colonies of North Africa* –*noun* (person) **colonist.**

**color** /ˈkʌlər/ *noun*
**1** a shade of something and the type of light it sends to the eye: *Red, yellow, and blue are colors.*
**2** paint, ink, pastel, chalk, etc., used to create color
**3** skin color as related to race: *Some people are prejudiced against other because of their color.*
**color** *verb*
to put color on: *The child colored the picture yellow and red.*

**colorblind** /ˈkʌl ərˌblaɪnd/ *adjective*
not able to see the difference between some or all colors: *He could not fly for the air force because he was colorblind.* –*noun* **colorblindness.**

**colorful** /ˈkʌlərfəl/ *adjective*
having bright colors: *She wore a colorful dress with red and orange flowers on it.*

**column** /ˈkɑləm/ *noun*
**1** in some buildings, a tall, thick piece used as support or decoration: *Those stone columns hold up the roof.*
**2** a row, especially a vertical one: *He added up a column of numbers.*

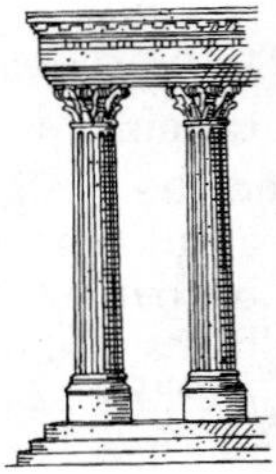
columns

**3** an article in a newspaper or magazine written regularly by a writer (called a *columnist*): *She writes a weekly column about politics for* The New York Times.

**coma** /'koʊmə/ *noun*
a medical condition like a long, deep sleep, *(synonym)* unconsciousness caused by disease or injury: *He injured his head in a fall and fell into a coma for a month.* *–adjective* **comatose.**

**comb** /koʊm/ *noun*
a flat piece of plastic (wood, metal) with teeth used to neaten the hair

**comb** *verb*
to pass a comb through the hair or something else: *I washed my face and combed my hair.*

**combat** /'kɑm,bæt/ *noun*
a violent struggle: *Soldiers shoot at each other in combat.* *–verb* **to combat.**

**combination** /,kɑmbə'neɪʃən/ *noun*
two or more things, ideas, or events put together: *Chicken soup is a combination of pieces of chicken, vegetables, and water.*

**combine** /kəm'baɪn/ *verb* **combined, combining, combines**
to join together: *Rain and freezing temperatures combine to make snow.* *(antonym)* separate.

**come** /kʌm/ *verb* **came** /keɪm/, **come, coming, comes**
**1** to move toward the speaker or a certain place: *Come here and look at this!*||*He came to my party.*
**2** to arrive: *The train comes at 9:09.*
**3** to be located in a certain position: *Five comes before six.*
**4** to be available: *Ice cream comes in many flavors.*||*Do those shoes come in my size?*
**5** to result in: *The cost of those shoes comes to $40.*
**6** to have importance: *For him, his job always comes first.*||*His family comes before anything else.*
**Come on:** **a.** an expression of encouragement: *Come on, you can do it!* **b.** an expression of doubt: *Oh come on, you don't really believe that!*
**How come:** *informal* why: *How come you got a salary increase and I didn't?*
**to come apart:** to fall into pieces: *That car is so old that it is coming apart.*
**to come down with something:** to contract a disease: *I came down with a cold yesterday.*
**to come from something** or **somewhere:** **a.** to be a native or citizen of: *He comes from London (Texas, Japan, etc.).* **b.** to be produced by: *Honey comes from bees.*
**to come over:** *My friend came over (to my house) to play cards.*
**to come through:** to do what is needed or expected, especially after a wait: *My citizenship papers finally came through.*
**to come up:** **a.** to come to someone's attention, be spoken of: *His need of money came up in our conversation.* **b.** to approach: *A man came up (to me) on the street and asked for money.* *(antonym)* go.

**comedy** /'kɑmədi/ *noun, plural* **comedies**
a funny movie, play, piece of writing, etc.: *That movie I saw was a really good comedy.* *–noun* (person) **comedian.** *(antonym)* tragedy.

**comfort** /'kʌmfərt/ *noun*
**1** a peaceful feeling of freedom from pain or worry: *People like to live in comfort.*
**2** kind and gentle care: *Nurses give comfort to sick people.*

**comfort** *verb*
to make pain or worry less bad: *Mothers comfort their sick children.*

**comfortable** /'kʌmftəbəl/ *adjective*
**1** relaxed and restful: *I sat on the big, soft sofa and made myself comfortable.*
**2** enough to be satisfied and happy: *She earns a comfortable living.* *–adverb* **comfortably.**

**comic** /'kɑmɪk/ *noun*
a comedian: *We watched a comic on TV.*

**comic** *adjective*
funny: *a comic play See:* comics.

**comical** /'kɑmɪkəl/ *adjective*
funny: *Everyone laughed at her comical remarks.*

**comic book** *noun*
a book of comic strips (color drawings that tell a story): *Children love to read*

*about the adventures of their favorite people and animals in comic books.*

**comics** /'kɑmɪks/*noun plural* or **comic strip**
picture stories of fun and adventure in newspapers: *He reads the comics every morning.*

**comma** /'kɑmə/ *noun*
the punctuation sign (,): *The comma is used to separate parts of a sentence.*

**command** /kə'mænd/ *noun*
**1** an instruction on what to do, *(synonym)* an order: *An army officer gave a command to the soldiers to shoot at the enemy.*
**2** one's skill or ability to do something: *She has a good command of English.*
**3** a signal containing instructions given to a machine or device: *She typed a command into the computer.*

**command** *verb*
**1** (in the military) to have control over a person or group: *The general commands the Third Army.*
**2** *formal* to demand with authority that someone do something: *He commanded the dog to sit.*

**commence** /kə'mɛns/ *verb formal* **commenced, commencing, commences**
to begin: *Our company commenced business on January 2 last year.*

**comment** /'kɑ,mɛnt/ *noun*
a remark, opinion: *The teacher wrote a comment on the student's paper about how good it was.* –*verb* **to comment.**

**commercial** /kə'm ɜrʃəl/ *noun*
a radio or television advertisement: *Television programs are often interrupted by commercials for cars.*

---

**USAGE NOTE:** Compare *commercial* and *advertisement. Commercials* are a kind of advertising on TV or radio. *Advertisements* in newspapers, magazines, billboards, and on the *World Wide Web* are not called *commercials.*

---

**commission** /kə'mɪʃən/ *noun*
**1** an amount of money paid, especially to a sales representative
**2** an act: *commission of a crime*
**3** a group of people authorized, usually by a government, to do something

**commit** /kə'mɪt/ *verb* **committed, committing, commits**
to do something: *He committed a crime.*
**to commit oneself:** to promise to do something: *The priest committed himself to a life of poverty.*

**commitment** /kə'mɪtmənt/ *noun*
a promise: *The mayor made a commitment to speak at the celebration.*

**committee** /kə'mɪti/ *noun*
a group of people organized for a purpose: *The company has a committee to handle employee problems.*

**common** /'kɑmən/ *adjective*
happening often, *(synonym)* frequent: *Car accidents are a common event.*|| *"Smith" is a very common name.*

**common sense** *noun, (no plural)*
the understanding of something from thinking intelligently and from everyday experience: *He knows about the harmful effects of smoking cigarettes, so it is common sense to stop.*

**communicate** /kə'myunɪ,keɪt/ *verb* **communicated, communicating, communicates**
to give information to others: *People communicate with each other by spoken or written language or by body movements.* –*noun* **communication.**

**Communism** /'kɑm yə,nɪzəm/ *noun*
a political system in which all businesses and other property are owned by the government for the use and good of the people: *Communism grew in Europe and Asia after World War II.* –*noun* (person) **Communist.**

**community** /kə'myunəti/ *noun, plural* **communities**
**1** the people as a group in a town, city, or other area: *The community is concerned about crime.*
**2** people forming a group in a racial, religious, business, etc., way: *The Dominican community in New York City is very large.*

**community college** *noun*
in the USA, a two-year college: *She is studying at a community college.*

**commute** /kə'myut/ *verb* **commuted, commuting, commutes**
to travel to and from one's work or

school regularly: *He commutes between his house in the country and his office in the city every day.* –*noun* (person) **commuter.**

**commute** *noun*
a regular trip, usually between home and workplace: *He has a long commute to work from home.*

**compact** /kəm'pækt/ *adjective*
**1** small compared with other things, taking up little space: *That compact suitcase is easy to carry.*
**2** close together: *The equipment in that case is packed in a compact way.*

**compact** *noun* /'kɑm,pækt/
a small case used to hold face powder and a mirror –*noun* **compactness.**

**compact disc** /'kɑm,pækt/ or **CD** *noun*
a disc used to record music, other sounds, images, and other information (that is read by a laser): *We use compact discs to play music on our stereo.*

**companion** /kəm'p ænyən/ *noun*
a person who goes with another person: *a traveling companion*||*John was her companion at the party.* –*noun* **companionship.**

**company** /'kʌmpəni/ *noun, plural* **companies**
**1** visitors, guests, often to a home: *We had company over for dinner.*
**2** a business: *She owns a company that makes fancy clothes.*
**3** a military unit: *a company of 50 soldiers*

**to keep someone company:** to go with someone for companionship: *He kept her company while she went to the doctor.*

**comparative** /kəm'pærətɪv/ *adjective*
**1** as compared with something else: *The comparative worth of a car is much greater than that of an old bicycle.*
**2** being the form of an adjective or adverb that compares one thing with another: *"Taller" (not "tallest") is the comparative form of "tall."* –*adverb* **comparatively.**

**compare** /kəm'pɛr/ *verb* **compared, comparing, compares**
to look for similarities and differences between two or more things, ideas, people, etc.: *The company's sales this year are excellent compared to* (or) *compared with last year's.* –*noun* **comparison.**

**compartment** /kəm'pɑrtmənt/ *noun*
an enclosed space within something larger: *Some trains have sleeping compartments.*

**compass** /'kʌmpəs/ *noun, plural* **compasses**
a device to tell direction (north, south, east, west, etc.): *Sailors use a compass to know where their ship is headed.*

compass

**compassion** /kəm'pæʃən/ *noun*
sympathy for someone, especially in doing something kind for him or her

**compatible** /kəm'pætəbəl/ *adjective*
capable of working or living well together –*noun* **compability.**

**compensation** /,kɑmpən'seɪʃən/ *noun*
**1** *singular* payment in money: *Her compensation from the company is $50,000 per year.*
**2** payment in satisfaction: *That teacher is not paid much, but he gets compensation from his love of teaching.* –*verb* **compensate.**

**compete** /kəm'pit/ *verb* **competed, competing, competes**
to participate in a contest: *Our basketball team competed against another team and won.*

**competent** /'kɑmpətənt/ *adjective*
having the ability to do something well, having good or excellent skills: *She is competent in accounting.*||*He is a competent manager.* –*noun* **competence;** –*adverb* **competently.**

**competition** /,kɑmpə'tɪʃən/ *noun*
an organized event in which people try to do something better than everyone else: *She is an excellent runner, and she enters every competition that she can.* –*noun* (person or business) **competitor.**

**competitive** /kəm'pɛtətɪv/ *adjective*
liking to compete: *He is very competitive in football; he likes to win.*

**complain** /kəm'pleɪn/ *verb*
to speak about pain or something that is

wrong: *She complains that her back hurts.* –*noun* (person) **complainer.**

**complaint** /kəm'pleɪnt/ *noun*
an expression of unhappiness or annoyance about something: *I went to the doctor with a complaint about my bad back.*

**complete** /kəm'plit/ *adjective*
**1** finished, done: *Repair of the bridge is now complete.*
**2** whole, having all its parts: *He has a complete collection of Elvis Presley records.* –*verb* **to complete.**

**complex** /kəm'plɛks/ *adjective*
having many parts or details that make something hard to understand or deal with: *Finding a cure for cancer involves complex scientific research.*

**complex** /'kɑm,plɛks/ *noun, plural* **complexes**
a group of buildings and parking lots: *That shopping complex has five restaurants, ten stores, and a day care center.*

**complexion** /kəm'plɛkʃən/ *noun*
the appearance and condition of the skin of the face: *She has a good complexion.*

**complication** /,kɑmplə'keɪʃən/ *noun*
a difficulty, problem: *A serious complication came up during the operation; her heart stopped beating.* –*verb* **to complicate;** –*adjective* **complicated.**

**compliment** /'kɑ mpləmənt/ *noun*
**to pay someone compliments:** an expression of praise, admiration, or congratulations: *People paid her compliments on her pretty dress.*

**compliment** *verb* /'kɑmplə,mɛnt/
to express praise, admiration, etc., to someone: *She complimented the boy on his good manners.* –*adjective* **complimentary** /,kɑmplə'mɛntri/.

**compose** /kəm'poʊz/ *verb* **composed, composing, composes**
**1** *formal* to put together with care, especially writing: *She composed a letter to her lawyer.*
**2** to create art: *to compose music or poetry* –*noun* (person) **composer.**

**composition** /,kɑmpə'zɪʃən/ *noun*
the writing of something: *She began composition of a letter to her mother.*

**comprehend** /,kɑ mprɪ'hɛnd/ *verb*
to get the meaning of something, to understand: *That student comprehends that he must improve his work, or fail the course.* –*noun* **comprehension.**

**compromise** /'kɑ mprə,maɪz/ *noun*
an agreement reached where each side gets some, but not all, of what it wants: *My boss and I reached a compromise on my raise where I get what I asked for, but I have to wait six months for it.*

**compromise** *verb* **compromised, compromising, compromises**
to reach a compromise: *We compromised, so I get the increase I asked for, but I have to wait for it.*

**compulsory** /kəm'pʌlsəri/ *adjective*
related to something that must be done, *(synonym)* required

**compute** /kəm'pyut/ *verb* **computed, computing, computes**
to do arithmetic or other calculations: *He computed the cost of building a new house.* –*noun* **computation.**

**computer** /kəm'pyutər/ *noun*
an electronic device that stores information and allows changes in it through the use of instructions (programs) to do various types of tasks, like word processing and accounting: *She uses her computer to write her books. See:* PC; art on page 8a.

**computerize** /kəm'pyutə,raɪz/ *verb* **computerized, computerizing, computerizes**
**1** to equip a business (or person) with computers: *The owner computerized the business; now, all of the accounting is done on computer.*
**2** to put information into a computer: *We did our accounting by hand for years, then we computerized it.*

**conceal** /kən'sil/ *verb*
to hide something: *The thief concealed a gun under his coat.* –*noun* **concealment.**

**conceive** /kən'siv/ *verb* **conceived, conceiving, conceives**
**1** to think of something: *I can't conceive of why he did such a stupid thing!*
**2** *formal* to become pregnant: *She conceived and had a son.*

**concentrate** /'kɑnsən,treɪt/ *verb* **concentrated, concentrating, concentrates**
to think hard about something: *During*

*exams, students concentrate hard on answering the questions.*

**concentration** /ˌkɑnsənˈtreɪʃən/ *noun* total attention to something: *He studies his textbook with total concentration.*

**concept** /ˈkɑnˌsɛpt/ *noun* a general idea that usually includes other ideas: *Democracy is a concept that includes the ideas of individual freedom and the right to vote.* –*adjective* **conceptual.**

**concern** /kənˈsɜrn/ *noun*
**1** care, attention: *He shows constant concern about how his mother is feeling.*
**2** worry: *When she was sick, he regarded her condition with great concern.*

**concern** *verb* to be about: *This letter concerns payment for my new TV.*

**concert** /ˈkɑnsərt/ *noun* a musical event: *I went to a rock concert last night.*

concert

**conclude** /kənˈklud/ *verb* **concluded, concluding, concludes**
**1** to bring to an end, *(synonym)* to finish: *The concert concluded with an exciting song. (antonym)* begin.
**2** to form an opinion: *After not getting a salary increase, I concluded that I must find a new job.*

**conclusion** /kənˈ kluʒən/ *noun*
**1** the end of something, the finish: *At the conclusion of the show, everyone clapped their hands.*
**2** an opinion, a judgment: *The doctor reached the conclusion that the woman needed some tests.*

**concrete** /kɑnˈkrit/ *noun* a building material made of cement: *Workers poured concrete to build the bridge.*

**concussion** /kənˈ kʌʃən/ *noun* an injury to the head and brain: *He got a concussion while playing football.*

**condemn** /kənˈdɛm/ *verb* to find guilty or unfit: *The judge condemned the criminal to life in prison.* –*noun* **condemnation.**

**condense** /kənˈdɛns/ *verb* **condensed, condensing, condenses**
**1** to shorten: *The writer condensed his letter from six pages to two pages.*
**2** to make thicker, especially by removing water: *condensed orange juice* –*noun* **condensation.**

**condition** /kənˈd ɪʃən/ *noun*
**1** the state of something (good, bad, weak, strong): *The condition of his health is excellent.*
**2** a disease, medical problem: *My grandmother has a heart condition.*
**3** a requirement: *Our apartment lease has two special conditions in it: we must take out the garbage and shovel the snow.* –*adjective* **conditional.**

**condom** /ˈkɑndəm/ *noun* a covering for the male sex organ worn during sex to prevent disease or pregnancy: *Wearing a condom reduces the chances of a woman becoming pregnant. See:* contraception.

**condominium** /ˌkɑndəˈmɪniəm/ *noun* housing, usually in an apartment building, in which each apartment is privately owned *See:* cooperative.

**conduct** /ˈkɑnˌdʌkt/ *noun* behavior: *Good conduct is expected of students in school.*

**conduct** *verb* /kənˈdʌkt/
**1** to behave: *The students conducted themselves well in class today.*
**2** to direct an orchestra, band, etc.: *He conducts the London Orchestra.*

**conductor** /kənˈd ʌktər/ *noun*
**1** a person who sells and checks tickets on a train, bus, etc.
**2** a person who directs an orchestra

**cone** /koʊn/ *noun* an object pointed at one end and then becoming wider at the other end: *An ice-cream cone is wide at the top and pointed at the bottom.*

**conference** /'kɑ nfrəns/ *noun*
**1** a professional meeting, convention, usually at a big hotel
**2** a private business meeting among people: *Mr. Smith cannot talk to you now; he is in a conference with his boss.*

**conference call** *noun*
a telephone call made between three or more people: *We organized a conference call among employees in New York, Chicago, and Denver.*

**confess** /kən'fɛs/ *verb* **confesses**
to admit something, especially something bad: *The criminal confessed his guilt in committing the robbery.*

**confession** /kən' fɛʃən/ *noun*
the admission of guilt: *The criminal gave a confession of guilt.*

**confidence** /'kɑ nfədəns/ *noun*
**1** belief in one's abilities: *That salesman has a lot of confidence in his ability to sell to difficult customers.*
**2** a secret, especially one told to another person that one trusts: *I told my friend in confidence how much money I have in the bank.*||*He kept that confidence and told no one.* –*verb* **to confide.**

**confident** /'kɑnfədənt/ *adjective*
with strong belief in one's ability or that something will definitely happen: *She behaves in a confident way.*||*He is confident that next year's sales will be excellent. (antonym)* unsure.

**confidential** /ˌkɑnfə'dɛnʃəl/ *adjective*
intended for only a few people to know, almost secret: *The doctor keeps his patients' records confidential; only his nurse and the patient can see them.*

**confirm** /kən'fɜrm/ *verb*
**1** to make sure something is correct by checking it again: *I made my airline reservations last month, and I called the airline to confirm them today.*
**2** to make something certain that was only suspected before: *The police came to our house and confirmed my worst fears that my son was in a car accident.* –*noun* **confirmation.**

**conflict** /'kɑnˌflɪkt/ *noun*
a difference, disagreement: *There is a conflict between what you are saying and what the contract says.*

**conflict** *verb* /kən'flɪkt/
to differ, disagree: *What the contract says and what you say conflict.*

**confront** /kən'frʌnt/ *verb*
to deal with something difficult or dangerous: *I confronted the problem of losing my job by working hard to find another one.* –*noun* **confrontation.**

**confuse** /kən'fyuz/ *verb* **confused, confusing, confuses**
to mix things up: *He sent the wrong reports because he confused them with other ones.* –*noun* **confusion.** *See:* art on page 18a.

**congratulate** /kən'grætʃəˌleɪt/ *verb* **congratulated, congratulating, congratulates**
to praise for something well done or important: *I would like to congratulate you on your graduation from high school.*

**congratulations** /kənˌgrætʃə'leɪʃənz/ *noun plural*
an expression of praise or pleasure for something well done or important: *Congratulations on the new baby!*

**congress** /'kɑŋgrɪs/ *noun, plural* **congresses**
in the USA, a governing group made up of the elected members of the House of Representatives and the Senate: *Congress passes laws for the nations.*

**conic** /'kɑnɪk/ *adjective*
cone-shaped: *An ice-cream cone is conic.* –*adjective* **conical.** *See:* cone.

**conjugate** /'kɑndʒəˌgeɪt/ *verb* **conjugated, conjugating, conjugates**
to give the forms of a verb: *I conjugated "to be" as "I am, you are, he/she/it is."* –*noun* **conjugation** /ˌkɑndʒə'geɪʃən/.

**conjunction** /kən'dʒʌŋkʃən/ *noun*
a type of word that joins other words, phrases, etc.: *"And," "but," and "whereas" are conjunctions.*

**connect** /kə'nɛkt/ *verb*
**1** to put or join together: *I connected the TV antenna to the TV.*
**2** to put into an electrical supply: *Then I connected the TV to an outlet. See:* disconnect.
**3** to reach someone by telephone: *After waiting ten minutes, I was connected with my boss.*

**4** (transportation) to join for another part of a trip: *The bus line connects with the trains at the railroad station.*
**5** to understand how one thing goes with another: *The police connected that man to the robbery.* *–adjective* **connected.**

**connection** /kəˈnɛkʃən/ *noun*
**1** an attachment, a joining together: *I fixed the loose connection between the TV antenna and the TV.*||*a bad connection on the telephone*
**2** a change to another vehicle or kind of transportation: *She got off the bus and made her connection with the train.*
**3** a relationship (between people, actions, ideas): *She has connections with officials in the government.*

**conquer** /ˈkɑŋkər/ *verb*
to fight and take control: *A huge army conquered that country.* *–noun* (person/nation) **conqueror.**

**conquest** /ˈkɑŋˌkwɛst/ *noun*
a military victory: *the Roman conquest of Gaul (early France)*

**conscience** /ˈkɑnʃəns/ *noun*
one's sense of right and wrong: *After he stole the money, he had a guilty conscience and returned it.*

**conscientious** /ˌkɑnʃiˈɛnʃəs/ *adjective*
careful about doing things one is supposed to do and doing them well: *She does all her work in a conscientious manner.* *–adverb* **conscientiously.**

**conscious** /ˈkɑnʃəs/ *adjective*
**1** awake: *The boxer was knocked out, but he was conscious again after one minute.*
**2** knowing or noticing something: *He feels very conscious of his foreign accent.* *–adverb* **consciously.**

**consciousness** /ˈkɑnʃəsnɪs/ *noun*
the state of being awake: *The boxer returned to consciousness after a minute.*

**consent** /kənˈsɛnt/ *verb*
**1** to agree to something: *She consented to marry John.*
**2** to approve: *Her father consented to her marrying John.*

**consent** *noun*
**1** agreement: *She gave John her consent.*
**2** approval: *John asked for her father's consent.*

**conservation** /ˌkɑnsərˈveɪʃən/ *noun*
keeping something from getting into bad condition: *Conservation of forests keeps them looking beautiful.* *–verb* **to conserve.**

**conservative** /kənˈsɜrvətɪv/ *adjective*
**1** having a political view toward keeping old ways of doing things: *In the USA, Republicans are the conservative party.* *(antonym)* liberal.
**2** slow to change, cautious
**3** not too much or too high: *She is conservative in her spending. She spends little.*

**conservative** *noun*
a person who is a conservative *–adverb* **conservatively.** *See:* Republican, USAGE NOTE.

**consider** /kənˈsɪdər/ *verb*
**1** to think about something: *I will consider your offer and tell you my decision tomorrow.*
**2** to have an opinion about something: *He considers this to be the best book on the subject.* *See:* considering.

**considerable** /kənˈsɪdərəbəl/ *adjective*
much, a lot: *That family owns a considerable amount of land.* *–adverb* **considerably.**

**considerate** /kə nˈsɪdərɪt/ *adjective*
sensitive to the feelings and comfort of others: *He is always considerate of others; he is kind and caring.* *–adverb* **considerately.**

**consideration** /kənˌsɪdəˈreɪʃən/ *noun*
careful thought: *The buyer gave the offer careful consideration and said, "Yes."*

**considering** /kənˈsɪdərɪŋ/ *preposition*
in view of: *Considering how sick he is, he should go to the doctor.*

**consist** /kənˈsɪst/ *verb*
to be made up of: *The problem consists of two parts.*

**consistent** /kənˈ sɪstənt/ *adjective*
**1** in agreement with: *His description of the accident is consistent with what the police reported.*
**2** repeated in the same way: *His high*

*performance is consistent day after day.* *–adverb* **consistently.**

**consolidate** /kən'sɑlə,deɪt/ *verb* **consolidated, consolidating, consolidates**
to group together to reduce in number: *I had so many bank accounts at different banks that I consolidated them all into one bank.* *–noun* **consolidation.**

**consonant** /'kɑnsənənt/ *noun*
any letter of the alphabet that is not a vowel: *The letters "b," "c," "d," "f," etc., are consonants.*

**constant** /'kɑnstənt/ *adjective*
**1** happening all the time, *(synonym)* continuous: *I can't sleep because of the constant noise of trucks on the street.*
**2** unchanging: *For 15 years, I have had a constant problem with a bad back.*

**constant** *noun*
a quantity or quality that does not change: *When I drive my car, I drive at a constant 55 miles per hour, no slower, no faster.* *–adverb* **constantly.**

**constipation** /,kɑnstə'peɪʃən/ *noun*
difficulty in moving waste from one's bowels: *He suffers from constipation because he doesn't eat fruit.* *–verb* **to constipate** /'kɑnstə,peɪt/; *–adjective* **constipated.**

**constitution** /,kɑnstə'tuʃən/ *noun*
the written principles and rules, governing a country: *The American constitution guarantees that the people have certain rights.* *–adjective* **constitutional.**

**construct** /kən'strʌkt/ *verb*
to build, to put together piece by piece: *Builders construct buildings.* *–noun* (business) **constructor.**

**construction** /kən'strʌkʃən/ *noun*
**1** the act(s) of building something: *That house has been under construction for two months now.*
**2** the way in which something is built: *The finest materials are being used, so the house will be of solid construction.*

construction

**consult** /kən'sʌlt/ *verb*
to ask the opinion of someone: *The President consults with top officials.*

**consultant** /kən'sʌltnt/ *noun*
a person who provides advice for pay: *The professor acts as a consultant to the government.* *–noun* (act) **consultation.**

**consume** /kən'sum/ *verb* **consumed, consuming, consumes**
to use up: *Her work consumes most of her time and energy.||He consumed of a big lunch.*

**consumer** /kən'sumər/ *noun*
the ordinary person who buys and uses goods and services

**contact** /'kɑn,tækt/ *noun*
**1** touch: *My clothes come in contact with my skin.*
**2** an electrical point: *The contact on the car battery is broken.*
**3** communication with someone: *He made contact by telephone with his friend.* *–verb* **to contact.**

**contact lens** or **contact lenses** *noun*
a small, round lens put directly on top of the eye to improve one's eyesight

**contagious** /kən'teɪʤəs/ *adjective*
(a disease) able to be given to others through physical contact or by air: *The common cold is a contagious disease.* *–noun* **contagion.**

**contain** /kən'teɪn/ *verb*
**1** to hold within a container: *That can contains peanuts.*
**2** to hold back, stop: *The students could not contain their laughter in class.*

**container** /kən't eɪnər/ *noun*
an object for holding things, such as a can, carton, box, or bottle: *I went to the store to buy a container of milk.*

**contemporary** /kən'tɛmpə,rɛri/ *adjective*
of today, *(synonym)* modern: *We like contemporary furniture in our apartment.* *(antonym)* antique.

**content (1)** /'kɑn,tɛnt/ *noun*
**1** *usually plural* things contained inside something: *A customs official examined the contents of my suitcase.*
**2** the ideas or meanings expressed in a speech or piece of writing, *(synonym)* subject matter: *The teacher returned his*

*paper and said the content was very interesting.*

**content (2)** /ˈkɑnˌtɛnt/ *adjective*
satisfied, pleased: *He is content with his good life.*

**contest** /ˈkɑnˌtɛst/ *noun*
**1** a competition: *The teacher organized a spelling contest in her English class.*
**2** a struggle or fight

**contest** *verb* /kənˈtɛst/
to disagree formally: *to contest a dead person's will in court*

**contestant** /kənˈ tɛstənt/ *noun*
a competitor in a competition: *She is the youngest contestant in the piano competition.*

**continent** /ˈkɑntənənt/ *noun*
one of the seven great land masses in the world: *The North American continent is made up of the United States of America, Canada and Mexico.* –*adjective* **continental** /ˌkɑntəˈnɛntl/.

**continual** /kənˈtɪnyuəl/ *adjective*
happening without stopping: *That dog's barking is a continual annoyance.*

**continue** /kənˈtɪnyu/ *verb* **continued, continuing, continues**
**1** to carry on for a period of time: *The storm continued for three days.*
**2** to start again after a pause: *The movie on TV continued after the news.* –*noun* **continuation.**

**continuing education** *noun*
education taken, especially by adults, on a part-time basis, adult education: *That college offers continuing education courses in foreign languages, accounting, etc.*

**contraception** /ˌkɑntrəˈsɛpʃən/ *noun*
the use of any method that prevents a woman from becoming pregnant, birth control –*noun, adjective* **contraceptive.**

**contract (1)** /ˈkɑnˌtrækt/ *noun*
an agreement, usually written and signed by those making it: *I signed a contract to buy a new car.* –*adjective* **contractual.**

**contract** *verb*
to make a written agreement: *I contracted for delivery of a new car.*

**contract (2)** /kənˈtrækt/ *verb*
**1** to become smaller: *When you bend your arms, your muscles contract.*
**2** to develop or catch a disease: *He contracted cancer.*

**contraction** /kənˈtrækʃən/ *noun*
a shortened word or words, as in "can't" for "cannot" and "I'm" for "I am": *Contractions are common in spoken English.*

**contractor** /ˈkɑ nˌtræktər/ *noun*
a business or person who agrees to do something under contract, especially a builder: *He is a contractor who builds small houses.*

**contrary** /ˈkɑnˌtrɛri/ *adjective*
different from, opposite: *He holds an opinion contrary to mine.*

**contrary** *noun*
**on the contrary:** the opposite of what has been said: *"You hate jazz." "On the contrary, I love it."*

**contrast** /ˈkɑnˌt ræst/ *noun*
a difference in color or meaning: *The photograph has good contrast between the blue lake and green hills.*

**contrast** *verb* /kənˈtræst/
to differ in color or meaning: *The blue and gold colors in the painting contrast beautifully with each other.*

**contribute** /kənˈtrɪbyut/ *verb* **contributed, contributing, contributes**
**1** to give money, time, etc.: *She contributes money to her church.*
**2** to participate in something: *Everyone on the team contributed to winning the game.* –*noun* **contributor.**

**contribution** /ˌkɑntrəˈbyuʃən/ *noun*
**1** a giving of money, one's time, etc.: *That rich man makes big contributions to help the poor.*
**2** positive or helpful participation: *Her good work made an important contribution to the company's success.*

**control** /kənˈtroʊl/ *noun*
**1** the power to decide or tell others what to do: *The owner has control over the company.*
**2** a device used to guide a vehicle: *The pilot is at the controls of the airplane.*
**in control: a.** in charge: *She is in control of the company.* **b.** managing one's behavior: *She gets upset, but keeps her anger in control.*

C

**out of control:** behaving badly: *The airplane went out of control and crashed.*||*When he gets angry, he gets out of control.*

**control** *verb* **controlled, controlling, controls**
**1** to have power: *Mr. Shin controls the company, but he cannot control his anger.*
**2** to guide something: *The pilot controls the airplane. –adjective* **controllable.**

**convenience** /kən'vinyəns/ *noun*
a situation agreeable to one's time or needs: *She has the convenience of being able to walk to work.*

**convenient** /kən' vinyənt/ *adjective*
**1** acceptable and suitable to one's time or needs: *Is it convenient that I meet you in your office at noon today?*
**2** easy and comfortable to do or get to: *We live in a neighborhood that is convenient to the stores and subway. –adverb* **conveniently.** *(antonym)* inconvenient.

**convention** /kən' vɛnʃən/ *noun*
a gathering of people of similar interests who listen to speakers: *We go every year to the convention of English teachers at a big hotel.*

**conversation** /ˌkɑnvər'seɪʃən/ *noun*
a talk: *I had a conversation about the party with my friend.*

**to make conversation:** to talk in a friendly and polite way: *While waiting at the bus stop, I made conversation with a stranger about the weather. –adjective* **conversational.**

**convert** /kən'vɜrt/ *verb*
to change the condition of something: *The owner converted the hotel into an apartment building.*||*He wants to convert to Catholicism. –noun* (act) **conversion.**

**convert** /'kɑnˌvɜrt/ *noun*
a person who changes religions: *He was Catholic, but now he is a convert to Buddhism.*

**convertible** /kən'vɜrtəbəl/ *noun*
a car that has a top that can be rolled or folded down

**convict** /kən'vɪkt/ *verb*
to find someone guilty of a crime in a court of law: *He was convicted of murder.*

**convict** /'kɑnˌvɪkt/ *noun*
a person going to jail for a crime: *The police are searching the area for an escaped convict.*

**conviction** /kən' vɪkʃən/ *noun*
**1** the act of finding someone guilty in a court of law for committing a crime: *He received a murder conviction from the jury.*
**2** a strong belief: *She has strong convictions about being honest and working hard.*

**convince** /kən'vɪns/ *verb* **convinced, convincing, convinces**
to cause someone to believe something is worth doing or true: *The young man convinced the beautiful woman to marry him.*||*He convinced her that he loves her.*

**cook** /kʊk/ *verb*
to prepare food either cold or by heating it in various ways (frying, boiling, etc.): *She cooks dinner for us every evening.*

**cook** *noun*
a person who prepares and cooks food: *My mother is a terrific cook! See:* art on page 19a.

**cookie** /'kʊki/ *noun*
a small, flat, sweet, often crisp cake: *I like chocolate-chip cookies.*

**cooking** /'kʊkɪŋ/ *noun*
the art and practice of preparing and serving food: *She studied cooking in Paris.*

**cookout** /'kʊkaʊt/ *noun*
a meal prepared and eaten outside with a group of people, often including hamburgers, hot dogs, and potato salad *See:* barbecue.

**cookout**

**cool** /kul/ *adjective*
**1** not warm or cold, but more cold than hot: *San Francisco has a cool climate.*
**2** calm, not angry: *My boss never gets angry; she has a cool manner.*
**3** not friendly: *He made a cool reply to a question.*
**4** *slang* excellent: *He's a cool guy!*

C

**cool** *noun*
one's calm
**to keep one's cool:** to stay calm: *The house was on fire, but the mother kept her cool and led her children to safety.*
**cool** *verb*
**1** to lose or take away heat, *(synonym)* to chill: *The soda is cooling in the refrigerator.*
**2** to become unfriendly, distant: *Relations between the two countries cooled.*
**to cool down** or **off: a.** to stop sweating: *Let's go for a swim and cool off.* **b.** to calm down: *Two men argued, and a friend told them to go outside and cool off.*

**cooperate** /koʊ'ɑpəˌreɪt/ *verb* **cooperated, cooperating, cooperates**
to agree to help someone toward a common purpose or goal: *The workers cooperated with each other to fix the broken pipe.*

**cooperation** /koʊˌɑpə'reɪʃən/ *noun*
the act of working with someone toward a common goal: *It takes cooperation between employees to make a business run well.*

**cooperative** /koʊ'ɑprətɪv/ *adjective*
willing to do what is needed or being asked: *My neighbor was cooperative and helped me clean the yard.*
**cooperative** *noun*
an apartment building owned by the people who live there: *She owns a two-bedroom cooperative.*

**coordinate** /koʊ 'ɔrdneɪt/ *verb* **coordinated, coordinating, coordinates**
to bring together various people and activities for a common purpose: *She coordinated a study by telling each scientist what to do and sharing the results with all of them.*
**coordinate** /koʊ'ɔrdnɪt/ *noun*
a point of location on a map or graph: *The teacher asked us to find the coordinates of Iceland on a map.* –*noun* (person) **coordinator.**

**coordination** /koʊˌɔrdn'eɪʃən/ *noun*
**1** bringing together people and activities for a purpose: *The coordination of that school play is done by the teacher.*
**2** the ability to move the body well in athletics: *Baseball players need to have good coordination; their eyes, arms, and legs need to work together.*

**cop** /kɑp/ *noun slang*
a police officer: *After he hit me, I called the cops to come get him.*

**copier** /'kɑpiər/ *noun*
a machine used to make copies of something, a photocopier: *The copier in our office gets heavy use.*

**copper** /'kɑpər/ *noun*
a brownish red metal and basic chemical element: *The pipes in that building are made of copper.*

**copy** /'kɑpi/ *noun, plural* **copies**
**1** something made to look like another: *I made three copies of my report on the copy machine.* *See:* duplicate.
**2** a fake: *What a mistake! That museum paid $1,000,000 for a fake; it was only a copy, not the original.*
**3** one of a number of identical books, magazines, newspapers, etc.: *This book has sold over 50,000 copies.* *See:* cc, USAGE NOTE.
**copy** *verb* **copied, copying, copies**
**1** to make something look like another: *I copied into my notebook what the teacher said.*
**2** to fake
**3** to steal someone else's written work *See:* plagiarize.
**to copy down:** to write down: *Students copy down what professors say and write in class.*

**copyright** /'kɑp iˌraɪt/ *noun*
ownership of written or picture material (books, music, paintings) by authors, composers, and painters

**cord** /kɔrd/ *noun*
strong string or rope: *I tied the package with some cord.*

**corduroy** /'kɔrdəˌrɔɪ/ *noun*
strong, thick cloth with soft raised lines, used to make pants, jackets, and suits: *Those corduroy pants will last for years.*

**core** /kɔr/ *noun*
**1** the center of some fruits, containing the seeds: *an apple core*
**2** the center of anything: *the earth's core*

**cork** /'kɔrk/ *noun*
a bottle stopper: *The waiter pulled the cork out of the wine bottle.*

**corn** /kɔrn/ *noun*
in the USA, a tall green plant with large, yellow seeds, fed to cattle or eaten cooked by people *See:* art on page 2a.

**corner** /ˈkɔrnər/ *noun*
the area where two streets, walls, etc., meet: *I will meet you on the corner of Main St. and 3rd Ave. at noon. See:* art on page 4a.

**corner** *verb*
to force someone or something into a position from which escape is impossible

**corporation** /ˌkɔrpəˈreɪʃən/ *noun*
a business with a legal right (incorporated) to operate *–adjective* **corporate.**

**corpse** /kɔrps/ *noun*
a lifeless human body (as compared with a dead animal): *The accident victim's corpse lay in the street.*

**correct** /kəˈrɛkt/ *verb*
**1** to make (something) accurate: *The teacher corrected the student's spelling mistake.*
**2** to change someone's or one's own behavior to the right way: *He was lazy but two weeks in army camp corrected his behavior.*

**correct** *adjective*
**1** accurate: *The student gave the correct answer to the question.*
**2** honest, proper: *She found the man's wallet and returned it to him because that is the correct thing to do. –adverb* **correctly;** *–noun* **correctness.**

**correction** /kəˈr ɛkʃən/ *noun*
a change made to fix a mistake: *I spelled that word incorrectly, but have made the correction now.*

**correspondence** /ˌkɔrəˈspɑndəns/ *noun*
**1** mail sent between people: *She answers the correspondence from her customers every day.*
**2** an agreement, matching: *There is a correspondence between spending less money and saving more. –verb* **to correspond;** *–noun* (person) **correspondent.**

**corrupt** /kəˈrʌpt/ *adjective*
dishonest: *That official is corrupt because he takes bribes. –verb* **to corrupt.**

**cosmetics** /kɑzˈm ɛtɪks/ *noun*
a beauty preparation, like makeup, lipstick, and skin cream

**cost** /kɔst/ *noun*
**1** the price of something: *What is the cost of a loaf of bread in the store?*
**2** *usually used in the singular* the waste of time, effort, or hurt of something: *That war was won at a cost of 50 million lives.*

**cost** *verb* **cost, costing, costs**
**1** to have as its price: *That car costs $30,000.*
**2** to cause a loss: *That car accident cost five lives.*

**costly** /ˈkɔstli/ *adjective* **costlier, costliest**
**1** expensive: *Their dinner was costly but wonderful.*
**2** hurtful in time, effort, money, or pain: *I lost my wallet and that was a costly mistake.*

**cost of living** *noun, (no plural)*
the cost of necessities of life, such as food, housing, clothes, transportation, etc.: *The cost of living in cities like New York, Paris, and Tokyo is very high.*

**costume** /ˈkɑsˌtum/ *noun*
a style of clothes worn especially by an actor or for entertainment: *We went to a Halloween party where everyone wore funny costumes. –verb* **to costume.**

**cot** /kɑt/ *noun*
a simple bed that can be folded up and moved easily: *I took a cot out of the closet for my friend to sleep on.*

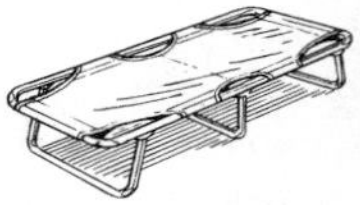
cot

**cottage** /ˈkɑtɪʤ/ *noun*
a small, simple house usually in the country: *She lives in a cottage by the lake.*

**cotton** /ˈkɑtn/ *noun*
**1** a plant whose seeds are covered with soft, white material that is made into thread and cloth
**2** cloth made from this material: *His shirts are made of cotton.*

**couch** /kaʊʧ/ *noun, plural* **couches**
a piece of furniture for sitting or lying on, a sofa: *The couch in our living room is soft and comfortable.*

couch

**cougar** /'kugər/ *noun*
a large cat found in mountains of western North, Central, and South America: *Cougars attack sheep and cows.*

**cough** /kɔf/ *verb*
to push air out of the throat suddenly with a sharp sound: *I was coughing quite a bit because of my cold. –noun* **cough.** *See:* art on page 11a.

**could** /kʊd/ *auxiliary verb and past tense of* can
**1** used to indicate that something is possible: *Everyone could hear the radio program.*
**2** used to make a suggestion or give permission: *You could go to the movie, if you want to.*
**3** used to ask for something: *Could you pass me the salt and pepper, please? See:* can; may; would.

**council** /'kaʊnsəl/ *noun*
a group of officials: *The city council advises the mayor on what to do. –noun* **councilor** /'kaʊnslər/.

**counsel** /'kaʊnsəl/ *noun*
**1** advice, usually given by an expert
**2** a lawyer *–verb* **to counsel.**

**counselor** /'kaʊnslər/ *noun*
**1** an advisor: *The school counselor and I talked about which courses I should take.*
**2** a lawyer
**3** someone who takes care of children at a summer camp: *The camp counselor taught the children a new song.*

**count** /kaʊnt/ *verb*
**1** to add up, calculate: *I counted my suits one by one.*
**2** to say numbers in order: *to count to three*
**3** to consider, think of: *I count her as one of my best friends.*
**4** to be of importance, to matter: *Having money counts because you can't do much without it.*
**to count on someone** or **something:** to be sure of: *You can count on her to do a good job.*

**count** *noun*
**1** a total, a sum: *I made a count of all my sweaters: 12 to be exact.*
**2** a legal charge against someone: *She was guilty on all counts.*
**to keep count:** to note, keep track of: *I must keep count of how many students are in class every day.*
**to lose count:** to not know the exact number: *She's lost count of how many grandchildren she has. –adjective* **countable.**

**countdown** /'kaʊnt,daʊn/ *noun*
a counting of numbers from higher to lower: *The countdown for a space rocket goes, "... 5, 4, 3, 2, 1, Blast off!"*

**counter** /'kaʊntər/ *noun*
a flat, table-like surface: *The waiter put my hamburger on the counter in front of me.*
**over-the-counter:** referring to something that can be sold without a doctor's permission (prescription): *Aspirin and cold medicine are sold over-the-counter. See:* art on page 10a.

**counter** *prefix*
**1** in response to: *counterattack*
**2** similar to: *counterpart*
**3** in the opposite direction: *counterclockwise*

**counterclockwise** /,kaʊntər'klɑk,waɪz/ *adverb*
moving in the direction opposite to which the hands of a clock move: *I turn my key counterclockwise to open my door. See:* clockwise.

**counterfeit** /'kaʊntər,fɪt/ *adjective*
fake, false, especially money *–verb* **to counterfeit;** *–noun* (person) **counterfeiter.**

**country** /'kʌntri/ *noun, plural* **countries**
**1** a nation: *the country of Canada*
**2** an area outside cities and towns: *We drive to the country to relax.*

**country** *adjective*
typical of the country, especially in being simple, rough, or old fashioned: *country furniture*

**county** /'kʌʊnti/ *noun, plural* **counties**
(in the USA) a smaller political and geographical area within states: *County governments are often responsible for some of a state's highways.*

**couple** /'kʌpəl/ *noun*
**1** two people (usually one female and one male) who are married, living to-

gether, or in a relationship: *Jane and Tom are a couple that love to go dancing.*
**2** several, usually two: *Can you lend me a couple of dollars? Yes, for a couple of days.* –*verb* **to couple.** *See:* pair.

**coupon** /'ku,pɑn/ *noun*
a piece of paper that offers a payment, service, or lowering in the price: *He gives coupons to the supermarket cashier who takes money off the price of the food.*

coupons

**courage** /'kɜrɪʤ/ *noun*
bravery, the strength of mind and/or body to face and overcome danger: *The fire fighter showed courage by jumping into the cold lake to save a drowning boy.* –*adjective* **courageous** /kə'reɪʤəs/; –*adverb* **courageously.**

**course** /kɔrs/ *noun*
**1** a series of lessons in a subject, usually at a school: *I took a college course in English literature.*
**2** a planned route: *That ship headed for China is on course/off course.*

**of course:** naturally, clearly: *Of course I'll come to your wedding.*

**court (1)** /kɔrt/ *noun*
a government building with rooms where a judge and often a jury hear cases: *The murder trial took place in a court of law.*

**to go** or **take someone to court:** to make a legal, written complaint against someone: *When the company would not pay the money it owed us, we went to court to get it. See:* sue.

**court (2)** *noun*
**1** an area marked off for sports: *We played on a tennis (volleyball, handball, etc.) court. See:* course.
**2** the place where a king or queen lives or meets with others: *the royal court in London*

**courteous** /'kɜr tiəs/ *adjective*
having good manners, polite: *The taxi driver is very courteous to his customers. (antonym)* rude. –*adverb* **courteously.**

**courtesy** /'kɜrt əsi/ *noun, plural* **courtesies**
good manners, politeness: *The telephone operator treats all callers with courtesy.*

**courthouse** /'kɔrt,haʊs/ *noun*
the building in which courts of law and other legal activities are located: *I went to the courthouse to get a copy of my birth certificate.*

**courtyard** /'kɔrt, yɑrd/ *noun*
an outdoor area next to a house or building: *Cars drive into the courtyard to let people out at the building's front door. See:* patio.

**cousin** /'kʌzən/ *noun*
a child of an aunt or uncle: *My cousins live in Florida.*

**cover** /'kʌvər/ *noun*
**1** a removable top of something: *a cover for a jar*
**2** a layer of cloth or other material: *The bed covers have a pretty flower design.*
**3** the strong outer part of a book, magazine
**4** a place to hide
**5** shelter or safety: *When it started to rain, I ran for cover under a tree.*

**cover** *verb*
**1** to put something on or over something else: *She covered the table with a cloth.*
**2** to report an event: *That newspaper reporter covered the story about the fire.*
**3** to travel a distance: *We covered 30 miles (48 km) on bicycles yesterday.*
**4** to be enough money to pay for something: *This $400 will cover the cost of a new coat.*

**to cover something up:** to hide something, keep others from knowing about it: *The company covered up the scandal about stealing money.* –*noun* **coverage.**

**cow** /kaʊ/ *noun*
the adult female of cattle and some other large animals: *Farmers get up early to milk the cows. See:* calf; art on page 14a.

**coward** /'kaʊərd/ *noun*
a person without courage: *She was a coward when she ran out of the burning house and left her children to die.* –*adjective* **cowardly;** –*noun* **cowardice.**

**cowboy** /ˈkaʊˌbɔɪ/ *noun*
a man who works on a cattle ranch or rodeo, taking care of the cattle

**cowgirl** /ˈkaʊˌgɜrl/ *noun*
a woman who works on a cattle ranch or rodeo, taking care of cattle

**coyote** /kaɪˈoʊti/ *noun, plural* **coyotes** or **coyote**
a kind of wolf similar to a medium-sized dog found mainly in western North and Central America: *Coyotes often hunt rats and mice at night.*

coyote

**cozy** /ˈkoʊzi/ *adjective* **cozier, coziest**
warm, friendly, and comfortable: *We had dinner at a cozy restaurant with a fireplace.*

**crab** /kræb/ *noun*
a sea animal with a flat shell, four pairs of legs, and two claws

**crack** /kræk/ *noun*
a line of separation in a material, a split: *That drinking glass has a crack.*

**crack** *verb*
to break without coming apart: *A small stone hit the window and cracked it.*

**cracker** /ˈkrækər/ *noun*
a small, thin piece of unsweetened baked dough: *She likes to eat cheese on crackers.*

**cradle** /ˈkreɪdl/ *noun*
a baby's bed, especially one that moves back and forth

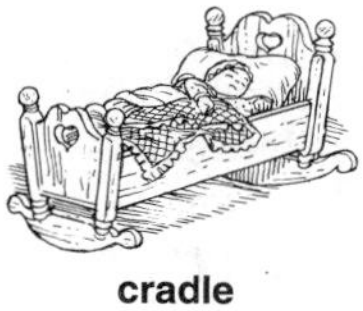
cradle

**cradle** *verb* **cradled, cradling, cradles**
to hold gently: *She cradled the baby in her arms.*

**craft** /kræft/ *noun*
**1** a skilled trade: *the craft of furniture making*
**2** skill in making things by hand: *the craft of basketweaving, the craft of making pottery*
**3** a boat, airplane, or space vehicle: *water craft, aircraft, spacecraft*
**4** skill in tricking people *See:* crafty.

**craft** *verb*
to make something with skill: *He crafts fine furniture by hand.* –*noun* **craftsman** /ˈkræftsmən/, **craftsmanship.**

**cramp** /kræmp/ *noun*
a painful tightening of a muscle: *After running, he got a cramp in his leg.*

**cramped** /kræmpt/ *adjective*
small and uncomfortable: *She lives in a cramped little apartment.*

**cranberry** /ˈkræn ˌbɛri/ *noun, plural* **cranberries**
a small, sour red berry that grows in wet land especially in New England, or the plant it grows on: *Cranberries are cooked and made into jelly that is eaten with turkey on Thanksgiving. See:* art on page 3a.

**crane** /kreɪn/ *noun*
**1** a large waterbird with long legs and neck
**2** a large machine used to lift heavy loads

crane

**crane** *verb* **craned, craning, cranes**
to lift one's head like a crane: *People craned their necks to see the accident scene.*

**crash** /kræʃ/ *noun, plural* **crashes**
**1** a violent hit against something, usually with damage, an accident: *a car crash, a plane crash*
**2** the loud, violent sound of a crash: *Cars hit together with a loud crash.*

**crash** *verb* **crashes**
**1** to smash against something: *The bus went out of control and crashed against cars and telephone poles.*
**2** to fail or collapse: *The computer crashed and all its data was lost.*

**crate** /kreɪt/ *noun*
a box made of wood used to send things: *That store has crates of oranges and tomatoes.* –*verb* **to crate.**

**crater** /ˈkreɪtər/ *noun*
a large hole in the ground: *the crater of a volcano*

crater

**crawl** /krɔl/ *verb*
to move slowly and close to the ground: *Babies crawl on their hands and knees.* –*noun* **crawl.**

**crayon** /ˈkreɪˌɑn/ *noun*
a stick made of colored wax used for drawing: *Children love to draw with colored crayons.*

**craze** /kreɪz/ *noun*
a popular style that passes soon: *Wearing black shoes with thick soles was the craze this year. See:* fad.

**craze** *verb* **crazed, crazing, crazes**
to become insane, crazy: *Fighting in the jungle crazed many soldiers.*

**crazy** /ˈkreɪzi/ *adjective* **crazier, craziest**
**1** sick in the mind, insane: *The crazy man talks to himself all the time.*
**2** making no sense, foolish: *He is crazy. He thinks he will make $1 million this year!*
**3** wildly enthusiastic: *When she saw that new car, she went crazy over it.*
**like crazy:** actively, hard: *She ran like crazy to catch the bus.* –*adverb* **crazily;** –*noun* **craziness.**

**cream** /krim/ *noun*
**1** the fatty part of milk that goes to its surface: *Butter is made from cream.*
**2** a thick, smooth substance used in cosmetics and medicine: *She put cold cream on her face.* –*verb* **to cream.**

**cream cheese** *noun*
a soft, white, smooth cheese made of milk and cream: *She put cream cheese on her toast.*

**creamy** /ˈkrimi/ *adjective* **creamier, creamiest**
**1** (food) smooth and thick like cream: *I like a creamy salad dressing.*
**2** (appearance) light colored and smooth like cream: *She has a creamy complexion.* –*noun* (business) **creamery.**

**crease** /kris/ *noun* **creased, creasing, creases**
a fold in cloth or paper *The cleaners put a crease in my pants with an iron.* –*verb* **to crease.**

**create** /kriˈeɪt/ *verb* **created, creating, creates**
**1** to give life to: *Parents create their children. (antonym)* destroy.
**2** to make something in a special way, usually with skill or artistry: *That artist created great paintings.*

**creation** /kriˈeɪ ʃən/ *noun*
**1** the beginning of existence of something: *the creation of the universe*
**2** the making of something: *That statue is a great artistic creation.*
**the Creation:** (in religion) the creating by God of the world

**creative** /kriˈeɪ tɪv/ *adjective*
**1** showing artistic skill and imagination: *That artist has the creative ability to paint beautiful pictures.*
**2** having the ability to think well and solve problems: *a creative solution to a problem* –*adverb* **creatively;** –*noun* **creativity** /ˌkrieɪˈtɪvəti/.

**creator** /kriˈeɪt ər/ *noun*
a person who creates something: *He was the creator of television many years ago.*
**the Creator:** God

**creature** /ˈkritʃər/ *noun*
a living being: *The creatures on earth include humans and animals.*

**credentials** /krɪˈdɛnʃəlz/ *noun plural*
**1** identity papers: *That government official carries his credentials with him to show who he is.*
**2** papers (diplomas, awards, references of good employment) that show one's achievements: *She has excellent credentials for the job.*

**credit (1)** /ˈkrɛdɪt/ *noun*
a cause for admiration, honor, etc.: *Her many good grades in school are a credit to her skill.*
**to give credit:** to give admiration for something: *I give the teacher credit for explaining things so clearly.*||*I give him credit for looking so healthy.*
**to take credit for something:** to accept admiration or feel pleasure for something well done: *The teacher takes credit for her students' doing well on exams.* –*verb* **to credit.**

**credit (2)** *noun*
**1** the ability to buy now and pay later: *Our company has credit with other companies, so we buy now and pay them in 30 days.*||*I bought this new suit on credit.*
**2** a unit of a course at a school, college, etc.: *I earned three credits in my English course.*

**credit** *verb*
(in accounting) to add a sum to someone's account: *When I sent a $300 check, the bank credited my account for that amount.*

**credit card** *noun*
a small, flat plastic card that allows a person to buy goods and services on credit: *I used my credit card to pay for dinner. See:* charge card.

credit card

**creek** /krik/ *noun*
a small stream: *We went fishing in the creek.*

**creep** /krip/ *verb* **crept** /krεpt/, **creeping, creeps**
to move slowly: *Cars creep through a traffic jam.*

**creep** *noun*
a slow movement

**creole** /ˈkriˌoʊl/ *noun*
a language that has developed from a mixture of two languages and has become the native language of people in a place: *She speaks Haitian creole. See:* dialect.

**crept** /krεpt/ *verb*
*past tense and past participle of* creep

**crest** /krεst/ *noun*
the top of something: *the crest of a hill, the crest of a wave*

**crew** /kru/ *noun*
**1** the workers on a ship, airplane, train, space vehicle, etc.: *the captain and crew on a ship*
**2** a group of workers: *the stage crew in a theater*

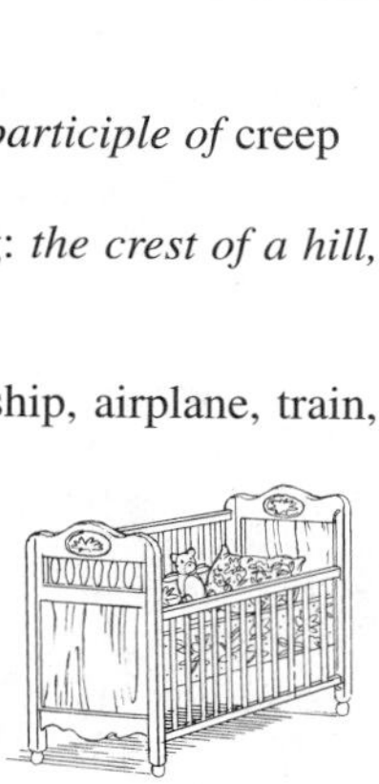
crib

**crib** /krɪb/ *noun*
a baby's bed with high sides: *The baby cannot fall out of her crib.*

**cricket** /ˈkrɪkɪt/ *noun*
**1** a small, dark brown insect that makes a high-sounding noise: *I can hear the crickets at night.*
**2** an outdoor ball game popular in the British Commonwealth

**crime** /kraɪm/ *noun*
**1** a serious, illegal act: *the crime of murder*
**2** serious illegal acts in general: *The police fight crime: murder, theft, and drug dealing.*
**3** a bad situation that should not happen: *It is a crime that such a nice man has so much trouble in his life. See:* misdemeanor.

**criminal** /ˈkrɪmənəl/ *noun*
a person who commits a serious crime

**crimson** /ˈkrɪmzən/ *adjective*
a deep, dark red: *Red roses have crimson flowers.*

**cripple** /ˈkrɪpəl/ *noun*
a person or animal unable to walk or use arms and legs normally: *The taxi driver had a car accident and now he is a cripple.* –*verb* **to cripple.**

**crisis** /ˈkraɪsɪs/ *noun, plural* **crises** /-ˌsiz/
an emergency: *The hurricane caused a crisis as people are without houses or food.*

**crisp** /krɪsp/ *adjective*
**1** having a fresh, firm feel: *crisp lettuce*
**2** cool, refreshing: *crisp sea air* –*adverb* **crisply;** –*noun* **crispness;** –*adjective* **crispy.**

**critic** /ˈkrɪtɪk/ *noun*
a person who criticizes something or someone: *That critic of government laws was put in jail.*||*a movie critic*

**critical** /ˈkrɪtɪkəl/ *adjective*
**1** pointing out problems: *The teacher wrote critical remarks on my paper about mistakes that I made.*
**2** very important: *It is critical that you study for the exam or you will fail it.*
**3** dangerous, urgent: *Her illness is at the critical stage where she may die.* –*adverb* **critically.**

**criticize** /ˈkrɪt əˌsaɪz/ *verb* **criticized, criticizing, criticizes**
**1** to give opinions about art, music, theater, etc. as a profession: *The newspaper's critic criticized the new movie as boring.*
**2** to point out faults in someone or something: *The teacher criticized the student's poor spelling.* *–noun* (act) **criticism.** *(antonym)* praise.

**crocodile** /ˈkrɑkəˌdaɪl/ *noun*
a very long, thin animal (reptile) with hard skin and a long mouth with sharp teeth

**crook** /krʊk/ *noun*
a criminal, especially a thief or cheat: *There are crooks everywhere ready to cheat you.*

**crooked** /ˈkrʊkɪd/ *adjective*
**1** bent, not straight: *a crooked stick*
**2** criminal, dishonest: *a crooked businessman*

**crop** /krɑp/ *noun*
a planting of food (grain, vegetables, or fruit): *Farmers had a good crop of wheat this year.*

**crop** *verb* **cropped, cropping, crops**
to cut something short: *Sheep cropped the grass in the field.*

**cross** /krɔs/ *noun, plural* **crosses**
**1** a wooden pole with a piece of wood running across it near the top, on which people were killed in ancient times
**2** a sign made like a + or an X

**cross** *adjective*
**1** horizontal: *a cross bar used in building*
**2** angry: *She is very cross today; she complains about everything.*

**cross** *verb* **crosses**
**1** to go over or across something: *I crossed the street to catch the bus.*
**2** to pass while going in opposite directions: *Our letters crossed in the mail.*
**3** to oppose, to anger someone: *He crossed his friend by not paying back the money that he owed him. See:* double-cross.
**to cross one's fingers:** to wish for good luck: *I have my fingers crossed that I pass the exam today.*
**to cross someone** or **something off** or **out:** to remove, draw a line through: *I make a list of things to do, then cross off/out the ones that are done.*

**crossing** /ˈkrɔsɪŋ/ *noun*
a place where a street, river, etc. can be crossed: *The school crossing is on the next corner.*

**cross-reference** *noun*
a note telling a reader about related information in another part of a book, file, index, etc. *–verb* **to cross-reference.**

**crossroad** /ˈkrɔsˌroʊd/ *noun* or **crossroads** *plural noun used with a singular verb*
the place where one road crosses another road: *I will meet you at the crossroads of Main St. and First Ave.*

**crosswalk** /ˈkrɔsˌwɔk/ *noun*
a place on a street marked with lines for people to cross while vehicles stop: *Children are told to cross the street only at the crosswalks. See:* art on page 4a.

**crossword puzzle** /ˈkrɔsˌwɜrd/ *noun*
a printed word game with numbered squares to be filled in with answers from numbered ideas: *Crossword puzzles are fun to do if you like words.*

**crossword puzzle**

**crow** /kroʊ/ *noun*
**1** a large black bird with a loud cry
**2** the cry made by a rooster

**crow** *verb*
**1** to make the sound of a rooster: *The rooster crows every morning at sunrise.*
**2** *figurative* to boast about something: *She is crowing about how beautiful her new baby is.*

**crowd** /kraʊd/ *noun*
**1** a large group of people close together: *the crowd at the football game*
**2** a group of friends, similar people: *That crowd likes rock music.*

**crowd** *verb*
to form into a crowd: *The people crowded into the theater.*

**crowded** /ˈkraʊdɪd/ *adjective*
full of people: *That subway train is so crowded no one else can get on.*

**crown** /kraʊn/ *noun*

crown

**1** a decoration for the head made of gold and jewels to show high position: *The queen of England wears her crown for special ceremonies.*
**2** the top back part of the head or a hat

**crown** *verb*
**1** to place a crown on someone's head: *The high priest crowned the new king.*
**2** to declare someone a winner: *She was crowned Miss Universe in a beauty contest.*

**crude** /krud/ *adjective* **cruder, crudest**
**1** rough, unfinished: *He lives in a cabin with crude chairs.*
**2** behaving badly: *The child was sent to his room because of his crude behavior* *–adverb* **crudely;** *–noun* **crudeness.**

**cruel** /ˈkruəl/ *adjective*
**1** willing to cause others mental or physical pain, mean: *She makes cruel remarks about her husband being too fat.*
**2** painful, very difficult: *Cancer is a cruel disease because of the suffering it causes.* *–noun* **cruelty.** *See:* kind

**cruise** /kruz/ *noun*
a pleasure trip on a boat or ship: *We took a cruise in the Caribbean.*

**cruise** *verb* **cruised, cruising, cruises**
**1** to sail on a boat or ship in a pleasant, comfortable manner: *We cruised down the coast in our sailboat.*
**2** to move in a vehicle or airplane at its best, fast, comfortable speed: *Jet planes cruise at 600 miles (960 km) per hour.*

**crumb** /krʌm/ *noun*
a small piece of bread or cake: *She feeds bread crumbs to the birds.*

**crumble** /ˈkrʌmbəl/ *verb* **crumbled, crumbling, crumbles**
to fall into pieces, especially from age: *Over many years, that old church crumbled into ruins.* *–adjective* **crumbly.**

**crunch** /krʌntʃ/ *noun, plural* **crunches**
**1** a sound like teeth biting an apple: *You hear the crunch when she bites into a fresh apple.*
**2** a difficult, high-pressure situation: *Two employees did not come to work today, so we are in a crunch to do their work, too.* *–adjective* **crunchy;** *–verb* **to crunch.**

**crush** /krʌʃ/ *verb* **crushes**
**1** to push, press hard: *She crushed a piece of paper in her hand.*
**2** to smash: *The roof fell in and crushed the furniture in the building.*

**crust** /krʌst/ *noun*
**1** a hard covering: *the earth's crust*
**2** a firm outer layer (of food): *a pie crust*

**crutch** /ˈkrʌtʃ/ *noun, plural* **crutches**
a support made of metal or wood to help people walk: *He broke his foot and is on crutches now.* *See:* art on page 11a.

**cry** /kraɪ/ *noun, plural* **cries**
**1** a loud sound made by living things: *a cry of pain, a cry for help*
**2** a normal sound made by some animals and birds: *the cry of a bird*
**3** an act or period of tears running from the eyes from strong emotion: *She had a good cry when the nice person died at the end of the movie.*

**cry** *verb* **cried, crying, cries**
**1** to make a loud sound from the mouth in pain or fear: *The swimmer cried out for help.*
**2** to have tears running from the eyes because of sadness, pain, or strong emotion: *He cried when his mother died.*

**crystal** /ˈkrɪstəl/ *noun*
**1** clear, high quality glass: *Those fine wine glasses are made of crystal.*
**2** a clear mineral
**3** a small regular shape of some substance: *ice crystals*

**cub** /kʌb/ *noun*
the young of some wild animals (bear, wolf, fox, etc.): *Lion cubs depend on their mother to feed them.*

**cube** /kyub/ *noun*
a square object with four sides, a top and a bottom: *an ice cube*

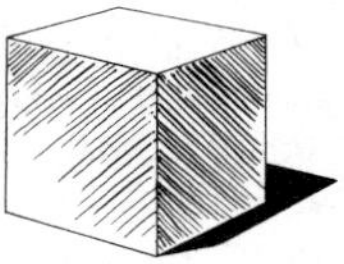

cube

**cube** *verb* **cubed, cubing, cubes**
**1** to cut into cubes: *The cook cubed a piece of cheese to put on a salad.*

**2** to multiply a number by itself twice: *Two cubed is 2 x 2 x 2 = 8, or 2³.* –*adjective* **cubic.** *See:* art on page 16a.

**cucumber** /ˈkyu,kʌmbər/ *noun*
a long, round vegetable with green skin and crisp white flesh, or the plant it grows on: *Cucumbers are cut in pieces for salads.* *See:* art on page 2a.

**cuddle** /ˈkʌdl/ *verb* **cuddled, cuddling, cuddles**
to hold tenderly and close: *The mother cuddled her baby in her arms.* –*adjective* **cuddly.**

**cue** /kyu/ *noun*
a sign or signal, especially one used to start an action: *The film director pointed at the actors as a cue for them to start acting.* –*verb* **to cue.**

**cuff** /kʌf/ *noun*
**1** an upward fold at the bottom of a pair of pants
**2** the bottom part of a long sleeve: *I unbuttoned my shirt cuffs.*
**3** *plural* **cuffs:** handcuffs

**cuff** *verb*
**1** to make cuffs on shirts or trousers
**2** to put handcuffs on someone: *A police officer captured a thief and cuffed him.*

**cultivate** /ˈkʌlt ə,veɪt/ *verb* **cultivated, cultivating, cultivates**
**1** to prepare the land to grow food (to plow, plant seed, water, and fertilize the land): *From ancient times, people have cultivated crops, like wheat, for food.*
**2** to develop an understanding, such as of art, music, books, etc.: *She has cultivated her knowledge of art.*

**cultivated** *adjective*
well-educated: *She is a cultivated woman.* –*noun* **cultivation.**

**culture** /ˈkʌltʃər/ *noun*
**1** the ideas, activities (art, foods, businesses), and ways of behaving that are special to a country, people, or region: *In North American culture, men do not kiss men when meeting each other. They shake hands.*
**2** the achievements of a people or nation in art, music, literature, etc.: *The Chinese have had a high culture for thousands of years.* –*adjective* **cultural.**

**cultured** /ˈkʌltʃərd/ *adjective*
having knowledge of art, music, books, etc.: *He is a cultured man who knows a lot about music and dance.*

**cup** /kʌp/ *noun*
**1** a small, round, open container, usually with a handle, for drinking liquids: *She drinks coffee from a cup.*

cup

**2** a measure of 8 fluid ounces (or 16 tablespoons): *The recipe called for a cup of flour.*
**3** a prize for winning a sports competition *See:* trophy.

**one's cup of tea:** (often used negatively) a favorite thing: *Driving in a bad snowstorm is not my cup of tea.* *See:* art on page 5a.

**cupboard** /ˈkʌbərd/ *noun*
a piece of furniture or a closet with shelves and doors, especially for dishes and containers of food: *I put the cans of beans in the cupboard.*

**curable** /ˈkyʊrəbəl/ *adjective*
able to be cured: *Tuberculosis is a curable disease.*

**curb** /kɜrb/ *noun*
the edge and border area of a sidewalk: *Two boys sat on the curb and watched the cars go by.*

**cure** /kyʊr/ *verb* **cured, curing, cures**
**1** to make someone healthy by using medicines and treatments: *A doctor cures sick people.* *See:* heal.
**2** to solve problems or bad conditions: *The government cured poverty by giving jobs to poor people.*

**cure** *noun*
healing of a disease: *a cure for cancer*

**curfew** /ˈkɜrfyu/ *noun*
a period of time ordered by the government when people may not go outdoors: *Some cities enforce a 10 P.M. curfew for teenagers.*

**curiosity** /,kyʊriˈɑsəti/ *noun, plural* **curiosities**
interest in knowing about things: *He has a natural curiosity about how machines work.*

**curious** /ˈkyʊriəs/ *adjective*
**1** interested in knowing about things: *I am curious; where did you buy that beautiful dress?*

**2** strange, unusual: *His curious behavior has many people worried.* –*adverb* **curiously.**

**curl** /kɜrl/ *noun*
hair that turns round and round in circles: *Her hair is full of pretty curls.*

**curl** *verb*
to form hair into curls: *The hairdresser curled her hair.* –*adjective* **curly.**

**currency** /ˈkɜrənsi/ *noun, plural* **currencies**
the money used to pay for goods and services in a country: *The currency in the USA is made up of dollar bills and coins.*

**current** /ˈkɜrənt/ *noun*
a flow of something, such as electricity or water: *The current in the river is slow.*

**current** *adjective*
**1** belonging to present time: *The current situation is peaceful.*
**2** being up-to-date with obligations: *All our bills are current; we owe nothing.*

**currently** /ˈkɜrəntli/ *adverb*
at this time, now: *We are currently painting our old house.*

**curriculum** /kəˈrɪkyələm/ *noun, plural* **curricula** /-lə/
the courses offered at an educational institution (school, college, etc.): *The curriculum at that college has a lot of science and engineering.*

**curse** /kɜrs/ *noun*
**1** a request or prayer for harm to be done to someone: *That evil man put a curse on his neighbor.*
**2** dirty word(s), swear word(s)

**curse** *verb* **cursed, cursing, curses**
**1** to put a curse on someone
**2** to speak or write dirty words: *That guy curses all the time! See:* swear.

**curtain** /ˈkɜrtn/ *noun*
a cloth covering usually hanging in front of a window or theater stage: *We have a shower curtain to keep water in the bathtub. See:* art on page 22a.

**curve** /kɜrv/ *noun*
a line or surface that bends without angles: *There is a curve in the road ahead.*

**curve** *verb*
to bend in a curved line: *The highway curves to the left about a mile from here.* –*adjective* **curvy.**

**cushion** /ˈkʊʃən/ *noun*
a type of soft head rest (pillow) or soft support for the body: *The cushions on the sofa are covered with silk.*

**custodian** /kʌˈst oʊdiən/ *noun*
a person who cleans and makes repairs in a building, *(synonym)* janitor –*adjective* **custodial.**

**custody** /ˈkʌstədi/ *noun*
**1** safekeeping, protection: *After the parents divorced, the mother got custody of the children.*
**2** being held under arrest by the police **in custody:** *The police found the criminal; he is in custody in jail now.*

**custom** /ˈkʌstəm/ *noun*
**1** a way of behaving that is special to a person, people, region, or nation: *It is his custom to smoke a cigar after dinner.*
**2 customs:** taxes on goods brought into a country and the branch of government that tracks the goods brought into a country

**customer** /ˈkʌstəmər/ *noun*
a person or business that buys from another person or business: *Our company treats its customers well with fast service and good products. See:* client; purchaser; art on page 5a.

---

**USAGE NOTE:** Businesses have *customers.* Providers of services, such as lawyers, have *clients.* Doctors, dentists, etc. have *patients.* A person who stays at a hotel (or motel) is a *guest.* Business people and companies that sell to others are called *vendors* or *suppliers.*

---

**cut** /kʌt/ *noun*
**1** an injury (wound) caused by a knife or other sharp edge: *I have a cut on my finger.*
**2** a hole or opening made by something sharp (knife, saw, scissors): *He made cuts in the fabric for buttonholes.*
**3** less of something: *He was given a cut in salary.*

**cut** *verb* **cut, cutting, cuts**
**1** to open with a knife by accident: *She cut her finger with a knife.*
**2** to divide into pieces or parts with a knife: *She cut the apple pie into six pieces.*

**3** to remove completely: *He cut (or) cut out meat from his diet. (He no longer eats meat.)*||*That company cut 100 employees from its staff.*
**4** to stop or interrupt something: *A storm cut off the electricity.*

**to cut someone** or **something apart:** to put into pieces with a knife: *The cook cut apart the chicken by cutting off the legs and wings.*

**to cut back** or **on something:** to reduce something: *Our company cut back the number of employees from 100 to 75.*

**to cut something down:** **a.** to reduce the amount of something: *She cut down on the number of cigarettes that she smokes from 30 to 10 a day.* **b.** to chop down: *He cut down a tree.*

**Cut it out!:** to stop annoying (or) bad behavior: *I told you to stop playing that radio so loudly. Cut it out!*

**to cut off** **a. (something):** to remove: *A doctor cut off the man's diseased foot.* **b. (someone):** *I got cut off the telephone when there was trouble on the line.*

**to cut something out:** **a.** to remove: *The doctor cut out the woman's cancerous tumor.* **b.** *informal* to stop doing something: *I cut out smoking cigarettes. See:* art on page 11a.

**cute** /kyut/ *adjective* **cuter, cutest** pleasing to look at: *a cute baby* *–noun* **cuteness.** *See:* handsome, USAGE NOTE.

**cycle** /'saɪkəl/ *noun*
**1** an event or activity that changes from time to time from one characteristic to another and then back to the first one: *We have weather cycles of good rainfall, then dry weather, then rain again.*||*a business cycle*
**2** a bicycle or motorcycle

**cycle** *verb* **cycled, cycling, cycles**
**1** to go through a cycle (weather, business)
**2** to ride on a bicycle or motorcycle: *He cycles to work on his motorcycle.* *–adjective* **cyclical** /'saɪklɪkəl/, **cyclic.**

**cyclist** /'saɪklɪst/ *noun* a person who rides a bicycle or motorcycle: *Cyclists pedal around the park.*

cyclist

**cylinder** /'sɪləndər/ *noun*
**1** a shape or object with a flat, circular top and bottom and straight sides
**2** a usually hollow metal object with this shape, especially a mechanical part: *One of the cylinders in my car engine does not work.* *–adjective* **cylindrical.**

# D, d

**D, d** /di/ *noun* **D's, d's,** or **Ds, ds**
the fourth letter of the English alphabet

**'d** *contraction*
**1** would: *He said he'd eat with us.*
**2** had: *He said he'd already eaten.*
**3** did: *Where'd he eat? McDonalds.*

**dab** /dæb/ *noun*
a small amount of something: *I put a dab of butter on my bread.* *–verb* **to dab.**

**dad** /dæd/ *noun informal*
*short for* daddy *See:* daddy.

**daddy** /ˈdædi/ *noun, plural* **daddies**
one's father: *My daddy works for the government.*

**daffodil** /ˈdæfəˌdɪl/ *noun*
a yellow flower: *Daffodils are among the first flowers to come up in the spring.* *See:* art on page 1a.

daffodil

**daily** /ˈdeɪli/ *adverb*
each day: *I take a walk daily.* *–adjective* **daily.**

**dairy** /ˈdɛri/ *noun, plural* **dairies**
a building in which cows are kept and milked: *Cows are milked at the dairy each morning.*

**daisy** /ˈdeɪzi/ *noun, plural* **daisies**
a flower with a flat wheel of long, thin white or yellow petals: *Daisies grow wild in many places.* *See:* art on page 1a.

**dam** /dæm/ *verb* **dammed, damming, dams**
to build a type of wall across a river to stop or limit its flow: *Governments dam rivers to produce electrical power.* *–noun* **dam.**

**damage** /ˈdæmɪʤ/ *verb* **damaged, damaging, damages**
to hurt (someone's property, reputation, etc.): *They damaged the car badly in the crash.* *–noun* **damage;** *–adjective* **damaging.**

**damp** /dæmp/ *adjective*
a little wet: *He cleaned the tables with a damp cloth.* *–noun* **dampness;** *–verb* **to dampen.**

**dance** /dæns/ *verb* **danced, dancing, dances**
to move the body in tune with music: *She dances every Saturday night at the disco.* *–noun* **dance.**

**dandruff** /ˈdændrəf/ *noun*
dry skin that forms on the head and drops in little white pieces: *Every winter he has a problem with dandruff in his hair.*

**danger** /ˈdeɪnʤər/ *noun*
a physically harmful situation: *Driving too fast puts people in danger. (antonym)* safety.

**dangerous** /ˈdeɪnʤərəs/ *adjective*
harmful, risky: *Smoking cigarettes is dangerous to your health.* *–adverb* **dangerously.**

**dare** /dɛr/ *verb* **dared, daring, dares**
**1** to ask someone if they have courage

enough to do something difficult or dangerous: *His friend dared him to do it.*
**2** to have enough courage, nerve: *His mother said, "Don't you dare do that again!"* –*noun* **dare;** –*adjective* **daring.**

**dark** /dɑrk/ *adjective* **darker, darkest**
**1** without light: *a dark cave*
**2** not light in color: *He wore a dark blue suit.*||*She has dark eyes.*

**dark** *noun*
nighttime, darkness: *Don't try to work in the dark.* –*verb* **to darken.**

**darkness** /ˈdɑrknɪs/ *noun*
nighttime, a condition without light: *We enjoyed sitting outdoors in the darkness of night.*

**darling** /ˈdɑrlɪng/ *adjective*
lovable, sweet: *a darling little girl*||*my darling son* –*noun* (person) **darling.**

**darn** /dɑrn/ *verb*
to sew repairs in worn or torn cloth: *You should darn those socks.*

**darn** *noun exclamation*
a mild expression of anger: *Darn! I burned the food!*||*Darn it! I forgot my keys!*

**dart** /dɑrt/ *verb*
to move quickly: *A child darted out in front of the car.*

**dart** *noun*
a small object with a sharp point to be thrown, blown, or shot: *Some people blow poison darts to kill animals for food.*

**dash** /dæʃ/ *verb* **dashes**
**1** to run quickly over a short distance: *I dashed into the house to get out of the rain.*
**2** to leave quickly: *I have to dash now; see you later!*

**dash** *noun* **dashes**
**1** a short, rapid run, especially in an athletic event: *He runs the 100-meter dash.*
**2** a short line used for punctuation in writing or printing: (-) *or* (—)
**3** a small amount of something: *Put a dash of pepper in the soup.*

**dashboard** /ˈdæʃˌbɔrd/ *noun*
in a vehicle, the front part inside, covered with instruments: *On the dashboard of a car, you can see the gas level, the mileage, etc.*

dashboard

**data** /ˈdeɪtə/ *noun plural*
*used often with a singular verb* organized information: *Scientists gather data, then study it for its meaning.*||*Computers process data to create information.*

**date** /deɪt/ *noun*
**1** a specific day, month, or year: *The date of their marriage was June 24, 1996.*||*The date on the building was 1910.*
**2** a social appointment, usually of a couple: *The boy and girl went on their first date last night.*
**3** the person with whom one has a social appointment: *She introduced her date to everyone at the party.*

**date** *verb* **dated, dating, dates**
**1** to show a date: *The letter was dated May 1, 1895.*
**2** to go out on dates with: *She dates several young men.*

**daughter** /ˈdɔtər/ *noun*
a female child: *They are married and have two daughters. See:* son. *See:* art on page 13a.

**daughter-in-law** /ˈdɔtərɪnˌlɔ/ *noun, plural* **daughters-in-law**
the wife of one's son: *She became our daughter-in-law last year.*

**dawn** /dɔn/ *noun*
the appearance of the sun in the morning, *(synonym)* sunrise: *We see the light of dawn in the east.*

**dawn** *verb*
to come up: *The sun is dawning over the land.*

**day** /deɪ/ *noun*
the time period between the appearance of the sun (sunrise) and its going down at night (sunset): *Most people work during the day and sleep at night.*

**day care** *noun*
a service of caring for pre-school-aged children while the parents work: *She drops her child off at day care on her way to work.*

**daydream** /ˈdeɪˌdr im/ *noun*
thoughts that are pleasant but not real: *The boy has daydreams about being a baseball star.* –*verb* **to daydream;** –*noun* (person) **daydreamer.**

**daylight** /ˈdeɪˌla ɪt/ *noun*
the light from the sun during the day: *She opened the curtains to let the daylight in.*

**daytime** /ˈdeɪˌtaɪm/ *noun, (no plural)*
the daylight hours: *During the daytime, I play tennis and at nighttime, I work in a restaurant.*

**DC** /ˈdiˌsi/
*abbreviation of* direct current *See:* AC.

**D.C.** /ˈdiˈsi/ *noun*
*abbreviation of* District of Columbia, location of US capital city of Washington

**dead** /dɛd/ *adjective*
**1** lifeless, no longer living: *The old man is dead; he died yesterday.*
**2** not working, without power: *The batteries in this flashlight are dead.*

**dead end** *noun*
a road without an exit: *We live on a dead end street.*

**deadline** /ˈdɛdˌlaɪn/ *noun*
a time or date by which something must be finished: *The deadline for the project is two o'clock tomorrow.*

**deadly** /ˈdɛdli/ *adjective* **deadlier, deadliest**
**1** so dangerous as to cause death: *deadly weapons, deadly poison*
**2** *figurative* destructive, terrible: *His deadly remark about her work made her want to quit her job.*

**deaf** /dɛf/ *adjective* **deafer, deafest**
unable to hear: *He is deaf in one ear.* *–verb* **to deafen.**

**deal** /dil/ *verb* **dealt** /dɛlt/, **dealing, deals**
to give, especially cards to players of a card game: *First, deal each player five cards.*
**to deal with someone** or **something: a.** to work with someone or something, especially in business: *Have you ever dealt with this company before?* **b.** to treat, to manage: *Her job is dealing with customer complaints.* **c.** to concern, to be about: *This book deals with tax laws.*

**deal** *noun*
**1** an agreement, especially in business: *We have made a deal to buy that building.*
**2** *informal* a good buy, *(synonym)* a bargain: *You paid only $5 for this? Wow, what a deal!*
**3** a turn to give out the playing cards in a game: *Give me the cards; it's my deal.*

**dealer** /ˈdilər/ *noun*
**1** a person who deals cards: *She's a dealer in a casino in Las Vegas.*
**2** a businessperson who buys from producers and sells to customers: *a car dealer, a drug dealer –noun* (business) **dealership.**

**dealt** /dɛlt/ *verb*
*past participle of* deal

**dean** /din/ *noun*
in a school or college, a manager in charge of an important group: *He is the dean of students at a small college.*

**dear** /dɪr/ *adjective* **dearer, dearest**
loved, cared for: *She's a dear friend.* *–noun* **dear.**
**Dear:** *salutation* a polite word to greet someone in a letter: *Dear Mr. Lee, I am writing this letter to ask for your help.*

**death** /dɛθ/ *noun*
the end of life: *His death came in his sleep.*

**debate** /dɪˈbeɪt/ *verb* **debated, debating, debates**
**1** to argue, present differing views on a question: *The two political parties debated the value of their programs.*
**2** to consider, discuss: *She debated with herself about going to college. –noun* **debate.**

**debris** /dəˈbri/ *noun, (no plural)*
remains of something broken, *(synonym)* trash: *Old newspapers, dead leaves, and tin cans formed the debris in the park.*

**debt** /dɛt/ *noun*
**1** an amount of money owed to another: *He owes a debt of $50 to a friend.*
**2** a need to thank someone for their help: *I owe a debt of thanks to you for helping me.*

**debtor** /ˈdɛtər/ *noun*
a person, business, or government that owes money: *The debtors of the bank had trouble making payments.*

D

**decade** /'dɛkeɪd/ *noun*
a period of 10 years: *the decade of the 1990s||The development of the park took a decade to complete.*

**decay** /dɪ'keɪ/ *verb*
**1** become soft and bad: *Fallen leaves decay into the ground over time. See:* rot.
**2** to fall into ruin or poor condition: *The Roman Empire slowly decayed and lost its power.* *–noun* **decay.**

**deceased** /dɪ'sist/ *verb*
*past participle of* decease

**deceased** *adjective*
dead *–noun* (person(s)) **the deceased.**

**deceit** /dɪ'sit/ *noun*
dishonesty, trickery: *The salesman disappeared before people learned of his deceit. See:* deception. *–adjective* **deceitful;** *–adverb* **deceitfully.**

**deceive** /dɪ'siv/ *verb* **deceived, deceiving, deceives**
to fool, *(synonym)* to mislead: *He deceived me when he said he loved me, because he really doesn't.*

**December** /dɪ'sɛmbər/ *noun*
the 12th and last month of the year: *Christmas comes on December 25.*

**decency** /'disənsi/ *noun*
respectful concern for doing the right thing: *As a matter of common decency, you should tell him the truth.*

**decent** /'disənt/ *adjective*
**1** proper, correct (behavior, attitude): *To help the poor is the decent thing to do.*
**2** well-behaved and kind: *a decent human being* *–adverb* **decently.**

**deception** /dɪ'sɛpʃən/ *noun*
something that causes someone to believe what is not true, *(synonym)* trickery: *His deception of the people who trusted him was a shock to them all.* *–adjective* **deceptive;** *–adverb* **deceptively.**

**decide** /dɪ'saɪd/ *verb* **decided, deciding, decides**
**1** to make a choice, judgement about what to do: *We've decided to go on vacation August 1.*
**2** to determine, to bring to a certain end: *One point decided the football game.*

**decimal** /'dɛsəməl/ *noun*
a part of something (fraction) expressed in tens written to the right of a dot: *.1=1/10, .01=1/100, .001=1/1000*

**decimal** *adjective*
related to decimals: *a decimal fraction*

**decimal point** *noun*
a dot placed to the left of a decimal: *In .23, the dot to the left of the 2 is a decimal point.*

**USAGE NOTE:** The number *.23* is read as *"point two three."*

**decision** /dɪ'sɪʒən/ *noun*
a choice made: *She made a decision to go on vacation.*

**decisive** /dɪ'saɪsɪv/ *adjective*
**1** showing a clear result, unquestionable: *The team had a decisive victory by winning 20 to 2.*
**2** able to make decisions quickly and follow them firmly: *a decisive leader* *–adverb* **decisively.**

**deck** /dɛk/ *noun*
**1** the various levels of a ship: *the main deck, quarter deck*
**2** a pack of playing cards: *A deck has 52 cards.*
**3** a wooden platform attached to a house: *Let's have lunch out on the deck.*

**deck**

**declaration** /ˌdɛklə'reɪʃən/ *noun*
a serious spoken or written statement: *He made a quiet declaration of his love for her.* *–adjective* **declarative.**

**declare** /dɪ'klɛr/ *verb* **declared, declaring, declares**
to state something, usually formally: *She declared her love to him in a letter.*

**decline** /dɪ'klaɪn/ *verb* **declined, declining, declines**
**1** to refuse, usually politely: *He declined our invitation to dinner.* *(antonym)* accept.
**2** to move downward: *Prices have declined to new lows.* *–noun* **decline.**

**decontamination** /ˌdikənˌtæmə'neɪʃən/ *noun*
the process of removing poisons, (radiation, germs, etc.) from something: *After touching rat poison, the workers had to*

*go through decontamination.* *–verb* **to decontaminate.**

**decorate** /ˈdɛkəˌreɪt/ *verb* **decorated, decorating, decorates**
**1** to beautify, put up decorations: *We decorated our house for the holidays.*
**2** to present a mark or medal to someone: *They decorated the soldier for her bravery.* *–noun* **decorating,** (person) **decorator;** *–adjective* **decorative.**

**decrease** /dɪˈkris/ *verb* **decreased, decreasing, decreases**
**1** to grow smaller in number: *The population decreased last year.*
**2** to lessen in strength or force: *Light decreases as the sun goes down at sunset.* *–noun* **decrease.** *(antonym)* increase.

**dedicate** /ˈdɛdəˌkeɪt/ *verb* **dedicated, dedicating, dedicates**
**1** to give completely: *She dedicated herself to her career.*
**2** to formally open in honor of someone: *The park is dedicated to a poet named Walt Whitman.* *–adjective* **dedicated.**

**deduct** /diˈdʌkt/ *verb*
to take away, subtract: *They offered a discount: they said they would deduct 20 percent from the price.* *–adjective* **deductible;** *–noun* **deduction.**

**deed** /did/ *noun*
the official paper showing ownership of real estate: *This is a photocopy of the deed to my house and land.* *–verb* **to deed.**

**deep** /dip/ *adjective* **deeper, deepest**
**1** going far below something: *a deep river, a deep hole* *(antonym)* shallow.
**2** serious, strong: *in deep thought, in deep trouble, a deep sleep*
**3** (of sound) low, *a radio announcer with a deep voice*
**4** (of color) rich and dark: *the deep green of the forest* *–adverb* **deeply.**

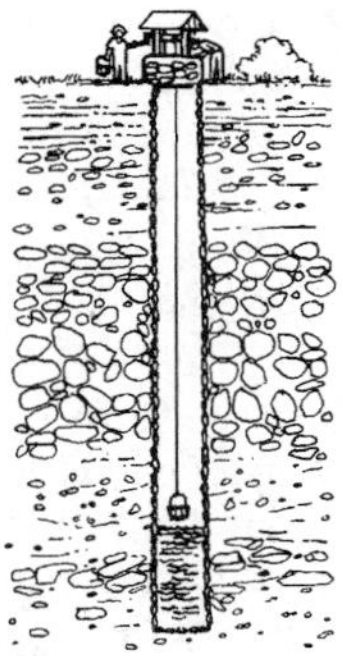
deep

**deep** *adverb*
**1** below the surface of something: *The water here is only two feet deep.*
**2** far down or in: *They live deep in the jungle.*||*We talked deep into the night.*

**deepen** /ˈdipən/ *verb*
to make deeper: *We deepened the hole by digging more.*||*The student deepened her knowledge of mathematics.*

**deer** /dɪr/ *noun, plural* **deer**
a four-footed animal with horns: *There are many deer in the woods behind our house.* *See:* art on page 14a.

**default** /dɪˈfɔlt/ *verb*
**1** to fail to pay money owed on time: *He defaulted on the loan by missing three payments.*
**2** to fail to perform: *They defaulted on our contract when they didn't deliver the materials promised.* *–noun* **default.**

**defeat** /ˈdɪˌfit/ *verb*
**1** to beat, win a victory over: *They defeated the enemy after a long war.*
**2** to make fail: *Taking work with you defeats the purpose of a vacation.* *–noun* **defeat.**

**defect (1)** /dɪˈfɛkt/ *verb*
to leave a country, group, political party, etc., to go to another: *He defected to the enemy.* *–noun* **defection,** (person) **defector.**

**defect (2)** /ˈdifɛkt/ *noun*
something wrong with a product: *Don't buy that tie; there's a defect in the material.*

**defective** /dɪˈfɛktɪv/ *adjective*
having something wrong, *(synonym)* imperfect: *A defective part stopped the machine from working.*

**defend** /dɪˈfɛnd/ *verb*
**1** to protect against attack: *The army defended the city.*
**2** (in law) to protect the rights of someone accused of a crime: *You'll need a lawyer to defend you in court.*
**3** to explain, argue in support of: *to defend one's views (opinion, position, etc.)*

**defendant** /dɪˈfɛndənt/ *noun*
a person or group (business, organization, etc.) accused of wrongdoing and called into court: *The defendant in this*

*trial is accused of stealing a car. See:* plaintiff.

**defense** /dɪˈfɛns/ *noun*
**1** a protection against attack: *This football team has a strong defense.*
**2** (in law) the protection of a person accused of wrongdoing (a defendant): *The lawyer presented a strong defense.*
**3** an explanation, an argument to support a position, a choice, etc. *–adjective* **defensive;** *–adverb* **defensively.**

**defer** /dɪˈfɜr/ *verb formal* **deferred, deferring, defers**
to delay, move to a later time: *We wish to defer our decision until next week.* *–noun* **deferral.**

**deficiency** /dɪˈfɪʃənsi/ *noun, plural* **deficiencies**
a lack, an amount that is not enough: *The child became sick because of a vitamin deficiency in her food.* *–adjective* **deficient.**

**deficit** /ˈdɛfəsɪt/ *noun*
a lack of money created by spending more than one's income: *Our business did poorly last year; we must reduce our deficit this year!* (*antonym*) surplus.

**define** /dɪˈfaɪn/ *verb* **defined, defining, defines**
**1** to explain the meaning of: *Dictionaries define words.*
**2** to describe exactly: *Please define the terms of the agreement.*
**3** to show the shape of: *Can you define the limits of the property on this map?*||*She defined her eyes with make-up.*

**definite** /ˈdɛfənɪt/ *adjective*
**1** sure, without doubt: *Do you have a definite date for their arrival?*
**2** clear, easy to see: *a definite improvement in his health* *–adverb* **definitely.**

**definition** /ˌdɛfəˈnɪʃən/ *noun*
**1** an exact explanation: *The teacher gave definitions of the new words.*
**2** clearness of an image (picture, photo, etc.): *a small TV screen with poor definition*

**deform** /dɪˈfɔrm/ *verb*
to force something out its normal shape or appearance: *An earthquake deformed parts of a bridge.*||*The child was deformed.* *–noun* **deformation, deformity.**

**defraud** /dɪˈfrɔd/ *verb*
to steal money by trickery or deceit: *He defrauded the government by cheating on his taxes.*

**defrost** /dɪˈfrɔst/ *verb*
to cause ice to melt, such as from a refrigerator's freezer or frozen food: *You can defrost a frozen cake by putting it in a microwave oven.* *–noun* **defroster.**

**defy** /dɪˈfaɪ/ *verb* **defied, defying, defies**
to oppose openly, refuse to obey: *The union defied management and went on strike.*

**degradable** /dɪˈgreɪdəbəl/ *adjective*
to be able to be broken down: *This plastic bag is degradable.*

**degrade** /dɪˈgreɪd/ *verb* **degraded, degrading, degrades**
**1** to lower in the opinion of others or in self-respect: *Don't degrade yourself by accepting such a poor job offer.*
**2** to break down and lose quality: *Medicine can degrade over time* *–adjective* **degrading;** *–noun* **degradation** /ˌdɛgrəˈdeɪʃən/.

**degree** /dəˈgri/ *noun*
**1** a unit of measurement, such as for temperature, angles, or direction and location: *Water freezes at 32 degrees Fahrenheit (32° F).*||*The corner of a square is a 90 degree angle.*
**2** amount or force: *a high degree of intelligence*
**3** a diploma from a college or university: *She has a degree in chemistry.*

**delay** /dɪˈleɪ/ *verb*
**1** to slow or stop for a time: *We must delay our decision for a day.*
**2** to cause to be late: *Heavy car traffic delayed me an hour.*
**3** to move to a later time: *They have delayed the court hearing until next month.* *–noun* **delay.**

**delegate (1)** /ˈdɛləˌgɪt/ *noun*
a representative (of a government, political party, etc.) with the power to speak, act, or vote: *Many nations send delegates to the United Nations.*

**delegate (2)** /ˈdɛlə,geɪt/ *verb* **delegated, delegating, delegates**
to give (power or authority to someone to act in one's place): *The president delegates authority to his vice-presidents.*

**delegation** /,dɛləˈgeɪʃən/ *noun*
**1** a group of official representatives: *He is a member of the Brazilian delegation to the United Nations.*
**2** the act of giving (power or authority to someone to act in one's place): *Her delegation of so much authority to her assistant upset her business partners.*

**delete** /dɪˈlit/ *verb* **deleted, deleting, deletes**
to take out: *By mistake, the secretary deleted a paragraph from the letter he was typing.* –*noun* **deletion.**

**deli** /ˈdɛli/ *noun informal*
*short for* delicatessen.

**deliberate (1)** /dəˈlɪbərɪt/ *adjective*
done on purpose: *That was no accident; it was deliberate!* –*adverb* **deliberately.**

**deliberate (2)** /dəˈlɪbə,reɪt/ *verb* **deliberated, deliberating, deliberates**
to discuss, in a serious manner: *Congress is deliberating whether to pass that law.* –*noun* **deliberation;** –*adjective* **deliberative.**

**delicacy** /ˈd ɛləkəsi/ *noun, plural* **delicacies**
special food that tastes great and is hard to get: *Fresh, garden-grown tomatoes are a delicacy.*

**delicate** /ˈdɛləkɪt/ *adjective*
**1** easily broken or hurt: *This cup is made of delicate china. (antonym)* sturdy.
**2** made in a fine, sensitive manner: *These china plates have a lovely, delicate flower pattern.*
**3** needing sensitive treatment: *He is upset at failing the course, so talking to him about it is a delicate matter.* –*adverb* **delicately.**

**delicatessen** /,dɛləkəˈtɛsən/ *noun*
a food market and sandwich shop featuring high quality cooked meats and other fine foods: *Many people like to go to a delicatessen for lunch. See:* deli.

**delicious** /dəˈlɪʃəs/ *adjective*
good-tasting, *(synonym)* tasty: *Thank you for the delicious meal.*

**delight** /dɪˈlaɪt/ *verb*
to make happy, bring joy to: *Their beautiful gift delighted her.* –*noun* **delight;** –*adjective* **delighted.**

**delightful** /dɪˈl aɪtfəl/ *adjective*
very enjoyable, pleasing: *We had a delightful time at your party.* –*adverb* **delightfully.**

**delinquent** /dɪˈl ɪŋkwənt/ *adjective*
late in paying a bill: *The company has too many delinquent customers.*

**delinquent** *noun*
a lawbreaker, especially a youth: *Juvenile delinquents can be sent to a special school by the courts.*

**delirious** /dɪˈlɪriəs/ *adjective*
suffering from confusion and wild imaginings: *She was delirious from a high fever.* –*noun* **delirium.**

**deliver** /dəˈlɪvər/ *verb*
**1** to take goods to a place of business, a home, etc.: *Trucks deliver food to supermarkets.*
**2** to give, pass on: *to deliver a speech, deliver a message*
**3** to help (a baby) to be born: *Which doctor delivered your baby?*

**delivery** /dəˈlɪvəri/ *noun, plural* **deliveries**
**1** the taking of goods to a place of business, a home, etc.: *This company promises fast delivery.*
**2** giving or passing on something: *delivery of a message*
**3** the act of giving birth: *She had a difficult delivery, but the baby is fine.*

**deluge** /ˈdɛlyuʤ/ *noun*
a heavy rain, usually brief and sudden: *The deluge caused flooding.*

**deluge** *verb figurative* **deluged, deluging, deluges**
to come down on in a heavy outpouring: *Reporters deluged the President with questions.*

**deluxe** /dɪˈlʌks/ *adjective*
representing the finest quality: *They had deluxe rooms in an expensive hotel.*

**demand** /dəˈmænd/ *verb*
**1** to ask for very strongly, *(synonym)* to command: *They demand payment today.*
**2** to require, have a strong need for: *This problem demands immediate attention.* –*noun* **demand.**

**demanding** /də'mændɪŋ/ *adjective*
**1** requiring high performance: *My boss is very demanding of others.*
**2** requiring great effort: *Climbing a mountain is a demanding job.*

**demerit** /də'mɛrɪt/ *noun*
a bad mark against a person's record: *The captain gave a soldier 10 demerits for not cleaning his gun correctly.*

**democracy** /dɪ'mɑkrəsi/ *noun, plural* **democracies**
a government based on a written constitution and laws made by representatives elected by the people: *Democracy guards the rights of the individual. –adjective* **democratic;** *–verb* **to democratize** /dɪ'mɑkrəˌtaɪz/.

**Democrat** /'dɛməˌkræt/ *noun*
in the USA, a member of the Democratic Party: *She has voted Democrat all her life. See:* Republican.

**democratic** /ˌdɛmə'krætɪk/ *adjective*
related to a democracy and democratic ideas *–adverb* **democratically.**

**Democratic Party** *noun*
in the USA, a political party begun in 1828 and considered liberal

---

**USAGE NOTE:** The two main political parties in the USA are the *Democratic Party* and the *Republican Party.* Democrats are more liberal than Republicans and generally believe in greater government involvement in social issues. The symbol of the *Democratic Party* is the donkey.

---

**demolish** /də'mɑlɪʃ/ *verb*
to pull down, destroy: *Workers demolished the old building. –noun* **demolition** /ˌdɛmə'lɪʧən/.

**demon** /'dimən/ *noun*
an imaginary evil creature, a devil: *demons in a nightmare –adjective* **demonic** /dɪ'mɑnɪk/.

**demonstrate** /'dɛmənˌstreɪt/ *verb* **demonstrated, demonstrating, demonstrates**
**1** to show (how something works, its advantages, etc.): *I'll demonstrate how our new computer works.*
**2** to march in protest: *Students demonstrated in the streets outside the government building.*

**demonstration** /ˌdɛmən'streɪʃən/ *noun*
**1** a display or explanation of something: *Workers watched a demonstration of a new machine.*
**2** a public show of opinion, especially a protest: *A demonstration against the war was held in front of the government building. –noun* (person) **demonstrator.**

**demote** /dɪ'moʊt/ *verb* **demoted, demoting, demotes**
to lower in position or rank: *The editor was angry when the manager demoted her to assistant editor. –noun* (act) **demotion.** *(antonym)* promote.

**den** /dɛn/ *noun*
**1** the home of certain animals: *a bear's (lion's, fox's) den*
**2** a room for relaxation and study: *Our family watches TV in the den.*

**denial** /dɪ'naɪəl/ *noun*
**1** a statement saying that something is not true: *The politician made a denial of the story connecting her to a crime.*
**2** refusal, rejection: *I was angry at his denial of my request for a day off. –adjective* **deniable.**

**denomination** /dəˌnɑmə'neɪʃən/ *noun*
**1** a religious group with its own beliefs within a larger religion: *Within Christianity, there are many denominations, such as Roman Catholics, Protestants, and the Eastern Orthodox Church.*
**2** an amount (of money): *The bank robbers got only bills in small denominations, such as fives and tens.*

**denominator** /dɪ'nɑməˌneɪtər/ *noun*
the number below the line in a fraction: *In 4 divided by 2, 2 is the denominator.*

**dense** /dɛns/ *adjective* **denser, densest**
crowded together: *a dense forest, dense traffic –adverb* **densely;** *–noun* **density** /'dɛnsɪti/.

**dent** /dɛnt/ *noun*
a hole made by a hit: *The accident left a dent in my car door. –verb* **to dent.**

**dent**

**dental** /'dɛntl/ *adjective*
related to teeth

and dentistry: *She works in a dental office.*

**dentist** /'dɛntɪst/ *noun*
a person qualified in dentistry: *The dentist examined my teeth. –noun* **dentistry.**

**deny** /dɪ'naɪ/ *verb* **denied, denying, denies**
**1** to say something is not true: *She denied that she stole the watch.*
**2** to refuse, reject: *They denied their son permission to go.*

**deodorant** /di'oʊdərənt/ *noun*
a substance that contains a perfume to hide unpleasant smells, especially of the human body: *She puts on deodorant after a bath. –verb* **to deodorize.**

**depart** /dɪ'pɑrt/ *verb*
to leave, begin a trip: *The plane to Tokyo will depart at 3:00.*

**department** /dɪ'p ɑrtmənt/ *noun*
**1** a division (of a business, college, organization, etc.) with a specific function: *He works for a newspaper in the advertising department.*
**2** a branch of government: *the Department of Defense –adjective* **departmental** /ˌdipɑrt'mɛntl/.

**department store** *noun*
a store that sells a wide variety of goods, such as clothes, furniture, dishes, etc.: *Macy's in New York City is a famous department store. See:* art on page 4a.

**departure** /dɪ'pɑrʧər/ *noun*
an act of departing, a leaving: *My departure for Los Angeles is at 8:00* A.M. *tomorrow. (antonym)* arrival.

**depend** /dɪ'pɛnd/ *verb*
**1** to rely on, trust: *I depend on you to be on time.*
**2** to need (for support): *Her family depends upon her salary from that job.*
**3** to be controlled by: *Tomorrow's picnic depends on our having good weather. –noun* **dependence.**

**dependable** /dɪ'pɛndəbəl/ *adjective*
able to be trusted, responsible: *A good friend must be dependable.*||*The trains are dependable; they run on time. –adverb* **dependably.**

**dependent** /dɪ'pɛndənt/ *adjective*
**1** in need of support from: *A dog is dependent upon its owner for food.*
**2** controlled by, varying with: *Our wages are dependent on good profits.*

**deport** /dɪ'pɔrt/ *verb*
to force someone, usually a foreigner or criminal, to leave a country, especially by taking away his or her citizenship: *The government deported the criminal. –adjective* **deportable** /dɪ'pɔrtəbəl/; *–noun* **deportation.**

**deportee** /ˌdipɔr 'ti/ *noun*
a person who is deported: *Deportees must find a country prepared to take them.*

**deposit** /dɪ'pɑsɪt/ *verb*
**1** to place something valuable, such as money, in a bank: *I deposit my paycheck in the bank.*
**2** to place valuables for safekeeping: *to deposit jewelry in a safe*
**3** to come down: *Sand deposits slowly on the ocean bottom.*

**deposit** *noun*
the act of placing money in an account: *I made a deposit of $500 at the bank this morning.*

**depreciate** /dɪ'priʃiˌeɪt/ *verb* **depreciated, depreciating, depreciates**
to go down in value: *This house has depreciated since we bought it. –noun* **depreciation.**

**depress** /dɪ'prɛs/ *verb*
**1** to make someone feel sad: *The loss of his job depressed him.*
**2** to press down *–adjective* **depressed, depressing;** *–adverb* **depressingly.**

**depressed** /dɪ'prɛst/ *adjective*
saddened, in low spirits: *I feel depressed in bad weather.*

**depression** /dɪ'prɛʃən/ *noun*
**1** a feeling of sadness: *She's in a depression over the death of her husband.*
**2** a mental illness: *The doctor is treating him for depression.*
**3** a long period of economic slowdown and much unemployment: *the Great Depression of the 1930's*

**deprive** /də'praɪv/ *verb* **deprived, depriving, deprives**
**1** to take something away from: *Poverty deprived him of good food and medicine.*
**2** to keep something from, *(synonym)* to deny: *Her illness deprived her of a chance to go to college.* *–adjective* **deprived** /də'praɪvd/; *–noun* **deprivation.**

**depth** /dɛpθ/ *noun*
**1** a distance below a surface: *The swimmer went down to a depth of five meters.*
**2** a large amount: *I admire her depth of knowledge.*
**3** a distance measured backwards from a line: *a building on a piece of land with a depth of 100 feet*

**deputy** /'dɛpyəti/ *noun, plural* **deputies**
a person, usually in a police function, given power to act as an official: *The deputy police chief arrested a thief.*

**descend** /dɪ'sɛnd/ *verb*
to go down: *He descended the stairs.*||*A plane descends in preparation for landing. (antonym)* ascend.
**to descend from:** to be a descendant of: *She says she's descended from the first English settlers in America.*

**descendant** /dɪ's ɛndənt/ *noun*
someone born into a certain family line: *She is a descendant of our first President.*

**describe** /dɪ'skraɪb/ *verb* **described, describing, describes**
**1** to explain: *The teacher described how to solve the problem.*
**2** to tell what something looks like, to report: *The reporter described the house fire as it was happening.*

**description** /dɪ' skrɪpʃən/ *noun*
an explanation: *His book gives a description of how to build a house.*

**desert (1)** /'dɛzərt/ *noun*
a dry place with little or no rain, making large areas of sand and rock with few plants or animals: *The Sahara Desert is in Africa.*||*Southern California has a large desert.*

desert

**desert (2)** /dɪ'zɜrt/ *verb*
to leave forever: *People deserted the old town because the river flooded it.* *–noun* (act) **desertion,** (person) **deserter.**

**deserve** /dɪ'zɜrv/ *verb* **deserved, deserving, deserves**
to be worthy of, earn something good or bad: *A good worker deserves good pay.*

**design** /dɪ'zaɪn/ *noun*
**1** the form or style in how something looks: *Their house was built in a modern design.*
**2** a picture to show how something will be made: *Here is the design for our next magazine cover.*
**3** the art of making designs: *She studies fashion design.*
**4** a pattern that decorates: *I like the design on his tie.* *–verb* **to design;** *–noun* (person) **designer.**

**desirable** /dɪ'zaɪrəbəl/ *adjective*
**1** worthwhile, valuable: *They own a desirable piece of property by the sea.*
**2** attractive: *She is a beautiful and intelligent woman; any man would think she is desirable.* *–noun* **desirability.**

**desire** /dɪ'zaɪr/ *verb formal* **desired, desiring, desires**
**1** to wish, want: *The President desires that we leave tomorrow.*
**2** to want very strongly: *She desires to succeed in business, no matter the cost.* *–noun* **desire.**

**desk** /dɛsk/ *noun*
a piece of furniture like a table, usually with drawers and used to write on: *She works at her desk every day. See:* art on page 8a.

**desktop computer** or **desktop** /'dɛsk,tɑp/ *noun*
a computer small enough to fit on top of a desk: *We have three desktops in our office. See:* laptop.

**despair** /dɪ'spɛr/ *noun*
sadness without hope: *When she learned that she had cancer, she fell into despair.* *–verb* **to despair.**

**desperate** /'dɛspərɪt/ *adjective*
**1** in immediate, very strong need: *Those poor people are desperate for food.*
**2** wild and dangerous: *a desperate criminal willing to kill anyone to escape* *–adverb* **desperately;** *–noun* **desperation.**

**despite** /dɪ'spaɪt/ *preposition*
even though, in spite of: *Despite the fact that she is short, she is an excellent basketball player.*

**dessert** /dɪ'zɜrt/ *noun*
the last course in a meal, usually a sweet dish, such as cake, fruit, etc.: *We had apple pie and coffee for dessert.*

**destination** /ˌdɛstə'neɪʃən/ *noun*
the place where someone is going or something is being sent: *The destination of our trip is San Francisco.*

**destiny** /'dɛstəni/ *noun, plural* **destinies**
**1** the influence of uncontrollable forces on your life: *It was destiny, not an accident, that brought the two friends together.*
**2** the future, final result: *The destiny of the Earth depends on how humans control themselves.*

**destroy** /dɪ'strɔɪ/ *verb*
**1** to pull or break down: *The storm destroyed every house near the ocean.*
**2** to ruin, put an end to: *to destroy one's reputation, hopes, chances* *–noun* **destruction.**

**destruction** /dɪ' strʌkʃən/ *noun*
terrible and complete ruin: *A hurricane causes great destruction to buildings and trees.*

**destructive** /dɪ' strʌktɪv/ *adjective*
causing great damage: *Hurricanes bring the destructive force of high winds.* *–adverb* **destructively.**

**detach** /di'tæʧ/ *verb* **detaches**
to remove, separate, disconnect: *We need a carpenter to detach this bookshelf from the wall.* *–adjective* **detachable;** *–noun* (act) **detachment.**

**detail** /'diˌteɪl/ *noun*
**1** a small matter, usually of little importance: *There is one detail in the plan that is unclear to me.*
**2** small, fine parts: *This painting is rich with detail.* *–verb* **to detail.**

**detect** /dɪ'tɛkt/ *verb*
to uncover, find: *They detected a problem in the computer and fixed it.* *–noun* (act) **detection.**

**detective** /dɪ'tɛktɪv/ *noun*
a police officer (or private investigator) whose work is getting information about crimes: *a police detective*

**detector** /dɪ'tɛktər/ *noun*
a device used to locate the presence of something: *Metal detectors are used in airports to find guns.*

**detergent** /dɪ'tɜrʤənt/ *noun*
a strong soap that removes dirt and stains caused by grease, tea, blood, etc.: *This laundry detergent can remove grass stains from clothes.*

**deteriorate** /dɪ'tɪriəˌreɪt/ *verb* **deteriorated, deteriorating, deteriorates**
to fall into bad condition, become weak: *The old man's health has deteriorated.* *–noun* **deterioration.**

**determination** /dɪˌtɜrmə'neɪʃən/ *noun*
**1** strong will: *She has great determination to succeed.*
**2** a finding, conclusion: *The police made a determination as to the cause of the car accident; the engine exploded.*

**determine** /dɪ'tɜrmɪn/ *verb* **determined, determining, determines**
**1** to decide: *The judge determined that the accused (defendant) was guilty.*
**2** to influence or control: *The weather will determine if we have the party outdoors or not.* *–noun* **determiner.**

**determined** /dɪ't ɜrmɪnd/ *adjective*
of strong will: *The workers are determined to finish the job on time.*

**detour** /'diˌtʊr/ *noun*
a second road used while the main road is closed for repair: *Signs directed traffic to a detour.* *–verb* **to detour.**

**devastate** /'dɛvəˌsteɪt/ *verb* **devastated, devastating, devastates**
to destroy completely: *A storm devastated the island.* *–noun* **devastation.**

**develop** /də'vɛləp/ *verb*
**1** to happen, occur: *Before making any plans to travel, let's see what develops when the storm arrives.*
**2** to change a place by building stores, houses, etc.: *They're going to develop this open land into a shopping center.*
**3** to process: *to develop photographic film*

**development** /də 'vɛləpmənt/ *noun*
growth, progress: *We are responsible for the development of our students' minds.*

**device** /dɪ'vaɪs/ *noun*
**1** an electrical or mechanical machine: *The computer is an electronic device.*
**2** a tool or implement: *An electric can opener is also a device.*

**devil** /'dɛvəl/ *noun*
**1** (in some religions) the most powerful of evil spirits and enemy of God
**2** a person who has caused trouble, especially a child: *That little devil has eaten all the cookies again!*

**devise** /də'vaɪz/ *verb* **devised, devising, devises**
to make, develop: *She has devised a plan for the company's future.*

**devote** /dɪ'voʊt/ *verb* **devoted, devoting, devotes**
to give: *He devotes a lot of time to working in his garden.*

**devotion** /dɪ'voʊʃən/ *noun*
**1** loyalty, working hard for something: *The teacher won praise for his devotion to his students.*
**2** loving attention: *She is full of devotion to her family.* –*adjective* **devoted.**

**devout** /dɪ'vaʊt/ *adjective*
deeply religious: *She is a devout Catholic (Baptist, Jew, Muslim, etc.).*

**dew** /du/ *noun*
drops of water, especially on grass, that come from night air

**diabetes** /'daɪə'bitɪs/ *noun*
a disease caused by too much sugar in the blood: *She has had diabetes since childhood.* –*noun* (person) **diabetic.**

**diagnose** /'daɪəg,noʊs/ *verb* **diagnosed, diagnosing, diagnoses**
to discover and name a disease, sickness: *Doctors diagnose illnesses.*

**diagnosis** /,daɪəg'noʊsɪs/ *noun, plural* **diagnoses** /-siz/
a finding, and naming of a disease: *The doctor has made a diagnosis of the illness as diabetes.* –*adjective* **diagnostic.**

**diagonal** /daɪ'ægənəl/ *noun adjective*
a line connecting two opposite corners of a four-sided figure, such as a square –*adverb* **diagonally.**

**diagram** /'daɪə,græm/ *noun*
a drawing with markings to show how something is put together or works: *The engineer drew a diagram of a machine.* –*verb* **to diagram.**

**dial** /'daɪəl/ *noun*
a surface, usually round, divided into markings with meaning: *the dial of a watch*

**dial** *verb*
to make a call by pressing numbers: *If you want to phone long distance, dial the operator. See:* dial tone.

**dialect** /'daɪə,lɛkt/ *noun*
a way of speaking a language that is different from others speaking the same language: *The characters in the movie spoke in a Scottish dialect that was strange to the American audience.*

**dialogue** or **dialog** /'daɪə,lɔg/ *noun*
conversation between people in a book, play, etc.: *You should read this story; the dialogue is very funny.* –*verb* **to dialogue.**

**dial tone** *noun*
a sound made when a telephone receiver is picked up: *There's no dial tone, so I guess the phone isn't working.*

**diameter** /daɪ'æmətər/ *noun*
the width of a circle, measured by a straight line through its center from side to side: *She drew a circle two inches in diameter.*

**diamond** /'daɪəmənd/ *noun*
**1** the hardest jewel and very valuable: *What a beautiful diamond ring!*

diamonds

**2** a figure with four straight sides and pointed at the top, bottom, and sides
**3** a playing card with one or more red diamonds: *the six of diamonds*

**diaper** /'daɪəpər/ *noun*
a soft thick cloth (or thick paper with a plastic covering) used to cover the area between the legs, especially for babies: *Parents put diapers on their babies.*

**diarrhea** /ˌd aɪəˈriə/ *noun*
an illness in which bowel movements are too watery and too frequent: *He ate too much fruit and has diarrhea now.*

**diary** /ˈdaɪəri/ *noun, plural* **diaries**
a personal record written about one's activities and feelings: *She has written in a diary since she was a child.*

**dice** /daɪs/ *noun*
*plural of* die
small blocks of plastic (bone, wood) with one to six dots on each side and rolled in games of chance: *With one roll of the dice, he won $50.*

dice

**dictate** /ˈdɪkˌteɪt/ *verb* **dictated, dictating, dictates**
**1** to speak words to be written down by someone: *He dictated a letter to his secretary.*
**2** to command, say what someone must do: *The winner of a war can dictate to the loser the terms for peace.*

**dictation** /dɪkˈt eɪʃən/ *noun*
a communication spoken so that it can be written down: *The manager gave dictation to her secretary for an hour.*

**dictator** /ˈdɪkˌteɪtər/ *noun*
a ruler with total power: *The leader of that country is a dictator and no one can speak against him. –adjective* **dictatorial;** *–noun* **dictatorship.**

**dictionary** /ˈdɪkʃəˌnɛri/ *noun, plural* **dictionaries**
a book or computer program listing words in alphabetical order with their meanings: *For a definition of that word, look in the dictionary.*

**did** /dɪd/ *verb*
**1** *past tense of* do: *I did all my work yesterday.*
**2** past auxiliary verb: *Did she go home?*

**didn't** /ˈdɪdnt/
*short for* did not

**die** /daɪ/ *verb* **died, dying, dies**
**1** to stop living: *He died of a heart attack.*
**2** to stop working (said of an object): *My car died on the way to work.*

**to die out:** to pass out of existence: *Dinosaurs died out millions of years ago. (antonym)* live.

**diet** /ˈdaɪɪt/ *noun*
**1** one's regular foods: *The boy lives on a diet of junk food (hamburgers, ice cream, potato chips).*
**2** a weight loss program: *I have to go on a diet to lose 15 pounds.*

**diet** *verb*
to lose weight by eating less: *My friend diets all the time. –adjective* **dietary;** *–noun* (person) **dietician.**

**differ** /ˈdɪfər/ *verb*
**1** to be different from: *Our new product differs from others and it costs less, too.*
**2** to hold a different opinion, disagree

**difference** /ˈdɪf ərəns/ *noun*
**1** a way of being different: *What is the difference between the new product and the old one?*
**2** the amount by which two numbers differ: *The difference between 7 and 9 is 2.*

**it makes no difference:** it doesn't matter, it's not important

**to make a difference:** to bring a change (for the better): *She received an increase in pay and it has made a big difference in how she feels. (antonym)* agreement.

**different** /ˈdɪfərənt/ *adjective*
**1** unlike, not the same: *The new and old computers are very different from each other. The new ones are much faster.*
**2** several: *This dress comes in different colors; which one would you like?*
**3** strange, unusual: *I agree that he's different, but I like him. –adverb* **differently.** *(antonym)* similar.

**difficult** /ˈdɪfɪˌkʌlt/ *adjective*
**1** hard, needing effort (mental or physical): *We have a difficult problem to solve.*
**2** causing trouble or worry: *She's having a difficult time finding a job. (antonym)* easy.

**difficulty** /ˈdɪfɪˌkʌlti/ *noun, plural* **difficulties**
**1** something requiring effort or time: *I had difficulty understanding the directions.*
**2** something that causes problems:

*There's one difficulty in the plan, and that is, it costs too much.*
**3** trouble: *in difficulty with the law*

**dig** /dɪg/ *verb* **dug** /dʌg/, **digging, digs**
to make (a hole or opening) by taking away earth: *A worker digs holes to plant flowers.*

**to dig for: a.** to look for by digging: *to dig for gold* **b.** to look for (information), to search for: *A newspaper reporter digs for the facts.*

**dig** *noun*
a place where scientists dig: *They're on a dig in Egypt.*

**digest** /daɪ'ʤɛst/ *verb*
to change food in the body (stomach and intestines), so the body can use it: *Meat digests slowly.*||*He can't digest milk.* –*adjective* **digestible.**

**digestion** /daɪ'ʤɛsʧən/ *noun*
the process of changing food in the body (stomach and intestines), so the body can use it: *She has good digestion; she can eat anything!*

**digit** /'dɪʤɪt/ *noun*
**1** one of the Arabic numbers (numerals) from 0 to 9: *The sum 1,234 is a four-digit number.*
**2** *formal* a finger or toe: *The hand has five digits.* –*adjective* **digital.**

**dignified** /'dɪgn əˌfaɪd/ *adjective*
with a formal, serious, and calm manner: *The students listened in dignified silence to the college president.* –*verb* **to dignify;** –*noun* **dignity.**

**dike** /daɪk/ *noun*
something built to hold back sea water, a river, etc.: *We visited the dikes of Holland.*

dike

**dilemma** /də'lɛmə/ *noun*
a difficult choice between two usually difficult ideas: *She was in a dilemma over staying in her little apartment or taking the time and trouble to move.*

**diligent** /'dɪləʤənt/ *adjective*
hardworking: *He raised his grades by being a very diligent student.* –*adverb* **diligently;** –*noun* **diligence.**

**dilute** /daɪ'lut/ *verb* **diluted, diluting, dilutes**
to weaken a liquid by adding something: *My tea was too strong, so I diluted it with more water.* –*noun* (act) **dilution.**

**dim** /dɪm/ *verb* **dimmed, dimming, dims**
to lower the strength of, especially a light: *The driver dimmed the headlights on her car.*

**dim** *adjective*
**1** (of light) weak: *Don't work in dim light. (antonym)* bright.
**2** not very possible, *(synonym)* unlikely: *His chances of recovery (from illness) are dim.*

**dime** /daɪm/ *noun*
in the USA, a 10-cent coin: *Ten dimes equal one dollar.*

**dimension** /də'mɛnʃən/ *noun*
**1** a measurement of something in one direction: *The dimensions of a room are its length, width, and height.*
**2** size: *a problem of great dimension*

**diminish** /də'mɪnɪʃ/ *verb*
to lessen in force, number, or quality: *The need to take action has diminished. (antonym)* increase.

**dine** /daɪn/ *verb formal* **dined, dining, dines**
to eat a meal, especially a special or formal one: *They dined at a fancy restaurant.*

**diner** /'daɪnər/ *noun*
**1** a person who dines: *There are few diners in the restaurant tonight.*
**2** a type of restaurant with low prices, fast service, and simple food: *Truck drivers stop to eat at diners on the highway.*

**dining** /'daɪnɪŋ/ *adjective*
related to eating: *We ate in the dining room.*

**dinner** /'dɪnər/ *noun*
the main meal of the day (in the USA, usually in the evening): *We go out to dinner one evening a week.*

**dinosaur** /'daɪnəˌsɔr/ *noun*
many small to huge reptiles that lived millions of years ago: *Tyrannosaurus Rex was a large, meat-eating dinosaur.*

dinosaur

**dip** /dɪp/ *noun*
**1** a small decrease: *There has been a dip in the price of sugar.*
**2** a short swim: *We went for a dip in the ocean.*
**3** a creamy mixture for dipping chips, crackers, vegetables, etc.: *Try this delicious dip!*

**dip** *verb* **dipped, dipping, dips**
**1** to go down a little: *The price of oil dipped today by $1.00 a barrel.*
**2** to put something into a liquid for a moment: *The artist dipped his brush in the paint.*

**diploma** /dɪ'ploʊmə/ *noun*
an official paper stating that someone has passed a course of study: *He has a high school diploma. See:* degree.

**diplomacy** /dɪ'ploʊməsi/ *noun*
**1** skill in handling personal, business, and governmental affairs: *You must use diplomacy in asking someone to do a difficult job.*
**2** the formal business between countries: *the art of diplomacy between foreign nations*

**diplomat** /'dɪplə,mæt/ *noun*
a person who acts as an official representative of a nation's government *–adjective* (polite) **diplomatic.**

**direct** /də'rɛkt/ *verb*
**1** to guide, control: *The police officer directed traffic.*
**2** to manage and guide in the arts: *She directed a film (orchestra, play).*
**3** to order, command: *The teacher directed the students to open their books. –noun* **director.**

**direct** *adjective*
**1** straight, without interruptions: *We have little time, so we must go the most direct way home.*
**2** open and honest: *She liked his direct answers to her questions.*
**3** without anyone or anything coming between: *direct sunlight, a direct result, direct knowledge of an event*

**direct current** *noun*
electrical current that flows in only one direction: *Direct current is used in Europe. See:* AC; DC.

**direction** /də'rɛkʃən/ *noun*
**1** a line of movement: *We walked in the direction of our hotel.*
**2** leadership, guidance toward a purpose: *The new manager gave direction to the company's work.*
**directions: a.** instructions (how to do something), guidance: *The teacher gave us directions for taking the exam.* **b.** instructions (how to go somewhere): *We followed the police officer's directions and got to the museum. –adjective* **directional.**

**directly** /də'rɛktli/ *adverb*
**1** in a direct manner: *Go directly to school and do not stop on the way.*
**2** openly and honestly: *He answers questions directly and honestly.*

**directory** /də'rɛktəri/ *noun, plural* **directories**
a listing of items, such as names, addresses, businesses, etc., usually in alphabetical order: *You can find my phone number in a telephone directory.*

**dirt** /dɜrt/ *noun*
**1** loose earth: *I planted flowers in the dirt.*
**2** something unclean: *What's that dirt on your shirt? See:* art on page 9a.

**dirty** /'dɜrti/ *adjective* **dirtier, dirtiest**
**1** unclean: *The girl came home from playing wearing a dirty shirt.*
**2** dishonest: *Your hiding his book when he needed it was a dirty trick.*
**3** not polite, offensive: *dirty jokes, dirty language*

dirty

**dirty** *verb* **dirtied, dirtying, dirties**
to make or become dirty: *She dirtied her hands in the garden.*

**disability** /,dɪsə'bɪləti/ *noun, plural* **disabilities**
something that takes away a normal ability, especially as a result of an accident, or disease: *She has a hearing disability. –verb* **to disable.**

**disabled** /dɪs'eɪbəld/ *adjective*
**1** having a (mental or physical) disability: *He is disabled and can't work.*
**2** not working, damaged: *We saw a disabled vehicle on the side of the road.*

**disadvantage** /ˌdɪsəd'væntɪʤ/ *noun*
something that hurts or gets in the way (of success): *The high cost of living is a disadvantage to living in a big city.*
**at a disadvantage:** in a bad position: *The team was at a disadvantage because their star player was sick. –adjective* **disadvantageous.**

**disadvantaged** /ˌdɪsəd'væntɪʤd/ *adjective*
without the normal benefits of society, especially because of poverty or racial prejudice: *He comes from a disadvantaged family and had to leave school at age 16 to get a full-time job.*

**disagree** /ˌdɪsə'gri/ *verb* **disagreed, disagreeing, disagrees**
**1** to differ, hold a different opinion: *I disagree with what you say.*
**2** to show differences: *Those two reports diagree on the facts.*

**disagreeable** /ˌdɪsə'griəbəl/ *adjective*
**1** unfriendly (uncooperative, difficult to deal with): *She is so disagreeable that no one will work with her.*
**2** unpleasant: *a disagreeable job to do –adverb* **disagreeably.**

**disagreement** /ˌdɪsə'grimənt/ *noun*
**1** a difference of opinion: *We are in disagreement about what to do.*
**2** an argument: *They had a disagreement over money.*

**disappear** /ˌdɪsə'pɪr/ *verb*
**1** to go out of sight: *The little dog was just here, then he disappeared.*
**2** to pass out of existence: *Dinosaurs disappeared from the earth long ago. –noun* **disappearance.**

**disappoint** /ˌdɪs ə'pɔɪnt/ *verb*
**1** to make people sad or unhappy by not doing what they hoped for: *I was disappointed when she told me she could not go to the movies with me.*
**2** to keep something from happening, to block: *Our hopes for a picnic were disappointed by the rain storm. –adjective* **disappointing; –***noun* **disappointment.**

**disappointment** /ˌdɪsə'pɔɪntmənt/ *noun*
sadness over the loss of something expected or hoped for: *He suffered disappointment when she refused to marry him.*

**disapproval** /ˌdɪsə'pruvəl/ *noun*
**1** bad opinion, objection: *The teacher showed her disapproval by making the class stay after school.*
**2** refusal: *His request for a larger office received disapproval.*

**disapprove** /ˌdɪsə'pruv/ *verb* **disapproved, disapproving, disapproves**
**1** have a bad opinion of: *Her father disapproved of her behavior.*
**2** to refuse to accept: *The bank disapproved his request for money.*

**disarm** /dɪs'ɑrm/ *verb*
to take away weapons: *The police officer disarmed the criminal by taking away her gun. –noun* (act) **disarmament.**

**disaster** /dɪ'zæstər/ *noun*
**1** a large act of destruction and loss: *The earthquake created a disaster.*
**2** *figurative* a total failure: *The party was a disaster; the food was bad and the music was too loud. –adjective* **disastrous.**

**disbelief** /ˌdɪsb ə'lif/ *noun*
a refusal or unwillingness to believe: *When the explosion was announced, the people reacted with shock and disbelief. –verb* **to disbelieve.**

**disc** /dɪsk/ *noun*
*variation of* disk, a thin flat circular plate: *Her collection includes compact discs of music. See:* disk, diskette.

**discard** /dɪ'skɑrd/ *verb*
to throw away as useless: *We must discard this old food.*

**discern** /dɪ'sɜrn/ *verb formal*
**1** to see differences between: *He discerned major differences between the two job offers.*
**2** to see and understand: *He discerned the importance of those differences in the two jobs. –noun* **discernment.**

**discharge** /dɪs'ʧɑrʤ/ *verb* **discharged, discharging, discharges**
**1** to ask or allow someone to leave their employment: *Management discharged*

*100 workers.*||*The navy discharged the sailor.*
**2** to fire, explode (guns, cannons, bombs, etc.): *A gun discharged by accident.*
**3** to let or send out: *The cut discharged blood.*||*The volcano discharged smoke.* *–noun* **discharge** /'dɪsˌʧarʤ/.

**disciple** /dɪ'saɪpəl/ *noun*
a student of a teacher or school of thought who spreads their teachings

**discipline** /'dɪs əˌplɪn/ *noun*
**1** obedience to rules of good behavior and order: *The students were quiet because their teacher demanded discipline in the classroom.*
**2** control of the mind and body to do things that must be done: *Students need self-discipline to succeed in their studies.*
**3** a field of study: *In which discipline does that teacher work? She teaches mathematics.* *–adjective* **disciplinary.**

**discipline** *verb* **disciplined, disciplining, disciplines**
**1** to punish for breaking the rules: *The student behaved badly in class, so the teacher disciplined him by giving him extra work to do.*
**2** to train to control the mind and body: *He disciplined himself to run fast.*

**disc jockey** *noun*
*See:* disk jockey.

**disclose** /dɪs'kloʊz/ *verb* **disclosed, disclosing, discloses**
to tell or show, especially something hidden or secret: *He disclosed new information on the project.* *–noun* (act) **disclosure.**

**disco** /'dɪskoʊ/ *noun*
*short for* discotheque, a dance hall with recorded popular music: *We like to go to a disco on Saturday nights.*

**discomfort** /dɪs' kʌmfərt/ *noun*
(mental or physical) pain that is not serious: *The patient felt discomfort in her legs.*||*He had some discomfort about asking his boss for a raise in pay.*

**disconnect** /ˌdiskə'nɛkt/ *verb*
to take apart a connection: *Disconnect the wires from the machine before you try to fix it.* *–noun* **disconnection.**

**discontinue** /ˌdɪskən'tɪnyu/ *verb* **discontinued, discontinuing, discontinues**
to stop, end, or interrupt: *The company has discontinued making that item.* *–noun* **discontinuation.**

**discotheque** /'dɪ skəˌtɛk/ *noun*
*See:* disco.

**discount** /'dɪsˌka ʊnt/ *noun*
an amount (percentage) subtracted from a price: *The discount on this item is 10 percent off the retail price.*

**discount** *verb*
to reduce a price by an amount: *The store discounted the item by 10 percent.*

**discourage** /dɪ's kɜrɪʤ/ *verb* **discouraged, discouraging, discourages**
**1** to take away one's confidence or hope: *Low exam grades discouraged her.*
**2** to advise against, try to prevent: *I discouraged him from driving his car too fast.* *(antonym)* encourage. *–noun* **discouragement;** *–adjective* **discouraging.**

**discover** /dɪ'skʌvər/ *verb*
**1** to learn, find out: *When she got to her door, she discovered she had lost her key.*
**2** to find, see, or learn of (something no one knew before): *Galileo discovered the planet Jupiter.*

**discovery** /dɪ'skʌvəri/ *noun, plural* **discoveries**
**1** the finding of something new: *Since the discovery of penicillin, it has saved millions of lives.*
**2** something that is discovered or learned: *His discoveries in science made him famous.*

**discriminate** /dɪ'skrɪməˌneɪt/ *verb* **discriminated, discriminating, discriminates**
to see the differences (between): *The expert discriminated between two periods of art.*

**to discriminate (against):** to treat someone unfairly, especially because of prejudice based on race, sex, religion, etc.: *Some whites discriminate against blacks.* *–noun* **discrimination;** *–adjective* **discriminatory.**

D

D

**discuss** /dɪ'skʌs/ *verb* **discusses**
to talk about: *Please discuss the problem with the other employees.*

**discussion** /dɪ'skʌʃən/ *noun*
**1** a talk, serious conversation: *We had a discussion about solving the problem.*
**2** a formal meeting (conference): *They are holding a discussion about international banking.*

**disease** /dɪ'ziz/ *noun*
**1** a sickness: *Disease destroys many lives in poor parts of the world.*
**2** *figurative* a bad social condition: *The love of money can spread like a disease.*

**disgrace** /dɪs'greɪs/ *noun*
dishonor, a state of shame (for an offense): *He suffered disgrace for stealing.*

**disgrace** *verb*
to dishonor, bring shame to: *The official disgraced himself by his dishonesty.* *–adjective* **disgraceful;** *–adverb* **disgracefully.**

**disguise** /dɪs'gaɪz/ *verb* **disguised, disguising, disguises**
**1** to change one's appearance to fool others: *The secret agent disguised his appearance to look like a farmer.*
**2** to hide, cover up: *She disguised her evil purpose by pretending to be friendly.* *–noun* **disguise.**

**disgust** /dɪs'gʌst/ *verb*
to cause feelings of strong dislike: *Trash on the streets disgusts everyone.*

**disgust** *noun*
a feeling of strong dislike: *The terrible smell filled me with disgust.*

**dish** /dɪʃ/ *noun, plural* **dishes**
**1** plates, bowls, and platters used to serve and hold food: *Please put the dishes on the table for dinner.*
**2** an amount of food: *a dish of ice cream*
**3** a type of cooked food: *She made his favorite dish for dinner.*
**to do** or **wash the dishes:** to wash dirty dishes, plates, etc.: *I'll do the dishes tonight, since you cooked.*

**dishcloth** /'dɪʃˌklɔθ/ *noun*
a cloth used to wash dishes, dishrag: *Leave the dishcloth to dry on the hook.*

**dishonest** /dɪs'ɑnɪst/ *adjective*
not honest, untruthful: *That company is dishonest; it cheats on its taxes.* *–adverb* **dishonestly;** *–noun* **dishonesty.**

**dishtowel** /'dɪʃˌtaʊəl/ *noun*
a cloth towel used to dry dishes after washing: *Pass me the dishtowel, so I can dry the dishes.*

**dishwasher** /'dɪʃˌwɑʃər/ *noun*
**1** a machine used to wash dishes: *Our dishwasher uses a lot of water.*
**2** a person whose job is washing dishes: *He's a dishwasher in a Chinese restaurant. See:* art on page 7a.

**disillusioned** /ˌdɪsɪ'luʒənd/ *adjective*
unhappy from a loss of belief or faith: *He doesn't vote anymore because he's disillusioned with politics.* *–noun* **disillusionment.**

**disinfect** /ˌdɪsɪn'fɛkt/ *verb*
to clean by killing germs or bacteria: *He disinfected the bathroom with a disinfectant.* *–noun* **disinfectant.**

**disintegration** /dɪˌsɪntə'greɪʃən/ *noun*
a breakdown into small pieces: *Leaves begin a process of disintegration after they fall.* *–verb* **to disintegrate.**

**disk** /dɪsk/ *noun*
**1** *variation of* disc, a thin flat circular plate: *A computer disk is for storing information. See:* diskette.
**2** a soft layer between two bones in the spine: *A slipped disk is causing the pain in her back.*

disk

**disk drive** *noun*
the place (in a computer or compact disc player) where the disk is put in

**disk jockey** or **DJ** /'diˌdʒeɪ/ *noun*
a person who plays recorded music on the radio or in a disco: *Some disk jockeys on the radio talk and tell jokes.*

**diskette** /dɪs'kɛt/ *noun*
(in computers) a plastic plate on which computer information is stored and read: *We use three-inch diskettes in our computer.*

**dislike** /dɪs'laɪk/ *verb* **disiked, disliking, dislikes**
to not like or enjoy: *He dislikes apples, so he never eats them.*

**dislike** *noun*
a feeling of not liking: *She has a dislike for fruits and vegetables.*

**dismiss** /dɪs'mɪs/ *verb*
**1** to send away: *The teacher dismissed the students at the end of class.*
**2** to ignore as unimportant: *She dismissed the proposal as not worth thinking about. –noun* **dismissal.**

**disobedience** /ˌdɪsə'bidiəns/ *noun*
refusal to follow an order or rule: *Disobedience of orders is a serious offense in the military. –adjective* **disobedient;** *–adverb* **disobediently.**

**disobey** /ˌdɪsə'beɪ/ *verb*
to refuse to follow an order, not to do what one is told: *The girl disobeyed her mother and broke the rule.*

**disorder** /dɪs'ɔrdər/ *noun*
**1** a state of confusion, a lack of order: *Her room was in a state of disorder with magazines and clothes on the floor.*
**2** a sickness or disturbance (of the mind or body): *a stomach disorder*

**disorderly** /dɪs 'ɔrdərli/ *adjective*
**1** using violence in public: *The protesters became disorderly and were arrested.*
**2** disorganized, messy: *His disorderly way of leading a meeting causes confusion.*

**disorganized** /dɪs'ɔrgəˌnaɪzd/ *adjective*
confused, not in order: *She is so disorganized that she can never find anything.*

**dispense** /dɪ'spɛns/ *verb* **dispensed, dispensing, dispenses**
to distribute, give out: *The Red Cross dispensed medical supplies to the hurricane victims.*||*The law court dispenses justice to the people. –noun* **dispenser.**

**display** /dɪs'pleɪ/ *verb*
**1** to place in a position to be seen, to show: *The store displays goods in glass cases.*
**2** to allow something to be seen: *He displayed his anger by shouting at me.*

**display** *noun*
a presentation, showing: *What a beautiful display of clothing in that store window!*

**displeasure** /dɪs'plɛʒər/ *noun*
annoyance, irritation: *She showed her displeasure at his bad manners by criticizing him. –verb* **to displease.**

**disposable** /dɪ'spoʊzəbəl/ *adjective*
capable of being thrown away after use: *Paper napkins are disposable.*

**dispose** /dɪ'spoʊz/ *verb* **disposed, disposing, disposes**
**to dispose of: a.** to throw away, put in a trash container: *After your picnic, please dispose of the trash (garbage, litter, etc.).* **b.** to deal with something and bring to an end: *At the meeting, the committee quickly disposed of the first matter on the list. –noun* **disposal.**

**dispute** /dɪ'spyut/ *noun*
an argument: *The couple had a dispute over money.*

**dispute** *verb* **disputed, disputing, disputes**
to argue against: *One person disputes what the other says.*

**disqualification** /dɪsˌkwɑləfə'keɪʃən/ *noun*
a forcing out of a person or group, such as a sports team, from participation: *When the soccer team suffered a disqualification for breaking the rules, they couldn't play for the rest of the season. –verb* **to disqualify.**

**disrupt** /dɪs'rʌpt/ *verb*
**1** to interrupt, cause a break in the flow of: *The storm disrupted our telephone service, so we could not make phone calls for two days.*
**2** to cause a disorder in, upset: *A protester disrupted a meeting by shouting at the officials. –noun* **disruption;** *–adjective* **disruptive.**

**dissatisfy** /dɪs'sætɪsˌfaɪ/ *verb* **dissatisfied, dissatisfying, dissatisfies**
to not satisfy, not please: *The teacher was dissatisfied with my work and told me so. –noun* **dissatisfaction;** *–adjective* **dissatisfying;** *–adjective* **dissatisfied; dissatisfying.**

D

**dissolve** /dɪ'zɑlv/ *verb* **dissolved, dissolving, dissolves**
**1** to put something, like sugar or powder, into a liquid and make it seem to disappear: *The powder dissolved in water.*
**2** to end (an association, group, or contract): *to dissolve a marriage*

D

**distance** /'dɪstəns/ *noun*
amount of space between two points: *What is the distance between the earth and the moon?*||*The distance between Boston and New York is 250 miles (400 km.).*
**in the distance:** far away: *We saw dark clouds in the distance.*
**to keep one's distance:** **a.** to stay away because of safety: *When I'm out walking, I keep my distance from strange dogs.* **b.** to be unfriendly: *Since our argument, she's kept her distance from me and never even says hello.*
**distance** *verb* **distanced, distancing, distances**
to put or keep at a distance: *After he became rich, he distanced himself from old friends.*

**distant** /'dɪstənt/ *adjective*
**1** far away: *She's studying the distant stars. (antonym)* nearby.
**2** not friendly, cold: *She used to have a close relationship with her sister, but now they are distant toward each other.* –*adverb* **distantly.**

**distill** /dɪ'stɪl/ *verb*
to make (a liquid) into gas by boiling it and then collecting the remaining liquid, especially to make alcohol: *Whisky is distilled from grain.* –*noun* **distillation.**

**distinct** /dɪ'stɪŋkt/ *adjective*
**1** clear, easy to see: *Medical care has made a distinct improvement in his health.*
**2** separate, different: *Those two types of birds are quite distinct (from each other).* –*adverb* **distinctly.**

**distinction** /dɪ'stɪŋkʃən/ *noun*
**1** a clear difference: *The history teacher made a distinction between the customs of long ago and today.*
**2** excellence: *She achieved distinction in the field of history.*
**3** *singular* something that sets someone apart, especially an honor: *She had the distinction of graduating first in her class.* –*adjective* **distinctive;** –*adverb* **distinctively.**

**distinguish** /dɪ'stɪŋwɪʃ/ *verb* **distinguishes**
**1** to see or understand differences: *That child cannot distinguish between right and wrong!*
**2** to show as different, set apart: *What distinguishes our company from other companies is our excellent record of customer satisfaction.*

**distinguished** /dɪ'stɪŋgwɪʃt/ *adjective*
famous for excellent achievement: *She is a distinguished writer.*

**distort** /dɪ'stɔrt/ *verb*
to twist, bend out of shape: *Anger distorted his face.* –*noun* **distortion.**

**distracted** /dɪ'stræktɪd/ *adjective*
having one's attention pulled away: *Distracted from her reading by a noise outside, she ran to the window.*

**distraction** /dɪ'strækʃən/ *noun*
something that interrupts, a disturbance: *Noise is a distraction when I'm trying to study.* –*verb* **to distract.**

**distress** /dɪ'strɛs/ *noun, plural* **distresses**
**1** emotional pain or suffering: *We could see her distress over the death of her aunt.*
**2** difficulty, danger: *That ship is in distress; it is sinking.*
**distress** *verb*
to cause emotional pain: *Her aunt's death distressed her deeply.*

**distribute** /dɪ'strɪbyut/ *verb* **distributed, distributing, distributes**
**1** to give out: *The government distributes free food to the poor.*
**2** to spread out, place at separate points: *The population in the desert is distributed over a wide area.*

**distribution** /ˌdɪstrɪ'byuʃən/ *noun*
a giving or dealing out (of something): *The Red Cross was responsible for the distribution of medical supplies.* –*noun* (person) **distributor.**

**district** /'dɪstrɪkt/ *noun*
**1** an area of special character where a type of business is located: *Wall Street is in the big banking district of New York.*

**2** an area officially marked for a purpose: *a postal district, a political district*

**district** *verb*
to divide into districts

**district attorney** /'di'eɪ/ *noun abbreviation:* **D.A.** the chief lawyer for a government who works to send criminals to jail and punish other wrongdoers

**distrust** /dɪs'trʌst/ *verb*
to lack trust in, doubt the honesty, or ability of: *The two nations have distrusted each other for years.*

**distrust** *noun, (no plural)*
doubt, lack of trust: *Enemies have a distrust for each other.* –*adjective* **distrustful.**

**disturb** /dɪ'stɜrb/ *verb*
**1** to interrupt, bother: *Bad dreams disturbed her sleep.*
**2** to worry, upset: *The bad news disturbed him.* –*noun* **disturbance;** –*adjective* **disturbed.**

**ditch** /dɪʧ/ *noun, plural* **ditches**
a long narrow hole dug in the earth, especially to hold or carry water: *I fell into the ditch by the side of the road.*

ditch

**dive** /daɪv/ *verb* **dove** /doʊv/, or **dived, diving, dives**
**1** to jump into the water head first: *The swimmer dove into the pool.*
**2** to go down sharply: *The airplane dove suddenly.*

**dive** *noun*
**1** a headfirst jump into the water: *She made a graceful dive.*
**2** a fast downward movement: *a dive in the price of gold* –*noun* (person) **diver.**

**diversity** /dɪ'vɜrsɪti/ *noun, plural* **diversities**
**1** a condition of many different things, *(synonym)* variety: *Diversity, such as eating vegetables, fruit, fish, and grains, is important for good health.*
**2** differences among people in race, ethnic group, religion, etc.: *the diversity of the American people* –*verb* **to diversify.**

**divide** /dɪ'vaɪd/ *verb* **divided, dividing, divides**
**1** to figure how many times one number contains another: *4 divided by 2 is 2.*
**2** to separate (into parts), break up: *They have divided the first floor into five rooms.*||*The huge business divided into smaller companies.*
**3** to break up, cause to disagree: *Arguments over politics divided the two brothers.* –*adjective* **divisible.**

**divine** /dɪ'vaɪn/ *adjective*
**1** heavenly, related to a godly force: *Do you believe in a divine power that controls all life?*
**2** *figurative* excellent, wonderful: *We attended a divine party last night.* –*adverb* **divinely.**

**diving** /'daɪvɪŋ/ *noun*
various underwater sports: *My friend has gone scuba diving in the Caribbean Sea.*

**diving board** *noun*
a flat, flexible board used for the fun or sport of springing into water: *Swimmers run onto the diving board and jump into the pool.*

diving board

**division** /dɪ'vɪʒən/ *noun*
**1** a separation, breaking up (into parts, shares, etc.): *We need to agree on a fair division of labor.*
**2** the mathematical operation of dividing one number by another: *An example of division is "4 divided by 2 equals 2."*

**divorce** /dɪ'vɔrs/ *noun*
a legal ending of a marriage: *She asked her husband for a divorce.*

**divorce** *verb* **divorced, divorcing, divorces**
**1** to end a marriage by law: *He divorced his wife.*
**2** to separate: *She believes in divorcing her personal life from her life as a businessperson.*

**divulge** /dɪ'vʌldʒ/ *verb* **divulged, divulging, divulges**
to tell something that was secret: *He divulged his feelings to his closest friend.*

**dizziness** /'dɪzinɪs/ *noun*
lightheadedness, a feeling of losing consciousness and balance: *Her high fever caused dizziness and she fell.*

**dizzy** /'dɪzi/ *adjective* **dizzier, dizziest**
lightheaded, faint: *He felt dizzy from the heat.*

**DJ** /'diˌdʒeɪ/ *noun*
*See:* disk jockey.

**do (1)** /du/
*auxiliary verb* **do, does, did** or their negatives **don't, doesn't, didn't**

**1** (used to form simple present or past tense questions): *Do they speak English?*||*Where did he go?*||*Don't you like this music?*

**2** (used so as not to repeat words): *He likes jazz and I do too.*||*She works in Miami and so does her brother.*||*I didn't call her and he didn't either.*

**3** (used to give another verb more force): *He really does need a haircut.*||*But I did tell you the truth!*

**do (2)** *verb* **did** /dɪd/ or **done** /dʌn/ or **doing, does** /dʌz/

**1** to perform (an action): *The doctor did everything to help the sick person.*||*What should we do?*

**2** to perform (a job): *He's doing the cooking.*

**3** to complete (a job): *I did my homework.*

**4** to work at (for a living): *What do you do (for a living)?*||*He does accounting.*

**5** to get along, progress: *The patient is doing poorly today.*||*She has done well as a lawyer.*

**6** to be enough: *A small piece of cake will do for me, thanks.*

**7** to act or behave: *Do as your teacher tells you.*

**8** to produce or act (in a play): *Our college theater group did Shakespeare.*

**9** to cover (a distance): *He can do 100 miles (160 km) a day on his bicycle.*

**10** to arrange or put in order: *do one's hair, make-up, etc.*

**to do for (someone** or **something): a. someone:** to care for someone: *His grandfather is sick, so a nurse does for him.* **b. something:** to be acceptable for: *This shirt is old, but it'll do fine for working in the garden today.*

**to do one's (own) thing: a.** to do as one pleases: *At the shopping center, we each did our own thing for an hour before we met for lunch.* **b.** to perform something one is good at: *He's a great dancer, so I love to watch him do his thing.*

**to do something over: a.** to do again, redo (something done badly): *His teacher asked him to do over the problems she had marked.*||*He did them over.* **b.** to redecorate, redo: *The new vice president had her office done over in blue and white.*

**to have to do with: a.** to be about, *(synonym)* to concern: *This letter from a customer has to do with the prices of our products.* **b.** to have a connection with: *His influence had nothing (something, a lot, etc.) to do with my getting the job.*

**doable** /'duəbəl/ *adjective*
possible, capable of being done: *Building a dam across that river will take a lot of work, but it is doable.*

**dock** /dɑk/ *noun*
a type of pier where boats or ships stop for (un)loading or repairs: *We got on our boat at the dock.*

dock

**dock** *verb*

**1** to approach and then tie a boat to a dock: *We docked our boat.*

**2** to attach a space vehicle to another one: *The two spacecraft docked over Africa.* –*noun* (person) **dockworker.**

**doctor** /'dɑktər/ *noun*

**1** a person trained in medicine with a license to treat people for sickness: *I visited the doctor yesterday for a medical examination. See:* physician.

**2** a person with an advanced university degree: *The English professor's name is Dr. Smith.* –*verb* **to doctor.** *See:* PhD.

**document** /'dakyəmənt/ *noun*
**1** a paper, such as a formal letter, contract, record, etc.: *The official documents showing who owns land are kept in the courthouse.*
**2** a letter, report, etc., created on a computer: *Documents can be stored on diskettes or on the computer's hard drive.* –*noun* **documentation.**

**document** *verb*
to give written evidence: *The police documented their case with accounts of the accident by people who saw it.* –*adjective* **documentary.**

**dodge** /dadʒ/ *verb* **dodged, dodging, dodges**
**1** to move quickly out of the way: *The boxer dodged the punch.*
**2** to avoid (a responsibility): *Politicians dodge hard questions from reporters.*

**doe** /doʊ/ *noun*
a female deer: *Does give birth to baby deer, called fawns.*

**doer** /'duər/ *noun informal*
someone who takes action rather than just talking: *She is a doer; she gets things done.*

**does** /dʌz/ *verb*
*third person singular, present tense of* do: *He does carpentry for a living.*

**doesn't** /'dʌzənt/
*auxiliary verb, contraction of* does not: *She doesn't like vegetables.*

**dog** /dɔg/ *noun*
four-legged meat-eating animal usually kept as a pet or to work (for farmers, police, etc.): *Americans have a saying, "A dog is man's best friend."*
**to work like a dog:** *informal* to work hard without rest: *We worked like dogs to finish the job on time. See:* art on page 14a.

**dogma** /'dɔgmə/ *noun*
a statement of belief made by an authority that people are supposed to accept without question: *Church dogma has not changed for many, many years.* –*adjective* **dogmatic.**

**doll** /dal/ *noun*
a child's toy that looks like a baby: *Many little girls play with dolls.*

doll

**dollar** /'dalər/ *noun*
the unit of money of the United States of America, Canada, and Australia: *The price of oil is given in US dollars.*

**dollar sign** *noun*
the symbol ($) used to mean the US dollar: *I bought that coat for $100.*

**dolphin** /'dalfɪn/ *noun*
an intelligent ocean animal that can swim at great speed: *Dolphins are a delight to watch as they perform in the water.*

**domain** /doʊ'meɪn/ *noun*
**1** a land area controlled by someone: *The lion looks out over his domain.*
**2** an area of responsibility or knowledge: *Deciding on accounting matters is the boss's domain.*

**dome** /doʊm/ *noun*
a rounded roof: *The dome on the capitol building in Boston is painted gold.*

**domestic** /də'mɛstɪk/ *adjective*
**1** related to one's home life: *The couple has a happy domestic life.*
**2** related to national concerns (not foreign relations): *The President concerns herself with domestic matters.* –*adverb* **domestically.**

**domestic** *noun*
a person employed as a household servant: *She works as a domestic for a rich family.* –*noun* **domesticity** /ˌdoʊmɛs'tɪsɪti/.

**domesticate** /də 'mɛstɪˌkeɪt/ *verb*
to train an animal that was wild for human use or life in a household: *Cats and dogs are domesticated animals.*

**dominant** /'damənənt/ *adjective*
having greater power or influence: *She is dominant in her relationship with her younger brother.* –*noun* **dominance.**

**dominate** /ˈdɑmɪˌneɪt/ *verb* **dominated, dominating, dominates**
to have the most important place or greatest influence in: *She is the greatest opera singer in the world; she dominates the field.* *–noun* **domination.**

**domino** /ˈdɑməˌnoʊ/ *noun, plural* **dominoes**
a black rectangular game piece with one to six white dots on each half of one surface: *We like to play dominoes during a quiet evening.*

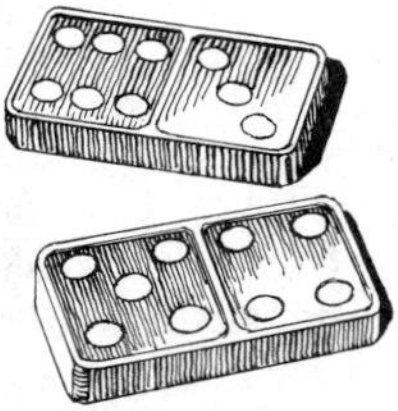
dominoes

**donate** /ˈdoʊˌneɪt/ *verb* **donated, donating, donates**
to give without charge: *She donated blood when the Red Cross asked people for it.* *–noun* (person) **donor.**

**donation** /doʊˈneɪʃən/ *noun*
a gift, *(synonym)* a contribution: *The company makes donations of its products and also gives money for poor families.*

**done** /dʌn/ *adjective* and *past participle of* do
**1** finished, completed: *The job is done.*
**2** cooked: *My meat is too well done.*

**donkey** /ˈdɑŋki/ *noun*
a type of horse, a long-eared animal: *Donkeys are used for transportation and for carrying loads.*

**don't** /doʊnt/
*auxiliary verb, contraction of* do not: *Don't forget to call!*

**donut** /ˈdoʊˌnʌt/
*See:* doughnut.

**doom** /dum/ *verb*
to send to an unhappy end: *Heavy rains and floods doomed the corn crop to failure.*

**doom** *noun*
an unhappy end, especially death: *A sense of doom spread across the land at the start of war.* *–noun* **doom.**

**door** /dɔr/ *noun*
a movable part that allows someone to enter or leave a building, a room or a vehicle, etc.: *I opened the refrigerator door and took out the milk.*
**to answer the door:** to go to open the door when someone knocks or rings the doorbell *See:* art on page 6a.

**doorbell** /ˈdɔrˌbɛl/ *noun*
a bell rung to show someone is at a door: *I rang the doorbell and waited for someone to come to the door.*

**doorknob** /ˈdɔrˌnɑb/ *noun*
a round handle used to open and close a door: *I turned the doorknob and entered the room.*

**doormat** /ˈdɔrˌmæt/ *noun*
a small rug placed before a door to catch dirt: *We have "Welcome" written on our doormat.*

**doorstep** /ˈdɔrˌstɛp/ *noun*
the top step of a staircase, especially to a house

**doorway** /ˈdɔrˌweɪ/ *noun*
the opening through a door: *The doorway is blocked by a guard.*

**dope** /doʊp/ *noun*
an illegal drug (cocaine, heroin, marijuana, etc.): *He takes dope; in fact he's on dope now.*

**dorm** /dɔrm/ *noun*
*short for* dormitory

**dormitory** /ˈdɔrmɪˌtɔrɪ/ or **dorm** /dɔrm/ *noun, plural* **dormitories**
a college or university building where students live: *The dormitories can be noisy places to live because many students play loud music.*

**dosage** /ˈdoʊsɪʤ/ *noun*
an amount of medicine: *The doctor decided on the dosage for the patient. See:* dose.

**dose** /doʊs/ *noun*
**1** an amount (of medicine): *The doctor ordered a large dose of 20 pills for the disease.*
**2** an amount (of something bad) that one receives: *an accidental dose of radiation*

**dot** /dɑt/ *noun*
**1** a small point: *the dot over an "i"*
**2** a round figure, large or small, in a pattern: *She wore a blouse with large polka dots on it.*

**dot** *verb* **dotted, dotting, dots**
to mark with a dot or dots: *The writer dotted an "i."*||*Small towns dot the map in farm country.*
**on the dot:** *informal* exactly on time: *He arrived at 9:00 on the dot.*

**double** /'dʌbəl/ *verb*
to make two times as much: *She doubled her savings in a year.*||*In summer the demand for electricity doubles because of air conditioners.*
**double** *noun*
someone who looks like someone else: *Without his glasses, he's a double for the President, don't you think?*
**double** *adjective*
**1** two times as much: *I'd like a double order of mashed potatoes.*
**2** made for two people: *a double bed, a double room*
**3** having two parts: *a double door, a word with a double meaning*

**double-check** *verb*
to look carefully at something twice for correctness: *I double-checked the numbers and found no mistakes.*

**double-cross** *verb informal*
to trick someone by agreeing to do something but then not doing it, especially to cause someone harm: *The criminal's partner agreed not to talk to the police, then she did talk; she double-crossed her partner.*

**double negative** *noun*
the use of two negatives in speaking or writing: *"I don't have no money" contains the double negative of "don't" and "no." Correct English is: "I don't have any money."*

---
**USAGE NOTE:** Use of the *double negative* is considered incorrect in English.

---

**double-park** *verb*
to park a vehicle in the street beside another one already parked at the curb: *He double-parked his car, and the police gave him a parking ticket.*

**double-space** *verb* **double-spaced, double-spacing, double-spaces**
to leave two spaces between lines: *The professor expects all student papers to be typed and double-spaced.*

**doubt** /daʊt/ *verb*
to be unsure and feel you cannot believe something: *I doubt that the economy will get better soon.*
**doubt** *noun*
uncertainty, lack of sureness: *Our doubts about the weather made us not have the picnic.*
**beyond** or **without (a) doubt:** certainly, without question: *He is without a doubt the best-looking man I've ever seen!*

**doubtful** /'daʊtfəl/ *adjective*
questionable, causing doubt: *The accuracy of that information is doubtful.*

**doubtless** /'daʊtlɪs/ *adjective*
without doubt, certainly: *She will doubtless keep her promise.* –*adverb* **doubtlessly.**

**dough** /doʊ/ *noun*
a mixture of flour, liquid(s), and other ingredients to be baked: *A baker makes dough for pie crusts (bread, pizza, etc.).* –*adjective* **doughy.**

**doughnut** or **donut** /'doʊˌnʌt/ *noun*
a small O-shaped cake deep-fried in oil: *This morning we went out for coffee and doughnuts.*

**dove (1)** /dʌv/ *noun*
a bird similar to a small pigeon that makes a soft call and is a symbol of peace and harmony: *The white dove is a symbol of the international peace movement.*

dove

**dove (2)** /doʊv/ *verb*
*past tense of* dive

**down (1)** /daʊn/ *adverb*
toward a lower place or level: *I slipped and fell down.*
**down** *preposition*
**1** toward a lower level of: *He went down the stairs.*
**2** at a distance along: *The post office is down the street from here.*
**down** *adjective*
**1** *figurative* in low spirits, sad: *She's feeling down, so let's try to cheer her up.*
**2** lower in amount: *Sales are down, and the company is in trouble.*

**3** (of computers) not working: *Without power, our computer is down now.*
**4** completed: *The students are almost finished with their exams, with three down and one to go.*

**down (2)** *noun, (no plural)*
small, soft feathers of a bird: *Some winter jackets are filled with (goose) down.* –*adjective* **downy.**

D

**downhill** /'daʊn'h ɪl/ *adverb*
in a downward direction: *We walked downhill toward the river.*

**down payment** *noun*
a part payment at the time of buying something: *We made a down payment on the refrigerator and agreed to make monthly payments on the rest.*

**downsize** /'daʊn,saɪz/ *verb* **downsized, downsizing, downsizes**
to make smaller, especially a work force or business: *The management downsized the work force from 2,700 to 400 employees.*

**downstairs** /'daʊn'stɛrz/ *adverb*
in the direction of the floors below: *I walked downstairs to answer the doorbell.*

**downtown** /,daʊn'taʊn/ *adverb*
to or in the business center of a city: *Our business moved downtown last year.*
**downtown** *adjective*
located in the city's center: *We have an excellent downtown location.*

**downward** /'daʊnwərd/ *adverb*
toward a lower place: *Prices moved downward.*

**dozen** /'dʌzən/ *noun*
a group of 12: *I bought a dozen eggs.*

**Dr.** /'dɑktər/ *noun*
*abbreviation of* doctor

**drab** /dræb/ *adjective* **drabber, drabbest**
dull in color, uninteresting: *She wears drab clothes.*

**draft** /dræft/ *noun*
**1** the first, second, (etc.) time something is written before it is final: *the first draft of a letter, the final draft of a report*
**2** a system of requiring people by law to serve in the military: *The army relies on the draft for new soldiers.*
**3** air currents that chill the body: *This room has a cold draft in it.*
**draft** *verb*
**1** to write a draft of something: *I drafted a letter and showed it to my lawyer.*
**2** to require military service of someone: *The government drafted him into the army.*

**drafty** /'dræfti/ *adjective* **draftier, draftiest**
with unwanted cool air currents: *Please close the window; this room is too drafty for me!*

**drag** /dræg/ *verb* **dragged, dragging, drags**
**1** to pull with difficulty: *I dragged the sofa across the room.*
**2** to search or sweep the bottom (of a lake, river, etc.): *They dragged the river for the sunken car.*
**drag** *noun informal, (no plural)*
something that is boring or disliked: *She hates to shop, so shopping is a drag for her.*

**dragon** /'drægən/ *noun*
a large angry, imaginary animal usually able to fly and breathe fire: *Children's stories sometimes tell of fire-breathing dragons.*

dragon

**drain** /dreɪn/ *verb*
(of a liquid) to pass or flow out: *The water drained slowly out of the sink.*
**drain** *noun*
**1** a pipe that carries away liquid waste: *With all the rain, the drains in the streets are full.*
**2** something that uses up strength, energy, or resources: *Emergency repairs to my car have been a drain on my bank account.*
**to go down the drain:** to be wasted or lost: *We worked for months on that project, and when it was stopped, all that time and effort went down the drain.* –*adjective* **draining.**

**drama** /ˈdræmə/ *noun*
**1** a play, especially a serious one, for acting on a stage: *Our theater group is producing a drama by Shakespeare.*
**2** the writing and performance of plays: *She's studying drama.* *–noun* (writer) **dramatist.**

**dramatic** /drəˈmætɪk/ *adjective*
**1** related to drama: *He has written dramatic plays for the theater.*
**2** related to a high emotional point: *a dramatic scene in a play* *–adverb* **dramatically.**

**dramatization** /ˌdræmətɪˈzeɪʃən/ *noun*
a theatrical presentation (on film, radio, television, etc.) of a real-life situation: *The play is a dramatization of her family's difficult move from Europe to Argentina.* *–verb* **to dramatize.**

**drank** /dræŋk/ *verb*
*past tense of* drink

**drape** /dreɪp/ *noun*
*plural* **the drapes:** draperies, curtains: *In the morning we open the window drapes to let the sunlight in. See:* art on page 6a.

**drape** *verb* **draped, draping, drapes**
to hang something loosely: *He draped his coat over the back of a chair.*

**draperies** /ˈdreɪpəri/ *noun plural only*
long heavy curtains: *We have red draperies over the windows in the living room.*

**drastic** /ˈdræstɪk/ *adjective*
sudden, extreme, and severe: *We must take drastic steps to stop the disease.* *–adverb* **drastically.**

**draw** /drɔ/ *verb* **drew** /dru/ or **drawn** /drɔn/, **drawing, draws**
**1** to make a picture: *The artist drew a picture of a boat.*
**2** to take out, remove: *The nurse drew blood from the patient for testing.*
**3** to take in (air): *He drew a deep breath and announced he was getting married.*
**4** to pull closer: *The woman drew her husband to her for a kiss.*
**5** to attract: *The sidewalk musician drew a crowd to hear him play his violin.*

**to draw back:** **a.** to move back to avoid: *The boy drew back in fear of the snake.* **b.** to refuse to complete or fulfill: *At the last minute, the workers' union drew back from signing the contract.*

**to draw near:** to come close (in time), approach: *The time for paying taxes is drawing near.*

**to draw the line:** to fix a limit on what one is willing to do: *I'll help her organize her term paper, but there I draw the line; I won't write it for her.*

**to draw up:** **a.** to prepare (something written): *The lawyer drew up a contract for the sale of the property.* **b.** (of a vehicle) to arrive and stop: *A taxi drew up in front of the hotel.*

**draw** *noun*
**1** a tie in a competition: *The game ended in a draw, with a score of 12 to 12.*
**2** the removal of a playing card from a deck: *It was my draw, so I took a card from the deck.*
**3** something that attracts customers: *There are four good films at that theater, but the horror movie is the biggest draw.*

**drawback** /ˈdrɔˌbæk/ *noun*
something that can create a problem: *The house is far from public transportation, which is a drawback since I don't own a car.*

**drawer** /drɔr/ *noun*
a box-like container that slides in and out of a piece of furniture: *The letters are in the top drawer of that desk. See:* art at dresser.

**drawing** /ˈdrɔɪŋ/ *noun*
a picture, piece of art: *The artist did a drawing in pencil of a house.*

**drawn** /drɔn/ *verb*
*past participle of* draw

**dread** /drɛd/ *verb*
to fear (some future event or experience): *I always dread going to the dentist to have a tooth pulled.*

**dread** *noun, (no plural)*
a strong fear of something in the future: *She is full of dread about moving to a strange city.* *–adjective* **dreadful;** *–adverb* **dreadfully.**

**dream** /drim/ *verb* **dreamed** or **dreamt** /drɛmt/
**1** to experience imaginary things while asleep: *I dreamed last night that I was on an ocean voyage.*
**2** to imagine and hope for: *She dreams about owning her own business.*

**dream** *noun*
**1** imaginary ideas experienced while asleep: *The child has bad dreams.*
**2** something hoped for: *She has a dream about being an engineer.*
**3** a beautiful person or thing: *They're building their dream house.* –*noun* (person) **dreamer.** *See:* daydream.

**dreamy** /ˈdrimi/ *adjective* **dreamier, dreamiest**
soft and pleasant as in a good dream: *That beautiful island has a dreamy feel to it.*

**dreary** /ˈdrɪri/ *adjective* **drearier, dreariest**
dark and sad: *That old house has such a dreary look.*

**drench** /drɛntʃ/ *verb* **drenches**
to make completely wet: *The heavy rain drenched our clothes.* –*noun* **drenching.**

**dress** /drɛs/ *verb* **dresses**
to put clothes on, get dressed: *I dressed quickly.*||*She dresses her boys each morning for school.*
**to dress up:** to put on special, good clothes: *We dressed up for the wedding.*
**to dress up:** to put on special, more formal clothes: *She dressed up in her nicest suit to attend the wedding.*

**dress** *noun, plural* **dresses**
**1** a piece of girl's or woman's clothing: *She wears dresses to work.*
**2** a style of clothes: *Soldiers march in military dress.*

**dress** *adjective*
(of clothing) formal: *a dress shirt, a dress suit, a dress uniform See:* art on page 12a.

**dress code** *noun*
requirements as to how one must dress: *The school dress code requires white tops and blue bottoms (skirts/pants) for all students.*

**dresser** /ˈdrɛsər/ *noun*
a piece of bedroom furniture for storing clothes: *I keep underwear and sweaters in my dresser. See:* art on page 22a.

dresser

**dressing** /ˈdrɛsɪŋ/ *noun*
**1** a bandage: *The nurse put a dressing on the man's cut.*
**2** sauce for salad: *That restaurant bottles their "house" (own) salad dressing.*
**3** stuffing cooked with chicken, fish, etc.: *dressing for a Thanksgiving turkey*

**dressy** /ˈdrɛsi/ *adjective* **dressier, dressiest**
formal, stylish: *The opening night at the opera is always a dressy occasion.*

**drew** /dru/ *verb*
*past tense of* draw

**dribble** /ˈdrɪbəl/ *verb* **dribbled, dribbling, dribbles**
to pour out in small amounts: *The baby dribbled milk from her mouth.*

**drier** /ˈdraɪər/ *adjective*
*comparative of* dry

**drier** *noun*
*See:* dryer.

**drift** /drɪft/ *verb*
to move slowly, carried by wind or water: *An empty boat drifts with the current.*

**drift** *noun*
snow or sand blown into a pile by the wind: *We had to dig the car out of the snow drift.*

**drill** /drɪl/ *noun*
**1** a tool with a long, sharp metal piece that turns to make holes: *a carpenter's drill, a dentist's drill*
**2** a practice exercise done over and over: *School children do arithmetic drills.*

**drill** *verb*
**1** to make holes with a drill: *A carpenter drills holes for screws with an electric drill.*

**2** to perform practice exercises: *Soldiers drill with their rifles.*

**drink** /drɪŋk/ *noun*
**1** an amount of liquid for drinking: *I need a drink of water.*
**2** an alcoholic beverage: *She's had too many drinks.*

**drink** *verb* **drank** /dræŋk/ or **drunk** /drʌŋk/, **drinking, drinks**
**1** to swallow a liquid: *He drinks water with his meals.*
**2** to drink alcoholic beverages: *It's dangerous to drink and drive a car.* *–noun* (person) **drinker.** *See:* art on page 18a.

**drinkable** /ˈdrɪŋkəbəl/ *adjective*
OK to drink: *Is this drinkable water?*

**drip** /drɪp/ *noun*
a series of small drops of liquid or one of these drops: *The kitchen faucet has a drip.*

**drip** *verb* **dripped, dripping, drips**
to pour in drips: *The sink has dripped water for a week now.*

**drive** /draɪv/ *verb* **drove** /droʊv/ or **driven** /ˈdrɪvən/, **driving, drives**
**1** to control and steer (a vehicle): *She's 16 and learning to drive the family car.*
**2** to travel or take someone in a vehicle: *We drove across the country on vacation.*||*He's driving her home.*
**3** to force in some direction: *The increase in prices has driven away customers.*||*The carpenter drove a nail into the wood with a hammer.*
**4** to cause forcefully: *Her parents have driven her to study hard.*

**to drive at something:** to mean something without openly saying it: *I don't understand what you're driving at when you say that. Please explain.*

**drive** *noun*
**1** a trip in a vehicle: *We went for a drive in the mountains.*
**2** a road or driveway
**3** high energy, force of mind and spirit: *He works very hard; he has a lot of drive.*
**4** a strong, organized group effort to gain something: *The Red Cross held a blood drive.*
**5** the part of a computer where a disk goes: *the disk drive*

**driver** /ˈdraɪvər/ *noun*
the person in control of a vehicle: *The driver of the car sits behind the steering wheel.*

**driveway** /ˈdraɪvˌweɪ/ *noun*
a roadway leading to a garage or house: *We parked the car in the driveway and walked into the house.*

**drizzle** *verb* **drizzled, drizzling, drizzles**
to rain lightly: *It drizzled all day.* *–noun* **drizzle.**

**drool** /drul/ *verb*
to let liquid (saliva) pass from the mouth: *The dog drooled when he smelled his dinner.* *–noun* **drool.**

**droop** /drup/ *verb*
to lean over or hang down with tiredness or weakness: *The flowers drooped from lack of water.*

**droop** *noun*
a hanging down: *The droop of her shoulders told me that she was tired.*

**drop** /drɑp/ *verb* **dropped, dropping, drops**
**1** to fall: *Apples drop from trees.*
**2** to let fall by mistake: *She dropped her keys on the floor.*
**3** to suddenly stop and leave unfinished: *I dropped what I was doing and ran to help.*

**to drop by** or **drop in (on someone):** to make an informal visit without an appointment: *Drop by to see me whenever you can.*

**to drop out:** to leave or stop taking part in: *She dropped out of the race because of an injury. See:* dropout.

**to drop off:** **a.** *informal* to fall asleep: *I dropped off on the sofa while watching TV.* **b.** to lessen, decrease: *Sales have dropped off sharply.*

**to drop someone** or **something off:** **a. someone:** to take someone to a place in a vehicle: *The bus dropped off its passengers in front of the library.* **b. something:** to deliver: *We dropped off their order at noon.*

**drop** *noun*
**1** a very small amount of liquid: *I put a drop of medicine in my eye.*
**2** a fall or a sharp movement down:

D

*There was a 20-degree drop in the temperature last night.*
**3** a small candy: *A lemon cough drop eased my sore throat.*

**drop-in** *adjective*
without an appointment: *She hurt her hand and went to a drop-in medical center.*

**dropout** /ˈdrɑpˌaʊt/ *noun*
a student who leaves school without graduating: *He is a high school dropout.*

**drought** /draʊt/ *noun*
a time of little or no rainfall: *The farming region is experiencing a bad drought.*

**drove** /droʊv/ *verb*
*past tense of* drive

**drown** /draʊn/ *verb*
to die by breathing in water or other liquid: *The swimmer drowned in the lake.*

**drowning** /ˈdraʊnɪŋ/ *noun*
an act of death by breathing in water or other liquid: *The drowning took place in the swimming pool.*

**drug** /drʌg/ *noun*
**1** a medicine: *The doctor gave the patient a new drug.*
**2** an illegal drug: *Cocaine is a hard drug.*
**on drugs:** under the influence of drugs: *She is on drugs for the pain.*

**drug** *verb* **drugged, drugging, drugs**
to place under the influence of a drug

**drug dealer** *noun*
a person who buys and sells illegal drugs: *He is a major drug dealer in North America.*

**druggist** /ˈdrʌgɪst/ *noun*
the owner of a drugstore (or the pharmacist at a drugstore): *I'm going to ask the druggist for her advice about that new medicine.*

**drugstore** /ˈdrʌgˌstɔr/ *noun*
in the USA, a store that sells medicine approved by doctors, as well as health and beauty supplies: *She went to the drugstore to buy her medicine. See:* pharmacist; prescription.

**drum** /drʌm/ *noun*
**1** a musical instrument made of a round, hollow tube with a skin stretched tightly over one or both ends to be struck with a drumstick or by hand: *My brother plays the drums in a band.*
**2** a large drum-shaped container: *an oil drum –noun* (musician) **drummer.**

**drum** *verb* **drummed, drumming, drums**
**1** to play the drums
**2** to make a drum-like sound: *When she's thinking, she drums her fingers on her desk. See:* art on page 15a.

**drunk** /drʌŋk/ *verb*
*past participle of* drink

**drunk** *adjective* **drunker, drunkest**
under the influence of alcohol: *She has had too much to drink; in fact, she's drunk.*

**drunk** *noun*
a person who must have alcohol: *He's never sober; he's a drunk. –noun* **drunkard.** *See:* addict.

**drunken** /ˈdrʌŋkən/ *adjective*
related to drinking too much alcohol: *a drunken man –adverb* **drunkenly.**

**dry** /draɪ/ *adjective* **drier, driest**
**1** lacking water: *I have dry skin in the winter. (antonym)* wet.
**2** where alcoholic drinks are not permitted, especially in public places: *In a dry town, stores can't sell alcohol.*
**3** (of wine) not sweet or fruity: *dry champagne –noun* **dryness.**

**dry** *verb* **dried, drying, dries**
to remove wetness from something: *Dry the dishes with a dish towel.*

**dry-clean** *verb*
to clean clothes, curtains, etc. by passing a cleaning fluid through them: *The dry cleaner dry-cleans men's and women's suits.*

**dryer** /ˈdraɪər/ *noun*
electrical devices used to dry (hair, clothes, etc.): *Hand-held blow dryers are popular for drying hair.*

**dual** /ˈduəl/ *adjective*
double, having two parts: *He uses his car for a dual purpose, for business and personal use. –noun* **duality** /duˈælɪti/.

**duck** /dʌk/ *noun*
water birds with short bodies, rounded beaks, and feet made for swimming: *There are ducks nesting in the pond nearby.*

**duck** *verb*
to lower (one's head or body) quickly to avoid being hit by something: *The tall man ducked his head to avoid a low tree branch.*

**duckling** /ˈdʌklɪŋ/ *noun*
a baby duck: *The ducklings are swimming close to their mother.*

**duct** /dʌkt/ *noun*
**1** a tube in living things: *Tears pass through tear ducts near the eyes.*
**2** in buildings, a tube or passage especially for air

**due** /du/ *adjective*
**1** required to be finished, submitted, paid, etc. at the stated time: *The report is due next week.||The rent is due tomorrow.*
**2** expected, scheduled: *The plane is due to arrive at 4:00.*
**due to:** because of, as a result of: *Her good grades are due to her hard work.*

**duel** /ˈduəl/ *noun*
in the past, a fight with swords or guns over a question of honor: *The two men fought a duel and one was killed.*

**duel** *verb*
to fight a duel: *The two men dueled in the early morning.*

**dues** /duz/ *noun plural*
the cost to be a member in some organizations: *Doctors, lawyers, and teachers pay yearly dues to their associations.*

**duet** /duˈɛt/ *noun*
music sung by two voices or played by two performers: *The sopranos sang a duet in the opera.*

**dug** /dʌg/ *verb*
*past tense and participle of* dig

**dull** /dʌl/ *adjective* **duller, dullest**
**1** not shiny or bright: *I need to polish that dull table top.*
**2** not sharp: *a dull knife, a dull pain*
**3** boring, tiresome: *That movie (lecture, party, etc.) was very dull.*

**dull** *verb*
to make less bright or sharp: *Does watching too much TV dull the mind?*

**duly** /ˈduli/ *adverb formal*
in the correct way, properly: *The prisoner was duly advised of her rights by the arresting police officer.*

**dumb** /dʌm/ *adjective* **dumber, dumbest**
**1** incapable of speaking
**2** stupid: *We have a dumb dog. (antonym)* smart.

**dump** /dʌmp/ *noun*
**1** a place where unwanted trash is put: *A truck picks up our trash and takes it to the dump.*
**2** *figurative* a dirty, messy place: *This apartment is a dump!*
**down in the dumps:** sad, depressed: *He failed his exam and is down in the dumps about it.*

**dump** *verb*
**1** to drop or unload quickly or carelessly: *The truck dumped a load of sand in the road.*
**2** *informal figurative* to suddenly end a personal relationship with: *She dumped her boyfriend for another man.*

**dune** /dun/ *noun*
a small hill of sand: *The sand dunes on the desert are formed by the wind.*

dungeon

**dungeon** /ˈdʌndʒən/ *noun*
a prison or hole in the bottom of a building to keep prisoners

**dunk** /dʌŋk/ *verb*
**1** to dip into a liquid: *I like to dunk bread in my coffee.*
**2** (in basketball) to drop the ball through the basket from above: *She's not very tall, but she can jump high enough to dunk the ball.*

**duo** /ˈduoʊ/ *noun, plural* **duos**
a pair of people, usually musicians: *She and her husband are a singing duo.*

**duplex** /ˈduplɛks/ *noun, plural* **duplexes**
an apartment or house that has two living quarters: *Our house is a duplex, and we rent the other half to some students.*

**duplicate** /ˈduplɪkɪt/ *noun*
an exact copy: *I'll make a duplicate of his letter and send it to you.*

**duplicate** *verb* /ˈduplɪˌkeɪt/ **duplicated, duplicating, duplicates**
**1** to make an exact copy: *I duplicated that letter for him.*
**2** to repeat: *I duplicated the original experiment, and it worked. See:* photocopy.



**duplication** /ˌduplɪˈkeɪʃən/ *noun*
**1** a copy of an original: *The picture is a duplication of a very expensive painting.*
**2** doing the same thing one more time: *Her work is an unnecessary duplication of my effort.*

**durable** /ˈdʊrəbəl/ *adjective*
long-wearing: *Those shoes have lasted a year; they are quite durable.* *–noun* **durability** /ˌdʊrəˈbɪləti/.

**during** /ˈdʊrɪŋ / *preposition*
**1** for all the time of: *We took shelter in a store during the rainstorm.*
**2** at some point (in a period of time): *I hope to see him during the next few days.*

**dusk** /dʌsk/ *noun*
the period late in the day between sunset and night just after the sun goes down: *It's hard to see at dusk, so I drive carefully.*

**dust** /dʌst/ *noun*
fine dry particles like powder: *There's dust on the bookshelves.*

dust

**dust** *verb*
**1** to remove dust: *I dusted my bookshelves.*
**2** to cover with a light coat of something: *The cook dusted the cake with powdered sugar.*

**dusty** /ˈdʌsti/ *adjective* **dustier, dustiest**
covered with dust: *My clothes are dusty from cleaning my apartment.*

**dutiful** /ˈdutɪfəl/ *adjective*
doing what you are supposed to do: *He is a dutiful son to his parents.* *–adverb* **dutifully.**

**duty** /ˌduti/ *noun, plural* **duties**
**1** what you must do, responsibility: *Her duty is to see that the business runs well.*
**2** special service: *jury duty, military duty*

**dwarf** /dwɔrf/ *noun, plural* **dwarfs** /dwɔrvz/
a small person with dwarfism: *"Snow White and the Seven Dwarfs" is a classic movie.* *–noun* (condition) **dwarfism.**

**dwarf** *verb*
to make something seem small by comparison: *The World Trade Center Towers dwarf even the tall buildings around them.*

**dwell** /dwɛl/ *verb* **dwelt** /dwɛlt/ or **dwelled, dwelling, dwells**
*formal* to live: *The king and queen dwell in a castle.*
**to dwell on:** to continue thinking or speaking about: *The professor dwelt on the topic for a long time.*

**dwelling** /ˈdwɛlɪŋ/ *noun formal*
a place where people live: *She lives in an old dwelling on the edge of town.*

**dwelt** /dwɛlt/ *verb*
*past tense and past participle of* dwell

**dye** /daɪ/ *noun*
a liquid used to color cloth or hair: *He used a blue dye to color the curtains.*

**dye** *verb* **dyed, dyeing, dyes**
to color with dye: *She dyes her hair red.* *–noun* **dyestuff.**

**dynamic** /daɪˈnæmɪk/ *adjective*
energetic, very active: *She is manager with lots of energy.* *–adverb* **dynamically.**

**dynamite** /ˈdaɪnəˌmaɪt/ *noun*
an explosive: *a stick of dynamite*

**dynamite** *adjective slang*
wonderful, excellent: *She is a dynamite rock star.*

**dynamite** *verb* **dynamited, dynamiting, dynamites**
to blow up with dynamite: *They dynamited the old building to make way for a new one.*

**dynasty** /ˈdaɪnəsti/ *noun, plural* **dynasties**
a series of family members who hold power in politics or business: *The Kennedys have a dynasty in American politics.*

# E, e



**E, e** /i/ *noun* **E's, e's** or **Es, es**
the fifth letter of the English alphabet

**each** /itʃ/ *adverb*
for one: *Those toys cost $1.00 each.*

**each** *adjective*
every: *Each toy is a different color.*

**each** *pronoun*
every one: *Each of the toys has a different shape. See:* every; all.

---

**USAGE NOTE:** Always use a singular verb with *each* because it refers to one of a group of things or people: *Each of the students has to meet with the teacher.*||*Each of the cars is blue.*

---

**eager** /ˈigər/ *adjective*
full of interest, *(synonym)* enthusiastic: *We are eager to go on vacation. –adverb* **eagerly;** *–noun* **eagerness.**

**eagle** /ˈigəl/ *noun*
a large strong bird that kills smaller animals for food and can be found in North America and elsewhere: *The symbol of the USA is the bald eagle.*

eagle

**ear** /ɪr/ *noun*
one of the two organs in the head for hearing and balance: *Rabbits have big ears. See:* art on page 21a.

**earache** /ˈɪrˌeɪk/ *noun*
a pain inside the ear

**early** /ˈɜrli/ *adverb* **earlier, earliest**
**1** at the beginning: *early in the morning*
**2** before the expected time: *The plane landed 15 minutes early.*

**early** *adjective* **earlier, earliest**
happening toward the beginning of a period of time: *Early morning is a good time to exercise. (antonym)* late.

**earn** /ɜrn/ *verb*
to get money or other things by working: *She earns her living as a doctor.* ||*She earned good grades at school. See:* salary.

**earnest** /ˈɜrnɪst/ *adjective*
wanting to do right, *(synonym)* sincere: *She is earnest in her wish to help the poor. –adverb* **earnestly.**

**earnings** /ˈɜrnɪŋz/ *noun plural*
wages, salary, or income: *We pay 30 percent of our earnings in taxes.*

**earphone** /ˈɪrˌfoʊn/ *noun*
a device placed over or in the ear to provide sound: *I use earphones to listen to audio tapes.*

earphones

**earring** /ˈɪrɪŋ / *noun*
jewelry worn on the earlobe: *She wore silver earrings and a silver necklace. See:* art on page 12a.

**earth** /ɜrθ/ *noun, (no plural)*
**1 Earth** or **earth:** the planet we live on: *Earth is the third planet from the sun.*
**2** the land: *The workers dug a hole in the earth.*

E

**earthquake** /ˈɜrθ,kweɪk/ *noun*
sudden, strong movements of the earth: *The western area of North America often has earthquakes.*

**ease** /iz/ *noun*
a lack of difficulty or worry: *She climbed the mountain with ease.* –*verb* **to ease.**

easel

**easel** /ˈizəl/ *noun*
a stand with three legs and a narrow shelf in front that holds flat things: *an artist's easel*

**easily** /ˈizəli/ *adverb*
without difficulty: *She can fix that car easily.*

**east** /ist/ *noun, (no plural)*
the direction straight ahead when facing a sunrise: *The sun rises in the east.*

**east** *adverb*
moving toward the east: *We are flying east.*

**east** *adjective*
located in the east: *The east side of Manhattan has some very expensive apartments.*

**Easter** /ˈistər/ *noun*
the Christian religious holiday celebrating Jesus Christ's return to life

**eastern** /ˈistərn/ *adjective*
in the east: *Denver, Colorado, is on the eastern side of the Rocky Mountains.*

**Eastern Standard Time** *noun*
*abbreviation:* **EST**, used in the part of the world that is in the fifth time zone to the west of Greenwich, England: *Miami, New York, and the rest of eastern North America are on Eastern Standard Time.*||*The President's speech is on television at 7:00* P.M. *EST.*

**easy** /ˈizi/ *adjective* **easier, easiest**
**1** simple: *It was easy to fix the lock.* *(antonyms)* hard; difficult.
**2** relaxed, smooth: *She is very pleasant; she has an easy manner.*
**3** pleasant, calm: *He has an easy life with few worries.*
**as easy as pie:** very easy to do: *The test was as easy as pie.* –*adverb* **easily.**

**easy** *adverb*
**to take it easy:** to relax: *After work, I watch TV and take it easy.*

**easygoing** /ˈizi,goʊɪŋ/ *adjective*
relaxed: *Nothing bothers him; he is easygoing.*

**eat** /it/ *verb* **ate** /eɪt/, **eaten** /ˈitn/, **eating, eats**
**1** to take (food) into the mouth, chew, and swallow: *He eats anything you give him. See:* art on page 19a.
**2** to have a meal: *Let's go out to eat.*
**to eat out:** to dine in a restaurant: *He lives alone and eats out frequently.*
**to eat something up:** *informal slang* to delight in something: *When his girlfriend praises him, he just eats it up.*
**to have one's cake and eat it too:** to spend something or use it up, but also try to keep it: *She wants to save money but also have expensive cars, vacations, and parties; she wants to have her cake and eat it, too.*

**eaten** /ˈitn/ *verb*
*past participle of* eat

**eavesdrop** /ˈivz,drɑp/ *verb* **eavesdropped, eavesdropping, eavesdrops**
to listen secretly: *He liked to eavesdrop on his neighbors' conversations.* –*noun* (person) **eavesdropper.**

**ebony** /ˈɛbən i/ *noun, (no plural)*
a black hardwood from Asia: *The dark keys on the piano are made of ebony.*

**eccentric** /ɪkˈsɛntrɪk/ *adjective*
strange, unusual: *The students laugh at the professor's eccentric habit of scratching his head while he talks.* –*noun* (person) **eccentric.**

**echo** /ˈɛkoʊ/ *noun, plural* **echoes**
a sound that repeats itself as it bounces off a hard surface: *The echoes of our voices in the caves were scary.*

**echo** *verb* **echoed, echoing, echoes**
to repeat as an echo: *Our shouts echoed in the canyon.*

echo

**eclipse** /ɪ'klɪps/ *noun*
the blocking out of one object when another passes in front: *We saw a eclipse of the sun by the moon.* –*verb* **to eclipse.**

**ecology** /ɪ'kɑlədʒi/ *noun*
the study of the natural connections among plants, animals, people, and the environment: *We must understand ecology to keep our planet safe.* –*noun* (person) **ecologist;** –*adjective* **ecological.**

**economical** /ˌɛkə'nɑməkəl/ *adjective*
getting good value: *That car burns so much gasoline that it is not economical to own it.* –*adverb* **economically;** –*verb* **to economize.**

**economics** /ˌɛkə'nɑmɪks/ *noun*
*used with a singular verb* the study of how society uses resources, such as money, labor, raw materials, and factories: *Economics is at the center of most governmental concerns.*

**economy** /ɪ'kɑnəmi/ *noun, plural* **economies**
the economic conditions on a worldwide, national, or regional scale: *The national economy is strong now.*

**ecstasy** /'ɛkstəsi/ *noun, plural* **ecstasies**
great delight: *When she agreed to marry him, he went into a state of ecstasy.* –*adjective* **ecstatic** /ɛk'stætɪk/.

**edge** /ɛdʒ/ *noun*
**1** the border where two surfaces meet: *He looked over the edge of the cliff.*
**2** a sharp, thin side of a blade or cutting tool: *She tested the edge of the knife blade.* –*verb* **to edge.**

edge

**edgy** /'ɛdʒi/ *adjective* **edgier, edgiest**
nervous: *She is edgy about her grades on the examination. (antonym)* relaxed.

**edible** /'ɛdə bəl/ *adjective*
able to be eaten: *The fruit of that tree is not edible.*

**edit** /'ɛdɪt/ *verb*
to correct and improve written or recorded works: *A copy editor edits the manuscripts of books.* –*noun* (person) **editor.**

**edition** /ə'dɪʃən/ *noun*
a specific printing of a book or periodical: *the evening edition of the newspaper*

**editorial** / ˌɛdɪ'tɔriəl/ *adjective*
about editing: *The student works in the editorial department of a newspaper.*

**editorial** *noun*
an opinion published in a newspaper or magazine or broadcast on radio or television: *An editorial on the economy was printed in today's newspaper.* –*adverb* **editorially.**

**educate** /'ɛdʒəˌkeɪt/ *verb* **educated, educating, educates**
to give someone knowledge through schooling: *He was educated in the public schools of Chicago.* –*noun* (teacher) **educator.**

**educated** /'ɛdʒəˌkeɪtɪd/ *adjective*
literate, having education: *She went to school through the tenth grade and considered herself educated.*

**education** /ˌɛdʒə'keɪʃən/ *noun, (no plural)*
basic instruction in schools: *The public schools in our neighborhood offer a good education.* –*adjective* **educational;** –*adverb* **educationally.**

**eel** /il/ *noun*
a snake-like fish: *Many people like to eat eels.*

eel

**effect** /ɪ'fɛkt/ *noun*
**1** a result: *One effect of being poor is not having enough food for your family.*
**2** an influence, *(synonym)* an impact: *Lowering taxes had a strong effect on the taxpayers, who definitely liked it!*

**in effect:** in reality: *This new law is, in effect, an increase in taxes.*

**effect** *verb*
to cause, especially by law: *The governor effected many changes to improve services. See:* affect, USAGE NOTE.

**effective** /ɪ'fɛktɪv/ *adjective*
having the result that one wants: *The medication is effective; it kills pain quickly.* –*adverb* **effectively;** –*noun* **effectiveness.**

**efficient** /ə'fɪʃənt/ *adjective*
productive: *She performs her job well and quickly; she is very efficient. –adverb* **efficiently;** *–noun* **efficiency.**

**effort** /'ɛfərt/ *noun*
**1** physical or mental work: *The workers made a great effort to finish the building on time.*
**2** an attempt, a try: *Most students made an effort to improve their grades.*



**EFL** /ˌiˌɛf'ɛl/ *abbreviation of*
English as a Foreign Language: *Students study EFL to learn English.*

**egg** /ɛg/ *noun*
an almost round (oval-shaped) shell in which a baby bird, reptile, or insect grows: *Chickens lay eggs, as do other birds. See:* art on page 19a.

eggs

**to put** or **have all of your eggs in one basket:** to risk all that one has in one investment or situation: *We used all our money to buy a house, then its value went way down. We shouldn't have put all our eggs in one basket.*

**eggplant** /'ɛgˌplænt/ *noun*
a plant with edible fruit shaped like a pear, usually with purple skin. *See:* art on page 2a.

**eggshell** /'ɛgˌʃɛl/ *noun*
the hard outer covering of an egg

**eight** /eɪt/ *noun*
the cardinal number 8

**eight** *adjective*
eight of something: *An octopus has eight legs.*

**eighteen** /eɪ'tin/ *noun*
the cardinal number 18

**eighteen** *adjective*
eighteen of something: *She is eighteen years old.*

---

**USAGE NOTE:** At age 18, Americans are allowed to vote in elections and can join the military forces.

---

**eighty** /'eɪti/ *noun, plural* **eighties**
the cardinal number 80

**eighty** *adjective*
eighty of something: *She is eighty years old.*

**either** /'iðər/ *adjective*
one or the other: *We can follow either road to go there.*

**either** *pronoun*
one or the other: *I'd like tea or coffee; either is fine.*

**either** *conjunction*
**either . . . or:** used to introduce two or more possibilities: *Either we take a vacation this month or not at all.*

**either** *adverb*
(used with a negative) also: *He doesn't smoke and she doesn't either.*

**elaborate** /ɪ'læbərɪt/ *adjective*
complex, detailed: *It was an elaborate plan involving many steps. –adverb* **elaborately;** *–noun* **elaboration.**

**elastic** /ɪ'læstɪk/ *adjective*
able to be stretched: *These rubber gloves are elastic and will fit any size hand.*

**elbow** /'ɛlboʊ/ *noun*
the middle joint in the arm between the wrist and shoulder. *See:* art on page 21a.

**elder** /'ɛldər/ *adjective noun*
older than another person: *Hans is the elder brother of the children in his family.*

**elderly** /'ɛldərli/ *adjective*
old, aged: *My aunt is elderly; she is 88 years old now. See:* old.

**elderly** *noun plural*
**the elderly:** old people: *The elderly are taken care of by their children in most parts of the world.*

**eldest** /'ɛldɪst/ *adjective*
oldest: *She is the eldest child in the family. (antonym)* youngest.

**elect** /ɪ'lɛkt/ *verb*
to choose by voting: *The people elected her to the Senate.*

**election** /ɪ'lɛkʃən/ *noun*
an event when people vote: *The Presidential election is held every four years in the United States of America.*

---

**USAGE NOTE:** *Election Day* in the USA is the first Tuesday following the first Monday in November. This is when general *elections* are held; primary *elections* happen earlier.

---

**electric** /ɪ'lɛktrɪk/ *adjective*
related to electricity: *an electric charge*

**electrical** /ɪˈlɛktrəkəl/ *adjective*
related to electricity: *electrical engineering* –*adverb* **electrically.**

**electrician** /ɪˌlɛkˈtrɪʃən/ *noun*
a person trained to work with electrical wiring and devices: *She is an electrician who works for the telephone company.*

**electricity** /ɪˌlɛkˈtrɪsəti/ *noun, (no plural)*
flow of energy used as a power source: *Before we moved into the new house, we had the electricity turned on.*

**electron** /ɪˈlɛkˌtrɑn/ *noun*
a part of the atom with a negative charge: *Electrons are parts outside the nucleus of an atom.*

**electronic** /ɪlɛkˈtrɑnɪk/ *adjective*
related to electronics: *TVs and radios are electronic devices.* –*adverb* **electronically.**

**electronic mail** or **E-mail** /ˈiˌmeɪl/ *noun*
messages sent and received electronically by computers over telephone lines or computer networks: *Our sales people use electronic mail to send in orders. See:* Internet; World Wide Web.

---

**USAGE NOTE:** *Electronic mail* is a rapidly growing form of communication using the computer. It is popular because messages, documents and computer programs can be sent anywhere in the world in a few seconds or minutes.

---

**elegant** /ˌɛləgənt/ *adjective*
stylish, graceful: *The living room has elegant furniture.* –*noun* **elegance;** –*adverb* **elegantly.**

**element** /ˈɛləmənt/ *noun*
**1** a part: *The most negative element of the project is its high cost.*
**2** any of more than one hundred basic chemical substances: *The elements hydrogen and oxygen combine to form water.*

**elementary** /ˌɛləˈmɛntəri/ *adjective*
simple, basic: *She is studying elementary mathematics. (antonym)* complex.

**elementary school** *noun*
in the USA, the lower grades of schooling: *He has two children in elementary school; one is in the first grade and the other is in sixth grade. See:* grade school.

**elephant** /ˈɛləfənt/ *noun*
the largest animal (mammal) that lives on land, with four legs, usually gray skin, a trunk, and long tusks –*adjective* **elephantine.** *See:* white elephant; art on page 14a.

elephant

**elevate** /ˈɛləˌveɪt/ *verb* **elevated, elevating, elevates**
to lift: *The machine elevated the heavy load off the ground.* –*adjective* **elevated.**

**elevated train** or **railway** *noun*
in the USA, a subway system that runs on tracks elevated above the street on a bridge-like structure sometimes called "the elevated": *The elevated railway runs across the city.*

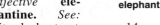

elevated train

**elevation** /ˌɛləˈveɪʃən/ *noun*
**1** a place or height above sea level: *Mountain goats live in the higher elevations above the valley.*
**2** an upward angle: *The line is drawn at an elevation of 45 degrees.*

**elevator** /ˈɛləˌveɪtər/ *noun*
a box-like car used to carry people and things between floors in a building: *We took the elevator to the tenth floor.*

**eleven** /ɪˈlɛvən/ *noun*
the cardinal number 11

**eleven** *adjective*
eleven of something: *She is eleven years old.*

**elf** /ɛlf/ *noun, plural* **elves** /ɛlvz/
a small, funny imaginary person in stories (folktales)

**eligible** /ˈɛlɪʤəbəl/ *adjective*
having the right to do or be chosen for something, qualified: *He graduated from high school with good grades, so*

*he is eligible to go to the state college.* –*noun* **eligibility** /ˈɛlɪʤəˈbɪləty/.

**eliminate** /ɪˈlɪməˌneɪt/ *verb* **eliminated, eliminating, eliminates**
to remove, exclude: *The losing team was eliminated from the rest of the competition.* –*noun* **elimination.**

**elite** /ɪˈlit/ *noun*
the leaders and professionals in the highest levels of a society

**elope** /ɪˈloʊp/ *verb* **eloped, eloping, elopes**
to marry secretly without the permission of one's parents –*noun* **elopement.**

**eloquence** /ˈɛləˌkwɪns/ *noun, (no plural)*
clear and persuasive speech or writing: *The senator often speaks with eloquence.* –*adjective* **eloquent;** –*adverb* **eloquently.**

**else** /ɛls/ *adjective*
other, different: *I did not do that; someone else did.*

**else** *adverb*
in a different time, way, or location: *Where else can I go?*

**or else:** **a.** or get bad results: *You do what I say, or else!* **b.** used to introduce an unpleasent or unwanted possibility: *We have to leave now or else we'll be late.*

**elsewhere** /ˈɛlsˌwɛr/ *adverb*
in some other place: *She doesn't live here; she must live elsewhere.*

**ELT** /ˌiˌɛlˈti/ *abbreviation of*
English Language Teaching

**E-mail** or **e-mail** /ˈiˌmeɪl/ *noun*
*short for* electronic mail

**emancipate** /ɪˈmænsəˌpeɪt/ *verb* **emancipated, emancipating, emancipates**
to free from slavery, liberate: *The Civil War emancipated the slaves in the USA.* –*noun* **emancipation.** *(antonym)* enslave.

**embargo** /ɛmˈbɑrgoʊ/ *verb* **embargoed, embargoing, embargoes**
to stop trade with another nation: *The United Nations voted to embargo that country.* –*noun* **embargo.**

**embarrass** /ɛmˈbærəs/ *verb*
to make someone to feel self-conscious or ashamed: *Her boyfriend embarrassed her by making fun of her new hairstyle in front of her friends.* –*adjective* **embarrassing, embarrassed;** –*noun* **embarrassment.** *See:* art on page 18a.

**embassy** /ˈɛmbəsi/ *noun, plural* **embassies**
the offices of a country's ambassador and employees in a foreign country: *I visited the US Embassy in Paris.*

**emblem** /ˈɛmbləm/ *noun*
a sign or symbol for decoration or for a purpose: *Her shirt has the company emblem on it.*

emblem

**embrace** /ɛmˈbreɪs/ *verb* **embraced, embracing, embraces**
to hold in one's arms as a sign of love: *He embraced his wife when she came home from work.* –*noun* (act) **embrace.**

**embroider** /ɛmˈbrɔɪdər/ *verb*
to decorate with needlework: *She embroiders tablecloths.* –*noun* **embroidery.**

**embryo** /ˈɛmbriˌoʊ/ *noun*
an egg in the early stage of growth before birth

**emerald** /ˈɛmərəld/ *noun*
a precious, green stone: *She wore a ring of diamonds and emeralds.*

**emerge** /ɪˈmɜrʤ/ *verb* **emerged, emerging, emerges**
to appear: *The hunter emerged from the forest and walked toward us.*

**emergency** /ɪˈmɜrʤənsi/ *noun, plural* **emergencies**
a bad situation that requires immediate attention: *Call the police; this is an emergency!*

**emergency room** or **ER** *noun*
part of a hospital that takes care of sick or injured people who need immediate attention: *The woman hurt in the accident went to the emergency room in an ambulance. See:* art on page 000.

**emigrant** /ˈɛməgrənt/ *noun*
a person who leaves his or her native country to live in another: *My assistant is an emigrant from Romania. See:* immigrant.

**USAGE NOTE:** Compare *emigrant* and *immigrant.* A person who goes to live permanently in another country becomes both an *emigrant* and an *immigrant.* This person is an *emigrant from* the homeland left behind and an *immigrant to* the new country.

**emigrate** /ˈɛməˌgreɪt/ *verb* **emigrated, emigrating, emigrates**
to leave one's country to live in another *–noun* **emigration.**

**emissary** /ˈɛməˌsɛri/ *noun, plural* **emissaries**
a representative on a special mission, especially from one government to another government: *The President sent his personal emissary to the Middle East to talk to the leaders there.*

**emission** /ɪˈmɪʃən/ *noun*
something that is sent out, such as smoke or dirty water: *Automobiles and trucks create emissions that pollute the air.* *–verb* **to emit.**

**emotion** /ɪˈmoʊʃən/ *noun*
a feeling, such as love, hate, happiness, or sorrow: *He felt strong emotions when he thought of his old girlfriend.* *See:* art on page 18a.

**emotional** /ɪˈmoʊʃənəl/ *adjective*
**1** related to feelings: *Her emotional health is good; she's happy.*
**2** full of strong feelings, excited with emotion: *When he disagrees with you, he becomes emotional.* *–noun* **emotionalism;** *–adverb* **emotionally.**

**empathize** /ˈɛmpəˌθaɪz/ *verb* **empathized, empathizing, empathizes**
to understand another's feelings: *He's afraid about his illness, and I empathize with him; it's scary when you're ill.* *–adjective* **empathetic** /ˌɛmpəˈθɛtɪk/.

**emphasis** /ˈɛmfəsɪs/ *noun, plural* **emphases** /-ˌsiz/
special importance placed on something: *She put great emphasis on beginning work immediately.*

**emphasize** /ˈɛmfəˌsaɪz/ *verb* **emphasized, emphasizing, emphasizes**
to place importance on: *The manager emphasized the need to cut expenses.*

**empire** /ˈɛmˌpaɪr/ *noun*
a group of nations ruled by a central government and usually an emperor: *the ancient Roman Empire*

**employ** /ɛmˈplɔɪ/ *verb*
**1** to give paid work to people: *That company employs 1,000 workers.*
**2** to use: *The company employs computers to keep track of expenses.*

**employable** /ɛmˈplɔɪəbəl/ *adjective*
ready and able to be employed: *She has computer skills and a positive outlook; she's employable.* *–noun* **employability.**

**employee** /ɛmˈplɔɪi/ *noun*
someone who works for a person, business, or government: *She is an employee of this company.*

**employer** /ɛmˈplɔɪər/ *noun*
a person, business, or government that employs people: *My employer is United Chemical Company.*

**employment** /ɛmˈplɔɪmənt/ *noun, (no plural)*
a job paying a salary or wages: *He lost his job and is looking for employment.*

**empower** /ɛmˈpaʊər/ *verb*
to give power to: *The judge empowered the police to look in the house for stolen property.* *–noun* **empowerment.**

**empty** /ˈɛmpti/ *adjective* **emptier, emptiest**
having nothing or no one inside: *There is nothing in the box; it is empty.* *(antonym)* full.

empty

**empty** *verb* **emptied, emptying, empties**
**1** to take out the contents of: *I emptied the drawer by taking my clothes out of it.*
**2** to become empty: *The movie theater emptied after the film ended.* *–noun* **emptiness.**

**enable** /ɛnˈeɪbəl/ *verb* **enabled, enabling, enables**
to make possible for: *Their savings enabled them to retire early.* *–adjective* **enabling.**

**enact** /ɛnˈækt/ *verb*
to make or pass a law: *The Congress enacted a new tax law.* *–noun* **enactment.**

**enclose** /ɛn'kloʊz/ *verb* **enclosed, enclosing, encloses**
to place within, put inside: *I enclosed a check in the envelope with my rent bill.*

**enclosure** /ɛn'kloʊʒər/ *noun*
an area with a fence around it: *During the day, the cattle are kept in an enclosure next to the barn.*

E

**encounter** /ɛn'kaʊntər/ *verb*
to meet by chance: *We encountered our friends at the store.* –*noun* **encounter.**

**encourage** /ɛn'kɜrədʒ/ *verb* **encouraged, encouraging, encourages**
to give strength or hope: *She encouraged her son to go to college.* –*noun* **encouragement;** –*adjective* **encouraging.**

**encyclopedia** /ɛn,saɪklə'pidiə/ *noun*
a group of articles that give information on general and specific topics in book form or on CD-ROM (usually arranged in alphabetical order): *I began research for my history paper by looking in the encyclopedia.*

**end** /ɛnd/ *noun*
**1** the last part of something: *the end of a street‖the end of a year*
**2** *formal* a goal, purpose: *The company wanted to improve its image, so to that end, it hired a popular athlete to appear in its advertisements.*

**to make ends meet:** to get enough money to pay for necessities of life: *I make just enough money to make ends meet, to pay the rent and buy food.*

**end** *verb*
to make stop, bring to an end: *We ended our conversation with a promise to see each other again.*

**to end in something:** to result in: *The meeting ended in an agreement on what to do. (antonym)* start.

**endanger** /ɛn'deɪndʒər/ *verb*
to place in danger: *They went swimming in the ocean in stormy weather and endangered their lives.* –*noun* **endangerment.**

**endangered species** *noun*
*used with a singular or plural verb* a plant or animal whose population is so small that it may die out: *The wildlife fund protects endangered species.*

**endorse** /ɛn'dɔrs/ *verb* **endorsed, endorsing, endorses**
to sign one's name on the back of a check or note: *He endorsed his paycheck and deposited it in his bank.* –*noun* **endorsement.**

**endurance** /ɛn'dʊrəns/ *noun, (no plural)*
the ability to do something for a long period of time: *Olympic runners have great endurance.*

**endure** /ɛn'dʊr/ *verb* **endured, enduring, endures**
to last, exist for a long time: *Great art endures for centuries.‖Athletes endure pain to win races.* –*adjective* **endurable; enduring.**

**enemy** /'ɛnəmi/ *noun, plural* **enemies**
a person, military, or nation that wants to hurt another: *During the US Civil War, the Northern and Southern states were enemies.*

**energetic** /,ɛnər'dʒɛtɪk/ *adjective*
having energy, active: *She is a very energetic woman with many interests.* –*adverb* **energetically.**

**energize** /'ɛnər,dʒaɪz/ *verb* **energized, energizing, energizes**
to give power to: *The battery energized the motor and made it run.* –*noun* **energizer.**

**energy** /'ɛnərdʒi/ *noun, plural* **energies**
**1** the power to do work: *Energy to run machines sometimes comes from electricity.*
**2** the power to be active (work, play): *He is full of energy and is active all the time.*

**enforce** /ɛn'fɔrs/ *verb* **enforced, enforcing, enforces**
to make people obey (laws, rules, etc.): *The police enforce the law by arresting criminals.* –*adjective* **enforceable;** –*noun* (action) **enforcement;** (person) **enforcer.**

**engage** /ɛn'geɪdʒ/ *verb formal* **engaged, engaging, engages**
**1** to make things fit and move together: *The driver engaged the car's gears.*
**2** to participate: *She didn't want to engage in conversation.*

**engaged** /ɛn'geɪdʒd/ *adjective*
**1** having an agreement to get married:

*The engaged couple plan to get married in the spring.*
**2** busy: *My boss is engaged right now, but she should be free in an hour.*

**engagement** /ɛn'geɪʤmənt/ *noun*
an agreement to marry: *We announced our engagement last week.*

**engine** /'ɛnʤɪn/ *noun*
**1** a machine that produces force and motion: *The engine in my car drives the wheels to make it move.*
**2** a machine that pulls a train, a locomotive

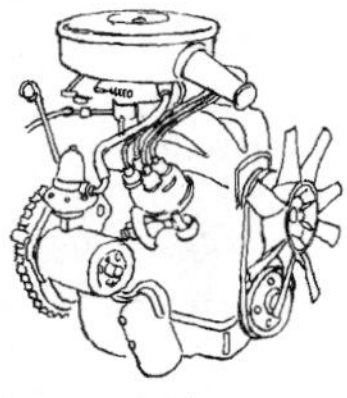
engine

**engineer** /ˌɛnʤə'nɪr/ *noun*
**1** a person trained in science and mathematics who plans the making of machines (mechanical engineer, electrical engineer), roads and bridges (civil engineer), etc.: *She is an electrical engineer who works for a computer company.*
**2** the person who drives a train: *The engineer stopped the train as it neared the station.* *–verb* **to engineer.**

**engineering** /ˌɛnʤə'nɪrɪŋ/ *noun*
**1** the profession of an engineer: *She studies electrical engineering.*
**2** the scientific planning of a machine, road, bridge, etc.

**English** /'ɪŋglɪʃ/ *noun, (no plural)*
**1** the people of England: *The English are proud of their history.*
**2** the English language: *Kristin speaks English, German, and Mandarin.*
**3** related to the English: *English woolens||the English language –noun* **an Englishman; an Englishwoman.**

---

**USAGE NOTE:** *English* is used around the world as a language of international communication. Today there are many more people who speak *English* as a second or foreign language than people who speak *English* as a first or native language.

---

**enjoy** /ɛn'ʤɔɪ/ *verb*
to get pleasure from, to like: *He enjoys music.*
**to enjoy oneself:** to have fun: *We enjoyed ourselves at their wedding. –noun* **enjoyment.**

**enjoyable** /ɛn'ʤɔɪəbəl/ *adjective*
pleasant: *We had an enjoyable day at the picnic.*

**enlarge** /ɛn'lɑrʤ/ *verb* **enlarged, enlarging, enlarges**
to make larger, expand the size of: *We enlarged our house by adding two new rooms. –noun* **enlargement, enlarger.**

**enlighten** /ɛn'laɪtn/ *verb*
to make someone understand: *The instructor enlightened his students on how to use adjectives in English. –noun* **enlightenment.**

**enlist** /ɛn'lɪst/ *verb*
to join the military voluntarily: *I enlisted in the army when I was 18. –noun* (act) **enlistment.**

**enormous** /ɪ'nɔrməs/ *adjective*
extremely big, huge: *The Sears Tower in Chicago is enormous; it's more than 100 stories tall! –noun* (size) **enormity;** *–adverb* **enormously.**

**enough** /ɪ'nʌf/ *adjective*
as much or as many as needed: *We have enough money to pay the bills.||Do we have enough books for everyone?*

**enough** *adverb*
to the amount necessary: *She plays the piano well enough.*

**enough** *noun, (no plural)*
a satisfactory amount: *The basketball game was boring; we saw enough and went home.*

**enough** *exclamation*
Stop!: *Enough! I don't want to hear anymore!*

**enroll** /ɛn'roʊl/ *verb*
to become a member of an organization: *I enrolled in college this fall; I will graduate in four years.*

**enrollment** /ɛn'roʊlmənt/ *noun*
the number of students in a class or school: *My English literature course has an enrollment of 200 students.*

**ensure** /ɛn'ʃʊr/ *verb* **ensured, ensuring, ensures**
to make sure: *He ensured that all the doors were locked before he left his apartment. See:* insure.

**enter** /'ɛntər/ *verb*
**1** to go into: *I entered the classroom.*
**2** to begin: *She will enter college in the fall.*

**3** to write down, record: *The computer screen told me to enter my name, so I typed it in. (antonym)* exit.

**enterprise** /ˈɛntərˌpraɪz/ *noun*
**1** the qualities of courage, hard work, and intelligence, especially in business: *Her business is doing well because of her enterprise.*
**2** a business *–adjective* **enterprising.**

**entertain** /ˌɛntərˈteɪn/ *verb*
to amuse: *She is a singer who entertains the audience.* *–noun* **entertainment;** *–adjective* **entertaining.** /ˌɛntərˈteɪnɪŋ/

**enthusiasm** /ɛnˈθuziˌæzəm/ *noun*
strong interest, good feeling: *You can see the workers' enthusiasm in that company.*

**enthusiastic** /ɛnˌθuziˈæstɪk/ *adjective*
eager, excited: *She is enthusiastic about beginning her new job.* *–adverb* **enthusiastically.**

**entire** /ɛnˈtaɪr/ *adjective*
complete, whole: *She ate the entire cake, not just one piece!* *–adverb* **entirely.**

**entitle** /ɛnˈtaɪtl/ *verb* **entitled, entitling, entitles**
**1** to allow, authorize: *That pass entitles you to enter the concert for free.*
**2** to call, name: *That book is entitled* Gone with the Wind.

**entitlement** /ɛnˈtaɪtlmənt/ *noun*
a right, especially for governmental aid: *The man has entitlements to Social Security and medical care.*

**entrance** /ˈɛntrəns/ *noun*
**1** a door, gate, or other opening allowing one to enter: *We walked through the entrance to the museum.*

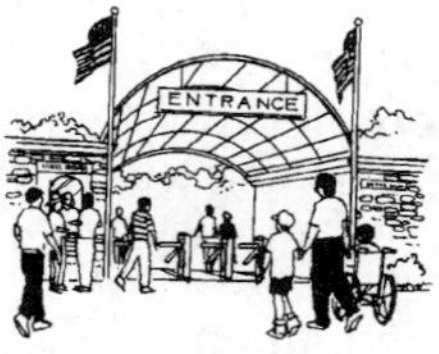

entrance

**2** an act of entering: *He has formally announced his entrance into the race for President. (antonym)* exit. *See:* art on page 8a.

**entrée** /ˈɑntreɪ/ *noun*
in the USA, the main part of the meal: *We started with soup and had steak as the entrée.*

**entrepreneur** /ˌɑntrəprəˈnɜr/ *noun*
a person who starts a business: *She is an entrepreneur who built a company around a new computer product.*

**entry** /ˈɛntri/ *noun, plural* **entries**
**1** an act of entering: *Many people opposed the entry of the USA into the war.*
**2** a record of a sale or event, such as a birth: *The clerk made an entry of the sale in the company books.*
**3** a word and its definition in a dictionary: *College dictionaries have about 200,000 entries.*

**entry-level:** (of a job) in the lowest category

---

**USAGE NOTE:** Jobs that require the least experience are called *entry-level positions.* Many people begin their careers at *entry-level* positions and work their way eventually into high-level positions: *She began at the entry level as a clerk and became president of the company.*

---

**envelop** /ɛnˈvɛləp/ *verb*
to cover completely: *Fog enveloped the airport.*

**envelope** /ˈɛnvəˌloʊp/ *noun*
a paper cover for letters: *We put our bills in envelopes to mail to our customers.*

envelope

**envious** /ˈɛnviəs/ *adjective*
wanting what someone else has: *He is envious of my new car and wants one like it.* *–adverb* **enviously.** *See:* envy.

**environment** /ɛnˈvaɪrənmɛnt/ *noun*
the air, land, water, and surroundings that people, plants, and animals live in: *The environment in big cities is usually polluted.* *–adjective* **environmental;** *–adverb* **environmentally.**

**envy** /ˈɛnvi/ *verb* **envied, envying, envies**
to want the same things someone else has: *He has a wonderful job; I envy him.*

**envy** *noun, (no plural)*
a desire to have what belongs to another: *She is full of envy of her friend's good looks.* *See:* jealous.

**epidemic** /ˌɛpəˈdɛmɪk/ *noun adjective*
a disease that spreads quickly among many people: *There are epidemics of influenza every winter.*

**episode** /ˈɛpəˌsoʊd/ *noun*
one in a series of events: *I watched an episode of a soap opera on television.*

**e pluribus unum** /ˈiˈplʊrəbəsˈyunəm/ *adverbial phrase*
Latin for "out of many, one"; used as the motto of the USA to express the ideal of unity among the many peoples living in the country

**equal** /ˈikwəl/ *noun*
the same (in amount, size, appearance, power, etc.): *Those two managers are equals; both are managers of the company.*

**equal** *adjective*
being the same, equivalent, alike: *The two tables are of equal length (importance, height, etc.).* –*adverb* **equally.**

**equal** *verb*
**1** to be the same as: *The two horses equal each other in speed.*
**2** to result in (from adding, multiplying, etc.): *Two plus two equals four.*

**equality** /ɪˈkwɑləti/ *noun, plural* **equalities.**
a condition of being equal in importance, power, etc.: *Some countries are working toward economic equality.*

**equal sign** *noun*
the symbol (=) that means terms on either side of it are equivalent: 2 + 2 = 4.

**equation** /ɪˈkwɛɪʒən/ *noun*
a mathematical statement that two amounts are equal: *The following is a simple equation: 2 + 2 = 4.*

**equator** /ɪˈkweɪtər/ *noun, (no plural)*
an imaginary line around the middle of the earth that is equal in distance from the North and South Poles: *Countries that are on or near the equator have very hot temperatures.* –*adjective* **equatorial** /ˌikwəˈtɔriəl/.

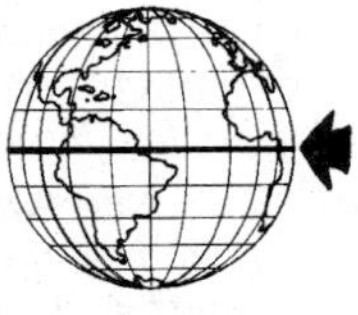
equator

**equinox** /ˈikwəˌnɑks/ *noun, plural* **equinoxes**
the two days each year (around March 21 and September 22) when day and night are of equal length

**equip** /ɪˈkwɪp/ *verb* **equipped, equipping, equips**
to provide with equipment: *Our office is equipped with two powerful computers.*

**equipment** /ɪˈkwɪpmənt/ *noun, (no plural)*
items needed for a purpose: *I have sports equipment that includes golf clubs, tennis rackets, and ice skates.*

**equity** /ˈɛkwəti/ *noun, (no plural)*
fairness, justice

**equivalent** /ɪˈkwɪvələnt/ *adjective*
equal, the same: *The two runners are equivalent in speed.*

**era** /ˈɪrə/ *noun*
a time period with a general character: *The Eisenhower era in the USA was one of peace and a good economy.*

**erase** /ɪˈreɪs/ *verb* **erased, erasing, erases**
to clean off: *The teacher erased the blackboard.*

eraser

**eraser** /ɪˈreɪsər/ *noun*
a small piece of rubber used to remove pencil, ink, or other marks: *I like to use pencils with erasers on top.* *See:* art on page 8a.

**erect** /ɪˈrɛkt/ *adjective*
standing up, straight: *She is old but she stands erect.*

**erect** *verb*
to build, construct: *A construction company erected a large building across the street.* –*noun* **erection;** –*adverb* **erectly.**

**erode** /ɪˈroʊd/ *verb* **eroded, eroding, erodes**
to wear away: *Rain and wind eroded the topsoil from the farmland.* –*noun* **erosion.**

**erotic** /ɪˈrɑtɪk/ *adjective*
about sexual desire

E

**errand** /ˈɛrənd/ *noun*
a short trip made for a specific purpose: *I have to put money in the bank, go to the post office, and do some other errands.*

**erratic** /ɪˈrætɪk/ *adjective*
not working in a regular manner: *Her heartbeat is erratic; it misses beats. –adverb* **erratically.**

**error** /ˈɛrər/ *noun*
a mistake: *He made an error in arithmetic.*

**erupt** /ɪˈrʌpt/ *verb*
to explode: *A volcano erupts.*||*The audience erupted with laughter. –noun* **eruption.**

**escalate** /ˈɛskəˌleɪt/ *verb* **escalated, escalating, escalates**
to raise: *The disagreement between the two countries escalated into war. –noun* **escalation.** *(antonym)* decline.

**escalator** /ˈɛskəˌleɪtər/ *noun*
a moving staircase: *The escalators in the department store run to all six floors.*

escalator

**escape** /ɪˈskeɪp/ *verb* **escaped, escaping, escapes**
to get away: *The lion escaped from its cage.*||*We escaped to an island in the Pacific for our vacation.*

**escape** *noun*
**1** an act of escaping: *The criminal made an escape from prison.*
**2** a temporary break from cares or worries: *They enjoyed an escape from the city at their country house. –noun* (person) **escapee.**

**escort** /ˈɛsˌkɔrt/ *noun*
someone who goes with another as a guide, guard, or companion: *The Prime Minister's car has a police escort. –verb* **to escort.**

**ESL** /ˌiˌɛsˈɛl/ *abbreviation of*
English as a second language: *Many students study ESL to improve their English.*

**especially** /ɪˈspɛʃəli/ *adverb*
**1** just (for a special purpose): *I bring this present especially for you.*
**2** to a large degree: *He is especially fond of chocolate.*

**essay** /ˈɛseɪ/ *noun*
a short, written work on a topic that gives the author's opinion: *I wrote an essay on Shakespeare for my English class. –noun* (writer) **essayist.** *See:* fiction, USAGE NOTE.

**essence** /ˈɛsəns/ *noun, (no plural)*
the main point of a subject: *The essence of the matter is that the two people really love each other.*

**essential** /ɪˈsɛnʃəl/ *adjective*
necessary, required: *It is essential that you deliver the message this morning. –adverb* **essentially.**

**establish** /ɪˈstæblɪʃ/ *verb*
to create: *The English established a colony in Africa.*||*Over many years, she established a reputation as a good lawyer. –noun* **establishment.**

**estate** /əˈsteɪt/ *noun*
**1** a large house with much land
**2** the wealth (money, property) left by a dead person: *His estate was worth a million dollars.*

**esteem** /əˈstim/ *noun, (no plural)*
honor, respect: *These students hold their English professor in high esteem.*

**estimate** /ˈɛstəˌmeɪt/ *verb* **estimated, estimating, estimates**
**1** to make a judgment about (the price of something): *They estimated the value of my painting at $1,000.*
**2** to figure the amount of, *(synonym)* to calculate: *I estimated that the trip would take about two hours.*

**estimate** /ˈɛstəmɪt/ *noun*
a calculation or approximation of the value of something: *The mechanic gave me a rough estimate of three hundred dollars for the repairs to my car.*

**etc.** /ɛtˈsɛtərə/ *adverb*
*abbreviation of* et cetera and other similar things, and so on: *I told the carpenter all about the table that I need: the color, the width, the height, etc.*

---

**USAGE NOTE:** The term *et cetera* is used in its full-length form in speaking but not in writing. Its abbreviation, *etc.*, is used in writing.

---

**eternal** /ɪ'tɜrnəl/ *adjective*
lasting forever: *People of many religions believe that God is eternal.* –*adverb* **eternally.**

**eternity** /ɪ'tɜrnəti/ *noun, (no plural)*
a time period without end: *A billion years is an eternity.*

**ethic** /'εθɪk/ *noun*
**1** moral or correct behavior: *The priest spoke about the Christian ethic: "Love your neighbor as yourself."*
**2** *plural* ethics: a system of moral or correct actions and principles: *Her ethics in business are excellent.*

**ethical** /'εθɪkəl/ *adjective*
related to moral or correct behavior: *He found a woman's wallet and did the ethical thing: he returned it to her.* –*adverb* **ethically.**

**ethnic** /'εθnɪk/ *adjective*
related to group characteristics, such as race, country of origin, religion, or culture: *The USA has many different ethnic groups.* –*noun* **ethnicity** /εθ'nɪsəti/.

**etiquette** /'εtəkɪt/ *noun, (no plural)*
the correct way to behave: *Good etiquette tells a bride and groom to write thank-you notes for wedding gifts.*

**Europe** /'yʊrəp/ *noun, (no plural)*
the world's sixth largest continent: *Spain, Germany, and Greece are countries in Europe.*

**European** /ˌyʊrə'piən/ *noun*
a person from Europe: *He is a European.*
**European** *adjective*
related to Europe: *Many Americans like European culture.*

**evade** /ɪ'veɪd/ *verb* **evaded, evading, evades**
to avoid: *The politician evaded the reporter's question by changing the subject. (antonym)* seek.

**evaluate** /ɪ'vælyuˌeɪt/ *verb* **evaluated, evaluating, evaluates**
to study and make a judgment about: *The committee evaluated the reports and made a decision.*

**evaluation** /ɪˌvælyu'eɪʃən/ *noun*
a study of worth (value, ability) and a judgment about it: *My boss did an evaluation of my job performance.*

**evaporate** /ɪ'væpəˌreɪt/ *verb* **evaporated, evaporating, evaporates**
to change from a liquid into a part of the air: *Water evaporates from lakes and oceans.* –*noun* **evaporation.**

**evasion** /ɪ'veɪʒən/ *noun*
a statement or action that avoids what should be said or done: *tax evasion*

**evasive** /ɪ'veɪsɪv/ *adjective*
not direct or clear: *He's always evasive and never gives a clear answer.*

**eve** /iv/ *noun, (no plural)*
the evening before an event, especially a holiday: *New Year's Eve.*

**even** /ivən/ *adjective*
**1** the same in measurement (distance, height, etc.), equal: *The pieces of wood are even in length.*
**2** the same in place, score, etc. in a contest: *The two runners were even at the finish line.*
**3** (of numbers) that can be exactly divided by two: *The numbers 2, 4, and 6 are even; 1, 3, and 5 are odd numbers.*
**4** *figurative* on equal terms after repayment of a debt: *Here's the $20 that I owe you; now we're even.*
**even** *adverb*
**1** more, to a greater extent: *He makes things even harder than they were by acting the way he does.*
**2** so little as: *She left him without even a word of explanation.*
**3** used to make a comparison stronger: *Even a child would know what to do.*
**even if:** although: *He says he'll finish the job even if it kills him!*
**even** *verb*
to make equal: *I'll even the surface of this table by sanding it down.* –*adverb* **evenly;** –*noun* **evenness.**

**evening** /'ivnɪŋ/ *noun*
the period between 6:00 P.M. and midnight: *We went to a movie yesterday evening. (antonym)* morning.

**event** /ɪ'vεnt/ *noun*
**1** a happening, especially an important one: *The events that led to the war were complex.*
**2** a competition, contest: *I entered the*

*ten mile (16km) race, an event in which I specialize.*

**eventual** /ɪ'vɛntʃuəl/ *adjective*
happening later, *(synonym)* ultimate: *The tennis match was long, but he was the eventual winner. –adverb* **eventually.**

**ever** /'ɛvər/ *adverb*
at any time: *Is he ever on time?*||*Don't ever do that again!*||*It was the best movie I've ever seen.*

**ever-** *prefix* always: *the ever-popular chocolate chip cookie*

**evergreen** /'ɛvər,grin/ *noun adjective*
a tree with needles as leaves that stay green all year: *The pine on our lawn is an evergreen.*

**every** /'ɛvri/ *adjective*
**1** each: *Every driver must have a license.*
**2** once in each period of time: *You must take your medicine every two hours.*

**every now and then** or **every so often:** once in a while, occasionally: *She stops by to see me every now and then.*

**everybody** /'ɛvri,badi/ *pronoun*
everyone, all persons: *Everybody who wants to go fishing should let me know.*

**everyone** /'ɛvri,wʌn/ *pronoun*
everybody, all persons: *Everyone must eat to live. (antonym)* no one.

**everything** /'ɛvri,θɪŋ/ *pronoun*
**1** all things: *Everything in the kitchen was destroyed by the fire.*
**2** all that is important in life: *Her health is everything to her. (antonym)* nothing.

**everywhere** /'ɛvri,wɛr/ *adverb*
in all places: *I lost my keys and looked everywhere for them. (antonym)* nowhere.

**evict** /i'vɪkt/ *verb*
to force out of a property by threat, law, or physical force: *They did not pay their rent on their apartment for three months, so the owner evicted them. –noun* **eviction.**

**evidence** /'ɛvədəns/ *noun*
words or objects that support the truth of something: *The lawyer showed the murder gun as evidence in court.*

**evident** /'ɛvədənt/ *adjective*
plain, clear: *It is evident that he is guilty.*

**evil** /'ivəl/ *adjective*
extremely bad, wicked: *He tries to hurt people; he's evil. –noun* **evil.** *(antonym)* good.

**evolution** /,ɛvə'luʃən/ *noun, (no plural)*
the development of living things

**evolve** /i'valv/ *verb* **evolved, evolving, evolves**
to develop, change: *Farming evolved slowly over thousands of years.*

**ex** /ɛks/ *noun, plural* **exes**
**1** the letter *x*
**2** *slang short for* ex-wife or ex-husband: *My ex and I are still friends.*

**ex-** *prefix* former: *She is ex-treasurer of the company, now retired.*

**exact** /ɪg'zækt/ *adjective*
accurate: *He gave me the exact measurements of the table. –noun* **exactness;** *–verb* **to exact.**

**exactly** /ɪg'zæktli/ *adverb*
accurately: *The job must be done exactly as she wants it done.*

**exaggerate** /ɪg'zædʒə,reɪt/ *verb* **exaggerated, exaggerating, exaggerates**
to say something is better, worse, more important, etc., than it really is: *He said he caught a fish as long as his arm, but he was exaggerating. –noun* **exaggeration.**

**exam** /ɪg'zæm/ *noun*
*short for* examination, *(synonym)* test

**examination** /ɪg,zæmə'neɪʃən/ *noun*
**1** a test of one's knowledge: *I took an examination in English yesterday.*
**2** a close look (an inspection): *The doctor gave me a physical examination. –verb* **to examine.** *See:* test, USAGE NOTE.

**example** /ɪg'zæmpəl/ *noun*
a sample, or event showing something: *The sales representative showed an example of her new product.*

**for example:** as a model of what I mean: *He wants an expensive car, a Mercedes, for example.*

**to set an example** or **a good example:** to behave in the way others should: *She is an excellent worker; she sets a good example for others in her company.*

**exceed** /ɪk'sid/ *verb*
to be or do more than what is expected: *Sales of the new product exceeded our estimates.*

**excel** /ɪk'sɛl/ *verb* **excelled, excelling, excels**
to do very well: *She excels at swimming.*

**excellent** /'ɛksələnt/ *adjective*
very high in quality: *The violinist gave an excellent performance; everyone applauded loudly.* –*noun* **excellence;** –*adverb* **excellently.**

**except** /ɪk'sɛpt/ *preposition*
excluding: *Everyone was invited except me.* *(antonym)* including.

**except** *conjunction*
but: *I would lend you the money except that I don't have any.*

**exception** /ɪk'sɛpʃən/ *noun*
something unusual: *He is usually on time; his lateness today is an exception.*

**exceptional** /ɪk'sɛpʃənəl/ *adjective*
unusual and excellent

**excess** /ɪk'sɛs/ *noun*
more than what is needed or wanted: *We have an excess of paperwork in this office.* –*adjective* **excessive.**

**exchange** /ɪks'ʧeɪnʤ/ *noun*
a trade: *I gave him $50 for his power saw, and we made the exchange at his house.*||*I gave him $50 in exchange for his saw.*

**exchange** *verb* **exchanged, exchanging, exchanges**
**1** to trade: *People exchange money for goods in stores.*
**2** to return something to a store and get another in its place: *She went back to the store and exchanged the shirt because her husband didn't like the color.*
**3** to communicate: *We exchanged ideas during the meeting.*

**exchange rate** *noun*
the price at which one country's money may be traded for another's: *For years, the exchange rate for the Danish crown was seven crowns to one US dollar.*

**excitable** /ɪk'saɪtəbəl/ *adjective*
easily excited, emotional: *He is excitable; he gets angry very quickly.*

**excite** /ɪk'saɪt/ *verb* **excited, exciting, excites**
to make someone to feel delight: *The band played louder and excited the audience.* –*noun* **excitement.**

**exclamation point** *noun*
a punctuation symbol (!) used for emphasis surprise, delight, etc.: *Ouch! I hit my finger with the hammer!*

**exclude** /ɛk'sklud/ *verb* **excluded, excluding, excludes**
**1** to leave or keep out: *I put all but one vegetable into the soup; I excluded the corn.*
**2** to keep out, *(synonym)* to prohibit: *The restaurant excludes anyone who is not properly dressed from entering.* –*noun* **exclusion.** *(antonym)* include.

**exclusive** /ɪk'sklusɪv/ *adjective*
limited to people with a lot of money and high social position: *an exclusive club*||*an exclusive neighborhood* –*adverb* **exclusively.**

**excuse** /ɪk'skyuz/ *verb* **excused, excusing, excuses**
**1** to forgive: *She excused him for being late.*
**2** to allow to leave: *The teacher excused the students, and they left class.*

**Excuse me:** an expression used to get someone's attention: *Excuse me, is this seat free?*

**excuse** /ɪk'skyus/ *noun*
a reason that explains an offense: *He had a good excuse for not doing his homework; his father had died.*

**execute** /'ɛksəˌkyut/ *verb* **executed, executing, executes**
**1** to kill, especially by government or military: *Soldiers executed the traitor by shooting him.*
**2** to perform: *A computer executes the commands given to it.*

**execution** /ˌɛksə'kyuʃən/ *noun*
the act of putting someone to death: *The execution of the murderer will take place tomorrow.*

**executive** /ɪk'zɛkyətɪv/ *noun*
a manager (or administrator) in a company or institution: *She is an executive with a bank.*

**executive** *adjective*
**1** related to the responsibilities of an executive: *As a bank officer, she has the executive authority to approve loans.*
**2** in the USA, related to the President,

his or her powers, cabinet, and staff: *the Executive branch of government*

**exemption** /ɪg'zɛmpʃən/ *noun*
**1** something that lets a person not pay taxes: *You can claim these expenses as exemptions on your income taxes.*
**2** freedom from a duty, requirement, or restriction: *He received an exemption from military duty because he is disabled.* –*verb* **to exempt.**



**exercise** /'ɛksər,saɪz/ *verb* **exercised, exercising, exercises**
to do physical activities to strengthen the body: *I exercise by lifting weights and running.*

exercise

**exercise** *noun*
**1** physical movements to strengthen the body: *Every morning, I do sit-ups and other exercises.*
**2** a question or task for mental training: *The teacher gives the students exercises in math.*

**exertion** /ɪg'zɜrʃən/ *noun*
physical work: *Walking up stairs requires exertion.* –*verb* **to exert.**

**exhale** /ɛks'heɪl/ *verb* **exhaled, exhaling, exhales**
to let out air from the lungs: *The doctor told me to exhale as she listened to my heartbeat.* –*noun* **exhalation** /,ɛkshəleɪʃən/. *(antonym)* inhale

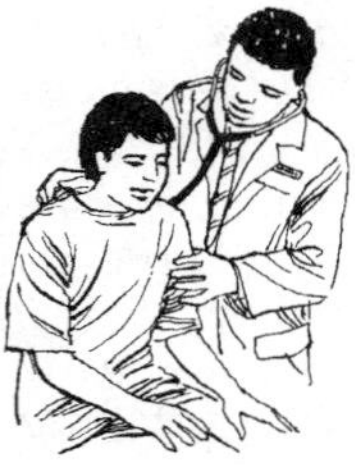
exhale

**exhaust** /ɪg'zɔst/ *verb*
**1** to use completely: *We have exhausted our supply of pencils and must order more.*
**2** to make very tired: *She got up three times a night to feed her baby and that exhausted the new mother.*

**exhaust** *noun*
smoke, steam, bad air that comes out of pipes: *Exhaust from a car's engine escapes through the tailpipe.*

**exhibit** /ɪg'zɪbɪt/ *verb*
to show, display: *A museum exhibits art for people to see.*

exhibit

**exhibit** *noun*
a display: *We visited an art exhibit at the museum.* –*noun* (person) **exhibitor.**

**exhibition** /,ɛksə'bɪʃən/ *noun*
a display (of art, products, etc.): *I enjoyed the art exhibition at the museum.*

**exile** /'ɛg,zaɪl/ *verb* **exiled, exiling, exiles**
to force someone out of his or her home country: *The government exiled him because they did not like his political opinions.* –*noun* (person/place) **exile.**

**exist** /ɪg'zɪst/ *verb*
**1** to be present: *Poverty and hatred exist all over the world.*
**2** to live with difficulty: *Poor people exist on very little money.*

**existence** /ɪg'zɪstəns/ *noun*
**1** the presence of something in the real world: *The company has been in existence for 20 years.*
**2** *singular* a type of life: *People in the mountains lead a simple existence.* –*adjective* **existent.**

**exit** /'ɛgzɪt/ *verb*
to leave, depart: *We exited the building through a side door. (antonym)* enter.

**exit** *noun*
a door leading outside: *A movie theater has exits on three sides. (antonym)* entrance. *See:* art on page 10a.

**exotic** /ɪg'zɑtɪk/ *adjective*
unusual and attractive: *The exotic plants from the jungle are beautiful.*

**expand** /ɪk'spænd/ *verb*
to grow larger: *The balloon expanded, then exploded.* –*noun* **expansion.**

**expect** /ɪk'spɛkt/ *verb*
**1** to think something will happen or someone will come: *I expect him very soon.*
**2** to want and believe (that someone will do something): *The mother told her son that she expected him to behave in school.*

**to be expecting (a baby):** *She is expecting a baby in May.*

**expectation** /ˌɛkspɛk'teɪʃən/ *noun*
hope, desire: *He has expectations that he will make a lot of money.*

**expel** /ɪk'spɛl/ *verb* **expelled, expelling, expels**
to send away for a reason: *The principal expelled the disrespectful student from school.*

**expenditure** /ɪk'spɛndətʃər/ *noun*
the spending or using of money, time, energy, etc.: *The company has made several big expenditures on new equipment.*

**expense** /ɪk'spɛns/ *noun*
a cost, price: *The expense of moving from one house to another is high.*

**expensive** /ɪk'spɛnsɪv/ *adjective*
costly, high priced: *He gives expensive gifts to his family for Christmas. –adverb* **expensively.** *(antonym)* cheap.

**experience** /ɪk'spɪriəns/ *noun*
**1** an event: *Our visit to Alaska was a pleasant experience.*
**2** understanding gained through doing something: *She has years of experience in teaching.*

**experience** *verb* **experienced, experiencing, experiences**
to feel or know by personal involvement in: *She has experienced difficulties (satisfaction, success, etc.) in her new job.*

**experiment** /ɪk'spɛrəmənt/ *noun*
a test done to see if something works or happens: *We do experiments in chemistry class each week.*

**experiment** *verb*
to test, try something: *The school experimented with different textbooks to see which one is best. –noun* **experimentation.**

**expert** /'ɛkˌspɜrt/ *noun*
a master at something: *She is an expert with computers.*

**expiration** /ˌɛkspə'reɪʃən/ *noun*
a date at which something is no longer useable: *The expiration of my passport meant I had to get a new one.*

**expire** /ɪk'spaɪr/ *verb* **expired, expiring, expires**
to stop being valid: *My driver's license expires in June.*

**explain** /ɪk'spleɪn/ *verb*
to give information about, make clear: *The instructor explained the causes of the French Revolution.*

**explanation** /ˌɛksplə'neɪʃən/ *noun*
information given to help someone understand: *The computer salesperson gave an explanation of how to use that computer. –adjective* **explanatory.**

**explode** /ɪk'sploʊd/ *verb* **exploded, exploding, explodes**
to blow apart with force: *A bomb exploded on the battlefield.*

**exploit** /ɪk'splɔɪt/ *verb*
to treat unfairly, take advantage of: *He exploited workers by paying them very little. –adjective* **exploitive;** *–noun* **exploitation** /ˌɛksplɔɪ'teɪʃən/.

**exploration** /ˌɛksplə'reɪʃən/ *noun*
a journey of discovery, a search: *the exploration of space –adjective* **exploratory** /ɪk'splɔrəˌtɔri/.

**explore** /ɪk'splɔr/ *verb* **explored, exploring, explores**
**1** to travel into in order to learn about, *(synonym)* to scout: *The children went to explore the playground.*
**2** to study *–noun* (person) **explorer.**

**explosion** /ɪk'sploʊʒən/ *noun*
a blowing apart with force: *A bomb explosion damaged the building.*

explosion

**explosive** /ɪk'sploʊsɪv/ *noun*
a substance (such as dynamite), used to make explosions: *Soldiers used explosives to blow up a bridge.*

**export** /ɪk'spɔrt/ *verb*
to ship something from one country to another for sale: *Canada exports a lot of wheat and wood.*

**export** *noun*
/'ɛkˌspɔrt/ an act of exporting or the item that is exported: *Wheat is a big export for Canada. –noun* (person) **exporter.** *(antonym)* import.

E

**expose** /ɪk'spoʊz/ *verb* **exposed, exposing, exposes**
to make known: *A politician exposed a secret plan for a revolution.*

**exposition** /ˌɛkspə'zɪʃən/ *noun*
a show where manufacturers display their products: *We went to a food and cooking exposition at the Trade Center.*

**exposure** /ɪk'spoʊʒər/ *noun*
**1** being unprotected, especially from weather: *The lost mountain climbers suffered from exposure to the cold.*
**2** a section of photographic film: *That roll of film contains 36 exposures.*

**express** /ɪk'sprɛs/ *verb* **expressed, expressing, expresses**
**1** to speak about: *She expressed her worries about money to her friend.*
**2** *informal* to send something the fastest way: *I expressed the package overnight.*
**to express oneself:** to show one's ability to communicate: *She expresses herself well in English.*
**express** *adjective*
nonstop, fast: *an express train*

**expression** /ɪk'sprɛʃən/ *noun*
**1** the look on one's face: *He had an expression of delight when we gave him a surprise party.*
**2** a sign: *He sent her roses as an expression of his love.*
**3** a group of words: *When you tell someone to "break a leg," it is an expression meaning "good luck."*

**expressive** /ɪk'sprɛsɪv/ *adjective*
showing emotion: *His laughter was very expressive of the happiness he felt.* –*adverb* **expressively.**

**expressly** /ɪk'sprɛsli/ *adverb*
with clear purpose: *He sent flowers expressly for you.*

**expressway** /ɪk'sprɛsˌweɪ/ *noun*
a highway usually with six to eight paths (lanes): *The expressway takes you into Boston quickly and avoids the back streets.*

**expulsion** /ɪk'spʌlʃən/ *noun*
a sending out: *You could see expulsion of dust from the volcano from miles away.*||*The child's bad behavior resulted in her expulsion from school.*

**extend** /ɪk'stɛnd/ *verb*
to make longer: *I extended the antenna on my radio to its full length.*||*We're extending our vacation from two to three weeks.* –*adjective* **extended.**

**extended family** *noun*
an entire family including parents, grandparents, children, aunts, uncles and many other relatives who may live in other households: *Our entire extended family will be here for Thanksgiving dinner. See:* family.

**extension** /ɪk'stɛnʃən/ *noun*
**1** more time: *The student asked the teacher for an extension on his paper.*
**2** one of many connected telephone lines: *Call the company's main number, 555-2000, and ask for my extension, 245 (said "extension 2-4-5").*

**extent** /ɪk'stɛnt/ *noun, (no plural)*
an amount, degree: *The economy has slowed to a great extent.*

**exterior** /ɪk'stɪriər/ *noun*
the outside of something: *The exterior of the house needs painting.*

**exterminate** /ɪk'stɜrməˌneɪt/ *verb* **exterminated, exterminating, exterminates**
to kill all of a group of people or other living things: *Some people exterminate garden insects by spraying poison on the plants.* –*noun* (action) **extermination,** (person) **exterminator.**

**external** /ɪk'stɜrnəl/ *adjective*
outside: *The external surface of the airplane is very smooth and shiny.* –*adverb* **externally.** *(antonym)* internal.

**extinct** /ɪk'stɪŋkt/ *adjective*
no longer in existence, especially a kind of plant or animal: *The passenger pigeon is an extinct species.* –*noun* **extinction.**

**extinguish** /ɪk'stɪŋgwɪʃ/ *verb*
to stop: *Firefighters extinguished a fire.*

**extinguisher** /ɪk'stɪŋgwɪʃər/ *noun*
*short for* a fire extinguisher, a device that shoots out liquid to stop a fire

extinguisher

**extra** /'ɛkstrə/ *adjective*
**1** more than the usual: *That store charges an extra amount for home delivery.*
**2** duplicate: *We keep extra light bulbs in the closet.*
**3** more than needed: *After the party was over, we had extra food.* *–noun* **extra.**

**extract** /ɪk'strækt/ *verb*
to remove, pull out (something firmly fixed): *The dentist extracted a bad tooth.*

**extracurricular** /ˌɛkstrəkə'rɪkyələr/ *adjective*
outside (or) after school: *His extracurricular activities include playing football and singing in the choir.*

---

**USAGE NOTE:** *Extracurricular activities* are strongly encouraged for high school and college students in the USA because they help students develop many different skills and abilities. Common activities are playing sports, writing for a school newspaper, joining a science or language club, playing in a band, or running for student government.

---

**extraordinary** /ɪk'strɔrdnˌɛri/ *adjective*
**1** outstanding, wonderful: *The violinist gave an extraordinary performance.*
**2** uncommon: *She is a woman of extraordinary strength.* *–adverb* **extraordinarily.**

**extravagant** /ɪk'strævəgənt/ *adjective*
too generous or expensive: *She gives extravagant gifts to her family for their birthdays.* *–adverb* **extravagantly.**

**extreme** /ɪk'strim/ *adjective*
the farthest away: *Our house is at the extreme end of the road.*

**extremely** /ɪk'strimli/ *adverb*
very: *That movie was extremely funny.*

**eye** /aɪ/ *noun*
**1** the organ of sight: *She has beautiful brown eyes.*
**2** the center of something: *the eye of a hurricane*
**3** the hole in a needle

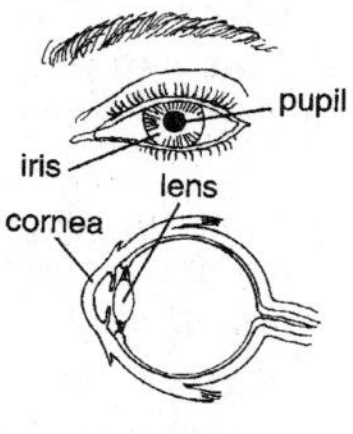

eye

**to catch someone's eye:** to get someone's attention: *I tried to catch the waiter's eye.*

**to keep an eye on someone or something:** to watch in a protective way: *When we went away on vacation, I asked the neighbors to keep an eye on our house.*

**to see eye to eye (with someone):** to agree: *We see eye to eye on the matter, so let's sign a contract.* *See:* art on page 21a.

**eyeball** /'aɪˌbɔl/ *noun*
the entire ball-shaped eye: *The eyeball is a delicate organ.*

**eyeball** *verb slang*
to look at closely, examine: *What you are telling me about the place is interesting, but I want to go there and eyeball it for myself.*

**eyebrow** /'aɪˌbraʊ/ *noun*
the line of hair over the eye. *See:* art on page 21a.

**eye contact** *noun*
a look directly at the eyes of another person: *They are angry at each other and do not make eye contact when they meet.*

---

**USAGE NOTE:** In American culture, a person who does not use *eye contact* might be considered rude or dishonest. On the other hand, someone who *looks you in the eye is* believed to be honest and truthful.

---

**eyeglasses** /'aɪglæsɪz/ *noun plural*
a pair of lenses in a frame used for better sight: *She wears eyeglasses for reading.*

**eyelash** /'aɪˌlæʃ/ *noun, plural* **eyelashes**
a hair from the row of hairs on the eyelids: *She wears false eyelashes that are long and black.*

**eyelid** /'aɪˌlɪd/ *noun*
the folds of skin over the eyeballs: *She carefully applied make-up to her eyelids.*

**eyesight** /'aɪˌsaɪt/ *noun, (no plural)*
ability to see, *(synonym)* vision: *He lost his eyesight in an accident. (antonym)* blindness.

# F,f

F

**F, f** /ɛf/ *noun* **F's, f's or Fs, fs**
**1** the sixth letter of the English alphabet
**2** a grade you receive when you fail an exam: *He was shocked when he got an F on his history test. See:* Fahrenheit.

**fable** /ˈfeɪbəl/ *noun*
a story or poem, usually with animals that often teaches a lesson

**fabric** /ˈfæbrɪk/ *noun*
cloth material: *She made a dress out of the cotton fabric.*

**fabulous** /ˈfæbyələs/ *adjective*
great, wonderful: *We had a fabulous vacation!*

**facade** /fəˈsɑd/ *noun*
the front or outside part of a building: *The facade of that building is made of wood.*

**face** /feɪs/ *noun*
**1** the front of the head: *That young woman has a pretty face. See:* art on page 21a.
**2** the front or outside part of something: *the face of a clock (building, mountain, etc.)*

**to make a face:** to show that one doesn't like something by the expression on one's face: *My son makes a face when I tell him to eat his vegetables.*

**face** *verb* **faced, facing, faces**
**1** to present a front to someone or something: *I sat in the first row and faced the teacher.*||*My apartment faces the park.*
**2** to meet with courage: *I decided finally to stand up and face my enemy.*

**face-lift** *noun*
a surgical operation on the face to make a person look younger: *At age 60 the actor decided to have a face-lift.*

**facial** /ˈfeɪʃəl/ *adjective*
related to the face: *Her facial expression changed to happiness when she heard the good news.*

**facial** *noun*
a treatment to improve the face's skin: *She went to a beauty salon to have a facial.*

**facilitate** /fəˈsɪləˌteɪt/ *verb* **facilitated, facilitating, facilitates**
to help, make easier: *The tourist office sent us a guide who facilitated our travel through Japan.*

**facility** /fəˈsɪləti/ *noun, plural* **facilities**
service(s), including the physical area that an organization provides: *The sports facility at that club includes tennis courts and a swimming pool.*

**facsimile** /fækˈsɪməli/ *noun*
*See:* fax.

**fact** /ˈfækt/ *noun*
something that is real (not opinion) such as an event, date, physical object, or number: *The news reporter went to find out the facts behind the story. –adjective* **factual.**

**the facts of life** or **a fact of life: a.** a usually unpleasant part of life that one must accept: *Having to work for a living is a fact of life for most people.* **b.** *figurative* information about sex: *The mother explained the facts of life to her daughter.*

**faction** /ˈfækʃən/ *noun*
a group of people within a larger group: *One faction within the Liberal Party wants a tax freeze.*

**factor** /ˈfæktər/ *noun*
**1** a fact that one needs to consider: *The high cost of labor is an important factor in the price of steel.*
**2** a number by which a larger number can be divided: *Two and four are factors of eight.*

**factory** /ˈfæktəri/ *noun, plural* **factories**
a building or group of buildings where people work, usually with machines, to make things

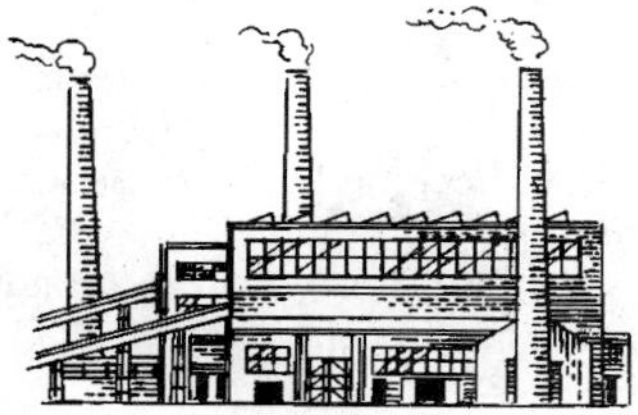

factory

**faculty** /ˈfækəlti/ *noun, plural* **faculties**
**1** special ability: *She has the faculty to express herself well.*
**2** *plural* powers of the mind: *The old man has lost his faculties and cannot take care of himself.*
**3** *used with a singular or plural verb* the teaching staff at a school: *That university has an excellent faculty.*

**fad** /fæd/ *noun*
a fashion that lasts a short time: *The current fad among young people is to wear baseball caps. –adjective* **faddish.**

**fade** /feɪd/ *verb* **faded, fading, fades**
to lose the original color, grow pale: *The wallpaper has faded from red to pale pink.*

**Fahrenheit** /ˈfær ən,haɪt/ *adjective*
a system of measuring temperature in which water freezes at 32° and boils at 212°: *The temperature is 90 degrees Fahrenheit this afternoon; it's really hot! See:* Centigrade, Celsius.

**fail** /feɪl/ *verb*
**1** to not succeed: *He failed his math test.*
**2** to not work when needed: *The automobile brakes failed when he tried to stop.*
**3** to lose strength and ability: *The old man is failing rapidly and may die soon.*

**failing** /ˈfeɪlɪŋ/ *noun*
a fault: *The student's failing is that he does not study enough.*

**failure** /ˈfeɪlyər/ *noun*
**1** a person who fails: *He cannot keep a job, so he feels he is a failure in life. (antonym)* success.
**2** a situation in which something stops working: *A failure in the electrical system caused the lights to go out.*
**3** not carrying out one's responsibilities: *Her failure to act in time caused the company to suffer a big loss.*

**faint** /feɪnt/ *verb*
to fall unconscious, *(synonym)* to pass out: *She fainted from the sun's heat.*

**faint** *adjective*
**1** unclear, weak: *The image is too faint to see what it is.||We heard a faint cry for help from the bottom of the mountain.*
**2** dizzy, weak: *I feel faint from the heat.*

**fair** /fɛr/ *adjective*
**1** just, not favoring one side (group, person, etc.) over another: *The judge's decision was fair to both sides.*
**2** honest: *He offered me a fair price for the car.*
**3** light-haired and light-skinned: *Both she and her brother are fair.*
**4** bright, sunny: *We have fair weather so we can work in our garden.*
**5** neither good nor bad, average: *The student's grades were just fair now.*

**fair** *noun*
an event where people show, buy, and sell products: *One of our pigs won first prize at the county fair.||There is a famous book fair in Frankfurt, Germany.*

**fair** *adverb*
**fair and square:** justly and honestly: *I won the race fair and square. –noun* **fairness.**

**fairly** /ˈfɛrli/ *adverb*
**1** justly, not favoring one side (group, person, etc.) over another: *The boss acts fairly toward all her employees.*
**2** not too much or too little: *He should arrive here fairly soon. See:* kind of, USAGE NOTE.

**fairy** /ˈfɛri/ *noun, plural* **fairies**
a small, imaginary creature with magical powers: *When children lose their baby*

*teeth, the Tooth Fairy puts money under their pillows.*

**fairy tale** *noun*
a children's story with magical creatures and interesting adventures: *Parents read fairy tales to their children before bedtime.*

**faith** /feɪθ/ *noun*
**1** strong belief, not based on facts, that an event will have a good result: *I have faith that she will completely recover from her illness.*
**2** great trust in someone: *He has faith that his family will always help him.*
**3** a specific religion: *The school is open to children of all faiths.*

**to have faith in someone** or **something:** to believe in someone or something, especially in God: *My husband has faith in God.*

**faithful** /ˈfeɪθfəl/ *adjective*
**1** true to a religion: *Churchgoers are faithful to their religious beliefs.*
**2** loyal to one's husband, wife, boyfriend, or girlfriend by not having a sexual relationship with someone else: *He has always been faithful to his wife.*
**3** according to the facts: *Her book was a faithful account of the years she spent in jail as a political prisoner.* –*adverb* **faithfully.**

**faithless** /ˈfeɪθlɪs/ *adjective*
immoral, disloyal: *The wife rejected her faithless husband.*

**fake** /feɪk/ *noun*
**1** a copy, usually of something valuable: *That painting is a fake.*
**2** person claiming to be someone or something he or she is not: *That man pretends to be a cop, but he's a fake.*

**fake** *verb* **faked, faking, fakes**
to make or write something in order to deceive: *He faked his wife's signature on a check.*

**falcon** /ˈfælkən/ *noun*
a bird that can be trained to hunt small animals –*noun* (person) **falconer,** (activity) **falconry.**

**fall** /fɔl/ *noun*
**1** a sudden move to the ground from a standing position: *He took a bad fall and broke his ankle.*
**2** a severe loss of status or power: *The political leader had a fall from power.*
**3** the season between summer and winter, *(synonym)* autumn: *In the fall, the leaves change to bright colors. See:* rainfall; snowfall; waterfall.

**fall** *verb* **fell** /fɛl/, **fallen** /ˈfɔlən/, **falling, falls**
**1** to move suddenly to the ground from a standing position: *She fell and hurt her head.||He fell into the pool (out the window, down the stairs, etc.).*
**2** to suffer a large loss of status or power: *The government fell and was replaced by another.*
**3** to drop, become less: *The price of oil fell sharply.*
**4** to pass into a new state or condition: *He fell asleep while watching TV.||She fell ill for a month.*

**to fall all over oneself:** to try hard, be eager: *He fell all over himself trying to please his new boss.*

**to fall back on someone** or **something:** to depend on in case of need: *When she lost her job, she fell back on piano playing for money.*

**to fall behind someone** or **in/on something:** to be unable to continue at the same level or rate: *One marcher fell behind the others.||The woman fell behind in her rent payments.*

**to fall flat on one's face:** **a.** to move completely to the ground from a standing position: *He was ice skating and fell flat on his face.* **b.** to fail completely: *She tried to become an actress in New York but fell flat on her face.*

**to fall for someone:** to fall in love with: *She was so beautiful that he fell for her right away.*

**to fall in love:** to suddenly form deep feelings of love for someone or something: *He fell in love with her the first time they met.||She fell in love with California on a trip there.*

**to fall through:** to fail to happen: *The deal that we made fell through at the last minute.*

**fallen** /ˈfɔlən/ *verb*
*past participle of* fall

**falling-out** *noun*
a disagreement between people resulting

in an end to their friendship: *The two men had a falling-out over a woman and didn't speak to each other for years.*

**false** /fɔls/ *adjective* **falser, falsest**
**1** incorrect, untrue: *The test consisted of questions that had to be answered as either true or false.*
**2** disloyal, unfaithful: *She pretended to be my friend, but her friendship was false.*
**3** not real: *He has false teeth. –noun* **falsehood.**

**false alarm** *noun*
the setting off of an alarm when there is no real danger: *False alarms anger firefighters, who have to answer them.*

**falsify** /ˈfɔlsəˌfaɪ/ *verb* **falsified, falsifying, falsifies**
to make something false by changing it, to lie about: *He falsified his past in order to get the job. –noun* **falsification.**

**fame** /feɪm/ *noun, (no plural)*
the state of being well-known and talked about: *The rock singer enjoyed wealth and fame for many years. –adjective* **famous.**

**familiar** /fəˈmɪlyər/ *adjective*
**1** knowing about (something): *I'm familiar with that neighborhood because I lived there for many years.*
**2** more friendly than is proper: *When he tried to kiss her, she told him that he was getting too familiar. –noun* **familiarity;** *–verb* **to familiarize.**

**family** /ˈfæməli/ *noun, plural* **families**
**1** one's closest relatives, usually parents, children, brothers, and sisters: *His family consists of his mother, a sister in Florida, and himself.*
**2** a group related by blood or marriage: *Most of my family lives on the West Coast, but I have some cousins in Chicago. See:* extended family; nuclear family.

**family name** *noun*
one's last name: *His family name is Cruz.*

**family tree** *noun*
a drawing that shows the relationship of a large number of family members: *The couple has their family tree hanging on a wall in their living room.*

**famine** /ˈfæmɪn/ *noun*
a serious lack of food: *Famine is sometimes caused by a long period without rainfall.*

**famous** /ˈfeɪməs/ *adjective*
very well-known: *She is a famous Hollywood actress. –adverb* **famously.**

**fan** /fæn/ *noun*
**1** a person who is very interested in someone or something, such as a sport, a type of music, an actor, etc.: *She is a great fan of that rock group and never misses their concerts.*
**2** a handheld or mechanical device that creates a current of air in order to cool: *In the summer, we use the fan to keep cool. See:* art on page 22a.

fan

**fan** *verb* **fanned, fanning, fans**
to move air with a fan: *I fanned the flames in the fireplace.*

**fanatic** /fəˈnætɪk/ *noun*
a person who shows too much enthusiasm for something: *He is a political fanatic who is in favor of violent revolution. –adjective* **fanatical;** *–noun* **fanaticism.**

**fancy** /ˈfænsi/ *adjective* **fancier, fanciest**
**1** not plain or simple: *They wear fancy clothes and live in a fancy neighborhood.*
**2** of high quality, special: *He enjoys eating and buys fancy foods at expensive shops.*

**fang** /ˈfæŋ/ *noun*
a long, sharp, pointed tooth

**fanny** /ˈfæni/ *noun slang, plural* **fannies**
the part of the body on which a person sits: *I slipped while roller skating and fell on my fanny.*

**fanny pack** *noun*
a small bag worn around the waist for carrying money, keys, etc.: *When Pedro rides his bike to school, he puts his money and some crackers in his fanny pack.*

fanny pack

**fantasize** /ˈfænt əˌsaɪz/ *verb* **fantasized, fantasizing, fantasizes**
to have imaginary desires and experiences: *She fantasizes that she is a famous singer.*

**fantastic** /fænˈt æstɪk/ *adjective*
**1** *informal* wonderful, fabulous: *We had a fantastic time on our vacation in the Rocky Mountains.*
**2** imaginative, strange, and unreal: *The movie was filled with fantastic, strange-looking animals.* –*adverb* **fantastically.**

**fantasy** /ˈfæntəsi/ *noun, plural* **fantasies**
an imaginative, unreal picture, thought or story: *He has fantasies about meeting a beautiful movie star.*

**far** /fɑr/ *adverb* **farther** /ˈfɑrðər/ **farthest** /ˈfɑrðɪst/
**1** to a great distance: *We had to walk far to get to the nearest gas station.*
**2** for a long time: *The effects of the disaster will last far into the future.*
**3** much more: *He failed the test but promises to do far better next time.*

**as far as: a.** to a specific point in space: *From the hill, we could see as far as the nearest village.* **b.** as much as: *As far as I know, the trains are running on time.*

**by far:** greatly, very much: *He is by far the best football player in the league.*

**far from:** not at all: *We are far from happy with the results of the election.*

**far off: a.** in the distant future: *The date of our departure is not far off.* **b.** incorrect: *He is not far off when he says that the economy is improving.*

**so far, so good:** everything has been fine until now: *I was worried that my math course was going to be difficult, but so far, so good.*

**farce** /fɑrs/ *noun*
(in the theater) a type of humorous play filled with foolish situations

**fare** /fɛr/ *noun*
**1** the cost of a ride, such as on a bus, train, or boat: *You pay the fare when you get on the bus.*
**2** a passenger: *The bus has 20 fares on it.*

**Far East** *noun, (no plural)*
the countries of eastern Asia: *I travel on business to the Far East once a year.*

**farewell** /ˌfɛrˈwɛl/ *interjection old usage*
good-bye (for a long time or forever): *He said farewell to his family and boarded the ship.*

**farewell** *adjective*
relating to a person's leaving: *We had a farewell party* or *farewell dinner for him before he left.*

**farm** /fɑrm/ *noun*
a piece of land for raising crops and animals, usually with a farmhouse, barn(s), and equipment: *As a boy, I lived on a farm in Maine.*
–*noun* (person) **farmer.**

farm

**farm** *verb*
to raise crops and animals: *Her family has farmed their land for a hundred years.* –*noun* (activity) **farming.**

**farmland** /ˈfɑrmˌ lænd/ *noun*
land used in farming

**far-sighted** *adjective*
able to see clearly only at a distance: *He is far-sighted, so he needs glasses for reading. (antonym)* near-sighted.

**farther** /ˈfɑrðər/ *adjective*
*comparative of* far: more distant: *He moved farther away from the table and stood up.*

**farthest** /ˈfɑrðɪst/ *adjective*
*superlative of* far: *Of all our friends, the Nelson family lives farthest away.*

**fascinate** /ˈfæsəˌneɪt/ *verb* **fascinated, fascinating, fascinates**
**1** to interest greatly, hold the attention of someone: *The customs and traditions of other societies often fascinate people.*
**2** to strongly attract: *She fascinates friends with her intelligence and charm.*
–*adjective* **fascinating;** –*noun* **fascination.**

**fashion** /ˈfæʃən/ *noun*
**1** any style of dress popular for a period of time: *It was the fashion for women to wear gloves when they went out.*

**2** *(no plural)* a manner, way: *The children formed a line in an orderly fashion.*
**in fashion** or **out of fashion:** popular or unpopular at a particular time: *Although the writer died over fifty years ago, his ideas are still in fashion.*

---

**USAGE NOTE:** New York is the center of the USA's *fashion* industry.

---

**fashionable** /'fæʃənəbəl/ *adjective*
in the latest style: *Her clothes are very fashionable.*

**fast** /fæst/ *adverb*
**1** rapidly, quickly: *That athlete can run fast. (antonym)* slow.
**2** faster than normal speed: *My watch is running five minutes fast.*
**3** deeply, completely: *The baby is fast asleep now.*

**fast** *adjective*
**1** rapid, quick: *We took a fast train from New York to Boston.*
**2** done quickly: *He finished the job in half an hour, which was fast work!*

**fast** *verb*
to eat and drink little or nothing: *From time to time, I fast for a day to lose weight. –noun* **fast.**

**fasten** /'fæsən/ *verb*
**1** to attach: *He fastened pictures on the wall with tape.*
**2** to close (button, tie, etc.): *She fastened the buttons on her blouse. –noun* (thing) **fastener.**

**fast food** *noun*
food prepared in advance, kept warm or covered until ordered, and served rapidly as one pays for it: *I eat fast food every day at lunch.*

---

**USAGE NOTE:** An American invention, *fast food* is now sold in countries all over the world at restaurants such as McDonald's™ or Pizza Hut™.

---

**fastidious** /fæ'stɪdiəs/ *adjective*
very careful, paying (too) close attention to details: *Our English teacher is fastidious about our spelling.*

**fat** /fæt/ *adjective* **fatter, fattest**
weighing too much, heavy: *She exercises every day to avoid getting fat. See:* overweight, USAGE NOTE.

**fat** *noun*
**1** a soft, oily substance found under the skin of people and animals: *Some beef has a lot of fat in it.*
**2** this substance specially prepared for use in cooking: *There's a lot of butter in the cream sauce, so it's high in fat.*

**fatal** /'feɪtl/ *adjective*
**1** causing death: *The poor man had a fatal heart attack.*
**2** resulting in disaster, tragedy: *She made the fatal mistake of returning to her country just as the war began. –adverb* **fatally;** *–noun* **fatality.**

**fate** /feɪt/ *noun*
**1** a force or power that people believe determines in advance everything that happens: *Fate brought the two leaders together so that they might bring peace to the world.*
**2** a sad end: *It was while mountain climbing that he fell and met his fate (death).*

**father** /'fɑðər/ *noun*
**1** one's male parent: *His father lived to be 90 years old.*
**2 Father: a.** God: *Oh Father, please listen to my prayer.* **b.** the form of address for a Catholic or Anglican priest: *Father Tomkins comforts the poor. –adjective* **fatherly.** *See:* art on page 13a.

**father** *verb*
to cause a woman to give birth to a child: *He fathered two children. –noun* **fatherhood** /'fɑðər,hʊd/.

**father-in-law** /'fɑðərɪn,lɔ/ *noun, plural* **fathers-in-law**
the father of either one's husband or one's wife: *He and his father-in-law often go fishing together. See:* art on page 13a.

**fatherland** /'fɑ ðər,lænd/ *noun*
the country of one's birth

**Father's Day** *noun*
a day honoring fathers, held on the third Sunday in June: *We celebrated Father's Day by bringing Dad breakfast in bed.*

**fatigue** /fə'tig/ *noun*
**1** *(no plural)* the feeling of being very tired: *He is suffering from fatigue and wants to go to bed early.*

**2** *plural* military clothes: *Soldiers wear fatigues.*

**fatigue** *verb* **fatigued, fatiguing, fatigues**
to make someone tired: *Long car trips fatigue me.*

**fatten** /ˈfætn/ *verb*
**1** to make fat: *The farmer fattened the turkey in preparation for the Thanksgiving Day meal.*
**2** to grow fat: *That baby has really started to fatten up.*

F

**fatty** /ˈfæti/ *adjective* **fattier, fattiest**
containing a lot of fat: *I didn't buy the meat because it was too fatty.*

**faucet** /ˈfɔsɪt/ *noun*
a device that controls the flow of water or other liquids: *The plumber said that I needed to buy a new faucet.*

**fault** /fɔlt/ *noun*
**1** something that does not work properly, *(synonym)* an imperfection: *There is a fault in the computer system.*
**2** a weak point in someone's character: *He has some faults, such as sometimes talking too much.*
**3** blame, responsibility (for a mistake): *Nobody knew who was at fault for the train accident.*
**4** a large crack in the surface of the earth: *The San Andreas fault lies near San Francisco, where the fault line runs north and south.*

**to find fault with:** to criticize, usually too often: *He complained that his boss was always finding fault with his work.*

**fault** *verb*
to criticize, blame: *I fault him for not delivering the product on time. –adjective* **faultless;** *–adverb* **faultlessly.**

**faulty** /ˈfɔlti/ *adjective* **faultier, faultiest**
**1** not working properly: *The fire was caused by faulty electrical wiring.*
**2** incorrect: *Faulty thinking on his part caused the mistake.*

**favor** /ˈfeɪvər/ *verb*
to prefer: *I favor leaving today instead of tomorrow.*

**favor** *noun*
a helpful act: *He did me a favor by lending me his car.*

**in favor of:** on the side of, in support of: *The hospital workers voted in favor of the new contract.*

**favorable** /ˈ feɪvərəbəl/ *adjective*
approving, positive: *I received a favorable report from the doctor. –adverb* **favorably.**

**favorite** /ˈfeɪvərɪt/ *adjective*
most preferred: *Chocolate is my favorite candy. –noun* (person or thing) **favorite.**

**fawn** /fɔn/ *noun*
a young deer

**fax** /fæks/ *noun, plural* **faxes**
**1** a document sent electronically through telephone lines: *I sent a fax of my letter (order, illustration, etc.) to our Hong Kong office.*
**2** a machine used to send an electronic document, a fax machine. *See:* art on page 20a.

**fax** *verb* **faxed, faxing, faxes**
to send a fax: *I faxed it this morning. See:* facsimile.

**FBI** /ˌɛfbiˈaɪ/ *noun*
*abbreviation of* Federal Bureau of Investigation in the USA, the government agency that investigates crimes in which a national law has been broken: *The FBI discovered that the man was selling secrets to a foreign government.*

---

**USAGE NOTE:** People usually refer to government agencies, such as the *FBI* (Federal Bureau of Investigation) by their initials because their names are so long. Others are the *FDA* (Food and Drug Administration), *EPA* (Environmental Protection Agency), and *IRS* (Internal Revenue Service).

---

**fear** /fɪr/ *noun*
a strong feeling of fright or worry that something bad will happen: *a fear of dogs||He has a fear that the economy will become worse.*

**fear** *verb*
**1** to feel a strong fright: *He fears snakes.*
**2** to view with anxiety: *She fears that something terrible will happen to her children on their way to school. –adjective* **fearful;** *–adverb* **fearfully.**

**fearless** /ˈfɪrlɪs/ *adjective*
without fear, *(synonym)* courageous: *Even though her fight for women's rights*

*is unpopular, she is fearless in continuing it.* –*adverb* **fearlessly;** –*noun* **fearlessness.**

**feast** /fist/ *noun*
a large, rich meal: *Every Thanksgiving, my whole family gets together and has a feast.* –*verb* **to feast.**

**feat** /fit/ *noun*
an impressive act, showing strength, courage, or unusual ability: *The soldier's feats of courage were extraordinary.*

**feather** /ˈfɛðər/ *noun*
one of the many soft, thin parts of a bird that covers its body: *That bird has colorful feathers.*

feather

**a feather in one's cap:** an honor for others to admire: *His graduating first in his class is a feather in his cap.* –*verb* **to feather;** –*adjective* **feathery.**

**feature** /ˈfitʃər/ *noun*
**1** an important part or special quality of a product or service: *The salesman described to us the car's many features.*
**2** *plural* **features:** the mouth, chin, nose, eyes, etc. of the human face: *That model has beautiful features.*

**feature** *verb* **featured, featuring, features**
to advertise as important: *The department store featured lamps and rugs in its annual sale.*

**February** /ˈfɛbyu͵ɛri/ *noun*
the second month of the year, between January and March

**fed** /fɛd/ *verb*
*past tense and past participle of* feed
provided with food: *You can see from his big stomach that he is well fed.*

**fed up:** annoyed or angry about a bad situation that has existed for a long time, *(synonym)* disgusted: *I am fed up with his constant lateness.*

**federal** /ˈfɛdərəl/ *adjective*
(in the USA) related to the national government: *The federal government is providing money for a job training program.* –*adverb* **federally.**

**Federal Bureau of Investigation** *noun*
*See:* FBI.

**federation** /͵fɛdəˈreɪʃən/ *noun*
a group of organizations or states: *A federation of teachers' unions is working hard to improve the educational system.*

**fee** /fi/ *noun*
a charge, cost or payment: *We pay all sorts of fees: a parking fee, a registration fee, tuition fees, and doctors' fees.*

**feeble** /ˈfibəl/ *adjective*
weak, without power or energy: *The elderly lady has become feeble and unable to care for herself.*||*His feeble attempts at solving the problem are worthless.* –*adverb* **feebly.**

**feed** /fid/ *noun*
food that one gives to animals: *Each morning the farmer gives the cows their corn or hay feed.*

**chicken feed:** a small amount of money (said with strong disapproval): *He's crazy to think we will work on Sundays for chicken feed.*

**feed** *verb* **fed** /fɛd/, **feeding, feeds**
**1** to give food: *She gets up early every morning to feed her baby.*||*The farmer feeds his cows.*
**2** to take in as food: *Big fish feed on smaller fish.*
**3** *figurative* to supply with something, such as information or material: *The accounting department feeds information to the other departments in the company.*||*A worker feeds wood into the machine.*

**feedback** /ˈfid͵bæk/ *noun*
criticism of one's ideas (plans, actions, etc.): *The radio station decided to cancel the show after receiving negative feedback from its listeners.*

**feel** /fil/ *verb* **felt** /fɛlt/, **feeling, feels**
**1** to experience a sensation (warmth, cold, pain, hunger, etc.) or emotion: *I feel a little cold.*||*She felt nervous on her wedding day.*
**2** to touch in order to find or learn something: *He felt around in his pocket for the key.*||*The doctor could feel that the bone was broken.*

F

**3** to experience a condition: *The patient feels better today.*||*She felt ill yesterday.*
**4** to have an opinion: *He feels that smoking is bad for his health, so he quit.*
**to feel for someone:** to have sympathy for: *I felt for Tom when his wife died.*
**to feel free:** to be invited to do something: *My friend told me, "Feel free to help yourself to coffee or tea."*
**to feel like:** to have a desire for something: *I feel like having some ice cream.*
**to feel up to something:** to be ready to do something difficult or unpleasant: *He feels up to cleaning out the garage today.*||*She is still not well and doesn't feel up to going out.*

**feel** *noun*
**1** a touch: *I gave the paint a feel to see if it was still wet.*
**2** an understanding, a special skill: *My daughter does well in math; she seems to have a real feel for numbers.*
**3** the way something feels when you touch it: *The feel of fine leather is smooth and soft.*
**to get the feel of something:** to become used to or comfortable with: *She drove around to get the feel of the new car.*

**feeling** /ˈfilɪŋ/ *noun*
**1** *(no plural)* ability to recognize touch: *His hands are so cold that he has lost feeling in them.*
**2** an emotion: *The mother has a strong feeling of love for her family.*
**3** a belief that something is true: *I have a feeling that he's an excellent teacher.*
**4** *plural* one's general attitude toward hurt, criticism, etc.: *Her strong criticism hurt her daughter's feelings.*

**feet** /fit/ *noun*
*plural of* foot

**feline** /ˈfiˌlaɪn/ *adjective*
related to cats: *The feline world includes lions, tigers, and house cats.*

**fell** /fɛl/ *verb*
*past tense of* fall

**fellow** /ˈfɛloʊ/ *noun*
*informal* a man or boy: *Charles is a friendly fellow.*

**fellow** *adjective*
referring to people with whom one has something in common: *He lunches with some of his fellow workers (students, scientists, etc.) each day.*

**felony** /ˈfɛləni/ *noun, plural* **felonies**
a major crime, such as murder or rape: *He was sentenced to jail for committing two felonies.* –*noun* (person) **felon.**

**felt (1)** /fɛlt/ *verb*
*past tense and past participle of* feel

**felt (2)** *noun*
a fabric made by pressing together wool and other materials: *His hat is made of felt.*

**female** /ˈfiˌmeɪl/ *noun*
a human or animal of the sex that can produce young: *In the past, females were not permitted to join that club.* –*adjective* **female.**

---

**USAGE NOTE:** Many people avoid the use of *female* as a noun for a person and use *woman* instead.

---

**feminine** /ˈfɛmənɪn/ *adjective*
**1** having characteristics people usually consider typical of women, such as warmth and softness: *The dress she wore made her look feminine.*
**2** (in grammar) referring to a certain class of words: *The word for "house" is feminine in Spanish.* –*noun* **femininity.**

**feminist** /ˈfɛmənɪst/ *noun*
a person who believes that women should have the same rights, opportunities, and treatment as men –*noun* **feminism.**

**fence** /fɛns/ *noun*
a structure made of various materials, such as wood or wire, that is used to prevent people or animals from entering or leaving an area: *The fence around the factory is ten feet (three meters) tall. See:* art on page 9a.
**on the fence:** undecided: *She was on the fence about buying a new car.*

**fence** *verb* **fenced, fencing, fences**
**1** to put a fence around an area: *We fenced the property around the lake.*
**2** to fight with a sword as a sport: *He liked to fence for exercise.*

**fender** /ˈfɛndər/ *noun*
the outer covering above the tire of a car: *The right front fender on my car needs to be repaired.*

**ferocious** /fə'ro ʊʃəs/ *adjective*
violently cruel: *The ferocious attack of the hungry lions left three zebras dead.* –*adverb* **ferociously;** –*noun* **ferocity.**

**Ferris wheel** /'fɛrɪs/ *noun*
an amusement park ride consisting of a large wheel with chairs rising to the top as the wheel goes around

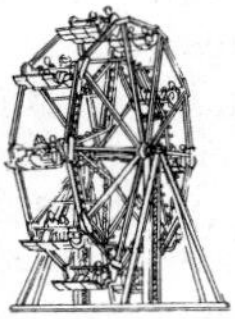
Ferris wheel

**ferry** /'fɛri/ *noun, plural* **ferries**
a type of boat used to carry passengers and goods. –*noun* **ferryman;** –*verb* **to ferry.**

**fertile** /'fɜrtl/ *adjective*
**1** able to produce new plants: *The farmland in Iowa is very fertile.*
**2** able to produce young: *The doctor performed tests to see if she was fertile.* –*noun* **fertility.**

**fertilizer** /'fɜrtl,aɪzər/ *noun*
food for plants, either natural or chemical: *That farmer uses natural fertilizer from his cows.* –*verb* **to fertilize.**

**festival** /'fɛstəvəl/ *noun*
a public celebration, usually of some special occasion: *On Norwegian independence day, the Norwegians in my town hold a festival with singing and dancing.*

**festive** /'fɛstɪv/ *adjective*
joyful, with much food and good spirits: *Our birthday parties are festive occasions with food, wine, and friends.* –*noun* **festivity.**

**fetch** /fɛʧ/ *verb* **fetches**
to get something and bring it back: *If I throw a stick, my dog will fetch it.*

**fetus** /'fitəs/ *noun, plural* **fetuses**
an unborn human or other animal: *The pregnant woman went to the doctor to make sure that the fetus was healthy.*

**feud** /fyud/ *noun*
a disagreement or feeling of strong dislike (between persons, families, groups, etc.): *The feud between the families has gone on for almost seventy years.* –*verb* **to feud.**

**fever** /'fivər/ *noun*
higher than normal body temperature, usually due to infection –*adjective* **feverish.** *See:* headache, USAGE NOTE.

**few** /'fyu/ *adjective*
**1** (with "a") not many: *Those plastic rings cost only a few cents to make.*||*Most students come on time, but a few are always late.*
**2** (without "a") not many, not enough: *Few people registered for the course, so the college canceled it.*

**few and far between:** rare: *Shoppers are few and far between today because of the bad weather.*

---

**USAGE NOTE:** Compare: *He has a few friends* with *he has few close friends.* We use "a" before "few" if we want to say that he has at least some friends, though not many. We leave out "a" if we want to say that he has almost no close friends.

---

**fiancé** /,fiɑn'seɪ/ *noun*
a woman's future husband: *Her fiancé is Brazilian.* –*noun* (female) **fiancée.**

**fiber** /'faɪbər/ *noun*
**1** natural or artificial threads used to make cloth, or rope: *cotton, wool, nylon, silk fiber*
**2** *(no plural)* the part of a plant taken in as food that helps food pass quickly through the body: *Doctors say you should eat food that is high in fiber.*

**fiction** /'fɪkʃən/ *noun, (no plural)*
**1** stories that a writer imagines, as opposed to true stories: *The author's new novel is a fine work of fiction.*
**2** something unreal, a lie: *What that man says about his past is pure fiction.* –*adjective* **fictional.**

---

**USAGE NOTE:** *Novels* and *short stories* are works of *fiction.* The class of *nonfiction* includes *essays, biographies,* and *history books.*

---

**fiddle** /'fɪdl/ *noun*
a violin used for folk or popular music: *My friend plays the fiddle in a country band.*

**fiddle** *verb* **fiddled, fiddling, fiddles**
to move something around a little with

one's fingers: *He fiddled with the wires and got the radio to work again.*

**field** /fild/ *noun*
**1** an area of land used for a specific purpose: *a field of corn, an oil field, a baseball (football, soccer) field*
**2** an area of activity, interest, or study: *His daughter has always been interested in the field of medicine. See:* art on page 9a.

**field trip** *noun*
a trip one takes outside the classroom, laboratory, or office for purposes of study

**fiend** /find/ *noun*
an evil person, *(synonym)* monster *–adjective* **fiendish.**

**fierce** /fɪrs/ *adjective* **fiercer, fiercest**
**1** cruelly violent: *Fierce animals, such as the lion and bear, are very frightening when they attack.*
**2** very strong: *The government ran into fierce opposition to its proposal. –adverb* **fiercely;** *–noun* **fierceness.**

**fiery** /'faɪəri/ *adjective* **fierier, fieriest**
**1** full of fire: *The building became a fiery trap for the firefighters.*
**2** full of emotion: *a fiery speech*

**fiesta** /fi'ɛstə/ *noun*
a public celebration in Latin countries, frequently for a religious holiday, with food, music, and dancing: *During the fiesta, there was dancing in the street.*

**fifteen** /ˌfɪf'tin/ *noun*
the cardinal number 15

**fifteen** *adjective*
fifteen of something: *Fifteen students failed the exam.*

**fifteenth** /ˌfɪf'tinθ/ *adjective*
the ordinal number 15

**fifth** /fɪfθ/ *adjective*
the ordinal number 5: *She is the fifth child in the family* (or) *the fifth.*

**fifth** *noun*
a liquid measure of one fifth of a gallon: *He bought a fifth of Scotch for the celebration.*

**fiftieth** /'fɪftiɪθ/ *adjective*
the ordinal number 50

**fifty** /'fɪfti/ *noun, plural* **fifties**
the cardinal number 50

**fifty** *adjective*
fifty of something: *He lost fifty pounds.*

**fifty-fifty:** an equal share or chance: *The plan has a fifty-fifty chance of succeeding.*

**fig** /fɪg/ *noun*
a soft, sweet fruit with many small seeds: *Figs grow in the Mediterranean region.*

**fig.** *abbreviation of*
**1** figurative, not real
**2** figure, as in a picture in a book: *See fig. 4 on page 237.*

**fight** /faɪt/ *verb* **fought** /fɔt/, **fighting, fights**
**1** to argue: *That couple fights continually over* (or) *about money.*
**2** to make a great effort to get something: *Political parties fight each other for votes.*||*Women fought for the right to vote.*
**3** to make a great effort to stop something: *That organization was formed to fight poverty.*
**4** to use physical force: *The two children fought each other with sticks.*||*As a soldier, he fought bravely for his country.*

**to fight a losing battle:** to fight with no chance of winning: *She fought a losing battle against cancer.*

**to fight back:** **a.** to defend oneself: *When the company accused her of stealing, she fought back by hiring a lawyer.* **b.** to hold back: *She fought back her tears.*

**fight** *noun*
**1** an argument, quarrel: *Two friends had a fight over money.*
**2** a physical struggle, a battle: *The two teenagers had a knife fight. –noun* **fighter.**

**figurative** /'fɪgyərətɪv/ *adjective*
related to a word or phrase that expresses meaning in an interesting way, usually through comparison: *When you call a fearful person a mouse, you are using figurative language. –adverb* **figuratively.**

**figure** /'fɪgyər/ *noun*
**1** a number, sum: *The cost figure for that project is a million dollars.*
**2** a person's shape: *That actor has a good figure.*
**3** the form of a person: *In the moonlight, we could see two figures in the distance.*
**4** an important person: *Martin Luther King, Jr. is a famous historical figure.*

**5** a drawing in a book: *The figure on page 63 shows how a car engine works.*

**figure** *verb* **figured, figuring, figures**

**1** to believe, predict: *I figure that it will take us about two hours to climb the mountain.*

**2** to be a part of: *He figures largely in her dreams for the future.*

**That figures!:** something one expects: *That figures! He's always late.*

**to figure on:** to plan, expect: *You can figure on spending $800 for the plane fare.*

**to figure out:** to solve or understand: *The student figured out the solution to the math problem.*

**figure skating** *noun*

the sport of ice skating in various patterns (or figures): *People love to go figure skating on frozen lakes.* –*noun* (person) **figure skater.**

**file (1)** /faɪl/ *noun*

a piece of hard metal with a rough edge used to smooth objects: *She uses a nail file to shape her fingernails.* –*verb* **to file.**

file

**file (2)** *noun*

a folder, box, cabinet, space on a computer disk, etc. used for holding information: *The head office keeps a file on each employee. See:* art on page 20a.

**on file:** existing in a file: *The interviewer promised to keep my job application on file.*

**file (3)** *verb* **filed, filing, files**

to place something in a file: *I filed the daily reports in that cabinet.*

**file (4)** *noun*

a line of people or objects: *The children walked in single file.* –*verb* **to file.**

**file clerk** *noun*

a person employed to get files for use and then put them back: *Computers have replaced file clerks in some businesses.*

**filet** /fɪˈleɪ/ *noun*

*variation of* fillet

**fill** /fɪl/ *verb*

**1** to use all available space: *Children filled the hole with sand.*||*The church was filled with people.*

**2** to pour liquid or pack a substance into a container: *A waiter filled my glass with water.*

**3** to cause someone to experience strong emotion: *The child fills her mother's heart with joy.*

**to fill 'er up** or **fill it up:** to fill a gasoline tank in a car or truck: *I told the gas station attendant to fill 'er up for our trip.*

**to fill in:** **a.** to replace someone temporarily: *The boss was ill, so his assistant filled in for him at the meeting.* **b.** to complete, supply information as on a form: *I filled in the blanks on a job application.*

**to fill out:** to complete: *I filled out a form to apply for a driver's license.*

**to fill someone in on:** to give someone information, to inform about, apprise: *I filled him in on all the details.*

**fill** *noun*

**to have had one's fill of someone** or **something:** to be dissatisfied: *I have had my fill of bad weather and am going to Florida for a vacation.*

**fillet** or **filet** /fɪˈleɪ/ *noun*

a boneless piece of fish or meat: *Fillet of sole is my favorite fish recipe.*

**filling** /ˈfɪlɪŋ/ *noun*

**1** a usually soft food put inside a cake, candy, or sandwich: *Those chocolate candies have a creamy filling.*

**2** a substance used to fill a hole in a tooth: *The dentist replaced two fillings I had lost.*

**filling** *adjective*

(of food) making one feel full: *Spaghetti is very filling.*

**filling station** *noun*

a gas station: *We stopped the car at a filling station to buy some gasoline.*

**USAGE NOTE:** At a *full-service filling station* a worker puts gas in your car and will, if asked, clean the windshield, check the oil, and put air in the tires. A *self-service* station may have no worker to do that, so you must pump the gas and do any other tasks yourself.

**filly** /ˈfɪli/ *noun, plural* **fillies**

a young, female horse

**film** /fɪlm/ *noun*

**1** a thin surface layer of a substance: *I*

F

*washed away a film of grease on the frying pan.*
**2** *(no plural)* material one puts into a camera to take pictures
**3** a movie, motion picture *–noun* **filmmaker.**

**film** *verb*
to make a movie: *The cameraman filmed a scene for a motion picture.*

**filter** /ˈfɪltər/ *noun*
a device used to catch unwanted matter as liquids and gases pass through it: *I use a filter in my coffee machine.* *–verb* **to filter.**

**filth** /fɪlθ/ *noun, (no plural)*
**1** disgusting dirt: *The city streets were filled with filth.*
**2** *figurative* offensive books, pictures, and films, usually related to sex: *That magazine contains filth.*

**filthy** /ˈfɪlθi/ *adjective* **filthier, filthiest**
**1** covered with dirt, disgustingly dirty: *The beggar's clothes are filthy.*
**2** *figurative* offensive, usually in a sexual way: *That store sells filthy magazines.* *–noun* **filthiness.**

**fin** /fɪn/ *noun*
the flat wing-like part of a fish that it uses for movement and balance: *One of the fish's fins got caught in a net.*

fin

**final** /ˈfaɪnl/ *noun*
**1** the last contest in a series (often *plural* **finals**): *The world tennis final will be played tomorrow.*
**2** end of term examination: *I have my chemistry final tomorrow.*

**final** *adjective*
**1** last: *I sat in the final row of the airplane.*
**2** will not change: *The judge's decision is final.* *–adverb* **finally.**

**finally** /ˈfaɪnəli/ *adverb*
in the end, at last: *He finally arrived after driving for ten hours.*

**finance** /fəˈnæns/ *noun*
**1** the science and art of raising and managing large sums of private and public money: *My friend works in finance at an international bank.*
**2** *plural* **finances:** the money that an individual, company, or institution has: *He has difficulty managing his finances and is always in debt.*

**finance** *verb* **financed, financing, finances**
to provide money: *His bank just financed a large building project in India.*||*She is financing her child's college education.* *–adjective* **financial.**

**find** /faɪnd/ *verb* **found** /faʊnd/, **finding, finds**
**1** to discover, either by chance or by searching: *I found $10 on the sidewalk.*
**2** to learn from experience: *She finds that she can lose weight just by eating less.*
**3** to arrive at: *The arrow found its target.*||*I was lost but finally found my way back to the hotel.*
**4** to express a reaction to someone or something: *She found the museum fascinating.*
**to find it (odd, unusual, unlikely, etc.) that:** to make an observation that something is strange: *I find it odd that my friend hasn't called recently; I hope he's not ill.*
**to find something out:** to learn: *I just found out that the payment is due tomorrow.*||*I found this out today.*

**find** *noun*
a valuable discovery: *The deep sea treasure was an exciting find.*||*The new secretary in my office is a real find.*

**fine** /faɪn/ *noun*
money one pays as a punishment for breaking a rule or law: *He paid a fine for parking illegally.*

**fine** *verb* **fined, fining, fines**
to order payment for breaking a rule or law: *The court fined the company for dumping garbage illegally.*

**fine** *adjective* **finer, finest**
**1** excellent: *Now is a fine time to buy property.*
**2** high quality: *That store sells fine jewelry.*||*She has fine taste in clothes.*||*She is a person of fine character.*
**3** deeply felt: *He has a fine sense of hearing (smell, touch, etc.).*
**4** very thin or small: *That knife has a fine edge on its blade* (or) *a fine point on its tip.*

**5** made of thin threads or very small pieces: *That shirt is made of a fine silk.*
**6** well, healthy: *I feel fine today.*

**fine** *adverb informal*
well: *You did fine on your exam.* *–noun* **fineness.**

**finger** /'fɪŋgər/ *noun*
one of the parts of the hand that moves *She told her son not to eat with his fingers. See:* art on page 21a.

**to keep one's fingers crossed:** to wish strongly for something: *I hope it doesn't rain tomorrow; let's keep our fingers crossed.*

**to not lift a finger:** to make no effort to help: *She made all the preparations for the party; her husband didn't lift a finger.*

**to put one's finger on something:** to say exactly what something is: *There's something strange about that man, but I can't put my finger on it.*

**finger** *verb*
to touch or rub with the fingers: *The buyer fingered the cloth to check the quality.*

**fingernail** /'fɪŋgər,neɪl/ *noun*
the hard covering at the end of each finger: *She puts red polish on her fingernails. See:* art on page 21a.

**fingerprint** /'fɪŋgər,prɪnt/ *noun*
the set of narrow lines made by a person's fingertips when they are covered with ink and pressed against paper: *The police keep these fingerprints of criminals for their records.* *–verb* **to fingerprint.**

fingerprint

**finish** /'fɪnɪʃ/ *verb* **finishes**
**1** to complete, to end: *I finished my work in three hours. (antonyms)* begin, start.
**2** to cover the surface of something: *The carpenter finished the table with furniture oil.*

**finish** *noun, plural* **finishes**
**1** the end, termination of an activity or event: *We were present at the finish of the race. (antonym)* start.
**2** a covering or surface: *That table has a smooth and shiny finish.*

**finish line** *noun*
the line that marks the end of a race: *Our horse crossed the finish line far ahead of the others.*

finish line

**fir** /fɜr/ *noun*
a type of tall pine tree with thin pointed leaves found in cool climates: *Firs are often used as Christmas trees.*

**fire** /faɪr/ *noun*
the process of burning, which produces heat and light: *The fire in the stove is hot enough to cook now.||We sat around the fire to keep warm.||The restaurant was closed because of a fire.*

fire

**on fire:** burning, in flames, *(synonym)* ablaze: *The house next door is on fire.*

**to be under fire:** to be under attack: *The soldiers on the bridge are under fire from enemy aircraft.*

**to catch (on) fire:** to start to burn *If you're not careful, the curtains will catch fire from that candle.*

**to fight fire with fire:** to use the same methods as someone else: *He complains to the boss about us, so we'll fight fire with fire and complain to the boss about him.*

**to set fire to** or **to set on fire:** to start something burning: *She accidentally set the bed on fire* (or) *set fire to the bed with a cigarette.*

**fire** *verb* **fired, firing, fires**
**1** to shoot a weapon: *The soldier fired his gun at the enemy.*
**2** to dismiss from employment, to take away someone's job: *The boss fired two workers. See:* quit, USAGE NOTE.

**fire alarm** *noun*
a device that makes a loud sound to warn people of a fire: *Everyone left the build-*

F

*ing when the fire alarm sounded. See:* smoke detector.

**firecracker** /'faɪr,krækər/ *noun*
a light, often colorful explosive used at celebrations: *Some people like to set off firecrackers on Independence Day. See:* fireworks.

**fire department** *noun*
the organization responsible for putting out unwanted fires in a city or town: *We called the fire department when we smelled smoke.*

**fire drill** *noun*
a time at which all people leave a building as practice for a real fire: *The schools have fire drills every month.*

**fire engine** *noun*
a truck with equipment used to put out fires: *A fire engine with six firefighters arrived and put out the grass fire.*

fire engine

**fire escape** *noun*
a metal stairway attached outside a building to provide escape from a fire: *We can reach the fire escape by going out our living-room window.*

**fire extinguisher** *noun*
a container with chemicals under pressure that are shot through a hose to put out fires: *We keep a fire extinguisher in the kitchen.*

**firefighter** /'faɪr,faɪtər/ *noun*
a person employed to put out fires: *The firefighter went into the burning building to save the child.*

**firehouse** /'faɪr,haʊs/ *noun*
a building where fire engines and equipment are kept, often with living space for firefighters

**fire hydrant** *noun*
an upright metal container that has a pipe inside, which is connected to an underground water supply, *(synonym)* fireplug: *Fire-fighters connected their hoses to the nearest fire hydrant.*

fire hydrant

**fireman** /'faɪrmən/ *noun* **firemen** /-mən/
*variation of* firefighter

**fireplace** /'faɪr,pleɪs/ *noun*
a space built into the wall of a building, made of brick or stone, in which fires are set: *Our family sits around the fireplace on cold winter nights.*

**fireplug** /'faɪr,p lʌg/ *noun*
*See:* fire hydrant.

**fireproof** /'faɪr, pruf/ *adjective verb*
not be able to be harmed by fire: *That apartment building is fireproof.*

**fire station** *noun*
*See:* firehouse.

**fireworks** /'faɪr, wɜrks/ *noun plural*
a show of light, colorful explosives for celebration: *The Independence Day fireworks are beautiful to see in the night sky. See:* firecracker.

**firing squad** *noun*
a small unit of soldiers who shoot to kill a prisoner on command: *The prisoner shook with fear as he stood before the firing squad.*

**firm** /fɜrm/ *adjective*
**1** quite solid: *His muscles are firm from exercise.*||*The bed is firm.*
**2** fixed, definite: *Her decision is firm and will not be changed.*||*The price on that item is firm.*
**3** strong, not easily moved: *That house is built on a firm ground.*||*She gave him a firm handshake.*

**firm** *noun*
a business of professionals: *He belongs to a law firm* (or) *an accounting firm.*

**first** /fɜrst/ *adjective*
in the position of number one in a series: *She is the first person in line. (antonym)* last.

**at first glance:** seen or considered quickly, on the surface: *At first glance, the jewels looked real.*
**first things first:** The most important or necessary things must be done before any others: *First things first, you must earn the money to pay for the trip before you go.*
**in the first place:** to be considered before other matters (often used to express frustration): *In the first place, I don't understand what you are talking about, so how can I make a decision?*

**first** *pronoun*
number one in a series: *She was the first to hear the news.*
**at first:** in the beginning in comparison to later events: *At first, I thought he was lying, but I later learned that he was telling the truth.*

**first** *adverb*
occurring before any other action, person, or thing: *He cleaned the floors first before doing the windows.||The horse I picked finished first in the race.||This meeting will cover three issues: first, we shall discuss last year's sales; second, this year's new products; third, new ways of selling our product.*

**USAGE NOTE:** Some prefer to use *firstly, secondly, thirdly,* etc. Either is correct.

**first aid** *noun*
emergency medical treatment that an injured or sick person receives before he or she gets the necessary treatment: *When the worker received a bad cut on his hand, a co-worker gave hm first aid and then took him to the hospital.*

**first base** *noun*
(in baseball) the base that must be reached first by the runner: *The player hit the ball and ran to first base.*

**first-class** *adjective*
referring to the best quality: *They stayed at a first-class hotel.*

**first-class** *adverb*
by rapid mail: *I will send the letter first-class.*

**first cousin** *noun*
the son or daughter of one's aunt or uncle: *Two of my first cousins live in Chicago.*

**first floor** *noun*
the entry-level floor of a house or building: *Our office is on the first floor.*

**USAGE NOTE:** In the USA, the first floor is usually at sidewalk ground level.

**first-generation** *adjective*
being the first children of immigrants to be born in the new country: *My parents came from Italy to America, and I was born in America; I am a first-generation American.*

**first lady** or **First Lady** *noun, plural* **Ladies**
the wife of a leader of a country: *The first lady gave a speech against drugs.*

**USAGE NOTE:** As the wife of the President, the *First Lady* of the USA serves as the official hostess of the White House. She also accompanies her husband on state visits, campaigns for his reelection, and usually gives attention to a social issue such as literacy, drug abuse, or child welfare.

**first name** *noun*
the name that comes before the name of one's family: *His first name is Thomas, but I can't remember his last name.*

**first name** *adjective*
**first-name basis:** referring to a friendly, informal relationship: *The owner and I are on a first-name basis.*

**first person** *noun*
(in grammar) the form of a pronoun or verb that refers to the speaker(s): *For the verb "to be," "I am" is the first person singular and "we are" is the first person plural form.*

**first-rate** *adjective*
excellent, among the best: *She is a first-rate lawyer; she wins cases often.*

**fish** /fɪʃ/ *noun, plural* **fish** or **fishes**
an animal that lives in water and uses openings on the side of its head (gills) to breathe: *I love to eat fish that I catch in the ocean.* *See:* art on pages 14a and 17a.
**to be** or **feel like a fish out of water:** to feel awkward, in the wrong place: *I felt like a fish out of water at that fancy restaurant since I usually eat at fast-food places.*

F

**to drink like a fish:** to drink large amounts of alcohol: *He used to hate beer, but now he drinks like a fish.*

**fish** *verb* **fishes**

**1** to try to catch fish: *When I was little, my uncle used to fish with me.*

**2** *figurative* to search for something with the hand: *She fished in her bag for a pen.*

**to fish someone** or **something out:** to pull out: *Two women fished a little boy out of the water.*||*She opened her handbag and fished out a small key.*

**fish and chips** *noun*

fried pieces of fish served with French fries: *Every Friday, he enjoys fish and chips for lunch.*

**fishbowl** /ˈfɪʃˌboʊl/ *noun*

**1** a bowl used to keep pet fish are kept: *There are two goldfish in the fishbowl.*

**2** *figurative* a place with little or no privacy: *The President lives in a fishbowl; he has no privacy.*

**fisherman** /ˈfɪʃərmən/ *noun* **fishermen** /-mən/

**1** a person who enjoys fishing for sport

**2** a person who earns his living by fishing: *The fisherman takes his boat out to sea early in the morning.*

**fishhook** /ˈfɪʃˌhʊk/ *noun*

a curved piece of thin metal with a sharp, pointed end designed to catch fish by the mouth: *I put a worm on the end of the fishhook.*

fishhook

**fishing** /ˈfɪʃɪŋ/ *noun, (no plural)*

**1** the sport of fishing: *We like to go fishing during our vacation.*

**2** the business of catching and selling fish: *Fishing can be a difficult way to make a living.*

**fishing rod** *noun*

a long, metal stick, fitted with cord or plastic line and used to catch fish: *We use a very strong fishing rod to go deep-sea fishing.*

**fishstick** /ˈfɪʃstɪk/ *noun*

finger-sized pieces of fried fish: *We have fishsticks for dinner once a week.*

**fishy** /ˈfɪʃi/ *adjective* **fishier, fishiest**

**1** smelling like a fish: *The trash has a fishy smell that is making me sick.*

**2** *figurative* strange, possibly dishonest: *Strangers keep going in and out of that house; there is something fishy going on there.*

**fist** /fɪst/ *noun*

the closed hand, especially when used for hitting someone or something: *He hit the table with his fist to get everyone's attention.*

**fit** /fɪt/ *verb* **fitted** or **fit, fitting, fits**

**1** to be the right size and shape: *These shoes fit well; I'll buy them.*||*The key fits into the lock.*

**2** to be suitable for a specific purpose: *That telephone system fits our needs.*

**if the shoe fits, wear it:** if the description of someone is true, then you must accept it: *My friend said, "My girlfriend just told me that I lived like a pig." I said, "Well, if the shoe fits, wear it; your apartment is a complete mess."*

**to fit like a glove:** to fit closely and comfortably, almost perfectly: *These shoes fit like a glove.*

**to fit the bill:** to satisfy or provide just what is needed: *The new paint job really fits the bill in brightening up the house.*

**fit** *noun*

**1** a sudden strong display of anger: *He nearly had a fit when he got a parking ticket.*

**2** the way that something fits: *That suit looks good on you; it has a nice fit.*

**3** a sudden attack of a disease: *a coughing fit*

**fit** *adjective* **fitter, fittest**

**1** in good physical condition, healthy: *He looks fit after his vacation.*

**2** suitable, proper: *Because of his dishonesty, he isn't fit to be mayor.*

**fit to be tied:** very frustrated: *When she heard that her son had crashed the car again, she was fit to be tied.*

**fitness** /ˈfɪtnɪs/ *noun*

**1** a person's physical condition: *To im-*

*prove her fitness, she runs two miles every day.*
**2** suitability: *His poor performance as assistant manager made us doubt his fitness for the position of manager.*

**fitting** /ˈfɪtɪŋ/ *noun*
the act of trying on clothing in order to get the proper size: *The costume designer asked the actor to come in for a fitting this week.*

**fitting** *adjective*
suitable, *(synonym)* proper: *It was a fitting end to the story.*

**five** /faɪv/ *noun*
the cardinal number 5

**five** *adjective*
five of something: *He gave me five dollars.*

**fix** /fɪks/ *verb* **fixes**
**1** to repair: *The mechanic fixed the brakes on my car.*
**2** to correct: *He fixed the mistakes in the report, before giving it to his boss.*
**3** *figurative* (of a competition) to arrange in advance who will win: *The horse race had been fixed.*
**4** to prepare: *He fixed dinner for his wife.*

**fix** *noun, plural* **fixes**
difficulty, a troublesome situation: *He used his credit card too freely and has gotten himself into a fix with high payments.*

**fixture** /ˈfɪkstʃər/ *noun*
parts inside a building, such as faucets, sinks, or bathtub

**fizz** /fɪz/ *verb* **fizzes**
to bubble

**flab** /flæb/ *noun*
loose, fatty flesh: *That man has flab around his waistline.* –*adjective* **flabby.**

**flag** /flæg/ *noun*
a piece of fabric, usually with a design, used as a symbol: *The flags of many countries fly near the United Nations building.*

flags

**flag** *verb* **flagged, flagging, flags**
**to flag down:** to make something (usually a vehicle) stop by waving: *I flagged down a taxi cab to take me to the airport.*

**flagpole** /ˈflægˌpoʊl/ *noun*
a tall pole from which flags are hung

**flake** /fleɪk/ *noun*
a small piece of something, light in weight with a rough or smooth surface: *Americans love breakfast cereals in the form of flakes.* –*adjective* **flaky.**

**flake** *verb* **flaked, flaking, flakes**
to fall off in flakes

**flame** /fleɪm/ *noun*
a hot, bright light produced by burning: *The flames from the fireplace give off a pleasant warmth.*
**to go up in flames:** to burn completely: *The fire spread quickly, and the house went up in flames.*

**flame** *verb* **flamed, flaming, flames**
to produce a flame: *The campfire flamed brightly when we added wood.*

**flamingo** /fləˈmɪŋgoʊ/ *noun, plural* **flamingos** or **flamingoes**
a tall, long-legged, pink water bird

**flammable** /ˈflæməbəl/ *adjective*
capable of catching fire

**flannel** /ˈflænl/ *noun*
a soft wool or cotton fabric: *He wears gray flannel suits.*

**flap** /flæp/ *verb* **flapped, flapping, flaps**
to move up and down, or sideways: *Birds flap their wings.*

**flash** /flæʃ/ *noun, plural* **flashes**
**1** a sudden quick show of light: *There was a flash of lighnting in the storm.*
**2** (in photography) a device for adding light: *The flash on my camera needs batteries.*
**in a flash:** very quickly: *I'll be back in a flash.*

**flash** *verb* **flashes**
**1** to appear suddenly, especially light or fire: *Lightning flashed in the distance.*
**2** to show very briefly: *The gambler flashed a roll of $100 bills.*

**flashbulb** /ˈflæʃˌbʌlb/ *noun*
a bulb that gives off a short strong light used for photography

**flash card** *noun*
a small card with writing on both sides, used for memorizing information: *Those flash cards have a question on one side and the answer on the other.*

**flashlight** /ˈflæʃˌlaɪt/ *noun*
a hand-held light that runs on batteries: *When the lights went out, we used a flashlight to find the exit.*

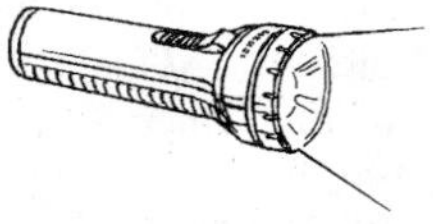
flashlight

**flashy** /ˈflæʃi/ *adjective* **flashier, flashiest**
showy: *He wears flashy clothes and drives an expensive sports car.*

**flat** /flæt/ *adjective* **flatter, flattest**
**1** level, with no higher and lower points: *The farmland near the river is very flat.*
**2** lying full length: *He is flat on his back with the flu.*
**3** without bubbles: *the Coca-Cola™ is flat.*
**a flat tire** or **a flat:** a tire that has lost air: *During our trip across the country, we had a flat* (or) *a flat tire.*

**flat** *adverb*
**1** completely, firmly: *When I asked him for a favor, he turned me down flat.*
**2** (of time) exactly: *He ran the race in six minutes flat.* –*adverb* **flatly;** –*noun* **flatness.**

**flatten** /ˈflætn/ *verb*
to make lower and thinner: *The cook flattens the chopped beef into hamburgers.*

**flatter** /ˈflætər/ *verb*
to praise someone usually in order to win favor: *He flatters his boss by telling her how intelligent she is.* –*noun* (person) **flatterer,** (act) **flattery.**

**flavor** /ˈfleɪvər/ *noun*
a specific taste: *That steak has an excellent flavor.*

**flavor** *verb*
to add a specific taste to something: *She flavored the sauce with salt and pepper.* –*adjective* **flavorful.**

**flavoring** /ˈfleɪvərɪŋ/ *noun*
any ingredient added to food to give it a specific taste: *The company added chocolate flavoring to its ice cream.*

**flaw** /flɔ/ *noun*
something wrong, a fault, imperfection: *a flaw in a diamond.* –*adjective* **flawed.**

**flea** /fli/ *noun*
a very small jumping insect that feeds on blood: *His dog has fleas.*

**flea market** *noun*
an informal outdoor marketplace where people sell things at low prices: *The flea market in our area sells used clothing.*

**flee** /fli/ *verb* **fled** /flɛd/, **fleeing, flees**
to run away, escape

**fleet** /flit/ *noun*
**1** all the ships in a navy or a group of ships: *Honolulu is a major port for the US naval fleet.*
**2** a group of airplanes, trucks, or cars: *American Airlines™ has a large fleet of planes.*

**flesh** /flɛʃ/ *noun*
the skin and the soft substance beneath it: *The doctor cut into the flesh to remove the bullet.*
**flesh and blood:** **a.** the human body: *Those soldiers are made of flesh and blood; be careful with their lives.* **b.** one's closest relatives (parents, brothers, sisters, children): *I must help those children, for they are my own flesh and blood.* –*adjective* **fleshy.**

**flew** /flu/ *verb*
*past tense of* fly

**flexible** /ˈflɛksəbəl/ *adjective*
**1** capable of bending easily: *Rubber and plastic are flexible materials.*
**2** *figurative* able to change easily in a new situation: *She is flexible and always open to new ideas.* –*noun* **flexibility.**

**flick** /flɪk/ *noun*
a quick movement of a finger or wrist: *He removed the piece of dust from the chair with a flick of his finger.*

**flicker** /ˈflɪkər/ *verb*
to shine unsteadily: *The flames of the campfire flickered in the night.*

**flier** or **flyer** /ˈflaɪər/ *noun*
**1** a person who travels on an airplane: *Frequent fliers receive free flights from airlines.*
**2** a pilot: *He is a flier in the Air Force.*
**3** a small printed notice that gives information or advertises something

**flight** /flaɪt/ *noun*
**1** the act of traveling through the air: *The flight of birds seems very easy.*
**2** a trip by air: *Our flight from Chicago to Seattle was pleasant.*
**3** escape: *The television program showed the flight of families from the war.*
**4** a set of stairs: *The women's dress department is up one flight.*
**in flight: a.** running away, especially to escape punishment: *The escaped prisoner is in flight from the law.* **b.** to be in the air: *We arrived late at the airport; our plane was already in flight.*
**to take flight:** to fly: *Birds take flight in the morning to look for food.*

**flight attendant** *noun*
a person who serves passengers on a plane and is responsible for their safety

**flimsy** /ˈflɪmzi/ *adjective* **flimsier, flimsiest**
**1** poorly made, thin: *The jacket is made of flimsy cloth.*
**2** not strong: *That house was built with flimsy materials.*
**3** *figurative* weak: *Erika gave a flimsy excuse for being late. –noun* **flimsiness.**

**fling** /flɪŋ/ *verb* **flung,** /flʌŋ/ **flinging, flings**
to throw, forcefully: *He flung his jacket off angrily.*
**fling** *noun*
a forceful throw: *He gave the ball a fling toward his friend.*

**flip** /flɪp/ *verb* **flipped, flipping, flips**
**1** to turn end over end: *He flipped a coin into the air.*
**2** to throw lightly and quickly: *He flipped the ball to me.*
**3** to turn over suddenly: *The truck flipped over on its side on the icy road.*
**4** *slang* to explode in anger or lose self-control: *He flipped when the teacher told him that he had failed the exam.*
**5** *slang* to show great happiness: *She flipped when she learned that she had won the prize.*

**flirt** /flɜrt/ *verb*
to smile and talk with someone in a way that invites interest in love: *He flirts with every woman he meets. –noun* (person) **flirt;** *–adjective* **flirtatious.**

**float** /floʊt/ *verb*
**1** to rest or move on the top of water or other liquid: *Logs floated downstream on the river.*
**2** to rest or move in the air: *A balloon floats by us. (antonyms)* sink, fall.
**float** *noun*
**1** an object resting on the surface of the water that holds a fishline or net: *The fisherman left early in the morning to set up his floats.*
**2** a flat, unmovable structure in a lake or pond: *People sun themselves on a float near the beach.*
**3** a colorful display set on wheels in a parade: *Clowns wave from a float in the Easter parade.*

**flock** /flɑk/ *noun*
a group of certain animals, such as sheep, goats, chickens, and geese: *a flock of sheep. –verb* **to flock.**

**flood** /flʌd/ *verb*
**1** to cover dry land with water: *The river ran over its banks and flooded the town.*
**2** *figurative* to provide too much of something: *The President was flooded with questions about the scandal. –noun* **flood.**

**floor** /flɔr/ *noun*
**1** the bottom surface area inside a building: *The floor in her apartment is made of wood.*
**2** a level of a building: *That tall building has 50 floors. See:* art on pages 6a and 7a.

**flop** /flɑp/ *verb* **flopped, flopping, flops**
**1** to move awkwardly: *A fish flopped about on the beach.*
**2** to drop heavily: *He was so tired that he flopped on the sofa and fell asleep.*
**3** *figurative* to fail: *The new play flopped and was closed promptly.*
**flop** *noun figurative*
a failure: *The play was a flop.*

**florist** /ˈflɔrɪst/ *noun*
a person who owns or runs a flower shop: *The florist sent flowers for Mother's Day.*

**floss** /flɔs/ *noun*
soft thread used to clean teeth: *I bought some dental floss at the drugstore.*
**floss** *verb* **flosses**

to use dental floss: *He flosses twice daily.*

**flounder** /'flaʊndər/ *noun*
a common type of flatfish

**flour** /'flaʊər/ *noun*
a brown or white powder made from grain used in cakes, bread, cookies, etc.

**flow** /floʊ/ *verb*
to move smoothly, like water: *The river flows to the sea.*

**flow** *noun*
a steady movement: *The flow of the water from the pipe is slow.*

**flower** /'flaʊər/ *noun*
the colorful part of a plant or the plant itself: *We planted flowers—roses and tulips—in the garden.*

flower

**flown** /floʊn/ *verb*
*past participle of* fly

**flu** /flu/ *noun*
*short for* influenza

**fluent** /'fluənt/ *adjective*
able to easily speak or write a language: *She speaks fluent Japanese.* –*noun* **fluency;** –*adverb* **fluently.**

**fluffy** /'flʌfi/ *adjective* **fluffier, fluffiest**
soft and airy: *The pillows are fluffy.*||*The new snow is fluffy.* –*noun* **fluff.**

**fluid** /'fluɪd/ *noun*
a liquid: *The mechanic put fluid in the brake system.*

**flung** /flʌŋ/ *verb*
*past tense and past participle of* fling

**flunk** /flʌŋk/ *verb*
to not pass, to fail: *He flunked a test.*

**flurry** /'flɜri/ *noun, plural* **flurries**
**1** a rush of activity: *a flurry of buying at a department store sale*
**2** a light snowfall: *A snow flurry left a thin layer of snow on the ground.* –*verb* **to flurry.**

**flush** /flʌʃ/ *verb* **flushes**
**1** to wash with water: *A doctor will flush the man's injured eye.*
**2** to become red in the face: *His face flushed after working in the heat.* –*noun* **flush.**

**flute** /flut/ *noun*
a long, tube-shaped musical instrument made of metal with holes along the side –*noun* (musician) **flutist.** *See:* art on page 15a.

**flutter** /'flʌtər/ *verb*
to wave very quickly and lightly: *The flag fluttered in the wind.*||*You could hear birds' wings flutter in the tree.* –*noun* **flutter.**

**fly** /flaɪ/ *verb* **flew** /flu/, **flown** /floʊn/, **flying, flies**
**1** to move through the air: *Birds fly north in the spring.*
**2** to pilot an aircraft: *He flies planes for Swiss Air™.*
**3** *figurative* to move quickly, hurry: *He was late and flew out the door to his next appointment.*

**to fly into a rage** or **off the handle:** to explode in anger: *When he doesn't get what he wants, he flies into a rage* (or) *off the handle.*

**fly** *noun, plural* **flies**
**1** a small, usually two-winged insect: *A fly landed on the table.*
**2** an opening in pants held together by a zipper or buttons: *He zipped up the fly on his jeans.*

**flyer** /'flaɪər/ *noun*
*variation of* flier

**foam** /foʊm/ *noun, (no plural)*
a liquid substance full of air bubbles acting as a covering: *Ocean waves are covered with white foam.* –*verb* **to foam;** –*adjective* **foamy.**

foam

**focus** /'foʊkəs/ *noun, plural* **focuses**
**1** a change (an adjustment of the eye, camera lens, microscope, etc.) to get a clear picture: *I adjusted the focus of the camera to six feet (two meters).*
**2** an object of attention: *The focus of the*

*news report was the state of the economy.*

**focus** *verb* **focuses**

**1** to change in order to get a clear picture: *The photographer focused her camera on the child's face.*

**2** to center one's attention on: *The Senator's speech focused on health care improvement.*

**to be in** or **out of focus:** to have a clear or unclear picture: *We couldn't see their faces; the photograph was out of focus.*

**foe** /foʊ/ *noun*

someone who is against you, enemy: *She was no longer sure if Marco was a friend or foe.*

**fog** /fɔg/ *noun*

a heavy gray cloud near the ground that makes it difficult to see: *The heavy morning fog made driving difficult.*

**fog** *verb* **fogged, fogging, fogs**

to cover or become covered with fog: *The roads are fogged tonight; it will be difficult to drive.||The front window is fogged up, so the driver can't see well.* –*adjective* **foggy.**

**foil** /fɔɪl/ *noun*

a very thin sheet of metal used to wrap or line things: *The cook wrapped the chicken in foil.*

**fold** /foʊld/ *verb*

**1** to turn one part of something over another part: *I folded a piece of paper in half.*

**2** to push movable parts of something together: *We folded the chairs together and set them against the wall.* –*noun* **fold.**

**folder** /ˈfoʊldər/ *noun*

a container for documents, made of a folded piece of heavy paper: *She kept the old newspaper articles in a folder on her desk.*

**folk** /foʊk/ *noun, plural* **folks** or **folk**

**1** *used with plural verb* ordinary people: *His family are country folk; hers are city folk.*

**2** *plural informal* **folks:** parents: *Her folks live in New England.*

**3** *plural informal* **folks:** used when speaking directly to friends, guests: *You folks come in and sit down.*

**folktale** /ˈfoʊkˌteɪl/ *noun*

a well-known story, often by an unknown author, passed down through earlier generations: *Folktales make good bedtime stories for children.*

**follow** /ˈfɑloʊ/ *verb*

**1** to go after someone or something, to chase: *A dog followed its owner down the street. (antonym)* lead.

**2** to go along a path, road, trail, etc.: *We followed the dirt road until we reached the lake.*

**3** to happen after another event: *Rain followed the dark clouds and lightning.*

**4** *figurative* to understand: *I follow what you are saying.*

**5** to obey: *Most members of the political party followed the orders of their leader.*

**6** to pay attention to: *She follows the news closely.*

**to follow in someone's footsteps** or **tracks:** to do the same as the person before you: *She followed in her mother's footsteps and became a musician.*

**to follow something through:** to complete a task after you have finished doing most of it: *He always follows through on projects he begins.*

**follower** /ˈfɑloʊər/ *noun*

person who follows a leader: *The religious leader and his followers entered the temple. (antonym)* leader.

**following** /ˈfɑloʊɪŋ/ *adjective*

next: *She then moved to Mexico the following year.||Write down the following address: 123 Center Street.*

**following** *noun, (no plural)*

**1** a group of admirers or followers: *The writer has a following among college students.*

**2** people or items (in a list): *Bring one of the following as identification: a birth certificate, or a driver's license.*

**following** *preposition*

after: *Following the graduation ceremony, there was a party.*

**fond** /fɑnd/ *adjective*

**1** having warm feelings toward someone or something: *She is fond of children.||He has fond memories of his vacation.*

**2** having a liking, or a preference for: *He*

*is fond of food and drink.* –*adverb* **fondly;** –*noun* **fondness.**

**fondle** /ˈfɑndl/ *verb* **fondled, fondling, fondles**
to touch tenderly, gently: *The mother fondled her baby in her arms.*

**food** /fud/ *noun*
the things that people, animals, and plants eat to keep them alive and help them grow: *She likes to eat spicy food.*

**food processor** *noun*
a machine that cuts and mixes food

**food stamps** *noun plural*
in the USA, tickets provided by the government and used by people of low income to buy food: *She pays for her food at the local supermarket with food stamps.*

**fool** /ful/ *verb*
**1** to deceive: *He fooled her into paying money for the fake necklace.*
**2** to surprise or do something unexpected: *I thought that the exam would be difficult, but it fooled me—it was easy.*
**3** to pretend: *He appeared to be angry but said he was only fooling.*

**to fool around with someone** or **something: a.** to play with: *On weekends he fools around with old cars for fun.* **b.** to be unfaithful in marriage: *Everyone but his wife knows that he fools around.* **c.** to joke or have fun: *Stop fooling around and do some work.*

**to fool with:** to handle something dangerous: *Guns are dangerous; don't fool with them.*

**fool** *noun*
**1** a person with poor judgment: *He is a fool who gambles his money away.*
**2** a person who makes a silly mistake –*adverb* **foolishly;** –*noun* **foolishness.**

**foolish** /ˈfulɪʃ/ *adjective*
showing poor judgment: *She was foolish to spend all her savings on an expensive vacation.*

**foot** /fʊt/ *noun, plural* **feet** /fit/
**1** the body part attached to the lower leg and used for walking: *My right foot hurts. See:* art on page 21a.
**2** a length of measurement equal to 12 inches (approx. 26 cm): *That table is seven feet* (or) *7′ long. See:* art on page 16a.
**3** the lowest part: *He stood at the foot of the stairs (foot of the mountain, hill, etc.).*

**to get cold feet:** to become too nervous to act: *She was about to ask her boss for a raise but then got cold feet.*

**to put one's foot down:** to insist on something: *When her son was getting poor grades in school, she put her foot down and made him study every night.*

**foot** *verb*

**to foot the bill:** to pay the cost of something: *I footed the bill for my daughter's wedding.*

**football** /ˈfʊtˌbɔl/ *noun*
**1** in the USA, a sport played by two 11-person teams with the object of carrying or passing the ball over the other team's goal line: *My friends and I watch football on TV on weekends.*
**2** (non-USA) soccer: *Football is an international sport followed by millions of fans.*
**3** the ball used in either sport

**footprint** /ˈfʊtˌprɪnt/ *noun*
the mark left by a bare foot or shoe on a surface, such as dirt, sand, or a floor: *We followed the footprints along the beach.*

footprints

**footstep** /ˈfʊtˌstɛp/ *noun*
the sound of feet moving on a surface: *We could hear footsteps in the hallway.*

**footwear** /ˈfʊtˌwɛr/ *noun*
shoes and boots, etc.: *This shoe store has a large selection of footwear.*

**for** /fər/ *preposition*
**1** with the purpose of: *I am cutting some wood for fire.*||*She needs glasses for reading.*
**2** in exchange: *I'll give you twenty dollars for that watch.*
**3** in relation to: *The child is tall for his age.*

**4** because of: *San Francisco is famous for its fog.*
**5** in the interest of, to the benefit of: *Mr. Chen speaks for all of us.*||*I baked a cake for you.*
**6** in favor of: *The Senator is for raising taxes.*
**7** in the direction of, as a destination: *Our plane is headed for Taipei.*
**for nothing:** **a.** with no payment in return: *I did some work for a friend for nothing.* **b.** with no gain, uselessly: *My computer failed, so I did a lot of work today for nothing.*

**for** *conjunction*
for the reason that, because: *The government provided food, for the people were hungry.*

**forbid** /fər'bɪd/ *verb* **forbade** /-'bæd/ **forbidden** /-'bɪdn/, **forbidding, forbids**
to not permit: *The law forbids selling alcohol to anyone under the age of twenty-one.*

**force** /fɔrs/ *noun*
**1** power, energy: *The force of the wind knocked over a tree.*
**2** the use of power to make someone do something: *The police took the suspect to jail by force.*
**3** a military, police, or other unit organized to use physical power: *New York City has a large police force.*
**4** political power or influence: *The Congresswoman is a force for change in the government.*
**in force:** (in law) to be in effect, active: *The law that says one cannot smoke in public buildings is in force* (or) *is no longer in force.*

**force** *verb* **forced, forcing, forces**
**1** to use power or energy: *Strong winds forced boats onto the beaches.*
**2** to use power to make someone do something: *The police forced a confession from a suspect.*
**3** to use physical strength to open something: *The police forced open the door.* –*adjective* **forceful;** –*adverb* **forcefully;** –*noun* **forcefulness.**

**forecast** /'fɔr,kæst/ *noun*
a statement about what one thinks will happen in the future: *According to the weather forecast, it's going to snow tonight.* –*verb* **to forecast.**

**forehead** /'fɔrɪd/ *noun*
the part of the face above the eyebrows: *The child had a cut on his forehead.*

**foreign** /'fɔrɪn/ *adjective*
(from) outside one's own country: *This country imports a great variety of foreign goods.*

**foreigner** /'fɔrənər/ *noun*
someone from outside one's own country: *Many foreigners from Europe and Asia enjoy visiting Disneyland.*

**foreman** /'fɔrmən/ *noun, plural* **foremen** /-mɛn/
a boss of a group of workers: *He is a foreman in that factory.*

**forest** /'fɔrɪst/ *noun*
a large area with many trees: *In some national parks, the forest continues for miles and miles.*

**forever** /fə'rɛvər/ *adverb*
**1** always, for an endless period of time: *Our love will last forever.*
**2** continually, constantly: *The little boy is forever asking questions.*

**forge** /fɔrdʒ/ *verb* **forged, forging, forges**
to make a fake copy of something: *She forged her husband's signature on the check.*||*An artist forged a painting.* –*noun* (thing) **forgery;** (person) **forger.**

**forget** /fər'gɛt/ *verb* **forgot** /-'gɑt/, **forgotten** /-'gɑtn/, **forgetting, forgets**
**1** to not remember: *I've forgotten how to play the piano.*||*I forgot my keys (my purse, a ten o'clock appointment, etc.)!*
**2** to stop thinking about something: *You should forget about going to Europe on vacation; it costs too much.*

**forgetful** /fər'gɛtfəl/ *adjective*
often not remembering things –*adverb* **forgetfully;** –*noun* **forgetfulness.**

**forgive** /fər'gɪv/ *verb* **forgave** /-'geɪv/, **forgiven** /-'gɪvən/, **forgiving, forgives**
to not feel angry towards someone who did something wrong: *He forgot his wife's birthday, but she forgave him.* –*noun* **forgiveness.**

**fork** /fɔrk/ *noun*
**1** an instrument for eating, with a handle and at least two long points: *The dinner table is set with knives, forks, and spoons. See:* art on pages 5a and 7a.

fork

**2** a division into two parts: *To get to the town, turn left at the fork in the road.* –*verb* **to fork.**

**form** /fɔrm/ *verb*
**1** to shape or make an object: *She formed a dish from clay.*
**2** to become the shape of: *The children formed a circle.*
**3** to arrange something or put it together: *The manager formed a committee to study the project.*
**4** to come into existence: *Ice forms on the river in the winter.*
**5** to make up: *Good eating habits form the basis of a healthy diet.*

**form** *noun*
**1** the shape of something: *The candy was shaped in the form of a ring.*
**2** a type, kind: *People live under different forms of government, such as democracies or dictatorships.*
**3** a printed paper with spaces to be filled in: *When you apply for a passport, you must fill out some forms.*

**formal** /'fɔrməl/ *adjective*
**1** according to rules, laws, customs, etc.: *I received a formal invitation to the wedding today.*
**2** very or too proper: *He's a difficult person to get to know because he's always so formal. (antonym)* informal.

**formality** /fɔr'mæləti/ *noun, plural* **formalities**
**1** customary behavior (usually **to observe the formalities):** *We must observe the formalities and introduce ourselves to the other guests at the party.*
**2** the meaningless observance of a rule or custom: *All visitors must sign in at the front desk as a formality.*

**format** /'fɔrˌmæt/ *noun*
**1** the arrangement and style of print on a page: *That magazine's new format makes it easier to read.*
**2** any general arrangement of something: *The format of the lesson was a short lecture followed by a discussion.* –*verb* **to format.**

**formation** /fɔr'meɪʃən/ *noun*
**1** a bringing together, creation: *The formation of a committee on health issues took several days.*
**2** a group of people or things arranged a certain way: *Soldiers marched by in military formation.*

**former** /'fɔrmər/ *adjective*
**1** previous, past: *He is a former employee of this company.*
**2** referring to the first thing or person named in a pair

**former** *noun*
the first thing or person named in a pair: *We eat lots of fish and chicken, but we prefer the former* (meaning "the fish"). *See:* latter.

**formerly** /'fɔrmərli/ *adverb*
in the past, some time ago: *She was formerly president of that organization.*

**formula** /'fɔrmyələ/ *noun, plural* **formulas** or **formulae** /-ˌli/
**1** (in math) a rule expressed in symbols: $a^2 + b^2 = c^2$ *is a mathematical formula.*
**2** (in chemistry) a group of symbols representing a chemical: *The chemical formula for water is* $H^2O$*.*
**3** artificial milk for growing babies

**fort** /fɔrt/ *noun*
a group of buildings surrounded by high walls and used for military purposes

**forth** /fɔrθ/ *adverb*
*formal* forward, ahead: *Explorers went forth to discover a new world.*
**and so forth:** and other similar things: *She complained that the city was dirty, dangerous, expensive, and so forth.*

**fortieth** /'fɔrtiɪθ/ *adjective*
the ordinal number 40

**fortress** /'fɔrtrɪs/ *noun, plural* **fortresses**
a building, group of buildings, or town well-protected against attack *See:* fort.

**fortunate** /'fɔrt ʃənɪt/ *adjective*
**1** lucky at a particular time: *We were fortunate to escape the accident without injury.*
**2** lucky in general –*adverb* **fortunately.**

**fortune** /ˈfɔrtʃən/ *noun*
**1** wealth, riches: *He made a fortune in the oil business.*
**2** chance, (good or bad) luck: *Then he had the bad fortune to fall ill.*

**fortune teller** *noun*
a person who tells one's future

**forty** /ˈfɔrti/ *noun, plural* **forties**
the cardinal number 40

**forty** *adjective*
forty of something: *He is forty years old.*

**forward** /ˈfɔrwərd/ or **forwards** /ˈfɔrwərdz/ *adverb*
ahead (in space or time): *We are moving forwards with our plans to open a new store.*||*Walk three steps forward and turn left. (antonym)* backward or backwards.

**forward** *adjective*
**1** front: *Our room is in the forward area of the ship.*
**2** bold: *The little boy is forward in asking for favors even from strangers.*

**forward** *verb*
to send ahead to someone's new or other address: *While we are away in the summer, our neighbor forwards our mail to us. –noun* **forwardness.**

**fossil** /ˈfɑsəl/ *noun*
the remains of ancient animal or plant life found in rock: *We know about dinosaurs from fossils they left behind.*

**foster** /ˈfɔstər/ *adjective*
related to a system in which adults receive money from the government to take care of children who are not their own: *That woman cares for three foster children.*||*She is a foster parent.*

**fought** /fɔt/ *verb*
*past tense and past participle of* fight

**foul** /faʊl/ *adjective*
**1** rude, offensive: *When she gets angry, she sometimes uses foul language.*
**2** very unpleasant: *She's been in a foul mood all day.*

**found** *verb*
*past tense and past participle of* find

**foundation** /faʊnˈdeɪʃən/ *noun*
the base of a building: *The foundation for our house is made of cement.*

**founder** /ˈfaʊndər/ *noun*
a creator of something: *The founder of that college was a wealthy businessman.*

**fountain** /ˈfaʊntn/ *noun*
**1** an ornamental structure that sends water into the air to please people: *The water fountain in the square attracts tourists each summer.*
**2** a device usually found in public buildings that provides water for drinking

fountain

**four** /fɔr/ *noun*
the cardinal number 4

**four** *adjective*
four of something: *The child had four toys.*

**fourteen** /ˌfɔrˈti n/ *noun*
the cardinal number 14

**fourteen** *adjective*
fourteen of something: *Only fourteen (of the) passengers survived the plane crash. –noun* **fourteenth.**

**fourth** /fɔrθ/ *adjective*
the ordinal number 4: *She is the fourth child in the family.*

**Fourth of July** *noun*
(in the USA) Independence Day: *The Fourth of July is a day of great celebration across the United States.*

**fowl** /faʊl/ *noun, plural* **fowls** or **fowl**
birds such as chickens, ducks, and geese

**fox** /fɑks/ *noun, plural* **foxes** or **fox**
a small dog-like animal with a thick furry tail, considered to be clever

fox

**foxy** /ˈfɑksi/ *adjective* **foxier, foxiest**
clever, tricky: *He is a foxy old man.*

**foyer** /ˈfɔɪər/ *noun*
an entrance room: *I met my guest in the foyer of our office building.*

**fraction** /ˈfrækʃən/ *noun*
**1** a small part of something: *She spoke so quickly that I understood only a fraction of what she said.*
**2** a part of a whole number, expressed in symbols: *The fraction one-half can also be expressed as .5 or 1/2.* *–adjective* **fractional;** *–adverb* **fractionally.**



**fracture** /ˈfræktʃər/ *verb* **fractured, fracturing, fractures**
to break or crack: *She fractured her leg while skiing.* *–noun* **fracture.**

**fragile** /ˈfrædʒəl/ *adjective*
easily broken, delicate: *That dish is fragile, so be careful.* *–noun* **fragility.**

**fragment** /ˈfrægmənt/ *noun*
a bit or piece of something: *The clay pot had broken into fragments long ago.*

**fragrance** /ˈfreɪgrəns/ *noun*
**1** pleasant smell: *The fragrance of roses filled the air.*
**2** perfume *–adjective* **fragrant;** *–adverb* **fragrantly.**

**frail** /freɪl/ *adjective*
physically weak: *His mother has grown old and frail.* *–noun* **frailty.**

**frame** /freɪm/ *noun*
a border placed around something: *She put the photo in a plastic frame.*||*The window frames need painting.*

**frame** *verb* **framed, framing, frames**
**1** to place a frame around something: *She framed the painting and hung it in the living room.*
**2** *figurative* to arrange the proof of a crime so that an innocent person appears guilty: *The accused murderer said that he was framed by his brother.*

**framework** /ˈfreɪm,wɜrk/ *noun*
a structure used to support other things: *The framework of that house is made of wood.*

**frank (1)** /fræŋk/ *adjective*
open, direct, unafraid to express the truth: *The rock star was frank about his drug problem.* *–noun* **frankness.**

**frank (2)** *noun*
*short for* frankfurter

**frankfurter** /ˈfræŋkfərtər/ *noun*
a meat mixture usually made with beef or pork in the shape of a tube: a hot dog

**frankly** /ˈfræŋkli/ *adverb*
with openness and honesty: *The official spoke frankly about the region's problems.*

**frantic** /ˈfræntɪk/ *adjective*
**1** very rushed: *Rescuers made a frantic effort to save the drowning man.*
**2** almost crazy with fear (grief, anxiety, etc.) *–adverb* **frantically.**

**fraud** /frɔd/ *noun*
**1** trickery with the purpose of gaining another's money or property: *The company offered property for sale in Arizona, but it was a fraud; the property didn't exist.*
**2** someone who isn't really the person he or she appears to be: *He said he was an Italian prince, but he was a fraud.* *–adjective* **fraudulent.**

**freak** /frik/ *noun*
a person or animal with an abnormal shape: *The animal was a freak, born with two heads.*

**freak** *adjective*
strange, as when something unusual happens: *In New York, there was a freak snowstorm last year in June.*

**freckle** /ˈfrɛkəl/ *noun*
a small light brown spot on the skin, often from being in the sun: *She develops freckles in the summer.* *–verb* **to freckle;** *–adjective* **freckled; freckle-faced** /ˈfrɛkəl,feɪst/.

freckle

**free** /fri/ *adjective* **freer, freest**
**1** not under the control of another person or institution: *After twenty years in prison, he was a free man.*
**2** completely without: *The property is free of any debt.*||*The river is not yet free of pollution.*
**3** without payment: *Admission to the concert is free.*
**4** not in use, available: *The telephone (hotel room, bathroom, etc.) is free now.*

**5** not busy: *Are you free to talk now, or should I come back later?*

**free** *verb* **freed, freeing, frees**

**1** to let go, release from something unpleasant: *The jailer freed the prisoner.*||*Winning the lottery freed him of money worries forever.*

**2** to clear away or remove a barrier: *The workers freed the road of the fallen trees.*

**free** *adverb*

moving around without being stopped: *The children can run free in the park.* –*adverb* **freely.**

**freebie** or **freebee** /'fribi/ *noun informal*

a gift, something free: *My friend gave me a concert ticket and other freebies.*

**freedom** /'fridəm/ *noun*

**1** having the power to act and speak without being stopped: *The boy has the freedom to go where he wants to go.*

**2** a set of legal rights protected by the government, such as freedom of speech or religion: *Our various freedoms are the bases of our nation.*

**3** release from prison or slavery: *The jury found the suspect not guilty, and the judge gave him his freedom. (antonym)* captivity.

**freeway** /'fri,weɪ/ *noun*

a wide road for high-speed travel *See:* expressway; highway.

**freeze** /friz/ *verb* **froze** /froʊz/**, frozen** /'froʊzən/, **freezing, freezes**

**1** to become very hard or turn into ice because of low temperature: *The water in the pond freezes in winter.*

**2** to have the temperature drop below the freezing point (32°F/0°C): *It's going to freeze tonight.*

**3** to preserve food by keeping it very cold: *We froze the soup we made yesterday.*

**4** to stop and stand completely still: *A man pointed a gun at me and told me, "Freeze or I'll shoot!"*

**5** to stop the movement of something: *The Senator wants to freeze government spending.*||*The bank froze my account for two days, so I couldn't use it.*

**to freeze over:** to turn into ice: *The surface of the pond froze over last night.*

**to freeze up: a.** to be unable to move or function because of ice: *We had no water last night because the pipes froze up.* **b.** to be unable to perform because of nervousness: *As soon as she saw the large audience, she froze up and couldn't make her speech.*

**freeze** *noun*

**1** a condition of freezing by a temperature below 32°F or 0°C: *The freeze last night destroyed the farmer's oranges.*

**2** an action that stops movement: *The company put a freeze on salaries; nobody is going to get a raise.*

**freezer** /'frizər/ *noun*

the part of a refrigerator that keeps food frozen: *We put some steaks in the freezer for future use.*

**freight** /freɪt/ *noun, (no plural)*

goods that trucks, ships, trains, etc. take from one place to another: *A truck brought a load of freight to the warehouse.*

**French fries** *noun plural*

pieces of potatoes fried in fat: *Americans love hamburgers with French fries.*

**frenzy** /'frɛnzi/ *noun, plural* **frenzies**

a state of panic, causing a wild show of emotion –*adjective* **frenzied.**

**frequency** /'frikwənsi/ *noun, plural* **frequencies**

the time at which something happens: *The buses stop here with regular frequency.*

**frequent** /'frikwənt/ *adjective*

often: *Car theft is a frequent happening in this area.* –*adverb* **frequently.**

**fresh** /frɛʃ/ *adjective*

**1** recently picked, (prepared, baked, etc.), not frozen or from a can: *We enjoy fresh vegetables and fruit, straight from the garden.*

**2** bright, new: *a fresh coat of paint*

**3** different, exciting, original: *New people with fresh ideas joined the company.*

**4** pleasantly cool: *fresh breeze*

**5** rude: *The little boy was fresh to the teacher.* –*adverb* **freshly;** –*noun* **freshness.**

**freshen** /'frɛʃən/ *verb*

to make or become fresher: *I'll freshen*

F

*your drink with more soda and ice cubes.*||*She freshened up the room with some flowers.*

**freshman** /ˈfrɛʃmən/ *noun, plural* **freshmen** /-mɛn/
a student in the first year of high school or college: *She is a freshman at the university.*

**USAGE NOTE:** First-year high school and college students are called *freshmen;* second-year students are *sophomores;* third-year students are *juniors*; and fourth-year students are *seniors.*

**fret** /frɛt/ *verb* **fretted, fretting, frets**
to worry or express anxiety

**friction** /ˈfrɪkʃən/ *noun*
**1** difficult movement that results when two surfaces are rubbed together: *When you rub your hands together rapidly, the friction produces heat.*
**2** conflict: *The friction between the two secretaries created tension in the office.*

**Friday** /ˈfraɪdeɪ/ *noun*
the sixth day of the week between Thursday and Saturday

**fridge** /frɪʤ/ *noun informal*
*short for* refrigerator

**fried** /fraɪd/ *verb*
*past tense and past participle* of fry

**friend** /frɛnd/ *noun*
**1** a person whom one likes and trusts: *She's a good (=close) friend of mine.*||*Anna and Paul are just friends (=not lovers). (antonym)* enemy.
**2** a person who supports a particular cause or group: *The Senator, who is from a farm state, is a friend of the farmer.*
**to make friends with someone:** to form a relationship with someone one likes and trusts: *She made friends with some of her co-workers.* –*adjective* **friendless;** –*noun* **friendship.**

**friendly** /ˈfrɛndli/ *adjective* **friendlier, friendliest**
**1** helpful, pleasant, agreeable: *She has a friendly manner with customers.*||*This bar has a friendly atmosphere.*
**2** referring to the relationship of fondness and trust between people who like each other: *He is friendly with his boss; they often go out to lunch together.* –*noun* **friendliness.**

**fright** /fraɪt/ *noun*
sudden fear, shock: *A tree fell on the house and gave him a fright.* –*verb* **to frighten;** –*adjective* **frightful;** –*adverb* **frightfully.**

**frightened** /ˈfraɪtnd/ *adjective*
feeling afraid: *The child is frightened of dogs.*

**frightening** /ˈfraɪtnɪŋ/ *adjective*
making (a person or animal) afraid: *The war movie was very frightening.* –*adverb* **frighteningly.**

**frigid** /ˈfrɪʤɪd/ *adjective*
freezing, very cold

**fringe** /frɪnʤ/ *noun*
**1** the border of a piece of clothing, rug, tablecloth, etc., made of hanging threads or other material: *His jacket had fringes on the arms.*
**2** the outer edge or limit of something: *The building is located on the fringes of the city.*

**frisky** /ˈfrɪski/ *adjective* **friskier, friskiest**
full of energy, playful: *My cat feels frisky this morning.* –*adverb* **friskily.**

**frog** /frɔg/ *noun*
a small usually green or brown animal with long, powerful legs

**from** /frəm/ *preposition*
**1** showing where something started or its origin: *She moved from Los Angeles to Chicago.*||*This beer is imported from Mexico.*||*The letter is from my sister.*
**2** showing a beginning point in time: *We worked on the project from May to July.*||*I'll meet with you again a week from Friday* (=showing a future time).||*The two of them have been friends from that day on* (=since that day).
**3** showing the material something is made of: *Coffee comes from beans.*||*Those gloves are made from leather.*
**4** showing distance: *Those boats are two miles from the shore.*||*Boston is 250 miles (400 km) from New York.*
**5** showing a range, especially of sizes

and numbers: *That type of fish measures from three to six feet in length (one to two meters).*
**6** showing a reason or cause: *His death from heart failure was shocking news.*
**7** showing difference: *I don't know one type of computer from another.*
**8** showing separation: *He removed his hand from her arm.*

**front** /frʌnt/ *noun*
**1** the forward area or side of something: *The front of the store has a toy display.*||*To enter the building, you have to go around to the front.*
**2** the way a person appears to others: *He is a funny, relaxed man, but always puts on a serious front for strangers.*
**3** in war, the area where there is fighting: *The general sent fresh troops to the front. (antonym)* back.

**front** *adjective*
forward: *The front windows of our house overlook the park.*||*The front row of seats in the theater is full.*

**in front of:** **a.** directly ahead of: *In the class photo, Maria is sitting in front of Tony.*||*There are some trees in front of the building.* **b.** facing: *He stood in front of the mirror.* **c.** in the presence of: *Don't talk about that in front of the children.*

**frontier** /frʌn'tɪr/ *noun*
**1** the outer edge of settled land that is close to the wilderness: *The American West was still a frontier a century ago.*
**2** the border between two countries: *There have been reports of fighting on the frontier.*

**frost** /frɔst/ *noun*
white icy covering on a surface that forms when small drops of water in the air freeze: *There was frost on my window this morning. –adjective* **frosty.**

**frosting** /'frɔstɪŋ/ *noun*
a sugary covering, such as on cakes: *That cake has chocolate frosting.*

**frown** /fraʊn/ *noun*
a look of disapproval (doubt, annoyance, etc.) made by pulling the eyebrows downward and tightening the mouth: *He had a frown on his face after being unfairly criticized.*

**frown** *verb*
to have a frown on one's face: *She frowned when she heard the bad news.*

**to frown on:** to disapprove of: *The teacher frowns on students talking in the classroom.*

**froze** /froʊz/ *verb*
*past tense of* freeze

**frozen** /'froʊzən/ *adjective*
*and past participle of* freeze

**fruit** /frut/ *noun*
the part of a plant that contains the seed, especially when used as food: *Apples, pears, and oranges are some common types of fruit.*

**fruitful** /'frutfəl/ *adjective*
producing a lot of something, successful: *Representatives from the hospital and labor union had a fruitful discussion concerning the new contract. –adverb* **fruitfully;** *–noun* **fruitfulness.**

**frustrate** /'frʌˌstreɪt/ *verb* **frustrated, frustrating, frustrates**
**1** to prevent someone from doing something: *Their attempts to climb the mountain were frustrated by winter storms.*
**2** the feeling you get when something or someone stops you from doing, having, or being what you want: *She felt frustrated when she didn't get a salary increase after all her hard work. –noun* **frustration.**

**fry** /fraɪ/ *verb* **fried, frying, fries**
to cook in a fatty substance, such as butter or vegetable oil: *He fried eggs in a frying pan.*

**frying pan** *noun*
a shallow pan with a handle used for frying food

**frying pan**

**fuel** /'fyuəl/ *noun*
a substance, such as coal, oil, or gasoline, that is used to provide energy and power: *Gasoline is the fuel used in most motor vehicles. –verb* **to fuel.**

**fugitive** /'fyuʤətɪv/ *noun*
a person who is running away

**fulfill** /fʊl'fɪl/ *verb*
**1** to perform or complete: *He fulfilled*

*his requirement by making loan payments on time.*
**2** to satisfy: *She fulfilled her dreams of becoming an actress.* –*noun* **fulfillment.**

**full** /fʊl/ *adjective*
**1** filled to the limit: *That bottle won't hold any more water; it's full.*||*I'm not going to order dessert; I'm full.*
**2** containing a large number amount of something, filled with: *The report is full of errors.*||*That meat is full of fat.*
**3** complete: *We've already spent a full week on this project.*||*I need to get a full night's sleep.*
**4** to the maximum: *The ship traveled at full speed.*

**to be full of baloney (it, beans):** to be all wrong: *He's full of it; he doesn't know what he's talking about.*

**full** *adverb*
forcefully, completely: *A bullet hit the soldier full in the chest.*

**in full:** with the complete amount: *I've paid him back the money in full.* *(antonym)* empty.

**full-length** *adjective*
**1** complete: *This is her first full-length novel (film, play, etc.).*
**2** floor-length, from head to toe: *She wore an elegant full-length dress to the dance.*

**full moon** *noun*
the moon when fully lit by the sun so that it appears completely round

**full-time** *adverb*
35–40 hours a week: *He works full-time.*||*He is a full-time employee during the day and goes to school at night. See:* part-time.

**fully** /ˈfʊli/ *adverb*
completely: *I didn't fully understand your question.*

**fumble** /ˈfʌmbəl/ *verb* **fumbled, fumbling, fumbles**
**1** to struggle with something, or to handle something in an awkward way: *She fumbled with the keys as she tried to open the front door.*
**2** to drop or lose control of: *The baseball player fumbled the ball.*

**fume** /fyum/ *noun*
*usually plural* **fumes:** the gas, smoke, or odor given off usually from a chemical –*verb* **to fume.**

**fun** /fʌn/ *noun, (no plural)*
**1** pleasurable activity, enjoyment: *We had fun at the picnic.*
**2** a source of pleasure: *She's a lot of fun at parties.*||*Going to the dentist is no fun.*

**to make fun of someone** or **something:** to laugh at someone or something in an unkind way: *He often makes fun of his sister by imitating her.*

**fun** *adjective informal*
giving pleasure or enjoyment: *Water-skiing is a fun sport.*

**function** /ˈfʌŋkʃən/ *verb*
**1** to perform a task or serve as: *She functions as both student advisor and teacher.*
**2** to work (well, poorly, etc.): *The new computer has been functioning well.*

**function** *noun*
**1** purpose, use: *The computer has a number of important functions.*
**2** a formal social occasion –*adjective* **functional.**

**fund** /fʌnd/ *noun*
**1** a sum of money for a specific purpose: *The school received government funds for buying computers.*
**2** a large amount of something: *We were surprised by his fund of knowledge.*

**fund** *verb*
to provide money for a purpose: *The school lunch program is funded by the government.*

**fundamental** /ˌfʌndəˈmɛntəl/ *adjective*
**1** basic, most important: *Honesty is a fundamental principle in dealing with others.*
**2** essential, necessary: *Food, shelter, and clothing are fundamental needs.*

**fundamental** *noun*
**1** the basic, most important principle (matter, concept): *Openness to new ideas is a fundamental in business.*
**2** an essential, necessity: *Having work is a fundamental in life.*

**funeral** /ˈfyunərəl/ *noun*
the ceremony for the burial or burning of a dead person

**fungus** /ˈfʌŋgəs/ *noun, plural* **fungi** /ˈfʌnˌʤaɪ/ or **funguses**
an organism that feeds on living or dead

plants or animals and cannot live apart from them: *Mushrooms are a type of fungus.* –*adjective* **fungal** /ˈfʌŋgəl/.

**funnel** /ˈfʌnl/ *noun*
a tool with a wide opening on top leading into a narrow bottom and used to control the flow of a liquid: *She used a funnel to pour water from a bowl into a bottle.*

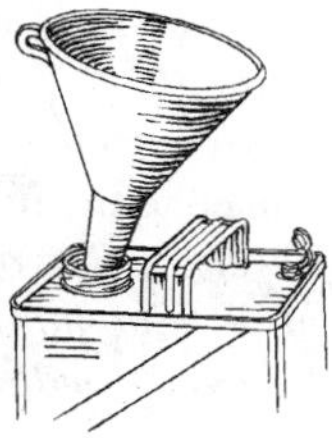
funnel

**funny** /ˈfʌni/ *adjective* **funnier, funniest**
**1** making one smile or laugh: *Her story was so funny that we couldn't stop laughing.*||*She's a funny person.*
**2** odd, strange: *Something funny is going on in that house next door.*
**3** a little sick: *I started to feel funny about an hour after I ate lunch.* –*noun* **funniness.**

**fur** /fɜr/ *noun*
**1** the hairy coat of an animal: *The cat's fur is soft and shiny.*
**2** clothing made from this

**furious** /ˈfyʊriəs/ *adjective*
very angry: *He is furious because he missed his plane.* –*adverb* **furiously.**

**furnace** /ˈfɜrnɪs/ *noun*
a heavy container for burning fuel especially to provide heat: *That old house has a coal furnace.*

**furnish** /ˈfɜrnɪʃ/ *verb* **furnishes**
**1** to provide or give something: *The travel agency furnished me with the information that I needed for my trip.*
**2** to provide with furniture, lamps, curtains, etc.: *She furnished the apartment with modern furniture.* –*noun* **furnishings.**

**furniture** /ˈfɜrnɪʧər/ *noun, (no plural)*
articles such as tables, chairs, beds, sofas, and other objects for homes and offices: *We need to buy furniture for the living room.*

**furry** /ˈfɜri/ *adjective* **furrier, furriest**
having a coat of fur: *Furry animals grow long coats in winter.*

**further** /ˈfɜrðər/ *adverb*
**1** more, additionally: *We can discuss the plan further tomorrow.*
**2** *comparative of* far more ahead, more distant: *I can't walk any further.*||*He is further away from his goals than ever.*

**further** *adjective*
more, additional: *Have you received any further news about the accident?*

**further** *verb*
to help move forward: *He is taking business courses to further his career.*

**USAGE NOTE:** *Further* (and *furthest*) may be used instead of *farther* (and *farthest*) to express physical distances, as in *"He has moved his business farther* (or) *further from town."* However, you cannot substitute *farther* for *further* to express abstract meanings, as in *"After further consideration, he accepted the plan."*

**furthest** /ˈfɜrðɪst/ *adjective*
*superlative of* far; most distant, farthest away: *Luis is the student who lives furthest from the school. See:* further.

**fury** /ˈfyʊri/ *noun, plural* **furies**
violent anger: *The storm attacked the coast with the fury of a hurricane.*

**fuse** /fyuz/ *noun*
**1** a safety device that breaks if too much electricity passes through it: *The air conditioner caused a fuse to blow.*
**2** a string attached to an explosive that one lights to set it off: *The soldier lit the fuse that set off the bomb.*
**to blow a fuse: a.** to cause a fuse to break: *When we had the electric heater and the microwave on at the same time, we blew a fuse.* **b.** to become angry suddenly: *He blew a fuse when his flight was canceled.*

**fuse** *verb* **fused, fusing, fuses**
to melt together or become one: *The two political parties fused to increase their power.* –*noun* **fusion.**

**fuss** /fʌs/ *noun*
a show of great concern over something unimportant: *What a fuss over such a small mistake!*
**to make a fuss:** to complain noisily about something unimportant: *He makes a fuss if his breakfast eggs aren't cooked right.*
**to make a fuss over** or **fuss over someone:** to pay a lot of attention to: *Every time her son comes to dinner, his mother makes a fuss over* (or) *fusses over him.*

**fuss** *verb* **fusses**
to act anxious or to handle something nervously: *Stop fussing with your hair; it's time to go.*

**fussy** /ˈfʌsi/ *adjective* **fussier, fussiest**
**1** critical, difficult to please: *He is so fussy about what he eats that nothing pleases him.*
**2** very careful when choosing something: *She is quite fussy about her clothes and shops only in the best stores.* *–adverb* **fussily;** *–noun* **fussiness.**

F

**futile** /ˈfyutl/ *adjective*
useless, unsuccessful: *He made a second and futile attempt to pass the examination.* *–adverb* **futilely;** *–noun* **futility.**

**future** /ˈfyutʃər/ *noun*
**1** the state of life and events ahead, things to come: *No one knows what will happen in the future. (antonym)* past.
**2** one's life ahead in time, especially a career: *She is planning for a future in medicine.*

**future** *adjective*
related to the future: *Future relations between the two countries should improve.*||*She introduced him as her future husband.* *–adjective* **futuristic.**

**fuzzy** /ˈfʌzi/ *adjective* **fuzzier, fuzziest**
**1** covered with short, soft hair or threads: *The surface of that cloth feels fuzzy.*
**2** unclear, *(synonym)* blurry: *The image in that picture is fuzzy.* *–adjective* **fuzzily;** *–noun* **fuzziness.**

# G,g

**G, g** /dʒi/ *noun*
**G's, g's** or **Gs, gs** the seventh letter of the English alphabet

**gadget** /ˈgædʒɪt / *noun*
any small or unusual, useful object (an electronic device, machine, tool, etc.): *She has many electronic gadgets in her house, from computers to an electric toothbrush.*

**gadgetry** /ˈgædʒɪtri/ *noun, (no plural)*
a group of small or unusual and useful objects: *The engineer has a house full of gadgetry.*

**gag** /gæg/ *noun*
**1** tape or other material that covers, or is put into, the mouth to stop someone from speaking
**2** *informal* a joke: *A friend told some funny gags at lunch today.* –*verb* **to gag.**

**gage** /geɪdʒ/ *noun*
*See:* gauge.

**gaiety** /ˈgeɪəti/ *noun, (no plural)*
laughter and good feelings: *The gaiety at the party made everyone feel good.*

**gain** /geɪn/ *verb*
**1** to obtain, receive: *Students gain useful knowledge by taking a computer course.*
**2** to make money: *A person gains by buying a house that goes up in value.*
**3** to come closer to someone or something: *The runner gained on the other runners and finally won the race.*
**4** to go up, increase: *He gained a lot of weight this winter. (antonym)* to lose.

**gain** *noun*
**1** a profit: *I made a big gain on the value of my house.*
**2** an increase, advance: *The discovery of a new kind of star was a gain for science. (antonym)* loss.

**gait** /geɪt/ *noun*
the way a person (or horse) walks

**gal** /gæl/ *noun old usage*
(used in a friendly conversation) a girl or woman: *She's a wonderful gal; everyone loves to talk with her.*

**galaxy** /ˈgæləksi/ *noun, plural* **galaxies**
a large system of stars: *Our galaxy is called the Milky Way.* –*adjective* **galactic** /gəˈlæktɪk/.

**gale** /geɪl/ *noun adjective*
a strong wind (of about 60 miles or 96 km per hour): *The gale knocked over trees in our area.*

**gallbladder** /ˈgɔlˌblædər/ *noun*
an organ attached to the liver that stores and sends out a liquid bile that helps with digestion: *The gallbladder helps the body digest fat. See:* art on page 21a.

**gallery** /ˈgæləri/ *noun, plural* **galleries**
a room or building used to show or sell art, usually smaller than a museum

**gallon** /ˈgælən/ *noun*
in the USA, a liquid measurement equal to four quarts of 32 ounces each: *Yesterday, I bought five gallons of juice for the party.*

---

**USAGE NOTE:** A *gallon* is equal to 3.8 liters. Gasoline, paint, wine and other liquids are commonly sold in gallons: *My car is old, but gets about 20 miles to the gallon.* A *quart* equals one-fourth of a gallon or .95 liters: *We need eggs, bread, and a quart of milk.*

---

**gallop** /ˈgæləp/ *noun*
the fastest run of four-legged animals, especially horses: *The horse raced at full gallop.* –*verb* **to gallop.**

**gallows** /ˈgælouz/ *noun, plural* **gallows**
a raised, wooden structure used to hang criminals: *A murderer was sent to the gallows to die.*

**gamble** /ˈgæmbəl/ *noun*
a risk: *She took a gamble that it would not rain when she planned an outdoor party in cloudy weather.*

**gamble** *verb* **gambled, gambling, gambles**
**1** to play games of chance for money: *He gambles on horse races.*
**2** to take a risk: *She gambled that he would fall in love with her.*

**gambler** /ˈgæmblər/ *noun*
a person who plays games of chance

**game** /geim/ *noun*
**1** an activity or sport, often with rules, that people play: *The game of tennis has grown in popularity.*
**2** a particular sporting event: *Our team won the football game last night.*
**3** wild animals, such as deer, birds, and fish captured or killed for sport: *The hunters captured deer and other wild game.*

**game show** *noun*
a television program where people play a game for prizes: *Her friend won a new car on the game show.*

**gang** /gæŋ/ *noun*
**1** (usually used in a negative way) a group of (young) people joined together for support and protection: *She joined a street gang when she was 12 years old.*
**2** a group of criminals
**3** a group of friends: *Where is the gang going on Friday night?*

**gang** *verb*
**to gang up on someone:** to join together and act against someone or something: *A group of older boys ganged up on the child and asked him for money.*

**gangrene** /ˈgæŋˌgrin/ *noun, (no plural)*
a disease that causes the death of flesh in parts of the body

**gangster** /ˈgæŋstər/ *noun*
a member of an organized group of criminals

**gap** /gæp/ *noun*
an empty space between two things

**garage** /gəˈrɑʒ/ *noun*
**1** a building where a vehicle is kept: *I keep my car in the garage next to my house. See:* art on page 4a.
**2** a place where cars can be repaired

**garage** *verb* **garaged, garaging, garages**
to park in a garage: *We garaged our car for the winter.*

**garage sale** *noun*
a sale of used household items (old lamps, tables, etc.) inside or near a person's garage

**garbage** /ˈgɑrbɪʤ/ *noun, (no plural)*
**1** things you do not want any more (old newspapers, empty cans, etc.): *I put the garbage from last night's party in the trash can this morning.*
**2** ideas and opinions that are considered stupid or worthless:
**to take out** or **put out the garbage:** to take garbage outside so that it can be picked up by garbage trucks: *I take out the garbage every day.*

**garbage can** /ˈgɑrbɪʤ kæn/ *noun*
a container that you put trash (garbage) into, and put outside to be picked up by garbage trucks

garbage can

**garden** /ˈgɑrdn/ *noun*
an area of land used to grow flowers and vegetables: *We have a small flower garden behind our house.*

**garden** *verb*
to work in a garden –*noun* (person) **gardener;** (activity) **gardening.**

**gargle** /ˈgɑrgəl/ *verb* **gargled, gargling, gargles**
to clean the throat and mouth with a liquid: *Each morning, he gargles with a mixture of salt and water.* –*noun* **gargling.**

**garlic** /ˈgɑrlɪk/ *noun, (no plural)*
a type of onion used as seasoning in

food: *This tomato sauce needs more garlic.* –*adjective* **garlicky.**

**garment** /ˈgɑrmənt/ *noun adjective*
a general term for a piece of clothing: *He removed some shirts and other garments from the suitcase. See:* apparel.

**garment bag** *noun*
a thin luggage bag used to carry suits and dresses: *She carries a garment bag right on the airplane when she travels.*

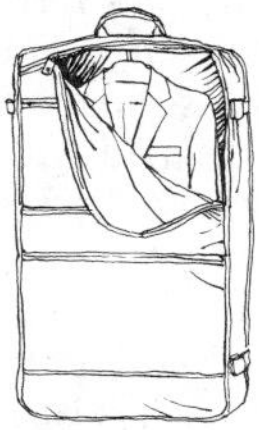
garment bag

**gas** /gæs/ *noun, plural* **gases**
**1** any air-like substance, which usually cannot be seen, that is not a liquid or solid: *Oxygen is a gas that exists in large amounts in the air.*
**2** a substance used for cooking and heating: *She turned on the gas* (or) *gas stove to boil some water.*
**3** *informal short for* gasoline: *I stopped the car for gas at the gas station.*
**4** *informal* wind from the stomach or lower body: *Eating onions gives me gas.*

**to run out of gas: a.** to have no more gasoline: *Our car ran out of gas on the highway.* **b.** to become very tired, unable to continue: *I worked very late last night; then I ran out of gas and went to bed.*

**gas** *verb* **gassed, gassing, gases**
to kill or injure with poisonous gas

**to gas something up:** to fill something with gasoline: *I'm going to gas up the car for our long trip.*

**gaseous** /ˈgæsiəs/ *adjective*
in the form of gas: *A gaseous cloud formed above the burning chemical factory. (antonym)* solid.

**gash** /gæʃ/ *noun, plural* **gashes**
a long, deep cut –*verb* **to gash.**

**gas main** *noun*
a pipe carrying gas under the streets

**gasoline** /ˌgæsəˈlin/ *noun, (no plural)*
a liquid produced from oil, used as an engine fuel. *See:* gas **3**.

**gasp** *verb*
to take short quick breaths usually with difficulty: *She gasped for air after she finished the long run.* –*noun* **gasp.**

**gas station** *noun*
a place that sells gasoline and repairs vehicles: *I stopped at the gas station to get some gas.*

gas station

**gate** /geɪt/ *noun*
a metal or wooden door that closes an open space in a wall, fence, city, etc.: *A gate in the fence opens into a flower garden.*

**gather** /ˈgæðər/ *verb*
**1** to bring together, collect: *He gathered his clothes together and packed them in the suitcase.*
**2** to come together: *Townspeople gathered in the town hall to talk about the new school.*
**3** to understand: *I gather from what I hear that your business is doing well.*
**4** to bring in, pick: *Farmers gather their corn when it is ready.||We gathered flowers by the river.*

**gathering** /ˈgæðərɪŋ/ *noun*
**1** a group of people: *A gathering of admirers formed near the movie star's hotel.*
**2** a meeting, social occasion: *We had a social gathering at the church last night.*

**gaudy** /ˈgɔdi/ *adjective* **gaudier, gaudiest**
too brightly colored: *The dancers in the show wore gaudy costumes.* –*adverb* **gaudily;** –*noun* **gaudiness.**

**gauge** or **gage** /geɪʤ/ *noun*
a device for measuring size, amount, etc.: *The gauge showed that the air temperature is normal.*

**gauge** or **gage** *verb* **gauged, gauging, gauges**
to measure: *to gauge one's success*

**gauze** /gɔz/ *noun*
a very thin, light material with very small holes, usually used as a covering

G

in medicine or as a curtain: *The doctor covered the cut with a piece of gauze.*

**gave** /geɪv/ *verb*
*past tense of* give

**gay** /geɪ/ *adjective*
**1** relating to the lives and concerns of homosexual people: *There are large communities of gay people in New York and San Francisco.*
**2** *old usage* joyful, happy: *Everyone at the party is having a gay time.*

**gay** *noun*
a person who is homosexual, usually a man: *American gays have formed political organizations.*

G

**gaze** /geɪz/ *verb* **gazed, gazing, gazes**
to look at someone or something for a long time: *He gazed out the window at the trees.*

**gazelle** /gə'zɛl/ *noun, plural* **gazelles** or **gazelle**
an animal like a small deer: *Most gazelles are found in Africa.*

**gear** /gɪr/ *noun*
**1** a flat, round piece of metal with teeth
**2** one of several speeds in a vehicle: *I put the car into high gear and drove away.*
**3** equipment, usually connected with sports: *The climber gathered up his gear and headed toward the mountain.*

**gearshift** /'gɪr,ʃɪft/ *noun*
a handle used to change from one speed to another in a vehicle: *The gearshift in a car is located on the floor to the driver's right.*

**GED** /,ʤii'di/ *noun*
*abbreviation of* General Equivalency Diploma an official document showing that a person has successfully completed his or her high school education: *She received her GED after attending evening classes.*

**USAGE NOTE:** The *GED* is needed for many jobs. Night school and television courses that lead to the *GED* make it possible for working people to complete a high school education.

**gee** /ʤi/ *exclamation*
an expression of surprise: *Gee, I didn't know that you found a new job!*

**geese** /gɪs/ *noun*
*plural of* goose: *One goose, two geese.*

**gee whiz** /'ʤi'wɪz/ *exclamation*
a mild expression of surprise (disappointment, annoyance): *Oh, gee whiz, my computer isn't working right again!*

**gel** /ʤɛl/ *noun*
a soft, clear substance between a liquid and a solid state, such as jelly: *She uses gel in her hair to keep the style in place.*

**gel** *verb* **gelled, gelling, gels**
**1** to form into a gel
**2** to come together: *After much discussion, our plans for the party started to gel. See:* jell.

**gelatin** /'ʤɛlətn/ *noun*
**1** a clear substance made from boiled animal bones that has no taste
**2** Jello™

**gem** /ʤɛm/ *noun*
a jewel or precious stone

**gemstone** /'ʤɛm,stoʊn/ *noun*
a jewel or precious stone, usually before it is cut into a shape: *South America exports many gemstones, including diamonds.*

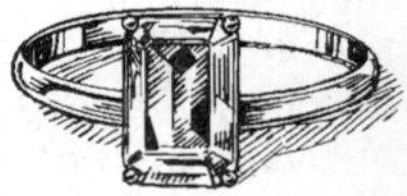
gemstone

**gender** /'ʤɛndər/ *noun*
**1** (in some languages) the grouping of words into masculine (male), feminine (female), and neuter (other) classes: *The gender of "la casa" is feminine.*
**2** The classification of male and female living things: *Most companies do not refuse to hire people based on their race, age, or gender.*

**gene** /ʤin/ *noun*
the basic part of a living cell that contains characteristics (eye color, hair, intelligence, etc.) of one's parents

**general (1)** /'ʤɛnərəl/ *adjective*
common to most, usually true: *The general feeling among her friends is that she is a kind person.*
**in general:** usually: *In general, he gets along well with people.* –*noun* **generality** /,ʤɛnə'raeləti/. *See:* generalization.

**general (2)** *noun*
a military officer (US Army, US Air

Force, US Marines) belonging to the highest level: *Generals in the army have great responsibility.*

**generalization** /ˌʤɛnərələ'zeɪʃən/ *noun* a general statement about something without reference to details or important differences: *Politicians are famous for making speeches full of generalizations.* *–verb* **to generalize.**

**generally** /'ʤɛnərəli/ *adverb*
**1** usually: *We generally take the bus to work.*
**2** without details, in general: *Generally speaking, the weather has been cool this summer.*

**generate** /'ʤɛnəˌreɪt/ *verb* **generated, generating, generates**
to produce or make: *The local power station generates electricity.*

**generation** /ˌʤɛnə'reɪʃən/ *noun*
**1** one of the different age levels in a family, such as grandparents, children, and grandchildren
**2** a group of people of approximately the same age: *The older generation is always complaining about the younger generation.*

**Generation X** /ɛks/ *noun, (no plural)* in the USA, the people born during the 1960s and early 1970s: *Many members of Generation X have a college education but are not hopeful about the future.*

---

**USAGE NOTE:** You may shorten *Generation X* to *Gen X* and refer to its members as *Generation Xers* or *Gen Xers.* Members of *Generation X* grew up watching the American dream of success on television, but have found the real world quite different. They are unhappy about the difficulty of finding jobs, the state of the national economy, world politics, and the environment.

---

**generator** /'ʤɛnəˌreɪtər/ *noun* a machine used to produce electricity: *The hospital has two emergency generators in case of a power cut.*

**generosity** /ˌʤɛnə'rɑsəti/ *noun, (no plural)* the willingness to give or the act of giving to others: *Her generosity allowed the museum to buy many new paintings.*

**generous** /'ʤɛnərəs/ *adjective*
**1** ready to give, giving: *My brother is very generous; he gave me $20,000 to buy a new car.*
**2** given freely: *The cook gave us generous amounts of food.* *–adverb* **generously.** *(antonym)* stingy.

**genius** /'ʤinyəs/ *noun, plural* **geniuses** a person of great intelligence and ability: *Albert Einstein was a genius in physics.*

**genre** /'ʒɑnrə/ *noun* a type of literature, art, or music grouped by style or subject: *Novels and poetry are different genres of literature.*

**gentle** /'ʤɛntl/ *adjective* **gentler, gentlest**
**1** kind, soft, not rough: *The mother is very gentle with her baby.*
**2** well-behaved: *My dog is very gentle; he would never bite.*
**3** light, slow: *A gentle breeze comes from the ocean.* *–noun* **gentleness;** *–adverb* **gently.** *(antonym)* rough.

**gentleman** /'ʤɛntlmən/ *noun, plural* **gentlemen** /-mɛn/ a polite and honorable man

**genuine** /'ʤɛnyuɪn/ *adjective*
**1** true, real: *That restaurant serves genuine Spanish food.*||*a genuine diamond*
**2** honest, *(synonym)* sincere: *Her sadness over the death of her cat is genuine; she cried all night.* *–adverb* **genuinely;** *–noun* **genuineness.** *(antonym)* fake.

**geography** /ʤi'ɑgrəfi/ *noun, (no plural)* the scientific study of the earth's surface, features, climate, people, etc.: *I bought a new set of maps for my geography class.* *–adjective* **geographic** /ˌʤiə'græfɪk/.

**geology** /ʤi'ɑləʤi/ *noun, (no plural)* the scientific study of the earth through its rocks, soil, etc.: *In geology we studied the rocks and deserts of California.*

–*noun* (person) **geologist;** –*adjective* **geologic** /ˌʤiəˈlɑʤɪk/.

**geometric** /ˌʤiəˈmɛtrɪk/ *adjective*
with regular shapes and lines: *wrapping paper with geometric designs*

**geometry** /ʤiˈɑmətri/ *noun, (no plural)*
the study in mathematics of lines, angles, shapes, etc.

**geranium** /ʤəˈreɪniəm/ *noun*
a garden plant with attractive red, pink, or white flowers: *His mother grows geraniums in her garden. See:* art on page 1a.

G

**germ** /ʤɜrm/ *noun*
a very small living thing (microorganism) that can cause illnesses or disease: *She washes her hands with soap before cooking to kill any germs.*

**German shepherd** /ˈʤɜrmən/ *noun*
a type of strong, large dog with a blackish-brown coat: *The German shepherd is often used as a police dog.*

**gesture** /ˈʤɛsʧər/ *noun*
a body movement to show something (a feeling, an idea, etc.): *She made a gesture to the right with her hand to show the direction of the park.*

**gesture** *verb* **gestured, gesturing, gestures**
to make a movement with your hand or head to show something: *He gestured to me to sit down.*

**get** /gɛt/ *verb* **got, gotten, gets**
**1** to receive, obtain: *I got a telephone call (letter, message, etc.).*
**2** to go for: *She went to get some food at the supermarket.*
**3** to become: *The weather is getting warmer.*
**4** to go, move, or arrive: *Call me when you get home.*||*I got in the house (down from the ladder, under the bed, etc.).*
**5** to cause someone to do something for you: *I got my hair cut.*
**6** to experience something: *She got her car stolen last night.*
**7** to catch an illness: *He's gotten the flu.*
**8** to understand: *She doesn't get it when I tell her she can't stay out late.*
**9** to annoy: *His behavior really gets to me sometimes.*

**to get ahead:** to succeed, improve oneself: *She has a good job and is getting ahead in life.*

**to get along with someone:** to have a friendly relationship with someone: *She doesn't get along with her boss.*

**to get away:** to escape: *The criminal got away from the police.*

**to get back:** **a.** to return: *She got back from vacation last week.* **b.** to reply, respond: *I will get back to you with an answer tomorrow.*

**to get behind:** **a.** to support, help succeed: *Many people got behind the politician and helped her win the election.* **b. in something:** to be late with one's work, payments, etc.: *He got behind in his rent payments and had to leave the apartment.*

**to get in:** to arrive: *The bus got in at 4 o'clock.*

**to get into something:** to put oneself or someone else into a certain situation, usually bad: *The children are always getting into trouble.*

**to get out:** **a.** to leave: *He will get out at 4 P.M. when his classes are finished.* **b.** to remove: *This new soap gets chocolate spots out.*

**to get over someone** or **something:** **a.** to return to a normal state after a bad experience or illness: *She still hasn't gotten over her mother's death.* **b. can't get over:** to be very surprised: *I can't get over how well he looks after his illness.*

**to get through:** **a. to someone:** to make contact, reach: *I was finally able to get through to my friend on the telephone.* **b. with something:** to finish: *After I got through with my work, I went to bed.*

**to get up:** **a.** to wake up: *I get up at 6 A.M. every morning.* **b.** stand up: *She got up from her seat and left the room. (antonym)* give.

**getaway** /ˈgetəˌweɪ/ *noun*
an escape: *The thief made his getaway in a stolen car.*

**get-together** *noun*
an informal meeting for fun, a gathering: *After work, some of us had a get-together at a friend's apartment.*

**geyser** /'gaɪzər/ *noun*
a natural hot spring that sends water into the air from time to time: *Many tourists come to photograph the geysers in the state park.*

geyser

**ghetto** /'gɛtoʊ/ *noun, plural* **ghettos**
an area in a city where many people of the same nationality, race, or religion live, usually a poor area: *He wrote about his experiences growing up in the ghetto.*

**ghost** /goʊst/ *noun*
the spirit of a dead person: *People say ghosts live in that old house.*

**giant** /'ʤaɪənt/ *noun*
a person, animal, plant, or object much larger than normal: *This plant is a giant.*||*a giant elephant (antonym)* tiny.

**gift** /gɪft/ *noun*
**1** something given freely to another, *(synonym)* a present: *My father gave me a watch as a birthday gift.*
**2** a special natural ability: *She has a gift for languages; she can speak five different languages.*

**gigabyte** /'gɪgə,baɪt/ *noun adjective*
(in computers) one billion bytes or approximately 1,000 megabytes

**gigantic** /ʤaɪ'gæntɪk/ *adjective*
very large, huge: *Elephants are gigantic creatures. (antonym)* small.

**giggle** /'gɪgəl/ *verb* **giggled, giggling, giggles**
to laugh in a silly, uncontrolled way

**gill** /gɪl/ *noun*
openings on the sides of a fish through which the fish breathes

**gimmick** /'gɪmɪk/ *noun*
an unusual method or object used to get attention: *The sales assistant gave me a free shopping bag as a sales gimmick when I entered the store.*

**gin** /ʤɪn/ *noun*
a strong, clear alcoholic drink made from grain and berries: *Gin and tonic is a popular before-dinner drink.*

**gipsy** /'ʤɪpsi/ *noun, plural* **gipsies**
*See:* gypsy.

**giraffe** /ʤə'ræf/ *noun*
an African animal with long legs, a very long neck, and a spotted coat: *Giraffes eat leaves located high in trees. See:* art on page 14a.

giraffe

**girdle** /'gɜrdl/ *noun*
a piece of women's underwear that fits very tightly around the hips and stomach to change her shape

**girl** /gɜrl/ *noun*
**1** a female child
**2** a daughter: *They have two boys and a girl. –adjective* **girlish.**

**girlfriend** /'gɜrl,frɛnd/ *noun*
**1** a male's female friend with whom he has a romantic relationship: *He bought his girlfriend a gold watch.*
**2** a female friend: *His wife goes bowling with her girlfriends once a week.*

**USAGE NOTE:** Women may use *girlfriend* to refer to any female friend, but when men use the term, it usually refers to a romantic relationship: *Bill said his girlfriend made him a sweater.* The term *boyfriend* always refers to a romantic relationship: *Mary's new boyfriend is very good-looking.*

**Girl Scout** *noun*
a member of the Girl Scouts, an international organization that trains girls in character building and healthy activities: *His daughter joined the Girl Scouts and loves to go camping.*

**give** /gɪv/ *verb*
**1** to pass to someone: *Please give me the car keys.*
**2** to pass to someone as a gift: *I gave my friend a birthday present.*
**3** to produce, provide: *Good food gives you energy.*
**4** to cause to have: *He gave his wife the flu.*||*The book gave him some good ideas.*
**5** to make or do something: *I will give you a phone call tomorrow.*
**6** to permit, allow (often of time): *Give yourself an hour to drive to the meeting.*

7 to perform: *Musicians give concerts.*

**to give something away:** to offer something freely, to make a gift of: *They are giving away prizes at the new store.*

**to give something back:** to return something: *My friend gave back the tools that he borrowed.*

**to give in (to someone** or **something):** to agree to do something you were unwilling to do: *The little boy cried so much that his mother finally gave in to him and bought some candy.*

**to give off something:** to send out (a smell, heat, light, etc.): *She gives off a smell of roses.*

G

**to give someone** or **something up:** **a.** to stop doing something: *I gave up smoking last year.* **b.** to accept defeat: *After spending an hour trying to solve the math problem, he gave up and asked for help. (antonym)* take.

**given** /gɪvən/ *verb*
*past participle of* give

**given name** *noun*
first name(s): *The given names of Mr. and Mrs. Smith's daughters are Jane and Nicole.*

**glacier** /'gleɪʃər/ *noun*
a large mass of ice that moves slowly, usually down a mountain: *Glaciers are similar to slow-moving rivers of ice.*

**glad** /glæd/ *adjective* **gladder, gladdest**
pleased, happy: *I am glad that you had a good time at the party. See:* happy, USAGE NOTE.

**gladly** /'glædli/ *adverb*
happily, willingly, eagerly: *I'll gladly help you with your French homework.*

**glamorous** or **glamourous** /'glæmərəs/ *adjective*
having an attractive and exciting appearance: *Marilyn Monroe was a glamorous movie star. –adverb* **glamorously;** *–noun* **glamour** or **glamor.**

**glance** /glæns/ *noun*
a quick short look at something: *She took a quick glance at her watch.*

**at a glance:** immediately, with one look: *I could tell at a glance that the numbers were wrong. –verb* **to glance**

**gland** /glænd/ *noun*
one of the many small organs in the body that sends out substances to change body chemistry: *the sweat glands –adjective* **glandular** /'glændʒələr/**.**

**glare** /glɛr/ *noun*
1 a strong light: *The sun's glare on the car's front window made driving difficult.*
2 a look of anger or hatred: *an angry glare (antonym)* smile.

**glass** /glæs/ *noun, plural* **glasses**
1 a hard clear material used in windows (buildings, ornaments, objects, etc.): *Be careful with that vase; it is made of glass.*
2 windows
3 a drinking container made of glass: *I had some bread and two glasses of milk for breakfast. See:* art on pages 5a and 7a.
4 *plural* **glasses:** two pieces of glass or plastic in a frame that one wears in front of the eyes to see better, *(synonym)* eyeglasses: *She wears glasses* (or) *eyeglasses for reading.*

**glassful** /'glæs͵fʊl/ *noun*
the amount contained in a glass: *The child had a glassful of milk at lunch.*

**glassware** /'glæs͵wɛr/ *noun, (no plural) used with a singular verb* household objects made of glass, such as drinking glasses and ornaments

**gleam** /glim/ *verb*
to shine brightly: *Diamonds gleam.*

**glee** /gli/ *noun, (no plural)*
a feeling of delight, joy: *He jumped up and down with glee when he won the prize. –adjective* **gleeful** /'glifəl/**.**

**glee club** *noun*
a group of singers: *The glee club practices every Thursday night.*

**glib** /glɪb/ *adjective* **glibber, glibbest**
able to talk easily and well with little thought or preparation: *a glib salesperson*

**glide** /glaɪd/ *verb* **glided, gliding, glides**
1 to fly through the air without power: *Birds can glide in the air.*
2 to move easily and quickly over a surface: *The sailboat glided across the lake.*

**glide** *noun*
a smooth motion or movement: *The airplane reached high in the sky, then went into a glide.*

**glider** /ˈglaɪdər/ *noun*
a type of airplane that rides air currents without an engine

glider

**glimpse** /glɪmps/ *noun*
a short look at something, often not very clear
**to catch a glimpse of something:** to see briefly: *I only caught a glimpse of the thief before he ran away.*
**glimpse** *verb* **glimpsed, glimpsing, glimpses**
to see something quickly, often not very well: *I glimpsed the house through the trees. See:* glance.

**glitch** /glɪʧ/ *noun, plural* **glitches**
a small (technical) problem: *A glitch in the computer is stopping the printer from working.*

**glitter** /ˈglɪtər/ *verb*
to shine brightly with flashes of light: *Her jewels glittered. –noun* **glitter.**
**all that glitters is not gold:** everything that looks or seems attractive is not always attractive in reality: *You can be rich and still be unhappy because all that glitters is not gold.*

**gloat** /gloʊt/ *verb*
to take or show great pleasure in oneself, usually in an offensive way: *The young boxer gloated over his defeat of the champion. –noun* **gloating.**

**global** /ˈgloʊbəl/ *adjective*
relating to all the world, *(synonym)* worldwide: *We have a global economy today. –adverb* **globally.**

**globe** /ˈgloʊb/ *noun*
**1** the earth, world: *Airplanes circle the globe in hours these days.*
**2** a round object with a map of the world on it: *The students used a globe to measure the distance between two cities. See:* art on page 8a.

globe

**gloom** /glum/ *noun, (no plural)*
**1** a feeling of sadness: *After the child's death, the house was full of gloom.*
**2** dark surroundings *–adjective* **gloomy.**

**glorify** /ˈglɔrəˌfaɪ/ *verb* **glorified, glorifying, glorifies**
to give honor, fame, and admiration: *Poets glorified the ancient kings in their poems. –noun* **glorification** /ˌglɔrəfəˈkeɪʃən/.

**glorious** /ˈglɔri əs/ *adjective*
full of great honor and fame: *England has a glorious history. –adverb* **gloriously.**

**glory** /ˈglɔri/ *noun, plural* **glories**
**1** great honor, fame, and admiration: *The candidate accepted the glory of winning the Presidency.*
**2** *plural* **glories:** great beauty, special attraction: *The Empire State building is one of New York City's glories. –adjective* **glorious;** *–adverb* **gloriously.**

**glossary** /ˈglɑs əri/ *noun, plural* **glossaries**
an alphabetical list of words and their meanings: *A glossary at the end of the book gives explanations of foreign words.*

**glossy** /ˈglɔsi/ *adjective* **glossier, glossiest**
smooth and shiny: *I washed and polished my car and now it is glossy.*
**glossy** *noun, plural* **glossies**
a photograph on shiny paper: *I had several glossies made of my favorite photo.*

**glove** /glʌv/ *noun*
a covering for the hand with a separate part for each finger and thumb: *In the winter, she wears leather gloves.*
**to fit like a glove:** to fit perfectly: *These new pants fit like a glove. See:* art on page 12a.

**glow** /gloʊ/ *noun*
**1** light from the sun or a fire: *The warm glow of a fire in the fireplace on a cold night gives comfort.*
**2** a slightly reddish color to the skin, usually in the face: *After her vacation, she has a glow of good health.*

G

**glow** *verb*
to give off light, usually without a flame: *The cigarette glowed in the dark.*

**glue** /glu/ *noun*
a sticky liquid or solid that joins things together: *I use glue to stick pictures on paper.*

**glue** *verb* **glued, gluing, glues**
to join things together with glue: *I glued the pictures to a piece of paper.*

**gnaw** /nɔ/ *verb*
to keep biting at something over a period of time: *Rats gnaw through containers to get at food inside.*

G

**GNP** /ˌʤiɛn'pi/ *noun*
*abbreviation of* gross national product

**go** /goʊ/ *verb* **went** /wɛnt/, **gone** /gɔn, gɑn/, **going, goes**
**1** to move from one place to another: *I go to my office every morning.*
**2** to leave a place: *I have to go* (or) *be going now, but I'll see you later.*
**3** to move somewhere to do something: *She likes to go swimming (shopping, driving, dancing, etc.).*
**4** to operate: *The engine is still going; shut it off.*
**5** to change from one condition to another, become: *He went crazy.*||*The value of the dollar is going down.*
**6** to reach to: *This highway goes to Washington.*
**7** to stop, break, or collapse: *The motor went; we have to buy a new one.*
**8** to perform, be: *Business (Life, My job, etc.) is going well.*||*How are things going?*
**9** to look good with: *That blue tie and green suit don't go together.*
**to go: a.** (of time) to remain: *I have four days to go before my vacation ends.* **b.** to buy food at a restaurant to eat at home: *I got some Chinese food to go and ate it at home.*
**to go after someone** or **something:** to try (hard) to obtain, chase: *The police went after the thief.*
**to go along with:** to agree with: *I go along with what you are saying.*
**to go away:** to leave, depart: *Please go away and don't bother me now.*
**to go back:** to return: *He left the country as a child and never went back.*
**to go by something** or **someone:** to be directed or guided by something or someone: *You can't go by what he says: he lies sometimes.*
**to go far:** to succeed: *He is very smart and will go far in life.*
**to go for: a. something:** to try to get: *She decided to go for the job of sales manager at her company.* **b. something** or **someone:** to like very much: *He really goes for blonde women.*
**to go off: a.** to leave, depart: *My friend went off and left me alone.* **b.** to shut off (said of mechanical devices): *The lights went off.* **c.** to explode: *A bomb went off in the post office.*
**to go on: a.** to happen: *What's going on at that meeting?* **b.** to continue: *She went on working even after the accident.*
**to go out: a.** to leave one's home in order to have fun: *That evening, she and a friend went out (to a movie, play, dinner, dance, etc.).* **b.** to have a romantic relationship with someone and spend time together: *They went out for two years before getting married.*
**to go through something:** to experience, usually something painful: *He went through a difficult time after his wife died.*
**to go together** or **with: a.** to be suitable together: *Those blue shoes and that blue skirt go well together.* **b.** to have a romantic relationship: *She has been going with him for a year now.*
**to have to go:** to need to go to the toilet: *I have to go badly. Where's the men's room?*

**go** *noun, plural* **goes**
a try, attempt at something: *I couldn't solve the problem, so I asked my friend to have a go at it.*
**to be on the go:** to be very busy: *I've been on the go all week and I'm tired.* *(antonym)* come.

**goal** /goʊl/ *noun*
**1** a score in some sports, such as soccer or hockey: *The player scored two goals during the last game.*
**2** the place used for scoring points
**3** purpose, aim: *Our goal is to increase company sales by ten percent this year.*

**goalie** /ˈgoʊli/ *noun informal*
a goalkeeper

**goalkeeper** /ˈgoʊlˌkipər/ *noun*
a player who stands in the goal and tries to stop the other team from scoring

**goat** /goʊt/ *noun*
a small four-legged animal, related to a sheep, that has horns and a rough coat and gives milk: *Many wild goats live in the mountains.*

**gobble** /ˈgɑbəl/ *noun*
the noise that a turkey makes

**god** /gɑd/ *noun*
**1 God:** the Supreme Being, Creator in many religions (Christianity, Islam, Judaism)
**2** one of the beings or spirits worshipped in various cultures: *Mars was the ancient Roman god of war.*

**godchild** /ˈgɑdˌʧaɪld/ *noun, plural* **godchildren** /-ˌʧɪldrən/
the child (**godson** or **goddaughter**) of someone else whom one promises to take care of if the natural parents die: *My best friend's daughter is my godchild.*

**goddaughter** /ˈgɑdˌdɔtər/ *noun*
*See:* godchild.

**goddess** /ˈgɑdɪs/ *noun, plural* **goddesses**
**1** a female god
**2** a beautiful woman: *Marilyn Monroe was a goddess among film stars.*

**godfather** /ˈgɑdˌfɑðər/ *noun*
**1** *See:* godparent.
**2** *figurative* the head or leader of a criminal organization (especially in the Mafia)

**godly** /ˈgɑdli/ *adjective* **godlier, godliest**
believing in God, very religious

**godmother** /ˈgɑdˌmʌðər/ *noun*
*See:* godparent.

**godparent** /ˈgɑdˌpɛrənt/ *noun*
a person (**godfather** or **godmother**) who promises to take care of someone else's child if the child's parents die: *My godparents are my mother's best friend and her husband.*

**godson** /ˈgɑdˌsʌn/ *noun*
*See:* godchild.

**goggles** /ˈgɑgəlz/ *noun plural*
plastic glasses that protect the eyes: *When she swims, she wears goggles.*

goggles

**gold** /goʊld/ *noun, (no plural)*
a precious yellow metal used for jewelry, coins, etc.: *Her rings are made of gold.*
**to have a heart of gold:** to be a kind and generous person
**worth one's** or **its weight in gold:** of great value: *She is an excellent worker; she's worth her weight in gold.*

**gold** *adjective*
made of or related to gold: *a gold ring*

**golden** /ˈgoʊldən/ *adjective*
**1** bright yellow, gold colored: *a golden apple*
**2** made of gold or gold leaf: *That picture has a golden frame.*
**3** very valuable, excellent: *She was accepted by the university; she has a golden opportunity to receive an excellent education.*

**Golden Rule** *noun*
a rule that you should treat others as you would like to be treated yourself: *Some people try to live by the Golden Rule.*

**goldfish** /ˈgoʊldˌfɪʃ/ *noun, plural* **goldfish** or **goldfishes**
small colorful fish kept in a bowl or tank by people: *She likes bright-colored goldfish.*

**gold mine** *noun*
**1** a place, usually underground, from which gold is taken
**2** *figurative* a business or activity that is very successful: *That business of his is a gold mine.*

**gold-plated** *adjective*
covered with gold –*noun* **gold plating.**

**golf** /gɑlf/ *noun, (no plural)*
a game in which people try to hit a small hard ball with a special stick (a club) into a small hole over a large area of land: *I like to play golf on weekends.* –*verb* **to golf;** –*noun* (person) **golfer.**

**golly** /ˈgɑli/
*exclamation* an expression of surprise

**gondola** /ˈgɑndələ/ *noun*
a long narrow boat with a flat bottom used on canals in Venice
–*noun* (person) **gondolier** /ˈgɑndəˈlɪr/.

gondola



**gone** /gɔn/
*verb*
*past participle of* go

**good** /gʊd/ *adjective* **better** /ˈbɛtər/, **best** /bɛst/
**1** (in general) having a pleasing quality, great, pleasurable: *She had a good time on her vacation.*||*That singer is very good.*||*You look good; I like your new hair style.*
**2** having the ability or skill to do something well: *He's good at (playing) the piano.*||*I am no good at numbers.*
**3** kind: *She's very good with children; they all love her.*
**4** important to one's health or character: *Milk and cheese are good for your bones and teeth.*||*Too much television is not good for children.*
**5** well-behaved: *Her son is very good; he never fights with other children.*
**6** fresh, not spoiled: *The bread from yesterday is still good.*
**7** real, not fake: *That coin is good, not a fake.*
**8** behaving in a moral way: *She is a good woman.*
**9** able to be used legally: *Her driver's license is good for five years.*
**10** *informal* **as good as:** almost: *I washed those old curtains and now they look as good as new.*

**good** *noun, (no plural)*
something that is morally correct or of value: *She always looks for the good in people.*||*There is some good in him; don't send him to jail.*
**for your own good:** in one's own best interest (said to someone who should do something difficult for his or her own benefit): *You should stay in school. I'm telling you this for your own good.*
**to do good:** to benefit others, perform a kindness: *The church does good by helping the poor.*

**good** *exclamation*
wonderful, excellent: *Good! The rain has stopped.*
**Good for you:** congratulations: *Good for you; I'm really happy that you won the tournament!*

**good** *adverb*
**to make good:** to succeed: *She made good in the banking business. (antonym)* bad.

---

**USAGE NOTE:** *Good* should not be used to describe a verb in formal speech or writing, such as in, *He did good on the test.* It should be: *He did well on the test.*

---

**good-bye** /gʊdˈbaɪ/ *noun*
an expression used when one is leaving: *When we finished our conversation, I said good-bye to her and left.*

**goodhearted** /ˈgʊdˈhɑrtɪd/ *adjective*
kind, generous: *She is a goodhearted woman.*

**good-looking** *adjective*
attractive, pleasing to the eye: *She is a good-looking woman.*

**good luck** *noun, (no plural)*
said to wish someone well: *"Good luck! Call me when you get back from your trip."*||*He wished me good luck in my new job.*

**goodness** /ˈgʊdnɪs/ *noun, (no plural)*
**1** the quality or state of being good: *People spoke of the priest's goodness and generosity.*
**2** *exclamation* **Goodness!** or **My Goodness!:** used to express surprise: *"My goodness! You're two hours early!" (antonym)* badness.

**goods** /gʊds/ *noun plural*
items that can be bought or sold: *The goods that you ordered have arrived in the store.*

**good will** or **goodwill** *noun, (no plural)*
friendliness or good feelings between

people: *The talks between the two countries took place in an atmosphere of good will.*

**goof** /guf/ *noun informal*
a stupid, careless mistake: *He made a goof and ordered the wrong part.*
**to goof off:** not to work hard, to waste time: *He goofs off all day when the boss is away.*

**goose** /gus/ *noun, plural* **geese** /gis/
**1** a water bird with a long neck, larger than the duck: *Geese fly south for the winter.*
**2** the female of this bird
**to cook someone's goose:** to ruin someone, get someone in trouble: *A witness cooked the thief's goose by telling the police where the thief was hiding.*

**GOP** /ˌʤioʊ'pi/ *noun*
*abbreviation of* Grand Old Party, the Republican Party in US politics

**gopher** /'goʊfər / *noun*
a small animal that makes holes in the ground: *Many gophers live in the flat grasslands of the USA.*

**gorge** /gɔrʤ/ *noun*
a high, narrow opening between mountains, usually with a stream

**gorgeous** /'gɔrʤəs/ *adjective*
beautiful: *She is a fashion model and a gorgeous woman.*||*The flowers in the window have a gorgeous color.* *(antonym)* ugly.

**gorilla** /gə'rɪlə/ *noun*
the largest of the great apes (man-like monkeys), found in western Africa: *There are only a few mountain gorillas left in the world.*

**gosh** /gɑʃ/ *exclamation*
expression of surprise or disappointment: *Gosh, that exam was difficult.*

**gosling** /'gɑzlɪŋ/ *noun*
a baby goose

**gospel** /'gɑspəl/ *noun*
an idea that one is not permitted to disagree with: *In that company, the owner's wishes are the gospel* (or) *gospel truth that everyone must follow.*
**Gospel:** any of the first four books of the New Testament in the Christian Bible

**gospel music** *noun*
a type of American religious music with a strong beat: *My mother sings gospel music in church.*

**gossip** /'gɑsəp/ *verb*
to talk or write about other people's actions or lives, sometimes in an untruthful way: *She is always gossiping about her neighbors.* *–noun* **gossip.**

**got** /gɑt/ *verb*
*past tense and participle of* get
**1** to be necessary, must do something: *I've got to leave now; it's very late.*
**2** to have something or someone: *I've got $100 to spend this evening.*

**gotten** /'gɑtn/ *verb*
*past participle of* get

**goulash** /'guˌlɑʃ/ *noun*
a thick soup of vegetables, meat, and seasonings (usually paprika), cooked together: *We had beef goulash with potatoes for dinner. See:* stew.

**gourd** /gɔrd/ *noun*
a fruit with a hard outer shell that usually cannot be eaten: *People use gourds to hold drinking water.*

**govern** /'gʌvərn/ *verb*
**1** to rule a country, city, etc.: *The President governs the USA.*||*The mayor governs the city.*
**2** to have influence over something, *(synonym)* to determine: *The weather governs the prices of fresh fruit and vegetables every year.*

**government** /'gʌvərmənt/ *noun*
**1** a system of political control of a country, city, etc.: *That country has a military government.*
**2** the people who rule: *The government decided to cut taxes for the middle classes.* *–adjective* **governmental** /ˌgʌvərn'mɛntl/.

**governor** /'gʌvənər/ *noun*
a government official in charge of a state in the USA: *The state governors meet each year to discuss common problems.*

**gown** /gaʊn/ *noun*
**1** a long, formal evening dress for women: *She wore a blue silk gown to the opera.*
**2** a long, usually black coat worn in spe-

cial ceremonies by judges, professors, students, etc.: *a school graduation gown*

**GPA** /ˌʤipi'eɪ/ *noun*
*abbreviation of* grade point average

**grab** /græb/ *verb* **grabbed, grabbing, grabs**
to take quickly and roughly: *A thief grabbed the woman's purse and ran.*

**grace** /greɪs/ *noun*
beauty of movement or style: *She dances with grace.*

**graceful** /'greɪsfəl/ *adjective*
with beauty of motion or style: *She is a graceful dancer.* *–adverb* **gracefully.** *(antonym)* awkward.

**gracious** /'greɪʃəs/ *adjective*
kind and polite: *She is a gracious woman who provides her guests with everything they need.* *–adverb* **graciously;** *–noun* **graciousness.**

**grad** /græd/ *noun informal*
*short for* graduate: *He is a high school grad.*

**grade** /greɪd/ *noun*
**1** an educational class level: *Her son goes into the seventh (first, 12th, etc.) grade this year.*
**2** a school or test score: *He makes good grades in school.*
**3** a level of quality: *That store sells an excellent grade of fruits and vegetables.*

**grade** *verb* **graded, grading, grades**
to score, mark: *The teacher grades tests every week.*

**grade point average** *noun*
the average of a student's marks in which 4.0 is considered perfect: *He has a 3.7 grade point average for his four years of college study.*

---

**USAGE NOTE:** Abbreviated as GPA. The numbers correspond to these letter grades: 4.0 = A, 3.0 = B, 2.0 = C, 1.0 = D, 0 = F

---

**grade school** *noun*
in the USA, elementary school; first through fifth or sixth grades: *Her eight-year-old daughter goes to grade school in the neighborhood.* *See:* secondary school.

---

**USAGE NOTE:** *Grade school* or *elementary school* is followed by two or three years of *middle school* or *junior high school;* sixth or seventh through eighth or ninth grades. *High school* begins in ninth or tenth grade and goes through twelfth grade. Tenth, eleventh, and twelfth grades are also called, respectively, *sophomore, junior,* and *senior year: Their son is a senior in high school, but their daughter is only in eighth grade.*

---

**gradual** /'græʤuəl/ *adjective*
happening slowly or by small steps

**graduate** /'græʤuˌeɪt/ *verb* **graduated, graduating, graduates**
to receive a degree from an educational institution: *He graduates from high school in June.* *–noun* (person) **graduate.**

**graduate school** *noun*
an educational institution where students study for a higher degree

**graduation** /ˌgræʤu'eɪʃən/ *noun*
a ceremony on completing a level of education (high school, college) where a degree is given by school officials to graduating students: *My family came to my college graduation in the summer.* *See:* diploma.

graduation

**graffiti** /grə'fiti/ *noun plural*
*used with a singular or plural verb*
rude, funny, or political writings and drawings on walls of public buildings

**grain** /greɪn/ *noun*
**1** a single seed of a plant (wheat, corn)
**2** the seeds in large amounts as food: *Russia buys grain from America.*
**3** a very small, hard piece of something: *Grains of sand form a beach.*
**4** a small amount of something: *There is not a grain of truth in what he says.*

**to take something with a grain of salt:** not to believe all that is said, to doubt: *You have to take what he says with a grain of salt because he doesn't always tell the truth.*

**gram** /græm/ *noun*
a measure of weight equal to one 1,000th of a kilogram or about .04 oz.

**grammar** /'græmər/ *noun, (no plural)*
a system of rules that apply to a language: *We study grammar in order to write good sentences.*

**grammatical** /grə'mætikəl/ *adjective*
**1** related to the rules of grammar: *My grammatical knowledge of Spanish is very poor.*
**2** correct according to the rules of grammar: *This sentence is grammatical.* –*adverb* **grammatically.**

**Grammy™** /'græmi/ *noun, plural* **Grammys** or **Grammies**
a small statue given each year for excellence in many areas of the recording industry, mainly for music: *Aretha Franklin, the singer, has won many Grammys™.*

**grand** /grænd/ *adjective*
**1** large and attractive: *a grand old house*
**2** *formal* pleasant, enjoyable: *We had a grand time on our vacation.* –*adverb* **grandly.**

**granddaughter** /'græn,dɔtər/ *noun*
a daughter of one's child

**grandfather** /'græn,fɑðər/ *noun*
the father of one's father or mother *See:* art on page 13a.

**grandfather clock** *noun*
a clock in a tall wooden frame that stands on the floor

grandfather clock

**grandma** /'græn,mɑ/ *noun informal*
*short for* grandmother

**grandmother** /'græn,mʌðər/ *noun*
the mother of one's father or mother: *My grandmother lives in Texas. See:* art on page 13a.

**grandpa** /'græn,pɑ/ *noun informal*
*short for* grandfather

**grandparent** /'græn,pɛrənt/ *noun*
a parent of one's father or mother

**grandson** /'græn,sʌn/ *noun*
the son of one's daughter or son

**grandstand** /'græn,stænd/ *noun*
rows of seats outdoors sometimes covered with a roof, for watching sporting events: *We sat in the grandstand.*

**granite** /'grænɪt/ *noun*
a hard, gray rock: *That building is made of granite and will last for hundreds of years.*

**grant** /grænt/ *verb formal*
**1** to give or allow what is asked for: *The politican granted my request for an interview for my newspaper.*
**2** to accept as true: *I grant what you say is correct, but you still owe me the money.*

**grant** *noun*
money given for a specific purpose: *The government gave the school a grant to teach computer skills.*

**grape** /greɪp/ *noun*
a small round fruit, usually green or dark purple, that grows in bunches and can be used to make wine: *Grapes are grown in great quantities in California and New York. See:* art on page 3a.

**grapefruit** /'greɪp,frut/ *noun, plural* **grapefruits** or **grapefruit**
a large round fruit, usually yellow with a thick skin, that has a sour taste: *I have a half grapefruit for breakfast. See:* art on page 3a.

**grapevine** /'greɪp,vaɪn/ *noun*
the climbing plant on which grapes grow

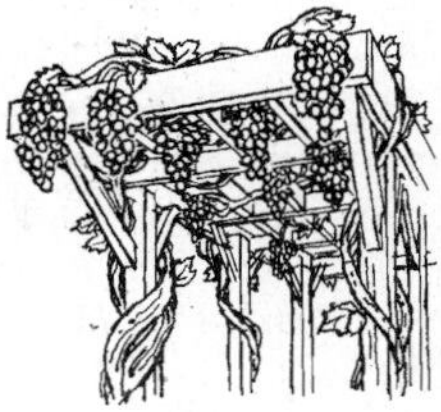
grapevines

**graph** /græf/ *noun*
a drawing that shows changes in quantities: *I made a line graph that shows sales increases from year to year.*

**graph** *verb*
to show changes in picture form –*adjective* **graphic;** –*adverb* **graphically.**

**graphics** /ˈgræfɪks/ *noun plural*
pictures such as photographs and drawings: *the graphics in an art book*

**grasp** /græsp/ *verb*
**1** to hold firmly, take hold of: *I grasped the door handle with both hands and pulled hard.*
**2** to succeed in understanding something often difficult: *After reading the book again, I finally grasped the main points of the story.* –*noun* **grasp.**

**grass** /græs/ *noun, plural* **grasses**
green plant that covers the ground: *I like to play tennis on grass. See:* art on page 9a.

G

**grasshopper** /ˈgræsˌhɑpər/ *noun*
a plant-eating insect that can jump high and makes a loud noise: *Grasshoppers got into our flower garden and ruined it.*

**grassy** /ˈgræsi/ *adjective* **grassier, grassiest**
covered with grass: *The grassy areas around the building make it an attractive place to work.*

**grate** /greɪt/ *noun*
**1** bars that hold the wood and coal in a fireplace
**2** bars put over a window to keep out thieves *See:* grating.

**grateful** /ˈgreɪtfəl/ *adjective*
thankful: *I am grateful for all your help.* –*adverb* **gratefully.**

**gratify** /ˈgrætəˌfaɪ/ *verb formal* **gratified, gratifying, gratifies**
**1** to give pleasure and satisfaction: *His children's success gratified him.*
**2** to satisfy a desire: *She gratified her hunger by eating chocolate cake.* –*noun* **gratification.**

**grating** /ˈgreɪtɪŋ/ *noun*
a covering of metal bars over a window, hole, etc.: *The grating over the hole in the road stops large objects from falling in.*

**gratitude** /ˈgrætəˌtud/ *noun, (no plural)*
thankfulness, *(synonym)* appreciation: *She showed her gratitude by saying, "Thank you!"*

**gratuity** /grəˈtuəti/ *noun, plural* **gratuities**
a gift of money for service, *(synonym)* a tip: *The standard gratuity at good restaurants is 15 percent of the bill.*

**grave** /greɪv/ *adjective* **graver, gravest**
serious, worrying: *The patient is very ill and in grave condition.*

**grave** *noun*
a place in the ground for placing a dead person: *He is buried in a grave next to his wife's. See:* gravestone.

**to turn over in one's grave:** said of a dead person who would not be happy with the actions of the living: *Their mother would be turning over in her grave if she could see how badly her children behave.* –*adverb* **gravely.**

**gravestone** /ˈgreɪvˌstoʊn/ *noun*
a stone over a grave that usually shows the name and dates of birth and death of the dead person

**graveyard** /ˈgreɪvˌyɑrd/ *noun*
an area of land, sometimes near a church, where dead people are buried

**gravity** /ˈgrævəti/ *noun, (no plural)*
**1** a natural force pulling objects to the ground: *Objects fall to earth because of the force of gravity.*
**2** seriousness: *When the shooting started, the gravity of the situation became clear.*

**gravy** /ˈgreɪvi/ *noun, (no plural)*
a warm thick liquid made of the juices and fats from cooked meat: *I like brown gravy on my potatoes.*

**gray** or **grey** /greɪ/ *noun*
the color black mixed with a little white: *The lady is dressed in gray.*

**gray** or **grey** *adjective*
**1** colored gray: *She is wearing a gray dress.*
**2** sad, depressing: *It is a gray day: rainy and cold.*

**gray** or **grey** *verb*
(of hair) to become gray: *My father's hair is graying.*

**graze** /greɪz/ *verb* **grazed, grazing, grazes**
**1** to feed on grass: *The sheep graze in the field.*
**2** to touch lightly against something and injure the skin: *The child fell and grazed her hand.*

**grease** /gris/ *noun, (no plural)*
**1** animal fat softened by cooking
**2** any thick oily substance

**grease** *verb* /gris/ **greased, greasing, greases**
to put grease on: *He greased the wheels.*

**greasy** /ˈgrisi/ *adjective* **greasier, greasiest**
having (too much) grease: *That meat is very greasy.*

**great** /greɪt/ *adjective*
**1** large, *(synonym)* huge: *A great big bear blocked our path. (antonym)* small.
**2** famous: *Alexander the Great never saw the Great Wall of China.*
**3** excellent, superior: *That company has a great reputation.*
**4** *informal* pleasant, wonderful: *We had a great time on our vacation. –noun* **greatness.** *(antonym)* bad.

**greatly** /ˈgreɪtli/ *adverb*
very much: *Crime has increased greatly in the city over the last year.*

**greed** /grid/ *noun, (no plural)*
a strong desire for money, food, etc.: *Greed made the child take the last piece of cake. –adjective* **greedy;** *–adverb* **greedily.**

**green** /grin/ *adjective*
**1** having the color of most plants, a mixture of blue and yellow: *After the rain, the grass looked very green. See:* art on page 16a.
**2** with little experience or training: *The general sent the green soldiers for more training.*

**green card** *noun*
a small plastic card from the US government allowing a non–US citizen to live and work in the USA legally: *The company couldn't hire her without a green card.*

**USAGE NOTE:** A *green card* may be obtained by the relative or employer of a non-US citizen. Foreigners who have green cards may apply for *citizenship* after living in the United States of America for five years, or after three years if they are married to a US citizen. A work permit may be an authorization card or a stamp in a passport from immigration. An F-1 visa is given to students.

**greenhouse** /ˈgrinˌhaʊs/ *noun, plural* **greenhouses** /-ˈhaʊzɪz/
a building with glass walls and a glass roof, used to grow and protect plants: *Those flowers were grown in a greenhouse during the winter.*

**greet** /grit/ *verb*
to say hello to someone: *When I met the president, she greeted me in a very friendly way. –noun* (person) **greeter.**

**greeting** /ˈgritɪŋ/ *noun*
**1** the first words or actions used on meeting someone, such as "Hello" or "Hi": *We passed on the street and gave each other a friendly greeting.*
**2** *plural* **greetings:** good wishes, usually written: *"Greetings on your birthday and Congratulations!"*

**greeting card** *noun*
a card, folded and printed with a message inside, such as "Get well soon" or "Happy Birthday": *I sent my friend a greeting card for her birthday.*

greeting card

**grew** /gru/ *verb*
*past tense of* grow

**grey** /greɪ/ *noun adjective*
*See:* gray.

**greyhound** /ˈgreɪˌhaʊnd/ *noun*
a thin racing dog with long legs: *People love to watch greyhounds race at the track.*

**grief** /grif/ *noun, (no plural)*
great sadness, sorrow: *Her brother's sudden death caused her a great deal of grief.*
**to give someone grief:** to make trouble for someone: *My boss gives me a lot of grief about my poor computer skills. –verb* **to grieve;** *–adjective* **grevious.**

**grievance** /ˈgrivəns/ *noun*
a complaint, especially of being treated unfairly: *Workers have a grievance over low wages.*

**grill** /grɪl/ *noun*
a frame of metal bars on which food is cooked, usually outside: *I put some hamburgers on the grill. See:* barbecue.

**grill** *verb*
to cook on a grill: *I grilled some burgers for lunch. See:* barbecue, USAGE NOTE.

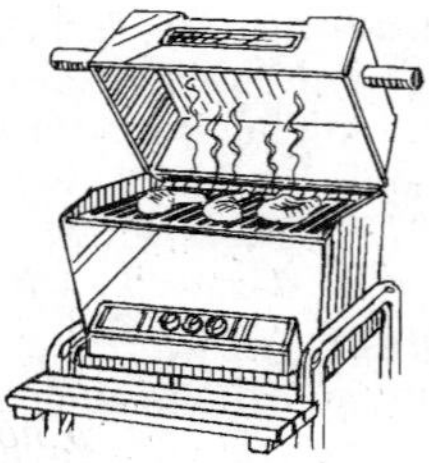
grill

**grim** /grɪm/ *adjective* **grimmer, grimmest**
**1** serious: *The prisoner has a grim look on his face.*
**2** expecting the worst: *He suffered a severe injury and his future looks grim.* –*adverb* **grimly;** –*noun* **grimness.**

**grimace** /ˈgrɪməs/ *verb* **grimaced, grimacing, grimaces**
to twist the face: *He grimaced at hearing the bad news.*

**grimace** *noun*
a twisting of the face, often in pain: *He has a grimace on his face.*

**grin** /grɪn/ *noun*
a big smile: *He greeted his friend with a big grin. See:* smile, USAGE NOTE.

**grin** *verb* **grinned, grinning, grins**
to give a big smile: *He grinned at his girlfriend.*

**to grin and bear it:** to suffer pain or embarrassment without complaining: *I know the work is hard, but you'll just have to grin and bear it. (antonym)* frown.

**grind** /graɪnd/ *verb* **ground** /graʊnd/, **grinding, grinds**
**1** to make into small pieces or powder by rubbing: *I ground the coffee beans.*
**2** to rub two hard surfaces together, usually to make smooth: *The worker is grinding metal parts.*

**grind** *noun*
**1** the process of grinding
**2** *informal figurative* a tiring job: *Her job is a daily grind; she works on the computer eight hours a day.*

**grinder** /ˈgraɪndər/ *noun*
any device used to grind substances: *We put beef in a meat grinder to make hamburger.*

**grindstone** /ˈgraɪnˌstoʊn/ *noun*
a piece of stone or other material used to smooth or sharpen metal

**to keep one's nose to the grindstone:** to work very hard and steadily

**gringo** /ˈgrɪŋgoʊ/ *noun slang, plural* **gringos**
a foreigner in Latin America, especially one who is white and speaks English (usually used in a negative way)

**grip** /grɪp/ *noun*
**1** a strong hold: *The thief had a firm grip on the money.*
**2** command, control: *He has a good grip on his emotions.*

**grip** *verb* **gripped, gripping, grips**
to hold firmly: *He gripped the club with both hands.*

**grizzly bear** or **grizzly** *noun, plural* **grizzlies**
a large gray and brown bear of western North America: *The grizzly bear frightens people because of its power and big size.*

grizzly bear

**groan** /groʊn/ *verb*
(to make) a deep sound from the throat to show pain, worry, disapproval, etc.: *He groaned as he lifted the heavy box.* –*noun* (sound) **groan.**

**grocer** /ˈgroʊsər/ *noun*
**1** a person who sells food and other household things
**2** a grocery store: *I'm going to the grocer to buy some groceries.*

**groceries** /ˈgroʊsəriz/ *noun plural*
food and other household things (soap, paper towels, etc.): *I buy groceries at the supermarket.*

**grocery** /ˈgroʊsəri/ *noun, plural* **groceries**
a food store: *The local grocery* (or) *grocery store is open seven days a week. See:* art on page 10a.

**groom** /grum/ *noun*
a man marrying a woman, *(synonym)* a bridegroom

**groom** *verb*
to dress well, keep the hair neat: *She is a well-groomed woman.*

**groove** /gruv/ *noun*
a long narrow hole for something to move smoothly in: *The doors on that cabinet slide open on grooves.*

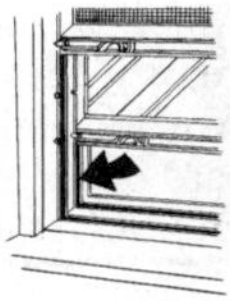
groove

**gross** /groʊs/ *adjective*
disgusting: *He behaved in a gross manner, so I left him.* *–noun* (condition) **grossness.**

**gross national product** *noun* *abbreviation* **GNP.** Total value in goods and services in a country's economy, usually for one year: *The GNP for the USA last year was four trillion dollars.*

**ground (1)** /graʊnd/ *noun*
**1** the earth, soil: *The ground is wet from the rain.*
**2** a safety wire on an electrical device

**ground** *verb*
to wire electrically into the earth for safety: *The lightning rod is grounded into the soil.*

**ground (2)** *verb*
*past tense and past participle of* grind

**ground floor** *noun*
in the USA, the first floor, one at ground level: *The reception is on the ground floor.*

**to get in on the ground floor:** to be present at the beginning of an excellent opportunity: *He got in on the ground floor with that small company and grew with it.*

**group** /grup/ *noun*
a number of people or things placed together: *A group of people protested against the new law.*||*a singing group*

**group** *verb*
**1** to put together in a group: *The students were grouped according to age.*
**2** to come together, gather: *People grouped on the street to watch the parade.*

**grove** /groʊv/ *noun*
a small grouping of trees: *An orange grove grows near the farmhouse.*

**grow** /groʊ/ *verb* **grew** /gru/, **grown** /groʊn/, **growing, grows**
**1** to plant and gather food: *A farmer grows corn and wheat.*
**2** to develop to full size: *The boy has grown into a man.*
**3** to become: *She grew sad (angry, etc.) with her child's rude behavior.*

**to grow by leaps and bounds:** to increase rapidly: *Our business is growing by leaps and bounds.*

**to grow out of something:** **a.** to become too old for something: *My son used to love to play with toy trains, but now he's grown out of it.* **b.** to become too large for something: *He has to buy new shoes because he's grown out of the old ones.*

**to grow up:** to develop from a child to an adult, *(synonym)* to mature: *Our daughter has grown up now.*||*She grew up in the San Francisco area.*

**growl** /graʊl/ *noun*
a low sound made in anger: *The dog let out a growl when the stranger came near.* *–verb* **to growl.**

**grown-up** /ˈgroʊnˌʌp/ *noun*
an adult: *Many grown-ups have dinner after the children are asleep.*

**growth** /groʊθ/ *noun*
**1** the process of growing, development: *The growth of trees in this area is helped by good weather.*
**2** an increase: *population growth*

**grumble** /ˈgrʌmbəl/ *verb* **grumbled, grumbling, grumbles**
to complain in a quiet, unhappy manner: *He grumbled about having to clean the bathroom.*

**grunge** /grʌndʒ/ *adjective*
a type of loud rock music originally from Seattle: *I listen to the Beatles, but my teenage children listen to grunge music.*

**grunge** *noun, (no plural)*
a style of dressing in old, inexpensive clothing worn by grunge musicians *–adjective* **grungy.**

**grunt** /grʌnt/ *verb*
to make a short deep sound from the throat, usually to show great effort, disgust, or boredom: *He grunted as he lifted the heavy rock.* *–noun* (sound) **grunt.**

**guarantee** /ˌgærənˈti/ *noun*
a written promise of satisfaction with a product or service: *The television comes with a guarantee that if it breaks within a year the company will fix it for free.* *See:* warranty.

**guarantee** *verb* **guaranteed, guaranteeing, guarantees**
**1** to give a guarantee: *The shipper guaranteed next-day delivery.*

G

**2** a strong promise: *I guarantee you'll enjoy the trip.*

**guaranty** *noun*
*See:* guarantee.

**guard** /gɑrd/ *noun*
**1** a person paid to protect property: *The building has guards at each entrance. See:* bodyguard.
**2** a person paid to keep prisoners from escaping:

**guard**



**guard** *verb*
**1** to protect property: *They guard against entry by strangers.*
**2** to be very careful: *Parents guard against anyone hurting their children.*
**3** to watch prisoners to keep them from escaping:
**to stand guard:** to perform guard duty: *A policeman stood guard at the door.*

**guarded** /ˈgɑrdɪd/ *adjective*
protected by a guard: *The President lives in a guarded building. –adverb* **guardedly.**

**guardian** /ˈgɑrdiən/ *noun*
**1** a person legally responsible for another, especially a child: *After the girl's parents died, her uncle became her guardian.*
**2** a guard: *Guardians watch over the museum's paintings. –noun* **guardianship.**

**guerrilla** /gəˈrɪlə/ *noun*
a member of an unofficial military group that is trying to attack and defeat the regular military: *Guerrillas hide in the jungle and attack government soldiers.*

**guess** /gɛs/ *noun, plural* **guesses**
a try at saying what might happen or is true: *I made a guess at the cost of that computer.*

**guess** *verb* **guessed, guessing, guesses**
**1** to make a guess: *I guess that it will rain today.*
**2** to say politely what one will do: *"Oh, I guess I'll go home now."*
**to keep someone guessing:** to not tell someone what is true or will happen: *She keeps him guessing by not saying whether she loves him.*

**guest** /gɛst/ *noun*
**1** a visitor who comes to someone's home for a short time: *We had guests for dinner last night.*
**2** someone who stays in a hotel: *Guests check out of the hotel each morning.*
**3** a person who is invited to a restaurant, the movies, etc., and who is paid for by the person inviting them: *"I'll pay; you're my guest this evening."*

**guidance** /ˈgaɪdns/ *noun, (no plural)*
**1** help, advice: *The teacher gave the student guidance on how to pass the exam.*
**2** an electronic device used to direct space vehicles (weapons, computers, etc.)

**guide** /gaɪd/ *noun*
**1** a person who shows the way and often gives information, especially to tourists: *A tour guide gave some history as we passed each important building.*
**2** a reference book: *a map guide*
**3** an idea (rule, measure, etc.) used to decide how to do something: *I use a ruler as a guide in drawing a straight line.*

**guide** *verb* **guided, guiding, guides**
**1** to show the way, give information: *A professor guided us through the museum.*
**2** to direct: *Religious teaching guides us to be kind to others. See:* guidelines.

**guidebook** /ˈgaɪdˌbʊk/ *noun*
a book with detailed information about a place or subject: *Tourists use guidebooks to find their way around cities.*

**guidelines** /ˈgaɪdˌlaɪnz/ *noun plural*
ideas or rules on what to do (or not to do): *The teacher gave us guidelines for writing our paper; it had to be typed and 10–12 pages long.*

**guilt** /gɪlt/ *noun, (no plural)*
**1** the state of having broken the law: *A jury decides the guilt or innocence of an accused person.*
**2** fault, blame for doing something wrong: *The guilt for stopping the talks lies with the lawyers.*
**3** a feeling of having done something

wrong or shameful: *It was guilt that finally caused him to admit to committing the crime. (antonym)* innocence.

**guilty** /'gɪlti/ *adjective* **guilter, guiltiest**
**1** having broken a law, at fault: *The jury found the man guilty of the murder.*
**2** having or showing a feeling of shame, of having done something wrong: *He feels guilty about hurting his friend. (antonym)* innocent. *–adverb* **guiltily.**

**guinea pig** /ˌgɪni/ *noun*
**1** a small animal that looks like a big rat
**2** *figurative* a person used for scientific or medical tests

**guitar** /gɪ'tɑr/ *noun*
a musical instrument with strings: *She plays the guitar beautifully.* *See:* art on page 15a.

guitar

**gulf** /gʌlf/ *noun*
a large area of a sea or ocean surrounded on three sides by land: *The Gulf of Mexico goes from Florida over to Texas and down to Mexico.*

**gull** /gʌl/ *noun*
a type of common seabird, a sea gull.

**gulp** /gʌlp/ *verb*
to swallow whole mouthfuls, usually quickly: *The thirsty man gulped (down) the water. –noun* **gulp.**

**gum** /gʌm/ *noun*
**1** a sticky substance from inside a tree
**2** chewing gum: *She offered me a piece of gum.*
**3** the pink flesh surrounding the teeth: *Her gums are bleeding.*

**gun** /gʌn/ *noun*
**1** a weapon that fires bullets or larger objects: *Hunters use guns to kill animals.*
**2** any device with barrels that shoot substances: *A worker used a paint gun to paint the wall.*
**to go great guns:** to make great progress: *Our new product is going great guns.*
**to jump the gun:** to act too soon: *He jumped the gun in advertising the new product because it is not ready for market yet.*
**to stick to one's guns:** to keep one's opinion or position in spite of opposition: *Everyone told him he was foolish, but he stuck to his guns and went ahead with his plans.*

**gun** *verb* **gunned, gunning, guns**
to cause an engine to run very quickly: *Racers gunned the engines of their cars.*
**to gun someone** or **something down:** to shoot someone or something with a gun, causing a fall to the ground or death: *The police gunned down a criminal in the street.*

**gunfire** /'gʌnˌfaɪr/ *noun, (no plural)*
a shooting of guns (rifles, pistols, etc.): *The sound of gunfire was heard in the hills.*

**gunman** /'gʌnmən/ *noun, plural* **gunmen** /-mɛn/
a criminal using a gun: *A gunman robbed the bank.*

**gunpoint** /'gʌnˌpɔɪnt/ *noun, (no plural)*
the end of a gun
**at gunpoint:** being forced to do something by someone who is pointing a gun at one: *I was robbed at gunpoint in the city.*

**gunpowder** /'gʌnˌpaʊdər/ *noun, (no plural)*
a mixture of chemicals that explodes, used to shoot bullets

**gunshot** /'gʌnˌʃɑt/ *noun*
the loud sound of a gun being fired: *The police heard a gunshot and ran after the criminal.*

**guru** /'guˌru/ *noun*
an Indian spiritual leader, a teacher

**gush** /gʌʃ/ *noun, plural* **gushes**
a sudden rush or flow of something: *a gush of oil, emotion, interest, etc. –noun* **gushing;** *–verb* **to gush.**

**gust** /gʌst/ *noun*
a sudden strong wind

**gut** /gʌt/ *noun*
**1** the food tubes in the stomach area
**2** *slang* stomach area: *He overeats and has a big gut.*
**3** *plural informal* **guts:** courage: *He's got guts to fight a man bigger than he is.*

**gut** *verb* **gutted, gutting, guts**
to completely empty or destroy the in-

G

side contents of a building: *The fire gutted the office building.*

**gut** *adjective informal*
(said of feelings) strong, often unexplained: *I can't explain it but I have a gut feeling that she's telling the truth.*

**gutsy** /'gʌtsi/ *adjective informal* **gutsier, gutsiest**
brave, *(synonym)* courageous: *She is gutsy; she defended herself against a robber.*

**gutter** /'gʌtər/ *noun*
a low, narrow area on the side of a street, or open pipe on a roof for water to run off: *Water runs along the gutter into the sewer.*

**guy** /gaɪ/ *noun informal*
a man: *He is a nice guy; he always helps me with my taxes.*

---

**USAGE NOTE:** In general, the word *guy* refers only to men. However, you may also use the word if you are speaking informally to a group of both males and females or only females.

---

**gym** /ʤɪm/ *noun*
*short for* gymnasium

**gymnasium** /ʤɪm'neɪziəm/ *noun*
a large sports hall, usually with seats for people to watch games: *The college gymnasium has seats for 15,000 visitors.*

**gymnast** /'ʤɪm,nəst/ *noun*
a person who does gymnastics: *She is a gymnast on the Olympic team.*

**gymnastics** /ʤɪm'næstɪks/ *noun plural used with a singular verb* the sport of doing different exercises to develop strength, balance, etc.: *Gymnastics is his favorite sport.*

**gynecology** /,gaɪnə'kɑləʤi/ *noun, (no plural)*
the branch of medicine that specializes in human females' sex organs: *Her doctor studied gynecology in medical school.* *–noun* (doctor) **gynecologist;** *–adjective* **gynecological.**

**gypsy** or **Gypsy** /'ʤɪpsi/ *noun, plural* **gypsies**
**1 Gypsy:** a people, especially of Eastern Europe, that live by going from place to place
**2** *figurative* a person who does not stay in one place for long

# H,h

H

**H, h** /eɪʧ/ *noun* **H's, h's** or **Hs, hs**
the eighth letter of the English alphabet

**ha** or **hah** /hɑ/ *exclamation*
used to show laughter: *Ha, ha, ha, that's a very funny joke!*

**habit** /ˈhæbɪt/ *noun*
something you do often: *He has the habit of going for a walk after dinner.*

**hack** /hæk/ *verb*
to cut or chop something: *A worker hacked branches off the trees with an ax.*

**hacksaw** /ˈhækˌsɔ/ *noun*
a saw used to cut metal: *The prisoner used a hacksaw to cut the bars of his cell. –verb* **to hacksaw.**

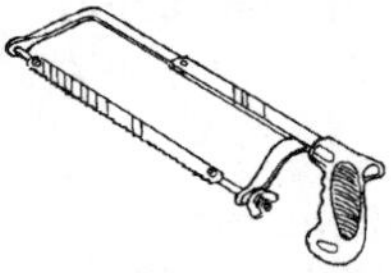
hacksaw

**had** /hæd/ *verb*
*past tense and past participle of* have: *I had a good time at the party.*

**hail** /heɪl/ *noun, (no plural)*
rain that freezes and falls as balls of ice: *Hail ruined the farmer's wheat crop. –verb* **to hail;** *–noun* (ice ball) **hailstone.**

**hair** /hɛr/ *noun, (no plural)*
a thin, fine covering on the skin of a person or an animal: *Most people have lots of hair on their heads. –adjective* **hairy.** *See:* art on page 21a.

**to let one's hair down:** to relax, act naturally, not formally

**hairbrush** /ˈhɛrˌbrʌʃ/ *noun, plural* **hairbrushes**
a brush for taking care of the hair: *She uses a hairbrush every morning. See:* art on page 23a.

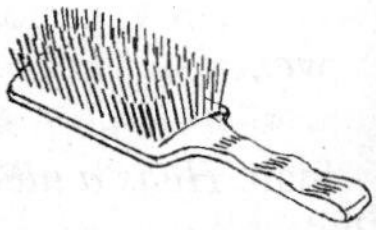
hairbrush

**haircut** /ˈhɛrˌkʌt/ *noun*
the cutting and usually styling of hair

**hairdo** /ˈhɛrˌdu/ *noun, plural* **hairdos**
*See:* hairstyle.

**hairdresser** /ˈhɛrˌdrɛsər/ *noun*
a person who cuts and styles hair

**hairstyle** /ˈhɛrˌstaɪl/ *noun*
the way that your hair is cut and shaped, *(synonym)* hairdo: *Her hairstyle is simple: short and straight. –noun* (person) **hairstylist.**

**half** /hæf/ *noun, plural* **halves** /hævz/
one of two equal parts of something: *I ate half a sandwich.*

**to go halves:** to split something (usually the price) in half: *My girlfriend and I went halves on a new TV.*

**half-hour** *noun*
30 minutes: *A flight to New York leaves from Washington every half-hour.*

**half-mast** *noun*
**to fly at half-mast:** to show respect for the dead by lowering the flag

half-mast

**halfway** /ˈhæfˈweɪ/ *adjective*
in the middle,

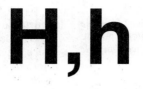

between two points: *New York is about halfway between Boston and Washington, D.C.*

**hall** /hɔl/ *noun*
**1** a big room which holds a lot of people for classes, meetings, or entertainment: *The concert hall was filled with people who came to see the show.*
**2** an area that connects the rooms in a building: *Your friend is waiting for you out in the hall.*
**3** a big building where students live: *What residence hall do you live in?*



**Halloween** /ˌhælə'win/ *noun*
(in the USA) October 31, when children wear costumes and visit neighbors' houses to ask for candy: *On Halloween, some children dress up as witches. See:* pumpkin.

**hallway** /'hɔlˌweɪ/ *noun*
an area that connects rooms in a building: *That hallway goes to the president's office.*

**halo** /'heɪloʊ/ *noun, plural* **halos** or **haloes**
a circle of light around the head: *Angels are often shown with halos around their heads.*

halo

**halt** /hɔlt/ *verb*
to stop: *The marching soldiers halted when their sergeant shouted, "Halt!"*||*The car halted at the traffic light.*

**halt** *noun, (no plural)*
an end or stop

**halve** /hæv/ *verb* **halved, halving, halves**
to cut something in half: *He halved the apple with a knife. See:* half.

**ham** /hæm/ *noun*
the meat of a pig, usually from the leg: *I would like a sandwich of sliced ham with cheese. See:* art on page 17a.

**hamburger** /'hæmˌbɜrgər/ *noun*
chopped beef, usually served as a sandwich: *I'd like a hamburger, fries, and a cola. See:* art on page 17a.

**hammer** /'hæmər/ *noun*
a tool with a handle and metal head used for hitting: *Carpenters use a hammer to pound nails.* –*verb* **to hammer.**

**hammock** /'hæmək/ *noun*
a bed made of net or strong material that you hang between two poles or trees: *After lunch, she likes to nap in her hammock in the yard.*

**hamster** /'hæmstər/ *noun*
a small animal that some people keep as a pet: *My hamster likes to eat carrots.*

**hand** /hænd/ *noun*
**1** a part of the human body at the end of the arm: *I write with my left hand. See:* art on page 21a.
**2** a moving part, as on a dial or clock: *On a watch, when the little hand is on 11 and the big hand is on 12, the time is 11 o'clock.*

**by hand:** made or done without a machine: *He washes his car by hand.*

**on hand:** nearby, ready to act or to use: *The store has plenty of toys on hand for the holiday sale.*

**on the one hand . . . on the other hand:** a way to show both the good and bad things about an idea, a suggestion or situation: *On the one hand, he is very intelligent, but on the other hand, he does not work very hard.*

**out of hand:** out of control: *The noisy kids were out of hand.*

**to give someone a hand:** to help: *Let me give you a hand with your bags.*

**hand** *verb*
to give something to someone with your hands: *I handed the cookies to my son.*

**to hand something down:** to give something to your children after you die: *His parents handed down a big house and land to their son.*

**handbag** /'hændˌbæg/ *noun*
a small bag for carrying things, purse

**handbook** /'hændˌbʊk/ *noun*
a book of information: *The Boy Scout Handbook is sold in many countries.*

**handcuff** /'hændˌkʌf/ *noun*
a short chain with round rings on each end that open and close around a prisoner's hands to hold them together: *A*

*policeman put handcuffs on a criminal.* –*verb* **to handcuff.**

**handcuff**

**handful** /ˈhændˌfʊl/ *noun* an amount of something you can hold in your hand, or any small amount: *I ate a handful of popcorn at the movies.*

**handicap** /ˈhændi ˌkæp/ *noun* something that keeps you from doing something well: *He lost a leg in an accident and now he has a handicap.*

**handicap** *verb* **handicapped, handicapping, handicaps** to cause someone to have problems doing something well: *A bad accident handicapped him for life.* –*adjective* **handicapped.**

**handicraft** /ˈhæn diˌkræft/ *noun* work that you do or make with your hands: *Some of the handicrafts that she makes are woven baskets.*

**handkerchief** /ˈhæŋkərʧɪf/ *noun* a square piece of cloth that you use for cleaning your nose or mouth: *He wiped his nose with a handkerchief. See:* art on page 12a.

**handle** /ˈhændl/ *noun* a part on an object that you use to pick it up or open it: *I pulled the handle and opened the refrigerator door.*

**handle** *verb* **handled, handling, handles**
**1** to touch or hold something in your hands: *Workers handle old paintings in the museum very carefully.*
**2** to take care of something: *I will handle some business, then go home early.*

**handlebars** /ˈhændlbɑrz/ *noun plural* the part of a bicycle or motorcycle that you hold when you are riding it

**handmade** /ˈhændˈmeɪd/ *adjective* made or done by hand without a machine: *Those sweaters are handmade from the best yarn.*

**handout** /ˈhænˌdaʊt/ *noun*
**1** a piece of paper that contains some kind of information: *The professor gave the class handouts that explained the homework.*
**2** something given for free: *That restaurant gives handouts of the food to poor.*

**handshake** /ˈhændˌʃeɪk/ *noun* a way people greet or leave each other, or agree, by holding each other's hand: *The two men greeted each other with a handshake.*

**handsome** /ˈhænsəm/ *adjective* good-looking, attractive –*adverb* **handsomely.** *(antonym)* ugly.

---

**USAGE NOTE:** Men are usually described as *handsome,* but women are usually called *beautiful* or *pretty.* People may also be called *good-looking.*

---

**handwriting** /ˈhæ ndˌraɪtɪŋ/ *noun* writing done by hand and not with a machine: *She has very clear handwriting.* –*adjective* **handwritten.**

**handy** /ˈhændi/ *adjective* **handier, handiest** nearby and ready for use: *He keeps his tools handy in a toolbox.*

**handyman** /ˈhændiˌmæn/ *noun, plural* **handymen** /-ˌmɛn/ someone who knows how to fix many things

**hang** /hæŋ/ *verb* **hung** /hʌŋ/, **hanging, hangs**
**1** to attach something from the top: *I hang my clothes in the closet every night.*
**2** *past* **hanged:** to put a rope around the neck to kill someone: *The authorities hanged a murderer.*

**to hang around:** to spend time doing nothing: *He hangs around the street corner every evening.*

**to hang on (to):** to hold someone or something tightly: *The swimmer hung on to the rope and was pulled to safety.*

**to hang up:** to put down the telephone to end a conversation: *He said good-bye and hung up.*||*She was angry yesterday and hung up on me.*

**hanger** /ˈhæŋər/ *noun* something you use to put clothes on: *She keeps her suits on hangers in the closet.*

**happen** /ˈhæpən/ *verb* to take place: *The accident happened this morning.*

**happiness** /ˈhæpinɪs/ *noun, (no plural)*
a feeling of joy or contentment

**happy** /ˈhæpi/ *adjective* **happier, happiest**
joyful, pleased: *His birthday party was a happy occasion. (antonym)* sad. *See:* art on page 18a.

**harbor** /ˈhɑrbər/ *noun*
a place where ships come to land

harbor

**hard** /hɑrd/ *adjective*
**1** firm, solid: *The surface of stone is hard and cold. (antonym)* soft.
**2** difficult to do or understand: *Poverty is a hard problem to solve. (antonym)* easy.
**3** not gentle or kind: *He's very hard on his students.*
**4** without happiness, full of problems: *She has had a hard life on a small farm.* –*noun* **hardness.**

**hard** *adverb*
with much force or effort: *She works hard every day.*

**hard disk** *noun*
the part of a computer where information is stored permanently: *His computer's hard disk has a lot of memory.*

**harden** /ˈhɑrdn/ *verb*
to make something hard or firm: *That glue hardens quickly.* –*noun* (a substance) **hardener.**

**hardhat** /hɑrdhæt/ *noun*
in the USA, a hat made of strong plastic worn by construction workers to keep them from being hurt

**hardly** /ˈhɑrdli/ *adverb*
almost not: *We have hardly any money left.*

**hardship** /ˈhɑrd͵ʃɪp/ *noun*
difficulty in your living conditions: *He suffered hardship after he lost his job because he had little money.*

**hardware** /ˈhɑrd͵wɛr/ *noun, (no plural)*
**1** tools and small building supplies (not wood): *She bought some hardware at a store.*
**2** machines, especially computer equipment: *That store sells computer hardware, such as PCs, printers, and modems. See:* software.

**harm** /hɑrm/ *noun, (no plural)*
hurt, *(synonym)* damage: *No harm came to the girl as she crossed a busy highway.*

**harm** *verb*
to hurt, injure, or damage: *A speeding car could harm her.*

**harmful** /ˈhɑrmfəl/ *adjective*
able to cause hurt or damage: *Smoking cigarettes can be harmful to your health.* –*adverb* **harmfully.**

**harmless** /ˈhɑrmlɪs/ *adjective*
not harmful: *Don't be afraid; that snake is harmless.* –*adverb* **harmlessly.**

**harmonica** /hɑrˈmɑnɪkə/ *noun*
a musical instrument played with the mouth

harmonica

**harmonize** /ˈhɑrmə͵naɪz/ *verb* **harmonized, harmonizing, harmonizes**
**1** (in music) to play or sing in harmony: *Our school's choir loves to harmonize.*
**2** to go together well: *She dresses beautifully and harmonizes her colors well.*

**harmony** /ˈhɑrməni/ *noun, plural* **harmonies**
**1** musical sounds that are pleasant together: *She is studying harmony in music school.*
**2** peaceful cooperation: *Harmony among the races exists throughout most of the great city.* –*adjective* **harmonious.**

**harness** /ˈhɑrnɪs/ *noun, plural* **harnesses**
leather belts and a collar that horses and other animals wear to pull something: *I put the harness on the horse so he can pull the wagon.* –*verb* **to harness.**

**harp** /hɑrp/ *noun*
a musical instrument that you play with

your fingers: *She plays the harp in a symphony orchestra. See:* art on page 15a.

**harsh** /hɑrʃ/ *adjective*
**1** rough, unpleasant or irritating: *The soap is too harsh for my skin.*
**2** cruel: *Winter in the Arctic is harsh.*||*The punishment was too harsh for such a young child. –adverb* **harshly;** *–noun* **harshness.**

**harvest** /ˈhɑrvɪst/ *verb*
to collect food from the fields: *We harvest corn in the early autumn.*

**harvest** *noun*
**1** the time when food is done growing and is ready to be collected: *Harvest is in September and October.*
**2** all the food that has been collected: *We picked hundreds of oranges in this year's harvest. –noun* (person or machine) **harvester.**

**has** /hæz/ *verb*
*third person, present tense of* have: *He has lots of money.*

**haste** /heɪst/ *noun, (no plural)*
speed or hurry: *He left in haste to catch a train. –adjective* **hasty.**

**hasten** /ˈheɪsən/ *verb*
to move or act quickly: *She is ill, so he hastened to her house to help.*

**hat** /hæt/ *noun*
a head covering: *He wears a warm hat in wintertime. See:* art on page 12a.
**to keep something under one's hat:** to keep something secret: *Keep this under your hat; don't tell the boss, but I am looking for a new job.*

**hatch** /hætʃ/ *verb* **hatches**
to come out of an egg: *Four chicks hatched yesterday.*

**hatchet** /ˈhætʃɪt/ *noun*
a small ax: *I use a hatchet to chop wood for the fire.*

**hate** /heɪt/ *verb* **hated, hating, hates**
to dislike someone or something strongly: *The two peoples have hated each other since the war began. –noun* **hate.** *(antonym)* love.

**hateful** /ˈheɪtfəl/ *adjective*
able to cause strong dislike: *She has a hateful attitude toward anyone who disagrees with her.*

**hatred** /ˈheɪtrɪd/ *noun, (no plural)*
hate: *The couple had feelings of hatred for many years before getting a divorce. (antonym)* love.

**haul** /hɔl/ *verb*
to carry a load: *Trucks haul sand to build a new road. –noun* **haul.**

**haunt** /hɔnt/ *verb*
to visit someone or something as a ghost: *When a ghost haunts a house, strange things can happen. –adjective* **haunted, haunting.**

**have** /hæv/ *verb* **had, having** /ˈhævɪŋ/, **has** /hæz/
**1** to own or possess something: *I have a new Ford™ car.*
**2** to be sick with something: *He has a bad cold.*
**3** to feel or experience something: *We have fun on weekends.*||*Our planners had a meeting on new products.*
**4** to allow, permit to happen: *I can't have a cat eating my plants!*
**5** to cause something to happen: *I had my house painted last year.*
**6** to order, choose: *I'll have the chocolate cake for dessert, please.*
**7** to give birth: *She had a baby boy.*
**had better:** must, ought to: *We had better get going, or we will be late.*
**to have on:** to wear: *He has on a jacket and boots.*
**to have to:** to be required to: *I have to pay the rent on the first of the month.*

**hawk** /hɔk/ *noun*
a large bird that hunts animals and birds: *Hawks fly overhead looking for rabbits.*

hawk

**hay** /heɪ/ *noun, (no plural)*
grass cut and dried for animal food: *The horses have plenty of hay to eat.*

**hay fever** *noun, (no plural)*
an illness that is a reaction to some trees and flowers, like a bad cold: *She has hay fever, and her nose won't stop running.*

H

**hazard** /ˈhæzərd/ *noun*
a danger: *A road being repaired is full of hazards to drivers.* –*adjective* **hazardous.**

**hazy** /ˈheɪzi/ *adjective* **hazier, haziest**
**1** filled with light fog, dust, or smoke: *The air in Los Angeles is nearly always hazy with pollution.*
**2** unclear: *His memory is hazy about the details of the accident.* –*noun* **haze.**

**he** /hi/ *pronoun*
third-person singular masculine: *Do you know Antonio? Yes, he and I went to school together. See:* who, USAGE NOTE.

**head** /hɛd/ *noun*
**1** the part of the body that contains the face, ears, hair, skull, and brain: *That boy shaved his head. See:* art on page 21a.
**2** leader, most important person: *She is the head of the finance committee.*
**3** the place at the beginning, top, or front: *He is at the head of the line.*
**Heads up!:** Watch out!: *Heads up; I'm coming through with boiling hot water!*
**to go to one's head: a.** to make you drunk: *The beer has gone to his head.* **b.** to cause you to become too pleased with yourself: *His new job has gone to his head; now he thinks he's better than everyone else.*

**head** *adjective*
first or most important: *She is sitting at the head table.*

**head** *verb*
**1** to lead, be in charge of something: *My father heads a large company.*
**2** go in a certain direction: *Let's head for home (Canada, port, etc.).*

**headache** /ˈhɛdˌeɪk/ *noun*
a pain in your head: *I have a headache and need to lie down. See:* art on page 11a.

**headlight** /ˈhɛdˌlaɪt/ *noun*
a light at the front of a car or truck used for night driving: *The headlights of the cars are very bright.*

**headline** /ˈhɛdˌlaɪn/ *noun*
a title printed in large type at the top of a newspaper or magazine story: *The headline in today's* Times *says "Peace declared!"*

**headphones** /ˈhɛdˌfoʊnz/ *noun plural*
earphones that you use to listen to a radio, TV, etc.: *I wear headphones to listen to music on my Walkman*™.

headphones

**headquarters** /ˈhɛdˌkwɔrtərz/ *noun plural*
*used with a singular or plural verb*
the main office for something: *The company's headquarters is in Chicago.*

**headway** /ˈhɛdˌweɪ/ *noun*
movement in a forward direction

**heal** /hil/ *verb*
to cure, to become or make someone become well: *A doctor heals patients.*||*The soldier's wounds gradually healed.* –*noun* (person) **healer.**

**health** /hɛlθ/ *noun, (no plural)*
how well your body and mind are: *Although she is 84 years old, my mother is in excellent health.* –*adjective* **healthful.**

**health care** *noun, (no plural)*
medical care: *Health care in the USA is very expensive. See:* health maintenance organization.

**health maintenance organization** *noun*
a business that provides medical care: *Our company pays for medical insurance at a health maintenance organization.* -*abbreviation* **HMO.** *See:* health care.

**healthy** /ˈhɛlθi/ *adjective* **healthier, healthiest**
in good health: *His wife had a healthy baby boy. (antonym)* ill; sick.

**heap** /hip/ *noun*
a lot of things that are on top of each other, usually in a messy way: *The garbage dump contains heaps of trash.*

**heap** *verb*
to put things on top of each other: *The party guests heaped gifts on the table.*

**hear** /hɪr/ *verb* **heard** /hɜrd/, **hearing, hears**
to get sound with your ears: *I hear the sound of traffic on the street.*

**to hear about:** to learn about: *He was surprised when he heard about my new job.*

**to hear from someone:** to have news from someone: *She heard from her parents this morning.*

**to hear of someone** or **something:** to know about someone or something: *I've never heard of Grand Island before. See:* listen, USAGE NOTE.

**hearing** /ˈhɪrɪŋ/ *noun, (no plural)*
the ability to hear: *His hearing is not good; he's becoming deaf.*

**hearing aid** *noun*
a very small machine placed in or near your ear to make sound louder: *Since she wears a hearing aid, my grandmother can hear the phone ring in another room.*

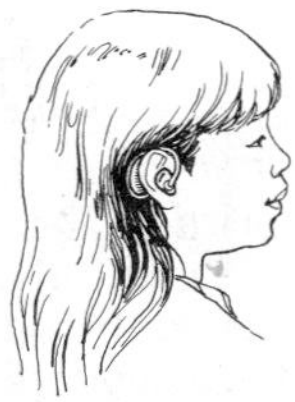
**hearing aid**

**heart** /hɑrt/ *noun*
**1** the organ in the chest that pumps blood through the body: *He has a weak heart and must not exercise too hard.*
**2** kindness, goodness: *She has a kind heart; she helps the poor.*
**3** the important or central part of something: *the heart of the city*
**4** one of the four kinds of playing cards with this shape ♥ on them

**by heart:** by memory: *She learned the names of all 50 states by heart.*

**heart attack** *noun*
a serious illness when your heart stops beating properly: *He had a mild heart attack but won't need an operation.*

**heartbeat** /hɑrtbit/ *noun*
the sound and movement of your heart as it moves blood through your body: *You have a strong heartbeat.*

**heartbreak** /ˈhɑrt,breɪk/ *noun*
something that makes you feel very sad or disappointed: *Their child's death is a heartbreak for them.*

**heartless** /ˈhɑrtlɪs / *adjective*
cruel, unkind: *He is so heartless that he will not talk to his own parents.*

**hearty** /ˈhɑrti/ *adjective* **heartier, heartiest**
large: *We ate a hearty breakfast before starting the trip.*

**heat** /hit/ *noun, (no plural)*
a feeling of warmth, high temperature: *The heat from the fire feels good on a cold night.*

**heat** *verb*
to warm something, make something hot: *We heat our house with an oil burner.*

**heater** /ˈhitər/ *noun*
a machine that makes the temperature of something go up: *In winter, we use electric heaters under our desks.*

**heaven** /ˈhɛvən/ *noun*
(in some religions) the place where God, angels, and the souls of dead people live forever: *The woman died and went to heaven.*

**heavy** /ˈhɛvi/ *adjective* **heavier, heaviest**
**1** with a lot of weight: *The rock is very heavy.*
**2** more than what is usual: *There is always heavy traffic in the morning in my town. –noun* (condition) **heaviness.**

**hectic** /ˈhɛktɪk/ *adjective*
very busy or fast: *I had a very hectic week; I worked late every night, and my child was sick.*

**heel** /hil/ *noun*
the rounded back part of the foot: *My heels hurt from walking so far.*

**height** /haɪt/ *noun*
**1** a measurement from the top to the bottom of something: *The building has a height of six stories (of 60 feet, 19 meters, etc.).||The space vehicle flies at a height of 200 miles (320 km) above the earth.*
**2** strongest or most important part of something: *She is at the height of her career in law.*

**heighten** /ˈhaɪtn/ *verb*
to make something stronger: *The storyteller heightened the suspense in the mystery story. (antonym)* lower.

**heir** /ɛr/ *noun*
the person legally in line to receive property (or title of nobility) when someone dies: *Prince William is heir to the British throne. –noun* (female) **heiress.**

**held** /hɛld/ *verb*
*past tense and participle of* hold

**helicopter** /ˈhɛliˌkɑptər/ *noun*
a small aircraft with one or two motorized blades on its top: *A police helicopter rescued passengers on a sinking boat.*

helicopter

**hell** /hɛl/ *noun*
(in religion) the place where the souls of bad people go after death

**he'll** /hil/
*contracted form of* he will: *He'll be ready to leave in a few minutes.*

H

**hello** /həˈloʊ/ *exclamation*
a greeting: *Hello, how are you today?*

**helmet** /ˈhɛlmɪt/ *noun*
a protective head covering: *Bicyclists wear helmets to protect their heads.*

**help** /hɛlp/ *verb*
**1** to do something good for someone: *My neighbor helped me fix my roof.*
**2** to make something better: *What will help my upset stomach?*
**3** to keep from doing something: *He is sad and cannot help crying.*

**help** *noun, (no plural)*
aid, support: *I gave my friend help with his homework. –noun* (person) **helper.**

**helpful** /ˈhɛlpfəl/ *adjective*
useful: *The lawyer gave me some helpful advice. –adverb* **helpfully.**

**helping** /ˈhɛlpɪŋ / *noun*
an amount of food on your plate: *The cook gave me a big helping of potatoes.*

**helpless** /ˈhɛlplɪs/ *adjective*
unable to do something: *He's helpless at changing a tire. –adverb* **helplessly.**

**hem** /hɛm/ *noun*
the bottom edge of a piece of clothing, folded and sewn, *(synonym)* hemline: *The hem on her skirt needs sewing.*

**hemisphere** /ˈhɛməˌsfɪr/ *noun*
half of the earth: *The earth is divided by the equator into the Northern and Southern hemispheres.*

**hen** /hɛn/ *noun*
a female chicken, pheasant, etc.: *Hens lay the eggs we eat for breakfast.*

**her** /hɜr/ *pronoun*
**1** *object form of* she: *I saw her leave the room.*
**2** belonging to a woman or a girl: *She took her purse when she left.*

**herb** /ɜrb/ *noun*
a plant that you use for cooking or medicine: *People use herbs to make food taste good.*

**herd** /hɜrd/ *noun*
a group of animals of one kind: *Herds of horses run wild in the American West.*

**here** /hɪr/ *adverb*
**1** at, to, or in this place: *We have lived here (in this house) for ten years.*
**2** used to give or show something: *Here are the keys to my car.*

**heritage** /ˈhɛrətɪdʒ/ *noun, (no plural)*
one's beliefs, traditions, history, etc. passed from parents to children, teachers to students: *This country has a heritage of freedom and independence.*

**hero** /ˈhɪroʊ/ *noun, plural* **heroes**
a person who is famous for doing something brave or good: *Martin Luther King, Jr., was a hero in the fight for equality for all people. –noun* **heroism;** *–adjective* **heroic.**

**heroin** /ˈhɛroʊɪn/ *noun, (no plural)*
a strong, dangerous drug

**heroine** /ˈhɛroʊɪn/ *noun*
a woman who is famous for doing something brave or good: *Amelia Earhart was a courageous pilot and heroine.*

**hers** /hɜrz/
*possessive pronoun of* she, belonging to her: *The coat in the closet is hers.*

**herself** /hərˈsɛlf/
*feminine pronoun of* she
used to refer to the same woman or girl that you just referred to: *She does all the work herself.*

**he's** /hiz/ *verb*
*contracted form of*
**1** he is: *He's a great guy.*
**2** he has: *He's been to England twice in the last year.*

**hesitate** /ˈhɛzəˌteɪt/ *verb* **hesitated, hesitating, hesitates**
to stop before you do something because

you are not sure that it is right: *He hesitated before crossing the street.* –*noun* **hesitation** /ˌhɛzəˈteɪʃən/.

**hey** /heɪ/ *exclamation*
used to get someone's attention or show surprise, happiness, etc.: *Hey, I didn't know that you won first prize!*

**hi** /haɪ/ *exclamation informal*
a greeting, hello: *Hi, how are you today?*

**hiccup** or **hiccough** /ˈhɪkʌp/ *noun*
a sharp sound you make in your throat: *He had the hiccups from eating too fast.* –*verb* **to hiccup.**

**hid** /hɪd/ *verb*
*past tense and past participle of* hide (1), to put something where people can't find it: *She hid candy in a closet so the children could not find it.*

**hidden** /ˈhɪdn/ *adjective and past participle of* hide
in a place that cannot be seen: *Guests were hidden behind the door at the surprise party.*

**hide (1)** /haɪd/ *verb* **hid** /hɪd/, **hidden** /ˈhɪdn/ or **hid, hiding, hides**
**1** to put something where people can't find it: *She hides her jewelry in a drawer.*
**2** to be or go in a place where people can't find you: *The little boy hid under the bed.*

**hide (2)**
the tough skin of an animal, such as a cow: *His boots are made of cowhide.*

**hide-and-seek** *noun, (no plural)*
a game for children; they hide while one child closes his or her eyes, then tries to find the other children: *The children played hide-and-seek at the birthday party.*

**hideout** /ˈhaɪdˌaʊt/ *noun*
a secret place: *The criminals have a hideout in the country.*

**high** /haɪ/ *adjective*
**1** describing how far up something goes: *The statue is ten feet high (three meters).*‖*She has a high-pitched voice.* *(antonym)* low.
**2** very large, fast, or strong: *Emotions at the protest rally were high.*
**3** very important: *She is a high official in the government.* –*adverb* **highly.**

**high** *adverb*
a long way from the ground: *Cliffs stand high above the ocean.*

high chair

**high chair** *noun*
a tall chair that you use for feeding a young child: *The baby loves to throw food on the floor from his high chair.*

**highlight** /ˈhaɪˌlaɪt/ *verb* **highlighted, highlighting, highlights**
to show that something is important: *Students highlight important parts of their textbooks.*

**highlighter** /ˈhaɪˌlaɪtər/ *noun*
a pen used for marking important parts of a book or article

**high school** *noun*
in the USA, a school for grades 9-12 or 10-12 (ages 14–18): *He graduated from high school in 1996. See:* grade school, USAGE NOTE.

**highway** /ˈhaɪˌweɪ/ *noun*
a big road between two towns or cities: *An interstate highway passes near our town.*

**hijack** /ˈhaɪˌʤæk/ *verb*
to take control of an airplane, car or bus by threatening its pilot, usually with a gun: *A man hijacked a plane from New York to Cuba.* –*noun* (person) **hijacker,** (act) **hijacking.**

**hike** /haɪk/ *noun*
a long walk in the country: *We went for a hike* (or) *we took a hike in a national park.* –*noun* (person) **hiker.**

**hike** *verb* **hiked, hiking, hikes**
to take a long walk: *We hiked through the hills of Yosemite Park.*

**hill** /hɪl/ *noun*
a high piece of land shorter than a mountain: *The hills above the city offer a lovely view.* –*adjective* **hilly.**

**hilly** /ˈhɪli/ *adjective* **hillier, hilliest**
having many hills: *Parts of West Virginia are very hilly.*

**him** /hɪm/
*object pronoun of* he: *I gave him the book.*

H

**himself** /hɪm'sɛlf/
*masculine pronoun of* him
used to refer to the man or boy you just referred to: *He did all the work himself* (or) *by himself.*

**hinge** /hɪndʒ/ *noun*
a piece of metal with two parts that connect two parts of a box or door: *The hinges on doors allow them to open.*

**hint** /hɪnt/ *verb*
to say something in an indirect way: *He hinted to his wife that he wanted a new watch for his birthday.* –*noun* **hint.**



**hip** /hɪp/ *noun*
the part of the body where your leg joins the side of your body: *He fell and hurt his hip.*

**hippo** /'hɪpoʊ/ *noun, plural* **hippos**
*short for* hippopotamus

**hippopotamus**
/ˌhɪpə'pɑtəməs/ *noun, plural* **hippopotamuses**
a large African animal with a heavy body and gray skin: *Hippopotamuses live near rivers.*

hippopotamus

**hire** /haɪr/ *verb* **hired, hiring, hires**
to pay someone to do something, employ: *The company hired an accountant last week.*

**his** /hɪz/ *pronoun*
*possessive form of* he: *He hung his coat in the closet.*

**Hispanic** /hɪ'spænɪk/ *noun*
a person of Latin American or Spanish descent: *Hispanics come from all over the world to New York.*

**Hispanic** *adjective*
related to Spanish-speaking Latin America

**hiss** /hɪs/ *noun, plural* **hisses**
a low-pitched sound like the sound of the letter *s*: *The cat hissed at the dog.*

**historic** /hɪ'stɔrɪk/ *adjective*
important in history, famous: *We visited many historic places in Paris.*

**historical** /hɪ'stɔrɪkəl/ *adjective*
related to history: *The French Revolution was of great historical importance.* –*adverb* **historically.**

**history** /'hɪstəri/ *noun, plural* **histories**
the study of past events (people, civilizations, etc.): *She studied European history at college.* –*noun* (person) **historian.**

**hit** /hɪt/ *verb* **hit, hitting, hits**
to touch someone or something with a lot of force: *He hit the nail with a hammer.*||*The boxer hit his opponent with his right fist.*

**to hit the nail on the head:** to describe something accurately: *You hit the nail on the head when you said that debt will destroy the economy.*

**to hit the roof:** to become very angry: *When someone ran into his car, he hit the roof and shouted.*

**hit** *noun*
**1** touching someone or something hard: *The fighter plane got a hit from enemy fire.*
**2** someone or something that is a great success: *The new movie was a big hit.*

**hitch** /hɪtʃ/ *verb, plural* **hitches**
to attach, connect, especially to harness an animal: *The farmer hitched the horse to a wagon.*

**hitchhike** /'hɪtʃˌhaɪk/ *verb* **hitchhiked, hitchhiking, hitchhikes**
to stand on the road and ask for a ride from others: *I hitchhiked from Baltimore to Washington.* –*noun* (person) **hitchhiker.**

**HIV** /ˌeɪtʃaɪ'vi/ *abbreviation of*
human immunodeficiency virus: *The HIV virus causes AIDS. See:* AIDS.

**hive** /haɪv/ *noun*
a box where bees live: *Beekeepers keep bees in hives.*

**HMO** /ˌeɪtʃɛm'oʊ/ *abbreviation of*
health maintenance organization

**hoard** /hɔrd/ *verb*
to hide a lot of something so that you can use or sell it in the future: *People hoard food in wartime.* –*noun* (person) **hoarder.**

**hoard** *noun*
a hidden supply of something: *They keep*

their hoard of rice and beans in a safe place. *–noun* (thing) **hoarding.**

**hoarse** /hɔrs/ *adjective* **hoarser, hoarsest**
with a scratchy voice caused by being ill or tired: *The politician is hoarse from giving speeches.* *–adverb* **hoarsely;** *–noun* **hoarseness.**

**hoax** /hoʊks/ *noun, plural* **hoaxes**
something that is not true, trick: *The bomb threat turned out to be a hoax.*

**hobby** /'habi/ *noun, plural* **hobbies**
an activity that you do often for pleasure: *His hobby is gardening.*

**hockey** /'haki/ *noun, (no plural)*
a sport for two teams played on ice with a puck or on a field with a ball: *The team that makes the most goals in hockey wins the game.*

hockey

**hoe** /hoʊ/ *noun*
a digging tool with a metal blade on a long handle: *I use a hoe to get weeds out of my garden.*

**hog** /hɔg/ *noun*
a large pig: *Hogs are raised for meat: ham, pork, and bacon.*

**hoist** /hɔɪst/ *verb*
to lift and move an object: *The father hoisted his child onto his shoulders.*

**hold** /hoʊld/ *verb* **held** /hɛld/ **, holding, holds**
**1** to have something in your hand(s) or arms: *The worker held the hammer in his right hand.*
**2** to keep something in a certain position: *The dancer held his leg in the air for five seconds.*
**3** to have room for something: *That barrel holds 60 gallons of oil.*
**4** to have a meeting: *We held a conference in my office.*
**hold it:** **a.** to stop, something: *Hold it! I don't want any more trouble from you!* **b.** to keep something: *Here's some money; hold it for me for a week.*
**to hold on:** **a.** to keep something in your hand: *Hold on to your key or you will lose it.* **b.** to wait: *He was very ill, but held on and gradually recovered.*
**to hold someone** or **something up:** **a.** to make someone or something late: *She held up the project for three months.* **b.** to rob someone or something: *He held up a store owner with a gun.*

**hold** *noun*
holding something in your hand: *He has a good hold on the steering wheel.*
**to be on hold:** **a.** postponed, delayed: *The project is stopped now and is on hold until next year.* **b.** waiting for someone on the telephone: *Mr. Jones is on hold on line two.*



**holdup** /'hoʊl,dʌp/ *noun*
a robbery with a weapon (gun, knife, etc.): *A holdup at gunpoint happened in the local grocery store.*

**hole** /hoʊl/ *noun*
an empty place or opening in something: *I sewed a patch to fix the hole in my shirt.*||*A rabbit jumped into its hole.*

**holiday** /'halə,deɪ/ *noun*
a day when you don't go to work or school, for celebration or rest: *Many companies in the United States of America give their employees ten legal holidays.*

**hollow** /'haloʊ/ *adjective*
empty insides, with no center: *The tree trunk was hollow from insects feeding inside.*

**holy** /'hoʊli/ *adjective* **holier, holiest**
coming from or connected with God: *Christmas is a holy day.*

**home** /hoʊm/ *noun*
the place where you live, or were born: *My home is an apartment in Manhattan.*
**at home:** comfortable and welcome: *I feel at home at my friend's house.*

**homeland** /'hoʊm,lænd/ *noun*
your native country: *The USA (China, Poland, etc.) is my homeland.*

**homeless** /'hoʊmlɪs/ *noun plural*
people who have no home: *The government built shelters for the homeless.* *–adjective* **homeless.**

**homemade** /'hoʊm'meɪd/ *adjective*
made at home or without a machine: *That bread is homemade.*

**homesick** /'hoʊm,sɪk/ *adjective*
feeling sad when you are away from home: *After traveling for a month, I began to feel homesick.* *–noun* **homesickness.**

**hometown** /'hoʊm'taʊn/ *noun*
the city or town where you grew up: *Seattle is my hometown.*

**homework** /'hoʊm,wɜrk/ *noun, (no plural)*
schoolwork that students do at home: *Our teacher gives us a lot of homework.*



**homosexual** /,hoʊmə'sɛkʃuəl/ *noun*
a person who is attracted to people of the same sex: *Scientists estimate that 10% of the people in the world are homosexual.* *–adjective* **homosexual.** *–noun* **homosexuality** /,hoʊmə,sɛkʃu'æ ləti/.

**honest** /'ɑnɪst/ *adjective*
truthful and trustworthy: *He is honest in his business with others.* *–adverb* **honestly.**

**honesty** /'ɑnəsti/ *noun, (no plural)*
truthfulness and trustworthiness: *You can trust her honesty both in what she says and in her business dealings.* *See:* dishonest.

**honey** /'hʌni/ *noun, (no plural)*
the sweet liquid made by bees: *I like honey on toast in the morning.* *–adjective* **honeyed.**

---

**USAGE NOTE:** *Honey* is a common term of affection between two people.

---

**honeymoon** /'hʌni,mun/ *noun*
a trip people take after they get married: *We went to Paris on our honeymoon.*

**honk** /hɑŋk/ *verb*
**1** to make a sound like a goose: *Geese honk on their way south each autumn.*
**2** to blow a car horn: *I honked at another car to warn him.* *–noun* (act) **honk.**

**honor** /'ɑnər/ *noun*
**1** one's good reputation (for honesty, integrity, etc.): *He is a man of honor and is totally trustworthy.*
**2** praise and respect from other people: *It was an honor to win "salesperson of the year."* *–adjective* **honorable;** *–adverb* **honorably.**

**hood** /hʊd/ *noun*
**1** a cloth covering for the head and neck (as part of a robe, coat, or jacket): *It started to snow, and she put up the hood on her jacket.*
**2** the metal cover of the front of a car

**hoof** /hʊf/ *noun, plural* **hooves** /huvz/ or **hoofs**
the hard part of the feet of cattle and horses: *The hooves of horses are protected by horseshoes.*

hoof

**hook** /hʊk/ *noun*
a curved piece of metal or plastic that you use to catch things with or hang things on: *We catch fish with hooks and worms* *–verb* **to hook.**

**hooves** /huvz/ *noun*
*plural of* hoof

**hop** /hɑp/ *verb* **hopped, hopping, hops**
to move by making short jumps: *Rabbit hop very quickly.* *–noun* **hop.**

**hope** /hoʊp/ *noun*
**1** wanting something good to happen and believing that it will: *He has hop that his cancer will not be fatal.*
**2** someone or something that can make situation better: *That doctor is my las hope.*

**hope** *verb* **hoped, hoping, hopes**
to want something to happen: *I hope tha you feel better soon.*

**hopeful** /'hoʊpfəl/ *adjective*
believing that something good will hap pen: *She is hopeful that she will be bette soon.* *–adverb* **hopefully;** *–noun* **hope fulness.** *(antonym)* hopeless.

**hopeless** /'hoʊplɪs/ *adjective*
without hope: *The football game is hope less; we're going to lose.* *–adverb* **hope lessly;** *–noun* **hopelessness.**

**horizon** /hə'raɪzən/ *noun*
the place in one's view where the earth

surface forms a line with the sky: *Sailors could see another ship coming over the horizon.*

**horizontal** /ˌhɔrəˈzɑntl/ *adjective*
going from side to side parallel to the ground: *He was horizontal on the bed.* *–adverb* **horizontally.** *See:* vertical.

**horn** /hɔrn/ *noun*
**1** a pointed growth on the heads of some animals: *Goats have horns.*
**2** a musical instrument that you blow to play: *The French horn has a beautiful sound.*
**3** a device that gives a warning sound: *a car horn*

**horoscope** /ˈhɔrəˌskoʊp/ *noun*
(in astrology) something that tells your future using the planets and the time you were born: *My horoscope for today is full of good news.*

**horrible** /ˈhɔrəbəl/ *adjective*
very frightening, very unpleasant, or annoying: *We had a horrible time getting through traffic.* *–adverb* **horribly.**

**horrify** /ˈhɔrəˌfaɪ/ *verb* **horrified, horrifying, horrifies**
to make someone very frightened: *The sight of his dead friend horrified him.*

**horror** /ˈhɔrər/ *noun*
a feeling of fear or terror: *I felt horror when I saw the monster movie.*

**horse** /hɔrs/ *noun*
an animal with four feet and hard hooves that can carry people and pull things: *The Arabian horse is one of the earth's most beautiful animals. See:* art on page 14a.
**straight from the horse's mouth:** directly from the person who said something

**horsepower** /ˈhɔrsˌpaʊər/ *noun adjective*
a way of measuring the power of an engine: *His car has a 200-horsepower engine.*

**hose** /hoʊz/ *noun*
a long, soft, tube: *I use a garden hose to water the grass.*

hose

**hospital** /ˈhɑspɪtl/ *noun*
a place where doctors and nurses help people who are sick or hurt: *He went to the hospital to have an operation.*

**hospitality** /ˌhɑspɪˈtæləti/ *noun, (no plural)*
treating people in a friendly way when they visit you: *We enjoyed the hospitality of friends at their country home.*

**hospitalize** /ˈhɑspɪtlˌaɪz/ *verb* **hospitalized, hospitalizing, hospitalizes**
to place in a hospital: *She was hospitalized for chest pains.*

**host** /hoʊst/ *noun*
a person who invites people to a social event, such as a party: *He is the host of a party tonight.* *–noun* (female) **hostess.** *See:* art on page 5a.

**hostage** /ˈhɑstɪʤ/ *noun*
a person who is a prisoner until you get money or something else you want: *He is a political hostage.*

**hostile** /ˈhɑstəl/ *adjective*
very angry or unfriendly: *That driver has a hostile attitude; he blows his horn and yells at other drivers.* *–noun* **hostility.**

**hot** /hɑt/ *adjective* **hotter, hottest**
**1** having a high degree of heat, burning: *The water is very, very hot. (antonym)* cold.
**2** spicy, with a lot of seasoning: *My food is hot because I added lots of red peppers to it.*

**hot dog** *noun*
a sausage made of ground, spiced meat: *We had hot dogs for lunch today. See:* art on page 17a.

**hotel** /hoʊˈtɛl/ *noun*
a place you can eat and sleep when you are traveling: *We stayed in a big hotel in Montreal.*

---

**USAGE NOTE:** An *inn* is a small hotel, often in the country, offering rooms and food to travelers.

---

**hour** /ˈaʊər/ *noun*
a time period of 60 minutes: *My train ride to work takes an hour.*
**hours:** a time period when a certain activity happens: *Our office hours are from nine to five.*

H

**on the hour:** at exactly one o'clock, two o'clock, etc.: *A bus leaves for New York on the hour.*

**hourly** /'aʊərli/ *adverb*
happening every hour: *A train leaves for San Francisco hourly from here.*

**house** /haʊs/ *noun, plural* **houses** /'haʊzɪz/
**1** a place to live for one or a few families: *Our house is located on the corner.*
**2** a building for a special purpose: *Firefighters work in the fire house.*

house

**housekeeper** /'haʊsˌkipər/ *noun*
a person who takes care of a private house or is in charge of workers in hotel rooms: *Our housekeeper cleans, does the laundry, and makes the beds.* –*noun* (work) **housekeeping.**

**housewife** /'haʊsˌwaɪf/ *noun plural* **housewives** /-ˌwaɪvz/
a woman who does not work outside of the home: *She is a housewife who is very active in community affairs.*

**housework** /'haʊsˌwɜrk/ *noun, (no plural)*
work that you do to keep a house in order: *My housework is cleaning, cooking, and doing the laundry.*

**housing** /'haʊzɪŋ/ *noun, (no plural)*
a general word for houses, apartments, etc. that people live in: *Housing in this area is expensive.*

**how** /haʊ/ *adverb*
**1** in what way: *How do you fix this broken pipe?*
**2** for what reason: *How can you say such an awful thing?*
**3** in what condition: *How do you feel?*
**4** in what amount: *How much does this sofa cost?*
**5** as part of a greeting: *How do you do?*
**how about:** *informal* what do you think about (something): *I couldn't decide what to wear, then asked her, "How about this dress?"*
**How come?:** *informal* Why?: *How come you didn't call me yesterday?*

**however** /haʊ'ɛvər/ *conjunction*
in spite of, but: *He is intelligent; however, he is also difficult.*
**however** *adverb*
**1** to any degree or amount: *You may stay there however long you wish.*
**2** said to show surprise: *However did the cat get up that tree?*

**howl** /haʊl/ *verb*
to cry loudly: *Monkeys howl in the treetops.* –*noun* (sound) **howl,** (act) **howling.**

**how-to** /'haʊ'tu/ *adjective*
telling the practical steps needed to do something: *a how-to book on home repairs* –*noun* **how-to.**

**huddle** /'hʌdl/ *verb* **huddled, huddling, huddles**
to stand or sit close together: *Baby rabbits huddle together next to their mother.*

**hug** /hʌg/ *noun*
putting your arms around someone: *He gives his children a hug and a kiss as they leave for school.*
**hug** *verb* **hugged, hugging, hugs**
to put your arms around someone: *She hugged her children.*

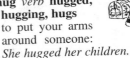

hug

**huge** /hyuʤ/ *adjective* **huger, hugest**
very large, enormous: *The country suffers from a huge debt.* –*adverb* **hugely.**

**hum** /hʌm/ *verb* **hummed, humming, hums**
**1** to make a sound of "M": *Bees hum when they fly.*
**2** to sing with your mouth closed: *He hummed a tune as he walked to work.*

**human** /'hyuman/ or **human being** *noun*
a person: *Humans live in almost every part of the earth.* –*adjective* **human;** –*adverb* **humanly.**

**humanity** /hyu'mænəti/ *noun, plural* **humanities**
**1** human beings as a group: *Humanity was threatened by nuclear war.*
**2** the state or condition of being human: *He showed his humanity by helping his neighbor. See:* man, USAGE NOTE.

**humble** /ˈhʌmbəl/ *adjective* **humbler, humblest**
**1** shy or weak: *He has a humble manner in the presence of important people.*
**2** modest, not wanting praise: *She is a great athlete, but is humble about her accomplishments.* –*verb* **to humble.**

**humid** /ˈhyumɪd/ *adjective*
having damp air (and uncomfortable weather): *Oh, it's so humid today; it's hard to breathe!* –*noun* **humidity.**

**hummingbird** /ˈhʌmɪŋˌbɜrd/ *noun*
a small colorful bird that beats its wings very quickly: *Hummingbirds move from flower to flower, drinking their sweetness.*

hummingbird

**humor** /ˈhyumər/ *noun, (no plural)*
something funny in written, spoken, or printed form: *That comedian's humor is often childish, so I don't think he's very funny.* –*adjective* **humorous;** –*adverb* **humorously.**

**hump** /hʌmp/ *noun*
round lump: *He has a hump on his back.*

**hundred** /ˈhʌndrɪd/ *noun, plural* **hundreds** or (after a number) **hundred**
the number 100: *I have a hundred dollars in my wallet.*
**hundreds:** lots of something: *Hundreds of people were on the beach last weekend.*

**hung** /hʌŋ/ *verb*
*past tense and past participle of* hang

**hunger** /ˈhʌŋgər/ *noun*
the need to eat: *That country suffers from hunger.* –*verb* **to hunger.**

**hungry** /ˈhʌŋgri/ *adjective* **hungrier, hungriest**
feeling that you want to eat: *I haven't eaten all day and feel very hungry.* –*adverb* **hungrily.**

**hunt** /hʌnt/ *verb*
to look for something: *I hunted for my hat and finally found it.* –*noun* **hunt,** (person) **hunter,** (activity) **hunting.**

**hurricane** /ˈhɜrəˌkeɪn/ *noun*
a large, violent rain and wind storm: *Hurricanes have winds up to 150 miles (240 km) per hour.*

**hurry** /ˈhɜri/ *verb* **hurried, hurrying, hurries**
to go somewhere or do something quickly: *We hurried, so as not to be late.* –*noun* **hurry.**

**hurt** /hɜrt/ *verb*
**1** to feel pain: *I fell, and my leg hurts.*
**2** to make someone feel pain: *The accident hurt him badly.* –*adjective* **hurtful.**

**husband** /ˈhʌzbənd/ *noun*
a man who is married: *He became her husband last year. See:* art on page 13a.

**hut** /hʌt/ *noun*
a small cabin: *People live in huts in that poor area.*

**hydrant** /ˈhaɪdrənt/ *noun*
a water outlet, fireplug: *Firefighters put hoses on water hydrants to get water to fight fires. See:* fire hydrant.

hydrant

**hydrogen** /ˈhaɪdrəʤən/ *noun adjective*
the lightest gas that you cannot see or smell

**hyena** /haɪˈinə/ *noun*
a meat-eating, wild, dog-like animal of Africa and southeast Asia: *Hyenas feed on small dead animals and birds.*

**hygiene** /ˈhaɪˌʤin/ *noun*
the science of keeping people and things clean: *Personal hygiene includes cleanliness, eating healthy foods, and exercising.* –*adjective* **hygienic;** –*noun* (person) **hygienist.**

**hymn** /hɪm/ *noun*
a religious song

**hyphen** /ˈhaɪfən/ *noun*
the punctuation mark (-): *A hyphen connects the parts of many words, such as "how-to."*

**hypnosis** /hɪpˈnoʊsɪs/ *noun*
a sleep-like state where a person's mind is open to suggestions: *Many people use hypnosis to stop bad habits, such as*

*smoking cigarettes.* –*noun* (person) **hypnotist;** –*verb* **to hypnotize.**

**hysterical** /hɪ'stɛrɪkəl/ *adjective*
**1** panicked, emotionally out of control: *The mother became hysterical when she realized her child was lost.*
**2** *figurative* very funny: *The jokes that he tells are hysterical.* –*adverb* **hysterically.**

H

# I, i

**I, i** /aɪ/ *noun* **I's, i's** or **Is, is**
the ninth letter of the English alphabet

**I, i** *pronoun*
first person singular, used in speaking or writing to refer to oneself: *I wish I could stay longer.*

**ice** /aɪs/ *noun, (no plural)*
frozen water: *Ice forms on the roads in winter.* *–adjective* **icy.**

**to break the ice:** to make people comfortable at a first meeting: *Let's play a game to break the ice. See:* icebreaker.

**ice** *verb*
to cover or decorate a cake with icing

**iceberg** /ˈaɪsˌbɜrg/ *noun*
a large piece of frozen ice in the sea

**icebreaker** /ˈaɪs ˌbreɪkər/ *noun*
**1** a powerful ship used to break paths in icy seas: *Our ship sailed in the path made by an icebreaker.*
**2** something said or done to help people start talking or feel comfortable: *John's funny story was a good icebreaker at the party. See:* ice.

**ice cream** *noun*
a frozen mixture of cream, milk, flavors, and sugar: *We enjoy eating chocolate ice cream for dessert.*

Ice-cream cone

**ice-cream cone** *noun*
a cookie-like food used to hold ice cream: *a chocolate ice-cream cone*

**ice hockey** *noun, (no plural)*
an ice-skating sport in which one team uses curved sticks to shoot a small, round object into the other team's goal

**ice skate** *noun*
a boot with a steel blade used to move over ice
*–verb* **to ice skate;** *–noun* (person) ice skater.

ice skates

**icicle** /ˈaɪsəkəl/ *noun*
a pointed piece of ice formed by water that freezes as it falls in small drops: *Icicles hang from tree branches in winter.*

**icing** /ˈaɪsɪŋ/ *noun*
a sweet, creamy covering on cakes: *The birthday cake had chocolate icing.*

**ID** or **ID card** /ˈaɪˈdi/ *noun*
*abbreviation of* identity card: a card, such as a driver's license, often with a photograph, that gives personal information, such as one's name, age, and address

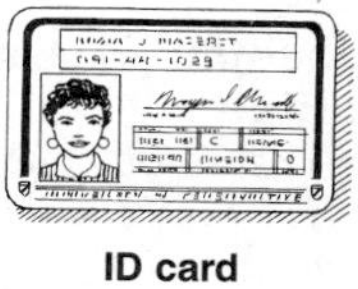

ID card

**idea** /aɪˈdiə/ *noun*
**1** a thought: *The speaker had very interesting ideas.*
**2** a plan, a way to do something: *She has an idea of how to solve the problem.*

**to have no idea:** to have no knowledge or information about something: *I have no idea where we are. I'm lost!*

**ideal** /aɪˈdiəl/ *noun*
the highest standard, something perfect:

*In an ideal world there would be no disease or hunger.*
**to have ideals:** to wish for perfection: *The priest has high ideals about saving the world.*

**ideal** *adjective*
most desirable, perfect: *Good weather means ideal conditions for the boat race today.* *–adverb* **ideally;** *–noun* **idealism,** (person) **idealist;** *–adjective* **idealistic.**

**idealize** /aɪ'diə,laɪz/ *verb*
to think of something as better than it really is: *He idealizes his job, even though it isn't perfect.*

**identical** /aɪ'dɛntəkəl/ *adjective*
exactly alike

**identification** /aɪ,dɛntəfə'keɪʃən/ *noun*
**1** something (such as a passport or driver's license) that proves who one is: *I showed my passport as identification.*
**2** recognition of someone or something: *The police officer made an identification of the criminal after talking to witnesses.*

**identification card** *noun*
*See:* ID.

**identify** /aɪ'dɛntə,faɪ/ *verb* **identified, identifying, identifies**
to recognize someone or something: *The children identified the bird from its picture in the book.*
**to identify with:** to feel connected to someone or something: *I identified with the girl in the movie.*

**identity** /aɪ'dɛntəti/ *noun, plural* **identities**
**1** who someone is or what something is: *The police still don't know the identity of the murderer.*
**2** a sense of oneself: *When she quit her job to raise her children, she lost her identity as a businesswoman.*

**ideology** /,aɪdi'ɑləʤi/ *noun, plural* **ideologies**
a set of beliefs shared by a political or social group: *In the USA, Democrats and Republicans have different ideologies.* *–adjective* **ideological.**

**idiom** /'ɪdiəm/ *noun*
an expression that does not mean the same as the individual words: *The words "to hit the roof" seem to mean "to hit against the top of a house," but it is actually an idiom that means "to become very angry."* *–adjective* **idiomatic.**

**idiot** /'ɪdiət/ *noun*
a stupid, foolish person *–noun* **idiocy;** *–adjective* **idiotic** /,ɪdi'ɑtɪk/.

**idle** /'aɪdl/ *adjective*
**1** not working, unemployed.
**2** worthless: *Don't listen to that idle talk.*

**idle** *verb* **idled, idling, idles**
**1** to run at lowest speed: *She lets her car engine idle to warm it up.*
**2** to waste time: *He idles away his time by watching television.* *–noun* (inactivity) **idleness.** *(antonym)* active.

**idol** /'aɪdl/ *noun*
**1** an object of religious worship, such as a statue: *Ancient peoples worshiped idols of their gods.*
**2** a famous person that many people admire, such as a film or music star *–verb* **to idolize.**

**i.e.** /'aɪ'i/ *abbreviation of*
the Latin *id est,* meaning "that is": *I like bright colors, i.e., red and yellow.*

**if** /ɪf/ *conjunction*
**1** used to show that the possibility that an event or situation will occur depends on the occurrence of another event or situation. These events or situations can be in the present, past, or future: *If you want to leave, let's go now.*||*If I had seen him, I would have spoken to him.*
**2** whether: *Please see if the children are dressed for school.*
**as if:** as though: *He acts as if he knew all the answers.*
**even if:** accepting that something is true: *I'm going to buy that shirt even if it's very expensive.*
**if only:** used to state a wish: *If only I had a million dollars!*

**igloo** /'ɪglu/ *noun, plural* **igloos**
a house made of icy snow blocks: *Eskimos make igloos for shelter.*

igloo

**ignite** /ɪg'naɪt/ *verb* **ignited, igniting, ignites**
to set on fire: *He ignited the wood with a match.* *–noun* **ignition.**

**ignorance** /ˈɪgnərəns/ *noun*
**1** lack of education: *Without schooling, children grow up in ignorance.*
**2** lack of knowledge: *Her ignorance of the speed limit made her drive faster than 65 miles per hour.*

**ignore** /ɪgˈnɔr/ *verb* **ignored, ignoring, ignores**
to pay no attention to: *At the party she ignored her old boyfriend.*

**ill** /ɪl/ *adjective*
sick, unwell: *He is ill; he has a bad cold.*
**to be ill at ease:** to feel awkward or uncomfortable

**ill** *adverb*
badly, unfavorably: *He is a bad man, and others think ill of him.* –*noun* **illness.**

**illegal** /ɪˈligəl/ *adjective*
against the law: *Stealing is illegal.* –*noun* **illegality** /ˌɪliˈgæləti/.

**illegible** /ɪˈlɛʤəbəl/ *adjective*
difficult to read: *The writing is illegible; I cannot read what it says.* –*noun* **illegibility** /ɪˌlɛʤəˈbɪləti/.

**illegitimate** /ˌɪləˈʤɪtəmɪt/ *adjective*
**1** not legal: *an illegitimate business*
**2** born to unmarried parents –*noun* **illegitimacy.**

**illiterate** /ɪˈlɪtərɪt/ *adjective*
unable to read or write –*noun* **illiteracy.**

---

**USAGE NOTE:** The word *illiterate* generally describes someone who can't read or write. Today people also speak of being *computer literate* or *computer illiterate*. People who have a very low level of literacy may be called *functionally illiterate*, because they can't get jobs that require much reading or writing.

---

**illuminate** /ɪˈlumɪˌneɪt/ *verb* **illuminated, illuminating, illuminates**
to give light to: *Streetlights illuminated the roads.* –*noun* **illumination.**

**illustrate** /ˈɪləˌstreɪt/ *verb* **illustrated, illustrating, illustrates**
**1** to give examples, explain: *She illustrated her point by speaking of her own experiences.*
**2** to provide with pictures, drawings, etc.: *The history book was illustrated with many maps and photographs.* –*adjective* **illustrative** /ɪˈlʌstrətɪv/; –*noun* **illustration,** (artist) **illustrator.**

**I'm** /aɪm/ *verb*
*contraction of* I am: *I'm a doctor.*

**image** /ˈɪmɪʤ/ *noun*
**1** a picture in the mind of someone or something: *His image of the city changed soon after his arrival.*
**2** picture, copy: *The image on the photograph is not clear.*

**imagery** /ˈɪmɪʤri/ *noun, (no plural)*
use of images, especially in art and literature: *The imagery in his writing is so detailed that the characters seem real.*

**imaginary** /ɪˈmæʤəˌnɛri/ *adjective*
existing only in the mind, unreal: *The child has an imaginary friend.*

**imagination** /ɪˌmæʤəˈneɪʃən/ *noun*
**1** the act of forming images in the mind: *His stories show that he has a good imagination.*
**2** ability to think of new ideas: *It will take a lot of imagination to solve the problem.* –*adjective* **imaginative.**

**imagine** /ɪˈmæʤɪn/ *verb* **imagined, imagining, imagines**
**1** to form (a picture, idea) in one's mind: *She imagined what it is like to be rich and famous.*
**2** to believe that something unreal is real: *The little girl imagined that she heard strange sounds in the middle of the night.*||*The little boy imagined he was a famous football player.*

**imitate** /ˈɪməˌteɪt/ *verb* **imitated, imitating, imitates**
**1** to act the same way as another: *The boy imitates his father's way of talking.*
**2** to copy, duplicate: *That manufacturer imitates the designs of a competitor.*
**3** to copy someone's speech to make fun of them: *My sister likes to imitate a famous singer.* –*noun* **imitation,** (person) **imitator;** –*adjective* **imitative.**

**immature** /ˌɪməˈʧʊr/ *adjective*
**1** not ripe or fully formed: *When oranges are green, they are immature; when they are orange, they are ripe.*
**2** like a child, not an adult: *His immature behavior annoys people.* –*noun* **immaturity.**

I

**immediate** /ɪ'midiət/ *adjective*
**1** right now: *People hurt in an earthquake have an immediate need for help.*
**2** nearby, close to: *Damage occurred in the immediate area of the earthquake's starting point.* *–noun* **immediacy;** *–adverb* **immediately.**

**immense** /ɪ'mɛns/ *adjective*
very large, *(synonym)* huge: *There is an immense statue in the park.* *–noun* **immensity.** *(antonym)* tiny.

**immerse** /ɪ'mɜrs/ *verb* **immersed, immersing, immerses**
to put something in water until it's covered: *The cook immersed the potatoes in boiling water.* *–noun* **immersion** /ɪ'mɜrʒən/; *–adjective* **immersible.**

**immigrant** /'ɪməgrənt/ *noun*
a person who moves to another country to live: *Millions of immigrants came to the United States of America for religious freedom.*

**immigrate** /'ɪmə͵greɪt/ *verb* **immigrated, immigrating, immigrates**
to leave one's own country to live in another: *John F. Kennedy's grandparents immigrated to the USA from Ireland.* *–noun* (person) **immigrant, immigration** /͵ɪmə'greɪʃən/. *(antonym)* emigrate. *See:* emigrant, USAGE NOTE.

**immoral** /ɪ'mɔrəl/ *adjective*
against most people's moral principles, evil: *Murder is immoral.* *–noun* **immorality** /͵ɪmɔ'rælǝti/.

**immortal** /ɪ'mɔrtl/ *adjective*
**1** living forever: *Ancient peoples believed their gods were immortal.*
**2** lasting forever: *Beauty and truth are immortal qualities.* *–noun* **immortality.**

**immunity** /ɪ'myunəti/ *noun, plural* **immunities**
**1** protection from disease: *Today there is more immunity to many diseases than in the 1950s.*
**2** protection from (punishment): *The criminal was given immunity because she gave information about other criminals to the police.* *–adjective* **immune;** *–verb* **to immunize.**

**impact** /'ɪm͵pækt/ *noun*
**1** a forceful hit, blow: *The car made a loud impact when it hit the wall.*
**2** effect, result: *Poverty has a bad impact on people's health.*

**impact** *verb informal*
to affect: *The Senator talked about how the new tax laws will impact middle class families.*

**impair** /ɪm'pɛr/ *verb*
to weaken, damage: *A blow to the ear impaired her hearing.* *–noun* **impairment.**

**impartial** /ɪm'pɑrʃəl/ *adjective*
treating all sides fairly: *The judge gave an impartial decision that did not favor either side.* *–noun* **impartiality** /ɪm'pɑrʃi'ælǝti/; *–adverb* **impartially.**

**impeach** /ɪm'pitʃ/ *verb*
to accuse a public official of a crime or wrongdoing: *The Congress impeached the President for criminal activity.* *–noun* (act) **impeachment.**

**imperative** /ɪm'pɛrətɪv/ *adjective*
necessary, urgent: *It is imperative that you call home immediately.*

**imperative** *noun*
(in grammar) a command form: *"Go home immediately!" shows the imperative of the verb "to go."*

**imperfect** /ɪm'pɜrfɪkt/ *adjective*
**1** having mistakes: *The diamond is pretty, but that crack makes it imperfect.*
**2** a verb tense indicating past action in progress: *"We were talking when you arrived" shows the imperfect tense of "talk."* *–noun* (condition) **imperfection.**

**imperialism** /ɪm'pɪriə͵lɪzəm/ *noun, (no plural)*
one nation controlling the political or economic life of other nations *–adjective* **imperial.**

**imperil** /ɪm'pɛrəl/ *verb formal*
to put in danger: *A storm imperiled the passenger ship.*

**impersonal** /ɪm'pɜrsənəl/ *adjective*
lacking in feeling or sympathy, unfriendly: *People often complain that government agencies are impersonal.*

**impersonate** /ɪm 'pɜrsə͵neɪt/ *verb* **impersonated, impersonating, impersonates**
act like someone else, sometimes using

clothes, voices, or makeup: *That actor impersonates famous politicians to make fun of them.* –*noun* **impersonation.**

**implement** /ˈɪmpləmənt/ *verb*
to start, put into action: *The meat company implemented a new advertising plan for low-fat beef.*

**implement** *noun*
a tool or piece of equipment: *With the right implements, I can unlock a door without a key.* –*noun* **implementation.**

**imply** /ɪmˈplaɪ/ *verb* **implied, implying, implies**
to suggest only indirectly: *My boss implied I would get a raise if I continue doing good work.*

**impolite** /ˌɪmpəˈlaɪt/ *adjective*
showing bad manners, rude –*noun* **impoliteness.**

**import** /ɪmˈpɔrt/ *verb*
**1** to bring products into one country from another: *The jeweler buys diamonds from Africa and imports them into the USA.*
**2** (in computers) to move data from one system to another –*noun* **importation, import.** *(antonym)* export.

**important** /ɪmˈpɔrtnt/ *adjective*
having great meaning or influence: *She is an important person in government.* –*noun* **importance.**

**impose** /ɪmˈpoʊz/ *verb* **imposed, imposing, imposes**
**1** to place upon, usually against one's will: *The government imposes new taxes on people.*
**2** to bother, take advantage of: *Relatives imposed upon us when they stayed for a whole week.* –*noun* (act) **imposition.**

**impossible** /ɪmˈpɑsəbəl/ *adjective*
**1** not able to be done: *Flying by waving your arms is impossible.*
**2** extremely difficult, unbearable: *You are impossible today! You disagree with everything I say.* –*noun* **impossibility;** –*adverb* **impossibly.**

**impostor** /ɪmˈpɑstər/ *noun*
a person who pretends to be someone else: *The impostor had a false passport, but the police knew his real name.*

**impractical** /ɪm ˈpræktəkəl/ *adjective*
not practical, not sensible: *He has intelligent solutions to problems, but their high cost makes them impractical.*

**imprecise** /ˌɪmpr əˈsaɪs/ *adjective*
not exact (vague): *The price of the trip is imprecise until we know the cost of airplane tickets.*

**impress** /ɪmˈprɛs/ *verb*
**1** to create and give an image of someone or something: *He impresses me as a nice man.*
**2** to cause others to admire: *Her excellent ideas impressed her boss.* –*noun* **impression.**

**impressive** /ɪmˈp rɛsɪv/ *adjective*
causing admiration: *That girl's ability is very impressive; she can jump high.*

**imprison** /ɪmˈprɪzən/ *verb*
to send to jail

**improbable** /ɪmˈprɑbəbəl/ *adjective*
not likely to happen: *Rain is improbable today because there are no clouds in the sky.* –*noun* **improbability.**

**improper** /ɪmˈprɑpər/ *adjective*
**1** showing poor manners, impolite
**2** incorrect, not suitable

**improve** /ɪmˈpruv/ *verb* **improved, improving, improves**
**1** to make better: *He improved his appearance by dressing more carefully.*
**2** to become better: *Her health improved when she began eating fruits.*
**3** to advance, progress: *He improved himself by getting a better job.*

**improvement** /ɪmˈ pruvmənt/ *noun*
something that is better or makes something else better: *They made improvements to the house by building a fancy kitchen and a new roof.*

**improvise** /ˈɪmprəˌvaɪz/ *verb* **improvised, improvising, improvises**
to create and perform (a song, speech, etc.) with no preparation

**impulse** /ˈɪmpʌls/ *noun*
a sudden desire, urge: *He had an impulse to run, but he kept on walking.* –*adjective* **impulsive;** –*adverb* **impulsively.**

**impunity** /ɪmˈpyunəti/ *noun, (no plural)*
a situation without risk or fear of punishment: *The king killed people with impunity.*

I

**impure** /ɪm'pyʊr/ *adjective*
**1** mixed with something, usually bad or dirty: *That water is impure; don't drink it.*
**2** morally or sexually wrong *–noun* **impurity.**

**in** /ɪn/ *preposition*
**1** used to show where someone or something is contained: *I left my keys in the car.*||*I saw his photograph in a magazine.*
**2** used to show location (room, building, city, country): *Students are in the classroom.*||*He was born in Cuba, but grew up in Miami, Florida.*
**3** used to show time (month, year, season): *My son was born in 1970.*||*I am going to take a two-week vacation in the summer.*
**4** at or by the end of a certain period of time: *I will call you in a week.*
**5** into: *We put the gift in a box.*
**6** used to refer to a particular condition or situation: *That child is always in trouble at school.*||*We walked to the bus station in the rain.*
**7** in between: located or existing in the middle of two things: *Hartford is a city in between Boston and New York.*

**in** *adverb*
present, here: *Dr. Smith is in today.*
**in for: a.** about to experience: *He is in for a big surprise.* **b.** in jail: *The prisoner is in for robbery.*
**in on:** aware of something others are not: *She is in on the secret.*

**in** *adjective*
**the in crowd:** fashionable social group: *The less popular students cannot join the in crowd.*

**in** *noun*
**the ins and outs of:** the details of something: *That lawyer knows all the ins and outs of criminal law.*

**USAGE NOTE:** We use *in* with a particular year or month, but we use *on* with a particular day: *She was born in 1965.*||*She was born in February.*||*She was born on February 6, 1965.* Also, we use *in* with a city, state, or country, but we use *on* with a street or avenue: *I live in San Francisco.*||*I live in California.*||*I live on Market Street.* When we give an exact address, *at* is used: *I live at 122 Market Street.*

**inability** / ˌɪnə'bɪləti/ *noun*
lack of power or ability to do something: *He needed someone to help him because of his inability to walk.*

**inaccessible** /ˌɪnæk'sɛsəbəl/ *adjective*
impossible or difficult to reach: *The road is blocked, so the town is now inaccessible.* *–noun* **inaccessibility.**

**inaccuracy** /ɪn'ækyərəsi/ *noun, plural* **inaccuracies**
something that is not correct, an error, mistake: *The inaccuracy of the numbers makes them useless.* *–adjective* **inaccurate.**

**inactive** /ɪn'æktɪv/ *adjective*
not working or moving: *He has been inactive since his retirement.* *–noun* (condition) **inaction.**

**inadequate** /ɪn'ædəkwɪt/ *adjective*
not enough: *There is an inadequate supply of food, so people are dying.*

**inappropriate** /ˌɪnə'proʊpriət/ *adjective*
**1** not suitable for the situation: *His dark wool suit was inappropriate in the Florida heat.*
**2** not proper, impolite

**inasmuch as** /ˌɪnəz'mʌtʃəz/ *conjunction formal*
because of the fact that, since: *Inasmuch as the patient is now feeling strong, he can leave the hospital.*

**inauguration** /ɪnˌɔgyə'reɪʃən/ *noun*
**1** a ceremony putting a US president or state governor into office: *The inauguration brings guests from all over.*

inauguration

**2** beginning, opening ceremony: *The inauguration of the holiday celebration included a speech by the mayor.* *–adjective* **inaugural;** *–verb* (action) **to inauguarate.**

**USAGE NOTE:** Presidential elections are held every four years in November. The *inauguration* of a US President takes place on the following January 20. It is not a national holiday.

**inbound** /ˈɪnˌbaʊnd/ *adjective adverb* headed toward or into a place from the surrounding area: *Inbound flights to the city are delayed because of the snow.*

**incapable** /ɪnˈkeɪpəbəl/ *adjective*
**1** not able: *Our small garage is incapable of holding three cars.*
**2** without ability or talent: *My boss is completely incapable; I don't know how he keeps his job.*

**incense** /ˈɪnˌsɛns/ *noun, (no plural)* substance (often in a stick form) that has a pleasant smell when burned

**incense** *verb* /ɪnˈsɛns/ **incensed, incensing, incenses** to make very angry: *The child's lies incensed her mother.*

**incentive** /ɪnˈsɛntɪv/ *noun* something that makes someone work harder, a reward: *The man promised his son $100 as an incentive for good grades.*

**inch** /ɪntʃ/ *noun* a measure of length equal to 1/12 of a foot or 2.54 centimeters: *My ruler is 12 inches long.*

**If you give him (her) an inch, he (she) takes a mile:** if you give someone a little opportunity, that person will take too much: *I loaned him my car for the evening, and he has kept it for a week. If you give him an inch, he takes a mile.* *See:* art on page 16a.

**inch** *verb* to move very slowly: *Traffic is so bad that cars are just inching along.*

---

**USAGE NOTE:** There are 12 *inches* in a *foot* (30.48 cm) and three feet to a *yard* (91.44 cm). Today both the US system (inches, feet, pounds, ounces, etc.) and the metric system are taught in school, but most Americans are more comfortable with the US system: *He's six feet four inches tall.*||*I bought ten yards of curtain material.*

---

**incident** /ˈɪnsədənt/ *noun* an event, occurrence, especially a bad one: *an incident where two men fight*

**incidentally** /ˌɪnsəˈdɛntli/ *adverb* used to introduce a new thought, *(synonym)* by the way: *Yes, I know she's from Japan. Incidentally, did you know that I speak Japanese?*

**incinerator** /ɪnˈsɪnəˌreɪtər/ *noun* a machine used to burn things, especially trash *–verb* **to incinerate;** *–noun* (act) **incineration.**

**inclination** /ˌɪnkləˈneɪʃən/ *noun* desire to do something, preference

**incline** /ɪnˈklaɪn/ *verb* **inclined, inclining, inclines**
**1** to move at an angle: *He inclined his easy chair to a nearly flat position.*
**2** to bend forward or backward: *Listeners inclined forward to better hear the speaker.*

**incline** *noun* a hill: *A train went up an incline through the mountains.* *(antonym)* decline.

**include** /ɪnˈklud/ *verb* **included, including, includes**
**1** to make something a part of something else: *She included some of her friends on the party guest list.*
**2** to put with, to attach: *She included some chocolate in each child's lunch bag.* *–noun* (act) **inclusion;** *–adjective* **inclusive.** *(antonym)* exclude.

**incoherent** /ˌɪnkoʊˈhɪrənt/ *adjective* not able to be understood: *The little girl was so frightened that her speech was incoherent.* *–noun* **incoherence.**

**incombustible** /ˌɪnkəmˈbʌstəbəl/ *adjective* not able to burn or be burned

**income** /ˈɪnˌkʌm/ *noun* money earned from working or other ways (pensions, investments, etc.)

**income tax** *noun* an amount (percentage) of individuals' and businesses' earnings paid to the government: *The company moved out of the state because of its high income tax.*

**incompatible** /ˌɪnkəmˈpætəbəl/ *adjective* not able to work or be together

**incompetent** /ɪn ˈkɑmpətənt/ *adjective* without the skill or talent to do something: *The first lawyer we hired was incompetent.* *–noun* **incompetence.**

**incomplete** /ˌɪnk əmˈplit/ *adjective* lacking, something unfinished: *My mother feels her life is incomplete without grandchildren.*

**incomprehensible** /ˌɪnkɑmpriˈhɛnsəbəl/ *adjective*
not able to be understood

**inconvenient** /ˌɪnkənˈvinyənt/ *adjective*
not at a good time, at an awkward time: *Seeing you tomorrow is inconvenient because I have another appointment.* –*noun* **inconvenience.**

**incorporate** /ɪnˈkɔrpəreɪt/ *verb* **incorporated, incorporating, incorporates**
**1** to include, contain: *The new tax laws incorporate ideas from Democrats.*
**2** to form a business into a corporation

**incorrect** /ˌɪnkəˈrɛkt/ *adjective*
**1** containing mistakes, wrong
**2** not acceptable, bad

I

**increase** /ˈɪnˌkri s/ *noun*
a larger amount of something: *Mr. Kim got a salary increase of 10 percent; he was earning $40,000 per year, so now he will earn $44,000.*

**increase** *verb* /ɪnˈkris/ **increased, increasing, increases**
**1** to go up in number, rise: *The temperature increased ten degrees.*
**2** to make bigger: *We increased the size of our house by adding another bedroom.*

**incredible** /ɪnˈkrɛdəbəl/ *adjective*
**1** wonderful: *We had an incredible time on our vacation!*
**2** unbelievable: *He told us an incredible story about his escape from prison.* –*adverb* **incredibly.**

**incriminate** /ɪnˈkrɪməˌneɪt/ *verb* **incriminated, incriminating, incriminates**
to show that someone participated in a crime

**incubate** /ˈɪnkyəˌbeɪt/ *verb* **incubated, incubating, incubates**

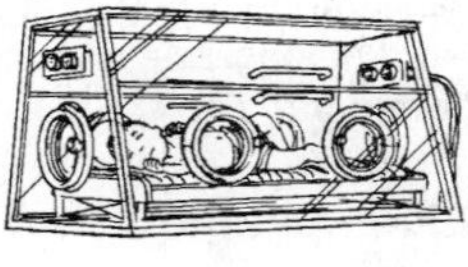
incubator

**1** to keep eggs warm until babies are born: *Birds incubate eggs by sitting on them.*
**2** to put a newborn baby in a special machine so it can grow –*noun* (act) **incubation,** (thing) **incubator.**

**indebted** /ɪnˈdɛtɪd/ *adjective*
owing money or thanks to someone: *I am indebted to you for saving my life.* –*noun* **indebtedness.**

**indecent** /ɪnˈdisənt/ *adjective*
**1** not good or proper: *It was indecent of him to lie to his mother.*
**2** not wearing clothes or behaving improperly in a sexual way: *The man took off his clothes in public and was arrested for indecent behavior.* –*noun* **indecency.**

**indeed** /ɪnˈdid/*exclamation*
used to express surprise or disbelief: *"I will earn a million dollars next year." "Indeed?"*

**indeed** *adverb*
**1** truly, factually so: *It was indeed the largest elephant in the world.*
**2** used to express something strongly: *Do I love my husband? Yes, indeed!*

**indefinite** /ɪnˈdɛfənɪt/ *adjective*
not specific about time, place, or detail: *We know the meeting is on July 12, but the time is indefinite.*

**indefinite article** *noun*
(in grammar) "a" or "an," used before a noun: *A tree fell in a forest.*

**indefinite pronoun** *noun*
a word, such as "either," "any," or "some," that replaces a noun in a nonspecific way: *He needs some (money) because he doesn't have any.*

**indent** /ɪnˈdɛnt/ *verb*
to start writing or typing a short distance in from the other type on the page: *When I begin a new paragraph, I indent five spaces.* –*noun* **indent.**

**independence** /ˌɪndəˈpɛndəns/ *noun, (no plural)*
**1** freedom: *Many former African colonies fought for independence from France, Portugal, and other European countries.*
**2** state of taking care of oneself: *She felt a sense of independence when she left home to go to college.* –*adjective* **independent;** –*adverb* **independently.**

**Independence Day** *noun*
in the USA, July 4, the holiday marking independence from Great Britain (also called the Fourth of July) *See:* Fourth of July.

**independent** /ˌɪndəˈpɛndənt/ *adjective*
**1** free: *The USA became an independent nation after 1776.*

**2** taking care of oneself: *He is independent of his parents but still asks for their advice.* –*adverb* **independently.**

**index** /ˈɪnˌdɛks/ *noun, plural* **indexes** or **indices** /-dəˌsiz/
a list of subjects in alphabetical order with page numbers in the back of the book: *Look for "World War II" in the index of your history book.*

**Indian** /ˈɪndiən/ *noun*
**1** a person born in India or with parents from India: *Many Indians practice the Hindu religion.*
**2** a person related to any of the original people of America, *(synonym)* Native American or Original American: *Her father is an Indian from South Dakota.*

**Indian** *adjective*
related to Indians: *She traveled to Calcutta to study Indian Music.*

---

**USAGE NOTE:** The preferred term for American Indians is *Native Americans* or *Original Americans.*

---

**indicate** /ˈɪndəˌkeɪt/ *verb* **indicated, indicating, indicates**
**1** to show where or what something is: *The girl indicated her choice of dessert by pointing to the chocolate cake.*
**2** to mean something: *Those black clouds indicate that it might rain soon.* –*noun* **indication, indicator** /ˈɪndəˌkeɪtər/; –*adjective* **indicative** /ɪnˈdɪkətɪv/.

**indict** /ɪnˈdaɪt/ *verb*
(in law) to formally accuse someone of a crime or wrongdoing –*noun* **indictment.**

**indigestion** /ˌɪndəˈʤɛsʧən/ *noun, (no plural)*
pain in the stomach because of something one has eaten: *He ate three hamburgers with beans and had indigestion.* –*adjective* **indigestible** /ˌɪndəˈʤɛstəbəl/.

**indirect object** *noun*
(in grammar) a noun receiving indirect action from a verb—for example, "him" in this sentence: *I loaned him money.*

**individual** /ˌɪndəˈvɪʤuəl/ *noun*
one person: *Three individuals walked away from the crowd.*

**individualist** /ˌɪndəˈvɪʤuəlɪst/ *noun*
a person who thinks and behaves according to his or her own beliefs: *Be an individualist; don't become a doctor like the rest of your family.* –*adjective* **individualistic;** –*noun* **individualism.**

**individualize** /ˌɪndəˈvɪʤuəˌlaɪz/ *verb* **individualized, individualizing, individulizes**
to make something for a person's special needs: *That company is very large, but it individualizes its services for each customer.*

**indivisible** /ˌɪndəˈvɪzəbəl/ *adjective*
not able to be forced apart, solid: *That family is indivisible; they stay together even during troubled times.*

**indoor** /ˈɪnˌdɔr/ *adjective*
located inside a building: *Some rich people have indoor swimming pools.* *(antonym)* outdoor.

**indoors** /ɪnˈdɔrz/ *adverb*
inside a building: *When it started to rain, we moved the party indoors.*

indoors

**indulge** /ɪnˈdʌlʤ/ *verb* **indulged, indulging, indulges**
**1** to take or eat something good (sometimes too much): *I indulged and had chocolate cake for dessert.*
**2** to allow someone to do something, even if it is not sensible: *Carlos indulged his son's wish to learn to fly an airplane.* –*adjective* **indulgent;** –*noun* (act) **indulgence.**

**industrialize** /ɪnˈdʌstriəˌlaɪz/ *verb* **industrialized, industrializing, industrializes**
to make a nation or region use and develop industry: *Many developing countries wish to industrialize their economies by building factories.* –*noun* **industrialization** /ɪnˌdʌstriəlɪˈzeɪʃən/.

**industrious** /ɪn ˈdʌstriəs/ *adjective*
hardworking, busy: *She started her own business and is now very industrious.*

**industry** /'ɪndəstri/ *noun, plural* **industries**
**1** the making and selling of products: *Industry grew quickly after the discovery of electricity.*
**2** a specific type of manufacturing: *The US auto industry is centered in the city of Detroit.*
**3** hard work: *His industry in college resulted in high grades. –adjective* **industrial.**

**ineffective** /ˌɪnɪ'fɛktɪv/ *adjective*
**1** not good enough to make something happen: *Shouting at people is ineffective; talking works better.*
**2** not good at doing something *–noun* **ineffectiveness.**

**inefficient** /ˌɪnɪ'fɪʃənt/ *adjective*
not using time well: *The factory is inefficient because its machinery is slow and old. –noun* **inefficiency.**

**ineligible** /ɪn'ɛlɪʤəbəl/ *adjective*
not able to do something for some reason (too young, not skilled, etc.), *(synonym)* unqualified: *He is ineligible to enter college because he has not finished high school. –noun* **ineligibility.**

**inequality** /ˌɪni'kwɑləti/ *noun, plural* **inequalities**
a condition in which there is a difference in opportunity, wealth, size, treatment, etc.: *There is a problem of inequality here; I make $20,000 a year and you make $30,000, but we do the same job.*

**inevitable** /ɪn'ɛvətəbəl/ *adjective*
definitely going to happen, unavoidable, certain

**inexpensive** /ˌɪnɪk'spɛnsɪv/ *adjective*
low-priced, cheap: *We had a difficult time finding an inexpensive apartment.*

**inexperience** /ˌɪnɪk'spɪriəns/ *noun*
**1** lack of experience in the world: *His inexperience with city life showed when he didn't know how to use the subway.*
**2** limited knowledge: *We laughed at her inexperience in the kitchen; she can't even prepare a simple meal.*

**infamous** /'ɪnfəməs/ *adjective*
famous because of something bad: *That city is infamous for its high crime rate. –noun* (condition) **infamy.**

**infancy** /'ɪnfənsi/ *noun, (no plural)*
**1** the part of a baby's life before he or she starts to walk: *Many parents choose to work at home during their child's infancy.*
**2** *figurative* early in time, beginning: *That business is still in its infancy; it opened last month.*

**infant** /'ɪnfənt/ *noun*
a baby: *A mother held an infant in her arms.*

infant

**infantile** /'ɪnfənˌtaɪl/ *adjective*
childish, stupid

**infantry** /'ɪnfəntri/ *noun, (no plural)*
soldiers who fight on foot: *The infantry moved forward through the fields.*

**infect** /ɪn'fɛkt/ *verb*
**1** to give someone a sickness or disease: *A flu virus has infected everyone in the office.*
**2** *figurative* to spread through a place: *Crime has infected the entire neighborhood.*

**infection** /ɪn'fɛkʃən/ *noun*
a disease or sickness received by someone or something: *The doctor is treating the child for an ear infection. –adjective* **infectious.**

**inferior** /ɪn'fɪriər/ *adjective*
lower in quality: *Most wine from Switzerland is inferior to wine from France. (antonym)* superior.

**inferior** *noun*
a person of lower rank or ability: *The army general is unkind to his inferiors. –noun* **inferiority.**

**infest** /ɪn'fɛst/ *verb*
to fill with insects or animals that cause trouble: *Ants infest our garden.*

**infinite** /'ɪnfənɪt/ *adjective*
going on forever, never-ending, limitless: *There are an infinite number of stars in the night sky.*

**infinitive** /ɪn'fɪnɪtɪv/ *noun*
(in grammar) the main form of a verb, usually used with "to": *"To go" is the infinitive form of the verb "go."*

**infinity** /ɪn'fɪnəti/ *noun, (no plural)*
a limitless number, thing, or place, such as outer space and time

**infirmary** /ɪn'fɜrməri/ *noun, plural* **infirmaries**
a place where people get medical care

**inflame** /ɪn'fleɪm/ *verb* **inflamed, inflaming, inflames**
**1** to cause great emotions, usually anger or excitement: *The king's evil actions inflamed the slaves.*
**2** to make red and sore: *The boy's knee became inflamed after he hurt it.*

**inflammable** /ɪn'flæməbəl/ *adjective*
able to burn

**inflammation** /ˌɪnflə'meɪʃən/ *noun*
a condition from an injury or disease, usually with redness, heat, and swelling: *He has an inflammation in his right eye from too much dust.*

**inflate** /ɪn'fleɪt/ *verb* **inflated, inflating, inflates**
**1** to fill with air: *A mechanic inflated the car's tires.*
**2** to raise above the normal or proper level: *Some stores inflate prices.*

**inflation** /ɪn'fleɪʃən/ *noun*
**1** a rise in prices and lowering of money's value: *Inflation was so great that bread cost twice as much in June as it did in May.*
**2** filling with air: *The inflation of the balloon was easy with a gas tank. –adjective* **inflationary.**

**inflict** /ɪn'flɪkt/ *verb*
to cause something bad, give someone a problem: *My father inflicts his old war stories on the whole family. –noun* **infliction.**

**influence** /'ɪnfluəns/ *noun*
the power to change or persuade others

**influence** *verb* **influenced, influencing, influences**
to change someone's mind, have an effect on: *Weather often influences how people feel. –adjective* **influential.**

**influenza** /ˌɪnflu'ɛnzə/ *noun*
an illness caused by viruses easily spread to other people

**inform** /ɪn'fɔrm/ *verb*
**1** to tell someone: *I informed my friends of my new address.*
**2** to report someone's wrongdoing: *He is a spy who informs on others to the government. –adjective* **informed.**

**informal** /ɪn'fɔrməl/ *adjective*
ordinary, not formal: *Dress at the party was informal, with no neckties or fancy dresses. –noun* **informality.**

**information** /ˌɪnfər'meɪʃən/ *noun, (no plural)*
knowledge, news, facts: *The library provided me with useful information.*

**information superhighway** *noun*
a worldwide computer system of facts, news, electronic mail, etc. *See:* E-mail; Internet; World Wide Web.

---

**USAGE NOTE:** People travel the *information superhighway* as a car travels on a good road: at top speed. They can get information on their computers from all over the world without leaving their homes or offices by using the *Internet* and *World Wide Web.*

---

**informative** /ɪn'fɔrmətɪv/ *adjective*
providing knowledge: *That television news show is very informative.*

**informer** /ɪn'fɔrmər/ *noun*
a spy: *He is a police informer about crimes committed in his neighborhood.*

**infrequent** /ɪn'frikwənt/ *adjective*
not often: *His visits to his parents are infrequent because he lives far away.*

**ingenious** /ɪn'ʤinyəs/ *adjective*
very good at making things or solving problems: *The campers thought of an ingenious way to cross the river without a bridge. –noun* (skill) **ingenuity.**

**ingratitude** /ɪn 'grætɪˌtud/ *noun, (no plural)*
not showing thanks

**ingredient** /ɪn'gridiənt/ *noun*
**1** a food item included with others: *Flour, milk, butter, and salt are some ingredients in bread.*
**2** a part of something: *Hard work is an ingredient of success.*

**inhabit** /ɪn'hæbɪt/ *verb*
to live in an area: *Lions inhabit those mountains. –noun* **inhabitant;** *–adjective* **inhabited.**

I

**inhale** /ɪn'heɪl/ *verb* **inhaled, inhaling, inhales**
to breathe in: *She inhaled the fresh mountain air.* *–noun* **inhalation** /ˌɪnhə'leɪʃən/. *(antonym)* exhale.

inhale

**inherit** /ɪn'hɛrɪt/ *verb*
to receive something after someone (usually a relative) dies: *He inherited his grandfather's watch.* *–noun* **inheritance.**

**inhuman** /ɪn'hyumən/ *adjective*
without good human qualities: *Not giving food to prisoners is inhuman.*

**inhumane** /ˌɪnhyu'meɪn/ *adjective*
not kind to animals or people, cruel: *Some people think that doing scientific experiments on animals is inhumane.* *–noun* **inhumanity** /ˌɪnhyu'mænəti/.

**initial** /ɪ'nɪʃəl/ *adjective*
beginning, first: *My initial good opinion of him changed with time.*

**initial** *noun, plural* **initials**
the first letters of one's names: *John Smith's initials are J.S.*

**initial** *verb*
to write one's initials on something: *He initialed a page to show that he had read it.*

**initiate** /ɪ'nɪʃiˌeɪt/ *verb* **initiated, initiating, initiates**
**1** to cause something to start, to begin: *The group was quiet until she initiated conversation by asking a question.*
**2** to bring someone into an organization with a ceremony or activity: *The young man was initiated into a club.* *–noun* **initiation** /ɪˌnɪʃi'eɪʃən/.

**initiative** /ɪ'nɪʃətɪv/ *noun*
the first step, usually an action that shows a serious desire to achieve one's goals: *He showed initiative by learning Spanish before traveling to South America on business.*

**inject** /ɪn'ʤɛkt/ *verb*
to force a substance, usually liquid, into a person or thing: *The doctor injected some medicine into the patient with a needle.* *–noun* **injection.**

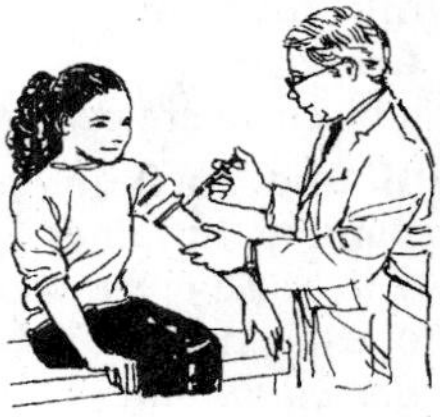
inject

**injure** /'ɪnʤər/ *verb* **injured, injuring, injures**
**1** to hurt, cause damage: *He injured his knee when he ran in a long race.*
**2** to hurt (feelings), *(synonym)* to offend: *Her unkind words injured my pride.* *–adjective* **injurious** /ɪn'ʤʊriəs/; *–noun* **injury.**

**injustice** /ɪn'ʤʌstɪs/ *noun*
an unfair act, a lack of fairness: *During the Civil War, many fought against the injustice of slavery.*

**ink** /ɪŋk/ *noun*
a colored liquid used in pens *–adjective* **inky.**

**in-law** /'ɪnˌlɔ/ *noun*
a person related by marriage: *My wife's father and mother are good in-laws; they treat me like a real son.* *See:* art on page 14a.

**in-line skates** or **inline skates** /'ɪnˌlaɪn/ *noun plural*
boots with one row of rubber wheels and a brake for stopping, used to move quickly over a road or other hard surface *–noun* **in-line skating** or **inline skating.** *See:* roller skates.

in-line skates

**inmate** /'ɪnˌmeɪt/ *noun*
a person in jail, a prisoner

**in memoriam** /'ɪnmə'mɔriəm/ *adverb phrase* (Latin for) in memory of (usually used to mark graves): *I saw a baby's gravestone that read "In Memoriam Robert White 1950-1951."*

**inn** /ɪn/ *noun*
a small hotel, usually in the country, often serving meals: *We like to stay at*

*small country inns.* *–noun* (owner) **innkeeper.** *See:* bed and breakfast, USAGE NOTE.

**inner** /ˈɪnər/ *adjective*
**1** existing or located within: *She doesn't show her inner feelings.*
**2** located inside, farther away from walls or doors: *an inner courtyard*

**inner city** *noun, plural* **inner cities**
a city's central area, especially a poor area

**innermost** /ˈɪnərˌmoʊst/ *adjective*
**1** deepest within: *Police found the missing child in the innermost part of the forest. (antonym)* outermost.
**2** *figurative* most secret, private: *innermost feelings*

**innocence** /ˈɪnəsəns/ *noun*
**1** lack of guilt: *You proved your innocence by showing you were at home when the crime happened.*
**2** a lack of knowledge and experience of the real world: *Small children have a wonderful innocence before they learn about evil.* *–adjective* **innocent.**

**innovation** /ˌɪnəˈveɪʃən/ *noun*
something new made or improved with new and different ideas: *Car telephones were an innovation in the 1980s.* *–verb* **to innovate;** *–adjective* **innovative** /ˈɪnəˌveɪtɪv/.

**inoculate** /ɪˈnɑkyəˌleɪt/ *verb* **inoculated, inoculating, inoculates**
to give a shot of medicine through a needle to prevent disease

**inoffensive** /ˌɪnəˈfɛnsɪv/ *adjective*
not causing anger or other bad feelings: *I let my little boy watch an inoffensive TV show on Saturday morning.*

**inoperative** /ɪnˈɑpərətɪv/ *adjective*
not working, broken: *The telephones are inoperative due to a bad storm.*

**inpatient** /ˈɪnˌpeɪʃənt/ *noun*
a person who stays overnight for medical care in a hospital: *inpatient services* *–adjective* **inpatient.**

**input** /ˈɪnˌpʊt/ *verb* **inputted** or **input, inputting, inputs**
to type information into a computer: *A worker inputs the company's sales figures every month.*

**input** *noun*
**1** information or advice from someone: *We would like your input, because you always have good ideas.*
**2** information typed into a computer: *My daily input includes letters, checks, and dates of meetings.*

**inquire** /ɪnˈkwaɪr/ *verb* **inquired, inquiring, inquires**
**1** to ask about something: *My friend inquired about my health.*
**2** to ask for (public or official) information, *(synonym)* to investigate: *A neighborhood group inquired into the plans for a new park.* *–noun* (act) **inquiry.** *See:* ask, USAGE NOTE.

**insane** /ɪnˈseɪn/ *adjective*
**1** mentally ill, crazy: *The doctors knew the man was insane when he heard voices in an empty room.*
**2** *figurative* ridiculous, foolish: *She has insane ideas about how to get rich overnight.* *–noun* **insanity** /ɪnˈsænəti/.

**insect** /ˈɪnsɛkt/ *noun*
a small animal with six legs, a body in three parts, and sometimes wings: *We have a lot of ants and other insects in our garden in the summer.*

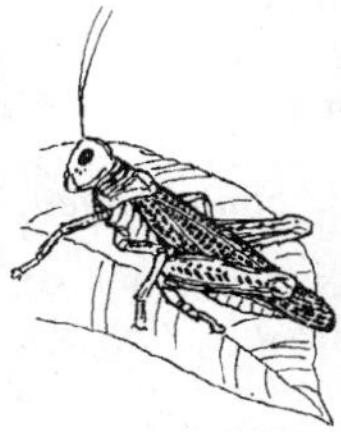
insect

**insecticide** /ɪnˈsɛktəˌsaɪd/ *noun*
a chemical or other substance used to kill insects

**insecure** /ˌɪnsəˈkyʊr/ *adjective*
**1** afraid, uncertain: *She feels insecure at home alone at night.*
**2** not steady, unsafe: *The fire escape is insecure; it moves in the wind.*

**insensitive** /ɪn ˈsɛnsətɪv/ *adjective*
unkind because someone is not aware of others' feelings: *She said insensitive things to the overweight woman.*

**inseparable** /ɪnˈsɛpərəbəl/ *adjective*
unable to be separated

**insert** /ɪnˈsɜrt/ *verb*
to put something into something else: *She inserted the letter into an envelope.* *–noun* **insertion** /ɪnˈsɜrʃən/.

**inside** /ˈɪnˌsaɪd/ *noun*
**1** the part (of a building) within walls: *The inside of the house looks better than the outside.*
**2** *plural* the parts of the body in the stomach: *My insides hurt from laughing too much.*

**inside** *preposition*
into: *He carried the painting inside the museum.*

**inside** /ɪnˈsaɪd/ *adverb*
toward the inside (of a building): *We walked inside to get out of the rain.* *(antonym)* outside.

**inside out:** (of clothing) having the wrong or inner side on the outside: *Her jacket was inside out.*

**inside** *adjective*
related to the inside of something: *The inside pockets of the coat are silk.*

**insider** /ˈɪnˌsaɪdɛr/ *noun*
a person belonging to a group in power: *That newspaper reporter is a Washington insider; he and the President have been good friends for many years.* *(antonym)* outsider.

**insight** /ˈɪnˌsaɪt/ *noun*
ability to see or know the truth, intelligence about something: *By moving to Washington, the senator gained insight into how politics really work.* *–adjective* **insightful** /ɪnˈsaɪtfʊl/.

**insignia** /ɪnˈsɪgniə/ *noun*
an official mark or design showing membership, rank, or honor: *I have a sweatshirt with my school's insignia.*

**insignificant** /ˌɪnsɪgˈnɪfəkənt/ *adjective*
not important, without meaning: *We thought the book had too many insignificant details about George Washington's life and not enough history.* *–noun* **insignificance.**

**insincere** /ˌɪnsɪnˈsɪr/ *adjective*
not showing one's true feelings or opinions: *He said he was happy you won the tennis match, but I think he was insincere.* *–noun* **insincerity** /ˌɪnsɪnˈsɛrəti/.

**insist** /ɪnˈsɪst/ *verb*
to demand, show strong opinion: *I insist that you go to the hospital immediately; you are very ill!*

**insist on:** to accept only certain things, to require: *The cook insists on the finest meat and fish.* *–noun* **insistence.**

**insomnia** /ɪnˈsɑmniə/ *noun (no plural)*
not able to sleep on a regular basis: *My father's insomnia went away when he stopped drinking coffee.* *–noun* (person) **insomniac.**

**inspect** /ɪnˈspɛkt/ *verb*
to look at something closely, examine: *Automakers inspect their cars to make sure they are safe.* *–noun* (person) **inspector.**

**inspection** /ɪnˈspɛkʃən/ *noun*
a close, careful look, examination: *Inspection of the old house shows that it needs a new roof.*

**inspiration** /ˌɪnspəˈreɪʃən/ *noun*
someone or something that makes a person work hard or gives them new ideas: *The story of her grandmother's difficult life was the inspiration for her latest book.* *–adjective* **inspirational;** *–verb* **to inspire.**

**install** /ɪnˈstɔl/ *verb*
**1** to put something (such as a piece of machinery) in place and make it work: *Our expert installed a new computer and we began using it Friday.*
**2** to employ someone, put someone in a job: *The new mayor was installed in office last week.* *–noun* (act) **installation,** (worker) **installer.**

**installment** /ɪnˈstɔlmənt/ *noun*
**1** one part of something that has been divided: *The story appeared in the magazine in three installments.*
**2** a partial payment: *He is paying off a $1,200 debt in twelve monthly installments of $100.*

**instance** /ˈɪnstəns/ *noun*
a single happening, situation: *In this instance, we will lend you money, but usually we can't.*

**for instance:** for example: *There are many things I would like to learn; for instance, I have always wanted to fly a plane.*

**instant** /ˈɪnstənt/ *noun*
a very quick period of time, less than a second: *Lightning struck a tree, and it fell in an instant.*

**instant** *adjective*
**1** very fast, immediate: *We can't give instant answers to such difficult questions.*
**2** easily mixed or prepared: *He added water and ice to the instant tea.* –*adverb* **instantly.**

**instantaneous** /ˌɪnstənˈteɪniəs/ *adjective*
with sudden, immediate effect: *The pain was instantaneous when I hit my head on the wall.*

**instant replay** *noun*
(in television) a filmed or taped moment, especially in sports, shown just after it happens

**instead** /ɪnˈstɛd/ *preposition*
in place of, rather than: *I got some roses, instead of chocolates for my girlfriend.*

**instinct** /ˈɪnˌstɪŋkt/ *noun*
a natural, unlearned behavior or ability: *Birds fly south each winter by instinct.* –*adjective* **instinctive.**

**institute** /ˈɪnstəˌtut/ *verb formal* **instituted, instituting, institutes**
to begin: *Since we instituted the new rule, fewer people have been late to work.*

**institute** *noun*
an organization, especially one for education or research

**institution** /ˌɪnstəˈtuʃən/ *noun*
**1** an organization that helps or serves people in the area of health, education, or work: *My aunt cannot pay for a private nurse, so she lives in a state institution.*
**2** an important, common custom in society: *The institution of marriage is important in most Western religions.*

**instruct** /ɪnˈstrʌkt/ *verb*
**1** to teach: *The Spanish professor instructs her students in the language and culture of Mexico.*
**2** to direct, tell someone what to do: *My sister instructed me to take out the trash.* –*adjective* **instructive;** –*noun* (teacher) **instructor.** *See:* teacher, USAGE NOTE.

**instruction** /ɪnˈstrʌkʃən/ *noun*
**1** education, teaching: *I receive instruction in computers at school.*
**2** *plural* information about how to do something, directions: *The mechanic gave us instructions on how to fix our car's lights.*

**instrument** /ˈɪnstrəmənt/ *noun*
**1** a tool that helps someone do work: *The doctor used an instrument to look in the girl's ears.*
**2** an object for making music, such as a violin, piano, or horn: *She plays two musical instruments.*

**insulation** /ˌɪnsəˈleɪʃən/ *noun*
any material that keeps out cold, heat, and/or sound: *My winter coat has soft feathers as insulation.* –*verb* **to insulate.**

insulation

**insult** /ˈɪnˌsʌlt/ *noun*
a very unkind remark about someone: *It was an insult to tell your brother that he's stupid. (antonym)* compliment.

**insult** /ɪnˈsʌlt/ *verb*
do or say bad, unkind things to someone: *You insulted me by saying I have ugly clothes.* –*adjective* **insulting.**

**insurance** /ɪnˈʃʊrəns/ *noun*
**1** an agreement in which you make regular payments to a company and this company will pay for a loss, accident, or illness: *I have insurance, so I can buy another car if someone steals mine.*
**2** any protection against a possible problem: *Do you carry an umbrella as insurance against getting wet in the rain?*

**insurance policy** *noun*
the legal contract or agreement that explains the type, details, and conditions of insurance: *I have a health insurance policy that tells me which doctors I can use.*

**insure** /ɪnˈʃʊr/ *verb* **insured, insuring, insures**
**1** to buy insurance for protection: *The company has insured all the workers who use dangerous machines.*
**2** to make sure, make certain: *I insured that the house was protected by locking all the doors.* –*noun* (business) **insurer.** *See:* ensure.

**intact** /ɪnˈtækt/ *adjective*
whole, not in pieces: *The eggs were in the bottom of the bag, but they did not break; they are still intact.*

**integer** /'ɪntəʤər/ *noun*
any positive or negative whole number, such as 1, 2, 3, 4, 5, etc., including 0 (zero), but not fractions: *If you add 2 and 1, you will get an integer, 3.*

**integral** /'ɪntəgrəl/ *adjective*
necessary, essential: *Rice is an integral part of Chinese food.*

**integrate** /'ɪntə,greɪt/ *verb* **integrated, integrating, integrates**
to put different groups of people together: *My school is integrated; it has African American, white, and other groups.* *–noun* **integration.**

**integrity** /ɪn'tɛgrəti/ *noun, (no plural)*
**1** strong morals, honesty: *Her integrity made her call the police when she found illegal drugs in her son's room.*
**2** completeness, strength: *The integrity of our nation depends on working together.*

**intellect** /'ɪntə,lɛkt/ *noun*
the ability to think logically and remember knowledge: *My sister is a person of great intellect; she teaches economics and advises the President.*

**intellectual** /,ɪntə'lɛkʧuəl/ *adjective*
related to thinking (not emotion) and learned knowledge: *If you read more books, you will increase your intellectual powers.*

**intelligence** /ɪn'tɛləʤəns/ *noun*
the ability to learn, understand, and use information: *He used his intelligence to win the science contest.*

**intelligent** /ɪn'tɛləʤənt/ *adjective*
**1** able to learn, understand, and use information well: *She gave an intelligent answer.*
**2** showing good judgment, wise: *Eating well and exercising are intelligent things to do.*

**intend** /ɪn'tɛnd/ *verb*
**1** to plan to do something: *I intend to visit Australia this year.*
**2** to mean to be for someone or something: *Don't read that letter; it is intended for my boyfriend.*

**intense** /ɪn'tɛns/ *adjective*
**1** strong (in feeling or emotion): *She felt intense pain when she broke her leg.*
**2** bright, strong: *an intense red*||*intense sunlight*

**intensify** /ɪn'tɛnsə,faɪ/ *verb* **intensified, intensifying, intensifies**
to get stronger, make something stronger, to increase: *The noise from the party intensified as more people arrived.*

**intensity** /ɪn'tɛnsəti/ *noun, (no plural)*
the degree, strength of something: *He showed the intensity of his love for her with roses and poems.*

**intensive** /ɪn'tɛnsɪv/ *adjective*
a lot in a short time: *I took an intensive English course and learned the language in three months.*

**intent** /ɪn'tɛnt/ *noun*
purpose, plan, *(synonym)* intention: *It was his intent to leave at 6:30, but he stayed until 8:00.*

**intentional** /ɪn'tɛnʃənəl/ *adjective*
done on purpose: *I am sorry I stepped on your foot; it was not intentional.*

**interact** /,ɪntər'ækt/ *verb*
to communicate with someone through conversation, looks, or action: *The children playing in the park interact well together.* *–adjective* **interactive;** *–noun* **interaction.**

**intercom** /'ɪntər,kɑm/ *noun*
a small machine that lets people talk to each other from different rooms or areas of a building: *From the kitchen, I heard my baby cry on the intercom.*

**interconnect** /,ɪntərkə'nɛkt/ *verb*
to relate to something, connect: *Railroad tracks interconnect at the train station.* *–noun* **interconnection.**

**interdependent** /,ɪntərdə'pɛndənt/ *adjective*
needing something from someone who also needs something in return: *The farmer and his cows are interdependent; he gives them food and shelter, and they give him milk.* *–noun* **interdependence.**

**interest** /'ɪntrɪst/ *noun*
**1** something one wants to know more about: *I have an interest in learning about computers.*
**2** an activity or thing that one likes, *(synonym)* hobby: *He plays piano because he has an interest in music.*
**3** right to know, concern: *She is my*

*daughter, so I have an interest in where she goes to college.*
**4** (percentage) of money paid on money that is borrowed: *Many credit cards have high interest rates.*

**interest** *verb*
to attract someone's attention: *Does chemistry interest you, or do you prefer biology?*

**interested** /'ɪntrɪstɪd/ *adjective*
having curiosity, wanting to know more: *He is interested in travel, so he visits a different country every year.*

---

**USAGE NOTE:** If someone or something excites your interest, you are *interested: I'm interested in reading more of her books.* The person or thing itself is *interesting: Her ideas are interesting.*||*She's an interesting writer.*

---

**interesting** /'ɪntrɪstɪŋ/ *adjective*
causing a wish to know more: *I think American children find TV to be more interesting than books. (antonym)* boring.

**interfere** /ˌɪntər'fɪr/ *verb* **interfered, interfering, interferes**
to enter or interrupt a situation or discussion, usually without permission: *Sandra didn't want to interfere in family problems, but she had important information about Shu-min's sick son. –noun* **interference.**

**interior** /ɪn'tɪriər/ *noun*
the inside of something: *From the outside, the house looks terrible, but the interior is beautiful.*

**interior** *adjective*
of or about the inside of something: *The interior walls are painted white. (antonym)* exterior.

**interjection** /ˌɪntər'ʤɛkʃən/ *noun*
**1** a comment that interrupts a conversation: *My teacher likes our questions and interjections during class.*
**2** a word that expresses a strong emotion (exclamation), such as *Oh!* or *Ouch!*

**intermarry** /ˌɪntər'mæri/ *verb* **intermarried, intermarrying, intermarries**
to marry someone of a different race, religion, etc. *–noun* **intermarriage** /ɪntər'mærɪʤ/.

**intermission** /ˌɪntər'mɪʃən/ *noun*
the time between acts (of a play, opera, etc.): *During intermission, I left my seat for a drink of water.*

**intern** /'ɪnˌtɜrn/ *noun*
**1** a doctor working in a hospital who is completing his or her medical training
**2** a person who works for little or no money in order to gain experience in a business or profession

**intern** /ɪn'tɜrn/ *verb*
to contain in an area, usually as a prisoner of war: *Japanese Americans were interned in California during World War II. –noun* **internment.**

**internal** /ɪn'tɜrnəl/ *adjective*
**1** inside, within: *Internal organs include the heart and liver.*
**2** related to an organization's or country's own rules, interests, and activities: *This President thinks more about internal affairs, such as unemployment and education, than about foreign affairs.*

**Internal Revenue Service** *noun*
in the USA, the government agency that collects taxes and makes sure that tax laws are obeyed: *The Internal Revenue Service is very busy in the spring when people must pay their yearly income taxes. See:* IRS.

**international** /ˌɪntər'næʃənəl/ *adjective*
of or about two or more nations: *We went to an international conference on computers. –adverb* **internationally.**

**International Phonetic Alphabet** *noun, abbreviation* **IPA**
symbols that show how to pronounce all human sounds for any language: *The IPA is used in many dictionaries. See:* page 561 for explanation of the IPA.

**Internet** /'ɪntərˌnɛt/ *noun, (no plural)*
a huge computer network of electronic mail and information, used by millions of people and organizations all over the world *See:* E-mail; information superhighway; World Wide Web, USAGE NOTE.

**interpret** /ɪn'tɜrprɪt/ *verb*
**1** to express the meaning of words in one language in another language, *(syn-*

*onym)* translate: *She interprets French for American tourists in Paris.*
**2** to decide on the meaning of something that is not very clear: *How would you interpret that dream? –adjective* **interpretative;** *–noun* (person) **interpreter.**

**interpretation** /ɪn,tɜrprə'teɪʃən/ *noun* an explanation about what something means: *I have a different interpretation of the poem.*

**interrupt** /,ɪntə'rʌpt/ *verb* to stop something from continuing: *A bad storm interrupted telephone communications.*||*Our little boy always interrupts our conversations by asking questions. –noun* **interruption.**

**intersection** /'ɪntər,sɛkʃən/ *noun*
**1** a crossing of roads: *Traffic lights control the movement of cars on streets.*
**2** a point or area that two shapes or figures share: *The intersection of two lines can form four angles. –verb* **to intersect.** *See:* art on pge 4a.

**interstate** /'ɪntər,steɪt/ *adjective* in the USA, or between states: *You can travel on Interstate Highway 20 from Atlanta, Georgia, to Columbia, South Carolina.*

**interstate** *noun* a major highway: *We drove off a small country road onto the interstate.*

**interval** /'ɪntərvəl/ *noun*
**1** a time period between events: *I always get hungry in the interval between breakfast and lunch.*
**2** an amount of distance or time, occurring regularly: *We stopped the car at 100-mile intervals to use the bathroom.*

**interview** /'ɪntər,vyu/ *verb*
**1** to get information by questioning someone: *A TV reporter interviewed the mayor about the city's problems.*
**2** to meet with and question someone to decide if that person is right for a job: *She interviewed 12 people before she found a good secretary. –noun* **interview,** (person) **interviewer.**

**intestine** /ɪn'tɛstɪn/ *noun* the tube in the body that carries food from the stomach to the waste opening between the legs (including the small and large intestines): *Drinking water helps your food move more easily through the intestines. –adjective* **intestinal.** *See:* art on page 21a.

**intimate** /'ɪntəmɪt/ *adjective*
**1** emotionally close: *We have had an intimate friendship since we were young.*
**2** close sexually: *I just want to be a friend; I don't want to be intimate with you.*
**3** deep and complete: *He has an intimate knowledge of plants and how to grow them. –noun* **intimacy;** *–adverb* **intimately.**

**intimate** *verb* /'ɪntə,meɪt/ **intimated, intimating, intimates** to suggest but not say clearly: *My boss intimated I may get a salary increase.*

**intimidate** /ɪn'tɪmə,deɪt/ *verb* **intimidated, intimidating, intimidates** to make someone fearful by showing power or making threats: *An older boy intimidated the little children when he took their lunch money. –noun* **intimidation.**

**into** /'ɪntu/ *preposition*
**1** to the inside of something: *We walked down the street and into the movie theater.*
**2** showing involvement: *She puts a lot of effort into her piano playing.*
**3** showing a change toward a condition or state: *The seed grew into a tall tree.*
**4** against, having contact with: *The car ran into a fence.*
**5** (in math) showing division: *Four into 12 is three.*
**6** *informal* very interested in: *He is really into playing basketball these days.*

**intolerable** /ɪn'tɑlərəbəl/ *adjective*
**1** too difficult or painful: *The heat in August is intolerable.*
**2** offensive: *Her bad language is intolerable to her parents.*

**intolerance** /ɪn 'tɑlərəns/ *noun* lack of kindness or understanding toward people who are different

**intoxicate** /ɪn'tɑksə,keɪt/ *verb* **intoxicated, intoxicating, intoxicates**
**1** to make drunk: *Drinking beer and whiskey intoxicates him.*
**2** to excite greatly: *The queen was intoxicated with her own power. –noun* (condition) **intoxication.**

**introduce** /ˌɪntrəˈdus/ *verb* **introduced, introducing, introduces**
**1** to present one person to another for the first time: *A friend introduced me to the woman I later married.*
**2** to put in something new: *The Mayor introduced a new job training program.*

**introduction** /ˌɪntrəˈdʌkʃən/ *noun*
**1** a first meeting, in which people learn each other's names: *She wants to meet that guest; will you make the introduction?*
**2** an opening statement before a speech or performance: *The vice president made an introduction before the president spoke.* –*adjective* **introductory.**

**intuition** /ˌɪntuˈɪʃən/ *noun*
a feeling, a guess about something without certain facts: *He used his intuition, not a map, to find my house.* –*adjective* **intuitive.**

**invade** /ɪnˈveɪd/ *verb* **invaded, invading, invades**
**1** to enter by force: *A foreign army invaded my country.*
**2** to enter without permission: *Loud music from next door invaded the quiet of our home.* –*noun* (person) **invader, invasion.**

**invalid** /ɪnˈvælɪd/ *adjective*
**1** not correct, lacking proof: *Your ideas about the politics are interesting but invalid.*
**2** not able to be used, illegal: *His driver's license is too old and is invalid.*

**invalid** /ˈɪnvəlɪd/ *noun*
a person unable to care for himself or herself because of sickness or disability: *A bad car accident made him an invalid.*

**invalidate** /ɪnˈvæləˌdeɪt/ *verb* **invalidated, invalidating, invalidates**
to make illegal or unusable: *Airport workers invalidated the drug dealer's passport so she could not leave the country.* –*noun* **invalidation.**

**invaluable** /ɪnˈvælyuəbəl/ *adjective*
extremely valuable, worth a great deal: *Your help in moving the big sofa was invaluable.*

**invent** /ɪnˈvɛnt/ *verb*
**1** to create something new: *Trains were invented long before cars.*
**2** to make up a story or to lie: *A little girl invented an imaginary friend to play with.* –*noun* **invention,** (person) **inventor.**

**invention** /ɪnˈvɛnʃən/ *noun*
something useful created by someone: *After the invention of the wheel, people could travel faster.*

**inventory** /ˈɪnvənˌtɔri/ *noun, plural* **inventories**
the items that are available for sale in a store: *The bookstore has a large inventory of cookbooks.*

**inventory** *verb* **inventoried, inventorying, inventories**
**to take inventory:** to count the items in a store to find out what has been sold and what needs to be replaced

**invertebrate** /ɪnˈvɜrtəbrɪt/ *noun*
an animal without a backbone: *Ants are invertebrates.*

**invest** /ɪnˈvɛst/ *verb*
to put money into a business, idea, or activity in the hope of making more money if it is successful: *We invested in a computer company and became rich as it grew.* –*noun* (person) **investor.**

**investigate** /ɪnˈvɛstəˌgeɪt/ *verb* **investigated, investigating, investigates**
**1** to look at something carefully, examine: *My car was stolen last week; the police are investigating.*
**2** to look at (choices): *We investigated three towns before we decided where to buy a house.* –*noun* (person) **investigator.**

**investigation** /ɪnˌvɛstəˈgeɪʃən/ *noun*
a search for facts and information, especially by people with power: *Police began an investigation of the crime.*

**investment** /ɪnˈvɛstmənt/ *noun*
money spent on something in the hope of making more money *See:* invest.

**invisible** /ɪnˈvɪzəbəl/ *adjective*
not able to be seen: *Music is invisible; we can hear it and feel it, but not see it.* –*noun* **invisibility.**

**invitation** /ˌɪnvəˈteɪʃən/ *noun*
a card or spoken request asking someone to come to an event: *The couple sent out wedding invitations to family and friends.*

**invite** /ɪn'vaɪt/ *verb* **invited, inviting, invites**
**1** to ask someone to come to an event: *I invited my friends to a birthday party.*
**2** to attract attention and a reaction: *The violinist's beautiful playing invited loud applause.*

**invoice** /'ɪnˌvɔɪs/ *noun*
(in business) a list of items or services and their cost, *(synonym)* a bill: *Our company sends invoices to customers after they order from us.*

**invoice** *verb* **invoiced, invoicing, invoices**
to prepare and send a bill: *We invoice our customers after we send them the books they have ordered.*

**involuntary** /ɪn'vɑlənˌtɛri/ *adjective*
**1** not done by choice, forced: *His leaving the job was involuntary; the company moved to another state.*
**2** done without thinking, automatic: *The human heartbeat is involuntary.* *–adverb* **involuntarily.**

**involve** /ɪn'vɑlv/ *verb* **involved, involving, involves**
**1** to need something to complete an action: *Getting a driver's license involves learning how to drive, studying the rules of the road, and taking a test.*
**2** to cause to participate: *If you have problems with money, don't involve your relatives by borrowing from them.* *–noun* **involvement.**

**inward** /'ɪnwərd/ *adverb*
toward the inside: *When he read the hate-filled letter, he stayed quiet and directed his anger inward.*

**inward** *adjective*
located on the inside, within something: *The inward side of the fence needs painting.* *–noun* **inwardness.** *(antonym)* outward.

**inwardly** /'ɪnwərdli/ *adverb*
within oneself, privately: *Inwardly, he loves her, but he can't tell her.*

**IOU** /'aɪoʊ'yu/ *abbreviation of*
I owe you: a written promise to pay back money

**IPA** /'aɪpi'ei/ *abbreviation of*
International Phonetic Alphabet

**Irish setter** *noun*
a breed of dog with long, silky, brownish-red fur

Irish setter

**iron** /'aɪərn/ *noun*
**1** *(no plural)* a common metal, used in making tools, machinery, furniture, and other strong items; also present in small amounts in the blood and some foods: *Eat more meat to get more iron.*
**2** a small household machine used to smooth wrinkles: *My mother uses an iron to press my cotton shirts. See:* art at ironing board.

iron

**to strike while the iron is hot:** to act while the opportunity is there

**iron** *verb*
to smooth with an iron: *She ironed two shirts and a pair of pants.*
**to iron something out:** to solve problems, reach agreement: *My sister and I were angry, but we ironed out our differences.*

**ironing** /'aɪərnɪŋ/ *noun, (no plural)*
the activity of smoothing out clothes, etc. with an iron: *My mother did the washing and ironing once a week.*

**ironing board** *noun*
a flat, covered surface on legs, used to spread out items for ironing

ironing board

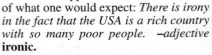

**irony** /'aɪrəni/ *noun, (no plural)*
a situation that shows the opposite of what one would expect: *There is irony in the fact that the USA is a rich country with so many poor people.* *–adjective* **ironic.**

**irrational** /ɪ'ræʃənəl/ *adjective*
**1** done without thinking: *I had the irrational wish to laugh loudly in church.*
**2** crazy, insane *–noun* **irrationality.**

**irregular** /ɪ'rɛgyələr/ *adjective*
**1** not occuring at set times: *She has ir-*

*regular work hours; sometimes she works during the day and sometimes at night.*
**2** not smooth or even: *The paper was torn, not cut, with an irregular edge.*
**3** not accepted standards, perhaps wrong or illegal *–noun* **irregularity.**

**irrelevant** /ɪ'rɛləvənt/ *adjective*
not important to the situation: *It is irrelevant to me whether you are rich or poor, as long as you are kind. –noun* **irrelevance.**

**irresponsible** /ˌɪrə'spɑnsəbəl/ *adjective*
not careful about one's duty or behavior: *The irresponsible mother left her baby alone for two hours. –noun* **irresponsibility.**

**irrigate** /'ɪrəˌgeɪt/ *verb* **irrigated, irrigating, irrigates**
to supply with water collected in another location *–noun* **irrigation.**

**irritable** /'ɪrɪtəbəl/ *adjective*
annoyed, bothered by something: *She felt irritable after waiting an hour for a bus in the rain. –noun* **irritability.**

**irritate** /'ɪrəˌteɪt/ *verb* **irritated, irritating, irritates**
**1** to annoy, bother: *Your messy bedroom irritates your mother.*
**2** to make something worse, especially a physical condition: *She irritated her skin by scratching too much. –noun* **irritation, irritant.**

**IRS** /'aɪɑr'ɛs/ *abbreviation of*
Internal Revenue Service, the USA's national tax collection agency: *The IRS sent me a letter saying I made a mistake on my tax form.*

**Islam** /ɪs'lɑm/ *noun, (no plural)*
**1** the Muslim religion: *Our cousin in North Africa is a follower of Islam.*
**2** the Muslim nations *–adjective* **Islamic.**

**island** /'aɪlənd/ *noun*
a piece of land completely surrounded by water: *She lived on an island that was connected to the coast by a bridge.*

island

**isle** /aɪl/ *noun*
an island

**isolate** /'aɪsəˌleɪt/ *verb* **isolated, isolating, isolates**
to separate from others, cause to be alone: *Some students isolated themselves from the rest of the class. –noun* **isolation** /ˌaɪsə'leɪʃən/.

**isolationism** /ˌaɪsə'leɪʃəˌnɪzəm/ *noun, (no plural)*
a political idea of avoiding involvement with other countries: *Isolationism is easier for countries that are surrounded by water.*

**issue** /'ɪʃu/ *verb* **issued, issuing, issues**
**1** to give or send out: *Between 1941 and 1945, the White House issued news about the war nearly every day.*
**2** to give or provide in a formal or official way: *The motor vehicle office issues drivers' licenses after people pass a test.*

**issue** *noun*
**1** a matter of concern: *The main issues we are discussing today are tax increases and military spending.*
**2** a particular copy of a magazine or newspaper: *Libraries keep old issues of newspapers and magazines.*

**it** /ɪt/ *pronoun*
**1** third person singular pronoun, used to refer to something that is neither male nor female, and usually not alive: *We just had a vacation, and it was very relaxing.*
**2** the subject of an impersonal verb: *It is raining today.*
**3** the subject or object of a verb, often introducing a more important part of the sentence: *It was in this room that I first saw you.*
**4** the object of a verb referring to something mentioned before: *I explained the grammar, so he understands it now.*

**That's it!: a.** that's all I can suffer (showing anger, frustration): *That's it; I'm leaving if you don't be quiet!* **b.** Yes! (showing delight, discovery): *That's it; what a wonderful idea!*

**to get it:** to understand: *He didn't laugh at your joke because he didn't get it.*||*This homework is hard; I don't get it.*

I

**italic** /aɪ'tælɪk/ *noun*
a style of type in which the letters lean to the right: *The sentence you are reading is in italic type or in italics.* –*verb* **to italicize** /aɪ'tæləˌsaɪz/.

**itch** /ɪʧ/ *noun, plural* **itches**
**1** a feeling on the skin causing an urge to scratch: *He has an itch on his leg from an insect bite.*
**2** a desire, a wish: *I have an itch to play tennis tonight.*

**itch** *verb*
to have an itch: *His head itches from the new soap.* –*adjective* **itchy.**

**item** /'aɪtəm/ *noun*
**1** a general term for a thing or object: *That stores has a wide choice of items on sale.*
**2** something on a list, a separate topic: *We have four items to discuss today; we'll start with item one.*
**3** a short piece of news: *an item in the newspaper*

**itemize** /'aɪtəˌmaɪz/ *verb* **itemized, itemizing, itemizes**
to list thing by thing: *I itemized the equipment that we need for the office.*

**itinerary** /aɪ'tɪnəˌrɛri/ *noun, plural* **itineraries**
a travel plan, showing places to visit and transportation times: *Look on our vacation itinerary to find out when we are flying to London.*

**itself** /ɪt'sɛlf/ *pronoun*
**1** third person singular pronoun used to refer back to a subject: *The problem solved itself; we did nothing.*
**2** used to make a noun stronger or more definite: *The neighborhood is dangerous, but the house itself is safe.*

**ivory** /'aɪvəri/ *noun, plural* **ivories**
the hard, white-yellow substance of elephant tusks: *My grandmother has some jewelry made of ivory.*

ivory

**ivy** /'aɪvi/ *noun, plural* **ivies**
a green plant with shiny leaves that can cover the ground or climb the walls of buildings: *The walls of my brick house are green with ivy.*

# J, j



**J, j** /ʤeɪ/ *noun* **J's, j's** or **Js, js**
the tenth letter of the English alphabet

jack

**jack** /ʤæk/ *noun*
a tool for lifting: *The mechanic used the jack to lift the car.*

**to jack something up:**
*verb* **a.** to lift with a jack **b.** to make the price of something go up, *(synonym)* to raise: *The snow in Florida jacked up the price of oranges.*

**jacket** /ˈʤækɪt/ *noun*
a short coat made of cloth, leather, or other material *See:* art on page 12a.

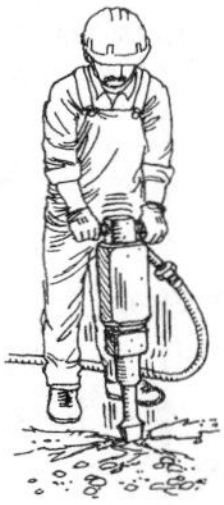

jackhammer

**jackhammer** /ˈʤækˌhæmər/ *noun*
a powerful, handheld tool used to break up rocks and cement

**jackknife** /ˈʤækˌnaɪf/ *noun, plural* **jackknives**
a knife with one or more blades that fold into the handle

**jackpot** /ˈʤækˌpɑt/ *noun*
a large amount of money or a big prize a person can win by playing games

jackknife

**to hit the jackpot:**
to win the big prize

**jagged** /ˈʤægɪd/ *adjective*
with a lot of small uneven sharp points *(antonym)* smooth.

**jaguar** /ˈʤægˌwɑr/ *noun*
a wild, large cat mainly of South America that has yellow fur and black spots: *Jaguars are fast and strong.*

**jail** /ʤeɪl/ *noun*
a building where people who break the law spend time as a punishment, *(synonym)* a prison: *The man is in jail because he killed a police officer.* **–***verb* **to jail.**

jam

**jam (1)** /ʤæm/ *noun*
a soft, sweet food spread containing small pieces of fruit: *She put some jam on her bread. See:* jelly.

**jam (2)** *noun*
a lot of people, cars, etc. in one place, so that it is difficult to move: *My bus got stuck in a traffic jam.*

jam

**to be in a jam:**
to be in a difficult situation: *I'm in a real jam. I just lost my job and can't pay my rent.*

**jam** *verb*
**jammed, jamming, jams**
**1** to push hard into something: *She*

*jammed the key into the door and then couldn't pull it out.*
**2** to fill with many people, cars, etc., *(synonym)* to crowd: *Workers jammed into the room to hear the mayor.*

**jamb** /ʤæm/ *noun*
the sides of a window or door frame

**Jane Doe** /'ʤeɪn'doʊ/ *noun*
**1** a name used for an imaginary average woman
**2** a woman with no known name: *The dead woman was a Jane Doe. See:* John Doe.

**janitor** /'ʤænətər/ *noun*
a person who cleans and fixes things in a building, *(synonym)* custodian

**January** /'ʤænyuˌɛri/ *noun*
the first month of the year



**jar** /ʤɑr/ *noun*
a container made of glass, plastic, etc. with a top: *a jar of face cream*

jar

**jargon** /'ʤɑrgən/ *noun, (no plural)*
the special words used in particular areas of work or study: *People who work with computers use jargon, such as "log on" and "on line."*

**jaw** /ʤɔ/ *noun*
the top and bottom bones of the mouth that hold the teeth *See:* art on page 21a.

**jaywalk** /ʤeɪwɔk/ *verb*
to cross the street illegally: *A policeman stopped her for jaywalking across Main Street.*

**jealous** /'ʤɛləs/ *adjective*
frightened or unhappy because someone might take someone or something you love away from you: *He gets jealous when other men talk to his girlfriend.* –*adverb* **jealously;** –*noun* **jealousy.** *See:* art on page 18a.

**jeans** /ʤinz/ *noun plural*
pants made of strong cotton material, usually blue

**Jeep™** /ʤip/ *noun*
a kind of strong car that can travel well over difficult ground: *The tourists drove a Jeep™ up the mountain road.*

**Jell-O™** or **jello** /'ʤɛloʊ/ *noun*
a soft sweet dessert with a fruit flavor that shakes when you move it

Jell-o™

**jelly** /'ʤɛli/ *noun*
**1** a soft, sweet food spread made by cooking fruit juice and sugar together: *The children love to eat peanut butter and grape jelly sandwiches for lunch. See:* jam (1).
**2** any soft material that looks like jelly: *Some skin medicine is in jelly form.*

**jellybean** /'ʤɛliˌbin/ *noun*
a small, fruit-flavored candy in the shape of a bean: *The children ate a lot of jellybeans at the party.*

jellybeans

**jerk** /ʤɜrk/ *noun*
**1** a quick, sharp pull or movement: *The train started with a jerk and I fell down.*
**2** *slang* a stupid, annoying person

**jerk** *verb*
to make a quick, sharp movement: *The little girl jerked her arm away when she touched the hot stove.*

**jersey** /'ʤɜrzi/ *noun*
a light, soft shirt: *a cotton jersey*

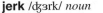

jersey

**jet** /ʤɛt/ *noun*
**1** an airplane that travels very fast because its engines push out hot gas
**2** gas, steam, liquid, etc. that comes out of a hole very fast: *We saw a big jet of gas come from the airplane engine.*

**jet lag** *noun*
a tired feeling you may have after a long trip by airplane into different time zones

**Jew** /ʤu/ *noun*
**1** a person who practices the Jewish religion: *Jewish people celebrate Chanukah.*
**2** a person whose family is Jewish: *The religion of the Jews is Judaism.* –*adjective* **Jewish.**

**jewel** /ˈʤuəl/ *noun*
a stone that is very valuable: *Diamonds are beautiful jewels.*

**jeweler** /ˈʤuələr/ *noun*
**1** a person who makes, repairs, and/or sells jewelry
**2** a jewelry store: *I am taking my watch to the jeweler to be fixed.*

**jewelry** /ˈʤuəlri/ *noun, (no plural)*
decorative items that people wear like rings, bracelets, and necklaces: *Her favorite piece of jewelry is a diamond ring.*

**jewelry**

**jigsaw puzzle** *noun*
a game made of a picture on cardboard or wood, cut into pieces and put back together again for fun

**jigsaw puzzle**

**job** /ʤɑb/ *noun*
**1** work that you do for money: *She found a job as an accountant.*
**2** a piece of work: *We have a big job to do at home today: we need to paint the kitchen and living room.*

---

**USAGE NOTE:** Both *work* and *job* refer to how people earn money. You can say: *What type of work do you do?* or *What type of job do you have?* However, *work* can also have a more general meaning. It can refer to school work or housework or other activities that people are not paid for: *Learning a new language (raising a child, planting a garden, etc.) is hard work. Job* is usually used to refer to a specific task or responsibility: *She's looking for a job in computer sales.*||*I work in an office.*||*My job is to answer the phones and make appointments.*

---

**jog** /ʤɑg/ *verb* **jogged, jogging, jogs**
to run slowly: *He jogged around the park. –noun* **jog,** (person) **jogger,** (sport) **jogging.**

**John Doe** /ˌʤɑnˈdoʊ/ *noun*
**1** a name used for an imaginary average man
**2** a name used for a man who has no known name or identity *See:* Jane Doe.

**join** /ʤɔɪn/ *verb*
**1** to become a part or a member of a group: *I joined a local church when I moved to the USA.*
**2** to come together with others: *She joined the line of people who were waiting to see a movie.*
**3** to put something together: *The mechanic joined the two pieces of metal together (with a screw, glue, etc.).*
**to join in something:** to do something with others, *(synonym)* to participate

**joint** /ʤɔɪnt/ *noun*
**1** a place where two pieces of material (wood, metal, etc.) come together: *You can see the joints in that wooden bookcase.*
**2** a point in the body where two moving parts come together: *The leg has the knee joint.*

**joint**

**joint** *adjective*
done together, shared: *My brother and I are joint owners of a small store. –adverb* **jointly.**

**joke** /ʤoʊk/ *noun*
something you do or say that is funny: *I laughed when I heard the joke.*

**joke** *verb* **joked, joking, jokes**
to say or do something funny: *We joke a lot when we are together; we always have fun!*

**jolly** /ˈʤɑli/ *adjective* **jollier, jolliest**
happy: *He is a jolly old man. (antonym)* sad.

**jolt** /ʤoʊlt/ *noun*
**1** a sudden, heavy movement: *The driver felt a jolt when the truck hit his car.*
**2** a sudden shock of electricity

**jot** /ʤɑt/ *verb* **jotted, jotting, jots**
to write down short pieces of information quickly: *I jotted down his phone number.*

**journal** /ˈʤɜrnl/ *noun*
**1** a written record of the day's events or one's thoughts and feelings: *She wrote in her journal that she was in love.*
**2** a magazine about one special thing: The New England Journal of Medicine *is for doctors and nurses.*

**journalism** /ˈʤɜrnlˌɪzəm/ *noun, (no plural)*
**1** the work of collecting and reporting the news
**2** the study of that field: *She is studying journalism so that she can become a reporter for a newpaper. –noun* (person) **journalist.**

**journey** /ˈʤɜrni/ *noun*
a trip, especially a long one: *Our journey from Vietnam to the USA took a long time.*



**joy** /ʤɔɪ/ *noun*
a feeling of great happiness: *I felt great joy when I saw my grandmother again after many years. –adjective* **joyful, joyous.** *(antonym)* despair.

**judge** /ʤʌʒ/ *noun*
**1** a person in charge in a court of law who decides how guilty people must be punished: *The judge sent the murderer to jail for 30 years.*
**2** a person who decides the person or thing that wins a competition: *The judge gave first prize to my painting.*

**judge** *verb* **judged, judging, judges**
**1** to make a decision in a court of law: *The man was judged not guilty.*
**2** to think about someone or something and form an opinion: *I judged her to be an honest person.*
**3** to decide the person or thing that wins a competition: *The school music teacher judged the piano contest.*

**judgment** or **judgement** /ˈʤʌʤmənt/ *noun*
what you think or decide to do about something: *In my judgement, you made the right decision.*

**jug** /ʤʌg/ *noun*
a container for liquid with a handle and a narrow opening: *a jug of milk (wine, water, etc.) See:* pitcher.

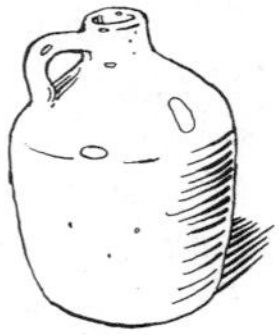
jug

**juggle** /ˈʤʌgəl/ *verb* **juggled, juggling, juggles**
to throw and catch two or more things in the air quickly: *The clown juggled five tennis balls. –noun* **juggler.**

juggler

**juice** /ʤus/ *noun*
**1** the liquid in fruits, vegetables, or meat: *orange juice, tomato juice, etc.*
**2** *slang* gas, electricity, etc.: *We need to change the car battery. There's no juice left in it.*

**juicy** /ˈʤusi/ *adjective* **juicier, juiciest**
full of juice: *This orange is juicy.*

**jukebox** /ˈʤukˌboks/ *noun, plural* **jukeboxes**
a coin-operated machine that plays music: *She put money in this jukebox and picked three songs.*

**July** /ʤʊˈlaɪ/ *noun*
the seventh month of the year, between June and August

**jumbo** /ˈʤʌmboʊ/ *adjective*
very big, *(synonym)* huge

**jump** /ʤʌmp/ *verb*
**1** to move quickly into the air, using your feet and legs to push you up: *The basketball player jumped up to catch the ball.*
**2** to go down: *The little boy jumped down from the tree.*
**3** to make a quick movement when you are frightened or surprised: *I jumped when I heard the gunshot.*
**4** *figurative* to go up quickly and suddenly: *The price of oil jumped when the war started.*
**to jump out of one's skin:** to be frightened suddenly: *I nearly jumped out of my skin when I saw the lion. –noun* **jump.** *See:* art on page 24.

**jumpy** /ˈʤʌmpi/ *adjective* **jumpier, jumpiest**
nervous: *I'm a little jumpy about flying on airplanes. (antonym)* calm.

**junction** /ˈʤʌŋkʧən/ *noun*
a place where two roads or railroad lines meet: *The car stopped at the junction and then turned left.*

**June** /ʤun/ *noun*
the sixth month of the year, between May and July: *My birthday is in June.*

**jungle** /ˈʤʌŋgəl/ *noun*
a hot, wet place where there are many trees and plants: *He visited the jungles of Guatemala. See:* forest.

**junior** /ˈʤunyər/ *adjective*
**1** shortened to **Jr.** to show that the son has the same first and last name as his father: *Philip Jones, Jr. is the son of Philip Jones, Sr. (Senior).*
**2** referring to a less important position in a company: *I am a junior manager at the new fast-food restaurant.*

**junior** *noun*
a student in his or her third year (out of a total of four years) of college or high school: *My daughter is a junior in high school. See:* freshman; sophomore; senior.

**junior college** *noun*
in the USA, a two-year college, *(synonym)* community college: *My brother attends Santa Rosa Junior College.*

**junior high school** *noun*
in the USA, a school for grades six through eight or seven through nine: *Our 13-year-old son goes to Kennedy Junior High School. See:* grade school; secondary school; high school.

**junk** /ʤʌŋk/ *noun, (no plural)*
things that are old or not useful anymore: *Their house is full of junk, such as old toys and broken lamps.*

**junk food** *noun, (no plural)*
food that is quick to prepare and tastes good, but is bad for your health: *He eats junk food, such as potato chips.*

**junkie** or **junky** /ˈʤʌŋki/ *noun slang, plural* **junkies**
**1** a person who cannot stop taking drugs: *The junkie robbed people to buy drugs.*
**2** a person who likes something very much that is usually not good for him or her: *I am a fast-food junkie. I love eating hot dogs, hamburgers, french fries, and ice cream.*

**junk mail** *noun, (no plural)*
letters, brochures, flyers, etc. received in the mail that try to sell you things you usually don't want: *Some people find junk mail annoying.*

**jury** /ˈʤʊri/ *noun, plural* **juries**
a group of usually 12 people who sit in a court of law, listen to information about a crime, and decide if a person, business, or institution has done something illegal or not: *The jury decided that the company was guilty of stealing money so the top executives went to jail. –noun* (person) **juror.**

**jury duty** *noun*
a period of time when a US citizen must serve on a jury, if called: *I can't go to work this week because I am on jury duty. See:* jury.

**just (1)** /ʤʌst/ *adverb*
**1** a very short time ago: *The train just left two minutes ago.*
**2** at this or that moment: *We're just having dinner* (or) *just about to have dinner; can you call me back in 30 minutes?*
**3** by a short moment of time, almost not: *You just missed him; he left five minutes ago.|| We arrived just in time to catch our airplane.*
**4** only: *I have just enough money to pay the bills.*

**just about:** *(synonyms)* almost, nearly: *I have just about finished this letter.*

**just as:** **a.** exactly the same as: *The new cook was told to leave the kitchen just as clean as it was before he started cooking.* **b.** when: *We arrived at the station just as the train was leaving. We had to wait an hour for the next train.*

**just now:** at this moment: *I can't go the movies with you, I am working just now.*

**just (2)** /ʤʌst/ *adjective*
fair and right, usually as the law says: *It is not just that someone only goes to prison for two years for murder. (antonym)* unfair, unjust.

**justice** /ˈʤʌstɪs/ *noun, (no plural)*
being fair and right, usually as the law says: *There is no justice if that murderer does not go to prison.*

**justice of the peace** *noun, plural* **justices**
a person who works for the government who can marry people and judge small crimes such as driving too fast, etc.: *My wife and I were married by a justice of the peace.*

**juvenile** /'ʤuvə,naɪl/ *noun*
a young person or child, especially under the age of 16: *Juveniles must be looked after by an adult.* –*adjective* **juvenile.**

**USAGE NOTE:** *Young adult* is a more common way of talking about people between the ages of 12 and 18: *My 13-year-old daughter thinks that she is a young adult, not a child.*

J

# K, k

**K, k** /keɪ/ *noun* **K's, k's** or **Ks, ks**
**1** the 11th letter of the English alphabet
**2** *singular informal* 1,000: *That house costs $100K* (or) *$100k ($100,000).*
**3** (in computers) *abbreviation of* kilobyte
**4** *abbreviation of* kilometer

**kangaroo** /ˌkæŋgəˈru/ *noun, plural* **kangaroos**
an animal from Australia with two legs, a long tail, and can jump very high

**kangaroo**

**karate** /kəˈrɑti/ *noun, (no plural)*
a traditional Asian sport where you use your hands and feet to fight

**kayak** /ˈkaɪˌyæk/ *noun*
a light, narrow, boat for one person *–verb* **to kayak.**

**kayak**

**keep** /kip/ *verb* **kept** /kɛpt/, **keeping, keeps**
**1** to have something and not give to someone else: *My parents gave us $30. I kept $20 and gave $10 to my sister.*
**2** to put away: *She keeps her money in a savings account.*
**3** to continue doing something or do something many times: *She keeps forgetting her homework.*
**4** to make something or someone stay in the same place or condition: *Please keep the window open. It's very hot.*
**5** to write down information: *She kept a diary of what she did every day.*
**6** to look after, care for: *He keeps his work clothes very clean.*
**7** to stay fresh: *That milk won't keep in this hot weather unless you keep it cold.*
**to keep on:** to continue doing something, or do something many times: *She kept on driving even though she was lost.*
**to keep to yourself:** to not mix much with other people: *My sister keeps to herself. She doesn't like meeting people.*
**to keep up with someone** or **something:** to do something as fast or as well as someone else so that you are equal: *The other runner was so fast I couldn't keep up with him. He finished before me.*

**keeper** /ˈkipər/ *noun*
a person who is paid to do something: *The grounds keeper cuts the grass.*

**kennel** /ˈkɛnəl/ *noun*
a place where you can leave your dog when you go away somewhere

**kept** /kɛpt/ *verb*
*past tense and past participle of* keep

**kernel** /ˈkərnəl/ *noun*
a seed of a plant, usually one that can be eaten: *a kernel of corn (wheat, rice, etc.)*

**kernel**

**kerosene** /'kɛrəˌsin/ *noun, (no plural)*
a thin oil with no color that is made from petroleum, used for heating, lighting, etc.

**ketchup** /'kɛʧəp/ *noun, (no plural)*
a thick, red sauce made from tomatoes: *He put ketchup on his hamburger.*

**kettle** /'kɛtl/ *noun*
a large cooking pot, usually with a cover *See:* art on page 7a.

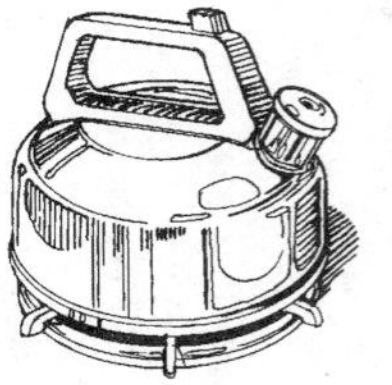
kettle

**key** /ki/ *noun*
**1** a thin piece of metal that opens or closes a lock, starts or stops an engine, etc.: *I opened the front door with my key.*
**2** a part of a machine or musical instrument that you press down with your fingers: *She pressed a computer key and typed a letter.*
**3** information that explains the meaning of something: *This key shows you the names of the different parts of the machine in Spanish.*

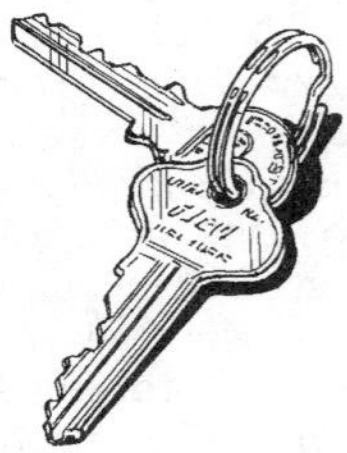
keys



**key** *adjective*
very important: *a key industry*

**keyboard** /'kibɔrd/ *noun*
all the keys on a piano, computer, etc.

keyboard

**keyhole** /'kiˌhoʊl / *noun*
the hole for the key in a lock

**key ring** *noun*
a ring that holds keys

**Kg or kg** *abbreviation of*
kilogram

**khaki** /'kæki/ *adjective*
light brown color: *I like to wear khaki pants to school in the summer.*

**khaki** *noun, plural* **khakis**
light brown, loose pants that men and women wear informally

**kick** /kɪk/ *verb*
to hit someone or something with the foot or feet: *The football player kicked the ball down the field.*
**to kick off:** to start something, especially a game of football: *We kicked off the meeting with coffee and tea. –noun* **kick-off.**
**to kick someone out:** to make someone leave: *Our landlord kicked our neighbors out of their apartment because they didn't pay their rent each month.*

**kick** *noun*
**1** hitting someone or something with the foot or feet: *to give a football a kick*
**2** strength, force: *That coffee is strong. It has a real kick.*
**for kicks** or **just for kicks:** *informal* just for fun: *I go skiing with some friends every year just for kicks.*
**to get a kick out of something:** to get pleasure from doing something: *I got a kick out of repairing that car.*

**kid** /kɪd/ *noun*
**1** *informal* a child
**2** a young goat

**kid** *verb* **kidded, kidding, kids**
to make jokes: *She often kids him about his bright red hair.*

**kid** *adjective*
*informal* younger: *My kid brother just got his driver's licence.*

---

**USAGE NOTE:** Adults in the USA often refer to young people as *kids* and college students as *college kids* in a friendly way.

---

**kidnap** /'kɪdˌnæp/ *verb* **kidnapped, kidnapping, kidnaps**
to take someone away by force, and to ask for money from family or friends before you free them: *–noun* (act) **kidnapping,** (person) **kidnapper.**

**kidney** /'kɪdni/ *noun*
one of two parts in your body that clean your blood, located in the lower part of your back. *See:* art on page 21a.

**kill** /kɪl/ *verb*
**1** to make someone or something stop

living: *The dog was killed when it ran under the bus.*||*The bad weather killed all my tomato plants.*
**2** to hurt badly: *My back (tooth, foot, etc.) is killing me. I need to see a doctor. See:* murder. *–noun* (person) **killer, killing.**

**kilo** /ˈkiloʊ/ *noun*
*short for* kilogram

**kilobyte** /ˈkɪləˌbaɪt/ *noun*
approximately 1,000 bytes, a measure of computer memory space *–abbreviation* K. *See:* megabytes.

**kilogram** /ˈkɪləˌgræm/ *noun*
1,000 grams, or 2.2 pounds (lbs.): *She bought two kilograms (kg)* (or) *kilos of bananas. –abbreviation* kg.

**kilometer** /kɪˈlɑmɪtər/ *noun*
1,000 meters, or 0.62137 mile: *It is 400 kilometers (km) from Boston to New York City. –abbreviation* km.

**kilowatt** /ˈkɪləˌwɑt/ *noun*
*–abbreviation* kW or Kw (1,000 watts)

**kind** /kaɪnd/ *adjective*
friendly and helpful to people *–noun* **kindness.** *The woman who stopped to help us when our car broke down was very kind.*

**kind** /kaɪnd/ *noun*
someone or something that is the same as someone else in some way; a sort, type: *He has the same kind of leather jacket as mine.*||*What kind of animal is that?*
**kind of:** a little bit: *I stayed up late last night so I am kind of tired.*

---

**USAGE NOTE:** Both *kind of* and *sort of* mean "a little bit" before adjectives: *That restaurant is kind of expensive.*||*I feel sort of nervous telling you about this problem.*

---

**kindergarten** /ˈkɪndərˌgɑrtn/ *noun*
classes for four- and five-year-old children. Children go to these classes before they begin first grade at school.

**kindly** /ˈkaɪndli/ *adverb*
please: *Would you kindly hold the door open for me?*

**king** /kɪŋ/ *noun*
a man who rules a country and who is from a royal family: *The king gave a feast to celebrate the victory. –noun* (place) kingdom. *See:* queen.

king

**king-size** /ˈkɪŋˌsaɪz/ or **king-sized** /ˌsaɪzd/ *adjective*
**1** bigger than queen-size: *All four children slept in the king-size bed.*
**2** bigger than the normal size: *My grandfather smokes king-sized cigarettes.*

**kiss** /kɪs/ *noun, plural* **kisses**
**1** a touch with the lips to show that you like or love someone or something: *The child gave his dog a big kiss.*
**2** a small candy: *She gave her brother a bag of chocolate kisses for his birthday.*

**kiss** *verb* **kisses**
to give someone or something a kiss to show happiness or love: *He kissed her when she gave him the beautiful flowers.*

**kit** /kɪt/ *noun*
**1** a group of tools, supplies, etc. kept together, often in a box, and used to make or do something: *a mechanic's kit, a carpenter's kit, a make-up kit, etc.*
**2** a group of small pieces to be put together to make something: *My brother made a model airplane from a kit.*

**kitchen** /ˈkɪtʃən/ *noun*
a room where you can prepare food, and usually find a stove, sink, and refrigerator: *See:* art on pages 5a and 7a.

**kite** /kaɪt/ *noun*
a light toy made from paper and wood with a long string to fly in the air.

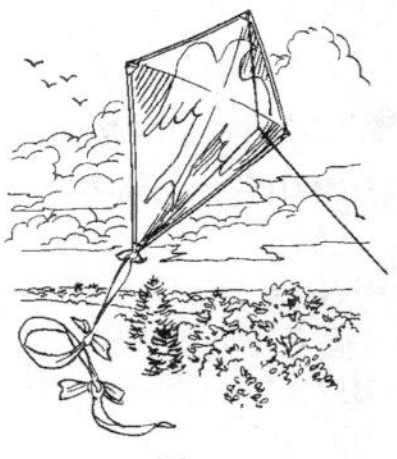
kite

**kitten** /ˈkɪtn/ *noun*
a baby cat: *Our cat has four new kittens.*

**KKK** *abbreviation of* Ku Klux Klan

**Kleenex™** /ˈkliˌnɛks/ *noun, plural* **Kleenexes**
a name of a kind of soft paper, usually used on the face, *(synonym)* tissue: *People use Kleenex™ to wipe their eyes (nose, glasses, etc.).*

**Km** *abbreviation of* Kilometer

**knack** /næk/ *noun, (no plural)*
a special talent for doing things: *He has a knack for fixing cars.*

**knapsack** /ˈnæpˌsæk/ *noun*
a bag that you can carry on your back, *(synonym)* a backpack: *When I travel, I always carry my tickets and passport in my knapsack. See:* art at backpack.

knapsack

**knead** /nid/ *verb*
to press something with your fingers and hands: *The baker kneads the flour and milk together to make bread.*

**knee** /ni/ *noun*
the part of your body that joins the top part and bottom part of your leg. It is in the middle of your leg: *The runner hurt his knee when he fell down. See:* art on page 21a.

**kneel** /nil/ *verb* **knelt** /nɛlt/ or **kneeled, kneeling, kneels**
to move down to the ground onto your knees or to stay on your knees

**knelt** /nɛlt/ *verb*
*past tense and past participle of* kneel

**knew** /nu/ *verb*
*past tense of* know

**knife** /naɪf/ *noun, plural* **knives** /naɪvz/
a piece of metal with a handle that you hold. It has a sharp blade that you use to cut things: *The cook cut the meat with the knife. See:* art on page 7a.

knife

**knit** /nɪt/ *verb* **knit** or **knitted, knitting, knits**
to make clothes from mainly wool with long sticks called knitting needles *–noun* **knitting,** (tool) **knitting needle.**

**knob** /nɑb/ *noun*
a round handle on a door or machine: *He turned the door knob and opened the door.*

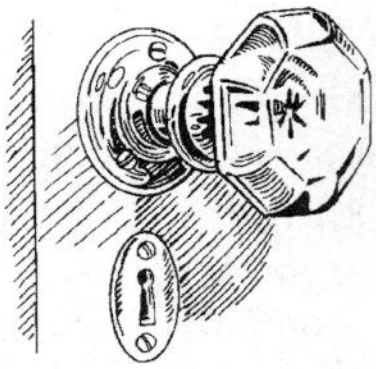
knob

**knock** /nɑk/ *verb*
**1** to hit something to make noise: *The boy knocked on the door, but his father didn't hear him.*
**2** to hit something with a hard blow: *The child knocked the plate off the table and it broke.*
**to knock someone** or **something down:** to make someone or something fall to the ground
**to knock someone out:** to hit someone so hard that they fall down and cannot get up again for some time
**to knock oneself out:** to work very hard: *She knocked herself out staying up all night to finish the job.*

**knockout** /ˈnɑkˌaʊt/ *noun*
(in boxing) when you hit the other boxer to the ground and finish the fight *See:* KO.

**knot** /nɑt/ *noun*
a fastening made of pieces of thread (rope, wire, etc.) that you tie tightly so they cannot move: *The sales assistant put string around the package and tied it with a knot.*

knot

**to tie the knot:** *informal* to get married: *My brother and his girlfriend have been dating for years, and now they're finally tying the knot.*

**knot** *verb* **knotted, knotting, knots**
to make or tie a knot: *He knotted his tie and then went to work.*

**know** /noʊ/ *verb* **knew** /nu/, **known** /noʊn/, **knowing, knows**
**1** to have information about something because you have learned it: *My sister*

*knows a lot about South America. She lived there for ten years.*

**2** to have met or seen someone or something before: *She knows the people who live next door. She has visited them many times.*

**to get to know:** to spend time learning about a person you met or a place you are visiting or living in: *She got to know him well when they worked together.*

**to know how to:** to be able to do something: *She knows how to write computer programs (speak French, fly airplanes, etc.).*

**to know of:** to have some knowledge of someone or something: *I know of the new store, but I have never been there.* *See:* learn, study, find out.

**knowledge** /'nɑlɪʤ/ *noun*
the information and understanding you have about something: *He has knowledge of the accident and how it happened. (antonym)* ignorance. *–adjective* **knowledgeable.**

**known** /noʊn/ *verb*
*past participle of* know

**known** /noʊn/ *adjective*
famous, *(synonym)* recognized: *Brazil is known for its coffee.*

**knuckle** /'nʌkəl/ *noun*
one of the bones in your hand that connects your fingers with your hand. It is the place where your fingers bend.

**KO** /'keɪ'oʊ/ *noun*
*abbreviation of* knockout: *The boxing match ended with a tenth round KO.*

**koala** or **Koala bear** /koʊ'ɑlə/ *noun*
a small animal from Australia that looks like a little bear and lives in trees

**Koran** /kə'ræn/ *noun, (no plural)*
the holy book of Islam: *Muslims believe that the Koran contains the things that Allah told Mohammed.*

**kosher** /'koʊʃər/ *adjective*
**1** (from Jewish religious law, especially about food) clean, pure: *He eats only kosher meat.*
**2** *informal* done in a correct and honest way

**Kph** *abbreviation of*
kilometers per hour

**kudos** /'ku,doʊz/ *noun singular*
good reaction or comments, *(synonym)* praise: *My restaurant received kudos from the food critic.*

**Ku Klux Klan** /'ku'klʌks'klæn/ also **KKK** or **the Klan** *noun*
a secret group of people who think that white people are better than others. It is found mostly in the southern USA: *The KKK is devoted to having white Christian people rule the world.*

**kung fu** /'kʌŋ'fu/ *noun, (no plural)*
a Chinese way of fighting with your hands and feet

**kw or KW** /'keɪ'dʌbəl,yu/ *abbreviation of*
kilowatt(s)

K

# L, l

**L, l** /ɛl/ *noun* **L's, l's** or **Ls, ls**
the 12th letter of the English alphabet

**lab** /læb/ *noun*
*See:* laboratory.

**label** /ˈleɪbəl/ *noun*
**1** a small piece of paper or cloth attached to something to identify it: *The label on this shirt says, "Made in United States of America."*
**2** a marker on a product used to give its name and contents

**label** *verb*
**1** to mark with a label: *The teacher labeled the grade cards with each student's name.*
**2** to name someone or something: *His teachers have labeled him a troublemaker.*

**labor** /ˈleɪbər/ *noun, (no plural)*
**1** work, especially difficult physical work: *He is well paid for his labor.*
**2** the work force, workers in general

**a labor of love:** work done not for pay but out of love for it

**labor** *verb*
to work hard

**to go into** or **be in labor:** to begin giving birth

**laboratory** /ˈlæbrəˌtɔri/ *noun, plural* **laboratories**
a room with special equipment for doing experiments and other exploratory work

**Labor Day** *noun*
in the USA and Canada, a holiday observed on the first Monday in September in honor of workers

**labor union** *noun*
an organization of workers formed to protect the interests of its members such as by getting them more money and benefits

**lace** /leɪs/ *noun*
**1** *(no plural)* material, such as silk, made by hand or machine into fine decorative patterns: *She has a tablecloth made of beautiful lace for her dining room table.*

lace

**2** strings used to tie shoes and boots

**lace** *verb* **laced, lacing, laces**
to close together or fasten with laces: *I laced up my boots.*

**lack** /læk/ *noun, (no plural)*
to be without something: *There is a lack of rain this summer.*

**lack** *verb*
to be without (something needed): *She lacks the skill for the job.*

**ladder** /ˈlædər/ *noun*
**1** a piece of equipment used for climbing: *A worker climbed a ladder to fix the roof.*
**2** a series of upward steps: *She climbed the ladder of success at her company.*

ladder

# Flowers

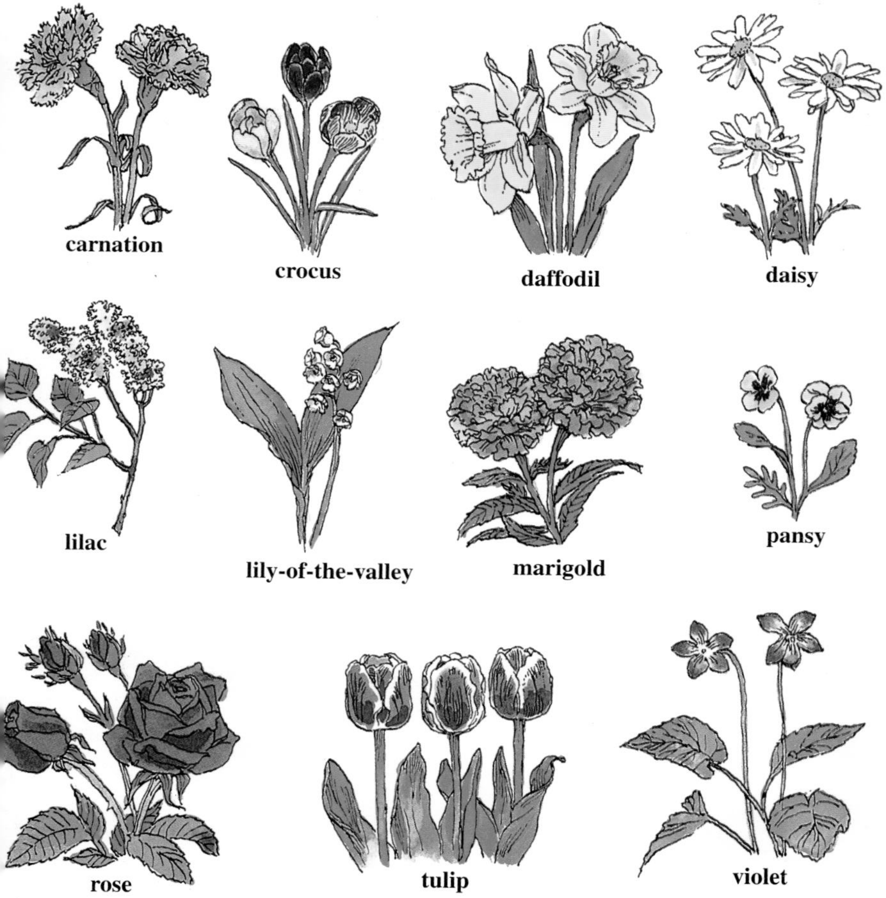


# Tree Leaves

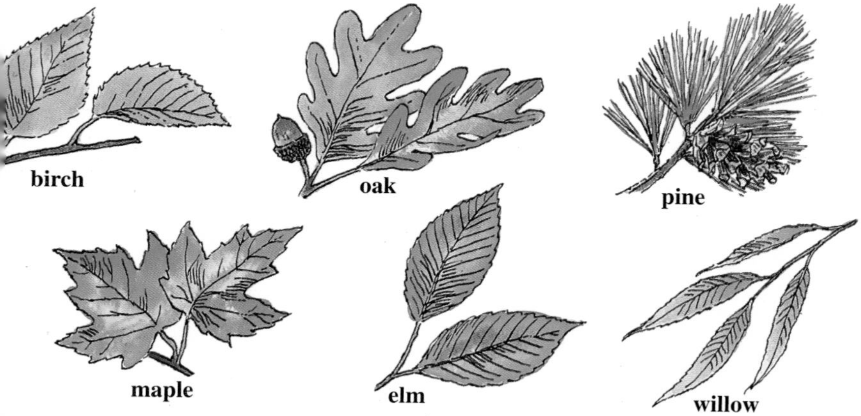

# Vegetables

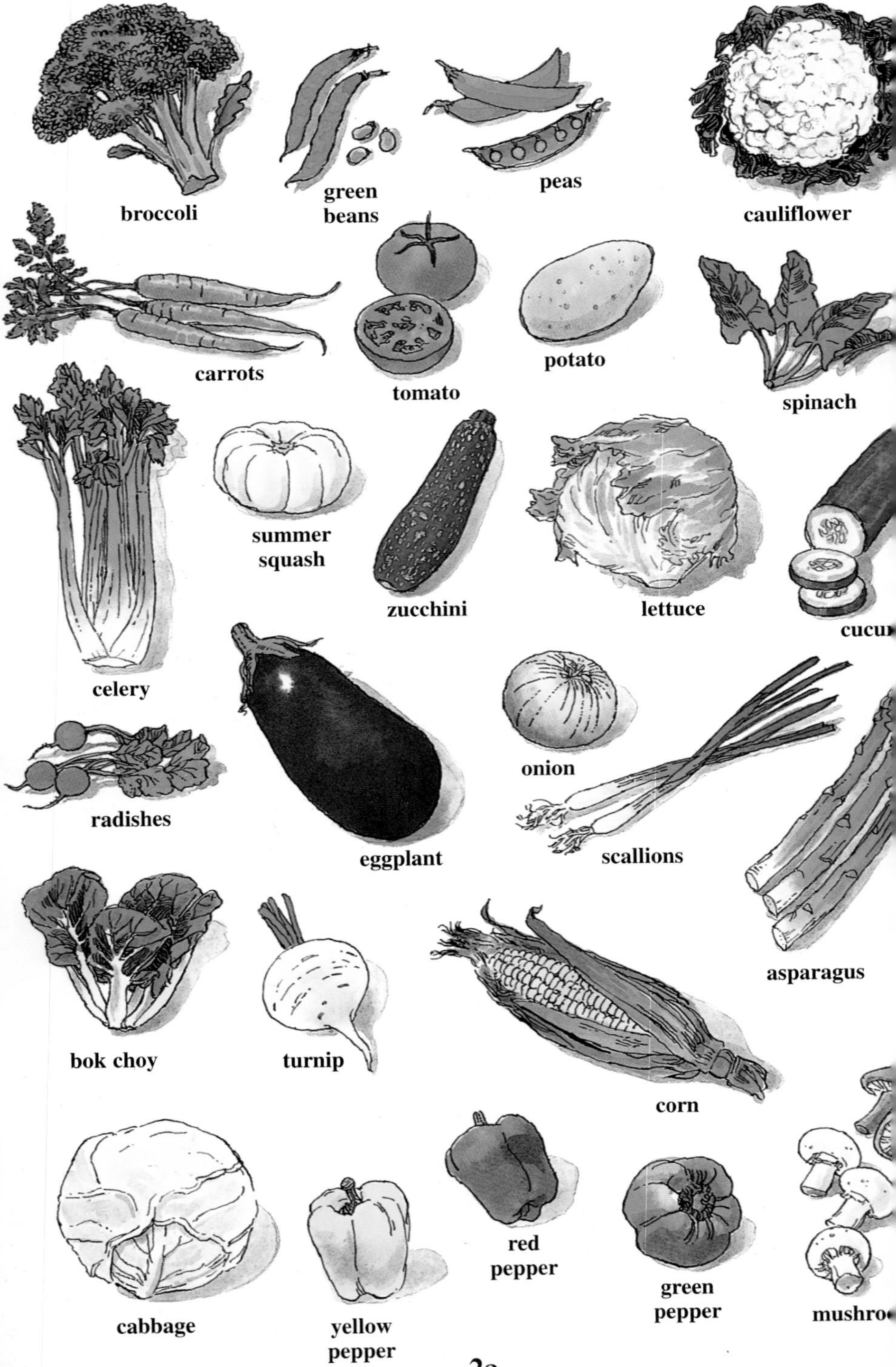

broccoli
green beans
peas
cauliflower
carrots
tomato
potato
spinach
celery
summer squash
zucchini
lettuce
cucu
radishes
eggplant
onion
scallions
asparagus
bok choy
turnip
corn
cabbage
yellow pepper
red pepper
green pepper
mushro

# Fruits

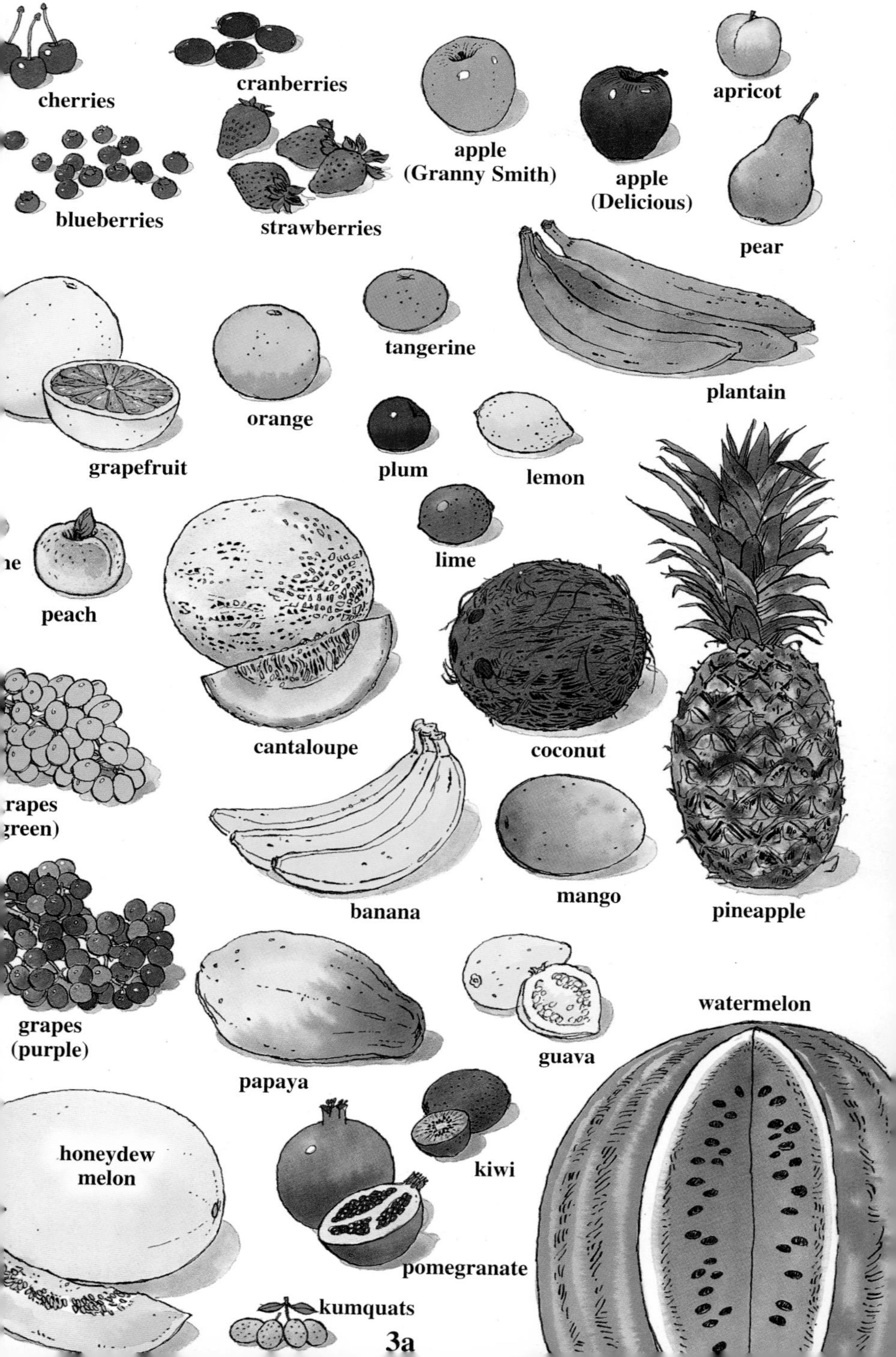

cherries
cranberries
apple (Granny Smith)
apple (Delicious)
apricot
blueberries
strawberries
pear
tangerine
plantain
orange
grapefruit
plum
lemon
ne
lime
peach
cantaloupe
coconut
rapes
reen)
banana
mango
pineapple
grapes (purple)
papaya
guava
watermelon
honeydew melon
kiwi
pomegranate
kumquats

# Downtown

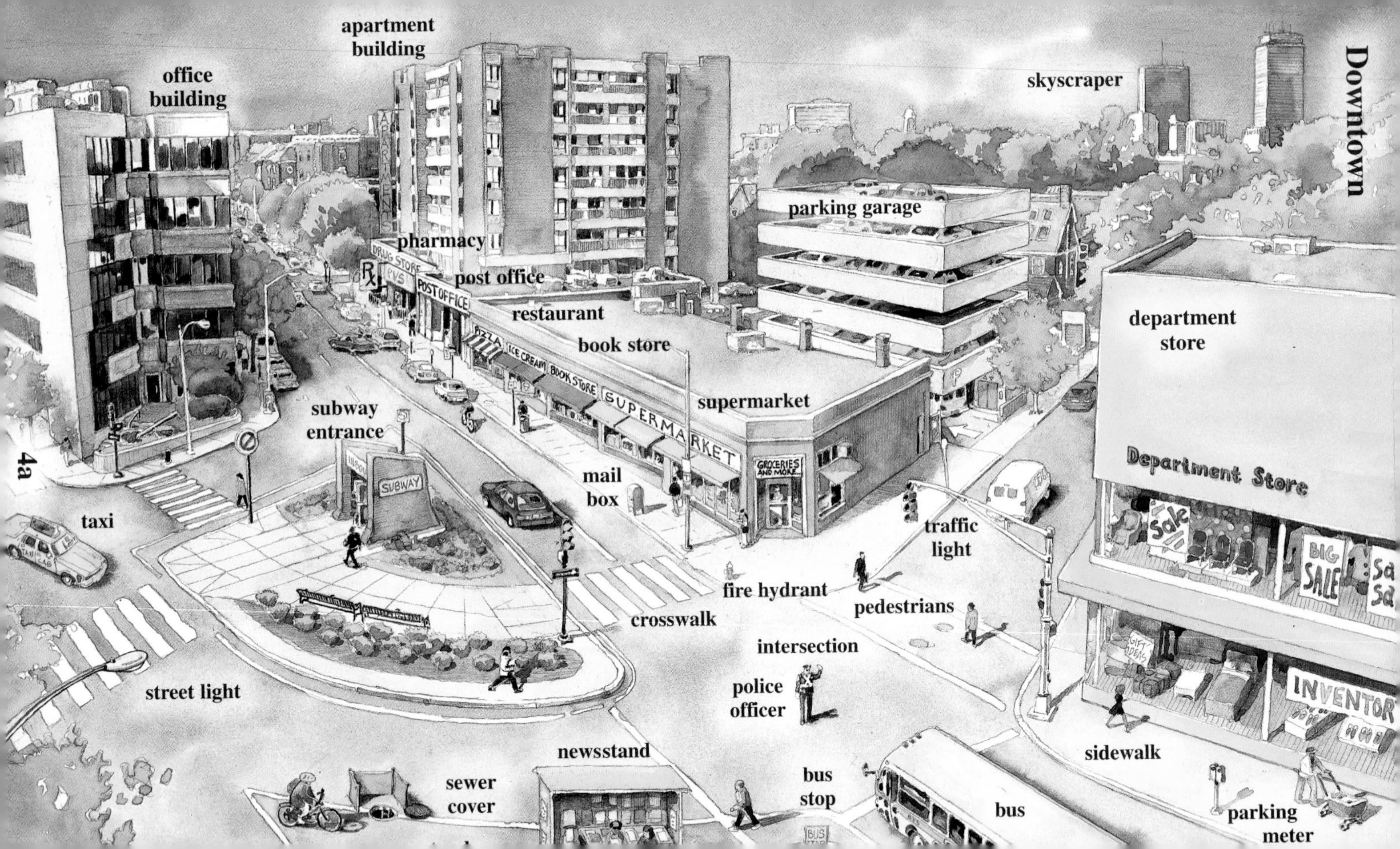
apartment building
office building
skyscraper
parking garage
pharmacy
post office
restaurant
book store
department store
supermarket
subway entrance
mail box
traffic light
taxi
fire hydrant
pedestrians
crosswalk
intersection
street light
police officer
newsstand
sidewalk
sewer cover
bus stop
bus
parking meter

Restaurant
chef
host(ess)
server or waitress
server or waiter
salad bar
customer
chair
napkin
tablecloth
soft drink
menu
plate
glass
placemat
salt & pepper
candle
fork
cup
5a

# Living Room

ceiling
wall
ceiling light
picture
window shade
window
television
thermostat
door
drapes
bookcase
VCR
stereo
floor
lamp
light
switch
end
table
lamp
speaker
sofa
coffee table
floor
rug
telephone
easy chair

# Kitchen

wall
cabinets
window
microwave oven
kettle
pot
pan
electric outlet
sink
toaster
paper towels
coffee pot
door
refrigerator
stove
dishwasher
chair
spoon
cup
glass
table
plate
knife
saucer
fork
floor

# Classroom

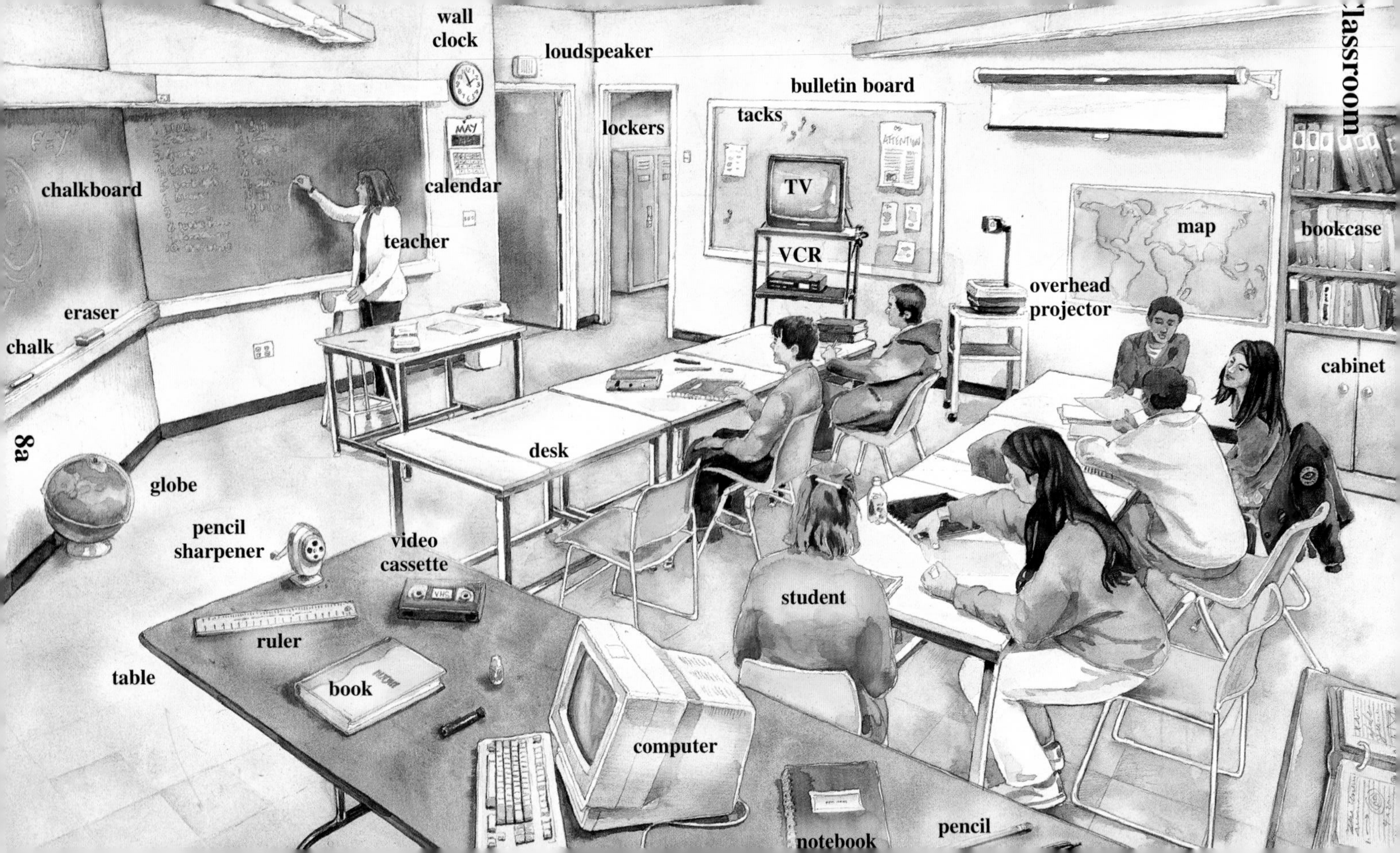
wall clock
loudspeaker
bulletin board
tacks
lockers
chalkboard
calendar
TV
map
bookcase
teacher
VCR
overhead projector
eraser
chalk
cabinet
desk
globe
pencil sharpener
video cassette
student
ruler
table
book
computer
pencil
notebook

# Playground

swing set
jungle gym
fence
basketball court
school
playing field
baseball diamond
tennis court
seesaw
swing
grass
ball
slide
bucket
shovel
sandbox
dirt

# Supermarket

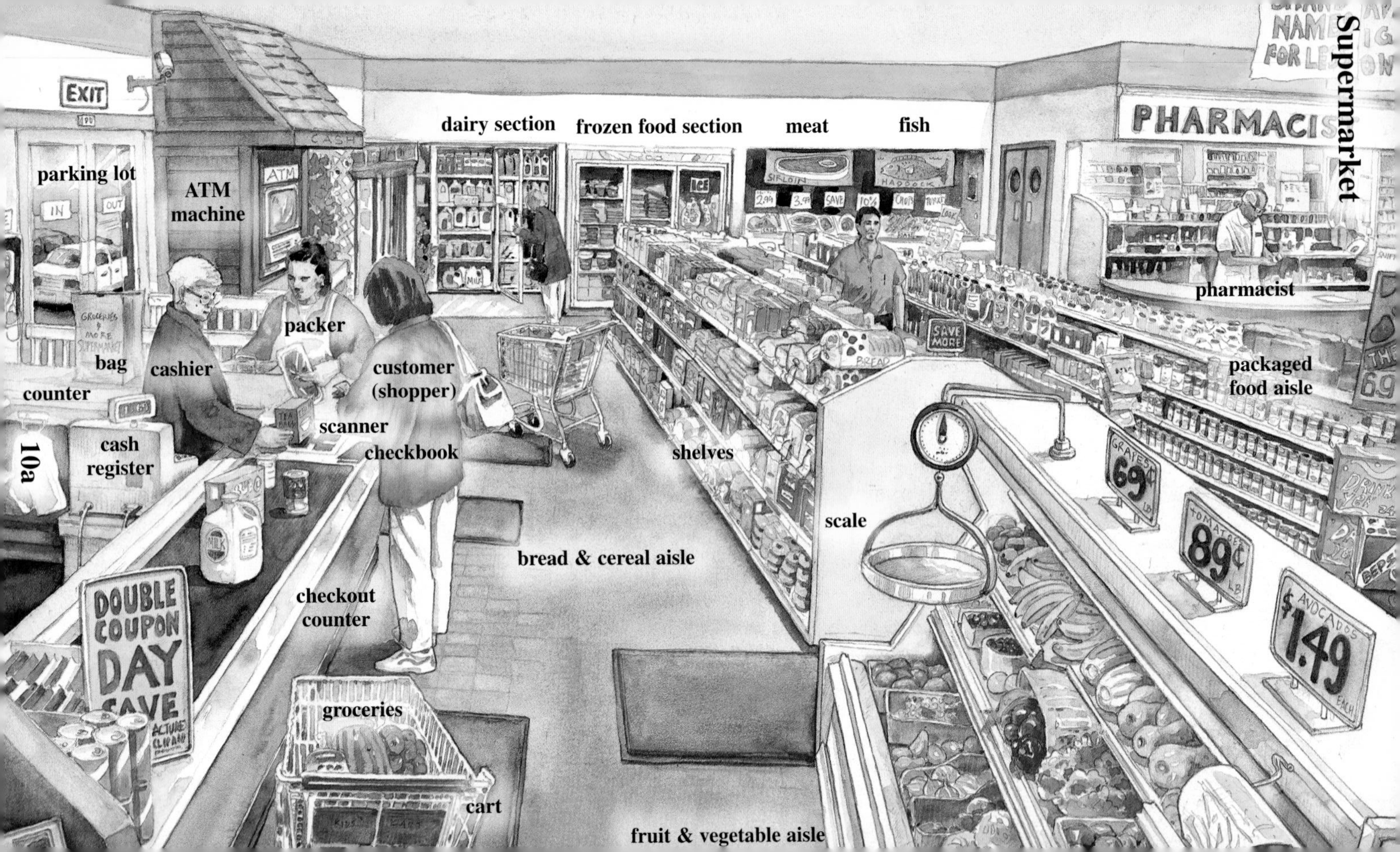
EXIT
parking lot
IN
OUT
ATM
machine
ATM
CASH
dairy section
frozen food section
meat
fish
ICE
SIRLOIN
HADDOCK
SAVE MORE
BREAD
PHARMACIS
pharmacist
packaged
food aisle
bag
cashier
packer
customer
(shopper)
counter
scanner
checkbook
cash
register
shelves
scale
bread & cereal aisle
checkout
counter
DOUBLE
COUPON
DAY
SAVE
MILK
groceries
cart
fruit & vegetable aisle
GRAPES 69¢ LB
TOMATOES 89¢ LB
$ AVOCADOS 1.49 EACH

# Emergency Room/Doctor's Office

# Clothing

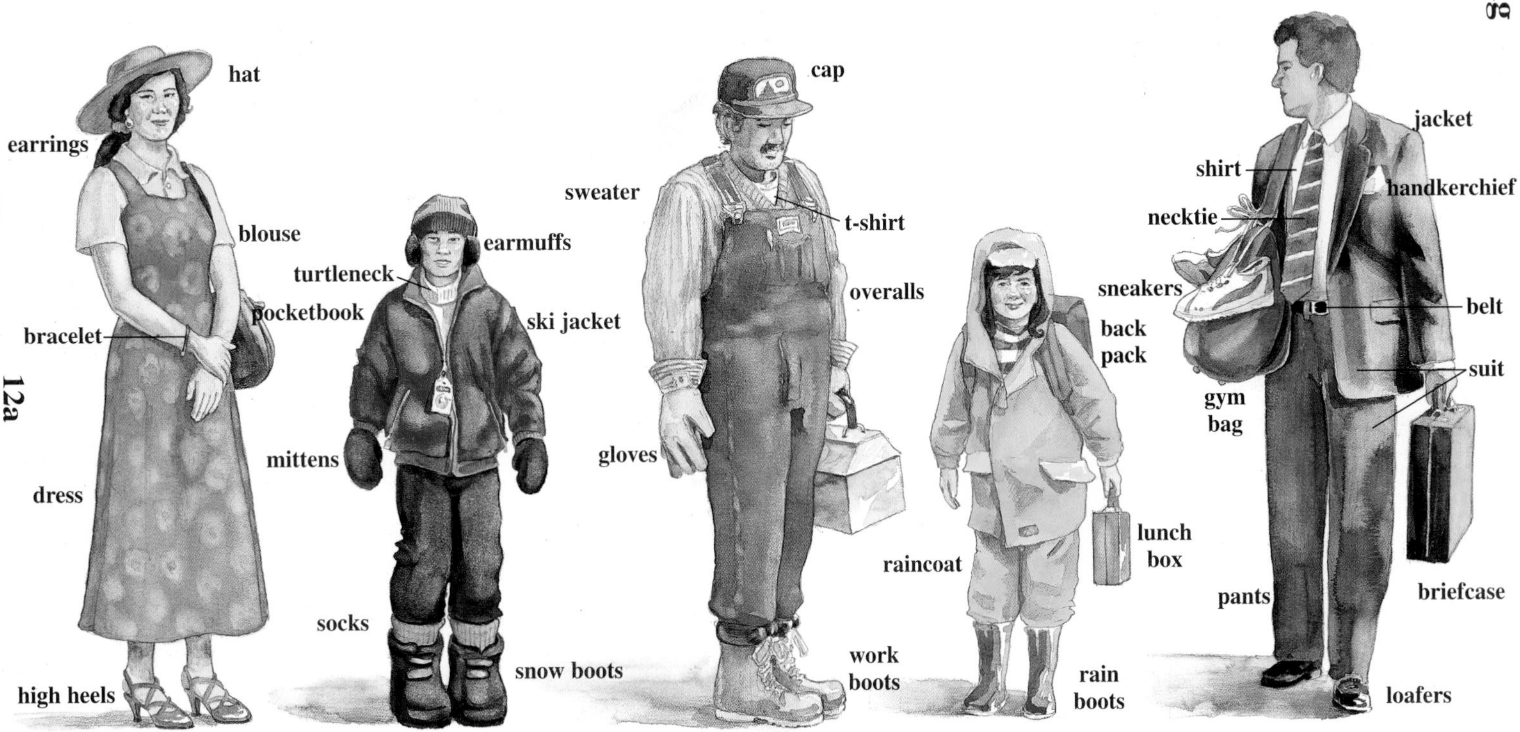
hat
earrings
blouse
pocketbook
bracelet
dress
high heels
turtleneck
earmuffs
ski jacket
mittens
socks
snow boots
sweater
cap
t-shirt
overalls
gloves
work boots
sneakers
back pack
raincoat
lunch box
rain boots
jacket
shirt
handkerchief
necktie
belt
suit
gym bag
pants
briefcase
loafers

# Family Relationships

# Animals

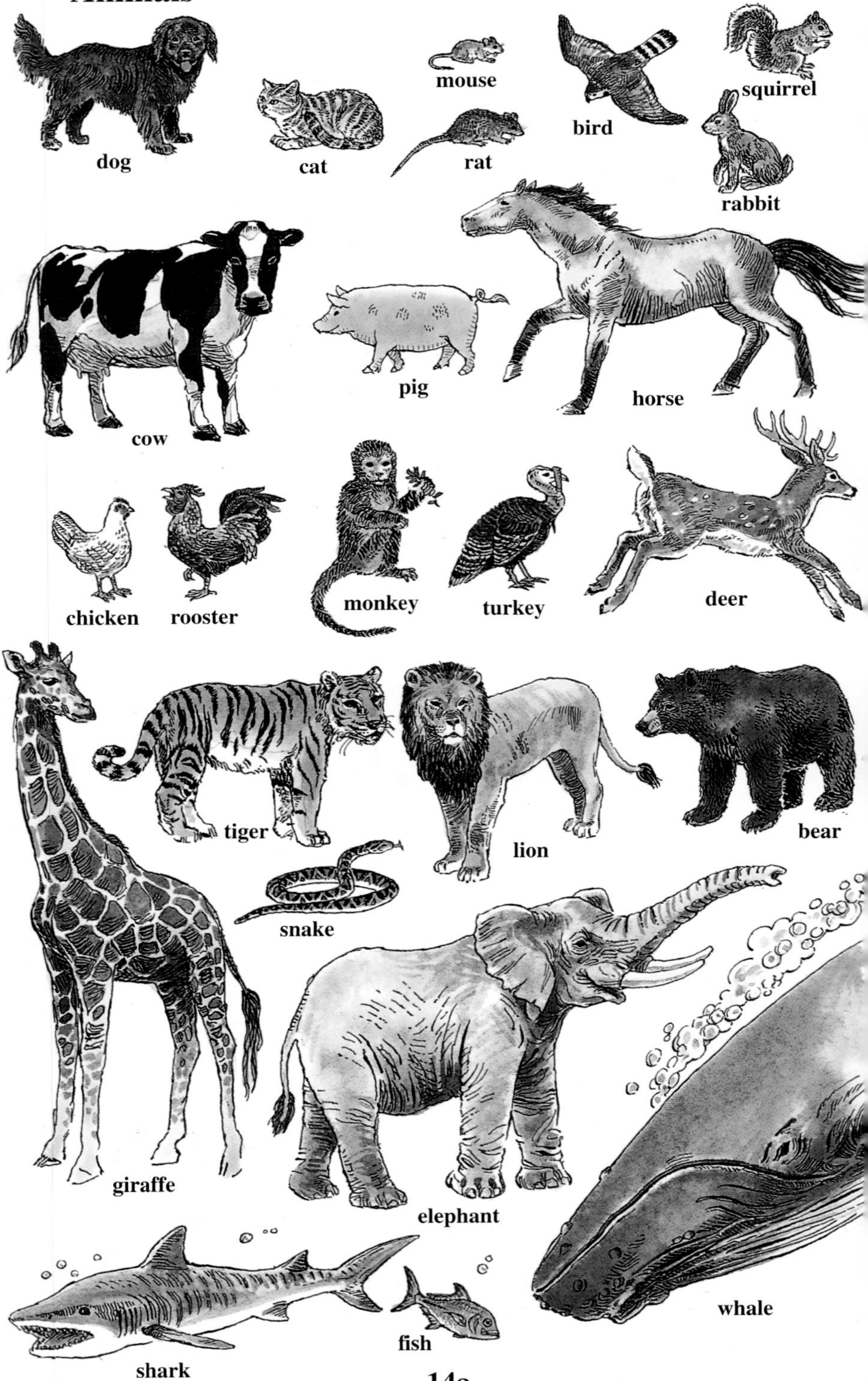
dog
cat
mouse
rat
bird
squirrel
rabbit
cow
pig
horse
chicken
rooster
monkey
turkey
deer
giraffe
tiger
lion
bear
snake
elephant
whale
shark
fish

# Musical Instruments

# Measurements

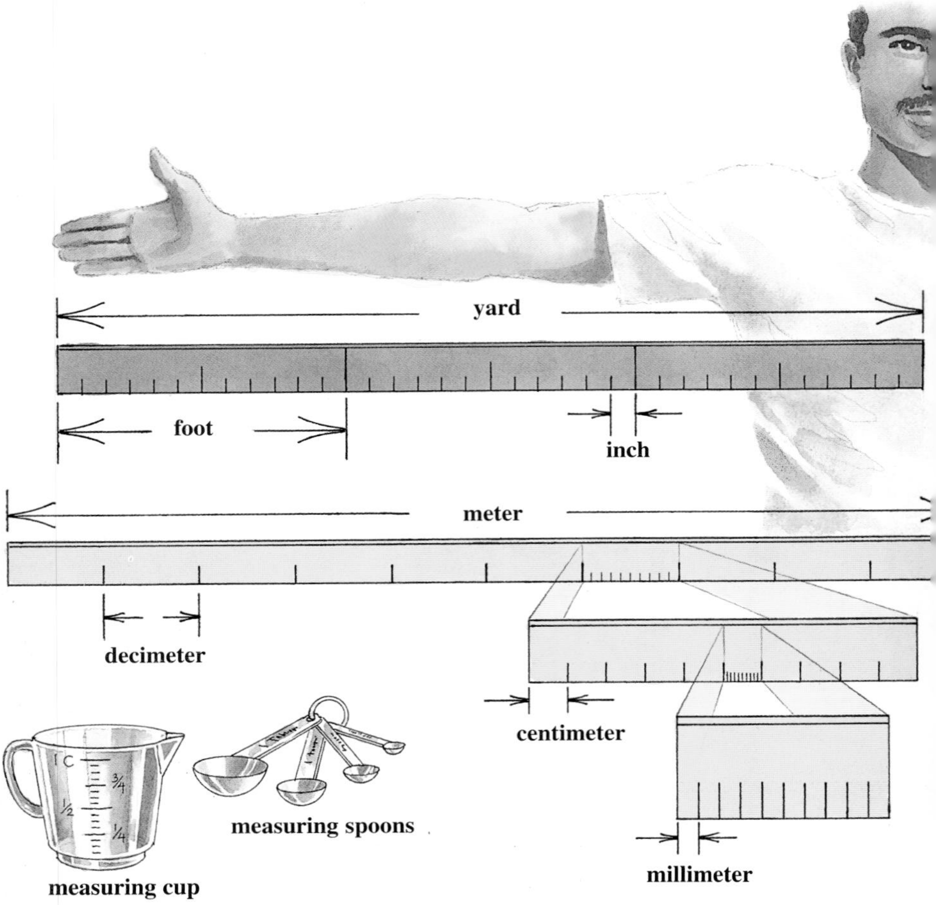


# Shapes

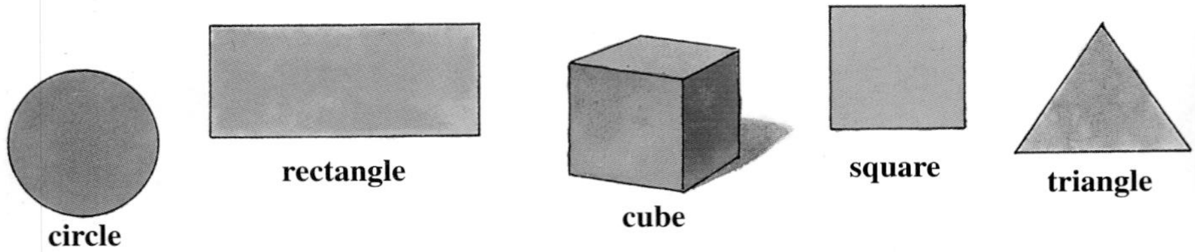


# Colors

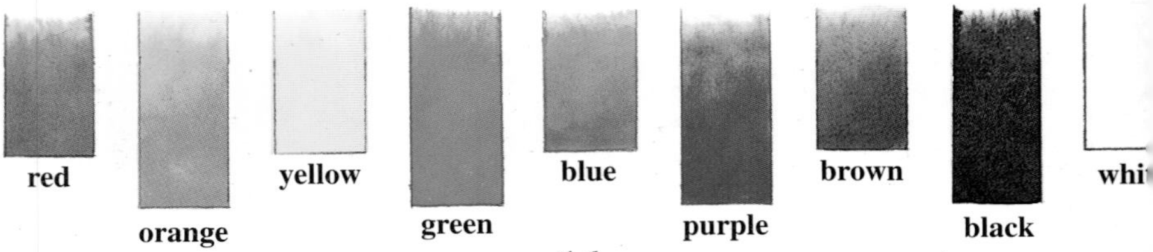

# Breads and Cereals

cereal

bread

bagel

rice

muffin

noodles

spaghetti

# Dairy

butter

cheese

milk

yogurt

eggs

# Meat and Fish

bacon

fish

chicken

ham

hamburger

hot dog

steak

# Emotions and feelings

embarrassed

happy

jealous

angry

excited

bored

confused

surprised

scared/frightened

stressed

tired

worried

# Verbs of everyday living

to wake up

to brush your teeth

to shave

to shower

to dress/
to put on your clothes

to cook

to eat and drink

to go to work

to work

to go home

to go to sleep

to sleep

# Office

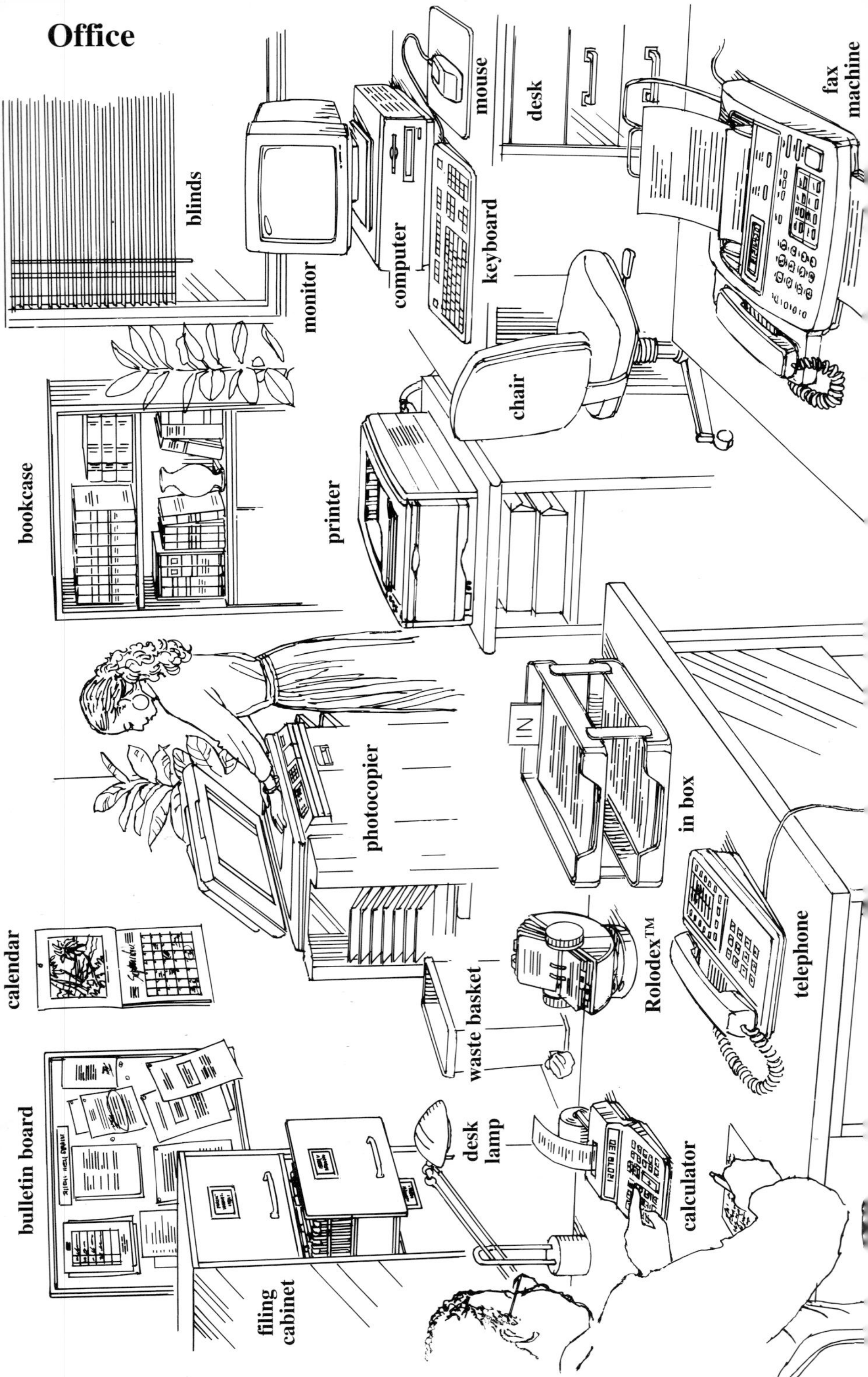

blinds
bookcase
calendar
bulletin board
monitor
computer
keyboard
mouse
desk
fax machine
chair
printer
photocopier
in box
Rolodex™
telephone
waste basket
desk lamp
calculator
filing cabinet

# Parts of the body

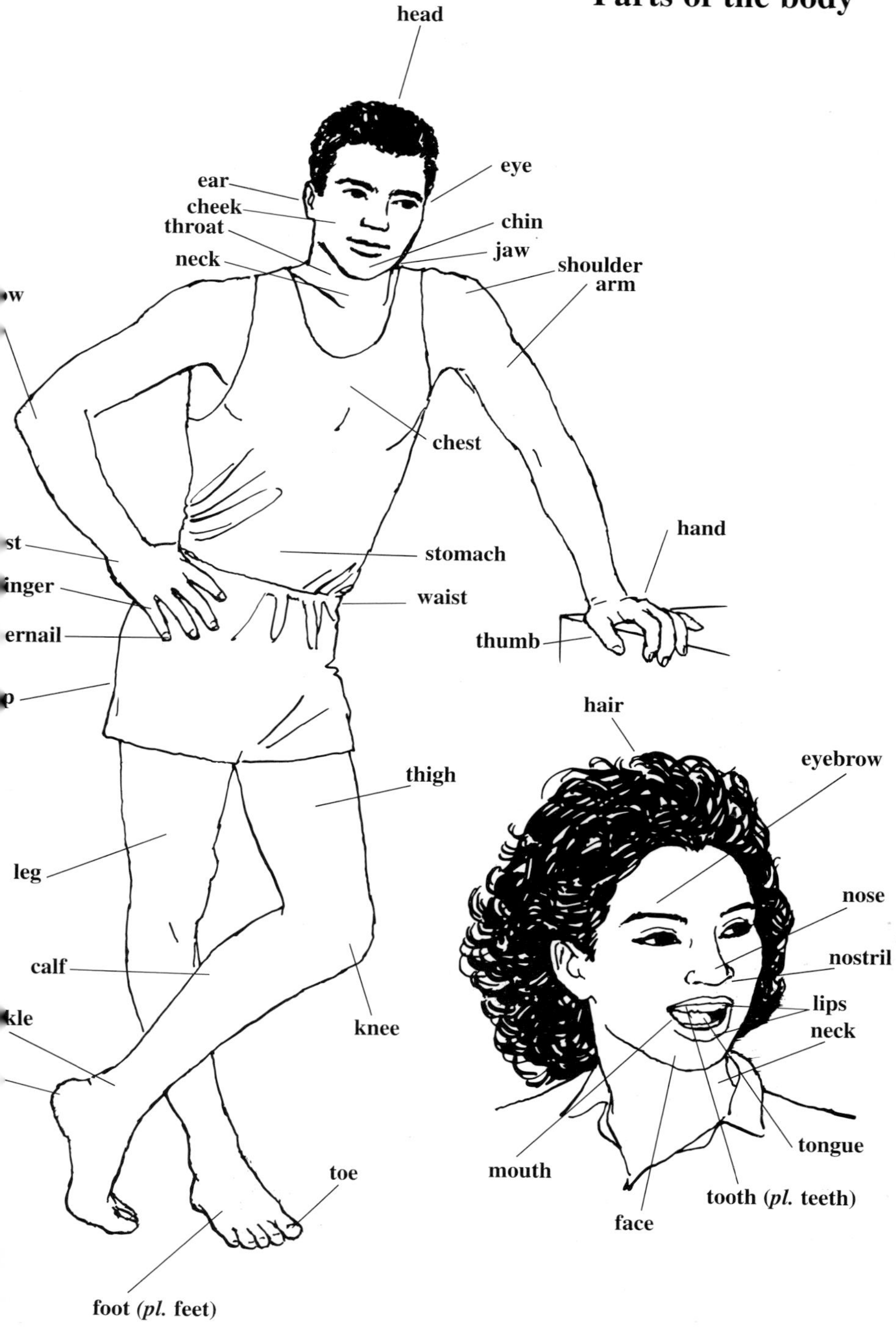

# Bedroom

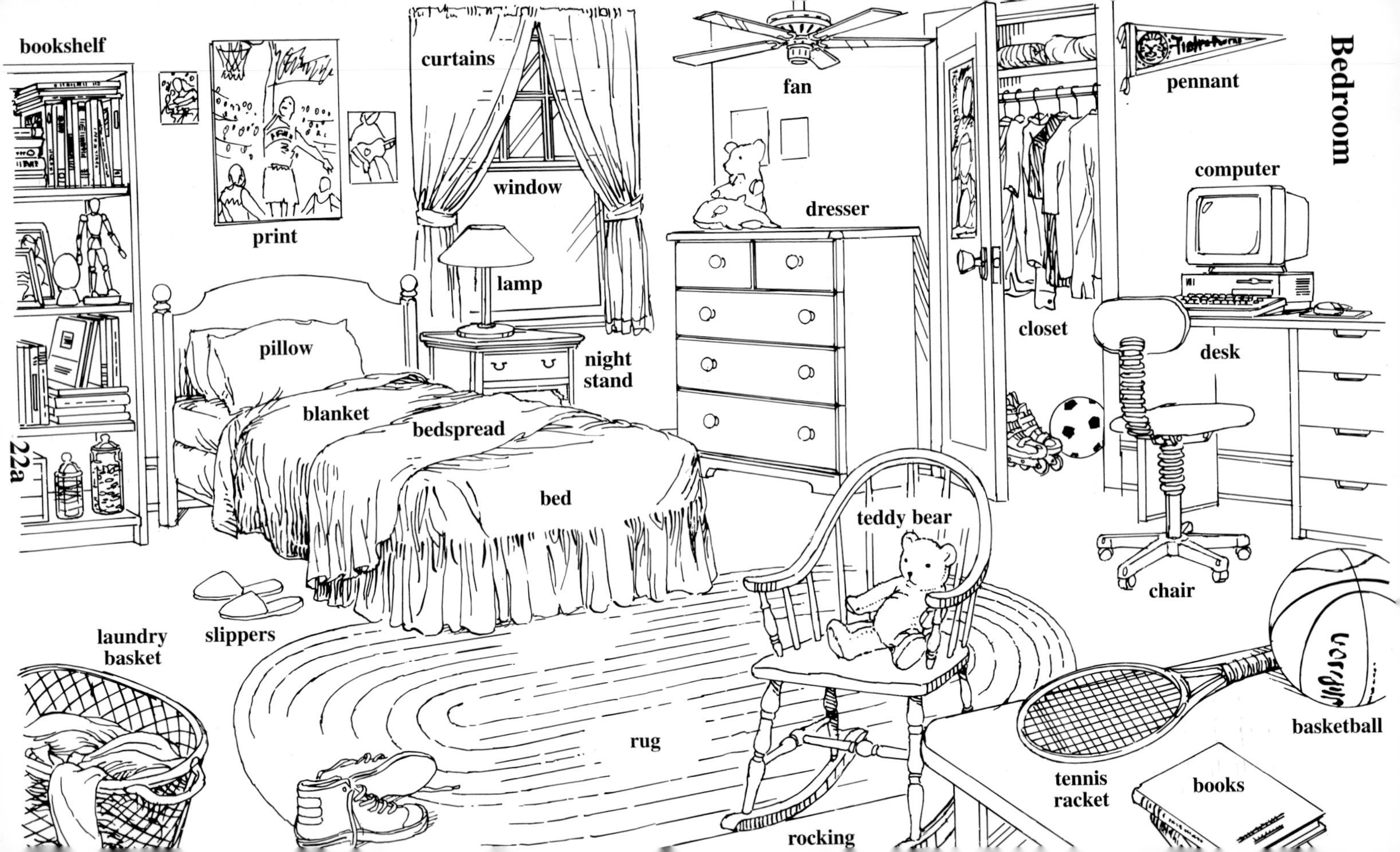
bookshelf
print
curtains
window
lamp
fan
dresser
closet
pennant
computer
desk
chair
pillow
blanket
bedspread
bed
night
stand
teddy bear
laundry
basket
slippers
rug
rocking
tennis
racket
books
basketball

# Bathroom

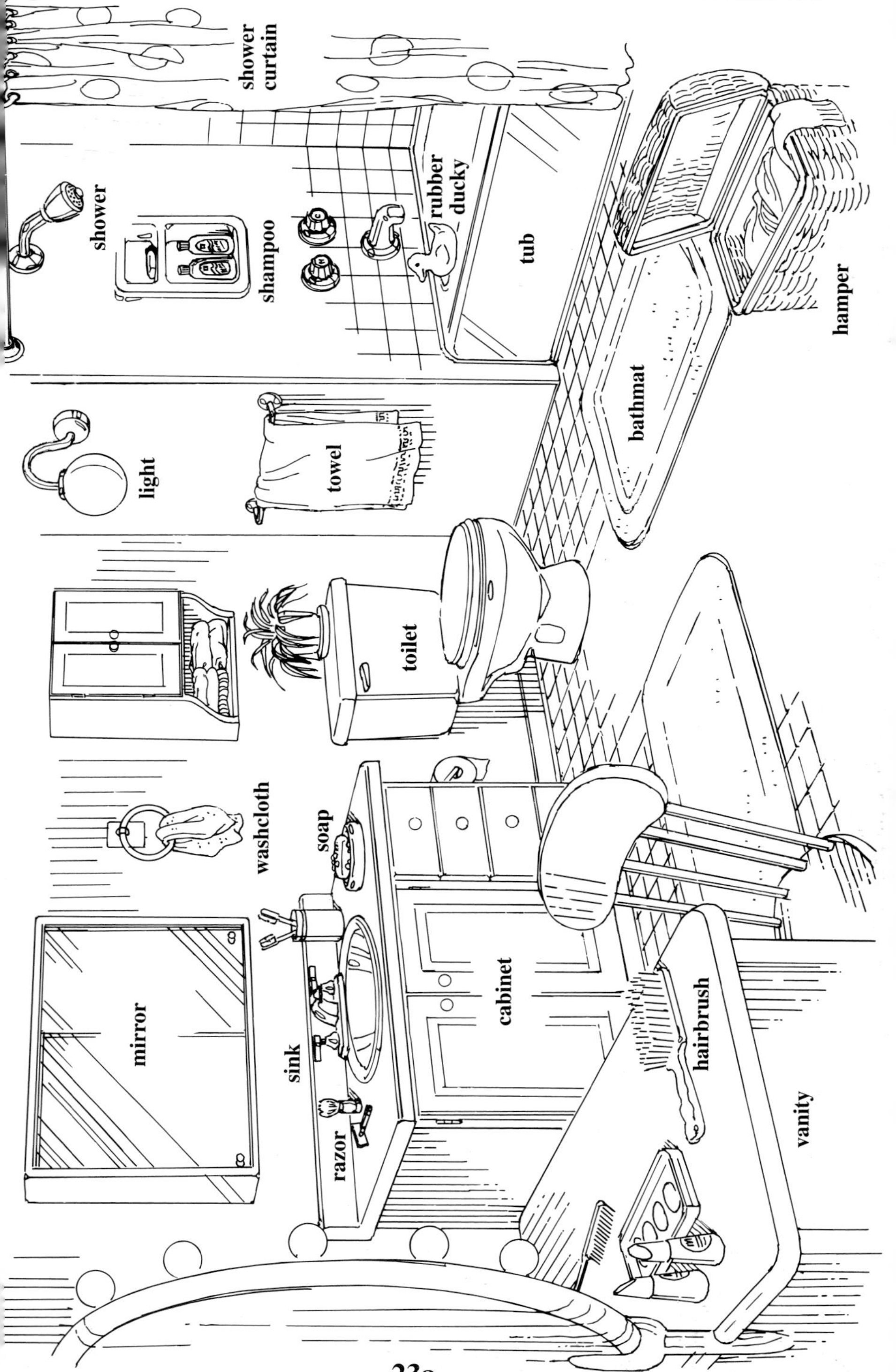
shower curtain
shower
shampoo
rubber ducky
tub
hamper
bathmat
light
towel
toilet
washcloth
soap
mirror
sink
razor
cabinet
hairbrush
vanity

# Transportation

to walk

to run

to jump

to bicycle

to skateboard

to Rollerblade™

subway

train

plane

bus

motorcycle

car

cab/taxi

**ladies' room** *noun*
a toilet for women *See:* bathroom, USAGE NOTE.

**lady** /'leɪdi/ *noun, plural* **ladies**
(polite word for) a woman: *"Ladies and gentlemen, may I have your attention, please."*

**lag** /læg/ *noun*
a delay, slowness: *There was a lag in communications, so he did not hear the news until many days later.*

**lag** *verb* **lagged, lagging, lags**
to not keep up, to delay: *The little boy lagged behind the others on the walk.*

**lagoon** /lə'gun/ *noun*
an area of sea water almost completely surrounded by land

**laid** /leɪd/ *verb*
*past tense and past participle of* lay

**laid-back** *adjective informal*
relaxed, calm: *My boss is easy to work for because he's so laid-back.*

**lain** /leɪn/ *verb*
*past participle of* lie (2)

**lake** /leɪk/ *noun*
a large body of fresh water

**lakefront** /'leɪk,frʌnt/ *noun*
land next to and around a lake: *We swim in the lake.*

**lamb** /læm/ *noun*
a young sheep or the meat from one

**lame** /leɪm/ *adjective* **lamer, lamest**
unable to walk normally due to some injury or disability

**lament** /lə'mɛnt/ *verb formal*
to feel sadness or cry for: *Her friends lamented the death of the dear old lady.*

**lamp** /læmp/ *noun*
a lighting device using electricity, oil, or gas *See:* art on page 6a.

**land** /lænd/ *noun*
**1** soil, earth: *The land in this area is good for farming.*
**2** an area owned as property: *We own our house and the land around it.*
**3** a nation, country: *The boy dreamed of travel to a foreign land.*

**land** *verb*
to reach land: *Our airplane landed at New York's Kennedy Airport.*

**landing** /'lændɪŋ/ *noun*
arrival of an aircraft or a boat on land *(antonym)* takeoff.

**landlord** /'lænd,lɔrd/ *noun*
a man or business that owns buildings or land that he rents to others: *The landlord of our apartment building is a huge real estate company.* *–noun* (female) **landlady.**

**landmark** /'lænd,mɑrk/ *noun*
**1** something easy to see and usually important, such as a tall building or mountain: *The tallest mountain in the area is a famous landmark.*
**2** an important event: *The invention of the radio is a landmark in technology.*

**landscape** /'lænd,skeɪp/ *noun*
**1** a wide view of the land: *The landscape seen from the mountains is beautiful.*
**2** a picture showing such a view: *She paints landscapes.*

**landscape** *verb* **landscaped, landscaping, landscapes**
to improve (the ground around a building) with trees, plants, etc.

**landslide** /'lænd,slaɪd/ *noun*
**1** a large fall of rocks and earth down a slope: *A landslide blocked the main road.*
**2** a very big win, especially in an election

**lane** /leɪn/ *noun*
**1** a short street, often narrow with little traffic: *They live on a little country lane outside of town.*
**2** one of several paths marked by painted lines on a highway: *He drives slowly in the right lane of the highway.* *See:* street, USAGE NOTE.

**language** /'læŋgwɪʤ/ *noun*
**1** human communication by systems of written and spoken words, and body movements: *She studies language development in children.*
**2** a particular communication system shared by a people: *He knows three languages: French, English, and American Sign Language.*
**3** a type of speech or wording: *He uses bad language.*
**4** any system for giving instructions to a

computer: *PASCAL and COBOL are computer programming languages.*

**lantern** /ˈlæntərn/ *noun*
a light or flame inside a container usually of metal and glass: *They took a lantern on their camping trip.*

**lap** /læp/ *verb* **lapped, lapping, laps**
to lick with the tongue in order to drink: *A cat laps milk from a bowl.*

**lap** *noun*
**1** the area formed by the top of the legs in a seated position: *The baby sat on his mother's lap.*
**2** a complete turn around a track or a length of a swimming pool

**lapel** /ləˈpɛl/ *noun*
the front area of a jacket, blouse, etc. that is folded back, then continues to the back collar: *He wears a flower in his lapel.*

lapel



**lapse** /læps/ *verb* **lapsed, lapsing, lapses**
(of agreements, rights, benefits) to end or be no longer valid: *My driver's license has lapsed; I can't drive a car now.*

**lapse** *noun*
the passing of a period of time: *There was a lapse of nine years before he saw her again.*

**laptop computer** or **laptop** /ˈlæp,tap/ *noun*
a small computer that is easy to carry: *The reporter used a laptop to write the story. See:* desktop.

**larceny** /ˈlarsəni/ *noun*
(in law) stealing of property *–adjective* **larcenous.**

**large** /larʤ/ *adjective* **larger, largest**
big or bigger than usual in size, amount, etc.: *She works for a large computer company. (antonym)* small.

**largely** /ˈlarʤli/ *adverb*
mostly, to a great degree: *He is largely responsible for the success of the business.*

**lark** /lark/ *noun*
a gray and brown songbird

**on a lark:** a carefree good time: *They decided just this morning to go on a weekend lark in the mountains.*

**laser** /ˌleɪzər/ *noun*
a device that focuses a powerful light in a specific place for many uses, from surgery to metal cutting

**lash** /læʃ/ *verb*
to hit with a whip: *The man lashed the horse to make it run faster.*

**lash** *noun*
a type of short whip: *He used a lash to punish the prisoner. See:* eyelash.

**last** /læst/ *adjective*
**1** behind all others in position: *He was the last in line because he arrived very late.*
**2** (of a time period) the most recently passed: *All the bills were paid last month (week, year).*
**3** final, at the end: *His last days before his death were peaceful.*
**4** least desirable: *Washing windows is the last thing that I want to do.*

**last but not least:** at the end but still important

**last** *adverb*
**1** behind all others: *My favorite horse ran last in the race.*
**2** in the recent past: *When he last visited his mother, she was well.*

**last** *noun, (no plural)*
a person or thing after all others: *He was the last to arrive.*

**last** *verb*
**1** to continue to exist: *The old stone wall has lasted for hundreds of years.*
**2** to remain in good condition: *Well-made shoes last a long time.*
**3** to live longer than: *The sick patient is not expected to last the night.*
**4** to be enough: *That pile of wood should last the winter.*

**lasting** /ˈlæstɪŋ/ *adjective*
continuing for a long time: *She makes a good, lasting impression on people.*

**last name** *noun*
a family name: *His full name is Sam Jones; his last name is Jones. See:* surname.

**latch** /læʧ/ *noun*
a type of lock

**late** /leɪt/ *adjective* **later, latest**
**1** arriving after the expected time: *She was late for our meeting.*
**2** happening near the end (of a period of time): *in the late afternoon||the late 1800s*
**3** dead: *A church service was held for the late Mr. Jones.*

**late** *adverb*
after the expected time: *The movie started five minutes late.*

**lately** /ˈleɪtli/ *adverb*
recently: *Lately, her health has been much better.*

**latest** /ˈleɪtɪst/ *adjective*
**1** most recent: *We just heard the latest news.*
**2** most modern or current: *She wears the latest fashions.*

**Latin (1)** /ˈlætn/ *noun, (no plural)*
the language of Romans: *Latin was spoken throughout the Roman Empire.*

**Latin (2)** *noun adjective*
referring to the peoples of France, Italy, Spain, Mexico, and Central and South America, whose languages come from Latin: *There are ten Latins and ten Asians in my English class.*

**Latin America** *noun*
the countries of Central and South America

**Latino** /ləˈtinoʊ/ *adjective*
a Latin American person living in the USA

**latitude** /ˈlætəˌtud/ *noun*
an imaginary line of measurement of the earth's surface running parallel to the equator: *New York City is located at a latitude of about 41 degrees north of the equator and at a longitude of 74 degrees west of Greenwich, England. See:* longitude.

**latter** /ˈlætər/ *noun, (no plural)*
the second of two people or things named: *We eat lots of fish and chicken, but we prefer the latter (chicken). See:* former.

**latter** *adjective*
later, nearer the end: *I disliked the latter part of the book.*

**laugh** /læf/ *noun*
**1** a sound of happiness, made with the voice: *When he heard my funny story, he gave a loud laugh.*
**2** something that deserves no respect: *That performance was so bad that it was a laugh.*

**laugh** *verb*
to make sounds of happiness: *You never laugh at my jokes. See:* smile, **USAGE NOTE.**

**laughter** /ˈlæftər/ *noun, (no plural)*
the sound of laughing: *Laughter from the audience lasted for several minutes.*

**launch** /lɔntʃ/ *verb*
**1** to push into the water: *We launched our boat into the lake.*
**2** to send up into the air: *The spacecraft will be launched tomorrow. –noun* **launch.**

**launder** /ˈlɔndər/ *verb*
to clean with soap and water: *She launders her clothes at the Laundromat.*

**Laundromat™** /ˈlɔndrəˌmæt/ *noun*
a business with washing machines and driers that people pay to use to clean their clothes

**laundry** /ˈlɔndri/ *noun, plural* **laundries**
**1** a business that washes, dries, and irons clothes for people: *A big laundry supplies restaurants with uniforms and tablecloths.*
**2** clothes and linen that need to be washed or have just been washed: *She put the dirty laundry into the washer. See:* art on page 22a.

**lava** /ˈlɑvə/ *noun, (no plural)*
hot liquid rock: *Lava flowed down the sides of the volcano.*

**lavatory** /ˈlævəˌtɔri/ *noun formal, plural* **lavatories**
a room with toilets and sinks, bathroom

**law** /lɔ/ *noun*
**1** a rule made by a government that people must follow: *In the United States of America, laws are written by Congress and by state legislatures.*
**2** *(no plural)* such rules as a group: *Lawyers must know the law.*
**3** *(no plural)* the officials and courts of the legal system: *The man is in jail because he got into trouble with the law.*
**4** (in many religions) a commandment from God

**5** a statement describing what happens under certain conditions: *the law of gravity*

**law** *adjective*
related to law: *She has a law degree.*

**lawbreaker** /ˈlɔˌbreɪkər/ *noun*
a person who disobeys a law

**lawful** /ˈlɔfəl/ *adjective*
permitted by law, according to law

**lawn** /lɔn/ *noun*
an area of cut grass: *The lawn in the front yard is kept very neat.*

**lawn mower** *noun*
a machine used to cut grass: *He uses a lawn mower to cut his front lawn.*

**lawn mower**

**lawsuit** /ˈlɔˌsut/ *noun*
a legal action bringing a problem or claim to be decided in a court of law: *John's lawyer filed a lawsuit against the company where he had the accident.*

**lawyer** /ˈlɔyər/ *noun*
a professional who practices law: *She called a lawyer to handle the divorce. See:* attorney.

**laxative** /ˈlæksətɪv/ *noun adjective*
a medicine to help move blocked waste from the lower body: *The doctor recommended a gentle laxative.*

**lay (1)** /leɪ/ *verb*
*past tense of* lie

**lay (2)** *verb* **laid** /leɪd/, **laying, lays**
**1** to put down: *I laid my keys on the table.*
**2** to prepare, set: *She lays the table for dinner each night.*
**3** to form, create: *He's laying plans for a new business.*
**4** to produce (eggs): *Birds and insects lay eggs.*
**to lay off someone** or **something: a.** to fire workers from their jobs, but with the understanding they may be called back to work and can receive unemployment pay: *My company laid off 200 workers due to the poor economy.* **b.** *informal* to stop: *I told you to lay off bothering my little brother!*
**to lay to rest: a.** to bury: *The old man was laid to rest in the town where he was born.* **b.** *figurative* to stop or make disappear: *The politician announced his plans to retire, laying the recent rumors about his plans to rest.*

**layer** /ˈleɪər/ *noun*
**1** a coating, covering: *A layer of mud lies on the lake bottom.*
**2** a thickness, usually one of several: *The birthday cake had two layers of chocolate cake with chocolate icing between them.*

**layer** *verb*
to arrange in layers *–noun* **layering.**

**layoff** /ˈleɪˌɔf/ *noun*
a dismissal from employment, especially temporary: *When the economy is bad, there are often layoffs of factory workers.* *–verb* **to lay; to layoff.**

**layout** /ˈleɪˌaʊt/ *noun*
**1** a drawing or design, such as for a building or advertisement
**2** an arrangement, such as of rooms or furniture, etc: *I prefer the layout of the first house we looked at.*

**lazy** /ˈleɪzi/ *adjective* **lazier, laziest**
**1** disliking and avoiding work: *He's so lazy that he avoids any kind of work.*
**2** lacking energy or activity: *He spent a lazy afternoon reading and sleeping.*

**lb.** /paʊnd/ *noun*
*abbreviation for* pound(s): *I bought a 2 lb. piece of beef.*||*It weighed 2 lbs.*

---

**USAGE NOTE:** A *pound* is equal to 16 ounces, which is abbreviated as *oz.*:*She gave birth to a healthy baby girl, who weighed seven pounds and six ounces (7 lbs. 6 oz.).*

---

**lead (1)** /lɛd/ *noun, (no plural)*
**1** a heavy soft basic metal used in industry: *Plumbers use lead to close the spaces in pipes.*
**2** in pencils, the round, dark part that makes marks: *I need a pencil with a softer lead.* *–verb* **to lead (pipes).**

**lead (2)** /lid/ *verb* **led** /lɛd/, **leading, leads**
**1** to go first, to show the way: *She led the visitors on a tour through the museum.*
**2** to be ahead of, in front of: *He leads the others in the race by several meters.*

**3** to direct, control: *She led the orchestra (the discussion, the team, etc.).*
**4** to be a route to: *That road leads to the river.*
**5** to experience, live (a life): *He leads an exciting life.*
**to lead to something:** to result in: *Use of illegal drugs can lead to death.*
**lead** *noun*
**1** a distance one is ahead: *That race horse has a big lead over the others.*
**2** a piece of information useful in a search: *My friend gave me a lead on a new job opening.*

**leader** /ˈlidər/ *noun*
**1** a person who directs others: *Our leader tells us what to do.*
**2** one who is in front of others: *The Senator is the leader in the Presidential race.* –*noun* **leadership.**

**leading** /ˈlidɪŋ/ *adjective*
**1** ahead of others: *The Senator is the leading candidate for President.*
**2** most important: *That singer has the leading role in the opera.*
**leading lady** or **man:** person playing an important role in a play or film

**leaf** /lif/ *noun, plural* **leaves** /livz/
**1** a part of a plant, usually flat and green, growing from its stem or a branch

leaf

**2** a thin sheet of metal, such as gold: *The frame of the mirror is covered with rich-looking gold leaf.* –*verb* **to leaf.** *See:* turn (over a new leaf).

**leaflet** /ˈliflɪt/ *noun*
a folded paper printed with information or advertising

**league** /ˈlig/ *noun*
**1** a group of sports teams that compete against each other: *Our local team belongs to the National Football League.*
**2** a group of people, businesses, or nations joined together in a shared interest: *The League of Nations was founded in 1919 to promote world peace.*

**leak** /lik/ *noun*
**1** an unwanted opening that lets out small or large amounts of liquid or gas: *The boat has a leak and is filling up with water.*

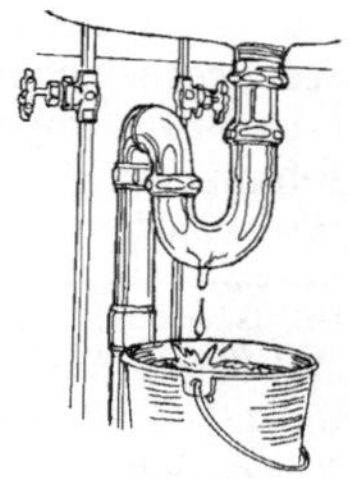
leak

**2** a giving out of secret information: *A leak from inside the government spread the news of the President's decision.*
**leak** *verb*
**1** to let in or out unwanted liquid or gas: *The kitchen sink leaks water onto the floor.*
**2** to give information secretly: *An official inside the government leaked a story to the newspapers.* –*noun* **leakage;** –*adjective* **leaky.**

**lean** /lin/ *verb*
**1** to rest against for support: *He leaned against a wall.*
**2** to bend from the waist: *He then leaned over and picked a flower.*
**to lean on** or **upon someone:** to depend on for help: *Her children lean on her, even though they are adults.*
**to lean toward(s):** to favor, prefer: *She leans toward going on vacation in July, not August.*
**lean** *adjective* **leaner, leanest**
**1** (of a person) thin, not fat: *Professional dancers are usually lean.*
**2** (of meat) with little fat: *They eat lean meat with the fat cut off.*
**3** producing little: *The country is going through lean times now because of the bad economy.*

**leap** /lip/ *noun*
**1** a jump into the air: *The dancer made several leaps around the stage.*
**2** *figurative* **by leaps and bounds:** with fast progress: *That company is growing by leaps and bounds.*
**leap** *verb* **leaped** or **leapt** /lɛpt, lipt/, **leaping, leaps**
to jump into or through the air: *Monkeys leaped from branch to branch.*

**learn** /lɜrn/ *verb* **learned** /lɜrnd/ or **learnt** /lɜrnt/, **learning, learns**
to gain knowledge or a skill in: *She*

*learned some American history in high school.*

**to learn the ropes:** to learn how to do a job by doing it: *To be successful in business you first need to learn the ropes.*

---

**USAGE NOTE:** Compare the verbs *study* and *learn.* When you *study* something, like algebra or biology, you try to learn it. You may or may not be successful. If you say you *learned* something, it means that you studied it and now you know it. For example, "I *studied* Italian for many years, but never *learned* to speak it until I spent a year in Rome."

---

**learning** /ˈlɜrnɪŋ/ *noun, (no plural)* knowledge or understanding gained through study: *He is a professor of great learning.*

**lease** /lis/ *verb* **leased, leasing, leases** a contract to pay to use property (a building, equipment, etc.) for a period of time: *Our business has leased its offices for five years.* *–noun* **lease.** *See:* rent.



**leash** /liʃ/ *noun* a cord used to hold a dog: *She walks her dog on a leash.*

**leash** *verb* to tie up with a leash

leash

**least** /list/ *noun, (no plural)* the smallest amount of something: *She is paid the least of all the office employees.*

**in the least:** in the smallest amount, at all: *I don't care about that matter in the least.*

**least** *adjective* about the smallest amount: *He is paid the least amount of all the workers.*

**leather** /ˈlɛðər/ *noun* the skin of cattle, sheep, etc. used to make shoes, belts, gloves, etc. *–adjective* **leathery.**

**leave** /liv/ *verb* **left** /lɛft/, **leaving, leaves**

**1** to go away (from): *I leave at 8:00 to go to work.*

**2** to go away from someone and never return: *He has left his wife (his job, college, etc.).*

**3** to cause to stay when one goes away: *They left their children with a babysitter.*

**4** to fail to bring when one goes away: *Oh, no, I left the keys inside the car!*

**5** to put in the care of: *I'll leave a message with your secretary.*

**6** to have as a result: *Drinking tea will leave yellow spots on your teeth.*

**to leave no stone unturned:** to make every possible effort: *The police left no stone unturned to solve the crime.*

**to leave off something: a.** not to include: *The airline left off several passengers' names, so they had no seats.* **b.** to stop (talking, reading, writing, etc.): *He surprised me by leaving off in mid-sentence.*

**to leave someone** or **something out:** not to include: *To shorten the lecture, the professor left out the less important parts.*

**to leave something to someone: a.** to give something to someone after one's death: *In her will, she left all her property to her children.* **b.** to depend on someone to manage something: *Just leave the travel arrangements to me.*

**to leave something up to someone:** to allow someone else to decide: *He often leaves decisions involving the children up to his wife.*

**to leave word:** to leave a message

**leave** *noun* a period away from work or the military

**on leave:** temporarily away from work or the military by official permission

**lecture** /ˈlɛktʃər/ *verb* **lectured, lecturing, lectures**

**1** to give a talk on a topic

**2** to give a long, serious talk with a warning: *The boy's mother gave him a lecture on bicycle safety.* *–noun* (person) **lecturer.** *See:* teacher, USAGE NOTE.

**ledge** /lɛdʒ/ *noun* a flat area like a shelf in rock formations and below windows

ledge

**ledger** /ˈlɛdʒər/ *noun*
a book in which numbers are recorded: *Every business should keep a ledger of its income and expenses.*

**left (1)** /lɛft/ *adjective*
on or by the side of the body containing the heart: *Fewer people write with the left hand than with the right.*

**left** *adverb*
toward the left: *We headed to the corner and turned left.*

**left** *noun*
**1** a left-hand turn: *We made a left at the corner.*
**2** *(no plural)* the liberal or socialist parties in politics: *He believes the New Left will win the election.* *–adjective* **leftist.**

**left (2)** *verb*
*past tense and past participle of* leave

**left-handed** *adjective*
favoring the use of the left hand: *She is a left-handed tennis player.* *–noun* (person) **left-hander.**

**leftovers** /ˈlɛft,oʊvərz/ *noun plural*
what remains, such as some food after a meal: *We ate leftovers of the turkey on Sunday evening.*

**leg** /lɛg/ *noun*
**1** one of the lower limbs of humans and many animals, used for walking, running, etc.: *Runners need strong legs.*
**2** one of the supports of a piece of furniture: *Don't sit on that chair; one of the legs is broken.*

**to cost an arm and a leg:** to cost much more than expected: *The new car cost her an arm and a leg, but she loves it.*

**to pull someone's leg:** to play a trick on someone: *She was pulling my leg when she said she had won $1 million in the lottery.* *See:* art on page 21a.

**legacy** /ˈlɛgəsi/ *noun*
something passed on or left by older people: *We must not let destruction of the environment be our legacy to our children.*

**legal** /ˈligəl/ *adjective*
**1** related to law: *The legal system works to protect those who are innocent and punish those who are guilty.*
**2** permitted or created by law: *He has a legal right to vote.*

**legal holiday** *noun*
a holiday made by the federal or state government on which businesses, institutions, etc. often close: *Christmas and New Year's Day are legal holidays in the USA.*

**legalize** /ˈligə,laɪz/ *verb* **legalized, legalizing, legalizes**
to make something legal that was illegal before *–noun* **legality.**

**legend** /ˈlɛdʒənd/ *noun*
a story from the distant past: *Each country has its legends about the past.*

**legendary** /ˈ lɛdʒən,dɛri/ *adjective*
**1** based on stories from the distant past: *Legendary stories are passed down from parents to children.*
**2** famous

**legible** /ˈlɛdʒəbəl/ *adjective*
able to be read, clear: *The photocopy is weak but legible.*

**legion** /ˈlidʒən/ *noun*
a mass of people or things: *Legions of people filled the streets to celebrate independence.*

**legislate** /ˈlɛdʒɪs,leɪt/ *verb* **legislated, legislating, legislates**
to write, argue about, and pass laws *–noun* (person) **legislator.**

**legislation** /,lɛdʒɪsˈleɪʃən/ *noun*
**1** an act of making a law: *Congress has approved legislation of a new tax on cigarettes.*
**2** the law itself: *tax legislation*

**legislative** /ˈlɛdʒɪs,leɪtɪv/ *adjective*
related to making laws: *Congress is the legislative branch of the US government.*

**legislature** /ˈlɛdʒɪs,leɪtʃər/ *noun*
a governmental body with the power to make laws for a nation or state

**legitimate** /ləˈdʒɪtəmɪt/ *adjective*
**1** legal, lawful: *He has a legitimate claim to part of the profits.*
**2** honest, genuine: *She runs a legitimate business.*
**3** reasonable: *She has a legitimate concern about her daughter's health.*
**4** born to parents legally married to each other *–noun* **legitimacy;** *–verb* **to legitimize.**

L

**leisure** /'liʒər/ *noun, (no plural)*
relaxation free from work: *They enjoy their leisure at the seashore.*

**leisurely** /'liʒ ərli/ *adjective*
without hurry: *a leisurely bath*

**lemon** /'lɛmən/ *noun*
**1** a sour yellow fruit: *She squeezed some lemon on the fish.*
**2** *informal* a badly made machine that constantly breaks down and needs repair
*–adjective* **lemony.** *See:* art on page 2a.

**lemonade** /ˌlɛmən'eɪd/ *noun*
a drink made of lemon juice, water, and sugar: *We like lemonade on hot days.*

**lend** /lɛnd/ *verb* **lent** /lɛnt/, **lending, lends**
to permit the use of for a period of time, *(synonym)* loan: *Banks lend money to people.*
**to lend a hand:** to help
**to lend an ear:** to listen

**length** /lɛŋkθ/ *noun*
**1** the measurement of something from end to end: *The length of the highway is 100 miles (160 km). See:* width; depth.
**2** the amount of time something takes: *The length of the trip was four hours.*
**at length:** in great detail, over a long time: *The speaker talked at length about his political views.*

**lengthen** /'lɛŋkθən/ *verb*
to become or make longer (in space or time)

**lengthwise** /'lɛŋkθˌwaɪz/ *adverb*
in the direction of the length of something: *We measured the table lengthwise at six feet and across at three.*

**lengthy** /'lɛŋkθi/ *adjective* **lengthier, lengthiest**
long in distance, time, or coverage

**lenient** /'liniənt/ *adjective*
not punishing bad behavior: *That mother is too lenient with her noisy children.*
*–noun* **leniency.**

**lens** /lɛnz/ *noun, plural* **lenses**
a clear curved piece of glass or plastic that makes images smaller or larger: *Cameras and eyeglasses have lenses.*

**leopard** /'lɛpərd/ *noun*
a large member of the cat family, often light brown with black spots

**lesbian** /'lɛzbiən/ *noun*
a female homosexual: *Lesbians are physically and romantically attracted to other women. See:* gay.

**less** /lɛs/ *adjective*
not so much (in amount): *She makes less money at her new job. But she also has to work less.*

**lessen** /'lɛsən/ *verb*
to make less, *(synonym)* to reduce: *The medicine lessened the patient's pain.*

**lesser** /'lɛsər/ *adjective*
*comparative of* less.
not as much: *We ordered a lesser amount of food this month.*

**lesson** /'lɛsən/ *noun*
**1** something to be learned: *She studied the first five lessons in her French book for an exam.*
**2** a class or period of instruction: *Her piano lesson is at 4:00.*

**let** /lɛt/ *verb* **let, letting, lets**
**1** to allow, permit: *I let my dog run free in the yard.*
**2** to rent: *He lives with his family in one of his apartments and lets the other.*
**let alone:** even less: *I can't afford a nice apartment, let alone a house!*
**to let off steam:** to to talk about one's troubles, then to feel better: *She had a bad day at the office and let off steam at home telling her husband about it.*
**to let on:** to tell that one knows something secret: *She learned about the surprise party planned for her but didn't let on that she knew.*
**to let out: a.** to allow to go out: *I let the cat out at night.* **b.** to allow (a sound) to come out, express: *I let out a shout when I hurt my finger.* **c.** (in sewing) to make larger: *The waist in these pants needs to be let out. (antonym)* to take in
**to let someone off:** to set free with little or no punishment: *The judge let the young man off with only a warning not to steal apples again.*
**to let up:** to become less strong or forceful: *The rain is letting up now.*

**lethal** /ˈliθəl/ *adjective*
able to kill

**let's** /lɛts/
*contraction of* let us (used to express a wish or liking): *Let's go out for lunch!*

**letter** /ˈlɛtər/ *noun*
**1** a part of an alphabet: *The letter* B *follows the letter* A.
**2** a written message, usually sent by mail: *She sent a letter to her mother.*

**letter** *verb*
to draw or write letters on

**letter carrier** *noun*
*See:* mail carrier.

**lettuce** /ˈlɛtəs/ *noun*
a leafy salad plant: *I like a salad made with dark green lettuce. See:* art on pge 1a.

**letup** /ˈlɛtˌup/ *noun*
a slowdown, becoming less strong: *It has been raining all day with no letup.*

**leukemia** /luˈkimiə/ *noun*
cancer of the white blood cells, often leading to death

**level** /ˈlɛvəl/ *adjective*
**1** flat, smooth: *We can't put the picnic table here because the ground isn't level.*
**2** at the same height, even: *The building is level with its neighbor.*

**level** *noun*
**1** height, distance from the ground upward: *The land around here is mainly at sea level.*
**2** an amount of something, quantity: *a low level of production||a government official at a very high level*

**to be on the level:** to be honest and sincere: *He is not on the level when he says that he'll be able to pay because he owes everyone money.*

**level** *verb*
to pull down to the ground, flatten: *The town decided to level the old train station and build a new one.*

**to level with someone:** to tell someone what the real situation is, honestly and completely

**lever** /ˈlɛvər/ *noun*
a piece of metal used to push things upwards: *A worker used a steel rod as a lever to lift a rock.* –*noun* **leverage.**

**lexicon** /ˈlɛksəˌkɑn/ *noun*
a dictionary –*adjective* **lexical.**

**liability** / ˈlaɪəˈbɪləti/ *noun*
**1** a legal requirement, such as to pay debts: *Insurance companies had huge liabilities to pay because of the hurricane damage to buildings.*
**2** a disadvantage: *That business has excellent products, but its debt is a big liability. (antonym)* asset.

**liable** /ˈlaɪəbəl/ *adjective*
**1** legally responsible for something
**2** likely (to do or experience): *If you drive in a bad storm, you are liable to have an accident.*

**liar** /ˈlaɪər/ *noun*
a person who doesn't tell the truth

**libel** /ˈlaɪbəl/ *noun, (no plural)*
(in law) a published statement or picture that unfairly damages a person's good name

**liberal** /ˈlɪbərəl/ *adjective*
**1** generous, large: *She puts liberal amounts of food on the table.*
**2** (in politics) proposing change: *The liberal politicians wanted to spend more money on helping poor people.* –*noun* **liberalism;** –*verb* **to liberalize.**

---

**USAGE NOTE:** The two largest political parties in the USA are the *Democrats* and the *Republicans.* Democrats are often called *liberals* and Republicans are often called *conservatives.*

---

**liberal arts** *noun plural*
(in education) study of subjects mainly of a non-scientific type, such as literature, languages and history

**liberty** /ˈlɪbərti/ *noun, plural* **liberties**
**1** freedom from control, especially from governmental laws that make people's lives difficult
**2** freedom from prison, slavery, etc.: *Prisoners gain their liberty after serving their sentences.*

**library** /ˈlaiˌbrɛri/ *noun*
**1** a building where a collection of books and other reference materials is kept: *Public libraries are found all over the USA.*
**2** a collection of books and other refer-

L

ence materials: *The couple has a library of travel books in their house.* –*noun* **librarian.**

**lice** /laɪs/ *noun,*
*plural* of louse, blood-sucking insects: *The child had lice in his hair.*

**license** /ˈlaɪsəns/ *noun*
a permit given by an official organization, usually to someone who passes an examination: *She has a driver's license (hairdresser's license, license as a registered nurse, etc.).*

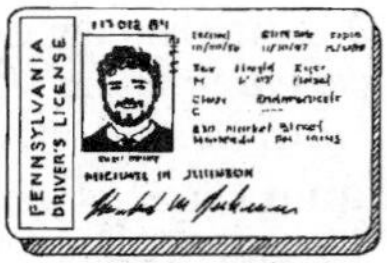

license

**license** *verb*
to give a permit to or for: *This restaurant is licensed to sell beer and wine.*

**licensed practical nurse** *noun*
*abbreviation of* **LPN**
a nurse who has passed an examination and can provide nursing care if supervised by a doctor or registered nurse

**lick** /lɪk/ *verb*
**1** to rub the tongue over: *Children like to lick ice cream cones.*
**2** *slang* to win easily: *The soccer team licked their opponents.*

**lick** *noun*
a stroke of the tongue

**lid** /lɪd/ *noun*
a covering of a container, a top: *I took the lid off the coffee can.*

**lie (1)** /laɪ/ *noun*
a statement that is not true: *His excuse for being late was a lie.*
**a (little) white lie:** a small lie told to save someone's feelings from being hurt

**lie** *verb* **lied, lying, lies**
to tell something that is not true: *He lied when he said he didn't steal.*

**lie (2)** *verb* **lay** /leɪ/, **lain** /leɪn/, **lying, lies**
**1** to rest in a horizontal position: *She lay down on the grass to enjoy the sun.*
**2** to be located: *The river lies near the town.*

**lieutenant** /luˈtɛn ənt/ *noun*
**1** (in the USA) an officer of the lowest military rank
**2** (in many governmental positions) a rank below: *He was elected Lieutenant Governor of Louisiana.*

**life** /laɪf/ *noun, plural* **lives** /laɪvz/
**1** the state of being alive of a plant or animal: *When the doctor arrived, the life had already gone out of the old man.*
**2** living things: *Is there life on other planets?*
**3** one's time from birth to death

**lifeboat** /ˈlaɪfˌbout/ *noun*
a small boat used in emergencies

**lifeguard** /ˈlaɪfˌgɑrd/ *noun*
a person whose job it is to save swimmers from drowning

**life insurance** *noun*
a contract paying money after the death of its owner

**life jacket** *noun*
a piece of equipment worn around the upper body to keep a person above water

life jacket

**life preserver** *noun*
equipment, especially a doughnut-shaped ring, used to keep a person above water

**life raft** *noun*
an air-filled lifeboat

**lifestyle** /ˈlaɪfˌ staɪl/ *noun*
the manner in which one lives

**lifetime** /ˈlaɪfˌt aɪm/ *noun*
the total amount of time of a person's life

**lift** /lɪft/ *verb*
**1** to raise to a higher level: *He lifted his little girl up to his shoulders.*
**2** to remove, end: *The government lifted laws against bringing foreign wheat into our country.*
**3** to go up and disappear: *The clouds lifted in the morning sun.*
**4** *informal* to steal: *Someone lifted my wallet while I was leaving the train station.*

**lift** *noun*
**1** an act of raising to a higher level: *A worker gave the box a lift onto a shelf.*
**2** a raising of feelings to happiness: *The good news gave us all a lift.*

**3** a free ride: *My friend gave me a lift to the store in his car.*

**lift-off** *noun*
the sending up of a space vehicle from Earth: *The space vehicle is scheduled for lift-off at 7:03 A.M.*

**light** /laɪt/ *noun*
**1** *(no plural)* energy from the sun, electric lights, fire, etc., that allows us to see
**2** *(no plural)* sunshine, daylight: *He walked out of the house and into the light.*
**3** something that produces light, such as light bulbs or lamps: *When it is dark, we turn on the lights.*
**4** something that can start a fire, such as a match: *She took out a cigarette and asked her friend for a light.*
**5** a traffic signal: *Turn right at the next light.*
**6** a way of understanding: *He now looks back on his life and sees it in a new light.*
**to make light of:** to treat as if unimportant: *He made light of his illness, but we knew it was serious.*

**light** *verb* **lighted** or **lit** /lɪt/, **lighting, lights**
**1** to set on fire: *We light a fire in the fireplace on cold winter nights.*
**2** to give light to: *At night, we light the sides of the house to keep strangers away.*
**to light up: a.** to brighten, as with happiness: *Her eyes lit up at the good news.* **b.** to make a cigarette burn

**light** *adjective* **lighter, lightest**
**1** having little weight, not heavy: *An empty suitcase is light.*
**2** pale in color, not dark: *She wore a light blue dress.*
**3** not forceful, or strong: *a light rain, a light sleep*
**4** gentle, delicate: *Dancers move with light steps. See:* art on page 23a.

**light bulb** *noun*
the round glass part of an electric light

light bulb

**lighter** /ˈlaɪtər/ *adjective*
*comparative of* light: not as heavy in weight or dark in color as something else: *A feather is lighter than a rock.*||*White is lighter than gray.*

**lighter** *noun*
a device for making cigarettes, cigars burn: *a cigarette lighter*

**lightheaded** *adjective*
feeling faint or dizzy: *The hot weather sometimes makes him feel lightheaded.*

**lighthouse** /ˈlaɪtˌhaʊs/ *noun*
a tall building with a powerful light on top to guide ships

lighthouse

**lighting** /ˈlaɪtɪŋ/ *noun, (no plural)*
**1** the system for producing light in a room or the quality of that light: *The lighting in that restaurant is soft and pleasant.*
**2** starting of a fire: *The lighting of a wood fire begins with small pieces of wood.*

**lightly** /ˈlaɪtli/ *adverb*
gently, softly
**to take something lightly:** to treat with a lack of seriousness or concern: *He took his illness lightly.*

**lightness** /ˈlaɪtnɪs/ *noun*
**1** a small degree of weight or color: *The lightness of the colors in the room made it cheerful.*
**2** lack of seriousness: *The lightness of the conversation pleased everyone.*

**lightning** /ˈlaɪtnɪŋ/ *noun*
a flash of light between clouds in the sky or between sky and earth (especially during a thunderstorm): *The lightning hit the tree and started a fire.*

**lightning rod** *noun*
a device for directing lightning harmlessly into the ground

**likable** /ˈlaɪkəbəl/ *adjective*
(of a person) easy to like, pleasant: *He's a likable boy, always friendly.*

**like** /laɪk/ *verb* **liked, liking, likes**
**1** to enjoy, find pleasant, approve of: *He likes to watch television.*||*I don't like my son's new girlfriend.*
**2** to be attracted to: *The boy and girl like each other very much.*

**would like:** want, desire: *I would like coffee, please.*

**like** *adjective*
**1** similar to: *The girl is like her mother.*
**2** *suffix* **-like** seeming to be, typical of: *homelike, childlike*

**likes and dislikes:** *noun plural* personal preferences: *We all have our likes and dislikes.*

**likelihood** /'laɪkli,hʊd/ *noun*
probability (of something happening): *In all likelihood, it will rain today.*

**likely** /'laɪkli/ *adjective* **likelier, likeliest**
probable, to be expected: *Accidents are likely to happen.*

**likeness** /'laɪknɪs/ *noun*
sameness or similarity: *The daughter has a likeness to her mother.*

**likewise** /'laɪk,waɪz/ *adverb*
**1** in addition, also: *My friend ordered a hamburger, and I did likewise.*
**2** in the same way or manner

L

**liking** /'laɪkɪŋ/ *noun*
fondness, having a taste for: *She has a liking for French perfume.*

**lilac** /'laɪ,læk/ *noun*
a bush or shrub, with white or purple flowers and pleasant smell *See:* art on page 1a.

**lily** /'lɪli/ *noun, plural* **lilies**
a green plant usually with white flowers *See:* art on page 1a.

**lily pad** *noun*
leaf of a water lily

**limb** /lɪm/ *noun*
**1** *formal* an arm, leg, or wing of an animal: *People have four limbs: two arms and two legs.*
**2** a tree branch

**lime** /laɪm/ *noun*
a small green fruit: *He drinks soda with a little lime (juice). See:* art on page 2a.

**limit** /'lɪmɪt/ *noun*
**1** the greatest amount allowed: *The speed limit is 55 MPH on some roads.*
**2** the farthest point of, border: *The limits of the property are marked by a fence.*
**off limits:** where someone is not permitted to go

**limit** *verb*
to keep within limits, restrict: *I limited the amount of candy each child had so they would still be hungry for dinner.* –*adjective* **limiting;** –*noun* **limitation.**

**limo** /'lɪmoʊ/ *noun*
*short for* limousine

**limousine** /,lɪmə'zin/ *noun*
a large, expensive car, usually with a driver

limousine

**limp** /lɪmp/ *adjective* **limper, limpest**
lacking firmness or stiffness: *The flowers are limp from lack of water.*

**limp** *noun*
an uneven walk as from an injury to the leg or foot

**limp** *verb*
to walk with a limp

**line** /laɪn/ *noun*
**1** a long narrow, continuous mark, such as on a piece of paper: *My notebook has thin blue lines printed on each page.*
**2** a stripe: *Two yellow lines painted on a highway mean that drivers should not pass cars ahead of them.*
**3** a row of people or things: *A line of people waited outside the passport office.*
**4** a limit or border: *A sign at the state line said, "Welcome to Florida."*
**5** a rope or cord: *We hang clothes on the line to dry them in the sun.*
**6** a wire: *Power lines carry electricity.*
**7** an electronic connection, such as a telephone line: *Mr. Sanchez is on the line and wants to talk with you.*
**between the lines:** in an indirect way, not written or said openly: *The letter from his mother said that everything was fine at home, but reading between the lines he knew there was a problem.*
**in the line of duty:** while performing one's work, especially as a police officer or firefighter: *A firefighter was injured in the line of duty.*
**on line:** *See:* online.
**to draw the line:** *See:* draw.

**to get in line:** **a.** to join with others in a line: *I got in line and waited to buy my ticket for the movie.* **b.** *figurative* to act in the desired or approved way: *After the teacher punished the student, he got in line and behaved well.*
**to hold the line:** to wait for someone on the telephone: *The bank clerk asked the customer to hold the line while he checked the account.*
**line** *verb* **lined, lining, lines**
**1** to mark lines on
**2** to form a border: *Tall trees line the street.*
**3** to put an inner layer on: *Her fur coat is lined with silk.*
**to line up:** to form a line
**linen** /ˈlɪnən/ *noun adjective*
**1** *(no plural)* cloth made from a soft, strong plant (flax): *She wore a summer dress made of linen.*
**2** a type of cloth product such as bedsheets and tablecloths
**liner** /ˈlaɪnər/ *noun*
**1** a ship or airplane: *an ocean liner*
**2** an inner layer in clothing: *In winter, he puts the wool liner into his coat for warmth. See:* cruise ship.
**lineup** /ˈlaɪnˌʌp/ *noun*
**1** (in sports) a list of players who will play a game: *The starting lineup includes the team's best players.*
**2** *figurative* any listing of people, events, products, etc.: *The fall lineup of television programs (new fashions, social events, etc.) looks interesting.*
**lingerie** /ˌlɑnʒəˈreɪ/ *noun, (no plural)*
women's underwear (bras, slips, panties, and stockings)
**lining** /ˈlaɪnɪŋ/ *noun*
an inner layer, such as in a jacket or coat
**every cloud has a silver lining:** an expression that means that something good can be found in every bad situation: *My car got a new paint job because of the accident; every cloud has a silver lining.*
**link** /lɪŋk/ *noun*
**1** one connection in a series, such as a ring in a chain: *Her bracelet has 25 gold links.*
**2** part of a communication or transport system: *Railroads and buses are links in a transportation system.*
**3** a relationship: *That crime has a link to other crimes committed by the same person.*

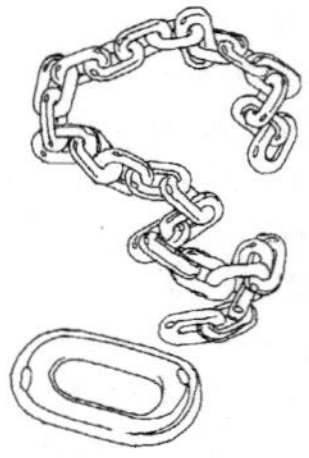
link

**link** *verb*
to connect: *Workers linked the railroad cars together.*
**to link something up:** to put together, connect
**linoleum** /lɪˈnoʊliəm/ *noun, (no plural)*
a smooth, strong floor covering: *We have linoleum on our kitchen floor.*
**lion** /ˈlaɪən/ *noun*
a large member of the cat family, found mainly in Africa *See:* art on page 14a.
**lip** /lɪp/ *noun*
**1** one of two outer parts of the human mouth: *Your lips form an "o" when you say the word "food."*
**2** the top edge of something: *There is a gold line around the lip of the teacup.*
**3** *suffix* **-lipped:** having lips as described: *She was white-lipped with fear.*
**lipstick** /ˈlɪpˌstɪk/ *noun*
a coloring that women put on their lips
**liquefy** or **liquify** /ˈlɪkwəˌfaɪ/ *verb* **liquefied, liquefying, liquefies**
to change into liquid form: *Ice liquefies into water as it melts.*
**liquid** /ˈlɪkwɪd/ *noun*
the substance that is neither a gas nor a solid: *Water is a liquid that covers most of the earth.*
**liquid** *adjective*
neither solid nor gas: *When it is frozen, water is no longer liquid.*
**liquor** /ˈlɪkər/ *noun*
a strong alcoholic drink: *Vodka, whiskey, and scotch are types of liquor.*
**list** /lɪst/ *noun*
a series of items written in a downward row: *I made a list of things to buy at the store: milk, cheese, chicken, and bread.*

**list** *verb*
to make a list of

**listen** /ˈlɪsən/ *verb*
**1** to hear, sense with the ears: *I like to listen to birds sing in the trees.*
**2** to pay attention to and follow: *I listened to the advice of my friend.*

**to listen in (on something):** **a.** to listen to: *She listens in on the private conversations of others.* **b.** to listen, such as to a radio program

**to listen up:** to pay attention: *Listen up, children! See:* hear.

---

**USAGE NOTE:** We *hear* (passively) because we have ears, and we *listen* (actively) when we focus our attention on something: *I was listening to the radio, so I didn't hear you come in.*

---

**listener** /ˈlɪsənər/ *noun*
a member of an audience, such as for a radio program



**listing** /ˈlɪstɪŋ/ *noun*
**1** a list of items: *I made a listing of the new clothes that I need.*
**2** an advertisement

**list price** *noun*
the regular price of an item: *The list price was $100, but I got it for $80.*

**lite** /laɪt/ *adjective slang*
a nonstandard spelling of **light** used mainly in advertising low-calorie food products: *lite beer, lite yogurt*

**liter** /ˈlitər/ *noun* or *British* **litre**
a liquid measure equal to 33.824 ounces or 1.057 quarts

**literacy** /ˈlɪtərəsi/ *noun, (no plural)*
the ability to read and write: *The literacy level in that country is high.*

**literal** /ˈlɪtərəl/ *adjective*
keeping to the exact meaning of a word or words: *We translate the French "S'il vous plaît" as "Please," but a literal translation would be "If it pleases you."*

**literally** /ˈlɪtərəli/ *adverb*
according to the exact words: *I know he told you to get lost, but he didn't mean it literally; he just wanted you not to bother him.*

**literate** /ˈlɪtərɪt/ *adjective*
**1** able to read and write: *He couldn't read the sign because he isn't literate.*
**2** well-educated: *She is a very literate woman. See:* illiterate.

**literature** /ˈlɪtərəʧər/ *noun, (no plural)*
**1** written works, such as novels, poems, and plays
**2** written information about a specific field: *The current literature on medicine is highly technical. –adjective* **literary.**

**litre** /ˈlitər/
*British See:* liter.

**litter** /ˈlɪtər/ *noun*
**1** *(no plural)* pieces of unwanted things (trash) on the ground: *Empty bottles, newspapers, and other litter lay on the sidewalks.*
**2** a group of animals born together: *Our dog had a litter of four puppies.*

litter

**litter** *verb*
to drop unwanted things on the ground: *People littered the park with bottles.*

**little** /ˈlɪtl/ *adjective*
**1** small in size: *Little children played in the school yard.*
**2** small in amount: *He gets little pay for the work he does.*
**3** young or younger: *their little boy, her little brother*
**4** unimportant: *She leaves the little decisions to her assistants. See:* few.

**little** *adverb* **less** /lɛs/, **least** /list/
**1** not much: *He cared little about his job.*
**2** not at all: *Little did I know what trouble lay ahead.*
**3** to some degree: *I was a little angry.*

**little** *pronoun*
**1** a small amount: *She has little to do.*
**2** a short distance or time: *I moved my chair a little to the left.*

**Little League** *noun*
a group of children's baseball teams supported by local families and businesses

**livable** /ˈlɪvəbəl/ *adjective*
satisfactory, comfortable enough to be lived in

**live** /lɪv/ *verb* **lived, living, lives**
**1** to have life, be or stay alive, exist: *He is badly hurt, but the doctors say he'll live.*
**2** to have one's home located (in a place): *She lives in Boston.*
**3** to lead one's life in a certain way: *to live dangerously*
**to live and let live:** to not criticize or oppose others just because they are different from you
**to live on something: a.** to have as one's only means of support: *She can't live on her salary.* **b.** *figurative* to continue to live: *After her death, she lived on in our hearts.*

**live** /laɪv/ *adjective*
**1** living, alive: *The science teacher brought a live snake to class.*
**2** able to explode: *live bullets (ammunition)*
**3** (of a performance) viewed or heard by an audience as it happens, not recorded earlier

**live-in** /ˈlɪvˌɪn/ *adjective*
living in the house where one works: *a live-in maid*

**livelihood** /ˈlaɪvliˌhʊd/ *noun*
way of earning money to live: *He makes his livelihood as a waiter.*

**lively** /ˈlaɪvli/ *adjective*
quick and full of energy

**liver** /ˈlɪvər/ *noun*
**1** the organ in the body that helps in making sugar for energy and cleaning the blood
**2** this organ from certain animals as a food: *cow's liver, chicken livers*

**livestock** /ˈlaɪvˌstɑk/ *noun*
farm animals, such as cattle, sheep, and chickens

**living** /ˈlɪvɪŋ/ *noun, (no plural)*
**1** *singular* way of making money to live on: *He earns his living as a cook.*
**2** the getting of things necessary for life, such as food and housing: *the high cost of living*||*a rising standard of living*

**living** *adjective*
alive: *Who is the world's greatest living artist?*

**living room** *noun*
the room in a home where people sit, often to talk, read, or entertain *See:* art on page 8a.

**lizard** /ˈlɪzərd/ *noun*
a type of animal (reptile) with four legs and a long tail: *The chameleon, which changes colors, is a type of lizard. See:* art on page 14a.

**llama** /ˈlɑmə/ *noun*
a South American animal, like a small camel, used to carry loads

llama

**load** /loʊd/ *noun*
**1** an amount to be carried, lifted, etc.: *Trucks can carry heavy loads of materials.*
**2** an amount of work, responsibility, etc.: *That department has a heavy load of work.*

**load** *verb*
**1** to put a load into or on: *Workers loaded the truck with sand.*
**2** to put bullets into a gun or film into a camera: *Soldiers loaded their guns.*
**3** to put into position: *She loaded new software onto the computer.*
**to load (someone** or **something) up: a.** to fill (with goods to be moved): *The driver loaded up his truck and left.* **b.** to give too much work: *The boss loaded her up with extra work. –adjective* **loading.**

**loaf** /loʊf/ *noun, plural* **loaves** /loʊvz/
an amount of baked bread: *We buy loaves of bread at the bakery.*

**loaf** *verb*
**1** to spend time in a carefree way: *During vacation we loafed at the beach.*
**2** to waste time instead of work: *He loafs on the job by talking all day.*

**loafer** /ˈloʊfər/ *noun informal*
**1** a person who avoids work: *She is a loafer who works as little as she can.*
**2** *trademark* for a type of shoe with no strings (laces): *Loafers are comfortable footwear. See:* art on page 12a.

**loan** /loʊn/ *noun*
**1** a sum of money borrowed at a rate of interest: *I applied at the bank for a loan at 7% interest.*
**2** the act of lending something: *I thanked him for the loan of his car.*
**loan** *verb*
to lend: *I loaned my car to a friend for the weekend.*

**lobby** /ˈlɑbi/ *noun, plural* **lobbies**
**1** an entrance area to a building
**2** a person or group working to influence people (especially politicians)
**lobby**
—*verb* **lobbied, lobbying, lobbies**
to try to influence someone in power (especially politicians) to support one's interests and needs: *All major industries lobby for favor in the nation's capital.* –*noun* (person) **lobbyist.**

**lobster** /ˈlɑbstər/ *noun*
an ocean animal with large claws and a hard shell that lives on the ocean bottom

L

**local** /ˈloʊkəl/ *adjective*
located nearby, as in your neighborhood, town, or area: *We have plenty of local stores to choose from.*
**local** *noun*
a train or bus that makes all stops: *That train is a local.*

**locate** /ˈloʊˌkeɪt/ *verb* **located, locating, locates**
**1** to find the location of: *The student located Moscow, Paris, and London on a map.*
**2** to be placed: *The company's new office building is located outside the city.*

**location** /loʊˈke ɪʃən/ *noun*
**1** the place where something is located: *The location of the capital is in the center of the state.*
**2** a piece of property: *We moved our offices to a new location in the city.*

**lock** /lɑk/ *noun*
**1** a device for preventing a door, suitcase, etc., from being opened except with a key: *After the robbery, we changed the locks on our doors.*
**2** an area in a waterway where the water level can be raised and lowered so that ships can pass through it: *They opened the gates to the next lock in the canal.*
**lock** *verb*
to close with a lock: *I locked my apartment door before leaving for work.*
**to lock (someone** or **something) up: a.** to close and lock a house, office, store, etc.: *I was the last to leave the warehouse, so I locked up.* **b.** to put someone in jail

**locker** /ˈlɑkər/ *noun*
a storage container, such as one in a row of metal cabinets used for keeping work clothes, athletic equipment, etc. *See:* art on page 8a.

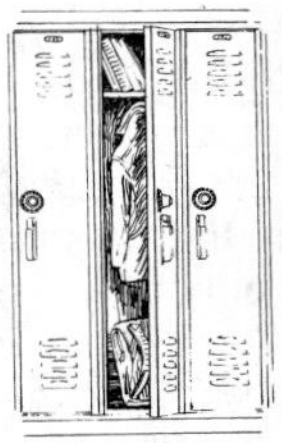
locker

**locksmith** /ˈlɑkˌsmɪθ/ *noun*
someone who puts in and repairs locks

**locomotive** /ˌloʊkəˈmoʊtɪv/ *noun*
a large railroad vehicle with an engine

**locust** /ˈloʊkəst/ *noun*
an insect of the grasshopper family flying in large groups and destroying crops

**lodge** /lɑʤ/ *noun*
a cabin or other small country house
**lodge** *verb* **lodged, lodging, lodges**
to present formally or officially: *A dissatisfied customer lodged a complaint.*

**lodger** /ˈlɑʤər/ *noun*
a paying guest, especially of a house where people rent rooms –*noun* (place) **lodging.**

**loft** /lɔft/ *noun*
**1** an open work area or part of one in a factory: *Many lofts in New York have been changed to artists' apartments.*
**2** a platform above a main floor, such as a sleeping loft in an apartment: *A narrow staircase leads to a loft with a bed.*
**loft** *verb*
to send or be sent into the air: *The football lofted into the air.* –*adjective* **lofty.**

**log** /lɔg/ *noun*
**1** a large piece of a tree that has fallen or been cut down: *The man cut trees into logs with a saw.*
**2** a journal or other record of information: *He keeps a log of all the work he does each day.*

**log** *verb* **logged, logging, logs**
**1** to cut trees into logs: *He logs trees for a big paper company.*
**2** to enter into a written record: *The captain logs (in) the name of each soldier as he arrives at camp.*
**to log on to something:** to enter into a computer system: *I logged on to an information service that helped me with my report.*

**logic** /ˈlɑʤɪk/ *noun*
a system of reasoning: *She uses logic—not emotion—in all her decisions.*

**logical** /ˈlɑʤəkəl/ *adjective*
**1** using a system of reasoning: *She has a very logical mind.*
**2** showing good sense, reasonable: *It is logical to want to save money.*

**lollipop** /ˈlɑli ˌpɑp/ *noun*
a ball or flat round piece of hard candy on a stick: *Children enjoy lollipops.*

**lone** /loʊn/ *adjective*
only, by oneself or by itself: *He was the lone person to discover the secret.*||*a lone wolf*

**loneliness** /ˈloʊnlinɪs/ *noun, (no plural)*
a condition of being alone and feeling sad

**lonely** /ˈloʊnli/ *adjective* **lonelier, loneliest**
**1** alone and feeling sad: *Without friends, he felt lonely in a new city.*
**2** empty of people, deserted

**lonesome** /ˈloʊnsəm/ *adjective*
feeling sad and in need of a friend

**long** /lɔŋ/ *adjective* **longer, longest**
**1** having a certain length: *The table is six feet long, or about two meters long.*
**2** lasting a certain amount of time: *Our conversation was only five minutes long.*
**3** having great distance: *It is a long way from New York to Hong Kong.*
**4** lasting a great amount of time: *The Senator made a long speech on taxes.*
**in the long run:** over many months or years: *The economy is weak now, but in the long run it will improve.*
**long** *adverb*
(for) a long time: *Have you been waiting long?*
**as** or **so long as:** if, provided that, on condition that: *So long as it does not rain, we can go fishing.*
**So long:** *informal* Good-bye: *So long for now! See you tomorrow!*
**long** *noun*
(in clothes) a length and cut for a tall person: *In suits, he wears a long.*
**before long:** soon, shortly: *Clouds appeared, and before long it began to rain.*
**long** *verb*
to want very much: *She longs to take a vacation.*

**long ago** *adverb*
in the distant past: *Long ago, people believed the earth was flat.*

**long-distance** *adjective*
between distant places: *I had to make many long-distance (telephone) calls when I was far away from home.*

**longer** /ˈlɔŋgər/ *adjective*
*comparative of* long
**no longer** or **not any longer:** not now, not anymore: *He no longer works there; he retired.*||*I won't wait any longer; I'm leaving.*

**longhand** /ˈlɔŋˌhænd/ *noun, (no plural)*
ordinary writing by hand: *She writes letters in longhand to her friends.*

**longitude** /ˈlɔnʤəˌtud/ *noun*
the distance from an imaginary line called the Prime Meridian, which runs north and south from pole to pole and divides the earth's surface into east and west *–adjective* **longitudinal.** *See:* latitude.

**look** /lʊk/ *verb*
**1** to use one's eyes to see: *Look! There's a beautiful bird in that tree.*
**2** to look very closely at, *(synonym)* to examine: *I stood and looked at the painting for a long time.*
**3** to appear, seem to be: *She looked tired after the race.*
**4** to face, have a view of: *These windows look south.*
**It looks like** or **It looks as if:** it seems probable that: *It looks like (it's going to) snow.*
**to look after someone** or **something:** to take care of someone or something: *She stayed home to look after the baby.*

**to look ahead:** to think about and plan for the future: *She's got a good job now and looks ahead to a bright future.*

**to look around (something): a.** to examine an area: *Getting off the train, he looked around to see if his friends were there.* **b. something:** to consider a number of choices, especially before buying something: *We looked around at many houses before we found this one.*

**to look forward to something:** to be eager for something enjoyable in the future: *I'm looking forward to my vacation next month.*

**to look into something:** to try to find the truth about something: *The police looked into the crime and solved it.*

**to look on:** to stand by and watch: *A crowd looked on as two men fought.*

**to look on** or **upon someone** or **something:** to think of or consider someone or something: *She looks on him as the brother she never had.*

**to look out (for someone** or **something): a.** to be careful: *Look out! You'll fall!* **b.** to be careful about someone or something dangerous: *Look out for that car!* **c.** to care for or protect someone or something: *A mother needs to look out for her children when they play outside.*

**to look out on** or **over something:** to face or have a view of something: *Our apartment looks out on a park.*

**to look over something:** to examine something: *We looked over the contract before signing it.*

**to look (someone** or **something) up:** to try to find something in a dictionary or other reference: *Look up the number in the telephone book.*

**to look up to someone:** to respect or admire someone

**look** *noun*

**1** an act of looking: *The girl gave a look in my direction.*

**2** an appearance: *That lady has a fashionable look.*

**3** a facial expression, especially one used to communicate a feeling: *He gave me an angry look.*

**4** *plural* **looks:** one's general appearance, especially a good one: *That actor is known more for his looks than for his acting.*

**loom** /lum/ *verb*

to appear large and dangerous: *We saw the storm looming in the distance.*

**loom** *noun*

a frame or machine used to weave cloth and rugs

loom

**loon** /lun/ *noun*

a water bird with a laugh-like cry: *I could hear the loons late at night.*

**loop** /lup/ *noun*

a shape in the form of a circle made by a line, string, wire, etc.: *The cowboy threw a loop of his rope over the horse's neck.*

**loop** *verb*

to make a loop (in, over, or with): *The cowboy looped his rope over the cow's horns.*

**loophole** /ˈlupˌhoʊl/ *noun figurative*

a way out (of an agreement), especially a fault in a law that allows people to avoid following it: *There is a loophole in the new tax law that allows the rich not to pay higher taxes.*

**loose** /lus/ *adjective* **looser, loosest**

**1** not firmly fixed or attached: *A button came loose and fell off my jacket.*

**2** escaped, free: *The farmer's horse got loose, and he had to catch it.*

**3** not tight-fitting: *She wears loose clothing in summer.*

**4** careless, too relaxed: *The bookkeeping (attendance, discipline, etc.) in that company is loose.* –*noun* **looseness.**

**loose-leaf** *adjective*

containing individual sheets of paper that can usually be removed or replaced: *Students keep their notes in a loose-leaf binder. See:* art on page 8a.

**loosen** /ˈlusən/ *verb*

to make or become less tight or firm: *A worker loosened the screws on the TV and opened the back of it.*

**loot** /lut/ *verb*

to rob, steal from: *People looted stores during the riot.* –*noun* **lost.**

L

**lord** /lɔrd/ *noun*
a man of high rank in society: *She reads books about English lords and their ladies.*
**the Lord:** in Christianity. a term for God or Jesus Christ: *O Lord, hear my prayer.*

**lose** /luz/ *verb* **lost** /lɔst/, **losing, loses**
**1** to become unable to find: *He lost his keys.*
**2** to fail to win: (in a competition or war): *Our team lost the basketball game.*
**3** to have something valuable taken away: *Because of the storm, they lost time (their ship, their lives, etc.).*
**4** to be unable to keep, no longer control (one's balance, patience, etc.): *She lost her temper and began shouting.*
**5** to have less of: *lose weight, lose interest in something*
**6** to escape from (someone who is following): *The thief managed to lose the police in the crowded street.*
**7** to fail to make someone understand: *I'm afraid you've lost me; would you repeat the instructions?*

**loser** /ˈluzər/ *noun*
a person or team that has lost a competition: *Our team was the loser in the volleyball game.*

**loss** /lɔs/ *noun, plural* **losses**
**1** a failure to win: *Our team has a record of five wins and two losses.*
**2** an amount of money that is lost or taken away: *She suffered a large loss when the price of her house went down.*
**3** the fact of losing someone or something valued, especially because of a death: *The loss of his mother caused him great pain.*
**to be at a loss for words:** to not know what to say: *When she learned she had won a big prize, she was at a loss for words and could only smile.*

**lost** /lɔst/ *verb*
*past tense and participle of* lose
**lost** *adjective*
**1** unable to be found, misplaced: *His keys are lost.*
**2** not knowing where one is located: *The lost child asked a police officer for help.*
**3** killed or destroyed: *Several sailors were lost at sea in the storm.*
**Get lost!:** angry request for others to leave: *Get lost and stop annoying me!*

**lot** /lɑt/ *noun*
**1** a piece of land: *We own a small lot next to our house.*
**2** *(no plural)* one's condition in life: *It was his lot to become priest.*
**3** *informal* **a lot (of)** or **lots (of):** a large amount or number: *I like her a lot.*‖*He has lots of money, problems, etc.*

**lotion** /ˈloʊʃən/ *noun*
a liquid used to clean, soften, or protect skin: *People use sunscreen lotion to protect against sunburn.*

**lottery** /ˈlɑtəri/ *noun, plural* **lotteries**
a game of chance in which people buy tickets with numbers and the winner is the one whose numbers match the numbers picked by the lottery organizer: *Many states have a lottery to raise money.*

**lotto** /ˈlɑtoʊ/ *noun*
a lottery: *I play lotto once a week.*

**loud** /laʊd/ *adjective* **louder, loudest**
having a strong sound, noisy: *The sound of city traffic is loud.* –*noun* **loudness.**

**loudspeaker** /ˈlaʊdˌspikər/ *noun*
a device for making sound louder: *Loudspeakers in the train station announce departures and arrivals. See:* art on page 8a.

**lounge** /laʊndʒ/ *noun*
a place with seats where people can wait
**(cocktail) lounge:** a barroom often with comfortable seats and tables: *We met in the lounge for a drink before dinner.*
**lounge** *verb* **lounged, lounging, lounges**
to rest in a relaxed position: *We lounged on the beach.*

**louse** /laʊs/ *noun, plural* **lice** /laɪs/
a bloodsucking insect that lives on people and animals

**lousy** /ˈlaʊzi/ *adjective slang*
awful, no good: *That repair shop did a lousy job of fixing my car.*

**lovable** /ˈlʌvəbəl/ *adjective*
easy to love: *a lovable child*

**love** /lʌv/ *verb* **loved, loving, loves**
**1** to like with great feeling: *I love my wife with all my heart.*
**2** to enjoy very much, find very pleas-

ing: *He loves to play golf, but his wife loves gardening.*

**love** *noun*

**1** *(no plural)* very strong liking for someone: *She shows her love for her children every day.*

**2** strong enjoyment or pleasure: *a love of music*

**3** a lovable person: *That little boy is such a love!*

**to fall** or **be in love (with someone):** to begin to feel or to have a strong attraction to someone: *He fell in love with her the moment he saw her; it was love at first sight. (antonym)* hate.

**lovely** /ˈlʌvli/ *adjective* **lovelier, loveliest**

**1** attractive, pretty: *The girl on the magazine cover is lovely.*

**2** pleasant, delightful: *We had a lovely time at the wedding.* *–noun* **loveliness.**

**loving** /ˈlʌvɪŋ/ *adjective*

having or showing love: *The children's mother is a loving woman.*

**low** /loʊ/ *adjective* **lower, lowest**

**1** below something else in level: *The land is low in this area; it is near sea level.*

**2** near the floor or ground: *Those flowers grow low to the ground.*

**3** (of a sound) quiet or deep: *They spoke in low voices so as not to disturb anyone.*

**4** morally bad, dishonest: *He stole from his friend, and that was a low thing to do.*

**5** sad, depressed: *She is feeling low about the death of her father.*

**to be low on something:** to have only a little of something left: *We were low on gas, so we drove into a gas station.*

**low** *adverb*

**1** in, at, or to a lower position or level: *She scored low on the test.*

**2** near the floor or ground: *He bent low to pick up the child.*

**low** *noun*

a low level: *Winter temperatures there reach extreme lows. (antonym)* high.

**lower** /ˈloʊər/ *adjective*

*comparative of* low

**lower** *verb*

**1** to let down to a level nearer to the ground: *A sailor lowered a rope over the side of the ship.*

**2** to make less in amount or degree: *The salesman lowered the price of the car.*

**lowercase** /ˈloʊərˌkeɪs/ *adjective*

in small rather than capital letters: *This sentence is in lowercase letters, except for the capital "T" of "This."*

**loyal** /ˈlɔɪəl/ *adjective*

faithful to others, especially one's friends or country: *He is a loyal soldier.*

**loyalty** /ˈlɔɪəlti/ *noun, plural* **loyalties**

faithfulness, a strong feeling of support: *The loyalty of dogs to their owners is well-known.*

**LPN** /ˈɛlpiˈɛn/ *noun*

*See:* licensed practical nurse.

**lubricant** /ˈlubrəkənt/ *noun*

oil, grease, or other substance used to smooth surfaces that rub against each other: *Oil is used as a lubricant in engines.* *–verb* **to lubricate.**

**luck** /lʌk/ *noun, (no plural)*

**1** something that happens by accident, not by control, *(synonyms)* chance, fortune: *She had good luck in finding a new job quickly.*

**2** good fortune, success: *He wished me luck.*

**in** or **out of luck:** to have or not have good fortune: *You're in luck today; there's a new job opening.*

**to luck out:** *informal* to have good fortune: *These shoes are usually expensive, but I lucked out and bought them on sale.*

**lucky** /ˈlʌki/ *adjective* **luckier, luckiest**

having or bringing good luck, fortunate: *He was lucky not to hurt himself when he fell.||Seven is my lucky number.*

luggage

**luggage** /ˈlʌgɪʤ/ *noun, (no plural)*

suitcases and bags used to carry clothes while traveling, *(synonym)* baggage:

*We checked our luggage in at the airport ticket counter.*

**lullaby** /ˈlʌləˌbaɪ/ *noun, plural* **lullabies**
a quiet song to help a child to sleep: *She sings sweet lullabies to her baby at bedtime.*

**lumber** /ˈlʌmbər/ *noun, (no plural)*
wood cut to different lengths and sizes for building houses, furniture, etc.: *I bought some lumber at the lumberyard to make bookshelves.*

**lumber** *verb*
**1** to cut trees for lumber: *People lumber for a living in the Pacific Northwest.*
**2** to walk or run in an awkward, heavy way: *He lumbered up the steps with a heavy suitcase in each hand.* –*noun* **lumbering.**

**lumberjack** /ˈlʌmbərˌʤæk/ *noun*
a person who cuts down trees or transports them: *His father was a Canadian lumberjack.*

**lump** /lʌmp/ *noun*
**1** a round mass: *An artist shaped a lump of clay into a pot.*
**2** a hard growth: *She felt a lump in her chest and called the doctor.*
**3** a small block of sugar: *One lump or two in your coffee?*
**a lump sum:** an amount of money paid at one time: *We paid for the car in a lump sum: $25,000.* –*adjective* **lumpy.**

**lunch** /lʌnʧ/ *noun,* **lunches**
the meal eaten at noon time between breakfast and dinner: *I have just a sandwich for lunch.*

**lunch** *verb formal*
to have lunch: *We lunched at a nice restaurant today.*

---

**USAGE NOTE:** Most workers in the USA have only 30 minutes to one hour for *lunch*, so they usually eat a small, informal meal, often just a sandwich. Typically, people eat lunch any time between noon and 2:00 P.M. *Dinner,* usually the big meal of the day, is served between 6:00 and 7:30 P.M. in most American homes.

---

**lunch counter** *noun*
a restaurant counter where one sits for quick service: *We sat at the lunch counter today rather than at a table.*

**luncheon** /ˈlʌnʧən/ *noun formal*
lunch

**luncheonette** /ˌlʌnʧəˈnɛt/ *noun*
a restaurant that serves inexpensive meals

**lunchroom** /ˈlʌnʧˌrum/ *noun*
an area in a business or school where employees or students can eat: *We had lunch in the company lunchroom today.*

**lung** /lʌŋ/ *noun*
one of two breathing organs in the chest that supply oxygen to the blood: *Her lungs are in bad condition from smoking.*

**lunge** /lʌnʤ/ *verb* **lunged, lunging, lunges**
to move forward with sudden force: *She lunged at the basketball and stole it from the opposing player.* –*noun* **lunge.**

**luscious** /ˈlʌʃəs/ *adjective*
juicy and delicious: *Ripe pears have a luscious taste.*

**lush** /lʌʃ/ *adjective*
(of plants) having thick, healthy growth: *The garden is lush with new spring growth.*

**luster** /ˈlʌstər/ *noun, (no plural)*
**1** a shine, such as bright polish on a surface: *The luster of wax made the table shine.*
**2** a special quality: *Wonderful costumes added luster to the performance of the opera.* –*adjective* **lustrous.**

**luxury** /ˈlʌgʒəri/ *noun, plural* **luxuries**
**1** *(no plural)* great comfort at great expense: *That family lives in luxury, enjoying costly clothes, high-priced cars, and a beautiful house.*
**2** something pleasant that is expensive and not a necessity: *We can't afford luxuries, such as overseas vacations.* –*adjective* **luxurious.**

**lying** /ˈlaɪɪŋ/ *verb*
*present participle of* lie

**lying** *noun*
saying something that is not true: *His lying will get him into trouble someday.*

**lynch** /lɪntʃ/ *verb*
(of a crowd) to attack and hang someone accused of a crime, without any legal process: *Cowboys lynched the cattle thief after they caught him.*

**lyrics** /ˈlɪrɪks/ *noun plural*
the words of a song: *The lyrics to that song are funny.* *–noun* (writer) **lyricist.**

L

# M, m

**M, m** /ɛm/ *noun* **M's, m's** or **Ms, ms**
the 13th letter of the English alphabet

**M.A.** /ˌɛm'eɪ/
*abbreviation of* Master of Arts, the advanced university degree: *He has an M.A. in English literature. See:* B.A.

**ma'am** /mæm/ *noun*
*short for* madam: *Yes, ma'am. How would you like to pay for this? Cash or credit card?*

**macaroni** /ˌmækə'rouni/ *noun, (no plural)*
a type of food (pasta) made from wheat flour in the shape of small tubes *See:* spaghetti, USAGE NOTE.

**machete** /mə'ʃɛti/ *noun*
a long knife

**machine** /mə'ʃin/ *noun*
a device made of separate parts that uses power to do work: *A car is a machine used for transportation.* –*noun* (worker) **machinist.**

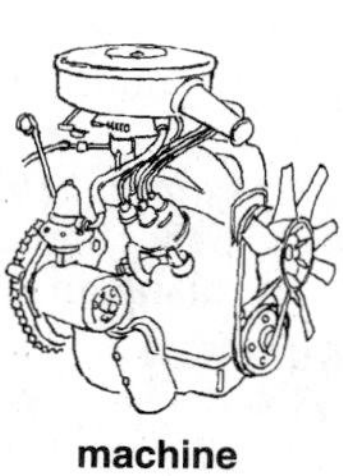
**machine**

**machine gun** *noun*
a weapon that fires many bullets fast

**machinery** /mə'ʃinəri/ *noun, (no plural)*
machines as a group: *Machinery in that factory is used to make cotton fabric.*

**machismo** /mɑ'tʃizmoʊ/ *noun, (no plural)*
an attitude or behavior that values male strength and courage: *He believes in machismo and acts like a big man.*

**macho** /'mɑtʃoʊ/ *adjective*
strong, tough, virile (said of men): *He tried to act macho to hide his fear.*

**mad** /mæd/ *adjective* **madder, maddest**
**1** angry, upset: *She was mad when her boyfriend was late without calling her. (antonym)* happy.
**2** liking something very much: *He is mad about fast cars.*
**3** crazy, *(synonym)* insane: *He went mad when his wife died. (antonym)* sane.

**madam** /'mædəm/ also **ma'am** /mæm/ *noun*
a polite way to speak to a woman: *The store clerk said, "Madam, how may I help you?"*

**made** /meɪd/
*adjective and past participle of* make

**madly** /'mædli/ *adverb*
totally, completely against all reason: *He is madly in love with her.*

**madman** /'mædˌmæn/ *noun, plural* **madmen** /-ˌmɛn/
a crazy, dangerous person: *A madman is loose in the city.* –*noun* **madwoman.**

**madness** /'mædnɪs/ *noun, (no plural)*
**1** a serious mental illness, *(synonym)* insanity: *In his madness, he thought he was the President.*
**2** a foolish, crazy idea: *It was madness to drive in that bad snowstorm.*

**Mafia** /'mɑfiə/ *noun*
a violent, criminal organization most active in Italy and the USA: *The Mafia*

*controls the sale of illegal drugs in some places.*

**magazine** /ˌmægəˈzin/ *noun*
a small weekly, or monthly, publication that usually includes news, stories, and photos: *We read* Time *magazine.*

**magic** /ˈmæʤɪk/ *noun, (no plural)*
**1** the use of forces outside the laws of nature to make something happen: *The old woman used magic to change the girl into a bird.*
**2** the use of tricks to entertain people: *That magician uses magic to pull rabbits out of a hat.||He does magic tricks. –adjective* **magical.**

**magician** /məˈʤɪʃən/ *noun*
a person who does magic tricks

**magistrate** /ˈmæʤəˌstreɪt/ *noun*
a low-level government official

**magnet** /ˈmægnɪt/ *noun*
a metal object that attracts iron and steel: *I have a magnet on my desk that holds paper clips. –verb* **to magnetize;** *–adjective* **magnetic** /mægˈnɛtɪk/.

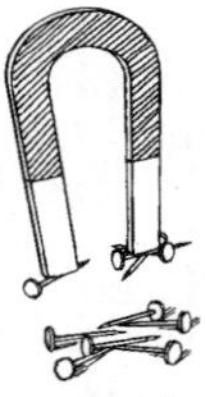
magnet

**magnetism** /ˈmægnəˌtɪzəm/ *noun, (no plural)*
the study of magnets and their forces

**magnification** /ˌmægnəfəˈkeɪʃən/ *noun*
the power to make something appear larger: *With the magnification on the copy machine, you can make a document larger than its original size.*

**magnificent** /mægˈnɪfəsənt/ *adjective*
very beautiful or impressive: *The Taj Mahal in India is a magnificent building. –noun* **magnificence.**

**magnify** /ˈmægnəˌfaɪ/ *verb* **magnified, magnifying, magnifies**
to make something look larger: *His eyeglasses magnify words so he can read them.*

**magnifying glass** *noun*
a curved piece of clear glass or plastic used to make images or objects look larger

magnifying glass

**magnitude** /ˈmægnəˌtud/ *noun, (no plural)*
**1** the size or importance of something: *You don't seem to understand the magnitude of the problem.*
**2** (in science) the degree of brightness of a star or force of an earthquake

**maid** /meɪd/ *noun*
a female cleaning woman: *Maids clean the rooms in hotels.*

**maiden name** *noun*
a woman's family name before she marries: *Mrs. Silveri's maiden name was Rodriguez.*

**mail** /meɪl/ *noun, (no plural)*
**1** letters, packages, etc., sent through the postal system: *The mail arrives at noon every day except Sunday.*
**2** the postal system: *I put letters into the mail every evening.*

**mail** *verb*
to send by mail: *I mailed a package to my friend in Seattle. See:* electronic mail.

**mailbox** /ˈmeɪlˌbɑks/ *noun, plural* **mailboxes**
**1** large blue metal box on the street in which people put mail: *She dropped a letter into the mailbox.*
**2** a metal box into which mail carriers put people's mail *See:* art on page 4a.

**mail carrier** *noun*
a person who delivers mail: *Our mail carrier arrives around 10:00 A.M. See:* letter carrier; mailman.

mail carrier

**mailman** /ˈmeɪlˌmæn/ *noun, plural* **mailmen** /-ˌmɛn/
a male letter carrier *See:* letter carrier.

**mail order** *noun*
the system of selling products by mail: *She shops for clothes by mail order.*

**main** /meɪn/ *adjective*
central, most important: *Our teacher talked about the main idea of the story.*

**main clause** *noun*
the main clause in a sentence is a group of words with a subject, verb, and often

an object that can stand by itself as a sentence: *In the following sentence, the main clause goes from "the" to "over": When we arrived, the party was almost over.*

**mainframe** /'meɪn, freɪm/ *noun*
a powerful, central computer

**mainland** /'meɪn,lænd/ *noun, (no plural)*
land on one of the seven great land areas (continents) of the world, not including islands: *mainland* (or) *mainland China*

**mainly** /'meɪnli/ *adverb*
usually, mostly: *Farmers plant seeds mainly in the spring.*

**mainstream** /'meɪn,strim/ *noun*
the group of ideas accepted by most people, the most popular way of thinking: *Her ideas are in the mainstream of American political thought.*

**mainstream** *verb*
to mix a person into a main group: *Some non-native students take bilingual classes and are mainstreamed into regular classes later.*

**maintain** /meɪn'teɪn/ *verb*
**1** to keep in good condition: *People maintain their houses well in this neighborhood.*
**2** to keep something going, continue: *She maintains a friendship with her friend who lives in another state.*

**maintenance** /'meɪntənəns/ *noun, (no plural)*
keeping something in good condition, such as by cleaning, painting, and fixing it: *maintenance of a building*

**majestic** /mə'ʤɛstɪk/ *adjective*
**1** causing admiration: *The Rocky Mountains in the western United States are majestic. (antonym)* small.
**2** proud, dignified: *The Queen acts in a majestic manner. –adverb* **majestically.**

**majesty** /'mæʤəsti/ *noun, plural* **majesties**
**1** a title for a king or queen and the power connected to the position: *Her Majesty the Queen will visit a hospital today.*
**2** impressive appearance because of size, beauty, etc.: *The majesty of the Alps mountains in Switzerland takes people's breath away.*

**major** /'meɪʤər / *adjective*
main, most important: *The major reason for working is to make money to live. (antonym)* minor.

**major** *noun*
**1** a military rank above captain and below colonel: *She is a major in the Air Force.*
**2** one's main subject of study in college: *My major is Spanish literature.*

**major** *verb*
to study as one's major field in college: *He majored in economics at the university.*

**majority** /mə'ʤɔrəti/ *noun*
more than half, but not all of something

**Major League** *noun*
(in baseball) the highest-level organization of teams in professional baseball: *He plays baseball in the major league. –adjective* **major-league.**

**make** /meɪk/ *verb* **made** /meɪd/ **, making, makes**
**1** to build, create: *Our company makes computers.*
**2** to do, perform: *Nobody likes to make mistakes.||A doctor made a cut in the patient's stomach.*
**3** to earn money: *She makes a good salary (living, income) as an accountant.||That company makes a big profit.*
**4** to cook, prepare: *He made chicken with rice for dinner.*
**5** to choose someone for a particular job: *The boss made her sales manager.*
**6** to pass laws: *Congress makes the laws of the country.*
**7** to force, order someone to do something: *Her mother made her brush her teeth.*
**8** to cause something to happen: *You're making me nervous.*

**to make a big deal of something:** to make something seem more important than it is

**to make believe:** to pretend that something is true: *The father makes believe that he is a dog and tells his children stories in a funny voice.*

M

**to make do:** to live or work at a minimum level: *When I started my business, I made do with old equipment until I had enough money to buy new things.*
**to make ends meet:** to have enough money to pay one's bills, but with little left over: *She makes ends meet by working two jobs.*
**to make fun of someone:** to laugh at in an unkind way: *The other students made fun of the old-fashioned way she dressed.*
**to make it:** **a.** to succeed: *She owns a good business and has made it* (or) *made it big in life.* **b.** to attend a particular event: *I'm sorry I couldn't make it to your party on Saturday.*
**to make out:** **a.** to see something and recognize it: *The sailors could not make out the shore through the fog.* **b.** to result in something, succeed: *A woman had a job interview and later her husband asked how she made out.* **c.** to kiss and hug: *A couple was making out on a park bench.*
**to make sense:** to be reasonable, logical: *His explanation doesn't make sense.*
**to make something up:** to lie
**to make up:** to agree to be friends again: *The couple had a fight, but then kissed and made up.*

**make** *noun*
the name of the company that made a particular product: *What make is your car?* *–noun* (person) **maker.**

**make-believe** *noun, (no plural)*
not real, pretend: *He said the story wasn't true; it was just make-believe.*

**makeup** /ˈmeɪkˌʌp/ *noun*
lipstick, face powder, etc., especially used by women and actors, *(synonym)* cosmetics

**malaria** /məˈlɛriə/ *noun, (no plural)*
a jungle disease carried by a type of mosquito, that causes weakness, fever, etc.: *Malaria is still a dangerous disease in some parts of the world.*

**male** /meɪl/ *noun*
a human, animal or insect that carries the seed to make babies: *Human males are fully grown by 18 years of age.* *–adjective* **male.**

**mall** /mɔl/ *noun*
a building or group of buildings with connected hallways with shops, restaurants, theaters, etc.: *We can shop at many different stores at the mall.*

mall

**malnutrition** /ˌmælnuˈtrɪʃən/ *noun, (no plural)*
a sick condition caused by lack of food: *Malnutrition is common in some poor countries.* *–adjective* **malnourished.**

**malpractice** /mælˈpræktɪs/ *noun, (no plural)*
wrong treatment by a professional, especially a doctor: *The doctor was taken to court (sued) for malpractice after the patient died.*

**mama** or **mamma** /ˈmɑmə/ *noun informal*
mother: *Mama, would you please hold my hand to cross the street?*

**mammal** /ˈmæməl/ *noun*
a type of animal. Female mammals produce milk which they feed to their young: *Whales, horses, mice, and humans are all mammals.* *–adjective* **mammalian** /məˈmeɪliən/.

**man** /mæn/ *noun, plural* **men** /mɛn/
**1** the adult male of the human species: *Who was that handsome man you were dancing with?*
**2** people in general: *Man lives in almost all parts of the earth.* *See:* USAGE NOTE below and at mankind.
**3** *slang exclamation of* surprise, admiration, or anger: *Man! It's cold outside today!*||*Man! She can really sing!*

**man** *verb* **manned, manning, mans**
to operate something (guns, machinery): *Soldiers man guns and shoot at the enemy.*

---

**USAGE NOTE:** Many people don't like the use of *man* for all people because it does not include women; they prefer to use the term *humanity.*

---

**manage** /'mænɪʤ/ *verb* **managed, managing, manages**
**1** to direct the business of an organization: *She manages a legal department in a large company.*
**2** to struggle but succeed at doing something: *He managed to carry the heavy box into the house by himself.*

**manageable** /'mænɪʤəbəl/ *adjective* able to be done: *Work is difficult, but manageable.* *–noun* **manageability.**

**management** /'mænɪʤmənt/ *noun*
**1** the art and science of directing an organization, especially in business
**2** the people who are in control in an organization: *Management met with the workers to discuss salary increases.*

**manager** /'mænɪʤər/ *noun* a person who runs a business on a day-to-day basis: *Two customers complained to the manager of the restaurant about the waiter.* *–adjective* **managerial.**

**mandatory** /'mændə,tɔri/ *adjective* required, necessary by law

**maneuver** /mə'nuv ər/ *noun* a movement made in a particular direction: *The pilot turned the airplane to the west in a maneuver to get back on course.* *–verb* **to maneuver.**

**maniac** /'meɪni,æk/ *noun* an insane person; a wild, dangerous person *–adjective* **maniacal** /mə'naɪəkəl/.

**manicure** /'mænɪ,kyʊr/ *noun* a treatment to make fingernails and hands beautiful: *My wife had a manicure at the beauty salon.* *–noun* (person) **manicurist;** *–verb* **to manicure.**

**manipulate** /mə'nɪpyə,leɪt/ *verb* **manipulated, manipulating, manipulates**
**1** to change the position of something: *A worker manipulates the handles of a machine to turn it in different directions.*
**2** to influence someone or something secretly, especially for one's own advantage: *He manipulated the price of wheat so he could buy it cheaply.* *–noun* **manipulation;** *–adjective* **manipulative.**

**mankind** /,mæn'kaɪnd/ *noun, (no plural)* humanity, people in general: *Mankind has existed for thousands of years.* *See:* man, **2.**

---

**USAGE NOTE:** Many people consider the use of *mankind* (meaning all people) to be unfair to women because it has only the word *man* in it; a more general term is *humankind* or *humanity.*

---

**manly** /'mænli/ *adjective* **manlier, manliest** having characteristics, such as strength and courage, that are traditionally associated with men

**man-made** *adjective* not natural, *(synonym)* artificial: *Plastic is a man-made substance.*

**manner** /'mænər/ *noun*
**1** behavior, a way of acting: *Some children have good (or bad) manners.*
**2** *singular* a type of action, a way of doing something: *"Hit the ball in this manner," said the tennis coach as she showed her student how to do it.*

**all manner of:** all kinds of: *There was all manner of food at the party.*

**mannerism** /'mænə,rɪzəm/ *noun* a particular motion of the body, such as a facial expression, etc., that someone often uses: *One of his mannerisms is waving his hands when he talks.*

**mansion** /'mænʃən/ *noun* a large, expensive house with land

**manual** /'mænyuəl/ *noun* a small book that explains how to do something, especially how to use a machine: *The manual for my computer shows how to set it up and program it.*||*a driver's manual*

**manual** *adjective* done using the hands rather than by machine *–adverb* **manually.**

**manufacture** /,mænyə'fækʧər/ *verb* **manufactured, manufacturing, manufactures** to make something for sale, usually using machinery: *Our company manufactures furniture.*

**manufacture** *noun, (no plural)* the act of making products using machinery: *The manufacture of that type of gun is illegal now.* *–noun* (person or business) **manufacturer, manufacturing.**

**manure** /mə'nʊr/ *noun, (no plural)*
animal waste that is put on fields to make plants grow bigger

**manuscript** /'mæn yəˌskrɪpt/ *noun*
a handwritten or typed document before it is printed: *The author's book manuscript was written on a typewriter.*

**many** /'mɛni/ *adjective* **more** /mɔr/, **most** /moʊst/
related to a lot of something: *Many people attended the concert.*
**a good** or **great many:** a lot of: *A good many people should exercise more.*
**how many:** used to ask about the number of something: *How many books do you have?||How many do you have?*

**many** *noun*
*singular used with a plural verb* used with *of,* a large number of something: *Many of us eat too much sugar.*

**many** *pronoun*
a large number of something: *When the babies heard a loud noise, many began to cry.||How many cried? (antonym)* few.

**map** /mæp/ *noun*
a picture of locations, such as countries, cities, towns, mountains, rivers and flat lands with roads: *We looked at a map to find the best roads to Chicago. –verb* **to map.** *See:* art on page 8a.

map

**maple** /'meɪpəl/ *noun*
a tall shade tree that produces a sugary liquid *See:* art on page 1a.

**marathon** /'mærəˌθɑn/ *noun*
**1** a foot race of over 26 miles (42.9 km): *Thousands of runners come to the Boston Marathon every April.*
**2** any event or test that lasts a long time: *an all-night marathon meeting –noun* (runner) **marathoner.**

**marble** /'mɑrbəl/ *noun*
**1** *(no plural)* a type of stone that is cut and polished for use in floors, walls, statues, etc.
**2** *plural* **marbles:** a game children play by rolling small balls of marble or glass on the floor: *When it rains, the children stay in and play marbles.*

**march** /mɑrʧ/ *verb* **marches**
**1** to step in a formal way, such as soldiers or musical band members in a parade: *My high school band marched in a parade.*
**2** to progress, move ahead: *The seasons march on. See:* walk, USAGE NOTE.

**march** *noun, plural* **marches**
**1** a military piece of music with a happy beat: *The band played marches that cheered everyone up.*
**2** a trip made on foot by soldiers: *Soldiers made a long march from their camp to the mountains. –noun* (person) **marcher.**

**March** /mɑrʧ/ *noun*
the third month of the year, between February and April

**Mardi Gras** /'mɑrdiˌgrɑ/ *noun*
the Tuesday before the beginning of Lent and a time of public celebration in many countries: *Mardi Gras in New Orleans is a big party with dancing, music, and fun.*

**mare** /mɛr/ *noun*
a female horse or donkey

**margarine** /'mɑrʤərɪn/ *noun, (no plural)*
a food that looks like butter made from vegetable oils

**margin** /'mɑrʤɪn/ *noun*
**1** the side border of a printed page: *The margins on a newspaper are blank.*
**2** the degree or amount more than what is needed: *She won by a margin of 5,000 votes. –adjective* **marginal.**

**marijuana** /ˌmærə'wɑnə/ *noun, (no plural)*
an illegal drug that is smoked, *(synonym)* pot

**marine** /mə'rin/ *adjective*
related to the ocean and ships: *She studied marine science in high school.*

**Marine Corps** *noun*
US military trained to fight on land and sea *–noun* (person) **marine** or **Marine.**

**marital** /'mærətl/ *adjective*
related to marriage: *"What is your marital status?" "I am single."*

**mark** /mɑrk/ *noun*
**1** a stain or spot: *There is a mark on the wall where I hit it with a ball.*
**2** a grade, such as on an examination or for a course: *She got high marks in high school.*
**3** a symbol, a sign of high status: *Young people stand up as older people enter the room as a mark of respect.*
**4** something one aims at: *He shot an arrow and it hit the mark.*
**to be off the mark** or **to miss the mark:** wrong, inaccurate: *The weather reporter missed the mark when she said it would rain today, because it's sunny!*
**mark** *verb*
**1** to make a spot or stain: *The broken plate marked the floor where it broke.*
**2** to show a specific place: *I marked the page you should read with a piece of paper.*
**3** to write down, note: *He marked the price on a piece of paper.*
**4** to correct homework or examinations: *The teacher marked the students' exams.*
**5** to celebrate: *The USA marks its independence from Britain with Fourth of July celebrations.*

**market** /ˈmɑrkɪt/ *noun*
**1** a place or store that sells things *See:* art page 10a.
**2** the combination of makers, sellers, and buyers of a product or service on a local, national, or international level: *There is a good market for healthy foods these days.*
**market** *verb*
to offer goods and services for sale: *That company markets meat in the New York area.* *–noun* (business) **marketer.**

**marketplace** /ˈmɑrkɪtˌpleɪs/ *noun*
**1** an open area in a city or town for selling products, especially food: *The marketplace is in the center of the city.*
**2** the combination of all makers, sellers, and buyers of a product or service

**marmalade** /ˈmɑrməˌleɪd/ *noun, (no plural)*
a fruit mixture that is put on bread, rolls, etc.: *orange marmalade*

**maroon (1)** /məˈrun/ *adjective noun*
a dark purplish red: *He wears a maroon baseball cap.*

**maroon (2)** *verb*
to leave someone in a distant place with little or no hope of escape: *Our ship sunk and we were marooned on an island.*

**marriage** /ˈmærɪʤ/ *noun*
**1** a legal union of a man and woman: *The couple enjoyed a long and happy marriage.*
**2** a wedding: *My sister had a private marriage with only a small ceremony.*

**marry** /ˈmæri/ *verb* **married, marrying, marries**
**1** to join each other in marriage: *Jane and Joe were married last Saturday.*
**2** to perform the ceremony that joins two people in marriage: *They were married by a minister.* *–adjective* **married.** *(antonym)* unmarried.

**Mars** /mɑrz/ *noun*
the fourth planet from the sun, between Earth and Jupiter

**marsh** /mɑrʃ/ *noun, plural* **marshes**
a low, wet area of land: *Marshes have ponds where ducks build nests and feed.* *–noun* (area) **marshland;** *–adjective* **marshy.**

**marshal** /ˈmɑrʃəl/ *noun*
a type of police officer, especially an officer of the US government: *A US marshal arrested a criminal.*

**marshmallow** /ˈmɑrʃˌmɛloʊ/ *noun*
a soft, white candy made of sugar: *We cooked marshmallows over a fire.*

**Martin Luther King Day**
*See:* nonviolence, USAGE NOTE.

**martyr** /ˈmɑrtər/ *noun*
a person who dies for a cause and whose death encourages others to continue it: *Martin Luther King, Jr. is a martyr who died for the advancement of blacks in America.* *–verb* **to martyr;** *–noun* (act) **martyrdom.**

**marvelous** /ˈmɑrvələs/ *adjective*
wonderful, excellent: *We had a marvelous time on vacation.*

**masculine** /ˈmæskyəlɪn/ *adjective*
**1** related to male qualities: *That actor has a very masculine image in his films.*
**2** related to the male gender of nouns in

M

some languages: *The words for "work" in French and Spanish are masculine:* le travail *and* el trabajo. *(antonym)* feminine.

**mash** /mæʃ/ *verb* **mashes**
to crush into a mass: *She mashed bananas to feed to her baby.*||*mashed potatoes* –*noun* **mash.**

**mask** /mæsk/ *noun*
a covering for the face used especially to hide one's identity or for a ceremony: *Skiers use masks to keep their faces warm in the cold.*

**mask** *verb*
to hide one's face: *Robbers masked themselves to avoid being identified. See:* art on page 11a.

**masquerade** /ˌmæskəˈreɪd/ *noun adjective*
a party or dance where people wear costumes and masks

masquerade

**masquerade** *verb* **masqueraded, masquerading, masquerades**
to pretend to be someone else: *He masquerades as a big businessman, but he really isn't one.*

**mass** /mæs/ *noun, plural* **masses**
**1** a group of people, things, etc.: *A mass of people were in the town center for the concert.*
**2** a shapeless amount of matter: *A mass of rock fell down the mountain.*
**3** the amount of matter of an object: *Spaceships have no weight in space but do have mass and could cause damage if they hit each other.*

**mass** *verb* **masses**
to come together in a mass: *Hundreds of people massed in front of the ball park.*

**massacre** /ˈmæsəkər/ *verb* **massacred, massacring, massacres**
to kill many people or animals in a cruel way: *Hunters massacred elephants to get ivory (from their tusks).* –*noun* **massacre.**

**massage** /məˈsɑʒ/ *noun*
the act of rubbing and moving the muscles of the body for relaxation and relief of pain: *He gave me a relaxing massage for half an hour.* –*verb* **to massage.**

**massive** /ˈmæsɪv/ *adjective*
huge, great: *A massive amount of information is available now with computers.*

**mass media** *noun, (no plural)*
*used with a singular or plural verb* television, radio, and large city newspapers used to communicate with people daily

**master** /ˈmæstər/ *noun*
**1** a person who has control over people or animals: *The dog's master ordered it to lie down.*
**2** a skilled person: *He is a master at the game of tennis.* –*adjective* **masterful.**

**master** *verb*
to learn how to do something well: *He finally mastered typing.*

**master of ceremonies** *noun*
a person who introduces others, especially entertainers at a public event

**masterpiece** /ˈmæstərˌpis/ *noun*
one of the best works of art, music, literature, etc.: *The painting* Mona Lisa *by Leonardo da Vinci is considered a masterpiece.*

**master's** or **master's degree** *noun*
*abbreviation:* **M.A.** a college degree above a Bachelor's and below a Ph.D.: *Her master's degree is in literature. See:* B.A., M.A., USAGE NOTE.

**mat** /mæt/ *noun*
a piece of material with many uses, such as under plates on tables, in front of doors, on floors, etc.: *We wipe our feet on the mat in front of our door to remove dirt from our shoes.*

**mat** *verb* **matted, matting, mats**
to press down and together: *The rain matted the dog's hair.*

**match** /mætʃ/ *noun, plural* **matches**
**1** a competition: *We played a tennis match and then watched a soccer match on TV.*
**2** people or things that go well together: *There is a nice match between the color of his suit and his tie.*||*Jack and my sister are a good match; they have many interests in common.*
**3** a small stick used to light fires: *He struck a match to light the candle.*

**match** *verb* **matches**
to be similar to something else: *One of his socks is blue and the other is brown; they don't match.*

**matchbook**
/ˈmætʃˌbʊk/ *noun*
a piece of thick paper (cardboard) covering a set of matches: *Businesses advertise their products on matchbook covers.*

matchbook

**mate** /meɪt/ *noun*
**1** one of a pair of animals: *The male bird found food for its mate.*
**2** a husband or wife: *The old woman's mate died last week.*
**3** either of a matched pair: *I lost the mate to my glove.*

**-mate:** *suffix* friend, companion, usually with other words: *roommate, classmate, housemate*

**mate** *verb* **mated, mating, mates**
to become a pair to produce babies (said about animals): *Animals mate in the springtime.*

**material** /məˈtɪriəl/ *noun*
**1** cloth, fabric: *Her suit is made out of fine wool material.*
**2** any physical substance, such as rock, wood, glass, plastic, etc. used to make something: *Building materials include wood, bricks, and pipes.*
**3** tools and supplies: *Art materials include paint, brushes, and paper.*
**4** information in many forms that can be used, such as for a book or a speech: *Our teacher put together material for a textbook.*

**material** *adjective*
related to the physical, not the spiritual

**maternity** /məˈtɜrnəti/ *adjective noun*
related to the condition of producing and caring for a baby: *She took three months' maternity leave from work to take care of her baby.* –*adjective* **maternal.**

**math** /mæθ/ *noun*
*short for* mathematics

**mathematics** /ˌmæθəˈmætɪks/ *noun*
*plural used with a singular verb* the study of numbers, symbols, and forms that follow strict rules and laws: *Mathematics is a difficult area of study.* –*adjective* **mathematical;** –*adverb* **mathematically;** –*noun* (person) **mathematician.**

**matrimony** /ˈmætrəˌmoʊni/ *noun, (no plural)*
the state of marriage: *Religions see matrimony as a relationship blessed by God.* –*adjective* **matrimonial.**

**matter** /ˈmætər/ *noun*
**1** subject of interest or concern: *We met to discuss business matters.*
**2** problem or difficulty (used with *the*): *What's the matter?*‖*There is nothing the matter.*
**3** a general word for the physical substances that make up the world: *Air, water, rocks, and trees are all forms of matter.*

**a matter of:** **a.** an unknown but small amount: *The train arrives in a matter of minutes.* **b.** a decision, a situation: *It's a matter of whether you want to get home early or late.*

**as a matter of fact:** actually, in reality: *As a matter of fact, I do speak Spanish.*

**matter** *verb*
to be of importance: *What you think matters.*

**mattress** /ˈmætrɪs/ *noun, plural* **mattresses**
a rectangular pad of wool, cotton, etc., to put on a bed for sleeping

**mature** /məˈtʃʊr/ *verb* **matured, maturing, matures**
to grow to full size and full mental abilities: *Human babies mature slowly.*

**mature** *adjective*
**1** adult, fully grown: *There are tall mature trees on each side of our street.*
**2** capable of doing what is right, responsible: *Mature teenagers can be excellent babysitters for small children. (antonym)* young.

**maturity** /məˈtʃʊrəti/ *noun, (no plural)*
the state of being fully grown, adulthood: *Some people say girls reach maturity earlier than boys do. (antonym)* youth.

**maximum** /ˈmæksəməm/ *noun adjective* the most of something: *Race cars run at the maximum* (or) *maximum speed.* *(antonym)* minimum.

**may** /meɪ/ **might** /maɪt/ or **may have, may** *auxiliary verb used with other verbs without the infinitive "to"*
**1** expressing possibility of something happening: *I may go to the movies tonight if I'm not too tired.*
**2** asking or giving permission: *May I go to the movies?||You may go to the movies, but you have to wash the dishes first.*

**may as well:** having no reason not to do something: *We may as well go home, this party is so boring. See:* can, might, modal auxiliary.

---

**USAGE NOTE:** *May* is used with the base form of another verb: *I may go away for the weekend.||You may leave when you finish your work.*

---

**May** /meɪ/ *noun* the fifth month of the year, between April and June



**maybe** /meɪbi/ *adverb* possibly, perhaps: *Maybe it will rain today.||Maybe I will go to the movies tonight.*

**Mayflower** /ˈmeɪˌflaʊər/ *noun* the name of a ship that brought British people to North America in 1620

**mayonnaise** /ˈmeɪəˌneɪz/ *noun, (no plural)* a sauce made of eggs, oil, and lemon juice

**mayor** /ˈmeɪər/ *noun* the elected head of a city's government

**maze** /meɪz/ *noun* a system of passages designed to confuse people or animals as they move through it

maze

**MD** /ˈɛmˈdi/ *abbreviation of* Doctor of Medicine:*Jerry Christopher, MD*

**me** /mi/ *pronoun* the object form of *I*: *The teacher praised me for my speech.*

**meadow** /ˈmɛdoʊ/ *noun* land with grass and few trees

**meal** /mil/ *noun* a daily time for eating, known as breakfast, lunch, supper, or dinner, or all the food served at such a time

**mealtime** /ˈmilˌtaɪm/ *noun* a time when meals are eaten

**mean** /min/ *verb* **meant** /mɛnt/, **meaning** /ˈminɪŋ/, **means**
**1** to have a purpose, to intend to say: *That red light means to stop your car and wait for the train to go by.||What does this word mean?*
**2** to intend to do, want to do something: *I meant to call home, but forgot to do it.*

**mean** *noun* a number in the middle between two groups of numbers: *The age of students in our class ranges from 18 to 30; the mean age is 24.*

**mean** *adjective* unkind, wanting to hurt someone *(antonym)* kind.

**meaning** /ˈminɪŋ/ *noun* the idea that a word, sentence, sign, etc. is expressing: *Can you tell me the meaning of that sentence? –adjective* **meaningful.**

**means** /minz/ *noun plural*
**1** wealth and influence: *They are a family of means in this town.*
**2** the skill, tools, money, etc., necessary to do something: *Our company has the means to develop new products.*

**by all means:** **a.** definitely, absolutely: *By all means, I would like to see you this evening!* **b.** using everything and everyone available to get something done: *Citizens of the town put out the fire by all means available.*

**measles** /ˈmizəlz/ *noun used with a singular verb* a disease caused by a virus that can be given to others. It causes red spots on the body.

**measure** /ˈmɛʒər/ *verb* **measured, measuring, measures** to find the size,

measure

weight, speed, etc., of something: *I measured the size of the floor for a new rug.*
**to measure up to something:** to meet standards: *The new student's work measures up to the level of the other students.*
**measure** *noun*
**1** finding the size, weight, speed, etc., of something: *The measure of the floor is 15' by 20' (approx. 4.6 m x 6.1 m).*
**2** an amount of something: *a ten-pound (approx. 4.5 kilos) measure of grass seed*
**3** an action taken for a particular purpose: *The city took measures to make the park safer at night.* –*adjective* **measurable.**

**measurement** /ˈmɛʒərmənt/ *noun*
a calculation of the size, weight, speed, etc., of something: *A tailor took the man's measurements for a new suit.*

**meat** /mit/ *noun*
**1** the muscle and flesh of animals: *We often eat meat, either chicken or lamb.*
**2** *figurative* something important, meaningful: *Our meetings were not just talk; there was some meat to them.* –*adjective* **meaty.**

**meatball** /ˈmitˌbɔl/ *noun*
a small ball of chopped beef: *spaghetti and meatballs*

**Mecca** /ˈmɛkə/ *noun*
**1** a city in western Saudi Arabia considered the most holy city to Muslims
**2** *figurative* a place that attracts people

**mechanic** /məˈkænɪk/ *noun*
a person who repairs and maintains machinery: *car mechanic*

**mechanical** /məˈkænɪkəl/ *adjective*
related to machines and systems: *The air conditioner stopped because of a mechanical problem.* –*adverb* **mechanically.**

**mechanism** /ˈmɛkəˌnɪzəm/ *noun*
parts of a machine that move and perform a function: *A lock has a mechanism that opens and closes.* –*verb* **to mechanize.**

medal

**medal** /ˈmɛdl/ *noun*
an award shaped in a circle: *Olympic athletes can win gold, silver, or bronze medals.* –*noun* (person) **medalist.**

**media** /ˈmidiə/ *noun*
*used with a singular or plural verb* used with *the* to mean the combination of television, radio, news magazines, and large newspapers

**medic** /ˈmɛdɪk/ *noun*
a person trained to give emergency medical help to the sick or injured until they can see a doctor

**Medicaid** /ˈmɛdɪˌkeɪd/ *noun, (no plural)*
in the USA, a health-care program for poor people paid for by the government

**medical** /ˈmɛdɪkəl/ *adjective*
related to medicine: *a medical emergency* –*adverb* **medically.**

**Medicare** /ˈmɛdɪˌkɛr/ *noun, (no plural)*
in the USA, a public health care program for people 65 years old or older that is paid for by the government

**medication** /ˌmɛdɪˈkeɪʃən/ *noun*
drugs, such as pills, shots, etc., used to treat or cure an illness: *He has to take medication for high blood pressure twice a day.* –*verb* **to medicate.**



**medicine** /ˈmɛdəsən/ *noun, (no plural)*
**1** the art and science of curing sick people and preventing disease: *Modern medicine can now cure many diseases that used to kill people.*
**2** substances used to treat illnesses, *(synonym)* medication: *She gave her baby cough medicine.* –*adjective* **medicinal.**

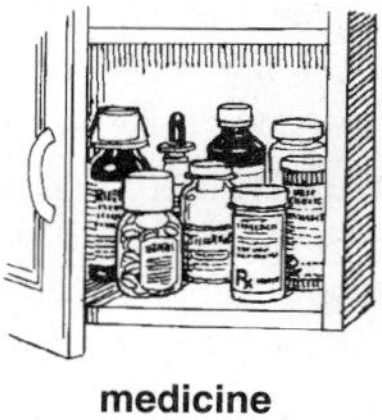
medicine

**medieval** /ˌmid ˈivəl/ *adjective*
related to the Middle Ages: *Medieval times lasted about 1,000 years, from about 476 to 1450 A.D.*

**mediocre** /ˌm idiˈoʊkər/ *adjective*
not good or bad, inferior –*noun* **mediocrity** /ˌmidiˈɑkrəti/. *(antonym)* excellent.

**medium** /ˈmidiəm/ *adjective*
average-sized: *He wears medium-sized sweaters.*

**meet** /mit/ *verb* **met** /mɛt/, **meeting, meets**
**1** to see someone you know without planning to do so: *On the street, I met an*

*old friend whom I had not seen in over 20 years.*
**2** to plan to see someone at a certain time or place: *I will meet you tonight at your place at eight (8:00 P.M.).*
**3** to wait for and greet someone: *I met my friends at the airport and took them to their hotel.*
**4** to join, come together: *Two highways meet near the town.*
**5** to be introduced to someone for the first time: *I would like you to meet my friend Kim.*
**6** to reach a desired goal: *Our company met its sales goal for the year.*
**7** to satisfy: *Governments try to meet the needs of their people for law and order.* *(antonym)* to part.

**meet** *noun*
a sports competition: *Our college had a running (track) meet with another college.*

**meeting** /'mitɪŋ/ *noun*
a gathering of two or more people for a specific purpose: *Our department holds a meeting every Monday morning.*

M

**megabyte** /'mɛgə,baɪt/ *noun*
a unit of computer memory of about one million bytes: *That computer has a hard disk memory of 500 megabytes. See:* gigabyte; kilobyte; megs.

**megs** /mɛgz/ *noun plural*
*short for* megabytes: *My computer has 800 megs of memory. See:* megabytes; kilobytes.

**melancholy** /'mɛlən,kɑli/ *adjective*
very sad: *Listening to the sad music on a rainy day made her feel melancholy.* –*noun* **melancholy.**

**mellow** /'mɛloʊ/ *adjective*
smooth and pleasing: *Some coffees have a mellow taste.*||*mellow music*

**melodic** /mə'lɑdɪk/ *adjective*
having melody, pleasant: *The violin music they played was melodic.*

**melodious** /mə'loʊdiəs/ *adjective*
pleasing to the ear: *The folk singer had a melodious voice.*

**melodrama** /'mɛlə,drɑmə/ *noun*
a story of strong emotion usually about love, danger, and death: *We saw a melodrama on TV where war separates a couple forever.* –*adjective* **melodramatic.**

**melody** /'mɛlədi/ *noun, plural* **melodies**
a song or other piece of music: *He played some of his old favorite melodies on the piano.*

**melon** /'mɛlən/ *noun*
a sweet, juicy, thick-skinned fruit (such as cantaloupe, honeydew, or watermelon) *See:* art on page 3a.

**melt** /mɛlt/ *verb*
**1** to change from a solid to liquid state: *Ice melts to water quickly in warm weather.*
**2** *figurative* to feel warmth and love: *He melts when he sees a beautiful baby.* *(antonym)* freeze.

**melting pot** *noun*
**1** a container in which metals are melted
**2** *figurative* a place in which immigrants mix into the main culture: *New York City is called a melting pot where people from all over the world live together.*

**member** /'mɛmbər/ *noun*
a person who belongs to an organization, club, family, etc.: *She is a member of a tennis club.*

**membership** /'mɛmbər,ʃɪp/ *noun*
**1** the state of being a member: *My membership in the health club ends next month.*
**2** all members of a group: *The membership of a health club includes both men and women.*

**memo** /'mɛmoʊ/ *noun, plural* **memos**
*short for* memorandum

**memorable** /' mɛmərəbəl/ *adjective*
unforgettable, worth remembering: *We took some memorable vacations in Alaska in the past.*

**memorandum** /,mɛmə'rændəm/ *noun, plural* **memorandums** or **memoranda** /-də/
a written note used inside a company to inform others, ask for information, etc., *(synonym)* memo: *I sent my boss a memorandum to inform her of the situation and ask for her suggestions.*

**memorial** /mə'mɔriəl/ *noun*
**1** a statue, building, etc. built in memory of the dead: *The Lincoln Memorial in Washington, D.C., has a big statue of President Abraham Lincoln.*
**2** a service held to remember the dead

memorial

**Memorial Day** *noun*
in the USA, a national holiday on the last Monday in May in memory of people killed in wars

**memorize** /'mɛmə,raɪz/ *verb* **memorized, memorizing, memorizes**
to study something in order to remember it exactly: *Students memorize the verb forms of a new language.*

**memory** /'mɛməri/ *noun, plural* **memories**
**1** the ability of the brain to remember: *He has an excellent memory for faces.*
**2** past event that you remember: *She has pleasant memories of her vacations.*
**3** the capacity of a computer to hold information: *My computer has a four gigabyte memory.*

**men** /mɛn/ *noun*
*plural of* man

**menace** /'mɛnɪs/ *verb* **menaced, menacing, menaces**
**1** to threaten someone with harm: *A thief menaced the store owner with a gun.*
**2** to put in danger, be harmful: *Heavy rainstorms menace the farmers' crops.* *–noun* **menace.**

**mend** /mɛnd/ *verb*
to fix, repair, such as holes in fences or clothes: *He mended a hole in his sock with a needle and thread. (antonym)* tear.
**to mend one's ways:** to show better behavior, improve: *After she failed the math exam, she mended her ways and studied more.*

**menopause** /'mɛnə,pɔz/ *noun, (no plural)*
the time when women around ages 45 to 50 can no longer have babies: *She went through menopause recently.*

**men's room** *noun*
a public toilet for men: *After the movie, he went to the men's room.*

**USAGE NOTE:** *Men's room* is a polite term for *restroom,* a bathroom in a public place. *Bathroom* and *toilet* are considered less polite terms.

**menstruation** /,mɛnstru'eɪʃən/ *noun, (no plural)*
in females, the bleeding that occurs every month: *Menstruation begins in many girls at the age of 11 or 12. See:* period. *–verb* **to menstruate;** *–adjective* **menstrual.**

**mental** /'mɛntl/ *adjective*
related to the mind: *He's old, but his mental abilities are still strong. –adverb* **mentally.** *(antonym)* physical.

**mentality** /mɛn'tæləti/ *noun, plural* **mentalities**
a way of thinking, attitude toward life or a situation: *He's 30 years old, but has the mentality of a teenager.*

**mention** /'mɛnʃən/ *verb*
to say or write something briefly or informally: *I mentioned to my friend that he needs a haircut.*
**Don't mention it.:** You're welcome; it's no trouble: *He thanked her for her help and she said, "Don't mention it."*

**menu** /'mɛnyu/ *noun, plural* **menus**
**1** a list of foods available in a restaurant: *We read the menu and chose a main dish.*
**2** (in computers) a display of operations or files: *I chose a file from the main menu. See:* art on page 5a.

**meow** /mi'aʊ/ *noun*
a sound made by a cat *–verb* **to meow.**

**merchandise** or **merchandize** /'mɜrʧən,daɪz/ *noun, (no plural)*
items, goods for sale, such as clothes, furniture, etc.: *That department store has a large selection of merchandise for sale.*

**merchandise** or **merchandize** *verb* /'mɜrʧən,daɪz/ **merchandised, merchandising, merchandises**
to buy, display, advertise, and sell goods at retail: *Department stores merchandise*

*clothes by advertising them in newspapers.* –*noun* (activity) **merchandising,** (business or businessperson) **merchant.**

**merciful** /'mɜrs ɪfəl/ *adjective*
showing kindness: *He suffered so much pain from cancer that his death was merciful.* –*adverb* **mercifully.**

**merciless** /'mɜr sɪlɪs/ *adjective*
cruel, without pity: *The cat was merciless, playing with the mouse until he killed it.* –*adverb* **mercilessly.**

**mercury** /'mɜrky əri/ *noun, (no plural)*
liquid metal known for its shiny appearance at room temperature: *(In thermometers) the level of mercury rises as the temperature goes up.*

**Mercury** /'mɜrkyəri/ *noun, (no plural)*
the closest planet to the sun: *The surface of Mercury is very hot.*

**mercy** /'mɜrsi/ *noun*
forgiveness, willingness to let someone avoid punishment: *The governor showed mercy to the prisoner sentenced to death.*

M

**merely** /'mɪrli/ *adverb*
only, nothing more than: *I merely asked how he felt, and he started shouting.*

**merge** /mɜrʤ/ *verb* **merged, merging, merges**
to combine: *The two companies decided to merge into one company.*

**meridian** /mə'rɪdiən/ *noun*
on a map or globe, a line (of longitude) that makes a half circle of the earth from the North to the South Pole: *The prime meridian runs through Greenwich, England.*

**merit** /'mɛrɪt/ *verb*
to be worthy of, deserve attention because of the quality of someone or something: *That business proposal merits careful consideration.*

**merit** *noun*
**1** high quality, excellence: *Her poetry is of great merit.*
**2** a good quality of something: *We discussed the merits of the plan.*

**merry** /'mɛri/ *adjective* **merrier, merriest**
happy, lively: *We had a merry time at the party last night.* (*antonym*) sad.

**to make merry:** to celebrate cheerfully: *We made merry at my brother's wedding.* –*noun* **merriment.**

**merry-go-round** *noun*
a type of ride with models of horses on a platform that goes around to music, *(synonym)* carousel

merry-go-round

**mess** /mɛs/ *noun*
**1** a bad condition where things are disorderly or disorganized: *His office is always a mess because he never throws anything away.*
**2** a dirty condition: *An egg fell on the floor and made a mess.*
**3** trouble, a difficult situation: *She's in a mess because she quit school and cannot find a job.* –*verb* **to mess.**

**message** /'mɛsɪʤ/ *noun*
**1** a short piece of information that one person says or writes to another: *I left a message on her answering machine to call me.*
**2** the central meaning: *The message of that speech was that drugs are dangerous.*

**messenger** /'mɛsənʤər/ *noun*
a person who brings a message, letter, package, etc.

**messy** /'mɛsi/ *adjective* **messier, messiest**
**1** in bad condition with too many things in wrong places: *Her room is always messy with magazines and clothes everywhere.*
**2** dirty, soiled: *The kitchen floor is messy with spilled food.*

**met** /mɛt/ *verb*
*past tense and past participle of* meet: *We met in the park last week and went for a walk.*

**metal** /'mɛtl/ *noun*
hard, shiny substances that can be melted, shaped, and cut to make things such as iron, copper and steel: *Steel is a metal that is used a lot in building and manufacturing.*

**metal** *adjective*
made of metal: *a metal door* –*adjective* **metallic.**

**metaphor** /ˈmɛtəˌfɔr/ *noun*
a way of describing something in a colorful way by showing its similarity with something else: *When you say that someone has "a heart of stone" you are using a metaphor to express that this person is cold and uncaring.* –*adjective* **metaphorical.**

**meteor** /ˈmitiər/ *noun*
a mass of rock or metal from outer space that burns up when it enters the earth's atmosphere –*adjective* **meteoric.**

**meteorite** /ˈ mitiəˌraɪt/ *noun*
a small meteor that lands on Earth

**meteorology** /ˌmitiəˈrɑləʤi/ *noun*
the study of the earth's atmosphere and weather conditions –*noun* (person) **meteorologist;** –*adjective* **meteorological.**

**meter** /ˈmitər/ *noun*
**1** a measurement of 39.37 inches (3.37 inches more than a yard)
**2** a machine that measures things, such as the use of water, electricity, and gas *See:* art on page 16a.

**method** /ˈmɛθəd/ *noun*
a way of doing something: *The teacher is using a new method to teach math.*

**methodical** /məˈθɑdɪkəl/ *adjective*
careful, in a step-by-step manner: *He is very methodical in his work habits.*

**methodology** /ˌmɛθəˈdɑləʤi/ *noun*
a group of methods for doing something: *Teachers use different methodologies to teach language to students.* –*adjective* **methodological** /ˌmɛθədəˈlaʤ əkəl/.

**metric system** *noun*
the system of measurement based on the meter, kilogram, and second –*adjective* **metric.**

**metropolitan** /ˌmɛtrəˈpɑlətən/ *adjective*
related to a city and its surrounding area (suburbs): *Metropolitan Miami covers a much larger area than the city of Miami itself.* –*adjective informal* **metro.**

**mice** /maɪs/ *noun*
*plural of* mouse

**microcomputer** /ˈmaɪkroʊkəmˌpyutər/ *noun*
a computer smaller than minicomputers

**microfilm** /ˈmaɪk rəˌfɪlm/ *noun*
a small film of highly reduced images of things: *Old newspapers on microfilm can be found in the library.*

microphone

**microphone** /ˈmaɪ krəˌfoʊn/ *noun*
an electronic device used for recording on tape, or for making the sound louder

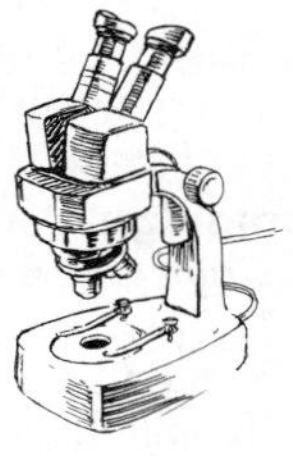
microscope

**microscope** /ˈmaɪ krəˌskoʊp/ *noun*
an instrument that uses lenses to make small objects appear larger –*noun* **microscopy** /maɪˈkrɑskəpi/.

**microscopic** /ˌmaɪkrəˈskɑpɪk/ *adjective*
very small, can be seen only with a microscope: *Viruses are microscopic in size.*

**microwave** /ˈmaɪk rəˌweɪv/ *noun*
**1** a short electromagnetic wave: *Radar uses microwaves.*
**2** a microwave oven

**microwave** *verb* **microwaved, microwaving, microwaves**
to cook with a microwave oven: *She microwaved her dinner. See:* art on page 7a.

**mid** or **mid-** /mɪd/*prefix*
referring to the middle of something: *The temperature was in the mid-90s.*||*She paused in mid-sentence.*

**middle** /ˈmɪdl/ *noun*
**1** the center of something: *The seeds of an apple are in its middle.*
**2** *informal* the waist: *He wears a belt around his middle.*
**in the middle of:** in the process of doing something: *We were in the middle of a meeting when the phone rang.*

**middle age** *noun, (no plural)*
the period of human life between the ages of 40 and 65 –*adjective* **middle-aged.** *(antonym)* young.

**Middle Ages** *noun plural*
*used with a singular verb* the (medieval) period of history from the fall of Rome in 476 A.D. to about 1450: *The*

*Middle Ages lasted for about 1,000 years.*

**middle class** *noun*
the social level of people between the working class and upper class: *The USA has a large middle class.*

**middle school** *noun*
in USA, a school between elementary and high school, usually with grades five through eight *See:* grade school, secondary school, **USAGE NOTE.**

**midget** /ˈmɪʤɪt/ *noun*
a very small, short person: *Children do not like to be called midgets.*

**midnight** /ˈmɪdˌnaɪt/ *noun*
12:00 P.M., the end of the day: *A new day begins at one second after midnight.*

**to burn the midnight oil:** to work through the night: *I burned the midnight oil getting my report ready.*

**Midwest** /ˌmɪdˈwɛst/ *noun*
*short for* the Middle West of the USA, states from Ohio, Michigan, and Indiana in the east to Kansas and Nebraska in the west *–noun* (person) **Midwesterner.**

**midwife** /ˈmɪdˌwaɪf/ *noun, plural* **midwives** /-ˌwaɪvz/
a person who is not a doctor but is trained to help women in giving birth to babies *–noun* **midwifery** /ˌmɪdˈwɪfəri/.

**might** /maɪt/ *verb*
*auxiliary and past tense of* may
**1** helping verb used to express possibility: *I might go shopping this afternoon if I have time.*||*She might have been a good doctor if she hadn't quit school.*
**2** as a suggestion: *You might visit the Metropolitan Museum of Art when you go to New York. See:* modal auxiliary.

**might** *noun*
strength, power: *He pushed the rock with all his might, but couldn't move it.*

---

**USAGE NOTE:** *Might* is used with the base form of another verb to express possibility in the present, future, or past: *I might go to the beach tomorrow, if it doesn't rain.* Also, *might* can be used when you want to suggest something in a polite way: *You might want to take the train instead of the bus. It's much faster.*

---

**mighty** /ˈmaɪti/ *adjective* **mightier, mightiest**
having great strength, power: *Mighty armies fought in World War II.*

**mighty** *adverb informal*
very, greatly: *I'm mighty pleased to see you.*

**migraine** /ˈmaɪˌgreɪn/ *noun*
a severe headache

**migrant** /ˈmaɪgrənt/ *noun*
an animal or person who moves from one place to another, especially farm workers who pick crops: *Migrant workers pick fruit in Florida each year.*

**migrate** /ˈmaɪˌgreɪt/ *verb* **migrated, migrating, migrates**
to move from one place to another, as animals, such as birds, and fish do: *Some birds migrate from North America to South America in the winter. –noun* (act) **migration** /maɪˈgreɪʃən/; *–adjective* **migratory.** *See:* emigrate.

**mike** /maɪk/ *noun informal*
*short for* microphone

**mild** /maɪld/ *adjective*
**1** moderate, not cold or hot: *We had mild weather this summer, except for one week of heat.*
**2** not sharp or strong-tasting: *Those peppers are mild, not hot.*
**3** gentle, calm: *She is good with children because she has a mild manner.*

**to put it mildly:** to state something in a way that makes it sound much less extreme than it is: *The temperature is warm today, to put it mildly; it's over 100 degrees. (antonym)* strong.

**mile** /maɪl/ *noun*
a distance equal to 5,280 feet (1.6 km): *A marathon is 26.8 miles (42.9 km) long.*||*A nautical mile of 6,076 feet is used in air and sea navigation.*

**mileage** /ˈmaɪlɪʤ/ *noun, (no plural)*
the distance in miles between two points: *The mileage between San Francisco and Los Angeles is approximately 400 (640 km).*

**milestone** /ˈmaɪlˌstoʊn/ *noun*
**1** a marker, such as a stone beside a road with the distance in miles on it
**2** *figurative* an important achievement,

event: *Getting her college degree was a milestone in her life.*

**military** /'mɪlə,tɛri/ *noun (no plural)*
a group of armed forces (army, air force, navy, etc.) of a nation: *In the USA, the military is headed by politicians.* –*adjective* **military.**

**milk** /mɪlk/ *noun, (no plural)*
a white liquid produced by women and some female animals: *Cows' milk feeds their young and is food for humans, too.* –*adjective* **milky.**

**milk** *verb*
to take milk from (cows, goats, etc.) *See:* art on page 17a.

**mill** /mɪl/ *noun*
**1** a factory where raw material is made into something, such as grain made into flour: *The steel mills in Pittsburgh were famous for their large size.*
**2** a small machine for crushing or cutting food into small pieces: *She puts beef through a mill to make hamburger meat.*

**mill** *verb*
to crush grain into flour: *A worker milled wheat into flour for making bread. See:* grind.

**milligram** /'mɪlə,græm/ *noun*
-*abbreviation:* **mg.** 1/1,000th of a gram

**milliliter** /'mɪlə,litər/ *noun*
-*abbreviation:* **ml.** 1/1,000th of a liter

**millimeter** /'mɪlə,mitər/ *noun*
-*abbreviation:* **mm.** 1/1,000th of a meter *See:* art on page 16a.

**million** /'mɪlyən/ *noun, plural* **million** or **millions**
1,000,000 of something: *She made a million dollars* (or) *$1,000,000 last year.* –*adjective* **millionth.**

---

**USAGE NOTE:** The plural of *million* is not used after a number: *He has six million dollars.* BUT *Millions of people love rock and roll music.*

---

**millionaire** /,mɪlyə'nɛr/ *noun*
a rich person who has a million dollars or more: *He is a millionaire from Texas.*

**mime** /maɪm/ *noun*
an entertainer who imitates actions and expresses emotions without speaking –*verb* **to mime.**

**mimic** /'mɪmɪk/ *noun* **mimicked, mimicking, mimics**
a person who copies the speech and body movements of others, to make fun of them: *My sister is a very funny mimic; she mimics our friends and famous people.* –*noun* **mimicry;** –*verb* **to mimic.**

**mind** /maɪnd/ *noun*
**1** the part of a person that thinks and feels: *He is very old, but his mind is still clear.*
**2** the mental processes of learning, thinking, and applying knowledge: *She has a good mind and is an excellent student.*
**3** beliefs, ideas, feelings: *He speaks his mind and lets you know what he thinks.*

**to be out of one's mind:** *informal* to be crazy: *You're out of your mind to drive in this storm.*

**to change one's mind:** to change a plan, intention: *He keeps changing his mind about which car to buy.*

**to lose one's mind:** to go insane, crazy: *He lost his mind and is in a mental hospital now.*

**to make up one's mind:** to make a decision: *She can't make up her mind about whether or not to marry him. (antonym)* body.

**mind** *verb*
**1** to take care of, watch over: *I mind the children at home.*
**2** to pay attention to something: *Mind how you pronounce your words.*
**3** not to like something, be annoyed at: *He minds the noise of trucks in the street.*
**4** to obey, do as one is told: *The boy's mother told him to mind the teacher.*

**never mind:** it doesn't matter; don't worry: *Never mind the dishes, we'll wash them later.*

**would or do you mind:** *informal* used to make a polite request: *Would you mind turning down the radio a little?*

**mindful** /'maɪndfəl/ *adjective*
careful in doing things: *She is mindful of her need to study hard.* –*noun* **mindfulness.**

**mine (1)** /maɪn/ *possessive pronoun*
belonging to me: *That umbrella is mine.*||*Those boots are mine.*

**mine (2)** *noun*
a hole made in the ground to remove minerals (coal, gold, etc.): *Some big gold mines go for miles under the earth.*

**mine** *verb* **mined, mining, mines**
to remove minerals from under the earth's surface *–noun* (worker) **miner.** *See:* gold mine.

**mine (3)** *noun*
a hidden bomb or explosive device, land mine: *Roads to the battlefield are loaded with mines. –verb* **to mine.**

**minefield** /ˈmaɪnˌfild/ *noun*
**1** an area where explosives are hidden
**2** *figurative* a situation that can lead to conflicts, lawsuits, etc.: *Any politician who takes away programs for old people is walking on a political minefield.*

**mineral** /ˈmɪnərəl/ *noun*
a substance, such as copper, iron, or diamonds, etc. found naturally in the earth

**mingle** /ˈmɪŋgəl/ *verb* **mingled, mingling, mingles**
to move around in a group of people: *I mingled at the party and talked with many people.*

mingle

**mini** /ˈmɪni/ *noun*
a small type of something, such as a miniskirt: *In winter, she wears long skirts and in summer, she wears minis.*
**mini-** *prefix* miniature, referring to a small or short copy of something: *We took a minicourse on English grammar.*

**miniature** /ˈmɪniəʧər/ *noun*
a small original or copy of something: *She paints miniatures* (or) *miniature portraits of people. –verb* **to miniaturize.**

**minicomputer** /ˈmɪnikəmˌpyutər/ *noun*
a small, powerful computer

**minimal** /ˈmɪnəməl/ *adjective*
related to a least amount of something

**minimum** /ˈmɪnəməm/ *noun adjective*
the least amount of something: *The couple cut their household expenses to the minimum. (antonym)* maximum.

**minimum wage** *noun, (no plural)*
in the USA, the minimum hourly rate that employers must pay to workers: *It is difficult to support a family on the minimum wage because it is so low.*

**mining** /ˈmaɪnɪŋ/ *noun, (no plural)*
the business and process of taking minerals out of the earth: *Mining requires a big investment in land, equipment, and labor.*

**miniskirt** /ˈmɪniˌskɜrt/ *noun*
a short skirt from the waist to above the knee

**minister** /ˈmɪnəstər/ *noun*
**1** a Protestant clergyman or clergywoman: *The new minister of the local church is a woman.*
**2** a high government official (not in the USA): *The Minister of Public Housing belongs to the Prime Minister's Cabinet. –verb* **to minister;** *–adjective* **ministerial.**

**ministry** /ˈmɪnəstri/ *noun, plural* **ministries**
**1** *(no plural)* the profession of the Christian clergy: *He wanted to join the ministry at an early age.*
**2** a government department (not in the USA): *The Ministry of Education sets standards for the school in the country.*

**minor** /ˈmaɪnər/ *adjective*
**1** not important: *We agreed on everything in the contract, even minor points.*
**2** not well known, obscure: *Minor poets are not read much by students.*

**minor** *noun*
a person under a legal age, such as 18, to vote, drink alcohol in bars, etc.

**minority** /məˈnɔrəti/ *noun, plural* **minorities**
**1** a number or group that is less than half of the total: *The Senator's "no" vote was in the minority, as the law was passed by a vote of 63 to 37.*
**2** people of a different race, background, or religion from those of the majority of people in a nation: *New York City has been a home to minorities for centuries. –adjective* **minority.**

**mint (1)** /mɪnt/ *noun*
**1** a plant with a cool, fresh taste: *Mint is often used in tea to make it taste better.*
**2** a candy made of sugar and mint, sometimes covered with chocolate: *We had a mint after dinner. –adjective* **minty.**

mint

**mint (2)** *noun*
a building owned by the government where coins are made and paper money is printed: *The USA has mints in Denver and other cities. –verb* **to mint.**

**minus** /'maɪnəs/ *noun, plural* **minuses**
**1** a minus sign (–): *The accountant put a minus beside the $100 expense.*
**2** something missing or bad: *Not having a college degree is a minus for him in looking for a job. (antonym)* plus.

**minus** *preposition*
to subtract, take away something: *Seven minus three equals four.*||*4 – 2 = 2.*

**minus sign** *noun*
*See:* minus, **1**.

**minute (1)** /'mɪnɪt/ *noun*
**1** 60 seconds: *I like an egg boiled for three minutes.*
**2** a moment, brief time period: *When you have a minute, I would like to talk with you.*
**3** a unit of measurement equal to 1/60th of a degree, in an angle

**minute (2)** /maɪ'nut/ *adjective*
very small: *Bacteria are minute organisms.*

**miracle** /'mɪrɪkəl/ *noun*
an event that cannot be explained by the laws of nature: *All the passengers on the plane died in the crash except one who was saved by a miracle. –adjective* **miraculous** /mɪ'rækyələs/; *–adverb* **miraculously.**

**mirror** /'mɪrər/ *noun*
a highly polished surface or glass that gives off light and images: *She looks in the mirror as she puts on makeup.*

mirror

**mirror** *verb*
to copy, agree with: *He mirrors his wife's opinions about most things. See:* art on page 23a.

**mis-** /ˌmɪs/*prefix*
indicating something negative: *I misunderstood your question.*

**misbehave** /ˌmɪsb ɪ'heɪv/ *verb* **misbehaved, misbehaving, misbehaves**
to act badly, be impolite *–noun* (act) **misbehavior** /ˌmɪsbɪ'heɪvyər/.

**misc.** *adjective*
*abbreviation of* miscellaneous

**miscarriage** /mɪs'kærɪʤ/ *noun*
accidental birth of a baby before the proper time, resulting in its death *–verb* **to miscarry.**

**miscellaneous** /ˌmɪsə'leɪniəs/ *adjective*
referring to various objects or ideas that are not connected: *She keeps miscellaneous items in her garage, such as a bicycle, an old table and a broken TV. –noun* (different things) **miscellany** /'mɪsəˌleɪni/.

**mischief** /'mɪsʧɪf/ *noun, (no plural)*
small, annoying acts or behavior, usually by children *–adjective* **mischievous.**

**misconduct** /mɪs'kɑnˌdʌkt/ *noun, (no plural)*
misbehavior, not acting according to the rules

**miser** /'maɪzər/ *noun*
a person who tries not to spend any money, even on necessities: *When the old miser died, his relatives found a million dollars in a box under his bed. –adjective* **miserly.**

**miserable** /'mɪzrəbəl/ *adjective*
**1** very unhappy: *After their dog died, the couple felt miserable for weeks.*
**2** feeling physical pain: *She has a bad cold and feels miserable.*
**3** poor quality or bad conditions: *Poor children can lead miserable lives. –adverb* **miserably.**

**misery** /'mɪzəri/ *noun, plural* **miseries**
**1** *(no plural)* sadness, a state without hope: *Ever since his wife died, he's been in misery.*

**2** physical suffering, bad conditions

**misfortune** /mɪs' fɔrʧən/ *noun*
**1** *(no plural)* bad luck: *Misfortune follows her wherever she goes.*
**2** a terrible event: *The earthquake was a misfortune for thousands of people.*

**mislead** /mɪs'lid/ *verb* **misled** /-'lɛd/, **misleading** /-'lidɪŋ/, **misleads**
to lead one to the wrong idea, action, or direction, *(synonym)* to deceive: *The book's title misled me into thinking it was a story book, but it was about cars.*

**misplace** /mɪs'pleɪs/ *verb* **misplaced, misplacing, misplaces**
to put something where you can't find it: *I misplaced my keys somewhere.*

**misrepresent** /mɪs'rɛprɪ'zɛnt/ *verb*
to say something incorrect or untrue on purpose: *He misrepresented the job as working in an office when it is actually an outside sales position.* *–noun* **misrepresentation** /mɪs'rɛprɪzɛn'teɪʃən/.

**miss** /mɪs/ *verb* **misses**
**1** to fail to hit something: *The tennis player missed the ball.*
**2** to fail to arrive in time for something: *I missed the bus this morning.*
**3** to fail to attend something: *I'm sorry you missed the party.*
**4** to fail to understand: *She missed the main point the teacher made.*
**5** to feel a sense of loss: *When the student went to college in a new city, he missed his family.*
**6** not to recognize or notice something: *The shoe store is on the corner straight ahead; you can't miss it.*

**to miss out:** not to participate in something, not enjoy: *Be sure to come to the picnic because if you don't, you will miss out on the fun.*

**miss** *noun*
**1** the failure to hit something *(antonym)* hit.
**2** **miss** or **Miss:** a form of address for an unmarried woman or girl, used alone or before her last name: *The waiter said, "How may I help you, miss?"*||*"How do you do, Miss Jones?"* *See:* Ms., USAGE NOTE.

**missile** /'mɪsəl/ *noun*
**1** an object that is thrown or shot, such as a bullet, arrow, stone
**2** a cigar-shaped weapon (rocket) with explosives: *A missile struck the ship and sank it.* *–noun* **missilery** /'mɪsəlri/.

**missing** /'mɪsɪŋ/ *adjective*
not there, absent: *He is missing from class; maybe he's sick.*

**mission** /'mɪʃən/ *noun*
**1** a purpose: *The priest's mission is to work for peace with other countries.*
**2** a group of people sent to another country for a specific purpose: *a trade mission*
**3** a religious settlement: *Many towns in California were originally missions of the Catholic church.*

**missionary** /'mɪʃə,nɛri/ *noun, plural* **missionaries**
a person, especially a member of the clergy, sent to another country to persuade others to accept his or her religion

**mist** /mɪst/ *noun, (no plural)*
very fine drops of water forming a cloud

**mist** *verb*
to form mist, especially a very fine rain: *It is misting outside now.* *–adjective* **misty.**

**mistake** /mɪ'steɪk/ *noun*
something wrong, incorrect, *(synonym)* error: *The waiter made a mistake in adding up the bill.*

mistake

**mistake** *verb* **mistook** /mɪ'stʊk/, **mistaken, mistaking, mistakes**
to have a wrong idea, to identify someone incorrectly: *I mistook that woman for a friend of mine, but she's a stranger.*

**mistaken** /mɪ'ste ɪkən/ *adjective*
*& past participle of* mistake: incorrect, wrong: *He was mistaken when he thought I was on vacation; I wasn't.*

**mister** /'mɪstər/ *noun*
*abbreviation*: **Mr.** a form of address for a

man: *Excuse me, mister, can you tell me what time it is?*||*Mr. Smith is in his office.*

**mistress** /'mɪstrɪs/ *noun, plural* **mistresses**
**1** *old usage* the female head of a household: *Is the mistress of the house at home?*
**2** a woman in a sexual relationship with a married man who is not her husband

**misunderstanding** /ˌmɪsʌndər'stændɪŋ/ *noun*
**1** a mistaken idea: *We had a misunderstanding about the time of our meeting.*
**2** an argument, disagreement

**mitten** /mɪtn/ *noun*
a covering for the hand (glove) that covers the fingers together and the thumb separately *See:* art on page 12a.

**mix** /mɪks/ *verb* **mixes**
**1** to stir together: *I mixed the milk and the flour to make bread.*
**2** to meet and talk with other people, *(synonym)* to socialize: *Guests mixed with each other at the party.*
**to mix someone** or **something up or to get mixed up:** to confuse, replace one thing with another by mistake: *My teacher mixed my test up with another person's who has the same last name.*||*The tests got mixed up. See:* mix-up.

**mix** *noun, plural* **mixes**
**1** a combination of different things or people: *There is an interesting mix of people in my class.*
**2** a food preparation that comes in a package: *She made a cake from a mix by adding water and an egg and then baking it.*
**mixed up:** confused: *In a hurry, I got all mixed up and left my keys at home.*

**mixture** /'mɪkstʃər/ *noun*
a combination of things, especially foods or chemicals

**mix-up** *noun*
a confused situation: *There was a mix-up at the office where my paycheck was given to another person by mistake.*

**moan** /moʊn/ *verb*
**1** to make low sounds of pain or pleasure: *He cut his thumb with a knife and moaned in pain.*
**2** to complain: *She is always moaning about how much work she has.* –*noun* **moan.**

**mob** /mɑb/ *noun*
a large group of people, often angry about something: *A mob gathered in the town square to protest new tax increases.*

**mob** *verb* **mobbed, mobbing, mobs**
to act like a mob: *Shoppers mobbed the stores for big holiday sales.*

**mobile** /'moʊbəl/ *adjective*
movable, capable of going from one place to another: *She broke her leg but is now mobile and can walk with a cane.* –*noun* **mobility.**

**mobile home** /'moʊbəl/ *noun*
a small house made of metal that often can be pulled by a car or truck *See:* trailer; motor home.

mobile home

**moccasin** /'mɑkəsən/ *noun*
a soft shoe without a heel: *Moccasins are often decorated with pretty beads.*

moccasins

**modal auxiliary** /'moʊdl/ *noun*
(in grammar) a verb that is used with another verb. Modals can express various meanings, such as ability, probability, and permission: *Some modal auxiliaries are "can," "may," and "might." See:* mood, **2**; tense, *noun.*

USAGE NOTE: Modal auxiliaries in English include: *can, could, may, might, must, shall, should, will, would.* The modal auxiliary is used before the base form of the main verb as with *will* and *can*: *I will be home late tonight. Can you make dinner for me?*

M

**model** /ˈmɑdl/ *noun*
**1** a small copy of something: *We made a one-foot-tall model of the new office building.*
**2** a person who is paid for artists to paint or by companies to wear their clothes or show their products: *a clothes model*
**3** a specific type of product from a manufacturer: *Car makers produce new models of their car every year.*

model

model

**model** *adjective*
**1** a good example: *He is a model student and always does his homework.*
**2** referring to a small copy of something: *My son likes to build model airplanes.*

**model** *verb*
**1** to serve as a model for artists: *He models for painting students.*
**2** to shape as with the hands: *She models clay into pots.*
**3** to make a model of something: *He models designs of buildings.*

**modem** /ˈmoʊdəm/ *noun*
(in computers) an electronic device for sending or receiving computer information over telephone lines: *We send orders from our office to the factory by modem.*

**moderate** /ˈmɑdəˌreɪt/ *verb* **moderated, moderating, moderates**
**1** to become less in strength or severity: *The hurricane's high winds moderated (slowed) as it reached the shore.*
**2** to be in charge of a discussion group: *The news reporter moderated a discussion between politicians.* *–noun* (person) **moderator.**

**moderate** *adjective* /ˈmɑdərɪt/
**1** in the middle, not large or small: *He makes a moderate income.*
**2** not high or low, comfortable: *warm, moderate weather*

**modern** /ˈmɑdərn/ *adjective*
**1** related to today's life, current: *Most modern women work outside the home.*
**2** new, the latest of something: *Modern computers keep getting faster and faster.* *–noun* **modernism, modernity** /məˈdɜrnəti/. *(antonym)* old.

**modernize** /ˈmɑdərˌnaɪz/ *verb* **modernized, modernizing, modernizes**
to improve something by replacing old things with new ones: *We modernized our computer systems with the newest equipment.* *–noun* **modernization** /ˌmadərnəˈzeɪʃən/.

**modest** /ˈmɑdɪst/ *adjective*
**1** describing a person who does not talk much about his or her achievements or abilities
**2** not large, *(synonym)* moderate: *He lives on a modest income in a modest house.* *–noun* **modesty.**

**modifier** /ˈmɑdəˌfaɪər/ *noun*
(in grammar) a word or phrase that describes another: *Adjectives are modifiers that describe nouns, such as "good" in "We had a good time."*

**modify** /ˈmɑdəˌfaɪ/ *verb* **modified, modifying, modifies**
**1** to change something
**2** (in grammar) to describe something: *In the sentence, "She's wearing a blue sweater," the word "blue" modifies "sweater."* *–noun* (act) **modification.**

**moist** /mɔɪst/ *adjective*
slightly wet, *(synonym)* damp. *(antonym)* dry.

**moisten** /ˈmɔɪsən/ *verb*
to make a little bit wet

**moisture** /ˈmɔɪsʧər/ *noun, (no plural)*
very small amount of liquid: *The moisture in the air makes it feel hot.*

**moisturize** /ˈmɔɪsʧəˌraɪz/ *verb* **moisturized, moisturizing, moisturizes**
to add liquid: *She moisturizes her hands with cream.* *–noun* (liquid) **moisturizer.**

**mold (1)** /moʊld/ *noun*
an empty form into which materials are put to shape objects, such as tools, toys, candy, etc.: *Workers pour hot plastic into molds to make toys.*

M

**mold** *verb*
**1** to form into a shape: *She molded the clay into a pot with her hands.*
**2** to strongly influence the development of a person's character: *Her personality was molded by her strict parents.*

**mold (2)** *noun, (no plural)*
a bad-smelling, destructive plant (fungus) that grows on materials: *green mold on bread –adjective* **moldy.**

**mole** /moʊl/ *noun*
**1** a small, dark, growth on the skin
**2** a small animal (rodent) that digs in the earth

**molecule** /ˈmɑlɪˌkyul/ *noun*
(in chemistry) the smallest unit of the elements of a substance *–adjective* **molecular** /məˈlɛkyələr/.

**molest** /məˈlɛst/ *verb*
**1** to harm sexually: *He molested children and was sent to jail for 30 years.*
**2** *old usage* to annoy, disturb *–noun* **molestation** /ˌmoʊlɛˈsteɪʃən/.

**mom** /mɑm/ *noun informal*
*short for* mommy, mother

**mom-and-pop store** *noun informal*
a small family business: *He runs the mom-and-pop store on the corner.*

**moment** /ˈmoʊmənt/ *noun*
**1** a brief period of time, such as a few seconds to several minutes
**2** a short period: *World War II was a terrible moment in world history. –adverb* **momentarily;** *–adjective* **momentary.**

**momentum** /moʊˈmɛntəm/ *noun*
the speed at which something moves: *The big ship started to move slowly and then gradually reached full momentum.*

**momma** /ˈmɑmə/ *noun informal*
mother

**mommy** /ˈmɑmi/ *noun informal, plural* **mommies**
mother

**monarchy** /ˈmɑnərki/ *noun*
a government run by a king or queen (monarch) usually with limited powers: *The monarchy in England plays an important role in British society. –noun* (person) **monarch;** *–adjective* **monarchal.**

**monastery** /ˈmɑnəˌstɛri/ *noun, plural* **monasteries**
a place where monks live, work, and pray: *Some monasteries are open to the public as a place to rest. –adjective* **monastic.** *See:* convent.

**Monday** /ˈmʌnˌdeɪ/ *noun*
the day of the week between Sunday and Tuesday

**money** /ˈmʌni/ *noun, (no plural)*
paper bills and coins used to buy things: *Money can't buy you love.*
**for my money:** in my opinion: *For my money, that movie we saw last night was great.*
**money's worth:** to receive good value: *I have worn these shoes for two years and really got my money's worth.*
**to make money:** to earn money or profit

**monitor** /ˈmɑnətər/ *noun*
a screen, as on a television or computer, that shows information

**monitor** *verb*
to observe the actions of others: *The boss monitors the quality of her employees' work. See:* art on page 20a.

**monk** /mʌŋk/ *noun*
a member of an all-male religious group who lives in a monastery

**monkey** /ˈmʌŋki/ *noun*
an animal with a human-like face, long tail, and excellent climbing ability *See:* art on page 14a.

**monolingual** /ˌmɑnəˈlɪŋgwəl/ *adjective*
having only one language: *Most Americans are monolingual in English. (antonym)* bilingual.

**monologue** /ˈmɑnəˌlɔg/ *noun*
a long talk by only one person *(antonym)* dialogue.

**monopoly** /məˈnɑpəli/ *noun, plural* **monopolies**
the control of an entire market by only one person, business, or organization: *The government has laws against monopolies in many industries. –verb* **to monopolize.**

**monster** /ˈmɑnstər/ *noun*
**1** a frightening, imaginary creature, usually a person, animal, or plant: *The monster in the film looked like a giant insect.*
**2** a very cruel person or animal

**monster** *adjective figurative*
something unusually big or violent: *monster hurricane* –*adjective* **monstrous.**

**month** /mʌnθ/ *noun*
a time period of about 30 days as one of 12 months that make a year: *His rent costs $500 a month, and he pays it on the first of the month.*

**monthly** /ˈmʌnθli/ *adverb*
done each month: *She washes her car monthly.*

**monthly** *noun, plural* **monthlies**
a magazine published monthly

**monument** /ˈmɑnyəmənt/ *noun*
a statue, building, etc., built in memory of a person or historical event

**monumental** /ˌmɑnyəˈmɛntl/ *adjective*
large in size or importance: *The Bible is a monumental book in human history.*

**moo** /mu/ *noun*
the sound made by a cow –*verb* **to moo.**

**mood** /mud/ *noun*
an emotional state or feeling, such as happiness or sadness: *She is in a good mood today and smiles a lot.* –*adjective* **moody.**

**moon** /mun/ *noun*
**1** the natural round object (satellite) that goes round the Earth: *The moon is Earth's nearest neighbor in space.*
**2** any similar body that goes around the other planets
**once in a blue moon:** rarely, almost never: *She works all the time and takes a vacation once in a blue moon.*

**moonlight** /ˈmunˌlaɪt/ *noun, (no plural)*
light from the moon, especially a full moon: *When the moon is full, you can see well in the moonlight.* –*adjective* **moonlit** /ˈmunˌlɪt/.

**moonlight** *verb informal* **moonlighted, moonlighting, moonlights**
to have a second job (often at night) in addition to regular work –*noun* **moonlighting.**

**moose** /mus/ *noun, plural* **moose**
the largest member of the deer family living in northern North America, Europe, and Asia *See:* art on page 14a.

**mop** /mɑp/ *noun*
cleaning equipment made of rope-like pieces at the end of a long stick: *A worker wet the mop to clear the floor. See:* broom.

mop

**mop** *verb* **mopped, mopping, mops**
**to mop something up:** to use a mop: *A worker mopped up the floor this morning.*

**moral** /ˌmɔrəl/ *adjective*
related to what is right or wrong: *She is a very moral person who acts correctly all the time; she never steals or lies. (antonym)* immoral. –*adverb* **morally.**

**moral** *noun*
an idea about correct living, especially an idea shown by a story: *"The truth will out" is a moral that means that the truth will eventually be told.*

**morale** /məˈræl/ *noun, (no plural)*
the level of enthusiasm and confidence a person or group has for what they are doing: *Morale in our company is high after a good sales last year.*

**morality** /məˈræləti/ *noun, (no plural)*
standards of behavior, beliefs about what is right and wrong: *Religious people often talk about the need for greater morality.* –*noun* (person) **moralist.**

**more** /mɔr/ *adjective*
*comparative of* many *and* much: additional, added: *She needs to make more money if she wants to buy a car.*

**more** *adverb*
additionally, to a greater degree or amount: *He should study more than he does.*
**more and more:** to an increasing degree: *She is becoming more and more interested in going into politics.*
**more or less:** approximately, about: *That table is more or less six feet (two meters) long.*

**more** *noun*
a greater number, degree, etc.: *The more who come to the party, the more fun we'll have, or as they say, "The more, the merrier." See:* less; fewer.

**moreover** /mɔr'oʊvər/ *adverb*
in addition: *She is rich; moreover, she is beautiful and generous.*

**morning** /'mɔrnɪŋ/ *noun*
the hours between sunrise and noon: *Children go to school in the morning.*

**mortal** /'mɔrtl/ *adjective*
living until death: *All of us are mortal.* –*adverb* **mortally;** –*noun* **mortality.**

**mortgage** /'mɔrgɪʤ/ *noun*
a loan from a bank for buying property, which is paid back over a number of years: *We make monthly payments on our house mortgage.*

**mortgage** *verb* **mortgaged, mortgaging, mortgages**
to borrow money against the value of one's house: *He mortgaged his house in order to have enough money to start his own business.*

**mosquito** /mə'ski toʊ/ *noun, plural* **mosquitoes** or **mosquitos**
small, biting, blood-sucking insects: *Mosquitoes spread disease in many parts of the world.*

**moss** /mɔs/ *noun*
a short, soft plant that grows on the ground and on trees –*adjective* **mossy.**

**most** /moʊst/ *noun*
the highest degree, amount, number, etc.: *I liked Paris the most of all the cities I have ever visited.*

**at most:** at the greatest degree, amount, etc.: *Those fancy shoes should cost at most $100.*

**most** *adjective*
*superlative of* many, much, more: related to the highest degree, amount, number, etc.: *Last year, he made the most money that he has ever made.*

**most of all:** regarding the greatest amount, degree, etc.: *I like to eat ice cream most of all.* –*adverb* **mostly.**

**most** *adverb*
for the most part, usually: *I like to vacation mostly in the fall. (antonym)* least.

**motel** /moʊ'tɛl/ *noun*
a hotel next to a highway where people park their cars in front of the rooms *See: bed and breakfast, hotel* USAGE NOTES

**moth** /mɔθ/ *noun, plural* **moths**
an insect with wings that is active at night

**mother** /'mʌðər/ *noun*
the female parent: *My mother lives in New Hampshire.*

**mother** *verb*
to take care of: *She mothers her two children with loving care.* –*adjective* **motherly.** *See:* art on page 13a.

**motherhood** /'mʌðər,hʊd/ *noun, (no plural)*
the state of being a mother: *Motherhood came late to her. She had her first child at age 40.*

**mothering** /'mʌðərɪŋ/ *noun, (no plural)*
care given by mothers: *Her child is sickly, so he needs a lot of mothering.*

**mother-in-law** /'mʌðərɪn,lɔ/ *noun, plural* **mothers-in-law**
the mother of one's husband or wife *See:* art on page 13a.

**Mother Nature** *noun*
a term for nature and its power

**Mother's Day** *noun*
in the USA, a holiday on the second Sunday in May that honors mothers

**mother tongue** *noun*
the first language one speaks as a child: *Her mother tongue is Spanish.*

**motion** /'moʊʃən/ *noun*
**1** *(no plural)* movement, going from one place to another: *That child is always in motion; she never sits still.*
**2** a movement of the head, hand, arm, etc.: *I made a motion with my hand to get the attention of the waiter.*

**motion** *verb*
to move the hand, arm, etc.: *She motioned with her hand to get the waiter's attention.*

**motivate** /'moʊtə,veɪt/ *verb* **motivated, motivating, motivates**
to give a reason to do something: *A desire to go to medical school motivates her to study hard every day.* –*noun* **motivation;** –*adjective* **motivational.**

**motive** /'moʊtɪv/ *noun*
a reason, purpose for doing something: *Money was the thief's motive in robbing.*

**motor** /ˈmoʊtər/ *noun*
a machine that creates power, such as the engine in a car: *An air conditioner uses an electric motor to cool the air.* *–verb* (to travel) **to motor,** (to provide with motors) **to motorize.**

**motorbike** /ˈmoʊtərˌbaɪk/ *noun*
a lightweight motorcycle similar to a bicycle, often with a powerful motor

**motorboat** /ˈmoʊtərˌboʊt/ *noun*
a boat with a motor usually without sails: *Our friends have a motorboat that they take on the lake on weekends.*

**motorcycle** /ˈmoʊtərˌsaɪkəl/ *noun*
a two-wheeled vehicle larger than a motorbike, with a powerful engine *–verb* **to motorcycle.** *See:* art on page 24a.

**motorcycle**

**motor home** *noun*
a metal house on wheels pulled by another vehicle or driven by itself *See:* mobile home.

**motor inn** *noun*
a type of hotel for people traveling by car, *(synonym)* motel: *On our trip, we stayed at motor inns.* *See:* hotel, **USAGE NOTE.**

**motorist** /ˈmoʊtərɪst/ *noun*
a person who drives or rides in a car, truck, or motorcycle

**motor vehicle** *noun*
a general term for a car, bus, truck, etc.

**motto** /ˈmɑtoʊ/ *noun, plural* **mottoes** or **mottos**
a short saying that states a basic belief of a nation, organization, etc.: *The motto on the US dollar says "in God we trust."*

**mound** /maʊnd/ *noun*
a rounded pile, in the shape of a hill

**mount** /maʊnt/ *verb*
**1** to increase, go up: *Costs of products are mounting every week.*
**2** to climb on: *The cowboy mounted his horse and rode away.*
**3** to put on display, hang up: *We mounted new pictures on the wall.*||*The theater mounted a production of the new play.*

**Mount:** mountain (used in names of places): *Mount McKinley*

**mountain** /ˈmaʊntn/ *noun*
**1** a tall piece of land and rock higher than a hill: *The mountains south of San Francisco make a pretty picture.*
**2** *figurative* a large amount: *There is a mountain of dishes to wash.*

**to make a mountain out of a molehill (a small dirt pile):** to become angry over a small concern: *She made a mountain out of a molehill about getting a B on her exam instead of an A.* *–adjective* **mountainous.**

**mountain lion** *noun*
a large cat with a long tail and light brown coat, found from western Canada to the tip of South America, *(synonym)* a cougar

**mountain range** *noun*
a group of mountains in a general area

**mourn** /mɔrn/ *verb*
to feel sad at the death of someone: *The family mourned the death of their grandfather.* *–noun* (person) **mourner;** *–adjective* **mournful.**

**mourning** /ˈmɔrnɪŋ/ *noun, (no plural)*
a traditional way of expressing sorrow for a dead person: *Wearing black clothes is a sign of mourning.*

**mouse** /maʊs/ *noun, plural* **mice** /maɪs/
**1** a small gray or brown animal found around the world: *Mice steal food and carry diseases.* *See:* art on page 14a.
**2** (in computers) a small device for controlling computer operations *See:* art on page 20a.

**mousetrap** /ˈmaʊsˌtræp/ *noun*
a device used to catch mice

**mouth** /maʊθ/ *noun, plural* **mouths** /maʊðz/
**1** the opening on the face used for eating food: *With a spoon, the mother put food in her baby's mouth.*
**2** an entrance or opening: *People entered the mouth of the cave.*

**by word of mouth:** through people talking to each other: *That new store never advertised; its business grew by word of mouth.*

**to take the words out of someone's mouth:** to say the same thing someone else is about to say: *"It's a perfect day for sailing." "You took the words right out of my mouth." See:* art on page 21a.

**mouthful** /'maʊθˌfʊl/ *noun*
**1** an amount equal to the size of one's mouth: *I'm so full I can't eat another mouthful.*
**2** *figurative* something difficult to pronounce: *The teacher's last name is a mouthful, so the children call her Mrs. B.*

**mouthwash** /'maʊθˌwɑʃ/ *noun, plural* **mouthwashes**
a liquid that cleans and freshens the mouth: *I use a mouthwash each morning.*

**movable** /'muvəbəl/ *adjective*
capable of being moved: *Those heavy boxes on wheels are movable. (antonym)* immovable.

**move** /muv/ *verb* **moved, moving, moves**
**1** to go from one place to another: *I moved closer to the window to get some fresh air.*
**2** to change a home or office: *We moved from the city to the country.*
**3** to put something in a different place or position: *I moved my arms over my head.*
**4** to create emotion in someone: *We were deeply moved by the words of the song.*
**to move away:** **a.** to go live in another place: *We moved away from New York and live in Florida now.* **b.** to step back: *Firefighters told people to move away from the fire.*
**to move in:** to go live in: *We bought a new house and moved in last week.*
**to move out:** to leave a place permanently, usually a home: *We moved out of our old house into a small apartment.*

**move** *noun*
**1** a change of position: *The police officer told the thief not to make a move or he would shoot.*
**2** a change of homes: *We made a move from a city apartment to a house.*
**3** a player's action: *(in games) Each player makes one move at a time.*

**movement** /'muvmənt/ *noun*
**1** going from one place to another, motion: *Movement of traffic is very slow during rush hour.*
**2** the ability to move: *The worker injured his hand and has no movement in it.*
**3** a political or social cause

**mover** /'muvər/ *noun*
a business or person who moves furniture, etc.: *Movers came in and moved our things to a new apartment.*

**movie** /'muvi/ *noun*
**1** a motion picture, film: *I saw a great movie last night about cowboys.*
**2** *plural* **the movies:** films in general: *We like to go to the movies once a week.*

**mow** /moʊ/ *verb* **mowed** or **mown** /moʊn/, **mowing, mows**
to cut with a machine (mower) or blade: *I mowed the grass yesterday.*

**mower** /'moʊər/ *noun*
a machine with sharp blades used to cut grass: *an electric mower to cut the grass*

**mower**

**MPH**
*abbreviation of* miles per hour: *The speed limit is 55 MPH on that road.*

**USAGE NOTE:** Said as "miles per hour," not "MPH."

**Mr.** /'mɪstər/
*abbreviation of* Mister, *plural* **Messrs.** /'mɛsərz/: *Mr. Jones is here to see you.*

**Mrs.** /'mɪsɪz/
*abbreviation of* Mistress, *plural* **Mmes.** /meɪ'dɑm/ a title before the name of a married woman: *Mrs. Jones visited the doctor. See:* Ms., USAGE NOTE.

**Ms.** /mɪz/
*abbreviation of* Miss or Mrs.
a title for a woman that does not say whether she is married or single: *Ms. Smith is the director of accounting here.*

**USAGE NOTE:** Use of the title *Ms.* avoids mistakenly calling a married woman *Miss* or a single woman *Mrs.* Many people prefer *Ms.* because it does not say whether a woman is married or not, as *Mr.* does not for men.

---

**much** /mʌʧ/ *adjective* **more** /mɔr/ **, most** /moʊst/
related to a lot of something: *We haven't had much snow this winter.*
**how much:** used to ask about the amount of something: *How much gasoline is left?||How much is left?*

**much** *noun*
a lot, plenty of something: *I had too much to eat at the party!*

**much** *adverb*
**1** more of something, a lot: *She is feeling much better.*
**2** often, frequently: *I asked him if he played tennis much.*
**3** to the degree, amount that: *He said that he plays as much as he wants to. (antonym)* little.

**mud** /mʌd/ *noun*
earth that is wet and sticky

**muddy** /'mʌdi/ *adjective* **muddier, muddiest**
**1** full of or covered with mud: *My boots are muddy after walking in the woods.*
**2** unclear, confused: *Her writing is muddy and difficult to understand. –verb* **to muddy.**

**muffin** /'mʌfɪn/ *noun*
a small, sweet bread often made of a grain, such as corn, bran, oats, etc. *See:* English muffin. *See:* art on page 17a.

muffin

**mug** /mʌg/ *noun*
a thick cup with a handle: *She drinks a mug of coffee at lunch. See:* glass.

mug

**mug** *verb* **mugged, mugging, mugs**
to attack someone to rob him or her: *He was mugged in the park. –noun* (act) **mugging.**

**mugger** *noun*
a criminal who robs others in public

**muggy** /'mʌgi/ *adjective* **muggier, muggiest**
of damp, hot air: *Muggy weather makes people feel uncomfortable. See:* humid.

**mule** /myul/ *noun*
an animal that comes from a female horse bred with a donkey

**multi-** /ˌmʌlti/ *prefix*
many of something: *Her business has made her a multimillionaire.*

**multiple** /'mʌltəpəl/ *adjective*
many, a number of: *She has multiple reasons for not marrying him.*

**multiple-choice** *adjective*
having many choices for answers, as on a test: *The multiple-choice questions on that test had four possible answers.*

**multiplication** /ˌmʌltəplə'keɪʃən/ *noun, (no plural)*
**1** the arithmetic operation of multiplying one number by another: *2 times 2 equals 4 is an act of multiplication.*
**2** an increase in number, intensity, variety, etc.: *The multiplication of problems at the company continues.*

**multiply** /'mʌltəˌplaɪ/ *verb* **multiplied, multiplying, multiplies**
**1** in arithmetic, to increase a number by a certain number of times: *If you multiply 20 five times, you get 100.*
**2** to increase in number: *Mice multiply very rapidly by having babies every three weeks. See:* divide.

**mumble** /'mʌmbəl/ *verb* **mumbled, mumbling, mumbles**
to speak unclearly in a low voice: *He mumbles when he talks, so it's hard to understand him. –noun* (person) **mumbler, mumble.**

**munch** /mʌnʧ/ *verb informal* **munches**
to chew strongly and steadliy on something

**municipal** /myʊ'nɪsəpəl/ *adjective*
related to a city, town, etc.: *There is a municipal parking lot near the town hall. –noun* (city/town) **municipality.**

**mural** /'myʊrəl/ *noun*
a painting done directly on a wall: *Two huge murals decorated the entrance hall of that building. –noun* (artist) **muralist.**

**murder** /'mɜrdər/ *noun*
the killing of someone illegally and on

purpose: *A criminal committed murder when he shot the woman.*

**murder** *verb*
to kill someone (not in military battle): *The criminal murdered the woman for her money and jewels. –noun* (criminal) **murderer;** *–adjective* **murderous.**

**murmur** /'mɜrmər/ *noun*
a low, unclear sound: *A murmur of conversation went through the classroom after the teacher announced the exam.*

**murmur** *verb*
to speak in a low voice

**muscle** /'mʌsəl/ *noun*
**1** a part of the body on the bones that makes the body move and give it size: *The muscles in my legs hurt after walking a long distance.*
**2** *figurative* power, force: *Help me move this sofa, and let's put some muscle into it!*

**muscular** /'mʌskyələr/ *adjective*
having well developed, strong muscles: *He is a strong, muscular man.*

**museum** /myu'ziəm / *noun*
a place that displays valuable, and important art or historical objects

**mush** /mʌʃ/ *noun, (no plural)*
a soft, wet mass, especially corn or oat meal: *The farmer had cornmeal mush and coffee for breakfast. –adjective* **mushy.** *(antonym)* solid.

**mushroom** /'mʌʃˌrum/ *noun*
a type of small plant (fungus) with a thick round top. Some mushrooms can be eaten. *See:* art on page 2a.

**music** /'myuzɪk/ *noun, (no plural)*
the art of putting sounds together in a pleasing way: *I prefer classical music to jazz.*
**music to my ears:** to learn good news: *When my wife told me we were going to have a baby, I told her it was music to my ears.*

**musical** /'myuzɪkəl/ *adjective*
**1** related to music: *She has musical ability and plays the piano well.*
**2** pleasant-sounding: *Her voice has a musical quality.*

**musician** /myu'zɪʃən/ *noun*
a person who writes, sings, or plays music: *Many misicians played at the jazz concert.*

**must** /mʌst/
*auxiliary verb used with other verbs without the infinitive "to"*
**1** expressing duty, what one has to do: *I must go to work tomorrow.*
**2** expressing the probability of something: *Her car is gone, so she must have left already. See:* modal auxiliary.

**must** *noun, (no plural)*
something necessary: *A warm winter coat is a must in Chicago, where it gets cold and windy.*

---

**USAGE NOTE:** The past tense of *must* is usually *had to*: *I had to go to work yesterday.*

---

**mustache**
/'mʌˌstæʃ/ *noun*
hair growing above the mouth: *His new mustache makes him look older. See:* sideburns.

**mustache**

**mustard** /'mʌstərd/ *noun, (no plural)*
a hot yellow or brown sauce made from the seeds of a plant: *I like to put mustard on my hot dogs.*

**mutual** /'myuʧuəl/ *adjective*
**1** having the same feeling or behavior towards each other: *I was happy to see my friend, and he said the feeling was mutual.*
**2** sharing a feeling or interest: *They have a mutual interest in Japanese art.*

**my** /maɪ/
*possessive pronoun of* I: *My head aches; I'm going to my room.*

**my**
*exclamation* to express surprise: *My goodness, (my word, oh my, etc.) it's starting to rain again!*

**myself** /maɪ'sɛlf/
*reflexive pronoun of* I
**1** done by oneself: *I poured myself a glass of milk.*||*I cut myself by accident.*
**2** alone: *I live by myself.*
**3** one's usual condition: *I'm not feeling myself today; I didn't sleep well last night.*

**mysterious** /mɪ'stɪriəs/ *adjective* having no known cause

**mystery** /'mɪstəri/ *noun, plural* mysteries

**1** an event that has no known cause: *How the universe was created is still a mystery.*

**2** a secret: *Why she left home without saying where she was going is still a mystery.*

**3** a story in which someone commits a crime and the reader doesn't find out this person's identity until the end: *My friend likes to read murder mysteries. –verb* **to mystify.**

**myth** /mɪθ/ *noun*

**1** a story from ancient societies about history, gods, and heroes

**2** an untrue or unproved story: *His stories about his great successes in sports are myths. –adjective* **mythical.** *(antonym)* fact.

**mythology** /mɪ'θɑləʤi/ *noun, (no plural)*

**1** the stories of ancient peoples

**2** the study of myths and ancient societies *–verb formal* **to mythologize;** *–adjective* **mythological** /ˌmɪθə'lɑʤɪkəl/.

# N, n

**N, n** /ɛn/ **N's, n's** or **Ns, ns**
the 14th letter of the English alphabet

**NAACP** /ˈɛnˌdʌbəlˌeɪsiˈpi/
*abbreviation of* National Association for the Advancement of Colored People, an organization that protects the rights of African-Americans and works to provide them with equal opportunities for a good education and jobs

**nag** *verb* **nagged, nagging, nags**
to tell someone many times to do something in an annoying way: *She's always nagging her son to get a haircut.*

**nag** *adjective* **nagging**
constantly bothered by something: *a nagging backache*

**nag** *noun*
a person who nags another

**nail** /neɪl/ *noun*
**1** a small, thin, metal rod with a sharp point on the end, used to hold things together or to keep them in place: *She used nails to put bookshelves on the wall.*

nails

**2** the hard smooth surface at the end of a finger or toe: *She has long nails. See:* fingernail.

**nail** *verb*
to attach with a nail: *Workers nailed wooden boards together.*

**nail clipper** *noun*
a small metal tool with sharp edges for cutting fingernails or toenails

**nail file** *noun*
a thin, flat piece of metal with a rough surface used to smooth and shape fingernails

**nail polish** *noun*
paint used to cover and beautify fingernails and toenails: *She put red nail polish on before she went out to dinner.*

**naive** /nɑˈiv/ *adjective*
having or showing a childlike, simple view of the world, because of a lack of experience: *He was naive to trust a friend with so much money.* –*adverb* **naively;** –*noun* (condition) **naiveté.**

**naked** /ˈneɪkɪd/ *adjective*
without clothes

**name** /neɪm/ *noun*
**1** a word by which a person, place, or thing is known: *Her name is Diane Daniel.*||*What is the name of that flower?*
**2** *usually singular* an important person: *He is a big name in banking (entertainment, city politics, etc.).*
**3** *usually singular* the way other people think of you, *(synonym)* reputation: *She has a good name in the local community.*
**not a penny to one's name:** very poor
**to call someone names:** to address someone using an offensive word, *(synonym)* to insult: *He became angry and called me names like "stupid" and "fool."*

**name** *verb* **named, naming, names**
to give someone a name: *She named her daughter Mary.*

**namely** /ˈneɪmli/ *adverb*
to be exact, specifically: *I would like to buy a new car, namely a Mercedes.*

**nanny** /'næni/ *noun, plural* **nannies**
a person hired to take care of a child: *She works as a nanny for a rich family.*

**nap** /næp/ *verb* **napped, napping, naps**
to sleep for a short period of time: *I napped for an hour this afternoon.* –*noun* **map.**

**napkin** /'næpkɪn/ *noun*
a square piece of paper or cloth used when eating to wipe the mouth, protect the lap, and clean up spills: *We need to buy some paper napkins for the party. See:* art on page 3a.

napkin

**narcotic** /nɑr'kɑtɪk/ *noun*
a drug that reduces pain and causes sleep: *He is on narcotics.*

**narcotic** *adjective*
related to drugs: *Marijuana has a narcotic effect.*

**narrate** /'nær,eɪt/ *verb* **narrated, narrating, narrates**
to tell a story in writing or speech: *He narrated a television show on the history of Mexico.* –*noun* (act) **narration** /næ'reɪʃən/, **(person) narrator.**

**narrative** /'nærətɪv/ *noun*
a story, a description of events: *a narrative about a lost dog finding its home*

**narrow** /'nærou/ *adjective*
**1** not wide, less wide than usual: *The big truck can't fit in the narrow street.*||*Little light came through the narrow windows.*
**2** almost unsuccessful: *The thief got away, but only by a narrow escape.*

**narrow** *verb*
to become less wide: *The road narrows in the mountains.* –*adverb* **narrowly;** –*noun* **narrowness.** *(antonym)* wide.

**narrow-minded** /'nærou'maɪndɪd/ *adjective*
showing or having no interest in the ideas and opinions of others: *No one accepted his narrow-minded political views.*

**NASA** /'næsə/
*abbreviation of* National Aeronautics and Space Administration, the agency of the US federal government responsible for space exploration

**nasty** /'næsti/ *adjective* **nastier, nastiest**
**1** unkind, offensive: *a nasty person*||*a nasty comment*
**2** not nice, unpleasant: *nasty weather*||*a nasty smell (antonym)* friendly.

**nation** /'neɪʃən/ *noun*
**1** the people living in a country or region: *When the war ended, there was joy throughout the nation.*
**2** a country with its own government: *Spain is one of many nations in the European Union.*
**3** a group of Native American tribes that together form a union: *the Sioux nation*

**national** /'næʃənəl/ *adjective*
**1** about a nation: *national pride*||*national holidays*
**2** all over the country, *(synonym)* nationwide: *The story about the murder received national attention in the news.*

**national** *noun*
a person who is a citizen of a particular country: *She is an American national living in Brazil.* –*adverb* **nationally.**

**nationalism** /'næʃənə,lɪzəm/ *noun*
a feeling of loyalty to a country –*noun* (person) **nationalist;** –*adjective* **nationalistic.**

**nationality** /,næʃə'næləti/ *noun, plural* **nationalities**
the state of being a citizen of a particular country: *"What nationality is she?"—"Peruvian."*

**national monument** *noun*
a historic statue or building, owned by the national government: *The Lincoln Memorial in Washington, D.C., is a national monument.*

**national park** *noun*
a large park kept by the national government in its natural condition for people to use: *Yellowstone and Yosemite are famous national parks in the USA.*

---

**USAGE NOTE:** There are about 375 *national parks* and monuments in the USA, and about 175 national forests. The public can use the national parks for free or a low cost. People visit the parks to see natural beauty, to hike, and to camp.

---

**native** /ˈneɪtɪv/ *noun*
**1** a person who is born in a certain place: *She is a native of Texas.*
**2** *pejorative* one of a group of people living in a place before the arrival of Europeans: *They forced the natives to leave their land by burning their villages.*
**native** *adjective*
**1** born in a certain place: *She's a native New Yorker.*
**2** being the language one first learned as a child: *She speaks English fluently, but her native language is Italian.*
**native speaker:** a person who speaks a particular language as his or her first language: *a native speaker of Spanish*

---

**USAGE NOTE:** The opposite of a *native speaker* is a *nonnative speaker*, a person who does not speak a particular language as his or her first language: *Since Han came to the US from Taiwan at age 20, he's a nonnative speaker of English. He is a native speaker of Chinese.*

---

**Native American** *adjective*
of or about American Indians: *Native American history*||*a Native American poet* *–noun* (person) **Native American.** *See:* Indian, USAGE NOTE.
**natural** /ˈnætʃərəl/ *adjective*
**1** formed by nature, not made or changed by people: *We admired the natural beauty of the forest.*
**2** true to life, not fake: *A good actor must seem very natural.*
**3** born with a particular ability, without need of education or training: *He is a natural athlete who is excellent at many sports.*
**naturalize** /ˈnætʃərəˌlaɪz/ *verb* **naturalized, naturalizing, naturalizes**
to become a citizen of a country
**naturalized** *adjective*
*Born and raised in Hong Kong, she has become a naturalized citizen of the USA.* *–noun* **naturalization.**
**naturally** /ˈnætʃərəli/ *adverb*
**1** in a natural way: *Animals grow up naturally in a forest (not in a zoo).*
**2** as to be expected, of course: *Naturally, I would like to go to bed; I'm tired.*

**nature** /ˈneɪtʃər/ *noun, (no plural)*
**1** the part of our world not made by people, such as the sky, trees, fields, rivers, plants, animals, etc.
**2** the forces that control the natural part of the world: *Hurricanes and earthquakes show the dangerous power of nature.*
**3** a person's character, personality: *It is his nature to be kind.*
**Mother Nature:** the forces that control the natural world: *We had bad weather this year; Mother Nature has not been kind to us.* *–noun* (person) **naturalist.**
**naughty** /ˈnɔti/ *adjective* **naughtier, naughtiest**
badly behaved (usually used with children): *That boy is a naughty child.* *–noun* **naughtiness.**
**nausea** /ˈnɔziə/ *noun, (no plural)*
a feeling like you are going to vomit, sick to one's stomach: *She has a feeling of nausea from eating too much.* *–verb* **to nauseate.**
**nautical mile** *noun*
6,076 feet or 1,852 meters, used in sea and air travel: *The airplane is traveling at 600 nautical miles per hour.*
**naval** /ˈneɪvəl/ *adjective*
related to the navy and sailors: *He is in charge of the naval officers.*
**navigate** /ˈnævəˌgeɪt/ *verb* **navigated, navigating, navigates**
**1** to plan the path of a ship or airplane, using maps and mechanical aids (a compass)
**2** to guide the path of a ship or airplane: *The captain navigated his boat carefully up the river.* *–noun* **navigation,** (person) **navigator.**
**navy** /ˈneɪvi/ *noun, plural* **navies**
a country's sailors and fighting ships with their related equipment: *The US Navy keeps ships in many parts of the world.* *See:* army; air force.
**near** /nɪr/ *adjective*
**1** close in distance or time: *Go to the nearest hospital.*||*I'll see you in the near future.*
**2** almost happening: *a near accident (loss, disaster, etc.)*

N

**near** *adverb*
close to: *There's a supermarket near my house. (antonym)* far.

**nearby** /ˌnɪrˈbaɪ/ *adjective*
close: *We walked to a nearby town.*

**nearby** *adverb*
close: *Is there a post office nearby?*

**nearly** /ˈnɪrli/ *adverb*
almost, not completely: *He has nearly finished his meal.*||*That table costs nearly $500.*

**nearsighted** /ˈnɪrˌsaɪtɪd/ *adjective*
unable to see things that are far away: *She always wears glasses because she's very nearsighted. (antonym)* farsighted.

**neat** /nit/ *adjective*
**1** in good order, *(synonym)* tidy: *His house is always neat and clean.*
**2** skillfully done: *a neat way of saying something*
**3** *informal* great, wonderful: *We had a neat time at the party. –adverb* **neatly;** *–noun* **neatness.**

**necessarily** /ˌnɛsəˈsɛrəli/ *adverb*
as is always true, as must be: *Traveling in that country isn't necessarily expensive; you can find low-priced hotels and restaurants.*

**necessary** /ˈnɛsəˌsɛri/ *adjective*
required, needed: *Do you have the skills necessary to do the job?*||*It isn't necessary for me to attend the meeting.*

**necessity** /nəˈsɛsəti/ *noun, plural* **necessities**
**1** a basic need or requirement in order to live: *Water is a necessity for all life.*
**2** something that must be done: *I would like you to come with me, but it is not a necessity.*

**neck** /nɛk/ *noun*
**1** the part of the body that joins the head and the shoulders: *She wore a scarf around her neck.*
**2** a narrow part of something: *This bottle has a long neck. See:* art on page 21a.
**a pain in the neck:** a bother, an annoyance: *That job is a pain in the neck.*||*That guy is a pain in the neck with his constant complaints.*
**neck and neck:** even or very close in a competition, such as a race: *The horses ran neck and neck toward the finish line.*
**to nearly break one's neck:** to nearly get seriously hurt: *I tripped on the stairs and nearly broke my neck.*
**to risk one's neck:** to put oneself in danger, especially physical harm: *That man risked his neck when he jumped into the icy river to save the boy.*
**up to one's neck in:** very occupied with, struggling to manage: *She's up to her neck in financial problems.*

**neck** *verb old usage*
to kiss and touch lovingly: *A young couple is necking in the car over there. See:* art on page 21a.

**necklace** /ˈnɛklɪs/ *noun*
a string of jewels or a chain of gold, silver, etc., worn around the neck: *She always wears gold necklaces when she goes out in the evening.*

necklace

**necktie** /ˈnɛkˌtaɪ/ *noun*
a long, narrow piece of cloth worn under one's shirt collar and tied in front, *(synonym)* a tie: *She bought him some neckties for Christmas. See:* art on page 12a.

**nectarine** /ˌnɛktəˈrin/ *noun*
an orange-yellow fruit with a smooth skin *See:* art on page 3a.

**need** /nid/ *noun*
**1** *usually singular* something that is required or wanted: *The company has a need for computer programmers.*
**2** *usually singular* a desire, wish: *He feels a need for love (a new car, vacation, etc.).*
**3** *usually singular* something that is necessary: *There's no need for you to sign this.*
**4** something one must have to live, such as food and clothing: *Our needs are simple.*

**need** *verb*
to require, be necessary: *Everyone needs food.*||*The baby needs love and affection.*

**needle** /ˈnidl/ *noun*
**1** a thin, pointed piece of metal or plastic for sewing or knitting: *She looked for a*

*needle and thread to sew the button. See:* knitting needle.

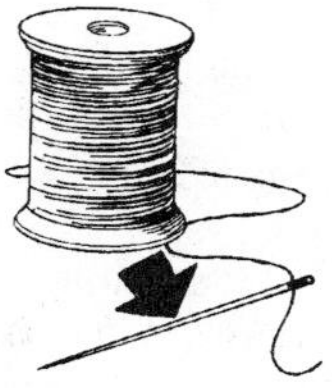

needle

**2** a thin, pointed object used in measuring instruments, radios, etc.: *The needle on my stereo is broken, so I can't listen to music.*

**3** a sharp, hollow medical instrument used to put liquid into or take liquid out of one's body (hypodermic needle): *The nurse used one hypodermic needle to take blood. See:* shot; injection.

**needless** /'nidlɪs/ *adjective*
not necessary: *This long meeting is a needless waste of time. –adverb* **needlessly.**

**needy** /'nidi/ *adjective* **needier, neediest**
**1** without the basic things necessary to live, such as food, clothing, and housing; poor: *That needy man has no money or food.*
**2** *plural* **the needy:** poor people in general: *The needy are helped by the churches in our town. (antonym)* wealthy.

**negative** /'nɛgətɪv/ *adjective*
**1** expressing no: *He received a negative response to his question.*
**2** lacking positive qualities: *She has a negative attitude toward other people.*
**3** showing a dislike of someone or something: *She had a negative opinion of the film.*
**4** always seeing the bad side of a situation or person, *(synonym)* pessimistic: *He has a negative way of looking at life.*

**negative** *noun*
**1** an expression of no: *She received a negative in response to her request.*
**2** a problem: *One of the negatives of this plan is that it costs a lot of money.*
**3** (in photography) film that shows light images as dark and dark images as light: *Photographs are made from negatives. –adverb* **negatively.** *(antonym)* positive.

**neglect** /nɪ'glɛkt/ *verb*
**1** to not give enough care or attention to someone or something: *Working every weekend, he neglected his family.*
**2** to forget to do something: *She neglected to pay a bill (mail a letter, telephone her mother, etc.).*
**3** to not do something that is one's duty or responsibility: *He neglected to make repairs in his house. –noun* **neglect;** *–adjective* **neglectful.**

**negotiate** /nɪ'goʊʃiˌeɪt/ *verb* **negotiated, negotiating, negotiates**
to talk in order to reach an agreement: *The labor union is currently negotiating with the company.*||*The two countries negotiated a peace agreement. –noun* (person) **negotiator,** (act) **negotiation.**

**neighbor** /'neɪbər/ *noun*
**1** a person or family that lives next to or near one's house, apartment, etc.: *Our neighbors are very friendly.*
**2** the person next to another person: *Please pass the paper to your neighbor. –adjective* **neighboring.**

**neighborhood** /'neɪbərˌhʊd/ *noun*
the people, buildings, land, etc., where one lives: *We are friends with many of the families in our neighborhood.*

**neither** /'niðər/ *conjunction*
not also: *"I don't know the answer."—"Neither do I."*

**neither . . . nor:** not one and not the other: *Neither you nor I can attend tonight's meeting.*||*She has neither friends nor family to help her.*

**neither here nor there:** not important: *We haven't received the official report yet, but that's neither here nor there; we all know what it's going to say.*

**neither** *adjective*
not either of two: *Neither plan is acceptable.*

**neither** *pronoun*
not either one of two: *We invited both of them, but neither can come.*||*Neither of us prepared for the exam.*

**nephew** /'nɛfyu/ *noun*
the son of one's brother or sister, or the son of one's husband or wife's brother or sister: *My nephew Luke is my sister's son. See:* niece; art on page 13a.

**nerd** /nɜrd/ *noun informal*
a boring person with poor social skills: *Why did you invite that nerd to the party? –adjective* **nerdy.**

**nerve** /nɜrv/ *noun*
**1** a long fiber that carries messages be-

tween the brain and other parts of the body: *Nerves can carry messages from the brain to move a muscle, or send feelings of pleasure or pain back to the brain.*

**2** *(no plural)* courage: *It takes nerve to skydive.*

**to have a lot of** or **some nerve:** to act in a rude way, take advantage: *He had a lot of* (or) *some nerve stealing my parking space.*

**to get on someone's nerves:** to annoy, irritate someone: *His constant complaining gets on my nerves.*

**to hit a nerve:** to bring up a painful subject for someone: *I hit a nerve when I asked him how his wife was; she divorced him last month.*

**nervous** /'nɜrvəs/ *adjective*

**1** worried about a future event, *(synonym)* anxious: *The student is very nervous about taking her exams next week.*

**2** easily upset, always worried and tense: *He's a nervous person who can't sit still for a minute.*

**3** related to the nerves: *the nervous system*||*a nervous habit (antonym)* calm. *–adverb* **nervously;** *–noun* **nervousness.**

N

**nest** /nɛst/ *noun*

a place where birds or other animals, such as insects, raise their young: *There was a bird's nest high up in the tree.*

nest

**nest** *verb*

to build a nest and raise young in it: *Birds nest in the spring.*

**net** /nɛt/ *noun*

a material made of string, wire, etc., knotted together. There are many different kinds of nets: *A fisherman uses a net to catch fish.*||*A hair net is used to hold hair in place.*||*In tennis, a player must hit the ball over a net.*

net

net

**net** *verb* **netted, netting, nets**

to catch with a net: *The fisherman nets fish in the river.*

**network** /'nɛt,wɜrk/ *noun*

**1** a system of connected roads, railways or communication lines: *a network of highways*||*a network of telephone lines*||*a computer network*

**2** a large television or radio company with stations across the country: *ABC, CBS, and NBC are the three major television networks.*

**neutral** /'nutrəl/ *adjective*

**1** not on either side in a disagreement, war, etc.: *That politician is neutral, neither for nor against a tax increase.*||*Switzerland remained neutral during World War II.*

**2** not clearly one thing or another: *Her face has a neutral expression.*

**3** (of colors) dull: *Gray is a neutral color. –noun* **neutrality.**

**never** /'nɛvər/ *adverb*

at no time, not ever: *My husband and I never go to the movies.*||*She's never been to China.*||*I'll never see you again.*

**nevertheless** /,nɛvərðə'lɛs/ *adverb*

in spite of that, however: *We spent too much money on our vacation; nevertheless, we had fun.*

**new** /nu/ *adjective*

**1** recently made, bought, arrived, etc.: *Is that a new shirt you're wearing?*||*I'm new in the neighborhood.*||*There are some new leaves on the plant.*

**2** of the latest type, design, etc.: *Have you seen the new car that company is selling?*

**3** not known, not existing before: *a new cure for the disease*||*a new idea –noun* **newness.** *(antonym)* old.

**newcomer** /'nu,kʌmər/ *noun*

a person who arrived recently from another place: *He is a newcomer to our town.*

**newlywed** /'nuli,wɛd/ *noun*

a person who has just been married: *We gave a party for the newlyweds.*

**news** /nuz/ *noun plural*

*used with a singular verb*

**1** a report on the latest major events in one's own city and country and in other parts of the world. We can find the news

on television, on the radio, and in newspapers and magazines: *I watched the evening news on television.*
**2** information about recent events or changes in someone's personal or business life: *She read a letter with news from her son.*

**newscast** /ˈnuzˌkæst/ *noun*
a radio or TV program reporting current events: *This newscast is coming to you direct from Tokyo.* –*noun* (person) **newscaster.**

**newspaper** /ˈnuzˌpeɪpər/ *noun*
a printed paper containing daily or weekly news: *We read the newspaper every morning.*

**newsstand** /ˈnuzˌstænd/ *noun*
a small store often with one side open, that sells newspapers and magazines: *The newsstand on the corner also sells candy.*

newsstand

**New Testament** *noun*
the section of the Bible that contains the earliest Christian writings, including the story of the life of Christ.

**New World** *noun*
the Western Hemisphere (North, Central, and South America): *Columbus sailed to the New World from Spain.* *(antonym)* Old World.

**new year** *noun*
the year that is coming soon (said at the end of the year before): *We are making vacation plans for the new year.*

**New Year's Day** *noun*
January 1: *New Year's Day is a holiday for most people.*

**New Year's Eve** *noun*
the evening up to 12 midnight of December 31: *We're going to a party on New Year's Eve.*

---

**USAGE NOTE:** The most well-known *New Year's Eve* celebration in the USA takes place in Times Square in New York City. Thousands of people go there at midnight to watch a ball of lights slowly fall down from the top of a large building. People all over the world watch this on TV.

---

**next** /nɛkst/ *adjective*
**1** the one after the present: *The next time that you're late, you'll be in trouble.*||*Her next book was a great success.*
**2** closest to where one is: *Turn right at the next traffic light.*

**next** *adverb*
after the present one: *I will answer your question next.*

**next** *preposition*
**next to:** beside: *He's sitting next to his sister.*

**next door** *adverb*
located beside, to the left or right of a building, office, apartment, etc.: *The shop next door always looks busy.*

**nice** /naɪs/ *adjective* **nicer, nicest**
**1** kind, friendly, pleasant: *She is such a nice person. Everyone likes her.*
**2** pretty, attractive: *That is a nice dress.*
**3** proper, well-behaved: *Your son is such a nice boy.*
**4** pleasing, enjoyable: *We had a very nice time on our vacation.* –*noun* **niceness.**

**nicely** /ˈnaɪsli/ *adverb*
**1** well, excellently: *The patient was sick, but is now doing nicely.*
**2** properly, politely: *Speak nicely to your mother.*

**nickel** /ˈnɪkəl/ *noun*
**1** *(no plural)* a hard, silver-colored metal
**2** in the USA and Canada, a five-cent coin *See:* penny; dime; quarter.

**nickname** /ˈnɪkˌneɪm/ *noun*
a name used by family and friends: *James's nickname is Jim.*

**nicotine** /ˈnɪkəˌtin/ *noun, (no plural)*
the poisonous chemical in tobacco: *It is difficult for people to stop smoking because nicotine is habit-forming.*

**niece** /nis/ *noun*
the daughter of one's brother or sister, or the daughter of one's husband or wife's brother or sister: *My niece Michelle is my brother's daughter. See:* nephew; art on page 13a.

**night** /naɪt/ *noun*
**1** the time without sunlight between sunset and sunrise: *I couldn't sleep all night.*||*We walked in the dark of night.*
**2** evening: *We went to the movies last night.*

**nightclub** /ˈnaɪtˌklʌb/ *noun*
a place where people can eat, drink, and dance or watch a show: *We go to a nightclub on Saturday nights. See:* bar, **USAGE NOTE.**

**nightgown** /ˈnaɪtˌgaʊn/ *noun*
a loose, comfortable dress that women or girls wear for sleeping: *Put on your nightgown and go to bed.*

**nightly** /ˈnaɪtli/ *adverb*
every night: *The store is open nightly until eight.*

**nightmare** /ˈnaɪtˌmɛr/ *noun*
**1** a frightening dream: *The poor child had a nightmare.*
**2** a terrible experience *–adjective* **nightmarish.**

**night shift** *noun*
**1** a work period at night: *She's a nurse who works on the night shift at a local hospital.*
**2** the people who work at this time

**night school** *noun*
a division of a school or college that gives classes in the evenings and on weekends: *After work she goes to night school to finish her degree in English.*

**nighttime** /ˈnaɪtˌtaɪm/ *noun, (no plural)*
the period of darkness between sunset and sunrise: *It was nighttime and the children were asleep.*

**nine** /naɪn/ *adjective*
the cardinal number 9: *nine apples*

**nine** *noun*
*Nine of the children were at the park.*

**nineteen** /ˌnaɪnˈtin/ *adjective*
the cardinal number 19: *She's 19 years old.*

**nineteen** *noun*
*Nineteen of the soldiers were killed. –adjective* **nineteenth** /ˌnaɪnˈtin θ/.

**ninety** /ˈnaɪnti/ *noun, plural* **nineties**
the cardinal number 90: *The film is 90 minutes long.*

**ninety** *noun*
*Ninety out of a hundred people voted for her. –adjective* **ninetieth** /ˈnaɪntiɪθ/.

**ninth** /naɪnθ/ *adjective*
the ordinal number 9: *She was my ninth customer today.*

**ninth** *noun*
*She is the ninth in line.*

**nip** /nɪp/ *noun*
a sharp, shallow bite: *The little boy got a nip on the hand from a dog. –verb* **to nip.**

**nipple** /ˈnɪpəl/ *noun*
**1** the tip of the breast, through which mother's milk is passed to babies
**2** the top rubber part of a baby's bottle

**nitpick** /ˈnɪtˌpɪk/ *verb*
to find problems with small, unimportant details, usually in someone else's work: *Instead of helping us write the report, he just kept nitpicking. –noun* (person) **nitpicker.**

**nitrogen** /ˈnaɪtr əʤən/ *noun, (no plural)*
a gas which makes up most of the earth's air and is essential to plant and animal life

**nitty-gritty** /ˌnɪtiˈgrɪti/ *noun, (no plural) informal*
the specific details or basic facts of a situation
**to get down to the nitty-gritty:** to begin discussing the most important aspects or specific details to reach an agreement: *Let's get down to the nitty-gritty so that we can come to an agreement on how to solve this problem.*

**no** /noʊ/ *adverb*
used to tell someone you do not agree or do not want to do something: *"Do you want to go?"—"No, I don't."*||*No, don't say that because it's not true.*

**no** *adjective*
**1** not any: *to have no time (no money, no fear, etc.)*
**2** not at all: *She's no cook.*||*The sign says "No smoking."*||*We are no closer to the truth.*

**no** *noun*
an answer to a question: *She gave my request a solid no. (antonym)* yes.

**Nobel Prize** /noʊˈbɛl/ *noun*
an award given each year in the following areas: physical sciences, medicine, economics, literature, and efforts towards world peace: *She won the Nobel Prize in chemistry.*

**nobility** /noʊ'bɪləti/ *noun, (no plural)*
**1** the group of people of high social rank: *a member of the French nobility*
**2** the quality of being noble

**noble** /'noʊbəl/ *adjective*
having or showing strength of character, high ideals, and honorable intentions: *noble ambitions to help the poor||a noble cause* *–noun* (person) **noble;** *–adverb* **nobly.**

**nobody** /'noʊ,badi/ *noun*
no one, no person: *The house was empty; nobody was there.*

**nobody** *noun, plural* **nobodies**
an unimportant person, someone without money, education, or social position: *How did that nobody get to be president of a company?*

**nod** /nad/ *verb* **nodded, nodding, nods**
to move the head up and down a little to show that you agree or to greet another person: *When the waiter asked if he wanted more coffee, he nodded "Yes."*

**noise** /nɔɪz/ *noun*
a sound, especially an unpleasant one: *We heard a strange noise.||Street noise keeps me awake all night.||The children were told not to make any noise.*

**noisy** /'nɔɪzi/ *adjective* **noisier, noisiest**
**1** full of noise and sounds: *a noisy restaurant*
**2** making loud noise: *a noisy machine*

noisy

**nomad** /'noʊ,mæd/ *noun*
a member of a group with no permanent home that moves often in search of water and grassy land for its animals: *We passed desert nomads watching over their goats.* *–adjective* **nomadic.**

**nominate** /'namə,neɪt/ *verb* **nominated, nominating, nominates**
**1** to officially suggest someone for election to a position: *The Republican Party nominated him for President.*
**2** to appoint someone to a position: *The manager nominated me to attend the conference.* *–noun* (act) **nomination.**

**nominative** /'namənətɪv/ *noun*
a grammatical word form referring to the subject of something: *The pronoun "we" is nominative.*

**non-** /nan/
*prefix* not, lack of: *Nonfat milk is milk with no fat.*

**noncredit** /,nan 'krɛdɪt/ *adjective*
(in education) referring to a course offered for no school credit: *I take the noncredit reading course.*

**nondiscriminatory**
/,nandɪ'skrɪmənə,tɔri/ *adjective*
not basing one's judgement of a person on race, religion, sex, or nationality: *The company has nondiscriminatory hiring practices.* *–noun* **nondiscrimination.**

**none** /nʌn/ *pronoun*
**1** not any: *We wanted some coffee, but there was none left.*
**2** no one: *None of the children had enough to eat.*

**nonetheless** /,nʌnðə'lɛs/ *adverb*
however, in spite of that: *The soldiers were cold, tired, and hungry; nonetheless, they continued to march.*

**nonfat** /,nan'fæt/ *adjective*
containing no fat: *Athletes often buy nonfat milk.*

**nonfiction** /,nan'fɪkʃən/ *noun*
stories, books, and articles about real people and events: *The author writes only historical nonfiction. See:* fiction, USAGE NOTE.

**nonflammable** /,nan'flæməbəl/ *adjective*
referring to something that cannot burn or be set on fire: *The furniture is covered with nonflammable material.*

**nonpolluting** /,nanpə'lutɪŋ/ *adjective*
not causing any kind of pollution: *Sun and wind power are nonpolluting producers of energy.*

**nonprescription** /,nanprɪ'skrɪpʃən/ *adjective*
(of medicine) not requiring a doctor's prescription, *(synonym)* over-the-counter: *Aspirin is a nonprescription drug.*

**nonprofessional** /ˌnɑnprəˈfɛʃənəl/ *adjective noun*
referring to a person who works at, but is not an official member of, a particular profession or trade: *We hired nonprofessional carpenters to save money.*

**nonprofit** /ˌnɑn ˈprɑfɪt/ *adjective*
(of businesses and organizations) not intended to make a profit

---

**USAGE NOTE:** *Nonprofit organizations* do not have to pay tax on money they receive. Churches, charities, museums, and schools are usually nonprofit.

---

**nonrefundable** /ˌnɑnrɪˈfʌndəbəl/ *adjective*
referring to money (paid for something) that will not be returned for any reason: *We made a nonrefundable deposit toward buying a house.*

**nonresident** /ˌnɑnˈrɛzədənt/ *noun*
a person who does not permanently live in an area. This word usually relates to one's legal address or foreign citizenship: *She is a nonresident living in New York on a student visa.*

**nonreturnable** /ˌnɑnrɪˈtɜrnəbəl/ *adjective*
referring to something bought that may not be returned to get one's money back or to exchange for another product: *We threw away the nonreturnable beer and soda cans.*

**nonsense** /ˈnɑnˌsɛns/ *noun, (no plural)*
**1** words that have no meaning: *The baby spoke nonsense.*
**2** speech or writing that is foolish or untrue: *His ideas are pure nonsense.*
**3** an act or behavior that doesn't make sense: *That company wants us to pay a bill that we've already paid. That is nonsense!*

**nonstop** /ˌnɑnˈstɑp/ *adverb*
without stopping: *He worked nonstop for 24 hours.*

**nonviolence** /ˌnɑnˈvaɪələns/ *noun, (no plural)*
a belief that forbids the use of force in bringing about political change: *Mahatma Gandhi favored nonviolence in India's struggle to gain independence from Great Britain.*

---

**USAGE NOTE:** Following the ideas of Mahatma Gandhi, Dr. Martin Luther King Jr., led *nonviolent* protests during the *civil rights* movement in the 1950s and 1960s. Later the antiwar and women's movements also held nonviolent protests. One popular type of protest was the *sit-in*, in which people would sit down somewhere and refuse to move. Police had to carry the people away from the protest area.

---

**nonviolent** /ˌnɑnˈvaɪələnt/ *adjective*
peaceful, without the use of force: *It is always best to try to find nonviolent solutions to problems. (antonym)* violent.

**noodle** /ˈnudl/ *noun*
**1** a long, narrow or wide flat strip of pasta made from a mixture of flour, egg, and water: *Boil the noodles first.*
**2** *informal* head: *You can figure it out; just use your noodle! See:* art on page 17a.

**noon** /nun/ *noun*
12 o'clock during the day: *We stopped work at noon for lunch.*

**no one** *pronoun*
not one person, nobody: *No one is in the office; everyone has left.*

**noontime** /ˈnuntaɪm/ *noun*
the period surrounding 12 o'clock during the day: *I go out for lunch at noontime.*

**noose** /nus/ *noun*
a rope tied at one end in a loop with a knot that allows the loop to tighten for the purpose of hanging someone by the neck

**nope** /noʊp/ *adverb informal*
no: *"Are you coming with me?"—"Nope, I can't leave now."*

**nor** /nɔr/ *conjunction*
and not: *I can't afford to buy a house, nor can you.*
**neither . . . nor:** not that one either: *Neither you nor she plans to attend the meeting.*

**normal** /ˈnɔrməl/ *adjective*
as expected, typical, average: *Hot weather is normal for the summer.*||*My temperature was above normal this morning.*||*She had a normal childhood.* –*noun* **normality** /nɔrˈmæləti/.

**normally** /ˈnɔrməli/ *adverb*
ordinarily, usually: *Normally, I would go fishing, but the weather is bad.*

**north** /nɔrθ/ *noun, (no plural)*
**1** the direction to the right when facing a sunset
**2** the northern part of a country: *Minnesota is in the north; Texas is in the south.*
**The North:** in the USA, the former Union states in the Civil War: *The North defeated the South in the Civil War.*

**north** *adjective*
**1** referring to the area towards the north: *the north side of the street*
**2** (of wind) coming from the north: *a cold north wind*

**north** *adverb*
towards the north: *The plane (car, boat, etc.) is going north.*

**northern** /ˈnɔrðərn/ *adjective*
located in the north: *the northern part of the United States*||*northern California*

**northerner** /ˈnɔr ðərnər/ *noun*
someone originally from or living in the northern part of a country: *He was a northerner from Boston traveling in the southwest.*

**North Pole** *noun*
the point on earth that is furthest north and the land around it: *The scientist is studying bird life at the North Pole.*

**nose** /noʊz/ *noun*
**1** the part of the face above the mouth that contains two holes (called nostrils) for smelling and breathing: *She has a long straight nose.*
**2** sense of smell: *Dogs have good noses.*
**3** too much interest or interference in the affairs of others: *He'd better keep his nose out of my business.*
**4** the forward part of certain things: *the nose of a plane (boat, gun, etc.)*
**on the nose:** exactly right: *His estimate of the cost of the project was on the nose.*
**under one's nose:** very near someone, easy to see: *Your keys are right under your nose! See:* art on page 21a.

**nosebleed** /ˈnoʊzblid/ *noun*
a condition of blood running from the nose: *He got a nosebleed after being hit in the face by a baseball.*

**nostril** /ˈnɑstrəl/ *noun*
one of the two holes in the nose *See:* art on page 21a.

**nosy** /ˈnoʊzi/ *adjective* **nosier, nosiest**
too curious about the affairs of others: *She's so nosy; she's always asking me personal questions which I refuse to answer.* –*noun* **nosiness.**

**not** /nɑt/ *adverb*
used to express a negative statement or question, often shortened to *-n't* after auxiliary verbs: *He will not pay his bill.*||*You shouldn't say that.*||*"Are you ready?"—"No, I'm not."*||*Don't leave yet.*||*She doesn't believe that he's guilty. (= She believes that he isn't guilty.)*||*Can't you see I'm busy?*
**not at all:** a response when someone thanks you for something: *"I really appreciate your help."—"Not at all, it was no trouble."*

**notarize** /ˈnoʊtəˌraɪz/ *verb* **notarized, notarizing, notarizes**
to have a notary public state that a signature on a document is real (and not fake): *I had my signature on the contract notarized at the bank.* –*noun* **notarization** /ˌnoʊtərəˈzeɪʃən/.

**notary public** or **notary** /ˈnoʊtəri/ *noun, plural* **notaries public** or **notary publics**
a person with the legal authority to state that a signature on a document is real (and not fake): *The lawyer is also a notary public.*

**note** /noʊt/ *noun*
**1** a short written message: *She sent me a thank-you note for the gift.*
**2** *usually plural* **notes:** words, phrases, or short sentences that help one remember what one heard or read: *I studied my class notes before the history exam.*
**3** a piece of paper representing a promise to pay a sum of money: *She received a bank note for $1000.*
**4** (in music) a single sound or the symbol used to represent it: *She played the first few notes of the song.*

notes

**to take** or **make notes:** to write down words, phrases, or short sentences to remember what one heard or read: *He took notes during the meeting.*

**note** *verb* **noted, noting, notes**
**1** to write down: *I noted the most important information on a piece of paper.*
**2** to observe, pay attention to: *Note the "For Sale" signs in front of the houses.*

**notebook** /'noʊt-bʊk/ *noun*
**1** a book with blank or lined pages to make notes in: *Students carry their notebooks to class.*
**2** a small computer *See:* art on page 8a.

notebook

**nothing** /'nʌθɪŋ/ *noun, (no plural)*
**1** not anything: *There is nothing to eat in the kitchen.*||*She said nothing to me about the problem.*
**2** not anything important, interesting, valuable, etc.: *There is nothing in the newspaper (on TV, the radio, etc.) today.*

**nothing but:** only: *The company makes nothing but toys.*||*That child is nothing but trouble.*

**to have nothing to do with someone** or **something:** to avoid completely: *She will have nothing to do with her former husband.*

**notice** /'noʊtɪs/ *verb* **noticed, noticing, notices**
to observe, to look at with interest: *I noticed that there was a hole in my sweater.*||*She noticed him as soon as he entered the room.*

**notice** *noun*
**1** a written message: *I received a notice that the rent was unpaid.*||*There was a notice on the door that the store had moved.*
**2** a statement or warning about a future event: *When she decided to quit her job, she gave the company two weeks' notice.*

**noticeable** /'noʊtɪsəbəl/ *adjective*
easy to see, obvious: *There has been a noticeable increase in sales.*||*His weight loss is noticeable. –adverb* **noticeably.**

**notify** /'noʊtəˌfaɪ/ *verb* **notified, notifying, notifies**
to give information to, to state officially: *A man notified the police that his store had been robbed.*

**noun** /naʊn/ *noun*
(in grammar) a name of a person, place, thing, action, or quality. It is used as the subject or object of a sentence or the object of a preposition: *In the sentence, "People buy stamps at the post office," "People," "stamps," and "post office" are nouns.*

**nourish** /'nɜrɪʃ/ *verb* **nourishes**
to feed, especially with healthful food: *Children should be nourished with good meals.*

**nourishment** /'nɜrɪʃmənt/ *noun, (no plural)*
food, especially healthy things to eat: *A child needs nourishment to grow strong.*

**novel** /'nɑvəl/ *noun*
a book-length story that is a product of the imagination: *She wrote a novel about the war. See:* fiction, USAGE NOTE.

**novel** *adjective*
new and different: *He thought of a novel solution to the problem.*

**novelist** /'nɑvəlɪst/ *noun*
a person who writes novels: *The novelist has written several best-sellers.*

**novelty** /'nɑvəlti/ *noun, plural* **novelties**
**1** something new and unusual: *It is a novelty to visit Disney World for the first time.*
**2** a small, unusual item: *The store sold novelties (small statues, baseball caps) to tourists.*

**November** /noʊ'vɛmbər/ *noun*
the eleventh month of the year: *November has 30 days.*

**now** /naʊ/ *adverb*
**1** at this time: *I used to take the bus, but now I take the subway.*
**2** immediately, (synonym) at once: *Go now, or you'll be late to work.*
**3** (used in telling or writing stories) then, next: *She heard a knock at the door. Now she was frightened.*

**now and then** or **now and again:** occasionally, once in a while: *I still see him now and then.*

**now that:** *conjunction* since: *Now that everyone's here, we can begin the meeting. (antonym)* later.

**NOW** /naʊ/ *noun*
*abbreviation of* National Organization for Women, an organization in the USA that works to improve the lives and protect the rights of women

**no way** *interjection informal*
no, definitely not: *He wants me to lend him $1,000. No way!*

**nowhere** /ˈnoʊˌwɛr/ *adverb*
not anywhere, in no place: *My wallet is nowhere to be found.*

**nowhere** *noun*
**in the middle of nowhere:** in a place where few people live: *Our car broke down in the middle of nowhere and we couldn't find a phone. (antonym)* somewhere.

**nuclear energy** *noun, (no plural)*
power produced by the splitting of the atom: *Nuclear energy is used to produce electricity.*

**nuclear missile** *noun*
a military weapon containing a nuclear explosive device

**nucleus** /ˈnukliəs/ *noun, plural* **nuclei** /-kliˌaɪ/
**1** the center of something: *Those three people are the nucleus of the organization.*
**2** (in physics) the center of an atom: *The nucleus of an atom is composed of protons and neutrons.*
**3** (in biology) the central part of a cell: *The nucleus of a cell controls its growth.*

**nude** /nud/ *adjective*
without any clothes, *(synonym)* naked: *Some people like to sleep nude.*

**nude** *noun*
(in a painting, picture, or other works of art) a person without clothes: *The artist was famous for his nudes. –noun* **nudity.** *(antonym)* clothed.

**nuisance** /ˈnusəns/ *noun*
a bother, someone or something that causes annoyance: *It's a nuisance, but we need to do the report over again and correct the errors.‖She's a real nuisance, always calling when we're eating dinner.*

**numb** /nʌm/ *adjective*
**1** without feeling: *My hands are numb from the cold.*
**2** unable to feel any emotion: *After the death of my brother, I felt numb. –noun* **numbness.**

**number** /ˈnʌmbər/ *noun*
**1** a symbol, such as "3," or a word, such as "five," that expresses a quantity or a position in a series: *The average number of students in a class is 25.‖She is number 21 on the waiting list.*
**2** a group of people or things: *A large number of people visit this museum every year.‖She gave me a number of (=several) suggestions.*
**3** a total: *The number of inches in a foot is 12.*
**4** a number used to identify someone: *a social security number‖a checking account number*
**5** a performance of a song, dance, piece of music, etc. in a series: *Her first number was a song from a popular musical.*

**number** *verb*
**1** to give a number to something: *I numbered the pages of the report.*
**2** to include, consider: *She numbered him among her closest friends.*
**3** to total: *The crowd numbered in the thousands.*



**numeral** /ˈnumərəl/ *noun*
a symbol that represents a number: *The Roman numeral for "9" is "IX."*

**numerator** /ˈnuməˌreɪtər/ *noun*
the symbol over the line in a common fraction: *The numerator in the fraction 2/3 is 2. See:* denominator.

numerator

**numerical** /nuˈmɛrɪkəl/ *adjective*
related to numbers: *The report provided us with the necessary numerical information. –adverb* **numerically.**

**numerous** /ˈnumər əs/ *adjective*
many: *Numerous people attended the concert.*

**nun** /nʌn/ *noun*
a female member of a religious order: *She is a nun who is studying to be a nurse. See:* monk.

**nurse** /nɜrs/ *noun*
**1** a person specially trained to take care of sick, injured, or old people: *The nurse gave the patient some pills.*
**2** a person employed to take care of young children: *The wealthy family hired a nurse for their child.*

**nurse** *verb* **nursed, nursing, nurses**
**1** to give care to sick or old people: *He nursed his wife back to health.*
**2** to feed a baby through the breast: *She nursed the baby for six months. See:* art on page 11a.

**nursery** /ˈnɜrsəri/ *noun, plural* **nurseries**
**1** a room specially set up for children: *The children were playing in the nursery.*
**2** a place you can buy plants and trees: *a tree nursery*

**nursery rhyme** *noun*
a story for children in the form of a short poem: *The nursery rhymes of Mother Goose are popular with children.*

**nursery school** *noun*
a school for children before they enter kindergarten

**nursing** /ˈnɜrsɪŋ/ *noun*
the profession of caring for the ill: *She chose a career in nursing after high school.*



**nursing home** *noun*
a private institution for the care of the elderly: *My 80-year-old father went into a nursing home last fall.*

**nut** /nʌt/ *noun*
**1** a fruit with a hard shell or its seed: *a candy made from fruit and nuts*
**2** *informal* a person who seems very odd or crazy: *Stop acting like a nut!*
**3** a small piece of metal with a hole in the middle used with a bolt.

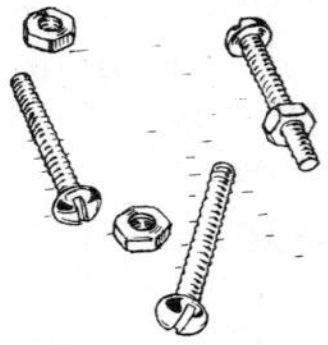
**nuts and bolts**

**nutrient** /ˈnutriənt/ *noun adjective*
one of the substances contained in food that is essential to life, such as protein, vitamins, and minerals: *Fruit, vegetables, and whole grains are high in nutrients.*

**nutrition** /nuˈtrɪʃən/ *noun, (no plural)*
**1** the study of how the body needs and uses food: *She's taking a course in nutrition in college.*
**2** the processes by which the body uses food: *The body requires proper nutrition in order to stay healthy. –adjective* **nutritional;** *–noun* (person) **nutritionist.**

**nutritious** /nuˈtrɪʃəs/ *adjective*
(of food) containing substances that are necessary for good health: *Fruit is more nutritious than cake.*

**nuts** /nʌts/ *adjective informal*
crazy, foolish: *You're nuts to try to climb that mountain; it's too dangerous.*
**to be nuts about** or **over:** very enthusiastic about, very fond of, *(synonym)* crazy about: *She's just nuts about her new boyfriend.*

**nutshell** /ˈnʌtˌʃɛl/ *noun*
the hard outer covering of a nut
**in a nutshell:** in the fewest possible words: *The situation in a nutshell is that I don't love you anymore and I want a divorce.*

**nutty** /ˈnʌti/ *adjective* **nuttier, nuttiest**
**1** tasting like or containing nuts: *The almonds give the pie a nutty flavor.*
**2** crazy, foolish: *What a nutty idea!*

**nylon** /ˈnaɪˌlɑn/ *noun, (no plural)*
a strong, artificial material used in making cloth, thread, and stockings: *Women wear stockings made of nylon.*
**nylons:** *plural* stockings, usually worn by women with a skirt or dress: *I always wear black nylons with my black dress when we go out to a nice place.*

# O,o

**O, o** /oʊ/ *noun* **O's, o's** or **Os, os**
**1** the 15th letter of the English alphabet
**2** zero (especially in saying numbers): *My telephone number is 456-00 (oh-oh) 22.*

**oak** /oʊk/ *noun*
a tall hardwood tree that grows small nuts called acorns, or the wood of such trees *See:* art on page 1a.

**oar** /ɔr/ *noun*
a piece of wood with a flat end used to row a boat

oar

**oasis** /oʊ'eɪsɪs/ *noun, plural* **oases** /oʊ'eɪˌsiz/
a place with trees and water in the desert

**oath** /oʊθ/ *noun, plural* **oaths** /oʊðz/
a promise to do something: *The soldiers took an oath of loyalty to their country.*

**oatmeal** /'oʊtˌmil / *noun*
crushed oats made into cookies and breakfast cereal

**oats** /oʊts/ *noun plural*
a type of grain eaten by animals and people *–adjective* **oat.**

**obedient** /ə'bidiənt/ *adjective*
willing to follow or obey (rules, orders, etc.) *(antonym)* disobedient. *–adverb* **obediently;** *–noun* **obedience.**

**obey** /oʊ'beɪ/ *verb* **obeyed, obeying, obeys**
to do what someone or something asks or orders you to do *(antonym)* disobey.

**object** /'ɑbʤɪkt/ *noun*
**1** a thing, especially one you can see or touch: *A pencil was one of the objects left on the table.*
**2** (in grammar) the focus of a verb's action: *The word "answers" is the object in the sentence: "Students give answers to questions."*

**object** /əb'ʤɛkt/ *verb*
to not like or agree with something: *She objects to the death penalty.* *–noun* (person) **objector.**

**objection** /əb'ʤɛkʃən/ *noun*
a statement or feeling that you do not like or agree with: *I have an objection to high prices.*

**objective** /əb'ʤɛktɪv/ *noun*
a goal, purpose: *My objective in going to school is to get a degree.*

**obligation** /ˌɑblə'geɪʃən/ *noun*
something you must do, especially because of a rule or law: *She has a family obligation to visit her sick aunt.*

**oblige** /ə'blaɪʤ/ *verb* **obliged, obliging, obliges**
required because of law, etc.: *We are obliged to stop the car at a red light.*

**obnoxious** /əb'nɑkʃəs/ *adjective*
very unpleasant: *He has an obnoxious habit of cleaning his teeth during meals.* *–adverb* **obnoxiously.**

**obscure** /əb'skyʊr/ *verb* **obscured, obscuring, obscures**
to block from view, hide: *Fog obscured the airport, so our plane could not land.*

O

**obscure** *adjective*
difficult to see or understand: *That professor's writing is so obscure that it is very hard to understand.* *–adverb* **obscurely;** *–noun* **obscurity.**

**observation** /ˌɑbzərˈveɪʃən/ *noun*
**1** watching someone or something
**2** a remark, opinion: *My friend made an observation that I seem nervous today.*

**observe** /əbˈzɜrv/ *verb* **observed, observing, observes**
to watch someone or something *–noun* (person) **observer.**

**obsess** /əbˈsɛs/ *verb* **obsesses**
to have something control your thoughts: *He is obsessed with being clean; he's always washing his hands.* *–adjective* **obsessed;** *–noun* **obsession.**

**obsolete** /ˌɑbsəˈlit/ *adjective*
no longer used, replaced by something better: *Tape will soon be obsolete, now that compact discs are popular.*

**obstacle** /ˈɑbstɪkəl/ *noun*
something that gets in your way and keeps you from doing something: *A tree fell across the road and became an obstacle for cars and trucks.*



**obstruct** /əbˈstrʌkt/ *verb*
to keep someone from doing something: *A tree fell across the road and obstructed traffic.* *–noun* **obstruction;** *–adverb* **obstructively.**

**obtain** /əbˈteɪn/ *verb*
to get something: *She obtained the house with money from her parents.* *–adjective* **obtainable.**

**obvious** /ˈɑbviəs/ *adjective*
easy and clear to see or understand: *It is obvious that it is going to rain from those black clouds.* *–adverb* **obviously;** *–noun* **obviousness.**

**occasion** /əˈkeɪʒən/ *noun*
**1** a time when something happens: *On occasion, he smokes a cigarette after dinner.*
**2** a special time or event: *Their wedding was a happy occasion.*

**occasional** /əˈkeɪənəl/ *adjective*
happening sometimes, not often *–adverb* **occasionally.**

**occupation** /ˌɑkyəˈpeɪʃən/ *noun*
**1** one's means of making a living, job: *Her occupation is as a doctor.*
**2** any activity on which you spend time: *Her chief occupation at school was reading.*
**3** taking control of something: *The enemy's occupation of the city lasted a year.* *–adjective* **occupational.**

**occupy** /ˈɑkyəˌpaɪ/ *verb* **occupied, occupying, occupies**
**1** to be, live, or work in a place
**2** to take control of something: *Soldiers occupied the town.*
**3** to take someone's time or space: *Children occupy their free time with their toys and games.* *–noun* (person) **occupier.**

**occur** /əˈkɜr/ *verb* **occurred, occurring, occurs**
to happen: *The accident occurred at 10:00 A.M.* *–noun* **occurrence.**
**to occur to someone:** to come to (someone's) mind: *It suddenly occurred to me that I knew how to solve that problem!*

**ocean** /ˈoʊʃən/ *noun*
the great body of salt water covering more than 70 percent of the earth's surface: *the Atlantic Ocean* *–adjective* **oceanic** /ˌoʊʃiˈænɪk/.

**o'clock** /əˈklɑk/ *adverb*
a way of saying the time: *11 o'clock*

**October** /ɑkˈtoʊbər/ *noun*
the 10th month of the year: *October is harvest time in many parts of the USA.*

octopus

**octopus** /ˈɑktəpəs/ *noun, plural* **octopuses**
a sea animal with eight arms and a soft body

**odd** /ɑd/ *adjective*
**1** (about numbers) not able to be divided by two. The numbers 1, 3, 5, and 7 are odd numbers.
**2** strange, unusual: *He is never late and it's odd that he's not here now.*
**3** part of a pair or set: *There is a box of odd socks in the laundry room.*

**odd jobs:** small jobs that are not full-time or regular: *She does odd jobs, such as painting rooms and fixing cars.* –*adverb* **oddly.** *(antonym)* usual.

**oddity** /'ɑdəti/ *noun, plural* **oddities**
something unusual: *Black roses are oddities.*

**odds** /ɑdz/ *noun plural*
the possibility that something will happen: *The doctors have given him good odds for a full recovery.*

**odor** /'oʊdər/ *noun*
a bad smell or scent: *The odor of old fish filled the air.*

**of** /ʌv/ *preposition*
**1** showing who or what owns something: *That old car of mine gives me trouble all the time.*
**2** showing what something is made of: *That necklace is made of pearls.*
**3** used with numbers, especially times and dates: *It is five minutes of eight (o'clock).*
**4** showing that someone or something is in a group: *All of the students understood.*
**5** showing who or what does or has something: *It is nice of her to help.*

**off** /ɔf/ *preposition*
**1** from or away from something: *He took his coat off the hanger.*
**2** down from something: *Water drips off the roof in a rain storm.*
**3** at a distance from a time or a place: *Ships fish off the coastline.*

**off** *adverb*
**1** not being used: *Turn the radio off, please.*
**2** not at school or work: *She asked for a week off.*

**to be better off:** having a better life: *She has a good job and is better off now than she was when unemployed. (antonym)* on.

**offend** /ə'fɛnd/ *verb*
to hurt someone's feelings –*noun* (person) **offender.**

**offense** /ə'fɛns/ *noun*
an act that is against the rules or laws

**to take offense:** to feel unhappy or angry: *They took offense at our suggestions.* –*adjective* **offensive;** –*adverb* **offensively.**

**offer** /'ɔfər/ *verb*
to say you will do something or give something (to somebody) if somebody wants you to: *We offered to help clean the house.*||*He offered me a cup of coffee.*

**offer** *noun*
an act or object that is done for or given to somebody if he or she wants it: *They made me an offer of a new job.*

**office** /'ɔfɪs/ *noun*
**1** a place of business (building or room) with desk, chair, telephone, etc.: *His office is in a tall building.*
**2** an official or government position: *The President has the highest office in government.*
**3** a place where you can get something or find some information: *the post office*||*the airline ticket office*

**officer** /'ɔfəsər/ *noun*
**1** a person in the military or police who commands others
**2** a person who has power or responsibility in a business or government

**official** /ə'fɪʃəl/ *noun*
a person who works for a government or other organization: *Labor officials met to discuss a new contract.*

**official** *adjective*
of or related to a position of power or authority: *Presidents of two nations signed the official documents for a peace agreement.* –*adverb* **officially.**

**off-season** *noun*
not during the height of the tourist season *(antonym)* in-season.

**offshore** /ˌɔf'ʃɔr/ *adjective*
away from the land in the water *(antonym)* onshore.

**often** /'ɔfən/ *adverb*
many times, frequently

**every so often:** occasionally: *He only washes his car every so often. (antonym)* seldom.

**oh** /oʊ/
an expression of emotion, like surprise, fear, or disgust: *Oh, I forgot my eyeglasses!*

**oil** /ɔɪl/ *noun*
**1** a thick liquid (petroleum) found under the sea or the earth and that we can use in machines or burn for heat or energy
**2** the fatty liquid that comes from some plants, or animals: *People cook with olive oil.*

oil

**oil** *verb*
to put oil into or onto something: *I oiled the wheel on my bicycle. See:* grease.

**oil painting** *noun*
a painting done with paints made from oil

**oil well** *noun*
a hole dug for oil: *Oil wells are found in many parts of Texas.*

**oily** /ˈɔɪli/ *adjective* **oilier, oiliest**
covered by or containing oil: *The salad was very oily. –adjective* **oiled.**

**ointment** /ˈɔɪntmənt/ *noun*
cream that contains medicine: *ointment for sore muscles*

ointment

**OK** or **okay** /oʊˈkeɪ/ *adjective informal*
all right, well: *I feel OK today.*

**OK** or **okay** *verb informal* **OK'd, OK'ing, OK's** or **okayed, okaying, okays**
to give approval: *They okayed the proposal in just five minutes.*

**OK** or **okay** *noun informal*
permission, approval: *They gave it an OK.*

**old** /oʊld/ *adjective*
**1** indicating a specific age: *His brother is 20 years old.*
**2** indicating long life or existence: *Their grandfather is very old.*
**3** in use for a long time: *She was wearing an old hat.*
**4** past, before now: *He met his old roommate for dinner last week.*
**5** known for a long time: *It was good to see my old friends again. (antonym)* new.

**old** *noun*
**the old:** *plural* elderly people, the aged: *The old have special medical needs.*

**USAGE NOTE:** When describing people, it is more common and polite to use the word *elderly: She takes care of two elderly women.*

**old-age** /oʊld eɪdʒ/ *noun*
the time in your life when you are old

**old-fashioned** /ˌoʊldˈfæʃənd/ *adjective*
no longer used, out-of-date: *His clothes are old-fashioned.*

**olive** /ˈɑlɪv/ *noun*
**1** (the small green or black oval fruit of) a tree that comes from southern Europe
**2** a yellow-green color

**Olympic Games** /əˈlɪmpɪk/ or **Olympics** *noun plural*
the international sports competitions held every four years

**omelet** or **omelette** /ˈɑmlɪt/ *noun*
a fried dish made of eggs often served folded over a filling, such as cheese

**omit** /oʊˈmɪt/ *verb* **omitted, omitting, omits**
to leave out something, not include it *–noun* **omission.** *(antonym)* include.

**on** /ɑn/ *preposition*
**1** on the surface of (supported by, touching, connected to): *We have a rug on the floor.*
**2** indicating location: *Their house is located on the seashore.*
**3** indicating days or dates: *We'll be there on Sunday, June 19th.*
**4** indicating something that is in process: *I'm on vacation now.*
**5** referring to a subject, about: *We watched a video tape on exercise.*
**6** by means of, using: *I talked to the doctor on the phone.||She is on penicillin.||We went to church on foot.*

**on** *adverb*
**1** working, being used: *He turned the television on.*

**2** continuing, more distant: *He arrived in Newark and drove on to Baltimore.*
**3** covering the body: *She put her shoes on.*
**on and on:** for a long time, without stopping: *The speaker talked on and on.*
**on** *adjective*
working, being used: *The TV is on. (antonym)* off.

**once** /wʌns/ *adverb*
**1** occurring one time only: *I told him what to do just once.*
**2** occurring in the past: *I once visited California many years ago.*
**at once:** immediately, right now
**just for once:** for this time only
**once in a while:** sometimes
**once more** or **once again:** one more time, again
**once** *conjunction*
when, as soon as: *Once he understood, he did what he was told to do.*

**one** /wʌn/ *noun*
the cardinal number 1: *Turn to page one in your book.*||*Let's meet at one (= one o'clock).*||*I owe you one (= one dollar).*
**one** *pronoun*
**1** any person, you: *One can only try.*
**2** someone or something that has already been said: *He looked for a pen and found one in his pocket.*
**3** a single person, thing, or animal: *She's the one he wants to meet.*
**one another:** each other: *She told her children to be kind to one another.*
**one** *adjective*
**1** being a single person, thing, or animal: *He has only one dollar in his wallet.*
**2** related to a unified group: *Our children returned home and we are one family again.*
**one by one:** in single file, one at a time

**oneself** /wʌn'sɛlf/ *reflexive pronoun*
**1** alone or without help: *There are many things one must do by oneself.*
**2** (used to make something sound stronger): *One must believe oneself that anything is possible.*
**to be oneself:** to act normally or in a relaxed manner

**one-way** *adjective*
allowing travel in only one direction: *a one-way street*||*a one-way ticket*

**onion** /'ʌnyən/ *noun*
a round vegetable with a strong smell and taste *See:* art on page 2a.

**online** or **on-line** /ˌɑn'laɪn/ *adjective*
**1** having, offering, or using a connection to a network of computers (by direct wiring or modem)
**2** (of computers and electrical equipment) working properly: *The system was down earlier, but now it's online again. (antonym)* off-line.

**only** /'oʊnli/ *adjective*
**1** with no others in its group: *I gave my only pencil to a friend.*
**2** in a subgroup of a whole: *They were the only students who passed the exam.*
**3** most worthy of consideration, *(synonym)* superior: *She's the only candidate for this position.*
**an only child:** with no brothers or sisters
**only** *adverb*
**1** with nobody or nothing else: *I can only say how sorry I am.*
**2** at least: *If they would only try to understand.*
**only** *conjunction*
except, but: *The sky is clear, only it is too hot to go for a walk.*|| *You may go bicycle riding, only watch out for cars.*

**on-the-job** *adjective*
happening during work, such as learning a skill: *She received on-the-job training on how to use a computer.*

**onto** /'ɑntu/ *preposition*
on top of, something: *The horse left the field and walked onto the road.*

**onward** /'ɑnwərd/ or **onwards** *adverb adjective*
in a forward direction: *After landing in Los Angeles, the plane flew onwards to Hawaii. (antonym)* backward(s).

**ooh** /u/ *exclamation*
an expression of pleasure, surprise, or disgust: *Ooh, he's a terrific actor!*

**oops** /ʊps/ *exclamation*
an expression of surprise or apology said after making a mistake, dropping something, etc.: *Oops, I spilled some coffee.*

**open** /'oʊpən/ *adjective*
**1** not closed or locked: *The front door is open; please come in!*

**2** without trees, buildings, etc.: *They built their house in an open field.*
**3** ready for business: *She looked everywhere before she found a drugstore that was open. (antonym)* closed. *–adverb* **openly.** *See:* open-minded.

**open** *verb*
**1** to move something so that people or things can pass: *She opened the door before I could knock.*
**2** to unfold something so you can see it: *She opened the map on the table.*
**3** to start, begin: *The movie opens in a theater next week.*
**4** to make something ready for business: *Most stores open at noon on Sundays.*

**open** *noun*
the outdoors, outside: *I like sleeping in the open.*

**opener** /ˈoʊpənər/ *noun*
a person or thing that opens: *She uses an electric can opener to open cans.*

**opening** /ˈoʊpənɪŋ/ *noun*
**1** a way through something: *An opening in the trees leads to a large garden.*
**2** an available job: *We have an opening in our sales department.*
**3** becoming open: *We celebrated the opening of the store with a party.*

O

**opening** *adjective*
beginning, starting: *Her opening comments at the meeting were short.*

**openly** *adverb*
in a way that is easy to see: *She smiled openly when she saw me.*

**opera** /ˈɑprə/ *noun*
**1** a play with a story which is set to music
**2** a theater where you can listen to these plays: *The opera is located up the avenue from our offices. –adjective* **operatic** /ˌɑpəˈrætɪk/.

**operate** /ˈɑpəˌreɪt/ *verb* **operated, operating, operates**
**1** to work: *Her new computer operates at a high speed.‖He operates out of his home.*
**2** to be in charge of something: *He operates a food business in the city.*
**3** to cut open a person's body to remove or repair a part inside, such as a muscle or a bone: *The doctor operated on her this morning and removed her appendix.*

**operation** /ˌɑpəˈreɪʃən/ *noun*
**1** a way or process of working something, such as a machine: *The operation of that machine is simple; just press the green buttons to make it work.*
**2** (in surgery) an act of cutting open a person's body to remove or repair something inside: *She had an operation to remove her appendix.*
**3** something that needs to be done or planned: *The company planned a secret operation to improve its products.*

**operator** /ˈɑpəˌreɪtər/ *noun*
**1** a person who operates a machine: *the operator of a big truck*
**2** a person who makes and answers telephone calls: *I didn't know how to make an overseas call, so I asked an operator to help me.*

**opinion** /əˈpɪnyən/ *noun*
what someone believes, something not proven in fact: *His opinion is that life on earth will improve next year.*

**opinionated** /əˈpɪnyəˌneɪtɪd/ *adjective*
believing that your own opinions are the only ones that are true

**opossum** /əˈpɑsəm/ *noun, plural* **opossums** or **opossum**
an American animal with a pointed nose and a long bare tail that is active mostly at night and may pretend to be dead when in danger

**opponent** /əˈpoʊnənt/ *noun*
a person who is on the opposite side in a fight, game, contest, etc.: *She was the mayor's opponent in the last election.*

**opportunity** /ˌɑpərˈtunəti/ *noun, plural* **opportunities**
a good time to do something: *I had the opportunity to visit my relatives this summer.*

**oppose** /əˈpoʊz/ *verb* **opposed, opposing, opposes**
to be against something or someone: *I am opposed to your spending the rent money on a new TV.*

**opposite** /ˈɑpəzɪt/ *preposition*
in a position across from someone or something: *My friend sat opposite me at dinner.*

**opposite** *adjective*
**1** across from one another, facing each other: *The restaurant and my apartment are on opposite sides of the street.*
**2** disagreeing: *opposite opinions –noun* **opposition.** *(antonym)* same.

**optician** /ɑp'tɪʃən/ *noun*
a skilled person who makes eyeglasses and examines eyes *–noun* **optometry.**

**optimism** /'ɑptəˌmɪzəm/ *noun*
the belief that good things will happen: *Even though she is often sick, she has kept her optimism. (antonym)* pessimist. *–noun* (person) **optimist;** *–adjective* **optimistic.**

**option** /'ɑpʃən/ *noun*
a choice: *She has two options: she can stay here or leave. –adjective* **optional.**

**or** /ɔr/ *conjunction*
**1** referring to choices or alternatives: *You can go today or tomorrow.*
**2** if not: *Take care of your car or else you'll have problems.*
**or so:** more or less, *(synonym)* approximately: *The car cost $19,000 or so.*

**oral** /'ɔrəl/ *adjective*
**1** related to the mouth: *Dentists give their patients oral examinations.*
**2** spoken, not written: *He had to give an oral report at the meeting. –adverb* **orally.**

**orange** /'ɔrɪnʤ/ *noun*
**1** a round, orange-colored fruit with thick skin *See:* art on page 3a.
**2** the color made by mixing red and yellow *See:* art on page 16a.

**orbit** /'ɔrbɪt/ *noun*
a path in space of a planet, moon, or spacecraft

**orbit** *verb*
to move around something in space: *Planets orbit the sun. –adjective* **orbital.**

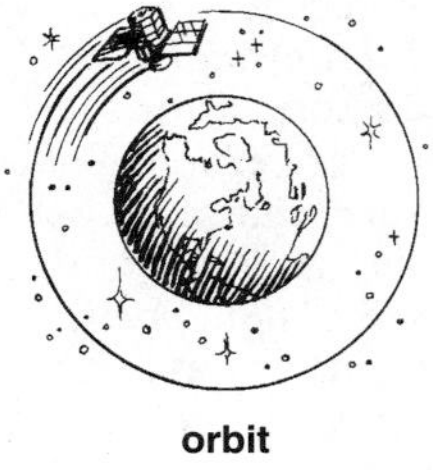
orbit

**orchard** /'ɔrʧərd/ *noun*
a place where fruit trees grow

**orchestra** /'ɔrkəstrə/ *noun*
a large group of musicians who play music on instruments, such as the violin and horns

orchestra

**ordeal** /ɔr'dil/ *noun*
a painful experience or a struggle that tests one's abilities

**order** /'ɔrdər/ *noun*
**1** the way that you place people or things in time or space, organization: *She put the newspapers in order by their dates.*
**2** a direction to do something, *(synonym)* a command
**3** asking someone to sell, make, or bring you something: *She placed an order with our company for new computers.*
**in order to/that:** so that you can do something else: *He moved to a smaller apartment in order to save money.*
**out of order:** broken, not working

**order** *verb*
**1** to tell someone what to do
**2** to request that something be supplied: *I've ordered new curtains.*

**orderly** /'ɔrdərli/ *adjective*
neatly arranged, organized

**ordinal** /'ɔrdnəl/ *adjective*
referring to ranking or place in a series: *First, second, third, and fourth, etc. (also written 1st, 2nd, 3rd, 4th) are ordinal numbers. See:* cardinal.

**ordinarily** /ˌɔrdn'ɛrəli/ *adverb*
under normal conditions, usually

**ordinary** /'ɔrdnˌɛri/ *adjective*
normal or regular: *She wears an ordinary pair of shoes to go for a walk.*

**ore** /ɔr/ *noun*
earth or rock from which you can get

metals: *Workers find gold in ore taken from deep in the earth.*

**organ (1)** /ˈɔrgən/ *noun*
a part of an animal or plant that has a specific purpose: *The eyes, tongue, and heart are human organs.*

**organ (2)** *noun*
a musical instrument played like a piano that makes music by electronic sounds or by wind blowing through pipes *–noun* (person) **organist.**

**organic** /ɔrˈgænɪk/ *adjective*
**1** related to living things: *Plants and animals are made of organic matter.*
**2** (of food) grown without using chemicals: *organic fruits and vegetables –adverb* **organically.**

**organism** /ˈɔrgəˌnɪzəm/ *noun*
a living creature: *Bacteria are very small organisms.*

**organization** /ˌɔrgənəˈzeɪʃən/ *noun*
**1** a group of people working together for a specific purpose, such as a business or a hobby: *We belong to an organization that gives food to the poor.*
**2** an arrangement of people, things, or functions for a specific purpose: *The organization of books is by subject matter. –adjective* **organizational.**

O

**organize** /ˈɔrgəˌnaɪz/ *verb* **organized, organizing, organizes**
**1** to make a group for a specific purpose
**2** to plan or arrange something *–noun* (person) **organizer.**

**origin** /ˈɔrəʤɪn/ *noun*
the start of beginning of something: *The origin of that folk song is France.*

**original** /əˈrɪʤənəl/ *adjective*
**1** first, earliest: *The original draft of her novel has been lost.*
**2** new, different from what has come before: *That book has many original ideas.*
**3** not a copy or translation: *The original painting is in a museum; this is just a copy.*

**original** *noun*
something that cannot be or has not been copied or translated: *She wants to study English, so she can read Shakespeare's plays in the original.*

**originally** /əˈrɪʤənəli/ *adverb*
previously, before: *He originally came from Florida but lives in Chicago now.*

**ornament** /ˈɔrnəmənt/ *noun*
something that is beautiful rather than useful: *His grandmother's living room is full of little china ornaments.*||*Christmas tree ornaments –adjective* **ornamental;** *–noun* **ornamentation.**

ornament

**orphan** /ˈɔrfən/ *noun*
a child whose parents have died

**orphan** *verb*
to become an orphan: *He was orphaned at an early age. –noun* (place) **orphanage.**

**Oscar** /ˈɑskər/ *noun*
an award given each year to actors, directors, and other people for great work in American movie making *See:* Emmy.

**ostrich** /ˈɑstrɪʧ/ *noun, plural* **ostriches**
a large African bird with long legs and neck, which cannot fly

ostrich

**other** /ˈʌðər/ *adjective*
**1** different from, not this or these: *I don't like this book, so I'm going to read the other one first.*
**2** second: *We play cards every other Tuesday night.*
**3** more of the same kind: *He was at the library with two other students.*

**other than:** except for, besides: *There isn't anything to do other than to wait to see what happens.*

**the other day:** on a day not long ago: *He called me just the other day.*

**other** *pronoun*
**1** something that remains: *You take one end, and I'll take the other.*

**2** someone or something that is uncertain: *They promised to take us out to dinner sometime or other.*

**otherwise** /ˈʌðər,waɪz/ *adverb*
**1** in every other way, except for: *Their plane was late, but otherwise they had a good trip.*
**2** if not, or else: *You must pay your taxes on time; otherwise, you will be punished.*

**ouch** /aʊʧ/ *exclamation*
an expression of pain and surprise: *Ouch! I hit my finger with the hammer!*

**ought** /ɔt/ *auxiliary verb*
**1** used to say what is right to do: *You ought to drive more slowly.||It's after 11:00; I ought to go to bed.*
**2** used to say what you think will happen: *The wind has stopped blowing; so it ought to be warmer now. See:* might; must; should.

**ounce** /aʊns/ *noun*
**1** *abbreviation:* **oz.** a measurement of weight equal to 1/16 of a pound (28 g): *Several ounces of pepper will last a long time.*
**2** a liquid measurement equal to 1/16 of a pint (29.6 ml)
**3** *figurative* a very small amount: *She told me the news without an ounce of emotion.*

**our** /ˈaʊər/*possessive adjective*
belonging to us: *Our house is on the corner.*
**ours:** *possessive pronoun*
*That house is ours.*

**ourselves** /ɑrˈsɛlvz/
*reflexive pronoun*
**1** referring to us: *We bought ourselves a new car.*
**2** used to make "we" stronger: *We didn't believe his story ourselves.*
**by ourselves: a.** alone: *We went there by ourselves because nobody wanted to go with us.* **b.** without help: *We were surprised to be able to finish the work by ourselves.*

**out** /aʊt/ *adjective*
**1** not in one's office, house, etc., *(synonym)* absent: *The boss is out now, but will be back in an hour.*
**2** not working, broken: *The electricity was out for a week after the hurricane.*

**out** *adverb*
**1** away from the inside, middle, or center: *The children ran out of the house to play in the yard.*
**2** in(to) a place where something can be seen: *The moon comes out at night.*

**out** *preposition*
from inside, away from: *Our cat jumped out the window.*
**out of:** not having something: *I'm out of time now and must leave.||The car is out of gas.*
**to talk someone out of something:** to get someone to change an opinion on something: *We talked them out of moving to a larger house. (antonym)* in.

**outbreak** /ˈaʊt,br eɪk/ *noun*
a sudden appearance of a disease or something negative, such as crime: *an outbreak of the flu*

**outcome** /ˈaʊt,kʌm/ *noun*
the effect, result of something: *The outcome of the election was a surprise.*

**outdoor** /ˈaʊt,dɔr/ *adjective*
located outside or used outside: *That singer gives outdoor concerts in the summer.||an outdoor dance (antonym)* indoor(s).

**outdoors** /,aʊtˈdɔrz/ *adverb*
outside a building: *The weather was good, so they held the concert outdoors.*

**outdoors** *noun*
**the outdoors:** the world of nature (forests, lakes, etc.): *She likes to hike in the outdoors. (antonym)* indoor(s).

**outer** /ˈaʊtər/ *adjective*
at a greater distance, farther from the middle or center: *outer islands||outer space (antonym)* inner.

**outfit** /ˈaʊt,fɪt/ *noun*
a set of clothing you wear for a special reason *–verb* **to outfit.**

**outing** /ˈaʊtɪŋ / *noun*
a short trip to have fun

**outlaw** /ˈaʊt,lɔ/ *noun*
a criminal being chased by the police

**outlaw** *verb*
to make something illegal: *Most states have outlawed the use of marijuana.*

**outlet** /'aʊt,lɛt/ *noun*
**1** a device in a wall that supplies electricity: *He plugged the lamp into an outlet.*
**2** a way out or opening for something

**outline** /'aʊt,laɪn/ *noun*
**1** a line that shows the outer shape of something: *The children drew the outline of flowers on paper, then colored them.*
**2** the main ideas of something: *She made an outline of the book she read. See:* flow chart. *–verb* **to outline.**

**outlook** /'aʊt,lʊk/ *noun*
**1** a statement of what will probably happen: *The outlook for the economy is good for this year.*
**2** your point of view

**out-of-date** *adjective*
no longer useful *(antonym)* modern.

**outpatient** /'aʊt,peɪʃənt/ *noun*
a person who receives medical treatment at a hospital or clinic but does not stay there overnight in bed: *He cut his hand and was treated as an outpatient at a local hospital. (antonym)* inpatient.

**output** /'aʊt,pʊt/ *noun*
**1** something that has been made or done: *That state's annual agricultural output has increased.*
**2** information, data, produced by a computer *See:* input.

**outrage** /'aʊt,reɪʤ/ *noun*
a cruel or evil act, serious offense: *The mayor's decision to close the hospital is an outrage.*

**outrageous** /aʊt' reɪʤəs/ *adjective*
**1** very bad, insulting: *Her outrageous behavior at the party offended everyone.*
**2** shocking: *That hotel charges outrageous prices. –adverb* **outrageously.**

**outside** /,aʊt'saɪd/ *noun*
**1** the outdoor or exterior surface of something: *The outside of the house needs painting.*
**2** outdoors

**outside** *adverb*
to or toward the outside: *She stepped outside and breathed the fresh air.*

**outside of:** except for, other than: *Outside of you and me, no one else knows the secret.*

**outside** *adjective*
outdoor, exterior in location: *The paint on the outside walls of the house is falling off.*

**outside** *preposition*
**1** on or to the outside of: *Leave my mail outside my door.*
**2** except, other than: *He has no interests outside his family. (antonym)* inside.

**outskirts** /'aʊt,s kɜrts/ *noun plural*
the outer area of something: *Our car broke down on the outskirts of the city.*

**outstanding** /,aʊ t'stændɪŋ/ *adjective*
excellent, very good

**outward** /'aʊtwərd/ *adjective*
moving away from, going out

**outward** *adverb*
(or **outwards**) away from the center, toward the outside: *Move your arms outward as you breathe out. (antonym)* inward(s).

**oval** /'oʊvəl/ *noun*
anything that is shaped like an egg: *an oval picture frame||an oval face*

**ovary** /'oʊvəri/ *noun, plural* **ovaries**
**1** the organ of a woman or a female animal that produces eggs
**2** the part of a flowering plant that produces seeds *–adjective* **ovarian.**

**oven** /'ʌvən/ *noun*
any usually box-shaped device used for cooking, baking, and heating food

**over** /'oʊvər/ *adverb*
**1** from an upright position: *She stood up quickly and knocked the chair over.*
**2** so as to show another side: *Turn the steaks over or they will burn.*
**3** across a distance, open space: *Come over here and sit with me!*
**4** above the surface or top of something: *A hot air balloon flew over early this morning.*
**5** so as to cover completely: *She painted over the ugly wallpaper.*
**6** another time, again: *My homework assignment was so bad that my teacher made me do it over.||We were supposed to leave on Thursday, but the bad weather forced us to stay over (the weekend).*

**over and over:** many times: *She plays the same songs over and over.*

**over** *adjective*
**1** done, finished: *By the time they arrived, the party was over.*
**2** above the amount: *Our trip cost over $2,000.*

O

**all over:** completely finished: *The movie was terrible, but he stayed in the theater until it was all over.*
**over with:** finished, completed, usually of something unpleasant: *I have to have a tooth pulled and I want to get it over with as soon as possible.*
**over** *preposition*
**1** at a higher level than, above, but not touching: *The flag was flying over the entrance to the building.*
**2** in order to cover: *We put plastic over the furniture to protect it.*
**3** from one side to the other, across: *A dog jumped over the fence. (antonym)* under.

**overall** /ˌoʊvərˈɔl/ *adverb*
in general, considering everything: *Overall, his job performance is quite good.*
**overall** /ˈoʊvərˌɔl/ *adjective*
including everything, total: *The overall length of that table is nine feet (three m).*

**overalls** /ˈoʊvərˌɔlz/ *noun plural*
loose work pants with straps over the shoulders, usually worn over other clothes *See:* jeans; art on page 12a.

**overboard** /ˈoʊvərˌbɔrd/ *adverb*
over the side of a boat or ship and into the water
**to go overboard:** to do too much of something: *They went overboard and spent $30,000 on their wedding.*

**overcharge** /ˌoʊvərˈʧɑrʤ/ *verb* **overcharged, overcharging, overcharges**
to charge someone too much money for something

**overcoat** /ˈoʊvərˌkoʊt/ *noun*
a long winter coat that you wear over other clothes

**overcome** /ˌoʊvərˈkʌm/ *verb* **overcame** /-ˈkeɪm/**, overcoming, overcomes**
to fight against something successfully

**overcrowd** /ˌoʊvərˈkraʊd/ *verb* **overcrowded, overcrowding, overcrowds**
to allow too many people in one place *–adjective* **overcrowded.**

**overdo** /ˌoʊvərˈdu/ *verb* **overdid** /-ˈdɪd/**, overdone** /-ˈdʌn/**, overdoing, overdoes** /-ˈdʌz/
**1** to do too much of something: *She overdid it by rushing around in the summer heat and is ill now.*
**2** to cook something too long: *We overdid the meat and it didn't taste good.*

**overdose** /ˈoʊvərˌdoʊs/ *noun*
too much of a drug: *He took an overdose and was in the hospital for weeks.*

**overdue** /ˌoʊvərˈdu/ *adjective*
not arriving at an expected time, late

**overflow** /ˌoʊvərˈfloʊ/ *verb*
to flow over the edges of something: *After the heavy rains, the flooded river overflowed its banks.*

**overgrown** /ˌoʊvərˈgroʊn/ *adjective*
covered with plants: *When I came back from my long vacation, I found my garden overgrown.* *–verb* **to overgrow;** *–noun* **overgrowth.**

**overhead** /ˌoʊvərˈˌhɛd/ *adverb*
above your head: *Birds flew overhead on their way south.*

**overhear** /ˌoʊvərˈhɪr/ *verb* **overheard** /-ˈhɜrd/**, overhearing, overhears**
to hear something by accident: *I overheard the conversation of the couple eating at the next table.*

**overlap** /ˌoʊvərˈlæp/ *verb* **overlapped, overlapping, overlaps**
to have a part of one thing over another: *His sweater overlaps the top of his pants.*

**overload** /ˌoʊvərˈloʊd/ *verb*
to place too much work, weight, etc., on someone or something: *She has overloaded her schedule with work, study, and family responsibilities.* *–noun* **overload.**

**overlook** /ˌoʊvərˈlʊk/ *verb*
**1** to look down on something: *The cabin on the hill overlooks the valley below.*
**2** to not see or do something: *He overlooked important ideas in his report.*

**overnight** /ˌoʊvərˈnaɪt/ *adverb*
during or for a single night: *He stayed overnight at his friend's house.*

**overpass** /ˈoʊvərˌpæs/ *noun, plural* **overpasses**
a road that goes over another road, railroad, etc. by a kind of a bridge: *We left the main highway and used the overpass to the other side.*

**overreact** /ˌ oʊvərriˈækt/ *verb*
to react to something in a way that is stronger than necessary

**overseas** /ˌoʊvərˈsiz/ *adverb*
from or to a land across the sea: *That business ships its products overseas.*

**overshoes** /ˈoʊvərˌʃuz/ *noun plural*
rubber boots you wear over shoes to protect them from water: *Overshoes keep your feet dry in winter snow.*

**oversleep** /ˌoʊvərˈslip/ *verb* **overslept** /-ˈslɛpt/, **oversleeping, oversleeps**
to sleep too long or too late: *She overslept and missed her appointment.*

**over-the-counter** *adjective*
available without a doctor's prescription: *Most types of aspirin are available in over-the-counter form.*

**overtime** /ˈoʊvərˌtaɪm/ *noun*
time worked above normal working hours, usually beyond 40 hours per week: *Overtime (pay) is paid at a higher hourly rate.*

**overweight** /ˌoʊvərˈweɪt/ *adjective*
heavier than the normal or permitted weight: *He is a little overweight and needs to eat less.*

**USAGE NOTE:** In the USA, it is considered impolite to say that someone is *fat* or *obese.* It is more polite to say that someone is *overweight.*

**overwhelming** *adjective*
very strong: *There was an overwhelming smell of fish in the kitchen.*

**overwork** /ˌoʊvərˈwɜrk/ *verb*
to make someone work too hard or too long: *The new manager is overworking his employees.*

**ow** /aʊ/ *exclamation*
an expression of pain: *Ow! I hurt my finger.*

Ow!

**owe** /oʊ/ *verb* **owed, owing, owes**
to need to pay money to someone: *He owes the landlord last month's rent.*

**owl** /aʊl/ *noun*
a meat-eating bird active at night: *Owls catch mice at night.* *–adjective* **owlish.**

**own** /oʊn/ *adjective*
(used with *possessive adjectives*)
**1** belonging to oneself: *This is my own recipe for apple pie.*
**2** (used to emphasize): *She found the answer by her own efforts; no one helped her.*

**own** *pronoun*
belonging to oneself: *He said the car was his own.*
**on one's own:** without help
**to be on one's own:** to be independent

**own** *verb*
to have something that is only yours: *She owns a bookstore.*
**to own up to something:** admit that you did something

**owner** /ˈoʊnər/ *noun*
a person or business that owns something *–noun* **ownership.**

**ox** /ɑks/ *noun, plural* **oxen** /ˈɑksən/
a male cow which does farm work: *Oxen pull plows on many farms in the world.*

**oxygen** /ˈɑksɪʤən/ *noun, (no plural)*
a colorless, odorless gas present in air: *People must breathe oxygen in order to live.* *–verb* **to oxygenate** /ˈɑksɪʤəˌneɪt/.

**oz** *abbreviation of* ounce:
*Baby José weighed 8 lbs., 3ozs. when he was born.*

**ozone** /ˈoʊˌzoʊn/ *noun, (no plural)*
a poisonous gas found in parts of the earth's lower atmosphere: *If ozone is lost in the atmosphere, earth will be subjected to the sun's harmful rays.*

# P, p

**P, p** /pi/ *noun* **P's, p's** or **Ps, ps**
the 16th letter of the English alphabet

**pa** /pɑ,pɔ/ *noun*
*short for* papa, father

**Pablum™** /ˈpæbləm/ *noun, (no plural)*
a light, soft cereal made to feed babies

**pace** /peɪs/ *verb* **paced, pacing, paces**
to walk back and forth in a worried manner: *He paced in the hospital room, waiting for the birth of the baby.*

**pace** *noun*
**1** a single step or its length
**2** speed of an activity: *Runners in a long race kept up a steady pace.*

**to keep (up) the pace:** to maintain a steady level of activity; to meet expected standards: *I have worked seven days a week for several months, but I can't keep up that pace forever!*

**pacifier** /ˈpæsəˌfaɪər/ *noun*
a small round object made of rubber or plastic for babies to bite or suck: *The baby cried until his mother gave him a pacifier.* –*verb* **to pacify.**

**pacifist** /ˈpæsəfɪst/ *noun*
a person who believes it is wrong to use violence to settle conflicts: *He refused to join the army because he is a pacifist.* –*noun* (act) **pacifism.**

**pack** /pæk/ *verb*
**1** to place and/or to wrap objects in a container for transport or storage: *She packed two suitcases for her trip.*
**2** to crowd together or force things into a small space: *She packed the drawer so tightly she could not close it.*||*Thousands of people packed the stores during the holiday season.*

**to pack up:** to prepare to leave: *After the convention, we packed up and left the hotel.*

**pack** *noun*
**1** a group of several similar things wrapped together: *He bought a pack of cigarettes at the store.*||*a pack of gum*
**2** a group of animals: *A pack of wolves chased the deer.*
**3** a bag of cloth or leather for carrying personal items: *He carries a pack on his back for his schoolbooks. See:* backpack.

**package** /ˈpækɪʤ/ *noun*
**1** a container (a box, bag, or wrapped paper) holding one or more things: *a package of cookies*||*The mail carrier delivered a package for you.*
**2** a group of things that are taken or offered together: *The government provides a package of health services for poor people.*

**package** *verb* **packaged, packaging, packages**
to wrap in a package: *Toy companies package their products to make them attractive to children.*

**packed** /pækt/ *adjective*
crowded or filled with people or things: *The stadium was packed with people for the football game.*||*The boxes were packed and ready for shipment.*

**pact** /pækt/ *noun*
an agreement

**pad** /pæd/ *noun*
**1** a flat, thin piece of soft material used

for comfort or protection: *He put a pad on the garage floor to kneel on while he fixed his car.||The bicycle rider put a pad on her seat. –noun* (stuff) **padding.**
**2** a number of pieces of paper attached together at one end: *Each student was given a pad of paper to write on.*

**pad** *verb* **padded, padding, pads**
**1** to fill something with soft material: *The furniture maker padded the chair.*
**2** *figurative* to fill with unnecessary or untrue things: *She pads her speeches with boring stories.*

**paddle** /pædl/ *noun*
a tool with a handle attached to a wide, flat, or slightly curved surface: *The baker used a paddle to mix flour and butter together.||They moved the boat with paddles.*

**paddle** *verb*
to move a canoe or other boat with a paddle: *He paddled up the river.*

**padlock** /'pæd,lɑk/ *noun*
a lock with a movable U-shaped rod: *She locked her bike to the fence with a padlock.*

padlock

**page** /peɪʤ/ *noun*
one side of a single sheet of paper in a book, report, etc.: *People turn the pages of a book as they read.*

**page** *verb* **paged, paging, pages**
to call someone by loudspeaker or electronic device: *The manager's secretary paged her to remind her of a meeting.*

**pageant** /'pæʤənt/ *noun*
a colorful public entertainment, usually showing a famous historical event: *Each year they put on a pageant about the American Revolution.*

**pager** /'peɪʤər/ *noun*
a device used to contact someone quickly with an electronic signal: *The doctor wears his pager on his belt so the hospital can reach him.*

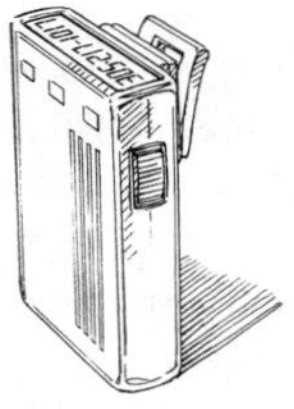
pager

**paid** /peɪd/ *verb*
*past tense and past participle of* pay

**pail** /peɪl/ *noun*
a large metal or plastic container, (synonym) a bucket: *A worker filled a pail with water to clean the floor.*

**pain** /peɪn/ *noun, (no plural)*
a hurt that results from physical injury or disease, or from mental or emotional suffering: *After the car accident, he had a pain in his right side.||The memory of her mother's illness caused her great pain.*

**a pain** or **a pain in the neck:** an annoying person or situation: *Traveling to work in big cities is often a pain* (or) *a pain in the neck.*

**pain** *verb*
to hurt: *My hand pains me from a fall.||It pains me to see food wasted.*

**painful** /'peɪnfəl/ *adjective*
causing pain, hurting: *Her broken ankle is a painful injury. –adverb* **painfully.**

**paint** /peɪnt/ *noun*
a liquid mixture of coloring matter (pigment) and oil or water, used to cover and color surfaces: *Workmen covered the floors with white paint.*

**paint** *verb*
**1** to apply paint (to walls, furniture, etc.): *She painted her room green.*
**2** to create a picture or work of art using paint: *She painted a picture of the mountains at sunset.*

**paintbrush** /'peɪnt,brʌʃ/ *noun, plural* **paintbrushes**
a brush used to apply paint: *House painters use large paintbrushes.*

**painter** /'peɪntər/ *noun*
a person who paints, such as a worker or artist: *A painter is painting our house this week.*

**painting** /'peɪntɪŋ/ *noun*
**1** *(no plural)* the process of painting: *Painting our house will take a long time.*
**2** a painted work of art: *Paintings hang in museums.*

**pair** /pɛr/ *noun, plural* **pairs** or **pair**
**1** two similar things that go together, such as a pair of shoes: *She bought a pair of gloves to wear in winter.*
**2** two people in close relation: *That man and woman make a good-looking pair.*

**pair** *verb*
to put together as a pair: *The teacher*

*paired me with the student next to me to do a project.*

**pajamas** /pəˈdʒɑməz/ *noun plural*
loose pants with a jacket made for sleeping and relaxing: *His pajamas are made of cotton.*

**pal** /pæl/ *noun informal*
a good friend: *I went to the movies with a group of my pals last night.*

**palace** /ˈpælɪs/ *noun*
**1** the official home of a king, queen, or other rich and powerful person: *The palace was filled for the prince's wedding.*
**2** a large and grand house: *The poor boy thought the big house was a palace.* –*adjective* **palatial.**

**pale** /peɪl/ *adjective* **paler, palest**
**1** light in color: *That wall is painted in a pale green.*
**2** unhealthy-looking: *She looks pale and sick.* –*noun* **paleness.**

**pale** *verb* **paled, paling, pales**
to turn pale: *He paled at the thought of seeing his enemy.*

**palm (1)** /pɑm/ *noun*
a type of tree found in tropical places with no branches and large, long leaves at the top: *Palm trees are a common sight in southern California.*

**palm (2)** *noun*
the inside of the central part of the hand: *He touched her head with his palm.*

**pamper** /ˈpæmpər/ *verb*
to give more attention and care to someone than is necessary: *She pampers her child by picking her up every time she cries.*

**pamphlet** /ˈpæmflɪt/ *noun*
a small book of a few pages containing advertising or useful information: *The hospital gives its patients a pamphlet that describes its services.*

**pan** /pæn/ *noun*
**1** a flat, round, metal container with low sides and a handle, used in cooking: *He uses a frying pan to cook eggs each morning.*
**2** a container for holding liquid: *a dish-pan||a paint pan See:* art on page 7a.

**pancake**
/ˈpæn,keɪk/ *noun*
a flat, round cake cooked until brown and made of flour, milk, eggs, and butter: *He likes pancakes for breakfast. See:* scrambled eggs, **USAGE NOTE.**

pancakes

**panda** /ˈpændə/ *noun*
a large animal from China that looks like a bear with black-and-white fur: *Pandas are an endangered animal. See:* endangered species.

**pane** /peɪn/ *noun*
a piece of glass as a part of a window

**panel** /ˈpænəl/ *noun*
**1** a part of a surface that is different from the area around it: *The wall was made from panels of wood.*
**2** a surface area that contains buttons, levers, and other controls for operating a machine or a system: *The pilot faced the airplane's control panel to prepare for takeoff.*
**3** a group of people chosen for a project or discussion of problems: *The panel discussed the pros and cons of the new law.*

**panel** *verb*
to cover a surface, such as a wall, with panels, especially of wood: *The dining room was paneled in fine wood.*

**panic** /ˈpænɪk/ *noun*
a condition of uncontrolled fear in response to danger: *The fire in the subway caused a panic.*

**panic** *verb* **panicked, panicking, panics**
to experience uncontrolled fear: *She panicked and ran out the door.* –*adjective* **panicky.**

**panorama** /ˌpænəˈræmə/ *noun*
**1** a wide, open view of an outdoor area: *We stood on a mountaintop and viewed the panorama of sea and sky.*
**2** a full view or complete picture: *That book presents a panorama of American history.* –*adjective* **panoramic** /ˌpænəˈræmɪk/.

**pant** /pænt/ *verb*
to breathe quickly: *Dogs pant with their tongues hanging out after running fast.*

P

**panther** /ˈpænθər/ *noun*
a large, wild type of cat, usually with black fur, known for its ability to hunt: *The hungry panther silently waited in the low bushes and then sprang to attack the deer.*

**panties** /ˈpæntiz/ *noun plural*
underpants worn by women or girls

**pantry** /ˈpæntri/ *noun*
a small room next to the kitchen

**pants** /pænts/ *noun plural*
a man's or woman's garment that runs from the waist to the ankles with two long parts for the legs: *Her legs were cold, so she put on a pair of pants.*

**pantyhose** /ˈpæntiˌhoʊz/ *noun*
*used with a plural verb* a tight, thin garment that goes from the waist, down the legs, and over the feet and is worn by women under other clothes: *Many women wear pantyhose for extra warmth in winter. See:* stockings; tights.

**papa** /ˈpɑpə/ *noun informal*
father

**papaya** /pəˈpaɪə/ *noun*
a tropical tree with large, greenish-yellow fruit, or the fruit itself: *I have never eaten a papaya before, are they tasty? See:* art on page 3a.

**paper** /ˈpeɪpər/ *noun*
**1** thin, smooth material made from wood or cotton and cut into sheets to be used for writing, wrapping, or covering: *I wrote a letter on a piece of paper.*
**2** a newspaper: *Have you read this morning's paper?*

**paperback** /ˈpeɪpərˌbæk/ *noun*
a book with a cover made of heavy paper: *Paperbacks are small and easy to carry. See:* hardcover.

**paperwork** /ˈpeɪpərˌwɜrk/ *noun, (no plural)*
**1** government or legal forms that must be filled out to complete some action or process: *Buying a house involves a lot of paperwork.*
**2** work that requires a lot of time for reading and writing reports, letters, or other documents: *She stayed up late to go through paperwork that she had brought home from the office.*

**parachute** /ˈpærəˌʃut/ *noun*
a large, lightweight sheet, attached to a falling person or thing, that unfolds in the wind and causes the person or thing to fall slowly: *The pilot always remembered to take his parachute.* –*verb* **to parachute.**

parachute

**parade** /pəˈreɪd/ *noun*
an orderly movement of people in colorful or formal dress or uniforms, usually to show pride or to honor a special day or event: *On Memorial Day, we saw a parade of soldiers marching in honor of those who died in war.*

**parade** *verb* **paraded, parading, parades**
to march in a parade, to celebrate: *On Thanksgiving Day, clowns, horses, children, and bands parade down Fifth Avenue in New York City.*

**paradise** /ˈpærəˌdaɪs/ *noun, usually singular*
**1 a.** in the Bible, the original home of the first human beings: *Adam and Eve were sent out of paradise because they disobeyed God.* **b.** heaven
**2** any place where everything is beautiful, delightful, and peaceful: *Parts of California seem like paradise to me. (antonym)* hell.

**paragraph** /ˈpærəˌgræf/ *noun*
a part of a piece of writing, signaled by a space or other break, that introduces a new thought or idea: *Newspaper articles use very short paragraphs to make reading easier and faster.*

**parakeet** /ˈpærəˌkit/ *noun*
a type of small parrot often kept in a cage: *I have a pet parakeet that has bright green and black feathers.*

**paralegal** /ˌpærəˈligəl/ *noun*
a worker (an assistant) in a law office who performs many of the lawyers' less important duties: *My sister worked for two years as a paralegal before going to law school.*

P

**parallel** /ˈpærəˌlɛl/ *adjective*
running side by side at an equal distance apart: *Railroad tracks are parallel to each other.*

**parallel** *noun*
a likeness or connection between two or more events: *The police officer saw a parallel between the two murder cases.*

**parallel** *verb*
to be similar or to occur at the same time: *The histories of the two countries closely parallel each other.*

**paralysis** /pəˈræləsɪs/ *noun, plural* **paralyses** /-ˌsiz/
**1** a loss of ability to move or feel part of the body: *After the car accident, he suffered from paralysis of both his legs.*
**2** an inability to act *–adjective* **paralytic;** *–verb* **to paralyze.**

**paramedic** /ˌpærəˈmɛdɪk/ *noun*
a person trained to provide emergency medical help when a doctor is not present: *Paramedics rushed to help the victims of the car accident. See:* art on page 11a.

**paraphrase** /ˈpærəˌfreɪz/ *verb* **paraphrased, paraphrasing, paraphrases**
to explain the meaning of something said or written by using different words or phrases: *The teacher asked his students to paraphrase the poem.*

**paraphrase** *noun*
a brief explanation

**parcel** /ˈpɑrsəl/ *noun*
a package or box that has been wrapped and closed with string or tape

**parcel post** *noun, (no plural)*
in the USA, fourth-class mail, a low-cost way of sending packages over long distances by means of trucks and trains: *She sent a package of clothes to relatives by parcel post.*

**pardon** /ˈpɑrdn/ *verb*
to forgive or excuse someone: *He asked me to pardon him for being late for the meeting.*

**pardon** *noun*
an act of forgiving someone and excusing him or her from punishment: *The governor gave the thief a pardon, and he was released from prison.*

**pardon me** or **I beg your pardon:** a polite way of saying "I am sorry. Please excuse me": *When the waiter bumped into our table, he said, "Oh! pardon me!"*

**parent** /ˈpɛrənt/ *noun*
the mother or father of someone: *His parents live in Florida. –adjective* **parental;** *–noun* **parenthood.**

**parenthesis** /pəˈrɛnθəsɪs/ *noun, plural* **parentheses** /-ˌsiz/
the curved signs ( ) that mark off extra information in a sentence

**park** /pɑrk/ *noun*
an area of land where people can exercise, play, or relax: *He took his dog for a walk in the park.*

**park** *verb*
to bring a car to rest in one place and leave it for a limited amount of time: *She parked her car in front of the store.*

**parka** /ˈpɑrkə/ *noun*
a short coat (with a hood)

parka

**parking** /ˈpɑrkɪŋ/ *noun, (no plural)*
the activity of bringing a car to rest and leaving it: *She was good at parking large cars in small spaces. See:* art on page 4a.

**parking lot** *noun*
a flat area used for parking cars, often guarded (by an attendant): *That shopping mall has a huge parking lot in front of the stores. See:* art on page 10a.

**parking meter** *noun*
a time clock set on a pole next to a parking space into which one puts coins to pay for parking: *He forgot to put money in the parking meter, so he had to pay a fine.*

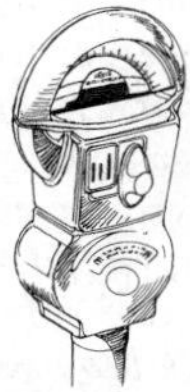
parking meter

**parkway** /ˈpɑrkˌweɪ/ *noun*
a wide highway with grass and trees in the middle and/or along the sides: *They liked to drive on the parkway because it was beautiful.*

**parliament** /ˈparləmənt/ *noun*
the group of elected officials that make or change laws in some countries, such as Great Britain: *The British Parliament has two divisions, the House of Lords and the House of Commons. –adjective* **parliamentary.**

**parlor** /ˈparlər/ *noun*
**1** a room in a house used for sitting and talking
**2** a store or business that sells a particular product or service: a beauty parlor

**parole** /pəˈroʊl/ *noun, (no plural)*
the early release of a prisoner who promises to be good and report regularly to a law officer: *After two years in prison, she was given parole, but she had to stay in this country. –noun* (person) **parolee.**

**parole** *verb* **paroled, paroling, paroles**
to give someone limited freedom; to put on parole: *He was paroled because he had been a good prisoner. (antonym)* jail.

**parrot** /ˈpærət/ *noun*
a type of tropical bird with a curved beak and colorful feathers, some of which can copy human speech: *He keeps a parrot in a birdcage in his living room.*

parrot

**part** /part/ *noun*
**1** a piece (section or portion) of something: *Part of that wall is falling down.||Part of what he says is true.*
**2** one of many other things that are put together to make a machine: *He bought some new parts for his bicycle.*
**3** a role or duty to perform in some activity or event: *She has a part in a new movie.||He did his part to help his friend.*
**4** one side of a conflict or disagreement: *He took her part because he thought she was right.*
**5** a line that separates the hair on a person's head: *She used a comb to make a part in her hair.*

**to take part in something:** to participate in something: *She takes part in after-school programs; she plays in the band.*

**part** *verb*
**1** to pull apart, separate, or divide: *She parted the curtains to let in the sunlight.*
**2** to go away from or leave a person or place: *After the party, my friend and I parted to go to our separate homes.*

**part** *adverb*
in part, partially: *The ice cream cake is part chocolate and part vanilla. (antonym)* whole.

**partial** /ˈparʃəl/ *adjective*
incomplete, only a part of something: *He owed me $1,000, and he made a partial payment of $500. –adverb* **partially.** *(antonym)* complete.

**participant** /parˈtɪsəpənt/ *noun*
a person who takes part in something: *He was a participant in the discussion.*

**participate** /parˈtɪsəˌpeɪt,/ *verb* **participated, participating, participates**
to take part or have a role in an activity or event: *She likes to participate in political campaigns. –noun* **participation /parˌtɪsəˈpeɪʃən/.**

**participle** /ˈpartəˌsɪpəl/ *noun*
the form of a verb that can be used as an adjective or as auxiliary verb to form certain verb tenses: *The past participle of "to cook" is "cooked," as in "The meat is cooked." The present participle is "cooking," as in "The food is cooking."*

**particular** /pərˈtɪkyələr/ *adjective*
**1** relating to a specific person, idea, item, etc.: *I like rock music in general, but not that particular group.*
**2** special, unusual: *There is nothing of particular interest on TV tonight.*
**3** very exact and demanding about what one wants: *He is very particular about the food he eats; everything has to be cooked just right.*

**particular** *noun, usually plural*
**particulars:** a specific fact or detail: *I can tell you briefly what happened, but I'll save the particulars for later.*

**in particular:** **a.** specifically, especially: *I thought the whole meal was good, but the soup in particular was delicious.* **b.** specific, special: *The salesclerk asked if I was looking for anything in particular.*

**particularly** /pərˈtɪkyəl/ *adverb*
especially, greatly: *She is particularly interested in modern art.*

**parting** /'pɑrtɪŋ/ *noun*
the act or moment of separating or leaving someone: *The lovers' parting was filled with tears.*

**partly** /'pɑrtli/ *adverb*
to some degree, in part: *He is partly right in what he says. (antonym)* wholly.

**partner** /'pɑrtnər/ *noun*
**1** a person who joins together with one or more people for a common purpose: *A husband and wife are partners in marriage.||He's my friend and tennis partner.*
**2** one of the owners of a business: *The partners in that company work hard.*
**3** a person with whom one dances: *His partner can really dance well. –noun* **partnership.**

**part of speech** *noun, plural* **parts of speech**
(in grammar) a class of words, such as noun, verb, adjective, or adverb, based on the way words are used in a sentence: *It is helpful to know the parts of speech to learn a new language.*

**part-time** *adjective*
taking up only part of a normal workday or workweek: *She has three part-time jobs.*

**part-time** *adverb*
for less than a full workday or work week: *While in school, he worked part-time as a waiter. (antonym)* full-time.

**party** /'pɑrti/ *noun, plural* **parties**
**1** a social event where people come to talk, drink, eat, dance, and have fun: *We have a party at our house on New Year's Eve.*
**2** a political group with a set of beliefs for the public good: *The liberal party wants to raise taxes.*

**party** *verb* **partied, partying, parties**
to participate in a social party: *Starting Saturday evening, we partied until four o'clock in the morning.*

**pass** /pæs/ *verb* **passes**
**1** to go forward or move along in a steady motion: *We watched the boat as it slowly passed up the river.*
**2** to move beyond someone or something: *He drove faster in order to pass the truck in front of him on the highway.*
**3** to move something from one place to another: *She asked me to pass her the dish of fruit.||I passed copies of the book to everyone in the room.*
**4** to succeed at or meet the standards of a test: *He passed the test at school.*
**5** to give official approval to someone or something: *Congress passed a law that will raise taxes.*
**6** to go by or through something: *She passed through the gate on the way to catch her train.||I always look in the windows when I pass that store.*
**7** (in sports) to throw or kick a ball from one player to another
**8** to change from one condition to another: *The season passed slowly from winter to spring.*

**to pass something along** or **down:** to give something (especially as an inheritance): *My grandmother passed along her wedding ring to me.*

**to pass away** or **on:** to die: *Her father passed away just last week.*

**to pass out:** to lose mental awareness, as from fear, tiredness, or too much alcohol: *He had too many drinks at the party and passed out on the floor.*

**pass** *noun, plural* **passes**
**1** a try at doing something: *She made a pass at writing the report.*
**2** a narrow path in a mountain range that allows travel from one side to another: *The hikers walked over the mountain pass into the valley.*
**3** a written or printed card or piece of paper that gives one the right to enter some place: *He showed his pass to the guard, who let him enter the building.||She gave us a free pass to see the new movie.*
**4** a result on a test that allows you to do something: *I earned a pass on my driver's test and was allowed to get my license.*
**5** (in sports) the act of passing a ball from one player to another: *He made a good pass to help score the goal.*

**passage** /'pæsɪʤ/ *noun*
**1** a narrow opening or way between two places: *He walked through the passage to the garden.*
**2** the act of moving from one place to another: *The constant passage of big trucks made the street noisy.*

**3** a trip on a ship or airplane: *We made reservations for passage from New York to London.*
**4** a section of writing or music: *The priest read a passage from the Bible.*
**5** the movement of time: *The passage of time goes fast.*

**passenger** /ˈpæsəndʒər/ *noun*
a person (other than the driver) who rides in a bus, boat, car, taxi, etc.: *The bus that crashed was carrying 20 passengers.*

**passer-by** /ˌpæsərˈbaɪ/ *noun, plural* **passers-by**
a person who passes by: *The passers-by took no notice of lovers kissing.*

**passing** /ˈpæsɪŋ/ *noun, (no plural)*
**1** a movement; flow: *The passing of time goes slowly in the hospital.*
**2** death: *The old man's passing saddened his family.*
**in passing:** said in the middle of saying something else: *While talking to his mother, he said in passing that he was feeling well and strong.*
**passing** *adjective*
lasting only a short time: *She gave him a passing look and walked on.*
**passing grade:** success in an examination or course: *I received a passing grade in my math course.*

P

**passion** /ˈpæʃən/ *noun*
**1** a very strong feeling, such as love, anger, or hatred: *He felt such passion that he forgot where he was.*||*She spoke with passion about the love of freedom.*
**2** strong interest in some activity: *She has a passion for painting.*

**passionate** /ˈpæʃənɪt/ *adjective*
about feeling or expressing passion: *She made a passionate speech in favor of the peace plan.*

**passive** /ˈpæsɪv/ *adjective*
**1** unwilling to take action
**2** (in grammar) a verb form in which the subject is affected by, rather than the performer of, the action, as in "He was hit by a car," or "The proposal was accepted." *–adverb* **passively;** *–noun* **passivity** /pæˈsɪvəti/. *(antonym)* active.

**passport** /ˈpæsˌpɔrt/ *noun*
a small book given to a citizen by a government as proof of nationality and permission to leave and reenter the country: *Before leaving for Japan, I had to get a passport.*

**password** /ˈpæsˌwɜrd/ *noun*
a secret word or phrase used get into a guarded place or a protected system: *I forgot my password, so I couldn't operate the computer.*

**past** /pæst/ *noun, usually singular*
**1** the time gone by, before the present: *In the past, he wrote with a pen; now he uses a computer.*
**2** history: *When she moved to America, she made an effort to study its past.*
**3** someone's personal history: *Before we hire him, we must learn about his past.*
**past** *adjective*
gone by in time: *In the past century, many things have changed.*||*It is 10:10 A.M.; that is, 10 past 10 in the morning.*
**past** *adverb*
to go by or beyond: *He drove past at a fast speed.*
**past** *preposition*
already later than: *It is past midnight now. (antonym)* future.

**pasta** /ˈpɑstə/ *noun, (no plural)*
**1** a general term for food made of flour, eggs, and water, formed in many shapes and cooked in boiling water: *Athletes often eat pasta because it is a good way to get quick energy.*

pasta

**2** a dish of food made from pasta: *My favorite pasta is spaghetti and meatballs.*

**paste** /peɪst/ *noun, (no plural)*
a thin, wet substance used to stick pieces of paper together
**paste** *verb* **pasted, pasting, pastes**
to stick things together with paste: *A child pasted her drawings onto a large sheet of paper.*

**pastime** /ˈpæsˌtaɪm/ *noun*
a pleasurable activity: *His favorite pastimes are playing golf and watching TV.*

**pastor** /ˈpæstər/ *noun*
a minister in charge of a church

**past participle** *noun*
a form of a verb indicating past action and used to form perfect tenses and the passive or as an adjective: *The verb*

*"seen" in "I have already seen that movie" is a past participle.‖The "fried" in "fried eggs" is a past participle used as an adjective. See:* participle.

**pastry** /ˈpeɪstri/ *noun, plural* **pastries**
**1** a rich mixture (dough) shaped into a shell to contain foods, such as fruit, cheese, or chicken
**2** a small, sweet cake baked from pastry dough: *We had cream-filled pastries for dessert.*

**past tense** *noun*
a verb form used to express an action or a state in the past: *The past tense of "to go" is "went," as in, "Yesterday I went to class in the evening."*

**pasture** /ˈpæstʃər/ *noun*
a field or other large open area where sheep and cattle feed on the grass

**pat** /pæt/ *noun*
**1** a soft, light touch: *The mother gave her son a pat on the head.*
**2** a small flat amount of something: *He spread a pat of butter on his bread.*
**a pat on the back:** an expression of encouragement or praise: *The teacher gave me a pat on the back for getting an "A" on the test.*

**pat** *verb* **patted, patting, pats**
**1** to press down repeatedly with a soft, light touch: *She patted the laundry after she folded it.*
**2** to tap lovingly: *The boy patted his dog on its head.*

**patch** /pætʃ/ *noun, plural* **patches**
a piece of material used to cover a hole or a weak spot

**patch** *verb* **patches**
to cover with a patch: *My favorite old jacket was torn, so I patched it.*

**patent** /ˈpætnt/ *noun*
the right given by a government to be the only person or company permitted to make, use, and sell an invention for a limited number of years: *He wanted a patent for his invention so no one else could copy it. –verb* **to patent.**

**path** /pæθ/ *noun, plural* **paths**
**1** a narrow way for walking or cycling, made by repeated use: *Paths made by animals go through the woods.*
**2** the direction of a movement: *He stood in the path of a moving truck.*

**pathetic** /pəˈθɛtɪk/ *adjective*
causing feelings of pity or compassion: *It was pathetic to see the families had lost their homes in the fire.*

**patience** /ˈpeɪʃəns/ *noun, (no plural)*
the ability to accept discomfort, pain, or troubles while waiting calmly for something: *She waited with patience until her baby stopped crying. (antonym)* impatience.

**patient** /peɪʃənt/ *adjective*
having or showing patience, calm, or being undisturbed: *His train was late, but he was patient. –adverb* **patiently.**

**patient** *noun*
a person cared for or treated by a doctor: *The doctor visited her patients in the hospital. See:* art on page 11a.

**patio** /ˈpætiˌoʊ/ *noun, plural* **patios**
an open area next to a house used for outdoor eating, sitting, etc. in good weather: *We relax and enjoy the sun on our patio in summer.*

**patriot** /ˈpeɪtriət/ *noun*
a person who is proud of his or her country and eager to defend it: *The patriots formed an army to fight the invading army. –adjective* **patriotic.**

**patriotism** /ˈpeɪtriəˌtɪzəm/ *noun, (no plural)*
a feeling of love, loyalty, and support for one's country, especially in defense against its enemies: *Patriotism caused him to join the army and fight for his country.*

**patrol** /pəˈtroʊl/ *verb* **patrolled, patrolling, patrols**
to make regular trips through an area or along its border to guard against trouble or crime: *A policeman patrols the park to prevent robberies. –noun* **patrol.**

**patter** /ˈpætər/ *noun*
**1** the sound of quick light taps or steps on a hard surface: *the patter of rain on the street‖the patter of little feet*
**2** fast talk: *The comedian's patter was very funny.*

**patter** *verb*
to make a pattering sound: *She pattered about the kitchen in her slippers.*

**pattern** /ˈpætərn/ *noun*
**1** an example or model to be followed: *Her writing shows a pattern of excellence.*
**2** a form or guide to follow when making something: *She made the dress herself from a pattern.*
**3** a design of regular shapes and lines: *The flower pattern in that dress is very pretty.*
**4** a repeated set of events, characteristics, or features: *There is a pattern to his behavior; he grows quiet when he's sad.* –*verb* **to pattern.**

**pause** /pɔz/ *noun*
a short break or moment of rest in the middle of an action or movement: *She took a brief pause in her speech while she drank some water.* –*verb* **to pause.**

**pave** /peɪv/ *verb* **paved, paving, paves**
to cover over a road, a path, or other area with tar, cement, etc., to make a hard, flat surface: *They paved the field with cement to make a parking lot.*
**to pave the way:** to be the first to do something so as to make it easier for those who follow: *Early settlers paved the way for those who arrived later.*

**pavement** /ˈpeɪvmənt/ *noun, (no plural)*
the covering of cement, tar, etc., on a sidewalk or road: *The pavement on the road is black tar.*
**to pound the pavement:** to walk for hours in search of business, work, etc.: *He is a salesman, and he really pounds the pavement looking for new customers.*

P

**paw** /pɔ/ *noun*
**1** the foot of an animal: *The cat cleaned its paws.*
**2** *slang* the human hand: *She told her son to keep his paws off the candy.*
**paw** *verb*
to touch, rub, or strike with a paw: *The lion pawed at its food.*

**pay** /peɪ/ *noun, (no plural)*
money paid in return for work done: *She refused to take the job because the pay was too low.*||*He earns good pay.*
**pay** *verb* **paid** /peɪd/, **paying, pays**
**1** to give money to someone in return for regular work: *That company pays its employees every two weeks.*
**2** to settle a bill, debt, or loan by giving what is owed: *She paid the doctor's bill by writing a check.*
**3** to be to one's advantage: *It pays to get to work on time.*
**to pay attention:** to look at and listen to closely: *The teacher told the students to pay attention to her in class.*
**to pay one's dues:** **a.** to pay for membership in a club or union **b.** to earn one's place in an organization through long and patient service: *He paid his dues as a traveling salesman, and now he has a good office job.*
**to pay one's way:** to support oneself, pay for food, rent, clothing, etc.: *She has a good job and pays her own way in life.*
**to pay someone** or **something back:** **a. someone:** to return an insult or injury: *He shouted at her, and she paid him back by not speaking to him for a week.* **b. something:** to return money that one owes: *I paid back the $10 that my friend loaned to me.*
**to pay someone** or **something off:** **a. someone:** to pay money to someone to persuade them to help you, especially by doing something dishonest: *The criminals paid off the judge and got away free.* **b. something:** to finish paying for something: *I finally paid off the 30-year mortgage on my house.* **c.** to produce good results: *Her hard work paid off when she got a big raise.*
**to pay up:** to pay money that is due: *He was three months late in paying the rent, and the landlord told him to pay up.*

**payable** /ˈpeɪəbəl/ *adjective*
that is to be paid (by a certain date or to a certain person or business): *The loan is payable on the first of each month.*||*Make the check payable to me.*

**paycheck** /ˈpeɪˌtʃɛk/ *noun*
a salary or wage check: *I went to the bank to cash my paycheck.*

**payday** /ˈpeɪˌdeɪ/ *noun*
the regular day when one is paid one's wage or salary: *Our payday is on the Thursday of every second week.*

**payment** /ˈpeɪmənt/ *noun*
**1** the act of paying: *I make a payment on my car loan each month.*
**2** the money paid: *The payment amounts to $300.*

**pay phone** *noun*
a public telephone operated by putting in coins or credit cards: *I called my friend from a pay phone in the hotel.*

pay phone

**payroll** /ˈpeɪˌroʊl/ *noun*
a list of employees to be paid and the amounts due to each: *We hired him and put him on the payroll.*

**pay telephone** *noun*
*See:* pay phone.

**PC** /ˌpiˈsi/ *noun, plural* **PCs** or **PC's**
*abbreviation of* personal computer: *I have a PC at home and one at the office. See:* desktop; laptop.

**pea** /pi/ *noun*
a small, round, green seed that grows (in long pods) and is eaten as a vegetable *See:* art on page 2a.

**peace** /pis/ *noun, (no plural)*
**1** a time without war: *After the last war, the country returned to peace.*
**2** a state of calm, with no conflict between peoples *(antonym)* war.

**peaceful** /ˈpisfəl/ *adjective*
calm, quiet, without troubles: *My life in a little house by a pond was peaceful. –adverb* **peacefully;** *–noun* **peacefulness.**

**peach** /piʧ/ *noun, plural* **peaches**
a juicy, round, yellowish-pink colored fruit with a large, rough seed: *Peaches grow well in hot weather. –adjective* **peachy.** *See:* art on page 3a.

**peacock** /ˈpiˌkɑk/ *noun*
a large male bird with large, showy, blue and green tail feathers

peacock

**proud as a peacock:** very pleased with oneself: *When he won the awards, he was as proud as a peacock.*

**peak** /pik/ *noun*
**1** the pointed top of a mountain: *The peak of the mountain is covered with snow.*
**2** the pointed end of something, such as the top of a roof: *Two birds were sitting on the peak of the barn.*
**3** the point of greatest activity, strength, or success: *That singer is now at the peak of her career.*

**peak** *verb*
to reach the highest point: *The price of gas has peaked and is now going down. (antonym)* valley.

**peanut** /ˈpiˌnət/ *noun*
a small, light-brown nut about the size of a pea, that grows underground and is a popular snack food: *She always eats peanuts at baseball games.*
**for peanuts:** very little money: *He works for peanuts as a clerk in a grocery store.*

**peanut brittle** *noun, (no plural)*
a hard, flat candy made with peanuts

**peanut butter** *noun, (no plural)*
a soft, creamy food made from crushed peanuts: *Sandwiches made with peanut butter are very popular for lunch.*

**pear** /pɛr/ *noun*
a sweet, juicy fruit with a green, yellow, or brownish skin that is narrow at the top and wide at the bottom *See:* art on page 3a.

**pearl** /pɜrl/ *noun*
a smooth, white, round object formed naturally (within oysters) and valued as a jewel: *She wears earrings made of pearls.*

P

**peasant** /ˈpɛzənt/ *noun*
a farmer of low social rank who lives and works on a small piece of land

**pebble** /ˈpɛbəl/ *noun*
a small stone made round and smooth by the action of water: *We threw pebbles into the ocean.*

**pecan** /pɪˈkɑn/ *noun*
a nut with a smooth, hard shell that grows on (hickory) trees, common in the southern states of the USA: *She uses many pecans in a pecan pie.*

**peck** /pɛk/ *verb*
to strike or pick up something with the beak: *Chickens peck at grain on the ground.*

**peculiar** /pɪˈkyu lyər/ *adjective*
**1** odd, strange: *His peculiar behavior puzzles everyone who knows him.*

**2** belonging only to one specific person, group of people, place, etc.: *Bright orange tail feathers are peculiar to that type of bird.* –*adverb* **peculiarly.**

**peculiarity** /pɪˌkyuli'ærəti/ *noun, plural* **peculiarities**
something odd or strange: *The old house has many peculiarities.*

**pedal** /'pɛdl/ *noun*
a flat part (lever) pushed with the foot to operate a machine or tool: *He stepped on the brake pedal to stop the car.*

**pedal** *verb*
to move by using pedals: *He pedals his bike to work every day.*

**peddle** /'pɛdl/ *verb* **peddled, peddling, peddles**
to sell small items from door to door or on the street: *He peddles watches on the street.* –*noun* (person) **peddler.**

**pedestrian** /pə'dɛstriən/ *noun*
any person walking on a sidewalk, across a street, or down a road: *Pedestrians crowd the sidewalks at noon.*

**pedestrian** *adjective*
related to walking: *pedestrian traffic* ||*a pedestrian crossing See:* art on page 4a.

**pediatrician** /ˌpidiə'trɪʃən/ *noun*
a doctor who treats children: *The pediatrician cured my baby's illness. See:* physician.

P

**peek** /pik/ *verb*
to look secretly at someone or something, especially when one is not supposed to: *A student peeked at the test questions before the test started.*||*He peeked through the crack in the door to see who was inside.*

peek

**peek** *noun*
a quick look: *Let's take a peek at this new video. See:* peep.

**peel** /pil/ *verb*
to take the skin off a piece of fruit or vegetable: *She peeled the apples before cooking them.*

**peel** *noun*
the skin of a fruit or vegetable: *She threw the orange peel in the trash.*

**peep** /pip/ *noun*
a brief look at something

**peer (1)** /pɪr/ *noun*
a person who is one's equal in age, rank, ability, or other quality

**peer (2)** /pɪr/ *verb*
to take a long, slow look as if to discover something: *He peered out the window to see who was coming.*

**peg** /pɛg/ *noun*
a small rod made of metal or wood that fits in a hole and is used to hang things on, hold things together, or mark a place: *He hung his hat on a peg near the door.*

**peg** *verb* **pegged, pegging, pegs**
**1** to attach or fasten using pegs: *He pegged a picture to the wall.*
**2** to set a value for something: *He pegged the price of his house at $200,000.*
**3** *informal figurative* to classify someone as a certain type of person: *I have him pegged as a lazy fellow.*

**pelican** /'pɛlɪkən/ *noun*
a large bird that lives near water and stores the fish it catches in a bag under its beak: *Pelicans dive into the ocean for fish.*

**pelt** /pɛlt/ *verb*
to attack by throwing things: *Protesters pelted the police with bottles and rocks.*

**pelt** *noun*
the fur and skin of an animal: *The hunters returned from the forest with fox pelts.*

**pelvis** /'pɛlvɪs/ *noun, plural* **pelvises**
the area of the body between the backbone and the legs, framed by the hip bones: *A woman's pelvis is wider than a man's.* –*adjective* **pelvic.**

**pen (1)** /pɛn/ *noun*
an instrument used to write or draw in ink: *She looked in her purse for a pen to sign her check. See:* pencil.

**pen** *verb* **penned, penning, pens**
to write with a pen: *She penned a personal letter to her lawyer. See:* art on page 8a.

**pen (2)** *noun*
a small area of land surrounded by a fence and used to keep animals in: *He built a pen for his sheep.* *–verb* **to pen.**

**penalize** /ˈpinəˌlaɪz/ *verb* **penalized, penalizing, penalizes**
**1** to punish
**2** to force penalties that seem unfair on a person or group: *The students complained that they were being penalized by the new rules.*
**3** to give a penalty to a player or team for breaking a rule: *He was penalized for kicking another player.*

**penalty** /ˈpɛnəlti/ *noun, plural* **penalties**
the punishment one receives for breaking a law or a rule, such as having to pay money (a fine) or going to prison: *In that country, the penalty for murder is death.*||*She had to pay a penalty for sending in her tax returns late.* *(antonym)* reward.

**pencil** /ˈpɛnsəl/ *noun*
a narrow, pointed instrument, usually made of wood with a black or colored center, used for writing or drawing: *He used a pencil to add up the total of his monthly bills. See:* pen **(1);** art on page 8a.

**penetrate** /ˈpɛnəˌtreɪt/ *verb* **penetrated, penetrating, penetrates**
to pass or cut a way into or through: *The child cried as the doctor's needle penetrated his skin.* *–noun* **penetration;** *–adjective* **penetrable** /ˈpɛnətrəbəl/.

**penguin** /ˈpɛŋgwɪn/ *noun*
a large black-and-white seabird (found mainly in the Antarctic), that stands upright on short legs and has wings for swimming, not flying

penguin

**penicillin** /ˌpɛnəˈsɪlɪn/ *noun, (no plural)*
a medicine that fights germs or bacteria that cause infection or diseases: *His doctor gave him a shot of penicillin to cure a sore throat. See:* antibiotic.

**peninsula** /pəˈnɪnsələ/ *noun*
a long, usually narrow strip of land surrounded by water and connected to the mainland: *Florida is a peninsula.*

**penknife** /ˈpɛnˌnaɪf/ *noun, plural* **penknives** /-ˌnaɪvz/
a small pocketknife with a folding blade: *He carries a penknife to open his mail.*

**penmanship** /ˈpɛnmənˌʃɪp/ *noun*
**1** the skill of writing by hand
**2** one's style or manner of writing by hand: *Her penmanship is round and clear.*

**penniless** /ˈpɛnɪlɪs/ *adjective*
having no money, poor: *a penniless beggar*

**penny** /ˈpɛni/ *noun, plural* **pennies** /pɛns/
a small coin worth one cent, or 1/100 of a US, Canadian, or Australian dollar or British pound: *Pennies in the USA are made of copper.*
**a penny for your thoughts:** a phrase used to ask someone what he or she is thinking

**pension** /ˈpɛnʃən/ *noun*
a regular payment made by a business or government to a person who has retired from a job: *She is 70 years old and receives a pension from her former employer.*

**pensioner** /ˈpɛnʃənər/ *noun*
a person who receives a pension

**penthouse** /ˈpɛntˌhaʊs/ *noun, plural* **penthouses** /-ˌhaʊzɪz/
an apartment built on the roof of a tall building: *Stephanie's penthouse in New York has a wonderful view of Central Park.*

**people** /ˈpipəl/ *noun, used with a plural verb*
**1** human beings in general: *People are the same all over the world.*
**2** the common persons of a nation: *The people are in favor of the government's programs.*
**3** the members of a nation or race as a group: *The peoples of Africa have a rich history.*

**pepper** /ˈpɛpər/ *noun, (no plural)*
a common hot-tasting powder used to flavor food and improve taste: *You always find salt and pepper on a restaurant table. See:* art on page 5a.

**peppermint** /ˈpɛpərˌmɪnt/ *noun*
**1** *(no plural)* a (herb) plant whose leaves

are crushed for oils used in medicines and as flavoring
**2** *(no plural)* the cool, fresh taste of this oil: *This ice cream tastes like peppermint.*
**3** a candy flavored with peppermint oil: *He gave out peppermints to all the children.*

**per** /pɜr/ *preposition*
for one, for each: *That bread costs $3.00 per pound.*
**as per:** according to, in agreement with: *As per your instructions, we are sending the package to your home address.*

**perceive** /pərˈsiv/ *verb formal* **perceived, perceiving, perceives**
**1** to become aware of something through the senses (sight, hearing, touch, etc.) or by thinking: *We could just perceive the first light of sunrise.*
**2** to understand: *She perceived my meaning right away. –adjective* **perceptive;** *–noun* **perception.**

**percent** /pərˈsɛnt/ *adjective*
for each hundred of something: *That loan charges 11 percent interest per year.*
**percent** *noun*
one part of each hundred: *The salesperson gave me a discount of 20 percent (20%) off the regular price.*

**percentage** /pərˈsɛntɪʤ/ *noun*
an amount of something understood as a part of a whole that equals 100: *A large percentage of the people favor the new President's policies.*
**percentage** *adjective*
related to parts per hundred: *The interest rate on that loan is 11 percentage points.*

**perch** /pɜrʧ/ *noun, plural* **perches**
**1** a place where a bird lands and rests: *Pigeons use the sunny side of the roof as a perch.*
**2** a seat or position high above everything around it: *From his perch on the ladder he watched the parade below. –verb* **to perch.**

**perfect** /ˈpɜrfɪkt/ *adjective*
**1** the best possible: *a perfect score* (or) *record||If only the world were perfect!*
**2** complete and faultless, with nothing wrong or missing: *This car is in perfect condition.*
**3** appropriate and satisfactory in every way: *The holiday decorations were perfect.*
**4** total, complete: *a perfect fool||a perfect stranger (antonym)* imperfect.
**perfect** /pərˈfɛkt/ *verb*
to make perfect, without fault: *She perfected her style of playing the piano by practicing eight hours a day.*

**perfection** /pərˈfɛkʃən/ *noun, (no plural)*
**1** the state of being perfect: *She demanded perfection from her employees.*
**2** the process of making something perfect: *They are working on the perfection of a car that runs on electricity.*
**3** a perfect example of something: *This garden is wonderful; it's perfection!*
**to perfection:** excellently, the best way possible: *The Thanksgiving turkey was cooked to perfection. –noun* (person) **perfectionist.**

**perfectly** /ˈpɜr fɪktli/ *adverb*
**1** without faults or mistakes: *The space flight went perfectly, without a problem.*
**2** *figurative* completely, absolutely, without question or doubt: *perfectly happy||a perfectly good reason*

**perform** /pərˈfɔrm/ *verb*
**1** to do or finish a task: *He performed his regular duties quickly and quietly.*
**2** to give, act out, or present a performance (of a play, piece of music, dance, etc.): *The actors performed a play for the queen.*

**performance** /pərˈfɔrməns/ *noun*

performance

**1** the action of doing or completing something: *The performance of his duties took all day.*
**2** the presentation before an audience of a ceremony or work of art (drama, music, dance, etc.): *The performance of the play lasted two hours.*
**3** the behavior or operation of a person or machine: *Her performance at school was excellent.||The computer's performance was better than we expected.*

**performer** /pərˈfɔrmər/ *noun*
a person who performs for an audience, such as a singer, dancer, actor, musician,

etc.: *The circus performers delighted the children.*

**perfume** /'pər,fyum/ *noun*
**1** a pleasant, attractive smell, *(synonym)* a fragrance: *The flowers had a strong perfume.*
**2** a pleasant-smelling liquid made from flowers used on the body to make a person smell good: *He gave her some perfume for her birthday.*

**perfume** *verb* **perfumed, perfuming, perfumes**
to apply perfume: *She perfumed her neck and wrists.*

**perhaps** /pər'hæps/ *adverb*
maybe, possibly: *Perhaps I'll go to the movies tonight; I'm not sure yet.*

**period** /'pɪriəd/ *noun*
**1** any time, long or short, that has particular qualities or characteristics: *the dangerous period of an illness||a rainy period in spring||a happy period in my life*
**2** a regular division of time in a school day or a game: *the lunch period||The team scored in the second period.*
**3** a woman's monthly menstruation: *She occasionally has pain when she gets her period.*
**4** a punctuation mark (.) that ends a sentence: *This sentence ends with a period.* *–adjective* **periodic.**

**permanent (1)** /'pɜrmənənt/ *adjective*
**1** lasting, or meant to last, forever or for a long time: *They hoped their marriage would be permanent.*
**2** firmly set, not expected to change soon: *This house is now my permanent address. (antonym)* temporary. *–adverb* **permanently;** *–noun* **permanence.**

**permanent (2)** *noun*
treatment of the hair with chemicals designed to produce curls and waves: *She had a permanent at the beauty shop this morning.*

**permissible** /pər'mɪsəbəl/ *adjective*
allowable, permitted: *The teacher said that it was not permissible to talk in class.*

**permission** /pər'mɪʃən/ *noun, (no plural)*
agreement to allow someone to do something: *She asked for permission to leave work early.*

**permit** /pər'mɪt/ *verb* **permitted, permitting, permits**
**1** to allow, let: *He would not permit us to leave the building.*
**2** to make possible or offer the opportunity: *If time permits, I will visit my uncle.*

**permit** *noun* /'pɜr,mɪt/
an official document giving someone the freedom to do something or go somewhere, such as a gun permit, driving permit, etc.

**persist** /pər'sɪst/ *verb*
to continue steadily in the same manner in spite of obstacles or opposition: *He persisted in asking her to marry him until she finally said, "Yes."* *–noun* **persistence;** *–adjective* **persistent.**

**person** /'pɜrsən/ *noun*
**1** a single human being, an individual: *There was just one person in the restaurant.*
**2** someone whose identity is not known: *That person stole my purse.*
**3** (in grammar) any of the three classes of pronouns or verb forms that indicate the speaker (first person), the one spoken to (second person), or the one spoken about (third person)
**in person:** physically present, face-to-face: *I have to go to New York to see him in person.*

**personal** /'pɜrsənəl/ *adjective*
**1** related to a particular person, private: *He receives personal telephone calls at the office.*
**2** done or carried out in person: *a personal visit||a personal conversation*

**personal computer** or **PC** *noun*
a small computer that can easily be moved, designed mainly for home use

**personality** /,pɜrsə'nælәti/ *noun, plural* **personalities**
**1** the total effect or character of a person's qualities (habits, behavior, attitudes, etc.): *She has a warm, lively personality.*
**2** an important or well-known person, especially in the entertainment business: *Movie personalities filled the audience at the award ceremony.*

**personally** /'pɜrsənəli/ *adverb*
**1** by oneself, not through others: *The President thanked the soldier personally by telephoning him.*
**2** in one's own opinion: *I, personally, am opposed to the plan, but my company is going ahead with it.*
**3** as a person: *I don't know him personally, but others speak well of him.*

**personal pronoun** *noun*
a pronoun that refers to a person or thing that is speaking, is spoken to, or is spoken about: *The personal pronouns are I, me, you, he, him, she, her, it, we, us, they, and them.*

**personnel** /ˌpɜrsə'nɛl/ *noun, (no plural)*
**1** all the people working in an organization (a business, school, etc.): *The company had to fire half of its personnel to save money.*
**2** the office in a business that handles employee affairs, such as hiring, records, and benefits: *I went to personnel to ask about the company retirement program.*

---

**USAGE NOTE:** The term *Human Resource Department* is often used instead of *Personnel Department.*

---

**perspire** /pər'spaɪr/ *verb* **perspired, perspiring, perspires**
to have drops of salty liquid form (sweat) on the skin because of heat or nervousness, *(synonym)* to sweat: *She perspires when she has to take a test.* *–noun* **perspiration.**

P

**persuade** /pər'sweɪd/ *verb* **persuaded, persuading, persuades**
to lead a person or group to believe or do something by arguing or reasoning with them: *I persuaded my friend to stop drinking alcohol.*

**persuasion** /pər'sweɪʒən/ *noun, (no plural)*
the act of persuading: *Instead of fighting, try persuasion to get what you want.*

**persuasive** /pər'sweɪsɪv/ *adjective*
**1** good at persuading others: *He is a persuasive salesman.*
**2** reasonable, sensible: *a persuasive argument* *–adverb* **persuasively.**

**pessimist** /ˌpɛsə'mɪst/ *noun*
a person who tends to see only the bad things in life and to expect that they are more likely to get worse than better: *Because he's such a pessimist, he never wants to try new things.* *–noun* **pessimism.** *(antonym)* optimist.

**pessimistic** /ˌpɛsə'mɪstɪk/ *adjective*
expecting something to become worse than it is: *a pessimistic view of the future* *–adverb* **pessimistically.**

**pest** /pɛst/ *noun*
**1** a small animal or an insect that causes damage to food or crops, or otherwise bothers human beings: *Rats, mice, and flies are some common pests.*
**2** an annoying person: *The little girl who demands attention all the time is a pest.* *–verb* **to pester.**

**pet** /pɛt/ *noun*
**1** an animal kept in the home and treated with kindness and love: *Dogs are very popular as pets.*
**2** a favorite person: *That smart girl is the teacher's pet.*

**pet** *adjective*
**1** kept or treated as a pet: *She has six pet cats.*
**2** favorite, special: *His pet topic is politics.*
**3** showing love: *My pet name for her is "Cookie."*

**pet** *verb* **petted, petting, pets**
to touch lightly and lovingly with the hand: *She pets her cat on its back.* *–noun* **petting.**

**petal** /'pɛtl/ *noun*
the colored or white leaf-like part of a flower: *The petals of a rose are soft.*

**petite** /pə'tit/ *adjective*
(said of women) small

**petition** /pə'tɪʃən/ *noun*
a formal request signed by many people to make a change: *The neighborhood signed a petition asking for more streetlights.* *–verb* **to petition;** *–noun* (person) **petitioner.**

**phantom** /'fæntəm/ *noun*
a ghost

**pharmacist** /'fɑrməsɪst/ *noun*
a person who has studied pharmacy and has a license to prepare and sell drugs, *(synonym)* a druggist: *The pharmacist*

*sold me some medicine for my cold. See:* art on page 10a.

**pharmacy** /ˈfɑrməsi/ *noun, plural* **pharmacies**
a drugstore, or the place where drugs are prepared and sold within a store: *She pointed me to the pharmacy in the back of the store. See:* art on page 4a.

**phase** /feɪz/ *noun*
**1** a period of time of change, a stage of development: *The time you spend in high school is an important phase of your education.*
**2** one of the regularly changing appearances of the moon: *We studied the phases of the moon in school.*

**phase** *verb* **phased, phasing, phases**
**to phase something in** or **out:** to introduce or remove something slowly, in steps: *They are phasing out that old model of TV.*||*They are phasing it out.*

**Ph.D.** /ˌpieɪtʃˈdi/ *noun*
*abbreviation for* Doctor of Philosophy, an advanced university degree above a master's degree: *She has a Ph.D. in English from Berkeley. See:* M.A., USAGE NOTE.

**philosopher** /fəˈlɑsəfər/ *noun*
a person who studies or teaches philosophy *–adjective* **philosophical.**

**philosophy** /fəˈlɑsəfi/ *noun, plural* **philosophies**
**1** the study of the most general truths and beliefs about the nature and meaning of human existence, the world, and of life: *Philosophy is a difficult subject.*
**2** *(no plural)* a way of living, especially a calm, patient attitude toward life: *His philosophy brings him peace of mind. –verb* **to philosophize.**

**phone** /foʊn/ *verb* **phoned, phoning, phones**
*short for* telephone: *I phoned my friend this morning. –noun* (device) **phone.**

**phone book** *noun short for* telephone book:
a book listing names, addresses, and telephone numbers of people, businesses, and institutions: *I looked in the phone book for the number for the police.*

**phone booth** *noun*
*short for* telephone booth

**phonetics** /fəˈnɛtɪks/ *plural noun, used with a singular verb*
the science and study of speech sounds

**phony** /ˈfoʊni/ *adjective* **phonier, phoniest**
not real, *(synonyms)* false, fake: *This ring was made with phony diamonds.*

**phony** *noun, plural* **phonies**
a person who is not sincere, or pretends to be different than he or she really is: *He says he is a rich businessman, but he is really a phony. (antonym)* genuine.

**photo** /ˈfoʊtoʊ/ *noun, plural* **photos**
*short for* photograph: *I took some photos of my kids.*

**photocopier** /ˈfoʊtəˌkɑpiər/ *noun*
a machine that makes copies of documents and pictures by photographing them, *(synonym)* Xerox™ machine: *The library in my town has three photocopiers for public use.*

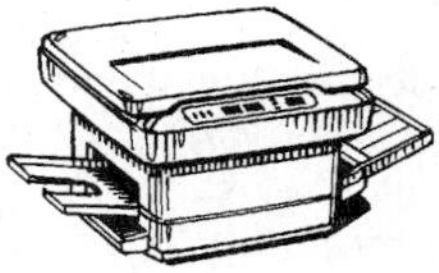
photocopier

**photocopy** /ˈfoʊtəˌkɑpi/ *noun, plural* **photocopies**
a photographic copy of a document, picture, etc., made by a photocopier: *I made a photocopy of a letter that I wrote.*

**photocopy** *verb* **photocopied, photocopying, photocopies**
to make photocopies of something: *I photocopied my letter.*

USAGE NOTE: The brand name *Xerox* ™ is also used as a verb to mean photocopy: *I need to Xerox* ™ *these papers.*

**photograph** /ˈfoʊtəˌgræf/ *noun*
a picture made from light passing through a camera onto film: *We took photographs of the children while on vacation. –adjective* **photographic.**

**photograph** *verb*
to take a photograph (or photographs) of something: *He photographed our wedding last year. –noun* (person) **photographer.**

**photography** /fəˈtɑgrəfi/ *noun, (no plural)*
the art and science of producing pictures with a camera: *The book is about early 19th century British photography.*

P

**phrase** /freɪz/ *noun*
a usually small group of words that is not a sentence but may form part of a sentence: *"Down the hill" is a phrase in "The ball rolled down the hill."*

**physical** /ˈfɪzɪkəl/ *adjective*
**1** related to things one can see and touch (as opposed to mental or spiritual things): *She studies the brain as a physical organ that works like a computer.*
**2** related to the body: *After falling from a ladder, he had many physical aches and pains.*
**3** related to the laws of nature: *There are physical limits to how fast we can travel.*

**physical** *noun*
*short for* physical examination, a medical examination performed by a doctor: *I had a physical before starting my new job.*

**physically** /ˈfɪzɪkli/ *adverb*
in or of the body: *The sight of blood makes her physically ill.*

**physician** /fɪˈzɪʃən/ *noun*
a doctor: *My physician told me to stop smoking cigarettes.*

**physics** /ˈfɪzɪks/ *noun plural*
*used with a singular verb* the study of the most basic forms of matter, energy, and motion, including heat, light, sound, and electricity: *The laws of physics are true throughout the universe.*



**pianist** /piˈænɪs/ *noun*
a person who plays the piano

piano

**piano** /piˈænoʊ/ *noun, plural* **pianos**
a large musical instrument built with a wooden frame and many small black and white levers (called "keys") that are struck by the player's fingers: *She has played piano since she was a child. See:* art on page 15a.

**pick** /pɪk/ *verb*
**1** to choose: *She picked a bright yellow dress to wear to the wedding.||They picked her to play on their team.*
**2** to gather fruits, flowers, vegetables, etc., by breaking them off from the plants they grow on: *He picked an apple from the tree.||She went into the garden to pick flowers.*
**3** to start, bring about: *He picked a fight with his brother.*
**4** to steal valuables from someone's purse or pocket: *A thief picked my wallet from my pocket.*
**5** to pull (pluck) the strings of a musical instrument with either the fingers or a small, flat piece of plastic or wood: *She picked her guitar with skill.*
**to pick on someone:** to choose to bother, hurt, or laugh at a person: *The older boys picked on him because he was new to the school.*
**to pick someone** or **something out: a. someone:** to see clearly: *She picked out her friend in the crowd.* **b. something:** to choose: *Will you pick out a book for me?*
**to pick someone** or **something up: a.** to go and get something or meet someone: *He picked up his date at her house.* **b.** to take passengers in a vehicle: *The bus picked us up on time.* **c.** to try to become sexy with someone one has just met: *He tried to pick up someone at the party, but he had no luck.* **d.** to lift or raise up: *I picked up a rock.||Pick up your feet!* **e.** to get, gain, or learn easily: *She picks up new languages easily.*

**pick** *noun*
**1** a choice or selection: *What's your pick from all the movies we can see tonight?*
**2** the best or finest choice among a group: *She's the pick of all the girls.*
**3** a small, sharp, pointed instrument: *an ice pick||a dentist's pick*
**4** a small, flat piece of wood or plastic used to pluck the strings of a musical instrument *–noun* (person) **picker.**

**picket** /ˈpɪkɪt/ *noun*
workers who stand in front of an office, factory, etc. to prevent others from entering to work, as part of a strike: *The striking workers formed a picket early in the morning.*

**picket** *verb*
to protest by standing or walking outside a company's building: *Protesters picketed outside the main entrance.*

**pickle** /ˈpɪkəl/ *noun*
a round green vegetable (cucumber) soaked in vinegar and spices: *I like a slice of pickle with my sandwich.*

**pickpocket** /ˈpɪk ˌpakɪt/ *noun*
a person who steals from the pockets or

purses of people in crowds or public areas: *A pickpocket on the bus stole his wallet.*

**pickup truck** *noun*
a light truck of medium size, with a driver's cabin in front, an open space in back, low side walls, and a rear gate that folds down; often used in everyday work: *The gardener carried tools in her pickup truck.*

pickup truck

**picky** /ˈpɪki/ *adjective* **pickier, pickiest**
difficult to please

**picnic** /ˈpɪknɪk/ *noun*
**1** a trip taken by a friendly group of people to a pleasant outdoor place to eat a meal that has been prepared ahead of time and carried along: *We went for a picnic in the park.*
**2** an outdoor meal eaten on a holiday or special occasion: *Our company gave a picnic for all employees.*

**picnic** *verb* **picnicked, picnicking, picnics**
to have a picnic: *We picnicked in the park.*

**picture** /ˈpɪktʃər/ *noun*
**1** a drawing, painting, or photograph: *The children draw pictures with colored pencils.||His picture is in the paper.*
**2** an example or perfect model: *She is a picture of good manners.*
**3** a movie: *We went to see a picture.*
**4** the future: *The picture looks good for the success of our business.*
**5** an explanation or mental image: *She tried to give us a picture of how a computer works.*
**6** (the quality of) an image on a TV or movie screen: *This TV gets a really good picture.*
**to get the picture:** to understand, see the meaning after some difficulty: *After she explained the solution to the math problem, I said, "Oh, now I get the picture."*

**picture** *verb* **pictured, picturing, pictures**
to give a certain image of: *The drawing pictured the man in an old chair.* *See:* art on page 6a.

**pie** /paɪ/ *noun*
fruit, meat or other foods baked in a pastry shell: *Would you like some apple pie for dessert?*
**as easy as pie:** very easy: *Riding a bike is as easy as pie.*

---

USAGE NOTE: Apple *pie* is a traditional American dessert. People say "as American as apple pie" to refer to something that is very American: *Baseball was invented in the United States; it's as American as apple pie.*

---

**piece** /pis/ *noun*
**1** a part of a whole thing that is separate from the rest: *He dropped the glass and it broke in pieces.*
**2** a single product of an activity that requires skill, especially a work of art: *a piece of music/poetry/work||That essay was an excellent piece of writing!*
**a piece of cake:** something very easy to do: *It will be a piece of cake to win this game.*

**piece** *verb* **pieced, piecing, pieces**
**to piece something together:** **a.** to put together, repair: *She pieced together the broken chair.* **b.** to make sense of something by putting together separate facts: *He tried to piece together what happened to all his money.*

**pier** /pɪr/ *noun*
a large, long, flat structure of wood or iron built over water, at which boats can load or unload passengers and cargo: *She waved goodbye from the boat to her friends who stood on the pier.*

**pierce** /pɪrs/ *verb* **pierced, piercing, pierces**
**1** to cut a hole in or through something with a pointed object: *The needle pierced my skin.||She had her ears pierced for earrings.*
**2** to break through the surface or into the deepest part of something: *The boat pierced the waves of the sea.||The searchlight pierced the darkness of night.*

**piercing** /ˈpɪrsɪŋ/ *adjective*
sharp and painful: *a cold, piercing wind||a piercing scream*

**pig** /pɪg/ *noun*
**1** a common farm animal, valued for its

meat, with a fat round body, thick skin, short nose, legs, and tail: *A big, fat pig cannot run fast.*

**2** a fat, impolite, or offensive person who eats too much: *I will never invite that man to dinner because he is a pig.*

**to pig out on something:** to take pleasure in eating too much: *After school, he pigged out on pizza and ice cream. See:* art on page 14a.

**USAGE NOTE:** When pig meat is eaten, it is called *pork, ham,* or *bacon;* it is not called *pig.*

**pigeon** /ˈpɪdʒən/ *noun*
a gray or white bird with a round body and small head, commonly found in cities: *People in the park threw small pieces of bread to the pigeons.*

**piglet** /ˈpɪglɪt/ *noun*
a baby pig

**pigtail** /ˈpɪgˌteɪl/ *noun*
a length of hair that hangs down the back of the neck and shoulders, formed by folding two or more ropes of hair (strands) around each other: *She made her hair into a pigtail before she went swimming.*

**pile (1)** /paɪl/ *noun*
a collection of similar things laid together, forming the shape of a small hill, *(synonym)* a heap: *A truck left a pile of sand near the road.*||*His clothes lay in a pile on the floor.*

**pile** *verb* **piled, piling, piles**
to make into a pile: *He piled the newspapers on his desk.*

**pilgrim** /ˈpɪlgrəm/ *noun*
a person who travels a long way to visit a holy place: *Pilgrims often travel together for comfort and support when faced with difficulties. –noun* **pilgrimage** /ˈpɪlgrəmɪdʒ/.

**USAGE NOTE:** In 1620, a group of people from England settled at Plymouth in Massachusetts. These people are often called the *Pilgrims* (with a capital P). The *Thanksgiving* holiday in the USA celebrates a 1621 harvest feast that the Pilgrims shared with Native Americans of the Massachusetts coast.

P

**pill** /pɪl/ *noun*
a small, round piece of medicine meant to be swallowed: *He takes a pill to reduce his high blood pressure.*

**pillar** /ˈpɪlər/ *noun*
a tall round piece of wood, stone, or metal used to support a building: *Rock pillars stood on either side of the doorway.*

**pillow** /ˈpɪloʊ/ *noun*
a square or rectangular cloth bag filled with soft material, used to support the head for comfort when lying in bed: *He sleeps with a soft pillow under his head. See:* art on page 22a.

**pilot (1)** /ˈpaɪlət/ *noun*
**1** a person who flies an aircraft
**2** a person who guides boats

**pilot** *verb*
to act as a pilot: *She piloted the ship to land.*

**pimple** /ˈpɪmpəl/ *noun*
a small, red swelling on the skin: *That young man has pimples on his face. –adjective* **pimply.**

**pin** /pɪn/ *noun*
**1** a short, straight, very thin piece of metal with a sharp point and a flat, round head, used to hold together things (made of cloth, paper, etc.) by sticking through them: *She kept a box of pins with her needles and thread for sewing.*

**2** a piece of jewelry attached to clothing with a pin: *She wore a diamond pin on her coat.*

**3** any object used to hold things in place (by piercing or clasping them): *She wore a hair pin to hold back her hair.*

**on pins and needles:** feeling worried and tense: *He was on pins and needles while waiting for the doctor.*

**pin** *verb* **pinned, pinning, pins**
**1** to fasten with a pin: *He pinned a flower to her dress.*||*She pinned up a notice on the board.*

**2** to hold something or someone in one place and be unable to move: *She was pinned against the door by the crowd.*||*They were pinned down by enemy gunfire.*

**pinch** /pɪntʃ/ *verb* **pinches**
**1** to press tightly between the thumb and

a finger: *She pinched (the skin of) his arm to get his attention.*
**2** to be caught and pressed between two hard objects that come together: *She pinched her finger in the desk drawer.*
**to pinch pennies:** to be very careful about spending money: *When she was a student, she had to pinch pennies.*

**pinch** *noun, plural* **pinches**
a pressing together of the thumb and a finger, especially of the skin to cause sharp pain: *My mother gave me a pinch to make me be good.*

**pine** /paɪn/ *noun*
**1** a tall, straight tree, found mainly in cool climates, with small, thin, sharp leaves (called "needles") that remain green throughout the year and woody, brown fruit (called "cones"): *We built a summer house among the pines* (or) *pine trees.*
**2** the soft, yellowish wood of this tree, very commonly used for furniture and houses: *We built our house out of pine.* *See:* art on page 1a.

**pineapple** /ˈpaɪˌnæpəl/ *noun*
a tropical plant with a fruit that is brown and rough on the outside and sweet, yellow, and juicy on the inside *See:* art on page 3a.

pineapple

**Ping-Pong** /ˈpɪŋˌpɑŋ/ *noun*™
a game two or four people play on a tabletop using wooden paddles and a small ball: *Ping Pong™ is a very fast game.*

Ping-Pong™

**pink** /pɪŋk/ *noun, (no plural)*
a light red color: *Pink roses are pretty.*

**pinkie** or **pinky** /ˈpɪŋki/ *noun informal, plural* **pinkies**
the little finger: *When she holds a teacup, she raises her pinkie.*

**pinnacle** /ˈpɪnəkəl/ *noun*
the pointed top of a mountain

**pint** /paɪnt/ *noun*
a unit of measure for liquids, equal to 16 ounces or one half quart (.47 liter): *He bought a pint of beer.*

**pioneer** /ˌpaɪəˈnɪr/ *noun*
one of the first people to enter new land to live and work there: *Pioneers crossed America to find new farm land.*

**pioneer** *verb*
to develop, explore, or settle something new: *She pioneered the political movement for women's rights.*

**pipe** /paɪp/ *noun*
**1** a tube through which liquids or gases pass from one place to another: *Pipes are used to carry water and gas into homes and buildings.*

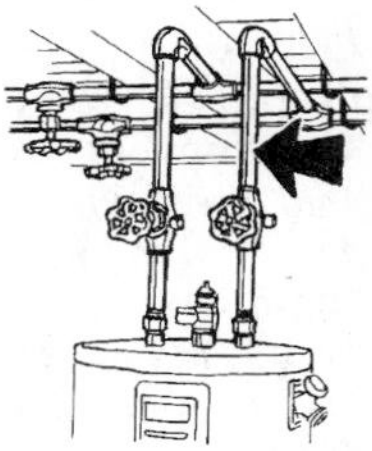
pipe

**2** a small tube with a bowl at one end and a mouthpiece at the other, for smoking tobacco: *Smoking a pipe is not allowed in this restaurant.*
*–verb* **to pipe.**

**pipeline** /ˈpaɪpˌlaɪn/ *noun*
a long system of connected pipes that carry gas, water, or oil over long distances: *The city's pipelines bring us water from the mountains.*

**piracy** /ˈpaɪrəsi/ *noun, (no plural)*
robbery (of boats or airplanes) that takes place at sea or in the air: *They would not sail across the ocean because they feared piracy.*

**pirate** /ˈpaɪrɪt/ *noun*
a person who steals sailing ships or airplanes or the goods they carry: *The pirates threatened to kill anyone who tried to stop them.*

**pistol** /ˈpɪstəl/ *noun*
a small gun that can be held and shot with one hand: *Most police officers carry a pistol.*

**pit (1)** /pɪt/ *noun*
**1** a large, open hole in the ground: *The builders dug a deep pit for the foundation of the new office building.*
**2** a large hole in the ground where people dig for minerals: *a coal pit*||*a sand pit*
**the pits:** something extremely bad, the worst: *This restaurant is the pits.*

**pit** *verb* **pitted, pitting, pits**
**1** to mark with pits: *The front of his truck was pitted by stones from the road.*
**2** to put in opposition to or competition with: *In the tennis match, I was pitted against my best friend.*

**pit (2)** *noun*
the hard seed of some fruits: *Cherries and peaches have pits.*

**pit** *verb* **pitted, pitting, pits**
to remove the pit: *I pitted some peaches before we ate them.*

**pitch** /pɪʧ/ *verb* **pitches**
**1** to throw or toss: *She pitched her bags into the trunk of the car.*||*They pitched hay onto the wagon.*
**2** (in baseball) to throw the ball to the batter: *My father taught me how to pitch when I was young.*
**3** to set up: *They pitched their tent near the river.*
**to pitch in:** to join with others or contribute to an activity: *We all pitched in to help homeless people.* –*noun* **pitch.**

**pitcher (1)** /ˈpɪʧər/ *noun*
a tall, round container with an open top and large handle, used for holding and pouring liquids: *A waiter poured water from a pitcher into my glass.*

pitcher



**pitcher (2)** *noun*
(in baseball) the player who throws the ball toward the batter, who tries to hit it: *Pitchers must have strong arms.*

**pitfall** /ˈpɪtˌfɔl/ *noun*
a hidden danger or difficulty that is a common cause of mistakes or errors: *Starting a new business has many pitfalls.*

**pitiful** /ˈpɪtɪfəl/ *adjective*
**1** worthy of pity, sad: *Many poor people live in pitiful conditions.*
**2** hopelessly bad, not worthy of much attention: *His attempts to win her love were pitiful.* –*adverb* **pitifully.**

**pity** /pɪti/ *noun, (no plural)*
**1** the feeling of sorrow or sympathy caused by the suffering or hardships of others: *She feels pity for the poor and the sick.*
**2** a sad situation: *It is a pity that your husband is ill.*
**to have** or **take pity on someone:** to help someone out of sympathy or kindness: *A soldier had (or took) pity on a wounded enemy and helped him to safety.*

**pity** *verb* **pitied, pitying, pities**
to feel sorry for someone: *He pities the poor and gives money to them.*

**pizza** /ˈpitsə/ or **pizza pie** *noun*
a flat, wide circle of bread dough, usually baked with tomato sauce and cheese: *I ordered a slice of pizza and a soda.* –*noun* (store) **pizzeria.**

**place** /pleɪs/ *noun*
**1 a.** a spot occupied by a person or thing: *Here is a good place to hang the picture.* **b.** *figurative* a position in relation to certain thoughts, ideas, feelings, etc.: *She has no place for him in her heart.*||*He has a place of honor in his country's history.*
**2** a particular location, area, or region on the earth, such as a city, state, island, etc.: *The city of Buenos Aires is a great place to visit.*
**3** a position in line: *He asked me to save him a place while he parked the car.*
**4** a final position in a race or competition: *She came in second place in the diving contest.*
**5** a room, building, or piece of land used for a particular purpose: *the workplace*||*a marketplace*||*a holy place*
**6** *informal* a room, apartment, house, or other shelter where people live: *After the movie, let's go back to my place.*
**in** or **out of place:** in or not in the position where (someone or something) belongs: *Everything is in place, so we are ready to go.*||*On his first trip away from home, he felt out of place.*
**in place of:** instead of, as a substitute for: *If you are sick, she will have to go in place of you.*
**to go places:** to be successful: *He's so smart; he is really going to go places.*
**to take place:** to happen: *The dance will take place on Saturday night.*

**place** *verb* **placed, placing, places**
to put in a specific location or position: *I*

*placed the bag of apples on the kitchen table.*||*She was placed on the school's board of directors.* –*noun* **placement.**

**placement office** *noun*
the office in a college or university that helps students find jobs: *He went to the placement office for a job interview.*

**plague** /pleɪg/ *noun*
a dangerous disease that spreads very fast and kills its victims quickly: *Before the modern age, plagues killed millions of people.*

**plaid** /plæd/ *noun*
a pattern of light- and dark-colored lines and rectangles often used for the fabric of clothes: *He wore a pair of pants with a bright plaid on the boat trip.* –*adjective* **plaid.**

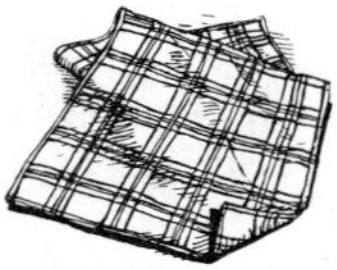
plaid

**plain** /pleɪn/ *noun*
**1** a wide area of flat land: *We drove over a plain that lay between two sets of hills.*
**2** *plural* **plains:** a large area of flat land: *In North America, the plains continue for hundreds of miles.*

**plain** *adjective*
**1** easy to see, hear, or understand: *in plain sight* (or) *language*||*Try to make your instructions plain.*
**2** simple, ordinary, not fancy: *He likes plain cooking.*||*They had a very plain wedding ceremony.* –*noun* **plainness.** *(antonym)* fancy.

**plainly** /ˈpleɪnli/ *adverb*
**1** clearly, obviously: *That is plainly the wrong way to do things.*
**2** in a plain manner: *They were dressed very plainly.*

**plan** /plæn/ *noun*
**1** a program of action for the future, usually including a series of steps toward a goal: *We made a plan for raising money to build a new library.*
**2** a drawing of something to be made, showing all its parts and their relations: *She drew a detailed plan of the house she wanted to build.*
**3** a map: *He made a plan of the city's subway lines.*

**to have plans:** **a.** to have a date or appointment: *I'm not free; I have plans for this evening.* **b.** to have goals, dreams, etc.: *She has big plans for her future as a doctor.*

**plan** *verb* **planned, planning, plans**
**1** to make a plan for: *They planned a big meeting to be held next year.*
**2** to intend to do something: *He planned to take a vacation in June.*

**plane** /pleɪn/ *noun*
an airplane: *Our plane landed at the airport. See:* airplane; jet.

**planet** /ˈplænɪt/ *noun*
a very large ball-shaped body (such as the earth) that moves around a star (such as the sun) in outer space: *People have always wanted to know if there is life on other planets.* –*adjective* **planetary** /ˈplænəˌtɛri/.

**plant** /plænt/ *noun*
**1** a living thing that usually grows in the earth and makes its own food from sunlight: *Humans and animals could not live without plants.*
**2** a factory, or the land, buildings, and machinery used to manufacture products: *My father worked in an automobile plant.*

**plant** *verb*
to put seeds, plants, or trees in the ground to grow: *Farmers planted wheat and corn this spring.*||*I planted my garden in April.*

**plantation** /plænˈteɪʃən/ *noun*
a large farm, usually in a warm climate, that grows a single major crop, such as tea, coffee, cotton, etc.: *There were many cotton plantations in the southern USA.*

**planter** /ˈplæntər/ *noun*
the owner of a plantation: *He was a wealthy coffee planter from Kenya.*

**plaster** /ˈplæstər/ *noun, (no plural)*
a mixture of water, (lime) and sand spread on walls to make a smooth surface after it dries: *The plaster on that old wall is yellow and cracked.*

**plaster** *verb*
to cover walls with plaster: *They plastered the wall before painting it.* –*noun* (worker) **plasterer.**

**plastic** /ˈplæstɪk/ *noun*
a strong, lightweight material made from chemicals, which can be shaped into many forms and is commonly used as a substitute for metal or wood: *Many things, such as toys, furniture, and computers, are made of plastic.*

**plastic** *adjective*
**1** easily shaped or formed by pressing: *Wet clay is very plastic.*
**2** made from plastic: *We ate with plastic forks and spoons.*

**plate** /pleɪt/ *noun*
**1** a flat dish with a raised border, used to hold food: *I put plates on the table for lunch.*
**2** a serving of food: *He had a plate of spaghetti for lunch.*
**3** a flat sheet of hard material: *She replaced a broken plate of glass in the window. See:* art on page 5a.

**plateau** /plæˈtoʊ/ *noun, plural* **plateaus** /-ˈtoʊz/
**1** a raised area of flat land with a steep drop on at least one side: *Plateaus can be hundreds of miles long.*
**2** *figurative* a stage or period in which there is no change or progress: *The economy kept improving, and then reached a plateau.*

**platform** /ˈplætˌfɔrm/ *noun*
**1** a flat raised structure, such as used for making speeches and boarding or exiting trains: *I stepped from the platform into the train.*
**2** a statement of beliefs and goals made by politicians: *Our candidate ran for reelection on a platform calling for political reform.*

**plating** /ˈpleɪtɪŋ/ *noun*
a thin covering of metal: *The silver plating on that knife is very shiny.*

**platinum** /ˈplætnəm/ *noun adjective*
a silvery white metal used in jewelry and traded as very valuable: *She collects platinum rings.*

**platter** /ˈplætər/ *noun*
a large, flat dish with a raised border, used to hold food: *He put the platter holding the roast turkey on the table.* –*noun* **platterful.**

**play** /pleɪ/ *noun*
**1** fun, amusement: *Children are at play in the park.*
**2** a theatrical production, such as a drama or musical: *Shakespeare's plays have been performed for centuries.*
**3** one's turn in a sport, game, or gambling: *I told my card partner that it was her play.*
**4** action in a game or event: *The play in that Ping-Pong™ match is very fast.*

**a play on words:** a word or phrase used with a double meaning: *A manufacturer of calculators used a play on words in its ads: "You can count on our products," meaning that you can rely on their quality and you can count with them.*

**play** *verb*
**1** to have fun, amuse oneself: *Children played with a ball on the beach.*
**2** to participate in a sport or game: *She plays tennis, and he plays cards.*
**3** to compete against in a sport or game: *Our school's football team is going to play the best team in the state tomorrow.*
**4** to perform on a musical instrument: *She played the piano while he played the violin.*
**5** to act a part in a movie or stage production: *She played the lead role in the film.*
**6** to take part in, have an effect on: *Education of the workforce plays an important role in a healthy economy.*
**7** to cause a radio, TV, tape player, etc., to produce sounds: *He plays the radio loudly.*

**to play by the rules:** to act in a correct, proper way: *She plays by the rules and does not cheat on her tests.*

**to play it cool:** to not get excited, remain dignified and calm: *When they offered her a salary higher than she expected, she just played it cool and accepted it.*

**to play it safe:** to take no risk, do the safest thing: *It's not supposed to rain, but I think I'll play it safe and take my umbrella.*

**to play something back:** to listen to or watch a recording again: *The singers made a recording, then played back their song to listen to it. (antonym)* work.

P

**playful** /'pleɪfəl/ *adjective*
**1** liking to play: *That dog is a playful little dog.*
**2** not serious, joking in a friendly way: *She gave him a playful hit on the arm and smiled.* –*adverb* **playfully;** –*noun* **playfulness.**

**playground** /'pleɪ,graʊnd/ *noun*
an area used by children to play in, especially one with permanent structures like swings: *Parents take children to the playground to have fun. See:* art on page 8a.

**playing card** *noun*
one of a set of usually 52 cards marked with the numbers one through ten or a picture, used for playing various games: *I bought a pack of playing cards.*

playing card

**playmate** /'pleɪ,meɪt/ *noun*
a child who plays with another child

**playwright** /'pleɪ,raɪt/ *noun*
a person who writes plays: *The playwright attended the opening night of his new play.*

**plaza** /'plɑzə/ *noun*
a public space in the shape of a square: *The town is built around a large plaza with a fountain in the middle.*

**plea** /pli/ *noun*
**1** an urgent request: *The hungry man's pleas for food were answered.*
**2** (in law) a response to an accusation: *The man's lawyer entered a plea of not guilty before the court.*

**plead** /plid/ *verb* **pleaded** or **pled** /plɛd/, **pleading, pleads**
to request urgently: *A hungry man pleaded for food.*

**pleasant** /'plɛzənt/ *adjective*
**1** enjoyable, pleasing: *This is a pleasant, sunny day.*||*The ice cream has a pleasant taste.*
**2** friendly, easy to like: *She has a pleasant personality.* –*adverb* **pleasantly;** –*noun* **pleasantness.** *(antonym)* unpleasant.

**please** /pliz/ *verb* **pleased, pleasing, pleases**
**1** to make someone feel happy, satisfy: *It pleases me that you are making such a big effort in this class.*
**2** to want, like, feel: *You should feel free to do what you please.*

**please** *interjection*
**1** a polite request, way of asking someone to do something: *Please sit down and take your coat off.*
**2** a polite way of saying yes: *"Would you like some butter?" "Please."*

**please** *adjective* **pleased**
**1** a polite greeting on first meeting someone: *I am pleased to meet you.*
**2** happy: *I was pleased that you could come to the party. (antonym)* displease.

**pleasing** /'plizɪŋ/ *adjective*
pleasant, enjoyable: *That food has a pleasing taste (smell, look).* –*adverb* **pleasingly.**

**pleasure** /'plɛʒər/ *noun*
enjoyment, feeling of happiness: *Good food is one of life's great pleasures.*

**pleat** /plit/ *noun*
a fold doubled over on itself in cloth –*adjective* **pleated.**

**pledge** /plɛʤ/ *noun*
a formal promise to do or give something: *He signed a pledge to stop drinking.* –*verb* **to pledge.**

**plentiful** /'plɛntɪfəl/ *adjective*
in good supply, more than enough: *Food is plentiful in the USA.* –*adverb* **plentifully.**

**plenty** /'plɛnti/ *noun adjective*
large quantity: *We have plenty of food for the party today. (antonym)* little.

**pliers** /'plaɪərz/ *noun plural*
a tool used for holding, twisting, or cutting: *I used a pair of pliers to pull a nail out of the wood.*

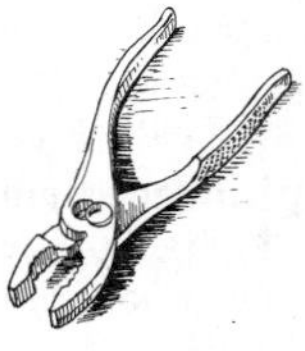
pliers

**plot** /plɑt/ *verb* **plotted, plotting, plots**
to plan in secret a way to cause harm: *Two employees of the bank were caught plotting to steal money.*

P

**plot** *noun*
**1** the main story in a novel or play: *The plot concerns a poor boy who moves to California and becomes an actor.*
**2** an area of land: *Her house is located on a small plot of land.*

**plow** /plaʊ/ *noun*
**1** a farm tool used to turn over ground for planting crops: *The farmer walked behind a plow pulled by a horse.*

plow

**2** a machine used to move snow, sand, etc.: *Snowplows remove snow from the streets.* –*verb* **to plow.**

**plug** /plʌg/ *noun*
**1** a device made of rubber, wood, etc. used to block an opening: *He pushed a wooden plug into the opening in the wine barrel.*
**2** a small plastic device at the end of an electrical cord with small metal parts that can be connected to an electrical supply: *The television set needs a new plug. See:* socket; outlet.

**plug** *verb* **plugged, plugging, plugs**
to block something with a plug: *Workers plugged the hole in the pipe.*

**to plug something in:** to connect something to a power supply by pushing a plug into an electrical socket: *Plug in the TV over here.*||*Plug it in.*

**plum** /plʌm/ *noun*
a round fruit with smooth, often deep purple skin and juicy flesh, or the tree it grows on: *My grandmother made delicious plum jelly. See:* art on page 3a.

**plumber** /'plʌmər/ *noun*
a worker who puts in and fixes pipes, sinks, bathtubs, etc.: *The plumber came to fix the broken toilet.*

**plumbing** /'plʌmɪŋ/ *noun, (no plural)*
**1** pipes for water and gas in a building: *The plumbing in that old house does not work well.*
**2** the work that a plumber does

**plump** /plʌmp/ *adjective*
(referring especially to women and children) round in shape, a little fat, but in a pleasing way *(antonym)* thin.

**plunge** /plʌndʒ/ *verb* **plunged, plunging, plunges**
to jump or fall fast and far: *A young boy plunged into the water from a cliff.*

**plunge** *noun*
a jump or fall: *She took a plunge into the ocean.*

**plural** /'plʊrəl/ *noun*
referring to more than one of something: *Potatoes is the plural of potato.*

**plus** /plʌs/ *preposition*
increased by adding: *Five plus nine is fourteen (5+9=14).*||*The bill came to thirty dollars plus tax.*

**plus** *conjunction*
in addition, and: *The job calls for patience plus an interest in children.*

**plus** *noun, plural* **pluses**
**1** the symbol (+), the plus sign
**2** an advantage: *One of the pluses of the job would be the opportunity to travel.*

**plus** *adjective*
**1** greater or more than said: *a grade of B plus (B+)*||*He has 20 plus years of experience.*
**2** referring to an advantage, positive: *The apartment is small, but on the plus side, it has a great view.*
**3** referring to a positive number *(antonym)* minus.

**plus sign** *noun*
the symbol (+), used to indicate addition (100+10=110) or a number above zero (+5)

**P.M.** or **p.m.** /ˌpi'ɛm/
*abbreviation of* post meridiem (after noon), used to refer to the time period between noon and midnight: *The plane leaves at 7:45 P.M.*

**P.O.** /ˌpi'oʊ/ *noun*
*abbreviation of* post office

**poach** /poʊtʃ/ *verb* **poaches**
**1** to cook gently in a hot liquid: *poached eggs, poached salmon*
**2** to hunt on someone's land without their permission

**P.O. Box** *noun*
*See:* post office box.

**pocket** /'pɑkɪt/ *noun*
a type of small bag sewn into garments for holding things: *He keeps his wallet in the back pocket of his jeans.*

P

**to pick someone's pocket:** to steal from someone: *Someone picked my pocket and stole my wallet.*

**pocketbook** /ˈpɑkɪtˌbʊk/ *noun*
a bag that women use to carry their personal possessions, (synonyms) handbag, purse: *She carries her wallet, keys, and makeup in her pocketbook. See:* art on page 12a.

**poem** /ˈpoʊəm/ *noun*
an arrangement of carefully chosen words in short lines that expresses rich images and often deep thoughts and feelings: *The subject of the poem was the joy and sorrow of love.*

**poet** /ˈpoʊɪt/ *noun*
a person who writes poems: *She is a poet who writes about the beauty of nature.*

**poetry** /ˈpoʊətri/ *noun, (no plural)*
poems in general or as a form of literature: *People have been writing poetry since ancient times. –adjective* **poetic.**

**point** /pɔɪnt/ *noun*
**1** the sharp tip of a knife, needle, or other tool or weapon: *She stuck the point of the needle through the cloth.*
**2** a location, spot: *We located Paris at a specific point on the map.*
**3** a small round mark: *A period is a point at the end of a sentence.*
**4** purpose: *What is the point of this meeting?*
**5** a unit of scoring in games and tests: *Our team scored seven points in the first quarter.*
**6** a decimal point: *She made a 4.0 (pronounced: four-point-oh) average this semester.*

**to get to the point:** to reach the most important part: *I wish he would get to the point and tell us what he wants.*

**point** *verb*
**1** to show the direction of something: *We asked her the way and she pointed toward the town.*
**2** to bring to someone's attention or notice: *She pointed out an error in the report.*
**3** to give a reason or fact in support of an opinion: *She pointed out that the company cannot continue to lose money.*

**to point the finger:** *figurative* to accuse, blame someone, often unfairly

**pointed** /ˈpɔɪntɪd/ *adjective*
having a point: *Needles are pointed.*

**pointer** /ˈpɔɪntər/ *noun*
**1** a long, narrow stick used to direct people's attention to something: *The teacher used a pointer to show where Moscow and New York are located on the map.*
**2** a needle on a measuring device: *The pointer on the scale showed the package weighed 20 pounds.*

**pointless** /ˈpɔɪntlɪs/ *adjective*
meaningless, not worth doing: *The storm was so bad that it was pointless to try to travel in it. –adverb* **pointlessly;** *–noun* **pointlessness.**

**point of view** *noun, plural* **points of view**
an attitude or set of beliefs, someone's way of looking at something: *I understand your point of view, but I see the problem differently.*

**poison** /ˈpɔɪzən/ *noun*
**1** any substance that harms or kills people, animals, or plants if they eat, drink, or touch it: *She tried to kill herself by drinking poison.*
**2** anything that harms or destroys: *Lies are poison to friendships.*

**poison** *verb*
**1** to harm or kill with a poison: *Workers poisoned rats living beneath the streets.*
**2** to have a bad influence on someone or something: *Disagreements over money poisoned the couple's marriage. –noun* (person) **poisoner.**

**poisonous** /ˈpɔɪzənəs/ *adjective*
**1** causing harm or death by poison: *The bite of certain snakes is poisonous.*
**2** harming or destroying relationships among people: *Keeping secrets can sometimes be poisonous to relationships. See:* toxic.

**poke** /poʊk/ *verb* **poked, poking, pokes**
to press with something pointed, such as a finger or a stick: *His wife poked him in the arm to wake him up.*

**to poke fun at someone** or **something:** to laugh at: *She poked fun at her friend by imitating her complaints.*

**poke** *noun*
a push with something pointed: *She gave him a poke to get his attention.*

**poker (1)** /'poʊkər/ *noun*
a pointed metal rod: *I used a poker to move wood and coals in the fire.*

**poker (2)** *noun*
a popular card game played for money: *She won $100 playing poker.*

**polar** /'poʊlər/ *adjective*
related to a pole, especially the earth's North or South Pole: *The polar climate is very cold, windy, and icy.*

**polar bear** *noun*
a large white bear living on the coasts of the northern arctic: *Polar bears feed mainly on seals.*

**polar bear**

**pole (1)** /poʊl/ *noun*
a long wooden or metal rod: *She raised a flag up the pole.*

**pole (2)** *noun*
either end of an imaginary line drawn through the center of the earth from north to south: *The North Pole is a cold and icy place.*

**police** /pə'lis/ *noun, (no plural)*
a department of city and state governments whose men and women in uniform keep peace, prevent crime, catch and jail criminals, etc. *–verb* **to police.**

**police force** *noun*
police officers as a group

**policeman** /pə'lismən/ *noun, plural* **policemen** /-mɛn/
a male police officer

**police officer** *noun*
a member of the police, a man or woman trained in police methods: *Police officers in this city have six months of training. See:* art on page 4a.

**police station** *noun*
a local building for police business: *Police officers report to the local police station and go on patrol from there.*

**policewoman** /pə'lis,wʊmən/ *noun, plural* **policewomen** /-,wɪmən/
a female police officer

**policy** /'pɑləsi/ *noun, plural* **policies**
**1** a rule or group of rules for doing business by industry and government: *The policy of that store is that personal checks are not accepted.*

**polio** /'poʊli,oʊ/ *noun, (no plural)*
a disease, especially of children, that can cause paralysis: *He had polio as a child.*

**polish** /'pɑlɪʃ/ *verb* **polishes**
**1** to rub something until it is smooth and shiny: *I polished my shoes.*
**2** to refine, perfect something: *Her manners are very polished.*

**polish** *noun* **polishes**
**1** a waxy substance used to shine objects: *I rubbed polish on my shoes.*
**2** perfection, smoothness: *His singing style has a lot of polish. –adjective* **polished.**

**polite** /pə'laɪt/ *adjective* **politer, politest**
**1** having good manners, *(synonym)* courteous: *He is a polite little boy who says "Thank you" and "Excuse me" often.*
**2** well mannered and well-educated: *People should not tell dirty jokes in polite company. –adverb* **politely;** *–noun* **politeness.** *(antonym)* rude.

**political** /pə'lɪtɪkəl/ *adjective*
related to politics: *The President's political views are liberal. –adverb* **politically.**

**politician** /,pɑlə'tɪʃən/ *noun*
a person who runs for elected office, such as president, governor, mayor, or congress: *She is a career politician and mayor of the city.*

**politics** /'pɑlə,tɪks/ *noun plural*
*used with a singular or plural verb*
the art or science of conducting government: *She has a strong interest in local politics.*

**polka** /'poʊlkə/ *noun*
a lively dance from Eastern Europe done by couples moving in a circle: *Dancing the polka is a lot of fun.*

**poll** /poʊl/ *noun*
**1** a set of questions people are asked to find out their opinion on a particular subject: *The poll showed that most people opposed a tax increase.*
**2** *plural* **the polls:** the places where people go to vote: *The polls close at 9:00 P.M. –verb* **to poll.**

**pollen** /'pɑlən/ *noun, (no plural)*
fine grains that are carried from one

flower to another, to start the development of new flowers: *Many plants drop their pollen in the fall as it grows cold.* –*verb* **to pollinate.**

**pollute** /pə'lut/ *verb* **polluted, polluting, pollutes**
to make impure or dirty, *(synonym)* to poison: *Factories pollute rivers by dumping poisonous chemicals into them.* –*adjective* **polluted;** –*noun* **pollutant.**

**pollution** /pə'luʃən/ *noun, (no plural)*
the process or result of polluting the air, water, or soil: *Many countries are making a strong effort to reduce pollution.*

**poncho** /'pɑntʃoʊ/ *noun, plural* **ponchos**
an outer garment shaped like a blanket with a hole for one's head: *He wears a plastic poncho in the rain.*

poncho

**pond** /pɑnd/ *noun*
a body of water smaller than a lake: *There are fish in the pond near our camp.*

**pony** /'poʊni/ *noun, plural* **ponies**
a type of small horse: *The little girl wanted to ride the pony.*

**ponytail** /'poʊni,teɪl/ *noun*
a hairstyle where the hair is gathered at the back of the head and hangs down: *She wears her long, red hair in a ponytail.*

ponytail

**pool** /pul/ *noun*
**1** a swimming pool, usually made of cement or stone: *They have a pool in their back yard.*
**2** any still body of water or other liquid: *A pool of oil lies beneath the oil field.*
**3** a game played with 15 balls that are knocked with a stick into side holes on a special table: *He likes to play pool once a week.*

**pool** *verb*
to form into a pool: *Rainwater pooled to form puddles on the street.*

**poor** /pʊr/ *adjective*
**1** with little or no money: *That family is so poor, they can't afford to buy food.*
**2** not good quality: *The actor gave a poor performance.*
**3** worthy of pity: *Poor Jane, her mother just died!*
**4** without the necessary characteristics: *The land around here is poor; crops won't grow.* –*adverb* **poorly.**

**the poor:** *noun plural* the class of people with little or no money: *Religions teach that people with money should give some to the poor. (antonym)* the rich.

**pop** /pɑp/ *noun*
the sharp sound of something bursting or exploding: *You could hear the pop of firecrackers during the celebration. See:* soda, USAGE NOTE.

**pop** *verb* **popped, popping, pops**
to burst suddenly with a loud noise: *The popcorn popped as it cooked.*

**pop** *adjective*
*short for* popular, related to ordinary people: *Pop culture includes television, movies, sports, and rock and roll music.*

**popcorn** /'pɑp,kɔrn/ *noun, (no plural)*
a type of corn that bursts into large white pieces when cooked: *I like to eat popcorn at the movies.*

**Pope** /poʊp/ *noun*
the head of the Roman Catholic Church: *The Pope lives in the Vatican in Rome.*

**popular** /'pɑpyələr/ *adjective*
well-liked, admired by a group of people: *She is very popular with her college classmates. (antonym)* unpopular.

**popularity** /,pɑpyə'lærəti/ *noun, (no plural)*
**1** widespread acceptance: *The popularity of that new computer is growing daily.*
**2** widespread admiration: *The President's popularity resulted in his reelection.* –*verb* **to popularize.**

**populate** /'pɑpyə,leɪt/ *verb* **populated, populating, populates**
**1** to fill an area with people: *People from Europe populated many parts of the Americas.*
**2** to live in an area: *People from all over the world populate New York City.*

**population** /,pɑpyə'leɪʃən/ *noun*
all of the people living in a specific area:

P

*The population of this city is eight million.*

**populous** /'pɑpyələs/ *adjective*
having many people: *Beijing and Tokyo are very populous cities.*

**porch** /pɔrʧ/ *noun, plural* **porches**
a covered structure outside the front or back entrance to a house: *We sit outside on the porch on summer evenings.*

porch

**pork** /pɔrk/ *noun, (no plural)*
the meat of a pig: *I enjoy roast pork for dinner. See:* pig, USAGE NOTE.

**port** /pɔrt/ *noun*
**1** a harbor, safe place for ships to load and unload goods and passengers: *Boats head for port when a storm arises.*
**2** a town or city where there is a harbor: *The ship stopped at several ports in the Caribbean.*

**portable** /'pɔrtəbəl/ *adjective*
movable, capable of being carried or moved around: *She uses a portable computer when she travels. –noun* **portability** /ˌpɔrtə'bɪləti/.

**porter** /'pɔrtər/ *noun*
**1** a person employed to carry luggage, as at a train station or hotel: *Porters carry passengers' luggage from the airport to a taxi outside.*
**2** a cleaning person: *A porter cleaned the hallway.*

**portion** /'pɔrʃən/ *noun*
**1** a small piece or section of a larger thing: *I put a portion of my salary in a savings bank each month.*
**2** a serving of food: *That restaurant serves large portions of meat and potatoes.*

**to portion something out:** *verb* to divide into pieces and give them to others: *My grandmother portioned out her property among her five children before she died.*

**portrait** /'pɔrtrɪt/ *noun*
**1** a painting, photograph, or other picture of a person: *A portrait of her grandmother hangs on the wall.*
**2** a written or spoken description of someone or something: *The reporter painted a portrait of the killer as a crazy animal.*

**portray** /pɔr'treɪ/ *verb formal*
**1** to describe someone or something in a certain way: *The writer portrays Americans after the war as happy and rich.*
**2** to act, play the part of someone: *The movie star portrays a beautiful woman gone mad. –noun formal* **portrayal.**

**pose** /poʊz/ *noun*
**1** a particular way of holding one's head and body, especially for a picture: *The model held a pose sitting on a chair.*
**2** a false representation of oneself: *The thief's pose as a rich man was discovered by the police.*

**pose** *verb* **posed, posing, poses**
**1** to hold still in a pose, so one's picture can be painted, drawn, or photographed: *The mayor and his family posed for a photograph.*
**2** to present something that confuses, such as a question

**position** /pə'zɪʃən/ *noun*
**1** a location: *The best position for that desk is against the wall.*
**2** the way the body is held, the way in which something is arranged: *He was sitting in an uncomfortable position.*||*She changed the position of the objects on the table.*
**3** a job, employment: *She has an excellent position as head of a school.*
**4** a rank among others, place in an order: *That student holds the top position in his class.*
**5** a point of view, opinion: *The President's position is that taxes must be cut.*

**position** *verb*
to place in a location: *The soldiers positioned themselves on either side of the President.*

**positive** /'pɑzətɪv/ *adjective*
**1** showing a belief that something is useful, meaningful or hopeful: *He has a positive attitude toward his work; he likes it and does it well.*
**2** certain, definite, without doubt: *The police are positive that they have the right man in jail.*

P

**3** meaning yes: *I received a positive reply to my job application.*
**4** (of the results of a medical test) showing that a condition, disease, etc., exists: *She had a pregnancy test and the result was positive.* –*adverb* **positively.**

**possess** /pə'zɛs/ *verb* **possesses**
to own, have possession of something: *She possesses wealth and power.*

**possession** /pə'zɛʃən/ *noun*
**1** ownership, control over something: *They will lose possession of their car if they don't make the monthly payments.*
**2** *often plural* **possessions:** a piece of property, something one owns: *He lost most of his personal possessions in the fire.*

**possessive** /pə'zɛsɪv/ *adjective*
indicating ownership or a similar relationship: *The "my" and "'s" in "my friend's house" are possessive forms.*

**possibility** /ˌpɑsə'bɪləti/ *noun, plural* **possibilities**
an occurrence, situation, etc. that could happen: *There is a possibility that it will rain tomorrow.*

**possible** /'pɑsəbəl/ *adjective*
**1** capable of existing, happening, or being done: *Is it possible to get there by bus?*
**2** reasonable, probable: *There are several possible solutions to the problem.*

**possibly** /'pɑsəbli/ *adverb*
**1** perhaps, maybe: *This is possibly the coldest winter we've ever had.*||*The package should arrive next week, possibly sooner.*
**2** by any possibility or chance: *I got here as soon as I possibly could.*||*What could she possibly have meant?*

**possum** /'pɑsəm/ *noun*
*See:* opossum.

**post (1)** /poʊst/ *noun*
**1** the place where the members of the military live, *(synonym)* a military base: *That sergeant lives on his army post.*
**2** a job, especially in government: *He has a post in the foreign service.*

**post (2)** *verb*
to put up (a sign) in a public place: *The school principal posted a notice on the bulletin board.*||*She posted a sign about the next town meeting outside the library.*
**to keep someone posted:** to keep someone informed: *Be sure to keep me posted on what is happening with you.* –*noun* **posting.**

**post (3)** *noun*
a long, strong piece of metal or wood stuck upright in the ground: *Those posts hold up the fence.*

**postage** /'poʊstɪʤ/ *noun, (no plural)*
the cost of sending something by mail: *The postage for that letter is $1.00.*

**postage stamp** *noun*
a piece of paper with a picture and postage amount on it, placed on mail: *Postage stamps are sold at the post office.* –*adjective* **postal.**

**postcard** /'poʊstˌkɑrd/ *noun*
a small paper card often with a picture on one side and space for a message, address, and stamp on the other

**poster** /'poʊstər/ *noun*
a large sheet of paper, usually with a picture and writing, telling the public about some event: *We saw a poster about a free jazz concert in the park.*

**postman** /'poʊstmən/ *noun, plural* **postmen**
a man who delivers the mail *See:* letter carrier.

**post office** *noun, abbreviation* **P.O.**
**1** a government building where people buy stamps and send letters and packages: *I'm going to the post office to mail a package.*
**2** the entire mail system of a country *See:* art on page 4a.

**post office box** *noun, plural* **boxes**
a rented box where people can receive mail: *The advertisement said to send your order to P.O. Box 123, Radio City Station, New York 10019.* –*abbreviation* **P.O. Box.**

**postpone** /poʊst'poʊn/ *verb* **postponed, postponing, postpones**
to move something to a later time: *Our meeting for today was postponed until next week.* –*noun* **postponement.**

**posture** /'pɑsʧər/ *noun*
the way the body is held, often referring

P

to how well one sits or stands: *He has poor posture; he doesn't stand up straight.*

**pot** /pɑt/ *noun*
a container made of metal, glass, or clay used for cooking: *The potatoes are boiling in a pot of water. See:* art on page 7a.

**potato** /pəˈteɪtoʊ/ *noun, plural* **potatoes**
a round or oval vegetable, usually white inside with brown, red, or yellow skin: *Potatoes are one of the most popular foods in the Western world.*
**small potatoes:** an unimportant matter, a small amount of money: *The money he made from selling his old car was small potatoes. See:* art on page 2a.

**potato chip** *noun*
a thin slice of potato fried in oil

**potential** /pəˈtɛnʃəl/ *noun*
**1** the possibility of something good: *That business has the potential to make a big profit next year.*
**2** ability: *She has the potential to be a top ice skater.*

**pottery** /ˈpɑtəri/ *noun, (no plural)*
**1** objects made of soft clay and then baked until hard: *Bowls are a common type of pottery.*
**2** the activity or skill of making such objects: *I'm taking a pottery class at an art school. –noun* (person) **potter.**

P

**poultry** /ˈpoʊltri/ *noun, (no plural)*
birds raised for food, such as chickens, turkeys, and ducks: *Poultry are raised on farms for their eggs and meat.*

**pound (1)** /paʊnd/ *verb*
**1** to hit something repeatedly with force: *The worker pounded nails into the wall with a hammer.*
**2** to beat strongly: *My heart was pounding with excitement.*

**pound (2)** *noun*
**1** a weight of 16 ounces or 453.6 grams: *She bought a pound of butter at the store.*
**2** the basic unit of money in Britain and several other countries: *He exchanged dollars for pounds in London.*

**pour** /pɔr/ *verb*
**1** to let flow in a steady stream: *She poured milk into her coffee.*
**2** to move in large numbers: *A crowd of people poured out of the movie theater.*
**3** to rain hard: *Wear your boots and take an umbrella; it's pouring out!*

**poverty** /ˈpɑvərti/ *noun, (no plural)*
the lack of money and property, the state of being poor: *There were very few jobs in the town, and many families lived in poverty.*

**powder** /ˈpaʊdər/ *noun, (no plural)*
a dry substance in the form of very small grains: *She always puts baby powder on herself after a bath. –adjective* **powdery.**
**powder** *verb*
to use powder: *The mother powdered her baby's bottom.*

**power** /ˈpaʊər/ *noun*
**1** the authority and ability to do something important: *As a manager, she has the power to hire and fire employees.*
**2** one's ability to function or to do something: *He's 90 years old, but his mental powers are as strong as ever.*
**3** a supply of energy, especially electricity: *The electric company has shut the power off.*
**4** (in mathematics) the number of times a number is multiplied by itself, such as: $10^2$, $10^3$, etc.: *10 to the power of 2= $10^2$= 100.*

**powerful** /ˈpaʊərfəl/ *adjective*
having a lot of power or influence: *He is a powerful man in the Senate. –adverb* **powerfully.**

**practical** /ˈpræktɪkəl/ *adjective*
**1** sensible, not acting foolishly: *They wanted to buy a white couch, but with three small children, it just wasn't practical.*
**2** useful: *A computer would be a practical gift for a student.*

**practically** /ˈpræktɪkli/ *adverb*
**1** nearly, almost: *He has practically finished his dinner.*
**2** in a practical way, reasonably: *You're not thinking practically.*

**practice** /ˈpræktɪs/ *verb* **practiced, practicing, practices**
**1** to do something repeatedly to perfect it: *She practices the piano every day.*
**2** to work in the professions of medicine, law, or accounting: *That doctor has practiced medicine for many years.*

**3** to do something regularly or as a habit: *to practice a certain custom or religion*

**to practice what one preaches:** to do yourself what you tell others to do: *The doctor stopped smoking cigarettes when he decided to practice what he preaches to his patients in telling them to stop, too.*

**practice** *noun, (no plural)*
**1** regular repetition of an activity, art, sport, etc.: *It takes practice to do almost anything well.*||*football practice*
**2** the work or business of a person in a profession: *She has a large law practice.*

**in practice** or **out of practice:** having or not having the skill produced by doing something repeatedly: *I used to play tennis pretty well, but I'm out of practice now.*

**practice makes perfect:** repetition leads to excellence: *She plays the piano every day because practice makes perfect.*

**prairie** /'prɛri/ *noun*
a large area of flat land with tall grasses and few trees, especially in the central part of North America

prairie

**praise** /preɪz/ *verb* **praised, praising, praises**
to express admiration and respect: *The store manager praised the employee for her good work.*

**praise** *noun*
an expression of admiration and respect: *The mayor gave praise to the firefighters for saving people from the burning building. (antonym)* criticize.

**pray** /preɪ/ *verb*
to speak to God or other gods: *He prays every night for the safety of his family.*

**prayer** /prɛr/ *noun*
an act of speaking to God or other gods: *She said a prayer that her sick mother would get better.*

**not to have a prayer:** to have no chance: *Our team is so bad that it doesn't have a prayer of winning the game.*

**preach** /priʧ/ *verb* **preaches**
**1** to give a talk on a religious subject: *The minister preached the word of God to the people in the church.*
**2** to give advice in a forceful way: *She is always preaching to her children about not talking to strangers. –adjective pejorative* **preachy.**

**preacher** /'priʧər/ *noun*
a person who preaches, usually a leader of a church: *He is a preacher in a Protestant church.*

**precaution** /prɪ'kɔʃən/ *noun*
a step taken in advance to prevent harm

**precede** /prɪ'sid/ *verb* **preceded, preceding, precedes**
to come before, appear earlier: *The dark skies preceded a thunderstorm.*

**precinct** /'priˌsɪŋkt/ *noun*
**1** one of a number of districts in a city or town under the authority of its own police unit: *He lives in the 112th precinct.*
**2** a local police station: *He went to the precinct to report that he had been robbed.*

**precious** /'prɛʃəs/ *adjective*
**1** extremely valuable, costly: *Gold is a precious metal.*
**2** *figurative* much loved: *That child is so sweet and precious.*

**precise** /prɪ'saɪs/ *adjective*
**1** exact: *I need the precise street address of the doctor's office.*
**2** with special care: *He spoke in a very precise manner. –adverb* **precisely.**

**precision** /prɪ'sɪʒən/ *noun*
attention to correctness, exactness: *Parts of machines are made to precision.*

**precision** *adjective*
made with or producing absolutely correct measurements: *Computers are precision instruments.*

**predicate** /'prɛdɪkɪt/ *noun*
in grammar, the part of a sentence that says something about the subject and that consists of a verb and words connected to the verb: *In the sentence, "We bought a new car," "bought a new car" is the predicate.*

**predict** /prɪ'dɪkt/ *verb*
to say what will happen in the future: *It's difficult to predict which path the storm will take.*

**prediction** /prɪ'dɪkʃən/ *noun*
a statement about what will happen in

P

the future: *The weather reporter's prediction that it would rain today was correct.* –*adjective* **predictable.**

**preface** /'prɛfɪs/ *noun*
the part of a book that comes before the beginning: *In the preface, the writer explains that the book is based on a true story.* –*adjective* **prefatory.**

**preface** *verb* **prefaced, prefacing, prefaces**
to say or write as a preface: *The speaker prefaced her remarks with a joke.*

**prefer** /prɪ'fɜr/ *verb* **preferred, preferring, prefers**
to like one thing better than another: *He prefers chocolate ice cream to vanilla.*

**preferable** /'prɛfərəbəl/ *adjective*
better or more suitable, to be preferred: *She found life in the city preferable to her quiet life in the country.* –*adverb* **preferably.**

**preference** /'prɛfrəns/ *noun*
a choice of one thing as better, more suitable than another: *She has a preference for vegetable dishes over meat.*

**prefix** /'priˌfɪks/ *noun, plural* **prefixes**
a letter or group of letters that has no meaning when used alone but, when it is put at the beginning of a word, it can change the word's meaning: *"Un-" is a common prefix meaning "not," as in "unnecessary" or "unfair."* *See:* suffix.

**pregnancy** /'prɛgnənsi/ *noun, plural* **pregnancies**
a condition of growing a child in one's body: *Her first pregnancy was not difficult.*

**pregnant** /'prɛgnənt/ *adjective*
when a child is growing inside one's body: *She is six months pregnant.*

**prejudice** /'prɛʤədɪs/ *noun*
an opinion based on general dislike or feelings, rather than fact or reason: *Prejudice based on race is one of society's great problems.* *See:* discrimination; racism.

**prejudice** *verb* **prejudiced, prejudicing, prejudices**
to feel or show unfair dislike based on someone's race, religion, sex, looks, etc.: *He prejudiced his co-workers against the new manager by telling them she was very strict.* *See:* prejudiced.

**prejudiced** /'prɛʤədɪst/ *adjective*
feeling or showing unfair dislike

**premier** /prɪ'mɪr/ *noun*
the head of the government in some countries: *The premier of Italy visited Malaysia.* –*adjective* **premier.**

**premium** /'primiəm/ *noun*
**1** the monthly, quarterly, etc. payment for an insurance policy: *The monthly premium on my car insurance is very high.*
**2** an extra amount, especially for something special: *He paid a premium for that house because of its beautiful view.*

**preparation** /ˌprɛpə'reɪʃən/ *noun*
**1** making something ready: *She is buying food and baking a cake in preparation for the dinner tonight.*
**2** the process of getting oneself ready for something mentally or physically: *She spent hours at the piano every day in preparation for the concert.* –*adjective* **preparatory.**

**prepare** /prɪ'pɛr/ *verb* **prepared, preparing, prepares**
to make arrangements for something, make ready: *He prepared for his trip by packing his clothes.*||*She prepared dinner for her guests.* –*adjective* **prepared;** –*noun* (act) **preparedness.**

**preposition** /ˌprɛpə'zɪʃən/ *noun*
(in grammar) a word that shows a relationship to another part of speech, especially to a noun: *In "I went to the movie with my friend," "to" and "with" are prepositions.* –*adjective* **prepositional.**

**prescribe** /pri'skraɪb/ *verb* **prescribed, prescribing, prescribes**
(by a doctor) to write an order (prescription) for medicine: *My doctor prescribed medicine for my sore throat.*

**prescription** /prɪ'skrɪpʃən/ *noun*
an order for medicine: *Her doctor wrote her a prescription for medicine to relieve the pain.*

**presence** /'prɛzəns/ *noun, (no plural)*
**1** attendance: *Your presence at the wedding is important to the bride and groom.*
**2** the area around a person: *She never spoke about the subject in my presence.*

**3** an appearance of importance: *The Army general has great presence.*

**present (1)** /prɪ'zɛnt/ *verb*
**1** to offer for consideration: *She presented her idea for a new product at the last sales meeting.*
**2** to give: *The mayor presented the doctor with an award for his work with children.*||*The lawyer presented his bill.*
**3** to cause or represent: *The snow was so deep that it presented a problem to people trying to walk.*
**4** to perform: *to present a play* –*noun* **presentation.**

**present (2)** /'prɛzənt/ *adjective*
**1** at this time, now: *The present situation is peaceful.*
**2** physically located here: *All students were present in today's class. (antonym)* absent.

**present** *noun*
the here and now, at this time: *The present is peaceful, but in the past there was trouble in this area. See:* present tense.

**present (3)** /'prɛzənt/ *noun*
a gift: *He gave me this nice pen as a birthday present.*

**present participle** /'prɛzənt/ *noun*
(in grammar) a form of a verb, in English ending in *-ing,* that typically shows that an action is continuing, used with *be* to form progressive tenses or used as an adjective: *In the sentences "The dog is sleeping" and "Let sleeping dogs lie," "sleeping" is a present participle.*

**present tense** *noun*
(in grammar) a verb tense representing the current time, not past or future: *In, "Today is Monday," "is" is the present tense of the verb "be."*

**preserve** /prɪ'zɜrv/ *verb* **preserved, preserving, preserves**
**1** to protect from harm or change: *The government preserves the rights of every citizen.*
**2** to keep in good condition: *She preserves her health by eating sensibly and exercising*
**3** to prevent food from spoiling: *Keeping food in the refrigerator preserves its freshness.* –*noun* **preservation** /ˌprɛzər'veɪʃən/.

**preserve** *noun*
an area of land used to protect wild animals from people, especially hunters: *Huge animal preserves in Africa help protect wild elephants.*

**presidency** /'prɛzədənsi/ *noun, plural* **presidencies**
the office and duties of a president: *He was elected to the presidency of the United States.*

**president** /'prɛzədənt/ *noun*
**1** a head of some governments, including that of the USA: *The president must handle many problems.*
**2** the head of a business or institution –*adjective* **presidential** /ˌprɛzə'dɛnʃəl/.

**President's Day** *noun*
the third Monday in February, observed as a holiday in the USA in honor of the birthdays of Abraham Lincoln and George Washington

**press** /prɛs/ *verb* **presses**
**1** to push against: *She pressed a button to turn on the radio.*
**2** to smooth clothes with an iron: *He has his suits cleaned and pressed at the cleaners.*

**press** *noun, plural* **presses**
**1** a pushing motion: *The door opened at the press of a button.*
**2** a smoothing of clothes: *The cleaner gave her skirt a press.*
**3** a machine or device for crushing something: *a wine press*
**4** a machine for printing books, newspapers, magazines, etc.: *a printing press*
**the press:** people who report the news for newspapers, magazines, radio and television: *The press covers the president's every move.*

**pressure** /'prɛʃər/ *noun*
**1** application of force against something: *The pressure of the wind forced the door open.*
**2** measurement of that force: *The pressure in that tire should be 32 pounds.*||*He has high blood pressure.*
**3** atmospheric pressure: *A low-pressure front moved into our area, bringing rain.*
**4** application of influence on someone, sometimes with the threat of punish-

ment: *The people put pressure on the government to lower taxes or be voted out of office.*
**5** tension, a feeling of being pushed to do things: *The pressure of trying to balance work and school caused her to sleep poorly.*
**under pressure:** in an atmosphere of tension: *Some people perform well under pressure, but I don't.*
**pressure** *verb* **pressured, pressuring, pressures**
to apply pressure to someone: *Her boss pressured her to finish the report by Friday.*

**prestige** /prɛ'stiʒ/ *noun, (no plural)*
such qualities as excellent reputation, wealth, and power, that bring admiration and honor: *Her job as a lawyer for a big corporation has a lot of prestige.* –*adjective* **prestigious** /prɛ'stɪʤəs/.

**pretend** /prɪ'tɛnd/ *verb*
to behave like actors in an imaginary situation, *(synonym)* to make believe: *When we were children, my brother and I pretended we were soldiers.* –*noun* (condition) **pretension.**

**pretty** /'prɪti/ *adjective* **prettier, prettiest**
attractive, pleasing to the eye, but not beautiful: *She has a pretty face. See:* handsome, USAGE NOTE.
**pretty** *adverb*
to a certain degree: *We had a pretty good time at the party.*

**pretzel** /'prɛtsəl/ *noun*
a hard or soft bread-like food, usually shaped like a knot and salted

**pretzels**

**prevent** /prɪ'vɛnt/ *verb*
**1** to stop from happening, avoid: *He prevented an accident by stopping his car just in time.*
**2** to stop someone from doing something: *The rain prevented me from going.*

**prevention** /prɪ'vɛnʃən/ *noun, (no plural)*
the act of preventing something from happening: *prevention of disease*

**previous** /'priviəs/ *adjective*
occurring before something else: *On the previous day, we had visited The Statue of Liberty.*
**previous to:** before, earlier than: *Previous to that, we had traveled by car to Boston.* –*adverb* **previously.**

**prey** /preɪ/ *noun, (no plural)*
animals killed for food by other animals: *The lion attacked and killed its prey.* –*verb* **to prey.**

**price** /praɪs/ *noun*
an amount of money charged for goods or services, cost: *The price of milk has gone up.*
**at any price:** no matter how great the suffering or loss needed to get something: *The general wanted to win the war at any price.*
**price** *verb* **priced, pricing, prices**
**1** to put a price on something: *The company priced its new products lower than any other.*
**2** to find out the price of, determine prices: *We priced a number of different cars before deciding to buy one.*

**priceless** /'praɪslɪs/ *adjective*
having such great value that no price would be high enough: *Some paintings by famous artists are priceless.*

**prick** /prɪk/ *noun*
a slight stabbing pain made by a sharp point: *I felt a prick from the doctor's needle when he gave me a shot.*
**prick** *verb*
to make a small hole in the skin with a sharp point: *I pricked my finger on the needle.*

**pride** /praɪd/ *noun, (no plural)*
**1** self-respect: *When she failed her exams, her pride was hurt.*
**2** satisfaction with personal characteristics and abilities: *He takes great pride in his ability to fix things.*
**pride** *verb* **prided, priding, prides**
**to pride oneself on something:** to feel good about oneself for something: *He prides himself on his writing ability.*

**priest** /prist/ *noun*
**1** in many religions of the world, a person who performs religious duties
**2** in some Christian religions, a person

with the authority to conduct religious ceremonies and who is often in charge of a church: *Catholic priests often dress in black.* –*adjective* **priestly.** *See:* minister; clergy.

**primarily** /praɪ'mɛrəli/ *adverb*
mainly, first of all: *He is primarily concerned with his work, not his family.*

**primary** /'praɪˌmɛri/ *adjective*
main, greatest: *My primary concern is about my wife's health, since she has cancer.*

**primary school** *noun*
(in the USA) the first three to six grades of elementary school: *My grandson is in the first grade in primary school. See:* grade school, USAGE NOTE.

**prime minister** or **PM** *noun*
(in many countries outside the USA) the chief officer of a government

**primitive** /'prɪmətɪv/ *adjective*
unchanged since ancient times: *Primitive tribes live along the Amazon River.*

**prince** /prɪns/ *noun*
**1** a son of a king or queen: *The prince refused to marry the woman his father had chosen for him.*
**2** any nobleman with the title of prince

**princess** /'prɪnsɪs/ *noun, plural* **princesses**
**1** a daughter of a king or queen: *The princess has private teachers.*
**2** any noblewoman with the title of princess

**principal** /'prɪnsəpəl/ *noun*
the head of a school: *Ms. Wu is the principal of our local high school.*
**principal** *adjective*
main, most important: *The principal reason they visited was to make an offer to buy your business.*

**principle** /'prɪnsəpəl/ *noun*
a standard, such as a guide to behavior, rule: *It is a matter of principle with him to have no debts.*

**print** /prɪnt/ *verb*
**1** to put words or images onto paper or other material, using a mechanical process: *He printed a letter on his computer's printer.*
**2** to make available in print, *(synonym)* to publish: *The newspaper printed an interview with the senator.*
**3** to write by hand using letters similar to those in printed material: *He printed his name on the application.*
**to print something out:** to print from a computer: *She printed out her report and made 10 copies of it.* –*adjective* **printable.**
**print** *noun*
**1** letters printed on paper or other material: *I can't read the small print on the package.*
**2** a pattern printed on cloth, or the cloth itself: *Her dress has a black and white print.*
**3** a photograph produced on paper *See:* art on page 22a.

**printer** /'prɪntər/ *noun*
**1** a person or business whose work is printing
**2** a device attached to a computer, used for making paper copies of material produced on the computer: *The printer sits on her desk next to her computer.*

**printing** /'prɪntɪŋ/ *noun, (no plural)*
the art or process of putting words and images on paper or other materials by a mechanical process: *Printing is a big business, including everything from newspapers and magazines to public signs.*

**printout** /'prɪntˌaʊt/ *noun*
a document printed from a computer: *He did a printout of the letter.*

**prison** /'prɪzən/ *noun*
a jail, a place where people found guilty or accused of a crime are kept under guard: *He was sent to prison for robbing a bank.*

**prisoner** /'prɪzənər/ *noun*
a person who must stay in prison as punishment for a crime: *The prisoner was jailed for committing a crime. See:* convict.

**privacy** /'praɪvəsi/ *noun, (no plural)*
**1** the state of being away from the unwanted presence of others: *After meeting with many people, she looked forward to the privacy of her hotel room.*
**2** a state of secrecy regarding personal

matters: *Lawyers and doctors are required to guard the privacy of the people who pay for their services.*

**private** /'praɪvɪt/ *adjective*
**1** secret, keeping personal matters to oneself alone: *Her sex life is private; no one else has the right to know about it.*
**2** not public, away from other people and their observation: *She had a private room at the hospital.*
**3** owned by a person or business rather than a government: *The land is private property and no one is allowed to hunt or fish on it. (antonym)* public. *–adverb* **privately.**

**privilege** /'prɪvəlɪʤ/ *noun*
a special right or benefit given to a person: *As a top manager, she has the special privileges of a big office and a private bathroom.*

**privileged** /'prɪvəlɪʤd/ *adjective*
**1** having special rights or benefits: *Only the privileged few could afford to send their children to private schools.*
**2** private, known only by certain people: *The letter he sent to his lawyer contained privileged information.*

**prize** /praɪz/ *verb* **prized, prizing, prizes**
to appreciate something greatly: *He prizes his new car above all his other possessions.*

**prize** *noun*
an award presented for winning a competition or lottery: *She won first prize in a short story competition.*

**probability** /ˌprɑbə'bɪləti/ *noun, plural* **probabilities**
the chance that something will happen: *The probability that it will rain today is high.*

**probable** /'prɑbəbəl/ *adjective*
likely to happen, having a good chance of occurring: *It is probable that it will snow tomorrow. –adverb* **probably.**

**problem** /'prɑbləm/ *noun*
**1** a difficult situation or person: *He has a problem with understanding chemistry.||She's having a problem with her boss.*
**2** a question that needs to be thought about and solved: *I'm having difficulty with this math problem. –adjective* **problematical.**

**procedure** /prə'siʤər/ *noun*
a detailed method of doing something: *He told me the procedure for changing the oil in my car. –adjective* **procedural.**

**proceed** /prə'sid/ *verb*
**1** to continue doing something after stopping for some reason: *The plane stopped in Chicago, and then proceeded to Los Angeles.*
**2** to go forward, move ahead: *He proceeded to tell a funny story and we all laughed.*

**process** /'prɑˌsɛs/ *verb*
**1** to apply a procedure to something: *A clerk processed my airline ticket.*
**2** to change something from one state to another: *That factory processes wood into paper.*
**3** to turn data (facts) into information by computer: *Early computers processed data very slowly.*

**process** *noun*
a procedure, specific method: *The process of filling out an application often takes time.*

**produce** /'proʊˌdus/ *noun, (no plural)*
food products, especially fruits and vegetables: *That market sells fresh produce.*

**produce** *verb* /prə'dus/ **produced, producing, produces**
**1** to create, invent from the mind (write, compose, paint, etc.): *The artist produced a beautiful painting.*
**2** to bring into being, give birth to: *Last year she also produced a baby boy.*
**3** to manufacture or grow something: *That factory produces shoes.||That region produces milk products.*

**producer** /prə'dusər/ *noun*
**1** a person or group of people that manufactures or grows something: *That company is a producer of television sets.*
**2** a person or company that provides money for and presents entertainment: *She is a producer of sporting events (movies, theater, etc.).*

**product** /'prɑdəkt/ *noun*
**1** anything that is manufactured or grown to be sold: *That store sells food products.*

P

**2** the total sum resulting from multiplication: *The product of 2 x 2 is 4.*

**production** /prə'dʌkʃən/ *noun, (no plural)*
**1** the process of manufacturing or growing a product: *The production of computers has increased in the last ten years.*
**2** the creation and presentation of a play, film, etc.: *The director is working on a new production of* Romeo and Juliet.

**productive** /prə'dʌktɪv/ *adjective* producing good results, useful: *We had a productive meeting that solved some problems. –noun* (action) **productivity.**

**profession** /prə'fɛʃən/ *noun* a job for which one needs an advanced university degree, such as for a doctor or lawyer: *Her profession is accounting.*

**professional** /prə'fɛʃənəl/ *adjective*
**1** related to a profession: *She decided to talk to a lawyer for some professional advice.*
**2** a person who makes his or her living as an artist or athlete: *Professional football players must train hard.*

**professional** *noun* a person with proven ability in his or her occupation: *She is an excellent office manager; she is a real professional. –noun* (quality) **professionalism.**

**professor** /prə'fɛsər/ *noun* a teacher, especially at the university level; the highest rank among instructors: *She is a professor of English at Cornell University. See:* teacher, USAGE NOTE.

**proficient** /prə'fɪʃənt/ *adjective formal* skillful, expert: *She is proficient at speaking French. –noun* (skill) **proficiency.**

**profile** /'proʊˌfaɪl/ *noun* the view of the face from the side: *The artist did a drawing of her profile. –verb* **to profile.**

profile

**profit** /'prɑfɪt/ *noun*
**1** money gained by a company after expenses are subtracted: *That business made a $1 million profit last year.*
**2** benefit, something useful: *There is no profit in drinking too much alcohol. (antonym)* loss.

**profit** *verb*
**1** to receive more money than one spends, gain money: *She profited from the sale of her business.*
**2** to benefit from something, gain some advantage: *I profited from going to the library because I learned something new. (antonym)* to lose.

**profitable** /'prɑfətəbəl/ *adjective*
**1** bringing in more money than is spent: *That business became profitable last year.*
**2** beneficial, advantageous: *We spent a profitable afternoon studying for our final exams. (antonym)* unprofitable.

**profound** /prə'faʊnd/ *adjective* emotionally deep, sincere: *I give you my profound thanks for saving my life.*

**program** /'proʊˌgræm/ *noun*
**1** any organized plan to achieve a goal: *The Senator supports a government program to help poor people find jobs.*
**2** a television or radio show: *All the news programs include weather reports.*
**3** a written list of events, such as for a church, sports, or theatrical event: *All the actors' names were listed in the program.*
**4** a set of instructions telling a computer how to process information: *This program lets you create drawings on your computer.*

**program** *verb* **programmed, programming, programs** to write a set of instructions for a computer: *She knows how to program in several computer languages.*

**programmer** /'proʊˌgræmər/ *noun* a person who programs computers: *Computer programmers must learn new programs as they appear on the market.*

**programming** /'proʊˌgræmɪŋ/ *noun, (no plural)*
**1** selection and organization of shows for television and radio or other events: *She does the programming of children's shows for television.*
**2** an act of writing instructions for a computer: *His programming experience includes working in hospitals and banks.*

P

**3** the set of programs in a computer system: *The programming in that computer is too old to be of use.*

**progress** /'prɑg,rɛs/ *noun, (no plural)* advancement, movement toward a goal: *Progress is being made in building a new highway around the city.*

**progress** *adjective*

**in progress:** happening now: *The meeting is in progress now.*

**progress** /prə'grɛs/ *verb* to move ahead: *He is progressing nicely in his study of Spanish.*

**progression** /prə'grɛʃən/ *noun, (no plural)* a series of related events: *A progression of disagreements has led to war between those nations.*

**progressive** /prə'grɛsɪv/ *noun* a person who believes in making changes and trying out new ideas in government, education, etc.: *She is a progressive in politics and a member of the Progressive Party.* –*adjective* **progressive.** *See:* Democratic Party, **USAGE NOTE.**

**prohibit** /proʊ'hɪbɪt/ *verb*

**1** to forbid, *(synonym)* to ban by order or law: *The law prohibits people from killing each other.*

**2** to prevent from happening: *A bad snowstorm prohibited people from going to work.* –*adjective* **prohibitive.** *(antonym)* to permit.

P

**project** /'prɑ,ʤɛkt/ *noun* a piece of work one plans to do: *His current project is to build a swimming pool.*

**project** /prə'ʤɛkt/ *verb*

**1** to reach beyond a surface: *The balcony projects out beyond the wall of the house.*

**2** to work out how much something will be in the future: *The government projects that food prices will go up five percent this year.*

**3** to shine an image against a surface: *A movie projector projects a film onto a screen.* –*noun* **projection.**

**projector** /prə'ʤɛktər/ *noun* a type of camera with a strong light used to shine films onto screens: *A movie projector can show a movie on a screen far away.*

**prominent** /'prɑmənənt/ *adjective* well-known and respected

**promise** /'prɑmɪs/ *noun* a strong statement saying that you will or will not do something: *She made a promise to write to him every week.*

**promise** *verb* **promised, promising, promises**

**1** to say with certainty that you will or will not do something: *He promised not to be late again.*

**2** to show signs of success in the future: *That new business promises to be big.*

**promote** /prə'moʊt/ *verb* **promoted, promoting, promotes**

**1** to advance in rank, give someone a better job: *Her boss promoted her to office manager.*

**2** to make goods and services known to the public: *The company promoted its new product on television.* –*adjective* **promotable.**

**promotion** /prə'moʊʃən/ *noun*

**1** movement to a new and better job: *He got a promotion to sales manager.*

**2** making something known to the public, advertising

**prompt** /prɑmpt/ *adjective*

**1** on time, *(synonym)* punctual: *He was prompt; he arrived at noon, as planned.*

**2** quick, done without delay: *I received a prompt response to my letter.* –*adverb* **promptly;** –*noun* **promptness.**

**pronoun** /'proʊ,naʊn/ *noun* (in grammar) a word used in place of a noun: *"I, you, he, she, it, we," and "they" are personal pronouns.*

**pronounce** /prə'naʊns/ *verb* **pronounced, pronouncing, pronounces** to say letters or words; to speak correctly: *She pronounces her words clearly.*

**pronunciation** /prə,nʌnsi'eɪʃən/ *noun*

**1** the way in which a word should be spoken: *The pronunciation of words is shown in the dictionary.*

**2** how correctly one pronounces words: *Her pronunciation is excellent.*

**proof** /pruf/ *noun, (no plural)* documents, statements by witnesses, etc. showing that something is true: *The police believed that the woman was guilty* *of murder, but they had no proof. See:* evidence.

**proofread** /'pruf,rid/ *verb* **proofread** /-,rɛd/ **, proofreading, proofreads**
to examine a piece of writing for mistakes, and correct it: *Proofreaders proofread the newspaper before it is printed. See:* edit.

**propaganda** /,prɑpə'gændə/ *noun*
information made public, especially by a government, to persuade people that something is true and worthy of support: *During the war, the government published propaganda saying that its military forces were winning when in fact they were losing battles. –verb* **to propagandize.**

**propeller** /prə'pɛlər/ *noun*
a device with curved blades used to move a ship or aircraft

**proper** /'prɑpər/ *adjective*
**1** correct, right as to how to do something: *I learned the proper way to write a business letter.*
**2** having good manners, correct behavior: *It's proper to say thank you when you receive a gift.*
**3** suitable: *In this rainy climate, you have to have a proper raincoat and boots.*
**4** in a specific area, not outside it: *She lives in Paris proper, not in the suburbs. –adverb* **properly.** *(antonyms)* improper.

**property** /'prɑpərti/ *noun, plural* **properties**
**1** physical objects owned by someone, *(synonym)* possessions: *His personal property consists of clothes, a few dollars, and a watch.*
**2** land and buildings: *She owns property in California.*
**3** a characteristic: *One property of wool is its warmth.*

**prophesy** /'prɑfə,saɪ/ *verb* **prophesied, prophesying, prophesies**
to tell what will happen in the future: *A wise man prophesied that I will be happy soon. –noun* **prophecy.**

**prophet** /'prɑfɪt/ *noun*
a religious person who predicts the future *–noun* (woman) **prophetess.**

**proportion** /prə'pɔrʃən/ *noun*
the relationship of one part of something to another part in size and shape *–adjective* **proportional.**

**proposal** /prə'poʊzəl/ *noun*
**1** an offer: *A competitor made a proposal to buy my business.*
**2** an offer of marriage: *She accepted his (marriage) proposal.*
**3** something that is suggested as a possible plan: *We discussed the Mayor's proposal to increase the police force.*

**propose** /prə'poʊz/ *verb* **proposed, proposing, proposes**
**1** to suggest, recommend: *I propose that we go to the beach this weekend.*
**2** to offer marriage: *He proposed to her a year after they met.*

**prose** /proʊz/ *noun, (no plural)*
written or spoken language that is not poetry

**prosecute** /'prɑsə,kyut/ *verb* **prosecuted, prosecuting, prosecutes**
to begin and carry through a lawsuit against someone: *The government prosecuted the criminal. –noun* (person) **prosecutor.**

**prosper** /'prɑspər/ *verb*
to grow in wealth: *Farmers prosper when good weather produces large crops. –noun* **prosperity.**

**prosperous** /'prɑspərəs/ *adjective*
successful in business: *That family grew prosperous as its business grew.*

**protect** /prə'tɛkt/ *verb*
to defend against harm or loss: *She protected her face from the sun with a hat.*

**protection** /prə'tɛkʃən/ *noun*
action taken against harm or loss, a defense: *She wore a heavy coat as protection against the cold.*

**protein** /'proʊtin/ *noun*
a substance, such as found in meat or fish, needed by people and animals to live: *Eggs and milk are high in protein.*

**protest** /prə'tɛst/ *verb*
**1** to complain, object to something as wrong: *She protested about not receiving a salary increase.*

**2** to publicly express opposition to something as a group: *Workers organized to protest against wage cuts.*

**protest** /'proʊ,tɛst/ *noun*
**1** a complaint, objection: *Despite my son's protests, I ordered him to take a bath.*
**2** a public expression of opposition by a group: *During the 1960's, there were student protests at colleges across the country.*

**proud** /praʊd/ *adjective*
**1** pleased, satisfied with someone's success: *She was proud that she had won the race.*

proud

**2** having self-respect: *That family is too proud to accept money from friends, even though they are very poor.*
**3** thinking oneself better than others: *He is too proud to be a good friend to anyone. See:* pride. *(antonym)* humble.

**prove** /pruv/ *verb*
**1** to show that something is true or real: *He proved how old he was by showing his driver's license.*
**2** to result in: *His guess that it would rain today proved to be correct.*

**proven** /pruvən/ *adjective*
shown to be true or correct: *She has proven ability as a lawyer.*

**proverb** /'pravərb/ *noun*
a short saying rich in meaning: *"Man's best friend is his dog" is a proverb.*

**provide** /prə'vaɪd/ *verb* **provided, providing, provides**
**1** to supply, give something: *Parents provide their children with food, clothes, and shelter.*
**2** to take care of someone: *They provide for their child.*
**3** to prepare for a present or future need: *She provides for her future by saving money each month.*

**provide** *conjunction*
**provided that** or **providing that**: if, on the condition that: *We will go to the beach today provided that it doesn't rain.* *–noun* **provision.**

**province** /'pravɪns/ *noun*
an area of a country with its own local government, similar to states in the USA: *Ontario and Quebec are two large provinces in Canada.* *–adjective* **provincial** /prə'vɪnʃəl/.

**provoke** /prə'voʊk/ *verb* **provoked, provoking, provokes**
to make someone angry: *He provokes her by telling her that she is too fat.*

**prowl** /praʊl/ *verb*
to search secretly, hunt quietly: *A lion prowled the forest looking for food.* *–noun* (bad person) **prowler.**

**prune** /prun/ *noun*
a dried plum: *He eats prunes with his cereal for breakfast.*

**pry** /praɪ/ *verb* **pried, prying, pries**
**1** to loosen or open something with force: *He pried off the top of a paint can with a knife.*
**2** to look into someone else's personal life closely: *He pried into his daughter's love life so closely that she stopped telling him anything.*

**P.S.** *noun*
*abbreviation of* postscript
information added at the end of a letter

**psychiatry** /sə'kaɪətri/ *noun*
the area of medicine that treats mental diseases: *That hospital has doctors who practice psychiatry.* *–noun* (doctor) **psychiatrist.**

**psychology** /saɪ'kalədʒi/ *noun, (no plural)*
study of human and animal behavior: *She is interested in the psychology of cats.* *–noun* (person) **psychologist;** *–adjective* **psychological.**

**pub** /pʌb/ *noun*
a bar that often serves simple food: *She went to a pub for a hamburger and beer. See:* bar, USAGE NOTE.

**puberty** /'pyubərti/ *noun, (no plural)*
the stage of human development when a girl can have a baby and a boy can father one

**public** /'pʌblɪk/ *noun, (no plural)*
the citizens, the people of a local area, state, or country: *The President asked the public to support his tax cut program.*

**public** *adjective*
related to the people of a particular area,

P

state, or country: *The government spends money on public building projects such as bridges and prisons.*

**to make something public:** to tell something to people: *A famous singer made public her plans to marry. (antonym)* private.

**publication** /ˌpʌbləˈkeɪʃən/ *noun*

**1** a book, magazine, newspaper, etc.: *She reads all the publications in the field of medicine.*

**2** an act of publishing something: *Publication of the book will take place next month.*

**publicity** /pʌbˈlɪsəti/ *noun, (no plural)*

information given in the media (TV, newspapers, etc.) that creates public interest in a person or product: *A famous actor received a lot of publicity when he was sent to jail.* –*verb* **to publicize.**

**public school** *noun*

**1** in the USA a school that is paid for by taxpayers and the government and is open to everyone: *Their children attend a public school near their home.*

**2** in Great Britain, a private school that is paid for by parents, where children often live

**public service** *noun, (no plural)*

government employment: *People who work for the government work in public service.*

**publish** /ˈpʌblɪʃ/ *verb* **publishes**

to print and distribute something to the public: *That newspaper publishes daily and weekend editions.*

**publisher** /ˈpʌblɪʃər/ *noun*

**1** a business that prints and sells newspapers, books, magazines, etc., to the public: *He works for a textbook publisher in San Francisco.*

**2** a person who runs a publication: *She is the publisher of a magazine for lawyers.*

**pudding** /ˈpʊdɪŋ/ *noun*

a sweet, smooth, dessert made with eggs and milk: *We had chocolate pudding for dessert.*

**puddle** /ˈpʌdl/ *noun*

a small, usually dirty pool of water: *There were puddles of water on the street after it rained.*

**puff** /pʌf/ *verb*

to blow air, such as through the lips in short breaths: *She puffed and puffed after she ran up the hill.*

**puff** *noun*

a short amount of air, smoke, clouds, etc.: *Puffs of smoke came out of the chimney.* –*adjective* **puffy.**

**pull** /pʊl/ *verb*

**1** to move something toward one: *A horse pulled a cart.*||*I pulled the television set closer to me.*

**2** to remove or tear: *I had a tooth pulled.*||*She pulled some dead leaves off the plant.*

**3** to take away from an activity: *The teacher pulled the student out of class to speak to him privately.*

**4** to show a weapon as a threat: *A robber pulled a gun on me and took my money.*

**to pull away:** to leave or go: *We shouted good-bye as the boat pulled away from us.*

**to pull back:** move back: *The army pulled back from the battle front.*

**to pull for someone:** to show support: *Sports fans pull for their favorite team.*

**to pull oneself together:** to get control of one's emotions, stop crying: *After his mother's death, he tried to pull himself together.*

**to pull in:** to arrive: *My train pulled in at 8:09* P.M.

**to pull through:** to manage to live through a serious illness or difficult situation: *She had a heart attack, but pulled through in the hospital.*

**pull** *noun*

a forceful movement: *He gave the fishing line a pull and caught a fish.*

**to have pull:** to have power, influence: *Some business leaders have pull with politicians who will do favors for them. (antonym)* push.

**pullover** /ˈpʊlˌoʊvər/ *noun*

a type of sweater without buttons down the front: *He put a pullover on in the cold weather.*

**pulse** /pʌls/ *noun*

the steady beating of blood as it is sent through the body by the heart: *The doctor put her fingers on my wrist to feel my pulse.* –*verb* **to pulse.**

P

**pump** /pʌmp/ *noun*
a machine that forces gases or liquids from one place to another: *I used an air pump to fill up my bicycle tire with air.*
**pump** *verb*
**1** to use a pump: *A worker pumped air into the tires of the car.*
**2** *figurative* to supply a lot of something: *The government pumped money into building a new airport.*

**pumpkin** /ˈpʌmpkɪn/ *noun*
a large orange fruit with a hard outside shell and soft insides. *See:* honey, USAGE NOTE.

---

**USAGE NOTE:** To celebrate *Halloween,* children in the USA cut scary faces into pumpkins. The pumpkins are lit from inside with candles and put outside the house in the evening.

---

**punch** /ˈpʌntʃ/ *noun, plural* **punches**
**1** a hit with the fist: *One fighter gave the other one a punch in the stomach.*

punch

**2** a tool used to make holes, such as in paper: *I used a punch to make three holes in my exam paper to put it into a notebook.*
**punch** *verb* **punches**
**1** to hit with the fist, strike: *The fighter punched his opponent in the nose.*
**2** to make holes: *I punched a hole in the can and poured myself some juice.*

**punctual** /ˈpʌŋktʃuəl/ *adjective*
arriving or leaving on time, prompt: *He was punctual; he arrived at exactly 9:00.* –*noun* **punctuality.**

**punctuate** /ˈpʌŋktʃuˌəɪt/ *verb* **punctuated, punctuating, punctuates**
to put punctuation marks (commas, semicolons, periods, etc.) in sentences: *I punctuated this sentence with a period at the end.*

**punctuation** /ˌpʌŋktʃuˈeɪʃən/ *noun*
the use of specific marks, such as commas and periods, to make ideas within writing clear: *Her writing is clear and her punctuation is accurate.*

**punctuation mark** *noun*
any of a set of marks used in writing to make it clear: *Punctuation marks include the comma (,), semicolon (;), and period (.).*

**puncture** /ˈpʌŋktʃər/ *noun*
a hole made by something pointed: *There is a puncture in my car's front tire.*
**puncture** *verb*
to make a hole with a pointed object: *A nail has punctured the tire.*

**punish** /ˈpʌnɪʃ/ *verb* **punishes**
to discipline, make someone pay for doing something wrong: *The father punished his son by sending him to his room early at night. (antonym)* to reward.

**punishment** /ˈpʌn ɪʃmənt/ *noun*
a payment for doing something wrong, *(synonym)* a penalty: *The punishment for stealing is going to jail.*

**punk** /pʌŋk/ *noun*
**1** a rough young person, especially a young man: *Some punks got into a fight outside a bar.*
**2** a popular culture movement of young people with shocking dress and loud rock music as a protest against middle class life in Britain and the USA: *Their son dyed his hair green and played in a punk band.*
**punk** *adjective*
related to punk culture

**pupil (1)** /ˈpyupəl/ *noun*
in the USA, a student in elementary school, about ages 6–11: *His pupils say that he is an excellent teacher.*

**pupil (2)** *noun*
the dark, round opening in the center of the eye that controls the amount of light that enters it: *The pupil grows larger in darkness and smaller in sunlight.*

**puppet** /ˈpʌpɪt/ *noun*
a type of doll moved by fingers, strings, or rods and used as actors in shows: *Puppets move and talk in funny ways.* –*noun* **puppeteer.**

**puppy** /ˈpʌpi/ *noun, plural* **puppies**
a young dog not fully grown: *Puppies love to play and eat.*

P

**purchase** /ˈpɜrʧəs/ *verb* **purchased, purchasing, purchases**
to buy something, to pay for goods and services: *She purchased a new car.*
**purchase** *noun*
an act of buying: *The purchase of the car took several days of deciding which one to buy.* –*noun* (person) **purchaser.**

**pure** /pyʊr/ *adjective* **purer, purest**
**1** clean, not dirty: *People must have pure water to drink.*
**2** not mixed with other things: *The dress is made of pure cotton.*
**3** total, complete: *It was pure luck that he found money lying on the street.*
**4** free from evil: *He thinks pure thoughts about blue skies and mountain lakes.* –*noun* (clean condition) **purity.**

**purify** /ˈpyʊrəˌfaɪ/ *verb* **purified, purifying, purifies**
to make something clean, pure: *The machine purifies the air of dirt and smoke.* –*noun* **purification.**

**purple** /ˈpɜrpəl/ *noun, (no plural)*
the color made by mixing red and blue: *Purple is an unusual color for a car. See:* art on page 16a.

**purpose** /ˈpɜrpəs/ *noun*
a goal, reason: *The purpose of going to school is to learn.*
**on purpose:** with intention, *(synonym)* deliberately: *She stepped on my foot on purpose, not by accident.*

**purposeful** /ˈpɜrpəsfəl/ *adjective*
with a goal in mind, with determination: *She studies in a purposeful way to earn her medical degree.*

**purr** /pɜr/ *noun*
the soft, low sound made by a happy cat: *You can hear the purr of my kitten after she has eaten.* –*verb* **to purr.**

**purse** /pɜrs/ *noun*
a small bag that women use to carry their personal possessions, *(synonyms)* handbag, pocketbook: *She keeps her money, keys, and a comb in her purse. See:* art on page 12a.

**pursue** /pərˈsu/ *verb* **pursued, pursuing, pursues**
**1** to chase, go after someone to catch them: *A police officer pursued the speeding car and stopped it.*
**2** to work hard towards achieving a goal: *She is pursuing a career in medicine.*

**pursuit** /pərˈsut/ *noun*
**1** a chase: *A police officer ran down the street in pursuit of the thief.*
**2** a career, occupation: *Her current pursuit is a career in advertising.*

**pus** /pʌs/ *noun, (no plural)*
the thick yellowish-white liquid that forms in an infected wound: *A nurse gently cleaned the pus from the injury on my hand.*

**push** /pʊʃ/ *verb* **pushes**
**1** to press against someone or something with force: *He pushed the door open and entered the room.*
**2** to press (a button): *She pushed the emergency button in the elevator.*
**3** to hurry, work extra hard: *We pushed to finish the job on time.*
**4** to urge others to take a certain action: *A politician pushed his party members for a new gun control law.*
**to push someone around:** to treat someone roughly or unfairly: *She tries to push the other committee members around.*
**to push (something) through: a.** to move through: *We pushed through the crowd to enter the building.* **b. something:** to finish something in a hurry: *Congress pushed through a new law to lower taxes. See:* shove.
**push** *noun, plural* **pushes**
**1** pressure or force against someone or something: *She gave the door a push to open it.*||*A man gave another a push and they started to fight.*
**2** hard work, a big effort: *Our company salespeople made a big push to sell a new product. (antonym)* pull.

**pusher** /ˈpʊʃər/ *noun slang*
a seller of illegal drugs: *Police arrested drug pushers on the street. See:* dealer.

**pushy** /ˈpʊʃi/ *adjective* **pushier, pushiest**
behaving in a rude and forceful way: *He is so pushy that he interrupts other students when they are speaking with the teacher.*

**pussycat** or **pussy** *noun informal*
a house cat: *A little pussycat rubbed against my ankle.*

**put** /pʊt/ *verb* **put, putting, puts**
**1** to place, move something: *I put the book on the shelf.||She put her paycheck in the bank.*
**2** to cause someone to experience something: *That class is so dull it almost puts me to sleep.*
**3** to arrange, organize something: *Before going on his trip, he put his affairs in order, like stopping delivery of the newspaper.*
**5** to apply, use: *She put her knowledge of accounting to use in doing her taxes.*
**6** to express, say: *Let me put it to you another way.*
**to put one's best foot forward:** to make one's best effort or appearance: *You should dress nicely and put your best foot forward when you go to a job interview.*
**to put something on:** to dress: *She put on her coat and hat.*
**to put something out: a.** to take outside: *He put out the trash.* **b.** to destroy a fire: *Firefighters put out the fire.*
**to put someone through something:** to cause someone to suffer something: *The doctor put him through some tests.*
**put** *adjective*
**put out:** angry with someone: *I am put out with my friend because he is late again.*
**to stay put:** not to move, stay still: *I told my friend to stay put while I went to the store to buy food.*

**puzzle** /ˈpʌzəl/ *noun*
**1** a game in which a picture on stiff paper (cardboard) that has been cut into pieces is put back together, *(synonym)* a jigsaw puzzle

puzzle

**2** a mystery, something not understood: *The cause of the plane crash is still a puzzle.*
**3** any game that involves solving a problem: *The children had fun with a book of puzzles.*
**puzzle** *verb* **puzzled, puzzling, puzzles**
to confuse, not understand: *I was puzzled by her strange behavior.*
**to puzzle over something:** to think hard: *He puzzled over why she never returned his phone calls.*

**pyramid** /ˈpɪrəmɪd/ *noun*
a very large building with sides shaped as triangles built in ancient Egypt and Mexico

**python** /ˈpaɪˌθɑn/ *noun*
a large snake that wraps itself around its victims and tightens its hold so that they can't breathe: *The python wrapped itself around a pig and killed it.*

P

# Q, q

**Q, q** /kyu/ *noun* **Q's, q's** or **Qs, qs**
the 17th letter of the English alphabet

**Q-tip™** /ˈkyu,tɪp/ *noun*
a little rod with a small amount of soft cotton wrapped around both ends: *A Q-tip can be used to clean inside your ear.*

Q-tip

**quack (1)** /kwæk/ *noun*
the sound made by a duck: *"Quack, quack!" said the duck.*

**quack (2)** *noun*
a fake doctor: *The quack told him that the medicine would make him live forever.* *–noun* **quackery.**

**quadruple** /kwɑˈ drupəl/ *noun*
something that has been multiplied by four: *He charges quadruple for coats when it is cold.*

**quadruple** *verb* **quadrupled, quadrupling, quadruples**
to multiply by four: *He quadruples the price of coats every January.*

**quail** /kweɪl/ *noun*
a small bird with black and brown feathers: *Quail often hide when people come near them.*

quail

**quaint** /kweɪnt/ *adjective* **quainter, quaintest**
**1** attractive, often because of being old: *What a quaint old house!*
**2** strange, unusual in a pleasing way: *She has a quaint way of speaking.* *(antonym)* modern.

**quake** /kweɪk/ *noun*
a sudden, violent movement of the ground, *(synonym)* an earthquake: *Our house was destroyed during the quake.*

**quake** *verb* **quaked, quaking, quakes**
to shake violently: *He quaked with fear.*

**qualification** /ˈkwɑləfɪˈkeɪʃən/ *noun*
an ability that makes someone suitable to do something: *That mechanic has the qualifications to fix your car.*||*One qualification for receiving a California driver's license is that you must live in California.*

---

**USAGE NOTE:** In job interviews in the USA, applicants describe their *qualifications*, including education, work experience, hobbies and interests: *He said he'd studied journalism in college, worked at a newspaper, and learned photography, so the interviewer at the newspaper was impressed with his qualifications.*

---

**qualifier** /ˈkwɑlə,faɪər/ *noun*
**1** someone or something that is suitable to do something: *She is a qualifier for the final race because she won her first three races.*
**2** (in grammar) a word that limits or adds to the meaning of another: *Adjectives and adverbs are qualifiers.*

**qualify** /ˈkwɑlə,faɪ/ *verb* **qualified, qualifying, qualifies**
to pass tests to show one's suitability for

something: *He qualified for the teaching job.*

**quality** /ˈkwɑləti/ *noun, plural* **qualities**
**1** the overall nature or general character of something: *This product is excellent; it is of the highest quality.*
**2** something that is typical of someone's character and personality: *His best qualities are kindness, hard work, and intelligence.*

**quality** *adjective*
excellent: *Her company makes a quality product.*

**quantity** /ˈkwɑntɪti/ *noun, plural* **quantities**
**1** a general amount, a supply: *She bought a quantity of apples (computers, dresses, etc.).*
**2** an exact amount: *100 was the quantity ordered.*
**3** a value in a mathematical problem: *"a" is a quantity in a + b = c.*

**in quantity:** in a large amount at a lower price: *Our company buys in quantity; we order thousands of pencils at one time.* –*verb* **to quantify.**

**quarantine** /ˈkwɔrənˌtin/ *verb* **quarantined, quarantining, quarantines**
to keep a person or animal away from everyone else because that person or animal has a dangerous disease: *That man has smallpox and will be quarantined.* –*noun* **quarantine.**



**quarrel** /ˈkwɔrəl/ *verb* **quarreled** or **quarreling** or **quarrels**
to argue very angrily

**quarrel** *noun*
**1** a very angry argument
**2** a feeling that someone is wronging you, *(synonym)* a complaint: *She has a quarrel with her company; they are not paying her enough.* –*adjective* **quarrelsome.**

**quarry** /ˈkwɔri/ *noun, plural* **quarries**
a large hole in the ground from which workers take stone or sand: *He works in a stone quarry.*

**quart** /kwɔrt/ *noun*
in the USA, a liquid measure equal to 32 ounces or two pints: *I bought a quart of milk. See:* gallon, USAGE NOTE.

**quarter** /ˈkwɔrtər/ *noun*
**1** one fourth of something: *I need a quarter of a pound of butter.*
**2** fifteen minutes: *It is quarter to five (o'clock). See:* quarter hour.
**3** a US or Canadian coin worth 25 cents, or a quarter of a dollar: *The pencil costs a quarter.*
**4** a three-month period or a quarter of a year: *Many businesses report how much money they make each quarter.*
**5** an area, especially in a city: *He lives in the old quarter of the city.*

**quarters:** *plural* housing, especially for the military: *She lives in the officers' quarters.*

**quarter hour** *noun*
15 minutes: *That trip takes a quarter hour. See:* quarter, *noun,* **2**.

**quarterly** /ˈkwɔrtərli/ *adverb*
during or at the end of a three-month period: *Many businesses report quarterly on how much money they have made.*

**quarterly** *adjective*
every three months: *She wrote a quarterly report.* –*noun plural* **quarterlies.**

**quartz** /kwɔrts/ *noun, (no plural)*
a hard, light-colored mineral or rock found worldwide: *Quartz looks pretty in the sunlight.*

**queasy** /ˈkwizi/ *adjective* **queasier, queasiest**
**1** feeling sick: *My stomach feels queasy.*
**2** nervous, anxious: *She felt queasy as she waited to dive off of the cliff.* –*adverb* **queasily;** –*noun* **queasiness.**

**queen** /kwin/ *noun*
**1** a female ruler or the wife of a king: *The queen sat on her throne.*
**2** a playing card with a picture of a queen –*adverb* **queenly;** –*noun* **queenship.**

queen

**queen-size** or **queen-sized** *adjective*
having to do with a bed that is 60 inches wide by 80 inches long

**queer** /kwɪr/ *adjective* **queerer, queerest**
different than normal, very strange: *He has been feeling queer lately; maybe he's sick.* –*adverb* **queerly;** –*noun* **queerness.** *See:* odd.

**query** /'kwɪri/ *noun, plural* **queries**
a question: *I have a query about your business plan for next year.*

**query** *verb* **queried, querying, queries**
to question something, especially if you are not sure if it is correct: *He queried a customer about an unpaid bill.*

**question** /'kwɛstʃən/ *verb*
**1** to look for an answer to something unknown or in doubt: *She questioned the teacher about a difficult problem.*
**2** to try to get information from someone: *The police questioned the prisoner.*
**3** to wonder if something is just, good, or legal: *Some people question the legality of that government.* –*noun* **question,** (person) **questioner.** *(antonym)* answer. *See:* ask, USAGE NOTE.

**questionable** /'kwɛstʃənəbəl/ *adjective*
**1** doubtful, uncertain: *It is questionable whether this report is true.*
**2** odd, wrong: *He goes on many questionable trips in the middle of the night.* –*adverb* **questionably.**

**question mark** *noun*
the symbol (?), showing that something is a question: *What do you think?*

**questionnaire** /ˌkwɛstʃə'nɛr/ *noun*
a list of questions about a subject: *He answered a questionnaire about his health.*

**quick** /kwɪk/ *adjective* **quicker, quickest**
**1** done fast, *(synonym)* rapid: *He made a quick response to my call.*
**2** short, *(synonym)* brief: *This is a quick meeting that will be over in ten minutes.*
**3** able to understand ideas right away, intelligent: *She has a quick mind.* *(antonym)* slow. –*noun* **quickness.**

**quickly** /kwɪkli/ *adverb*
fast: *Run as quickly as you can to catch the bus.*

**quicksand** /'kwɪkˌsænd/ *noun*
soft, watery sand found in wet areas in which people and animals can sink

**quiet** /'kwaɪɪt/ *adjective* **quieter, quietest**
**1** without noise, silent: *The house was quiet because everyone was asleep.*
**2** calm, peaceful: *I spent a quiet evening at home.* –*noun* **quiet.** *(antonym)* loud; noisy.

**quiet** *verb*
**1** to silence: *He quieted the noisy crowd.*
**2** to calm: *She quieted the child's fears.* –*adverb* **quietly.**

**quilt** /kwɪlt/ *noun*
a bed covering made of pieces of material sewn together and filled with cotton, feathers, etc.

quilt

**quintuple** /kwɪn'tʌpəl/ *verb* **quintupled, quintupling, quintuples**
to multiply by five: *She quintupled her money in one year; she had $10,000 last year, and now she has $50,000!*

**quit** /kwɪt/ *verb* **quit, quitting, quits**
**1** to leave, especially a job: *He quit his job because he wasn't being paid enough.*
**2** to stop doing something: *She quit working for the day and went home.*
**3** to stop an activity: *He quit smoking.*||*She quit dancing when she broke her leg.* –*noun* (person) **quitter.**

**quite** /kwaɪt/ *adverb*
**1** completely, totally: *He is not quite done with his report.*
**2** very, *(synonym)* extremely: *The weather is quite cold.*

Q

**quiz** /kwɪz/ *verb* **quizzed, quizzing, quizzes**
**1** to give a short test, such as those given by a teacher
**2** to question someone: *Her mother quizzed her about where she was last night.* –*noun* **quiz.** *See:* test, USAGE NOTE.

**quiz show** *noun*
a game played on television in which players win prizes for correctly answering questions

**quota** /'kwoʊtə/ *noun*
**1** an amount of something that is required in a certain period of time:

*Computer salespersons must sell many computers each month to reach their quotas.*
**2** a limit, a maximum amount: *The government put a quota on the number of foreign cars allowed to be sold in the USA.*

**quotation** /ˈkwoʊˈteɪʃən/ *noun*
**1** a small part taken exactly as it is written or spoken from something longer (a book, play, speech, etc.): *She put a quotation from a book in her speech.*
**2** a statement of prices for goods or services: *They called the store to get a quotation on the price of a new couch.* –*adjective* **quotable** /ˈkwoʊtəbəl/.

**quotation marks** or **quotes** *noun plural*
the symbols used to show that something is quoted from another person's written or spoken words, shown as (" "): *"To be or not to be" is a line by Shakespeare that we put quotation marks around.*

**quote** /kwoʊt/ *verb* **quoted, quoting, quotes**
**1** to repeat something that another has said or written: *In her speech, the mayor quoted a famous writer.*
**2** to state the price of something: *Before you fix my car, will you quote a price on the repairs for me?*

**quote** *noun*
**1** a quotation: *That was a quote from the mayor's speech.*
**2** a statement of a price: *She asked for a quote on the price of a gold ring.*

Q

# R, r

**R, r** /ɑr/ *noun* **R's, r's** or **Rs, rs**
the 18th letter of the English alphabet

**rabbi** /ˈræbɑɪ/ *noun*
a spiritual leader and teacher of Jewish religion and law

**rabbit** /ˈræbɪt/ *noun*
a small animal with long ears, and a small tail *See:* art on page 14a.

rabbit

**rabies** /ˈreɪbiz/ *noun plural used with a singular verb* a deadly disease that harms the brain and nervous system, usually passed on by animal bites

**raccoon** /ræˈkun/ *noun*
an animal with a gray furry body, a ringed tail, and dark rings around its eyes

raccoon

**race (1)** /reɪs/ *noun*
a contest to see who can go the fastest: *At a track meet, races are run such as the 100-meter and 1000-meter races.*

**race** *verb* **raced, racing, races**
to compete by going faster than someone else: *Bicycle riders race each year in Europe for big prizes.*

**race (2)** *noun*
**1** any of the groupings of human beings according to genes, blood types, color of skin, eyes, hair, etc.: *New York has many races among its population.*
**2** people in general: *the human race*

**racetrack** /reɪstræk/ *noun*
a race course and the area around it used for racing between runners, cars, horses, dogs, etc.: *Joe's sister loves to go to the racetrack and bet on the horses.*

**racism** /ˈreɪˌsɪzəm/ *noun*
prejudice or unfairness against people because of their race: *A black politician accused the white mayor of racism because of unfair hiring practices.* *–adjective* **racial.**

**racist** /ˈreɪsɪst/ *noun*
a person who believes that his or her race is better than other races: *A person who believes that white people are better than black people is a racist. (antonym)* unprejudiced.

**rack** /ræk/ *noun*
a type of shelf or holder: *Our library has racks of books.*

**racket** /ˈrækɪt/ *noun*
**1** a piece of sports equipment with a handle and rounded end used to hit balls: *I have two tennis rackets.*
**2** a loud noise

**radar** /ˈreɪˌdɑr/ *noun, (no plural)*
a machine that gives information about the object's location, speed, size, etc.: *Major airports use radar to control the safe flights of airplanes.*

**radiation** /ˌreɪdiˈeɪʃən/ *noun, (no plural)*
sending out of waves of light, heat, etc.: *Nuclear radiation can be very harmful.* *–verb* **to radiate.**

R

**radiator**
/ˈreɪdiˌeɪtər/ *noun*
**1** a set of metal pipes with hot steam running through them, used to heat rooms: *My radiator warms my room in winter.*
**2** part of the cooling system of an engine: *The radiator in my car overheated last night.*

radiator

**radical** /ˈrædəkəl/ *adjective*
**1** having strong beliefs, ideas different from most people: *Radical students protested the President's visit to their college.*
**2** very unusual, different from what is normal: *We noticed a radical difference in our son's behavior after he finished college and got a job.* *–noun* **radical;** *–adverb* **radically.** *(antonym)* conservative.

**radio** /ˈreɪdioʊ/ *noun*
an electronic device that gives out sound (voices, music): *She listens to the news on the radio each morning.* *–verb* **to radio.**

**radioactive** /ˌreɪdioʊˈæktɪv/ *adjective*
containing or giving off nuclear radiation *–noun* **radioactivity.**

**radius** /ˈreɪdiəs/ *noun, plural* **radii** or **radiuses**
a measurement or line between the center and edge of a circle: *In math class, we learned how to measure the radius of a circle.*

R

**raffle** /ˈræfəl/ *noun*
a game of chance in which people buy numbered tickets to get a prize: *Our church held a raffle to raise money.* *–verb* **to raffle.**

**raft** /ræft/ *noun*
a type of flat boat: *We floated in a raft down a river.* *–verb* **to raft.**

**rag** /ræg/ *noun*
an old piece of cloth: *I use a rag to clean the furniture.*

**rage** /reɪʤ/ *noun*
strong uncontrolled anger: *When he did not get what he wanted, he went into a rage.* *–verb* **to rage.**

**raid** /reɪd/ *noun*
a sudden attack, such as one made by police on criminals: *Police made a raid on a drug dealer's house.* *–verb* **to raid;** *–noun* (person) **raider.**

**rail** /reɪl/ *noun*
a long, I-shaped piece of metal that trains run on: *Rails are made of steel for a smooth train ride.*

**railing** /ˈreɪlɪŋ/ *noun*
**1** a bar used as support beside stairs: *My elderly uncle holds onto the railing as he goes downstairs.*
**2** a fence made of rails

**railroad** /ˈreɪlˌroʊd/ *noun*
transportation for goods and passengers in trains on rails: *I prefer to ride the railroad to work.* *–verb* **to railroad.**

**railway** /ˈreɪlˌwe ɪ/ *noun*
a railroad

**rain** /reɪn/ *noun*
drops of water falling from clouds: *Rain fell on the city last night.*

**rain** *verb*
to fall from the sky as drops of water: *It rains in northern California six or seven months of the year.*
**to rain cats and dogs:** to rain very hard and fast: *Last night it rained cats and dogs, so I stayed inside to keep dry.*

**rainbow** /ˈreɪnˌboʊ/ *noun*
a curve of bright colors that sometimes forms in the sky after a rainstorm: *A rainbow with its red, blue, and yellow colors is a pretty sight.*

rainbow

**raincoat** /ˈreɪnˌkout/ *noun*
a coat worn to stay dry when it rains: *I wear my raincoat when it rains.* *See:* art on page 12a.

**raindrop** /ˈreɪnˌdrɑp/ *noun*
a drop of water from a cloud: *Raindrops fell on my window.*

**rainfall** /ˈreɪnˌfɔl/ *noun, (no plural)*
**1** the rain that falls during a rainstorm: *Last night's rainfall should help the flowers to grow.*
**2** the measurement of the amount of rain

that falls during a specified time: *The yearly rainfall in the desert is only two inches.*

**rainy** /'reɪni/ *adjective* **rainier, rainiest**
full of rain: *We have rainy weather this week. (antonym)* sunny.

**raise** /reɪz/ *verb* **raised, raising, raises**
**1** to lift up: *A police officer raised her hand to stop traffic.*
**2** to help a child to grow up: *My parents raised two sons.*
**3** to grow plants or farm animals: *That farmer raises corn and cows.*
**4** to bring up, suggest in conversation: *I raised a question at our meeting. (antonym)* lower.

**raise** *noun*
an increase in salary: *My company gave me a raise last week.*

**raisin** /'reɪzən/ *noun*
a dried grape: *He puts raisins on his cereal for breakfast.*

**rake** /reɪk/ *noun*
a tool with metal or wooden teeth and a long handle: *I used a rake to gather leaves from the lawn.*

rake

**rake** *verb* **raked, raking, rakes**
to use a rake: *I raked up leaves fallen on the sidewalk.*

**rally** /'ræli/ *noun, plural* **rallies**
a meeting of people to excite them about an idea, product, or sports event: *The football coach called a rally to build up excitement for the next game. –verb* **to rally.**

**ram** /ræm/ *noun*
**1** a male sheep
**2 RAM:** *abbreviation of* random-access memory: *My new computer has 32 megabytes of RAM.*

ram

**ram** *verb* **rammed, ramming, rams**
to hit with great force: *A car went off the road and rammed into a tree.*

---

**USAGE NOTE:** A computer's *RAM* is the memory the computer uses to hold programs. A computer with more RAM can run larger, more complicated programs. Having a lot of RAM is like having a large desk on which you can organize all of your information to use it easily.

---

**ramp** /ræmp/ *noun*
**1** a road that runs on and off a highway
**2** a walkway or metal plate that goes between two levels of a building: *A woman rolled her wheelchair up the ramp to the doctor's door.*

**ran** /ræn/ *verb*
*past tense of* run

**ranch** /ræntʃ/ *noun, plural* **ranches**
a very large farm in the western USA and Canada: *My friend lives on a ranch and rides her horse every day. –noun* (person) **rancher.**

**ranching** /'ræntʃɪŋ/ *noun, (no plural)*
farming, the raising of crops and animals on a ranch: *He likes ranching and being outdoors.*

**random** /'rændəm/ *adjective*
happening at any time, unplanned: *Random rain showers will pass through our city today. –adverb* **randomly.**

**random-access memory** *noun*
*abbreviation* **RAM**. *See:* ram.

**range** /reɪndʒ/ *verb* **ranged, ranging, ranges**
to cover a wide area: *Cattle range over large fields.||That company's product line ranges from small televisions to ones with huge screens.*

**range** *noun*
**1** an open field
**2** *(no plural)* a variety of things: *My friend and I talked about a wide range of topics: our families, our jobs, politics, and so on.*
**3** a stove for cooking
**4** a group of mountains: *The Rockies are a mountain range in the western USA.*

**rank** /ræŋk/ *noun*
one's position in the military or business: *She has the rank of general in the Air Force. –verb* **to rank.**

**ransom** /'rænsəm/ *noun*
money paid for return of a person taken

by criminals (kidnappers): *The family paid a ransom of $100,000 for the return of their kidnapped daughter.* –*verb* **to ransom.**

**rap** /ræp/ *noun*
**1** a knock, loud tap: *I heard a rap on the door, and I opened it.*
**2** a type of music in which the artist speaks to a strong rhythm: *Rap became popular in the 1980s.* –*noun* (artist) **rapper.**

**rap** *verb* **rapped, rapping, raps**
to knock, tap loudly: *My friend rapped on my door, and I let her in.*

---

**USAGE NOTE:** People who perform *rap* music are called *rap artists*, not rap musicians, because a rap performance combines dancing, talking, and singing in rhyme.

---

**rape** /reɪp/ *noun*
the crime of forcing a person to have sex when she or he does not want to: *A rape happened in the park last night.* –*verb* **to rape;** –*noun* (criminal) **rapist.**

**rapid** /ˈræpɪd/ *adjective*
very fast, quick: *His rapid speech is difficult to understand.* –*noun* **rapidity;** –*adverb* **rapidly.** *(antonym)* slow.

**rare** /rɛr/ *adjective*
**1** not often heard or seen: *The famous movie star made a rare public appearance.*
**2** not completely cooked: *My father likes rare meat that is still pink inside.*
**3** very valuable: *a rare painting*

**rarely** /ˈrɛrli/ *adverb*
not often, *(synonym)* seldom: *That famous old movie star is rarely seen in person these days.*

**rascal** /ˈræskəl/ *noun*
a badly behaved child

**rash** /ræʃ/ *noun*
red spots on the skin: *That strong soap gives me a rash on my legs.*

**rash** *adjective*
quick and foolish, without thinking

**raspberry** /ˈræzˌbɛri/ *noun, plural* **raspberries**
a plant of the rose family and its red or black fruit: *I like to eat raspberries and cream.*

**rat** /ræt/ *noun*
a small animal (rodent) with a long hairless tail, a pointed nose, and very sharp teeth: *Rats look like mice, but are larger.* *See:* art on page 14a.

**rate** /reɪt/ *noun*
**1** an amount of something: *The rate of interest on my savings in the bank was seven percent.*
**2** the cost of something: *The rate for a trip on that bus is $10 per person.*
**3** a speed: *Jet airplanes travel at a great rate of speed.*

**at any rate:** no matter what happens: *I may get a C in math, but at any rate I learned a lot.*

**rather** /ˈræðər/ *adverb*
**1** to like one thing more than another: *I would rather go shopping tomorrow than today.*
**2** a little, somewhat, or very: *The weather is rather hot today.* *See:* kind, USAGE NOTE.

**rating** /ˈreɪtɪŋ/ *noun*
a measure of good or bad quality, usually compared with other like things: *That company has the highest rating.*

**ratio** /ˈreɪʃoʊ/ *noun*
a relationship between two numbers: *The ratio of women to men in our class is 3 to 1, that is, 3 women to 1 man.*

**ration** /ˈræʃən,ˈreɪ/ *verb*
to limit food and other items, especially by governmental order: *During the war, the government rationed food supplies.* –*noun* (amount) **ration.**

**rational** /ˈræʃənəl/ *adjective*
showing logical thought, reasonable: *The rational thing to do was to take the sick man to a doctor.* *(antonym)* irrational.

**rattle** /ˈrætl/ *noun*
**1** a toy that makes short, quick noises when shaken
**2** the sound of a series of repeated noises: *a rattle in a car*

**rattle** *verb* **rattled, rattling, rattles**
to shake and sound like a rattle: *The tailpipe on my car is loose and rattles.* –*adjective* **rattling.**

**rattlesnake** /'ræ tl,sneɪk/ *noun*
a dangerous, poisonous snake that lives in North and South America and has hard skin at the end of its body which the snake rattles when ready to bite

**rattlesnake**

**raven** /'reɪvən/ *noun*
a large black bird with shiny black feathers

**raw** /rɔ/ *adjective*
**1** natural, uncooked: *Eating raw carrots is good for your eyesight.*
**2** in a natural state, not yet manufactured: *Cotton and wool are raw materials from which cloth is made.*

**ray** /reɪ/ *noun*
a thin line of light, energy, or heat: *Rays of light shine from a burning candle.*

**razor** /'reɪzər/ *noun*
a sharp cutting instrument: *Men use razors to shave their beards. See:* art on page 23a.

**Rd.** /roʊd/
*abbreviation of* Road: *His address is 21 Fordham Rd. See:* street, USAGE NOTE.

**reach** /ritʃ/ *verb* **reaches**
**1** to stretch out one's arm and hand: *He reached across the table to get the salt.*
**2** to go as far as: *We reached Nashville before our car needed gas.*
**3** to make contact with someone: *We couldn't reach you by telephone, so we are writing this letter.*

**reach** *noun, plural* **reaches**
the length an arm can be stretched out

**react** /ri'ækt/ *verb*
**1** to speak or move when something happens: *When he heard the good news, he reacted with a smile.*
**2** to act in a different way because of something: *The teacher reacted to the student's bad grades by giving him more homework.* –*noun* **reaction.**

**read** /rid/ *verb* **read** /rɛd/, **reading, reads**
**1** to see and understand written words and symbols: *She reads books already at age five.*
**2** to say something written out loud: *The professor read an important part of the textbook to the students.*
**3** to understand something because of clues or hints: *She could read the feeling of happiness on his face.*
**to read someone his or her rights:** (in the USA), police must tell a person they are taking to jail what that person's legal rights are: *The police officer read the man his rights, then she took him to jail.* –*noun* (person) **reader.**

**readable** /'ridəbəl/ *adjective*
easily read, clear: *That story is full of action and quite readable.* –*noun* **readability.**

**readiness** /'rɛdinɪs/ *noun, (no plural)*
ready to act, the ability to act quickly: *A fire truck is always in a state of readiness to go to a fire.*

**reading** /'ridɪŋ/ *noun*
**1** the process of seeing and understanding written material: *Schools teach reading in the first grade.*
**2** an exact amount shown by measuring equipment: *A reading of the gas meter in our house is done every month.*

**ready** /'rɛdi/ *adjective* **readier, readiest**
**1** prepared to do something: *Our meal is ready, so let's eat.*
**2** easily available: *ready answer, ready cash, ready money*

**real** /'riəl/ *adjective*
true, not fake or imaginary: *His real name is Bob Smith, not John Jones.*

**real** *adverb*
*informal* very, extremely: *We had a real good time at the party last night.*

**real estate** *noun, (no plural)*
property that cannot be moved, such as land, houses, and office buildings: *She owns real estate in the country.* –*adjective* **real-estate.**

**realistic** /,riə'lɪstɪk/ *adjective*
**1** appearing true to life: *The movie showed realistic scenes of farm life of rain, mud, and taking care of cows.*
**2** a view of the good and bad in life, not believing that everything is perfect: *She is realistic about the fact that with no education, she will have difficulty finding a high-paying job.* –*adverb* **realistically.**

R

**reality** /ri'æləti/ *noun, (no plural)*
the real world of objects and living things as it is in fact and not an idealistic view of it: *People needed time to understand the reality of damage caused by the hurricane.*

**realization** /ˌriələ'zeɪʃən/ *noun, (no plural)*
understanding, belief that something is true: *After looking for work, he came to the realization that he needs more education to find a job.*

**realize** /'riəˌlaɪz/ *verb* **realized, realizing, realizes**
to understand, believe something is true: *He realizes now that he needs to go back to college for more education.*

**really** /'riəli/ *adverb*
**1** in fact, truly: *Are you really happy, or are you just smiling to be nice to me?*
**2** very: *I am really surprised to see you!*

**rear** /rɪr/ **(1)** *noun, (no plural)*
**1** the back area of something: *He sat in the rear of the church. (antonym)* front.
**2** *informal* the buttocks: *He fell on his rear.*

**rear (2)** *verb*
to help children or young animals to grow: *A mother rears her children to adulthood.*

**rearrange** /ˌriə'reɪnʤ/ *verb* **rearranged, rearranging, rearranges**
to put something in a new order: *I've rearranged my work schedule; I no longer will work on weekends. –noun* **rearrangement.**

**reason** /'rizən/ *noun*
**1** the ability to understand and think logically: *Scientists use reason to understand nature.*
**2** the purpose for something: *His reason for going back to school is to learn new things.*

**reason** *verb*
to think logically: *He reasoned out the math problem and got the correct answer.*

**to reason with someone:** to talk to someone, trying to make him or her think logically and reasonably: *It is not possible to reason with a two-year-old child.*

**reasonable** /'rizənəbəl/ *adjective*
**1** referring to a logical and right thing to do, *(synonyms)* acceptable, sensible: *That man works very hard, so it is reasonable for him to ask for more money.*
**2** not priced too high: *The price of the coat was very reasonable, so I bought it. –adverb* **reasonably.** *(antonym)* unreasonable.

**reassure** /ˌriə'ʃʊr/ *verb* **reassured, reassuring, reassures**
to make someone believe that something will be all right: *She reassured him that she still loves him. –noun* **reassurance.**

**rebate** /'riˌbeɪt/ *noun*
money given by a company to people who have bought a product: *The car manufacturer gave me a rebate of $1,000 on the price of my new car. –verb* **to rebate.**

---

**USAGE NOTE:** Compare *rebate* and *coupon.* A *rebate* is money returned to a buyer (often by mail) after the sale: *I sent in a form to get a $1.00 rebate on the shampoo I bought.* A *coupon* reduces the price of the item at the time of the sale: *I used a coupon to buy cereal for 75 cents less than the regular price.* Some stores will double or triple the value of a coupon to get more business.

---

**rebel** /'rɛbəl/ *noun*
a person who fights against a person or group in power, especially against a government: *Rebels attacked an army station. –noun* (action) **rebellion.**

**rebel** *verb* /rə'bɛl/ **rebelled, rebelling, rebels**
to fight against a person or group in power: *He rebelled against his parents and left home. –adjective* **rebellious.**

**recall** /rɪ'kɔl/ *verb*
**1** to remember something: *I don't recall your name; I don't have a good memory for names. (antonym)* forget.
**2** to ask that something be returned: *The company recalled a product because it was not safe.*

**recall** /'rikɔl/ *noun, (no plural)*
a request for the return of unsafe products by the company that made them

**receipt** /rɪ'sit/ *noun*
a piece of paper showing that a bill is paid: *I bought a hat and the clerk gave me a receipt.*

**receive** /rɪ'siv/ *verb* **received, receiving, receives**
to get or take something that is given or sent: *I received a gift on my birthday.* *(antonym)* to give.

**recent** /'risənt/ *adjective*
in the past, but not very long ago, such as yesterday, last week, last month: *I paid a recent visit to my parents, last month in fact.* *–adverb* **recently.**

**reception** /rə'sɛpʃən/ *noun*
**1** a type of party planned so people can meet a special guest
**2** the entrance of a business: *I met my friend at the reception of her office.*
**3** the quality of a TV or radio signal: *Cable TV gives good reception.*

**receptionist** /rə'sɛpʃənɪst/ *noun*
a person who greets and directs people at a business entrance: *I gave the receptionist my name and waited for my appointment.*

**recess** /'ri,sɛs/ *noun, plural* **recesses**
a short stop or break, such as in school classes: *The school children play in the schoolyard when they have recess outside.* *–verb* **to recess.**

**recession** /rə'sɛʃən/ *noun*
a time when economic activity is not strong: *In a recession, there are fewer jobs, so people have less money.*

**recharge** /ri'ʧɑrʤ/ *verb* **recharged, recharging, recharges**
to put energy back into something: *My car battery was not working, so the mechanic recharged it for me.*

**recipe** /'rɛsə,pi/ *noun*
directions for cooking food: *She used her favorite recipe to make chocolate cake.*

**recipe**

**reckless** /'rɛklɪs/ *adjective*
doing something dangerous without thinking: *He is reckless when he drives his car too fast.* *–adverb* **recklessly;** *–noun* **recklessness.** *(antonym)* careful.

**recognition** /,rɛkəg'nɪʃən/ *noun, (no plural)*
**1** credit, praise for doing something well: *An excellent employee was given recognition with an award for her good work.*
**2** signs that one remembers someone or something: *I saw an old friend, but he showed no recognition that he remembered me.*

**recognize** /'rɛkəg,naɪz/ *verb* **recognized, recognizing, recognizes**
to recall, remember someone or something when one sees or hears that person or thing: *I recognized an old friend in a crowd and waved to her.* *–adverb* **recognizably.**

**recommend** /,rɛkə'mɛnd/ *verb*
**1** to tell others about something one likes: *I recommend that restaurant to you because it has very good food.*
**2** to advise someone to do something: *My doctor recommends that I see a specialist for my skin problems.*

**recommendation** /,rɛkəmən'deɪʃən/ *noun*
written or spoken praise about something or someone's good points: *He gave his friend a recommendation on a good movie to see.*

**record** /'rɛkərd/ *noun*
**1** something (usually written) that proves that an event happened: *The records of our business are kept in our computer and in printouts.*
**2** the best time, distance, etc., in an athletic event: *She holds the world record for running the 100 meters.*
**3** a criminal's history of arrests: *That thief has a long record.*
**4** a flat disk on to which a sound recording, especially music, has been pressed: *He has a collection of Elvis Presley records from the 1950s.*

**record** /rɪ'kərd/ *verb*
**1** to make a written record of something: *The cash register recorded the $10 purchase and printed a receipt.*
**2** to make a sound or video recording of

something: *The concert was recorded on videotape for showing on TV.*

**recorder** /rɪ'kɔrdər/ *noun*
a device used to record sight or sound: *Most reporters have a tape recorder to use in interviews.*

**recording** /rɪ'kɔrdɪŋ/ *noun*
an electronic or magnetic copy of a spoken or visual event: *Recordings of music are often sold as CDs.*

**recover** /rɪ'kʌvər/ *verb*
**1** to become healthy after being sick: *He recovered from his illness and is well again.*
**2** to get control again: *Workers recovered a sunken boat from the lake.*
**3** to put a new cover (new material) on something: *to recover a sofa See:* reupholster.

**recovery** /rɪ'kʌvəri/ *noun, plural* **recoveries**
**1** return of one's good health: *She made a quick recovery after surgery.*
**2** finding something lost: *The recovery of the missing painting took several years.*

**recreation** /ˌrɛkri'eɪʃən/ *noun, (no plural)*
fun things to do, such as sports, hobbies, and amusements: *Her favorite recreation is playing tennis.*

**recruit** /rɪ'krut/ *verb*
to interview and choose people to join an organization or cause: *She recruits people to become sales representatives for her company. –noun* (person) **recruit.**

**recruiter** /rɪ'krutər/ *noun*
a person who recruits others

**recruitment** /rɪ'krutmənt/ *noun, (no plural)*
the process of interviewing and choosing people to do a job

**rectangle** /'rɛkˌtæŋgəl/ *noun*
any shape with four straight sides that make right angles: *My textbook is shaped like a rectangle. –adjective* **rectangular** /rɛk'tæŋgyələr/. *See:* art on page 16a.

R

**recycle** /ri'saɪkəl/ *verb* **recycled, recycling, recycles**
to process and reuse materials, especially waste: *New York City recycles newspapers, bottles, and other garbage, and makes them into new products. See:* biodegradable, USAGE NOTE.

recycle

**recycling** /ri'saɪklɪŋ/ *noun, (no plural)*
the collection, processing, and reuse of waste items, such as used bottles and newspapers: *Recycling of aluminum cans saves energy because less energy is used in recycling aluminum than in making new aluminum.*

**USAGE NOTE:** *Recycling* has become common in North America. At home, some people sort trash into paper, plastics, and metals and take them to a recycling center. In some communities special *recycling containers* and trucks pick up the recycling.

**red** /rɛd/ *noun*
a basic color like that of blood: *She likes to wear red. –adjective* **red.** *See:* art on page 16a.

**redeem** /rɪ'dim/ *verb*
to turn something in, such as a coupon, for cash, a discount, or products: *I redeemed coupons for cereal at the supermarket and saved $1.50.*

**redo** /ri'du/ **redid** /'dɪd/, **redone** /'dʌn/, **redoing, redoes** /'dʌz/ *verb*
to do something over again: *I redid my report to make it more complete.*

**reduce** /rɪ'dus/ *verb* **reduced, reducing, reduces**
to make something smaller or less important: *He reduced his weight by 20 pounds by eating less and exercising. –noun* **reduction.**

**reef** /rif/ *noun*
in the ocean, a long bar made of sand, coral, etc.: *A ship hit a reef and sank.*

**reelect** /ˌriɪˈlɛkt/ *verb*
to elect an official again: *The mayor was reelected for a third time.* –*noun* **reelection.**

**refer** /rɪˈfɜr/ *verb* **referred, referring, refers**
to direct one's attention to something or someone: *My doctor referred me to a specialist.*||*The company referred me to their customer service department to solve my problem.*

**referee** /ˌrɛfəˈri/ *noun*
a type of official who makes players follow the rules of a sport: *The football referee blew his whistle to stop the game.*

**referee** *verb*
to act as a referee for a game or match: *My friend referees basketball games.*

**reference** /ˈrɛfərəns/ *noun*
**1** a source of information: *That student used an encyclopedia as a reference for his term paper.*
**2** a recommendation, especially for employment: *My former boss said that I could use her as a reference.*

**referendum** /ˌrɛfəˈrɛndəm/ *noun, plural* **referendums**
a direct popular vote taken on an important question: *A national referendum was held to decide whether to pay off the national debt through increased taxes.*

**refine** /rɪˈfaɪn/ *verb* **refined, refining, refines**
to change something into a purer form that is ready to be used: *Oil companies refine crude oil into gasoline.* –*noun* **refinement.**

**reflect** /rɪˈflɛkt/ *verb*
**1** to give off a shine: *Sunlight reflected off the water.*
**2** to show an image of something in water, a mirror, etc.: *I like to watch clouds reflected in the water.*

reflection

**to reflect on:** to think deeply about: *An old man reflected on what he had done in his lifetime.* –*noun* **reflection.**

**reform** /rəˈfɔrm/ *verb*
to improve something that exists, especially government: *A new President reformed the nation's health care system.*

**refresh** /rɪˈfrɛʃ/ *verb*
to make strong and clean again: *Eight hours of sleep and a shower always refresh me.*

**refreshment** /rɪˈfrɛʃmənt/ *noun*
food and drink that refreshes: *He needed refreshment, so he drank a tall glass of cola.*

**refrigerator** /rɪˈfrɪʤəˌreɪtər/ *noun*
a storage box with cooling and freezing sections for food: *We keep all our vegetables in the refrigerator to keep them fresh.* –*noun* **refrigeration;** –*verb* **to refrigerate.**

**refuge** /ˈrɛfyuʤ/ *noun*
**to take** or **seek refuge**: a place of safety: *When it started to rain hard, I took refuge in the doorway of a building.*

**refugee** /ˌrɛfyuˈʤi/ *noun*
a person trying to leave bad living conditions (such as oppression, war, or hunger): *During the war, many refugees went to safer countries nearby to live better lives.*

**refund** /ˈriˌfʌnd/ *noun*
an amount of money returned to the person who bought something: *The new TV never worked well, so I brought it back to the store for a refund.* –*verb* **to refund.**

**refusal** /rəˈfyuz əl/ *noun*
an act of saying no: *Alice's refusal to marry Chandler made Chandler very sad. (antonym)* acceptance.

**refuse (1)** /rəˈfyuz/ *verb* **refused, refusing, refuses**
to say no: *He refused an invitation to a party.*||*She refuses to drink alcohol or eat meat. (antonym)* to accept.

**refuse (2)** /ˈrɛfyus/ *noun*
garbage, waste: *Refuse is collected every Tuesday in our town.*

**regain** /riˈgeɪn/ *verb*
**1** to gain again, to get back: *She regained the money that she lost.*
**2** to add back on: *She regained the 15 pounds that she lost.*

**regard** /rə'gɑrd/ *verb*
**1** to think about the importance of something: *He regards his job as the most important thing in his life.*
**2** to deal with a certain matter: *This letter regards the payment for your new car.*
**regard** *noun, (no plural)*
**1** respect, concern, for something or someone: *I have high regard for mothers who take good care of their children.*
**2** *noun plural* **regards:** best wishes: *Give my regards to Joe when you see him.*
**in** or **with regard to:** concerning: *In regard to our conversation yesterday, I am sending the book to you by mail.*

**regarding** /rə'gɑrdɪŋ/ *preposition*
about, concerning: *Regarding your order, we will ship it today.*

**reggae** /'rɛgeɪ/ *noun, (no plural)*
a kind of music that began in the West Indies: *Bob Marley was one of the most famous reggae artists.*

**regiment** /'rɛʤəmənt/ *noun*
a group of about 400 soldiers

**region** /'riʤən/ *noun*
a geographical area of a country: *The northeast region of the USA includes New York and the six New England states.* –*adjective* **regional.** *See:* area.

**register** /'rɛʤɪstər/ *verb*
**1** to write one's name on an official list, such as a voter list or a school's student list: *I registered to vote in the presidential election this year.*
**2** to show on instruments or faces: *The scales registered 120 pounds.*
**register** *noun*
**1** a list or other official record of people
**2** a cash register in a store

**registered mail** *noun, (no plural)*
a way to send important mail: *I sent an expensive watch to my friend in Seattle by registered mail. See:* certified mail.

**registered nurse** *noun*
a nurse who has a degree and has passed a state examination for nurses: *She earns a good salary as a registered nurse.* –*abbreviation* **RN.**

---

**USAGE NOTE:** In the USA, different kinds of nurses have different amounts of education. A nurse who has finished two years of nursing school is called a *licensed practicing nurse (LPN).* A *registered nurse (RN)* has a university degree and practical training. *Nurse practitioners (NP)* are *RNs* with additional training. They can give medical exams, prescribe some medicines, and do some jobs that doctors do.

---

**registration** /ˌrɛʤɪs'treɪʃən/ *noun*
**1** an act of registering for something: *I did my registration for classes on Monday.*
**2** a document that shows something is registered: *Here is the registration for my boat.* –*noun* (person) **registrar.**

**registry** /'rɛʤɪstri/ *noun, plural* **registries**
an office of official records: *He went to the registry of motor vehicles to get a new driver's license.*

**regret** /rɪ'grɛt/ *verb* **regretted, regretting, regrets**
**1** to feel sad because of something that happened: *I regret that your mother died and left you alone.*
**2** to feel guilty or sorry for something one has done: *He regrets that he was angry with his son.* –*noun* **regret.**

**regular** /'rɛgyələr/ *adjective*
**1** normal, usual: *The child's regular bedtime is 8:00* P.M.
**2** not unusual, average: *He has a regular build and an average weight.* –*noun* (person) **regular.**

**regulation** /ˌrɛgyə'leɪʃən/ *noun*
**1** a rule, statement about what can be done and what cannot: *The state board of health makes many regulations about the food, water, and cleanliness in restaurants and food stores.*
**2** the general condition of controlling any part of human life: *Regulation of the banks is done by the federal government.* –*verb* **to regulate.**

**rehearsal** /rə'hɜrsəl/ *noun*
a practice time, especially to prepare for an artistic performance: *She went to the rehearsal for the new play.*

**rehearse** /rə'hɜrs/ *verb* **rehearsed, rehearsing, rehearses**
to practice, prepare for a performance: *She rehearsed the songs in the new show.*

R

**reign** /reɪn/ *noun*
the time period that a king or queen rules a country: *The reign of King Louis XIV of France ended in 1715.* –*verb* **to reign.**

**reimburse** /ˌriɪm'bɜrs/ *verb* **reimbursed, reimbursing, reimburses**
to pay someone back for the money that they paid: *His company reimburses him for hotel, meal, and other travel expenses.* –*noun* **reimbursement.**

**reins** /reɪn/ *noun*
*used in the plural* long pieces of leather connected to an animal's head or mouth and used by the rider to control the animal: *A cowboy holds the horse's reins.* –*verb* **to rein.**

**reindeer** /'reɪnˌdɪr/ *noun, plural* **reindeer** or **reindeers**
a large, strong deer that lives in cold, northern areas, used for meat, milk, clothing, and transportation: *Reindeer can pull loads two times their own weight.*

**reject** /rɪ'ʤɛkt/ *verb*
to refuse, not accept: *He asked her to go to the movies four times, and each time she rejected him. (antonym)* to accept.

**rejection** /rɪ'ʤɛkʃən/ *noun*
something that is not accepted: *Of the 10 college applications Erica made, she received seven acceptance letters and three rejections.*

**rejoice** /rɪ'ʤɔ ɪs/ *verb* **rejoiced, rejoicing, rejoices**
to feel great joy: *When the war ended, the winners rejoiced.* –*noun* **rejoicing.**

**relate** /rə'leɪt/ *verb* **related, relating, relates**
to be connected with, deal with something: *Our teacher relates our class discussions to real life.*

**related** /rə'leɪtɪd/ *adjective*
**1** connected by blood or marriage: *He is related to the governor; they are cousins.*
**2** connected, dealing with: *My doctor says my headaches are related to reading in bad light.*

**relation** /rə'leɪʃən/ *noun*
**1** a relative by blood or marriage: *My mother, father, and brother are my closest relations.*
**2** a connection: *The relation between mathematics and physics is close.*

**relationship** /rə'leɪʃənˌʃɪp/ *noun*
a connection between ideas, people, or things: *Those two people like each other and have a close relationship.*

**relative** /'rɛləˌtɪv/ *noun*
a person connected by blood or marriage to someone: *My parents and brother are my only living relatives.*

**relative** *adjective*
comparing good and bad: *We discussed the relative advantages of buying a new or used car.* –*adverb* **relatively.**

**relax** /rə'læks/ *verb* **relaxes**
**1** to stop work and enjoy oneself: *She relaxes by riding her bicycle.*
**2** to stop being nervous, tense, angry, etc.: *Why don't you stop being angry and relax for a while!*

**relaxation** /ˌrilæk'seɪʃən/ *noun, (no plural)*
a process of relaxing, such as freeing the mind of worry: *For relaxation, he plays golf on the weekends.*

**release** /ri'lis/ *verb* **released, releasing, releases**
**1** to let something go, set it free: *He releases his pet birds from their cage each day.*
**2** to let something be used publicly: *That movie was released last month and is playing in neighborhood theaters.* –*noun* (freedom) **release.**

**relevant** /'rɛləvənt/ *adjective*
closely connected: *My classes about new kinds of computers are relevant to my plan to work in computer repair.* –*adverb* **relevantly;** –*noun* **relevance.**

**reliability** /rəˌlaɪə'bɪləti/ *noun, (no plural)*
ability to be trusted: *That bank has been in business for years and its reliability is the best.*

**reliable** /rə'laɪəbəl/ *adjective*
**1** regularly does what it should do, *(synonyms)* dependable, sure: *The train service in this area is very reliable.*
**2** can be trusted: *He is a reliable worker who is always on time.*

**relief** /rə'lif/ *noun, (no plural)*
**1** the taking away of pain: *Two aspirin gave him relief from a headache.*
**2** freedom from worry: *When she learned that her daughter was safe, she felt great relief.*
**3** help given in times of trouble, hunger, war, or natural disaster: *After the flood, we gave money for relief of the people who lost their homes.*

**relieve** /rɪ'liv/ *verb* **relieved, relieving, relieves**
**1** to lessen or take away something unpleasant: *Aspirin relieves my pains.*
**2** to take the place of someone who is working: *The guards relieve each other every four hours.*

**religion** /rə'lɪʤən/ *noun*
a system of beliefs in a god or philosophy of life: *Buddhism and Hinduism are two of the world's major religions.*

**religious** /rə'lɪʤəs/ *adjective*
**1** related to religion: *Her religious beliefs are highly developed.*
**2** having strong beliefs in religion: *He is very religious; he prays every day. –adverb* **religiously.**

**relocate** /ri'loʊ,keɪt/ *verb* **relocated, relocating, relocates**
to move to a new place: *My friend relocated from New York to Florida. –noun* **relocation** /,riloʊ'keɪʃən/.

**reluctant** /rɪ'lʌktənt/ *adjective*
concerned or afraid: *He is reluctant to spend much money because he thinks he may lose his job. –noun* **reluctance.**

R

**rely** /rə'laɪ/ *verb* **relied, relying, relies**
to depend on: *I rely on the train to take me to work each day.*||*You can rely on me! –noun* **reliance.**

**remain** /rə'meɪn/ *verb*
to stay: *He remained at the camp while others went to look for food.*

**remains** /rə'meɪnz/ *noun plural*
parts or things that are left after death or destruction: *We saw the remains of the old city.*

**remark** /rə'mɑrk/ *verb*
to say something: *He remarked that the flower garden looks beautiful.*

**remark** *noun*
**1** a statement about something: *She made a remark about his good appearance.*
**2** a negative statement, cutting criticism: *She made a remark that he behaves like a fool.*

**remarkable** /rə'mɑrkəbəl/ *adjective*
worthy of attention: *The sick man was near death but made remarkable improvement and got well. –adverb* **remarkably.**

**remarry** /ri'mæri / *verb* **remarried, remarrying, remarries**
to marry again: *After her husband died, she remarried. –noun* **remarriage** /ri'mærɪʤ/.

**remedial** /rə'midiəl/ *adjective*
corrective, designed to improve something: *She is doing well in remedial reading; she can read well now. –noun* **remediation.**

**remedy** *noun, plural* **remedies**
a medicine, something that makes an illness better: *She took a cold remedy to relieve her sneezing and headache. –verb* **to remedy.**

**remember** /rɪ'mɛmbər/ *verb*
to recall, bring something from the past to mind: *I still remember my first day at school as a little boy. –noun* **remembrance.** *(antonym)* to forget.

**remind** /rə'maɪnd/ *verb*
to tell someone about doing something, cause someone to remember: *My wife reminded me to buy a present for our daughter's birthday. –noun* **reminder.**

**remote** /rə'moʊt/ *adjective*
referring to a faraway place or time

**remote control** *noun*
a device that controls something from a distance: *I have three remote controls: one each for the TV, the stereo, and the VCR.*

remote control

**remove** /rə'muv/ *verb* **removed, removing, removes**
to move or take something away: *You should remove all furniture from the*

*room before you clean the rug.* –*noun* (act) **removal;** –*adjective* **removable.**

**renew** /rɪ'nu/ *verb*
**1** to agree to something again, continue an agreement: *We renewed our magazine subscription.*
**2** to make someone or something new, fresh, and better: *She renewed her energy with a long vacation.*

**renewable** /rɪ'nuəbəl/ *adjective*
able to be renewed or continued: *This library book is renewable after two weeks.*

**renewal** /rɪ'nuəl/ *noun*
an act of making something new: *Renewal means making old buildings in cities into good places to live.*

**renovate** /'rɛnə,veɪt/ *verb* **renovated, renovating, renovates**
to renew something, make something (especially a building) look like new: *He renovated an apartment building by cleaning it, painting it, putting in new windows, new kitchens, and a new elevator.* –*noun* **renovation.**

**renowned** /rə'naʊnd/ *adjective*
famous, well known and liked or criticized: *Switzerland is renowned for its beautiful mountains. (antonym)* unknown.

**rent** /rɛnt/ *noun*
the amount of money paid for the use of a piece of property: *She pays a low rent on that apartment.*
**for rent:** available to be rented: *That house is for rent.* –*noun* (person) **renter.**
**rent** *verb*
to pay to use a piece of property, but not own it: *She has rented the apartment for many years.*

**rental** /'rɛntl/ *noun*
a piece of property that is rented out to others: *He does not own that fancy car; it's a rental.* –*adjective* **rental.**

**repair** /rə'pɛr/ *verb*
to fix something: *A mechanic repaired the motor in my car; it was overheating.*
**repair** *noun*
state of being fixed: *The repairs on my car will be finished tomorrow.* –*adjective* **repairable.**

**repairman** /rə'pɛrmən/ *noun, plural* **repairmen** /mən/ or **repairperson**
a person who fixes things: *My refrigerator stopped working, so I called the repairman.*

**repay** /ri'peɪ/ *verb*
to pay back: *I loaned my friend some money and he repaid me.* –*noun* **repayment.**

**repeal** /rə'pil/ *noun*
(in government) the act of taking away the legal value of something, a cancellation: *The new Congress's first act was a repeal of all of the old Congress's laws.*
**repeal** *verb*
to cancel, make something have no legal power: *They repealed the tax law.*

**repeat** /rɪ'pit/ *verb*
to say or do something again: *He told me a story and then repeated it later to his wife.* –*noun* **repeat.**

**repetition** /,rɛpə'tɪʃən/ *noun*
the act of doing or saying something again: *Repetition of the words in that song makes the song easy to remember.* –*adjective* **repetitious, repetitive.**

**replace** /rə'pleɪs/ *verb* **replaced, replacing, replaces**
**1** to get something new to take the place of something old: *I replaced my old car with a new one.*
**2** to take the place of someone or something: *Her boss retired and she replaced him.* –*adjective* **replaceable.**

**replacement** /rə' pleɪsmənt/ *noun*
someone or something that takes the place of another: *A worker retired and his replacement started work today.*

**replay** /'ri,pleɪ/ *noun*
a second showing of an event, such as sports played on television: *On the evening TV news, I saw exciting replays from today's football game.* –*verb* **to replay.**

**reply** /rə'plaɪ/ *verb* **replied, replying, replies**
to answer something: *He replied to my letter that I sent last month.*
**reply** *noun, plural* **replies**
an answer, response: *I received his reply yesterday.*

**report** /rəˈpɔrt/ *noun*
a written or spoken statement about something: *He wrote a five-page report about the new computer system.*

**report** *verb*
**1** to describe something, tell about something (event, need, etc.): *The news program reported that an accident happened on Main Street.*
**2** to work for someone: *She reports directly to the company's president.* –*adverb* **reportedly.**

**report card** *noun*
a listing of a student's grades or scores at a school: *She received straight A's on her report card from high school.*

**reporter**
/rəˈpɔrtər/ *noun*
a person who reports on events, such as for a newspaper, magazine, radio, or television station: *She is a reporter who writes about city news for the local newspaper. See:* journalist.

**reporter**

**represent** /ˌrɛprəˈzɛnt/ *verb*
**1** to show, give a picture or symbol of something: *The Statue of Liberty represents the freedom immigrants want to find in America.*
**2** to be an example of: *This plant represents a rare kind of flower.* –*noun* **representation.**

**representative** /ˌrɛprəˈzɛntətɪv/ *noun*
**1** a person who represents someone or something: *She is a sales representative for a large company.*
**2** a member of the US House of Representatives: *We will elect a new representative in the next election.*

**reproduction** /ˌriprəˈdʌkʃən/ *noun*
**1** a copy of something: *That painting is a reproduction of one by a famous artist.*
**2** (in biology) production of babies –*verb* **to reproduce.**

**reptile** /ˈrɛpˌtaɪl/ *noun*
a group of cold-blooded animals that have backbones, live on land, and usually reproduce by laying eggs: *Snakes, lizards, turtles, and crocodiles are reptiles.*

**republic** /rəˈpʌblɪk/ *noun*
a form of government in which citizens vote for people to represent them and to make laws: *Long ago, the USA was a republic in which only men who owned property could vote.* –*adjective* **republican;** –*noun* **republicanism.**

**Republican** /rəˈpʌblɪkən/ *noun*
one of two major political parties in the USA: *Every four years, the Republicans choose a candidate to run for the presidency.*

**Republican** *adjective*
of the Republican party: *She is a Republican governor. See:* Democratic Party, USAGE NOTE.

**USAGE NOTE:** The US political system is basically a two-party system; most elected officials belong to either the *Republican* or *Democratic* party. *See:* liberal, USAGE NOTE.

**reputation** /ˌrɛpyəˈteɪʃən/ *noun*
an opinion about the quality of something, such as a person's character: *He has the reputation of being a smart businessperson.*

**request** /rəˈkwɛst/ *verb*
to ask for something: *Our teacher requested that the class be quiet.*

**request** *noun*
an asking for something: *The students couldn't hear the teacher's request because they were making too much noise.*

**require** /rəˈkwaɪr/ *verb* **required, requiring, requires**
to need: *This radio requires two batteries.*

**requirement** /rəˈkwaɪrmənt/ *noun*
a necessity, something needed: *A high school degree is a requirement for this job.*
**to meet the requirements:** to have or do what is necessary: *She meets the requirements for graduation from high school.*

**rerun** /ˈriˌrʌn/ *noun*
repeat of a TV program: *Late at night, he watches reruns of old comedy shows.* –*verb* **to rerun.**

R

**rescue** /'rɛskyu/ *verb* **rescued, rescuing, rescues**
to save from danger: *Firefighters rescued people from the burning building.*
**rescue** *noun*
an act of saving someone: *The newspaper had a story about the rescue.* *–noun* (person) **rescuer.**

**research** /rə'sɜrtʃ/ *verb* **researches**
to study something deeply: *He researched many books in the library for his term paper.*
**research** *noun, (no plural)*
a study of information about something: *She did research in a chemical laboratory.* *–noun* (person) **researcher.**

**resent** /rɪ'zɛnt/ *verb*
to feel anger at something, feel hurt about something: *I resent the unkind things he said about me.* *–adjective* **resentful;** *–noun* **resentment.**

**reservation** /ˌrɛzər'veɪʃən/ *noun*
**1** a place saved in a hotel, on an airplane, etc.: *He has a reservation for three nights at the hotel.*
**2** special land in North America for tribes of Native Americans to live on: *We visited a Native American reservation in Arizona.*

**reserve** /rə'zɜrv/ *verb* **reserved, reserving, reserves**
to save a place in a hotel room, on an airplane, etc.: *He reserved a room for three nights in the hotel.*
**reserve** *noun*
land kept for a special purpose: *You can sometimes see wild animals at that nature reserve.*
**in reserve:** to keep something for later use: *I keep a small radio in reserve, so I can listen to music if my stereo system breaks.*

**reserved** /rə'zɜrvd/ *adjective*
set aside for use by someone: *That seat in the theater is reserved for Mr. Jones.*

**reservoir** /'rɛzərˌvwɑr/ *noun*
a body of water saved for use: *This lake is the reservoir of drinking water for the city.*

**resident** /'rɛzədənt/ *noun*
a person who lives in a certain area: *She is a resident of San Francisco.* *–noun* (place to live) **residence;** *–adjective* **residential.**

**resign** /rə'zaɪn/ *verb*
to choose to leave one's job: *She resigned from her job because she wanted to travel.* *–adjective* **resigned.**

**resignation** /ˌrɛzɪg'neɪʃən/ *noun*
an act of choosing to leave one's job: *He handed in his resignation as office manager.*

**resist** /rə'zɪst/ *verb*
**1** not to allow something to touch or hurt: *She resisted his kisses.*||*Stainless steel resists rust.*
**2** to oppose, be against
**3** not to do something that you want to: *He resisted eating the chocolate cake because it is too fattening.* *–noun* (person) **resister, resistance.**

**resolution** /ˌrɛzə'luʃən/ *noun*
a solution to a problem: *Politicians tried to find a resolution to the problems between their countries.*
**New Year's resolution:** a promise to change something about one's behavior, a decision made on the first day of the new year: *I made a New Year's resolution to exercise each day.* *–verb* **to resolve.**

**resort** /rə'zɔrt/ *noun*
a hotel with sports areas (swimming pool, tennis courts, etc.) for rest and relaxation: *We went to a resort in Arizona for our vacation.*
**as a last resort:** the last choice for a way of doing something: *If I can't fly to Chicago, I can drive there as a last resort.*

**resource** /'riˌsɔrs/ *noun*
a useful way to find something, especially information: *The library is an important resource for learning.*
**resources** *noun plural*
**1** money, funds: *She has the resources to buy a vacation home.*
**2** useful things in general: *Our country is rich in natural resources, such as oil, gold, and farm land.*

**respect** /rə'spɛkt/ *noun*
**1** approval and honor for a person or thing: *I have respect for his high intelligence.*
**2** thoughtful concern about the importance of something: *He has no respect for my rights!*
**respect** *verb*
to have a high opinion of: *I respect her hard work and good ideas. (antonym)* to disrespect.

**respectable** /rə'spɛktəbəl/ *adjective*
**1** having a good place in society: *They are respectable people who are liked and trusted in their town.*
**2** clean and well-dressed: *He shaved and put on clean clothes to look respectable for his guests. –adverb* **respectably;** *–noun* **respectability.**

**respectful** /rə'spɛktfəl/ *adjective*
having politeness toward someone: *Students and teachers should have a respectful attitude toward each other. –adverb* **respectfully.**

**respond** /rɪ'spɑnd/ *verb*
**1** *formal* to answer, reply: *The company responded to my order by sending it quickly.*
**2** to react: *He responded to her gift by kissing her hand.*

**response** /rə'spɑns/ *noun*
**1** an answer, reply: *My friend sent a response to my letter.*
**2** a reaction to something: *He tried to kiss her, but her response was to slap his face.*

**responsibility** /rə,spɑnsə'bɪləti/ *noun, plural* **responsibilities**
something that someone must do because of moral or legal necessity, or because of a job, *(synonym)* duty

**responsible** /rə'spɑnsəbəl/ *adjective*
**1** required to do something: *He is responsible for taking care of his younger brother while his parents are away.*
**2** trusted to do something: *She is very responsible and is always on time.*
**3** at fault, guilty: *He had to pay to repair both cars, because he was responsible for the accident. –adverb* **responsibly.**

**rest (1)** /rɛst/ *verb*
**1** to relax, stop work: *A worker stopped working and rested for five minutes.*
**2** to take time to become healthy after an illness: *She rested for two weeks after being in the hospital.*
**rest** *noun*
**1** a pause from work: *The workers get a rest at lunch time.*
**2** a time for recovering from an illness: *After his operation, he needed some rest in bed.*
**3** sleep: *She had a good night's rest. –adjective* **restful.**

**rest (2)** *noun, (no plural)*
the part of something that is left: *It's noon now, and I am going to take the rest of the day off.*||*She had some cake and I ate the rest.*

**restaurant** /'rɛstərənt/ *noun*
a business that serves food: *It is expensive to eat at fine restaurants.* *See:* café, USAGE NOTE; art on page 4a.

**restaurant**

**restless** /'rɛstlɪs/ *adjective*
wanting a change: *She is restless in her present job and wants a new one.*||*Children are restless and want to run and play.*

**restore** /rə'stɔr/ *verb* **restored, restoring, restores**
to make something look like it did when it was new: *We want to buy an old house and live there while we restore it. –noun* (person) **restorer.**

**restrain** /rɪ'streɪn/ *verb*
to stop from doing something: *She restrains her dog by holding on to its collar. –noun* **restraint.**

**restrict** /rɪ'strɪkt/ *verb*
**1** to limit: *Restaurants restrict the use of their toilets to customers only.*
**2** to punish by limiting freedom: *The sol-*

*dier was restricted to his room because he didn't follow orders.*

**restriction** /rɪ'strɪkʃən/ *noun*
a rule that limits something: *Restrictions don't allow workers to use company cars for personal use.* –*adjective* **restrictive.**

**rest room** *noun*
a washroom, toilet, bathroom: *He used the rest room at the store.*

---

USAGE NOTE: Compare *rest room* and *bathroom.* People commonly refer to a public toilet and washroom as a *rest room. Bathroom* refers to the room in a home where the toilet and bath are located.

---

**result** /rə'zʌlt/ *noun*
an effect, something that happens because of an action: *The results of the election surprised everyone.*
**to get results:** to make good things happen: *The hard work he put into his job search got results, and he has a new, interesting job.*

**result** *verb*
to cause a result, happen: *When the weather is hot, heavy rains can result.*

**resume** /rɪ'zum/ *verb* **resumed, resuming, resumes**
to begin again, restart: *The TV show will resume after this commercial.*

**résumé** /'rɛzə,meɪ/ *noun*
a short statement of one's work history and education used to get a new job: *He wrote a two-page résumé for a job interview.*

**retail** /'ri,teɪl/ *verb*
to sell products or services directly to people and not to stores: *That store retails computers and office supplies.* –*noun* (store) **retailer.**

**retina** /'rɛtnə/ *noun*
the inner lining of the eye that contains many light-sensitive cells and sends messages about light and color to the brain

**retire** /rə'taɪr/ *verb* **retired, retiring, retires**
to leave the work force and stop working: *At age 70, he retired and moved to Florida.* –*noun* (person) **retiree.**

**retirement** /rə'taɪrmənt/ *noun*
an act of leaving or the time after one leaves the workforce: *He took early retirement and moved south.*

**retreat** /rɪ'trit/ *verb*
to move away from something, such as soldiers who move away from the enemy: *The enemy was shooting heavily, so the army had to retreat to safety.* –*noun* **retreat.**

**return** /rɪ'tɜrn/ *verb*
**1** to come back, as from a trip: *He returned to his office after lunch.*
**2** to give something back: *She returned an umbrella she had borrowed.*

**return** *noun*
**1** a coming or bringing back: *We were surprised by his sudden return from vacation.*
**2** a tax return, official government form for filing taxes: *His accountant filed his tax return for this year.*
**returns:** *noun plural* election results: *The election returns showed that the mayor was reelected.*

**return** *adjective*
answered quickly: *He sent an answer to my letter by return mail.*

**returnable** /rə'tɜrnəbəl/ *adjective*
related to a purchased item that a buyer may return to get money back or something better: *That sweater is returnable if it doesn't fit you.*

**reunion** /ri'yunyən/ *noun*
a time when people who have something in common (college, family) get together: *My grandmother was the oldest person at our family reunion.* –*verb* **to reunite.**

**reupholster** /,riə'poʊlstər/ *verb*
to put new material on furniture: *A worker reupholstered my sofa with new fabric.* –*noun* **reupholstery.** *See:* recover.

**Rev.** /'rɛvərənd/
*abbreviation of* Reverend: *Rev. Allen is the minister at that church.*

**reveal** /rə'vil/ *verb*
to uncover something hidden: *He re-*

*vealed his secrets to his friend.* –*noun* **revelation.** *(antonym)* to hide.

**revealing** /rə'vilɪŋ/ *adjective*
showing something hidden: *A revealing story explained all about the lies a politician told about her life.*

**revenge** /rə'vɛndʒ/ *noun, (no plural)*
a desire or an act to hurt someone in repayment for a wrong: *When his partner cheated him, he wanted revenge, so he had him put in jail.* –*verb* **to revenge.**

**revenue** /'rɛvə,nu/ *noun*
incoming monies, such as tax payments for the government: *The government has a huge need for tax revenue.*

**Reverend** /'rɛvərənd/ *noun*
**1** a minister
**2** a title of address for a minister: *Our minister is the Reverend Robert Smith. abbreviation* **Rev.**

**reverse** /rə'vɜrs/ *noun, (no plural)*
a backwards direction: *He put the car in reverse and backed up.*

**review** /rə'vyu/ *verb*
**1** to look something over again: *I reviewed the information you gave me.*
**2** to write about the good and bad points of an artistic work: *A critic reviewed the new Broadway play and wrote good things about it.*

**review** *noun*
**1** an article about the good and bad points of an artistic work: *A good review of the new play was in today's newspaper.*
**2** a repeat of something: *Our teacher did a review of last week's lesson before we took the test.* –*noun* (person) **reviewer.**

**revise** /rə'vaɪz/ *verb* **revised, revising, revises**
to read carefully to correct something, especially a written work: *The author revised her book several times before publishing it.*

**revision** /rə'vɪʒən/ *noun*
the process of improving something written: *In English class, we talked about how revision can help us improve our writing.*

**revive** /rə'vaɪv/ *verb* **revived, reviving, revives**
to reawaken, return someone to consciousness: *A doctor revived a man who had lost consciousness.*

**revolt** /rə'voʊlt/ *verb*
**1** to fight against a government or other power: *The unemployed people revolted against the government.*
**2** to make someone angry or sick: *His bad behavior and dirty clothes revolted everyone near him.*

**revolt** *noun*
a fight against authority: *Workers led a revolt against the rich and powerful.*

**revolution** /,rɛvə'luʃən/ *noun*
**1** a big change, sometimes caused by force or war, especially in a government, economy, or field of study: *The industrial revolution changed how people worked and lived.* –*noun* (person) **revolutionary.**
**2** a complete turn or circle made by something: *The large hand on a clock makes one revolution each hour.* –*verb* **to revolve.**

**revolutionize** /,rɛvə'luʃə,naɪz/ *verb* **revolutionized, revolutionizing, revolutionizes**
to change completely, cause a new way of doing something: *Discovery of electricity revolutionized the way people live.*

**revolver** /rɪ'vɑlvər/ *noun*
a handheld gun (a type of pistol with a revolving cylinder to hold bullets): *A thief used a revolver to steal money from a store.*

**reward** /rə'wɔrd/ *noun*
**1** an award, something pleasant for something well done: *She gave herself the reward of a vacation after working hard all year.*
**2** money paid for the capture of a criminal –*adjective* **rewarding;** –*verb* **to reward.**

**rewind** /ri'waɪnd/ *verb* **rewound** /'waʊnd/, **rewinding, rewinds**
to wind again: *We have to rewind the video before we take it back to the store.*

**rewrite** /ri'raɪt/ *verb* **rewrote** /-'roʊt/, **rewriting, rewrites**
to change the wording of something: *The student rewrote his paper after the teacher corrected it.* –*noun* **rewrite.**

R

**rheumatism** /ˈruməˌtɪzəm/ *noun, (no plural)*
pain or swelling of the body's joints, such as of the hands and knees: *Her rheumatism is bothering her today.*

**rhinoceros** /raɪˈnɑsərəs/ *noun, plural* **rhinoceroses**
a very large animal of Africa, India, and Southeast Asia with one or two horns on its nose: *The rhinoceros is often hunted for its horns.*

**rhyme** /raɪm/ *noun*
words that sound alike: *"Rhyme" and "time" form a rhyme. –verb* **to rhyme.**

**rhythm** /ˈrɪðəm/ *noun*
a regular beat, especially in music or movement: *When people dance, they move to the rhythm of the music. –adjective* **rhythmic.**

**rib** /rɪb/ *noun*
any of the many curved bones in the front of the chest that form the rib cage: *He fell and broke a rib.*

**ribbon** /ˈrɪbən/ *noun*
**1** a thin, colorful strip of material often used to tie things up: *He tied the gift for his wife with a bright red ribbon.*

ribbon

**2** a piece of ribbon given as a prize or award: *The horse won a blue ribbon for first prize.*

**rib cage** *noun*
the area of the upper body formed by the ribs

**rice** /raɪs/ *noun, (no plural)*
a grain of the cereal grass family that is used for food and grows in watery areas: *Records show that people grew rice over 4,000 years ago in China. See:* art on page 17a.

**rich** /rɪʧ/ *adjective*
having a lot of money, property, etc., (synonym) wealthy: *Rich people usually live in big houses. –noun* (condition) **richness;** *–adverb* **richly.**
**the rich:** *noun plural* rich people as a group: *The rich are often powerful because of their money. (antonym)* poor.

**rid** /rɪd/ *verb* **rid** or **ridded, ridding, rids**
to free: *She rid herself of bad habits, like smoking cigarettes.*
**to get rid of something** or **someone**: to free oneself of, throw away: *She got rid of her old clothes by giving them to the poor.*

**riddle** /ˈrɪdl/ *noun*
a puzzle, question that requires cleverness to answer: *I have a riddle for you. "What is white and black and read all over? Answer? A newspaper!"*

**ride** /raɪd/ *verb* **rode** /roʊd/, **ridden** /ˈrɪdn/, **riding, rides**
**1** to be carried in or on a vehicle such as a car, truck, bus, or bicycle: *He rides to work with a friend each day.*
**2** to be carried by a horse or other animal: *She rides her horse on weekends.*

**ride** *noun*
**1** a trip, such as in a vehicle or on a horse: *I take a ride to work with a friend each day.*
**2** a vehicle or horse: *I meet my ride at the corner each morning. –noun* (person) **rider.**

**ridge** /rɪʤ/ *noun*
any long, narrow, high piece of land: *You could see a deer standing on top of a ridge.*

**ridicule** /ˈrɪdəˌkyul/ *noun, (no plural)*
criticism: *The mayor received a lot of ridicule after she delivered an unpopular speech. –verb* **to ridicule.**

**ridiculous** /rɪˈdɪkyələs/ *adjective*
stupid, foolish: *He often has ridiculous ideas. –adverb* **ridiculously.**

**riding** /ˈraɪdɪŋ/ *adjective*
*and present participle of* ride, sitting in or on something moving: *He is riding in a car.*

**rifle** /ˈraɪfəl/ *noun*
a type of gun with a long barrel held up to the shoulder to shoot it: *Soldiers carry rifles into battle.*

**rig** /rɪg/ *verb* **rigged, rigging, rigs**
to cheat: *A politician rigged the election by having votes of dead people counted for him. –noun* (truck) **rig.**

**right** /raɪt/ *adjective*
**1** referring to the direction to the east

when facing north: *I walked to the corner and made a right turn.*
**2** correct, accurate, exact: *I made the right decision.*
**3** politically conservative: *He voted for a candidate with a political view to the right.*

**right** *noun*
**1** permission to do something guaranteed by law: *We have the right to free speech in this country.*
**2** morally correct behavior, good conduct: *He knows right from wrong even though he's only five years old.*
**3** ownership, an interest in something: *Authors have rights in the sales of their works.*
**4** a conservative political party or wing: *He belongs to the political right.*
**5** the direction or side of the body which is to the east when facing north: *Her son stood on her right.*

**right** *adverb*
**1** correctly, in the proper way: *He did the job right the first time. (antonym)* wrong.
**2** in a direction to the right: *She drove to the corner and turned right.*

**right away:** without waiting, immediately: *I will do the job right away; you can count on me.*

**right off** or **right off the bat**: immediately, without having to think: *I don't remember his name right off the bat, but it will come to me soon.*

**right angle** *noun*
a 90-degree angle: *A square has four right angles.*

**rightful** /ˈraɪtfʊl/ *adjective*
having a fair or legal claim to something: *As his father's only relative, he has a rightful claim to his dead father's property.* –*adverb* **rightfully.**

**right-handed** *adjective*
using the right hand most of the time: *She is right-handed and uses right-handed scissors.*

**rigid** /ˈrɪʤɪd/ *adjective*
firm, difficult to bend: *I need a rigid box that won't break when it is full of heavy books.* –*noun* **rigidity;** –*adverb* **rigidly.** *(antonym)* flexible.

**rigorous** /ˈrɪgərəs/ *adjective*
having strict or high standards: *Students must finish rigorous programs of study for many years to become doctors.* –*adverb* **rigorously.**

**rim** /rɪm/ *noun*
the outside edge or border of something (usually round): *A spoon rested against the rim of the bowl.* –*verb* **to rim.**

**rind** /raɪnd/ *noun*
the outer covering of sausages and fruits, such as oranges, watermelon, etc.: *I peeled off the rind and ate the orange.*

rind

**ring (1)** /rɪŋ/
*verb* **rang** /ræŋ/, **rung** /rʌŋ/, **ringing, rings**
to cause a bell to make a sound: *Her phone rings all day long.*

**to ring a bell:** to cause someone to remember or recall something: *John Smith? That name does not ring a bell with me.*

**ring** *noun*
**1** a sound like that of a bell: *The ring of the doorbell surprised me because it rang at midnight.*
**2** *singular* a telephone call: *I'll give you a ring this evening.*

**ring (2)** *noun*
**1** a circular metal band worn on a finger, usually made of expensive metal and often with gemstones: *She wears a diamond ring on her finger.*

ring

**2** any circular band of metal, plastic, or other material: *Doughnuts are shaped like rings.*
**3** a circular group of something: *A ring of people listened to a man play guitar in the park.*
**4** a group of criminals: *The police found out where five members of the drug ring live.*

**ring** *verb*
to make a ringing sound: *My telephone rings all day long.*

**rink** /rɪŋk/ *noun*
a place for roller-skating or ice skating that has a wall or fence around it: *We went to the rink to watch the game.*

rink

**rinse** /rɪns/ *noun*
an act of splashing or soaking: *I gave the clothes a rinse in cool water.* –*verb* **to rinse.**

**riot** /ˈraɪət/ *verb*
to act as part of a group in a violent or dangerous way, especially against power: *People rioted and ran through the streets breaking windows.*

**riot** *noun*
an act of violent behavior by a large group: *The riot caused a lot of damage to the city's shopping area.*

**rip** /rɪp/ *noun*
a tear, a place where something has been pulled or cut in pieces: *A sharp tree branch made a rip in my jacket.* –*verb* **to rip.** *See:* rip-off.

rip

**ripe** /raɪp/ *adjective* **riper, ripest**
at the best time to be used or eaten, *(synonym)* mature: *Fruit and cheese taste best when they are ripe.*

**ripen** /raɪpən/ *verb*
to become ready to use or eat: *Grapes ripen in autumn.*

**rip-off** *noun slang*
an example of being cheated or stolen from: *That advertisement for land in Florida was a rip-off because the land was under water.*

**ripple** /ˈrɪpəl/ *noun*
a little wave: *There was a small ripple when I threw a stone into the water.* –*verb* **to ripple.**

**rise** /raɪz/ *verb* **rose** /ˈroʊz/, **risen** /ˈrɪzən/, **rising, rises**
to move upwards: *The sun rises in the morning.*||*Prices of food are rising.*

**rise** *noun*
**1** an elevation, raised piece of land: *We walked up on the rise.*
**2** an increase: *a rise in prices (antonym)* decline.

**risk** /rɪsk/ *verb*
to put something important in danger: *If you put money into gambling or horse races, you risk losing it.*

**risk** *noun*
a chance of losing something important: *When you buy land, you take the risk that it will lose value.*

**risky** /ˈrɪski/ *adjective* **riskier, riskiest**
dangerous, harmful: *Driving a race car is risky because you can get killed.*

**ritual** /ˈrɪʧuəl/ *noun*
a ceremony that marks a serious or sacred event: *A common ritual at a wedding is giving wedding rings.* –*noun* **ritualism.**

**rival** /ˈraɪvəl/ *noun*
someone who wants to get something and keep someone else from getting it: *Two sports teams have been rivals for years.* –*noun* **rivalry.**

**rival** *verb*
to be as good as: *No city rivals Paris.*

**river** /ˈrɪvər/ *noun*
a large body of water that moves in one direction between two river banks: *The Nile and the Mississippi are among the largest rivers in the world.*

**R.N.** /ˈɑrˈɛn/
*abbreviation of* registered nurse: *My sister is an R.N. See:* registered nurse, USAGE NOTE.

**roach** /roʊʧ/ *noun, plural* **roaches**
a cockroach, any of over 1,000 kinds of a flat-bodied insect that lives in households: *Roaches can be killed with poison.*

**road** /roʊd/ *noun*
a place where cars, trucks, and buses can

travel, especially one narrower than a street or highway: *We live on a small country road. See:* street, USAGE NOTE.

**roam** /roʊm/ *verb*
to go freely over a large area: *We roamed through the woods after we had a picnic.*

**roar** /rɔr/ *verb*
**1** to make a loud, scary sound: *Lions roar.*
**2** to laugh loudly: *He roared when he heard the joke. –noun* **roar.**

**roast** /roʊst/ *verb*
to cook at a high temperature, as in an oven: *We roasted a turkey for four hours in a 325-degree oven.*

**roast** *noun*
a piece of meat that is roasted: *I have a pork roast in the oven.*

**rob** /rɑb/ *verb* **robbed, robbing, robs**
to steal something from someone: *A thief robbed three houses on our street.*

**robber** /ˈrɑbər/ *noun*
a thief: *Robbers held up the bank.*

robber

**robbery** /ˈrɑbəri/ *noun, plural* **robberies**
an act of stealing something: *There was a bank robbery this morning.*

**robe** /roʊb/ *noun*
a type of long, outer clothing that covers a person from shoulder to foot: *Judges wear black robes over their suits.*

**robin** /ˈrɑbɪn/ *noun*
a songbird with red feathers in front and a black upper body

**robot** /ˈroʊbɑt/ *noun*
a device often with some humanlike characteristics, programmed to do different things: *Carmakers use robots to do unpleasant jobs, such as painting cars in hot conditions. –verb* **to robotize.**

**rock** /rɑk/ *noun*
stone, such as granite or limestone: *The shoreline is covered with rocks.*

**rock** *verb*
to move something back and forth gently: *A mother rocks her baby in her arms.*

**rock and roll** or **rock 'n' roll** /ˈrɑkənˈroʊl/ *noun, (no plural)*
a type of modern American popular music: *Guitars and drums are the main instruments played in rock and roll.*

**USAGE NOTE:** It is also common to shorten the words *rock and roll music* to *rock* or *rock music*. In 1995 the *Rock and Roll Hall of Fame* was opened in Cleveland, Ohio. This museum shows photographs, instruments, and other exhibitions about rock and roll music.

**rocket** /ˈrɑkɪt/ *noun*
a cigar-shaped air craft sent into the air to destroy military targets or to send vehicles into space: *A rocket lifted a telescope into place around the earth.*

rocket

**rocky** /ˈrɑki/ *adjective* **rockier, rockiest**
having many rocks in the land's surface

**rod** /rɑd/ *noun*
a narrow, round piece of material (of metal, wood, or plastic): *Long steel rods are used to strengthen concrete floors in new buildings.*

**rode** /roʊd/ *verb*
*past tense of* ride

**rodent** /ˈroʊdnt/ *noun*
a class of animals that includes rats, mice, and squirrels: *Rodents carry diseases.*

**rodeo** /ˈroʊdiˌoʊ/ *noun, plural* **rodeos**
an entertainment event with horse riding and cattle roping: *Riding bulls and wild horses are always exciting events at a rodeo.*

**role** /roʊl/ *noun*
**1** a part played by an actor or actress: *She plays the leading role in a television show.*
**2** a part or job one takes in a group: *At our meeting, I took on the role of secretary.*

**roll** /roʊl/ *noun*
**1** a round piece of bread: *He ate a ham sandwich on a roll.*

R

**2** an amount of something in roll form: *a roll of carpet||a roll of toilet paper*
**3** a list of the names of people in a group: *There are 20 students on the roll in our class.*

**roll** *verb*
to turn over and over: *The ball rolled across the football field.*
**to roll something up:** to make something flat into a long round shape: *She rolled up the window shade.*

**roller coaster** *noun*
an amusement ride in which small cars travel very fast on a curving, hilly track to excite riders

**roller coaster**

**roller skate** *noun*
wheels on boots or shoes that let a person move forward (skate) quickly: *She bought a pair of roller skates and she skates every day.* *–noun* **rollerskating.**

**Roman** /'roʊmən/ *adjective*
related to ancient or modern Rome, the Roman Empire, or its people
**Romans:** *noun plural* the Roman people

**romance** /roʊ'mæns/ *noun*
a love affair with excitement, adventure, and happiness: *Jane's and Paul's life together is full of romance.*

**Roman numeral** *noun*
any of the symbols used by the Romans to indicate numbers: *In Roman numerals, M=1,000, D=500, C=100, L=50, X=10, V=5, and I=1.*

**romantic** /roʊ'mæntɪk/ *noun*
an idealistic person who believes in the natural goodness of people: *Many young people are romantics.*
**romantic** *adjective*
related to love or romance: *They met at a very romantic place and had a picnic.* *–adverb* **romantically;** *–verb* **to romanticize.**

**roof** /ruf/ *noun*
**1** the covering on top of a building: *The roof on that old house lets water in when it rains.*
**2** the top of something: *Chewing gum sticks to the roof of his mouth.*
**to go through** or **hit the roof**: to become very angry: *He hit the roof when he heard the bad news.*

**room** /rum/ *noun*
**1** a space with its own walls, door, ceiling, and floor: *That house has ten rooms.*
**2** space, area: *The elevator is so full of people that there is no room to move.*
**room** *verb*
to live in a room as in a rooming house or dormitory: *I room in a dormitory at college.* *–noun* (person) **roomer.** *See:* roommate.

**room and board** *noun*
a place to live and food to eat: *Her parents pay the cost of her room and board at college.*

---

**USAGE NOTE:** College students in the USA usually pay three kinds of fees: *tuition* (fees for classes), *books and supplies* (required for the classes), and *room and board.* Room and board fees pay for the cost of living in a college dormitory and eating in a cafeteria: *He received a scholarship that paid for his room and board.*

---

**roommate** /'rum,meɪt/ *noun*
a person who lives with one in a room, apartment, or house: *My roommate has his own bedroom, and we share a kitchen and bathroom.*

**roomy** /'rumi/ *adjective* **roomier, roomiest**
having plenty of room: *Our house is old but roomy and comfortable. (antonym)* crowded.

R

**roost** /rust/ *noun*
a place where birds sleep or rest

**rooster** /'rustər/ *noun*
a male chicken: *Roosters usually make a lot of noise early in the morning.* *See:* art on page 14a.

**rooster**

**root** /rut/ *noun*
the part of a plant that grows down into the soil and brings

food and water into the plant: *The roots of trees grow deep into the earth.*

**square root:** (in mathematics) the number that, when multiplied by itself, equals a given number: *The square root of 9 is 3.*

**root** *verb*

**1** to grow into the ground: *The tree rooted into good soil.*

**2** to dig with one's nose: *Pigs root in the ground.*

**to root for:** to follow a player or team and want them to win: *We root for the local high school baseball team.*

**root beer** *noun, (no plural)*

a nonalcoholic drink made from the roots of some trees: *Most root beer is now made with artificial flavoring.*

**rope** /roʊp/ *noun*

a thick cord used for tying or hanging things: *She hangs her wet clothes on a rope to dry.*

rope

**to know the ropes:** to know one's job very well: *Al has worked here for 25 years, so he really knows the ropes.*

**rope** *verb* **roped, roping, ropes**

to catch cattle and horses with a rope: *Cowboys rope horses.*

**rose** /roʊz/ *noun*

**1** a bushy plant that has round, shiny leaves, thorns and large red, pink, white or yellow flowers with many petals and a beautiful smell: *He gave his wife a dozen roses for her birthday.*

**2** a light red or dark pink color: *My favorite color is rose. See:* art on page 1a.

**rosy** /ˈroʊzi/ *adjective* **rosier, rosiest**

**1** having the pinkish-red color of a rose: *Rosy cheeks are a sign of good health.*

**2** full of optimism: *She always takes a rosy view of life.*

**rot** /rɑt/ *noun, (no plural)*

a state of decay, especially caused by disease, or after death: *Rot in the tree trunk caused the tree to fall.* *–verb* **to rot.**

**rotation** /roʊˈteɪʃən/ *noun*

a movement around something: *The earth makes a complete rotation around the sun about every 365 days.* *–verb* **to rotate.**

**rote** /roʊt/ *noun, (no plural)*

learning something by memory alone: *That boy learned the alphabet by rote.*

**rotten** /ˈrɑtn/ *adjective*

referring to something that has gone bad, *(synonyms)* decayed, spoiled: *Rotten trees decay slowly and make the earth rich for new plants.*

**rouge** /ruʒ/ *noun, (no plural)*

a powder or cream, usually red or pink, used to color the cheeks: *Women put rouge on their cheeks to make their faces pretty.*

**rough** /rʌf/ *adjective*

**1** not smooth, uneven: *When wood is first cut, it feels rough.*

**2** moving in a stormy or violent way: *Strong winds cause rough seas.*

**3** done quickly: *The artist did a rough drawing before doing a painting.*

**4** close to correct but not exact: *His drawing gives you a rough idea of what the final picture will look like.*

**5** difficult and unfair: *It's rough being a single parent.* *–noun* **roughness.** *(antonym)* smooth.

**roughly** /ˈrʌfli/ *adverb*

**1** with roughness, such as pushing and punching: *The police treated a criminal roughly because he tried to run away.*

**2** about, but not exactly, *(synonym)* approximately: *The trip to Chicago takes roughly three hours by airplane.*

**round** /raʊnd/ *adjective*

circular or curved in shape: *Balls are round.*

**round** *noun*

**1** a group of things: *He bought a round of drinks for everyone.*

**2** a period of time in a boxing match: *Boxers fight for 12 rounds.*

**3** bullets for guns: *He fired 12 rounds at the target.*

**rounds:** *used in the plural* a series of stops or a regular walk, such as that taken by a security guard, police officer, or doctor: *Every hour, the guard makes his rounds of the office building.*

**round trip** *adjective*

of a journey that starts and ends in the same place: *I bought a round-trip ticket to San Diego.*

**route** /raʊt/ *noun*
**1** a path along which one travels: *The airline route from Seattle to Tokyo goes over the North Pole.*
**2** a series of stops made regularly: *The newspaper delivery truck has a regular route for dropping off newspapers.*

**routine** /ru'tin/ *noun*
a series of things someone does regularly: *He has a different routine on Saturday and Sunday than he does on weekdays.*

**routine** *adjective*
normal, not unusual in any way: *My doctor wants to do some routine blood tests.* *–adverb* **routinely.**

**row (1)** /roʊ/ *noun*
**1** a line of things, people, pictures, etc., placed side by side: *A row of trees lines the street.*
**2** a line of seating as in a theater: *We watched the play from the eighth row.*

**row (2)** /roʊ/ *verb*
to move a boat in the water using oars: *He rowed his boat across the pond.* *–noun* **row.**

**rowboat** /'roʊˌboʊt/ *noun*
a small boat moved by people pulling oars: *He uses a rowboat to go fishing on the lake.*

**rowdy** /'raʊdi/ *adjective* **rowdier, rowdiest**
loud, difficult to control or make quiet: *A rowdy group of boys ran through the streets.* *–noun* **rowdiness.**

**royal** /'rɔɪəl/ *adjective*
related to a king or queen: *The royal family lives in a large castle.* *–adverb* **royally.**

**royalty** /'rɔɪəlti/ *noun, (no plural)*
**1** a king or queen and family
**2** kings, queens, princes, and princesses, and nobility in general: *Royalty from all over the world came to see the princess become queen.*

---

**USAGE NOTE:** *Royalty* is used only in the singular, whether for one person, such as a King or Queen, or for a group, as in sense 2 above.

---

**rub** /rʌb/ *verb* **rubbed, rubbing, rubs**
to touch something while moving backwards and forwards: *A mother rubbed her child's back.*

**rubber** /'rʌbər/ *noun, (no plural)*
a natural substance that bends easily, made from a white liquid that comes from rubber trees or from chemicals (artificial rubber): *Tires for trucks, cars, and bicycles are made of rubber.* *–adjective* **rubbery.**

rubber band

**rubber band** *noun*
a circular piece of rubber that can stretch around things to hold them together: *She put a rubber band around her pencils so they wouldn't get lost.*

**rubbish** /'rʌbɪʃ/ *noun, (no plural)*
trash; unwanted, broken, or dirty things: *I put the rubbish in a plastic bag and threw it away.*

**ruby** /'rubi/ *noun, plural* **rubies**
a precious red gemstone: *She loves to wear rubies.*

**ruby** *adjective*
a deep reddish color: *She has ruby lips.*

**rudder** /'rʌdər/ *noun*
something flat and moveable used to steer a boat: *A sailor uses the rudder to make the ship go in the correct direction.*

**rude** /rud/ *adjective* **ruder, rudest**
impolite, making people angry by one's bad behavior or unkind words: *It was rude to walk away while that customer was talking to you.* *–adverb* **rudely;** *–noun* **rudeness.**

**rug** /rʌg/ *noun*
a heavy fabric floor covering: *They have a beautiful rug on their floor. See:* art on page 6a.

**ruin** /'ruɪn/ *verb*
**1** to damage something: *She spilled coffee on her white silk dress and ruined it.*
**2** to spoil something, to take the fun or usefulness out of something, especially an event: *His stupid behavior ruined our party.*

**3** to cause someone to lose all of his or her money: *Losses in gambling ruined him, so he has no money.*

**ruin** *noun*
**1** a state of destruction: *After the fire, the museum lay in ruins.*
**2** broken parts of buildings that still exist after thousands of years: *We went to Greece to see the ruins of ancient temples.* –*adjective* **ruinous.**

**rule** /rul/ *noun*
a statement about what must or should be done: *Our school has a rule that students must not eat or drink in class.*

**rule** *verb* **ruled, ruling, rules**
**1** to govern, usually as a king or dictator: *Emperors ruled ancient Rome.*
**2** to decide officially, say what will be done: *The court ruled that the woman was guilty.*

**ruler** /'rulər/ *noun*
**1** a person, such as a king or queen, who guides or controls a country: *The rulers of England governed for hundreds of years.*
**2** a measuring stick: *I use a short ruler to draw straight lines. See:* art on page 8a.

ruler

**rum** /rʌm/ *noun, (no plural)*
a strong alcoholic drink made from sugar cane: *Puerto Rico is famous for its light and dark rum.*

**rumble** /'rʌmbəl/ *noun*
a low, powerful noise: *You can hear the rumble of a railroad train as it goes through a tunnel.* –*verb* **to rumble.**

**rumor** /'rumər/ *noun*
gossip, talk that comes from what other people say and not from true information or personal knowledge: *There is a false rumor going around that the water supply is unsafe.* –*verb* **to rumor.**

**run** /rʌn/ *verb* **ran** /ræn/, **run, running, runs**
**1** to move the legs and feet quickly across the ground: *Every morning, he runs around the high school track.*
**2** to race on foot: *The track star ran the 100 meters in record time.*
**3** to leave quickly: *I have to run now; I'm late for a meeting.*
**4** to do some job or task: *She runs errands, like taking her daughter to dance class on Saturday morning.*
**5** to try to get elected to political office: *She ran for the Senate and won.*
**6** to direct and make decisions about something, *(synonym)* manage: *She runs her own business.*
**7** to work or function in a certain way: *That engine runs smoothly.*
**8** to flow, move as water does: *Mountain streams run to the ocean.* **to run after someone** or **something:** to chase: *She ran after the bus, yelling for it to stop.*

**to run around: a.** to go to many places: *I had to run around today to do shopping.* **b.** to spend time with someone: *He's been running around with my cousin.*

**to run around like a chicken with its head cut off:** to hurry in a confused, worried way: *He ran around like a chicken with its head cut off, looking for someone who could repair his computer.*

**to run away:** to get away from quickly, *(synonym)* to escape: *Deer run away from hunters.*

**to run someone** or **something down: a.** to hit someone as with a car or truck: *A man was run down by a speeding car as he crossed the street.* **b.** to lose energy, stop functioning: *The batteries in my radio have run down; I need new ones.*

**to run into someone** or **something**: **a.** to meet someone by chance: *I ran into an old friend at the airport in Seattle.* **b.** to hit someone or something: *The two boys ran into each other when playing football.*

**to run low:** to use almost all of something: *My car is running low on gasoline.*

**to run off: a.** to do something without thinking about others, leave without having the right to do so: *A man ran off and left his wife and children.* **b.** to make copies of something: *She ran off ten copies of the story she wrote.*

**to run up against a stone wall:** to meet a problem that will not move, be blocked: *When I talked with him about our plans, I ran up against a stone wall because he just will not agree to work together with us.*

**run** *noun*

**1** an exercise period, like jogging: *She goes for a five-mile run in the park every morning.*

**2** moving one's feet faster than a walk, the motions of running: *Our dog broke into a run as he came up to us.*

**3** a hole or separation, as in pantyhose: *She has a run in her pantyhose.*

**in the long run:** from now far into the future: *Losing weight now is difficult, but you will feel better in the long run if you lose it.*

**to make a run for it:** to go quickly to get to safety: *The ceiling started to fall down in the old building, and the workers had to make a run for it. See:* walk, USAGE NOTE; art on page 24a.

**run-down** *adjective*

in poor condition, needing to be fixed: *That old house is run-down and needs repairs and painting.*

**rung (1)** /rʌŋ/ *noun*

a step on a ladder: *To be safe, you should go up a ladder one rung at a time.*

**rung (2)** *verbpast participle of*

ring: *The telephone had rung three times when I picked it up.*

**runner** /ˈrʌnər/ *noun*

a person who runs for fun or competitively: *She is a long-distance runner, and she likes to run marathons.*

**running** /ˈrʌnɪŋ/ *noun, (no plural)*

an act of moving the legs and feet quickly: *She likes to go running every morning.*

**running** *adjective*

moving like water moves, *(synonyms)* flowing, pouring: *That old house has running water in the kitchen and the bathroom.*

**runway** /ˈrʌn,weɪ/ *noun*

a place where airplanes take off and land: *A jet plane taxied down the runway and took off.*

**rupture** /ˈrʌptʃər/ *verb* **ruptured, rupturing, ruptures**

to burst or break open so that something comes out of its closed container: *A water pipe ruptured and flooded the street for nearly half a mile.* *–noun* (a break) **rupture.**

**rural** /ˈrʊrəl/ *adjective*

related to the countryside, not the city: *They live on a farm in a rural area of Montana.*

**rush** /rʌʃ/ *verb* **rushes**

to move about doing things quickly: *She rushed to get ready for an evening at the theater.*

**to rush in/into something:** **a.** to enter a place quickly, run into: *Firefighters rushed into the building to save people from the fire.* **b.** to make a decision too quickly, without thinking: *I don't think that you should rush into getting married so young.*

**rush** *noun*

**1** a hurry, the act of doing things quickly: *There is always a rush in the stores at holiday time.*

**2** to be in a rush: to hurry, do everything quickly: *She is always in a rush to go someplace.*

**rush hour** *noun*

a time when traffic is very heavy, especially when people are going to and from work: *Try not to drive between 4:00 and 6:00 P.M. because that's rush hour in this city.*

**rust** /rʌst/ *noun, (no plural)*

the reddish-brown material that forms on metal when oxygen reacts with it: *My car is very old so rust has made holes in the fenders and the floor.* *–verb* **to rust.**

**rusty** /ˈrʌsti/ *adjective* **rustier, rustiest**

**1** having rust, covered with rust: *My car is rusty and needs to be cleaned and painted.*

**2** *figurative* (usually of a skill) not as good as before: *His French is rusty because he hasn't spoken it for years.*

**rut** /rʌt/ *noun*

a deep mark or long hole made by

wheels in a road: *Ruts in the dirt road make it difficult to drive on.*

**to get into a rut:** to do the same boring things over and over: *I need a new job because I feel like I've gotten into a rut.* –*verb* **to rut.**

**ruthless** /'ruθlɪs/ *adjective*
without pity, not thinking about the feelings or health of other people: *He is a ruthless businessman who thinks money is more important than people.* –*noun* **ruthlessness.** *(antonym)* kind.

**Rx** /'ɑr'ɛks/ *noun*
*abbreviation of* prescription or remedy, medicine: *My doctor gave me an Rx for my high blood pressure.*

**rye** /raɪ/ *noun, (no plural)*
a cereal grain used to make flour and whiskey and to feed animals

# S,s

**S,s** /ɛs/ *noun* **S's, s's** or **Ss, ss**
the 19th letter of the English alphabet

**Sabbath** /ˈsæbəθ/ *noun*
the last day of the week, the day of rest and worship: *Christians observe the Sabbath on Sunday.*

**sack** /sæk/ *noun*
a bag made of cloth or paper: *The farmers put wheat into the big, brown sacks.* –*verb* **to sack.**

**sacred** /ˈseɪkrɪd/ *adjective*
holy: *For religious people, a wedding ceremony is sacred.*

**sacrifice** /ˈsækrəˌfaɪs/ *noun*
**1** loss, or giving up of something valuable, for a purpose: *The parents made many sacrifices, such as wearing old clothes, to pay for their children's education.*
**2** an offering to a god

**sacrifice** *verb* **sacrificed, sacrificing, sacrifices**
to suffer loss, pain, or injury to achieve a goal: *The father worked hard and made a lot of money, but he sacrificed his health.* –*adjective* **sacrificial** /ˌsækrəˈfɪʃəl/.

**sad** /sæd/ *adjective* **sadder, saddest**
full of sorrow, unhappy: *After her mother's death, she was sad for weeks.* –*adverb* **sadly;** –*noun* **sadness.** *(antonym)* happy.

**sadden** /ˈsædn/ *verb*
to make unhappy: *I was saddened by my father's death.*

**saddle** /ˈsædl/ *noun*
the leather seat used for riding animals –*verb* **to saddle.**

saddle

**safe** /seɪf/ *noun*
a strong metal box, with a lock, for protecting money and valuables: *She has a safe in her closet where she keeps her diamond ring.*

**safe** *adjective* **safer, safest**
protected: *She likes to feel safe, she does not go outside at night.*

**safety** /ˈseɪfti/ *noun*
the condition of being free or protected from harm: *When the floods came, the farmers moved to the safety of high ground. (antonym)* danger.

**safety belt** *noun*
a long, thin piece of material that holds and protects a person in a car (truck, airplane, etc.): *I was wearing my safety belt when we got into the accident, so I was not hurt when the car crashed. See:* seat belt, USAGE NOTE.

**safety pin** *noun*
a small piece of metal used to bring two pieces of cloth together: *Do you have a safety pin? The zipper on my pants is broken.*

safety pin

**sag** /sæg/ *verb*
to bend or sink from weight or pressure: *The tent sagged under the weight of the wet snow.*

**said** /sɛd/ *verb*
*past participle of* say: *He said that the meeting is today.*

**sail** /seɪl/ *noun*
the strong cloth that helps a boat move with the wind: *The sails on the ship were not moving; there was no wind.*

**sail** *verb*
to travel by boat: *We sailed across the lake and back. –noun* **sailing.**

**sailboat** /ˈseɪlˌb oʊt/ *noun*
a boat with one or more sails: *Our sailboat is small but moves fast on the pond.*

**sailor** /ˈseɪlər/ *noun*
a person who works on a ship: *The sailors learned how to tie ropes and use the sails.*

**saint** /seɪnt/ *noun*
**1** (in Christianity) a person chosen by God
**2** a good and kind person: *You were a saint to give money to the hungry child. –noun* **sainthood;** *–adjective* **saintly.**

**sake** /seɪk/ *noun*
**1** peace of mind, good: *For your brother's sake, don't be late to his wedding.*
**2** purpose: *For the sake of discussion, let's say the building will cost $1 million to build.*

**salad** /ˈsæləd/ *noun*
a mixture of cold vegetables, fruit, or other foods: *I made a salad of lettuce and tomatoes. See:* art on page 5a.

S

**salary** /ˈsæləri/ *noun, plural* **salaries**
a regular payment from a business or organization for work done: *My salary increases five percent this year. See:* wage, USAGE NOTE.

**sale** /seɪl/ *noun*
**1** the exchange of something for money: *the sale of a shirt (car, house, etc.)*
**2** the selling of things at a lower price than usual: *The pet store is having a sale on dog food.*
**for sale:** available for purchase: *We don't want our car anymore; it is for sale.*
**on sale:** available for a lower price than usual: *I bought this coat on sale, for $20 less than the usual price.*

**sales clerk** *noun*
a person who helps customers and sells things: *The sales clerk brought the pants to the dressing room for me to try on. See:* clerk.

**salesman** /ˈseɪlzmən/ *noun, plural* **salesmen** /-mən/
*See:* salesperson.

**salesperson** /ˈseɪlzˌpɜrsən/ *noun*
a man or woman whose job is to sell things: *My company gives a prize to the salesperson who sells the most.*

**sales representative** or **sales rep** *noun*
someone whose job is to sell goods and services, usually outside of a store: *A sales representative called and tried to sell me insurance.*

**sales tax** *noun*
a percentage added to the price of something and given to the local or state government: *In our state, we pay an eight percent sales tax on everything we buy except food.*

**saleswoman** /ˈseɪlzˌwʊmən/ *noun* **saleswomen** /-ˌwɪmən/
*See:* salesperson.

**salmon** /ˈsæmən/ *noun, (no plural)*
a fish with reddish-pink flesh: *I like to eat grilled salmon with potatoes.*

**salon** /səˈlɑn/ *noun*
a shop or place for business, usually related to fashion or beauty: *I get my hair cut at Andre's Hair Salon.*

**salt** /sɔlt/ *noun*
the chemical, sodium chloride, used to flavor food: *Would you pass the salt, please? See:* art on page 5a.
**to take something with a grain of salt:** to understand that something may not be completely true: *You told me there were 300 people at the party; I'll take that with a grain of salt. –verb* **to salt.**

**salty** /ˈsɔlti/ *adjective* **saltier, saltiest**
having the taste of salt: *This soup tastes too salty for me.*

**salute** /səˈlut/ *noun*
a hand, usually the right one, raised to

the forehead to recognize or honor someone: *Soldiers must give a salute to officers.* *–verb* **to salute.**

**same** /seɪm/ *adjective*
identical, alike, equal: *He wore the same suit today as yesterday. (antonyms)* different, unequal.

**same** *adverb*
identically, equally: *She was sick yesterday, and she feels the same today.*

**sample** /ˈsæmpəl/ *verb* **sampled, sampling, samples**
to try something: *I sampled each dessert on the menu.*

**sample** *noun*
a small amount of something to try: *The clerk gave me a sample of cheese to taste.*

**sand** /sænd/ *noun*
tiny pieces of rock, which form the surface of beaches and deserts: *At the beach, we like to dig for shells in the sand.* *–adjective* **sandy.**

**sand** *verb*
to smooth the surface of something with rough paper: *When you build a table, you should sand the wood before you paint it. See:* sandpaper.

**sandal** /ˈsændl/ *noun*
a shoe made of a flat piece with straps: *I like to wear sandals in the summer.*

**sandpaper** /ˈsænd ˌpeɪpər/ *noun*
a strong paper with a layer of sand on one side: *I used sandpaper to smooth the rough bookshelves.*

**sandwich** /ˈsændwɪtʃ/ *noun*
two pieces of bread with other foods (such as cheese, meat, or vegetables) between them: *Would you put mustard on my ham sandwich, please?*

sandwich

**sane** /seɪn/ *adjective*
mentally healthy: *Don't call me crazy; I am quite sane. (antonym)* insane.

**sanitary** /ˈs ænəˌteri/ *adjective*
**1** free from dirt and germs: *The bathroom is sanitary now; I cleaned it.*
**2** related to cleanliness and health: *We wash our hands before eating for sanitary reasons.* *–noun* **sanitation.**

**sanitize** /ˈsænəˌtaɪz/ *verb* **sanitized, sanitizing, sanitizes**
to make very clean

**sanity** /ˈsænəti/ *noun*
mental health: *He kept his sanity while he was in prison by imagining a happy, free future.*

**sank** /sæŋk/ *verb*
*past tense of* sink: *A ship sank in the storm.*

**sarcasm** /ˈsɑrˌkæzəm/ *noun, (no plural)*
an attitude or comments that hurt someone's feelings, often by saying the opposite of what is meant: *She said with sarcasm, "Oh, sure, I'd love to spend all day listening to him talk."* *–adjective* **sarcastic.**

**sardine** /sɑrˈdin/ *noun*
a small fish, usually sold packed tightly in cans

**Satan** /ˈseɪtn/ *noun*
the Devil, the enemy of God and ruler of Hell *–noun* **satanism.**

**satellite** /ˈsætl ˌaɪt/ *noun*
**1** a moon or other object in space that circles a larger object, such as a planet: *The moon we see at night is Earth's only satellite.*
**2** a human-made object that circles a larger one in space: *The satellite had a camera that took pictures of Venus and Mars.*

**satin** /ˈsætn/ *noun*
a fabric that is shiny and smooth on one side: *a dress made of satin* *–adverb* **satiny.**

**satisfaction** /ˌsætɪsˈfækʃən/ *noun*
pleasure at having enough, *(synonym)* content: *I get satisfaction from exercising every day. (antonym)* dissatisfaction.

**satisfactory** /ˌsætɪsˈfæktəri/ *adjective*
good enough, acceptable: *I would like to earn more money, but my pay is satisfactory.*||*His homework is satisfactory, so I gave him a grade of C.*

**satisfy** /ˈsætɪsˌfaɪ/ *verb* **satisfied, satisfying, satisfies**
to meet wants or needs, get enough: *She satisfied her hunger by eating a*

*steak.*||*He satisfied his curiosity by asking lots of questions.*

**Saturday** /ˈsætər,deɪ/ *noun*
the seventh day of the week, between Friday and Sunday

**sauce** /sɔs/ *noun*
a flavored liquid poured over food: *I love to eat chocolate sauce on vanilla ice cream.*

**saucer** /ˈsɔsər/ *noun*
a small plate, usually with a circular mark for holding a cup *See:* art on page 7a.

**sausage** /ˈsɔsɪʤ/ *noun*
a round section of seasoned meat: *We eat pork sausage for breakfast.*

**savage** /ˈsævɪʤ/ *noun*
a wild person: *The savages threw spears and killed their enemies.*||*The murderer is a savage who should to go jail.*

**savage** *adjective*
cruel, mean: *The enemy planned a savage attack and killed many children. (antonym)* civilized.

**save** /seɪv/ *verb* **saved, saving, saves**
**1** not to spend or use and to keep something, for the future: *I have saved all the photographs that I took when I was young.*
**2** to spend less than usual on something: *The shopper saved a lot of money by buying things on sale.*
**3** (in computers) to keep information in a file by using a "save" command: *Please save the paragraph on your screen so it will not be lost.*
**4** to prevent someone from being harmed: *The boy was drowning in the lake; a woman jumped in and saved him.*
**to save something for a rainy day:** to keep something or to save money for difficult times: *The girl wanted to spend a dollar on candy, but her uncle told her to save it for a rainy day.*

**savings** /ˈseɪvɪŋz/ *noun plural*
money saved: *I put my savings in the bank.*

**savings account** *noun*
a bank account that receives small interest payments: *I put $600 in my savings account last year and earned five percent annual interest.*

**saw (1)** /sɔ/ *verb*
to cut using a saw: *The woman sawed some wood for the fire.* –*noun* **saw.**

**saw (2)** *verb*
*past tense of* see.

**saxophone** /ˈsæksə,foʊn/ *noun*
a musical horn made of brass, with a reed in the mouthpiece, often U-shaped *See:* art on page 15a.

saxophone

**say** /seɪ/ *verb* **said** /sɛd/, **saying, says** /sɛz/
to express with words or nonverbally: *I said what I felt in a love letter.*||*Your eyes are saying you love me, too.*

**say** *noun*
an opinion to express, a vote: *I have a say in how much to spend; I think we should spend $90.*

**saying** /ˈseɪɪŋ/ *noun*
a wise thought: *There is a saying that "you can't teach an old dog new tricks."*

**scab** /skæb/ *noun*
blood that becomes hard on the skin: *I cut my knee when I fell, and now there's a scab.*

**scaffold** /ˈskæfəld/ *noun*
a temporary structure for working on a building: *The painters stood on a scaffold near the third-floor windows.*

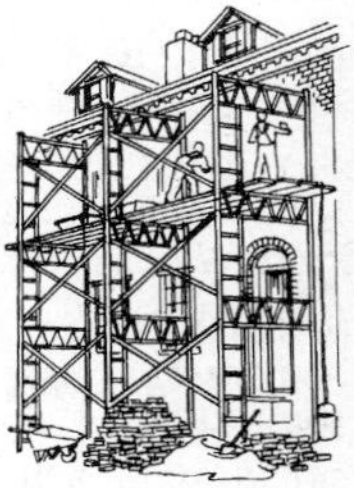
scaffold

**scale** /skeɪl/ *noun*
**1** an instrument for weighing things: *According to the scale, I've lost four pounds. See:* art on page 10a.
**2** a system of measurement or comparison: *On a scale of one to ten, I rate this movie a seven, quite good.*
**3** on a map, a small chart that shows the actual distance: *The scale for this map is one inch equals 100 miles.*

**scale** *verb* **scaled, scaling, scales**
**1** to climb something: *Monica scaled the ladder and painted her house.*

**2** to remove the skin of fish

**scalp** /skælp/ *noun*
the skin on the top of head, usually covered with hair: *Some shampoos make your scalp itch.*

**scam** /skæm/ *verb* **scammed, scamming, scams**
a plan to make money doing something wrong in a hidden way: *They ran a scam where they burned cars and collected insurance money.*

**scan** /skæm/ *verb* **scanned, scanning, scans**
to look at something and see as much as possible in a short time: *I scanned the newspaper.* –*noun* (quick look) **scan.**

**scandal** /ˈskændl/ *noun*
bad or embarrassing behavior (usually of a famous person) and the public's reaction to it: *The politician did not pay his taxes, and there was a scandal that lasted for months.* –*verb* **to scandalize.**

**scandalous** /ˈskæ ndləs/ *adjective*
causing shock or surprise

**scar** /skɑr/ *noun*
a mark left after a cut or wound heals

**scar** *verb* **scarred, scarring, scars**
to have or leave a scar: *She was scarred from the fire.*

**scarce** /skɛrs/ *adjective*
not available or plentiful: *Water is scarce in the desert.* –*noun* **scarcity.**

**scarcely** /ˈskɛrsli/ *adverb*
almost not, hardly: *I can scarcely live on the money I earn.*

**scare** /skɛr/ *noun*
a fear, a fright: *The little boy had a scare when his sister locked him in a closet. See:* art on page 18a.

**scare** *verb*
to cause fear: *The book about evil people scared me.*

**scarecrow** /ˈskɛrˌkroʊ/ *noun*
an object that looks like a person, made of old clothes and used to frighten birds away from a farm or garden: *Not many birds fly around our garden since we put up the scarecrow.*

**scarf** /skɑrf/ *noun, plural* **scarves** /skɑrvz/ or **scarfs**
a piece of cloth worn around the neck or on the head: *In winter, many people wear wool scarves.*

**scarlet** /ˈskɑrlət/ *noun*
a bright red color: *We have yellow, white, and scarlet roses in our garden.*

**scary** /ˈskɛri/ *adjective* **scarier, scariest**
causing fear, frightful: *We were lost in the dark, and it was very scary.*

**scatter** /ˈskætər/ *verb*
to go in all directions: *The old newspapers scattered in the wind.*

**scene** /sin/ *noun*
**1** a part of a film or play: *There is a very exciting car chase scene in that movie.*
**2** anger or embarrassing behavior, often in public: *She made a scene at the party by yelling at her boyfriend.*
**3** a place where something happens: *the crime scene*

**scenery** /ˈsinəri/ *noun*
**1** nature, such as trees, mountains, sky, etc.: *Each year, we vacation in the mountains and enjoy the scenery.*
**2** the decorations on a theater stage

**scenic** /ˈsinɪk/ *adjective*
with a pleasing view of nature: *The country road is very scenic in the autumn when the leaves are colorful.*

**scent** /sɛnt/ *noun*
a smell, usually pleasant: *The scent of flowers relaxes me.* –*verb* **to scent.**

**schedule** /ˈskɛʤul/ *noun*
a list of planned activities or events: *On the airline schedule, I saw that there is a flight to Tokyo at seven o'clock.*

**schedule** *verb* **scheduled, scheduling, schedules**
to plan activities: *We scheduled meetings for each day of our business trip.*

**scheme** /skim/ *noun*
**1** an ordered arrangement, plan: *The color scheme in the room is blue and yellow.*
**2** a secret or dishonest plan: *I think he had a scheme to cheat the customer.* –*verb* **to scheme;** –*noun* (person) **schemer.**

**scholar** /ˈskɑlər/ *noun*
**1** a person of great learning: *My teacher is a scholar of Shakespeare's writings.*

S

**2** a student on a scholarship: *My brother was a Rhodes scholar in England.*

**scholarship** /ˈskɑlər,ʃɪp/ *noun*
**1** study, learning, and knowledge: *The professor is famous for his scholarship.*
**2** a loan or grant that pays for study: *She got a $10,000 scholarship to go to college. See:* grant.

**school** /skul/ *noun*
**1** a place for teaching and learning: *I went to elementary school until I was 12. See:* art on page 9a.
**2** a group of fish: *a school of tuna*

**science** /ˈsaɪəns/ *noun*
knowledge related to the natural world, such as biology, chemistry, or physics

**scientific** /ˌsaɪənˈtɪfɪk/ *adjective*
related to natural sciences: *Space travel is a scientific advancement of the 20th century. –noun* (person) **scientist.**

**scissors** /ˈsɪzərz/ *noun plural*
a tool for cutting with two blades and a handle held with two fingers: *Hairdressers use scissors to cut people's hair.*||*My scissors are sharp.*

scissors

**scoop** /skup/ *noun*
a deep spoon used to hold an amount of something *–verb* **to scoop.**

**scorch** /skɔrʧ/ *verb*
to burn something and cause a mark or damage: *The fire scorched the walls of the house. –noun* (burn) **scorch.**

**score** /skɔr/ *noun*
**1** the number of points made in a game, contest, or test: *The student has a score of 99 out of a possible 100.*||*Our team made three scores and won the match.*
**2** music on paper that shows all the instruments' parts
**to keep score:** to see and record the number of points made: *She kept score with the help of a pen and paper.*

**score** *verb*
to make points in a sport or game: *Our basketball team scored in the last minute of the game.*

**scorn** /skɔrn/ *noun*
a feeling of disrespect, expressed in a strong way: *The scorn in your voice shows that you think I'm stupid. –verb* **to scorn.**

**scout** /skaʊt/ *noun*
**1** a person sent to collect information: *An army captain sends out scouts to see where the enemy is located.*
**2** a member of the Boy Scouts or Girl Scouts

**scout** *verb*
to collect information: *We scouted around for a new car. –noun* **scouting.**

**scramble** /ˈskræmbəl/ *verb* **scrambled, scrambling, scrambles**
**1** to move or climb quickly, especially on the hands and knees: *The children scrambled up the hill.*
**2** to mix together: *to scramble eggs*

**scrambled eggs** *noun plural*
eggs mixed and cooked in a frying pan

**USAGE NOTE:** A typical American breakfast might include *scrambled eggs,* bacon, toast, coffee, and orange juice. Other popular breakfast dishes are *cereal, oatmeal, pancakes,* and *waffles.* Some people have time to enjoy a big breakfast only on weekends, so on weekdays they eat a small breakfast of coffee and toast.

**scrap** /skræp/ *noun*
a small piece of something: *Write your phone number on this scrap of paper.*

**scrap** *verb* **scrapped, scrapping, scraps**
to get rid of: *With the bad weather, we scrapped our plans for a vacation.*

**scrape** /skreɪp/ *verb*
to rub against something rough and get a mark or injury: *I scraped my hand on the rusty doorknob. –noun* **scrape.**

**scratch** /skræʧ/ *noun, plural* **scratches**
a thin mark on a surface: *I made a scratch in the wall with a nail.*||*The little girl has a scratch on her hand from a pin.*

**scratch** *verb* **scratches**
**1** to stop an itch by rubbing it with the fingernails: *I scratched a mosquito bite with my fingernails.*
**2** to make a mark or sound with fingernails or claws: *The dog scratched at the door.*

S

**scratchy** /ˈskrætʃi/ *adjective* **scratchier, scratchiest**
with or able to cause scratches: *scratchy bark on a tree*

**scream** /skrim/ *noun*
a loud, high cry of strong feeling (pain, fear, anger, etc.): *She gave a scream when the man pulled out a knife.*
**scream** *verb*
to cry out in pain or fear: *He screamed for help.*

**screen** /skrin/ *noun*
**1** a movable divider in a room: *I undressed behind a screen in the bedroom.*
**2** a fine wire net in a window or door: *The screens on the windows keep the insects outside.*
**3** the surface on which a film or television show is seen: *a movie screen*||*a TV screen*
**screen** *verb*
to protect, divide, or hide an area: *My hat screened out the sun from my head.*

**screw** /skru/ *noun*
a small, nail-like object (with spiral indents): *The carpenter uses screws to put the table together.*
**screw** *verb*
to put a screw in something: *She screwed a shelf onto the bookcase.*

**screwdriver** /ˈskruˌdraɪvər/ *noun*
a tool for removing or putting in screws

**scribble** /ˈskrɪbəl/ *verb* **scribbled, scribbling, scribbles**
to write quickly and not neatly: *I scribbled "eggs, milk, cheese" on the grocery list.* –*noun* **scribble, scribbling.**

**script** /skrɪpt/ *noun*
**1** the written words for a speaker or actor: *The actors memorized the script.*
**2** handwriting in which the letters are connected: *He wrote a thank-you note in fancy script. See:* printing.

**scrub** /skrʌb/ *noun*
a complete washing: *Once a week, I give my dog a scrub in the bathtub.* –*verb* **to scrub.**

**sculptor** /ˈskʌlptər/ *noun*
an artist who makes non-flat art with stone, metal, and other substances: *A sculptor carved a statue of his lover in a piece of stone.* –*verb* **to sculpt.**

**sculpture** /ˈskʌlptʃər/ *noun*
three-dimensional art: *I walked around that sculpture of a ballet dancer by Degas.*

**sea** /si/ *noun*
a body of salt water, smaller than an ocean: *The Caspian Sea is between Europe and Asia.*

**seafood** /ˈsiˌfud/ *noun*
food (fish, lobster, seaweed, etc.) from the ocean or other body of water

**seal** /sil/ *noun*
**1** part of a lid or opening that must be broken to reach inside a container: *We broke the seal on the new aspirin bottle.*
**2** a brown water animal with flippers that lives in cold areas: *They saw many seals off the Coast of Alaska.*
**seal** *verb*
to close something firmly: *Please seal the envelope and mail it.*

**seam** /sim/ *noun*
the line where two pieces of cloth are sewed together: *There was a rip in the seam of his shirt.*

seam

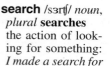

**search** /sɜrtʃ/ *noun, plural* **searches**
the action of looking for something: *I made a search for my lost sock.*
**search** *verb* **searches**
to look for something: *They searched three towns for the boy who ran away.*

**seashell** /ˈsiˌʃɛl/ *noun*
the hard outer covering of water animals, such as clams and oysters

**seashore** /ˈsiˌʃɔr/ *noun*
the area of land next to the sea, usually with a beach

**seasick** /ˈsiˌsɪk/ *adjective*
dizzy with an upset stomach caused by the motion of a boat: *Half the boat's passengers got seasick when it stormed.* –*noun* **seasickness.**

**season** /ˈsizən/ *noun*
a time of year or for a certain activity: *In some states the deer hunting season begins September 1.*

S

**season** *verb*
to add flavoring to food: *We season our vegetables with salt and garlic.*
**season** *adjective*
**in season:** available because of the time of year: *Here, tomatoes are in season in August.* *–adjective* **seasonal.**

**seat** /sit/ *noun*
a place to sit (a chair, sofa, bench, etc.): *We had wonderful seats in the front row at the theater.*
**seat** *verb*
to sit someone down: *The guests seated themselves at the table.*

**seat belt** *noun*
a long, thin piece of material that holds a person in a car seat for safety: *I wear my seat belt in case I have an accident. See:* safety belt.

seat belt

**USAGE NOTE:** Many states in the USA have strict *seat belt* laws, and drivers and passengers who do not wear their *seat belts* may have to pay a fine. Special car seats with *seat belts* are required for small children.

**second (1)** /'sɛkənd/ *adjective*
the position after first: *You were in second place in a race.*
**a second chance:** another opportunity to do something right: *The student failed the test, but the teacher gave him a second chance to pass.*
**second** *noun*
number 2 in a series: *I am second in line.*

**second (2)** *noun*
a unit of time, 1/60 of a minute: *The rocket will take off in 20 seconds.*

**secondary** /'sɛkən,dɛri/ *adjective*
not as important: *My job is of secondary importance to my health.*

**secondary school** *noun*
in the USA, a public or private high school, usually grades 9-12 or in some places 6-12: *Most students from my secondary school go to college when they finish.*

**USAGE NOTE:** *Secondary school* begins in sixth or seventh grade. It includes two or three years of *junior high school* or *middle school,* followed by three or four years of *senior high school.* Compare *grade school.*

**second class** *noun*
a less expensive part of a train, plane, etc.: *We like to travel in second class and use the extra money for nice hotels.*

**second-hand** *adjective*
used by someone else before: *We bought a second-hand car that had 25,000 miles on it. (antonym)* new.

**secrecy** /'sikrəsi/ *noun, (no plural)*
keeping information or knowledge private: *The plan was discussed quietly and in secrecy.*

**secret** /'sikrɪt/ *noun*
information or knowledge kept from others: *Your secret is safe; I won't tell anyone.* *–adverb* **secretly.**

**secretary** /' sɛkrə,tɛri/ *noun*
a person who works in an office, doing word-processing, filing, answering phones, and other jobs for a boss: *She asked her secretary to type a letter.*

**section** /'sɛkʃən/ *noun*
a piece or part of something: *They live in the section of town near the railroad station.*||*Would you like a section of this orange?*

**secure** /sə'kyʊr/ *adjective*
**1** protected from danger, safe: *He feels secure in the locked apartment.*
**2** sure, confident: *She is secure in knowing that her parents love her.* *–verb* **to secure.** *(antonym)* insecure.

**security** /sə'kyʊrəti/ *noun, plural* **securities**
**1** protection from danger or loss: *The owner put two locks on every door for better security.*
**2** people who help keep buildings and other areas safe, guards

**seduce** /sə'dus/ *verb* **seduced, seducing, seduces**
to convince a person to do something, often sexual, against his or her wishes

S

**see** /si/ *verb* **saw** /sɔ/, **seen, seeing, sees**
**1** to sense with the eye, to look: *I don't need glasses; I can see perfectly.*
**2** to understand: *The student sees what the professor is saying.*
**3** to meet: *I will see the dentist about my toothache.*||*I'll see you at the restaurant at noon.*
**4** (in saying good-bye) to meet later, in the future: *I'll see you later (soon, in a while, tomorrow, etc.).*
**to see someone off:** to go or be with someone to say good-bye: *Our friends like to see off all their friends who are traveling.*
**to see the light at the end of the tunnel:** to see hope or the end of a long and difficult situation: *After 12 years in school, we now see the light at the end of the tunnel, graduation.*

---

**USAGE NOTE:** Often Americans say goodbye to you with, "See you later." That expression does NOT mean that person expects to meet with you later in the day or evening. Instead it is only an informal way of saying "goodbye" or "until we meet again."

---

**seed** /sid/ *noun*
the part of a plant that is put into the ground and grows into another plant: *If you plant these seeds, they will grow into beans and corn.* *–verb* **to seed.**

**seek** /sik/ *verb* **sought** /sɔt/, **seeking, seeks**
to look for something: *The police are seeking a woman with blond hair and a blue dress.*

**seem** /sim/ *verb*
to appear: *He seems like a successful businessperson with his nice suit and big office.*

**seesaw** /ˈsiˌsɔ/ *noun*
a children's plaything, a piece of wood balanced on a bar, where a person sits on each end to move up and down *See:* art on page 9a.

**seize** /siz/ *verb* **seized, seizing, seizes**
to take something and hold it with force: *I seized his arm so he couldn't run away.*

**seizure** /ˈsiʒər/ *noun*
**1** the act of taking something by force or by law: *the seizure of property*
**2** a physical attack from a sickness or disease, such as heart failure: *The man had a seizure; he stopped breathing and started shaking.*

**seldom** /ˈsɛldəm/ *adverb*
not often: *I seldom go to the theater; I go two to three times a year.*

**select** /səˈlɛkt/ *verb*
to choose specific people or things: *The woman selected a vegetable dish from the menu.* *–adjective* **selective.**

**selection** /səˈlɛkʃən/ *noun*
**1** a group of things from which to choose: *The candy store had a selection of chocolates.*
**2** a choice: *I looked at the books in the library and made a selection of a mystery story.*

**self** /sɛlf/ *noun, plural* **selves** /sɛlvz/
**1** an entire person having his or her own character: *You showed your best self in helping the old people.*
**2** *prefix* **self-** related to oneself *See:* self-confident.

**self-confident** *adjective*
sure that one's actions are good and right: *He has a self-confident way of speaking, with a strong voice and clear opinions.* *–noun* **self-confidence.**

**self-control** *noun*
the ability to manage one's emotions and actions: *He drank too much and lost self-control; he started yelling.*

**self-defense** *noun*
the act of protecting oneself from harm: *The police officer acted in self-defense when he shot the criminal who tried to shoot him.*

**self-employed** *adjective*
related to working in a business that one owns: *She has been self-employed since she started that computer company years ago.* *–noun* **self-employment.**

**self-improvement** *noun, (no plural)*
the process of making oneself better (through study, hard work, changing one's appearance, etc.): *Many people try self-improvement by learning a new sport or language.*

**selfish** /ˈsɛlfɪʃ/ *adjective*
thinking about oneself more than others,

S

not sharing: *Your selfish brother took all the ice cream.* *–noun* **selfishness.**

**self-respect** *noun*
pride in oneself: *He had more self-respect when he went back to school and earned a high school diploma.*

**self-service** or **self-serve** *adjective*
(of a store or other business) choosing something oneself and paying for it at a cash register: *We buy gasoline for our car at a self-service gas station.*

---

**USAGE NOTE:** Many US gasoline stations offer *self-service* and *full-service* pumps. You can save money by going to the pumps marked "SELF" and pumping your own gas.

---

**sell** /sɛl/ *verb* **sold** /soʊld/, **selling, sells**
to take money in exchange for a product or service: *I'll sell you my CD player for $150. (antonym)* to buy.
**to sell oneself:** to talk about one's skills, to make oneself look good: *I really have to sell myself in this job interview.*

**seller** /ˈsɛlər/ *noun*
a person or business that takes money in exchange for something

**semester** /səˈmɛstər/ *noun*
half of the school year: *I took intermediate German in the fall semester and advanced German in the spring semester.*

---

**USAGE NOTE:** In the academic year, many colleges and universities have *two* terms called *semesters.* Some colleges operate on *quarters* or *trimesters* (three terms). *Semester* and *term* are often used to mean the same thing.

---

S

**semi-** /sɛmi/*prefix*
half

**semicircle** /ˈsɛmiˌsɜrkəl/ *noun*
half a circle

**semicolon** /ˈ sɛmiˌkoʊlən/ *noun*
the punctuation mark (;) *See:* colon, comma.

**seminar** /ˈsɛməˌnɑr/ *noun*
a meeting or short course on a specific topic: *I went to a two-day seminar on Native American art.*

**senate** /ˈsɛnɪt/ *noun*
an elected group of people in government, with the power to make laws: *The US Senate meets in Washington, D.C.* *–adjective* **senatorial** /ˈsɛnəˈtɔriəl/.

**senator** /ˈsɛnətər/ *noun*
an elected member of a senate: *Alma Perez is a senator from Oklahoma.*

**send** /sɛnd/ *verb* **sent** /sɛnt/, **sending, sends**
to cause to go or move: *Each week, I send a letter to my parents in England.*
**to send away for something:** to order by mail: *She sent away for flower seeds from a catalog.*
**to send for someone** or **something:** to ask for someone to come: *My boss sent for me.*||*She sent for a taxi.*
**to send someone away:** to make someone leave: *I sent away a stranger who knocked at my door. (antonym)* to receive.

**senile** /ˈsinaɪl/ *adjective*
mentally damaged from old age: *The old man cannot think clearly because he is senile.* *–noun* **senility** /səˈnɪləti/.

**senior** /ˈsinyər/ *noun*
**1** *abbreviation* Sr.: the father of a son with exactly the same name: *John Page Borden, Sr., is the father of John Page Borden, Jr.*
**2** someone in a higher position or longer in length of service
**3** in the USA, someone in the last (usually fourth) year of high school or college: *Mr. Yamamoto's son is a senior in high school. See:* freshman, USAGE NOTE.

**senior citizen** *noun*
someone usually over 60 years old: *My great-aunt can get a discount on bus tickets because she is a senior citizen.*

**seniority** /sinˈyɔrəti/ *noun*
the state of being higher in position or longer in length of service: *People with seniority will be laid off last.*

**sensation** /sɛnˈseɪʃən/ *noun*
**1** a physical feeling: *I sat on my foot, and now I have no sensation in it.*
**2** excitement, great interest: *The book on the politician's private life caused a sensation.*

**sensational** /sɛnˈseɪʃənəl/ *adjective*
very interesting or exciting: *The new play is sensational; you should see it!*

**sense** /sɛns/ *noun*
**1** a meaning or significance: *I looked up the sense of a word in* The Newbury House Dictionary.
**2** one of the five feelings of the body—sight, hearing, taste, smell, and touch
**3** *usually singular* a feeling: *She doesn't sleep enough, so she always has a sense of being tired.*
**4** intelligence, good judgment: *If you had any sense, you would get a better job.||It shows good sense to save money.*
**to make sense:** **a.** to be understandable: *Talk slowly; you're not making sense!* **b.** to be wise, to do the right thing: *It makes sense to take the train; it's faster.*

**sense** *verb* **sensed, sensing, senses**
to feel something

**sensible** /'sɛnsəbəl/ *adjective*
acting wisely: *You were sensible to wear boots in the mud. (antonym)* stupid.

**sensitive** /'sɛnsətɪv/ *adjective*
**1** sore or uncomfortable to the touch
**2** able to sense or feel in a stronger than normal way: *His skin is sensitive to wool.*

**sensitivity** /sɛnsə'tɪvəti/ *noun*
**1** the state of being easily hurt or affected emotionally: *He has great sensitivity; he always cries at sad movies.*
**2** sensing in a stronger than normal way: *My sensitivity to dust makes me sneeze.*
**3** great care or tact, so as not to cause unpleasant emotion: *The politician showed sensitivity to people of other races.*

**sent** /sɛnt/ *verb*
*past tense of* send

**sentence** /'sɛntns/ *noun*
**1** (in grammar) a thought expressed in words, usually with a subject and verb
**2** the punishment given by a court: *a prison sentence*

**sentence** *verb* **sentenced, sentencing, sentences**
to give a punishment: *The judge sentenced a criminal to 20 years in jail.*

**sentiment** /'sɛntəmənt/ *noun*
an emotional feeling

**sentimental** /sɛntə'mɛntl/ *adjective*
containing much emotion: *The movie has scenes full of love and loss; it is so sentimental! –noun* **sentimentality.**

**separate** /'sɛpərɪt/ *adjective*
**1** apart: *He and his wife sleep in separate beds.*
**2** different from something else: *The cost of making the product and the cost of selling it are two separate things.*

**separate** *verb*/'sɛpəˌreɪt/ **separated, separating, separates**
to move something apart or away from something else: *We separated the forks from spoons. –adverb* separately.

**separation** /sɛpə'reɪʃən/ *noun*
something that divides or separates, the act of separating: *The couple have a legal separation and live apart.*

**September** /sɛp'tɛmbər/ *noun*
the ninth month of the year, between August and October

**serene** /sə'rin/ *adjective*
(of a place) very calm, peaceful

**serenity** /sə'rɛnəti/ *noun, (no plural)*
calmness, peace: *He is not afraid to die; he feels serenity at the end of his life.*

**sergeant** /'sɑrʤənt/ *noun*
a middle-level officer in the army, air force, or marines, or on a police force

**series** /'sɪriz/ *noun*
**1** a group of similar things or events: *We heard a series of gunshots: three in a row.*
**2** a television show: *He acted in a TV series before he became a movie star.*

**serious** /'sɪriəs/ *adjective*
**1** thoughtful and quiet: *He is a serious man who works hard and doesn't smile. (antonym)* silly.
**2** important: *Cancer is a serious illness.*

**sermon** /'sɜrmən/ *noun*
a speech by a religious leader: *The sermon last Sunday was about Moses.*

**servant** /'sɜrvənt/ *noun*
a person who is paid to do household jobs: *One servant cleared the hallway, and another made dinner.*

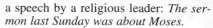

**serve** /sɜrv/ *verb* **served, serving, serves**
**1** to act as: *This table can serve as a desk.*
**2** to act as a servant, clerk, etc.: *The waitress served me coffee.*
**3** to be in public office: *The mayor served four years. See:* service.

S

**server** /ˈsɜrvər/ *noun*
**1** a person who serves: *a food server*
**2** the part of a computer that stores and serves information on command

**USAGE NOTE:** A *server* or *waitperson* may be a man or a woman. More and more, these terms are used in place of *waiter* and *waitress.*

**service** /ˈsɜrvɪs/ *verb* **serviced, servicing, services**
**1** to keep a machine in good working order: *The mechanic services our car every three months.*
**2** to provide goods and services: *We service our customers with a smile and a "thank you."*
**service** *noun*
**1** the care of a machine: *When our oven broke, we called a repairperson for service.*
**2** attention to customers' needs in a business: *The service at our favorite restaurant is excellent; the waiters are quick and polite.*
**3** religious worship: *Our temple has a service on Friday night.*

**service station** *noun*
a gas station, a car repair shop that sells gasoline and oil: *There are service stations located off the main highway.*

**session** /ˈsɛʃən/ *noun*
a meeting or other activity within a specific time period: *a one-hour exercise session*
**in session:** working, active: *The US Congress is in session until the summer.*

**set** /sɛt/ *noun*
**1** a group of related objects: *a set of pots and pans*
**2** a machine for watching or listening: *a TV set*
**3** scenery in a theater: *a stage set*
**set** *adjective*
**1** hardened: *The glue is set on the plate I am fixing.*
**2** agreed upon, decided: *We now have a set time for the meeting.*
**3** ready: *Get set to leave now.*
**all set:** prepared: *We have our tickets and our bags are packed, so we are all set for our vacation.*
**set** *verb*
**1** to put or place something: *I set the vase in the center of the table.*
**2** to become firm or hardened: *The gelatin has set, so we can eat it now.*
**3** to put a machine to a certain position: *Set the clock for 5:30 A.M.*
**4** to get something ready: *set the table*
**5** to go below the horizon: *The sun set in the west.*
**to set free:** to make free, let out: *We caught a butterfly in a net, but later we set it free.*
**to set up:** to get ready, arrange: *She set up chairs and tables for the party.*

**setting** /ˈsɛtɪŋ/ *noun*
**1** a place for an event or a story
**2** silverware and plates arranged on a table: *five place settings for five dinner guests*

**settle** /ˈsɛtl/ *verb* **settled, settling, settles**
**1** to agree: *We settled the details of the contract and signed it.*
**2** to go to the bottom: *The sand settled at the bottom of the lake.*
**3** to move in, to make a home: *Our family came from Russia and settled in New Jersey. –noun* (a place) **settlement,** (person) **settler.**

**seven** /ˈsɛvən/ *noun*
the cardinal number 7
**seven** *adjective*
seven of something: *We squeezed seven lemons for lemonade.*

**seventeen** /ˌsɛvənˈtin/ *noun*
the cardinal number 17
**seventeen** *adjective*
17 of something: *She is seventeen years old.*

**seventy** /ˈsɛvənti/ *noun, plural* **seventies**
the cardinal number 70
**seventy** *adjective*
70 of something: *He is seventy years old.*

**several** /ˈsɛvərəl/ *adjective*
a few, more than two: *Several people saw the accident, not just you.*

**USAGE NOTE:** *Several* describes a number greater than *two* but fewer than *many*: *There are several books on the table.* ||*I have several friends.*

**severe** /səˈvɪr/ *adjective*
very strong: *The severe storm blew down*

*a tree.*||*She has a severe case of the flu.* –*adverb* **severely.** *(antonym)* mild.

**sew** /soʊ/ *verb* **sewed** or **sewn** /soʊn/, **sewing, sews**
to put together with a needle and thread: *I lost a button, so I sewed a new one on.*

**sewage** /ˈsuɪʤ/ *noun, (no plural)*
waste and liquid that goes from toilets to pipes underground

**sewer** /ˈsuər/ *noun*
the tunnels and pipes that carry sewage underground

**sewing machine** *noun*
an electrical machine for sewing that works by pressing one's foot on a pedal

**sex** /sɛks/ *noun*
**1** the state of being male or female: *What sex is the new baby?*
**2** lovemaking

**sex** *adjective*
**1** related to being male or female: *sex differences*
**2** related to sex: *sex education*

**sexual** /ˈsɛkʃuel/ *adjective*
related to sexuality: *The couple has a strong sexual attraction for each other.*

**shabby** /ˈʃæbi/ *adjective* **shabbier, shabbiest**
worn, often dirty: *shabby old clothes*

**shack** /ʃæk/ *noun*
a small house or shed

**shade** /ʃeɪd/ *noun*
**1** an area that does not receive sunlight: *The sun is so hot; let's move into the shade under the tree.*
**2** a color that is only slightly different from a basic one
**3** a window covering: *I put down all of the window shades.* –*verb* **to shade.**

**shadow** /ˈʃædoʊ/ *noun*
the dark shape formed when someone or something blocks the sun or other light: *The houses made long shadows in the late afternoon.* –*adjective* **shadowy;** –*verb* **to shadow.**

shadow

**shady** /ˈʃeɪdi/ *adjective* **shadier, shadiest**
**1** out of the sunlight: *It's too hot in the sun; let's go under the shady tree.*
**2** dishonest: *The stranger who offered me a ride from the airport looks shady.*

**shaft** /ʃæft/ *noun*
**1** a round metal bar that turns, giving power in a long section of machinery: *the drive shaft of a truck*
**2** a hollow tube or tunnel: *a mine shaft*

**shake** /ʃeɪk/ *verb* **shook** /ʃʊk/, **shaken** /ˈʃeɪkən/, **shaking, shakes**
to make quick back-and-forth movements: *I shook the sand out of the towel.*||*An earthquake makes the ground shake.*

**to shake hands:** to join right hands with someone and move them up and down in greeting or agreement

**shake** *noun*
**1** a quick motion: *He gave the blanket a shake.*
**2** a handshake
**3** a drink made of milk, syrup, and ice cream, also called a milkshake

**shaky** /ˈʃeɪki/ *adjective* **shakier, shakiest**
**1** characterized by shaking: *During an earthquake, the ground is shaky.*
**2** *figurative* not firm or sure: *The company is doing badly; its future is shaky.*

**shall** /ʃæl/*auxiliary verb*
**1** used in formal writing to express a command: *The prisoner shall serve 20 years in jail.*||*The amount shall be $1,000.*
**2** used as part of a question when offering a suggestion: *Shall I go to the movies tonight?*||*Shall we leave now? See:* modal auxiliary, should, will.

**shallow** /ˈʃæloʊ/ *adjective*
not deep: *The pond is shallow; the water goes only up to my knees.*

**shame** /ʃeɪm/ *noun*
**1** a sad feeling because of knowing one has done wrong: *He stole money from the church and later felt great shame.*
**2** a sad situation, a pity: *It's a shame you can't go shopping with us.* –*verb* **to shame.** *See:* ashamed.

**shameful** /ˈʃeɪmfəl/ *adjective*
very bad: *It was a shameful lie to tell the old lady she had won a million dollars.*

**shampoo** /ʃæmˈpu/ *noun, plural* **shampoos**
**1** a liquid soap for cleaning the hair: *I use gentle shampoo on my baby's hair.*
**2** cleaning of the hair or other fibers: *The hairdresser gives me a shampoo before a haircut.*

**shampoo** *verb*
to clean with a liquid soap: *She shampoos her carpets once a month. See:* art on page 23a.

**shape** /ʃeɪp/ *noun*
**1** the form or outline of something: *The dollar bill is in the shape of a rectangle.*||*a human shape*
**2** physical condition, readiness: *She exercises every day to stay in shape.*

**shape** *verb* **shaped, shaping, shapes**
**1** to make into a shape: *He shaped the meat into hamburgers.*
**2** to have an effect, influence: *The struggle between countries shapes world events.*

**share** /ʃɛr/ *noun*
**1** one's own part of something: *I paid my share of the restaurant bill.*
**2** an equal portion of property or stock: *I own 12 shares in an oil company.*

**share** *verb* **shared, sharing, shares**
**1** to receive with others: *When we sold the business, my sister and I shared equally in the profits. (antonym)* to keep.
**2** to use or experience with others: *We shared a meal together.*||*The little girl shared her toys with her friend.*



**shark** /ʃark/ *noun*
a meat-eating fish, usually gray in color and with tough skin, sometimes dangerous *See:* art on page 14a.

shark

**sharp** /ʃarp/ *adjective* **sharper, sharpest**
**1** with a fine point or edge that is able to go through a surface or cut with ease: *a sharp knife*
**2** (of feeling) strong, intense: *a sharp pain in my stomach*
**3** *figurative* quick and intelligent: *She finds a lot of mistakes; she's sharp. –adverb* **sharply.** *(antonym)* dull.

**sharpen** /ˈʃarpən/ *verb*
to make pointed or to give a cutting edge: *sharpen a pencil*

**shave** /ʃeɪv/ *verb* **shaved** or **shaven** /ˈʃeɪvən/, **shaving, shaves**
**1** to cut off thin layers: *The carpenter shaved pieces off the door so it will close easily.*
**2** to cut hair close to the skin with a razor: *My brother's face is smooth after he shaves.*

**shave** *noun*
the act of cutting hair close to the skin: *Your beard is growing too long; you need a shave. –noun* **shaving.** *See:* art page 19a.

**shaving cream (gel, lotion)** *noun*
a semi-liquid substance put on the skin to make shaving easier: *My mother puts shaving cream on her legs before she shaves them.*

**she** /ʃi/ *pronoun*
third person feminine singular: *She is a brilliant woman. See:* who, USAGE NOTE.

**shed** /ʃɛd/ *noun*
a small building, often used for storage

**shed** *verb* **shed, shedding, sheds**
to lose hair or skin: *In the spring, animals shed their fur.*

**sheep** /ʃip/ *noun, plural* **sheep**
an animal kept for its wool and meat: *We made yarn from the wool of our sheep.*

**sheer** /ʃɪr/ *adjective* **sheerer, sheerest**
thin and able to be seen through: *We saw people moving behind the sheer curtains.*

**sheet** /ʃit/ *noun*
**1** a thin piece of cloth used as a bed covering
**2** a thin surface or piece of something: *a sheet of paper*

**shelf** /ʃɛlf/ *noun, plural* **shelves** /ʃɛlvz/
a flat piece of wood, metal, etc. that is used to hold objects: *My bookcase has six shelves. –verb* **to shelf.** *See:* art on page 10a.

**shell** /ʃɛl/ *noun*
**1** the hard, protective outer covering of

an animal, seed, or plant: *a turtle's shell||the shell of a nut*
**2** a bullet or other piece of ammunition: *shells from a gun*
**3** the outer structure of something: *Workers removed the interior walls and floors of a building and left the shell standing.*
**to come out of one's shell:** to be less shy: *The quiet boy came out of his shell at the party.*
**shell** *verb*
to remove the shell or covering: *We shelled peanuts and put them in a bowl.*

**shelter** /ˈʃɛltər/ *noun*
**1** any building or covering that gives physical protection: *When it started to rain, we found shelter under a tree. See:* art on page 4a.
**2** a place where homeless or abused people can sleep, eat, and be safe: *The woman moved to a shelter after her husband beat her.*
**shelter** *verb*
to protect someone or something: *The little house shelters us from the snow and cold.*

**shelve** /ʃɛlv/ *verb*
to place something on a shelf: *to shelve books*

**shepherd** /ˈʃɛpərd/ *noun*
a person who takes care of sheep in the fields *–verb* **to shepherd.**

**she's** /ʃiz/*contraction of*
she is

**shield** /ʃild/ *noun*
a piece of something, usually metal carried in one hand to protect oneself from flying objects: *The rocks bounced off the soldier's shield.* *–verb* **to shield.**

**shift** /ʃɪft/ *noun*
**1** a change in position or location: *a shift of money from one bank to another*
**2** an amount of work time: *The night shift begins at 11:00 P.M.*
**shift** *verb*
to change from one position to another: *The truck driver shifted gears to go up a hill.*

**shin** /ʃɪn/ *noun*
the frontal part of the lower leg

**shine** /ʃaɪn/ *noun, usually singular*
a brightness on something from smoothness or light: *He polished the knives and forks to a brilliant shine.*
**shine** *verb* **shone** /ʧoʊn/ or **shined, shining, shines**
to make something bright and clean: *He shines his shoes every day.*

**shingle** /ˈʃɪŋgəl/ *noun*
a small piece of wood or other material placed in overlapping rows on a building's roof or walls *–verb* **to shingle.**

**ship** /ʃɪp/ *noun*
**1** a large boat: *The ship is bringing silk from Hong Kong.*
**2** an airplane or rocket: *a space ship*
**ship** *verb* **shipped, shipping, ships**
to send something: *The mail-order company shipped my new boots by air.*

**shipment** /ˈʃɪpmənt/ *noun*
the act of sending something: *We sent the shipment of furniture by truck.*

**shipping** /ˈʃɪpɪŋ/ *noun, (no plural)*
**1** the act of sending a shipment: *We have workers who do the shipping from our warehouse.*
**2** the activities of ships: *Shipping is slowed by bad weather.*

**shipwreck** /ˈʃɪpˌrɛk/ *noun*
the loss or destruction of a ship: *The terrible storm caused a shipwreck.*

**shirt** /ʃɜrt/ *noun*
a piece of clothing worn on the upper body, often with sleeves: *He bought a tie to match his shirt. See:* blouse; sweat shirt; T-shirt; art on page 12a.

**shiver** /ˈʃɪvər/ *verb*
to shake in the body (from cold, fear, excitement, etc.): *She is shivering as she waits for a bus in the snow. –noun* **shiver.**

**shock** /ʃɑk/ *noun*
**1** a sudden psychological blow: *She got a terrible shock when she learned that her son was in the hospital.*
**2** strong, quick impact: *The car hit a wall, and the shock threw the driver against the windshield.*
**3** a quick pain caused by electricity: *I got a shock when I plugged in the lamp.* *–verb* **to shock.**

**shoe** /ʃu/ *noun*
a covering for the foot, often of leather and with a sole and heel: *My shoes have laces, and hers have high heels.*
**in someone's shoes:** to be in someone's place: *I wish that I was in your shoes when you met that famous rock star. See:* boot; sandal; sneaker.

**shoelace** /ˈʃu,le ɪs/ *noun*
the cloth or leather strings used to tie shoes

**shoeshine** /ˈʃu,ʃaɪn/ *noun*
cleaning and polishing the shoes: *I paid a man for a shoeshine at the airport.*

**shoot** /ʃut/ *verb* **shot** /ʃɑt/, **shooting, shoots**
**1** to use a gun: *to shoot a rifle*
**2** to hit someone or something with a bullet from a gun: *The hunter shot a deer.*
**3** to take pictures, use film: *I shot a roll of color film.*

**shoot** *noun*
**1** a gathering where there is a shooting contest: *a turkey shoot*
**2** a small, young plant growth: *a shoot of grass*

**shoot** *interjection*
used to express mild regret or annoyance: *Shoot, I left my wallet at home!*

**shop** /ʃɑp/ *noun*
**1** a store, usually small: *I bought some candy and gum in that little shop on the corner.*
**2** a place to work with one's hands: *My brother has a shop in the basement where he works with wood.*

**shop** *verb* **shopped, shopping, shops**
to go to stores, usually to buy: *We shop for food at the local supermarket.*
**to shop around:** to search for a certain item or the best price: *I shopped around until I found a purple dress in size 8.*

---

**USAGE NOTE:** Compare *shop* and *store.* Americans use the term *shop* for a small, specialized establishment like a *barber shop, coffee shop,* or *dress shop,* or a place that offers pleasant but nonessential items, like a *flower shop* or *gift shop.* The term *store* is a more general one, used for both small *and* large establishments. Most *shopping malls* have one or two big *department stores* as well as several shoestores, bookstores, clothing stores, and specialty shops.

---

**shopkeeper** /ˈʃɑp,kipər/ *noun*
a shop owner or manager

**shoplift** /ˈʃɑp,lɪft/ *verb*
to steal things from a store: *When no one was looking, she shoplifted two lipsticks and put them in her purse. –noun* (person) **shoplifter,** (action) **shoplifting.**

**shopper** /ˈʃɑpər/ *noun*
a person who shops: *Shoppers fill the grocery stores on Saturday. See:* art on page 10a.

**shopping** /ˈʃɑpɪŋ/ *noun, (no plural)*
the task of going to buy things in stores: *I did a little shopping during my lunch hour.*

**shopping center** *noun*
a group of different types of stores and restaurants with a large parking lot: *Does that shopping center have a bakery and a bookstore?*

**shopping mall** *noun*
a group of different types of stores and restaurants, all under one roof: *My teenage daughter likes to spend rainy days with her friends at the shopping mall.*

**shore** /ʃɔr/ *noun*
the sandy or rocky area of land next to a body of water: *She walked along the shore of Lake Michigan.*

**shoreline** /ˈʃɔr,laɪn/ *noun*
the line made when a body of water meets the land: *We followed the island's shoreline on our bicycles.*

**short** /ʃɔrt/ *adjective* **shorter, shortest**
**1** not long, high, or tall: *Philadelphia is a short distance from New York.*||*These pants are too short.*
**2** not having enough: *I can't go to the movies; I'm short on money.*
**3** a bit rude: *I tried to ask my boss a question, but he was very short with me. See:* short circuit. *(antonym)* long.

**short** *adverb*
**1** suddenly: *The bus stopped short, and some passengers fell off their seats.*

**2** less than or before a certain distance or time: *She threw the ball three feet short of my baseball glove.*

**shortage** /ˈʃɔrtɪʤ/ *noun*
a state of not having enough: *A shortage of oil made gasoline more expensive.*

**short circuit** *noun*
a problem in electrical wiring

**shortcut** /ˈʃɔrtˌkʌt/ *noun*
a shorter way to a place than usual: *We take a shortcut through a field instead of following the road.*

**shorten** /ˈʃɔrtn/ *verb*
to make shorter: *His speech lasted two hours; he should have shortened it. (antonym)* to lengthen.

**shortly** /ˈʃɔrtli/ *adverb*
soon: *We will be ready to leave shortly.*

**shorts** /ʃɔrts/ *noun plural*
**1** pants that end at or above the knee: *In the summer, we like to wear shorts to stay cool.*
**2** men's underpants: *boxer shorts*

---

**USAGE NOTE:** The word *shorts* is always used in the plural, like *pants: I'm wearing a T-shirt and shorts today because it's hot.*

---

**short story** *noun*
a piece of fiction that is shorter and usually simpler than a novel *See:* fiction, USAGE NOTE.

**shortwave** /ˈʃɔrtˈweɪv/ *adjective*
a radio wave or electronic wave having a length between 10 and 100 meters

**shot** /ʃɑt/ *noun*
**1** the shooting of a gun: *In the fight, you could hear shots being fired.*
**2** the use of a needle to put medicine into the body: *The doctor gave the little boy a shot in his right arm.*

**to give something a shot** or **to take a shot at something:** to try something: *You can't swim? You should give it a shot* (or) *take a shot at it.*

**shot** *verb*
*past tense* and *past participle of* shoot

**should** /ʃʊd/
*auxiliary verb and past tense of* shall
**1** helps express duty or obligation: *I should visit my grandmother because she is sick.*
**2** helps express something expected: *We should arrive in ten minutes if there is no traffic.* *See:* modal auxiliary; shall; USAGE NOTES.

**shoulder** /ˈʃoʊldər/ *noun*
the part of the body between the neck and upper arm: *The football player has big shoulders.*

**shout** /ʃaʊt/ *noun*
a loud cry, a yell: *A man gave a shout to call a taxi to pick him up.*

**shout** *verb*
to yell: *He shouted, "Hey, over here!"*

**shove** /ʃʌv/ *noun*
a hard push, usually with the hands: *The angry man gave another a shove.*

**shove** *verb* **shoved, shoving, shoves**
to push hard against something or someone: *He shoved the heavy rock off the road.*

**to shove off:** to leave (especially shore, in a boat): *We shove off at 9:00 A.M.*

**shovel** /ˈʃʌvəl/ *noun*
a curved metal or plastic surface with a handle used to pick up dirt, snow, etc.

shovel

**shovel** *verb*
to use a shovel: *He shoveled a hole in the sand.*

**show** /ʃoʊ/ *noun*
**1** a play, movie, TV program, or other entertainment: *We watched a show about African animals on TV.*
**2** a display or exhibition about a specific interest or product: *a horse show*/*a boat show*

**show** *verb* **showed, showing, shows**
**1** to cause someone to see: *Let me show you my new car.*
**2** to cause to be known: *Your tears show that you're sad.*
**3** to put before the public, display: *The downtown theater is showing movies from the 1950s.*
**4** to teach, demonstrate (often used with "how"): *She showed him how to eat a lobster.*

**to show (someone** or **something) off:** to act in a way that calls attention to oneself: *The boy shows off by telling people his father is very rich.*
**to show up:** to arrive (sometimes unexpectedly or late): *They finally showed up at 11:30.*

**show business** *noun, (no plural)*
the theater, film, TV, music, and other entertainment industries: *She works in show business as a singer.*

**shower** /'ʃaʊer/ *noun*
**1** a brief rain or snow: *After a shower in the morning, the sun came out at noon.*
**2** the act of bathing under a stream of water (or the place one does this): *I took a shower when I got home from running.*
**3** a party for someone who is getting married or having a baby
**shower** *verb*
to rain (or snow) for a short time: *It might shower this afternoon, so bring your umbrella. See:* art on page 19a and 23a.

**shred** /ʃrɛd/ *noun*
a small piece of something: *The police do not have a shred of evidence to prove he robbed your house. –verb* **to shred.**

**shrewd** /ʃrud/ *adjective*
tending to make smart decisions, *(synonym)* clever *–noun* **shrewdness.**

**shrimp** /ʃrɪmp/ *noun*
a small, edible water animal with a soft shell

**shrink** /ʃrɪŋk/ *verb* **shrank** /ʃræŋk/ or **shrunk** /ʃrʌŋk/, **shrinking, shrinks**
to make or become smaller: *My wool sweater shrank after I washed it.*
**shrink** *noun slang*
a psychiatrist or psychologist

**shrinkage** /'ʃrɪŋkɪʤ/ *noun, (no plural)*
a lessening of something's size: *shrinkage in a skirt||shrinkage in employment*

**shrub** /ʃrʌb/ *noun*
a plant with leaves, used especially for decoration around buildings and in parks: *We cut the shrubs in front of our house every month. –noun* **shrubbery.** *See:* bush.

shrub

**shrug** /ʃrʌg/ *verb*
to lift the shoulders upward as a sign of not caring or not knowing: *She shrugged when I asked her what time it was.*

**shudder** /'ʃʌdər/ *verb*
to shake for a moment (from fear, disgust): *I shudder when I think how bad that food tasted.*

**shuffle** /'ʃʌfəl/ *verb* **shuffled, shuffling, shuffles**
**1** to walk without lifting the feet: *The sad old man shuffled down the hall.*
**2** to mix in a different order: *We started a new game, so I shuffled the cards.*

**shut** /ʃʌt/ *verb* **shut, shutting, shuts**
to close something: *to shut one's mouth||to shut the door (antonym)* open.
**to shut up:** to cause someone to stop making noise: *The angry wife shut up her husband with a look.*
**to shut something off:** to make something stop working, moving or flowing: *I shut off the water in the sink.*
**shut** *adjective*
closed: *The oven door is shut.*

---

**USAGE NOTE:** To say *shut up* to someone is considered very rude. It is more polite to ask, "Would you please be quiet?"

---

**shutoff** /'ʃʌt,ɔf/ *noun*
a stoppage: *a shutoff of electricity (water, heat, etc.)*

**shutter** /'ʃʌtər/ *noun*
**1** a window covering that can be opened and closed: *A rainstorm began, and the woman closed the shutters.*
**2** the part of a camera that lets in or shuts out light
**shutter** *verb*
to close a window or a shutter

**shuttle** /'ʃʌtl/ *verb* **shuttled, shuttling, shuttles**
to travel back and forth: *Businesspeople shuttle between New York and Washington, D.C. every day.*
**shuttle** *noun*
a vehicle (plane, bus, van, etc.) used for traveling back and forth: *The shuttles leave the hotel for the airport every hour.*

**shy** /ʃaɪ/ *adjective* **shyer** or **shier, shiest** or **shiest**
not liking to talk to people: *The shy boy stood in a corner at the dance. –noun* **shyness.**

**shy** *verb* **shied, shying, shies**
to move away from something with fear or disgust: *The nervous horse shied away when I tried to climb onto her.*

**sibling** /ˈsɪblɪŋ/ *noun*
a person with the same parents as someone else, brother or sister: *I have two siblings: my brother and my sister.*

**sick** /sɪk/ *adjective*
**1** not well physically, ill, diseased: *He is sick with the flu. (antonym)* well.
**2** not well mentally: *She killed herself because she was extremely sick.*

**sickness** /ˈsɪknɪs/ *noun*
illness: *There is a lot of sickness in poor countries with few doctors.*

**side** /saɪd/ *noun*
**1** an edge or a surface of an object: *A box has six sides.*||*I have a pain in my right side.*
**2** a flat surface that connects top and bottom: *A sign hangs on the side of the building.*
**3** a particular location: *the south side of the city*
**4** a group or team: *My side won the soccer game.*

**side by side:** next to each other: *The students stood side by side for the class photo.*

**side** *verb*
to agree with someone: *He sided with me about whom to vote for.*

**sideburns** /ˈsaɪˌ bɜrnz/ *noun plural*
hair that grows on the side of a man's face, just in front of the ears

**side effect** *noun*
an effect of a medicine in addition to the expected effect: *The side effect of this pain pill was a dry mouth.*

**sidewalk** /ˈsaɪˌwɔk/ *noun*
the path next to a street, meant for walkers: *A woman walked her dog along the sidewalk. See:* art on page 4a.

sidewalk

**sideways** /ˈsaɪˌweɪz/ *adverb*
toward the side: *I had to turn sideways to fit through the opening in the fence.*

**sigh** /saɪ/ *verb*
to let out air from the mouth from fatigue or emotion: *He sighed with relief. –verb* **to sigh.**

**sight** /saɪt/ *noun*
**1** the physical sense of seeing: *My sight is good; I don't need glasses.*
**2** something or someone that is seen: *I like the sight of new snow in the winter.*

**sightseeing** /ˈsaɪˌsiɪŋ/ *noun, (no plural)*
the act of visiting places as a tourist: *We did some sightseeing at the Grand Canyon in Arizona.*

**sign** /saɪn/ *noun*
**1** a board or poster with information on it: *The sign on our store says "The Clothes Boutique."*|| *a stop sign*
**2** an action or other nonspoken way of communicating: *The wave of her hand was a sign of greeting.*
**3** a symbol: *The (X) is a multiplication sign.*

**sign** *verb*
**1** to write one's name on something: *He signed a check (letter, contract).*
**2** to use finger motions to communicate with people who can't hear: *My hearing-impaired sister signed "good-bye" to me.*

**to sign (someone) up:** to join, agree to do something, *(synonym)* to enroll: *I signed up for swimming lessons. –noun* (person) **signer.**

**signal** /ˈsɪgnəl/ *noun*
**1** an action or thing that sends a message: *A green light is a signal to go.*
**2** an electronic picture or sound: *The TV is very clear; there must be a good signal.*

**signal** *verb*
to send a signal: *Ships signal their positions by radio.*

**signature** /ˈsɪgn əʧər/ *noun*
one's name written by oneself: *My signature is on the birthday card.*

**significance** /sɪgˈnɪfəkəns/ *noun*
**1** the importance of something: *The end*

*of the war was an event of great significance.*
**2** the meaning of something: *I don't understand the significance of your wearing black all the time; are you sad?*

**significant** /sɪg'nɪfəkənt/ *adjective*
**1** important
**2** large, (*synonym*) substantial: *The company made a significant profit last year.*

**silence** /'saɪləns/ *noun*
quiet, no noise: *There was silence in the church as the people prayed.*

**silence** *exclamation* Quiet!: *Silence! This is a library. (antonym)* noise.

**silence** *verb* **silenced, silencing, silences**
to make quiet: *The teachers silenced the class before beginning to talk.*

**silent** /'saɪlənt/ *adjective*
quiet: *The forest was silent; even the birds were quiet. (antonym)* loud.

**silhouette** /ˌsɪlu'ɛt/ *noun,* **silhouetted, silhouetting, silhouettes**
an outline that is filled in with a dark color: *A silhouette of the side view of the boy's face shows the shape of his nose.* –*verb* **to silhouette.**

**silk** /sɪlk/ *noun*
the material made by silkworms: *She wears dresses made of silk.* –*adjective* **silken.**

**silky** /'sɪlki/ *adjective* **silkier, silkiest**
smooth, soft: *silky hair*

**silly** /'sɪli/ *adjective* **sillier, silliest**
foolish, stupid: *When he drinks wine, he starts acting silly.*

**silver** /'sɪlvər/ *noun*
a white, shiny metal used for making jewelry, knives, forks, spoons, and other objects

**silver** *adjective*
the color of silver: *My grandfather has silver hair.*

**silverware** /'sɪlvərˌwɛr/ *noun*
table tools, originally made from silver (knives, forks, spoons, etc.): *Please put the plates and silverware on the table.*

silverware

S

**similar** /'sɪmələr/ *adjective*
almost alike: *She has a blue dress similar to yours, but hers has a green collar. (antonym)* dissimilar. –*noun* **similarity.**

**simple** /'sɪmpəl/ *adjective*
without many details, not complex: *I drew a simple map.*

**simplify** /'sɪmpləˌfaɪ/ *verb* **simplified, simplifying, simplifies**
to make less complex: *Let's simplify the job by dividing it into smaller tasks.* –*noun* (condition) **simplicity.**

**simply** /'sɪmpli/ *adverb*
**1** easily: *The repair can be made simply, with just a screwdriver.*
**2** only, just: *Don't get angry; I was simply trying to help.*
**3** very, absolutely: *I was simply amazed when he finished the job in an hour.*

**simultaneous** /ˌsaɪməl'teɪniəs/ *adjective*
happening at the same time: *The two students gave a simultaneous answer.* –*adverb* **simultaneously.**

**sin** /sɪn/ *noun*
an act against religious beliefs: *The rabbi told the child that lying was a sin.* –*adjective* **sinful;** –*verb* **to sin.**

**since** /sɪns/ *conjunction*
**1** because: *The gas company turned your heat off, since you did not pay your bill.*
**2** after a certain time: *I haven't seen any snow since I moved to the South.*

**since** *adverb*
**1** between that time and now: *I quit my job last year and have not worked since.*
**2** before now: *She has long since stopped smoking.*

**since** *preposition*
from a specific time: *The company has been in business since 1941.*

**sincere** /sɪn'sɪr/ *adjective*
honest in one's thought and action: *Her love for you is sincere; she will stay with you in bad times.* –*noun* **sincerity.**

**sincerely** /sɪn'sɪrli/ *adverb*
**1** honestly, truly: *Please believe me; I am sincerely interested in helping you.*
**2** often used to close a letter: *See you soon. Sincerely, Joe Martin.*

**sing** /sɪŋ/ *verb* **sang** /sæŋ/ or **sung** /sʌŋ/, **singing, sings**
to make music with the voice: *She sings in a higher voice than her husband.* –*noun* (person) **singer.**

**single** /'sɪŋgəl/ *adjective*
**1** only one: *You can start a fire with a single match.*
**2** separate, individual: *Every single book in the library has a number.*
**3** unmarried: *She is single because she doesn't want a husband.*

**single** *noun*
**1** one person: *seat for a single*
**2** *usually plural* unmarried people: *The club had a party for singles.*
**3** a one-dollar bill: *The magazine cost $2.95, so I paid for it with three singles. See:* double.

**USAGE NOTE:** In American culture, it is not thought to be polite to ask a person you do not know well if he or she is *single* or *married.*

**singular** /'sɪŋgyələr/ *adjective*
special, unusual: *She has the singular honor of winning the Nobel Prize in chemistry.* –*adverb* **singularly.**

**singular** *noun*
(in grammar) only one, not the plural: *"Box" is the singular of "boxes."*

**sink** /sɪŋk/ *noun*
the container for running water, usually in a kitchen or bathroom: *He washed the dishes in the sink. See:* art on page 7a and 23a.

**sink** *verb* **sank** /sæŋk/ or **sunk** /sʌŋk/, **sinking, sinks**
to go or fall below the surface of water: *The boat had a hole, so it sank.*

**sinner** /'sɪnər/ *noun*
a person who acts against religious teaching

**sip** /sɪp/ *verb* **sipped, sipping, sips**
to drink a small amount at a time: *He sipped his tea.* –*noun* **sip.**

**sip** *noun*
a small amount of liquid: *He took a sip of tea.*

**sir** /sɜr/ *noun*
**1** a respectful word to use when talking to a man: *Would you like red or white wine, sir?*
**2** used to begin a formal letter to a man: *Dear Sir:*

**siren** /'saɪrən/ *noun*
a loud, alarm on a fire truck, ambulance, police car, etc.: *The fire engine's siren warned drivers to move out of the way.*

**sister** /'sɪstər/ *noun*
a daughter with the same parents as another daughter or son: *My brother wanted a sister, so he was happy that I was born a girl. See:* art on page 13a.

**sister-in-law** *noun, plural* **sisters-in-law**
the sister of a husband or wife, or the wife of a brother *See:* art on page 13a.

**sit** /sɪt/ *verb* **sat** /sæt/, **sitting, sits**
**1** to bend one's knees and rest on one's buttocks: *He sat on a chair.*
**2** to be located: *A computer sat on the desk.*

**to sit down:** to seat oneself: *I sat down on a bench in the park. (antonym)* to stand.

**site** /saɪt/ *noun*
an area or place: *a building site*

**situated** /'sɪʧuˌeɪtɪd/ *adjective*
in a certain place, located: *The church is situated in the center of the city.*

**situation** /ˌsɪʧu'eɪʃən/ *noun*
the way things are at a certain time, what's happening: *The leaders are meeting to talk about the situation in their countries.*

**six** /sɪks/ *noun, plural* **sixes**
the cardinal number 6

**six** *adjective*
six of something: *six cans of cola*

**six-pack** *noun*
six cans or bottles of a beverage, bought together: *a six-pack of beer*

**sixteen** /sɪks'tin/ *noun*
the cardinal number 16

**sixteen** *adjective*
16 of something: *sixteen years old*

**USAGE NOTE:** At age *16,* Americans are allowed to work legally and, in most states, to get a driver's license.

S

**sixty** /ˈsɪksti/ *noun, plural* **sixties**
the cardinal number 60

**sixty** *adjective*
60 of something: *I'm sixty years old!*

**sizable** or **sizeable** /ˈsaɪzəbəl/ *adjective*
large: *She spent a sizable amount of money.*

**size** /saɪz/ *noun*
**1** the physical measure of someone or something (bigness, smallness, etc.): *Look at the size of that baby; she's huge!*||*I would like the smaller size coffee, please.*
**2** a number that tells how big or small clothing items or shoes are: *After she lost weight, she went from a size 16 to a size 12.*||*His boots are a size 11.*
**3** *suffix* **-sized** /-ˌsaɪzd/ or **-size** /-ˌsaɪz/ related to the size of something: *a medium-sized meal*||*a king-size bed*||*a child-sized chair*

**skate** /skeɪt/ *noun*
**1** a boot with wheels or a blade attached, worn to slide along the ground
**2** metal ice skate, rollerskate
**3** a type of fish

**skate** *verb* **skated, skating, skates**
to move on ice or ground with skates: *I skate in the park each morning.* *–noun* **skating.** *See:* art on page 12a.

**skateboard** /ˈskeɪtˌbɔrd/ *noun*
a board with four wheels on which one stands and rolls along a surface *See:* art on page 24a.

**skateboard**

**skeleton** /ˈskɛlətn/ *noun*
a body's bones: *We studied the skeleton in biology class.*

**sketch** /skɛʧ/ *noun, plural* **sketches**
a drawing done without many details: *The artist drew a sketch of the woman's face in two minutes.* *–verb* **to sketch.**

**ski** /ski/ *noun*
**1** a long, narrow piece of wood, fiberglass, or plastic used for moving on snow: *After I fell, my ski came off and it slid down the mountain.*
**2** a waterski

**ski** *verb* **skied, skiing, skis**
to move on skis: *She skied in the mountains last week.*

**skiing** /ˈskiɪŋ/ *noun*
the sport of sliding down or across snowy surfaces on skis

**skid** /skɪd/ *verb* **skidded, skidding, skids**
to move across a surface, often sideways, with a sliding motion: *The truck skidded to a stop just before the fence.* *–noun* **skid.**

**skill** /skɪl/ *noun*
**1** an ability to do something well because of practice, talent, or training: *She has excellent musical skills.*
**2** a trade: *Carpentry is his skill.*

**skillful** /ˈskɪlfəl/ *adjective*
able to do something well: *He is skillful at building furniture.*

**skim** /skɪm/ *verb* **skimmed, skimming, skims**
**1** to read quickly: *I skimmed the magazine for the interesting articles.*
**2** to remove the top layer of something: *The cook skimmed the fat off the chicken soup with a spoon.* *–noun* (action) **skimming.**

**skin** /skɪn/ *noun*
the outer covering of a plant or animal's body: *His skin is very light, but it turns pink when he goes out in the sun.*||*a potato skin*||*the skin of an onion*

**skin** *verb* **skinned, skinning, skins**
to remove the skin: *The hunter skinned the dead bear.*

**there is more than one way to skin a cat:** there is more than one way to do something, to solve a problem: *If you can't reach your brother by phone, write a letter; there's more than one way to skin a cat.*

**skip** /skɪp/ *verb* **skipped, skipping, skips**
**1** to run in a hopping way: *The little girl skipped happily to her friend's house.*
**2** to use a jump rope: *to skip rope*
**3** to miss something that one usually does: *to skip a meal*||*to skip school for a day* *–noun* **skip.**

**skirt** /skɜrt/ *noun*
a piece of women's clothing that covers

the waist, hips, and part of the legs and has no leg dividers: *My mother wore pants to the party, but my sister wore a skirt and blouse.*

**skull** /skʌl/ *noun*
the bone part of the head

**skunk** /skʌŋk/ *noun*
a small animal with black fur and white stripes that gives off a bad-smelling liquid when frightened

**skunk**

**sky** /skaɪ/ *noun, plural* **skies**
the air we see above the earth: *The sky is blue today.*

**skyscraper** /ˈskaɪˌskreɪpər/ *noun*
a very tall building: *The Empire State Building is a famous skyscraper in New York. See:* art on page 4a.

**slab** /slæb/ *noun*
a thick, flat piece of something

**slacks** /slæks/ *noun*
pants, trousers: *Don't wear blue jeans to the wedding; put on slacks instead. See:* art on page 12a.

**slam** /slæm/ *verb* **slammed, slamming, slams**
**1** to hit something hard: *The angry man slammed his fist on the desk.*
**2** to close hard: *She slammed the door shut.* *–noun* **slam.**

**slander** /ˈslændər/ *noun*
the act of saying bad or untrue things about someone *–verb* **to slander.**

**slang** /slæŋ/ *noun*
informal language and expressions that are not used in formal speech and writing: *When we moved, I learned the slang of the local teenagers.*

**slant** /slænt/ *verb*
**1** to be at an angle straight up-and-down: *The flagpole is slanting; soon it will fall.*
**2** to allow one's opinion to show when telling a story: *The angry woman slanted the story of her divorce.* *–noun* **slant.**

**slap** /slæp/ *verb* **slapped, slapping, slaps**
to hit with a flat surface, especially with the hand: *The girl slapped her brother, and he started to cry.* *–noun* **slap.**

**slash** /slæʃ/ *verb*
to make a long cut with something sharp: *The knife slashed through the sack of flour.* *–noun* **slash.**

**slaughter** /ˈslɔtər/ *verb*
**1** to kill in a violent and bloody way, often in large numbers: *The army slaughtered the enemy.*
**2** to kill animals for food: *The farmer slaughtered cows for beef.* *–noun* **slaughter.**

**slave** /sleɪv/ *noun*
a person who is owned by someone else and who works for no money: *My grandmother's grandfather was a slave who was owned by a rich cotton farmer.*

**slave** *verb* **slaved, slaving, slaves**
to live and work as a slave: *Before the US Civil War, many people slaved for plantation owners.*

**slavery** /ˈsleɪvəri/ *noun*
the state of being owned by another person and working for no money

**sled** /slɛd/ *noun*
a vehicle that slides on runners over the snow: *Two kids sat on the sled and went down the hill.*

**sled** *verb* **sledded, sledding, sleds**
to travel by sled

**sleep** /slip/ *verb* **slept** /slɛpt/, **sleeping, sleeps**
**1** to rest in an unconscious state: *I have not slept all night, so I am very tired.*
**2** to have places to sleep: *A double bed sleeps two.*

**to sleep like a log:** to sleep well and deeply. *(antonym)* to awaken.

**sleep** *noun*
the state of resting unconsciously: *Sleep is important for good health. See:* art on page 19a.

**sleepy** /ˈslipi/ *adjective* **sleepier, sleepiest**
needing sleep, tired: *I feel sleepy; I'm going to rest. (antonym)* awake.

**sleet** /slit/ *noun*
frozen rain, a mixture of snow and rain: *If it gets colder, sleet may turn to snow.* *–verb* **to sleet.**

S

**sleeve** /sliv/ *noun*
the part of a piece of clothing that covers all or part of the arm: *In the summer, she likes blouses with short sleeves.*

**slender** /ˈslɛndər/ *adjective*
thin, slim: *She is very slender, so she can wear her teenaged daughter's clothes. (antonyms)* fat, obese.

**slept** /slɛpt/ *verb*
*past tense of* sleep

**slice** /slaɪs/ *verb* **sliced, slicing, slices**
to cut into thin pieces: *My father sliced the roast turkey for the family dinner.*

slice

**slice** *noun*
a thin, flat piece of something: *a slice of bread, tomato, meat, cake, etc.*

**slide** /slaɪd/ *verb* **slid** /slɪd/, **sliding, slides**
to move something across a surface: *Workers slid boxes across the floor.*

**slide** *noun*
**1** on a children's playground, a slope where one climbs up a ladder, sits, and moves down quickly *See:* art on page 9a.
**2** a photograph negative, shown against a screen: *We gathered in the living room and watched slides of my trip to Greece.*

**slight** /slaɪt/ *adjective* **slighter, slightest**
small: *a slight difference between two colors –noun* **slightness.**

**slim** /slɪm/ *adjective* **slimmer, slimmest**
**1** thin, slender: *He is slim because he runs five kilometers a day. (antonym)* fat.
**2** unlikely: *a slim chance of success –verb* **to slim.**

**sling** /slɪŋ/ *noun*
a cloth or leather support (as for a broken arm): *He broke his wrist, and it is in a sling. –verb* (to throw) **to sling.** *See:* art on page 11a.

**slip** /slɪp/ *noun*
**1** a small piece of something: *a slip of paper*
**2** a piece of women's underclothes that looks like a dress or skirt: *a silk slip under her dress*
**3** a mistake: *a slip in arithmetic||a slip of the tongue*
**4** a movement or fall caused by something slippery: *a slip on the ice*

**slip** *verb* **slipped, slipping, slips**
to fall or almost fall because of something slippery: *She slipped on the wet grass.*

**slipper** /slɪpər/ *noun*
a soft shoe worn only in the house: *I put on my warm slippers this morning. See:* art on page 22a.

**slippery** /ˈslɪpəri/ *adjective*
causing people or things to fall or slide: *The roads are very slippery with ice.*

**slit** /slɪt/ *verb* **slit, slitting, slits**
to make a narrow cut: *I slit open the envelope.*

**slit** *noun*
a narrow cut or opening: *You can see through a slit in the door.*

**slob** /slɑb/ *noun*
a dirty, messy person: *He eats with his fingers, drops food, and never takes a shower; what a slob. –verb* **to slobber.**

**slogan** /ˈsloʊgən/ *noun*
a saying or phrase that expresses a group's message: *"We bring good things to life" is the slogan of the General Electric Company.*

**slope** /sloʊp/ *noun*
a surface at an angle, especially of a hill or roof: *The slope is gentle, so children can ski down it. –verb* **to slope.**

**sloppy** /ˈslɑpi/ *adjective* **sloppier, sloppiest**
**1** dirty and wet: *We put on boots to walk through the sloppy mud.*
**2** messy, careless: *The living room was sloppy, with magazines all over the floor. –adverb* **sloppily.** *(antonym)* neat.

**slow** /sloʊ/ *adjective* **slower, slowest**
**1** not fast: *The traffic is very slow today.*
**2** not smart: *Repeat the directions; he is a bit slow.*
**3** not busy or active: *During the summer season, sales are slow for us.*
**4** behind the correct time: *My watch is slow; it says 3:00, but the time is 3:15. (antonym)* fast.

**slow** *verb*
to go less quickly: *Work has slowed this week, so we can go home earlier.*
**to slow something down:** to lessen the speed of something, to go less fast: *I put on the brakes and slowed the car down.* –*adverb* **slowly;** –*noun* **slowness.**

**slowdown** /ˈsloʊˌd aʊn/ *noun*
doing an activity more slowly, often by workers as a protest: *The factory has produced much less since the workers started a slowdown.*

**sluggish** /ˈslʌgɪʃ/ *adjective*
lacking energy, not completely awake: *She felt sluggish after only four hours of sleep.*

**slum** /slʌm/ *noun*
part of a city where poor people live in bad housing, often with lots of crime: *She saved money and moved away from the slums so her children could have a better life.*

**slump** /slʌmp/ *noun*
a sinking down: *She fell over in a slump.* –*verb* **to slump.**

**slur** /slɜr/ *verb*
**1** to say an unkind thing
**2** to speak unclearly: *She drank too much and started to slur her words.* –*noun* **slur.**

**slush** /slʌʃ/ *noun*
soft melting snow mixed with dirt: *slush on the sidewalk*

**smack** /smæk/ *noun*
a hit, usually with the hand: *to give someone a smack* –*verb* **to smack.**

**small** /smɔl/ *adjective* **smaller, smallest**
**1** little, not big: *a small child*||*a small car with two seats*
**2** not important, insignificant: *It's a small problem; don't worry. (antonym)* big.

**smart** /smɑrt/ *adjective* **smarter, smartest**
**1** able to think well, intelligent: *His son is a very smart boy; he has the best grades in his class. (antonym)* stupid.
**2** somewhat rude: *The child made a smart remark to her father, so she was sent to bed without dinner.*

**smart** *verb*
to hurt: *Putting alcohol on a cut smarts, but it cleans it.*

**smash** /smæʃ/ *verb* **smashes**
**1** to break into pieces with force: *The dish fell on the floor and smashed into little bits.*
**2** to crash: *The bicycle smashed into a fence, and the rider fell off.*
**to smash something up:** to break or ruin: *He smashed up his car in an accident.*

**smash** *noun*
the sound or act of smashing

**smear** /smɪr/ *noun*
a mark or spot made by spreading: *There was a smear on the glass from the child's dirty hands.* –*verb* **to smear.**

**smell** /smɛl/ *noun*
**1** the sense for which the nose is used: *My dog's sense of smell is excellent.*
**2** odor, scent, aroma: *The smell of soup cooking on the stove made me hungry.*

**smell** *verb*
**1** to sense an odor: *I smell the roses in the garden.*
**2** to have an odor: *This place smells like pine trees.*||*Something smells bad in the refrigerator.* –*adjective* **smelly.**

**smile** /smaɪl/ *verb* **smiled, smiling, smiles**
to turn the lips up at their corners, usually to show good feelings: *She smiles when she watches her kids play.*

**smile** *noun*
the expression of smiling: *He gave her the good news with a smile. (antonym)* frown.

**smog** /smɔg, smɑg/ *noun*
a mixture of smoke and fog, air pollution –*adjective* **smoggy.**

**smoke** /smoʊk/ *verb* **smoked, smoking, smokes**
**1** to use cigarettes, cigars, pipes, etc.: *I smoke cigarettes, but I'm trying to quit.*

smoke

**2** to give off small pieces of burned material and gas into the air: *The fire is smoking.*

**smoke** *noun*
the blackish-gray, gaseous substance from something burning: *Smoke comes from that chimney.*
**where there's smoke, there's fire:** if it seems like there's trouble, there probably is *-noun* (person) **smoker.**

**smoking** /ˈsmoʊkɪŋ/ *noun*
the use of tobacco: *Smoking is not allowed on many airplane flights.*

**smoky** /ˈsmoʊki/ *adjective* **smokier, smokiest**
**1** filled with smoke: *The kitchen is smoky from the stove.*
**2** tasting of smoke: *smoky bacon*

**smooth** /smuð/ *adjective* **smoother, smoothest**
without roughness or bumps: *The new road is smooth.* *–noun* **smoothness.**
**smooth** *verb*
to make flat, even, without bumps: *A carpenter smoothes the top of the table with sandpaper. (antonym)* to roughen.

**smother** /ˈsmʌðər/ *verb*
**1** to take away oxygen and kill
**2** to cover something completely: *She smothered her hot dog with ketchup.*

**smuggle** /ˈsmʌgəl/ *verb* **smuggled, smuggling, smuggles**
to bring things into or out of a country illegally: *Drug dealers smuggle cocaine into the USA.* *–noun* (person) **smuggler.**

**snack** /snæk/ *noun*
a small amount of food, usually eaten between meals: *My favorite snack is potato chips.*
**snack** *verb*
to eat a small amount: *We snacked on crackers and cheese.* *–noun* **snack bar.** *See:* bar, USAGE NOTE.

**snag** /snæg/ *noun*
**1** a tear in a piece of cloth: *Her stocking got a snag on a sharp corner.*
**2** a temporary problem: *We hit a snag when typing the addresses; the computer stopped working.*
**snag** *verb* **snagged, snagging, snags**
to catch on something: *He snagged his fish line on a log in the river.*

**snail** /sneɪl/ *noun*
a small, soft animal with a hard shell, noted for its slowness
**at a snail's pace:** very slowly: *The rush-hour traffic moved at a snail's pace.*

**snake** /sneɪk/ *noun*
a long, thin animal (reptile) without legs that moves with a winding motion *See:* art on page 14a.
**snake** *verb* **snaked, snaking, snakes**
to move in a winding way: *The river snakes through the forest to the ocean.*

**snap** /snæp/ *noun*
**1** a sudden sound and action like a crack or a pop: *the snap of two fingers||to close the notebook with a snap*
**2** a fastener for something, with one piece locking into another: *The baby's pants have snaps.*
**3** a period of cold weather: *During the cold snap, we wore thick sweaters.*
**snap** *verb* **snapped, snapping, snaps**
to break suddenly and with a sharp sound: *The pencil snapped in half.*

**snapshot** /ˈsnæp,ʃɑt/ *noun*
an informal photograph: *She took a snapshot of her kids around the picnic table.*

**snapshot**

**snarl** /snɑrl/ *verb*
to make an angry sound while showing one's teeth: *The dog snarled at a cat.* *–noun* **snarl.**

**snatch** /snætʃ/ *verb* **snatches**
**1** to take something quickly: *The boy snatched a piece of cake and ate it hungrily.*
**2** to steal: *to snatch a purse*

**sneak** /snik/ *verb* **sneaked** or (informal) **snuck** /snʌk/, **sneaking, sneaks**
to try not to be seen: *The boy sneaks into the movie without paying.*
**sneak** *noun*
a coward, a dishonest person

**sneaker** /ˈsnikər/ *noun*
a soft canvas or leather shoe, worn for sports or casual activities: *My daughter put on her sneakers and ran outside to play. See:* art on pages 12a and 22a.

---

**USAGE NOTE:** *Sneaker* is a general term for an athletic shoe, which can also be called a *tennis shoe, basketball shoe, running shoe,* etc., depending on its use.

---

S

**sneaky** /ˈsniki/ *adjective*
done in a secret or dishonest way

**sneeze** /sniz/ *verb* **sneezed, sneezing, sneezes**
to send air forcefully through the nose and mouth because of an irritation, cold, allergy, etc.: *She sneezes every time that she smells pepper.* *–noun* **sneeze.**

**snip** /snɪp/ *verb* **snipped, snipping, snips**
to cut something with a short, quick motion: *The gardener snipped off dead leaves from plants with scissors.* *–noun* **snip.**

**snob** /snɑb/ *noun*
a person who thinks he or she is better than others in intelligence, social class, etc.: *They are snobs who drink only expensive French wine and won't listen to rock music.* *–noun* **snobbery.**

**snobby** /ˈsnɑbi/ *adjective* **snobbier, snobbiest**
thinking of oneself as better than others *–adjective* **snobbish.** *(antonym)* friendly.

**snoop** /snup/ *verb*
to look around secretly in a place one doesn't belong: *He was snooping in his boss's desk drawer.* *–noun* (person) **snoop.**

**snooze** /snuz/ *noun informal*
a nap: *I'm going to lie down and take a snooze.* *–verb* **to snooze.**

**snore** /snɔr/ *verb* **snored, snoring, snores**
to make sounds from one's nose and mouth while sleeping: *He snores loudly, so his wife can't sleep.*

**snore** *noun*
the sound of snoring: *Her snores are so loud you can hear them downstairs.*

**snow** /snoʊ/ *noun*
the white flakes formed by frozen water that falls from the sky in cold weather: *mountains covered with snow*

**snow** *verb*
to fall from the sky in the form of snow: *It snowed all night and now the ground is covered.*

**to be snowed in:** to be unable to leave a place because of deep snow: *We were snowed in; the car was buried.*

**snowfall** /ˈsnoʊˌfɔl/ *noun*
an amount of fallen snow: *We had a heavy snowfall that covered our car.*

**snowstorm** /ˈsnoʊˌstɔrm/ *noun*
a heavy, serious fall of snow, usually with high winds: *We are having a snowstorm now, so there will be no school.*

**snowy** /ˈsnoʊi/ *adjective* **snowier, snowiest**
full of snow: *snowy weather*

**snug** /snʌg/ *adjective*
in a small, comfortable place: *The baby is snug in its mother's arms.*

**snuggle** /ˈsnʌgəl/ *verb* **snuggled, snuggling, snuggles**
to lie or sit close to someone and touch in a loving way: *On cold winter nights, they like to snuggle in bed.*

**so** /soʊ/ *adverb*
**1** to the degree or extent that: *He is so strong that he can bend a metal pipe.*
**2** to a great extent, very: *That elephant is so big!*
**3** in that way: *Why are you running so?*
**4** because, for that reason: *I was thirsty, so I drank.*
**5** also, in the same way: *She loves animals, and so does her husband.*

**or so:** about, nearly: *Meet us at 4:00 or so.*

**so** *adjective*
true, real: *She is getting married; I know it's so because I saw her engagement ring.*

**so** *conjunction*
with a result that: *She is unemployed, so she is looking for a job.*

**so** *interjection*
indicating surprise or disapproval: *So, there you are, late again!*

**soak** /soʊk/ *verb*
to be in water for a long time: *I soaked in the tub with bubble bath.* *–noun* **soak.**

**soap** /soʊp/ *noun*
a liquid or solid cleaning substance: *I washed my face with soap.*

**soap** *verb*
to use soap: *The boy stood under the shower and soaped himself all over.* *See:* art on page 23a.

**soap opera** *noun*
a television show, usually shown in the

S

afternoon, with love stories, high emotion, and unrealistic drama: *In that soap opera, two sisters died, came back to life, and married brothers.*

**soapy** /ˈsoʊpi/ *adjective* **soapier, soapiest**
full of soap: *soapy water*

**soar** /sɔr/ *verb*
to fly high through the air with no difficulty: *The birds soared above us.*

**sob** /sɑb/ *verb* **sobbed, sobbing, sobs**
to cry loudly with the body shaking: *She sobbed and screamed when she learned of her son's death. –noun* **sob.**

**sober** /ˈsoʊbər/ *adjective*
not drunk or affected by drugs: *He is sober enough to drive. –noun* **sobriety** /səˈbraɪəti/.

**soccer** /ˈsɑkər/ *noun*
a sport of two teams of 11 players each, who kick a ball into nets at either end of a rectangular field

**social** /ˈsoʊʃəl/ *adjective*
**1** about people and society: *social problems such as homelessness and unemployment*
**2** in a group: *social animals, like cattle and monkeys See:* socialize.

**socialism** /ˈsoʊʃəˌlɪzəm/ *noun*
a political philosophy that says the government should own and run factories, hospitals, schools, etc., with the people sharing in work and products: *Under socialism, the government pays for most education. –noun* (person) **socialist;** *–adjective* **socialist.**



**socialize** /ˈsoʊʃəˌlaɪz/ *verb* **socialized, socializing, socializes**
to be with other people in a friendly way, for talking, dining, etc.: *We socialize with two other couples almost every weekend. –adjective* (friendly) **sociable.**

**Social Security** *noun*
in the USA, a governmental program that pays a monthly amount of money to retired people and others who can't work: *My grandmother buys groceries with her check from Social Security.*

**social worker** *noun*
a person who works with poor or troubled people: *A social worker visited us every week after our parents died. –noun* **social work.**

**society** /səˈsaɪəti/ *noun, plural* **societies**
**1** a large group of people who share some of the same background and culture: *American society*
**2** a club or organization: *a musical society –adjective* **societal.**

**sock** /sɑk/ *noun*
a piece of clothing worn over the foot and under a shoe, and reaching partway up the leg *See:* stockings *See:* art on page 12a.

**socket** /ˈsɑkɪt/ *noun*
a place in a wall to connect an electrical wire: *We put the lamp on a table and plugged it into a socket.*

**soda** /ˈsoʊdə/ *noun*
a flavored, bubbly drink, *(synonym)* a carbonated beverage: *We bought two types of soda: ginger ale and root beer. See:* art on page 5a.

---

**USAGE NOTE:** *Soda* is also called *soda pop, pop,* and *tonic,* in different parts of the USA. It's considered a *soft drink* because it contains no alcohol.

---

**sofa** /ˈsoʊfə/ *noun*
a long, soft seat covered with cloth or leather with a back, arms, and room for two or more people: *We like to sit on the sofa and watch television. See:* art on page 6a.

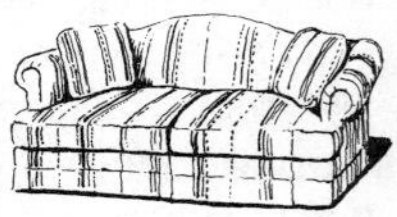

**sofa**

**soft** /sɔft/ *adjective*
**1** not hard; easy to bend or cut: *a soft pillow‖soft wood (antonym)* hard.
**2** not sharp or bright: *a soft shade of blue*
**3** not loud or strong, gentle: *soft flute music‖a soft breeze through the trees*
**4** (of consonants) making a less sharp or hard sound: *The "c" in "city" is soft, while the "c" in "cook" is hard.*

**soft-boiled** *adjective*
(of an egg) cooked in the shell for a short time in water so the inside stays soft

**soft drink** *noun*
a flavored, bubbly drink with no alcohol, such as cola or orange soda *See:* soda *See:* art on page 5a.

**soften** /ˈsɔfən/ *verb*
to make less hard: *He softened stale bread by dipping it in milk.*

**software** /ˈsɔftˌwɛr/ *noun, (no plural)*
in a computer, a set of instructions that lets a person do certain tasks, such as word processing, adding numbers, or using the Internet; software is not part of the machine itself: *I use communications software to exchange knowledge with other computer users.*

**soil** /sɔɪl/ *noun*
the top layers of earth in which plants grow: *The soil in Minnesota and Iowa is good for farming.*
**soil** *verb*
to make dirty: *to soil one's hands with grease*

**solar system** *noun*
the Sun, Earth, eight other planets, moons, comets, etc., that move around the sun: *Exploration of the solar system is fascinating.*

**sold** /soʊld/ *adjective & past participle of* sell
given in exchange for money: *If that house is not sold, I will buy it.*
**to be sold out:** to have no more left: *All the tickets for this show are sold out.*

**soldier** /ˈsoʊlʤər/ *noun*
a member of the military, especially in an army: *A soldier from the Vietnam War marched in the parade.*

**sole (1)** /soʊl/ *noun*
**1** the bottom of the foot: *The hot sidewalk burned the soles of my bare feet.*
**2** the bottom of a shoe: *The soles of my shoes have holes in them from walking a lot.*

**sole (2)** *noun, plural* **sole** or **soles**
a type of edible white fish similar to a flounder

**sole (3)** *adjective*
referring to only one of something, *(synonyms)* single, lone: *I don't have enough money; that's the sole reason I don't have a car.*

**solely** /ˈsoʊli/ *adverb*
alone, singly: *It was solely my fault that the cat ran out the door.*

**solemn** /ˈsɑləm/ *adjective*
serious: *A marriage ceremony is a solemn occasion.* –*noun* **solemnity.**

**solid** /ˈsɑlɪd/ *adjective*
**1** hard and difficult to break: *solid rock*
**2** not liquid or gas: *solid food*
**3** without holes or breaks, the same throughout: *The statue is solid marble.*
**4** trustworthy, reliable: *a solid reputation for honesty*
**solid** *noun*
something that is not liquid or gas: *The baby drinks milk and eats some solids, like bananas.* –*verb* **to solidify.**

**solitary** /ˈsɑləˌtɛri/ *adjective*
lone, single –*noun* **solitude.**

**solo** /ˈsoʊloʊ/ *adverb*
by oneself, alone: *I didn't want to go swimming, so my husband went solo.*
**solo** *adjective*
alone: *a solo performance*
**solo** *noun*
a piece of music written for one voice or instrument: *to sing a solo*||*a violin solo* –*noun* (singer or musician) **soloist.**

**so long** *interjection informal*
good-bye: *"So long for now; I'll see you later."*

**solution** /səˈluʃən/ *noun*
**1** an answer to a problem, a way of solving it: *The police found the solution to the mystery.*
**2** a mixture of a solid and a liquid, in which the solid can no longer be seen: *a solution of salt and water*

**solve** /sɑlv/ *verb* **solved, solving, solves**
to find an answer or solution for something: *We solved the problem by reading the directions.*

**some** /sʌm/ *adjective*
**1** an unknown amount, usually not a lot: *some bread*||*some money*
**2** unnamed, unknown: *Some neighbor left a cake on our front porch.*
**some** *pronoun*
part of something mentioned before: *We have coffee. Would you like some?*

**somebody** /ˈsʌmˌbɑdi/ *pronoun*
an unknown person: *Somebody telephoned but didn't give his name.*

S

**someday** /ˈsʌm,deɪ/ *adverb*
at a time in the future, not known now: *Someday you will be famous.*

**somehow** /ˈsʌm,haʊ/ *adverb*
in a way not known or understood: *Somehow, we will find water in the desert.*

**someone** /ˈsʌm,wʌn/ *pronoun*
an unknown person: *Someone should ask the police officer how to get to the park.*

**someplace** /ˈsʌm,p leɪs/ *adverb*
(at) an unknown place: *She left her purse someplace.*

**something** /ˈsʌm,θɪŋ/ *pronoun*
**1** an unknown thing: *Something in his eyes makes me think of my father.*
**2** *figurative* someone or something wonderful: *What a beautiful dress; it's really something!*

**sometime** /ˈsʌm,taɪm/ *adverb*
at an unknown time: *We can't stay here forever; we have to go sometime.*

**sometimes** /ˈsʌm,taɪmz/ *adverb*
not always, now and then: *Sometimes we go to the beach, but usually we go to the mountains.*

**someway** /ˈsʌm,weɪ/ *adverb*
*See:* somehow.

**somewhat** /ˈsʌm,wɑt/ *adverb*
to a small degree, *(synonyms)* a bit, rather: *Wear a sweater; it's somewhat cool today.*

**somewhere** /ˈsʌm,wɛr/ *adverb*
(at) an unknown place: *I can't find my glasses; I put them somewhere.*

**so much** *noun*
(of an amount) unknown: *Chicken costs so much a pound.*

S

**son** /sʌn/ *noun*
a male child: *They have two sons, so they want a daughter. See:* art on page 13a.

**song** /sɔŋ/ *noun*
a piece of music that is sung: *a love song||a bird's song*

**son-in-law** *noun, plural* **sons-in-law**
the husband of one's daughter

**sonnet** /ˈsɑnɪt/ *noun*
a poem with 14 lines and a specific pattern and rhythm: *a Shakespearean sonnet*

**soon** /sun/ *adverb*
**1** in the near future, not long from now: *We've been traveling all day and will arrive soon.*
**2** quickly, without delay: *She needs to get to the hospital as soon as possible.*

**soothe** /suð/ *verb* **soothed, soothing, soothes**
to soften mental or physical pain: *After playing tennis, she soothed her aching muscles by taking a warm bath.* *–adjective* **soothing.**

**sophisticated** /səˈfɪstə,keɪtɪd/ *adjective*
**1** with high-class tastes and understanding: *My cousins are very sophisticated, because they have lived in Paris and Rome.*
**2** complex: *sophisticated computer equipment* *–noun* **sophistication.**

**sophomore** /ˈsɑfə,mɔr/ *noun*
a student in the second year of high school or college

**soprano** /səˈprænoʊ/ *noun*
a woman or boy who sings in the highest voice range

**sore** /sɔr/ *adjective*
painful: *sore muscles* *–noun* **soreness.**

**sore throat** *noun*
a general feeling of pain in the throat, caused by a cold, infection, talking too much, etc.: *She coughed a lot, so she has a sore throat.*

**sorrow** /ˈsɑroʊ/ *noun*
deep sadness *(antonym)* joy.

**sorry** /ˈsɑri/ *adjective*
regretful, apologetic: *I'm sorry! I didn't mean to hurt you. (antonym)* glad.

**sort** /sɔrt/ *noun*
**1** a type, kind: *What sort of ice cream do you want? Vanilla?*
**2** a separation of various items: *a computer sort of our different accounts*
**sort of:** a little, somewhat: *I was sort of hungry, so I ate a banana.*

**sort** *verb*
to separate things into groups: *Would you sort these names alphabetically, please?*

**SOS** /ˈɛsoʊˈɛs/ *abbreviation of* save our ship:

a call for help: *The sinking ship sent an SOS over the radio.*

**sought** /sɔt/ *verb*
*past tense* and *past participle of* seek

**soul** /soʊl/ *noun*
the part of a person that is not the body; that is, the spirit, thoughts, emotions, etc.: *She believes the soul of her dead husband is in heaven.*

**sound** /saʊnd/ *noun*
**1** something that can be heard, a noise: *Stand still and don't make a sound.*||*I heard the sound of music.*
**2** the way something seems: *By the sound of your letter, it seems you're very happy.*

**sound** *verb*
**1** to make a sound: *The bell sounds at noon.*
**2** to appear: *You sound sad.*||*That idea sounds good to me.*

**soup** /sup/ *noun*
liquid food cooked, then served hot or cold, made from meat or vegetable juice, often with pieces of solid food: *chicken noodle soup*||*tomato soup*

**sour** /saʊr/ *adjective*
acid to the taste: *a sour lemon*||*sour milk* –*verb* **to sour.**

**source** /sɔrs/ *noun*
**1** beginning: *The source of our difficulties is not having enough money.*
**2** a place where information is obtained: *This history book is my source for accurate dates.*

**south** /saʊθ/ *noun*
the "down" direction on a compass and most maps, the direction to the left when facing a sunset: *Go toward the south to get to Mexico from Texas.*

**south** *adverb*
toward a southerly direction: *The birds flew south for the winter.*

**south** *adjective*
located to the south: *the south side of the city* –*adjective* **southerly.**

**southern** /'sʌðərn/ *adverb*
located in or about the south: *southern food*||*a southern accent*

**South Pole** *noun*
the southernmost part of the earth *(antonym)* North Pole.

**souvenir** /ˌsuvə'nɪr/ *noun*
an object bought to remember a place: *I bought a little Statue of Liberty as a souvenir of New York City.*

**sow (1)** /soʊ/ *verb* **sowed** or **sown** /soʊn/ **sowed, sowing, sows**
to plant seeds: *The farmer sowed his wheat in the spring.*

**sow (2)** /saʊ/ *noun*
an adult female pig

**soybean** /'sɔɪˌbin/ *noun*
a plant native to Asia, used for foods such as tofu, soy sauce, etc.

**spa** /spɑ/ *noun*
a hotel area with mineral springs

**space** /speɪs/ *noun*
**1** the area beyond earth in which planets, stars, moons, etc., exist: *The USA sent a spacecraft into space.*
**2** a blank or empty area: *the space between the sofa and the TV*
**3** a place used for something: *My car is in my parking space.*

**space** *verb* **spaced, spacing, spaces**
to put objects in order with empty areas in between: *I spaced the bottles neatly on the kitchen counter.*

**spacecraft** /'speɪsˌkræft/ *noun*
a vehicle that flies in space

**spacious** /'speɪʃəs/ *adverb*
large, with plenty of room: *a big, spacious room*

**spade** /speɪd/ *noun*
**1** a shovel for digging earth
**2** a black, pointed symbol found on playing cards of a particular suit: *the Queen of spades*

**spaghetti** /spə'g ɛti/ *noun, (no plural)*
long, thin food (pasta) *See:* art on page 17a.

**span** /spæn/ *noun*
the measure of time or space across, from one point to another: *The span of the roof from front to back is 20 meters.* –*verb* **to span.**

**spare** /spɛr/ *verb* **spared, sparing, spares**
**1** to save someone from harm: *The enemy soldier didn't shoot me; he spared my life.*
**2** to have enough to give or share: *Can you spare a few dollars to lend her?*

**spare** *adjective*
unused, extra: *a spare room for a guest*||*a spare tire in the car trunk*

**spark** /spark/ *noun*
a hot flash or bit of light caused by hard surfaces scraping together or from fire: *The train came to a quick stop and sparks flew from the wheels.*

sparks

**spark** *verb*
to produce sparks: *The electrical wires sparked.*

**sparkle** /ˈsparkəl/ *verb* **sparkled, sparkling, sparkles**
to give off bits of light: *diamonds that sparkle* –*noun* **sparkle.**

**spark plug** *noun*
a small part that causes an engine to start by firing a mixture of gasoline and air

**sparrow** /ˈspæroʊ/ *noun*
a small grayish-brown bird

**speak** /spik/ *verb* **spoke** /spoʊk/ or **spoken** /ˈspoʊkən/, **speaking, speaks**
**1** to say words, to talk: *I spoke with my friend on the telephone.*
**2** to know a language: *to speak Portuguese (Chinese, Spanish)*
**to speak out:** to protest: *He speaks out about problems in government.*
**to speak up:** to talk louder: *Will you speak up? I can't hear you.*

**speaker** /ˈspikər/ *noun*
someone who talks to an audience: *The speaker talked about the economy.*

**spear** /spɪr/ *noun*
a long, thin pole with a sharp point, used in hunting and war: *Hunters in India killed a tiger with a spear.*

**spear** *verb*
the act of hitting something with a spear

**special** /ˈspɛʃəl/ *adjective*
**1** important, meaningful: *A birthday party is a special occasion.*
**2** careful, greater than usual: *We gave the sick boy special attention.*

**special** *noun*
**1** a discount sale: *The grocery store is having a special on chicken.*
**2** a television show that is not part of the usual schedule: *We all watched a Christmas special.*

**specialist** /ˈspɛʃəlɪst/ *noun*
**1** a doctor who works in one area of medicine: *His family physician sent him to see a heart specialist.*
**2** a person with specific skills: *a specialist in computer design*

**specialize** /ˈspɛʃəˌlaɪz/ *verb* **specialized, specializing, specializes**
to study and work in a specific subject: *She specializes in cancer research.*

**specialty** /ˈspɛʃəlti/ *noun, plural* **specialties**
a job or subject about which one knows a lot: *As a manager, her specialty is starting new factories.*||*Surgery is that doctor's specialty.*

**species** /ˈspiʃiz/ *noun, plural* **species**
a grouping of living things: *the human species*

**specific** /spəˈsɪfɪk/ *adjective*
exact, definite: *The bank knows the specific amount of money in your account.*

**specific** *noun plural*
**the specifics:** the details: *Let's talk about the specifics of our vacation, like plane and hotel reservations.*

**specification** /ˌspɛsəfəˈkeɪʃən/ *noun, usually plural*
**1** the exact details (of a product or service), usually in writing or drawn plans: *Automobiles are built to exact specifications.*
**2** the act of specifying –*verb* **to specify.**

**speck** /spɛk/ *noun*
a tiny piece: *a speck of dust*

**spectacle** /ˈspɛktəkəl/ *noun*
a strange or amazing sight

**spectacular** /spɛk ˈtækyələr/ *adjective*
wonderful, exciting: *We had a spectacular time at the party.*

**spectator** /ˈspɛkˌteɪtər/ *noun*
an observer: *The football stadium is full of screaming spectators.*

**speech** /spitʃ/ *noun, plural* **speeches**
a talk about a subject to an audience: *The politician gave a speech to our union.*

**speed** /spid/ *noun*
**1** the rate at which something moves: *Traffic today is moving at a slow speed.*
**2** a gear in a vehicle: *With the car in a low speed, it is easier to climb hills.*

**speed** *verb* **sped** /spɛd/ or **speeded, speeding, speeds**
**1** to move quickly: *Ambulances speed sick people to the hospital.*
**2** to drive faster than the legal limit: *He was speeding at 75 mph (120 km), so the police stopped him.* *–noun* (person) **speeder.**

**speedboat** /'spid,boʊt/ *noun*
a powerful boat that can go very fast

**speeding** /'spidɪŋ/ *noun, (no plural)*
driving faster than the legal speed limit: *The driver was caught speeding.*

**speed limit** *noun*
the legal maximum speed, posted on signs along roads: *The speed limit in some states is 55 miles (88 km) per hour.*

**speedometer** /spɪ'dɑmətər/ *noun*
a device in a vehicle that shows a driver how fast he or she is going: *Your speedometer reads 80 kilometers per hour.*

**spell** /spɛl/ *noun*
**1** words or actions that cause a magic effect: *The witch's spell turned a frog into a prince.*
**2** *informal* a period of time: *You must have patience; you should wait a spell before doing anything.*

**spell** *verb* **spelled** or **spelt** /spɛlt/, **spelling, spells**
**1** to say or write the letters of a word in order: *"Dictionary" is spelled D-I-C-T-I-O-N-A-R-Y.*
**2** to be the letters of a word: *Y-E-S spells "yes."*

**spelling** /'spɛlɪŋ/ *noun*
**1** the ability to write words correctly: *Her spelling is excellent; she knows many difficult words.*
**2** how a word is spelled: *Can you tell me the spelling of "neighbor"?*

**spend** /spɛnd/ *verb* **spent** /spɛnt/, **spending, spends**
**1** to pay money for something: *He spent $400 to fix his car.*
**2** to use time and effort: *He spends a lot of time with his girlfriend.*

**spent** /spɛnt/ *verb*
*past tense & past participle of* spend

**sperm** /spɜrm/ *noun*
a male cell with a tail that can join with a female egg and make babies

**sphere** /sfɪr/ *noun*
a round object: *A ball is shaped like a sphere.*

**spice** /spaɪs/ *noun*
a flavoring for foods, such as pepper or cinnamon

**spicy** /'spaɪsi/ *adjective* **spicier, spiciest**
tasting of spices, *(synonym)* hot: *spicy tomato sauce*

**spike** /spaɪk/ *noun*
a long, sharp piece of metal, a large nail

**spill** /spɪl/ *verb* **spilled** or **spilt** /spɪlt/, **spilling, spills**
to cause or allow a liquid to fall from its container: *I spilled my coffee as I carried it to the table.*
**it's no use crying over spilled milk:** it doesn't help to be sad about something that happened in the past: *I'm sorry that I never went to college, but it's no use crying over spilled milk.*

**spill** *noun*
an act of spilling a liquid: *an oil spill from a ship*

**spin** /spɪn/ *verb* **spun** /spʌn/**, spinning, spins**
**1** to twist wool, cotton, etc. into thread: *to spin yarn*
**2** to turn around in a small circle: *He said, "Look behind you!" and I spun around.*

**spin** *noun*
a fast turning or spinning motion: *Give the wheel a spin.*

**spine** /spaɪn/ *noun*
**1** the connected bones in the back, backbone
**2** a sharp, pointed needle on living things: *the spines of a porcupine or cactus* *–adjective* **spiny.**

**spiral** /ˈspaɪrəl/ *noun*
something that curves in a circular way around a center point, like a screw or a winding staircase

**spiral** *verb*
to twist up or down: *The staircase spirals to the second floor.*

**spirit** /ˈspɪrɪt/ *noun*
**1** the nonphysical part of a person, made up of thoughts, emotions
**2** a ghost: *People think that old house is full of spirits that come out at night.* –*adjective* **spiritual.**

**spit** /spɪt/ *verb* **spat** /spæt/, **spit, spitting, spits**
to send liquid (saliva) or something else out of the mouth: *The little boy spit a baby tooth into my hand.* –*noun* **spit.**

**spite** /spaɪt/ *noun*
a feeling of wanting to hurt others: *That man broke our car window out of spite.*
**in spite of:** against what seems logical: *I write letters in spite of the fact that most people telephone.* –*adjective* **spiteful.**

**splash** /splæʃ/ *noun, plural* **splashes**
the movement and sound of a liquid as it falls: *I can hear the splash of water in the sink.*

**splash** *verb*
(of a liquid) to fly into the air: *Water splashed down a waterfall.*

**splendor** /ˈsplɛndər/ *noun*
great beauty: *the splendor of the Grand Canyon* –*adjective* **splendid.**

**splinter** /ˈsplɪntər/ *noun*
a small piece of wood or metal that breaks off from a larger piece: *I got a splinter in my foot from the old wooden floor.*

splinter

**splinter** *verb*
to break into little pieces: *The chair splintered when it fell from the truck.*

**split** /splɪt/ *verb* **split, splitting, splits**
**1** to divide something by cutting or breaking: *to split wood with an axe*
**2** to divide among people: *We split a large sandwich.*‖*They split $100: $50 each.*

**split** *noun*
a rip, break or division in something: *My old jeans have a split in the back.*

**spoil** /spɔɪl/ *verb* **spoiled** or **spoilt** /spɔɪlt/, **spoiling, spoils**
**1** (of food) to become bad or rotten: *The meat has spoiled; let's throw it out.*
**2** to give someone everything he or she wants: *They spoil their child by buying him a toy every time they go shopping.* –*adjective* **spoiled.**

**spokesperson** /ˈspoʊksˌpɜrsən/ *noun*
a person who communicates the ideas and opinions of another person, group, or company: *A spokesperson for the car company said that the new cars are the safest available.* –*noun* (man) **spokesman,** (woman) **spokeswoman.**

**sponge** /spʌnʤ/ *noun*
**1** a water animal with many holes in its skeleton and bodily tissues
**2** such an animal after it has died, or a similar-looking object, used to take up liquid or for cleaning: *Get a sponge; I spilled some juice.* –*verb* **to sponge.**

**sponsor** /ˈspɑnsər/ *noun*
a person, business, or group that helps pay for something (cultural or sporting event, TV show, etc.): *The sports store is the sponsor of the local baseball team; it pays for uniforms and transportation.*

**sponsor** *verb*
to act as a sponsor

**spontaneous** /spɑnˈteɪniəs/ *adjective*
not planned: *spontaneous laughter at a clown* –*noun* **spontaneity.**

**spool** /spul/ *noun*
a rounded object used for wrapping thread, rope, wire, etc.: *a spool of thread*

**spoon** /spun/ *noun*
an eating tool shaped like a small, shallow bowl with a handle: *He ate his cereal with a spoon. See:* art on page 5a.

**spoonful** /ˈspunfʊl/ *noun*
the amount that a spoon holds: *a spoonful of medicine*

**sport** /spɔrt/ *noun*
a game that involves physical exercise (football, baseball, tennis, etc.): *He uses his running and throwing skills in many sports.*

**spot** /spɑt/ *noun*
**1** a mark that looks different from its background: *She has a spot of lipstick on her dress.*
**2** a place, location: *We found a cool spot in the shade.*

**spot** *verb* **spotted, spotting, spots**
**1** to stain something: *to spot a dress with wine*
**2** to see: *I spotted a friend at the party and stopped to talk.*

**spotless** /ˈspɑtlɪs/ *adjective*
very clean: *The washed dishes are spotless.*

**spotlight** /ˈspɑtˌlaɪt/ *noun*
a powerful light that shines directly on someone or something: *A spotlight on our pool allows us to swim at night.*

**spotlight**

**spotty** /ˈspɑti/ *adjective*
covered with stains or spots: *a spotty tablecloth*

**spouse** /spaʊs/ *noun*
a husband or wife: *My spouse and I have been married for seven years.*

**sprain** /spreɪn/ *verb*
to hurt a body part by turning or putting too much pressure on it: *to sprain an ankle* –*noun* **sprain.**

**sprang** /spræŋ/ *verb*
*past participle of* spring

**spray** /spreɪ/ *verb*
to send something out over an area: *In summer, the kids spray each other with the water hose.*

**spray** *noun*
liquid that spreads in drops over an area: *a spray of perfume*

**spread** /sprɛd/ *verb* **spread, spreading, spreads**
**1** to cover a surface by pushing something all over it: *to spread butter on bread*
**2** to cause something to go a distance to many people: *to spread the news*||*to spread disease*
**3** to lay out smoothly and flat: *to spread a tablecloth*

**spread** *noun, (no plural)*
**1** a food that can be put on bread, crackers, etc. with a knife: *a cheese spread*
**2** movement over an area: *the spread of good news*

**spring** /sprɪŋ/ *noun*
**1** a piece of metal wire in a coil, that stretches and goes back to its original shape: *My sofa has springs, so it doesn't feel hard when I sit down.*
**2** a place where water comes naturally out of the ground: *We drank from a spring in the mountains.*
**3** the season between winter and autumn: *In the spring, we plant flowers and watch the days grow longer.*

**spring** *verb* **sprang** /spræŋ/ or **sprung** /sprʊŋ/**, springing, springs**
to jump by bending and then straightening the knees: *The deer springs across the field.*

**to spring a leak:** to get a hole and let air or water through: *The little boat sprang a leak and sank.*

**springtime** /ˈsprɪŋˌtaɪm/ *noun*
the season between winter and summer: *We enjoy fishing in the springtime.*

**sprinkle** /ˈsprɪŋkəl/ *noun*
**1** a short, light rainfall
**2** drops of liquid or tiny pieces of something falling: *a sprinkle of cheese*

**sprinkle** *verb* **sprinkled, sprinkling, sprinkles**
**1** to rain lightly: *Oh, it's sprinkling; I'll get my hat.*
**2** to cause to fall in drops or tiny pieces: *to sprinkle salt on meat* –*noun* (device) **sprinkler,** (act) **sprinkling.**

**sprung** /sprʌŋ/ *verb*
*past participle of* spring

**sputter** /ˈspʌtər/ *verb*
to make off and on sounds: *an engine that sputters*

**spy** /spaɪ/ *noun, plural* **spies**
a person who gains secret information and reports back to his or her government

**spy** *verb* **spied, spying, spies**
to collect information secretly: *He followed his wife and spied on her.*

**squad** /skwɑd/ *noun*
a small, organized group of people: *a football squad*

**squander** /ˈskwɑndər/ *verb*
to spend too much

**square** /skwɛr/ *noun*
**1** a shape with four equal sides: *The side of this box is a square.*
**2** (in math) the result of multiplying a number by itself: *The square of three is nine.*
**3** a place in a town where several streets meet: *There's a sandwich shop in the square.*

**square** *adjective* **squarer, squarest**
**1** having four equal sides: *a square mirror*
**2** a measurement for an area: *square meters*

**square** *verb* **squared, squaring, squares**
(in math) to multiply something by itself: *I squared 4 and got 16. See:* art on page 16a.

**squash (1)** /skwɑʃ/ *verb*
to make flat by pressing: *I squashed an insect with my foot.*

**squash (2)** *noun*
any of a variety of vegetables with a hard or firm skin and seeds inside: *zucchini squash||butternut squash See:* art on page 2a.

**squat** /skwɑt/ *verb* **squatted, squatting, squats**
to bend the knees and sit on the heels: *The boy squatted behind a chair so he wouldn't be seen.*

**squeak** /skwik/ *noun*
a sharp, high-pitched sound that is not very loud: *a squeak in a door –verb* **to squeak;** *–adjective* **squeaky.**



**squeal** /skwil/ *noun*
a high-pitched scream: *the squeal of a pig –verb* **to squeal.**

**squeeze** /skwiz/ *verb* **squeezed, squeezing, squeezes**
to press from two or more sides: *He put his arms around his girlfriend and squeezed her.||I squeezed lemon juice into my iced tea.*

**squeeze** *noun*
**1** the act of pressing from two or more sides: *She gave the beach ball a squeeze to let the air out.*
**2** a tight fit into something: *My car has room for four; five is a squeeze.*

**squid** /skwɪd/ *noun, plural* **squid** or **squids**
an edible water animal with ten legs

**squirrel** /ˈskwɜrəl/ *noun*
a small, usually gray animal with a long fluffy tail
**to squirrel something away:** to save: *Each week, he squirrels away $50 from his paycheck. See:* art on page 14a.

squirrel

**squirt** /skwɜrt/ *verb*
(of liquid) to send or come out in a thin line: *I squirted dishwashing soap onto the plate.*

**squirt** *noun*
a thin stream of liquid: *a squirt of window cleaner*

**stab** /stæb/ *verb* **stabbed, stabbing, stabs**
to cut with something sharp: *to stab someone with a knife*

**stab** *noun*
the motion of cutting into with something sharp: *He gave the meat a stab with his fork. –noun* (person) **stabber,** (act) **stabbing.**

**stable (1)** /ˈsteɪbəl/ *adjective*
**1** strong, steady: *a stable table with four thick legs*
**2** a calm, undisturbed state: *My life is more stable since I found a job and moved to the country. –noun* **stability.**

**stable (2)** *noun*
a building like a small barn for keeping horses, cows, etc. *See:* barn.

**stack** /stæk/ *verb*
to place one object upon another: *to stack boxes*

**stack** *noun*
a group of objects placed one upon the other: *a stack of newspapers*

**stadium** /ˈsteɪdi əm/ *noun, plural* **stadiums**
a playing area surrounded by seats, for sports, concerts, and other events: *We went to the football stadium on Saturday to see the game.*

**staff** /stæf/ *noun*
a group of workers: *the secretarial staff ||the sales staff*

**staff** *verb*
to interview and hire workers for jobs: *to staff a new office*

**stage** /steɪʤ/ *verb* **staged, staging, stages**
to put on entertainment for the public: *to stage a concert*

**stage** *noun*
**1** in a theater or auditorium, a floor that is higher than the audience's seats, used for performers
**2** a period of time in a process: *The river water is at a very high stage and will flood the land.*

**stagnant** /'stægnənt/ *adjective*
(of liquid) not moving, often with a bad smell: *We could not drink the water in the stagnant pond.* –*verb* **to stagnate** /'stægneɪt/; –*noun* **stagnation.**

**stain** /steɪn/ *verb*
to get a spot of color on something: *He stained his shirt with coffee.*

**stain** *noun*
**1** a spot of color (dirt, liquid, etc.): *a grass stain on pants*
**2** damage: *Her one grade of C was a stain on her good school record.*
**3** a type of thin paint through which wood is still visible

**stair** /stɛr/ *noun*
**1** a step in a flight of steps: *The girl stood on a stair and said goodnight.*
**2** *plural* **stairs:** several steps going up: *I took the stairs to the second floor.*

**staircase** /'stɛr,ke ɪs/ *noun*
a set of steps going up: *the staircase to the top floor*

**stairway** /'stɛr,weɪ/ *noun*
*See:* staircase.

**stake** /steɪk/ *verb* **staked, staking, stakes**
**1** to risk: *I'm telling the truth; I stake my life on it.*
**2** to give money for: *The company staked that new factory from last year's profits.*

**stake** *noun*
**1** a narrow, pointed piece of wood or metal used as a marker: *A stake in the ground shows where our yard ends.*
**2** an interest in something (often a financial one): *I have a stake in the restaurant's success, since my money helped start it.*

**stale** /steɪl/ *adjective*
not fresh or new: *stale bread||stale old war stories (antonym)* fresh.

**stalk (1)** /stɔk/ *verb*
to follow someone, usually waiting for a chance to attack: *a hunter who stalks deer in the woods*

**stalk (2)** *noun*
a stem of a plant: *a bean stalk*

**stall** /stɔl/ *verb*
**1** to keep something from happening, *(synonym)* to delay: *We're late meeting our friend; I think you're stalling by cleaning the house.*
**2** (of an engine) to stop working: *My car stalled and I couldn't get it started again.* –*noun* **stall.**

**stamina** /'stæmənə/ *noun*
the ability to exercise or work for a long time: *I don't have much stamina.*

**stammer** /'stæmər/ *verb*
to speak with many pauses and repeated words or syllables: *The shy boy stammered when he asked the pretty girl to the movies.* –*noun* **stammer.**

**stamp** /stæmp/ *noun*
**1** a small rectangle of paper with a picture and amount of money printed on it, used on things to be mailed: *I put a postage stamp on a letter and mailed it.*
**2** something that prints or causes a raised mark (on paper): *She has a rubber stamp of a flower.*

**stamp** *verb*
**1** to force a foot down to the ground: *The child stamped her foot and said, "I won't eat these carrots!"*
**2** to print or make a raised mark with something: *The lawyer stamped the paper to show it was legal.*

**to stamp something out:** to get rid of completely

**stampede** /stæm'pid/ *noun*
a rush forward as a group: *a cattle stampede* –*verb* **to stampede.**

**stand** /stænd/ *noun*
**1** a piece of furniture that holds or displays something: *a plant stand*
**2** a small area, often with just a table, for

selling things: *The children set up a lemonade stand for people walking by.*
**3** an opinion that one expresses firmly: *The mayor took a stand for the building of a new high school.*
**stand** *verb* **stood** /stʊd/, **standing, stands**
**1** to rise (from sitting or lying) to one's feet: *She got out of bed and stood.*
**2** to be on one's feet: *I'm tired of standing; let's find some chairs.*
**3** *informal* to like enough: *The ocean water is cold, but I can stand it enough to go swimming.*||*He can't stand the pressure of his job.*
**to know where one stands (with someone):** to know one's position (in the opinion of others): *I know where I stand with my boss; she likes me and my work.*
**to stand by:** at an airport, to wait to find out if there is space on a flight: *The ticket seller said we should stand by, and we did get on the flight. See:* standby.
**to stand by something** or **someone:** to not change, to stay faithful to: *I will always stand by you and be your friend.*
**to stand for something:** **a.** to have or represent an idea: *This country stands for life, liberty, and the pursuit of happiness.* **b.** to mean: *X in that math equation stands for an unknown amount.*
**to stand on one's own two feet:** not to need any help, to be self-supporting: *He can stand on his own two feet, without money from his parents.*
**to stand up:** **a.** to get on one's feet: *He was sitting, then he stood up.* **b.** to remain true: *After looking at the facts, his argument stands up.*

S

**standard** /ˈstændərd/ *noun*
**1** something against which other things or ideas are measured: *All new cars must meet the standard for pollution control.*
**2** *plural* **standards:** needs or expectations: *She has high standards; she dates only handsome, rich men.*
**standard** *adjective*
**1** commonly accepted as normal: *Sunny weather is standard in Southern California.*
**2** always part of something: *Seat belts are now standard on all new cars.*
**standard of living** *noun*
the way people live in terms of the quality of housing, food, buying power, recreational opportunities, etc.: *The standard of living in the poor country got better when more people became educated and found jobs.*
**standby** /ˈstænd,baɪ/ *noun*
someone or something that is always ready and available: *I have a new sports car, but this truck is my old standby.*
**on standby:** **a.** ready to work if needed: *The doctor is on standby in case of an emergency.* **b.** ready to go if space on an airplane becomes available: *We could not get a reservation on the flight that we wanted, so we were on standby.*
**standing** /ˈstændɪŋ/ *noun*
one's situation and place among others: *an employee in good standing*
**standing** *adjective*
related to standing: *Almost all the concert tickets are sold; standing room is all that is available at this performance.*
**staple** /ˈsteɪpəl/ *noun*
a small piece of metal whose ends bend to hold papers together *–verb* **to staple.**
**stapler** /ˈsteɪplər/ *noun*
a tool that holds staples and presses them through paper, etc.

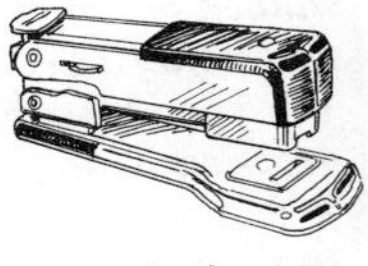
stapler

**star** /stɑr/ *noun*
**1** a bright, hot ball of gas in the sky, and the others seen at night as dots of light: *Our sun is a star.*
**2** a shape, usually with five or six points going in different directions from a central point
**3** very famous performer: *a movie star*
**star** *verb* **starred, starring, stars**
to have a large, important part: *He stars in a new film.*
**starch** /stɑrʧ/ *noun, plural* **starches**
**1** a liquid sprayed or put on clothes to make them stiff
**2** a part of many foods, including bread, potatoes, and rice
**starch** *verb* **starches**
to put starch on clothes: *I starched my dress.* *–adjective* **starchy.**
**stardom** /ˈstɑrdəm/ *noun*
the condition of being a famous performer: *The actress's goal is to achieve Hollywood stardom.*

**stare** /stɛr/ *verb* **stared, staring, stares**
to look at someone or something steadily: *I told my son to stop staring at the fat woman; it wasn't nice.* –*noun* **stare.**

**Star-Spangled Banner** *noun*
the national song of the USA

**start** /stɑrt/ *verb*
**1** to begin: *He started to cry.*
**2** to cause an action to begin: *She started the fashion for wearing plaid skirts.*
**3** to move one's body quickly and suddenly in surprise: *She started when the door slammed.*
**to start off:** to begin: *The speaker started off by describing her background.*
**to start something up: a.** to begin something: *He started up his company in 1990.* **b.** to turn on an engine: *The driver started her car up and drove away.*

**start** *noun*
a beginning: *I made a start on my homework. (antonym)* stop.

**startle** /'stɑrtl/ *verb* **startled, startling, startles**
to surprise, sometimes making someone jump: *I was studying when the phone rang and startled me.* –*adjective* **startled, startling.**

**starvation** /stɑr'veɪʃən/ *noun*
the state of having no food

**starve** /stɑrv/ *verb* **starved, starving, starves**
to feel pain or to die from lack of food: *The travelers got lost in the mountains and starved to death.* –*adjective* **starved, starving.**

**state** /steɪt/ *noun*
**1** a nation, country: *the state of Israel*
**2** a part of a country that has its own government and laws in addition to those of the country: *Rhode Island is the smallest state in the USA.*
**3** a situation or position, physical, mental, or emotional: *She has cancer, so the state of her health is bad.*

**state** *verb* **stated, stating, states**
to say, often in a formal way: *The law states that you cannot smoke on most airline flights.*

**stately** /'steɪtli/ *adjective*
very grand and serious: *The queen has a very stately manner.*

**statement** /'steɪtmənt/ *noun*
the act of saying or writing something: *People asked the mayor to make a statement about crime in the city.*

**static** /'stætɪk/ *noun*
the crackling noise on the radio or TV caused by electrical interference: *I can't hear the ball game through the static.*

**station** /'steɪʃən/ *noun*
**1** a place for the arrival and departure of transportation: *a railroad station*
**2** a place or building from which a service is provided: *a television station*||*a police station*

**station** *verb*
to place at a location: *to station a soldier at a training camp*

**stationary** /'steɪʃə,nɛri/ *adjective*
not moving or able to be moved: *The teacher asked us to remain stationary in our seats.*

**stationery** /'steɪʃə,nɛri/ *noun, (no plural)*
envelopes and paper for writing letters: *Her stationery has her name and address printed on it.*

**station wagon** *noun*
a long car with a covered back section: *We have a big family, but we can all fit in a station wagon.*

station wagon

**statistic** /stə'tɪstɪk/ *noun*
a number that represents something: *His death in a car accident was just another statistic in the death rate.* –*adjective* **statistical;** –*noun* (person) **statistician.**

**statistics** /stə' tɪstɪks/ *noun plural*
**1** *used with a singular verb* the study of numerical information: *Statistics is an easy subject for someone who is good at math.*
**2** *used with a plural verb* a collection of numerical information: *The statistics on AIDS deaths are frightening.*

**statue** /'stætʃu/ *noun*
the form of a person, animal, or thing, usually made from stone, wood, or metal: *a statue of George Washington*

**Statue of Liberty** *noun*
the huge statue of a woman holding a

S

torch, standing on an island near the southern tip of Manhattan in New York City; a famous symbol of freedom in the USA, and a popular tourist spot

**status** /ˈstætəs/ *noun*
**1** the condition of something at a particular time: *What is the status of our loan application with the bank?*
**2** one's position in society in terms of power and importance: *Doctors have more status than mechanics in US society.*
**3** a legal condition: *to have the status of a US citizen*

**stay** /steɪ/ *verb*
to continue to be in one place: *I can't stay long; I have to leave soon.*
**to stay at:** **a.** to visit, especially as a guest: *We stay at the same hotel on vacation.* **b.** to remain at the same level: *The temperature has stayed at zero for days.*
**to stay up:** to keep awake: *The student stayed up all night to study.*

**stay** *noun*
a visit: *a stay in a country hotel*

**steady** /ˈstɛdi/ *verb* **steadied, steadying, steadies**
**1** to make firm: *He held the ladder to steady it.*
**2** to make calm: *to steady one's nerves*

**steady** *adjective* **steadier, steadiest**
**1** firm, not going to fall over or break: *The chair is steady since I fixed it.*
**2** without interruption: *a steady rainfall||a steady diet of good food*
**3** calm, *(synonym)* dependable: *She is a steady person who thinks before she acts.*
**4** *informal* (of a girlfriend or boyfriend) regular or exclusive: *my steady girlfriend*

**steady** *noun*
a boyfriend or girlfriend with whom one is exclusive

**steak** /steɪk/ *noun*
a piece of meat or fish, usually about an inch (2 cm) thick: *Today, I'll have a broiled swordfish steak.*

**steal** /stil/ *verb* **stole** /stoʊl/, **stolen** /ˈstoʊlən/, **stealing, steals**
to take something that belongs to someone else without permission: *A thief stole my car.*

**steam** /stim/ *noun*
gas made by heated water under pressure: *Steam came out of the tea kettle.*
**to let off steam:** to show anger instead of holding it in: *He shouted and threw things to let off steam.*

**steam** *verb*
to give off steam: *a broken pipe that steams –adjective* **steaming.**

**steel** /stil/ *noun*
a hard metal made of carbon and iron: *a ship made of wood and steel*

**steep** /stip/ *adjective* **steeper, steepest**
at a high angle at which something or someone could easily fall: *We walked up a steep mountain road.*

**steeple** /ˈstipəl/ *noun*
the top, pointed section of a church

steeple

**steer (1)** /stɪr/ *verb*
to control the direction: *I steered my car into a parking space.||My dad steered me into his office and sat me down.*

**steer (2)** *noun*
a young ox that is raised for beef *See:* bull; ox.

**steering wheel** *noun*
in a vehicle, the circular object turned by a driver to control direction: *The driver turned the steering wheel to the left and the car went left.*

**stem** /stɛm/ *noun*
**1** thin part of a plant from which a flower grows: *the stem of a rose*
**2** a long part of something: *the stem of a wine glass*

**step** /stɛp/ *noun*
**1** a walking movement, the act of lifting the foot, moving it forward, and putting it down: *The baby took her first step today!*
**2** a short distance: *The shopping area is a few steps from the parking lot.*
**3** one in a set of stairs: *She came partway down to the bottom step.*
**4** *noun plural* **steps:** a set of stairs, staircase: *We put flower pots on the front steps of the house.*

**5** one action toward a goal: *the first step in our plan*

**step** *verb* **stepped, stepping, steps**
**1** to walk
**2** to place the foot: *to step on the sidewalk*

**to step out:** to leave for a moment: *He is not in his office; he stepped out but will be back shortly.*

**stepbrother** /ˈstɛpˌbrʌðər/ *noun*
the son of a parent's spouse who does not share a parent with oneself: *When my father remarried, his wife's sons became my stepbrothers.*

**stepchild** /ˈstɛpˌʧaɪld/ *noun, plural* **stepchildren** /-ˌʧɪldrən/
a son or daughter of one's spouse that is not one's own natural-born child

**stepdaughter** /ˈstɛpˌdɔtər/ *noun*
a daughter of one's spouse that is not one's own natural-born child

**stepfather** /ˈstɛpˌfɑðər/ *noun*
the husband of one's mother who is not one's own father

**stepladder** /ˈstɛpˌlædər/ *noun*
a ladder with a support section that is put into a locked position

**stepladder**

**stepmother** /ˈstɛpˌmʌðər/ *noun*
the wife of a child's father who is not the child's own mother

**stepparent** /ˈstɛpˌpɛrənt/ *noun*
a stepfather or stepmother

**stepsister** /ˈstɛpˌsɪstər/ *noun*
the daughter of a parent's spouse that is not one's own natural-born sister

**stepson** /ˈstɛpˌsʌn/ *noun*
a son of one's spouse that is not one's own natural-born son

**stereo** /ˈstɛriˌoʊ/ *noun*
*short for* stereophonic: a sound system (radio, CD player, etc.) that uses two speakers *See:* art on page 6a.

**stereotype** /ˈstɛriəˌtaɪp/ *noun*
**1** a person who is typical of a group: *The stereotype of a Wall Street banker carries a briefcase.*
**2** a simple and often mistaken idea about a group: *It is a stereotype that all women cry easily.* *–verb* **to stereotype.**

**sterile** /ˈstɛrəl/ *adjective*
**1** completely clean, with no bacteria: *A hospital's operating room is a sterile area.*
**2** unable to have children: *The couple adopted a baby because the man is sterile. (antonym)* fertile.

**sterilize** /ˈstɛrəˌlaɪz/ *verb* **sterilized, sterilizing, sterilizes**
to make completely clean: *to sterilize a needle with a match* *–noun* **sterilization.**

**sterling** /ˈstɛrlɪŋ/ *noun*
a metal that is more than 92 percent pure silver

**stew** /stu/ *noun*
a thick soup, usually a mixture of meat and vegetables: *beef stew*

**stick** /stɪk/ *verb* **stuck** /stʌk/, **sticking, sticks**
**1** to put in place with a pointed object: *He stuck a nail in the wood to mark the spot.*
**2** to attach with glue or tape: *The student stuck a poster on the wall with tape.*
**3** to make a hole with a thin or pointed object: *She accidentally stuck a needle in her finger.*
**4** to cause to move outward or forward: *The little girl stuck her tongue out.*
**5** not to move, even when pushed or pulled: *The top drawer sticks; I can't open it.*

**to stick someone** or **something up:** to rob with a gun or knife: *The thief stuck up a grocery store and stole $3,000.*

**to stick together:** to stay close or loyal to others, *(synonym)* to unite: *That family sticks together and helps each other.*

**stick** *noun*
**1** a small tree branch that has fallen off the tree: *to burn sticks in the fireplace*
**2** a long, thin piece of something: *a stick of dynamite*

**sticker** /ˈstɪkər/ *noun*
a label or small decoration with glue on the back: *She put a sticker on the envelope to mark it "airmail."*

**stickup** /ˈstɪkˌʌp/ *noun slang*
a robbery, especially by someone with a gun: *There was a stickup at the bank this morning.*

**sticky** /ˈstɪki/ *adjective* **stickier, stickiest**
**1** tending to attach because of a glue-like surface: *sticky wet paint*
**2** humid, hot: *sticky summer weather*

**stiff** /stɪf/ *adjective* **stiffer, stiffest**
**1** difficult to bend or move: *a stiff piece of wood*
**2** severe, serious: *a stiff fine for drunk driving –noun* **stiffness.**

**stiff** *adverb*
completely, totally: *scared stiff*

**stiffen** /ˈstɪfən/ *verb*
to grow hard or rigid, not easily moved: *a hip that has stiffened with age*

**still** /stɪl/ *verb*
to calm: *to still someone's fears*

**still** *adverb*
**1** motionless: *I stood still when I saw a deer in the field.*
**2** until a certain time, yet: *She was still asleep when I went to work.*
**3** all the same: *I don't eat much; still, I like to go to restaurants.*
**4** more, further: *We need still more time to finish the exam.*

**still** *adjective* **stiller, stillest**
**1** not moving, calm: *a still lake*
**2** silent, quiet: *The woods were still, with no wind in the trees. –noun* **stillness.**

**still** *noun*
**1** a piece of equipment for making liquor
**2** a photograph from a film

S

**stimulate** /ˈstɪmyəˌleɪt/ *verb* **stimulated, stimulating, stimulates**
to increase energy or activity: *Cold air stimulates me. –noun* **stimulant, stimulation.**

**stimulus** /ˈstɪmyələs/ *noun, plural* **stimuli** /-ˌlaɪ/
something that causes an action or response

**sting** /stɪŋ/ *verb* **stung** /stʌŋ/, **stinging, stings**
to cut into the skin, usually with poison: *This summer, I was stung by a bee.*

**sting** *noun*
**1** the act or result of stinging: *a bee sting*
**2** painful sensation: *the sting of alcohol on a cut*

**stingy** /ˈstɪndʒi/ *adjective* **stingier, stingiest**
not wanting to share or spend: *Don't be stingy; give me a bite of your sandwich. –noun* **stinginess.**

**stink** /stɪŋk/ *verb* **stank** /stæŋk/, **stunk** /stʌŋk/, **stinking, stinks**
**1** to smell bad: *a dirty refrigerator that stinks*
**2** to have a bad quality: *Don't read this book; it stinks.*

**stink** *noun*
a bad smell: *the stink from rotting vegetables*

**stir** /stɜr/ *verb* **stirred, stirring, stirs**
to move something (such as a spoon) in a circular motion through a liquid or mixture: *He stirred sugar into the tea.*

**stir** *noun*
a circular movement with something (such as a spoon): *to give the soup a stir*

**stitch** /stɪtʃ/ *verb* **stitches**
to sew together with thread: *I stitched a sleeve onto a dress with a sewing machine.*

**stitch** *noun, plural* **stitches**
one movement of a needle with thread in and then out of cloth or skin: *Her mother taught her to sew with tiny stitches.||He cut his hand and needed eight stitches.*
**a stitch in time saves nine:** something done now will save more work later: *He noticed a leaky pipe and fixed it immediately so it wouldn't cause a flood; a stitch in time saves nine. –noun* **stitching.**

**stock** /stɑk/ *verb*
to keep or have for sale: *The auto parts store stocks headlights.*

**stock** *noun*
**1** the items for sale in a store: *Some stock is on the shelves; the rest is in a back room.*
**2** a supply collected for the future: *We have a stock of candles in case the lights go out during a storm.*
**3** animals on a farm: *All the stock are in the barn for the night.*
**4** a piece of a business, bought in the form of shares: *She bought stock in a toy company. See:* share.

**in stock:** available for sale: *We have the paint that you need in stock.*
**out of stock:** not available for sale: *I'm sorry, but the dress that you want is out of stock.*

**stockings** /'stɑkɪŋ/ *noun plural*
a covering for a woman's foot and leg: *The woman bought nylon stockings. See:* nylons; pantyhose.

**stolen** /'stoʊlən/ *adjective and past participle of* steal
taken illegally: *The police followed a woman driving a stolen car.*

**stomach** /'stʌmək/ *noun*
the internal body part where food goes after being swallowed: *My stomach feels full after eating ice cream. See:* art on page 21a.

**stomachache** /'stʌmək,eɪk/ *noun*
pain in the belly or abdomen *See:* art on page 11a.

**stone** /stoʊn/ *noun*
**1** rock: *We live in a house made of stone.*
**2** a small piece of rock: *The little girl threw stones into the pond.*
**3** a jewel or gem: *How many stones are in your diamond ring?*

**stood** /stʊd/ *verb*
*past tense of* stand

**stool** /stul/ *noun*
a three- or four-legged seat without a back: *She sat on a stool.*

**stoop** /stup/ *verb*
to bend forward at the waist
**stoop** *noun*
**1** the act of bending forward with the head lowered: *to walk with a stoop*
**2** the stairs in front of a house or building: *Our neighbors sit on the stoop in the evening.*

**stop** /stɑp/ *verb* **stopped, stopping, stops**
**1** to end a movement: *I put on the brakes and the car stopped. (antonym)* to go.
**2** to end an activity: *Stop eating; you've had enough. (antonym)* to continue.
**3** to fill in an opening: *The plumber stopped a leak in a pipe*
**to stop at something:** to pause in a trip: *The bus stops at the corner.*
**to stop in:** to visit for a short time: *Our friend was passing by and stopped in to say hi.*
**stop** *noun*
**1** an end to motion: *The train came to a stop.*
**2** an end to activity: *There was a stop in work when lunchtime came.*
**3** a place for stopping: *a bus stop*

**stoplight** /'stɑp,laɪt/ *noun*
a traffic light: *You must wait when the stoplight turns red.*

**storage** /'stɔrɪʤ/ *noun, (no plural)*
a place for keeping things until they are needed: *Our business puts old financial records in storage until tax time.*

**store** /stɔr/ *noun*
**1** a place where things are bought and sold: *My friend worked in a grocery store in the fruit section.*
**2** a supply of something: *Dad has a store of batteries in a drawer.*
**in store:** about to happen: *There is a big surprise in store for you.*
**store** *verb*
to keep somewhere for future use: *We store meat in a freezer downstairs.* *–noun* **storing.**

**storm** /stɔrm/ *verb*
to rain or snow heavily, with strong winds: *We could not see across the street; it was storming so hard.*
**storm** *noun*
heavy rain or snow with high winds: *The storm lasted all night and now the river is flooded.*

**story (1)** /'stɔri/ *noun, plural* **stories**
**1** a piece of fiction (made up in one's mind; not true or real) written or told out loud: *He read the child a story about a rabbit who talks.*
**2** a real event, written or told out loud: *My aunt told the story of her childhood in Mexico.*
**3** a written tale, usually for adults *See:* short story.
**to make a long story short:** to give a short description of a complicated event
**What's the story?:** What is the situation now?: *You have been talking about the problem; what's the story? Do you have a solution?*

**story** or **storey (2)** *noun*
a level of a building: *Our house has three bedrooms on the second story.*

**stove** /stoʊv/ *noun*
a piece of kitchen equipment usually containing an oven, used to cook food: *Please turn down the heat on the stove or the soup will burn. See:* art on page 7a.

**straight** /streɪt/ *adjective* **straighter, straightest**
**1** in the form of a line without bending or curving: *a straight ruler*||*a straight line (antonym)* crooked.
**2** direct, clear: *a straight answer to a question*
**3** without interruption: *The storm lasted for three straight days.*
**4** not homosexual
**5** not taking or under the effects of drugs or alcohol

**straight** *adverb*
**1** with no water added: *to drink vodka straight*
**2** not bending: *to stand straight*
**3** without stopping: *I went straight to the bank when I got paid.*
**4** honestly: *Tell me straight.*

**straighten** /ˈstreɪtn/ *verb*
**1** to make straight, even: *The worker straightened a bent wire.*
**2** to make neat: *She straightened her messy closet.*

**to straighten someone** or **something out:** to solve problems, come to understand: *We are straightening the details out.*

**to straighten up: a.** to behave better: *You kids straighten up or we won't go out for ice cream.* **b.** to make neat and orderly: *The place was a mess after the party, so I straightened up.*

**strain** /streɪn/ *verb*
**1** to use great effort: *I strained to lift a heavy box.*
**2** to cause disagreement: *She married someone of a different religion, and that strained her relationship with her parents.*
**3** to stretch a part of one's body until there is pain or damage: *I strained a muscle in my back playing baseball.*
**4** to separate something from something else by passing or pouring it through holes: *She strained the chicken soup to take off some fat. –adjective* **strained;** *–noun* (kitchen tool) **strainer, strain.**

**strait** /streɪt/ *noun*
a narrow area of water joining two larger areas of water: *The Straits of Hormuz are between the Persian Gulf and the Gulf of Oman.*

**strange** /streɪndʒ/ *adjective* **stranger, strangest**
**1** unusual: *The girl picked a strange and beautiful flower.*
**2** difficult to understand: *We find it strange that your child doesn't like toys.*
**3** unknown: *His accent is strange to me; where is he from? –noun* **strangeness.**

**stranger** /ˈstreɪndʒər/ *noun*
an unfamiliar person, someone new to a place: *A stranger on the street asked for directions to the highway.*

**strangle** /ˈstræŋgəl/ *verb* **strangled, strangling, strangles**
to kill or harm by squeezing the throat, so no air can get through: *The murderer strangled the man. –noun* **strangulation.**

**strap** /stræp/ *verb*
to attach or hold someone or something: *She strapped herself into the car with a seat belt. –noun* **strap.**

**strategy** /ˈstræt ədʒi/ *noun*
planning to achieve a goal: *Our company's strategy is to make good products while keeping prices lower than the competition. –adjective* **strategic** /strəˈtidʒɪk/.

**straw** /strɔ/ *noun*
**1** dried grain stems without the grain, used for animal beds and for weaving mats, hats, and baskets: *She bought a straw hat from an island woman.*
**2** a thin tube of plastic or strong paper, used to draw a drink into the mouth: *She took a drink of cola through a straw. See:* art on page 5a.

**the last straw** or **the straw that broke the camel's back:** the final event, the last difficulty one can bear: *The TV picture jumps up and down, and now the sound is bad. That's the last straw; I'm buying a new TV!*

**strawberry** /ˈstrɔˌbɛri/ *noun, plural* **strawberries**
a small, red, sweet fruit with tiny seeds, high in vitamin C *See:* art on page 3a.

strawberries

**stray** /streɪ/ *verb*
to go beyond the limits of an area: *Our dog strayed into a neighbor's yard.*

**streak** /strik/ *verb*
**1** to move or run very fast: *The speedboat streaked across the lake.*
**2** to make marks or stains in the form of lines: *The windshield is so streaked with dirt that I can't see the road.*

**streak** *noun*
**1** a mark or stain in the form of a line, blur: *Let the ink dry, or it will make streaks when you touch it.*
**2** a period of time in which something happens: *I'm on a lucky streak: I found $5 on the street and won a free pizza!* –*noun* **streaking;** –*adjective* **streaky.**

**stream** /strim/ *noun*
**1** a flowing body of water, smaller than a river: *They had a picnic near a stream that ran down the mountain.*
**2** liquid moving steadily, without separating: *A stream of water came from the garden hose.*

stream

**stream** *verb*
to flow like a stream: *People streamed into the train station.*

**street** /strit/ *noun*
a road for cars and trucks, often with sidewalks for walkers: *The car turned right on Washington Street. See:* avenue, boulevard, road.

**USAGE NOTE:** We usually speak of *streets* in the city and *roads* in both the country and city: *The streets were crowded with shoppers.*||*My car almost hit a dog that was crossing the road.* An *avenue* is a wide street, often lined with trees: *Fifth Avenue is one of New York City's most famous streets.* A *boulevard* is a broad, tree-lined avenue, which may have a central island dividing the lanes of traffic: *Hollywood Boulevard is lined with palm trees.*

**streetlight** /ˈstritˌlaɪt/ *noun*
a light on a tall pole to make a street less dark at night *See:* art on page 4a.

streetlight

**strength** /strɛŋkθ/ *noun*
**1** muscle power: *I don't have the strength to move that table alone.*
**2** mental or emotional toughness: *She has the strength to help us with our problems.*
**3** not able to be gone through or broken: *the strength of a heavy wooden door*
**4** an activity at which one is skilled or talented: *Art is not one of her strengths.* *(antonym)* weakness.

**strengthen** /ˈstrɛŋkθən/ *verb*
to make or become stronger: *Exercising every day strengthens the heart.*

**stress** /strɛs/ *noun, plural* **stresses**
mental or physical strain or difficulty caused by pressure: *She is full of stress because her boss gives her too much work.*

**stress** *verb* **stresses**
to give strength to: *Her husband stressed the idea that she should change jobs and relax more. See:* art on page 18a.

**stressful** /ˈstrɛsfəl/ *adjective*
causing worry and tiredness

**stretch** /strɛʧ/ *verb* **stretches**
to make wider, longer, or larger by pushing or pulling: *If I wear my new shoes for a while, the leather will stretch.*||*The cat stretched her legs after her sleep.* –*noun* **stretch.**

**stretcher** /ˈstrɛʧər/ *noun*
a piece of hospital equipment used to carry patients who are lying down: *He had a heart attack and was carried to the ambulance in a stretcher. See:* art on page 11a.

S

**strict** /strɪkt/ *adjective* **stricter, strictest**
expecting rules to be followed: *The strict teacher makes us stay after school if we don't do our homework.* *–adverb* **strictly;** *–noun* **strictness.**

**strike** /straɪk/ *verb* **struck** /strʌk/, **struck** or **stricken** /ˈstrɪkən/, **striking, strikes**
**1** to hit hard: *She struck her brother and gave him a bloody nose.*
**2** to happen suddenly: *A good idea struck me as I was reading the newspaper.*
**3** to have an effect on: *The power of her words struck me.*
**4** to stop working because of disagreements with management: *The bus drivers are striking until the owners give them more vacation time.*

**to strike while the iron is hot:** to act quickly while the situation is good: *Dad is happy and relaxed and just got paid; let's strike while the iron is hot and ask if we can use the car. See:* struck.

**strike** *noun*
**1** a hard hit: *the strike of metal on metal*
**2** a discovery of something valuable: *a gold strike*
**3** a work stoppage because of disagreements with management: *During the strike, workers carried signs that read, "On strike: Better pay, shorter day!"*

**striker** /ˈstraɪkər/ *noun*
a worker who won't work because of disagreements with the employer: *Strikers walked in a circle near the factory gate.*

**string** /strɪŋ/ *noun*
**1** a rope-like cord made of thick threads: *We wrapped the box and tied a string around it.*
**2** a series of related or similar events: *a string of successes in business*
**3** a line of objects with a string pulled through them: *a string of pearls*
**4** *plural* **strings:** (in music) the instruments in the violin family (violin, viola, cello, bass fiddle, etc.)

**string** *verb* **strung** /strʌŋ/, **stringing, strings**
to put a string or strings on something: *to string a guitar||I strung some red and black beads for a necklace.*

**string bean** *noun*
a long, green bean

**string beans**

**strip** /strɪp/ *noun*
a thin, narrow piece of something: *a strip of bacon (cloth, leather, tape, etc.)*

**strip** *verb* **stripped, stripping, strips**
**1** to remove an outer layer: *to strip wallpaper off the wall*
**2** to take off one's clothes: *The boys stripped off their shirts and jumped into the pool.*

**stripe** /straɪp/ *noun*
a band of color against a background of a different color: *She wore a white blouse with pink stripes.* **–***verb* **to stripe.**

**stroke** /stroʊk/ *verb* **stroked, stroking, strokes**
to pass the hand lightly over something: *I like to stroke a baby's soft cheek.*

**stroke** *noun*
**1** a light rubbing motion: *one stroke of my hand*
**2** the hitting or sound of a bell, gong, or clock: *At the stroke of two, begin writing.*
**3** one mark with a writing tool: *She used four strokes of a pen to make an E.*
**4** a blocked or broken blood vessel in the brain that causes a lack of muscle control, difficulty speaking, and sometimes death

**stroll** /stroʊl/ *noun*
a relaxed, unhurried walk: *After dinner, we went for a stroll on the beach.*

**stroll** *verb*
to walk slowly: *We strolled through the park.*

**stroller** /ˈstroʊlər/ *noun*
a chair with four wheels used to hold and push a baby: *The boy's mother pushed his stroller into the shopping mall.*

**strong** /strɔŋ/ *adjective*
**1** having strength: *A strong man helped me push the car up the hill.*
**2** able to be easily sensed: *the strong smell of onions and garlic* *–adverb* **strongly.** *(antonym)* weak.

**struck** /strʌk/ *adjective and past participle of* strike
hit by: *The tree was struck by lightning and it caught fire.*

**structure** /'strʌktʃər/ *noun*
**1** a building of any kind: *A new structure is being built on the corner.*
**2** the way parts are put together or organized: *the structure of a song||a business's structure*

**structure** *verb* **structured, structuring, structures**
to put together or organize parts of something: *We are structuring a plan to hire new teachers.* –*adjective* **structural.**

**struggle** /'strʌgəl/ *noun*
**1** a difficult time or task using much effort and energy: *He has had a struggle all his life with bad health.*
**2** a conflict or war: *a struggle between two countries*
**3** a fight: *Two men got into a struggle outside a bar.*

**struggle** *verb* **struggled, struggling, struggles**
to use much physical or mental effort to do something: *I struggled to reach the seat belt behind me.*

**stub** /stʌb/ *noun*
a short piece of something broken or used: *This eraser is worn down to a stub.||a ticket stub*

**stubborn** /'stʌbərn/ *adjective*
unwilling to change one's mind: *My stubborn little boy would not put his coat on; he said, "No, no."*

**stuck** /stʌk/ *adjective informal and past participle of* stick
unable to continue: *I am stuck on this problem; I can't figure it out.*

**student** /'studnt/ *noun*
**1** a person who learns at any school, college, or university: *She is a high-school student and will start college next fall.*
**2** a person who studies something seriously, in or out of school: *a student of art See:* art on page 8a.

**studio** /'studioʊ/ *noun*
**1** a place where an artist works: *a ballet studio||photo studio*
**2** a one-room apartment: *My studio is too small; I'm moving to a one-bedroom apartment.*

**study** /'stʌdi/ *noun, plural* **studies**
**1** a room in a living space for reading, writing, and other quiet activities: *Her study is filled with books.*
**2** the act of learning: *the study of foreign languages*
**3** a report on a specific topic: *a governmental study on poverty*

**study** *verb* **studied, studying, studies**
**1** to learn, by practicing, reading, and listening: *She studied for the math test.||He studies African history.*
**2** to look at carefully, *(synonym)* to examine: *I study a contract carefully before I sign it.*

**stuff** /stʌf/ *verb*
to fill, usually tightly or completely, by pushing something into something else: *She stuffed her notebooks into a desk drawer.*

**stuff** *noun, (no plural)*
a general word for unnamed or unknown things: *There's some old, smelly stuff in the back of the refrigerator.||What's that stuff you're rubbing on your hands?*

**stuffy** /'stʌfi/ *adjective* **stuffier, stuffiest**
without fresh air –*noun* **stuffiness.**

**stumble** /'stʌmbəl/ *verb* **stumbled, stumbling, stumbles**
to trip or have trouble walking

**stump** /stʌmp/ *noun*
the part of a tree left after it has fallen or been cut: *She sat on a stump in the woods to rest.*

**stun** /stʌn/ *verb* **stunned, stunning, stuns**
**1** to make unconscious or senseless: *When I hit my head, the bump stunned me and I fell to the floor.*
**2** to surprise or shock: *The news of your friend's death stunned me.*

**stunning** /'stʌnɪŋ/ *adjective*
**1** very beautiful: *a stunning dress*
**2** very surprising: *Her mother's death was a stunning loss.*

**stung** /stʌŋ/ *verb*
*past tense and past participle of* sting

**stupid** /'stupɪd/ *adjective*
**1** not smart: *He makes the same mistakes over and over; he is so stupid!*
**2** not using one's brain or logic, foolish: *It was a stupid thing for her to leave her car keys in the car; it was stolen!* –*noun* **stupidity.** *(antonym)* intelligent.

**sturdy** /'stɜrdi/ *adjective* **sturdier, sturdiest**
strong, well-built: *He can walk for miles on his sturdy legs. (antonym)* weak.

**stutter** /'stʌtər/ *noun*
a problem with speaking in which the person repeats words or pauses *–noun* (person) **stutterer;** *–verb* **stutter.**

**style** /staɪl/ *noun*
**1** the particular way that something is done: *Her writing style is very simple and clear.*
**2** a sort, kind, type: *"What style of food does the restaurant serve?" "Italian."*
**3** fashion, the way of dressing or appearing: *I like the styles of the 1940s, with longer skirts and wide shoulders.*
**in style:** popular at that time: *My mom's old clothes are in style again!*
**out of style:** not popular at that time: *Big band music is out of style, but I still enjoy it.*

**style** *verb* **styled, styling, styles**
to make something in a special way: *to style men's clothes*||*to style a woman's hair* *–noun* (person) **stylist;** *–verb* **stylize** /'staɪlaɪz/.

**stylish** /'staɪlɪʃ/ *adjective*
fashionable, attractive: *The lady wears colorful, stylish dresses.*

**subject** /'sʌbʤɪkt/ *noun*
**1** an idea being thought, talked, or read about, a topic: *The subject of this book is teenage smoking of cigarettes.*
**2** something studied in school: *English is her favorite subject.*
**3** (in grammar) the noun that does the action in a sentence: *"Cat" is the subject of the sentence "The cat came home."*

**subject** /səb'ʤɛkt/ *verb*
to cause someone to receive an action: *The boss is unkind and he subjects his workers to his anger every day.*

**subject matter** /'sʌbʤɪkt/ *noun*
the topic being read about or discussed: *The subject matter of this class is international banking.*

**sublet** /'sʌbˌlɛt/ *verb* **sublet, subletting, sublets**
to rent from someone who is the original renter: *The tenant sublet an apartment to us for the summer.*

**submarine** /'sʌbməˌrin/ *noun*
a tube-shaped ship that can travel underwater

**submit** /səb'mɪt/ *verb* **submitted, submitting, submits**
**1** to pass in or give something, especially a piece of writing or artistic work, to someone: *When I finish this short story, I'll submit it to a magazine.*
**2** to give up to a greater power, *(synonym)* to surrender *–noun* (act) **submission.**

**subscription** /səb'skrɪpʃən/ *noun*
an agreement to buy a certain number of magazines or newspapers: *My subscription to that computer magazine runs out next month.* *–verb* **to subscribe.**

**substance** /'sʌbstəns/ *noun*
anything one can touch, material: *Tires are made of rubber and other substances.*

**substantial** /səb'stænʃəl/ *adjective*
**1** large: *The politician won the election by a substantial number of votes.*
**2** strong, durable: *substantial furniture*

**substitute** /'sʌbstɪˌtut/ *verb* **substituted, substituting, substitutes**
to replace: *I substitute olive oil for butter in cooking.*

**substitute** *noun*
a person or thing that acts in place of someone or something else: *Our teacher is having a baby, so we have a substitute.* *–noun* **substitution.**

**subtitles** /'sʌbˌtaɪtlz/ *noun plural*
in a foreign-language film, the words at the bottom of the screen that translate what the actors are saying

**subtle** /'sʌtl/ *adjective*
not obvious: *She gave me a subtle sign that she wanted to leave the party.* *–noun* **subtlety.**

**subtotal** /'sʌbˌtoʊtl/ *noun*
the sum of some, but not all, numbers being added: *I added up a subtotal of the items before adding the tax.*

**subtract** /səb'trækt/ *verb*
to take away a number (amount) from another: *Three subtracted from 6 equals 3.*

**subtraction** /səb'trækʃən/ *noun*
the act of subtracting: *The children*

S

*learned subtraction before multiplication.*

**suburb** /ˈsʌbˌɜrb/ *noun*
a small city or town outside a large city *–adjective* **suburban;** *–noun* **suburbia.**

**subway** /ˈsʌbˌweɪ/ *noun*
a public transportation system with trains that run underground: *In Boston, thousands of people take the subway to work every day. See:* art on page 24a.

subway

**succeed** /səkˈsid/ *verb*
**1** to accomplish a task or reach a goal: *She tried to quit smoking, and she succeeded. (antonym)* fail.
**2** to do well in life: *She has succeeded in business and is now a millionaire.*

**success** /səkˈsɛs/ *noun, plural* **successes**
accomplishment of a task, the reaching of a goal: *The meeting was a success; we agreed on everything. (antonym)* failure.

**successful** /səkˈsɛsfəl/ *adjective*
doing well, with success: *No one likes the new movie; it's not successful.*

**such** /sʌʧ/ *adverb*
to a large degree, very: *She was in such a terrible accident!*||*I have such great news! She's O.K.!*

**such** *adjective*
**1** of a certain kind: *I have never seen such children in my life.*
**2** used to refer to something being discussed: *You say you want to understand those people, but such people are impossible to understand.*

**such** *pronoun*
a person or thing in general: *His girlfriend left him; such are the risks of love.*

**such as:** for example: *He collects musical instruments, such as trumpets and guitars.*

**suck** /sʌk/ *verb*
to take liquid into the mouth

**sudden** /ˈsʌdn/ *adjective*
quick and unexpected: *We all jumped at the sudden loud noise. –adverb* **suddenly.**

**sue** /su/ *verb* **sued, suing, sues**
to make a claim in court that other people have violated one's legal rights and that the others should pay for one's suffering and damages: *She sued the company because it was unfair to women and racial minorities.*

**suffer** /ˈsʌfər/ *verb*
to experience pain, loss, hardship, etc.: *She suffered when her mother died.*

**to suffer from something:** to be ill with something, usually over a long period of time: *She suffers from arthritis. –noun* (person) **sufferer,** (pain) **suffering.**

**sufficient** /səˈfɪʃənt/ *adjective*
enough: *Our money was sufficient for a two-week vacation.*

**suffocate** /ˈsʌfəˌkeɪt/ *verb* **suffocated, suffocating, suffocates**
**1** to cause or have difficulty in breathing: *The smoky fire was suffocating us.*
**2** to kill by choking or smothering: *In the spy novel, the hero suffocated the murderer under a pillow. –noun* **suffocation.** *See:* smother.

**sugar** /ˈʃʊgər/ *noun*
a sweet substance, usually in the form of white crystals, obtained from plants, added to foods and drinks: *She put a teaspoon of sugar in her coffee. –adjective* **sugary.**

**suggest** /səgˈʤɛst/ *verb*
**1** to offer an idea for consideration: *He suggested that we have lunch at the hotel.*
**2** to bring (an idea) to mind: *The results of the test suggested that I was ill. –noun* (idea) **suggestion.**

**suicide** /ˈsuəˌsaɪd/ *noun*
the taking of one's own life: *to commit suicide –adjective* **suicidal.**

**suit** /sut/ *noun*
**1** a set of pieces of clothing, such as a coat and pants or a coat and skirt, made of the same material and worn together, usually for business or formal occasions: *Everyone wore his or her best suit to the company's annual meeting.*
**2** a lawsuit: *His suit against the phone company is not likely to succeed.*
**3** one of the four sets of cards used in games: *He arranged his cards by suits.*

**suit** *verb*
**1** to satisfy or please; to meet the needs of or be convenient for: *Your proposal suits my schedule.*
**2** to look good or well-matched with other things: *That big dress does not suit her slim figure. See:* art on page 12a.

**suitable** /'sutəbəl/ *adjective*
**1** convenient: *Please set a suitable time to meet.*
**2** appropriate: *You should wear clothes suitable for the occasion. –adverb* **suitably.**

**suitcase** /'sut,keɪs/ *noun*
a flat strong box with a handle for carrying; made to carry suits and clothes when travelling: *I carry one suitcase and a briefcase on business trips.*

suitcase

**sulfur** /'sʌlfər/ *noun*
a yellow substance found widely in nature as a powder and used in industry and medicine: *Eggs contain sulfur in the yolks. –adjective* **sulfuric.**

**sullen** /'sʌlən/ *adjective*
showing irritation or resentment by being silent and withdrawn: *When the group voted against his plan, he became sullen.*

**sulphur** /'sʌlfər/ *noun*
*variation of* sulfur

**sum** /sʌm/ *noun*
**1** the total reached by adding together numbers, things, or amounts: *The sum of our income is greater than the sum of our expenses.*
**2** an amount of money: *They spent a large sum for that house.*

**sum** *verb* **summed, summing, sums**
**to sum something up:** to summarize, to finish, especially a speech: *I would like to sum up my presentation by saying that we need to cut costs and increase sales.*

**summarize** /'sʌmə,raɪz/ *verb* **summarized, summarizing, summarizes**
**1** to give a summary: *He summarized a long report by giving its main ideas.*
**2** to finish, conclude: *The speaker summarized her talk by reviewing its main points.*

**summary** /'sʌməri/ *noun, plural* **summaries**
a brief statement of the most important features (ideas, facts, actions, etc.) of an event or a work: *He wrote a summary of his book to send to a publisher.*

**summer** /'sʌmər/ *noun*
the warm season between spring and autumn: *The gardens are beautiful in the summer. –adjective* **summery.**

**summertime** /'sʌmər,taɪm/ *noun*
the warm season, (in the northern hemisphere) the months of June, July, and August: *Children enjoy the summertime.*

**summit** /'sʌmɪt/ *noun*
the top of a mountain

**summon** /'sʌmən/ *verb formal*
to call or send for

**summons** /'sʌmənz/ *noun, plural* **summonses**
an order to appear in a court of law: *We received a summons to appear in traffic court on Monday.*

**sun** /sʌn/ *noun*
the star around which the Earth and other planets move and draw light, heat, and energy: *The sun rises every morning and sets every evening.*

**sun** *verb* **sunned, sunning, suns**
to bathe in the sunlight: *She loved to sun herself on the beach.*

**sunbathe** /'sʌn,beɪð/ *verb* **sunbathed, sunbathing, sunbathes**
to expose oneself to the sun's rays: *On vacation, we sunbathe on the beach. –noun* **sunbathing.**

**sunblock** *noun See:* sunscreen.

**sunburn** /'sʌn,bɜrn/ *noun*
the painful, reddened condition of the skin caused by too much sun: *She fell asleep on the beach and got a bad sunburn. –adjective* **sunburned.**

**sundae** /'sʌn,deɪ/ *noun*
a dish of ice cream topped with syrup chopped nuts and cherries: *I'll have a hot fudge sundae with vanilla ice cream.*

**Sunday** /'sʌn,deɪ/ *noun*
the first day of the week, between

Saturday and Monday, regarded by most Christians as the Sabbath, the day of worship and rest: *We spend Sundays in the park.*

**Sunday school:** religious teaching for children, usually held while their parents attend church service

**sunflower** /ˈsʌnˌflaʊər/ *noun*
a long-stemmed plant with large flowers

**sunflower**

**sunglasses** /ˈsʌn ˌglæsɪz/ *noun plural*
eyeglasses with colored lenses that protect the eyes from harmful rays of the sun: *In California, almost everyone wears sunglasses.*

**sunk** /sʌŋk/ *adjective informal and past participle of* sink
in big trouble, beyond help, a failure: *I forgot my car keys and now I'm sunk.*

**sunken** /ˈsʌŋkən/ *adjective and past participle of* sink
submerged: *a search for sunken treasure*

**sunlight** /ˈsʌnˌlaɪt/ *noun*
the natural light of the sun: *Let's move out of the shade and into the sunlight where it's warm.*

**sunny** /ˈsʌni/ *adjective* **sunnier, sunniest**
brightly lit with sunlight: *She showed me to the sunny greenhouse.*

**sunrise** /ˈsʌnˌraɪz/ *noun*
sunup, the moment when the sun appears in the east *(antonym)* sunset.

**sunscreen** /ˈsʌnˌskrin/ *noun*
a skin cream that keeps out the harmful rays of the sun: *Many people use sunscreen to protect themselves from skin cancer.*

**sunset** /ˈsʌnˌsɛt/ *noun*
sundown, the moment when the sun disappears in the west *(antonym)* sunrise.

**sunshine** /ˈsʌnˌʃaɪn/ *noun*
sunlight

**suntan** /ˈsʌnˌtæn/ *noun*
the browning (or darkening) of the skin from sunlight: *She went to the beach to get a suntan.*

**super (1)** /ˈsupər/ *noun*
*short for* superintendent, the head maintenance person in an apartment building

**super (2)** *adjective informal*
outstanding, excellent: *We had a super time on our vacation.*

**superb** /suˈpɜrb/ *adjective*
wonderful, first-class: *The designer did a superb job on the artwork.*

**Super Bowl** *noun*
(in USA) the national football championship: *The Super Bowl is the most important football game of the year.*

---

**USAGE NOTE:** The *Super Bowl* is played on a Sunday in January and is the most popular sporting event of the year, with millions of people watching the game on television and holding Super Bowl parties in their homes.

---

**superficial** /ˌsupərˈfɪʃəl/ *adjective*
lacking in serious thought, limited in understanding: *Her knowledge of the subject is very superficial.*

**superhighway** /ˌsupərˈhaɪˌweɪ/ *noun*
(in the USA) a wide, divided highway with two or more lanes in either direction, usually leading from one region or state to another: *You can drive fast on a superhighway.*

**superintendent** /ˌsupərɪnˈtɛndənt/ *noun*
**1** person who manages or directs a large project or public service organization: *the superintendent of schools*
**2** the person in charge of a large (especially apartment) building

**superior** /sʊˈpɪriər/ *noun*
a person who is higher in rank or importance: *My superiors at work have asked me to cut costs. (antonym)* inferior.

**superior** *adjective*
**1** better (than); above average; of high quality: *Our product is superior to our competitor's. (antonym)* inferior.
**2** of higher rank or position: *her superior officer –noun* **superiority.**

**superlative** /sʊ ˈpɜrlətɪv/ *noun*
(in grammar) the highest degree of comparison of an adjective or adverb: *"Best" is the superlative of "good."*

**superlative** *adjective*
of the highest quality: *He said that the painter did a superlative job. See:* comparative.

**supermarket** /'supər,markət/ *noun*
a large self-service store offering food and household items: *We go shopping at the supermarket every Thursday.*

**superstition** /,supər'stɪʃən/ *noun*
the belief in ghosts and strange happenings: *His mind is filled with superstition.* –*adjective* **superstitious.**

**supervise** /'supər,vaɪz/ *verb* **supervised, supervising, supervises**
to watch over the activity of others to maintain order and discipline: *She supervises an accounting department of 20 employees.* –*noun* (action) **supervision.**

**supervisor** /'supər,vaɪzər/ *noun*
a person who supervises others and their work –*adjective* **supervisory.**

**supplement** *verb* /'sʌplə,mɛnt/
to make an addition or additions to: *He supplemented his income by taking a night job.* –*adjective* **supplemental;** –*noun* **supplement.**

**supplier** /sə'plaɪər/ *noun*
a business that supplies goods or services to a buyer: *Our company has many suppliers who provide everything from office supplies, furniture, to cleaning services.*

**supply** /sə'plaɪ/ *verb* **supplied, supplying, supplies**
to give or provide something needed: *They supplied food to hungry people.*

**supply** *noun*
**1** a quantity of goods: *We need a supply of pens for school.*
**2** a system for delivering goods or services: *Their water supply is old and filled with leaks.*

**supplies:** *noun, plural* goods of a specific kind necessary for an operation: *That farm buys its supplies of feed and grain from the local feed store.*

**support** /sə'pɔrt/ *verb*
**1** to hold up or bear the weight of: *a beam that supports a roof*
**2** to provide the money for necessities of life: *She supports her family by working two jobs.*
**3** to contribute to by giving money to or working for: *We support our local hospital by giving blood regularly.*
**4** to agree with or express loyalty to: *He supports our efforts to end hunger.*

**support** *noun*
**1** the act of supporting something: *Can we have your support at the next meeting?*||*supports that hold up a roof*
**2** moral, emotional, or financial assistance: *Her family always gave her lots of support.*

**supporter** /sə'pɔrtər/ *noun*
a person or group that provides support: *The politician's supporters held a dinner in his honor.*

**supportive** /sə'pɔrtɪv/ *adjective*
helpful to another person, sympathetic: *a person with a supportive spouse*

**suppose** /sə'poʊz/ *verb* **supposed, supposing, supposes**
**1** to assume or imagine as if true; to consider possible: *Let's suppose that our plan fails—then what should we do?*
**2** to believe, conclude, or think: *She supposed she should go visit her mother.*

**be supposed to:** expected or required by custom, law, duty, or personal obligation: *You are supposed to pay income taxes.*

**supposing** /sə'po ʊzɪŋ/ *conjunction*
if, assuming that: *Supposing we do buy the house, how much will our monthly payments be?*

**supreme** /sʊ'prim/ *adjective*
highest in rank, authority, or power: *the Supreme Court*

**sure** /ʃʊr/ *adjective*
**1** without doubt, positive: *I'm sure that he will be here for dinner.*||*It is sure to be hot in July.*
**2** reliable, dependable: *I think you have found the sure solution to our problems.*
**3** okay, fine, yes: *"Would you like coffee?" "Sure."*

**be sure to:** don't forget to: *Be sure to lock the door before you leave.*

**sure** *adverb*
certainly: *This sure is a great dinner.*||*Sure you can!*

**for sure:** definitely, you can bet on it: *This is going to be a great party, for sure.*

**sure enough:** as expected: *Sure enough, everything turned out okay.*

**surely** /'ʃʊrli/ *adverb*
certainly, without doubt: *Surely, you don't believe that nonsense.*

**surf** /sɜrf/ *noun*
ocean waves as they come in and break on a shore: *At the beach, children played in the surf.*

**surface** /'sɜrfəs/ *noun*
**1** the outside layer of an object: *Rocks found on the beach usually have a smooth surface.*
**2** the flat top level of something: *the surface of a table (a pond, a mirror)*
**3** outward appearance: *On the surface, that looks like a good car, but the engine is bad.*

**surface** *verb* **surfaced, surfacing, surfaces**
**1** to rise to the surface
**2** to cover a road with paving material

**surfboard** /'sɜrf,bɔrd/ *noun*
a long, narrow board used for the sport of surfing

surfboard

**surgeon** /'sɜrdʒən/ *noun*
a doctor who performs surgery: *The surgeon operated on my broken leg.*

**surgery** /'sɜrdʒəri/ *noun, (no plural)*
the medical practice of treating injuries and disease by operating on (cutting into) the body: *My friend went into surgery today to have a growth on his arm removed.* –*adjective* **surgical.**

**surplus** /'sɜr,plʌs/ *noun, plural* **surpluses**
an amount more than what is needed or used: *When the party was over, we had a surplus of beer.*

**surprise** /sər'praɪz/ *noun*
an unexpected event that causes a feeling of pleasure or shock: *The court's decision was a surprise to us.*

**surprise** *adjective*
unexpected or unannounced: *They gave him a surprise birthday party.*

**surprise** *verb* **surprised, surprising, surprises**
**1** to cause or create a surprise: *He surprised us by saying that he was leaving the company.*
**2** to meet unexpectedly: *Last night he surprised a thief in the office. See:* art on page 18a.

**surrender** /sə'rɛndər/ *verb*
to admit defeat: *an army that surrenders to its enemy* –*noun* **surrender.**

**surround** /sə'raʊnd/ *verb*
to extend all around: *The stone wall surrounds our house.*

**surroundings** /sə'raʊndɪŋz/ *noun plural*
everything around or about the place or area in which one is located: *She lives in a pleasant neighborhood and enjoys her surroundings.*

**survey** /sər'veɪ/ *verb*
**1** to make an exact map of an area
**2** to find out the opinions of people by asking them questions and recording their answers: *The news agency surveyed voters about their opinions on taxes.*

**survey** *noun*
**1** the act of surveying
**2** the map of an area
**3** a set of questions designed to measure opinions: *She did a survey about immigration.*

**survival** /sər'vaɪvəl/ *noun*
the ability to continue to exist or live: *The poor man's survival depends on the help of others.*

**survive** /sər'vaɪv/ *verb* **survived, surviving, survives**
to continue to live or exist: *This tree has survived for many years.||She was lucky to survive the plane crash.*

**survivor** /sər'vaɪvər/ *noun*
a person who survives: *a survivor of a car crash*

**suspect** /sə'spɛkt/ *verb*
**1** to have an uncertain belief or expectation about something: *I suspect that rain is going to ruin our picnic.*
**2** to think that someone is guilty of something: *I suspect him of stealing the money.*

S

**suspect** /ˈsʌsˌpɛkt/ *noun*
a person thought to be guilty: *That man is the suspect in a murder.*

**suspend** /səˈspɛnd/ *verb*
**1** to hang from a point
**2** to stop for a period of time
**3** to take away someone's right or privilege, especially because of misbehavior: *My driver's license was suspended because I was speeding.* –*noun* **suspension.**

**suspense** /səˈspɛns/ *noun*
a state or feeling of anxiety and tension caused by uncertain expectations: *That action movie created a lot of suspense.* –*adjective* **suspenseful.**

**suspicion** /səˈsp ɪʃən/ *noun*
an act of suspecting

**suspicious** /səˈs pɪʃəs/ *adjective*
**1** having suspicions, distrustful of others: *He is suspicious of everyone who disagrees with him.*
**2** appearing guilty or worthy of distrust: *She was bothered by her husband's suspicious behavior.*

**swallow (1)** /ˈswɑloʊ/ *verb*
taking food or drink into the throat from the mouth: *He took big swallows of water.*

**swallow (2)** *noun*
a small bird with black top, white breast, brownish orange markings, and a double-pointed tail

**swamp** /swɑmp/ *noun*
soft wet land with thick plant growth: *Swamps are filled with natural wild life.* –*adjective* **swampy.**

**swamp** *verb*
to flood with water: *The storm caused high waves that swamped our boat.*

**swan** /swɑn/ *noun*
a large water bird, usually all white or all black, with a long, graceful neck

**swap** /swɑp/ *verb* **swapped, swapping, swaps**
to trade one thing for another, to exchange: *I swapped my bicycle for a guitar with a friend.*

**swap** *noun*
an instance of swapping: *The bicycle and the guitar both cost the same; so it was an even swap.*

**swarm** /swɔrm/ *noun*
a large number of insects or birds flying in a shapeless mass: *a swarm of bees* –*verb* **to swarm.**

**sway** /sweɪ/ *verb*
**1** to move back and forth, to rock: *The trees swayed in the strong breeze.*
**2** to influence: *He tried to sway my opinion in favor of new immigration laws.* –*noun* **sway.**

**swear** /swɛr/ *verb* **swore** /swɔr/, **sworn** /swɔrn/, **swearing, swears**
**1** to curse, use offensive language: *He swears when he is angry.*
**2** to declare or promise: *We swore to be loyal forever.*
**to swear by something:** to believe in, trust: *She swears by eating raw garlic to stay healthy.*
**to swear someone in:** to take an oath before beginning an elected position: *The judge swore in the new governor.*

**sweat** /swɛt/ *noun*
a salty moisture produced by the body through the skin: *The runner's sweat soaked through his shirt.* –*verb* **to sweat.**

**sweater** /ˈswɛtər/ *noun*
a garment with or without sleeves worn over the upper body and made of wool or cotton: *In winter, he wears a wool sweater over his shirt. See:* art on page 12a.

**sweat shirt** *noun*
a loose-fitting cotton garment with long sleeves, worn over the upper body for sports and leisure: *He dresses casually in a sweat shirt and jeans.*

sweat shirt

**sweat suit** *noun*
sportswear covering the upper body and legs

**sweep** /swip/ *verb* **swept** /swɛpt/, **sweeping, sweeps**
**1** to clear a surface such as a floor of dirt using a broom or brush: *She was sweeping the kitchen floor.*
**2** to move forcefully or quickly over or through: *The wind swept through the trees.*

**sweep** *noun*
**1** an act of sweeping
**2** a long, curving stretch of land
**3** a search: *The police made a sweep of the neighborhood.*

**sweepstakes** /'swip,steɪks/ *noun plural* a race or contest in which the entire prize goes to the winner: *He won the sweepstakes and became very rich.*

**sweet** /swit/ *adjective* **sweeter, sweetest**
**1** having a taste like sugar or honey: *This ice cream is very sweet.*
**2** pleasing, delightful: *She gave me a sweet smile when I arrived.*
**to be sweet on someone:** to like someone very much: *He is sweet on her.*
**sweet** *noun*
something sweet to eat, such as candy: *Would you like a sweet for dessert?||No, thank you, I don't eat sweets.* –*verb* **to sweeten.**

**sweetheart** /'swit,hɑrt/ *noun*
**1** someone who is loved with affection and feels the same: *They have been sweethearts for many years.*
**2** a person who is kind and cheerful to everyone: *She's a sweetheart and has no enemies.*
**3** a term of endearment: *"Hi, Sweetheart!"*

**swell** /swɛl/ *verb* **swelled, swollen** /'swoʊlən/, **swelling, swells**
to expand in size, usually from absorbing fluids: *I twisted my ankle and it swelled.* –*noun* **swelling.**
**swell** *adjective exclamation*
great!, wonderful!: *What a swell day to go to the beach!||Swell!*

**swept** /swɛpt/ *verb*
*past tense of* sweep

**swift** /swɪft/ *adjective* **swifter, swiftest**
quick, rapid: *The artist drew my portrait with a few swift movements of his pencil.* –*adverb* **swiftly.**

**swim** /swɪm/ *verb* **swam** /swæm/, **swum** /swʌm/, **swimming, swims**
to move through water by moving parts of the body: *He swam across the river and back again.*
**to sink or swim:** to do what is necessary to survive: *This company must stop losing money or go out of business; it's sink or swim.* –*noun* (sport) **swimming.**
**swim** *noun*
the act of swimming: *Let's go for a swim.*

**swimsuit** /'swɪm,sut/ *noun*
a bathing suit: *She put her swimsuit in the suitcase to go on vacation.*

**swindle** /'swɪndl/ *verb* **swindled, swindling, swindles**
to cheat someone out of money or property: *He swindled the old couple out of their life's savings.* –*noun* (thief) **swindler,** (act) **swindle.**

**swing** /swɪŋ/ *verb* **swang** /swæŋ/, **swung** /swʌŋ/, **swinging, swings**
**1** to move forward and backward: *The police officer was swinging keys on a keychain.||When the wind blew, the door swung shut.*
**2** to turn around quickly: *She swung around when he called her name.*
**swing** *noun*
**1** a swinging movement: *He took a swing at the ball, but he missed.*
**2** a seat suspended on ropes or chains that hangs from a tree branch, etc. and allows the seat to go forward and backward: *Children play on the swings in the park. See:* art on page 9a.

**switch** /swɪʧ/ *noun, plural* **switches**
**1** a device for turning on (or off) the electrical current to an appliance or machine: *Can you show me where the switch is on the TV?||This switch turns on the hall lights.*
**2** a shift or change: *There was a switch in the schedule, so we met in the morning instead of the afternoon.*
**switch** *verb* **switches**
**1** to use a switch: *She switched on the light.*
**2** to change or exchange: *He switched trains in Chicago.*

**switchboard** /'swɪʧ,bɔrd/ *noun*
a central telephone device where calls are sent to individuals: *Many companies have electronic switchboards that switch telephone calls automatically.*

**swollen** /ˈswoʊlən/ *verb*
*past participle of* swell
filled with liquid: *My sprained ankle is swollen.*

**sword** /sɔrd/ *noun*
a weapon with a handle and long steel blade: *Swords are not used in modern warfare.*

**swore** /swɔr/ *verb*
*past tense of* swear

**syllable** /ˈsɪləbəl/ *noun*
a part of a word as determined by vowel sounds and rhythm: *"Cat" is a word of one syllable; "hotel" has two syllables.*

**syllabus** /ˈsɪləbəs/ *noun, plural* **syllabuses** or **syllabi** /-ˌbaɪ/
an outline of topics for a course of study: *The syllabus for our course in American history included the colonial period, the Revolution, and the Constitution.*

**symbol** /ˈsɪmbəl/ *noun*
a sign, mark, picture, object, or event that represents something else: *The symbol of our country is our flag.*||*Road signs use symbols to give information and warnings. –verb* **to symbolize.**

**symmetrical** /sə ˈmɛtrəkəl/ *adjective*
balanced, with two parts that are mirror images of each other: *The symmetrical design of this church makes it very beautiful. –noun* **symmetry** /ˈsɪmətri/.

**sympathetic** /ˌsɪmpəˈθɛtɪk/ *adjective*
showing sympathy: *Sending flowers was a sympathetic thing to do.*

S

**sympathize** /ˈsɪm pəˌθaɪz/ *verb* **sympathized, sympathizing, sympathizes**
to express or feel sympathy: *The boy's mother sympathized with him when his dog died.*

**sympathy** /ˈsɪmpəθi/ *noun, plural* **sympathies**
**1** a feeling of pity and compassion: *I have no sympathy for criminals.*||*She felt sympathy for the war victims.*
**2** agreement in feeling or opinion: *I am in sympathy with the striking teacher's union.*

**symphony** /ˈsɪmfəni/ *noun, plural* **symphonies**
**1** a long and complex piece of music to be performed by an orchestra
**2** an orchestra: *We went to hear the symphony with other classical music lovers.*

**symptom** /ˈsɪmptəm/ *noun*
**1** a sign of disease: *A fever and muscle aches and pains are symptoms of the flu.*
**2** a sign of a larger development or problem: *Juvenile crime is a symptom of the failure of our schools.*

**synagogue** /ˈsɪnəˌgɑg/ *noun*
a place of religious study and worship for Jewish people: *They celebrated the Jewish new year at their synagogue.*

**synonym** /ˈsɪnəˌnɪm/ *noun*
a word that means the same as another word: *"Sympathy" and "compassion" are synonyms. See:* antonym.

**syntax** /ˈsɪnˌtæks/ *noun, (no plural)*
the order and relationship of parts of a sentence: *Each language has its own syntax.*

**synthetic** /sɪnˈθɛtɪk/ *adjective*
artificial, human-made: *Synthetic drugs are increasingly important for public health. (antonym)* natural.

**syringe** /səˈrɪnʤ/ *noun*
a hollow tube with a plunger, usually attached to a needle to take out or inject fluids into the body: *The nurse took a sample of my blood in a syringe.*

**syrup** /ˈsɪrəp/ *noun*
**1** a thick, sweet liquid made from sugar cane, maple sugar, or other natural sugars: *He poured syrup on his pancakes.*
**2** a medicine in the form of a sweet liquid: *cough syrup*

**system** /ˈsɪstəm/ *noun*
**1** a group of related parts that function together: *The air conditioning system in this building works very well.*
**2** an ordered, logical set of ideas: *She has a system for everything.*

**systematic** /ˌsɪstəˈmætɪk/ *adjective*
based on a system; orderly, methodical: *The scientist took a systematic approach to solving problems.*

# T,t

**T,t** /ti/ *noun* **T's, t's** or **Ts, ts**
the 20th letter of the English alphabet

**tab** /tæb/ *noun*
a marker, such as a piece of colored metal: *The doctor's files have a different colored tab for each letter of the alphabet.*

**table (1)** /ˈteɪbəl/ *noun*
a piece of furniture with a flat top on legs: *Our dining room table is large enough for six people.*

**to lay one's cards on the table:** to be honest, tell one's thoughts: *After much talk, he finally laid his cards on the table and told the truth. See:* art on pages 7a and 8a.

**table (2)** *noun*
a display of numbers or other information *See:* timetable.

**tablecloth** /ˈteɪbəlˌklɔθ/ *noun*
a covering of linen, cotton, etc., placed over a table: *That restaurant has pink tablecloths. See:* art on page 5a.

**tablespoon** /ˈteɪbəlˌspun/ *noun*
a large spoon used for measuring and eating food: *I put a tablespoon of oil in the pan to fry some eggs. –noun* **tablespoonful.** *See:* teaspoon.

**tablet** /ˈtæblɪt/ *noun*
**1** pieces of paper glued at the top edge into a block: *a tablet of writing paper*
**2** medicine or other substances pressed usually into a flat, round shape, a pill: *I take two aspirin tablets.*

**tack** /tæk/ *noun*
a small, sharp nail: *Workers nail carpets to floors with tacks. See:* thumbtack. *See:* art on page 8a.

**tack** *verb*
to nail something with tacks: *Workers tacked the carpet to the floor.*

**tackle** /ˈtækəl/ *noun, (no plural)*
**1** equipment used in a sport: *We take fishing tackle on camping trips.*
**2** (in US football) knocking a player carrying the ball to the ground *–verb* **to tackle.**

**tacky** /ˈtæki/ *adjective* **tackier, tackiest**
sticky, not dried: *The paint is still tacky on the wood.*

**tact** /tækt/ *noun*
consideration, care in dealing with others, especially not to offend: *She is a doctor who uses tact in her relationships with her patients. –adjective* **tactful;** *–adverb* **tactfully.** *(antonym)* rudeness.

**tag** /tæg/ *noun*
a marker, such as a sticker or label: *A clerk put red tags on items on sale in the store.*

tag

**to play tag:** a game where one child chases the others until one is touched or tagged as "it": *Children love to play tag.*

**tag** *verb* **tagged, tagging, tags**
**1** to put tags on things
**2** to touch another player in a game of tag: *The child who was "it" tagged her friend.*

**tail** /teɪl/ *noun*
a movable part of the bottom of many animals: *Dogs wag their tails in greeting.*

**taillight** /ˈteɪlˌlaɪt/ *noun*
the red, rear lights on vehicles: *When you step on the brakes, the taillights go on.*

**tailor** /ˈteɪlər/ *verb*
to cut, sew, alter, and repair clothes: *He tailors women's clothes.*

**tailor** *noun*
a person who makes, sews, or repairs clothes

**take** /teɪk/ *verb* **took** /tʊk/ or **taken** /ˈteɪkən/, **taking, takes**
**1** to hold: *He took the baby from his wife's hands.*
**2** to remove: *I took some money from my wallet.*
**3** to do: *We take a vacation every August.*
**4** to happen, occur: *The meeting took place yesterday.*
**5** to eat or drink: *He took some tea with his lunch.*
**6** to understand: *I take it from what you say that you don't feel well today.*
**7** to invite someone somewhere: *She took her daughter to lunch.*
**8** to lead to or bring: *That road takes you to the city.*
**9** to need: *That car takes expensive gasoline to run well.*||*It takes years of practice to become a great musician.*
**10** to subtract: *Take 90 from 100 and you have 10. (antonym)* to give.

**to be** or **get taken:** to be swindled, cheated: *I was overcharged and really got taken at that store.*

**to have what it takes:** to have the ability and desire to do something well: *He has what it takes to succeed in a hard business.*

**to take down someone** or **something: a.** to remove (from above): *She took down the decorations after the party.* **b. something:** to write, note: *Students take down what teachers say.*

**to take effect:** to become valid, go into effect: *The new law takes effect next month.*

**take ill** or **sick:** to become sick

**to take someone** or **something in: a.** to give shelter, care for: *She takes in stray cats who have no home.* **b. something:** to bring indoors: *He took in the laundry from the clothesline.*

**to take it from me:** believe me: *Take it from me, it will rain tomorrow.*

**to take it hard:** to suffer, react badly to something: *When he was fired from his job, he took it hard.*

**to take (something) off: a.** to remove clothes: *He took his clothes off and put on pajamas.* **b.** to lose weight: *He took off 20 pounds.* **c.** to go up into the air: *The airplane took off from the airport.* **d.** *figurative* to increase quickly: *Sales of the new product have taken off.* **e.** to leave quickly: *When the police arrived, the thief took off.*

**to take something up: a.** to shorten: *She took up the hem on her skirt.* ||*She took it up.* **b.** to do something new: *He took up tennis for the first time last week.*

**take-home pay** *noun, (no plural)*
the amount of money in one's paycheck after taxes and deductions are taken out

**taken** /ˈteɪkən/
*adjective and past participle of* take

**takeoff** /ˈteɪkˌɔf/ *noun*
a rise, as of an aircraft from the runway: *The takeoff of the jet went very smoothly. (antonym)* landing.

**takeout** /ˈteɪkˌaʊt/ *noun, (no plural)*
food ordered from a restaurant to be eaten elsewhere: *He owns a Chinese restaurant where customers come in and order takeout food.*

**tale** /teɪl/ *noun*
a story: *That book is a tale about the Old South.*

**talent** /ˈtælənt/ *noun*
an ability to do something well: *She has a talent for singing.* *–adjective* **talented.**

**talk** /tɔk/ *noun*
**1** speaking with someone: *Two friends had a good talk over coffee.*
**2** a speech to an audience: *The professor gave a talk on her new book at a conference.*

**talk** *verb*
to speak: *My friend and I talked about the future.*

**to talk back to someone:** to speak back rudely: *A student talked back to the teacher and said she is wrong and mean.*

**to talk someone into doing something:** to persuade: *I talked her into applying for the job, even though she didn't think she would get it.*

**to talk one's ear off:** to speak at great length and not allow the listener to speak: *She was so nervous that she talked my ear off for two hours.*

**to talk someone out of doing something:** to discourage someone from doing something: *A doctor talked the insane man out of jumping off the bridge.*

**to talk something over:** to discuss a matter, especially to reach an understanding: *We talked our budget over and decided to make an offer on a new house.*

**talkative** /ˈtɔkətɪv/ *adjective*
liking to talk: *He is a happy, talkative man.* *–noun* (person) **talker.**

**talk show** *noun*
a radio or television show where guests are interviewed by a host and listeners call in with questions or comments

**tall** /tɔl/ *adjective*
**1** referring to height: *That man is six feet (2 m) tall.*
**2** having above average height: *New York City is full of tall buildings.* *–noun* **tallness.** *(antonym)* short.

**tame** /teɪm/ *adjective* **tamer, tamest**
**1** friendly to humans: *Dogs and house cats are tame animals.*
**2** harmless: *The party was noisy but tame.* *(antonym)* wild.

**tame** *verb* **tamed, taming, tames**
to train: *She tamed a cat she found on the street.*

**tampon** /ˈtæmˌpɑn/ *noun*
a cotton plug used to stop blood, especially menstrual flow

**tan** /tæn/ *adjective*
a light brownish color: *She drives a tan car.* *See:* suntan.

**tan** *verb* **tanned, tanning, tans**
to make one's skin darker from the sun: *She tans easily.*

**tangerine** /ˌtændʒəˈrin/ *noun*
a small, sweet orange *See:* art on page 3a.

**tangle** /ˈtæŋgə l/ *verb* **tangled, tangling, tangles**
to knot up and not come apart easily: *Ropes on ships tangle.* *–noun* **tangle.**

**tank** /tæŋk/ *noun*
**1** a large closed container, such as for oil, gasoline, or water: *The oil tank in our basement holds 800 gallons of heating oil.*
**2** a military vehicle with a big gun on top *–adjective* **tanked.**

**tanker** /ˈtæŋkər/ *noun*
a large boat or truck used to carry liquid: *Oil tankers sail from the Middle East to Japan.*

**tanned** /tænd/ *adjective*
of skin darkened by the sun: *She came back from her vacation tanned and rested.* *(antonym)* pale.

**tap** /tæp/ *verb* **tapped, tapping, taps**
**1** to hit lightly as with the fingers: *A stranger tapped me on the shoulder and asked directions.*
**2** to listen secretly using a wiretap on a phone line

**tap** *noun*
**1** a light knock: *He gave me a tap on the shoulder to get my attention.*
**2** a faucet: *He took some water from the tap and drank.*
**3** device used to remove liquids: *A bartender put a tap in a barrel of beer.*
**4** an electronic listening device: *The FBI put taps in the cars of suspected criminal members.*

**tape** /teɪp/ *noun*
**1** strip of sticky material used to wrap or hold things down: *An electrician uses tape to cover wires.*
**2** recording material for sound and images: *I have the television program on tape.*

**tape** *verb* **taped, taping, tapes**
**1** to wrap or attach: *I taped the wire to the wall.*
**2** to record on tape: *He tapes television programs on his videocassette recorder.* *–noun* **taping.**

**tape deck** *noun*
a tape player and recorder, part of a larger sound system

**tape measure** *noun*
a flexible ruler made in a cloth or metal strip: *A tailor uses a tape measure to measure your waist.*

tape measure

**tape recorder** *noun*
a machine for recording and playing sounds: *I use a tape recorder to record my favorite music.* *–noun* **tape recording.**

**tapestry** /ˈtæpɪstri/ *noun, plural* **tapestries**
an artwork made of cloth that is woven of thread in designs or images: *They have a lovely gold and blue tapestry hanging on their living room wall.*

**tar** /tɑr/ *noun, (no plural)*
a black, sticky mass of dead plant matter: *Tar is used to cover roads and roofs.*

**tar** *verb* **tarred, tarring, tars**
to cover with tar: *Workers tarred the roof to waterproof it.*

**target** /ˈtɑrgɪt/ *noun*
**1** an object, animal, or person aimed at with a bullet, arrow, rock, etc.: *The police practice by shooting at paper targets.*
**2** a person chosen for investigation, punishment, or jokes: *The tall boy became the target of students' jokes.*
**3** a goal or objective: *Our target date for moving is January 1.* *–verb* **to target.**

**tariff** /ˈtærəf/ *noun*
a tax on imported goods

**tart** /tɑrt/ *noun*
a pastry with a sweet filling, a small pie: *I had an apple tart for dessert.*



**task** /tæsk/ *noun*
an assignment, job to do: *His boss gives him specific tasks to do each week.*

**taste** /teɪst/ *noun*
**1** the sense of flavor that comes from experiencing foods and liquids on the tongue: *I like the taste of bananas.*
**2** a small amount of something: *She had a taste of my chocolate cake.*
**3** a sense of style in manners, clothes, the arts, etc.: *She has good taste in clothes.* *–adjective* **tasteful;** *–adverb* **tastefully.**

**taste** *verb* **tasted, tasting, tastes**
to sense the flavor of food and liquids: *The food in that restaurant tastes good.*

**tasty** /ˈteɪsti/ *adjective* **tastier, tastiest**
flavorful: *That cook makes tasty food, rich in spices and seasonings.*

**tattoo** *noun*
a staining of the skin with decorations: *He wears a tattoo that says "Mom" on his chest.* *–verb* **to tattoo;** *–noun* **tattooing.**

**taught** /tɔt/ *verb*
*past tense of* teach

**tax** /tæks/ *noun, plural* **taxes**
a necessary payment on incomes, sales, etc., to the government: *We pay sales and income taxes.* *–adjective* **taxable.**

**tax** *verb* **taxes**
to put a tax on something: *Sales of all items except food are taxed by the city at 8.25 percent.* *–noun* **taxation.**

**taxi** /ˈtæksi/ *noun*
a taxicab or cab: *We take taxis to get to our business meetings. See:* art on pages 4a and 24a.

taxi

**taxi** *verb* **taxied, taxiing, taxies**
to travel a short distance: *Airplanes taxied onto the runway before taking off.*

**taxicab** /ˈtæksiˌkæb/ *noun*
a car with driver for hire: *Taxicabs fill the streets of the big city.*

**TB** /ˈtiˈbi/
*abbreviation of* tuberculosis

**tea** /ti/ *noun*
a bush with flowers and leaves that are made into a drink: *There are teas both with and without caffeine.*

**teach** /tiʧ/ *verb* **taught** /tɔt/, **teaching, teaches**
to instruct, educate: *She teaches mathematics to college students.*

**teacher** /ˈtiʧər/ *noun*
a person, such as a professor, whose job is to instruct others: *My music teacher has a lot of students. See:* art on pages 8a and 9a.

**USAGE NOTE:** *Teachers* work in schools up through twelfth grade (secondary school). At the university level, teachers are often called *lecturers* or *instructors* if they do not have a doctorate (PhD). Teachers with PhDs are usually called *professors.*

**teaching** /ˈtiʧɪŋ/ *noun*
the profession of instructing students: *Teaching requires time and patience.*

**teakettle** /ˈtiˌkɛtl/ *noun*
a metal pot used to boil water: *I heated the teakettle to make instant coffee.*

**team** /tim/ *noun*
two or more people working together, especially in sports: *Our high school football team won the state championship.* –*noun* (person) **teammate.**

**teamwork** /ˈtimˌwɜrk/ *noun*
a cooperative effort with each person working to reach a common goal

**teapot** /ˈtiˌpɑt/ *noun*
a clay pot with a cover to make and keep tea hot: *She put the teapot on a table.*

**tear (1)** /tɛr/ *verb* **tore** /tɔr/ or **torn** /tɔrn/, **tearing, tears**
to pull apart: *Lions tear at the zebra's flesh.*
**to tear someone** or **something down: a. someone:** to criticize: *He keeps tearing down others by criticizing them.* **b. something:** to destroy: *Workers tore down the old building.*
**to tear (something) off:** to take off quickly: *His clothes caught on fire and he tore them off.*
**to tear something up:** to rip into pieces: *She tore up a sheet of paper.*
**tear** *noun*
a hole: *He has a tear in his shirt after it caught on a nail. (antonym)* mend.

**tear (2)** /tɪr/ *noun*
a drop of salty liquid from the eye: *Tears ran down her cheeks as she watched a sad movie; she was in tears.* –*verb* **to tear.**

**tease** /tiz/ *verb* **teased, teasing, teases**
to make fun of someone in a friendly way: *The boys teased Jane about her funny hat.* –*noun* (person) **tease.**

**teaspoon** /ˈtiˌspun/ *noun*
a spoon holding about 1/3 of a tablespoon or 1/4 fluid ounce (5 ml): *People use teaspoons to stir coffee and tea.*

**technical** /ˈtɛknəkəl/ *adjective*
related to a specialized field of science or technology: *Technical skill is needed to fix that computer.* –*adverb* **technically.**

**technician** /tɛkˈnɪʃən/ *noun*
a worker trained in a specific area of technology: *She is a computer technician who knows how to fix computer equipment.*

**technique** /tɛkˈnik/ *noun*
**1** a method, procedure by which something is done: *Surgical techniques have developed, so that only small cuts are needed for many operations.*
**2** skill, ability to do something: *Her technique in ice skating is superb.*

**technology** /tɛkˈnɑləʤi/ *noun, plural* **technologies**
science and theoretical engineering used in practical applications: *That college offers courses in medical technology.* –*adjective* **technological.**

**teddy bear** /ˈtɛdi/ *noun*
a stuffed toy bear: *My four-year-old son has a brown teddy bear that he takes everywhere he goes. See:* art on page 22a.

**tedious** /ˈtidiəs/ *adjective*
boring, long and dull: *a tedious job*

**teen** /tin/ *noun*
a teenager

**teenager** /ˈtinˌeɪʤər/ *noun*
a person between the ages of 13 and 19: *Teenagers love to go shopping on weekends.* –*adjective* **teenage.**

**teeth** /tiθ/ *noun*
*plural of* tooth
hard, white dental structures in the mouth: *His teeth are white and shiny.*

**teethe** /tið/ *verb* **teethed, teething, teethes**
to grow teeth: *Babies teethe until they have all their teeth.*

**telecommunications** /ˌtɛləkəˌmyunəˈkeɪʃənz/ *noun, plural*
the sending of messages and images by

T

radio, television, cable, satellite, computer, etc.

**telegram** /'tɛlə,græm/ *noun*
a short written message sent by wire

**telegraph** /'tɛlə,græf/ *verb*
to send messages by wire or telephone: *People telegraphed messages before the telephone was used.*

**telegraph** *noun*
a telegraph machine: *The telegraph was the first means of long-distance electronic communication.*

**telephone** /'tɛlə,foʊn/ *noun*
an electronic device used for the communication of voice or electronic data: *He has a telephone in several rooms at home.*

**telephone** *verb* **telephoned, telephoning, telephones**
to communicate by telephone: *I telephoned my parents to tell them about my new job. See:* art on page 6a.

**telephone directory** *noun*
a book that has the names, addresses, and telephone numbers of people, businesses, etc.

**telescope** /'tɛlə,skoʊp/ *noun*
an instrument used to make distant objects seem larger: *Astronomers use giant telescopes to look at the stars.*

telescope

**televise** /'tɛlə,vaɪz/ *verb* **televised, televising, televises**
to send by television: *All TV networks televised the Presidential elections.*

**television** /'tɛlə,vɪʒən/ or **TV** /ti'vi/ *noun, (no plural)*
**1** the sending of images and sound via the airwaves or cable to a television set: *Most major sports events are shown on television.*
**2** a box-like device that receives and displays pictures and sound: *My favorite show is on television tonight. See:* art on page 6a.

**tell** /tɛl/ *verb* **told** /toʊld/, **telling, tells**
**1** to say in words: *She tells a story to her child each night.*
**2** to identify: *I can't tell where we are in the dark night.*
**to tell about someone** or **something:** to describe: *Our friends told us about their experiences on their vacation.*
**to tell someone** or **something apart:** to identify a difference: *It's hard to tell the sisters apart.*
**to tell it like it is:** to describe reality honestly: *His work is no good, so when you see him, tell it like it is.*

**teller** /'tɛlər/ *noun*
a person who takes in and pays out money at a bank: *I gave the teller my deposit and she gave me a receipt.*

**temp** /tɛmp/ *noun informal*
*short for* temporary worker: *We hire temps to work for us when our employees are on vacation.*

**temper** /'tɛmpər/ *noun*
one's emotional nature, often of anger: *He has a bad temper.*
**to keep** or **lose one's temper:** to keep or lose control of one's anger: *She's very patient; she never loses her temper.*

**temperature** /'tɛmpərətʃər/ *noun*
**1** the degree of heat or cold: *The temperature outside is cold today.*
**2** a fever: *My son has a cold and a temperature.*
**to take someone's temperature:** to measure the body's temperature using a thermometer

**temple** /'tɛmpəl/ *noun*
**1** a building for religious worship: *We entered the temple to worship.*
**2** a flat part of the face to the side and behind the eyes: *He gets headaches in his temples.*

**tempo** /'tɛmpoʊ/ *noun*
rate of speed of a piece of music: *That song has a fast tempo.*

**temporary** /' tɛmpə,rɛri/ *adjective*
passing, not permanent: *The side road is temporary until the main road is fixed.* –*adverb* **temporarily.**

**tempt** /tɛmpt/ *verb*
to attract: *Every time he sees chocolates in shop windows, they tempt him.* –*adjective* **tempting.**

**temptation** /tɛmp'teɪʃən/ *noun*
**1** a desire for something: *He gives in to*

T

*temptation when he sees a nice necktie and buys it.*
**2** an attraction, especially to something wrong, harmful, or evil: *An alcoholic gives in to temptation by taking a drink.*

**ten** /tɛn/ *noun*
the cardinal number 10

**ten** *adjective*
ten of something: *I have ten dollars.*

**tenant** /ˈtɛnənt/ *noun*
a person who pays rent for the use of an apartment, office, etc.

---

**USAGE NOTE:** *Tenant* usually refers to a person who rents an apartment or house from a *landlord,* owner of the property. In many states, tenants' rights are protected by the law.

---

**tend** /tɛnd/ *verb*
**1** to lean toward in attitude, action, etc.: *She tends to come to work early on Mondays.*
**2** to care for: *He tends his garden on weekends.*

**tendency** /ˈtɛndənsi/ *noun, plural* **tendencies**
leaning in attitude or behavior: *When he talks, he has a tendency to get lost in details.*

**tender** /ˈtɛndər/ *adjective*
**1** soft, gentle: *The father touched his child's cheek with tender strokes.*
**2** sore, painful when touched: *The sore on the girl's knee is tender to the touch.*
**3** (of food) soft and chewable: *That meat was tender and tasty.* –*adverb* **tenderly.** *(antonym)* tough.

**tenderness** /ˈtɛndərnɪs/ *noun*
**1** gentleness, kindness
**2** soreness to the touch

**tenement** /ˈtɛnəmənt/ *noun*
a crowded, low-quality house or apartment building: *City officials try to tear down tenements and build modern housing.*

**tennis** /ˈtɛnɪs/ *noun, (no plural)*
a game played on a court with two or four players who use rackets to hit the ball over a net, so that the opponent(s) cannot hit it back *See:* art on pages 9a and 22a.

tennis

**tense** /tɛns/ *adjective* **tenser, tensest**
nervous, jumpy: *He is very tense and irritable from too much work. (antonym)* calm.

**tense** *noun*
the part of a verb that shows the past, present, and future time: *Many English verbs like "go" and "do" are irregular in the past tense.*

**tense** *verb* **tensed, tensing, tenses**
to tighten up physically, become nervous: *As the argument got worse, each person tensed up.* –*adverb* **tensely.**

**tension** /ˈtɛnʃən/ *noun*
a state of stress, nervousness

**tent** /tɛnt/ *noun*
a movable shelter made of canvas, nylon, etc.: *We live in a tent when we go camping.*

tent

**term** /tɜrm/ *noun*
**1** a word or expression that describes something: *He used the terms "happy" and "relaxed" to describe his attitude.*
**2** a requirement as in a contract
**3** a time period, such as in elected office or education: *The senator is serving a six-year term in office.* –*verb* **to term.**

**terminal** /ˈtɜrmənəl/ *noun*
**1** a station (rail, bus, airline): *The bus terminal is on the city's west side.*
**2** the last stop on a transportation line
**3** an electrical post: *The terminals on the car battery are old and dirty.*
**4** a machine that works only by being connected to another computer

**terminate** /ˈtɜrməˌneɪt/ *verb* **terminated, terminating, terminates**
to end, stop: *The railroad line terminates at Central Station.* –*adjective* **terminable;** –*noun* **termination.**

**term paper** *noun*
a long essay or research study on a course topic: *I have five courses and have to do term papers for each one.*

**terrible** /ˈtɛrəbəl/ *adjective*
horrible, very bad: *There was a terrible car accident.* –*adverb* **terribly.**

**terrific** /tə'rɪfɪk/ *adjective*
**1** wonderful: *He did a terrific job in painting the kitchen.*
**2** powerful, tremendous: *The storm had terrific winds of 100 MPH (160 km).*

**terrify** /'tɛrə,faɪ/ *verb* **terrified, terrifying, terrifies**
to put strong fear in someone: *An ugly man terrified a small child. –adjective* **terrifying;** *–adverb* **terrifyingly.**

**territorial** /,tɛrə'tɔriəl/ *adjective*
related to a territory: *Cats are territorial animals that fight over their area.*

**territory** /' tɛrə,tɔri/ *noun, plural* **territories**
**1** an area or region of land: *The territory to the north of here is mountainous.*
**2** an area of land considered a state or province by a central government: *The island of Guam is a US territory.*

**terror** /'tɛrər/ *noun*
extreme fear, panic: *A thief at the window put terror into my heart. –noun* (criminal) **terrorist;** *–verb* **to terrorize.**

**terrorism** /'tɛrə,rɪzəm/ *noun, (no plural)*
the use of murder, bombs, kidnapping, etc., for political purposes: *Governments work together to stop terrorism.*

**test** /tɛst/ *noun*
**1** an examination to measure knowledge or ability: *Our teacher gave us a spelling test.*
**2** an experiment: *The laboratory reported the results of my blood test.*

**test** *verb*
**1** to examine someone: *The state tests people who want to get a driver's license.*
**2** to try out: *After his operation, he tested his strength by walking a few steps. –noun* **testing.**

---

USAGE NOTE: In school, a *test* is larger and more important than a *quiz,* but not as comprehensive as an *examination.*

---

**testify** /'tɛstə,faɪ/ *verb* **testified, testifying, testifies**
to tell what one knows, especially under oath in a court of law: *Two witnesses testified against the defendant.*

**testimony** /'tɛstə,mouni/ *noun, (no plural)*
formal, sworn facts given in court

**test tube** *noun adjective*
a hollow cylinder made of glass or plastic used for experiments: *Medical laboratories use large numbers of test tubes.*

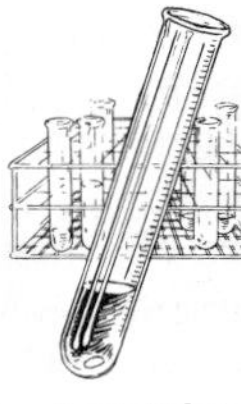
test tube

**text** /tɛkst/ *noun*
**1** written material: *The writer corrected the text of his letter.*
**2** a textbook: *The teacher told the students to look on page 10 of the text.*

**textbook** /'tɛkst,bʊk/ *noun*
a book written on a particular subject and used for study in courses: *Students study biology textbooks.*

**textile** /'tɛks,taɪl/ *noun*
cloth, fabric made by weaving: *Textiles are woven in textile factories.*

**texture** /'tɛkstʃər/ *noun*
the pattern and smoothness or roughness of touch of a material: *Wool flannel has a smooth, soft texture.*

**than** /ðən/ *conjunction*
used after adjectives and adverbs to show comparison: *The weather is hotter now than it was last year.*

**thank** /θæŋk/ *verb*
to express appreciation, gratitude: *I thanked my friend for taking me to dinner.*

**thanks** *noun plural*
gratitude, *(synonym)* appreciation: *He gives thanks to his professors for their patience.*
**thanks to:** because of: *Thanks to good weather, we had fun at the beach.*

**thankful** /'θæŋk fəl/ *adjective*
grateful, showing appreciation: *She is thankful to her doctor for saving her life. –noun* **thankfulness.**

**Thanksgiving Day** *noun*
a national holiday of celebration giving thanks for all good things observed in the USA on the fourth Thursday of November: *We had a turkey and pumpkin pie for dinner on Thanksgiving Day. See:* pilgrim, USAGE NOTE.

T

**thank-you** *noun*
an expression of appreciation: *She offered her thank-yous to the people who helped her.*

**that** /ðæt/ *pronoun*
referring to something or someone specific (but not nearby): *That person needs help.*

**after that:** then: *We ate dinner and after that we went to the movies.*

**that** *adverb*
so; as much as: *I'm not that hungry; I'll eat later.*

**that** *conjunction*
used to introduce clauses that refer to the sentence's subject: *The book that you wanted is out of the library right now. See:* those.

**thaw** /θɔ/ *noun*
a slow melting of ice: *During the spring thaw, ice melts on rivers and lakes.* *–verb* **to thaw.** *(antonym)* freeze.

**the** /ðə/ *definite article*
**1** referring to a specific singular or plural noun: *I closed the door and opened the windows.*
**2** used before a singular noun to form a group noun: *The poor need government help, but the politicians disagree on how to give it.*

**theater** /ˈθiətər/ *noun*
**1** the industry of writing and performing live musicals and dramas (not movie theaters): *Many people enjoy going to the theater.*
**2** a building, such as for movies, or outdoor shell with seats for the audience and a stage for performers: *Many theaters in New York are on or near Broadway.* *–adjective* **theatrical.**

theater

**theft** /θɛft/ *noun*
the act of stealing: *The theft of my wallet left me with no money.*

**their** /ðɛr/ *pronoun*
*possessive form of* they: *Their apartment is on the second floor.*

**theirs** /ðɛrz/ *pronoun*
*possessive form of* they: *The corner apartment on the second floor is theirs.*

**them** /ðəm;/ *pronoun*
*objective form of* they: *The corner apartment belongs to them.*||*She sent them a wedding gift.*

**theme** /θim/ *noun*
a central idea or main pattern: *The theme in that book is one of adventure in exploring the jungle.* *–adjective* **thematic** /θɪˈmætɪk/; *–adverb* **thematically.**

**themselves** /ðəmˈsɛlvz/ *pronoun*
*reflexive objective form of* they *and* them: *Farmers do a lot of the farm work themselves.*

**then** /ðɛn/ *adverb*
at that time: *I wasn't alive then.*

**then** *conjunction*
**1** an order of events: *I went to the drugstore, then to the supermarket, then home.*
**2** therefore, in that case: *If you don't feel well, then go home early.*

**theoretical** /ˌθiəˈrɛtəkəl/ *adjective*
in idea only: *His suggestions are only theoretical and have not been tested.* *–adverb* **theoretically.** *(antonym)* practical.

**theory** /ˈθiəri/ *noun, plural* **theories**
an idea, argument that something is true: *I have a theory that the earth is getting warmer, but I can't prove it.* *–noun* (person) **theorist;** *–verb* **to theorize.**

**therapist** /ˈθɛrəpɪst/ *noun*
**1** a person who heals disease or disorders: *He is a physical therapist who works with the disabled.*
**2** a psychiatrist or psychologist who helps patients for mental health: *She visits her therapist once a week to fight depression.*

**therapy** /ˈθɛr əpi/ *noun*
treatment of mental and physical illnesses and disorders: *She began therapy to treat her fear of crowds.*

**there** /ðɛr/ *adverb*
at or to a specific place: *The meeting is at the church and I promised to be there.*

**there** *adjective*
here, present: *That desk there needs repair.*

**there** *pronoun*
to begin a statement: *There is still time to finish the project. (antonym)* here.

**therefore** /'ðɛr,fɔr/ *adverb*
consequently, for that reason: *He practices the piano every day and therefore plays well.*

**thermometer** /θər'mɑmətər/ *noun*
a device that measures and shows temperature: *We put a thermometer outside our window.*

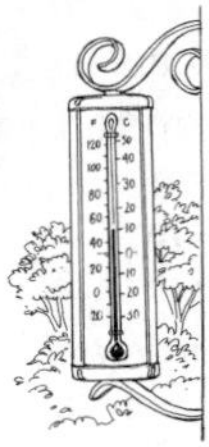

thermometer

**thermostat** /'θɜrmə,stæt/ *noun*
a device that controls temperature inside a building: *It's cold in here; turn up the thermostat! See:* art on page 6a.

**these** /ðiz/ *pronoun*
*plural of* this, referring to close things: *I am taking these flowers to my sick neighbor. See:* this.

**they** /ðeɪ/ *pronoun*
third person plural: *John and Jane have just married and they are on their honeymoon.*

**thick** /θɪk/ *adjective*
**1** having bulk, width, or depth: *The walls of the library are thick.*
**2** closely packed: *He has a thick head of hair. (antonym)* thin.
**3** stupid: *She loves her son, but knows that he's a bit thick.* *–adverb* **thickly.**

**thicken** /'θɪkən / *verb*
to make thicker (wider, deeper, etc.)

T

**thickness** /'θɪknɪs/ *noun*
the depth of something: *The thickness of the wood is two inches (5 cm).*

**thief** /θif/ *noun, plural* **thieves** /θivz/
a person who steals: *A thief stole my suitcase at the airport.*

**thievery** /'θivəri/ *noun, (no plural)*
an act of stealing

**thigh** /θaɪ/ *noun*
the part of the leg between the hip and knee *See:* art on page 21a.

**thin** /θɪn/ *adjective* **thinner, thinnest**
**1** slender, slim: *She is tall and thin.*
**2** not thick, wide, or deep: *A thin layer of dirt covers the rock.* *–adverb* **thinly.** *(antonym)* fat.

**thin** *verb* **thinned, thinning, thins**
to lessen: *His hair is thinning.*

**thing** /θɪŋ/ *noun*
a term for an unnamed material object, person, or animal: *We found a strange thing on the road.*
**first thing:** early, at the beginning
**the thing to do:** a proper, correct action: *The thing to do is to apologize right away.*

**things** *noun, plural*
**1** one's possessions: *When we moved, we took all of our things with us in a truck.*
**2** matters in general: *Things are bad now, but things will change soon.*

**think** /θɪŋk/ *verb* **thought** /θɔt/, **thinking, thinks**
**1** to reason, to use the brain: *She thinks of solutions to mathematical problems.*
**2** to remember: *He thinks that he sent the rent check to his landlord last week.*
**3** to believe, desire: *I think that I should go now.*
**4** to consider, have an opinion: *They thought that he acted like a jerk.*
**to think something over:** to consider for a while before deciding: *She thought over his marriage proposal for several weeks before accepting.* *–adjective* **thinkable;** *–noun* (person) **thinker.**

**third** /θɜrd/ *adjective*
the ordinal number 3: *She is the third child in the family.*

**third** *noun*
**1** of three equal parts: *one third, two thirds of a pound*
**2** number 3 in order: *She is third in line.*

**third person** *noun*
(in grammar) a person or thing in the singular as *he, she,* or *it* and in the plural as *they: In learning English, students often forget to add an "s" to the third person singular form of verbs in the present tense as in "speaks, walks, talks."*

**thirst** /θɜrst/ *noun, (no plural)*
the need to drink: *I satisfy my thirst by*

*drinking lots of water.* –*verb* **to thirst;** –*adverb* **thirstily;** –*adjective* **thirsty.**

**thirteen** /θər'tin/ *noun*
the cardinal number 13: *Thirteen is thought to be an unlucky number in many cultures.*

**thirteen** *adjective*
thirteen of something: *She bought thirteen eggs.*

**thirty** /'θɜrti/ *noun, plural* **thirties**
the cardinal number 30: *She is thirty today.*

**thirty** *adjective*
thirty of something: *Some months are thirty days long.*

**this** /ðɪs/ *pronoun*
referring to something close by: *You should read this book.*

**thorn** /θɔrn/ *noun*
sharp, pointed parts of the stems in some plants: *Roses are beautiful, but have thorns.*

**thorny** /'θɔrni/ *adjective* **thornier, thorniest**
**1** having thorns
**2** *figurative* difficult, complex, especially causing pain: *Raising taxes is always a thorny issue.*

**thorough** /'θɜroʊ/ *adjective*
complete: *The doctor made a thorough examination of the patient, then suggested a treatment.* –*adverb* **thoroughly;** –*noun* **thoroughness.**

**those** /ðoʊz/ *pronoun*
*plural of* that, referring to specific people or things not close by: *Those people caught in the flood need help.*

**though** /ðoʊ/ *conjunction*
even though, in comparison: *I enjoy playing tennis, though it is tiring.*

**though** *adverb*
despite the fact that: *Tennis is fun, though it's also tiring.*
**as though:** as if: *He acts as though he's stupid, but he's not.*

**thought** /θɔt/ *noun*
**1** an idea: *The thought of going out in the rain and fog discouraged him.*
**2** the process of reasoning: *He gave a lot of thought to moving to the country before doing so.*
**second thought(s):** changing one's opinion: *I said it would rain today, but on second thought, I think it won't.*

**thoughtful** /'θɔtfəl/ *adjective*
considerate, kind: *Her children were thoughtful and always took care of their elderly mother.* –*adverb* **thoughtfully;** –*noun* **thoughtfulness.**

**thousand** /'θaʊzənd/ *noun*
the cardinal number 1,000

**thousand** *adjective*
1,000 of something: *A thousand people came to the concert.*

**thread** /θrɛd/ *noun*
**1** a twisted fiber, such as cotton, wool, etc.: *A tailor sewed a hole with a needle and thread.*
**2** in a screw, the raised ridge that forms a spiral around it

thread

**thread** *verb*
to put thread through the eye of a needle

**threat** /θrɛt/ *noun*
a warning of harm: *They had to leave the building because of a bomb threat.*

**threaten** /'θrɛtn/ *verb*
to make threats: *A manager threatens to fire an employee unless her work improves.* –*adverb* **threateningly.**

**three** /θri/ *noun*
the cardinal number 3

**three** *adjective*
three of something: *The couple has three sons.*

**three-dimensional** or **3-D** /'θri'di/ *adjective*
having height, width, and depth: *A stone wall is three-dimensional.*

**thrift** /θrɪft/ *noun*
spending money carefully: *New Englanders are famous for their thrift.* –*adjective* **thrifty.**

**thrill** /θrɪl/ *noun*
a feeling of strong excitement, fear, or pleasure: *Riding a roller coaster gives you a thrill.* –*verb* **to thrill;** –*adjective* **thrilling.**

**thriller** /'θrɪlər/ *noun*
a mystery or adventure story

**throat** /θroʊt/ *noun*
the front of the neck between chin and chest; inside the mouth to the esophagus: *She has a sore throat. See:* art on page 21a.

**throne** /θroʊn/ *noun*
a decorated chair used especially by kings and queens in ceremonies as a symbol of power

**through** /θru/ *preposition*
in one side and out the other: *The boy walked through the backyard.*

**through** *adverb*
completely, from beginning to end: *He read through the magazine.*

**through** *adjective*
finished, done: *The maid is through cleaning the room now.*

**throughout** /θru'aʊt/ *preposition*
everywhere: *The rain spread throughout the city.*

**throughway** /'θru,weɪ/ *noun*
a major highway: *The throughway runs across the state into the city.*

**throw** /θroʊ/ *verb* **threw** /θru/ or **thrown** /θroʊn/, **throwing, throws**
**1** to send something through the air, *(synonym)* to toss: *One player throws the ball to the other.*
**2** to move something on a machine: *She threw a switch to start the assembly line moving.*
**to throw something away:** to discard, get rid of: *He threw away the old newspapers.*
**to throw out:** to put outside something no longer wanted: *I throw out the garbage every morning.*

**throw** *noun*
**1** the act of throwing
**2** the distance something is thrown: *a 50-foot (15.3 m) throw (antonym)* catch.

**thrust** /θrʌst/ *noun*
a quick forward motion as with the arm or feet *–verb* **to thrust.**

**thud** /θʌd/ *noun*
the sound that a falling heavy object makes when it hits the ground: *The big textbook fell on the floor with a thud.*

**thud** *verb* **thudded, thudding, thuds**
to fall heavily: *The big book thudded onto the floor.*

**thug** /θʌg/ *noun*
a criminal, a tough guy

**thumb** /θʌm/ *noun*
**1** on the hand, the digit opposite the index finger: *The thumb allows humans to hold things.*
**2** *plural* **thumbs up:** a sign of approval, support, or victory: *After I won the tennis match, my friends gave me thumbs up.*
**a rule of thumb:** a guideline, rule *–verb* **to thumb.** *See:* art on page 21a.

**thumbtack** /'θʌm,tæk/ *noun*
a small pin or tack used to put things on a wall or board

**thump** /θʌmp/ *verb*
to hit with a heavy sound: *A child thumped on a drum with her hands.*

**thunder** /'θʌndər/ *noun, (no plural)*
the loud, strong noise that follows lightning: *Thunder frightens some animals and people.*

**thunder** *verb*
**1** to create thunder
**2** *figurative* to sound like thunder: *A herd of cattle thundered by.*

**thunderstorm** /'θʌndər,stɔrm/ *noun*
a storm with heavy rain, thunder, and lightning

**Thursday** /'θɜrz,deɪ/ *noun*
the fifth day of the week, coming between Wednesday and Friday: *On Thursdays, she takes a computer course after work.*

**thus** /ðʌs/ *conjunction*
for that reason, therefore: *He does not watch television, thus he does not own a television set.*

**thus** *adjective*
in this way
**thus far:** so far, until now

**tick** /tɪk/ *noun*
**1** the sound of a clock in motion: *The grandfather clock in our front hall makes a loud tick.*
**2** a small insect that sucks the blood of larger animals: *Dog owners remove ticks from their pets.*

**tick** *verb*
to make the sound of a clock: *Old clocks tick away with the sound, "tick-tock tick-tock."*

T

**ticket** /ˈtɪkɪt/ *noun*

ticket

**1** a printed piece of paper bought for transportation or entertainment events: *I have two tickets to the theater tonight.*
**2** a written legal notice: *A traffic officer gave me a ticket for parking in an illegal spot.*

**ticket** *verb*
to write notices, such as traffic tickets: *A police officer ticketed a driver for speeding.*

**ticket office** or **box office** *noun*
a place that sells tickets: *The ticket office at the theater opens one hour before the performance begins.*

**tickle** /ˈtɪkəl/ *verb* **tickled, tickling, tickles**
to touch lightly the sensitive parts of the body so as to cause laughter: *The baby's father tickled its foot with his fingers.* –*adjective* **ticklish.**

**tide** /taɪd/ *noun*
the change in levels of sea and ocean water caused mainly by the moon's pull on the earth: *Boats go out to sea on the high tide.*

**tidy** /ˈtaɪdi/ *adjective* **tidier, tidiest**
neat, orderly: *The boy's room is never tidy. (antonym)* messy.

**tie** /taɪ/ *verb* **tied, tying, ties**
**1** to fasten together: *He tied his shoelaces.*
**2** to equal someone in a competition: *The tennis match is tied two to two.*
**to tie something up:** **a.** to fasten together: *I tied up old newspapers and put them outside.* **b.** to block: *We were tied up in traffic.* **c.** busy: *The manager can't talk to you now, as she's tied up in a meeting.*

**tie** *noun*
**1** a necktie: *I tied my tie.*
**2** a relationship: *He still has ties to his old neighborhood.*
**3** equality in competition: *The two teams had a two to two tie.*

**tiger** /ˈtaɪgər/ *noun*
large, wild yellow cat that lives in Asia: *Indian tigers have been hunted so much there are few left. See:* art on page 14a.

**tight** /taɪt/ *adjective*
**1** stretched firmly: *The belt is tight around his waist. (antonym)* loose.
**2** not allowing something, such as water or air to pass through: *Cans of food are air-tight.*
**3** rigid, firm: *The government keeps tight control over the people coming into the country.*
**4** close: *She held her baby tight.* –*adverb* **tightly;** –*noun* **tightness.**

**tighten** /ˈtaɪtn/ *verb*
**1** to fasten firmly: *He tightens his belt before he takes a walk.*
**2** to control more closely: *Border police tightened controls on foreign tourists. (antonym)* loosen.

**tights** /taɪts/ *noun, plural*
close-fitting stockings: *In the winter, I wear tights under my skirt.*

**tile** /taɪl/ *noun*
thin plates of clay, metal, etc., put down to cover a floor or wall: *A worker put new tiles on the bathroom floor.*

**tilt** /tɪlt/ *noun*
a leaning at an angle: *A rocket takes off straight up, then has a tilt in its path.*

**tilt** *verb*
to lean away from the vertical: *A computer operator tilts the screen into a comfortable position.*

**timber** /ˈtɪmbər/ *noun, (no plural)*
**1** wood for buildings: *Workers cut timber in the forest.*
**2** a wooden beam or support –*noun* **timberland** /ˈtɪmbərˌlænd/.

**time** /taɪm/ *noun, (no plural)*
**1** the length of existence, especially as measured in days, months, years, etc., or by clocks, etc.: *There is a saying that "time and tide wait for no man."*
**2** the exact hour, minute, or second in a day: *What time is it? The time is now 8:00 A.M.*
**3** a duration, period: *We have time to have lunch before the meeting.*
**4** an experience: *We had a good time at the party.*

**do you have the time:** to know what time it is: *"Excuse me, do you have the time?"—"Yes, it's two o'clock."*
**in time:** **a.** over a period of time: *In time, she will feel less sad about her mother's death.* **b.** on time, at the right time: *He arrived in time to get a good seat at the show.*
**one at a time:** in order, individually: *Please speak one at a time, not all at once.*
**on time:** at the planned moment (punctual): *The train left on time.*
**time off:** vacation, time not working: *He took time off and went to Mexico for a week.*
**Time out!:** (in sports) Stop play!: *The basketball referee shouted, "Time out!"*

**time** *verb* **timed, timing, times**
to measure the amount of time needed to do something: *We timed our trip to Boston; it took three hours.*

**time and a half** *noun, (no plural)*
pay at the regular hourly rate plus 50%, such as $20 per hour = $30: *She gets time and a half for overtime work.*

**time card** or **sheet** *noun*
a card on which a worker's hours at work are noted: *He puts his time card in a time clock when he gets to work and leaves work.*

**time limit** *noun*
a set period of time for doing something: *The time limit for the exam is two hours.*

**timely** /ˈtaɪmli/ *adjective* **timelier, timeliest**
fortunate, well-timed for a good result: *The arrival of help was timely because it saved everyone from starvation.*

T

**time-out** *noun See:* Time out!

**timer** /ˈtaɪmər/ *noun*
a clock or person who times events, usually to the minute or second: *She uses an egg timer in the kitchen to boil eggs.*

**times** /taɪmz/ *preposition*
multiplied by: *Ten times ten equals 100.*

**times** *noun plural*
**the times:** modern life, now: *These are good times.*
**behind the times:** outdated, old-fashioned

**time sheet** *noun*
*See:* time card.

**times sign** *noun*
the sign (x), which indicates multiplication: *10 x 15 = 150.*

**timetable** /ˈtaɪmˌteɪbəl/ *noun*
a printed display of transportation departure and arrival times: *I carry a commuter train timetable so I can check when my train leaves.*

**time zone** *noun*
one of 24 15-degree longitudinal divisions of the earth as measured from Greenwich, England: *When it is 11:00 A.M. in New York, it is 8:00 A.M. in the Pacific time zone of Los Angeles.*

**timid** /ˈtɪmɪd/ *adjective*
**1** easily frightened: *Many birds are timid and fly away as you come near them.* *(antonym)* bold.
**2** afraid of speaking to people, *(synonym)* shy: *The boy is timid about asking girls for dates.* *–adverb* **timidly.**

**tin** /tɪn/ *noun, (no plural)*
a grayish, flexible metal used as a protective coating and used with other metals: *My cup is made of tin.*

**tiny** /ˈtaɪni/ *adjective* **tinier, tiniest**
very small: *Cells are too tiny to see with the bare eye; one needs a microscope to see them. (antonym)* huge.

**tip** /tɪp/ *noun*
**1** the point of something: *The tip of a needle is very sharp.*
**2** advice, helpful information: *The coach gave a player a tip on how to improve her tennis game.*
**3** money given to someone for doing something: *I left the waiter a big tip.*

**tip** *verb* **tipped, tipping, tips**
**1** to leave money: *I tipped the waiter and left.*
**2** to lean: *She tipped the bucket and poured water out of it.*

**tipsy** /ˈtɪpsi/ *adjective* **tipsier, tipsiest**
a little bit drunk: *He drank too much and is a little tipsy.*

**tiptoe** /'tɪpˌtoʊ/ *verb* **tiptoed, tiptoeing, tiptoes**
to walk quietly on one's toes: *She tiptoed up the stairs, so as not to wake up her sleeping parents.*

tiptoe

**tire (1)** /taɪr/ *verb* **tired, tiring, tires**
to become fatigued: *He tires when he walks a long distance.* *–adjective* **tiring.**

**tire (2)** *noun*
the outer covering of a vehicle's wheel where air is put: *My bicycle got a flat tire this morning on my way to work.*

**tired** /taɪrd/ *adjective*
exhausted, fatigued: *She is tired after working all day. See:* art on page 18a.

**tissue** /'tɪʃu/ *noun*
**1** *(no plural)* a group of animal or plant cells that together make up an organ that performs a certain function: *Human liver tissue can grow again if it is injured.*
**2** paper products, such as toilet tissue or paper handkerchiefs: *After I sneezed, I wiped my nose with a tissue.*

**title** /'taɪtl/ *noun*
**1** the name of a book, musical piece, painting, etc.: *The title of that great novel is* War and Peace.
**2** legal proof, such as a document, of ownership of property: *I have title to two automobiles.*
**3** the name of a rank of nobility, academic degree, or office: *Dr. Jones has the title of Doctor of Medical Dentistry.*

**title** *verb* **titled, titling, titles**
to give a name or title to something: *The songwriter titled the song "Happy Days."* *–adjective* **titled.**

**to** /tu/ *particle*
**1** used to begin an infinitive of a verb, as in "to go" and "to know": *We have to go home now.*
**2** used in place of an infinitive: *He needs to fix his car but doesn't know how to.*

**to** *preposition*
**1** used to show an indirect object: *The sales clerk sold the dress to her.*
**2** used with many verbs to show motion: *A police officer came to our house.*
**3** including, between certain times, spaces, etc.: *He works from morning to evening (from 9 to 5).*
**4** regarding time, scores, and ratios: *Our team won 10 to 6.*
**5** relating, belonging to, fitting someone or something: *That is the key to the door.* *(antonym)* from.

**toad** /toʊd/ *noun*
a frog-like animal (amphibian): *Toads spend more time on land than frogs do.*

**toast** /toʊst/ *verb*
**1** to make bread or other foods brown with heat: *I toasted some white bread for sandwiches.*
**2** to honor someone, especially with a drink: *We toasted the guest of honor with a glass of wine.* *–noun* **toast.**

**toaster** /'toʊstər/ *noun*
an electrical device that browns food *See:* art on page 7a.

**tobacco** /tə'bækoʊ/ *noun, (no plural)*
a variety of leafy plants dried and cut for smoking or chewing: *People smoke tobacco in cigarettes.*

**today** /tə'deɪ/ *adverb*
**1** now, this present day: *Today, I'm not going to work.*
**2** these times: *Our government needs to do something about the economy today.*

**toe** /toʊ/ *noun*
each of five parts on the front of foot: *Her big toe hurts.*
**on one's toes:** ready to move or act: *The boss keeps everyone on their toes by checking their work. See:* finger. *See:* art on page 21a.

**toenail** /'toʊˌneɪl/ *noun*
the nail on each toe of the foot: *Toenails grow more slowly than fingernails.*

**together** /tə'gɛðɛr/ *adverb*
**1** as a group: *We went together to the party.*
**2** (to join) as a unit: *Carpenters nail pieces of wood together.* *–noun* **togetherness.** *(antonym)* apart.

T

**toilet** /ˈtɔɪlɪ t/ *noun*
**1** a bathroom fixture with a water tank, bowl, and drain pipe, used to send away bodily waste: *The toilet is stopped up.*
**2** a bathroom: *He excused himself to go to the toilet. See:* art on page 23a.

**toilet paper** *noun*
paper tissue used for cleaning oneself: *Toilet paper comes in rolls.*

**told** *verb*
*past tense of* tell

**tolerance** /ˈtɑl ərəns/ *noun, (no plural)*
**1** the ability to suffer something: *She has a high tolerance for pain.*
**2** acceptance, especially of different beliefs and behavior: *That city is famous for its tolerance of crime.* –*verb* **to tolerate.**

**tolerant** /ˈtɑlərənt/ *adjective*
accepting of different beliefs and behavior: *The boy's parents are tolerant of his bad manners. (antonym)* intolerant.

**toll** /toʊl/ *noun*
**1** money charged for passage: *Authorities charge a toll to use certain bridges and roads.*
**2** wear and tear: *Working many long days took its toll on her health.*

**toll** *verb*
to ring slowly: *The grandfather clock tolled 12 midnight.*

**tomato** /təˈmeɪtoʊ/ *noun, plural* **tomatoes**
a South American plant with large red fruit eaten as a vegetable: *Ripe tomatoes taste good. See:* art on page 2a.

**tomb** /tum/ *noun*
a burial room or grave with a monument over it: *Egyptian pyramids are tombs and monuments to dead rulers.*

**tombstone** /ˈtumˌstoʊn/ *noun*
a grave marker: *His tombstone is carved with the words, "Rest in Peace."*

**tomorrow** /təˈmɔroʊ/ *noun*
the day after today: *Tomorrow is Saturday.*

**tomorrow** *adverb*
indicating the day after today: *I have to work tomorrow.*

**ton** /tʌn/ *noun*
**1** a unit of measurement of weight, in the USA, 2,000 lbs.; in the British Commonwealth, 2,240 lbs.
**2** a metric ton: weight of 1,000 kilos

**tone** /toʊn/ *noun*
**1** the loudness or character of a voice: *He speaks to his baby in soft tones.*
**2** an electronic sound, such as the dial tone: *On the radio one hears, "At the sound of the tone, it will be 10 o'clock."*

**tongue** /tʌŋ/ *noun*
**1** the movable part in the mouth used for tasting and producing speech: *He drank hot tea and burned his tongue.*
**2** a language: *He speaks in a foreign tongue. See:* art on page 21a.

**tongue-twister** *noun*
words or phrases that are difficult to pronounce: *"Peter Piper picked a peck of pickled peppers" is a tongue-twister.*

**tonight** /təˈnaɪt/ *adverb*
the hours of darkness after this day: *The concert takes place tonight.*

---

**USAGE NOTE:** *Tonight* includes both *evening* and *night* of a given day: *Tonight at 7* P.M. *(=this evening), I'm having dinner with friends. Tonight at midnight (=late at night), I'm meeting a friend at a nightclub.*

---

**too** /tu/ *adverb*
**1** in addition, as well, also: *She went to the movie, and I decided to go, too.*
**2** not wanted as too troublesome: *That investment is too risky for us.*
**3** *informal* **too much:** extreme (often used humorously): *George, your bad jokes are too much.*

**took** /tʊk/ *verb*
*past tense of* take

**tool** /tul/ *noun*
an implement, such as a screwdriver, hammer, or saw, used to make or repair things: *He keeps his tools in a box.*

**tooth** /tuθ/ *noun, plural* **teeth** /tiθ/
**1** one of a set forming a dental structure in the mouth used for biting and chewing: *A dentist examines one tooth at a time.*
**2** pointed parts of something, such as teeth on a saw, rake, comb, etc. *See:* art on page 21a.

**toothache** /ˈtuθˌeɪk/ *noun*
a pain in a tooth or teeth

**toothbrush** /'tuθ,brʌʃ/ *noun, plural* **toothbrushes**
a brush with a handle used to clean teeth

**toothpaste** /'tuθ,p eɪst/ *noun, (no plural)*
flavored paste used to clean teeth: *She brushes her teeth with toothpaste.*

**top** /tɑp/ *noun*
**1** the highest part of something: *He touched the top of his head.*
**2** a lid, covering, cap: *The top of the jar is made of metal.*
**3** a shirt, a piece of clothing for the upper body: *She bought a new top to go with her skirt.*
**4** the best, first: *He is at the top of his class. (antonym)* bottom.
**off the top of my head:** quickly, without research or thought: *Off the top of my head, I don't know the answer, but I will find out.*

**top** *noun plural*
**1** the uppermost parts: *The tops of the trees move in the wind.*
**2** *figurative* excellent, terrific: *She is tops, just terrific!*
**3** *figurative* first: *He is tops in the country in his field.*

**topic** /'tɑpɪk/ *noun*
a subject of attention, writing, conversation: *Today's topic in math class was algebra. –adjective* **topical.**

**topic sentence** *noun*
a sentence that gives the main subject of concern: *The topic sentence began the first paragraph of her term paper.*

**torch** /tɔrʧ/ *noun, plural* **torches**
a lighting device with a flame atop a handle: *The Olympic torch is used to light the flame to begin the games.*

**torch** *verb* **torched, torching, torches**
to set afire: *Criminals torched buildings in the city.*

tornado

**tornado** /tɔr'neɪdoʊ/ *noun, plural* **tornadoes**
a twister; violent, fast-moving winds: *Tornadoes can lift houses and trees and put them down miles away.*

**tortoise** /'tɔrtəs/ *noun*
a land turtle with a high shell that moves in slow motion

**torture** /'tɔrʧər/ *noun*
**1** physical abuse that causes great pain: *Prisoners suffer torture from some military groups.*
**2** strong emotional pain

**torture** *verb* **tortured, torturing, tortures**
to harm: *Prison workers tortured captured soldiers during the war.*

**toss** /tɔs/ *verb* **tossed, tossing, tosses**
to throw: *The baseball player tossed the ball to the catcher. –verb* **to toss.**

**total** /'toʊtl/ *noun*
a sum, final adding up: *The total of this month's sales is up 20%.*

**total** *adjective*
**1** complete, entire: *That amount shows the total cost of the project.*
**2** absolute: *The house destroyed in the storm is a total loss.*

**total** *verb*
**1** to add up, reach a final figure: *The clerk totaled the bill.*
**2** to destroy, especially a car: *He drove too fast and totaled his car. –adverb* **totally.**

**totalitarian** /toʊ,tælə'tɛriən/ *adjective*
dictatorship by an individual or a group over a nation's people: *a totalitarian government –noun* **totalitarianism.**

**touch** /tʌʧ/ *verb* **touched, touching, touches**
**1** to feel with the skin, especially with the hand: *The doctor touched the patient's stomach to feel for problems.*
**2** to make contact: *The bookcase is touching the wall.*
**3** to move someone emotionally: *The music touched me and made me feel sad.*
**to touch down:** to land an aircraft: *Our plane touched down at San Francisco airport in a smooth landing.*
**to touch something off:** to start: *A spark touched off an explosion of a gas leak.*

**touch** *noun, (no plural)*
**1** a feeling of the skin: *The patient felt the touch of the doctor's hand.*

**2** physical contact: *The touch of her hand calmed him down.*
**3** a small amount: *Put a touch of salt in the soup.*
**in touch:** communication between people: *She stays in touch with her parents by telephoning them every week.*

**tough** /tʌf/ *adjective* **tougher, toughest**
**1** difficult, demanding: *Training to be a doctor is tough. (antonym)* easy.
**2** rubbery, difficult to chew, etc.: *The meat for dinner was tough. (antonym)* tender.
**3** mean: *Street gangs act tough.*
**4** strong: *Leather boots are tough.*
**tough** *noun informal*
a thug, criminal: *Many street toughs join gangs. –noun* **toughness.**

**toughen** /ˈtʌfən/ *verb*
to harden, make stronger: *Exercise toughened her muscles.*

**tour** /tʊr/ *noun*
a series of stops as on a trip: *The Secretary of State made a tour of four cities in Asia.*
**tour** *verb*
to make a tour: *We toured several countries in Europe on our vacation.*

**tourism** /ˈtʊrˌɪzəm/ *noun, (no plural)*
the tourist industry: *Tourism has increased between Europe and America.*

**tourist** /ˈtʊrɪst/ *noun*
a visitor who travels for pleasure: *Tourists go to beaches and the mountains in August.*
**tourist** *adjective*
related to tourism: *The Spanish consulate gave us a tourist visa.*



**tournament** /ˈtʊrnəmənt/ or **tourney** /ˈtʊrni/ *noun*
competition in a series of events leading to a winner, as in tennis, chess, and golf

**tow** /toʊ/ *verb*
to pull a boat, object, etc., behind another by a rope, chain, or metal bar: *My car broke down, and a truck towed it to the garage. –noun* **tow.**

**toward** /tɔrd/ or **towards** /tɔrdz/ *preposition*
**1** in the direction of, to: *The captain headed the boat toward home.*
**2** concerning: *His feelings towards his wife have stayed the same for 25 years.*
**3** soon before: *Toward the end of the play, my father fell asleep.*

**towel** /ˈtaʊəl/ *noun*
a piece of cloth or paper used to dry something: *People use a towel to dry the dishes. –verb* **to towel.** *See:* art on page 23a.

**tower** /ˈtaʊər/ *noun*
a tall round or square structure: *The radio tower is on top of the hill.*
**tower** *verb*
to rise over in size: *The tall man towers over his friends. –adjective* **towering.**

tower

**town** /taʊn/ *noun*
a settlement smaller than a city: *He comes from a small town in Vermont.*

**town hall** *noun*
a town's local government office building: *The old wooden town hall was replaced with modern brick buildings.*

**toxic** /ˈtɑksɪk/ *adjective*
poisonous: *Rat poison is toxic.*

**toy** /tɔɪ/ *noun*
a plaything: *Children like to play with toys, such as little cars and dolls.*
**toy** *adjective*
small, miniature: *a toy poodle*|*a toy gun*
**toy** *verb*
to treat someone or something lightly: *For a day or two, I toyed with the idea of going to Korea for vacation, then realized it would be too expensive.*

**trace** /treɪs/ *noun*
a very small amount: *Chemists found traces of poison in the food.*
**trace** *verb* **traced, tracing, traces**
**1** to follow something to its origin: *Police traced the illegal money from New York to London.*
**2** to copy onto thin paper from an image underneath: *Children trace letters of the alphabet to learn how to make them.*

**track** /træk/ *noun*
**1** an oval-shaped path used for running: *Competitors raced around the track.*

**2** metal rails or concrete paths for railroad, subway trains, etc.: *Railroad trains roll along steel tracks.*
**3** signs of movement of something, such as footprints, or tire marks: *Hunters followed the lion's tracks.*
**to keep** or **lose track of something:** to pay sharp attention to something, remain aware: *He keeps track of his expenses by writing them in a notebook.*||*I lost track of my old friend after he moved away.*
**track** *verb*
to follow the movement of something: *Hunters track deer.*

**tractor** /'træktər/ *noun*
a piece of farm machinery used for pulling things and for preparing the earth for planting: *The farmer uses a tractor for spring plowing.*

**tractor**

**trade** /treɪd/ *noun, (no plural)*
**1** business in general: *Trade between the two countries is active.*
**2** an exchange: *She made a trade of her bicycle to a friend for a CD player.*
**3** a type of work, skill: *Her trade is as a carpenter.*
**trade** *verb* **traded, trading, trades**
**1** to exchange: *I traded a computer for a bicycle.*
**2** to work in business: *She trades in farm equipment.*
**to trade something in:** to use property as part of payment: *He traded in his old car while buying a new one.*||*He traded it in.*

**trader** /'treɪdər/ *noun*
**1** a person who buys and sells stocks, bonds, etc.
**2** a person or business that buys and sells goods or services for other goods: *He is a silk trader who trades silk for spices and gold.*

**trade school** *noun*
in the USA, an educational institution for occupational skills, such as for auto mechanics, computer technicians, secretaries, or hairdressers: *She went to a trade school to learn how to be a computer technician.*

**tradition** /trə'dɪʃən/ *noun*
**1** the passing of customs and beliefs from one age group to another (parents to children): *The New Year's Eve tradition of watching the lighted ball fall happens every year in Times Square, New York.*
**2** a custom, a traditional way of celebrating a religious and cultural event and belief: *Thanksgiving dinner is an old tradition for many families in North America.* –*adjective* **traditional;** –*adverb* **traditionally.**

**traffic** /'træfɪk/ *noun, (no plural)*
the movement of vehicles, people, aircraft, etc., in a certain area: *Boat traffic on the river is heavy in summer.*
**stuck in traffic:** delayed: *An accident blocked the road, and I got stuck in traffic for an hour.*

**traffic jam** *noun*
vehicles blocking each other

**traffic light** or **signal** *noun*
a post with lights that control the flow of traffic: *We stopped at the red traffic light and waited for it to change to green. See:* art on page 4a.

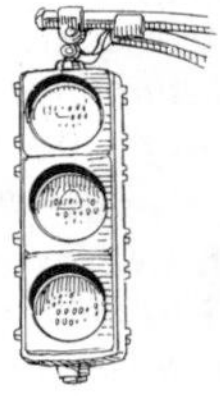
**traffic light**

**tragedy** /'trædʒədi/ *noun, plural* **tragedies**
a sad event, disaster: *The accidental death of their child is a tragedy.* –*adjective* **tragic** /'trædʒɪk/; –*adverb* **tragically.**

**trail** /treɪl/ *noun*
**1** a path, such as for hiking: *The Appalachian Trail goes for 2,050 miles (3,280 km) from Maine to Georgia.*
**2** tracks, such as footprints or pieces of information: *The criminal left a trail of evidence.*
**trail** *verb*
**1** to follow, track: *Police trailed the criminal to his home.*
**2** to grow along the ground

**trailer** /'treɪlər/ *noun*
a vehicle or house on wheels pulled by a

motorized vehicle: *We pulled a trailer across the state to a campground.*

**train (1)** /treɪn/ *verb*
to educate, instruct: *Trade schools train students in job skills.*

**train (2)** *noun*
a line of vehicles, such as railroad cars pulled by a locomotive, subway cars, etc.: *Passengers took the train from Los Angeles to Dallas. See:* art on page 24a.

**trainee** /treɪ'ni/ *noun*
a person in training, beginner: *She is a trainee at a bank.*

**training** /'treɪnɪŋ/ *noun, (no plural)*
a process of education, instruction: *He had training on how to use a computer.*
**in training:** preparing for an event or competition

**traitor** /'treɪtər/ *noun*
one who works against one's own country or other loyalty for another: *A traitor sold military secrets to an enemy country. (antonym)* patriot.

**tranquilizer** /'træŋkwəˌlaɪzər/ *noun*
a drug used to calm: *A doctor gave a tranquilizer to calm an upset patient. –verb* **to tranquilize.**

**transfer** /træns'fɛr/ *verb* **transferred, transferring, transfers**
**1** to move from one place to another: *We transferred our bags from the bus to the car.*
**2** to change ownership, as in a legal document: *After purchase, the deed to a house transfers it to new owners. –noun* **transfer.**

**transform** /træns'fɔrm/ *verb*
to change from one shape or appearance to another: *New paint transformed an old, dark house into a cheerful one. –noun* **transformation** /ˌtrænsfər'meɪʃən/.

**transistor** /træn'zɪstər/ *noun*
an electronic part that controls the flow of electricity in a machine (computer, TV, etc.): *My computer has hundreds of transistors inside on small boards.*

**transition** /træn'zɪʃən/ *noun*
a change from one condition to another: *The transition from high school to college can be difficult for students. –adjective* **transitional;** *–adverb* **transitionally.**

**translate** /'trænsˌleɪt/ *verb* **translated, translating, translates**
**1** to change, interpret as from one language to another: *He translated a letter from French into English.*
**2** to change into: *A 10% interest rate translated into a payment of $200 a month. –noun* **translation.** *See:* interpret.

**transmit** /træns'mɪt/ *verb* **transmitted, transmitting, transmits**
**1** to send: *He transmitted the package by messenger.*
**2** to broadcast: *That radio station transmits programs 24 hours a day.*

**transparent** /træns'pɛrənt/ *adjective*
allowing light to pass through so images can be clearly seen, clear: *Window glass is transparent. –adverb* **transparently.**

**transport** /træns'pɔrt/ *verb*
to move: *Trucks transport most of our goods to our customers.*

**transport** /'trænsˌpɔrt/ *noun, (no plural)*
transportation: *Transport in some countries is slow and unsafe.*

**transportation** /ˌtrænspər'teɪʃən/ *noun, (no plural)*
ways to move from one place to another: *Transportation by air, rail, and road is easily available in the USA. –noun* **transporter.**

**trap** /træp/ *noun*
**1** a mechanical device used to catch animals: *Hunters use traps to capture rabbits.*
**2** a surprise situation planned to harm or kill someone: *Soldiers entered a cave and fell into a trap as their enemy blocked the entrance shut. –noun* (person) **trapper.**

**trap** *verb* **trapped, trapping, traps**
**1** to hunt animals with traps
**2** to catch or harm someone in a trap: *The dogcatcher trapped a homeless dog.*

**trapezoid**
/træpəˌzɔɪd/ *noun*
a geometric figure with four sides, two of which are parallel: *A modern painter grouped bright-colored trapezoids on a canvas. –adjective* **trapezoidal.**

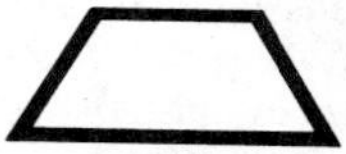

trapezoid

**trash** /træʃ/ *noun, (no plural)*
**1** waste, *(synonym)* garbage: *Once a week, we put out the trash for collection.*
**2** something of poor quality (or indecency, such as pornography): *A lot of the magazines sold in the store are trash.*

**trash** *verb* **trashed, trashing, trashes**
to destroy: *Rioters trashed stores as a protest.* –*adjective* **trashy.**

**trauma** /'traʊmə/ *noun*
**1** mental shock and pain: *The mother's trauma of losing her child still pains her.*
**2** an injury: *He suffered trauma to his head in the accident.* –*verb* **to traumatize.**

**traumatic** /traʊ'mætɪk/ *adjective*
shocking, harmful –*adverb* **traumatically.**

**travel** /'trævəl/ *verb*
to go to another place: *We traveled from Atlanta to New Orleans by bus.*

**travel** *noun*
**1** traffic, amount of traveling: *Travel along the busy highway is high.*
**2** touring, vacation: *During our travels in Europe, we enjoyed England most of all.*

**travel agency** *noun*
a business that organizes travel arrangements (hotel, transportation): *Our company arranges all of our business travel through a travel agency.* –*noun* (person) **travel agent.**

**traveler** /'trævələr/ *noun*
a person going somewhere: *Travelers rush through the train station.*

**traveler's check** *noun*
a substitute form of money that can be replaced if stolen or lost: *We buy traveler's checks instead of taking a lot of cash on our trips.*

**tray** /treɪ/ *noun*
a flat item with a raised edge for carrying food, displaying items, etc.: *Waiters bring food on trays.*

**tread** /trɛd/ *noun*
**1** a step, pace: *You could hear the tread of feet on the path.*
**2** that part of a tire that touches the road: *The tread on that car's tires is worn.* –*verb* **to tread.**

**treason** /'trizən/ *noun, (no plural)*
the crime of actions made against one's government: *Treason in time of war can be punishable by death.* –*adjective* **treasonous.**

**treasure** /'trɛʒər/ *noun*
**1** riches, such as gold and jewels: *Pirates stole treasure from ships.*
**2** valuable objects

**treasure** *verb* **treasured, treasuring, treasures**
to value greatly: *She treasures memories of her childhood.*

**treasurer** /'trɛʒərər/ *noun*
the person in charge of a business's money –*noun* **treasury.**

**treat** /trit/ *verb*
**1** to act toward: *She treats her children with loving care.*
**2** to give medical attention to: *The doctor treats her patients in her office.*
**3** to entertain, do something special for someone: *My friend treated me to a birthday dinner.*

**treat** *noun*
something special, such as a gift or pleasant occasion: *Seeing the rock star perform was a real treat.*

**treatment** /'tritmənt/ *noun*
**1** behavior toward someone: *His treatment of his friends is very kind.*
**2** medical attention, cure: *She went into the hospital for cancer treatment.*

**treaty** /'triti/ *noun, plural* **treaties**
a formal agreement between nations: *European countries signed a treaty on economic cooperation.*

**tree** /tri/ *noun*
a tall, woody plant with a trunk, branches, and leaves: *Trees line the avenues and make them pretty in autumn.*

**tremble** /'trɛmbəl/ *noun*
a shaking motion: *An earthquake hit with a jolt and a tremble.* –*verb* **to tremble.**

**tremendous** /trə' mɛndəs/ *adjective*
**1** huge: *A landslide left a tremendous pile of rocks on the road.*
**2** wonderful: *We had a tremendous time on our vacation.* –*adverb* **tremendously.**

**trend** /'trɛnd/ *noun*
**1** a fashion, current style: *Short skirts are the trend for summer this year.*
**2** a general curve or pattern: *The current trend of prices is up.* *–verb* **to trend.**

**trendy** /'trɛndi/ *adjective* **trendier, trendiest**
fashionable, stylish: *Her clothes are very trendy.*

**trespass** /'trɛs,pæs/ *verb* **trespassed, trespassing, trespasses**
to go illegally on private property: *Hunters trespassed onto the farmer's fields.* *–noun* (person) **trespasser.**

**trial** /'traɪəl/ *noun*
a legal process before a judge or judge and jury to establish facts and decide guilt or innocence: *The murder trial caused a sensation.*
**on trial:** to be a defendant in a court proceeding: *The state put the man on trial for theft.*

**triangle** /'traɪ,æŋgəl/ *noun*
a flat, three-sided geometric figure: *That road sign for danger is shaped in a triangle.* *–adjective* **triangular** /traɪ'æŋgyələr/. *See:* art on page 16a.

**tribal** /'traɪbəl/ *adjective*
related to a tribe: *Tribal customs are passed from parents to their children.*

**tribe** /traɪb/ *noun*
a group of people with common customs and ancestry: *Native American tribes once lived all over North America.* *–noun* **tribalism.** *See:* race **(2)**.

**trick** /trɪk/ *noun*
**1** an act meant to fool someone: *An undercover police officer bought illegal drugs in a trick to arrest a drug dealer.*
**2** magic: *Magicians do magic tricks.*

T

**trick** *verb*
to deceive, fool *–noun* **trickery.**

**trickle** /'trɪkəl/ *noun*
a drip, thin stream: *Water came from the faucet in only a trickle.*

**tricky** /'trɪki/ *adjective* **trickier, trickiest**
**1** wanting to fool others, deceitful: *He is a tricky guy who can't be trusted.*
**2** difficult: *Trying to repair an old wristwatch is tricky.* *–noun* **trickiness.**

**tricycle** /'traɪsəkəl/ *noun*
a cycle with three wheels: *Children ride tricycles before they learn how to ride a bicycle.*

tricycle

**tried** /traɪd/ *adjective and past participle of* try
**tried and true:** proven and dependable: *These methods are tried and true; we've used them for years.*

**trigger** /'trɪgər/ *noun*
**1** small, curved piece of metal pressed with the finger to fire a gun: *He pulled the gun's trigger and shot at the target.*
**2** any device used to set something off

**trigger** *verb*
to start an explosion: *The terrorist triggered the bomb.*

**trillion** /'trɪlyən/ *noun*
a thousand billions and written as 1,000,000,000,000: *The government spending went into the trillions of dollars.*

**trim** /trɪm/ *adjective*
in good physical condition, especially thin: *She exercises regularly and stays trim.* *(antonym)* fat.

USAGE NOTE: *Trim* or *slim* can describe someone in good physical shape, without a lot of fat. *Skinny* describes someone who is too thin and looks unhealthy.

**trim** *noun*
**1** good physical condition: *She is trim from running every day.*
**2** a haircut that cuts only the ends of the hair

**trim** *verb* **trimmed, trimming, trims**
to cut off, especially the outer section of something: *The butcher trims fat from the meat.* *–noun* **trimness.**

**trio** /'trioʊ/ *noun*
a group of three, especially musicians: *A trio sang old favorite songs.*

**trip** /trɪp/ *noun*
a journey, travel: *We took a trip north to see our cousin.*

**trip** *verb* **tripped, tripping, trips**
to lose one's balance by stepping badly on something: *I tripped over the loose rug and fell.*

**triple** /'trɪpəl/ *adjective*
threefold, three times

**triple** *verb* **tripled, tripling, triples**
to increase by three times: *The value of her house has tripled.*

**triumph** /'traɪəmf/ *noun*
**1** great success, victory: *His winning the tennis tournament was a triumph for him.*
**2** glory: *He has a feeling of triumph from winning.*

**triumph** *verb*
to win, succeed greatly: *As an unknown player, he triumphed over the champion.*

**trivia** /'trɪviə/ *noun plural*
unimportant details, things: *He pays attention to trivia and ignores important matters.* –*adjective* **trivial.**

**trolley** /'trɑli/ *noun, plural* **trolleys**
a streetcar

**trombone** /trɑm'boʊn/ *noun*
a brass horn with a slide: *Trombones make a rich sound.* –*noun* (person) **trombonist.** *See:* art on page 15a.

**troop** /trup/ *noun*
**1** a group of animals or people: *a troop of monkeys* ||*a Boy or Girl Scout troop*
**2** *plural* military personnel, especially soldiers: *The President sent in troops to guard our citizens.* –*verb* **to troop.**

**trooper** /'trupər/ *noun*
a state police officer: *A state trooper stopped a speeding driver.*

**trophy** /'troʊfi/ *noun, plural* **trophies**
a prize, such as a silver cup or bowl: *The race car driver held the trophy up high after he won the race.*

**tropics** /'trɑpɪks/ *noun, plural*
the hot region (Torrid Zone) of the earth lying between approximately 23 degrees north and 23 degrees south of the equator –*adjective* **tropical.**

**trot** /trat/ *noun*
a fast walk: *Horses moved in a trot around a racetrack.* –*verb* **to trot.**

**trouble** /'trʌbəl/ *noun*
**1** a public disturbance, crisis: *There is trouble at the American embassy.*
**2** difficulty, especially by accident: *Our friends are having car trouble.*

**to be** or **get in trouble:** to do illegal acts, unlawful behavior: *That thief is always in trouble with the law.*

**to make** or **cause trouble:** to create difficulty, annoyance: *The boy makes trouble for his parents by misbehaving.*

**trouble** *adjective*
physically ill: *She is troubled by a bad back.*

**trouble** *verb* **troubled, troubling, troubles**
to annoy, bother: *The street noise troubled him, so he couldn't sleep.*

**trousers** /'traʊzərz/ *noun, plural*
men's pants: *He had a pair of trousers cleaned and pressed.*

**truant** /'truənt/ *noun*
a student who doesn't go to school: *School authorities send officers to find truants.* –*noun* **truancy.**

**truce** /trus/ *noun*
a temporary stopping of fighting

**truck** /trʌk/ *noun*
a vehicle larger than a car used to carry things: *That big truck carries furniture from the store.* –*noun* (driver or business) **trucker.**

**true** /tru/ *adjective* **truer, truest**
**1** accurate, correct: *Reporters look for the true facts in a story, not rumor.*
**2** proven: *What she says is true because other people saw the same thing.*
**3** faithful, loyal: *He is true to his wife and does not go with other women.*
**4** sincere: *Our teacher has a true interest in her students.*

**to come true:** to happen as one desires or predicts: *When she won the national tennis contest, her childhood dreams came true. (antonym)* false.

**truly** /'truli/ *adverb*
**1** genuinely, really: *That is truly gold, not fake.*

T

**2** sincerely: *Many people finish their letters with "Yours truly" or "Truly yours."*

**trumpet** /ˈtrʌmpət/ *noun*
a horn (or brass musical instrument) with a high-pitched sound *–noun* (person) **trumpeter.** *See:* art on page 15a.

**trumpet**

**trunk** /trʌŋk/ *noun*
**1** a large piece of luggage: *I put my books and clothes in a trunk to sent them to my new house.*
**2** an elephant's nose
**3** the storage space in the back of a car: *She carries a blanket and boots in her trunk in case of emergencies.*
**4** the main stem of a tree: *a tree trunk*
**5** the central part of the body
**6** *plural* men's shorts, especially a bathing suit: *I put on my swim trunks and headed for the beach.*

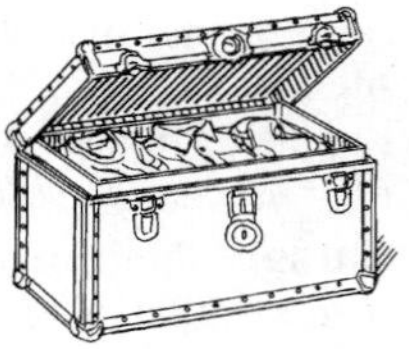

**trunk**

**trust** /trʌst/ *noun, (no plural)*
confidence in the honesty and reliability of someone or something: *I have complete trust in his ability to keep a secret.*

**trust** *verb*
**1** to have faith in someone: *I trust my friend completely.*
**2** to hope with confidence: *I trust that help will be here soon. (antonym)* distrust.

**trustful** /ˈtrʌstfəl/ or **trusting** /ˈtrʌstɪŋ/ *adjective*
believing in the honesty and reliability of someone: *He is very trustful of his older brother.*

**trustworthy** /ˈtrʌstˌwɜrði/ *adjective*
capable of being trusted; honest and reliable: *That guy looks strange, but he is very trustworthy. –noun* **trustworthiness.**

**truth** /truθ/ *noun, plural* **truths** /truðs/
**1** *(no plural)* accuracy, correctness: *She always speaks the truth.*
**2** something factual, proven: *The police brought out the truth about the crime. (antonym)* falsehood.

**truthful** /ˈtruθfəl/ *adjective*
**1** accurate, factual: *His story of the event is truthful.*
**2** honest and accurate: *He is a truthful person. –adverb* **truthfully.**

**try** /traɪ/ *verb* **tried, trying, tries**
**1** to attempt: *He tried to solve the math problem, but couldn't.*
**2** to test, experiment: *She tried eating spicy food but didn't like it.*
**3** (in law) to have a legal proceeding: *The state tried the criminal for theft.*
**to try something on:** to put on an item of clothing to see if it fits: *He tried on the shoes and they fit well.*

**try** *noun, plural* **tries**
an attempt: *His attempt to climb the high mountain failed, but it was a good try.*

**T-shirt** or **tee-shirt** /ˈtiˌʃɜrt/ *noun*
a lightweight, short-sleeved garment worn over the upper body: *T-shirts are cool and comfortable. See:* art on page 12a.

**tub** /tʌb/ *noun*
**1** a container with sides used to hold food, etc.: *a small tub of butter*
**2** a bathtub: *After working in the garden, she had a bath in the tub. See:* art on page 23a.

**tube** /tub/ *noun*
a hollow, flexible container: *I bought a tube of toothpaste.*

**tuberculosis** /təˌbɜrkyəˈloʊsɪs/ *noun, (no plural)*
a lung disease: *People used to go to health spas to recover from tuberculosis. –adjective* **tubercular.**

**tuck** /tʌk/ *noun*
a fold sewn in clothes, curtains, etc.: *She sewed tucks in the waist of her skirt.*

**tuck** *verb*
to put inside something else: *She tucked her shirt into her skirt.*

**Tuesday** /ˈtuzˌdeɪ/ *noun*
the third day of the week, between Monday and Wednesday

**tug** /tʌg/ *noun*
a hard pull: *I gave the rope a tug to be sure it was tied tightly. –verb* **to tug.**

**tugboat** /'tʌg,boʊt/ *noun*
a powerful, strong boat used to pull or push other boats and barges, especially in and out of harbors and docks

**tuition** /tu'ɪʃən/ *noun, (no plural)*
the cost of going to an educational institution: *In the USA, the cost of tuition at private colleges is very high.*

**tulip** /'tulɪp/ *noun*
a plant with bright bell-shaped flowers: *Red tulips are beautiful in the springtime. See:* art on page 1a.

**tumble** /'tʌmbəl/ *noun*
a fall: *He took a tumble down the stairs.*

**tummy** /'tʌmi/ *noun, plural* **tummies**
the stomach: *I ate a big dinner, and now my tummy hurts.*

**tumor** /'tumər/ *noun*
a growth of diseased tissue: *A doctor removed a tumor from the patient's stomach.*

**tuna** /'tunə/ *noun*
a large food and game fish: *I had a tuna sandwich for lunch.*

**tune** /tun/ *noun*
a song: *He played a tune on the piano.*

**tune** *verb* **tuned, tuning, tunes**
**1** to fix a musical instrument so it has the correct sound: *A piano tuner tuned my piano.*
**2** to set a radio, TV or stereo so it receives the desired station: *I tuned my radio to my favorite station.*

**to tune something up:** to clean and adjust a motor: *I tuned up my car myself.*

**tune-up** *noun*
a cleaning and adjustment of a motor: *I took my car in for a tune-up because it wasn't running well.*

**tunnel** /'tʌnəl/ *noun*
a passage under the ground: *dig tunnels for roads to go through mountains*

tunnel

**to see light at the end of the tunnel:** to get near the end of a long, difficult task: *We have experimented for years and now see light at the end of the tunnel for a new wonder drug.*

**turkey** /'tɜrki/ *noun*
a large food and game bird in North America: *Traditionally, many North Americans have a roast turkey for Thanksgiving dinner. See:* art on page 14a.

turkey

**turn** /tɜrn/ *verb*
**1** to move in a different direction: *The truck turned right onto a side street.*
**2** to change, transform: *The weather turned stormy today.*||*We turned an old barn into a pretty house.*
**3** to go around, spin: *The earth turns on its axis.*

**to turn loose:** to set free: *After the war soldiers turned prisoners loose and sent them home.*

**to turn over a new leaf:** to change, especially to correct one's bad behavior: *Managers who ignored their workers turned over a new leaf and worked closely with them.*

**to turn someone** or **something around:** to reverse direction: *He turned his car around and headed home.*

**to turn someone back:** to reverse direction, such as stop a trip: *The bad snowstorm made me turn back and go home.*

**to turn someone** or **something down: a. something:** to fold over: *The maid turned down the bedsheet and blanket for hotel guests each evening.* **b. someone** or **something:** to refuse, disapprove: *His manager turned down his proposal for a new project.*

**to turn (someone** or **something) in: a.** to go to bed, sleep: *I turned in at 11:00 P.M. last night.* **b. someone:** to surrender someone to the police: *A thief turned himself in to the police.* **c. something:** to hand in, give something to someone: *Students turned in their test papers when the class was over.*

**to turn someone or something off: a. someone:** to disgust, offend: *His unfriendly behavior turns off most people right away.* **b. something:** to shut off: *I turned off the light and went to sleep.*

**to turn someone** or **something on:** **a. someone:** to excite, cause enjoyment: *Playing tennis turns her on; she loves it!* **b. something:** to switch on, operate: *I turned on the lights in a dark room.*

**to turn out:** to develop into, become: *The young woman turned out well as the manager of a magazine.*

**to turn up:** **a.** to arrive: *She turned up at the meeting late.* **b.** to occur, happen, especially unexpectedly: *Something wonderful turned up. I won a prize!* **c. something:** to increase the sound: *Turn up the radio so we can hear the music better.*

**turn** *noun*
**1** a bend, curve: *The road makes a turn to the left at the crossroad.*
**2** a change of direction: *We took a turn at the next corner.*
**3** a time for a person to act: *It was my turn to wash the dishes (serve the tennis ball, speak in class, etc.).*

**to take turns:** one person does something, then the next person does it: *He and his wife take turns washing the dishes.*

**turnpike** /'tɜrn͵ paɪk/ *noun*
a main highway, usually with stops to pay tolls: *The turnpike from New York to Boston has stops for tolls.*

**turquoise** /'tɜr͵kwɔɪz/ *noun*
a light blue to blue-green semiprecious stone: *She loves to wear turquoise necklaces and silver rings.*

**turtle** /'tɜrtl/ *noun*
an animal (reptile) with a hard shell and strong beak: *People keep small turtles as pets. See:* tortoise. *See:* art on page 14a.

turtle

**turtleneck** /'tɜrtl͵nɛk/ *noun*
a pullover or sweater with a high, close-fitting neck: *He wears turtlenecks in the winter for warmth. See:* art on page 12a.

**tusk** /tʌsk/ *noun*
a long, thick front tooth, such as of elephants: *An elephant has two long tusks.*

**tutor** /'tutər/ *noun*
a teacher who helps students individually: *She is a tutor who helps foreign students improve their English.* –*verb* **to tuto;** –*noun* **tutorship.**

**tuxedo** /tʌk'sidoʊ/ *noun*
a black suit for formal occasions

**TV** /ti'vi/
*abbreviation of* television: *We watch the news on TV.*

**tweezers** /'twizərz/ *noun plural*
a small tool with two arms that are pushed together to remove something: *I used tweezers to take a piece of wood out of my foot.*

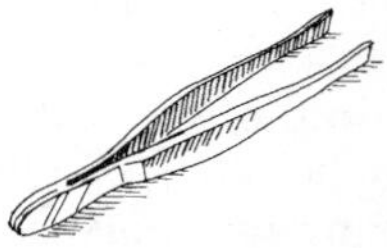
tweezers

**twelve** /twɛlv/ *noun*
the cardinal number 12

**twelve** *adjective*
12 of something: *There are 12 eggs in a carton.* –*noun* **twelfth** /twɛlfθ/. *See:* dozen.

**twenty** /'twɛnti/ *noun, plural* **twenties**
the cardinal number 20

**twenty** *adjective*
20 of something: *Twenty children lined up for lunch.*

**twenty-one** *noun*
the cardinal number 21

**twenty-one** *adjective*
**1** 21 of something: *He is 21 years old today.*
**2** the age of adulthood, which gives one the right to vote and drink alcohol: *Congress changed the voting age from 21 to 18.* –*noun* **twenty-first.**

---

**USAGE NOTE:** At age *21,* Americans are allowed to buy alcohol and drink in a public place such as a restaurant or bar.

---

**twice** /twaɪs/ *adverb*
two times: *She rang the doorbell twice.*

**twig** /twɪg/ *noun*
a small branch: *A hiker picked up twigs to build a campfire.*

**twilight** /'twaɪ͵laɪt/ *noun*
the period between sunset and darkness:

*The streetlights come on at twilight. See:* dusk.

**twin** /twɪn/ *noun*
one of two children born of the same mother at the same time: *The sisters are twins; both are blonde.*

**twin bed** *noun*
one of two single beds: *My brother and I sleep in twin beds.*

**twinkle** /'twɪŋkəl/ *verb* **twinkled, twinkling, twinkles**
to shine, off and on: *Stars twinkle in the night sky. –noun* **twinkle.**

**twist** /twɪst/ *verb*
**1** to turn: *I twisted the door knob, but the door wouldn't open.*
**2** to bend around each other: *I twisted two pieces of thread on a needle to sew a hole in my coat. –noun* **twist.**

**twitch** /twɪʧ/ *verb* **twitched, twitching, twitches**
to shake briefly or uncontrollably: *A nerve twitched in the man's cheek.*

**twitch** *noun, plural* **twitches**
a nervous reaction: *He has a twitch in his cheek.*

**two** /tu/ *noun*
the cardinal number 2

**two** *adjective*
two of something: *People have two eyes.*

**type** /taɪp/ *verb* **typed, typing, types**
to write on a typewriter, computer keyboard, etc.: *She types letters and memos on a computer.*

**type** *noun*
a category, characterization: *That type of steel is very strong.*

**typewriter** /'taɪpˌraɪtər/ *noun*
an electric machine used to print words in type: *Since he bought a computer, his old typewriter sits in the closet.*

**typhoid** /'taɪˌfɔɪd/ or **typhoid fever** *noun, (no plural)*
a disease with high fever caused by food or water dirty with bacteria: *Typhoid fever is still a great health threat.*

**typhoon** /taɪ'fun/ *noun*
a hurricane in Asia: *Typhoons are so powerful that they sink ships.*

**typical** /'tɪpɪkəl/ *adjective*
characteristic, representative: *The high quality of that machine is typical of all of that company's products.*||*Acting like a jerk is typical of my brother-in-law. –adverb* **typically.**

**typist** /'taɪpɪst/ *noun*
a person who types: *He works part-time as a typist in a computer office.*

**tyrant** /'taɪrənt/ *noun*
a ruler who uses terror and a police state to enforce his role *–adjective* **tyrannical** /tə'rænəkəl/; *–noun* (condition) **tyranny.**

**tzar** /zɑr/ *noun*
*variation of* tsar

# U,u

**U, u** /yu/ *noun* **U's, u's** or **Us, us**
**1** the 21st letter of the English alphabet
**2** something shaped like a *U See:* U-turn.

**UFO** /ˌyuɛfˈoʊ/ *noun, plural* **UFO's** *abbreviation of* Unidentified Flying Object, a space vehicle from another world

UFO

**ugly** /ˈʌgli/ *adjective* **uglier, ugliest**
very unpleasant to see: *His hand was burned in a fire, and it looks ugly. (antonym)* beautiful. *–noun* **ugliness.**

**uh-huh** /əˈhʌ/ *adverb slang*
yes, okay: *I asked her to go to dinner, and she said, "Uh-huh!" See:* yes, USAGE NOTE.

**ultimate** /ˈʌltəmɪt/ *adjective*
**1** greatest, most costly: *The soldier made the ultimate sacrifice by dying for her country.*
**2** most basic, fundamental: *The ultimate proof of his guilt was that someone actually saw him steal the money.*

**ultimate** *noun*
an extreme of any kind (best, worst, etc.): *A big diamond is the ultimate in expensive jewelry.*

**ultimately** /ˈʌltəmɪtli/ *adverb*
in the end, finally: *Ultimately, the war had to end; it cost too much in lives.*

**ultra-** /ˈʌltrə/ *prefix*
beyond the normal or usual: *That special telephone wire is ultrathin.*

umbrella

**umbrella** /ʌmˈbrɛlə/ *noun*
a foldable covering made of cloth on a handle to protect the head against rain and bright sunlight: *She opens her umbrella when it rains.*

**umpire** /ˈʌmˌpaɪr/ *noun*
a sports judge

**U.N.** /ˌyuˈɛn/ *noun abbreviation of* the United Nations

**unable** /ʌnˈeɪbəl/ *adjective*
**1** not able, incapable: *He is unable to walk because of a bad foot.*
**2** not skilled: *He is unable to do the job for lack of experience.*

**unacceptable** /ˌʌnɪkˈsɛptəbəl/ *adjective*
not acceptable because something is bad or wrong: *That student's bad behavior in class is unacceptable.*

**unaccustomed** /ˌʌnəˈkʌstəmd/ *adjective*
not used to: *People from the tropics are unaccustomed to cold winters.*

**unaffordable** /ˌʌnəˈfɔrdəbəl/ *adjective*
too expensive: *Houses in that rich neighborhood are unaffordable for most people.*

**unafraid** /ˌʌnəˈfreɪd/ *adjective*
not afraid, fearless: *She is a firefighter who is unafraid of danger.*

**unanimous** /yuˈnænəməs/ *adjective*
completely in agreement: *Everyone on the committee agreed in a unanimous decision.* –*adverb* **unanimously;** –*noun* (act) **unanimity.**

**unarmed** /ʌnˈɑrmd/ *adjective*
without a weapon: *Unarmed women and children were helpless in the war.*

**unavoidable** /ˌʌnəˈvɔɪdəbəl/ *adjective*
that which cannot be avoided or escaped: *Pain is unavoidable when you break a leg.* –*adverb* **unavoidably.**

**unaware** /ˌʌnəˈwɛr/ *adjective*
uninformed, not told about: *He was unaware that the meeting was this morning; no one told him.*

**unawares** /ˌʌnəˈwɛrz/ *adverb*
without warning, by surprise: *She was caught unawares by a sudden snowstorm.*

**unbearable** /ʌnˈbɛrəbəl/ *adjective*
not bearable, too much: *The ocean water is so cold that it is unbearable for swimming now.* –*adverb* **unbearably.**

**unbelievable** /ˌʌnbiˈlivəbəl/ *adjective*
**1** false, not worthy of belief: *That story is unbelievable.*
**2** *figurative* wonderful: *We had an unbelievable opportunity to go on a vacation to Brazil.* –*adverb* **unbelievably.**

**unbend** /ʌnˈbɛnd/ *verb* **unbent** /ˈbɛnt/ , **unbending, unbends**
**1** to straighten: *A branch unbends when the heavy snow melts from it.*
**2** to relax, to become less formal: *He learned to unbend a little in dealing with others and is more friendly.*

**unborn** /ʌnˈbɔrn/ *adjective*
not yet in existence, still inside the mother: *Unborn children are fed through a tube inside the mother.*

**unbuckle** /ʌnˈbʌkəl/ *verb* **unbuckled, unbuckling, unbuckles**
to open a buckle: *She unbuckled her seat belt when the plane landed.*

**unbutton** /ʌnˈbʌtn/ *verb*
to undo buttons: *He unbuttoned his shirt and took it off.*

**uncertain** /ʌnˈsɜrtn/ *adjective*
doubtful, unsure: *He has been out of work for a year; his future is uncertain.* –*adverb* **uncertainly;** –*noun* **uncertainty.**

**unchanging** /ʌnˈʧeɪnʤɪŋ/ *adjective*
the same always, without change: *It rains every morning; the weather seems unchanging here.*

**uncle** /ˈʌŋkəl/ *noun*
one's mother's or father's brother: *My Uncle John came to visit us.* *See:* art on page 13a.

**unclean** /ʌnˈklin/ *adjective*
dirty: *The floors are unclean; they haven't been washed.*

**unclear** /ʌnˈklɪr/ *adjective*
**1** poorly said or written, not clear: *Unclear writing is difficult to understand.*
**2** doubtful, uncertain: *It is unclear whether the economy will get better.*

**uncomfortable** /ʌnˈkʌmftəbəl/ *adjective*
feeling pain or discomfort: *She feels uncomfortable sitting on a hard chair.*

**uncommon** /ʌnˈkɑmən/ *adjective*
unusual, not commonly found or experienced: *Those birds are uncommon in this area.* –*adverb* **uncommonly.**

**unconscious** /ʌnˈ kɑnʃəs/ *adjective*
**1** senseless, knocked out: *A blow on the head made him unconscious.*
**2** unaware, not conscious of some event: *He was unconscious of the fact the bill was not paid because the check was lost.* –*adverb* **unconsciously;** –*noun* **unconsciousness.** *See:* K.O.

**unconstitutional** /ˌʌnkɑnstɪˈtuʃənəl/ *adjective*
(in law) found to be against the Constitution (of the US, any organization with a constitution): *The Supreme Court decided that the law is unconstitutional.* –*adverb* **unconstitutionally.**

**uncontrollable** /ˌʌnkənˈtroʊləbəl/ *adjective*
not capable of being controlled, out of control: *The weather is uncontrollable; no one can stop the rain.* –*adverb* **uncontrollably.**

**uncool** /ʌn'kul/ *adjective slang*
unacceptable and usually bad behavior: *He poured beer over everyone at the party, which was an uncool thing to do.*

**uncouple** /ʌn'kʌpəl/ *verb* **uncoupled, uncoupling, uncouples**
to pull apart, separate: *A worker uncoupled two railroad cars and one rolled away.*

**uncouth** /ʌn'kuθ/ *adjective*
badly behaved: *That uncouth man uses dirty language all the time.* –*adverb* **uncouthly.** *See:* crude.

**uncovered** /ʌn'kʌvərd/ *adjective*
**1** without a covering: *She became uncovered while asleep.*
**2** discovered, removed from hiding: *The thief uncovered by the detective was put in jail.*

**undecided** /ˌʌndɪ'saɪdɪd/ *adjective*
not decided, still under consideration: *She is undecided about where she wants to go on vacation.*

**under** /'ʌndər/ *preposition*
**1** beneath, below: *Roots are under the soil. (antonym)* over.
**2** directed by: *Those employees are under her management.*
**3** less than: *He is under the legal age (to drink alcohol, to vote, etc.).*

**under consideration:** being thought about: *The buyer has the offer under consideration and will decide tomorrow.*

**under control:** in control, being managed: *The fire is under control now and is not spreading.*

**under discussion:** being discussed and evaluated: *The new project is under discussion now.*

**under the influence of:** controlled by something, such as a drug or another person: *She was caught driving under the influence of alcohol.*

**underclass** /'ʌnd ərˌklæs/ *noun, plural* **underclasses**
the lowest class of people in a society: *The poor are an underclass who cannot escape poverty.*

---

**USAGE NOTE:** American society does not have clear social class distinctions; most people consider themselves to be *working, middle,* or *upper-middle class.* The *underclass* are people below the working class, who for many reasons have trouble finding work and who often need help from the government to live.

---

**underclassman** /'ʌndərˌklæsmən/ *noun, plural* **underclassmen** /-mən/
a male or female student in freshman or sophomore year of high school or college *See:* upperclassman.

**underdeveloped** /ˌʌndərdɪ'vɛləpt/ *adjective*
not developed economically: *Two underdeveloped countries worked together to improve their economies.* –*noun* **underdevelopment.**

---

**USAGE NOTE:** Instead of using *underdeveloped* to describe poorer nations, many people use the term *developing.* A *developing nation* is a country that is becoming economically stronger.

---

**underdog** /'ʌndərˌdɔg/ *noun*
a person or team with little chance of winning, especially in sports competition; the weaker competitor: *Our team was the underdog in the basketball game, but we won.*

**undergo** /ˌʌndər'goʊ/ *verb* **underwent** /-'wɛnt/, **undergone** /-'gɔn/, **undergoing, undergoes**
**1** to experience: *He will undergo an operation to remove a growth from his throat.*
**2** to suffer, survive: *To get the job, she had to undergo five tests and an interview.*

**undergraduate** /ˌʌndər'grædʒuɪt/ *noun*
a student in the first four years of college: *She is an undergraduate at the state university.*

**undergraduate** *adjective*
related to that level of college education: *She is taking undergraduate courses in English.*

**underground** /'ʌn dərˌgraʊnd/ *adjective*
located below the earth's surface: *We park our car into an underground parking garage.*

**undergrowth** /'ʌn dərˌgroʊθ/ *noun*
short plants growing under trees: *The undergrowth in that forest is very thick.*

**underline** /ˈʌndərˌlaɪn/ *verb* **underlined, underlining, underlines**
to draw a line under something: *He underlined words in this sentence with a pen.*

**undermine** /ˌʌndərˈmaɪn/ *verb* **undermined, undermining, undermines**
to ruin the efforts of someone: *She undermined her health by smoking cigarettes.*

**underneath** /ˌʌnd ərˈniθ/ *preposition*
below: *Potatoes grow underneath the ground.*

**undernourished** /ˌʌndərˈnɜrɪʃt/ *adjective*
starved, fed with poor food: *Undernourished children do not grow well.* *–noun* **undernourishment.**

**underpants** /ˈʌnd ərˌpænts/ *noun, plural*
short clothes worn around the waist under other clothes: *He wears cotton underpants. See:* (men) undershorts; (women) panties.

**underpass** /ˈʌndərˌpæs/ *noun, plural* **underpasses**
a roadway that passes under another road or structure: *An underpass runs under the highway.*

**underprivileged** /ˌʌndərˈprɪvəlɪʤd/ *adjective*
not getting the benefits others do from society: *The underprivileged get money from the government.*

**undershirt** /ˈʌnd ərˌʧɜrt/ *noun*
a T-shirt or sleeveless shirt worn under other clothing: *He wears an undershirt under his dress shirt.*

**undershirt**

**undershorts** /ˈʌn dərˌʃɔrts/ *noun, plural*
underpants for men: *His undershorts are white.*

**understand** /ˌʌnd ərˈstænd/ *verb* **understood** /-ˈstʊd/, **understanding, understands**
**1** to get the meaning of: *I understand exactly what you want.*
**2** to be informed: *I understand that you will leave tomorrow. Is that true?*
**3** to sympathize with, to sense another's feelings: *He understood her feelings when her cat died.*

**understanding** /ˌʌndərˈstændɪŋ/ *noun, (no plural)*
**1** an ability to get the meaning of: *I have a good understanding of the problem.*
**2** sympathy for: *Since your mother is dead, you have an understanding of how people feel when their parents die.*

**understood** /ˌʌndərˈstʊd/ *adjective*
agreed upon: *It is understood that the customer will pay half now and the other half on delivery of the flowers.*

**undertaker** /ˈʌndərˌteɪkər/ *noun*
a person or business that arranges funerals and burials for the dead: *The local undertaker is a serious person.*

**undertaking** /ˈʌndərˌteɪkɪŋ/ *noun*
a big task, big job, etc.: *To build a bridge across the river is a large undertaking.*

**underwater** /ˌʌndərˈwɔtər/ *adjective*
beneath the surface of water: *My boat is underwater after the bad storm.*

**underwear** /ˈʌndərˌwɛr/ *noun*
clothing, such as underpants, T-shirts, and slips, worn under other clothing: *He bought shorts in the store's underwear department.*

**underworld** /ˈʌnd ərˌwɜrld/ *noun*
the world of criminals

**undesirable** /ˌʌndɪˈzaɪrəbəl/ *adjective*
**1** unwanted, disagreeable: *Having black rings around your eyes is the undesirable result of being very tired.*
**2** unpleasant: *undesirable behavior*

**undo** /ʌnˈdu/ *verb* **undid** /-ˈdɪd/, **undone** /-ˈdʌn/, **undoing, undoes** /-ˈdʌz/
to unfasten: *He undid the buttons on his shirt. See:* undone.

**undoing** /ʌnˈduɪŋ/ *noun*
defeat: *He spent too much money, that was his undoing.*

**undone** /ʌnˈdʌn/ *adjective*
**1** unfinished, incomplete: *His work was left undone.*
**2** in a bad emotional condition: *She was completely undone by the death of her husband.*

**undoubted** /ʌn'da ʊtɪd/ *adjective* certain, unquestioned: *He is an employee who has undoubted loyalty.* –*adverb* **undoubtedly.**

**undress** /ʌn'drɛs/ *verb* **undresses** to remove one's clothing: *Her mother told her to undress and brush her teeth before bedtime.*

**uneasy** /ʌn'izi/ *adjective* **uneasier, uneasiest** nervous, worried: *He feels uneasy about taking the test today.* –*adverb* **uneasily.**

**uneducated** /ʌn'ɛʤə,keɪtɪd/ *adjective* without education: *She is an uneducated person who cannot read. See:* illiterate.

**unemployable** /,ʌnɪm'plɔɪəbəl/ *adjective* not able to have a job, usually because of bad health or not enough education or skills: *Her husband was unemployable after an accident broke his back.*

**unemployed** /,ʌnɪm'plɔɪd/ *adjective* without a job: *He was unemployed for three months.*

**unemployment** /,ʌnɪm'plɔɪmənt/ *noun, (no plural)*
**1** the general condition of having no job: *Unemployment now is five percent of the country's workers.*
**2** *informal* unemployment compensation: *He went on unemployment until he could find another job.*

**unemployment compensation** *noun* in the USA, regular payments made for a limited time by a state to qualified, unemployed workers: *He receives unemployment compensation, but it ends in six months.*

**unequal** /ʌn'ikwəl/ *adjective* not equal, different (in amount, quantity, size, time, etc.): *The legs on those pants are of unequal length.* –*adverb* **unequally.**

**uneven** /ʌn'ivən/ *adjective*
**1** not of the same height, length, size, width, etc.: *There are two pieces of wood of uneven length.*
**2** rough, unsmooth: *an uneven surface, an uneven performance*
**3** not equal in ability, intelligence, strength, etc.: *We watched an uneven competition where one team was much better than the other.* –*adverb* **unevenly.**

uneven

**unexpected** /,ʌnɪk'spɛktɪd/ *adjective* surprising: *An unexpected visitor arrived.* –*adverb* **unexpectedly.**

**unfair** /ʌn'fɛɪr/ *adjective* not fair or just to those concerned: *The boss was unfair in giving higher raises to his favorite employees.* –*adverb* **unfairly.**

**unfamiliar** /,ʌnfə'mɪlyər/ *adjective* strange, new: *He got lost in an unfamiliar neighborhood.*

**unfashionable** /ʌn'fæʃənəbəl/ *adjective*
**1** out of fashion, not admired now: *It is unfashionable to wear fur now.*
**2** lower-class: *They live in an unfashionable neighborhood.* –*adverb* **unfashionably.**

**unfasten** /ʌn'fæsən/ *verb* to undo: *He unfastened the buttons on his shirt.*

**unfavorable** /ʌn'feɪvərəbəl/ *adjective* bad, negative: *Unfavorable weather prevented the game from being played.* –*adverb* **unfavorably.**

**unfinished** /ʌn'fɪnɪʃt/ *adjective*
**1** uncompleted, undone: *When he died, the writer left several unfinished works.*
**2** without a finish, such as without paint: *The unfinished walls made the room look dirty.*

**unfit** /ʌn'fɪt/ *adjective*
**1** not in good condition: *That airplane is unfit to fly because one engine is broken.*
**2** lacking in good personal qualities: *Dishonest politicians are unfit to serve in office.*

**unfortunate** /ʌn 'fɔrʧənɪt/ *adjective*
**1** not lucky: *It is unfortunate that you just missed her.*
**2** sad: *How unfortunate that his wife died.* –*adverb* **unfortunately.**

**unfriendly** /ʌn'f rɛndli/ *adjective*
**1** cool toward someone, distant: *The unfriendly waiter made our meal unpleasant.*
**2** angry, rude: *That man made unfriendly comments to me; he's looking for a fight.*

**ungrateful** /ʌn'g reɪtfəl/ *adjective*
not thankful: *The ungrateful child did not write a "thank you" note for her gift.*

**unhappy** /ʌn'hæpi/ *adjective* **unhappier, unhappiest**
**1** sad: *His lack of friends makes him unhappy and lonely.*
**2** not satisfied: *She is unhappy with her job because of her low salary.* –*adverb* **unhappily.**

unhappy

**unhealthy** /ʌn'hɛlθi/ *adjective* **unhealthier, unhealthiest**
**1** sick, diseased: *He is an unhealthy person with a bad heart.*
**2** harmful: *He eats unhealthy foods full of fat.*

**unidentified flying object** /ˌʌnaɪ'dɛntəˌfaɪd/ *noun*
*abbreviated as* **UFO** a space vehicle from another world: *There are many sightings of unidentified flying objects each year.*

**uniform** /'yunəˌfɔrm/ *noun*
a special type of clothing worn by members of certain organizations: *Soldiers wear uniforms.*

uniform

**uniform** *adjective*
the same all through something: *Mix the milk well with the chocolate so the taste will be uniform.* –*noun* **uniformity** /ˌyunə'fɔrməti/; –*adverb* **uniformly.**

**unify** /'yunəˌfaɪ/ *verb* **unified, unifying, unifies**
**1** to unite: *The new President unified the people.*
**2** to bring together as a whole: *to unify separate ideas into one* –*noun* **unification** /ˌyunafə'keɪʃən/.

**unimportant** /ˌʌnɪm'pɔrtnt/ *adjective*
not important: *He left a comma out of the sentence, but that is an unimportant detail.*

**uninterested** /ʌn'ɪntrəstɪd/ *adjective*
not interested: *He is uninterested in buying our product; he doesn't need it.*

**union** /'yunyən/ *noun*
**1** an organization of workers: *She joined a union of hospital workers.*
**2** a marriage: *The union of two people in marriage is a wonderful thing.*

**unionize** /'yunyə ˌnaɪz/ *verb* **unionized, unionizing, unionizes**
to organize a group of workers into joining in a union: *A representative from a labor union unionized the workers in our company.* –*noun* **unionization.**

**unique** /yu'nik/ *adjective*
singular, one of a kind: *Each person in the world has a unique personality.* –*adverb* **uniquely.**

**unit** /'yunɪt/ *noun*
**1** a part or section of something: *a unit of information*||*a unit in a lesson*
**2** a standard of measurement: *An inch (foot, meter, mile, etc.) is a unit of measurement.*
**3** a bookcase or other piece of furniture: *That wall unit holds television equipment.*

**unite** /yʊ'naɪt/ *verb* **united, uniting, unites**
**1** to come together for a reason or purpose: *The nation united against its enemy.*
**2** to join in marriage: *A priest united a couple in marriage.*

**United Nations** *noun, plural*
*used with a singular verb* an international organization founded in 1945 and headquartered in New York City: *The United Nations works for cooperation and peace among nations. See:* U.N.

**unity** /'yunəti/ *noun, (no plural)*
a condition of oneness in belief (action, purpose): *Those two countries have a unity of purpose in wanting peace.*

**universal** /ˌ yunə'vɜrsəl/ *adjective*
found or practiced everywhere: *Poverty is a universal problem all over the world.* –*noun* **universality** /ˌyunəvər'sæləti/; –*adverb* **universally.**

**universe** /'yunə,vɜrs/ *noun*
the stars, planets, other bodies, and space taken together: *Scientists study the universe.*

**university** /,yunə'vɜrsəti/ *noun, plural* **universities**
a place of higher education that gives advanced degrees: *She got her Masters degree in science at a good university.*

---

**USAGE NOTE:** In the American educational system, after high school (secondary school) students can go to *college, university,* or a *technical institute.* The *university* is the largest of these institutions, and offers graduate degree programs in addition to undergraduate degrees. Most American students will say they go to *college*, rather than university, no matter which type of institution they attend.

---

**unjust** /ʌn'ʤʌst/ *adjective*
lacking justice, unfair: *He was not offered a job because of his race, and this is unjust. –adverb* **unjustly.**

**unjustified** /ʌn 'ʤʌstə,faɪd/ *adjective*
against common sense, without reason: *She makes bad, unjustified remarks about almost everyone.*

**unkind** /ʌn'kaɪnd/ *adjective*
**1** thoughtless, uncaring: *He was unkind to leave his wife alone when she was ill.*
**2** mean, bad: *The woman made unkind remarks about the man's weight and appearance. –adverb* **unkindly;** *–noun* **unkindness.**

**unknown** /ʌn'noʊn/ *adjective*
not known: *The location of his home is unknown.*

**unknown** *noun*
**1** something that is not known: *His location is an unknown.*
**2** (in math) a quantity that is not known: *Solve for the unknown in the equation.*

**unlawful** /ʌn'lɔfəl/ *adjective*
against the law: *It is unlawful to steal. –adverb* **unlawfully.** *See:* illegal.

**unless** /ʌn'lɛs/ *conjunction*
except that, on the condition that: *Unless he agrees to sign it, we have no contract.*

**unlike** /ʌn'laɪk/ *preposition*
**1** different from, not similar to: *Those black clouds are unlike any I've seen before.*
**2** not typical of: *It is unlike him to complain; he is usually quiet.*

**unlikely** /,ʌn'laɪkli/ *adjective*
doubtful, not probable: *It is unlikely that it will rain today.*

**unload** /ʌn'loʊd/ *verb*
**1** to remove something (from a vehicle): *A worker unloaded the chairs from the truck.*

unload

**2** to take bullets from a gun: *A soldier unloaded his rifle.*

**unlock** /ʌn'lɑk/ *verb*
to open: *She unlocked the door with a key.*

**unlucky** /ʌn'lʌki/ *adjective* **unluckier, unluckiest**
having bad luck that harms someone, such as having accidents: *He is unlucky: first, he breaks his arm, then someone steals his car.*

**unmarried** /ʌn'mærid/ *adjective*
not married, single: *I have two brothers; one is married and the other is unmarried.*

**unmistakable** /,ʌnmɪ'steɪkəbəl/ *adjective*
not able to be questioned, clear: *It is an unmistakable truth that the sky is blue. –adverb* **unmistakably.**

**unnecessary** /ʌn'nɛsə,sɛri/ *adjective*
needless, wasteful: *The salesperson got me to buy a lot of unnecessary things. –adverb* **unnecessarily** /,ʌnnɛsə'sɛrəli/.

**unoccupied** /ʌn'ɑkyə,paɪd/ *adjective*
empty, with no people: *The unoccupied building was falling apart.*

**unofficial** /,ʌnə'fɪʃəl/ *adjective*
informal, without official approval: *An unofficial statement was made that the company may close soon. –adverb* **unofficially.**

**unpack** /ʌn'pæk/ *verb*
to remove articles from a container: *She unpacked her suitcase and put her clothes away in drawers.*

U

**unpaid** /ʌn'peɪd/ *adjective*
not paid as yet, due: *He has many unpaid bills.*

**unpleasant** /ʌn'p lɛzənt/ *adjective*
**1** uncomfortable: *We had an unpleasant vacation because it rained all the time.*
**2** rude, offensive: *That man was very unpleasant to me.* –*adverb* **unpleasantly;** –*noun* **unpleasantness.**

**unplug** /ʌn'plʌg/ *verb* **unplugged, unplugging, unplugs**
**1** to remove (a plug), usually from an electrical supply: *The room went dark when he unplugged the lamp.*
**2** to clear, unblock: *The plumber unplugged a stopped-up sink.*

**unpopular** /ʌn'pɑpyələr/ *adjective*
not liked by many people: *The new tax on food is very unpopular.*

**unprepared** /ˌʌnp rɪ'pɛrd/ *adjective*
**1** unqualified, unskilled: *He is unprepared for the job; he needs more skills.*
**2** not ready: *Dinner is unprepared, but will be ready in an hour.*

**unprofessional** /ˌʌnprə'fɛʃənəl/ *adjective*
below the quality expected from a professional person or business: *The repair shop refused to fix the bad work that they did; both the work and the management were unprofessional.* –*adverb* **unprofessionally.**

**unprofitable** /ʌn'prɑfɪtəbəl/ *adjective*
not making a profit, losing money: *That is an unprofitable company; it's almost bankrupt.* –*adverb* **unprofitably.**

**unqualified** /ʌn 'kwɑləˌfaɪd/ *adjective*
unskilled, untrained: *He is unqualified for the job because of his lack of skills.*

**unquestionable** /ʌn'kwɛstʃənəbəl/ *adjective*
certain, without doubt: *The meeting was an unquestionable success; much was decided.* –*adverb* **unquestionably.**

**unreal** /ʌn'riəl/ *adjective*
**1** imaginary: *Her pains are unreal because they are in her imagination.*
**2** *slang* wonderful: *The salary that she makes is unreal, tremendous!*

**unreasonable** /ʌn'rizənəbəl/ *adjective*
**1** not reasonable, not sensible: *The old man makes unreasonable demands on his son to visit him every day.*
**2** too high, uneconomical: *The price of that new car is unreasonable.* –*noun* **unreasonableness;** –*adverb* **unreasonably.**

**unreliable** /ˌʌnrɪ'laɪəbəl/ *adjective*
not to be trusted: *You can't believe his promises because he's unreliable.*

**unrest** /ʌn'rɛst/ *noun, (no plural)*
discontent, unhappiness: *After the President was killed, there was unrest in the streets.*

**unripe** /ʌn'raɪp/ *adjective*
not ready for eating: *If you eat unripe fruit, you can get sick.*

**unroll** /ʌn'roʊl/ *verb*
to open, spread out: *A worker unrolled the rug onto the wood floor.*

unroll

**unruly** /ʌn'ruli/ *adjective*
disobedient, loud, and wild: *A group of unruly children ran through the hallway.* –*noun* **unruliness.**

**unsafe** /ʌn'seɪf/ *adjective*
in bad condition, dangerous: *That old building is unsafe to live in.* –*adverb* **unsafely.**

**unsanitary** /ʌn'sænəˌtɛri/ *adjective*
full of germs, not clean: *There are unsanitary conditions in that bathroom; it needs cleaning.*

**unsatisfactory** /ˌʌnsætɪs'fæktəri/ *adjective*
unacceptable, not meeting standards: *We received an unsatisfactory offer for the house, so we didn't sell it.* –*adverb* **unsatisfactorily.**

**unscrew** /ʌn'skru/ *verb*
**1** to loosen or remove a screw
**2** to turn or twist open: *He unscrewed (the top of) a jar of mustard.*

unscrew

**unskilled** /ʌn'skɪld/ *adjective*
without special skills or education: *Cutting the grass or sweeping the streets requires unskilled workers only. See:* blue-collar.

**unsnap** /ʌn'snæp/ *verb* **unsnapped, unsnapping, unsnaps**
to open (a snap): *He unsnapped his jacket and took it off.*

**unstable** /ʌn'ste ɪbəl/ *adjective*
**1** not behaving or thinking normally: *He is an unstable person who cries often at work.*
**2** shaky, unsteady, ready to fall into ruin: *an unstable company (bridge, situation)*

**unsteady** /ʌn'stɛdi/ *adjective*
subject to falling: *He is drunk and unsteady on his feet.* –*adverb* **unsteadily;** –*noun* **unsteadiness.**

**unsuccessful** /ˌʌnsək'sɛsfəl/ *adjective*
failed, disappointing: *She made an unsuccessful attempt to start her own business; it failed.* –*adverb* **unsuccessfully.**

**unsuitable** /ʌn'sutəbəl/ *adjective*
unacceptable, not what is wanted

**unsure** /nʃʊr/ *adjective*
not sure: *I am unsure about the weather. It may snow tomorrow.*

**untangle** /ʌn'tæŋgəl/ *verb* **untangled, untangling, untangles**
to take apart a knot, unknot: *She untangled a knot in a piece of string.*

**untidy** /ʌn'taɪdi/ *adjective* **untidier, untidiest**
messy: *Her untidy room has clothes all over the floor.* –*noun* **untidiness.**

**untie** /ʌn'taɪ/ *verb* **untied, untying, unties**
to undo (a necktie, knot, etc.): *He untied his shoes and took them off.*

**until** /ʌn'tɪl/ *preposition*
**1** up to a particular time: *We worked until noon, and then had lunch.*
**2** before a particular time: *We can't work again until Monday.*

**until** *conjunction*
up to the time that, before: *We will not be able to leave until our work is finished.*

---

**USAGE NOTE:** Many people drop the first syllable "un" from the word *until* when they pronounce it. This form is written as *till*, or contracted as *'til,* but in formal writing the complete word *until* is preferred.

---

**untimely** /ʌn'taɪmli/ *adjective*
happening too soon: *a young woman's untimely death*

**untrue** /ʌn'tru/ *adjective*
**1** false, incorrect: *What he said is untrue; he's lying.*
**2** not loyal: *He is a husband who is untrue to his wife.* –*adjective* **untruthful.**

**unused** /ʌn'yuzd/ *adjective*
not used, sitting idle: *He has unused equipment sitting in his garage.*

**unusual** /ʌn'yuʒuəl/ *adjective*
**1** not normal: *His unusual behavior shocks others.*
**2** special, very good: *She has an unusual talent for playing the piano.*

**unusually** / ʌn'yuʒuəli/ *adverb*
not usual, special: *We are having unusually good weather for this time of year.*

**unwilling** /ʌn'wɪlɪŋ/ *adjective*
**1** against: *She is unwilling to take a cut in pay.*
**2** forced: *She was an unwilling guest at the wedding; she did not want to go.* –*adverb* **unwillingly;** –*noun* **unwillingness.**

**unwind** /ʌn'waɪnd/ *verb* **unwound** /-'waʊnd/, **unwinding, unwinds**
**1** to undo: *She unwinds thread to sew something.*
**2** *figurative* to relax: *She likes to unwind at home after a hard day's work.*

**unwise** /ʌn'waɪz/ *adjective*
**1** stupid, dumb: *He was unwise to quit school.*
**2** not sensible: *It is unwise to buy a house at this bad time.* –*adverb* **unwisely.**

**unwrap** /ʌn'ræp/ *verb* **unwrapped, unwrapping, unwraps**
to uncover, to take the wrapping off something: *Children love to unwrap presents.*

U

**unzip** /ʌn'zɪp/ *verb* **unzipped, unzipping, unzips**
to undo the zipper on something: *She unzipped her jacket.*

unzip

**up** /ʌp/ *adverb*
**1** in a higher direction, upward: *He looked up at the sky and then walked up the hill.*
**2** to a higher level, more: *Prices are up.*||*The temperature is up another ten degrees.*
**3** finished, ended: *Your time is up.*
**4** built, put into use: *The building is up and ready for people to move in.*||*The new computer system is up and running.*
**5** out of bed, arisen: *I was up at 7:00 o'-clock this morning.*||*The sun was up at 6:32 A.M.*
**6** able to do: *Do you think he is up to the job (up to finishing school, up to finding a job, etc.)?*
**7** dependent on, responsible for: *It's up to you to decide.*||*It's up to me to finish the job.*
**8** doing, busy with: *What is he up to now?*||*He is up to something.*
**9** as far as, until: *Up to now, he's done a lot of work.*
**to come up:** **a.** to visit: *Come up and see us soon.* **b.** to prevent something: *Something has come up, and I cannot visit now.* **c.** to happen in the future: *What's coming up next week at the movies?*
**to hold up:** to delay: *The post office is on strike, and that is holding up our mail.*
**to hold someone up:** to rob at gun or knifepoint: *A robber held me up with a gun.*
**to be up a tree:** to be angry: *He is really angry; he's up a tree.*
**to be** or **keep up on what is happening:** to be current, informed: *I listen to the news to keep up on what is happening.*
**What's up?:** what is happening: *What's up? I bought a new stereo; otherwise, nothing's up.*
**up** *preposition*
to a higher place on: *(to be) up a tree, (to climb) up the stairs*

**upbeat** /'ʌpˌbit/ *adjective*
positive: *That teacher has an upbeat attitude toward his students. See:* enthusiastic. *(antonym)* depressed.

**upbringing** /'ʌpˌbrɪŋɪŋ/ *noun*
how parents, teachers, and others give a good or bad education and manners to a young person who is growing up: *Her good manners show she had an excellent upbringing.*

**update** /ˌʌp'deɪt/ *verb* **updated, updating, updates**
to make something current, up-to-date: *The TV updated a news story on the bad storm coming to our area. –noun* **update.**

**up-front** /ˌʌp'frʌnt/ *adjective*
**1** completely clear, honest: *I was up-front with him; I told him I needed money.*
**2** in advance, prepaid: *an up-front payment*
**up-front** *adverb*
**up front:** in the forward area: *When I'm a passenger in a car, I always like to sit up front.*

**upgrade** /'ʌpˌgreɪd/ *noun*
**1** land that heads upwards: *Trains travel slowly on upgrades into the hills.*
**2** something better, an improvement: *He got an upgrade from tourist to first class on the airplane. –verb* **to upgrade.**

**uphill** /ˌʌp'hɪl/ *adverb*
in an upward direction on land: *She had to walk her bicycle uphill.*

**upholstery** /ə'poʊlstəri/ *noun*
cloth, leather, or other covering on furniture: *The upholstery on that chair is worn.*

upholstery

**upkeep** /'ʌpˌkip/ *noun*
the cost and work needed to keep property and machines repaired and working

**upon** /ə'pɑn/ *preposition formal*
**1** on: *She sat upon the sofa.*
**2** at the time of: *Upon seeing her, I smiled and ran toward her.*

**upper** /'ʌpər/ *adjective*
located in a higher area or region: *His upper body hurts in the neck and chest.*

**upper class** *noun, plural* **classes**
**1** the highest social class: *Rich people belong to the upper class.*
**2** students in the last two years of high school or college: *Only the upper classes were allowed to have parties at the school.*

---

**USAGE NOTE:** Although American society is often called "classless," there is a small group of wealthy and powerful Americans who are the *upper class* of society.

---

**upperclassman** /ˌʌpər'klæsmən/ *noun, plural* **upperclassmen** /-mən/
a student in the last two years of high school or college: *The upperclassmen at my university include women and men who are juniors and seniors.*

**uppermost** /'ʌpərˌmoust/ *adjective*
highest: *After walking all day we finally reached the uppermost part of the mountain.*

**uppermost** *adverb*
most important: *Uppermost in his mind is the need for safety.*

**upright** /'ʌpˌraɪt/ *adverb*
standing up: *People walk upright, but cats don't.*

**upright** *adjective*
**1** standing up: *The tall lamp is standing in an upright position.*
**2** respectful of the law, honest: *He is an upright citizen who obeys the law.*

**uprising** /'ʌpˌraɪzɪŋ/ *noun*
a fight usually against the government: *An uprising of the people happened when there was no food available. See:* riot, revolt.

**uproar** /'ʌpˌrɔr/ *noun*
people complaining or shouting: *There was an uproar by the people over a tax increase. –adjective* **uproarious.**

**ups and downs** *noun, plural*
pleasant and unpleasant events: *Life has ups and downs.*

**upset** /ʌp'sɛt/ *adjective*
troubled, hurt emotionally: *He was upset by the bad news. –verb* **to upset.**

**upside down** /'ʌpˌsaɪd'daun/ *adverb*
turned with the bottom part at the top: *The dancer stood upside down on her hands. –adjective* **upside-down.**

**upstairs** /ˌʌp'stɛrz/ *adverb*
in the direction of the level above: *He climbed the steps to go upstairs.*

**upstate** /'ʌpˌsteɪt/ *adjective*
of the northern area of a state: *Syracuse and Rochester are in upstate New York.*

**up-to-date** /ˌʌptə'deɪt/ *adjective*
**1** done on time, not behind: *All my work is up-to-date.*
**2** modern: *Our business has the most up-to-date equipment.*

**uptown** /'ʌpˌtaun/ *adverb*
in or toward the upper part of a city: *I'm going uptown now, from 1st street to 125th street. (antonym)* downtown.

**upward** /'ʌpwərd/ or **upwards** /'ʌpwərdz/ *adverb*
up, rising: *He looked upward at the sky.||Sales are headed upwards. (antonym)* downward.

**uranium** /yʊ'reɪniəm/ *noun*
a chemical that is used in fuel for nuclear power plants and in nuclear bombs: *The government controls uranium closely.*

**Uranus** /yʊ'reɪnəs/ *noun, (no plural)*
the seventh planet from the sun: *Uranus is quite far from the sun.*

**urban** /'ɜrbən/ *adjective*
related to a city: *Many people move to urban areas to have the excitement of city life. –noun* (process) **urbanization.**

**urge** /ɜrʤ/ *verb* **urged, urging, urges**
to advise someone to do something in a serious way, to pressure: *I urge you to finish your education.*

**urge** *noun*
a desire: *I have an urge to eat some chocolates.*

**urgency** /'ɜrʤənsi/ *noun, (no plural)*
a strong need, an emergency: *He has a sense of urgency to act now and not wait.*

**urgent** /'ɜrʤə nt/ *adjective*
pressing, demanding immediate action:

*We have an urgent need for help; we are running out of food.* –*adverb* **urgently.**

**urine** /ˈyʊrɪn/ *noun*
liquid waste from the body: *Urine is flushed away in the bathroom toilet.* –*verb* **to urinate** /ˈyʊrəˌneɪt/.

**us** /ʌs/ *pronoun*
a group of two or more and that includes myself: *Let's keep the secret between us.*

**usable** or **useable** /ˈyuzəbəl/ *adjective*
able of being used: *The machine is usable now after repair.*

**usage** /ˈyusɪʤ/ *noun*
**1** the use of something: *The usage of heating oil increased during the cold winter.*
**2** the manner in which language is actually or correctly used: *It is important to learn proper usage of a language.*

**use** /yuz/ *verb* **used, using, uses**
**1** to employ for a purpose: *She used her intelligence to solve a problem.*
**2** /yus/ to feel something is normal: *As a man from the north, he is used to cold weather.*
**3** to satisfy a need: *She uses milk and sugar in her tea.*
**4** to get others to do what one wants: *He uses others to do his dirty work for him.*
**to use something up:** to use something completely: *She won the lottery last year, and used up the money in six months.*

**use** /yus/ *noun*
**1** a purpose: *The computer is of use to her in her work.*
**2** a right given by another: *She has the use of the office computer when she needs it.*
**3** the ability to use something again: *He hurt his hand, but he has the use of it again now.*
**in use:** being used: *That television is in use every day.*

**used** /yuzd/ *adjective*
not new, already in use: *a used car*

**useful** /ˈyusfəl/ *adjective*
**1** helpful, handy: *Tools, such as a hammer and saw, are useful when you want to fix something.*
**2** valuable: *Her language skills make her useful to our team.* –*adverb* **usefully;** –*noun* **usefulness.**

**user** /ˈyuzər/ *noun*
a person or group that uses something: *The user of that computer simply turns it on and starts typing.*

**user-friendly** *adjective*
easy to understand or use: *Our company buys user-friendly computers.*

**usual** /ˈyuʒuəl/ *adjective*
normal, customary: *To argue is not his usual behavior.*||*As usual, she is on time.* –*adverb* **usually.**

**utensil** /yuˈtɛnsəl/ *noun*
a tool or implement, especially for eating food: *Utensils for eating include knives, forks, and spoons.*

utensils

**utility** /yuˈ tɪləti/ *noun, plural* **utilities**
any basic necessity or service, such as running water, electricity, or gas

**utilize** /ˈyutlˌaɪz/ *verb* **utilized, utilizing, utilizes**
to use, to bring into use: *We utilized an old building to store our business files.* –*noun* **utilization.**

**utmost** /ˈʌtˌmoʊst/ *noun, (no plural)*
the greatest, without holding back: *She tries her utmost to do a good job.*

**utopia** /yuˈt oʊpiə/ *noun*
a place of ideal peace, cooperation, and good living: *Many people have written about living in a utopia.* –*adjective* **utopian.**

**utterly** /ˈʌtərli/ *adverb*
completely, totally: *She was utterly surprised when her lost friend suddenly appeared.*

**U-turn** /ˈyuˌtɜrn/ *noun*
a turn in the complete, opposite direction: *He was heading north and then made a U-turn and headed south.*

U-turn

# V,v

**V** or **v** /vi/ *noun* **V's, v's** or **Vs, vs,**
**1** the 22nd letter of the English alphabet
**2** shaped like a "V": *He raised two fingers and made the V sign for victory.*

**vacancy** /ˈveɪkənsi/ *noun, plural* **vacancies**
an empty room or building, such as a hotel room: *That office building has some vacancies on the first floor.*

**vacant** /ˈveɪkənt/ *adjective*
without a guest or someone staying in a room or building, empty: *There are two vacant apartments in that building. (antonym)* occupied.

**vacation** /veɪˈkeɪʃən/ *noun*
a time period away from work or one's regular activities, (*synonym*) a holiday: *We took a vacation in the mountains.*

**vacation** *verb*
to take time off for pleasure: *We vacationed in Italy.*

**vaccinate** /ˈvæks əˌneɪt/ *verb* **vaccinated, vaccinating, vaccinates**
medicine given through a needle put under the skin: *The nurse vaccinated the child against the flu. –noun* **vaccination.**

**vaccine** /vækˈsin/ *noun*
a medicine taken to prevent many diseases

**vacuum** /ˈvækˌyum/ *noun*
**1** an empty and airless space, such as in a bottle without air
**2** a state of being alone, usually without useful information or others to help: *When I work alone at home, I feel like I ...rk in a vacuum without people.*
... vacuum cleaner

**vacuum** *verb*
to clean with a vacuum cleaner: *He vacuumed the rug.*

**vacuum cleaner** *noun*
a machine that picks up dust and dirt in a strong current of air: *He used a vacuum cleaner to clean the rug.*

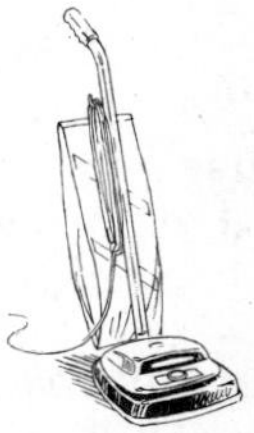
**vacuum cleaner**

**vagina** /vəˈʤaɪnə/ *noun*
a woman's sex organ: *The vagina opens into the uterus. –adjective* **vaginal.**

**vague** /veɪg/ *adjective* **vaguer, vaguest**
unclear: *He has some vague ideas about what to do, but nothing clear and exact. –noun* **vagueness;** *–adverb* **vaguely.**

**vain** /veɪn/ *adjective* **vainer, vainest**
overly concerned with how one looks: *He is always looking at himself in the mirror; he's so vain!*
**in vain:** for nothing, without success: *His long report was not approved, so he did all the work in vain. See:* vanity.

**valentine** /ˈvælənˌtaɪn/ *noun*
a love letter or greeting card given to a person to show friendliness or love on Saint Valentine's Day (February 14): *I sent my girlfriend a valentine for Valentine's Day.*

**valid** /ˈvælɪd/ *adjective*
**1** having a good reason for something: *He has a valid reason for being late; his car broke down.*
**2** legally usable for a set time period: *She has a passport that's valid for ten*

*years.* –*noun* **validity** /və'lɪdəti/; –*verb* **to validate.**

**valley** /'væli/ *noun*
a low area of land between hills and mountains: *Farmers plant crops in valleys.*

**valuable** /'v ælyuəbəl/ *adjective*
**1** having worth, value: *Gold jewelry is valuable.*
**2** useful, helpful: *a valuable piece of information*

**valuables** *noun plural*
personal objects, such as jewelry or art: *She keeps her valuables in a safe.*

**value** /'vælyu/ *verb* **valued, valuing, values**
**1** to think something is important: *I value my best friend's advice.*
**2** to put a price on something: *An expert valued the painting at $1 million.*

**value** *noun*
**1** worth: *The value of this home has doubled since we have owned it.*
**2** *plural* ideals, standards of a society: *We have tried to teach our children values like honesty and hard work.*

**vampire** /'væm,paɪr/ *noun*
an animal with wings (type of bat) that lives by drinking blood from other animals

**van** /væn/ *noun*
a box-like truck used for carrying large items: *People use moving vans to move their furniture to a new house.*

**vandal** /'vændl/ *noun*
a person who destroys property for fun: *The vandals destroyed some street lights and set fires in the park.* –*noun* **vandalism;** –*verb* **to vandalize.**

**vanilla** /və'nɪlə/ *noun*
a flavoring used in foods: *He likes vanilla ice cream.*

**vanish** /'vænɪʃ/ *verb* **vanishes**
to disappear: *The man vanished from sight.* –*adjective* **vanishing.**

**vanity** /'vænəti/ *noun*
too much concern with one's looks or importance

**vapor** /'veɪpər/ *noun*
a gas, usually one that cannot be seen: *Boiling water turns into vapor in the air.* –*verb* **to vaporize;** –*noun* (machine) **vaporization.**

**variable** /'v ɛriəbəl/ *adjective*
changing from one condition to another: *We will have variable weather with rain and sunshine today.*

**variable** *noun*
(in math) a factor, usually an unknown, in an equation or situation: *In the equation "3x=6," x is a variable.* –*noun* **variability.** *(antonym)* constant.

**varied** /'vɛrid/ *adjective*
& *past participle of* vary, of different kinds: *That store offers varied candies such as chocolates and jelly beans.*

**variety** /və'raɪəti/ *noun, plural* **varieties**
different types of things: *That store carries a wide variety of goods, from clothes to furniture.*

**various** /'vɛriəs/ *adjective*
a general number of people or things: *Various people attended the meeting.* –*adverb* **variously.**

**varnish** /'vɑrnɪʃ/ *noun, plural* **varnishes**
an oil-based liquid put on wood to give it a shiny finish: *He put a coat of varnish on the chair.* –*verb* **to varnish.**

**varsity** /'vɑrsəti/ *noun, plural* **varsities**
the school sports team playing at the highest level (not the junior varsity)

**vary** /'vɛri/ *verb* **varied, varying, varies**
to differ: *Costs of tickets vary from one airline to another.*

**vase** /veɪs/ *noun*
a decorated glass or clay container usually used to hold flowers: *The vase on the table has roses in it.*

**vast** /væst/ *adjective*
**1** wide in area: *Mr. Rockefeller owns a vast piece of land with two lakes.*
**2** important, great: *A good rainfall makes a vast difference in growing food crops.* –*noun* **vastness;** –*adverb* **vastly.**

**vault** /vɔlt/ *noun*
a large safe used to keep money, important papers: *a bank vault*

**VCR** /'visi'ɑr/ *noun*
*abbreviation of* videocassette recorder

**veal** /vil/ *noun*
meat from young cows

**vegetable** /ˈvɛʤtəbəl/ *noun*
many plants raised as food: *Lettuce, carrots, and string beans are vegetables.*

**vegetarian** /ˌvɛʤəˈtɛriən/ *noun*
a person who eats only plant foods

**vegetation** /ˌvɛʤəˈteɪʃən/ *noun, (no plural)*
the plant covering in an area: *Jungle vegetation is very thick.*

**vehicle** /ˈviɪkəl/ *noun*
a machine, such as a car or truck, that travels to transport people or goods: *We took our vehicle to the mechanic for a safety inspection.* –*adjective* **vehicular.**

**veil** /veɪl/ *noun*
a light, cloth covering worn over the face by women: *She wore a veil made of a light silk to the wedding.*

veil

**vein** /veɪn/ *noun*
any of many tubes that bring blood to the heart and lungs: *You can see the blue veins on the back of his hand. See:* vessel 1.

**velocity** /vəˈlɑsəti/ *noun, plural* **velocities**
speed, such as that measured in miles per hour or feet per second: *A bullet travels at a high velocity.*

**velvet** /ˈvɛlvɪt/ *noun*
a soft, thick cloth made of cotton, silk, etc.: *She wore a jacket made of blue velvet.* –*adjective* **velvety.**

**vending machine** *noun*
a machine that gives food, soft drinks, or other items after money is placed in it: *He often buys soft drinks from the vending machine.*

**venetian blind** /vəˈniʧən/ *noun*
a window shade with thin plastic or metal blades: *I closed the venetian blinds to keep the bright sunlight out.*

venetian blind

**...geance** ...nʤəns/ *noun*
...rmful act against someone who has ... something wrong to you: *He wants vengeance for the murder of his brother.* –*adjective* **vengeful.**

**venom** /ˈvɛnəm/ *noun*
the poison in some snakes and insects: *snake venom* –*adjective* **venomous.**

**vent** /vɛnt/ *verb*
**1** to make air or smoke escape: *to vent a room of smoke*
**2** to let go with force: *He vented his anger by screaming at his dog.*

**vent** *noun*
an opening used to let air escape

**ventilation** /ˌvɛntlˈeɪʃən/ *noun*
a system, such as air openings and blowers, used to change the air in a room or building: *The poor ventilation in my hotel room makes me feel sick.* –*noun* (thing) **ventilator;** –*verb* **to ventilate.**

**Venus** /ˈvinəs/ *noun*
the second planet from the sun: *Venus is between Mercury and Mars.*

**veranda** /vəˈrændə/ *noun*
a porch: *We often sit on the veranda on hot evenings. See:* porch.

veranda

**verb** /vɜrb/ *noun*
an action word: *"Be," "do," and "go" are verbs. See:* predicate.

**verbal** /ˈvɜrbəl/ *adjective*
related to written or spoken words: *She has good verbal skills.* –*verb* **to verbalize;** –*adverb* **verbally.**

**verdict** /ˈvɜrdɪkt/ *noun*
a decision of guilty or not guilty: *The judge gave a verdict of "not guilty" for the person accused of a crime. See:* defendant; jury.

**verify** /ˈvɛrəˌfaɪ/ *verb* **verified, verifying, verifies**
to prove something is true: *I verified the store's address by calling to check it.* –*noun* **verification.** *See:* confirm.

**versatile** /ˈvɜrsətl/ *adjective*
able to do many different things: *She is a versatile musician who can play many instruments.* –*noun* **versatility.**

**verse** /vɜrs/ *noun*
**1** poetry: *Poets write in verse.*
**2** a line of poetry or in the Bible

**version** /ˈvɜrʒən/ *noun*
an account of something: *He told his own version of the funny story.*

**versus** /ˈvɜrsəs/ *preposition*
against: *It was Argentina versus Germany in the World Cup match.*

**vertical** /ˈvɜrtɪkəl/ *adjective*
standing straight up: *A wall stands in a vertical position to the floor. –adverb* **vertically.** *(antonym)* horizontal.

**very** /ˈvɛri/ *adverb*
absolutely, extremely: *He was very pleased to see his friend.*

**very** *adjective*
absolute: *She is at the very beginning writing a long report.*

**vessel** /ˈvɛsəl/ *noun*
**1** a tube that carries fluid: *the blood vessels*
**2** a ship: *Vessels sail the Atlantic Ocean.*

**vest** /vɛst/ *noun*
piece of clothing without arms worn on the upper body: *He often wears a vest as part of a suit.*

**veteran** /ˈvɛtərən/ *noun*
any person leaving the military service with a record of good behavior: *She is a veteran of military service in Africa.*

**veteran** *adjective*
anyone with a lot of experience in a job, profession, or art: *He is a veteran newspaper reporter.*

**Veterans Day** *noun*
a holiday honoring soldiers who have fought in wars: *In the USA, Veterans Day is on November 11.*

**veterinarian** /ˌvɛtərəˈnɛriən/ *noun*
a doctor for animals: *The veterinarian came to see our sick horse. –adjective* **veterinary.**

**veto** /ˈvitoʊ/ *verb* **vetoed, vetoing, vetoes**
to cancel or stop the passage of a law: *The President vetoed the budget bill sent to him by Congress. –noun* **veto.**

**via** /ˈviə/ *preposition*
**1** by way of: *We flew to Rome via London.*
**2** through means of: *I sent a package via messenger.*

**vial** /ˈvaɪəl/ *noun*
a small, round container made of glass or plastic: *a vial of medicine*

**vibes** /vaɪbz/ *noun, plural slang*
*short for* vibrations, the unspoken good or bad feelings coming from a person or event: *I get good vibes from my new friend.*

**vibration** /vaɪˈbreɪʃən/ *noun*
**1** shaking: *I felt the vibration caused by a passing train.*
**2** *plural informal* the feelings given off by a person or event: *We had good vibrations from the successful business meeting. –verb* **to vibrate.**

**Vice President** /vaɪs/ *noun*
**1** the second in line to the President of the US government: *The Vice President represents the government at many official events.*
**2** (without capital letters) a title in other organizations given to those employees just below the rank of president: *Large corporations often have many vice presidents. –noun* **vice presidency.**

---

**USAGE NOTE:** The *Vice President* is an advisor to both the President of the USA and the president of the Senate. In the USA the Vice President and President run for office and are elected together.

---

**vice versa** /ˈvaɪsəˈvɜrsə/ *adverb*
the same in opposite order: *What may be too expensive for you may seem cheap to me or vice versa.*||*He loves her and vice versa. (She loves him.)*

**vicinity** /vəˈsɪnəti/ *noun, (no plural)*
the local area, places nearby: *Our house is located in this vicinity; it's three blocks away, in fact.*

**vicious** /ˈvɪʃəs/ *adjective*
cruel, wanting to hurt someone: *His vicious remarks are cruel and hurtful.*||*That vicious dog attacks and bites people. –noun* **viciousness;** *–adverb* **viciously.**

**victim** /ˈvɪktəm/ *noun*
someone or something that suffers from an accident, crime, illness, or bad luck: *The accident victim was helped by a doctor.*

**victimize** /'vɪkt ə,maɪz/ *verb* **victimized, victimizing, victimizes**
to trick another person, especially taking their money: *The dishonest man victimized an old lady by cheating her.*

**victor** /'vɪktər/ *noun*
the winner in a competition or battle: *The victor in the swimming competition won a prize. (antonym)* loser.

**victory** /'vɪktəri/ *noun, plural* **victories**
**1** winning a competition or battle: *Our country won victory in the war.*
**2** success: *He stopped smoking cigarettes and doing that was a big victory for him. –adjective* **victorious;** *–adverb* **victoriously.** *(antonym)* loss.

**video** /'vɪdioʊ/ *adjective*
related to television pictures: *The video part of the television broadcast was clear, but the sound was poor.*

**video** *noun*
television or videotape pictures: *We saw the movie on video.*

**video camera** *noun*
a camera used to record the pictures and sounds of events, using videotape: *Many families own a video camera today.*

**videocassette** /,vɪdioʊkə'sɛt/ *noun*
videotape in a plastic container used for playing in a videocassette recorder connected to a television set: *We often watch old movies on videocassette.*

**videocassette recorder** *noun*
usually called a **VCR**: an electronic machine that both records television programs on videotape and is used to play videotapes: *He watched a movie on our VCR. See:* art on page 6a.

**videodisc** /'vɪdioʊ,dɪsk/ *noun*
a flat, round object containing video and sound recording played on a disk player attached to a television set: *We watch movies on videodisc.*

**video game** *noun*
an electronic game played on a television set or machine: *Video games are fun to play.*

**videotape** /'vɪdioʊ,teɪp/ *noun*
...leo recording tape

...**otape** *verb* **videotaped, videotaping,** ...**otapes**
...ord on videotape: *We videotaped a* ...*ball game.*

**view** /vyu/ *verb*
**1** to look at: *We viewed the mountain scenery. –noun* (person/machine) **viewer.**
**2** to hold the opinion that, *(synonym)* to believe: *She views marriage as a serious matter.*

**view** *noun*
**1** a scene: *Our house has a view of the park.*
**2** opinion, belief: *Many people have views on how to fix the economy.*

**viewpoint** /'vyu,pɔɪnt/ *noun*
an opinion: *Her viewpoint is that she wants to get married, but not at this time.*

**vigorous** /'vɪgərəs/ *adjective*
strong and full of energy: *She does vigorous exercises, like running fast, every morning. –adverb* **vigorously.**

**villa** /'vɪlə/ *noun*
a country house: *They have a villa in the mountains.*

**village** /'vɪlɪʤ/ *noun*
a group of houses forming a settlement smaller than a town or city: *They live in a country village. –noun* (person) **villager.**

**villain** /'vɪlən/ *noun*
a bad person, especially a criminal: *Villains commit crimes. (antonym)* hero.

**vine** /vaɪn/ *noun*
a climbing plant, such as ivy or grape: *Vines cover the hills in wine country.*

**vinegar** /'vɪnəgər/ *noun*
an acid-tasting liquid made from wine

**vineyard** /'vɪnyərd/ *noun*
an area with grapevines: *Many vineyards are located near San Francisco.*

**vinyl** /'vaɪnəl/ *noun*
plastic used to make clothes and furniture covering: *The seat covering in my car is made of vinyl.*

**violate** /'vaɪə,leɪt/ *verb* **violated, violating, violates**
to break: *He violated the law by driving through a red light.*

**violation** /,vaɪə'leɪʃən/ *noun*
an act of breaking a law, contract, rule, etc.: *A violation of a law can bring punishment.*

**violence** /ˈvaɪələns/ *noun*
**1** injury or damage: *The criminal committed violence in shooting a man.*
**2** strong force, such as wind: *The violence of the hurricane caused great damage.* *–adjective* **violent;** *–adverb* **violently.**

**violet** /ˈvaɪələt/ *noun*
a plant with blue-purple flowers: *an African violet See:* art on page 1a.

**violet** *adjective*
a bluish-purple color: *She wore a violet dress.*

**violin** /ˌvaɪəˈlɪn/ *noun*
a stringed musical instrument played with a bow: *The violin is a great instrument to play by itself. See:* art on page 15a.

**VIP** /ˈviaɪˈpi/ *noun*
*abbreviation of* very important person: *She is a VIP in the government who works closely with the President.*

**viral** /ˈvaɪrəl/ *adjective*
related to viruses: *He has a viral infection, that is, viral pneumonia.*

**virtual** /ˈvɜrʧuəl/ *adjective*
nearly, almost but not quite

**virtual reality** *noun*
experiencing events that seem like real life by putting on special eyeglasses, hearing devices, and gloves attached to a computer: *Virtual reality can be used to view movies as though you were really taking part in them.*

**virtue** /ˈvɜrʧu/ *noun*
**1** moral goodness, such as honesty or clean living: *He is a man of great virtue.*
**2** advantage, special quality: *That new medicine has the virtue of being inexpensive.* *–adjective* **virtuous.**

**virus** /ˈvaɪrəs/ *noun*
any microorganism smaller than bacteria that causes such diseases as the common cold, influenza, measles, and HIV: *He caught a virus and was sick for a week. See:* viral.

**visa** /ˈvizə/ *noun*
a foreign travel authorization: *The American government gave me a six-month visa and stamped my passport.*

**Visa™** /ˈvisə/ *noun*
the name of a popular credit card: *When she travels, she charges her expenses on her Visa™* or *Visa™ card.*

**visibility** /ˌvɪzəˈbɪləti/ *noun*
clearness of the air and sky

**visible** /ˈvɪzəbəl/ *adjective*
easy to see: *Her health made a visible improvement.* *–adverb* **visibly.**

**vision** /ˈvɪʤən/ *noun*
**1** eyesight: *She has good vision.*
**2** an imaginary event: *to have a vision in a dream*
**3** ability to imagine the future: *There are leaders of vision in every industry.* *–noun* **visionary.**

**visit** /ˈvɪzɪt/ *verb*
to go to a place and stay for a time: *We visited my parents in the next town for two days.*

**visit** *noun*
a stay with someone or at a place: *We had a nice visit with our cousins in Ohio.*

**visitor** /ˈvɪzətər/ *noun*
**1** a person who visits other people: *Our company had some visitors yesterday.*
**2** tourists: *New York has many visitors.*

**visor** /ˈvaɪzər/ *noun*
the front of a hat that sticks out over the eyes: *A baseball cap has a long visor.*

visor

**visual** /ˈvɪʤuəl/ *adjective*
able to be seen: *A picture is a visual object.*

**visualize** /ˈvɪʤuəˌlaɪz/ *verb* **visualized, visualizing, visualizes**
to picture something in the mind, (*synonym*) to imagine: *When it snows, I like to visualize a vacation on a warm beach.*

**vital** /ˈvaɪtl/ *adjective*
**1** most important, absolutely necessary: *Water is vital to life.*
**2** energetic, lively: *She has a vital personality.* *–adverb* **vitally;** *–noun* **vitality.**

**vitamin** /ˌvaɪtəmɪn/ *noun*
any of many chemical substances necessary for good health: *Vitamin C is found in fruits, potatoes, etc.*

**vivid** /ˈvɪvɪd/ *adjective*
easy to see or imagine, clear: *The television reporter gave a vivid story about the hurricane.* *–noun* **vividness;** *–adverb* **vividly.**

**V-neck** /ˈviˌnɛk/ *noun*
a sweater, pullover, or other garment with the neckline shaped downward in a "V": *In winter, he wears a V-neck sweater and a warm coat.*

**vocabulary** /voʊˈkæbyəˌlɛri/ *noun*
**1** a group of words that forms a language: *She learns some new vocabulary every day.*
**2** the words used in a particular kind of work: *The vocabulary of computers is called "computerese."*

**vocal** /ˈvoʊkəl/ *adjective*
**1** related to speaking and the voice: *Words are formed in your throat with vocal chords.*
**2** loud, complaining: *A vocal group of protesters complained about bad air quality.* *–verb* **to vocalize;** *–adverb* **vocally.**

**vocalist** /ˈvoʊkəlɪst/ *noun*
a singer: *That vocalist sings with a local band.*

**vocation** /voʊˈkeɪʃən/ *noun*
one's work for pay: *His writing is not a vocation, he just does it for fun.*

**vocational** /voʊˈkeɪʃənəl/ *adjective*
related to work: *She is taking vocational training to learn to be a hairdresser.*

**vocational school** *noun*
a school where job skills are taught, such as auto mechanics, computer repair, or secretarial skills: *He goes to a vocational school and is learning computers.*

**vogue** /voʊg/ *noun, (no plural)*
a fashion for clothes, speech, or ideas: *Clothes in vogue this season will change next year.*

**voice** /vɔɪs/ *verb* **voiced, voicing, voices**
to speak, say: *He voiced his opinions about politics.*

**voice** *noun*
**1** the ability to speak: *She speaks in a clear voice.*
**2** a person who represents others, (*synonym*) a spokesperson: *She is a voice of support for the poor.*

**voice mail** *noun*
a telephone answering system on which one person leaves spoken messages for another: *John was not at his desk, but I left a message for him on his voice mail.*

**void** /vɔɪd/ *verb*
to stop something that was already done (ordered or planned), (*synonym*) to cancel: *I voided the check by writing "Void" over my signature.*

**void** *noun*
a dark, empty place: *a void of sadness*

**void** *adjective*
empty, barren: *The moon is void of life.*

**volcano** /vɑlˈkeɪnoʊ/ *noun, plural* **volcanos** or **volcanoes**
a hill or mountain formed by hot, melted rock escaping from beneath the earth: *Mt. Vesuvius in Italy is an active volcano.* *–adjective* **volcanic** /valˈkænɪk/.

**volleyball** /ˈvɑliˌbɔl/ *noun*
**1** a sport played by two to six players on each side of a net who score a point by grounding the ball on the opponent's side: *Volleyball is an Olympic sport.*
**2** the ball used in that sport

**volt** /voʊlt/ *noun*
a unit of measurement in electricity: *The electricity in our home is 120 volts.* *–noun* **voltage.**

**volume** /ˈvɑlˌyum/ *noun*
**1** a book or one of a series of books: *The dictionary is the largest volume on that shelf.*
**2** the strength of sound, loudness: *Turn up the volume on the radio.*
**3** amount of activity: *There is a large volume of traffic on the highways this summer.*

**voluntary** /ˈvɑlənˌtɛri/ *adjective*
done of one's own will without being forced or paid: *She gives money to the church on a voluntary basis, not because she has to.* *–adverb* **voluntarily.**

**volunteer** /ˌvalənˈtɪr/ *verb*
to agree to do something of one's own free will rather than by necessity: *He volunteers his time at the church.*

**volunteer** *noun*
a person who volunteers: *The USA has a military made up of volunteers. –noun* **volunteerism.**

**vomit** /'vamɪt/ *verb*
to have food and liquid from the stomach to go out of the mouth, (*synonym*) to throw up: *The child vomited when he had the flu. –noun* **vomit.**

**vote** /voʊt/ *verb* **voted, voting, votes**
to put "yes" or "no" beside a politician's name or "for" or "against" an idea: *I voted for Franklin Roosevelt for President. See:* cast.

**vote** *noun*
the act of voting for a person or idea: *She has my vote for governor. –noun* (person) **voter.**

**voucher** /'vaʊʧər/ *noun*
an official piece of paper used in place of money: *a travel voucher good for $500 on any airline.*

**vow** /vaʊ/ *verb*
to promise in a very serious way: *He vowed to repay the debt.*

**vowel** /'vaʊəl/ *noun*
in English, the letters a, e, i, o, u, and sometimes y

**voyage** /'vɔɪɪʤ/ *noun*
a long journey: *She took a voyage by boat from London to India. –noun* (person) **voyager; –***verb* **to voyage.**

**vulgar** /'vʌlgər/ *adjective*
unsuitable for polite company, (*synonym*) offensive, crude: *He uses vulgar language and dirty expressions. –verb* **to vulgarize; –***noun* **vulgarity** /vəl'gærəti/.

**vulnerable** /'vʌlnərəbəl/ *adjective*
**1** unprotected: *The soldiers were in a position vulnerable to attack by the enemy.*
**2** likely to be hurt or made to feel bad: *She has been feeling very vulnerable since her husband died. –noun* **vulnerability** /ˌvʌlnərə'bɪləti/.

**vulture** /'vʌlʧər/ *noun*
a type of bird that eats dead animals: *Vultures circled over the dying horse.*

V

# W,w

**W, w** /ˈdʌbəlyu,-yə/ *noun* **W's, w's** or **Ws, ws**
the 23rd letter of the English alphabet

**wade** /weɪd/ *verb* **waded, wading, wades**
to walk by forcing the legs through water or snow: *The hunter waded across the shallow river.*

**waffle** /ˈwɑfəl/ *noun*
a breakfast cake with a pattern of square holes, baked in a special pan called a waffle iron

waffle

**wag** /wæg/ *verb* **wagged, wagging, wags**
to shake back and forth: *A happy dog wags its tail.* –*noun* **wag.**

**wage** /weɪʤ/ *noun*
*usually singular* money paid for work done, usually by the hour: *That company pays a good wage to its workers.*

**wage** *verb* **waged, waging, wages**
to begin and continue (a war or military operation): *Countries waged war often in the 20th century.*

---

**USAGE NOTE:** A *wage* is money paid to an hourly worker, who by law has the right to overtime pay for extra hours worked beyond 40 hours per week. A *salary* is a fixed annual amount paid to a worker in a higher position, who does not get additional pay for extra hours worked. A salary can be paid weekly, every two weeks, or monthly, and often includes paid sick and vacation time.

---

**wager** /ˈweɪʤər/ *verb*
to risk money in games of chance (poker, dice, horse racing, etc.) gamble

**wagon** /ˈwægən/ *noun*
**1** a four-wheeled vehicle usually pulled by horses
**2** a child's cart pulled by a handle *See:* station wagon.

wagon

**wail** /weɪl/ *noun*
a loud crying sound: *the wail of a police siren* –*noun* **wailing;** –*verb* **to wail.**

**waist** /ˈweɪst/ *noun*
the middle section of a person's body: *She must have a small waist; look how small her belt is!*

**waistline** /ˈweɪst,laɪn/ *noun*
the line around a person's waist: *His waistline measures 36 inches (approximately 70 cm).*

**wait** /weɪt/ *verb*
**1** to stay in one place until something happens: *He waited in line to buy a theater ticket.*
**2** to serve food and drinks, to work as a waiter: *He waits (on) tables in a restaurant.*

**to wait up (for someone):** to delay going to bed: *He gets home so late; I am too tired to wait up for him.*

**wait** *noun*
the time spent waiting: *They had a long wait in the doctor's office.*

W

**waiter** /ˈweɪtər/ *noun*
a person who serves food and drinks to earn money: *She works as a waiter in a fancy restaurant. See:* restaurant. *See:* ;art on page 5a.

**waiting room** *noun*
a room where people can sit while waiting for a doctor (train, etc.): *The waiting room in the train station was hot and crowded. See:* art on page 11a.

**waitress** /ˈweɪtrɪs/ *noun, plural* **waitresses**
a woman who serves food and drinks to earn money: *She works as a waitress in a bar. See:* restaurant. *See:* art on page 5a.

**wake** /weɪk/ *verb* **woke** /woʊk/ or **waked** or **woken** /ˈwoʊkən/ or **waked, waking, wakes**
to stop sleeping, to awaken: *I woke (up) this morning at six o'clock.*||*Please don't wake the baby.*

**wake** *noun*
a watch over a dead person's body before burial

**waken** /ˈweɪkən/ *verb*
to wake, awaken: *He wakens early each morning.*

**walk** /wɔk/ *verb*
**1** to move forward by putting one foot in front of the other: *I walk to work each morning.*
**2** to go with: *The nurse walked the patient to the bathroom.*
**to walk on air:** to feel wonderful: *After she won the contest, she walked on air.*
**to walk out (of something): a.** to leave, usually suddenly: *She became so angry that she walked out.* **b.** to stop working in protest: *Workers walked out when their pay was cut.*
**to walk out on someone:** to leave suddenly, (*synonym*) to abandon *The husband walked out on his family one day and never returned. See:* art on page 24a.

**walk** *noun*
**1** exercise by walking: *I go for a walk* (or) *take a walk each morning.*
**2** a path, sidewalk: *The walk leading to the garden is covered with small stones.*

**walkie-talkie** /ˌwɔkiˈtɔki/ *noun*
a two-way radio small enough to carry by hand: *Some police officers use walkie-talkies to speak to each other from a distance.*

**wall** /wɔl/ *noun*
**1** the side of a room or building: *I have many pictures on my bedroom walls.*
**2** a high border between two areas, used to protect, divide, or enclose: *She built a stone wall around her garden.*
**3** a block: *The government met a wall of opposition.*
**4** *informal* **off the wall:** strange: *She's off the wall sometimes and does crazy things. See:* art on page 6a.

**wallet** /ˈwɑlɪt/ *noun*
a small, flat container made of leather that can be folded and put in one's pocket: *He carries cash and credit cards in his wallet. See:* purse.

wallet

**wallpaper** /ˈwɔlˌpeɪpər/ *noun*
paper for covering and decorating the walls of a room: *We are hanging new wallpaper in our dining room.*

**wall plug** *noun*
an electrical outlet: *I hooked the TV up to the wall plug.*

**walnut** /ˈwɔlˌnʌtˌ/ *noun*
**1** a nut
**2** the wood from a walnut tree

**walrus** /ˈwɔlrəs/ *noun, plural* **walruses** or **walrus**
a large sea animal, like a seal, with long teeth called tusks

**waltz** /wɔlts,wɔls/ *noun, plural* **waltzes**
a ballroom dance with a one-two-three beat *–verb* **to waltz.**

**wander** /ˈwɑndər/ *verb*
**1** to go from place to place without a fixed plan or purpose: *The travelers wandered from country to country.*
**2** to move away from a subject or clear idea: *He is old, and his mind wanders at times. –noun* (person) **wanderer.**

**wanna** /ˈwɑnə/ *verb slang*
*short for* want to: *I wanna go to the movies tonight.*

**want** /wɑnt/ *verb*
to desire: *I want to buy some food this morning.*||*The baby wants his mother.*

W

**wanted:** looked for by the police: *The police aren't arresting him; he is wanted only for questioning.*

**want** *noun*
**1** a desire, (*synonym*) a lack. *He has more wants than he can afford.*
**2** a need: *She is poor and in want of basic things like food and clothes.*

---

**USAGE NOTE:** *Would like* is used to ask politely for something that one *wants: I would like to go home now; I'm tired.*

---

**want ad** *noun*
an advertisement for jobs or things for sale: *He reads the want ads, looking for a job.*

**war** /wɔr/ *noun*
fighting with guns and other weapons between groups, armies, nations, etc.: *The war in that country lasted five years.*

**war** *verb* **warred, warring, wars**
to take part in war: *The two sides warred for years and never reached an agreement. –adjective* **warring.** *(antonym)* peace.

**ward** /wɔrd/ *noun*
a part of a hospital: *She is in the women's ward; she just had a baby.*

**-ward** /wərd/*suffix* in the direction of: *Look upward at the clouds.*

**warden** /ˈwɔrdn/ *noun*
the director of a prison

**wardrobe**
/ˈwɔrˌdroʊb/ *noun*
**1** a collection of clothing: *The rich lady has a large wardrobe of shoes, dresses, and coats.*
**2** a piece of furniture that acts as a place to keep clothes

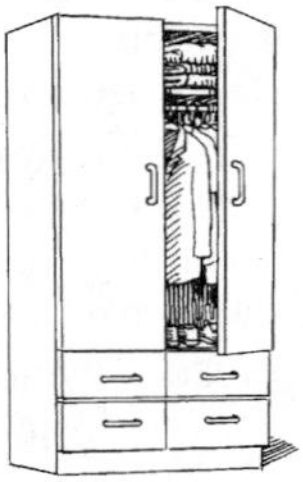
wardrobe

**warehouse**
/ˈwɛrˌhaʊs/ *noun, plural* **warehouses** /-ˌhaʊzɪz/
a building where goods are received, stored, and shipped: *Our warehouse has auto parts in it to sell.*

**warfare** /ˈwɔrˌfɛr/ *noun*
the way a war is fought: *The general knows everything about air warfare of bombers and fighter planes.*

**warm** /wɔrm/ *verb*
to heat, increase the temperature of: *We warmed ourselves near the fire.*

**to warm up someone** or **something:** to heat up: *He warmed up the coffee from earlier that day. See:* warm-up.

**to warm up to someone** or **something:** to grow to like someone or something: *We are warming up to our son-in-law; he's not so bad after all.*

**warm** *adjective*
**1** having heat, but not hot: *I like warm summer days.*
**2** friendly: *Her friends love her for her warm smile. –adverb* **warmly.** *See:* hot. *(antonym)* cold.

---

**USAGE NOTE:** In a range of temperatures, *warm* is between *hot* and *cold.*

---

**warm-blooded** /ˈwɔrmˌblʌdɪd/ *adjective*
with constant high body heat in any temperature: *Humans are warm-blooded, unlike snakes or spiders. See:* cold-blooded

**warmth** /wɔrmθ/ *noun, (no plural)*
**1** the state of being warm, a heated condition: *The warmth of the sun helped her relax.*
**2** friendliness: *Her warmth gives comfort and good feeling to others. (antonym)* coldness.

**warm-up** /ˈwɔrˌmʌp/ *adjective*
exercise done to prepare muscles for physical activity: *I do some warm-up exercises before running.*

**warn** /wɔrn/ *verb*
to tell that danger or trouble is near: *A sign warned us that the road was closed.*

**warning** /ˈwɔrnɪŋ/ *noun*
**1** a danger sign: *The pain in his chest was a warning about a heart attack.*
**2** a statement that something bad might happen: *The boss gave his workers a warning about being late.*

**warped** /wɔrpt/ *adjective*
bent out of shape: *a warped door*

W

**warranty** /ˈwɔrənti/ *noun, plural* **warranties**
a written promise of good quality of a product or service by its maker to replace it or give you your money back if anything is wrong with it: *The manufacturer gives a one-year warranty against any problems with its products. See:* guarantee.

**warrior** /ˈwɔriər/ *noun*
a fighter, soldier

**was** /wʌz/ *verb*
*past tense of* be

**wash** /wɑʃ/ *verb* **washes**
**1** to clean, usually with soap and water: *I washed the dishes this morning.*
**2** to pour over, spread: *Ocean waves washed over the rocks.*
**to wash up:** **a.** to clean oneself: *I am going to the bathroom to wash up.* **b.** to come onto shore: *The storm washed up garbage on the beach.*

**wash** *noun*
things to be cleaned, (*synonym*) the laundry: *I do the wash every Saturday morning.*

**washable** /ˈwɑʃəbəl/ *adjective*
able to be washed by usual methods: *That dress is washable in the washing machine.*

**washcloth** /ˈwɑʃˌklɔθ/ *noun, plural* **washcloths**
a small cloth used for cleaning the body *See:* art on page 23a.

**washer** /ˈwɑʃər/ *noun*
a machine for cleaning clothes, (*synonym*) a washing machine: *I put my dirty clothes in the washer.*

**washing** /ˈwɑʃɪŋ/ *noun, (no plural)*
dirty clothes to be washed, the laundry: *I do the washing once a week.*

**washing machine** *noun*
a machine for cleaning clothes: *I poured soap into the washing machine.*

**Washington's Birthday** /ˈWɑʃiŋtʌnz bɜrθˌdeɪ/ *noun*
February 22, birthday of George Washington, first US President. *See:* Presidents' Day.

**washroom** /ˈwɑʃˌrum/ *noun*
a bathroom: *I am going to the washroom to clean my hands.*

**wasn't**
*contraction of* was not

**wasp** /wɑsp/ *noun*
a flying insect with a narrow body and, in the females, a painful sting *See:* bee.

**waste** /weɪst/ *noun*
**1** a poor use (of effort, time, etc.): *He's too difficult, so dealing with him is a waste of time.*
**2** loss of something through improper use: *I had to throw away the extra spaghetti. What a waste of good food!*
**3** things that are not wanted and get thrown away, garbage: *Large trucks pick up household waste.*
**4** liquids or solids from the body: *Waste goes into toilets and is washed away.*
**to go to waste:** (of something good and useful) to not be used: *We cooked too much food for the party, and some of it will go to waste.*

**waste** *verb* **wasted, wasting, wastes**
**1** to make poor use of something valuable: *The builder wasted wood by ordering too much.*
**2** *slang* to kill
**to waste away:** to die slowly: *She has cancer and is slowly wasting away.* *–adjective* **waste, wasteful;** *–adverb* **wastefully;** *–noun* **wastefulness.** *(antonym)* save.

**wastebasket** /ˈweɪstˌbæskɪt/ *noun*
a container (barrel, bucket, basket, etc.) for unwanted items: *I throw old papers in the wastebasket.*

**wasteland** /ˈweɪstˌlænd/ *noun*
a place where nothing will grow or with no useful purpose: *The desert outside the village is wasteland.*

**wastepaper** /ˈweɪstˌpeɪpər/ *noun*
old or useless paper: *Offices have a lot of wastepaper from people's computer printers.*

**watch** /wɑʧ/ *verb* **watches**
**1** to look at: *The mother watched her children play.*
**2** to guard: *A guard watches prisoners.*
**to watch for:** to expect and look for: *The man watched for his bus to arrive.*

**to watch out (for someone** or **something):** to be aware of danger, be careful: *I told my son to watch out for ice on the road ahead.*

**watch** *noun, plural* **watches**
a small clock worn on the wrist: *I looked at my watch to see if I was late.*

**to keep watch:** a state of continuous attention or close observation: *The police kept a watch on the house to catch a criminal who lives there.* *–noun* (person) **watcher.**

**watchdog** /'waʧ,dɔg/ *noun*
a guard dog: *Two watchdogs guard the store at night.*

**watchful** /'waʧfəl/ *adjective*
always watching or looking: *The boy's mother keeps a watchful eye on him as he plays.* *–adverb* **watchfully;** *–noun* **watchfulness.**

**watchman** /'waʧmən/ *noun, plural* **watchmen** /-mən/
a security guard: *The night watchman checks on the building every hour.*

**water** /'wɔtər/ *noun*
**1** a colorless liquid that is necessary for life: *Most of the earth's surface is covered with water.*
**2** any body of water, such as a stream, lake, or ocean: *We like to vacation at the water.*
**3** *plural* **waters:** the sea near a country: *We fished in Canadian waters.*

**in hot water:** in trouble: *He's in hot water with the boss.*

**water** *verb*
to pour water on: *She waters the plants every day.*

**water buffalo** *noun, plural* **buffaloes** or **buffalo**
a large Asian animal with horns, often used to pull farm equipment

**water cooler** *noun*
a machine that keeps water cool and ready to drink in an office

**waterfall** /'wɔtər,fɔl/ *noun*
water falling from a high place: *Niagara Falls is a huge waterfall between New York and Canada.*

**water fountain** *noun*
a machine that gives cold water to drink in public places

**waterfront** /'wɔt ər,frʌnt/ *noun*
land that borders a body of water (sometimes with warehouses and docks): *The ships unloaded fish on the waterfront.*

**water lilly** *noun, plural* **lilies**
a water plant with pink or white folowers and large, floating leaves: *Water lilies covered the surface of the pond.*

water lilly

**water main** *noun*
a large underground pipe carrying drinking water: *The water main broke, and no water came into the house.*

**watermelon** /'wɔtər,mɛlən/ *noun*
a large, green, oval-shaped fruit with a sweet, juicy, pink interior *See:* art on page 3a.

watermelon

**water meter** *noun*
a machine for measuring the amount of water used in a house or building

**water pipe** *noun*
a metal or plastic tube used to move water from one place to another: *The hot-water pipe in the kitchen has a leak.*

**waterproof** /'wɔtər,pruf/ *verb*
to make something so water will not enter it: *Shoemakers waterproof boots to keep your feet dry.*

**waterproof** *adjective*
made so that water cannot pass through: *I can wear my watch when I swim because it is waterproof.* *–noun* **waterproofing.**

**water supply** *noun, plural* **supplies**
a central system that provides water, especially to homes, towns, and cities: *The city water supply comes from special ponds called reservoirs, in the country.*

**waterway** /'wɔtər,weɪ/ *noun*
a river, or other water passage

**watery** /'wɔtəri/ *adjective*
having or containing a lot of water: *Don't plant corn in that field; it's too watery.*||*The soup is watery and tasteless.*

**watt** /wɑt/ *noun*
a unit of measurement of electrical power: *My desk lamp uses a 60-watt light bulb.* –*noun* **wattage** /ˈwɑtɪʤ /.

**wave** /weɪv/ *verb* **waved, waving, waves**
**1** to move softly back and forth: *Flags waved in the wind.*
**2** to communicate with someone by raising and moving the hand: *She waved good-bye to her husband.*

wave

**3** to curl: *The hairdresser waved the woman's hair.*

**wave** *noun*
**1** a sign of greeting made by raising and moving the hand: *He gave me a wave of hello.*
**2** a long high mass of water moving across the surface of the sea: *The waves on the ocean are high today.*
**3** an electronic, light, or sound movement of energy: *Radio waves bring us music and news.*
**4** a sudden increase in an activity or a condition: *a crime wave*‖*a heat wave*

**wavy** /ˈweɪvi/ *adjective* **wavier, waviest**
having waves: *She has wavy hair.* –*noun* **waviness.**

**wax** /wæks/ *noun*
a soft, flexible, slightly greasy substance used in candles, furniture, and car polish, etc.: *Some wax comes from bees.*

**wax** *verb* **waxes**
to apply wax or polish to: *I waxed the table this morning.* –*adjective* **waxy.**

**way** /weɪ/ *noun*
**1** a method, manner, style: *One way to travel is by air.*‖*She speaks to people in a friendly way.*
**2** a direction: *Go that way, then to the right, and you will see the store.*
**3** a distance: *That store is a long way from here.*
**4** a path or road: *The way through the garden is covered with small stones.*
**5** the space or opening for a course of action: *The way is clear for our two companies to join together.*
**6** a manner or condition of living: *He is poor and in a bad way.*
**7** everyday habits, (*synonym*) customs: *We travel to other countries to learn the ways of other peoples.*‖*our way of life*

**by the way:** an expression used to change the subject in a conversation: *Oh, by the way, do you have my new address?*

**in** or **out of the way:** in or out of a position that blocks traffic or keeps people from passing: *The men stood in the way and would not let us enter the building.*

**no way:** an expression of strong disagreement or disapproval: *"Are you going out in this rain?" "No way."*‖*"No way am I going to lend him money."*

**to pay one's own way:** to pay one's expenses instead of depending on others: *My friend and I went on vacation, and we each paid our own way.*

**under way:** in progress: *The concert got under way at seven o'clock.*

**-way** *suffix*
**1** direction: *a one-way street*
**2** participant: *We made it a three-way partnership.*

**way** *adverb informal*
very, a lot: *We could see the birds in the sky way up high.*

**we** /wi/ *pronoun*
first person plural used by a speaker or writer to refer to himself or herself and one or more others: *We eat dinner together every evening.*

**weak** /wik/ *adjective*
**1** not physically strong: *The patient is losing blood and becoming weak.*
**2** not strong in character: *A weak leader doesn't have control of the situation.*

**weaken** /ˈwikən/ *verb*
to make or become less strong: *The sick lady weakens each day.*

**weakness** /ˈwiknɪs/ *noun*, *plural* **weaknesses**
**1** lack of strength: *The patient is suffering from weakness after the operation.*
**2** a desire for something that is not stopped easily: *She has a weakness for chocolate.*

**wealth** /wɛlθ/ *noun, (no plural)*
**1** a large amount of money and property: *They are a family of great wealth.*
**2** a large number or amount: *a wealth of*

*information* –*adjective* **wealthy;** –*noun* **wealthiness.** *(antonym)* poverty.

**weapon** /ˈwɛpən/ *noun*
a tool used to harm or kill: *Knives and guns are dangerous weapons.* –*noun* **weaponry** /ˈwɛpənri/.

**wear** /wɛr/ *verb* **wore** /wɔr/ or **worn** /wɔrn/, **wearing, wears**
**1** to have on one's body, such as clothes, glasses, or jewelry: *He wears suits to work.*
**2** to get smaller or lose quality through use: *The tires on my car are worn down.*
**3** to last a long time: *My heavy winter coat has worn well for five years.*
**4** to have as an expression on the face: *My father wore a smile when we arrived.*
**to wear off: a.** to lose effect: *The pain medication wore off after the operation.* **b.** to lose color, shine, etc., by rubbing, time, etc.: *Her lipstick wore off by noon.*
**to wear someone** or **something out: a. someone:** to tire: *He wore out his family with his complaining.* **b. something:** to make useless through use, use up: *I wear out a pair of shoes every six months.* –*adjective* **wearable.**

**weary** /ˈwɪri/ *adjective* **wearier, weariest**
**1** tired, without energy to do things: *She is weary from so much work.*
**2** having little patience, bored: *He is weary of arguing with you all the time.* –*adverb* **wearily;** –*noun* **weariness.**

**weasel** /ˈwizəl/ *noun*
a small, brown and white meat-eating animal: *Weasels sometimes eat chickens on farms.*

**weather** /ˈwɛðər/ *noun, (no plural)*
the conditions of the sky and air relating to rain, snow, heat, cold, etc.: *In good weather, we go outside.* –*verb* **to weather.**

**weather forecast** *noun*
a description of expected weather conditions: *She listens to the weather forecast on the radio each morning.* –*noun* (person) **weather forecaster.**

**weatherman** /ˈwɛðərmæn/ *noun, plural* **weathermen** /ˈwɛðərmɛn/ *See:* meteorologist.

**weather vane**
*noun*
a pointer on the top of a building, usually a barn, that shows wind direction

weather vane

**weave** /wiv/ *verb* **wove** /woʊv/or **woven** /ˈwoʊvən/, **weaving, weaves**
to make fabric by crossing threads or other material over and under one another: *My grandmother wove rugs from old pieces of cloth.*

**weave** *noun*
the pattern formed by the way a fabric is woven: *That cloth is made of a fine weave.* –*noun* (person) **weaver, weaving.** *See:* woven.

**web** /wɛb/ *noun*
a net of thin threads formed by a spider: *We could see a fly caught in the spider web.*

web

**we'd** /wid/
*contraction of* we had *or* we would

**wed** /wɛd/ *verb formal* **wedded** or **wed, wedding, weds**
to marry: *We wed and became husband and wife.*

**wedding** /ˈwɛdɪŋ/ *noun*
a marriage ceremony: *The wedding took place in a church.*

**wedge** /wɛʤ/ *noun*
a V-shaped piece of metal, wood, etc. used to separate two parts -*verb* **wedge.**

**wedlock** /ˈwɛdˌlɑk/ *noun formal*
a state of being legally married
**out of wedlock:** not legally married: *The child was born to a couple out of wedlock.*

**Wednesday** /ˈwɛnzdeɪ/ *noun*
the third day of the week, between Tuesday and Thursday

**weed** /wid/ *noun*
a wild plant that is not wanted in grass or garden: *My garden has more weeds than flowers.* –*adjective* **weedy.**

**week** /wik/ *noun*
**1** the seven-day period from Sunday through Saturday: *There are 52 weeks in the year.*
**2** seven days: *I'll see you one week from today.*

**weekday** /ˈwik͵deɪ/ *noun*
Monday, Tuesday, Wednesday, Thursday, or Friday are weekdays

**weekend** /ˈwik͵ɛnd/ *noun*
Saturday and Sunday: *I play sports on the weekend.*

**weekly** /ˈwikli/ *adjective*
happening once a week or every week: *This is a weekly newspaper.*

**weep** /wip/ *verb formal*
to cry: *The wife wept at her husband's funeral. –adjective* **weepy.**

**weigh** /weɪ/ *verb*
**1** to measure how heavy something is: *I weighed myself this morning.*
**2** to have a certain weight: *The apples weighed one pound.*

**weight** /weɪt/ *noun*
**1** the measure of how heavy something or someone is: *His weight is 220 lbs. (100 kilos).*
**2** a heavy object: *Some people lift weights for exercise.*
**3** *figurative* a responsibility that causes worry: *His mother's sickness is a weight on his mind. –adjective* **weighty.**

**weird** /wɪrd/ *adjective*
strange, (*synonym*) odd: *Sometimes we hear weird noises that sound like crying in the night. –adverb* **weirdly;** *–noun* **weirdness.**

**welcome** /ˈwɛlkəm/ *verb* **welcomed, welcoming, welcomes**
**1** to greet in a friendly way when someone arrives: *The woman giving the party welcomed her friends at the door.*
**2** to accept happily or with thanks: *He welcomed the idea of taking a vacation.*

**welcome** *noun*
a friendly greeting: *My friend shouted a welcome to me as I approached his house.*

**welcome** *adjective*
a polite response to "thank you": *"Thank you for the money." "You're welcome."*

**weld** /wɛld/ *verb*
to join metal things by melting them some and putting them together: *A worker welded steel pieces together for the new building. –noun* (person) **welder, welding.**

**welfare** /ˈwɛl͵fɛr/ *noun*
**1** one's general condition: *The mother is concerned about her son's welfare.*
**2** money from the government for food, housing, health services, etc.: *He lost his job and is now on welfare.*

---

**USAGE NOTE:** *Welfare* is an American governmental system that includes services such as unemployment compensation (money), food stamps, and housing assistance to the poor.

---

**well (1)** /wɛl/ *adverb* **better** /ˈbɛtər/, **best** /bɛst/
**1** in a good way: *She performs well as an actress.*
**2** very much: *He finished the exam well before the exam period ended.*
**as well as:** in addition to: *She has a dog as well as two cats.*
**well done:** I approve, congratulations: *You won the race. Well done! See:* well-done.

**well** *adjective*
in good health: *I hope you are well.*

**well** *interjection*
an expression to show surprise, doubt, etc.: *Well! That's an interesting idea!*

**well (2)** *noun*
a hole made in the ground (for water, oil, etc.): *Please fill this bucket from the water well.*

well

**we'll**
*contraction of* we will

**well-done** *adjective*
**1** skillfully done, excellent: *His test was well-done, so he got a good grade.*
**2** cooked thoroughly: *She likes her meat well-done.*

**well-known** *adjective*
**1** famous: *He is a well-known television actor.*
**2** part of common knowledge, widely

known: *It is a well-known fact that there are many rich people in our cities.*

**well-to-do** *adjective*
rich: *That well-to-do family lives in a big house with a swimming pool.*

**went** *verb*
*past tense of* go: *I went to work yesterday.*

**wept** /wɛpt/ *verb*
*past tense and past participle of* weep

**were** /wɜr/ *verb plural*
*past tense of* be

**we're** /wɪr/
*contraction of* we are

**weren't** /wɪrnt/
*contraction of* we are not

**west** /wɛst/ *noun*
**1** the direction in which the sun goes down at night
**2** the western part of a country: *California is in the west of the USA.*
**the West:** the western part of the world, especially Western Europe, the USA, and Canada
**the Wild West:** the western part of the USA during the 19th century: *In the Wild West, there was little law and order.*
**west** *adverb*
moving toward the west: *We are driving west on the main highway.*
**west** *adjective*
**1** located in the west: *We live on the west side of the park.*
**2** coming from the west: *a west wind*

**Western** /ˈwɛstərn/ *adjective*
of or belonging to the west: *Western clothes include cowboy hats and boots.*
**Western** *noun*
a story, movie, etc. about cowboys, Native Americans, etc. in the western USA: *The old Westerns are still popular movies today.*

**Westerner** /ˈwɛstərnər/ *noun*
someone from or living in the western part of a country: *He is a Westerner from Los Angeles.*

**Western hemisphere** *noun*
the half of the earth that includes North and South America

**wet** /wɛt/ *adjective* **wetter, wettest**
covered with or full of water or another liquid: *The ground is wet from today's rain. (antonym)* dry.
**to be all wet:** to be wrong, mistaken: *He's all wet; he doesn't know what he's talking about.*
**wet** *verb* **wet** or **wetted, wetting, wets**
to cover or fill with water: *We wet the dry ground with water. –noun* **wetness.**

**wetland** /ˈwɛtˌlænd/ or **wetlands** /ˈwɛtˌlændz/ *noun*
a watery area: *Wetlands near the ocean were made into a park to protect the birds.*

**wet suit** *noun*
a thick, waterproof body suit worn by swimmers and divers to keep warm in the water: *We put on wet suits and jumped into the cold ocean.*

**we've** /wiv/
*contraction of* we have

**whale** /weɪl/ *noun*
a very large animal shaped like a fish and found in the ocean: *The blue whale may reach 100 feet in length (25 m). See:* art on page 14a.

**whaling** /ˈweɪlɪŋ/ *noun*
the business of hunting and killing whales for their oil, bone, etc.: *Whaling is still done in some countries. –noun* (person or ship) **whaler.**

**wharf** /wɔrf/ *noun, plural* **wharves** /wɔrvz/ or **wharfs**
a long platform built over the water, where ships can pull up to load or unload: *Boats sailed up to the wharf, and the passengers got off. See:* dock; pier.

**what** /wʌt/ *pronoun*
**1** used in a question to get information about something: *What did you say?*||*What is your name?*
**2** used to show surprise, alarm: *What a terrible thing to have happen!*
**3** the thing or things that: *The teacher told the students what to do.*
**What do you do?:** What is your job, profession, etc.?
**What . . . for?:** why, for what reason: *What did you do that for?*||*"I'm going home." "What for?"*
**What if?:** What will happen if, supposing that: *What if we are wrong?*

**what it takes:** the necessary ability: *He has what it takes to succeed in business.*
**What's up?:** what is happening?: *What's up? You are holding your arm; did you hurt yourself?*
**what** *adjective*
(used in a question to get information about something): *What color is your car?*
**what** *interjection*
(used to show surprise, alarm): *"He broke his leg." "What!"*

---

**USAGE NOTE:** If you did not hear someone or would like to have something repeated, it is polite to say "Pardon me," "Excuse me," or "Would you please repeat what you said?" rather than just *"What?"*

---

**whatever** /wət'ɛvər/ *pronoun*
no matter what: *Whatever you decide, we need to leave soon.*

**wheat** /wit/ *noun*
a plant or grain usually made into flour to make bread, cake, pasta, etc.: *Wheat is a major food source, eaten throughout the world for 7,000 years.*

**wheel** /wil/ *noun*
a round piece of metal, rubber, wood, etc. allowing something to turn and roll: *Cars have four wheels; bicycles have two.* *–verb* **to wheel.**

**wheelbarrow** /'wil,bærou/ *noun*
a small cart with one wheel and handles for pushing, used to move small loads: *Gardeners put dirt into a wheelbarrow to move it across the garden.*

**wheelchair** /'wil,ʧɛr/ *noun*
a chair with wheels, used by a person who cannot walk: *He was angry when he couldn't get his wheelchair into the office building.* *See:* art on page 11a.

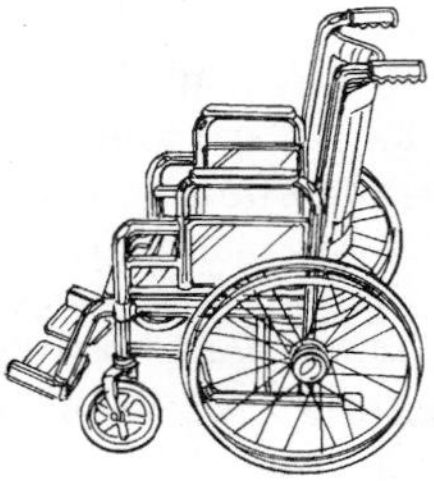
wheelchair

**when** /wɛn/ *adverb*
at what time: *When do you think that he will arrive?*

**when** *conjunction*
**1** at the time that: *It started to rain when we left the house.*
**2** considering that, although: *Why does he smoke when he knows it is so unhealthy?*
**3** immediately after, as soon as: *Please call us when you arrive.*

**whenever** /wɛ'nɛvər/ *conjunction*
at whatever time: *The roof leaks whenever it rains.*

**where** /wɛr;/ *adverb*
**1** at which place: *Where have you been for the last week?*
**2** to what place: *Where did you go after school?*
**where** *pronoun*
what place: *Where do they come from?*
**where** *conjunction*
**1** in which place: *He went to Dallas, where his parents live.*
**2** to which place: *I don't like the restaurant where we're going.*

**whereabouts** /'wɛrə,bauts/ *noun, plural*
a place where someone is: *His whereabouts are unknown.*

**whereas** /wɛr'æz/ *conjunction formal*
but, in fact: *He says that he paid me, whereas I have not received money from him.*

**wherever** /wɛr'ɛvər/ *adverb*
at or to any place: *We can eat wherever you would like to.*||*Wherever did you get that idea?*

**whether** /'wɛðər / *conjunction*
**1** if (shows choice): *Please tell me whether (or not) you want to go to the party.*
**2** no matter if (shows it is not important what one chooses or decides): *Whether you stay at home or come with me, I'm going to the party.*

---

**USAGE NOTE:** It is not necessary to use *or not* after whether: *I don't know whether to go out tonight since it's raining so hard.*

---

**which** /wɪʧ/ *adjective*
(used in questions) what one or ones in a group of people or things: *Which day is better for us to meet, Monday or Tuesday?*||*Which children in the class were absent?*

**which** *pronoun*
**1** (used in questions) what one or ones in a group of people or things: *Which of the movies did you like best?*
**2** (used to show the object or objects one is referring to): *This is the car (which* or *that) I want to buy.*
**3** (used to give more information about an object, objects, or the first part of the sentence): *This ring, which my brother gave me, is made of gold.*

**while** /waɪl/ *conjunction*
**1** at that time, during: *While you were away, the weather was terrible.*
**2** although: *While I do not agree with what you say, I understand your reasons for saying it.*

**while** *noun*
a short amount of time: *Let's stay for a while, then go home.*

**whim** /wɪm/ *noun*
a sudden desire, especially an unreasonable one: *She felt a whim for a new hat.*

**whine** /waɪn/ *verb* **whined, whining, whines**
**1** to give a long, soft, high cry: *The dog whined from pain.*
**2** to complain: *The child whined for more candy after her mother took it away.* –*noun* **whine.**

**whip** /wɪp/ *noun*
a long piece of rope or leather held in the hand, used to hit an animal or person: *Horse riders use whips to make their horses run faster.*

**whip** *verb* **whipped, whipping, whips**
**1** to hit with a whip
**2** to defeat badly or by a large amount: *Our team whipped our opponent by a score of 56 to 0.*

**whirlpool** /ˈwɜrlˌpul/ *noun*
water moving quickly in a circle: *Water forms a whirlpool as it runs down the drain of a sink.*

**whisker** /ˈwɪskər/ *noun*
**1** a long hair that grows near the mouth of some animals: *cat's whiskers*
**2** *plural* short hair on a man's face: *He shaves his whiskers every morning.*

**whiskey** /ˈwɪski/ *noun, (no plural)*
an alcoholic drink made from grain: *I ordered beer, and she ordered whiskey.*

**whisper** /ˈwɪspər/ *noun*
soft, quiet talking: *She didn't want the others to hear, so she spoke in a whisper.*

**whisper** *verb*
to speak in a soft, quiet voice: *She whispered secrets in his ear. (antonym)* shout.

**whistle** /ˈwɪsəl/ *noun*
**1** a musical sound made by blowing air through the lips: *We could hear the woman's happy whistle.*
**2** a loud sound: *a train whistle*
**3** a small pipe or instrument that makes a whistle –*verb* **to whistle.**

**white** /waɪt/ *noun*
**1** the lightest of all colors: *White is the color of snow and milk.*
**2** a person of a light-skinned race: *Many blacks and whites live in that neighborhood.*

**white** *adjective* **whiter, whitest**
**1** having a white color: *He wears white shirts to work.*
**2** of a light-skinned race, the white race –*verb* **to whiten.** *See:* art on page 16a. *(antonym)* black.

**white-collar** *adjective*
professional or working in an office: *I got a white-collar job as a computer programmer. See:* blue-collar.

**White House** *noun*
**1** in the USA, the President's house in Washington, D.C.: *Tourists can visit parts of the White House.*
**2** a symbol of the US government and its President

White House

**whitewash** /ˈwaɪtˌwɑʃ/ *noun*
a type of white paint: *A boy spread whitewash on the fence to make it look new.* –*verb* **to whitewash.**

**whittle** /ˈwɪtl/ *verb* **whittled, whittling, whittles**
to cut off small pieces (of wood) with a knife: *He whittles small toys for his sons.* –*noun* (person) **whittler,** (act) **whittling.**

**whiz** or **whizz** *noun, plural* **whizzes**
**1** a sound of fast motion

**2** a very smart and capable person: *She is a whiz in math.* *–verb* **to whiz.**

**who** /hu/ *pronoun*
**1** what or which person: *Who are you?*||*Who was that black-haired man?*
**2** the person or persons that: *I am the woman who just telephoned you.*
**3** used to give more information about a person or persons: *My sisters, who live in Denver, are coming to visit next week.*

---

**USAGE NOTE:** *Who* replaces *he, she, it,* or *they* in a sentence or question. *Who* agrees with the subject in number: *Who is that guy? Who are your friends? Whom* replaces the object of an action in a sentence or question: *I gave the book to her. To whom did you give the book? That is the woman to whom I gave the book.*

---

**whoa** /woʊ/
*exclamation* used to stop a horse

**who'd** /hud/*contraction of*
**1** who had
**2** who would

**whoever** /hu'ɛvər/ *pronoun*
any person that, no matter who: *Whoever arrives first unlocks the door.*

**whole** /hoʊl/ *adjective*
complete, all of something: *We ate the whole pie for dessert.* *–noun* **whole.**

**wholesale** /'hoʊl,seɪl/ *noun, (no plural)*
related to selling things in large amounts, and usually at lower prices, to stores and businesses: *Our company buys its office supplies wholesale.* *–noun* (business) **wholesaler.**

**wholesome** /'hoʊlsəm/ *adjective*
good for one's health, healthy: *Our family eats wholesome food, such as fresh fruits and vegetables.* *–noun* **wholesomeness.**

**who'll** /hul/
*contraction of* who will

**whom** /hum/ *pronoun formal*
a form of *who* used as the object of a verb or preposition: *She is the person to whom I have sent the letter.*||*He is a man whom we like. See:* who, USAGE NOTE.

**whoop** /hup/ *verb*
to let out a shout (of joy, surprise, etc.): *She whooped for joy.*
**to whoop it up:** to have fun and make a lot of noise: *We had a party and whooped it up all night.*

**who's** /huz/*contraction of*
**1** who is
**2** who has

**whose** /huz/ *pronoun and adjective*
possessive form of *who,* of which person?: *Whose coat is that?*||*Whose are these shoes?*

**why** /waɪ/ *adverb*
for what reason (need, cause, purpose, etc.): *Why are you crying?*||*I don't know why he is not here.*

**wicked** /'wɪkɪd/ *adjective*
very bad, evil: *A wicked man took the child from his parents.* *–noun* **wickedness.**

**wide** /waɪd/ *adjective* **wider, widest**
**1** related to the distance from side to side: *That table is three feet (9.2 m) wide.*
**2** with a great distance from side to side: *A long bridge crossed the wide river.*
**3** large: *She can play a wide range of musical instruments: the piano, guitar, and trumpet.* *–adverb* **widely;** *–noun* **wideness.** *(antonym)* narrow.

**wide** *adverb*
completely, fully: *wide-open*||*wide-awake*

**-wide** *suffix* going over or all through an area: *The President has a nationwide duty to the people.*

**widen** /'waɪdn/ *verb*
**1** to make wider, (*synonym*) to broaden: *Workers widened the road so more cars could pass. (antonym)* narrow.
**2** to make greater: *He widened his knowledge of the company by visiting all its offices.*

**widespread** /,waɪd'sprɛd/ *adjective*
covering a large area: *The forest fires were widespread through the mountains.*

**widow** /'wɪdoʊ/ *noun*
a wife whose husband has died

**widower** /'wɪdoʊər/ *noun*
a husband whose wife has died

**width** /wɪdθ/ *noun*
the distance across something: *The width of the floor is 12 feet (3.3 m).*

**wife** /waɪf/ *noun, plural* **wives** /waɪvz/
a woman who is married: *His wife is very busy; she has a job.* –*adjective* **wifely.** *See:* husband. *See:* art on page 13a.

**wig** /wɪg/ *noun*
a head covering made of false or human hair: *The actor wears a gray wig to look like an older man in the play.*

**wiggle** /ˈwɪgəl/ *noun*
a quick twisting and turning movement, usually from side to side: *The key was stuck, so he gave it a wiggle and it came out.* –*adjective* **wiggily;** –*verb* **to wiggle.**

**wigwam** /ˈwɪgˌwɑm/ *noun*
a kind of tent made of wood and covered with natural materials, used by Native Americans

wigwam

**wild** /waɪld/ *adjective*
**1** related to living in nature, not grown or cared for by humans: *Wild strawberries grow in the field behind my house.*
**2** exciting, unruly: *The college students had a wild time at the New Year's party.*
**3** misbehaving: *Her children are wild; they scream and run around all the time.*
**to be wild about:** to like very much: *She is wild about chocolate cake.* (*antonym*) tame.

**wild** *adverb*
**to go wild:** to act badly, out of control
**to run wild:** to live freely in nature: *Horses run wild in the hills of Wyoming.*

**wild** *noun* or *noun plural*
area away from people, towns, and cities: *I went on a trip in the wilds of Africa.*

**wildcat** /ˈwaɪldˌkæt/ *noun*
a small or medium-sized wild cat, such as the bobcat or lynx

**wilderness** /ˈwɪl dərnɪs/ *noun*
land in its natural state, especially a large area unspoiled by humans: *Wilderness is protected in many of our national parks.*

**wildflower** /ˈwaɪldˌflaʊər/ *noun*
a flower that grows without being cared for by humans: *In the spring, we pick wildflowers and put them in a basket on the table.*

**wildlife** /ˈwaɪldˌlaɪf/ *noun, (no plural)*
animals living in their natural setting: *There is much wildlife in the forests of Maine.*

**will (1)** /wɪl/ *auxiliary verb*
**1** (used to show future action): *I will see you at noon tomorrow.*
**2** (used to ask someone to do something) would, could: *Will you please pass the bread?*
**3** to be willing or ready to: *Please come in; the doctor will see you now.*
**4** (used to say what might happen in the future): *You will be sorry later if you quit school now.*
**5** (used to show what something can do): *This cake will serve 16 people.*

**will (2)** /wɪl/ *verb*
**1** to influence or control by the power of one's mind: *We didn't want rain, so we tried to will the clouds away.*
**2** to give (money or property) in one's will: *She willed her house and all she owned to her son.*

**will** *noun*
**1** the strength of the mind to control one's actions: *He has a very strong will; when he decides to do something, nothing can stop him.*
**2** a legal document that tells who will receive someone's money and property when that person dies: *My mother left me a gold watch in her will.*

**-willed** /wɪld/ *suffix* related to a person's desires or strengths: *He is a strong-willed man; he never changes his mind.*

**willful** or **wilful** /ˈwɪlfəl/ *adjective*
always wanting to have one's way: *He is a willful man who won't let anyone help him drive.* –*adverb* **willfully;** –*noun* **willfulness.**

**willing** /ˈwɪlɪŋ/ *adjective*
ready (to do something), (*synonym*) agreeable: *He is willing to help us paint the kitchen.* –*adverb* **willingly;** –*noun* **willingness.**

**willow** /ˈwɪloʊ/ *noun*
a tree with narrow leaves *See:* art on page 1a.

**willpower** /wɪlpaʊər/ *noun*
inner strength to do something difficult: *It takes willpower to stop smoking.*

**win** /wɪn/ *verb* **won** /wʌn/, **winning, wins**
**1** (in games) to make more points than another person or team, beat: *We won our tennis match today.*
**2** to get: *Our company won a contract to build offices for the government. (antonym)* lose.

**wind (1)** /wɪnd/ *noun*
**1** the natural movement of air outdoors: *The wind is strong, so the leaves are falling quickly.*
**2** breath, the power of breathing: *She had the wind knocked out of her when she fell.*

**wind (2)** /waɪnd/ *verb* **wound** /waʊnd/, **winding, winds**
**1** to wrap something around: *I wind string around packages before I mail them.*
**2** to turn and tighten: *You can wind a clock or a watch.*
**3** to curve, twist: *Roads wound through the hills.*
**to wind down:** to get slower, to decrease
**to wind something up:** **a.** to turn and tighten: *I wind up the grandfather clock once a week.* **b.** to finally arrive: *We got lost and wound up being two hours late. –adjective* **winding.**

**windmill** /ˈwɪndˌmɪl/ *noun*
a machine or building that gets its power from the wind turning its blades *See:* mill.

windmill

**window** /ˈwɪndoʊ/ *noun*
**1** an opening in a building, usually covered with glass: *Windows allow sunlight and air into buildings. See:* art on page 6a.
**2** a square place on a computer screen where information is shown: *Some computers can have several windows open at the same time.*

**window shade** *noun*
a window covering, such as a curtain or Venetian blind: *I pull down the window shades to keep out the afternoon sun. See:* art on page 6a.

**windshield** /ˈwɪndˌʃild/ *noun*
the glass across the front of a car that protects the driver and passengers from the wind: *The windshield on my car is dirty.*

**windshield wiper** *noun*
a thin rubber blade on a metal rod that clears a vehicle's windshield of rain, snow, and dirt

**windy** /ˈwɪndi/ *adjective* **windier, windiest**
with a lot of wind: *It is windy today, so hold on to your hat. –noun* **windiness.**

**wine** /waɪn/ *noun*
an alcoholic drink made from fruit, especially grapes: *We drink red wine with dinner every evening.*

**winery** /ˈwaɪnəri/ *noun, plural* **wineries**
a place where wine is made: *We took a tour of Spanish wineries.*

**wing** /wɪŋ/ *noun*
the part of a bird, insect, or airplane that helps it fly: *The bird had a broken wing and couldn't fly.*
**to take someone under one's wing:** to help or protect someone: *The dance teacher takes young dancers under her wing. –verb* **to wing.**

**wink** /wɪŋk/ *verb*
to close and open one eye quickly: *She winked and smiled at a guy she liked.*

**winner** /ˈwɪnər/ *noun*
**1** a person or team who gets more points or beats another: *She is the winner of the tennis match.*
**2** a good, fun, or successful thing: *That new TV show is a real winner. –noun* (act) **winning.** *(antonym)* loser.

**winter** /ˈwɪntər/ *noun*
the cold season between fall and spring: *The winters in the north are very cold.*

**wintry** /ˈwɪntri/ *adjective*
cold, snowy: *We are having wintry weather this week with snow and cold winds.*

**wipe** /waɪp/ *verb* **wiped, wiping, wipes**
to rub away (unwanted dirt, water, tears, etc.): *A waiter wiped the table clean with a cloth. –noun* (action) **wipe.**

**to wipe out:** to destroy, ruin: *The heavy rain wiped out the farmers' wheat crop.*

**wiper** /ˈwaɪpər/ *noun*
something used to wipe, especially a device for wiping a vehicle's windshield: *I always use the wipers when it rains.*

**wire** /waɪr/ *noun*
metal in the form of a thin string or of several strings twisted together: *Most metal fences are made of wire.*‖*A wire in my stereo is broken.* –*noun* **wiring.**

**wire** *verb* **wired, wiring, wires**
**1** to put electrical wire into buildings and machines: *Workers wired the house for electricity.*
**2** to send by means of a telephone or cable: *I wired money to my daughter in San Francisco.*

**wiretap** /ˈwaɪrˌtæp/ *noun*
a listening tool placed secretly on a telephone: *The FBI placed a wiretap inside each telephone.* –*verb* **to wire tap.**

**wisdom** /ˈwɪzdəm/ *noun, (no plural)*
**1** good sense learned from experience: *He is an old man of great wisdom.*
**2** knowledge, understanding: *There is much wisdom in religious writings.* *(antonym)* ignorance.

**wise** /waɪz/ *adjective* **wiser, wisest**
showing good judgment based on experience: *Taking care of your health is the wise thing to do.* –*adverb* **wisely.** *(antonym)* foolish.

**wish** /wɪʃ/ *verb* **wishes**
**1** to desire, want: *He wished that his girlfriend would marry him.*
**2** to express hope for something: *I wish you a happy birthday.*

**wish** *noun, plural* **wishes**
a desire, a want: *Marrying her is his fondest wish.* –*adjective* **wishful.**

**wit** /wɪt/ *noun*
**1** intelligence: *She has a sharp wit and understands quickly. See:* witty.
**2** an intelligent and amusing person: *She is a wit who writes funny plays.*

**witch** /wɪʧ/ *noun, plural* **witches**
a woman who practices magic: *Many people do not believe in witches and their magical powers.* –*noun* **witchcraft.**

**with** /wɪð/ *preposition*
**1** in the company of: *I will go with you to the zoo.*
**2** having, showing: *He wants a car with four doors.*
**3** by means of, using: *He ate the cake with a fork.*
**4** in support of: *Are you with us or against us?*
**5** in the same direction: *The car went with the traffic.*
**6** concerning: *My boss is very patient with me.*
**7** in spite of, despite: *With all his success, he was still not happy.*
**8** as a result of: *shaking with laughter*‖*eyes wet with tears*

**with it:** aware, up-to-date: *For an 80-year-old woman, she is really with it.*

**withdraw** /wɪðˈdrɔ/ *verb* **withdrew** /-ˈdru/ or **withdrawn** /-ˈdrɔn/, **withdrawing, withdraws**
**1** to move back: *Enemy forces withdrew from the city.*
**2** to take out: *I withdrew some money from the bank.*

**withdrawal** /wɪðˈdrɔəl/ *noun*
a removal, a taking out: *I made a withdrawal of $100 from my savings account.*

**to go through withdrawal:** to suffer effects from no longer using drugs: *The drug addict went through withdrawal in the hospital.*

**wither** /ˈwɪðər/ *verb*
to dry up and die: *Plants wither because they need water.*

**withhold** /wɪθˈhould/ *verb* **withheld** /-ˈhɛld/, **withholding, withholds**
**1** to not give: *She withheld approval of the plan until she understood it.*
**2** to subtract (taxes from a worker's pay): *The company withholds taxes from your paycheck.* –*noun* (action) **withholding.**

**within** /wɪˈðɪn/ *preposition*
inside (a person, container, time period, etc.): *He keeps his feelings within himself.*‖*The bill is due within 30 days.*

**without** /wɪˈðaut/ *preposition*
**1** not in the company of, *(synonym)* ab-

sent: *I went shopping without my husband.*
**2** not having, lacking: *a day without sunshine*

**without** *adverb*
**to do** or **go without:** to not have comforts, luxuries, etc.: *My parents did without to pay for my education.*

**witness** /'wɪtnɪs/ *verb* **witnesses**
**1** to see, observe something that happened: *He witnessed the auto accident and wrote a report.*
**2** to sign a document as a witness: *They asked me to witness their contract.*

**witness** *noun, plural* **witnesses**
a person who saw something and can tell about it: *I was a witness to the accident.*

**witty** /'wɪti/ *adjective*
humorous, funny: *She is very witty and bright.*

**wives** /waɪvz/ *noun*
*plural of* wife

**wiz** /wɪz/ *noun informal short for* wizard: *He is a math wiz.*

**wizard** /'wɪzərd/ *noun*
**1** a man who has magic powers
**2** a very capable or gifted person: *She is a wizard with computers. –noun* **wizardry** /'wɪzərdri/.

**woke** /woʊk/ *verb*
*past tense of* wake

**woken** /'woʊkən/ *verb*
*past participle of* wake

**wolf** /wʊlf/ *noun, plural* **wolves** /wʊlvz/
a wild, doglike animal that travels in groups: *Wolves hunt deer.*

wolf

**to keep the wolf from the door:** *informal* to have enough money to live on: *He is an unemployed manager who drives a taxi just to keep the wolf from the door.*

**wolf** *verb*
to eat very fast: *When he is very hungry, he wolfs his food.*

**woman** /'wʊmən/ *noun, plural* **women** /'wɪmən/
a mature female human: *A girl grows up to be a woman. –adjective* **womanly.**

**womb** /wum/ *noun*
the part of a woman's body where a baby can grow: *She has a healthy baby girl in her womb.*

**women** /'wɪmən/ *noun*
*plural of* woman

**women's rights** *noun, plural*
economic, social, and legal rights for women equal to those of men: *Women's rights include equal pay for equal work.*

**won** /wʌn/ *verb*
*past tense and past participle of* win

**wonder** /'wʌndər/ *verb*
**1** to express an interest in knowing: *I wonder if it will rain today.*
**2** to admire: *Many people wonder at the beauty of nature around them. –noun* (condition) **wonder.**

**wonderful** /'wʌnd ərfəl/ *adjective*
excellent, very pleasing: *We had a wonderful time on our vacation. –adverb* **wonderfully.**

**won't** /woʊnt/
*contraction of* will not

**wood** /wʊd/ *noun*
**1** the hard material that trees are made of: *The wood in that old oak tree is hard.*
**2** the material from trees used to make furniture, fuel, paper, etc.: *We used wood from our own land to build our house. See:* woods.

**wooden** /'wʊdn/ *adjective*
made of wood: *The house is full of wooden furniture.*

**woodland** /'wʊdlənd/ *noun*
an area with many trees: *The small town is surrounded by woodlands.*

**woodpecker** /'wʊd ˌpɛkər/ *noun*
a type of bird with a long, pointed beak used to knock holes in trees to find insects to eat and to make nests

**woods** /wʊdz/ *noun, plural*
a small forest: *We like to go for a walk in the woods.*

**woodwind** /'wʊdˌwɪnd/ *noun*
any of the wooden instruments in an orchestra that are played by blowing into them, such as the clarinet and oboe

**woodwork** /'wʊdˌwɜrk/ *noun*
floors, doors, furniture, and walls made from wood: *The woodwork in the library is made of oak and walnut.*

**woodworking** /ˈwʊ dˌwɜrkɪŋ/ *noun*
the art and craft of making things from wood, especially furniture

**wool** /wʊl/ *noun*
sheep's hair: *It is hard to cut wool from sheep.*||*My sweater is made of wool. –adjective* **woolen.**

**woozy** /ˈwuzi/ *adjective* **woozier, wooziest**
feeling faint, dizzy: *The summer heat made me feel woozy.*

**word** /wɜrd/ *noun*
**1** a written or spoken unit of language: *There are many words to describe the feeling of happiness.*
**2** speech in general, in written or spoken form: *The author put her thoughts into words.*
**3** a brief discussion: *I had a word with my secretary about him being late today.*||*I gave him a word of advice.*
**4** a promise: *I gave my word to my friend that I would help him.*||*You can trust her to keep her word.*
**5** message, news: *They sent word that they would be late.*
**word for word:** taken exactly from someone else's words: *She told me exactly what he said, word for word.*
**word** *verb*
to express in words: *He worded his introduction carefully.*

**wording** /ˈwɜrdɪŋ/ *noun*
the way words are arranged: *The wording of the contract is not right.*

**word processing** *noun*
**1** the typing, correction, and printing of words and numbers on a computer: *Word processing has taken the place of typing in most businesses.*
**2** the occupation (used with *to do*): *She does word processing at a bank. See:* input; output.

**word processor** *noun*
a small computer used for word processing: *The author writes her books on a word processor.*

**wordy** /ˈwɜrdi/ *adjective* **wordier, wordiest**
using lots of words: *His writing is very wordy and needs cutting. –noun* **wordiness.**

**wore** /wɔr/ *verb*
*past tense of* wear

**work** /wɜrk/ *verb*
**1** to be employed: *He works in a hospital.*||*He works as a machinist.*
**2** to repair, fix something: *The mechanic worked on the car to fix it.*
**3** to operate, cause to function: *He works on a computer all day.*||*Do you know how to work this camera?*
**4** to produce results: *That medicine works well in killing pain.*
**to be (all) worked up:** *informal* to be upset: *The student was all worked up about finishing her term paper on time.*
**to work against someone** or **something:** **a. someone:** to not help: *His lack of education works against him when he looks for a job.* **b. something:** to fight, battle: *Our political party worked against the opposing candidates.*
**to work at something:** to make great efforts: *He works at his studies and makes good grades.*
**to work like a dog:** to work very hard
**to work out:** **a.** to end in success: *The president worked out a solution to the company's problems.* **b.** to exercise: *She works out at the local health club.*
**work** *noun*
**1** employment: *Students will be looking for work after they finish college.*
**2** the change of energy into force: *Machines do the heavy work in our society.*
**3** an occupation, job type: *She has work as a store manager.*
**4** a creation, especially an artistic work: *The museum is showing the works of famous painters.*
**out of work:** lacking a job, unemployed

**workable** /ˈwɜrk əbəl/ *adjective*
practical, able to be done: *We made a workable agreement with another company to build a house together.*

**worker** /ˈwɜrkər/ *noun*
a person who works: *Steel workers are highly paid for their work.*

**workforce** /ˈwɜrkˌfɔrs/ *noun*
all workers employed nationally, regionally, or in an individual business: *The workforce in this area is well-educated and very reliable.*

**working class** *noun adjective*
the part of society that works for wages, especially work with the hands, such as blue collar and clerical workers: *Many people in the working class do not have a college education.*

**working papers** *noun plural*
**1** a written document saying that a young person is old enough to work: *In some states, young people must have working papers to get a job.*
**2** in the USA, a green card and Social Security number: *She is a legal immigrant and has working papers.*

**workings** /'wɜrkɪŋz/ *noun plural*
the way something works: *I don't understand the workings of a car.*

**workload** /'wɜrk,loʊd/ *noun*
the amount of work to be done: *The workload in the accounting department is very heavy.*

**workman** /'wɜrkmæn/ *noun, plural* **workmen** /'wɜrkmɛn/
a person who works with his or her hands: *Two workmen are digging up the garden to plant flowers.*

**workmanship** /'wɜrkmən,ʃɪp/ *noun, (no plural)*
the quality of work as seen in products: *The workmanship in my new car is excellent.*

**workout** /'wɜrk,aʊt/ *noun*
a period of physical exercise: *He goes to a gym for a daily workout.*

**work permit** *noun*
written permission given by a government to a foreigner to work in the country: *When a work permit expires, the immigrant often returns to his or her homeland.*

**workshop** /'wɜrk,ʃɑp/ *noun*
**1** a building or area with machinery and tools: *We make machine parts in our workshop.*
**2** a small group of students or professionals who study together: *My English workshop met this morning to discuss a new book.*

**workstation** /'wɜrk,steɪʃən/ *noun*
**1** a place within a workshop where a specific task is performed: *At my workstation, we make small TVs.*
**2** a computer on a network: *This network has 12 workstations that share the same printer.*

**workweek** /'wɜrk,wik/ *noun*
the number of days and hours from Monday to Sunday of a business or an employee: *Most US companies have a five-day workweek.*

**world** /wɜrld/ *noun*
**1** the earth: *It is possible to fly around the world in an airplane.*
**2** the state of affairs of humans and the planet in general: *What a wonderful (crazy, sad, etc.) world we live in.*
**3** a group of living things: *People are curious to know about the plant world.*

**world-class** *adjective*
related to the best in the world of something, especially in sports: *She is a world-class runner in the Olympics.*

**World Series** *noun*
the North American baseball championship: *The World Series winner must win four of the seven games in the series.*

**World War I** /wʌn/ *noun, (no plural)*
the great war (1914-1918) between the Allies (USA, Canada, Great Britain, France, Japan, et al.) and Germany, Austria, Hungary, et al.

**World War II** /tu/ *noun, (no plural)*
the great war (1939-1945) between the Allies (USA, Canada, Great Britain, France, et al.) and the Axis (Germany, Japan, et al.)

**worldwide** /,wɜrld'waɪd/ *adjective*
all over the world: *Interest in the computer business is now worldwide.*

**World Wide Web** *noun*
a way of moving around the Internet, viewing and saving information that can be text, graphics, sound, or video

**worm** /wɜrm/ *noun*
a small, crawling animal with a long, soft body and no legs: *Earthworms help the soil by digging holes in it.*

**worn** /wɔrn/ *verb*
*past participle of* wear

**worn** *adjective*
used: *The knees of my pants are worn.*

**worn out** *adjective*
**1** very tired, exhausted: *I am all worn out from working too hard.*

**2** no longer usable from wear: *The bottoms of my shoes are worn out.*

**worry** /ˈwɜri/ *noun, plural* **worries**
fear that something bad may happen: *He has worries about his health and his job.* *–adjective* **worrisome.**

**worry** *verb* **worried, worrying, worries**
to feel troubled or fearful: *She worries about the safety of her children at school.* *–adjective* **worried;** *–noun* (person) **worrier.** *See:* art on page 18a.

**worse** /wɜrs/ *adjective comparative of* bad
**1** lower in quality: *The weather was bad yesterday, but today it is even worse.*
**2** more harmful, more serious: *His health is getting worse every day.*

**worse** *adverb*
in a worse way: *The child behaved badly by day and worse at night.*

**worsen** /ˈwɜrsən/ *verb*
to become worse, decline: *His health worsens daily.*

**worship** /ˈwɜrʃɪp/ *verb* **worshiped, worshiping, worships**
to show great respect for: *Many people worship God.*

**worship** *noun*
(the act of showing) great respect: *The worship of God is common among the many people.* *–noun* (person) **worshiper;** *–adjective* **worshipful.**

**worst** /wɜrst/ *adjective superlative of* bad
**1** lowest in quality: *The movie was bad; it was the worst one I have ever seen!*
**2** most harmful: *This winter's weather is the worst in years.*

**in the worst way:** very much: *He needs a new car in the worst way. (antonym)* best.

**worth** /wɜrθ/ *noun, (no plural)*
**1** the value or cost of something: *That painting is an art object of great worth.*
**2** a quantity of something: *I would like $10 worth of gas, please.*

**worth** *adjective*
**1** equal in value to: *That dress is worth $100.*
**2** good enough for: *That book is worth reading.*

**worthwhile** /ˌwɜrθˈwaɪl/ *adjective*
worth doing, worth the trouble: *Seeing that art exhibit is worthwhile.*

**worthy** /ˈwɜrði/ *adjective* **worthier, worthiest**
deserving, due: *That new play is worthy of praise.* *–noun* **worthiness.**

**would** /wʊd/ *auxillary verb*
**1** used as past tense of *will*: *He said he would be here.*
**2** was willing to: *I asked her to change her mind, but she wouldn't.*
**3** (to ask someone to do something) will, could: *Would you please help me move this table?*

**wouldn't** /ˈwʊdnt/
*contraction of* would not

**wound (1)** /wʊnd/ *noun*
a cut or other hurt cutting into the body: *The police officer has a knife wound in her arm.*

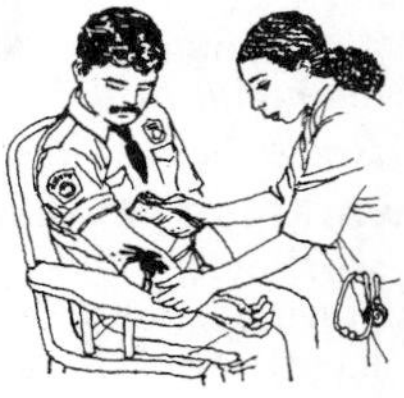
wound

**wound** *verb*
**1** to cause a wound: *The bullet wounded the soldier.*
**2** to hurt emotionally: *She left her boyfriend, and that wounded him.*

**wound (2)** /waʊnd/ *verb*
*past tense and past participle of* wind

**wove** /woʊv/ *verb*
*past tense of* weave

**woven** /ˈwoʊvən/
*past participle of* weave: *That cloth is finely woven.*

**wow** /waʊ/ *verb*
*exclamation* used to show surprise, delight: *Wow! What a great movie!*

**wrap** /ræp/ *verb* **wrapped, wrapping, wraps**
to cover (with material): *I wrapped the gift with colorful paper.*

**wrapper** /ˈræpər/ *noun*
a cover: *Candy bars have colorful wrappers.* *–noun* (material) **wrapping.**

**wrath** /ræθ/ *noun formal*
anger, hostility: *He feared his father's wrath.* *–adjective* **wrathful** /ˈræθfəl/.

**wreath** /riθ/ *noun, plural* **wreaths** /riðz/
a round arrangement of flowers or leaves used for decoration: *Many people hang wreaths of pine branches on their doors at Christmas.*

wreath

**wreck** /rɛk/ *verb*
to ruin, destroy: *He wrecked his car in an accident.* –*noun* (object) **wreck.**

**wreckage** /ˈrɛkɪʤ/ *noun*
what remains of something that has been destroyed: *wreckage after a hurricane*

**wren** /rɛn/ *noun*
a small brown bird: *I hear the wrens singing in the tree outside my window.*

**wrench** /rɛnʧ/ *noun, plural* **wrenches**
**1** a metal tool that tightens or loosens things: *He used a wrench to tighten the water pipes.*
**2** a sudden twisting movement: *With one wrench, he loosened the cap off the jar.* –*verb* **to wrench.**

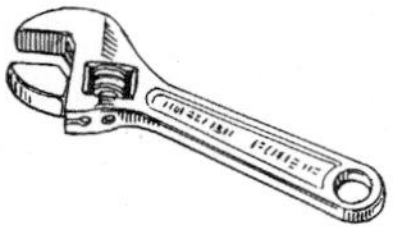
wrench

**wrestle** /ˈrɛsəl/ *verb* **wrestled, wrestling, wrestles**
**1** to fight with someone using the force of the body: *A police officer wrestled a criminal to the ground.*
**2** to do the sport of wrestling –*noun* (person) **wrestler,** (sport) **wrestling.**

**wretched** /ˈrɛʧɪd/ *adjective*
dirty, poor, and very unhappy: *To live in those old buildings must be wretched.* –*noun* **wretchedness.**

**wring** /rɪŋ/ *verb* **wrung** /rʌŋ/, **wringing, wrings**
to twist or squeeze forcefully, especially with hands: *He wrung the water from the clothes he had just washed.*

**wrinkle** /ˈrɪŋkəl/ *verb* **wrinkled, wrinkling, wrinkles**
to put lines or folds in something: *The back of her skirt was wrinkled from sitting on it.*

**wrinkle** *noun*
**1** a line or fold in something: *The old lady has wrinkles in her face.*
**2** a small problem

**wrist** /rɪst/ *noun*
the part where the hand attaches to the arm: *I always wear my watch on my left wrist.*

**wristwatch** /ˈrɪstˌwɑʧ/ *noun, plural* **wristwatches**
a watch worn on the wrist: *My wristwatch uses a small battery.*

**write** /raɪt/ *verb* **wrote** /roʊt/ or **written** /ˈrɪtn/, **writing, writes**
**1** to present ideas in words, such as on paper or electronically: *He has to write a term paper for his English class.*
**2** to communicate with someone in writing: *I wrote a letter to my brother about my new job.*
**to write something down:** to write information on paper: *I wrote down the doctor's address.*

**writer** /ˈraɪtər/ *noun*
someone who writes: *The writer of the letter expresses herself well.*

**writing** /ˈraɪtɪŋ/ *noun*
**1** the act of expressing ideas in words: *The writing of that report took many months.*
**2** handwriting: *Can you read her messy writing?*

**written** /ˈrɪtn/ *verb*
*past participle of* write

**wrong** /rɔŋ/ *adjective*
**1** incorrect, mistaken: *The price marked on those shoes is wrong.*
**2** related to bad behavior, not right: *It was wrong of him to cheat you.*

**wrong** *noun*
a mistake or bad action: *The boy broke his sister's toy because she broke his, but two wrongs don't make a right.*

**wrong** *adverb*
in a wrong way, incorrectly: *I wrote down the address wrong, so I could not find your house.* –*adverb* **wrongly.**

**wrongdoing** /ˈrɔŋˌduɪŋ/ *noun*
an act of breaking the law: *The police try to prevent people from wrongdoing.* –*noun* (person) **wrongdoer.**

**wrote** /roʊt/ *verb*
*past tense of* write

**wrung** /rʌŋ/ *verb*
*past tense and past participle of* wring
**wrung out:** very tired, *(synonym)* exhausted: *We were wrung out after a day in the hot sun.*

# X,x

**X, x** /ɛks/ *noun* **X's, x's** or **Xs, xs**
**1** the 24th letter of the English alphabet
**2** a mark for a location: *X marks the spot on the map where I live.*
**3** the Roman numeral for ten

**X, x** *verb*
to cross out with an X: *She X'd out a sentence in the letter. See:* ex.

**XL** /'ɛks'ɛl/
*abbreviation of* extra large size: *The size of that winter coat is XL.*

**Xmas** /'krɪsməs/ *noun informal*
*abbreviation of* Christmas: *This year I will spend the Xmas holidays with my family.*

**USAGE NOTE:** *Xmas* is used in informal writing but is not used in speaking.

**X-rated** /'ɛks,reɪtɪd/ *adjective*
in the USA, a rating for films that have nude sex scenes and often dirty language: *Children under the age of 17 cannot buy tickets for X-rated films.*

**x-ray** *noun* /'ɛksreɪ/
**1** a type of unseen radiation that passes through the soft parts of the body, but bounces off of the bones: *X-rays are used to make pictures of our bones.*
**2** a photograph taken with x-rays *See:* art on page 11a.

**x-ray** *verb*
to photograph using x-rays: *A doctor x-rayed my broken arm.*

**xylophone**
/'zaɪlə,foʊn/ *noun*
a musical instrument made of two rows of bars, each sounding a different note when hit with light wooden hammers

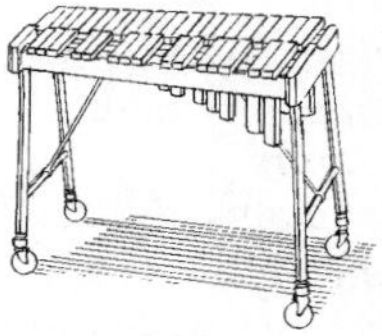

**xylophone**

# Y,y

**Y, y** /waɪ/ *noun* **Y's, y's** or **Ys, ys**
the 25th letter of the English alphabet

**the Y:** *noun abbreviation of* YMCA, the Young Men's Christian Association or YWCA, the Young Women's Christian Association: *He lives in a room at the Y.*

**yacht** /yɑt/ *noun*
an expensive boat used for pleasure or racing

yacht

**y'all** /yɔl/ *pronoun informal contraction of* you all

**yam** /yæm/ *noun*
a plant with a root, sweet potato: *Some people eat yams with their turkey for Thanksgiving dinner.*

**yank** /yæŋk/ *verb*
to give a strong, sharp pull on something: *He yanked a fish out of the water.*

**yank** *noun*
a strong pull: *He gave his fishing line a yank.*

**Yankee** /ˈyæŋki/ *noun*
an American as called by some foreigners: *My wife is from England and I am American. She calls me a Yankee.*

**yard** /yɑrd/ *noun*
**1** a length of three feet or 36 inches (0.91 meter): *I bought a yard of cloth to make a dress.*
**2** an area usually behind or in front of a house: *The children went outside to play in the yard. See:* inch. *See:* art on page 16a.

**yardage** /ˈyɑrdɪʤ/ *noun*
a general measure of length and width in feet and yards: *We measured the yardage of rug we needed to cover the floor.*

**yardstick** /ˈyɑrdˌstɪk/ *noun*
**1** a ruler 36 inches (0.91 meter) long
**2** *figurative* any measure of performance *See:* art on page 16a.

**yarn** /ˈyɑrn/ *noun*
threads of wool or other material made into thicker thread: *Wool yarn is used to make socks.*

**yawn** /yɔn/ *verb*
to open the mouth to show that one is tired: *She yawned at midnight because she was very tired. –noun* **yawn.**

**yd**
*abbreviation of* yard

**yeah** /ˈyɛə/ *adverb slang*
yes *See:* yes.

**year** /yɪr/ *noun*
**1** a time period of 12 months or 365 days: *He worked in Japan for a year.*
**2** a date: *the year 2001, 1939, or 1995*

**yearly** /ˈyɪrli/ *adverb*
during or at the end of a 12-month period: *Americans must pay their taxes yearly.*

**yearn** /yɜrn/ *verb*
to feel a strong desire or need for something or someone, (*synonym*) to long for: *He yearns for a better life.*||*She yearns for a pet dog. –noun* **yearning.**

**year-round** *adjective*
continuing throughout the year: *Tennis,*

*swimming, and golf are year-round activities in Florida.*

**yeast** /yist/ *noun*
part of a plant (a fungus) that causes chemical change with many uses, such as in making cheeses, wine, beer, and some breads *–adjective* **yeasty.**

**yell** /yɛl/ *verb*
to shout: *He yelled to a friend across the street. –noun* **yell, yelling.**

**yellow** /ˈyɛloʊ/ *noun*
a color, such as the yellow of a lemon *See:* art on page 16a.

**Yellow Pages** *noun*
a book that lists the telephone numbers and addresses of businesses and professionals arranged by their goods or services: *If you need to find a doctor, look under "Physicians" in the Yellow Pages.*

**yes** /yɛs/ *adverb*
**1** used to express agreement: *Would you like to go? Yes, I would.*
**2** very much so: *"Would you like to drive my new car?" "Oh, yes, I would!"*

---

**USAGE NOTE:** The use of *yes, yes, sir,* and *yes, ma'am* is formal. *Yeah, uh-huh, mm-hmm, yep,* and *yup* are informal, and are commonly used in everyday conversation: *"Do you know Ann?" "Uh-huh." "Have you seen her today?" "Mm-hmm." "Will she be at the meeting?" "Yup."* The body language for *yes* is a small, forward nod of the head.

---

**yesterday** /ˈyɛstər,deɪ/ *adverb*
the day before today: *It happened yesterday.*

**yesterday** *noun*
recently, in the recent past: *It seems like only yesterday that we talked, but it was a month ago. See:* today; tomorrow.

**yet** /yɛt/ *adverb*
**1** now, presently: *Don't go yet.*
**2** up to now, up to the present time: *The mail has not arrived yet.*
**3** in the future, still: *The mail may yet arrive before we leave.*

**yet** *conjunction*
nonetheless, still: *He said that he would pay, yet he didn't.*

**yield** /yild/ *verb*
**1** to produce something of value: *Her work yielded results.‖Our farm yields 20 truckloads of wheat each year.*
**2** to earn money, such as dividends or interest: *That savings account yields 8% interest.*
**3** to agree to, to give in: *to yield to someone's demands*
**4** to surrender: *to yield control of the company.*

**yield** *noun*
**1** production of various kinds: *an increase on crop yield of 20%*
**2** earnings of various kinds: *a savings account yield of 10%*

**YMCA** /ˈwaɪɛmsiˈeɪ/ *noun*
*abbreviation of* Young Men's Christian Association. *See:* Y.

**yoga** /ˈyoʊgə/ *noun*
a type of exercise that uses both the body and mind: *She learned yoga to relax.*

**yogurt** /ˈyoʊgərt/ *noun*
a thick, creamy food made from milk. It is available plain or with fruit flavor: *People eat yogurt for meals. See:* art on page 17a.

**yoke** /yoʊk/
*noun*
a piece of wood put around the necks of cattle to pull wagons and farm equipment *–verb* **to yoke.**

yoke

**yolk** /yoʊk/ *noun*
the yellow part of an egg: *The yolk in a chicken's egg has lots of vitamins.*

**you** /yu/ *pronoun*
the person or persons being spoken to: *Do you like my new hat?*

**you all** /yɔl/ *pronoun informal*
both of you or all of you: *I'm so glad to see you all.*

**you'd** /yud/ *contraction of*
**1** you would: *You'd be better off going tomorrow.*
**2** you had: *You'd better go now before it rains.*

**you'll** /yul/ *contraction of*
you will: *You'll receive it tomorrow.*

**young** /yʌŋ/ *noun, (no plural)*
**1** youth in general: *The young in Europe love American music.*

Y

**2** children, babies, usually of animals: *Most animals take care of their young for only a short time.*

**young** *adjective* **younger, youngest**
**1** not old, of few years: *young children*
**2** youthful, spirited: *Although she is 50, she looks young*
**3** inexperienced: *That child is too young to understand right from wrong.*

**young adult** *noun*
a person approximately 12–18 years old, (*synonym*) a youth: *Many young adults in our town work after school and on weekends. See:* juvenile; teenager; youth.

**youngster** /ˈyʌŋstər/ *noun*
a young girl or boy older than a baby and younger than a teenager: *That couple has two youngsters, ages eight and ten.*

**your** /yər/ *possessive pronoun*
belonging to the person being spoken to: *Is this your hat?*

**you're** /yʊr/
*contraction of* you are: *You're going with me, aren't you?*

**yourself** /yərˈsɛlf/ *reflexive pronoun, plural* **yourselves**
related to the person(s) being spoken to: *Are you doing the work yourself or having others do it?*

**yours** /yʊrz/ *possessive pronoun*
possessed by the person or persons being spoken to: *Is that car yours?*

**yours truly**
**1** an expression used to end a letter and placed above the signature: *Yours truly, Nancy Mann*
**2** *informal* me or I: *We were all at the party, including yours truly. See:* sincerely.

**youth** /yuθ/ *noun plural*
**1** young people: *The youth of today are worried about jobs.*
**2** a young man: *a youth involved in a crime*

**youthful** /ˈyuθfʊl/ *adjective*
typical of the young: *He has youthful good looks.*

**you've** /yuv/
*contraction of* you have: *You've made me feel better.*

**yo-yo** /ˈyoʊ/ *noun*
a toy that spins up and down on a string moved by the hand

**yucky** /ˈyʌki/ *adjective slang* **yuckier, yuckiest**
**1** bad, disgusting: *That food tastes yucky.*
**2** dirty: *Shoes covered with mud look yucky.*

**yummy** /ˈyʌmi/ *adjective slang* **yummier, yummiest**
good tasting: *This chocolate cake tastes yummy.*

**yup** /yʌp/ *adverb slang*
yes *See:* yes, USAGE NOTE.

**yuppie** /ˈyʌpi/ *noun informal*
*short for* young urban professional, a city person who makes a lot of money: *My son is a yuppie who works in a bank, owns a beautiful home, and drives a fancy car. See:* Generation X.

---

**USAGE NOTE:** *Yuppie* couples without children are sometimes called *DINKS,* which is an abbreviation for double-income, no kids.

---

**YWCA** /ˈwaɪˌdʌbə lyusiˈeɪ/ *noun*
*abbreviation of* Young Women's Christian Association

# Z,z

**Z, z** /zi/ *noun* **Z's, z's** or **Zs, zs**
the last and 26th letter of the English alphabet

**zealous** /ˈzɛləs/ *adjective*
having a strong desire to do something: *He is zealous about going to church everyday.* *–noun* **zeal;** *–adverb* **zealously.**

**zebra** /ˈzibrə/ *noun, plural* **zebras** or **zebra**
a horse-like animal with broad white and black stripes: *Lions like to eat zebras.*

zebra

**zenith** /ˈziniθ/ *noun, (no plural)*
the highest point in a curve: *The sun is at its zenith around noontime.*

**zero** /ˈzɪroʊ/ *noun, plural* **zeros** or **zeroes**
**1** the mathematical symbol (0) that means "nothing"
**2** 32 degrees below the freezing point on the Fahrenheit temperature scale, or the freezing point on the Celsius temperature scale
**3** nothing, the lack of something: *All our work came to zero when our computers stopped working.*

**zero** *adjective*
characterized by a total lack of something: *zero growth in sales*

**zero** *verb*
**to zero in on something:** to find out something exactly: *The doctor zeroed in on the exact cause of the pain.*

**zigzag** /ˈzɪg,zæg/ *verb* **zigzagged, zigzagging, zigzags**
to run to the left then right in a forward direction: *The bee zigzagged toward the flower.*

**zillion** /ˈzɪlyən/ *noun slang*
an amount too high to count: *I told you a zillion times not to do that!*

**USAGE NOTE:** Some people say *jillion* to mean the same thing: *He's got about a jillion cookbooks.*

**zinc** /zɪŋk/ *noun*
a basic metal with many practical uses

**zip** /zɪp/ *verb* **zipped, zipping, zips**
**1** to open, close, or fasten with a zipper: *She zipped her jacket.*
**2** to travel or move rapidly: *Cars zipped by on the highway.*

**zip** *noun*
**1** *abbreviation of* ZIP Code
**2** *informal figurative* enthusiasm, *(synonym)* vigor: *My mother has a lot of zip.* *–adjective* **zippy.**

**ZIP Code** *noun*
in the USA, five numbers or nine numbers added to addresses on letters and other items that indicate their location for mail delivery: *The Zip Code of our office in New York is 10019 or 10019-6845.*

**zipper** /ˈzɪpər/ *noun*
a metal or plastic fastener with teeth, used to open and close clothes, bags, etc.: *Jeans have zippers in the front.*

**zodiac** /ˈzoʊdi,æk/ *noun*
a circular picture divided into 12 equal

periods with names and signs related to the placement of stars and planets, often used in astrology: *The zodiac shows that a person born between November 22 and December 21 is called a Sagittarius.*

**zone** /zoʊn/ *noun*
an area of land or sky marked by a government, business, or person for a special purpose: *The city passed a law to create a business zone on some empty land. See:* time zone; jet lag.

**zone** *verb* **zoned, zoning, zones**
to say that an area is a zone: *The city zoned the land for business.*

**zucchini** /zu'kini/ *noun*
a long round green vegetable: *He ate meat with potatoes and zucchini for dinner.*

zucchini

# APPENDIXES

# I. Contemporary American Terms

African American
AIDS or acquired immune deficiency syndrome
American dream
associate degree
ATM or automatic teller machine
BA or Bachelor of Arts degree
Band-Aid ™
barbecue or BBQ
baseball
basketball
bed and breakfast
Bill of Rights
cable TV
civil rights
compact disc
cowboy
cowgirl
delicatessen
Democrat
Democratic Party
depression
disabled
disc jockey or DJ
district attorney or DA
dollar sign
electoral college
elevated train or railway
fanny pack
fast food
Father's Day
FBI or Federal Bureau of Investigation
Ferris wheel
filling station
first base
first lady or First Lady
Fourth of July
French fries
garage sale
GED or general equivalency diploma
Generation X
golden rule
granny
green card
greenhouse effect
grunge
Halloween
hamburger
hearing aid
high school
HMO or health maintenance organization
hometown
honeymoon
hot dog
in-line skates
information superhighway
IOU or "I owe you"
Jell-O™
junior college
junior high school
junk mail
laundromat
leftovers
Little League
living room
lobster
lollipop
loop
LPN or licensed practical nurse
lunch counter
MA or Masters Degree
Major League
Marine Corps
Mayflower

Medicaid
Memorial Day
mom-and-pop store
Mother Nature
MPH or miles per hour
Ms.
NAACP or National Association for the Advancement of Colored People
NASA or National Association of Space Aeronautics
national park
Native American
NOW or National Association of Women
Oscar
peanut butter
picket
primary school
rap
Republican
Republican Party
rock and roll or rock-n-roll
rodeo
roller coaster
secondary school
second-hand
self-service
service station
shopping mall
shrinkwrap
singles bar
skateboard
sneaker
soap opera
Social Security
soft drink
software
Star-Spangled Banner
Statue of Liberty
sundae
Super Bowl
supermarket
T-shirt
teddy bear
Thanksgiving Day
tongue-twister
trade school
traffic jam
trooper
vegetarian
vocational school
Washington's Birthday
Western
White House
World Series
Xmas or Christmas
y'all

# 2. Workplace Terms

account
acquisition
agent
allowance
analysis
applicant
application
apply
appointment
audit
bank
bank account
bankrupt
bankruptcy
bill
blue-collar
board
bookkeeper
branch
brand
budget
businessman
businesswoman
capacity
capital
cash
cc or carbon copy
charge
charge card
chargeable
clerical
clerk
client
clientele
clock
COD or cash on delivery
commercial
commission
company
competition
competitor
complaint
conference
conference call
consumer
contract
contractor
cooperative
copyright
corporation
cost
cost of living
count
coupon
cover
coverage
crash
credentials
credit
credit card
current
custodian
custom
customer
cutback
deadline
deal
dealer
dealership
debt
debtor
deed
deficit
delinquent
demote
depreciate
depreciation
depression
desktop computer
dictation
dilute
discount
distributing
dollar
downsize
file clerk
finance
financing
fire
firm
forgery
fraudulent
full-time
GNP or gross national product
guarantee
guarantor
insurance
insurance policy
insure
interest

inventory
invest
investor
invoice
IRS or Internal Revenue Service
itemize
job
journal
labor
Labor Day
labor union
landlady, landlord
larceny
laundromat
lawsuit
lawyer
ledger
legal holiday
lend
let
liability
life insurance
line
livelihood
lobby
loss
lot
marketplace
memo or memorandum
money
monopolize
off-line
offer
office
offshore
on-line or online
opening
organization
output
overcharge
overdue
overtime
partner
partnership
part-time
pay
paycheck
payday
payroll
personnel
policy
position
price
principal
product
productivity
profit
profitable
promote
promotion
public
savings account
standard of living
table
take-home pay
tariff
tax
technician
telecommunication
temp
term
time and a half
time card or time sheet
token
toll
trade
trade school
traffic
trainee
transfer
travel agency
travel agent
traveler's check
treasurer
trust
underdeveloped
underestimate
unemployed
unemployment
unemployment compensation
union
unionize
unprofessional
unprofitable
wage
welfare
white-collar
wholesale
work permit
worker
workforce
working class
working papers
workload
workweek
write
yield

# 3. Technology Terms

bug
byte
CD-ROM or compact disc – read only memory
chip or microchip
compatible
computer
computerize
data
desktop computer
disk
disk drive
diskette
document
down
drive
E-mail or electronic mail
gigabyte
hard disk
hardware
import
information superhighway
input
Internet
italic
k or K or kilobyte
keyboard
kilobyte
language
laptop
line
log
mainframe
megabyte or megs
modem
mouse
network
online or on-line
output
PC or personal computer
photocopy
print
printer
printout
process
program
programmer
programming
RAM or random access memory
server
software
technician
technology
telephone
terminal
transistor
type
typewriter
upgrade
user-friendly
VCR or videocassette recorder
virtual reality
window
word processor
WWW or World Wide Web

# 4. Countries/Nationalities/Languages

| Country | Nationality | Language(s) |
|---|---|---|
| Afghanistan | Afghan(s) | Pashtu, Afghan Persian |
| Albania | Albanian(s) | Albanian, Greek |
| Algeria | Algerian(s) | Arabic, French |
| American Samoa | American Samoan(s) | Samoan, English |
| Andorra | Andorran(s) | Catalan, French |
| Angola | Angolan(s) | Portuguese |
| Anguilla | Anguillan(s) | English |
| Antigua and Barbuda | Antiguan(s), Barbudan(s) | English |
| Argentina | Argentine(s) | Spanish, English, Italian |
| Armenia | Armenian(s) | Armenian, Russian |
| Aruba | Aruban(s) | Dutch, Papiamento |
| Australia | Australian(s) | English |
| Austria | Austrian(s) | German |
| Azerbaijan | Azerbaijani(s) | Azeri, Russian, Armenian |
| The Bahamas | Bahamian(s) | English, Creole |
| Bahrain | Bahraini(s) | Arabic, English, Farsi |
| Bangladesh | Bangladeshi(s) | Bangla, English |
| Barbados | Barbadian(s) | English |
| Belarus | Belarusian(s) | Byelorussian, Russian |
| Belgium | Belgian(s) | Flemish, French |
| Belize | Belizean(s) | English, Spanish, Maya |
| Benin | Beninese | French, Fon, Yoruba |
| Bermuda | Bermudian(s) | English |
| Bhutan | Bhutanese | Dzongkha |
| Bolivia | Bolivian(s) | Spanish, Quechua, Aymara |
| Bosnia and Herzegovina | Bosnian(s), Herzegovinian(s) | Serbo-Croatian |
| Botswana | Motswana (*sing.*), Batswana (*pl.*) | English, Setswana |
| Brazil | Brazilian(s) | Portuguese, Spanish, English |
| British Virgin Islands | British Virgin Islander(s) | English |
| Brunei | Bruneian(s) | Malay, English, Chinese |
| Bulgaria | Bulgarian(s) | Bulgarian |
| Burma | Burmese | Burmese |
| Burundi | Burundian(s) | Kirundi, French, Swahili |
| Cambodia | Cambodian(s) | Khmer, French |
| Cameroon | Cameroonian(s) | English, French |
| Canada | Canadian(s) | English, French |
| Cape Verde | Cape Verdean(s) | Portuguese, Crioulo |
| Cayman Islands | Caymanian(s) | English |
| Central African Rep. | Central African(s) | French |
| Chad | Chadian | French, Arabic |

| Country | Nationality | Language(s) |
| --- | --- | --- |
| Chile | Chilean | Spanish |
| China | Chinese | Chinese or Mandarin |
| Colombia | Colombian(s) | Spanish |
| Congo | Congolese | French, African languages |
| Costa Rica | Costa Rican(s) | Spanish |
| Croatia | Croat(s) | Serbo-Croatian |
| Cuba | Cuban(s) | Spanish |
| Cyprus | Cypriot(s) | Greek, Turkish, English |
| Czech Republic | Czech(s) | Czech, Slovak |
| Denmark | Dane(s) | Danish, Faroese |
| Djibouti | Djiboutian(s) | French, Arabic |
| Dominican Republic | Dominican(s) | Spanish |
| Ecuador | Ecuadorian(s) | Spanish |
| Egypt | Egyptian(s) | Arabic, English, French |
| El Salvador | Salvadoran(s) | Spanish |
| Eritrea | Eritrean(s) | Tigre and Kunama |
| Estonia | Estonian(s) | Estonian, Latvian, Lithuanian |
| Ethiopia | Ethiopian(s) | Amharic |
| Finland | Finn(s) | Finnish, Swedish |
| France | French | French |
| Georgia | Georgian(s) | Georgian, Armenian, Azerbaijani |
| Germany | German(s) | German |
| Ghana | Ghanaian(s) | English, African languages |
| Greece | Greek(s) | Greek, English, French |
| Haiti | Haitian(s) | French, Creole |
| Honduras | Honduran(s) | Spanish |
| Hong Kong | Chinese | Chinese, English |
| Hungary | Hungarian(s) | Hungarian |
| Iceland | Icelander(s) | Icelandic |
| India | Indian(s) | English, Hindi, Bengali, Telugu, Marathi, Tamil, Urdu, Gujarati, Malayalam, Kannada, Oriya, Punjabi, Assamese, Kashmiri, Sindhi, Sanskrit |
| Indonesia | Indonesian(s) | Bahasa Indonesia, English, Dutch |
| Iran | Iranian(s) | Persian, Turkic, Kurdish |
| Iraq | Iraqi(s) | Arabic, Kurdish, Assyrian |
| Ireland | Irish | Irish (Gaelic), English |
| Israel | Israeli(s) | Hebrew, Arabic, English |
| Italy | Italian(s) | Italian, German |
| Ivory Coast | Ivorian(s) | French |
| Jamaica | Jamaican(s) | English, Creole |
| Japan | Japanese | Japanese |
| Jordan | Jordanian(s) | Arabic |
| Kazakhstan | Kazakhstani(s) | Kazakh, Russian |

| Country | Nationality | Language(s) |
|---|---|---|
| Kenya | Kenyan(s) | English, Swahili |
| North Korea | Korean(s) | Korean |
| South Korea | Korean(s) | Korean |
| Kuwait | Kuwaiti(s) | Arabic |
| Kyrgyzstan | Kirghiz(s) | Kirghiz, Russian |
| Laos | Lao(s) or Laotian(s) | Lao, French, English |
| Latvia | Latvian(s) | Latvian, Lithuanian, Russian |
| Lebanon | Lebanese | Arabic, French |
| Lesotho | Mosotho (sing.), Basotho (pl.) | Sesotho, English |
| Liberia | Liberian(s) | English |
| Libya | Libyan(s) | Arabic, Italian, English |
| Liechtenstein | Liechtensteiner(s) | German |
| Lithuania | Lithuanian(s) | Lithuanian, Polish, Russian |
| Luxembourg | Luxembourger(s) | Luxembourgisch, German, French |
| Macedonia | Macedonian(s) | Macedonian, Albanian |
| Madagascar | Malagasy | French, Malagasy |
| Malawi | Malawian(s) | English, Chichewa |
| Malaysia | Malaysian(s) | Malay, English, Chinese |
| Malta | Maltese | Maltese, English |
| Martinique | Martiniquais | French, Creole patois |
| Mauritania | Mauritanian(s) | Hasaniya Arabic, Wolof |
| Mauritius | Mauritian(s) | English, Creole, French |
| Mexico | Mexican(s) | Spanish |
| Micronesia | Micronesian(s) | English, Trukese |
| Moldova | Moldovan(s) | Moldovan, Russian |
| Monaco | Monacan(s) | French, English, Italian |
| Mongolia | Mongolian(s) | Khalkha Mongol, Turkic |
| Morocco | Moroccan(s) | Arabic, Berber, French |
| Mozambique | Mozambican(s) | Portuguese |
| Namibia | Namibian(s) | English, Afrikaans, German |
| Nepal | Nepalese | Nepali |
| Netherlands | Dutch | Dutch |
| New Zealand | New Zealander(s) | English, Maori |
| Nicaragua | Nicaraguan(s) | Spanish, English |
| Niger | Nigerien(s) | French, Hausa |
| Nigeria | Nigerian(s) | English, Hausa |
| Norway | Norwegian(s) | Norwegian |
| Oman | Omani(s) | Arabic, English |
| Pakistan | Pakistani(s) | Urdu, English |
| Panama | Panamanian(s) | Spanish, English |
| Papua New Guinea | Papua New Guinean(s) | English |
| Paraguay | Paraguayan(s) | Spanish, Guarani |
| Peru | Peruvian(s) | Spanish, Quechua |
| Philippines | Filipino(s) | Pilipino, English |
| Poland | Pole(s) | Polish |
| Portugal | Portuguese | Portuguese |
| Puerto Rico | Puerto Rican(s) | Spanish, English |

| Country | Nationality | Language(s) |
|---|---|---|
| Qatar | Qatari(s) | Arabic, English |
| Romania | Romanian(s) | Romanian, Hungarian, German |
| Russia | Russian(s) | Russian |
| Rwanda | Rwandan(s) | Kinyarwanda, French |
| Saudi Arabia | Saudi(s) | Arabic |
| Senegal | Senegalese | French, Wolof |
| Serbia and Montenegro | Serb(s) and Montenegrin(s) | Serbo-Croatian, Albanian |
| Sierra Leone | Sierra Leonean | English, Mende, Temne |
| Singapore | Singaporean(s) | Chinese, Malay, Tamil, English |
| Slovakia | Slovak(s) | Slovak, Hungarian |
| Slovenia | Slovene(s) | Slovenian, Serbo-Croatian |
| Somalia | Somali(s) | Somali, Arabic, Italian |
| South Africa | South African(s) | Afrikaans, English, Zulu |
| Spain | Spaniard(s) | Castilian Spanish, Catalan |
| Sri Lanka | Sri Lankan(s) | Sinhala, Tamil |
| Sudan | Sudanese | Arabic, Nubian |
| Swaziland | Swazi(s) | English, Swati |
| Sweden | Swede(s) | Swedish |
| Switzerland | Swiss | German, French, Italian, Romansch |
| Syria | Syrian(s) | Arabic, Kurdish |
| Taiwan | Chinese | Mandarin Chinese, Taiwanese |
| Tajikistan | Tajik(s) | Tajik |
| Tanzania | Tanzanian(s) | Swahili, English |
| Thailand | Thai | Thai, English |
| Togo | Togolese | French, Ewe |
| Trinidad and Tobago | Trinidadian(s), Tobagian(s) | English, Hindi |
| Tunisia | Tunisian(s) | Arabic, French |
| Turkey | Turk(s) | Turkish, Kurdish, Arabic |
| Turkmenistan | Turkmen(s) | Turkmen, Russian |
| Uganda | Ugandan(s) | English, Luganda |
| Ukraine | Ukrainian(s) | Ukrainian, Russian, Romanian, Polish |
| United Arab Emirates | Emirian(s) | Arabic, Persian |
| United Kingdom | British, Welsh, Scottish | English, Welsh, Scottish form of Gaelic |
| United States of America | American(s) | English |
| Uruguay | Uruguayan(s) | Spanish |
| Uzbekistan | Uzbek(s) | Uzbek, Russian |
| Venezuela | Venezuelan(s) | Spanish |
| Vietnam | Vietnamese | Vietnamese, French, Chinese |
| Western Sahara | Sahrawi(s), Sahraoui(s) | Hassaniya Arabic |
| Western Samoa | Western Samoan(s) | Samoan, English |
| Yemen | Yemeni(s) | Arabic |
| Zaire | Zairian(s) | French, Lingala |
| Zambia | Zambian(s) | English |
| Zimbabwe | Zimbabwean(s) | English, Shona |

# 5. Information About U.S. Citizenship

1. This foreign affairs agency provides information on American foreign policy, American culture, and academic exchange programs:

   **United States Information Agency**
   301 4th St., SW
   Washington, DC 20547
   (202) 619-4700

2. This organization enforces U.S. immigration laws and processes immigrant visas and other paperwork needed to gain legal work and resident status:

   **Immigration and Naturalization Service (INS)**

   | | |
   |---|---|
   | For the recorded *Ask INS* line: | 1-800-375-5283 |
   | Forms request line: | 1-800-870-3676 |
   | To reach an INS counselor: | (202) 514-2000 |
   | Online: | http://www.ins.usdoj.gov |

3. U.S. Citizenship Test
   Contact your local INS office to learn how and when the test will be given. *U.S. Citizen Yes!* (Heinle & Heinle) is an excellent test preparation book.

4. ## Requirements to Become a Citizen

| | | |
|---|---|---|
| Age | 1. | You must be 18 years old or older. |
| Residency | 2. | You must be a lawful, permanent resident for five years.<br>OR |
| | 3. | You must be a lawful, permanent resident for three years if your spouse has been a citizen for three years and you have been living with him or her. |
| Literacy and Knowledge | 4. | You must understand, speak, read, and write simple English. |
| Loyalty | 5. | You must be willing to protect the United States. |
| Documents | 6. | You must file the N-400 form and other necessary documents, medical reports, fingerprints, and photographs with the INS. |

# 6. Common Irregular Verbs

| Simple Form | Past | Past Participle |
| --- | --- | --- |
| be | was, were | been |
| beat | beat | beaten |
| become | became | become |
| begin | began | begun |
| bend | bent | bent |
| bite | bit | bitten |
| blow | blew | blown |
| break | broke | broken |
| bring | brought | brought |
| build | built | built |
| buy | bought | bought |
| catch | caught | caught |
| choose | chose | chosen |
| come | came | come |
| cost | cost | cost |
| cut | cut | cut |
| do | did | done |
| draw | drew | drawn |
| drink | drank | drunk |
| drive | drove | driven |
| eat | ate | eaten |
| fall | fell | fallen |
| feel | felt | felt |
| fight | fought | fought |
| find | found | found |
| fit | fit | fit |
| fly | flew | flown |
| forget | forgot | forgotten |
| forgive | forgave | forgiven |
| freeze | froze | frozen |
| get | got | gotten |

| Simple Form | Past | Past Participle |
|---|---|---|
| give | gave | given |
| go | went | gone |
| grow | grew | grown |
| hang | hung | hung |
| have | had | had |
| hear | heard | heard |
| hide | hid | hidden |
| hit | hit | hit |
| hold | held | held |
| hurt | hurt | hurt |
| keep | kept | kept |
| know | knew | known |
| lay | laid | laid |
| lead | led | led |
| leave | left | left |
| lend | lent | lent |
| let | let | let |
| light | lit | lit |
| lie (down) | lay | lain |
| lie (untruth) | lied | lied |
| lose | lost | lost |
| make | made | made |
| mean | meant | meant |
| meet | met | met |
| pay | paid | paid |
| put | put | put |
| quit | quit | quit |
| read | read | read |
| ride | rode | ridden |
| ring | rang | rung |
| rise | rose | risen |
| run | ran | run |
| say | said | said |
| see | saw | seen |
| sell | sold | sold |

| Simple Form | Past | Past Participle |
|---|---|---|
| send | sent | sent |
| set | set | set |
| shake | shook | shaken |
| shine | shone | shone |
| shoot | shot | shot |
| shut | shut | shut |
| sing | sang | sung |
| sit | sat | sat |
| sleep | slept | slept |
| slide | slid | slid |
| speak | spoke | spoken |
| spend | spent | spent |
| split | split | split |
| spread | spread | spread |
| stand | stood | stood |
| steal | stole | stolen |
| stick | stuck | stuck |
| sting | stung | stung |
| sweep | swept | swept |
| swim | swam | swum |
| swing | swang | swung |
| take | took | taken |
| teach | taught | taught |
| tear | tore | torn |
| tell | told | told |
| think | thought | thought |
| throw | threw | thrown |
| understand | understood | understood |
| wake | woke | woken |
| wear | wore | worn |
| win | won | won |
| write | wrote | written |

# 7. Geographical Features: Continents, Mountains, Oceans and Seas

## The Continents

| Name | Area in sq. miles |
|---|---|
| Asia | 17,128,500 |
| Africa | 11,707,000 |
| North America | 9,363,000 |
| South America | 6,875,000 |
| Antarctica | 5,500,000 |
| Europe | 4,057,000 |
| Australia | 2,966,136 |

## Oceans and Major Seas

| Name | Area in sq. miles |
|---|---|
| Pacific Ocean | 64,186,000 |
| Atlantic Ocean | 31,862,000 |
| Indian Ocean | 28,350,000 |
| Arctic Ocean | 5,427,000 |
| Caribbean Sea | 970,000 |
| Mediterranean Sea | 969,000 |
| South China Sea | 895,000 |
| Bering Sea | 875,000 |
| Gulf of Mexico | 600,000 |
| Sea of Okhotsk | 590,000 |

## Principal Mountains

| Name | Country | Height in feet |
|---|---|---|
| Mt. Everest | China/Nepal | 29,028 |
| K-2 | China/Pakistan | 28,250 |
| Communism Peak | Tajikistan | 24,590 |
| Aconcagua | Argentina | 22,831 |
| Mt. McKinley | USA | 20,320 |
| Mt. Logan | Canada | 19,524 |
| Citlaltépetl | Mexico | 18,701 |
| Damavand | Iran | 18,606 |
| Mt. Elbrus | Russia | 18,510 |
| Jaya Peak | Indonesia | 16,503 |

# 8. Maps

## The World

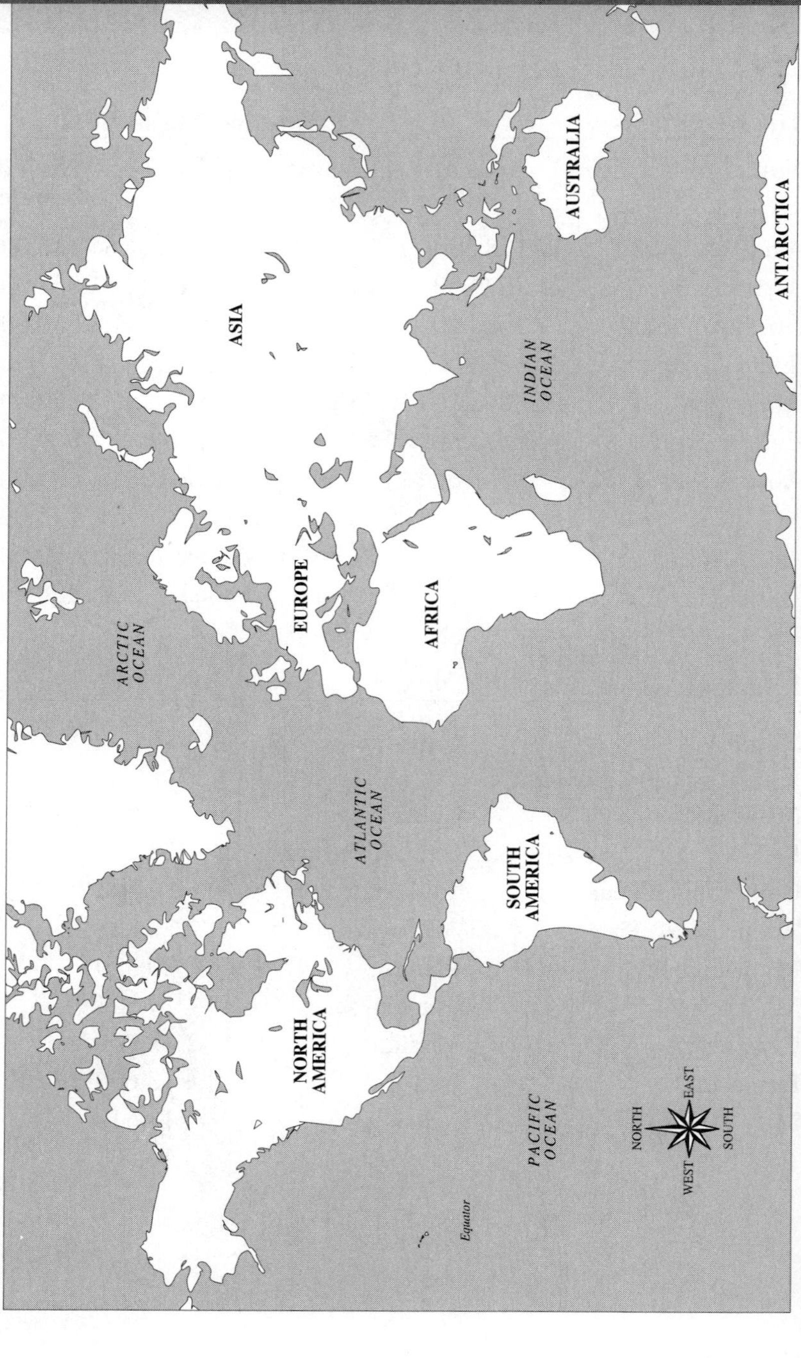

BAHAMAS
CUBA
GUATEMALA
DOMINICAN REPUBLIC
JAMAICA
PUERTO RICO
BELIZE
HONDURAS
HAITI
VIRGIN ISLANDS
DOMINICA
MARTINIQUE
ST. LUCIA
NICARAGUA
BARBADOS
GRENADA
EL SALVADOR
TRINIDAD & TOBAGO
COSTA RICA
VENEZUELA
FRENCH GUIANA
PANAMA
COLOMBIA
GUYANA
SURINAME
ECUADOR
PERU
BRAZIL
BOLIVIA
PACIFIC OCEAN
CHILE
PARAGUAY
URUGUAY
ARGENTINA
ATLANTIC OCEAN
NORTH
WEST
EAST
SOUTH

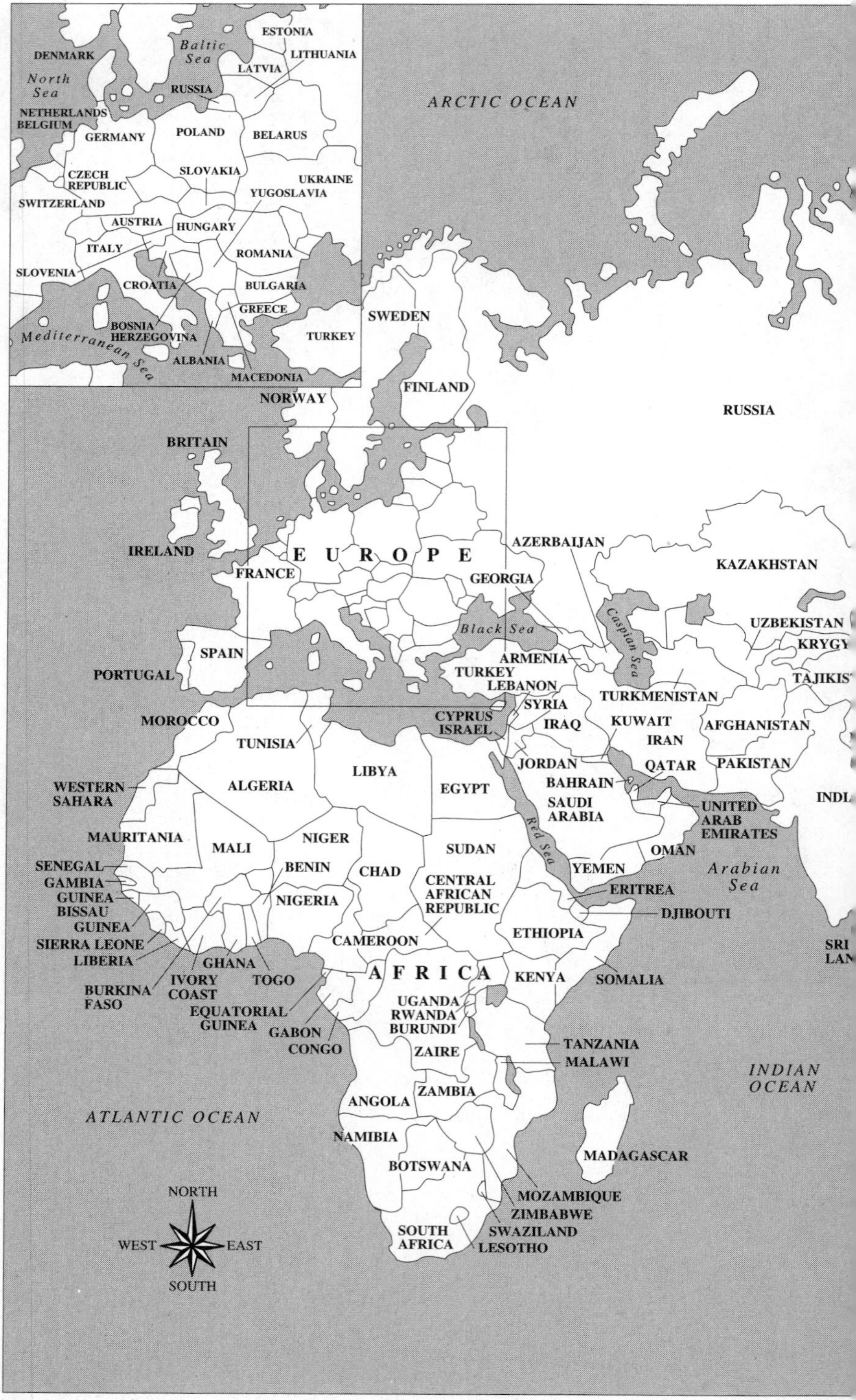
ESTONIA
Baltic Sea
LITHUANIA
DENMARK
North Sea
LATVIA
RUSSIA
NETHERLANDS
BELGIUM
GERMANY
POLAND
BELARUS
CZECH REPUBLIC
SLOVAKIA
UKRAINE
YUGOSLAVIA
SWITZERLAND
AUSTRIA
HUNGARY
ITALY
ROMANIA
SLOVENIA
CROATIA
BULGARIA
GREECE
BOSNIA HERZEGOVINA
TURKEY
Mediterranean Sea
ALBANIA
MACEDONIA
ARCTIC OCEAN
SWEDEN
FINLAND
NORWAY
RUSSIA
BRITAIN
IRELAND
E U R O P E
FRANCE
AZERBAIJAN
KAZAKHSTAN
GEORGIA
Caspian Sea
UZBEKISTAN
Black Sea
SPAIN
ARMENIA
PORTUGAL
TURKEY
LEBANON
TURKMENISTAN
SYRIA
MOROCCO
CYPRUS
ISRAEL
IRAQ
KUWAIT
AFGHANISTAN
TUNISIA
IRAN
JORDAN
QATAR
PAKISTAN
LIBYA
BAHRAIN
ALGERIA
EGYPT
WESTERN SAHARA
SAUDI ARABIA
UNITED ARAB EMIRATES
Red Sea
MAURITANIA
MALI
NIGER
SUDAN
OMAN
SENEGAL
BENIN
CHAD
YEMEN
Arabian Sea
GAMBIA
CENTRAL AFRICAN REPUBLIC
ERITREA
GUINEA BISSAU
NIGERIA
DJIBOUTI
GUINEA
ETHIOPIA
SIERRA LEONE
CAMEROON
LIBERIA
GHANA
A F R I C A
KENYA
SOMALIA
BURKINA FASO
IVORY COAST
TOGO
UGANDA
RWANDA
BURUNDI
EQUATORIAL GUINEA
GABON
CONGO
ZAIRE
TANZANIA
MALAWI
INDIAN OCEAN
ANGOLA
ZAMBIA
ATLANTIC OCEAN
NAMIBIA
MADAGASCAR
BOTSWANA
MOZAMBIQUE
ZIMBABWE
SOUTH AFRICA
SWAZILAND
LESOTHO
NORTH
WEST
EAST
SOUTH

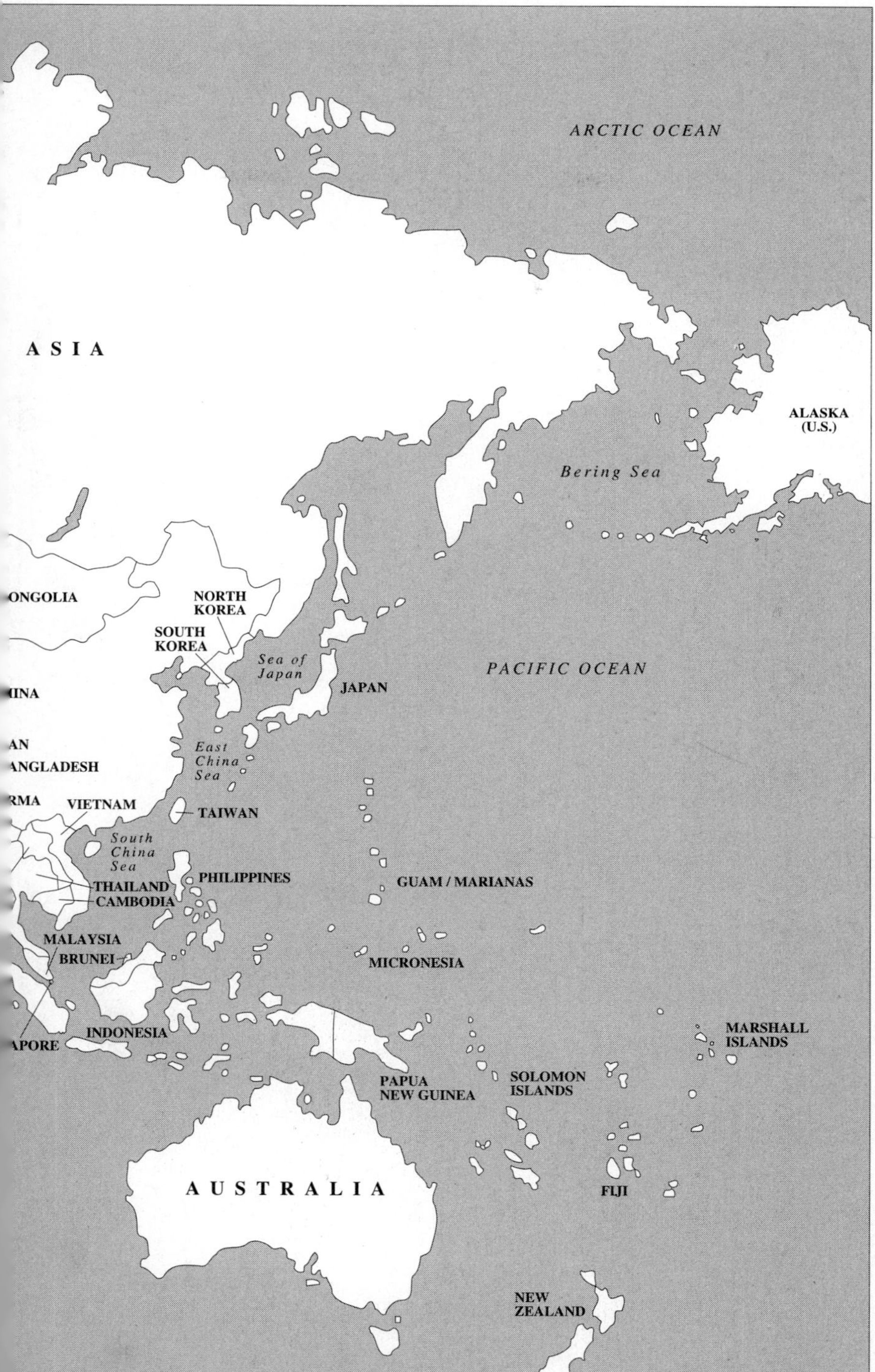
ARCTIC OCEAN
A S I A
ALASKA (U.S.)
Bering Sea
ONGOLIA
NORTH KOREA
SOUTH KOREA
Sea of Japan
JAPAN
PACIFIC OCEAN
HINA
AN
ANGLADESH
RMA
East China Sea
VIETNAM
TAIWAN
South China Sea
THAILAND
CAMBODIA
PHILIPPINES
GUAM / MARIANAS
MALAYSIA
BRUNEI
MICRONESIA
INDONESIA
APORE
MARSHALL ISLANDS
PAPUA NEW GUINEA
SOLOMON ISLANDS
A U S T R A L I A
FIJI
NEW ZEALAND

ARCTIC OCEAN
GREENLAND
Baffin Bay
Alaska (U.S.)
Yukon Territory
Northwest Territories
British Columbia
Alberta
CANADA
Saskatchewan
Manitoba
Hudson Bay
Ontario
Quebec
Newfoundland
Prince Edward Island
New Brunswick
Nova Scotia
Washington
Montana
North Dakota
Minnesota
Oregon
Idaho
Wyoming
South Dakota
Wisconsin
Michigan
New York
New Hampshire
Vermont
Maine
Massachusetts
Rhode Island
Connecticut
New Jersey
Maryland
Delaware
Washington, D.C.
Pennsylvania
Ohio
Indiana
Illinois
Iowa
Nebraska
Nevada
Utah
UNITED STATES
Colorado
Kansas
Missouri
West Virginia
Virginia
Kentucky
North Carolina
Tennessee
South Carolina
California
Arizona
New Mexico
Oklahoma
Arkansas
Mississippi
Alabama
Georgia
Texas
Louisiana
Florida
ATLANTIC OCEAN
PACIFIC OCEAN
Gulf of Mexico
MEXICO
Hawaii
PUERTO RICO
NORTH
WEST
EAST
SOUTH

# 9. Road Signs

There are hospital emergency services to the right.

Slow down. Children use this street to go to school.

This road is slippery when it is wet.

There is a railroad crossing ahead.

You may not turn left.

Slow down as you come to an intersection.
Be prepared to stop and let other cars go first.

You cannot park your car in this space.

This facility can be used by people with disabilities.

# 10. Days of the Week, Months of the Year, Ordinal and Cardinal Numbers

**Numbers**

| Cardinal | | Ordinal |
|---|---|---|
| 1 | one | first |
| 2 | two | second |
| 3 | three | third |
| 4 | four | fourth |
| 5 | five | fifth |
| 6 | six | sixth |
| 7 | seven | seventh |
| 8 | eight | eighth |
| 9 | nine | ninth |
| 10 | ten | tenth |
| 11 | eleven | |
| 12 | twelve | |
| 13 | thirteen | |
| 14 | fourteen | |
| 15 | fifteen | |
| 16 | sixteen | |
| 17 | seventeen | |
| 18 | eighteen | |
| 19 | nineteen | |
| 20 | twenty | |
| 21 | twenty-one | |
| 22 | twenty-two | |
| 23 | twenty-three | |
| 30 | thirty | |
| 40 | forty | |
| 50 | fifty | |
| 60 | sixty | |
| 70 | seventy | |
| 80 | eighty | |
| 90 | ninety | |
| 100 | one hundred | |
| 200 | two hundred | |
| 1000 | one thousand | |
| 10,000 | ten thousand | |
| 100,000 | one hundred thousand | |
| 1,000,000 | one million | |

**Days of the Week**

Sunday
Monday
Tuesday
Wednesday
Thursday
Friday
Saturday

**Months of the Year**

January
February
March
April
May
June
July
August
September
October
November
December

# II. Weights and Measures, Temperature: Celsius and Fahrenheit

## Weights and Measures

1 pound (lb.) = 453.6 grams (g.)
16 ounces (oz.) = 1 pound (lb.)
2,000 pounds (lb.) = 1 ton

1 inch (in. or ") = 2.54 centimeters (cm)
1 foot (ft. or ') = 0.3048 meters (m)
12 inches (12") = 1 foot (1')
3 feet (3') = 1 yard (yd.)
1 mile = 5,280 feet (5,280')

## Temperature chart: Celsius and Fahrenheit

degrees (°) Celsius (C) = (5/9 degrees Fahrenheit) –32

degrees (°) Fahrenheit (F) = (9/5 degrees of Celsius) +32

| C: | 100° | 30° | 25° | 20° | 15° | 10° | 5° | 0° | -5° |
|---|---|---|---|---|---|---|---|---|---|
| F: | 212° | 86° | 77° | 68° | 59° | 50° | 41° | 32° | 23° |

# 12. U.S. States, Capitals, and Postal Abbreviations

| State | Capital | P.A. | State | Capital | P.A. |
|---|---|---|---|---|---|
| Alabama | Montgomery | AL | Montana | Helena | MT |
| Alaska | Juneau | AK | Nebraska | Lincoln | NE |
| Arizona | Phoenix | AZ | Nevada | Carson City | NV |
| Arkansas | Little Rock | AR | New Hampshire | Concord | NH |
| California | Sacramento | CA | New Jersey | Trenton | NJ |
| Colorado | Denver | CO | New Mexico | Santa Fe | NM |
| Connecticut | Hartford | CT | New York | Albany | NY |
| Delaware | Dover | DE | North Carolina | Raleigh | NC |
| Florida | Tallahassee | FL | North Dakota | Bismarck | ND |
| Georgia | Atlanta | GA | Ohio | Columbus | OH |
| Hawaii | Honolulu | HI | Oklahoma | Oklahoma City | OK |
| Idaho | Boise | ID | Oregon | Salem | OR |
| Illinois | Springfield | IL | Pennsylvania | Harrisburg | PA |
| Indiana | Indianapolis | IN | Rhode Island | Providence | RI |
| Iowa | Des Moines | IA | South Carolina | Columbia | SC |
| Kansas | Topeka | KS | South Dakota | Pierre | SD |
| Kentucky | Frankfort | KY | Tennessee | Nashville | TN |
| Louisiana | Baton Rouge | LA | Texas | Austin | TX |
| Maine | Augusta | ME | Utah | Salt Lake City | UT |
| Maryland | Annapolis | MD | Vermont | Montpelier | VT |
| Massachusetts | Boston | MA | Virginia | Richmond | VA |
| Michigan | Lansing | MI | Washington | Olympia | WA |
| Minnesota | St. Paul | MN | West Virginia | Charleston | WV |
| Mississippi | Jackson | MS | Wisconsin | Madison | WI |
| Missouri | Jefferson City | MO | Wyoming | Cheyenne | WY |

**Capital of the USA**

District of Columbia, Washington, DC
(commonly abbreviated: Washington, DC)

# 13. Guide to Pronunciation Symbols

## Vowels

| Symbol | Key Word | Pronunciation |
|---|---|---|
| /ɑ/ | **hot** | /hɑt/ |
| | **far** | /fɑr/ |
| /æ/ | **cat** | /kæt/ |
| /aɪ/ | **fine** | /faɪn/ |
| /aʊ/ | **house** | /haʊs/ |
| /ɛ/ | **bed** | /bɛd/ |
| /eɪ/ | **name** | /neɪm/ |
| /i/ | **need** | /nid/ |
| /ɪ/ | **sit** | /sɪt/ |
| /oʊ/ | **go** | /goʊ/ |
| /ʊ/ | **book** | /bʊk/ |
| /u/ | **boot** | /but/ |
| /ɔ/ | **dog** | /dɔg/ |
| | **four** | /fɔr/ |
| /ɔɪ/ | **toy** | /tɔɪ/ |
| /ʌ/ | **cup** | /kʌp/ |
| /ɜr/ | **bird** | /bɜrd/ |
| /ə/ | **about** | /ə'baʊt/ |
| | **after** | /'æftər/ |

## Consonants

| Symbol | Key Word | Pronunciation |
|---|---|---|
| /b/ | **boy** | /bɔɪ/ |
| /d/ | **day** | /deɪ/ |
| /ʤ/ | **just** | /ʤʌst/ |
| /f/ | **face** | /feɪs/ |
| /g/ | **get** | /gɛt/ |
| /h/ | **hat** | /hæt/ |
| /k/ | **car** | /kɑr/ |
| /l/ | **light** | /laɪt/ |
| /m/ | **my** | /maɪ/ |
| /n/ | **nine** | /naɪn/ |
| /ŋ/ | **sing** | /sɪŋ/ |
| /p/ | **pen** | /pɛn/ |
| /r/ | **right** | /raɪt/ |
| /s/ | **see** | /si/ |
| /ʃ/ | **shoe** | /ʃu/ |
| /ʒ/ | **vision** | /'vɪʒən/ |
| /t/ | **tea** | /ti/ |
| /ð/ | **they** | /ðeɪ/ |
| /θ/ | **think** | /θɪŋk/ |
| /ʧ/ | **cheap** | /ʧip/ |
| /v/ | **vote** | /voʊt/ |
| /w/ | **west** | /wɛst/ |
| /y/ | **yes** | /yɛs/ |
| /z/ | **zoo** | /zu/ |

## Stress

/'/ **city** /'sɪti/

used before a syllable to show primary (main) stress

/ˌ/ **dictionary** /'dɪkʃəˌnɛri/

used before a syllable to show secondary stress

# 14. Terms and Labels Used

The terms and labels below are explained in the "Guide to the Dictionary," p. 5 GUIDE, or in the dictionary itself.

abbreviation of
adjective
adverb
antonym
auxiliary verb
conjunction
contraction of
especially
exclamation
formal
indefinite article
informal
interjection
no plural
noun
noun, no plural
past participle of
past tense of
phrase
plural
preposition
See:
short for
slang
someone
something
synonym
TM
USA
USAGE NOTE
usually
verb
vulgar